League Express

LEAGUE
Publications Ltd

RUGBY LEAGUE
2021-2022
Safe Passage

League Publications Ltd

First published in Great Britain in 2021 by
League Publications Ltd, Wellington House, Briggate, Brighouse, West Yorkshire HD6 1DN

A CIP catalogue record for this book is available from the British Library
ISBN 978-1-901347-40-1

Designed and Typeset by League Publications Limited
Printed by H Charlesworth & Co Ltd, Wakefield

Contributing Editor
Tim Butcher

Statistics, production and design
Daniel Spencer

Contributors

Thomas Alderson
Robson Andrews
David Ballheimer
Ryan Booth
Aaron Bower
Steve Brady
Tom Bramwell
Phil Caplan
Josh Chapman
Lewis Coleman
John Davidson
John Drake
Ian Golden
Sian Golden
Ryan Gould
Dan Hawkhead
Phil Hodgson
Ash Hope
Steven Hughes
Daniel Hunt
Mike Hyde
Stephen Ibbetson
Andrew Jackson
David Kuzio
Callum Linford
Lorraine Marsden
Bryn May
Josh McAllister
Keith McGhie
Ollie Mudd

Dave Musson
Dave Parkinson
Ian Pickles
Huw Richards
Ian Rigg
Martyn Sadler
Matthew Shaw
Steve Slater
Tom Smith
Andrew Steel
Sebastian Sternik
Mark Taylor
Doug Thomson
Callum Thorndike
Callum Walker
Gareth Walker
Jordan Weir
Chris Wilson
Gavin Wilson
Ian Wilson
Peter Wilson

Pictures
SWPix
Dean Williams
Matthew Merrick
Steve Jones (RLPix)
Richard Long
NRL Imagery
Catalans Dragons
Craig Cresswell
Simon Hall
Magi Haroun
Steve Gaunt
Steve Miller
Craig Thomas
David Greaves
Craig Hawkhead
Gareth Lyons
Steve McCormick
Gary McKeating
Peter Morley
Tom Pearson
Mark Cosgrove
Paul Cowan
Rob Terrace
Neville Wright
Bob Brough
Paul Clayton
Alex Coleman
Dave Jessop
Ian Lovell
Bernard Platt
Bernard Rieu
John Rushworth
Pete Smith
Jonny Tomes-Green

Main cover picture
SWPix

CONTENTS

ACKNOWLEDGEMENTS

The *League Express Yearbook 2021-2022* is the 26th of League Publications Ltd's annual series of Rugby League Yearbooks, which began in the first year of Super League in 1996.

This historical record of the Rugby League year would not be possible without the hard work and dedication of all the contributors to *Rugby Leaguer & Rugby League Express* and *totalrl.com* website.

We are able to include some wonderful action photography provided by, in particular SWPix, Dean Williams, Matthew Merrick, Steve Jones (RLPix), Richard Long and NRL Imagery in Australia.

Thanks to the Rugby Football League for their help during the year and to the historians and statisticians at clubs who help us resolve any anomalies.

Acknowledgement also to the Rothmans Yearbook 1999, compiled by our late friend Ray Fletcher, the British Rugby Records Book from London Publications and to the club officials, and some supporters, who helped us verify records.

Special thanks to Doug Thomson for the Championship round-up and to Lorraine Marsden, who wrote the League 1 and Women's sections.

The comprehensive statistical review is once again a work of wonder, compiled, under trying circumstances, by my colleague Daniel Spencer, who also designed the book.

TIM BUTCHER
Contributing Editor

INTRODUCTION

If the year 2020 was a nightmare for Rugby League, 2021 could easily have turned out to be a bad dream too. It is testament to the resilience of the game and those involved in it that it didn't, as the season drew to a satisfying conclusion on all fronts.

It wasn't perfect, the major disappointment being the postponement of the 16th World Cup scheduled for the end of the year, with the Australian and New Zealand Rugby Leagues' decision in July to withdraw from the tournament its death knell. With news coming daily out of the UK of quickly rising Covid-19 cases, the reluctance to let their top players travel was understandable, though nevertheless a huge letdown for League supporters. But the good news was that all the planning and hard work put in by tournament organisers would not go to waste and we could all look forward to the World Cup at the end of 2022. Fingers crossed.

Despite the ongoing take-up of vaccines against the virus and the UK government's lifting of restrictions to try to return to normal life, we had another dislocated domestic year in Rugby League.

The playing seasons got underway much later than usual because of the late finish in 2020 and was delayed again for two weeks because of Covid uncertainty. And fixture cancellations meant that only one Super League club - Wigan Warriors - managed to fulfil all its matches, a total of 17 games being postponed and never played. During the last part of July two consecutive Super League rounds had half of their fixtures wiped out.

Four clubs, Castleford, Huddersfield St Helens and Salford were hit with fines by the Rugby Football League for breaching its operational rules around postponing games. Two games were awarded with 24-0 scorelines. It was all threatening to fall apart.

Games in the first two months of the season were played in front of empty stands. When spectators were allowed to gather, with much limited capacities, many fans were reluctant to return to crowded places and attendances consequently took a hit. Magic Weekend, due to return and be played at St James' Park, Newcastle at the end of May, had to be put back to September. No scrums again, no reserves competition.

The spread of a new variant of Covid-19 and the lifting of restrictions leading up to July 19th led to the increase in postponements and there was a real worry at one stage that some clubs would not be able to play enough fixtures to qualify for the play-offs.

But it all turned out well in the end with some excellent games, as in every year, and a rip-roaring Grand Final at the end of it.

So aside from another year of disruption what will the year 2021 be remembered for?

For St Helens fans it couldn't have gone much better, Saints' 12-10 victory over Catalans Dragons at Old Trafford in October completing the double, ten weeks after their first Challenge Cup win since 2008 when they got the better of Castleford Tigers in another closely fought final. That 28-12 win at Wembley was played out in the sweltering heat of July, with the 40,000 fans allowed into the stadium creating a great atmosphere.

It was another vintage year for the Saints. They were consistent from start to finish and almost irresistible by the time the play-offs came around. And their women's side made a clean sweep of their trophies too.

St Helens and Catalans Dragons take to the field at Old Trafford ahead of the Super League Grand Final

Saints were pipped into second place in the table by the Dragons, who had an amazing successful season to win the League Leaders Trophy, their magnificent achievement coming only four years after they had clung on to their Super League place by beating Leigh in the Million Pound Game. It was no big surprise when Steve McNamara was named Coach of the Year at the end-of-season awards night. And to cap the night off, Sam Tomkins was unveiled as Steve Prescott Man of Steel.

Catalans' achievements were a huge step forward for the sport, facing a perpetual struggle to grab the attention of the French media. And by the end of the season Rugby League in France took another great leap forward when Toulouse Olympique, after a season in which they had to play all their regular-season games in England, won the Championship Grand Final to earn a place in Super League.

Sam Tomkins was a huge influence on the Dragons' success, along with Aussie stand-off James Maloney, with the blooding of some young French players an encouraging sign, utility Arthur Mourgue confirming his promise of the year before, as a superstar in the making.

Mourgue was one of a number of young talents to make their mark in Super League in 2021, along with the likes of Jack Welsby, who of course had already made a big impression the year before with his Grand Final winning try, Will Pryce at Huddersfield, Hull KR's Mikey Lewis, Leeds' Jack Broadbent, Wigan's Kai Pearce-Paul and Connor Wrench at Warrington.

At the other end of the career spectrum, two big-name signings came and went in a flash as Warrington's headliner, Greg Inglis and the returning Kyle Eastmond at Leeds managed less than a handful of games between them before calling it quits.

Introduction

The coaching merry-go-round went into overdrive in 2021, with half of the coaches in Super League having left their clubs by the end of the season, Wigan's Adrian Lam and Steve Price returning to Australia, Castleford Tigers' Daryl Powell taking Price's place at Warrington, Wakefield's Chris Chester and Leigh's John Duffy getting the sack mid-season and Salford's Richard Marshall suffering the same fate at the end of the season.

There was also a major exit in the back office as Super League Europe chief executive Rob Elstone quit his job. Elstone's departure brought to an end almost three years of Super League attempting to pull away from the RFL and carve out its own identity and its own financial future. It became increasingly obvious that a governance that was dominated by twelve Super League chairmen wasn't the road to strengthening the whole sport. A reduced broadcasting deal from Sky raised questions about SLE's value for money and at the start of the year a scheme to sell off part of the league to a private equity firm cost £750,000 even though the offer was rejected. Huddersfield Giants owner Ken Davy was appointed interim Executive Chairman of Super League and expressed his aim to bring the RFL and SLE closer together.

As always, the players and coaches produced some great entertainment and by the end of the season, TV viewing figures were reportedly showing a big increase on the last 'normal' season in 2019.

With St Helens doing the double, there were very few scraps to go around the rest of the clubs. But there were plenty of plus points for most fans at some time in the season. Even those of Leigh Centurions, who took up Toronto's place in Super League on the understanding they would receive almost half the funding of the rest of the clubs. They managed to compete in almost all their games and thoroughly deserved the two wins they recorded towards the end of the season, before accepting relegation gracefully.

We also saw two records set in 2021, Hull KR winger Ben Crooks scoring the fastest try in Super League in the round-three win over Huddersfield and Wakefield halfback Mason Lino kicking 37 consecutive goals to overtake Henry Paul and Hazem El Masri's Super League and NRL records.

At the end of the season, coach Shaun Wane finally got a full Test match under his belt as England beat France 30-10 in Perpignan and Jamaica also played a couple of World Cup warm-ups.

From start to finish, the Rugby League year is covered in the following pages. We hope you enjoy reliving it.

TIM BUTCHER
Contributing Editor

The 26th League Express Yearbook contains the full story of the domestic year, the Australian season and matchfacts for all Super League, Challenge Cup, Championship and League 1 games. Every player who has played Super League is also listed along with those players to have made their debuts this year. We have also selected five individuals who we judge to have made the biggest impact on Rugby League in 2021.

League Publications publishes the weekly newspaper Rugby Leaguer & Rugby League Express and the UK's most popular League website 'totalrl.com'.

1
THE 2021 SEASON

DECEMBER 2020
Seven is the number

After the strangest of seasons, the dislocation of Rugby League continued, as a consequence of the last game of the domestic programme taking place on November 27th. That was the date on which St Helens won their second consecutive Super League title in the most dramatic way when young star Jack Welsby scored a try after the hooter sounded at the KCOM Stadium that sealed an 8-4 win over League Leaders Wigan.

It was the hard-to-believe climax to a 302-day season. Testament was paid to the game's players, who had gone through salary cuts, a two-month extension to the playing season and restrictions and last-minute re-arrangements due to the coronavirus pandemic.

With the season ending around the time of year when players would usually be returning to pre-season training, there was no way that Super League XXVI could kick off on its usual slot at the start of February and a start date of 11th March, coincidentally the same date that the NRL was due to get under way in 2021, was announced.

Although by the end of the year a 'vaccine roll-out' had begun in the UK, the pandemic that was Covid-19 had by no means gone away. The government's plans to relax rules over the Christmas period were reversed at short notice and in the New Year the country was put into a third lockdown.

Clubs were having difficulties with recruitment because of uncertainties with budgets. And NRL players were tentative about coming to the UK, with the coronavirus infection rates in Australasia minuscule compared to Europe.

Catalans coach Steve McNamara was pleased that the start-date for Super League 2021 had been put back to March. 'Clearly, everybody needs a break following this season,' he said. 'It has taken its toll probably mentally more than physically. When you speak to players you can see the strain they have been through with all the uncertainty, testing procedures, confinements, its been really tough.'

The Super League Grand Final was scheduled for October 9th at Old Trafford. And the Magic Weekend was to return and be played at St James' Park, Newcastle, on 29th and 30th May. Clubs would play 13 home fixtures and 27 games overall. The later start meant a repeat of the six-team play-off format used in 2020.

The impact of Covid-19 stretched across all aspects of society and the consequences for Rugby League were serious.

Super League clubs were told on Thursday 17th December that the offer from Sky Sports for a new TV contract for the broadcasting rights to the competition would be around £20 million per year - roughly half the annual figure paid by Sky under the existing broadcasting contract.

A three-year deal with the BBC for the Challenge Cup was announced, covering also the Womens and Wheelchair Challenge Cups. And the BBC would also be covering every game from the World Cups due to be staged in England at the end of the year.

League Express revealed that a private equity company, Novalpina, had made a formal offer of £60 million to buy into Super League (Europe) Limited. Under the terms of the proposed deal, Novalpina would assume management rights for the competition and would be entitled to receive a third of Super League's broadcast income for as long as it held its stake in the competition. Super League would have to pay £750,000 to merchant bank Rothschilds for introducing a potential investor. All twelve Super League clubs, now including Leigh Centurions, had to give their consent. Any one club could cause the deal to fail by vetoing it.

Leigh Centurions were awarded the 12th place to play in Super League for the 2021 season, beating bids from five rival Championship sides, Featherstone Rovers, Halifax, London Broncos, Toulouse Olympique and York City Knights to replace Toronto Wolfpack, who withdrew in July and were then voted out by member clubs. An independent panel, led by Lord Jonathan Caine and comprising three members from the Rugby Football League governing body and three from Super League, made the decision.

The process resulted in some speculation that there could be a return to the licensing system previously used in Super League between 2009 and 2014 but RFL officials discounted it.

It had been previously agreed by the eleven Super League clubs that the promoted club would receive less central funding, although the Centurions had already begun assembling a strong squad. Their last season in Super League in 2017 ended with defeat in the Million Pound Game by Catalans Dragons.

Leigh's promotion left a vacant place in the second-tier Championship, which was also put out to a mini-licensing system and was won by Newcastle Thunder. Thunder were selected out of five applicants to be promoted from League 1 ahead of Barrow, Doncaster, Rochdale and Workington.

There was some significant signing activity towards the end of the year.

Incoming Hull FC head coach Brett Hodgson identified the halves as his main priority in the off-season, with Albert Kelly gone home to Australia, and the Black and Whites were willing to spend big in their pursuit of a new creative player. They made unsuccessful plays for Benji Marshall and Jackson Hastings in their pursuit of a marquee halfback.

Instead Hodgson turned to a familiar face and signed Wests Tigers halfback Josh Reynolds on a two-year deal with the option of a third. The pair spent the last several seasons together at the Tigers, where Hodgson was assistant to Michael Maguire. The 31-year-old made 160 NRL appearances and represented New South Wales four times.

The Airlie Birds were resigned to not having star fullback Jamie Shaul back until the back end of the season because of the ACL injury he sustained against Castleford in October and Jake Connor was tipped to fill the role.

There was a big exit of players over the river Hull and some big-name incomers in former England winger Ryan Hall, after a two-year stint with Sydney Roosters, Melbourne prop Albert Vete, Brisbane's Korbin Sims and Muizz Mustapha from Leeds. And by the end of the year the Robins had filled their final quota spot after completing the signing of Parramatta utility and Cook Island international Brad Takairangi.

There was a shock across the Channel when it was announced that captain Remi Casty had left the Catalans after not being offered a new contract. Casty, 35, had spent 15 seasons in Perpignan during two spells, either side of a one-year stint in the NRL with Sydney Roosters. A Super League Dream Team inductee in 2018, Casty had already attracted interest from other Super League clubs but ended up signing for Toulouse Olympique.

Casty's departure was the headline news in a shake-up of the Dragons' pack. Mikael Simon, Antoni Maria and Sam Moa all departed to play in the French league. And 22-year-old international halfback Lucas Albert announced he was leaving to join Carcassonne, while David Mead was strongly linked with a return to the NRL with Brisbane Broncos. Salford prop Gil Dudson and Castleford backrower Mike McMeeken were new arrivals.

The Dragons tied down promising playmaker Arthur Mourgue to a new three-year deal. The 21-year-old made four appearances for the Dragons as they reached the play-off semi-finals in 2020.

Hull FC's London-produced forward Lewis Bienek's signing was confirmed by Castleford before they made a double swoop for Huddersfield duo Suaia Matagi and Jordan Turner.

Richard Marshall, St Helens assistant, was unveiled as Salford Red Devils' new head coach, taking over from Huddersfield-bound Ian Watson.

Marshall's first signing was Newcastle Thunder prop, 24-year-old Scotland international Sam Luckley. The dynamic forward was set to join Ottawa Aces for the following season but their deferral saw him re-emerge on the market. Salford also confirmed the retention of Greg Burke, while Joe Burgess was unveiled for 2021, along with fullback Morgan Escare and second-rower Jack Wells from Wigan, with Harvey Livett and Matty Costello both joining the club from Warrington and St Helens respectively.

Danny Orr was also named the club's new assistant coach, with Paul Rowley to remain at the club in a development role.

Ian Watson's remodelling of Huddersfield Giants began with the signing of halfback Jack Cogger. The 23-year-old signed a two-year deal with the club. Cogger, a New South Wales representative at junior levels, had made 42 NRL appearances for Newcastle Knights and Canterbury Bulldogs. Former Toronto hooker James Cunningham had already joined the Giants and in December he was followed by Wolfpack teammate, former Cronulla Grand Final winner Ricky Leutele and Wigan back-rower Joe Greenwood.

And two days before Christmas the Giants announced the signing on a one-year contract of Great Britain forward Josh Jones from Hull FC, for an undisclosed fee. Watson had brought out the best of Jones during his time at Salford. Aussie workhorse prop Luke Yates also followed Watson to the John Smith's Stadium.

There had been a number of exits from Wigan. Ben Flower was confirmed as a signing for Leigh, while Chris Hankinson and Josh Woods were being offered to other clubs. Sean O'Loughlin had retired, leaving Wigan looking at a smaller squad for the 2021 season.

Staying put was Adrian Lam, the head coach having signed a 12-month contract extension. And veteran halfback, at age 35, Thomas Leuluai also signed a one-year extension, after playing 302 games for Wigan.

The Warriors were confident their youth production line would make them contenders again, although they did sign Parramatta halfback Jai Field.

Their biggest incoming was the re-signing of England forward John Bateman, who was persuaded to return from a stellar spell at Canberra to be nearer his family. Bateman would wear squad number 13, following on from long-serving club captain O'Loughlin. In the Super League era he would become only the third player to wear Wigan's number 13 shirt, after Andy Farrell (1996-2005) and O'Loughlin (2006-2020). Returning to Wigan for his second spell, after having enjoyed five seasons at the DW Stadium between 2014 and 2018, Bateman returned with much expectation after his NRL experience, including winning the Dally M second rower of the year award in 2019.

Former Leeds prop Rob Mulhern joined Warrington Wolves in a swap deal that saw Luis Johnson head the other way. Mulhern, who made his Super League debut with Leeds in 2014 before joining Hull KR in 2016, made his England debut in 2018 in the warm-up clash with France. He subsequently went on tour with England Knights that autumn.

The biggest story of the month by far was created by Kevin Sinfield's effort to raise money for and awareness of Motor Neurone Disease, driven by the disease's grip on Sinfield's former teammate Rob Burrow, by running seven marathons in the first seven days.

The Rhinos' director of rugby's initial aim was to raise £77,777 for the fund set up to support Burrow and his family, with his three children all aged under eight, plus additional funds for the Motor Neurone Disease Association (MNDA).

Seven was the number that Burrow wore throughout virtually all of his Leeds career, so Sinfield intended to run the seven marathons in seven days, finishing on the 7th December, with each run beginning at 7am.

Sinfield received worldwide acclaim for undertaking the challenge, in which he completed every run within three hours and 48 minutes. The BBC strongly promoted Sinfield's story and he was their first studio guest for many months on BBC Breakfast when he appeared on the programme.

The challenge saw over £2.5 million raised and a petition was launched to grant Sinfield a knighthood.

JANUARY
New year, new uncertainty

Rob Burrow and Keighley Chairman Mick O'Neill were awarded MBEs in the Queens New Year Honours List, while the Rugby Football League's former Chairman Brian Barwick was awarded the OBE.

Burrow, the former Leeds Rhinos, England and Great Britain player who had inspired so many through 2020, was recognised for services to Rugby League and to Motor Neurone Disease awareness during Covid-19.

O'Neill received his MBE for services to Rugby League, the community in Keighley and to charity during the Covid-19 pandemic. Having played a huge role in the successful Cougarmania days of the early 1990s, O'Neill returned to the Cougars, alongside his son Ryan and son-in-law Kaue Garcia in 2018 to save the club from extinction.

At the start of pandemic, the Cougars had donated thousands of face masks and other vital PPE equipment to the local NHS Trust, Hospice and several care homes throughout the area, while special-edition NHS shirts and branded face masks throughout the year also raised vital funds.

Barwick, who served two three-year terms as Chairman of the RFL from 2013-19 and retained a significant role in the sport as President of Rugby League World Cup 2021, received the OBE 'for services to sport and sports broadcasting', having previously worked as Head of Sport for the BBC, Controller of Sport for ITV and Chief Executive of the Football Association.

Warrington Wolves' Matty Ashton was named the Albert Goldthorpe Rookie of the Year for 2020. Ashton's electrifying pace caught the eye in his breakthrough Super League season in what was a continuation of a meteoric rise for the 22-year-old, who was playing amateur rugby just over two years before for Rochdale Mayfield.

The award was first created in 2008 to recognise the best player with ten or fewer Super League appearances at the start of the season. Previous winners included Sam Tomkins, Jermaine McGillvary and John Bateman. Ashton became the first Warrington Wolves player to ever win the award.

League Express confirmed that it would not awarding the Albert Goldthorpe Medal for the 2020 season, after the disrupted season meant players took part in a differing number of games.

Paul McShane was voted League Express Player of the Year by its readers. The Castleford hooker received an impressive 47.2% of results in the annual readers' poll, putting him considerably ahead of St Helens' Jonny Lomax and Wigan's Bevan French, who received 21.6% and 21.4% respectively. It capped a remarkable individual year for McShane, who had been named the Steve Prescott MBE Man of Steel.

In other Readers' Poll results, McShane's Castleford colleague Jacques O'Neill was voted the Young Player of the Year, while James Roby was the Mature Player of the Year for the third year in a row and also the Club Captain of the Year. Roby's team St Helens were the Club of the Year. The readers' Rookie of the Year was Ashton, while the Overseas Player of the Year was Saints' Lachlan Coote and the Best Overseas Newcomer Huddersfield's Aidan Sezer. The most entertaining player was Bevan French, while the player who readers said they would miss the most was James Graham.

In early January the Super League clubs turned their backs on the prospect of attracting private equity investment - at least for the time being.

The process had been a lengthy one, with arguments on both sides about its desirability. With several Super League clubs edging near to insolvency because of the chaos caused by the pandemic, the prospect of an investment of around £60 million into the game was attractive to some.

With Super League split broadly down the middle, some clubs were known to have opposed outside involvement because it would mean that the private equity firm, Novalpina, would effectively take control of Super League and would get its money back in five years out of the broadcast income generated by the competition.

League Express learned that St Helens and Leeds were joined by Huddersfield, Leigh and Warrington in rejecting the offer - it required the consent of all the twelve member clubs. And, given the long term opposition of St Helens Chairman Eamonn McManus and Leeds CEO Gary Hetherington, the likelihood of that happening had always seemed small.

Despite rejecting the proposal, Super League still had to pay a fee of around £750,000 to the merchant banker J Rothschild for introducing the investor.

Better news for SLE chief executive Rob Elstone was that that Sky had increased its offer for a new broadcasting contract, after initially offering £20 million per year. The new offer was thought to be much nearer to £30 million per year.

In the first week of January, the country was plunged into a third national lockdown and with Covid cases continuing to rise across the country, the Super League clubs were set to discuss pushing back the start of season by two weeks on health and safety grounds.

The clubs had the options of a 27, 25 or 23-game format, with England's preparation time for the World Cup a factor. Whatever option, there would be just two weeks between the Super League Grand Final and England's World Cup opener with Samoa at St James' Park, leaving England coach Shaun Wane facing the prospect of very little contact time with his squad.

The clubs were also considering the implementation of two-week player loans ahead of the 2021 season, following the abolition of dual-registration.

Dual-registration had been shelved because of Covid-19, with the prospect of players linking up with two 'bubbles' at once deemed a major hazard. Instead, loans were to be utilised throughout the year but with players unable to train with their parent clubs while playing for teams outside Super League.

That left young players facing the prospect of having to leave full-time environments to get first-grade experience, or potentially not play throughout the season while training with their parent clubs, with reserve-grade also abandoned for the 2021 campaign.

The Championship was set to start on the weekend of February 27-28th, consisting of 26 rounds, followed by a six-team play-off. But clubs from both divisions agreed to push back the season to the Easter weekend (2nd to 5th April), with League 1 to start on the weekend of May 8/9th. Championship clubs could return two weeks before that, with the first two rounds of the Challenge Cup set to take place on the weekends of March 20/21st and March 27/28th.

And League 1 clubs could return even earlier after a number of them also showed interest in entering the Challenge Cup.

The RFL's initial proposal envisaged the 13 UK-based Championship clubs entering the competition, with three byes added to make it a round of 16. They would then be whittled down to four clubs over two weeks, with those four clubs then automatically becoming the semi-finalists of the 1895 Cup, the final to be staged at Wembley.

Eventually, League 1 sides Barrow Raiders, Keighley Cougars and West Wales

Raiders joined 13 English clubs from the Championship. French side Toulouse Olympique did not enter either competition.

Wakefield Trinity condemned the actions of some of their players after they breached Covid-19 protocols by celebrating together on New Year's Eve. The UK was at the time edging towards a third lockdown, with gatherings banned. The players involved were understood to be club captain Jacob Miller, David Fifita, Kyle Wood and Tony Gigot. A day later, the club confirmed that French fullback Gigot had left the club by mutual consent.

Trinity's quiet off-season recruitment was completed with the signings of Eddie Battye and Mason Lino. Battye finally signed after the longest transfer saga of the off-season. Relegated London Broncos were keen to retain him but a deal was reached that would see the 29-year-old return to Wakefield after a successful loan spell at the end of the previous season.

New 26-year-old halfback Lino had played just 34 NRL games with New Zealand Warriors and latterly Newcastle Knights. Wakefield were badly lacking organisation in their attack in 2020.

Wigan Warriors continued to trim their squad as Chris Hankinson and Romain Navarrete joined London Broncos.

As clubs began pre-season training in January, Hull KR's signings had their first coming together. Ryan Hall, Korbin Sims, Muizz Mustapha and Luis Johnson all linked up with Tony Smith's side for the first time, although two of the club's other signings, Albert Vete and Brad Takairangi, were still awaiting visas.

Gareth Widdop returned to the UK ahead of Warrington Wolves' return to pre-season. Widdop, whose future had been the subject of intense speculation, returned to Australia for the winter and there was a strong belief in some quarters that he wouldn't return, cutting short his time in Super League. But his agent couldn't find him the right deal in the NRL and he was reportedly now committed to the Wolves.

Wolves forward Joe Philbin signed a contract extension keeping him at his hometown club until at least November 2024. The 26-year-old product of Warrington's Scholarship and Academy system had been at the Wolves since being 15 years old.

Leigh Centurions made their first signing following promotion to Super League, confirming the capture of Lewis Tierney from Catalans. The former Wigan winger had three years with the Dragons. Ryan Shaw left the Centurions to join his hometown club, Barrow.

Salford had lost Luke Yates, who followed coach Ian Watson to Huddersfield, but they gave their supporters some good news as Super League Dream Team member Krisnan Inu penned a new deal, while the club confirmed the signings of experienced overseas forward duo Elijah Taylor from Wests Tigers and former Toronto prop Darcy Lussick. Dec Patton, released by Warrington at the end of the season, also signed a short-term deal with the club. The 25-year-old was set to be the final piece in the jigsaw for new Red Devils coach Richard Marshall.

Covid was still proving a big disruption, Leeds Rhinos having had to abandon their pre-season for a number of days on 21st January after six players and one member of their training staff tested positive for the disease.

The Rhinos boosted their middle, confirming the marquee capture of Zane Tetevano and King Vuniyayawa from NZ Warriors. The 30-year-old New Zealander Tetevano signed for the club on a three-year deal after playing for Penrith Panthers in the 2020 NRL Grand Final, while Fiji international Vuniyayawa joined on a one-year deal and took up their final quota spot ahead of the 2021 campaign. As a result, the Rhinos released Ava Seumanufagai from his contract, allowing him to return to Australia to be closer to his family.

Liam Sutcliffe completed a U-turn by signing a new multi-year deal with the club, six months after handing in a transfer request. The England international asked to leave the club in search of a new challenge, claiming that he was keen to nail down a regular position, having spent the majority of his Leeds career as a utility.

Huddersfield suffered a major injury blow, with Ashton Golding being ruled out for several months after dislocating his shoulder in training. The fullback suffered the injury during a routine drill and was expected to miss between three to four months of action after surgery. The Giants then completed the signing of fullback Olly Ashall-Bott from London Broncos until the end of the season.

Catalans' pre-season preparations were on ice as the club continued to wait for guidance and financial support from the French government. Coach Steve McNamara had planned to restart training at Stade Gilbert Brutus in January but would have to wait until the end of the month at least before he could regather his squad.

McNamara said both French clubs, Dragons and Toulouse, were working closely on transport plans for the coming season as Covid continued to wreak havoc with international travel.

The Dragons found their first recruit of the new year with the signature of Penrith Panthers centre Dean Whare. The 31-year-old Kiwi international was a direct replacement for David Mead, who had returned to the NRL with Brisbane Broncos.

McNamara also denied reports that Israel Folau had turned his back on the second year of his contract. McNamara reacted furiously to media speculation that the 31-year-old former Australian dual-code international centre was considering moves to the NRL or rugby union, with twelve months still to run on his current deal in Perpignan.

In light of the current lockdown, the RFL's Rules Committee decided that, as in the post-lockdown 2020 season, there would be no scrums in 2021, as a result of health and safety concerns - it was thought that close contact of scrums increased the risk of transmission during a game.

It was hoped that scrums would return later in the year if and when the scale of the pandemic began to decline.

The World Cup was likely to retain scrums in accordance with the rules used in the international game.

FEBRUARY
Taking shape

Super League's 2021 season was finally set. It would kick off two weeks after the schedule announced in December, with six double-headers at Emerald Headingley Stadium on the weekend of 26-28th March, with all six games to be broadcast live on Sky Sports.

Super League club season ticket holders would also be able to watch all their teams' matches via the Our League App.

Because of Covid-19 restrictions there would be no fans in stadiums for the first six weeks of the competition.

The revised structure would see teams compete over 25 rounds as opposed to the initial plan of 27 rounds. The Magic Weekend was put back to to 4-5th September.

The domestic-season finale, the Super League Grand Final was to take place as originally scheduled at Old Trafford on Saturday 9th October.

The Championship was to return after a years absence on the Easter weekend in April, with a new club in Newcastle Thunder, a new name in Halifax Panthers, and a new modern stadium, the LNER Stadium in York.

The Championship clubs agreed to suspend golden point-extra time for drawn matches for the 2021 season, following concerns expressed for the welfare of players who would have gone more than a year since their last fixture, with the majority of players part-time. The intention was to reintroduce golden point for the 2022 campaign.

Meanwhile League Express revealed that Super League Executive Chairman Robert Elstone had set up an investigation into leaks from Super League board meetings.

During the pandemic, virtual board meetings had been held regularly using video messaging Zoom software and Elstone was alarmed by how often information from the meetings was revealed in media outlets. The directors discussed the issue among themselves, with Elstone urging them not to reveal any information to former League Express reporter Matthew Shaw.

'My advice to Super League is to engage with the media, rather than trying to stop news coming out,' said League Express editor Martyn Sadler. 'I would have thought that transparency is better than secrecy, particularly when we are talking about an organisation that is in the entertainment business.'

On 9th February, Elstone handed in his notice to the Super League board. The announcement was made to the media in a brief email, which said: 'Super League can confirm that it has received notice of Executive Chairman, Robert Elstones, intention to leave his position. The matter will be discussed by the Super League Board and no further comment will be made at this time.'

The matter was discussed by the Super League directors but there was general confusion because the majority of them appeared not to have had sight of Elstone's employment contract. The clubs appeared not to be sure how long his notice period was.

Elstone had been announced as Super League's chief executive officer in June 2018 and he was later made executive chairman, building a dedicated Super League staff at headquarters at Media City in Salford. External consultants were also brought in. He headed a board that was made up of each Super League chairman and one representative from the Rugby Football League, which proved largely unproductive. Observers witnessed an operation that cost millions of pounds a year to run achieving very little. A move back towards some kind of collaborative relationship with the Rugby Football League was thought sensible.

Elstone's departure brought to an end almost three years of Super League attempting to go in its own direction away from the RFL and carve out its own identity and its own financial future.

The RFL was confident that, with one governing body, the government would be more inclined to listen once more to arguments for further financial support. It had already had success in persuading the government to fund all the costs of Covid testing for all its clubs in 2021.

Wigan were hit by the announcement early in the month that marquee signing George Burgess would be leaving the club to undergo urgent hip surgery, to cure a problem that had badly disrupted his performances in his first season at the DW Stadium.

Burgess, 28, only played eight matches in 2020, making a home debut against Warrington in Round 1, when he clearly appeared to be carrying the effects of the condition, which he tried to shake off as the season went on. Coach Adrian Lam said there was no immediate hurry to find a replacement prop forward.

The Warriors also had their pre-season programme disrupted as their Robin Park training complex was shut down for ten days following an outbreak of Covid-19 within the first-team playing group. They returned on February 19th after Wigan's players had undergone two rounds of testing.

Catalans couldn't return to team training at all in February because of conditions attached to French government financial aid. The squad regrouped at Stade Gilbert Brutus on March 1st for a period of intense preparation before their first game against Hull KR at Headingley on Saturday 27th March.

Coach Steve McNamara was refusing to panic, insisting his side would be fully primed for the big kick-off. He was however resigned to the fact that Israel Folau would not be returning to the south of France. The controversial dual-code international had been forced to return home to Australia because of a serious family illness and was exploring options of resuming his career in the NRL.

Huddersfield Giants star Michael Lawrence was unveiled by the RFL as a player representative on a new body that the governing body hoped would help further diversify Rugby League while countering discrimination against members of ethnic minorities.

The new RFL Inclusion Board was to have eight members, including Lawrence and RFL non-executive director Dr Rimla Akhtar MBE, who was to chair the new board, as well as former Rugby AM owner Alex Simmons, Operations Director for the Jamaican Rugby League team.

Castleford Tigers gave no indication that they were considering releasing injured winger Sosaia Feki early from his contract after the former Cronulla star suffered a ruptured Achilles tendon in training. The injury was likely to keep Feki out for all or most of this season. It was the third injury blow Feki had suffered since joining the Tigers on a three-year contract from the Sharks before the start of the 2020 season.

Prior to the start of the 2020 season he ruptured a calf muscle, which kept him out of all Castlefords matches prior to the March lockdown. And when he returned in the Challenge Cup against Hull FC in September he suffered a knee injury that kept him out for the rest of the season.

Warrington Wolves confirmed that head coach Steve Price was to leave the club at the end of the 2021 season. Price joined the Wolves ahead of the 2018 campaign, reaching both domestic finals in his first season and going on to lead his side to Challenge Cup Final success against St Helens at Wembley in 2019.

Price was to remain in charge of the first team for the upcoming season, then return home to Australia with his wife and their three daughters once his contract expired.

Leigh Centurions coach John Duffy expressed his delight with his club's latest signing, utility back Brendan Elliot from Manly Sea Eagles.

Before the end of February the UK government was able to announce a planned lifting of lockdown restrictions due to falling infection rates and the progress of the mass vaccination programme.

Sports fans would be allowed back into stadiums from May 17th at the earliest. The first stage would allow up to 10,000 supporters or 25 per cent of capacity into grounds, whichever was the smaller. Several clubs switched their fixtures that weekend to Monday, 17th May to accommodate the return of supporters.

For Super League it would mean only a small, albeit significant number would be allowed into stadiums, with none of the stadiums boasting a capacity large enough to allow 10,000 fans in to attend.

But it did mean under the current plans the Challenge Cup Final in July would be played in front of a large crowd, while the Grand Final in October would hopefully see much larger numbers as restrictions were eased further.

MARCH
And...action!

The coronavirus, despite the success of the UK's vaccination programme and the planned gradual relaxation of lockdown measures, still created uncertainty for the game.

Early in March, three weeks before the season kick-off it was announced the Super League table would once again be determined using points percentages, to allow for the possibility of matches being postponed because of Covid issues. Championship and League 1 clubs had already agreed to use points percentage.

As with the other two divisions, Super League clubs would be required to have played a minimum of 70 per cent of their scheduled fixtures (18 out of 25 matches) to qualify for the top-six play-offs in September, unless they had accrued enough league points despite having played fewer than 18 matches.

The regulations surrounding postponements had been broadly carried forward from the 2020 season. Clubs would be permitted to withdraw from a fixture if they had seven or more of their top 25 players unavailable, either because of a positive Covid test or following test and trace analysis, or if they were prevented from playing or travelling to play as a result of government restrictions. The fixture would only be rearranged if both clubs had the same available match slot.

Win points percentage was calculated via the number of league points of a club divided by the number of matches played by that club, multiplied by fifty.

If four or more clubs had not played the minimum match requirement, the RFL Board had discretion to determine an alternative minimum figure.

Using this method Wigan had won the League Leaders' Shield in 2020.

The RFL Board also approved changes to the permitted movement between clubs during the 2021 season, again in response to Covid. Dual-registration was out but the minimum length of a loan period between clubs was halved from four weeks to two, with strict criteria regarding testing procedures.

Meanwhile, the deadline for clubs to advise players in the last year of their contracts of their intention with regard to contract offers was put back from April 30th to May 31st, to reflect the later start of the season. Players were still able to speak to other clubs from May 1st, as previously.

Huddersfield Giants owner Ken Davy was appointed the interim Executive Chairman of Super League and expressed his aim to bring the RFL and SLE closer together.

And Culture Secretary Oliver Dowden announced an additional £16.7 million in loan support to protect Rugby League. It followed the Government stepping in with £16 million in emergency support in 2020.

The big player news of the month came with Leeds Rhinos' signing of former St Helens halfback Kyle Eastmond. Rhinos coach Richard Agar said he was certain that Eastmond would enjoy great success on his return to Rugby League after almost ten years in the other code.

The signing could have been timely with Luke Gale and Robert Lui both picking up training injuries, with young halfback Callum McLelland, who underwent ankle surgery during the off-season, now dealing with a problematic hip complaint.

Wigan coach Adrian Lam was unconcerned at reports linking Jackson Hastings with a move to the NRL, saying the halfback was contracted to the Warriors and would be playing in Super League in 2021. Hastings gave an interview with Sydney newspaper The Daily Telegraph setting out his strong desire to go back to the NRL.

The 2019 Man of Steel winner, who was off-contract at the end of 2021, had yet to return to England to start pre-season with Wigan.

Meanwhile Thomas Leuluai was announced as the successor to Sean O'Loughlin as team captain.

Catalans would have to wait a while to get Penrith centre Dean Whare in training, as their new signing flew from down under and into French quarantine. Under current French virus-control measures, the 31-year-old Kiwi centre had to spend seven days in isolation before he could join his new team.

The Dragons, late starters to pre-season training, played two warm-up games, beating a French Federation Select 50-18 and the week after coming back from a 24-10 half-time deficit to beat Toulouse Olympique, who fielded new signings Mitch Garbutt, Dominique Peyroux and Joseph Paulo, by 40-28.

While most Super League clubs limited themselves to one pre-season trial, Leigh Centurions played two, a 79th-minute field goal from Ryan Brierley securing a 25-24 win at St Helens in Tommy Makinson's testimonial and a week later the Centurions going down 34-12 to a Gareth Widdop-inspired Warrington Wolves.

York City Knights played their first-ever match at the new LNER Community Stadium, which they were to share with the city's soccer club, in a pre-season game against Hull FC. The Super League side ran out 28-22 winners.

Salford's new signing Danny Addy stood out in the Red Devils' 20-6 home win over Wigan and Huddersfield beat Leeds 22-16.

And Michael Shenton and new signing Niall Evalds were tryscorers in Castleford's victory at Hull Kingston Rovers in a pre-season match that doubled as Adam Milner's testimonial game.

That week, Tigers' head coach Daryl Powell announced he was to leave the club at the end of the 2021 season, by which time he would have been in charge for more than eight years.

Round 1

The 26th season of Super League got underway on Friday 26th March, with all the round-one games being staged at Headingley Stadium.

St Helens started their title defence in convincing style with a 29-6 win over Salford Red Devils. Jonny Lomax and James Roby's relentless efforts alongside the kicking game of Theo Fages were central to an eventually comfortable win, as Red Devils errors cost them dear in what was head coach Richard Marshall's first match in charge. A brief spell after Ken Sio's second-half try apart, that with Krisnan Inu's conversion made it 13-6 after 55 minutes, they never looked likely to win.

Saints were missing fullback Lachlan Coote with a calf strain and he joined Morgan Knowles, who had not recovered from surgery on his thumb, in missing out. Jack Welsby deputised at the back, with coach Kristian Woolf handing debuts to his trio of NRL forward recruits in Joel Thompson, Sione Mata'utia and Agnatius Paasi, the latter on the bench.

Paasi was helped from the field after a huge collision with the ball-carrying Pauli Pauli at the start of the second half and he did not return. Centre Mark Percival limped off shortly after scoring on the hour mark, after having been restricted to just six matches 2020.

Salford fielded five debutants in former Wests Tiger Elijah Taylor, who was excellent at loose forward, Danny Addy and Harvey Livett, with Jack Wells and Declan Patton coming off the bench. New hooker Andy Ackers was self-isolating due to Covid-19 procedures.

A scrappy first half finished with the champions 13-0 in front. They were ahead within the first two minutes. Fages' first pinpoint high kick to the corner saw Tommy Makinson out-jump Kristian Inu in typical style to touch down. With Coote absent, Makinson also took on the kicking duties and landed an excellent conversion from out wide.

Salford responded well initially, with Kallum Watkins' spill from a Kevin Brown pass ending one of a couple of promising attacks. At the other end Mark Percival had a try ruled out for a forward pass from Jonny Lomax, who then had his own effort disallowed for a double movement.

Inu almost hit back but for a terrific Kevin Naiqama cover tackle, before Makinson slotted a penalty awarded for Jack Ormondroyd being offside when he picked up another mistake.

Another handling error saw Saints score their second, with Lomax scooping up the loose ball and sending Regan Grace to the corner.

An outstanding tackle from Dan Sarginson prevented Makinson getting his second but Saints extended their lead moments later when stand-in fullback Jack Welsby kicked a field goal after the half-time hooter had sounded.

The second half started in dramatic fashion when Paasi had to be helped from the field. Thompson was then held up over the line by outstanding defence from the Red Devils, who then wasted their own chance when Sarginson ran behind his own player on attack.

But Salford eventually hit back. Addy took them close with a dogged run from dummy-half, before Tui Lolohea picked his floated pass perfect for Sio to finish. Inu added a superb touchline conversion to reduce the gap to seven points.

But the comeback lasted a matter of minutes. Again a Fages kick created the try for Saints and this time Percival was the beneficiary for his first try since the 2019 Grand Final against the same opposition.

Inu saved another certain try by batting down Fages' pass after a Lomax and Grace long-range raid but then he made another crucial mistake when he spilled Fages' latest spiralling kick and Kevin Naiqama was on hand to collect and touch down. The scoring was completed when Alex Walmsley charged over.

The second game of the Friday night was much closer, as promoted Leigh gave neighbours Wigan a scare before succumbing to a 20-18 defeat.

Jake Bibby was the scoring hero after moved from the centre to the wing, when Aussie signing Jai Field was taken off in the 19th minute with a hamstring injury that was to rule him out for several months. Bibby thrived on the flank, scoring two tries to seal a memorable comeback win.

The Centurions threatened to pull off what would have been a sensational victory as they led 18-0 after dominating the first half hour.

Wigan were without inspirational Australian stars Jackson Hastings and Bevan French, still getting up to speed after returning Down Under for close-season breaks, and injured backs Oliver Gildart, Dom Manfredi and Liam Marshall. And Leigh were also missing a string of players - backs Brendan Elliot, signed from Manly, Jamie Ellis and Junior Sa'u and forwards James Bell, former Wigan prop Ben Flower and Tyrone McCarthy, with former New South Wales hooker Nathan Peats due to arrive in the UK that week after agreeing a one-year deal following his release by Gold Coast.

John Duffy's men really hit the ground running, racing into an 18-0 lead inside half an hour through tries by inspirational skipper Liam Hood, Iain Thornley and Ben Hellewell, all converted by Ryan Brierley.

And they might well have gone further ahead had motoring stand-off Joe Mellor

Leigh's Iain Thornley and Blake Wallace combine to halt Wigan's John Bateman

been able to pick up a kick through as Leigh counter-attacked after a Wigan move broke down.

Instead Wigan finally found a way through - twice in three minutes - with Bibby and Zak Hardaker, impressive at fullback in place of French, crossing to reduce the half-time deficit to ten points.

The first score of the second half was likely to be key and, after a spell of Leigh pressure proved fruitless, it went the way of Wigan, with Joe Bullock claiming a 63rd-minute try and Hardaker landing a conversion at the third attempt.

Within another three minutes, Adrian Lam's men, with Harry Smith busy in the halves in place of Hastings, were finally in front after Bibby, his side's scorer in the dramatic 8-4 Grand Final defeat by St Helens the previous November, claimed his second try of the evening and Hardaker tagged on the telling extra two points.

On the Saturday, Wakefield winger Tom Johnstone scored two long-range tries but it couldn't prevent Leeds emerging with a 28-22 win, in a game that was technically a home fixture for Trinity.

Johnstone's first, on nine minutes, after the Rhinos had shot into a 4-0 lead through a Luke Briscoe try and were threatening again, was a beauty. Wakefield spread the ball wide from their own '20' and Johnstone sped past Tom Briscoe and around fullback Richie Myler.

It sparked an eleven-minute spell that saw Trinity shoot into a 16-4 lead with tries through right winger Innes Senior and Matty Ashurst. Debutant scrum-half Mason Lino was looking a shrewd capture.

Catalans Dragons' Mike McMeeken looks for a way past Hull KR's Jordan Abdull

Leeds coach Richard Agar handed a debut to Zane Tetevano and, with the likes of Ash Handley, Robert Lui and Konrad Hurrell out injured, there were opportunities to impress for Academy graduates Jack Broadbent and Alex Sutcliffe, with elder brother Liam filling in at stand-off.

The Rhinos narrowed the deficit when a stunning break from Broadbent was eventually finished by Alex Sutcliffe, after a last-ditch pass from Briscoe when he appeared to be heading for touch.

Eight minutes later, Brad Dwyer dived over from dummy-half in typical fashion, catching the Wakefield defence off-guard close to the line. Then, three minutes before the interval, Myler scored after an inch-perfect Luke Gale pass. And, with Rhyse Martin converting all three tries, suddenly, Leeds were ahead by six at the break.

The second half was a much cagier, closely-fought contest. It remained thoroughly entertaining though, as underlined by the try which opened the scoring in the second half.

With Leeds pressing for further points, a high, hanging Gale kick seemed to be heading for Broadbent's hands. However, Johnstone plucked the ball from mid-air with a phenomenal leap, before racing away to touch down for his second of the game.

However, despite Lino converting to make it 22-22, Leeds soon hit back with a try of their own, as Myler sent Broadbent over in the corner after a rare Trinity error handed Leeds a fresh set on their opponents' line. Martin missed the touchline conversion, leaving the game finely poised at 26-22.

Leeds' scramble improved and denied Wakefield's incisive left-side attack and when

Martin added a late penalty with five minutes remaining to send Leeds six points ahead, it was enough to hang on for victory.

In the second Saturday game, a James Maloney golden-point field goal secured a 29-28 win for the Catalans over a Hull Kingston Rovers side that had battled back from an 18-4 half-time deficit, which was stretched to 28-4 on 50 minutes, to force extra time.

Up till then the Dragons had dominated the Robins in virtually every department, controlled by the outstanding Sam Tomkins. Rovers looked clunky and rusty but showed a never-say-die attitude to score 24-unanswered points late on, only to have their hearts broken by Maloney, who slotted the one-pointer over from 20 metres out following a vital break from Dragons' substitute Arthur Mourgue, who had sat on the bench for over 70 minutes.

Rovers, under new captain Shaun Kenny-Dowall, scored some classy tries of their own, including a hat-trick to Ryan Hall, after his two-year spell with the Roosters in the NRL had produced not one try, but were ultimately made to pay for starting both halves slower than their opponents.

The comeback started when young halfback Mikey Lewis weaved his way past three defenders to score a terrific solo try before Hall grabbed a double.

Things were unravelling for Catalans under intense pressure from the Robins, with errors and ill-discipline creeping in and things got worse for Steve McNamara's side when Julian Bousquet was sin-binned for his part in a scuffle.

Rovers set up a grandstand finish eight minutes from time as Hall collected a perfectly weighted Jordan Abdull kick behind the line to complete his hat-trick on debut, which Abdull converted from the touchline to cut the gap to six points.

Hull KR kept hammering the Catalans line and, moments after Tomkins left the field with a head knock, George King barged his way over under the posts for a converted try to level matters and send the game into golden point.

The Robins received the first possession of extra time but were limited to kicking from inside their own half before Mourgue's break out of nothing set up the perfect field position for Maloney to snap over the game-clinching field goal and break the hearts of Hull KR in a thoroughly dramatic night at Headingley.

Young Dragons centre Mathieu Laguerre, from Marseilles, scored on an outstanding debut, standing in for Samisoni Langi, with the suspended Micheal McIlorum and Joel Tomkins and injured Arthur Romano also missing. Dean Whare and Mike McMeeken also made debuts.

As well as Hall, Rovers had Korbin Sims and Albert Vete making debuts.

British Summer Time had begun by the time of the final two games on the Sunday afternoon.

Hull gave new coach Brett Hodgson the perfect start as they beat Huddersfield 22-10. With Jake Connor impressive at fullback - Jamie Shaul was sidelined by an ACL injury for much of the season - the Airlie Birds proved too good for the Giants, missing captain Aidan Sezer through injury.

NRL recruit Josh Reynolds also stood out and grabbed a try on debut. The former NSW stand-off was Hull's only debutant, whereas the Giants had six players pulling on the Claret and Gold for the first time in a first-class game - Ricky Leutele, Jack Cogger, Luke Yates, James Cunningham, Joe Greenwood and Josh Jones.

After a cagey opening, Hull were always in control from the moment they went ahead with two tries in the space of five minutes around the midpoint of the first half.

Connor weaved his way in on the right on 17 minutes and five minutes later centre Josh Griffin, also up against his former club, changed direction to crash over on the left.

Both were converted by captain Marc Sneyd, who then added an early second-half penalty. And it was Sneyd's clever close-range kick through that took Hull out of sight just past the hour, with Reynolds sharpest to react and touch down.

Sneyd added the goal, then another penalty to stretch the Black and Whites' lead to 22-0 before Huddersfield finally got on the scoreboard with 12 minutes left as former NRL

March

Grand Final winner Leutele got over on the left and then James Gavet ran in to score from the final play.

In the final game of the weekend, Castleford got off to a flyer with a 21-12 win over Warrington.

The Tigers had to overcome some adversity. Gareth O'Brien, who deputised for Danny Richardson, out with a hand injury, was forced from the field on 25 minutes with a head knock and didn't return. That meant 2020 Man of Steel Paul McShane moved to halfback alongside Jake Trueman and, together, they were key to the victory.

Trueman's kicking game, particularly from close range in the first half, was destructive. McShane was measured, calm and a telling influence in attack and defence, debutant Niall Evalds also impressing at fullback and another debutant Jordan Turner scoring two tries on the left wing.

Trueman, the Albert Goldthorpe Rookie of the Year in 2018, suffered a frustrating 2020 season disrupted by injury and coach Daryl Powell was tipping him for England selection.

Off-season signing Rob Mulhern made a debut off the bench for the Wolves but there was no place for Greg Inglis. Club chief executive Karl Fitzpatrick was cautious over when GI would make his Super League debut. Inglis had spent the past two years out of the sport and had been training with the Wolves for the past three months.

Castleford were on the front foot almost from the kick-off and within five minutes had taken the lead. When a deft kick from Trueman saw Josh Charnley miss not once, but twice in an attempt to swat the ball dead, Oliver Holmes was on hand to touch down just before the ball went out of play.

However, two minutes later, Warrington struck back when a towering kick from Stefan Ratchford tested Evalds and Toby King jumped highest to pluck the ball out of Evalds' grasp and touch down. Ratchford missed the conversion, though, leaving Castleford ahead by two.

As the half-hour mark approached, Evalds marked his Castleford debut with a brilliant individual try, bamboozling young centre Connor Wrench with some clever footwork to force his way through a gap and touch down. With O'Brien off the field, Peter Mata'utia took over the goal-kicking duties and was off-target, leaving the score at 10-4.

Then, a minute before the interval, after a Tigers penalty sprung them downfield, a wonderful cut-out pass from Evalds sent Turner over in the corner to extend the lead to ten points. It was a big moment, even if Mata'utia missed from the tee once again.

Ten minutes into the second half, Cheyse Blair had a try disallowed for a knock-on and, seconds later, the Wolves narrowed the gap as Jason Clark sent namesake Daryl through a gap with a well-timed pass. The hooker still had work to do, but he did it superbly, showing an impressive turn of pace. Ratchford again missed the conversion.

Seven minutes later, Evalds and Turner combined to send the latter over for his second try, though not without a bit of luck in the build-up, as a loose carry bounced into the hands of McShane. He took over the kicking duties, nailing it from the sideline to make it 20-8.

And as Warrington toiled away without any luck to try and claw back the gap once again, McShane stepped up when it mattered to kick the first field goal of his professional career and establish a three-score lead with nine minutes remaining. Warrington did register a consolation when a Ben Currie break was finished by Blake Austin but the damage had long since been done.

BETFRED SUPER LEAGUE
Sunday 28th March

	P	W	D	L	F	A	Diff %	Win %
St Helens	1	1	0	0	29	6	483.33	100.00
Hull FC	1	1	0	0	22	10	220.00	100.00
Castleford Tigers	1	1	0	0	21	12	175.00	100.00
Leeds Rhinos	1	1	0	0	28	22	127.27	100.00
Wigan Warriors	1	1	0	0	20	18	111.11	100.00
Catalans Dragons	1	1	0	0	29	28	103.57	100.00
Hull Kingston Rovers	1	0	0	1	28	29	96.55	0.00
Leigh Centurions	1	0	0	1	18	20	90.00	0.00
Wakefield Trinity	1	0	0	1	22	28	78.57	0.00
Warrington Wolves	1	0	0	1	12	21	57.14	0.00
Huddersfield Giants	1	0	0	1	10	22	45.45	0.00
Salford Red Devils	1	0	0	1	6	29	20.69	0.00

APRIL
A bigger picture

Round 2

The first weekend of April marked the Easter period, over which there was only one round of games in 2021.

That weekend across both the UK and Australia, Rugby League was dedicated to supporting stricken Hull KR star Mose Masoe, who had been diagnosed as tetraplegic, meaning partial or total loss of use of all four limbs and torso, after his tragic accident in a friendly match at the start of 2020.

Fans in the UK were urged to buy 'virtual tickets' for Super League's Mose Masoe round, whilst a 'We Stand With Mose' campaign was launched across the NRL by the Men of League Foundation.

All Super League clubs supported the cause and a number carried his name on their number ten shirts, which were then put up for auction. Other teams 'paid to play' and some stars auctioned their shirts and boots to further boost funds. Clubs and players shared videos on social media urging fans to back the campaign while sending messages to Masoe and his family.

Super League's Mose Masoe Round raised more than £100,000 for the recently-established Mose Masoe Foundation.

The Thursday night saw the two English clubs that Masoe represented meet in a round where all games were played at the Totally Wicked Stadium at St Helens.

'Home' team Hull KR, five days after their golden-point defeat to Castleford, were competitive for the majority of the game, bar lapses, first in the opening ten minutes and then when they were reduced to twelve men in the second half after George Lawler was sin-binned. But they never looked likely winners, as the likes of Theo Fages, Jonny Lomax and James Roby produced unstinting consistency to steer Saints to a 25-0 win.

Rovers had to overcome early adversity with the loss of prop Korbin Sims to concussion. And Elliot Minchella later suffered a season-ending knee injury. Sims had to be withdrawn after less than three minutes for a head injury assessment. By the time he was able to return his side was 10-0 down. He soon copped another head knock and was subsequently ruled out for the rest of the match.

Saints were again without fullback Lachlan Coote and were missing Mark Percival and Agnatius Paasi from their opening-round win over Salford, with Josh Simm coming in at left centre and Joe Batchelor onto the bench.

But they raced into a lead after three minutes when Regan Grace took a Lomax pass above his head and somehow stayed in the field when stepping past Adam Quinlan to score. Tommy Makinson added the conversion from the left touchline. And Saints crossed again shortly afterwards. The try was sparked by Matty Lee's offload to Roby, before Fages broke the Robins' defensive line and handed onto the supporting Jack Welsby - who was excellent throughout - to finish.

The Robins steadied and put together some attacks, with a bouncing ball just beating Ben Crooks to the dead-ball line and showed increased steel at the other end of the field, keeping Saints out during three consecutive sets.

After the break, it was a measure of Saints' respect for Rovers' defence when Makinson took the two points after a penalty for offside. That defence held up both Kyle Amor and Aaron Smith over the line, with Fages slotting a field goal for 13-0 in between.

The Robins' resistance eventually broke when Lawler was sin-binned for slowing down a play-the-ball on his own line. Moments later Smith scooped up an offload from Alex Walmsley and forced his way over. And the scoring was completed when Grace took a superb Welsby cut-out pass to collect his second.

The first game of the Thursday saw Wigan eventually run away to a 34-6 win over Wakefield.

Jake Bibby started on the right wing to maintain his bright scoring streak with a first career hat-trick as Wigan came from behind to win for the second match running. Zak Hardaker was another to shine for Adrian's Lam's depleted side as he continued to excel at fullback in the absence of Bevan French.

As in the defeat by Leeds in their first game of the new term, Trinity had periods of pressure but having notched 22 points against the Rhinos, they were limited to just a David Fifita try and Mason Lino conversion which gave them a 21st-minute lead.

The first-half loss of prolific winger Tom Johnstone, who failed a head assessment after a challenge by Willie Isa, blunted Trinity's attack and with second row James Batchelor moving into the centre, the Warriors exploited the defensive hesitancy ruthlessly.

At the time of Johnstone's exit, Wigan were back on level terms through Oliver Partington's try and the first of five Hardaker conversions from six attempts. And the Warriors stepped up a gear after the break, with Bibby's three tries sending him to the top of the tryscoring table. Hardaker and non-stop John Bateman also crossed.

On Good Friday, Warrington clicked into gear with a 44-12 win over Leigh, Tom Lineham and Toby King both scoring try-doubles.

The Wolves brushed aside a gallant challenge from the Centurions, leading 22-0 at half-time and going on to double their score in the second half, although Leigh did touch down twice and their spirit was demonstrated by Ryan Brierley scoring the last try of the game for them on 78 minutes.

Two tries in four minutes around the quarter-mark as good as settled the contest, some slick passing freeing up King for a simple score on the left and Josh Charnley then running inside to create space wide on the right for Jake Mamo to cleverly touch down. Gareth Widdop was in stunning form and his try in the 37th minute was a killer blow.

That week Warrington confirmed that Daryl Powell would take over as head coach at the end of the season.

The second Friday game was a much closer affair as Powell's current club Castleford edged Leeds 18-10. The Tigers went into the game celebrating four milestones, with Michael Shenton and Liam Watts marking 400 and 300 career games respectively. Paul McShane was playing his 150th game for the club while Peter Mata'utia was playing his 150th career game.

Leeds who, despite having Brad Dwyer coming off the bench for his 200th career appearance, had a largely youthful backline on display as injuries continued to hit them hard. Richie Myler had to pull out of the game earlier in the week with a hamstring injury, prompting Jack Broadbent to move to the unfamiliar position of fullback and handing Corey Hall, who came off the bench twice in 2020, a first Super League start in the centres.

The Tigers too were forced into changes from the team that beat Warrington five days earlier, with Danny Richardson and Watts coming into the starting line up to replace the unavailable Gareth O'Brien and George Griffin, with Tyla Hepi and Jesse Sene-Lefao on the bench. But despite all this Leeds still had enough in them to push Castleford all the way and it was only a late try by impressive new signing Jordan Turner that sealed the win.

Hull FC's Ligi Sao wrapped up by Salford's Harvey Livett and Elliot Kear

The Tigers edged the first-half scoring as Oliver Holmes and Niall Evalds tries gave them a 12-4 lead, with Luke Briscoe replying for the Rhinos. The second half was a fierce contest and Leeds threatened when Matt Prior stretched out from close range just after the hour mark. Rhyse Martin converted to cut the deficit to two points. But ten minutes later Turner finished off a slick move involving Evalds to give Cas a buffer late on.

On the Saturday, Hull FC dominated Salford in a 35-4 win. Josh Reynolds grabbed two tries as Hull made it two wins in two games as Jake Connor laid on scores for Andre Savelio and halfback Reynolds to help establish a 14-0 half-time lead.

Reynolds crossed again five minutes after the break and Josh Griffin followed four minutes later to kill off Salford. Ken Sio's try in the corner put the Red Devils on the board but they never looked like avoiding a second successive loss and Cameron Scott's try sealed Hull's victory.

Salford's misery was compounded by the loss of Dan Sarginson (ribs) and Elijah Taylor (shoulder) while Hull lost Reynolds (hamstring) and Marc Sneyd (dead leg) to injury in the second half.

In the final game of the round, Catalans also made it two from two with a 20-10 win over Huddersfield, orchestrated superbly by fullback Sam Tomkins.

Catalans led 20-6 at the break after three tries to Huddersfield's one, and the very fact the Giants kept their opponents scoreless after half-time underlined an improved display. It was, however, too late to win the game. And once again, the absence of Aidan Sezer was sorely felt.

A Tom Davies run from his own '20' set up the best and third of the Dragons' three tries. The break was matched by an equally superb covering tackle from Jake Wardle. However, Davies wriggled free, picked himself up and sent a charging Mike McMeeken over the line, with James Maloney converting to make it 20-6 at half-time, after Chris McQueen's converted try in reply to Matt Whitley's opener had levelled at 6-all on 12 minutes.

31

April

Benjamin Garcia got the Dragons' second, converted by Tomkins with James Maloney in the sin bin for a cannonball tackle. Maloney faced no charge from the Match Review Panel.

Sam Wood crossed for Huddersfield on 58 minutes from a superb cut-out pass from Lee Gaskell. But there was no way through after that and with five minutes remaining, Huddersfield's woes were compounded when Joe Greenwood was shown a red card following a high shot on Samisoni Langi. He got a three-match ban.

Challenge Cup Round 3

The opening rounds of the Challenge Cup were truncated as Covid-19 wreaked havoc on the lower league competitions.

Community clubs were unable to enter as no amateur Rugby League had taken place that year. With third-tier League 1 not scheduled to kick off until May, only Barrow, Keighley and West Wales Raiders decided to enter in the first round. All three were knocked out. Toulouse chose not to enter in the light of ongoing international travel restrictions.

By the time the Super League clubs entered in round three, four Championship clubs remained in Widnes, York, Swinton and Featherstone.

All were knocked out by Super League opposition. Salford got their first win of the year as former St Helens centre Matthew Costello and Morgan Escare celebrated their Salford debuts in style with two tries in a 68-4 rout of Widnes. Former Toronto prop Darcy Lussick also impressed on his Red Devils debut.

York City Knights suffered a 26-0 defeat to Wigan in an entertaining encounter at the LNER Community Stadium. There was a maiden first-team try for teenager Umyla Hanley, the 19-year-old son of ex-Wigan, Leeds and Great Britain star Ellery.

Warrington were made to work hard for their 32-8 win at Swinton Lions, three Wolves tries in the last seventeen minutes of the first half effectively deciding the tie, Toby King collecting a double.

And Hull FC had their tie at Featherstone sewn up by the break, Jake Connor doing most of the damage in a first half that finished 34-4, the Airlie Birds going on to win 34-14. Scrum-half Marc Sneyd missed the match because of a dead leg and partner Josh Reynolds was out for between four and six weeks with a hamstring injury.

There were two live games on BBC television on the Saturday and in the first there was an amazing performance from a Leeds Rhinos team shorn of several stars, including all of their halfbacks, against a St Helens side that was running hot. In the end Saints scraped through by 26-18 and this after Leeds' marquee player Zane Tetevano was sent off for a late challenge on Theo Fages. Tetevano was later banned for four games.

Saints led 20-6 after a strong start to the second half against twelve-man opposition - with Regan Grace bagging a try-double but allowed their visitors back into the tie and needed a late try by Tommy Makinson, his second, to put the game to bed.

Brad Dwyer led the Rhinos' fightback with two tries after he came off the bench. Fijian prop King Vuniyayawa and 17-year-old back-rower Morgan Gannon both made debuts in a side that had two back-rowers, Rhyse Martin and Cameron Smith, starting as the halfback pairing.

It was a very competitive game that prop Agnatius Paasi helped win when he came off the bench.

In the second match, Catalans had to produce their best game to emerge 26-6 winners over Wakefield.

Both sides went close in the early stages but, after forcing another set through a goal-line drop-out and beginning to build pressure, Catalans did manage to take the lead as Sam Tomkins picked up Josh Drinkwater's pass to step inside from the left and reach out to dot the ball down on the line.

Castleford's Jordan Turner races through the Hull KR defence to score a dramatic late try

However, Trinity hit back when they kept the ball alive on the last tackle and attacked the left flank, with Tom Johnstone sending a delightful kick back infield from the touchline for Mason Lino to dive over unopposed next to the sticks.

After Joe Westerman was then penalised for a high tackle on Ben Garcia directly in front of the posts, the French side opted to kick for goal, with James Maloney nudging Catalans two points ahead.

With a matter of seconds left on the clock until half-time, Trinity once again opted to go down the left flank and Johnstone attempted to finish the move acrobatically in the corner. But a superb cover tackle from Tom Davies forced him into touch and made sure the Dragons held a narrow 8-6 lead at the break.

After the turnaround, Lino kicked the ball out on the full and gifted Catalans good field position before Drinkwater dummied his way through the line and crashed over. Then Catalans once again earned a couple of repeat sets, shifting the ball well from left to right for Mike McMeeken to put Davies over in the corner.

The Dragons then added their fourth effort of the evening as Garcia managed to offload in the tackle to Gil Dudson, who had the simple task of finishing underneath the sticks for his first Catalans try.

On the Sunday, Huddersfield secured their first win under new coach Ian Watson, by beating Leigh 36-18, helped by a hat-trick of tries from winger Jermaine McGillvary.

The Giants raced to a 20-6 half-time lead but had to hold off a Leigh comeback late in the second half, while both teams had players yellow-carded for dubious tackles in a full-throttle encounter at the Leigh Sports Village. With Aidan Sezer still missing, Jack Cogger stepped up and controlled the game. Ben Flower and Nathan Peats both made their Centurions debuts.

April

The biggest drama had happened on the Friday night at Hull KR when Gareth O'Brien struck in the 99th minute of the game, with his field goal finally winning the tie 33-32 for Castleford - in the fourth period of golden point. It came five years after the 29-year-old kicked the winning field goal for Salford in golden point at the same ground in the Million Pound Game.

Castleford were behind 22-6 at half-time and then trailed 32-18 with ten minutes left but fought back both times to tie the score up with an unconverted Jordan Turner try right on full-time. Paul McShane was at the heart of Castleford's comeback on both occasions, with the reigning Man of Steel nabbing a close-range brace for his efforts.

The Tigers then fought in exhausting extra time to sensationally steal the victory after both sides had tried and failed to settle the outcome with a series of drop-goal attempts.

* There was a minute's silence at each Challenge Cup match over the weekend to commemorate the life of HRH Prince Philip, the Duke of Edinburgh who, on the Friday, died at the age of 99 years.

Round 3

Former St Helens and England halfback Kyle Eastmond made his Super League return in the Thursday game after a nine-year sojourn in rugby union, as Wigan continued their 100 per cent start to the season with a 19-6 win over Leeds at Headingley.

Eastmond was outshone by Wigan's Jackson Hastings, who produced the moments that mattered, including an impudent try that gave Wigan the lead for the final time on 59 minutes and two assists.

Fullback Zak Hardaker continued his great form, running for 184 metres and scoring a majestic solo try just after the half-hour, spotting young Leeds fullback Jack Broadbent up in the line and James Donaldson injured. Calling for the ball on the short side, Hardaker chipped over into the corner with supreme precision before out-sprinting the cover for a sublime pick-up and dot-down. He also capped off a tough win with a last-minute field goal.

Eastmond finally made his debut six weeks after signing a two-year contract with Leeds. After a quiet first half as he partnered second row Rhyse Martin in the halfbacks amid the Rhinos' halfback injury crisis, Eastmond grew into the game, defending solidly, producing a peach of pass for the Rhinos' sole score from Alex Mellor on 45 minutes, being vocal throughout and taking on the kicking role.

It was another valiant effort from a depleted Leeds side, led by Mikolaj Oledzki, who was fresh from his first England training camp two days before. Oledzki led the meterage stats for the game with 188, alongside making 44 tackles and playing for the majority of the 80 minutes.

Wigan were short of centres and backrower Liam Farrell continued in the left, finishing with two tries, including the game clincher eight minutes from time.

The Friday TV game produced a belter as Hull KR got their first win in dramatic fashion, a 25-24 home success over Huddersfield.

It was breathless from start to finish with Ben Crooks scoring the fastest try in Super League history and Jordan Abdull's seventy-seventh minute field goal ending a stirring second-half fightback from the Giants.

Crooks - recalled to the side in the place of the injured Greg Minikin at centre - etched his name into Rugby League record books after a colossal moment of miscommunication from the visiting side. At referee Liam Moore's whistle for kick-off, Abdull planted a looping kick towards the Giants' left flank. The returning Aidan Sezer appeared to call to Jake Wardle, heading in from the touchline to hold his position, Sam Wood overstepped on the wing and when the third rebound leapt back in-field, Crooks

Warrington's Blake Austin attempts a field goal against Hull FC

suddenly materialised to seize the loose ball and gleefully dive over the line. The clock read seven seconds.

Crooks then worked a second try prior to Mikey Lewis's score as the Robins, despite the loss of prop Korbin Sims early on with a head knock, shot into an 18-0 lead, Abdull kicking three conversions by the half hour.

But the Giants got a crucial try just before the break, Jermaine McGillvary moving clear of Luke Dorn into eighth outright on Super League's all-time tryscorer charts with 171 tries after benefitting from in a Kenny Edwards-Leroy Cudjoe combination wide on the right.

With Lee Gaskell off the bench in the second half, the Giants clicked into gear and scored some fine tries, from Darnell McIntosh, Jake Wardle and Chris McQueen, who was deemed to have fumbled the ball backwards chasing a kick in goal, giving Huddersfield a narrow lead.

A see-saw last act saw Kane Linnett seize the lead back for the hosts after McGillvary spilled a towering kick from Abdull, before Gaskell and Wardle combined to send McIntosh in for his brace with a half-field-length effort.

Sezer missed the goal kick before Abdull's field goal sealed it for Rovers, for whom forwards George King and George Lawler stood out.

On the same night Jack Welsby was again prominent as St Helens made it three wins from three with a 34-6 home win over Wakefield in the archetypal game of two halves.

The champions were held to 0-0 at the break by a Trinity team that stood tall up front and matched their much more fancied opponents physically. But an early second-half error as Ryan Hampshire and Lee Kershaw made a hash of collecting Saints' first downtown of the half changed the whole dynamic of the game and little over ten minutes later the contest was effectively over after three converted tries.

April

Youngster Welsby scored one and made another and later he added two more assists in another assured display. Kevin Naiqama and Regan Grace both finished with try-doubles.

Win-less Trinity were set to be without star winger Tom Johnstone until at least the middle of May after he suffered a succession of head knocks, concussed in successive games, against Wigan and in the Challenge Cup defeat by Catalans. Centre Bill Tupou and back row Matty Ashurst were also missing with injury.

Promoted Leigh were given a tough night at Castleford as they were outclassed 52-16 by the unbeaten Tigers. A Michael Shenton try on the half-time hooter to make it 34-0 ended the contest, with Paul McShane again in total control.

Lewis Bienek made his Tigers debut off the bench while James Bell and Josh Simm made their debuts for Leigh

The following night in Perpignan, Catalans Dragons also dominated from start to finish, emerging 42-6 winners over Salford.

James Maloney oozed class in a dominant role in the halves and with a near-perfect goal-kicking display, kicking seven from eight attempts. Fouad Yaha was the main beneficiary, collecting three second-half tries.

The sole game on the Sunday also provided a piece of history - a draw for the first time since golden point was introduced in Super League in 2019, with nothing to separate both Hull FC and Warrington after a frantic 90-minute contest in east Yorkshire.

Ten minutes of extra-time could not produce a single point as the game ended 14-all.

After a cagey and try-less first half, Marc Sneyd and Stefan Ratchford swapping penalty goals, the second half was anything but, with some exciting end-to-end action concluded by a converted Jake Mamo try on the final hooter to level up the game before a staggering nine missed attempts at field goals between both sides resulted in a share of the spoils for the first time since 2018.

Sneyd, who had so often got Hull over the line with his boot, missed four field-goal attempts, one of which was in regulation time, whilst his team-mate Jake Connor missed two hurried shots.

For the Wolves, Blake Austin missed three attempts, the last of which was blocked by a desperate charge down from Andre Savelio, whilst Gareth Widdop also dragged one wide in a game that had a bit of everything.

A converted second-half try from Jake Connor was cancelled out by Chris Hill but Carlos Tuimavave's try ten minutes from time looked to be enough for Hull, with back-rower Jordan Lane outstanding, to win a fourth straight game. But Mamo's last-gasp score saw Widdop land the goal to take the game into golden-point.

Round 4

St Helens kept their 100 per cent record intact in the Thursday-night TV game but were made to work hard for their 18-10 win at the so-far point-less Huddersfield Giants.

Saints could and probably should have been more than 12-0 to the good at half-time, with the help of tries by busy Theo Fages, supporting Jack Welsby's take of a high Lachlan Coote kick, and the returning Mark Percival.

Following the pattern of previous defeats, Huddersfield were once again better in the second half and a spell of pressure following a 40/20 by Jack Cogger was rewarded when Chris McQueen, playing in the centres rather than the second row, crossed from a smart handling move.

But Jonny Lomax's 63rd-minute score, after a galloping upfield run by Regan Grace and a lovely pass by the recently introduced Lewis Dodd, plus Lachlan Coote's third conversion from as many attempts, provided Saints with a 14-point cushion.

And while Jermaine McGillvary went over with eight minutes remaining and Aidan

Sezer added the goal, Saints saw the match out comfortably enough to make it five wins from five in all competitions

Something had to give on the same night as two one hundred per cent sides met at the DW Stadium and it was Castleford's record that took a hit as Wigan won a tight encounter 22-12. The result was in doubt right until Wigan hooker Sam Powell took advantage of some tired defending to touch down in the 76th minute and seal the victory for the Warriors.

Bevan French played his first game of the season and found himself on the wing due to Zak Hardaker's brilliant form at fullback. He didn't seem to mind as he scored a brace of tries. French played in place of Umyla Hanley, while Harry Smith also started for the first time this year with Tommy Leuluai missing out with a sternum injury.

Castleford opened the scoring after 15 minutes as the ball was spread wide and Peter Mata'utia produced a fine offload under pressure to send Derrell Olpherts in at the right corner. Paul McShane converted from the touchline. Hardaker converted his own try to level it up at 6-6.

Wigan's ill-discipline was becoming a problem as they conceded two penalties in quick succession and McShane calmed the situation down by slotting over a penalty to put the Tigers back in front.

Despite not playing well in the first half, the Warriors led at break after they spread the ball from right to left with Smith, Hastings and Liam Farrell all involved as French shot over in the corner for his first try of the season. Hardaker converted from the touchline for a 12-8 lead at half-time.

The Tigers levelled within seven minutes of the turnaround. It looked like French had produced an amazing try-saving tackle to stop Olpherts as referee Chris Kendall wiped it out. But after a word with his in-goal touch judge Kendall awarded the try. McShane failed to convert.

Wigan did not let that disappointment affect them as they hit back almost immediately to go back in front. Hastings showed some great vision to spot Olpherts out of position and sent a beautifully timed kick over for French to collect and score. Hardaker hit the post with the conversion attempt but Wigan led 16-12.

Castleford threw everything at Wigan heading into the final minutes but the home defence held firm as Olpherts was thwarted just yards short as he spied his hat-trick before Powell ensured the Warriors remained undefeated.

Another perfect record went on the Saturday as Warrington came back from an 8-0 deficit to record a deserved 24-8 win over Catalans at a wild and windy Stade Gilbert Brutus

Wolves coach Steve Price dropped Blake Austin from his travelling squad as Gareth Widdop and Stefan Ratchford teamed up in the halves. With fleet-footed Matty Ashton at fullback, Ratchford was given freedom in the middle of the pitch to wreak havoc with ball and boot.

A James Maloney penalty goal and converted try - a gift as Toby King's pass out of a tackle while clearing his line bounced up for the Aussie stand-off to canter over - had the Dragons 8-0 up after half an hour. But Warrington kept their feet on the ground and two tries before half-time put them in front.

Ben Currie was first to score after a break by Daryl Clark and then King collected a clever kick from Widdop, switching the angle of attack to the left and fooling the entire Catalan defence just before half-time.

The turnaround was complete when Jake Mamo tore 90 metres up the pitch after intercepting a Sam Tomkins pass five metres from his own line just two minutes into the second half. Then Widdop collected in a scramble from a towering Ratchford bomb and crossed on a 30-metre run in the 66th minute.

Salford got their first points of the season with a 34-8 home win over Leigh on the Friday night but it took a touch of class from Krisnan Inu and the rugby intelligence of

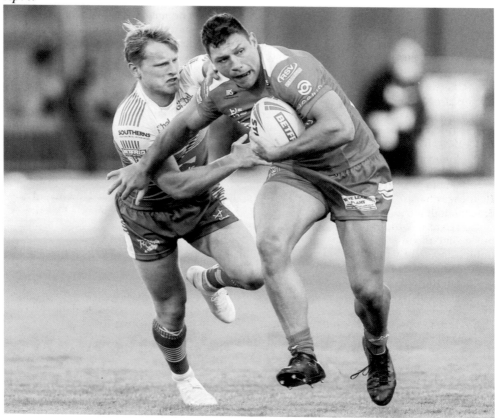

Hull KR's Ryan Hall fends off Leeds' Brad Dwyer

Kevin Brown to eventually ease them past Leigh.

The promoted Centurions were fully in the contest past the hour mark as they mounted a concerted attack while trailing by just four points. But a moment of magic from Inu turned the game decisively as he twice juggled an intercept before flicking the ball to Ken Sio, who raced 90 metres to touch down. Thirty-six-year-old Brown, the oldest player in the competition, scored his second try of the half moments later and two more tries, from Chris Atkin and Harvey Livett gave the scoreline a lopsided look.

Leigh, who handed a debut to recent signing Anthony Gelling, had an encouraging first half in which Iain Thornley scored one try and created another for a two-point half-time lead. But their late capitulation after an hour of promise spoiled their night.

In the Friday TV game, Hull kept up their unbeaten start to the season with a 20-14 home win over Wakefield. Win-less Trinity, led by the impressive Joe Westerman and busy halfback Mason Lino, caused Hull a multitude of problems, with the game only really decided by the final hooter. Wakefield didn't create the tries that their first-half pressure deserved and Hull led 8-0 from an Andre Savelio try and two Marc Sneyd goals.

But with three minutes to go to the break, right winger Lee Kershaw plucked out a cut-out pass from Jake Connor to run 95 metres and dot down under the posts. Lino's conversion made it 8-6 and it was a just reward for a Trinity side that had dominated proceedings in the first half.

Things got worse for Hull on the stroke of half-time when Bureta Faraimo was sent to the sin bin for a late shot on Max Jowitt, who was sent for a HIA and would not return. Faraimo received a two-match penalty notice the following Monday.

Wakefield picked up where they left off in the second half, forcing a drop-out in their first set but it was Hull that scored first just four minutes after the break. A pinpoint Sneyd chip was caught expertly by Adam Swift and he managed to crawl over in the corner. The halfback's conversion restored Hull's eight-point advantage against the run of play and whilst they were still down to twelve men.

Again, Wakefield refused to go away though and just five minutes later Ryan Hampshire, who played on despite suffering a broken jaw, stabbed through a lovely grubber which sat up nicely for James Batchelor, who was just able to ground the ball before he ran out of space. Lino was wayward with the conversion but Trinity were back to 14-10 with half an hour remaining.

Some big tackles managed to hold Wakefield out but the combination of Lino and Kelepi Tanginoa had the Hull defence in disarray several times.

Finally the pressure told and it was again from a Hull attack. This time Jordan Crowther charged down a Sneyd kick and the loose ball fell into the arms of Lino and the Samoan halfback ran 40 metres to the corner. Having been given the green light by the video referee, Wakefield were back level at 14-14.

Lino missed the important conversion though and Hull won it as Connor, impressing greatly at fullback, ran along the line before hitting Carlos Tuimavave with a superbly timed pass.

On the same night, Hull KR got their second win in a row, a 26-6 victory over Leeds at Craven Park.

Ryan Hall, against his old club, moved clear into second place on the all-time Super League tryscorer charts with his 200th as a Kane Linnett hat-trick helped Rovers record consecutive victories for the first time since 2019.

The injury-hit Rhinos were buoyed by the return of Ash Handley, Konrad Hurrell and Richie Myler, the latter notching up a 250th Super League career appearance. But it proved to be their own old boys club, led by Hall and Matt Parcell, who helped inspire their downfall on a sun-dappled spring evening.

The Rhinos' evening was best summed up in a flash of about-face play when Myler was sin-binned for dissent moments after his quick-tap penalty and breakaway ball for Brad Dwyer was called forward. Myler got a two-match penalty notice.

The deflation amid the Rhinos' ranks was palpable and when Linnett promptly ducked a challenge to scramble over for his third of the game shortly after, with eleven minutes left, their condemnation was complete.

Cook Islands and New Zealand forward Brad Takairangi, signed from Parramatta, was finally handed a Rovers debut after recovering from a hamstring injury picked up during pre-season.

Round 5

The last Thursday-night TV game of April provided controversy and drama, not just because home side Wigan edged Hull FC 16-14 with a Zak Hardaker penalty goal 14 minutes from the end.

Hull's Andre Savelio claimed to the referee that he was subject to a racist insult by Wigan's Tony Clubb during the first half of the game. The incident happened after 17 minutes but New Zealand-born Savelio, of Samoan descent, didn't report it straight away and took to social media after the game to explain his actions.

Wigan suspended Clubb from all club activities and joined with Hull FC to investigate the allegation. It was an embarrassment for the RFL. Rugby League took part that weekend in a sport-wide social media blackout aimed at tackling online abuse, while throughout the season players were being encouraged to make a stand against racism for 13 seconds before every game with the sport's 'Tackle It' initiative.

At the RFL tribunal the following Tuesday, Clubb accepted there had been an angry verbal altercation when the two players confronted each other at a play-the-ball and that he did use the word 'Polynesian'. But he claimed that it was in a different context to the one described by Savelio on social media.

Clubb was handed an eight-game ban, the lowest possible sanction he could have received after being found guilty of a Grade F offence of offensive language. The Wigan club fined him a further two weeks' wages which was put towards a training programme through the club's Education and Community departments targeted against abuse based on ethnicity.

The game itself was a bruising encounter between two unbeaten teams. The Warriors led 10-8 at half-time, with Jackson Hastings in irrepressible form, opening the scoring with a dummy near the Hull line that opened up a huge gap that even he seemed surprised about. Eight minutes later, Jake Connor went blind from dummy half close to the Wigan line and sent out a perfect long pass for Adam Swift to dive in the left corner.

Hull lost Scott Taylor to an ankle injury and then Connor to the sin bin for a high tackle on Hardaker but they led 8-6 after Marc Sneyd added a penalty to his earlier conversion.

But Wigan made their extra man count just before the hooter as they received another six and Liam Farrell was found on the left by Hastings, with the backrower-cum-centre evading the Hull defence over 20 metres to touch down. Hardaker was off target but the Warriors led 10-8 at half-time.

It was all Hull at the start of the second half and they went back in front when Mahe Fonua leapt the highest and picked Sneyd's kick out of the air ahead of Bevan French to score. Sneyd couldn't convert but Hull led by two again and went four points clear with Sneyd kicking another penalty after John Bateman was penalised for a late shot on Ligi Sao.

Within six minutes Jake Bibby touched down in the right corner after precision wide passing from Hastings, Harry Smith and Willie Isa. The conversion was missed, and the scores were locked up at 14-14.

Wigan got the winning points when more ill-discipline from Connor saw him slap Hastings as the Wigan halfback tried to play the ball near the Hull line. Hardaker kicked the easy goal from the penalty and there were no further scores.

St Helens remained the only other 100 per cent side the following night with a harder-than-expected 22-12 win at point-less Leigh.

Leigh dominated a first half that finished 6-all - Matty Russell's try cancelling out one from Sione Mata'utia a minute after Theo Fages was sent to the sin bin - winning eight penalties to Saints' two, and five set restarts to one.

The second half saw St Helens cruise into an 18-6 lead. Two set restarts created pandemonium for the Centurions' defence and Jonny Lomax capitalised, hot-footing forty metres on the left after 42 minutes before finding Lachlan Coote for the score. The Saints fullback goaled to make it 12-6 and when Jack Welsby found a way through from Coote's pass, the fullback was again on target.

But Anthony Gelling snatched an attempted wide pass from Coote and raced 65 metres for a try, with Ben Reynolds adding his second goal, although Saints found another way through when a cut-out ball from Coote put Kevin Naiqama into space for an unconverted try.

Saints were struck an injury blow late on, when James Bentley was taken from the field on a stretcher with a broken leg. He was out until August.

Catalans bounced back from their defeat to Warrington with a 38-18 win at Wakefield thanks to a late try flurry, with winger Tom Davies finishing with a hat-trick. With 13 minutes to go and with the score at 20-18 to the Dragons, win-less Trinity thought they had taken the lead when Liam Kay shot into the left corner. But Bill Tupou's pass was ruled forward.

Within a minute Dean Whare was putting Catalans 26-18 up, after James Maloney's conversion from out wide. Maloney converted two more tries to Davies and Samisoni Langi in the last four minutes of the game.

Leeds' King Vuniyayawa tries to halt the progress of Huddersfield's Aidan Sezer

Huddersfield fullback Olly Ashall-Bott and St Helens hooker Josh Eaves both made Trinity debuts as loan cover for injuries, with Ashall-Bott scoring a fine try.

In the Friday TV game, Castleford, who had announced that week the former Hull FC coach Lee Radford would be replacing Warrington-bound Daryl Powell at the end of the season, wore down the challenge of improving Salford to return to winning ways with a 28-18 success at the AJ Bell Stadium. There was little between the sides for lengthy periods of the game but interventions from Paul McShane, Danny Richardson and Jake Trueman were crucial in the final outcome.

The game went away from the home team in a minute either side of half-time, from two instances where they had possession. The final score of a nip-and-tuck first half came right on the hooter when Richardson slotted a long-range penalty, which had been awarded for Danny Addy not playing the ball correctly, that made it 14-12 to the Tigers.

Then a minute after the turnaround, Andy Ackers, a first-half try-scorer, was pulled up for a forward pass from dummy-half deep inside his own territory and, in the ensuing set, Trueman kicked perfectly for Cheyse Blair to finish.

Richardson's goal provided the first two-score lead of the game and he then added a second penalty before halfback partner Trueman got his name on the scoresheet, supporting a Peter Mata'utia offload before accelerating through a gap and over the line.

Salford's indiscipline cost them and they were temporarily reduced to twelve men when skipper Lee Mossop - moments after his own mistake gifted the Tigers an attacking chance - was shown a yellow card for a late hit on Richardson.

Instead of signalling a late Tigers flurry though, it resulted in Salford's third try, as Kevin Brown kicked intelligently for Tui Lolohea to touch down.

Brown added a rare drop-goal conversion to speed up the restart but time was running out and the Tigers closed the game out ahead of a repeat meeting in the Challenge Cup quarter-finals the following Saturday.

On the Saturday, Warrington were given a hard time by visitors Hull KR for an hour before pulling away for a 50-26 win.

In his first game in more than two years, Greg Inglis made a try-scoring debut - it was his 200th career try - starting in the centres before switching to fullback when Matty Ashton was forced off by an ankle injury in the second half.

With Jordan Abdull continuing his good form, Rovers led 18-12 at half-time as Shaun Kenny-Dowall, Ryan Hall and Abdull scored tries, with Toby King and Ben Currie replying for the Wire. Currie added his second after the break and Inglis went over before Hall's second for Rovers levelled at 22-all.

But the Wolves pulled clear through Daryl Clark, Jake Mamo - an interception that settled the game - Josh Charnley, twice, and Danny Walker scores, with Kane Linnett's try late on consolation for Rovers, whose two-game winning run came to an end.

Huddersfield got their first league points of the season in the only Sunday match, a Lee Gaskell field goal three seconds from time giving them a 14-13 win over Leeds at a showery John Smith's Stadium. Aidan Sezer ran the show for the Giants, picking up 13 of the 14 points registered by the home side.

Liam Sutcliffe came back in for Leeds following a knee injury and Kruise Leeming surprisingly filled in at halfback as Kyle Eastmond pulled up in the team run.

The Giants led 6-4 at the break, Sezer's self-converted close-range try coming in response to Bodene Thompson's unconverted opener.

From the second-half kick-off, the hosts shifted the ball to the left and Lee Gaskell scythed through the Leeds defence before offloading to Sezer, who cantered over from 30 metres. The halfback couldn't convert but when Kenny Edwards was taken out off the ball by Bodene Thompson, Sezer sent his side 12-4 up.

After soaking up heaps of pressure, the Rhinos hit back just before the hour. Sutcliffe skipped through a massive hole and managed to feed Ash Handley, who had enough pace to cross. Rhyse Martin added the goal to bring Leeds back to within two at 12-10. Martin levelled proceedings at 12-12 two minutes later as Huddersfield were found guilty of being offside.

It looked as though the Giants had won it with Josh Jones' try from a Gaskell kick. However, the linesman saw a push on a Leeds defender and the try was denied.

From the resulting penalty and next set, Sutcliffe sent a field-goal attempt wide, whilst Sezer's effort barely got off the ground.

It was third time lucky for Sutcliffe, who finally slotted home a one-pointer with six minutes to go to make it 13-12. But the Giants won the short kick-off and Sezer restored parity a minute later. Sutcliffe sent yet another one wide as the clock wound down. And it was a superb Gaskell field goal from 35 metres out that ended the tit for tat as the hooter sounded.

BETFRED SUPER LEAGUE

Sunday 2nd May

	P	W	D	L	F	A	Diff	% Win %
St Helens	5	5	0	0	128	34	376.47	100.00
Wigan Warriors	5	5	0	0	111	56	198.21	100.00
Castleford Tigers	5	4	0	1	131	78	167.95	80.00
Catalans Dragons	5	4	0	1	137	86	159.30	80.00
Hull FC	5	3	1	1	105	58	181.03	70.00
Warrington Wolves	5	3	1	1	144	81	177.78	70.00
Hull Kingston Rovers	5	2	0	3	105	134	78.36	40.00
Huddersfield Giants	5	1	0	4	68	98	69.39	20.00
Leeds Rhinos	5	1	0	4	63	99	63.64	20.00
Salford Red Devils	5	1	0	4	68	142	47.89	20.00
Wakefield Trinity	5	0	0	5	66	154	42.86	0.00
Leigh Centurions	5	0	0	5	66	172	38.37	0.00

* April 30th 2021 was the Rugby Football League's last day at Red Hall, its Leeds home since 1995. The RFL was relocating to Quay West in Salford until work on the new RFL headquarters at the Etihad stadium complex was completed later in the year.

MAY
The fans are back

Challenge Cup Quarter Finals

A first-half try-brace for Daryl Clark and the controlling presence of Gareth Widdop saw Warrington earn a fourth consecutive Challenge Cup semi-final berth, as they beat Catalans Dragons 16-6 at Headingley in the first quarter-final clash on the Friday.

Toby King cut the Catalans open with a slippery break inside the first three minutes, flicking on to Clark thirty metres out for the hooker to dot down under the posts. And Catalans' problems were then compounded when Gil Dudson, on his 250th career appearance, was sin-binned for a high shot.

Clark doubled his haul for the evening just before the half-hour mark, when a spell of intense pressure finally told, thanks to a short-range powerplay from Chris Hill that saw the prop manage to squeeze out a pass for his hooker to touch down. Clark's tries sandwiched a Widdop penalty and it was 14-0 at half-time.

A second Widdop penalty a handful of minutes into the second half further stretched Warrington's lead. It was their last score of the game as Dudson, Josh Drinkwater - with a pass between his legs - and Dean Whare combined to put Mike McMeeken over in the right corner to spark hope of a Dragons comeback.

But Warrington's mettle rose to the occasion in a herculean final stint that saw them clock up the best part of thirty consecutive tackles inside their own 20-metre area, repelling late breaks from McMeeken and young debutant Joe Chan to hold on.

Blake Austin was back for the Wolves. With Matty Ashton set for a three-month lay-off with an ankle injury sustained in the win over Hull KR, expectations were that Stefan Ratchford would return to fullback, paving the way for Austin's return. But only a late groin strain sustained by Ratchford in the warm-up ensured that Austin made the game, fuelling speculation about his future.

Warrington skipper Jack Hughes got a one-match ban for dangerous contact.

Regan Grace marked a new contract with a hat-trick of tries and James Roby produced another indefatigable display as St Helens moved a step closer to ending their Challenge Cup drought with a 23-18 win over Huddersfield. Skipper Roby was the only remaining member of the Saints side that last lifted the trophy in 2008 and played like a man determined to repeat history. Roby played the full 80 minutes, part of it at loose forward as Saints adapted to first-half injuries to Tommy Makinson and Louie McCarthy-Scarsbrook.

The Giants led 12-10 after a fascinating first half. Giants stalwart Michael Lawrence was the first try scorer, touching down a shrewd kick from Aidan Sezer, who then converted. Saints responded soon afterwards. Theo Fages grubbered on the last tackle, the ball bounced back off Josh Jones into the arms of Grace and he beat three Giants defenders to touch down.

Jones prevented a further try when he was first to touch down Kevin Naqaima's kick ahead but Saints were dominating and soon touched down again, Mark Percival taking Jonny Lomax's cut-out pass and pushing off Jermaine McGillvary on his way to the line.

Castleford's Gareth O'Brien takes on Salford's James Greenwood and Chris Atkin

It looked like Saints would take their lead into half-time but Huddersfield finished on a high. Building pressure through a penalty, two set restarts and a goal-line drop-out, they took advantage when Adam O'Brien attacked the blindside and good hands from Kenny Edwards and Ricky Leutele gave Darnell McIntosh just enough space to produce a spectacular corner-flag finish. Sezer converted from the left touchline to give his side their two-point interval advantage.

That was wiped out by an early second-half Lachlan Coote penalty, moments after Percival had stolen the ball from Lee Gaskell close to his own line.

And Saints were soon ahead. Smooth handling from Fages, Lomax and Coote gave Grace another opening that he took with both hands to slide over, despite Gaskell's attempted tackle. When Fages slotted a field goal ten minutes later, Saints' passage to the semi-finals was looking increasingly assured.

But another kick from Sezer caused problems for Saints and, when Naiqama couldn't gather, Joe Greenwood was on hand to send McIntosh over for his second. Sezer added a second touchline conversion to make it a five-point gap, with Huddersfield revived.

Ultimately St Helens - and Grace - would have the final say. Another fluid combination between Fages and Lomax again created the space and the Welsh winger made no mistake for a third time.

Saints coach Kristian Woolf was sweating over the extent of Makinson's foot injury, suffered in the win over Wakefield, as he lasted only three minutes of his comeback game.

On the Saturday - all the ties were played at Headingley - a spirited defensive display from Hull FC laid the platform for them to move to within a third Challenge Cup final in six seasons, following a 20-10 victory over Wigan. Two tries from prop Tevita Satae ultimately proved to be the main difference between the sides.

Wigan took the lead when a slick handling move to the right involving Harry Smith led to Willie Isa providing the decisive pass for Jake Bibby, who continued his fine early try-scoring form to dive over in the corner. Zak Hardaker, who was off colour all afternoon, missed the conversion.

However, just three minutes later, Hull hit the front - a lead they would not relinquish for the remainder of the afternoon. Their first try came when a short pass from Danny Houghton led to Satae barging over the top of two Wigan defenders, giving Marc Sneyd the simplest of conversions to make it 6-4.

Five minutes later, Hull extended their lead when Wigan were caught offside at the ruck, allowing Sneyd the opportunity to nudge the Black and Whites' lead out to four points.

That was all the scoring for the first half. But it wasn't the only drama. Hardaker missed another attempt at goal with a penalty just after the half-hour mark, ensuring Hull's four-point lead remained intact, before Hull's Jack Brown was sent to the sin bin for a dangerous tackle shortly afterwards.

Brown returned just after half-time and there was an encouraging moment for Wigan supporters when Dom Manfredi made his first appearance of the season off the bench. However, by the time he had marked his comeback with a try, Hull had extended their lead further.

Sneyd uncharacteristically missed a penalty when he pushed his attempt wide of the posts but, three minutes later, he found his range again to open up a six-point lead. In a game of tight margins, it was a significant moment.

Then, as the game entered the final quarter, Brett Hodgson's side struck another significant blow, as Satae crashed over for his second of the game and, with Sneyd converting to make it 16-4, it put real daylight between the sides for the first time.

Hull now had the advantage and their defensive resilience was paying off at the other end, too. Time and time again, they would deny the Warriors with some spirited defending, ensuring they held onto that two-score lead going into the final minutes.

However, Wigan were at least able to set up a grandstand finish with two minutes remaining, when Bevan French's clever kick was pouched by Manfredi, with Smith converting from out wide.

The Warriors had one last set and one last chance. However, as they chanced their arm following the hooter, Willie Isa spilled a pass into the arms of Adam Swift, who collected the ball, raced the length of the field and booked Hull's place in the final four.

Gareth O'Brien landed a field goal in the third minute of extra time to send Castleford into the Cup semi-finals after a 19-18 win over Salford.

After a bruising and tight 80 minutes where the Red Devils gave it everything, nothing separated the two teams at a rain-soaked Headingley thanks to a dramatic last-minute Lee Mossop four-pointer. But it was O'Brien who once again proved the golden-point hero after returning from the sin bin.

Salford twice led in the first half through Harvey Livett tries but the Tigers hit back both times through Daniel Smith and Peter Mata'utia and it was 12-all at half-time.

Michael Shenton put the Tigers in front on the hour mark after a smart Paul McShane break but, with Liam Watts in the sin bin for a late challenge on Elijah Taylor, Mossop scored with 18 seconds left to send the tie into extra time.

The Red Devils were the first to go for a field goal but McShane charged down Kevin Brown's attempt, which laid the platform for O'Brien to steal the show.

Liam Watts was banned the following Monday for two games for the late tackle. He was initially given a one-game ban but it was doubled when the former Hull man, having entered a guilty plea, challenged the grading, an action an independent tribunal described as 'frivolous'. And the Tigers also lost another prop in Grant Millington after he picked up a knee injury in the win.

May
Round 6

With limited capacity crowds allowed into sporting events in the UK from Monday 17th May, most games were switched to that day.

The exception was Leeds' clash with Wakefield, which was staged on the Friday to satisfy broadcasters and which the Rhinos won in golden-point extra time by 15-13.

Wakefield were understandably crestfallen, still winless in the cruelest of circumstances, the Rhinos ending a five-match losing run with a second close shave over their local rivals. Rhyse Martin's penalty from under the sticks - after Jay Pitts had been deemed to have illegally stolen the ball from King Vuniyayawa, following a marauding Konrad Hurrell run - was the difference between the sides.

Leeds coach Richard Agar asked for his senior players to stand up both before the game to stop the rot, Luke Gale returning after a month out but easing his way back.

But more notable were the performances of some of the next generation, their energy and craft behind a revival that saw the Rhinos come from 8-0 down, despite dominating the early exchanges. Jarrod O'Connor held the ship together in midfield and 17-year-old Morgan Gannon, off the bench, showed timing and strength to keep the visitors on the back foot.

Win-less Wakefield lost forwards Jordan Crowther and David Fifita to injury within the first half hour as Joe Westerman stood out amongst a huge team effort which had them 8-0 up after 33 minutes through Liam Kay and Mason Lino tries.

But on the back of a Matt Prior ball steal from Kelepi Tanginoa and a further set restart, the Rhinos took route one to open their scoring, Martin powering over three defenders and adding the goal. Then Prior illegally prevented Westerman getting a quick play the ball on the hosts' line, Lino kicking the penalty to make it 10-6 at the break.

Leeds put together their best attack on 54 minutes when Alex Mellor and O'Connor smartly kept the ball moving and Liam Sutcliffe's finely judged pass allowed Konrad Hurrell to cross, Martin's goal edging the Rhinos in front for the first time, although Lino levelled with another penalty after a Luke Briscoe tip tackle.

Luke Gale potted a field goal but mis-cued another after Lino had levelled with a one-pointer to force the extra time.

Monday night saw fans return for Super League games, with Hull KR providing the shock of the round at the Jungle as Jordan Abdull scored with barely seconds left to earn the Robins their third win, by 26-22.

The mostly home crowd was stunned as Castleford relinquished an early 14-point lead, as well as a 20-12 half-time advantage to crash on their return home.

James Clare and Michael Shenton had crossed inside the first quarter, with Danny Richardson converting both as well as adding a penalty. But Rovers were never far away and Ben Crooks got them back into it, scoring from a Brad Takairangi pass before Matt Parcell forced his way over just before the half-hour mark. Abdull converted both to bring Rovers back to within two points.

Despite the Robins' ascendancy, Derrell Olpherts found his way to the line two minutes before half-time and, with Richardson's conversion, Castleford were eight points up at the break.

Rovers kept the Tigers scoreless in the second half whilst adding 14 points themselves. Ryan Hall finally made the pressure tell on 48 minutes from an Adam Quinlan pass, with Crooks acrobatically diving in for his second just before the hour. Abdull failed with both conversions, leaving the scores locked at 20-20.

Richardson nudged Castleford back ahead with a penalty but the stage was set for Abdull to dummy and crash through to take home the points.

Catalans defied almost everybody's expectations to inflict a 27-10 defeat on Hull FC, who were at home for the first time since Lee Radford was infamously sacked on live television in March 2020. Over 5,500 spectators were allowed into the KCOM Stadium but

Catalans Dragons' Josh Drinkwater and Benjamin Garcia tackle Hull FC's Mahe Fonua

they were left bitterly disappointed, with the Dragons inspired by Sam Tomkins.

It was 4-4 at the break as James Maloney and Arthur Mourgue slotted over penalties for the Dragons whilst Mahe Fonua crossed for the hosts.

Maloney and Carlos Tuimavave were sent to the sin bin in a fractious first half for professional fouls but things lit up straight after the break as Josh Reynolds finished off a great move just a minute in. Sam Kasiano replied for Catalans on 54 minutes and then Mike McMeeken crashed over with 15 minutes to go to turn the game on its head. Maloney poked the Dragons seven points in front with a field goal before Tevita Satae was shown a yellow card for a high tackle.

Two further tries from Tom Davies in the last five minutes inflated the scoreline but the win was just deserts for the Dragons' overall performance.

Bevan French scored one and set up another two as Wigan remained unbeaten in Super League, whilst Leigh were still without a win after a 30-16 defeat at Leigh Sports Village.

To Leigh's credit they pushed their near neighbours all the way and even stormed into a 10-0 lead when Anthony Gelling and Nathan Mason crossed in the opening quarter. Ben Reynolds was wayward for Gelling's effort but converted Mason's, before Harry Smith cantered onto a brilliant French grubber.

Smith converted to bring Wigan back to 10-6 but the halfback was off target on 31 minutes when Dom Manfredi dived over in the corner off another French assist. Back at fullback, French was everywhere and he was next to register a four-pointer, stepping the Leigh defence as Smith's conversion sent Wigan 16-10 up.

But the Centurions would not lie down and, on the stroke of half-time, Jamie Ellis dotted down a superb Ryan Brierley kick. With Reynolds' conversion, Leigh were back level.

That was as good as it got for them, however, and Liam Farrell's try and Smith's conversion on 47 minutes gave the Warriors a 22-16 lead. Jake Bibby crossed just shy of the hour mark to extend the lead to ten and the threequarter was there again to dot down three minutes later. Smith couldn't convert either try but the damage had been done.

May

Halfback Theo Fages provided the piece de resistance as St Helens extended their unbeaten run in league and cup in 2021 to seven games with a 28-0 home win over Salford.

The wily halfback dominated the game with some brilliant touches but it was Alex Walmsley who provided the first points with a trademark score. Lachlan Coote's conversion made it 6-0.

Salford were already up against it at that point as Andy Ackers succumbed to a head injury in just the second minute, whilst Kallum Watkins dropped the ball with the line at his mercy. But the Red Devils kept Saints to just a 6-0 lead at half-time.

It didn't take long for the home side to assert their dominance after the break as Fages finished off a sweeping move that involved both Coote and Jack Welsby. At this point the game only seemed to be heading one way and Kevin Naiqama made sure of that just before the hour, flying in at the corner off a Coote pass.

Saints threatened to run away with it when Louie McCarthy-Scarsbrook and Regan Grace added another two tries in the final 13 minutes, with Coote converting four from five.

Salford fullback Dan Sarginson was handed a three-match ban for a dangerous throw.

Lee Gaskell was the man of the moment for Huddersfield as the Giants held off a Wolves fightback to win for the second time in the league in 2021, recording a 26-20 victory at Warrington.

Gaskell scored both his tries in the opening eleven minutes, with the second the pick of the bunch as he cut a huge hole through the Warrington defence.

Aidan Sezer converted both and was again on target on 34 minutes when Jermaine McGillvary finished off a wonderful move. Giants captain Sezer then added a penalty just before the break to make the score 20-0 at half-time.

Quite obviously shellshocked by some magnificent Huddersfield play and the booing from a section of their returning supporters, the Wolves came out firing in the second forty minutes.

Greg Inglis somehow grounded the ball just three minutes in and Gareth Widdop's conversion reduced the deficit to 14 points, though Inglis limped off the field moments later for what turned out to be the last game of his illustrious career.

Nonetheless, the try inspired the Wolves and, following a traditional Daryl Clark effort and then a Josh Thewlis try, they were back to within two points at 20-18 with a quarter of the game remaining.

The game belonged to the Giants however and Kenny Edwards' try settled their nerves on 67 minutes, even though the Wolves added a Widdop penalty. Sezer slotted over his own penalty two minutes before the end to extend the Giants' lead to six and round off a much-deserved victory.

Round 7

St Helens' 100 per cent start to the season was ended in a tight affair in Perpignan on the Saturday night as an under-strength Catalan side edged them by 20-16.

The Dragons lost Sam Tomkins and Samisoni Langi in the warm-up, leaving coach Steve McNamara to draft in Alrix Da Costa and Matthieu Laguerre, who had trained with the reserves that morning in preparation for the following day's Elite One clash at Lezignan.

Laguerre was again solid and Da Costa's inclusion allowed the electric Arthur Mourgue to switch from the bench to fullback. But the key man was stand-off James Maloney. With blood leaking from a bandaged head-wound, he struck a perfect four from four goals and scored an early try. But it was his ferocious tackling and non-stop chatter, cajoling his team-mates into action at crucial parts of the game, which had the Covid-limited 1,000 capacity crowd singing at the Gilbert Brutus.

Catalans Dragons' Benjamin Jullien and Fouad Yaha celebrate a try against St Helens

England second row Mike McMeeken also had a great game, using his powerful frame and subtle hands to create tries for Dean Whare and Benjamin Jullien and continue his impressive form since swapping Castleford for Perpignan.

Maloney scored all the points to put the Dragons 8-0 ahead before Lachlan Coote replied with a penalty just before half-time. Two minutes after the break, McMeeken scooped up Regan Grace's dropped ball on a kick-return and fed Whare with an astounding one-handed back flick pass as he fell to the ground in a tackle and Maloney converted. Mark Percival pulled a try back before Jullien benefitted from McMeeken's crabbing run and offload.

Saints fought hard and a series of penalties conceded towards the end of the match allowed them to progress upfield, Percival picking up his second try and Grace crossing five minutes from the end. But time ran out for the visitors, who hadn't been sharp enough to be in front at any stage in the game.

The result meant last year's regular-season leaders Wigan were the only side to maintain an unblemished record in 2021. But only just. On the same afternoon at the AJ Bell Stadium, after trailing Salford for almost the entire match, Jackson Hastings kicked a field goal with just three minutes left on the clock to clinch a dramatic 17-16 win.

Wigan trailed 14-10 at the break, Harvey Livett scoring a long-range interception try and three goals, while ex-Wigan forward Jack Wells also crashed over after prop Brad Singleton reached out to score for Wigan, before Harry Smith's long-range intercept and long pass sent in Liam Farrell.

Livett added his third penalty goal on the hour mark to make it 16-10 before Singleton crashed over for his second try with Smith converting to level.

Jackson Hastings shows his delight after kicking Wigan to victory against his former club Salford

As the match entered the final ten minutes, Morgan Escare attempted a field goal from around 20 metres out but the Warriors did well to get some bodies across and block it. There was no mistake when Wigan had a go, though, as Hastings slotted over the field goal and put the Warriors in front for the very first time with just three minutes left on the clock.

It was a win at a serious cost for Wigan, their key attacking star Bevan French suffering a hamstring injury that ended his season.

Also on the Saturday Gareth Widdop was in imperious form at the Halliwell Jones Stadium as Warrington swept away the challenge of Castleford in the last twenty minutes to win 38-14. The marquee halfback crossed for a hat-trick of tries and combined brilliantly with Blake Austin and Stefan Ratchford, who were also both in good form.

First-half tries from Josh Charnley - his 186th which moved him above Ryan Atkins into fifth in the all-time Super League list - Toby King and Widdop gave the Wire a 16-10 half-time edge, after the Tigers opened the scoring through Jake Trueman and Jordan Turner then levelled at 10-10.

Widdop crossed twice within three minutes around the hour mark to pull Warrington clear and collect his hat-trick. King and Daryl Clark stretched out the lead before Turner's consolation.

In a Sunday evening game, Josh Griffin put in a powerful performance, assisting one try and scoring another as Hull FC just about clambered over the line by 18-12 against a desperate Leeds side at Headingley.

It was a great defensive performance from the Airlie Birds that won the game. A key moment came just before the hour mark. With the scores locked at 18-8 since half-time, Adam Swift, twice, and Griffin scoring for Hull through Leeds' right-side defence against Liam Sutcliffe's converted opener and a Rhyse Martin penalty, substitute Brad Dwyer ignited the Rhinos' attack, creating a break before offloading to Tom Briscoe. Briscoe was felled and then remarkably rolled over one time too many to be held up by a desperate tackle from Carlos Tuimavave.

Leeds camped near the Hull line for most of the second half but they just couldn't breach the visitors' defence until the 77th minute. Tom Briscoe finally got over the line after a number of missed opportunities following great work by Dwyer, though Martin couldn't convert from out wide to leave it a six-point ball game.

The Rhinos were on the look-out for a new halfback after dual-code international Kyle Eastmond announced his retirement from professional rugby that week. The 31-year-old made just two appearances for the club. The ex-St Helens and England player returned to Rugby League with the Rhinos on a two-year contract in March after nine years playing rugby union with Bath, Wasps and Leicester.

Jermaine McGillvary moved ahead of Leon Pryce into standalone seventh place in the list of Super League's all-time tryscorers with 174 tries after his 73rd minute four-pointer in Huddersfield's fluent 44-6 win at still pointless Leigh.

Brendan Elliot made his debut, delayed by a knee injury, for the Centurions at fullback as Lewis Tierney gave the home side a 6-0 lead after quarter of an hour. And Leigh were still in the game until Jake Wardle scored the Giants' third try on 58 minutes.

But Giants centre Ricky Leutele was a thorn in Leigh's side all afternoon and he scored two tries, with Aidan Sezer the linchpin of the Giants' third successive win.

On the same Sunday afternoon the only other winless record went as Wakefield stunned in-form Hull KR by 28-12 as the crowds returned to Belle Vue.

Bill Tupou, who was returning to the side following injury, had the Robins' right-edge defence on the ropes throughout the game, as the returning Jacob Miller and Mason Lino clicked at halfback.

Winger Liam Kay scored two fine tries on the left and Lino kicked four from four goals to see Trinity lead 16-0 at half-time.

The game was decided three minutes after the break when Shaun Kenny-Dowall passed ten metres behind him to Trinity prop Tinirau Arona who couldn't believe his luck as he raced 50 metres to score.

Adam Quinlan finished off a superb break and offload from Jez Litten and Ben Crooks finished brilliantly in the corner after Hull KR chose to run the ball on the last tackle. Jordan Abdull kicked both conversions and the Robins looked capable of a comeback at 22-12.

However Korbin Sims had only just returned to the field from the bench when he was sent off on 70 minutes following a swinging arm on Max Jowitt and that seemed to take the sting out of a possible Robins' comeback.

Wakefield still had time for one more try. Again Tupou was the architect, storming through the Rovers defence before sending Miller over. Lino converted to maintain his perfect record with the boot. Sims was found not guilty the following Monday.

Round 8

The one remaining hundred per cent record of Super League XXVI was ended on the last Saturday of May as Catalans backed up recent wins over Hull FC and St Helens with a crushing 48-0 demolition of previously unbeaten Wigan at the Stade Gilbert Brutus.

The Dragons moved level at the top of the table, alongside St Helens and Wigan, with a seven-wins-from-eight-game record, after a blistering display, former Warriors players doing most of the damage. Ex-Wigan stars Michael McIlorum and Sam Tomkins scored early tries to put their old team on the back foot as Catalans set the tone from the start.

Two refusals from video-referee Ben Thaler for try-claims by James Maloney and Samisoni Langi then followed, sparing Wigan's blushes early in the game.

Those blushes turned into hot flushes in the 30-degree heat and humidity as Catalans began to boil. But Wigan held on until just before half-time when Tomkins scored his second following a sweeping move to the left.

Just 16-unanswered points at the interval didn't really reflect the home team's dominance but it didn't take long after the break for the full brutal reality to hit home for the Warriors.

May

Not even the return from injury of captain Thomas Leuluai could inspire Wigan as they fell further behind to a Maloney penalty following a dazzling midfield dash by Arthur Mourgue, which could only be stopped by a high tackle.

Two minutes later the electric young Frenchman was high-fiving after he dummied the Wigan defence and stepped over the line from five metres out.

At 24-0 Catalans could afford to turn down the heat but Josh Drinkwater switched on the afterburners with a simple grubber and touchdown through a gaping hole in the Wigan defence, Maloney's conversion making it 30-0.

Drinkwater, having his best game of the season, quickly doubled his tally with a powerful ten-metre surge over the line, Maloney again adding the conversion. Another former Wiganer, Tom Davies, then cut loose on a 40-metre run down the right wing and provided the pass for Mike McMeeken to crash over untouched.

Despite the best efforts of a brave but bewildered Jackson Hasting from scrum-half, Wigan lacked direction and too often possession was lost through careless handling or indiscipline.

This was exposed when an exasperated John Bateman threw the ball into the face of Benjamin Jullien and the penalty put Catalans on the offensive once more, with young French winger Matthieu Laguerre scoring a try in the left corner.

Wigan's frustration boiled over in the final minutes when Zak Hardaker appeared to head-butt his England fullback rival Sam Tomkins in a tackle. It was a red card for Hardaker and a yellow for a flurry of punches thrown in retaliation by Sam's big brother Joel.

Hardaker got two matches and Joel Tomkins four at the end of a week in which it was confirmed Wigan's international centre Oliver Gildart, yet to appear in 2021 because of a groin injury, was to join Wests Tigers on a two-year deal at the end of the season.

St Helens bounced back from their round-seven defeat in Perpignan with a 34-16 Friday night home defeat of Hull FC. The reigning champions showed their class, scoring six well-worked tries - Jack Welsby helping himself to a hat-trick on the left wing - in an attacking display that stretched fifth-placed Hull's so-far miserly defence in a contest the visitors never threatened to win.

Saints found their rhythm in the opening minutes and rarely let up on the back of some exceptional attacking play from Theo Fages, Jonny Lomax and Lachlan Coote, with Morgan Knowles and Alex Walmsley leading the charge through the middle.

In the Thursday TV game, in-form Warrington ran in ten tries against Salford as they posted a 62-18 win at the AJ Bell Stadium, where the home side were down to eleven players at one stage, after fullback Morgan Escare and prop Darcy Lussick were yellow-carded for high shots within six minutes of each other in the second half.

Salford had just one win from eight league games under new coach Richard Marshall and to compound their problems they lost Harvey Livett to a leg problem, adding to an injury list which already included halfback Kevin Brown, Danny Addy and centre Matt Costello, Marshall handing Newcastle product prop Sam Luckley a debut off the bench

England halfback Gareth Widdop continued his rich vein of form and Toby King marked his new four-year contract with a double as Warrington emphatically brushed aside Salford.

With hooker Danny Walker producing an outstanding display on a rare start, Stefan Ratchford and Blake Austin offering Widdop creative support and Jake Mamo also touching down twice, the Wolves had far too much for a disappointing Red Devils team.

On the Friday, a Jordan Turner try gave Castleford the lead after only two minutes in their eagerly awaited home clash with local rivals Leeds but 78 minutes later the Rhinos had completed an amazing 60-6 win.

Led by Kruise Leeming, Luke Gale and Richie Myler, Leeds utterly destroyed the Tigers in every possible aspect as Castleford were embarrassed on their own patch.

Wakefield's Liam Kay beats Huddersfield's Jermaine McGillvary to score in the corner

The Tigers conceded eleven tries, with the Rhinos carving them up left, right and down the centre in humiliating fashion. Leeming and Tom Briscoe both recorded braces, with 17-year-old back-rower Morgan Gannon getting his first professional try.

Castleford dropped out of the top-six play-off spots after Hull KR completed a 40-16 home win over Leigh on the Sunday afternoon.

Rovers had been derailed the round before at Wakefield, when seeming as though they would be looking up rather than down in 2021. Back in front of their fans after 441 days and on a glorious afternoon, the conditions and accompanying pent-up fervour from the home faithful were ideal additives to suit the Robins' style of play and they delivered, with Ryan Hall running in three of their eight tries, to already surpass their win ratio from 2020 as Leigh once more fell away in the second half.

The home halfbacks dominated, with Jordan Abdull maintaining his impressive start to the campaign and he was matched by Rowan Milnes. Brad Takairangi was a handful throughout and Matty Storton made a fine impact off the bench.

The Centurions' losing start to the Super League season now stretched to eight games and their brought-forward round-13 game at Wakefield the following Sunday was made even more significant after early relegation rivals Trinity won their second game in a row, this week an astounding 38-12 home victory over in-form Huddersfield.

The fact that the Giants only scored two tries in the last four minutes of the game summed up Wakefield's dominance. Trinity ran in five tries in a blistering first half - Bill Tupou's converted try just before the interval putting Wakefield 30-0 ahead and they were out of sight - and two in the second to blow away the Giants on a sunny Sunday afternoon. It was the first time Wakefield had recorded back-to-back victories since October and it pushed them away from the relegation zone. Mason Lino kicked four from five and Liam Kay grabbed a beautifully worked brace in a dominant team performance.

The only downside for Wakefield was a two-match ban given to back-rower Matty Ashurst the following Monday for a dangerous throw.

BETFRED SUPER LEAGUE
Sunday 30th May

	P	W	D	L	F	A	Diff %	Win %
St Helens	8	7	0	1	206	70	294.29	87.50
Catalans Dragons	8	7	0	1	232	112	207.14	87.50
Wigan Warriors	8	7	0	1	158	136	116.18	87.50
Warrington Wolves	8	5	1	2	264	139	189.93	68.75
Hull FC	8	4	1	3	149	131	113.74	56.25
Hull Kingston Rovers	8	4	0	4	183	200	91.50	50.00
Castleford Tigers	8	4	0	4	173	202	85.64	50.00
Leeds Rhinos	8	3	0	5	150	136	110.29	37.50
Huddersfield Giants	8	3	0	5	150	162	92.59	37.50
Wakefield Trinity	8	2	0	6	145	193	75.13	25.00
Salford Red Devils	8	1	0	7	102	249	40.96	12.50
Leigh Centurions	8	0	0	8	104	286	36.36	0.00

JUNE
On or off?

Challenge Cup Semi-finals

Leigh Sports Village hosted the Challenge Cup semi-finals double header on the first Saturday of June, with a restricted crowd of 4,000 in attendance, as Castleford Tigers and St Helens won the right to meet at Wembley in July.

In the first game, Castleford produced a stunning 35-20 win over Warrington, only eight days after the 60-6 Super League home humiliation by Leeds, utility back Jordan Turner finishing with a hat-trick against one of his former clubs.

Leading 19-0 at half-time, thanks to a near-faultless display, Castleford were well on their way to their first final since 2014 by the interval, though Warrington battled gamely after the break.

The Tigers rode out a fairly even first 15 minutes to move ahead when Gareth O'Brien, deputising at scrum-half for Danny Richardson, showed great initiative to weave his way across the line from close range.

Warrington's misery was compounded when, following a break from the Tigers, Jake Mamo was sin-binned for preventing Turner from a quick play-the-ball. That gave O'Brien the simplest of opportunities to make it 8-0 from the tee.

Turner managed to squeeze his way across the line to claim his first try of the evening, before the winger claimed another score shortly after, in the moments before Mamo returned to the field. It proved to be a damaging period without Mamo, who was set to join Castleford in 2022. Turner's second came courtesy of a wonderful cut-out ball from Niall Evalds, whose return to the Castleford side from a calf injury proved to be decisive.

If that wasn't enough of a half-time buffer, a field goal from the boot of Paul McShane put further daylight between the teams

There was some semblance of a fightback after half-time. Gareth Widdop's clever pass for Ben Currie three minutes in, shortly after Joe Philbin had been held up over the line, clawed back the deficit.

Then, two minutes later, Blake Austin turned provider as he threw an inch-perfect pass for Mamo to surge through the Castleford line. The centre still had work to do and he did it superbly, beating several Tigers defenders to touch down. Suddenly, it was game on.

However, Castleford responded impressively when Jesse Sene-Lefao crossed after Evalds' assist and that seemed to calm the Tigers' nerves.

Warrington kept fighting and when Toby King bombed his way over, despite the attention of several Castleford defenders, to cut the deficit to nine points with 25 minutes remaining, it raised the prospect of a thrilling grandstand finish going into the final quarter.

But Castleford held their nerve superbly. With just over 20 minutes remaining, Evalds was again influential as Turner went over for his hat-trick, before the outstanding McShane darted his way over to put daylight between the sides again.

A late try from Josh Charnley was nothing more than consolation for the Wolves.

Derrell Olpherts celebrates Castleford's victory against Warrington

St Helens knocked out Hull FC with a hard-earned 33-18 win. Saints were 20-2 up but then had to withstand a barrage of pressure from their opponents who, at one stage, cut the deficit to 21-18 and looked like they would take the lead before a crucial interception try from Regan Grace.

Grace's effort made it 27-18 and Lachlan Coote had just enough time to rub salt into the wounds.

There was controversy, as Saints halfback Theo Fages scored a key try, with Saints 8-2 up on 25 minutes, after picking up and racing away when Josh Griffin dropped the ball close to his line as he went down with a ruptured Achilles tendon.

Hull fans were furious at what they saw as a lack of sportsmanship. But no player or coach objected.

After the break, Jack Welsby gave Saints a 20-2 lead with just over 30 minutes to play and it looked all over. But Brett Hodgson's men showed tremendous resilience to claw their way back thanks to tries from Mahe Fonua, Danny Houghton and Cameron Scott.

St Helens' Jonny Lomax bursts past Hull FC's Jordan Lane and Danny Houghton

But with time running out and Hull pushing for a stunning victory, Jake Connor's pass was intercepted by Grace and the Welshman ran the length of the field to finally seal the win. Connor was then beaten to a high ball by Kevin Naiqama for Coote to pick up the tap back and Coote's sixth goal blew out the final scoreline.

Round 13

Wakefield and Leigh brought forward their clash to relieve the fixture congestion that was expected in the summer.

With the Centurions still winless after eight rounds and having parted ways with head coach Jon Duffy in midweek and Wakefield having hammered Huddersfield the week before, a home win for Trinity was predicted. But for concentrated periods, the hosts looked in serious risk of coming off second-best against their visitors, who delivered a spirited performance in a 30-20 defeat.

Assistant Kurt Haggerty was in caretaker charge as the Centurions started much the better, holding firm despite consecutive goal-line drop-outs forced by Trinity, before opening the scoring inside the first ten minutes after an inspired last-tackle solo play from Joe Mellor. The former Widnes halfback collected his own delightful chip-and-chase to skirt around three defenders and dot down next to the posts.

Two goals from Ryan Brierley gave Leigh an 8-0 lead but Jay Pitts and James Batchelor tries turned the game around at the break as Trinity, who lost Kelepi Tanginoa early on with a leg injury, led 12-8.

Gamestar Joe Westerman powered over to make it a century of tries on his 350th career appearance before Mellor and Lewis Tierney crossed to put the Centurions 20-18 ahead with 15 minutes to go.

But, with just under ten minutes on the clock, Liam Kay, who had been kept uncharacteristically quiet to that point, seized on the gap created by Junior Sa'u darting out of the line to dive over and restore Trinity's lead for the second time.

Then, with only two minutes to spare, Jacob Miller defused a chip with a barnstorming return, a play that laid the platform for the improving Mason Lino to cut a path to the posts from almost twenty metres out.

Anthony Gelling was a stand-out in his last game for Leigh before he returned home to New Zealand in the wake of him being found not guilty of assaulting his then wife in February of 2020.

Round 9

Hull FC had an early chance to bounce back after their Challenge Cup exit when they took on finalists Castleford at the Jungle the following Thursday.

And they did just that. The Airlie Birds scored five tries to two in a 30-12 victory, with Jake Connor in scintillating form against a much-changed Tigers line-up. Peter Mata'utia was selected at fullback to replace Niall Evalds, Alex Foster came into the centres and Paul McShane moved to halfback, with both Jake Trueman and Gareth O'Brien missing from the squad.

Seventeen-year-old Jason Qareqare made his debut on the wing, despite not having been named in the original 21-man Tigers squad. And it took him less than a minute to make a huge impression.

In the first set of the game, Castleford went down the short side and good work by Danny Richardson and Michael Shenton gave the young winger enough space to skin Bureta Faraimo and then round fullback Connor in spectacular fashion over 50 metres.

But Hull recovered with Adam Swift and Mahe Fonua tries, both converted by Marc Sneyd, to lead 12-8 at half-time. The same pair both scored in the second half before Connor's try made it safe, after Sneyd was sin-binned, before Oliver Holmes grabbed a consolation for the Tigers.

Hull coach Brett Hodgson was left with problems in the centres. With Josh Griffin out for the season due to the Achilles tendon injury sustained during the Challenge Cup semi-final, Carlos Tuimavave (hamstring) and Cameron Scott (shoulder) failed to finish the game.

The following night, Warrington too put their Challenge Cup semi-final disappointment behind them to eventually claim a 38-18 win against spirited but outgunned Wakefield Trinity, who, beset by traffic issues on the M62, only arrived 45 minutes before kick-off.

Gareth Widdop was in brilliant form, with a try and seven goals, as Josh Charnley finished with a hat-trick on the back of a dominant display by props Chris Hill and Mike Cooper.

Widdop's try put the Wolves ahead and Ben Currie cemented their advantage before David Fifita's reply. Jake Mamo extended the hosts' lead before Charnley crossed for his first.

Joe Arundel gave Wakefield hope of a comeback but Charnley ran in two more tries before Lee Kershaw scored a late consolation effort before the hooter.

The day after, Leigh Centurions gave Catalans a scare before the Dragons went home with a 36-30 victory.

Not for the first time this season, Leigh were the better team in the opening 40 minutes as they took the game to the Dragons and outscored them three tries to two.

Although two of those tries came from interceptions to Ben Reynolds and Brendan Elliot, there was no denying the class of the third as Matty Gee fooled the Catalans' defence by selling them a big dummy to split them open and score.

The Dragons looked slow and sluggish in the first half despite Josh Drinkwater's tenth-minute try but they were still in the game as they reduced the deficit to six points before the break, with James Maloney touching down.

Catalans levelled the game with a brilliant try eight minutes after the break. A seemingly poor kick was sent into Leigh's in-goal and, as it looked like it was going to bounce dead, the ball was flicked back infield by Drinkwater and Samisoni Langi was on hand to score. Maloney's goal made it all square.

The Catalans were now full of confidence and they hit the front for the first time in the 51st minute when Sam Tomkins and Dean Whare combined with fast hands to send Tom Davies in at the corner. Maloney converted from the touchline for a 24-18 advantage.

Leigh had completely fallen to pieces at the start of the second half and they

Leigh's Junior Sa'u meets Catalans Dragons' Samisoni Langi head on

conceded a third try in six minutes as Benjamin Jullien scythed through some poor defending to touch down.

Substitute Arthur Mourgue once again fizzed, as he stepped through the Centurions' defence to score a fine solo effort. Maloney converted that try and added a penalty not long afterwards for a 36-18 lead and it looked like the game was over.

But Leigh would have the final say and they finished the stronger with two late tries from Ben Hellewell and Ryan Brierley. Brierley converted both and Leigh trailed by six points with five minutes remaining.

A knock-on from the Dragons in their own half gave Leigh the opportunity to salvage something from the game but they could not get the final vital score.

On the Friday night, surprise package Hull KR had put the cleaners through Salford at Craven Park, emerging 40-4 victors, that after Salford had opened the scoring.

Shaun Kenny-Dowall was in strong form as Rovers cemented their place in the top six and made it three wins in their last four games. There were first tries of the season for George Lawler and Brad Takairangi, while Ryan Hall made it eleven for the year and Kane Linnett rounded off another hugely satisfying home outing with his eighth.

To compound the Red Devils' problems, they had only one win under their belt at this stage, Pauli Pauli was sent off in the last minute for a late challenge on Jordan Abdull, although he escaped further punishment.

The game was televised live after the scheduled game between Leeds and St Helens was postponed because of Covid issues in the Rhinos camp. The fixture between Huddersfield and Wigan went the same way after seven Huddersfield players test positive for Covid-19.

Round 10

A fast-spreading strain of Covid-19 was raising levels of coronavirus infection in the UK and the following Saturday's much-anticipated clash between Catalans and Leeds was also postponed after further outbreaks at the Rhinos.

The announcement came in the week that Kevin Sinfield, recently awarded the OBE for fundraising and services to Rugby League, confirmed he was to leave his Director of Rugby role at the Rhinos at the end of the season to join rugby union club Leicester Tigers as defence coach. News also broke that back-rower James Bentley had rejected a new contract offer at St Helens to move to Leeds on a two-year deal to run from next season.

On the Wednesday, Castleford ended their four-match losing league run with an 18-12 win at neighbours Wakefield, their 15th consecutive victory over Trinity.

The match came at a cost for both teams, with knee injuries for both Gareth O'Brien and Bill Tupou, although Trinity suffered the bigger blow as it was the end of their star centre's season.

Tupou was stretchered off just before half-time with a ruptured patella tendon suffered when turning awkwardly to catch a pass, which was a brutal blow on a night meant to herald the return of Tom Johnstone following successive concussions.

Wakefield made the livelier start in front of a boisterous home crowd but Castleford struck the first blow as a delicate Paul McShane grubber was pounced upon by George Griffin for the opening try, which was the only one converted by Danny Richardson.

The hosts hit back quickly when Trinity skipper Jacob Miller stepped between two defenders and managed to stretch out and dot the ball down. Mason Lino levelled with the conversion but parity would last only ten minutes before a moment of magic. After Max Jowitt kicked out on the full, gamestar Peter Mata'utia took in an O'Brien pass and set off on a stunning inside break, cutting through the Wakefield defence before spraying out wide for Jordan Turner to dive into the corner for his twelfth try in eleven matches, making it 10-6.

Tupou's replacement, Joe Arundel, did well to prevent Derrell Olpherts from scoring early in the second half but Castleford didn't have to wait too much longer to stretch their advantage. It came from another dabbed kick, this time from Richardson, which took a deflection at close range and then squirmed agonisingly through the body of Jowitt, providing a gift for captain Michael Shenton.

The contest remained keenly-contested and would not be over, even after the Tigers' fourth try on the hour. Joe Westerman's ball-steal proved costly as the Tigers pounced, with Mata'utia capping his fine display by taking in Turner's pass and squeezing through to score.

At 18-6 down, Wakefield finally found a way through, with Miller running onto the slick grubber of halfback partner Lino for his second of the night. Lino's conversion made it a one-score difference and a Richardson field-goal attempt was charged down to ensure it stayed that way. But Trinity would not get through again. Their final chance, which saw Ashurst fling a pass intended for Johnstone into touch, encapsulated their night.

Tigers coach Daryl Powell praised Mata'utia's performance, the day after it was revealed that both the Samoa international centre and backrower Oliver Holmes were to follow their coach to Warrington next season.

In the Thursday TV game, Ben Currie's first-half try proved decisive as Warrington emerged victorious on an attritional night that saw the Wolves show their defensive teeth with a 6-2 victory at St Helens.

Currie finished a rare moment of fluidity midway through the first half and it proved to be the only try of the night.

The first half played out like a game of chess, in which the Wolves were the more tactically astute. They had the better of the opening quarter, despite Lachlan Coote's 13th minute penalty, which was awarded for interference in the tackle after Alex Walmsley had gone close.

Warrington then responded with the best move of the evening. Gareth Widdop and Stefan Ratchford combined to release winger Tom Lineham from inside his own half and Currie supported on the inside for a fine try. Widdop added the conversion but failed with a penalty just before the break to leave his side 6-2 ahead.

The momentum of the clash shifted immediately after the break. Saints dominated virtually the entire third quarter, only to be kept at bay by Warrington's determined and well-organised defence.

The game became more open in the final quarter with both sides going close. St Helens' final chance slipped away when Jonny Lomax's try-making pass to Tommy Makinson was ruled forward, meaning they fell behind Catalans at the top of the table.

So did Wigan the next night after Hull KR recorded their sixth win out of ten games, this time a surprise 18-8 victory at the DW Stadium - their first win at Wigan in twelve years.

Rovers coach Tony Smith moved Brad Takairangi to stand-off to partner Mikey Lewis following Rowan Milnes standing down after a positive Covid test and Jordan Abdull failing head injury protocols. And the two halfbacks had standout games.

Oliver Gildart and Liam Marshall both made their first starts of the season for Wigan following knee and groin problems respectively, with Jackson Hastings moving to fullback as cover for the suspended Zak Hardaker.

There were tries for Ben Crooks, Ryan Hall and Adam Quinlan but the game was won deep inside Rovers' own half as they repelled attack after attack. George King was sin-binned for repeated infringements but Rovers took a vital six-point lead just before half-time when Takairangi put Ben Crooks into the corner with a superb looping pass. Crooks converted from the touchline.

Wigan's attack continued to be thwarted after the break and just after the hour mark Ryan Hall jumped higher than Jake Bibby to collect the ball and touch down from Lewis's towering bomb. Crooks converted for a 12-0 lead with less than a quarter of the game remaining.

Gildart registered a try in the corner following a neat inside ball from winger Marshall. Harry Smith failed to convert but the Warriors were back in the game at 12-4 and they made it back-to-back tries with Smith kicking ahead and Marshall picking the ball up before sending it inside for Gildart to grab his second.

Wigan trailed by four points heading into the final ten minutes. But just when it looked like Wigan would go on and win the game, Rovers made the game safe when Lewis's cute kick back inside saw Adam Quinlan scoop the ball up and touch down under the posts. Crooks' third conversion sealed the victory.

Wigan had waived the right to re-sign old boy George Williams. The 26-year-old England international moved to Canberra on a three-year contract ahead of the 2020 campaign, but his stay in the NRL was cut short amid reports of homesickness.

The deal with Canberra included a clause giving Wigan first refusal on their Academy product should he return from Australia. But the club issued a statement saying that while they could have taken legal action to force Williams to come back to them, they had opted not to.

On the same Friday night, Huddersfield coach Ian Watson claimed a 'huge' refereeing error contributed to his side's 9-8 defeat by his former club Salford, in the first match at the John Smith's Stadium since the return of spectators to grounds.

That was despite Salford playing with only twelve men for more than half the game following the 34th-minute dismissal of James Greenwood. Referee Scott Mikalauskas showed the second-rower a red card after Huddersfield hooker Adam O'Brien was the victim of a high tackle. But Watson, whose ninth-placed side had now suffered six defeats in nine Super League matches, insisted, the culprit was Dan Sarginson. He was right, and

Warrington's Ben Currie leaves St Helens' James Roby trailing

England squad call-up Sarginson was banned for three games the following Monday.

In Huddersfield's first game in a fortnight following the postponement of their home clash with Wigan under Covid protocols, the Giants lost halfback Jack Cogger to a knee injury only eight minutes in, as well as O'Brien, and had two tries disallowed, while Aidan Sezer hit an upright with a late field-goal attempt.

Salford survived 46 minutes with a man down to scrape only their second win of the season, Chris Atkin's field goal 15 minutes from time the clincher. And they did it without captain Lee Mossop, who was injured in the warm-up.

Salford announced that week that they had signed Tongan international halfback Ata Hingano until the end of the season, with an option for a further two years.

The round was completed on the Saturday afternoon as Leigh, who had shown signs of a first win, fell to their eleventh straight defeat. Their 64-22 home loss to Hull was the biggest of the season so far and, to add to their woes, Salford's win at Huddersfield left them further adrift at the foot of the table.

Hull FC put on a spectacular show, racking up their highest Super League points tally in eight years to reaffirm their play-off credentials, despite a host of injuries. Their pack was utterly dominant, with Tevita Satae, Ligi Sao and Manu Ma'u running rampant and Andre Savelio helping himself to a hat-trick. Fijian threequarter Mitieli Vulikijapani, signed from the Army, made his debut from the bench.

June
Round 11

The last weekend of June threw up problems in Super League, problems of their own making but made worse by the on-going disruption cause by Covid. Before the season began, a warm-up game for the England national side had been programmed in for that Friday against a Combined Nations All Stars team. It was to be England's only warm-up game for the World Cup before the season end.

Clubs had agreed that Super League fixtures would go ahead that week too. When the game came around several of them realised - with players drawn for both England and the Combined Nations - that their teams would be be severely weakened. There were rumours that some clubs were refusing to release players for the game.

In the end only one game was postponed, with the fixture at Hull KR, who were sixth in Super League, against St Helens on the Friday, falling victim to Covid issues in the Rovers camp, their next two fixtures against Hull FC (July 1st) and Catalans (July 5th) also postponed before the week was out.

In the Thursday-night TV game, Warrington made six changes to the team that had won at St Helens, with Stefan Ratchford, Daryl Clark, Mike Cooper, Ben Currie and Joe Philbin selected for England and Toby King ruled out with a knee injury. That handed chances to the likes of Connor Wrench, Ellis Longstaff, Riley Dean, Eribe Doro and Ellis Robson and they took their opportunities to shine in a 44-18 home win over Leigh, themselves missing hooker Nathan Peats on All Stars duty.

Hooker Danny Walker excelled at hooker and Gareth Widdop and Blake Austin pulled all the right strings from halfback as youthful Warrington eventually eased to victory.

Austin and Matt Davis went over in the first half for a 14-0 lead as Widdop kicked three goals. An early second-half try from Liam Hood brought it back to 14-6 but the Wolves ran away with the second half, Widdop finishing the night with 20 points of his own before having to go off towards the finish with an ankle problem.

On the same night, Catalans kept their place at the top of the table but they were made to fight hard for their 16-6 win at Castleford.

Castleford were without England international Paul McShane as well as Peter Mata'utia and Suaia Matagi who had been selected for the All Stars. On the other side, Catalans were missing England call-ups Tom Davies and Sam Tomkins.

The Tigers also had a host of injuries and with star halfback Jake Trueman nursing a back injury, prop Liam Watts played 65 minutes at stand-off.

Josh Drinkwater created two of the three tries with beautifully floated passes on each wing for Fouad Yaha and Mathieu Laguerre. Laguerre's try on 54 minutes to make it 14-0 effectively ended the contest. Samisoni Langi had forced his way over on the right for the Dragons on 20 minutes and the Tigers finally got a consolation when Derrell Olpherts crossed late on.

In the third Thursday-night game, Wakefield got their fourth win of the season with a 14-6 home victory over Wigan.

Both teams were severely depleted through international call-ups, suspension and injury. Wigan's Brad Singleton, Zak Hardaker and Tony Clubb were all missing through suspension. Liam Farrell and John Bateman were picked for England, while Jackson Hastings lined up for the All Stars. Youngsters Brad O'Neill and James McDonnell were recalled from loan spells, with McDonnell playing centre and O'Neill making a debut off the bench.

Wakefield captain Jacob Miller was out with a foot injury and Trinity were also missing Liam Kay and Kelepi Tanginoa, named in Tim Sheen's All Stars squad, while Reece Lyne and Joe Westerman were in Shaun Wane's 19-man squad.

Wakefield winger Tom Johnstone created the only two tries of the first half, the first for Ryan Hampshire after a great break on a kick return and then with a step and pass for

Wakefield's David Fifita and Eddie Battye bring down Wigan's Kai Pearce-Paul

Matty Ashurst. Mason Lino kicked a penalty after Umlya Hanley had crossed just after the hourmark to give Wigan some hope, but Trinity held on.

Johnstone and forward Jordan Crowther both left the field early with knee injuries, with both sidelined until the end of August.

On the Friday night, Hull FC fought back to beat Huddersfield at the re-christened MKM Stadium, formerly known as KCOM Stadium, by 17-10.

Neither club had any representatives for the national side but they lost eight players between them to the Combined Nations All-Stars team, with the Giants the worst affected with five. Huddersfield initially named just a 13-man squad due to injuries and enforced isolation, as well as international call-ups.

With Jake Connor and Jermaine McGillvary, not selected by coach Shaun Wane, staking their England claims over in Warrington playing for the All Stars, their ravaged clubs battled on with a fine second-half comeback earning Hull FC a third win on the bounce.

Giants coach Ian Watson was already without centre Jake Wardle, back-rower Joe Wardle, halfback Jack Cogger, hooker Adam O'Brien and captain Michael Lawrence due to injury. Centre Ricky Leutele, halfback Aidan Sezer, second-rower Kenny Edwards and loose forward Luke Yates were also in the All-Stars side.

The win continued Hull's solid form and there were plenty of positives to take from it, with Mitieli Vulikijapani excelling on the wing on his first start. Jack Logan returned to his boyhood club on loan from Batley Bulldogs and couldn't have been more delighted to score his 54th-minute try that levelled the scores. And another Hull youngster, Connor Wynne, scored the winner seven minutes later, Marc Sneyd adding a field goal four minutes from time.

June

Olly Ashall-Bott had given the Giants the lead in the eighth minute of the game and Oliver Russell's conversion and two penalty goals had sent Huddersfield in at half-time 10-0 up, although Russell was sin-binned for a high tackle on the stroke of half-time. Mahe Fonua's try nine minutes into the second half, which saw Darnell McIntosh have his season ended by an Achilles injury, changed the momentum of the game.

Leeds were due to play at Salford on the Friday, for their first outing since their 60-6 win at Castleford on May 28th. But the game was switched to the Sunday to ensure the game could be completed that weekend. The Rhinos had five players involved in the representative game with a further five players only cleared to return to playing over the weekend following positive Covid 19 tests the previous week. RFL regulations allowed for any team with four or more players selected for an international to be able to request a postponement. But both clubs faced congested fixture lists already in place for the remainder of the season.

The Rhinos fielded four players involved in the international and emerged comfortable 38-12 winners.

The first half was a real firecracker with Leeds amassing 22 points against eight in a half that brought two send-offs, a sin bin, a failed HIA and an intercept try, as Richie Myler scored two sparkling tries just before the break to tip the game the Rhinos' way.

The game blew up after 15 minutes when Lee Mossop punched Konrad Hurrell to the floor after a dispute at the play-the-ball. Mossop was red-carded, as was Bodene Thompson for running in and punching. Hurrell failed his HIA. Salford forward Jack Wells went to the sin bin for a dangerous tackle five minutes later.

Luke Gale and Ryan Lannon suffered the same fate following another fracas three minutes after the break. Tries by Jack Broadbent, Kruise Leeming and Gale took Leeds home, before Morgan Escare's consolation.

It was a busy Monday for the RFL's Match Review Panel. Mossop and Gale got two matches. Thompson and Salford winger Joe Burgess, not punished in the game, got one match each, also for punching.

Leeds Alex Mellor and Tom Briscoe were found guilty of making contact with the referee as they ran in, Mellor getting one match and Briscoe none. Wells got two matches for his tip tackle, while Lannon escaped a ban.

Round 12

Round 12 was heavily disrupted by Covid issues. Salford postponed their game at home to Wakefield and Hull KR the same with Hull FC. Both were re-scheduled for the week leading up to the Challenge Cup Final.

Castleford Tigers also pulled out of their home game with St Helens because they were unable to field a 17-man squad. However, they did not have the minimum seven players sidelined through Covid issues and St Helens were awarded the game 24-0.

So Wigan v Warrington was the standalone game of the Wednesday night with the Wolves completing a 40-14 victory, their sixth successive win.

Warrington's attacking strike was showcased on both sides of the field, with centre pairing Connor Wrench and Jake Mamo doing a lot of the damage, contributing four tries between them on the back of dominant go-forward from the Wolves pack.

It was Wigan's fourth defeat in a row and with Bevan French out for the rest of the season with a hamstring injury and Zak Hardaker missing with a neck problem, they could hardly afford the ankle injury picked up by John Bateman in the All Stars game.

Mamo's hat-trick was the result of anticipation and speed, with two long-range interceptions and the other from a messed up Wigan goal-line dropout. And his enthusiasm in defence stifled Wigan's left-side attack.

Warrington, missing Gareth Widdop, stormed ahead when Wrench touched down from Daryl Clark's grubber kick before Mamo ran in from 70 metres following an interception.

Warrington's Jake Mamo touches down despite the attentions of Wigan's Jake Bibby

Matt Davis extended their lead before Sam Powell cut the deficit but Mamo intercepted again after the break. Willie Isa and Oliver Gildart tries got Wigan back in it but Jack Hughes, Ben Currie and Mamo's third wrapped up the win.

The next night, Sam Tomkins-inspired Catalans put the cleaners through the down-at-heel Huddersfield Giants, heading straight back to France, as was the Dragons' norm in 2021, with a 50-12 win under their belts.

Giants coach Ian Watson made no bones about his limited options, having been quick to admit that many members of his matchday squad like Lee Gaskell and Chris McQueen were merely picked to make up much-needed numbers, with no intention of being fielded come the match itself.

The further blows of Darnell McIntosh's Achilles injury and a season-ending ankle problem for Aidan Sezer picked up on Combined Nations All-Stars duty had deepened their woes. Will Pryce, the 18-year-old son of former Great Britain stand-off Leon Pryce made his debut from the bench.

When James Maloney clipped a penalty over shortly before the twenty-minute mark, it was almost as if it unwrapped the spirit of the game, as the Dragons promptly put Benjamin Jullien over through an excellent Josh Drinkwater grubber on the left flank on the very next set. Mike McMeeken powered over on the right and one last try before the break - courtesy of Samisoni Langi - firmly put Catalans in control 20-0 up.

For a shining moment after the break, Huddersfield looked to have forced their way back into the game, winning a succession of six-again calls with their speed to eventually leave referee Ben Thaler with no choice but to sin bin offending Dragons defender Jason Baitieri.

The Giants promptly turned their one-man advantage into points, with Jake Wardle turning out some fancy footwork to speed away from his own half and hurl a pass inside off the right flank for Ashton Golding to collect and cross next to the posts, with Oliver Russell adding the conversion.

But any hopes of a resurgence from the hosts vanished when Catalans promptly came up with the ball from the restart a handful of yards from Huddersfield's try-line, where Benjamin Garcia promptly crawled his way over.

Wardle managed a final consolation score for Huddersfield, which was set up by the recently arrived Pryce with a delightful pass around two defenders, shortly before both Drinkwater and Gil Dudson were sin-binned for separate discipline issues. The Giants' rough night at the office was compounded when Tom Davies shot down the wing for a final try, despite the two-man disadvantage.

On the same night young threequarter Jack Broadbent scored four tries as Leeds chalked up a fifth win in ten Super League matches by beating Leigh 48-18 at Headingley.

The Centurions began well, against a side in the midst of a testing run and battling continued injury and suspension, as Matty Russell acrobatically finished a rippling move through the hands of James Bell, Ryan Brierley, Craig Mullen and Iain Thornley, with Brierley adding the touchline conversion.

But with Bell then in the sin bin for a tip-tackle on Mikolaj Oledzki, Leigh conceded two tries to an enthusiastic, youthful home side and never recovered.

The Rhinos' third win on the spin though, which took them to the edge of the play-off percentages, was built around the remaining core of experience in the ranks. Matt Prior, like the equally excellent Kruise Leeming, who played out of position again in the halves were standouts. Prior's charges and slipped passes in his third game in seven days were the foundation of victory.

When Leigh threatened a second wind just after the interval, taking the gap back to 12 points with Mark Ioane's close-in score, Prior, who was standing in as skipper, returned off the bench for a 15-minute spell to steady the ship and settle any thoughts of an upset.

It was 13 games without a win for Leigh, who were also hit by an injury to Brierley, in his third spell at the Centurions, who needed emergency surgery on an eye injury.

BETFRED SUPER LEAGUE
Thursday 1st July

	P	W	D	L	F	A	Diff %	Win %
Catalans Dragons	11	10	0	1	334	160	208.75	90.91
St Helens	10	8	0	2	232	76	305.26	80.00
Warrington Wolves	12	9	1	2	392	191	205.24	79.17
Hull FC	11	7	1	3	260	175	148.57	68.18
Wigan Warriors	11	7	0	4	186	208	89.42	63.64
Hull Kingston Rovers	10	6	0	4	241	212	113.68	60.00
Leeds Rhinos	10	5	0	5	236	166	142.17	50.00
Castleford Tigers	12	5	0	7	209	284	73.59	41.67
Wakefield Trinity	12	4	0	8	219	275	79.64	33.33
Huddersfield Giants	11	3	0	8	180	238	75.63	27.27
Salford Red Devils	11	2	0	9	127	335	37.91	18.18
Leigh Centurions	13	0	0	13	212	508	41.73	0.00

JULY
Playing the percentages

Round 13

As Super League tried to squeeze fixtures in, Round 13 became almost a ghost round. Wakefield's home game with Leigh had already been played and of the other five scheduled, three were victim to Covid and injury issues.

Hull KR and Salford postponed their Monday night games for Covid issues, Rovers' trip to Catalans and Salford's to Hull FC also due to be re-arranged.

Having 'lost' a game when they couldn't raise a side to play St Helens, Castleford were awarded a 24-0 win when Huddersfield Giants were unable to field a 17-man squad for their Tuesday-night game.

On the Sunday, there was a TV game when Wigan travelled to St Helens, as much in hope than in expectation, and fell to a 24-6 loss.

Saints piled on the agony for Wigan, inflicting the Warriors' fifth successive defeat, in a game played almost throughout in constant rain. Saints led 18-0 at half-time, with the Warriors hamstrung by conceding eleven penalties and suffering two sin bins.

St Helens kicked off and they were the first to put down a marker, as smart passing on the left led to Lachlan Coote being tackled just short of the line on the sixth tackle.

Coote's grubber almost saw Theo Fages touch down but Jackson Hastings just managed to kick the ball dead, before Ethan Havard's high tackle on Louie McCarthy-Scarsbrook saw Coote open the scoring with two points.

Shortly afterwards Jake Bibby was challenged by Mark Percival in trying to catch a Coote bomb and the ball rebounded for Regan Grace to score the opening try of the game, with Coote adding the conversion.

Another Saints penalty for a dangerous tackle allowed them to attack again and Lomax was just held short but Liam Farrell was caught offside again under his own posts and Coote kicked his third goal.

St Helens' next score came off the back of a great Morgan Knowles charge and after the ball went to ground Coote picked it up to touch down and pass 500 Super League points.

Wigan had a short spell of attack but Farrell conceded a penalty for a high tackle on Coote and yet another penalty, this time for offside, saw Coote kicking his fifth goal for an 18-0 lead.

Wigan's best chance came in the 38th minute when Hastings slotted a grubber to the left corner. But the ball just beat Oliver Gildart and Liam Marshall as it went into touch.

And with seconds remaining in the first half, Kai Pearce-Paul was penalised and sin-binned for a shoulder charge on Coote as he kicked the ball, giving Coote another chance to convert a penalty, which he missed.

After the turnaround, Willie Isa joined Pearce-Paul in the sin bin for a dangerous tackle on Jack Welsby - he was banned for two matches - and Saints extended their lead to 24 points when Percival touched down for another converted try.

St Helens' Alex Walmsley takes on Wigan's Thomas Leuluai and Kai Pearce-Paul

Wigan got a consolation from a Saints mistake when Farrell got over the line from Sam Powell's dummy-half pass.

Round 13 crept into Monday and Warrington's home fixture with Leeds was a tighter affair between two form teams, that the Rhinos won 22-16, with Matt Prior leading from the front in the absence of the suspended Luke Gale.

The Rhinos took the lead in the seventh minute when Robert Lui competed for a Liam Sutcliffe bomb that landed perfectly in front of the posts. Lui was able to beat stand-in fullback Josh Thewlis to collect the ball to touch down for a converted try.

Warrington equalised when Toby King made a charge to the line and almost got there before Danny Walker got the ball at dummy-half, deceived the defence and went over for the touchdown that Stefan Ratchford converted.

Leeds then scored a superb try, which featured Sutcliffe linking with winger Ash Handley, who gave a beautiful inside pass to Alex Mellor for the touchdown.

That persuaded Wolves coach Steve Price to introduce Daryl Clark into the game and the former Man of Steel almost immediately broke downfield but was unable to connect with Walker with what would have been a scoring pass.

Instead it was the Rhinos who were next to score through Handley, who took a fine pass from Tom Briscoe and showed great strength to force his way over, with Rhyse Martin kicking his third conversion, before adding a penalty for a 14-point lead going towards half-time.

At the start of the second half Thewlis conceded a penalty for a high tackle on James Donaldson and Martin kicked the penalty to put the Rhinos 16 points ahead.

And the Wolves probably realised that it wasn't going to be their night when Tom Lineham touched down. The referee signalled a try but his decision was overturned by video-referee Ben Thaler, who adjudged Lineham to have made a double movement.

But Warrington had renewed hope with ten minutes to go when Thewlis broke down the left and was tackled illegally by Sutcliffe, who earned a yellow card for his troubles. Less than a minute later Josh Charnley went over on the right after a quick Wolves passing movement.

Ratchford couldn't add the conversion but the Wolves got another penalty when Lui was sin-binned for a professional foul, meaning the Rhinos were down to eleven men.

Charnley was able to catch a Blake Austin bomb to the right corner for his second try, with Ratchford converting from the touchline to give the Wolves a glimmer of hope. But the game ended when Austin's pass was unable to find the supporting Daryl Clark.

Round 14

Two more games were postponed in round 14 because of Covid issues at both Hull clubs, the scheduled Sunday clashes between Hull FC and Leigh and Hull KR and Warrington not going ahead.

Another two form teams met on the Friday night at Headingley, league leaders Catalans Dragons putting on a second-half masterclass to win 26-18. After a patchy first half, James Maloney was the star, brilliantly setting up the two tries that swung the match and dictating where and how the game was played with his imperious kicking game, which included a critical 40/20 that set the position for the defining score.

Young Frenchman Arthur Mourgue impressed again, stepping into the shoes of Josh Drinkwater in the halves. Having already made a mark at fullback and as an auxiliary hooker, his speed and electrifying footwork struck constant fear into the Rhinos' defenders, epitomised by the opening try, when he shimmied and swayed past three would-be tacklers and then took Kruise Leeming over the line with him.

At the start of what looked like being a glittering career, he had Maloney alongside, playing his 300th career game.

After a great start, with Mourgue's try helping to establish an eight-point lead, the Dragons went into the break behind by ten and a man down, with Sam Kasiano part-way through his sin-binning for a high tackle on Luke Briscoe. Rhyse Martin, Bodene Thompson and Liam Sutcliffe were Leeds' tryscorers.

Matt Whitley pulled Catalans back into the game from Maloney's pass on 56 minutes and Mike McMeeken went over soon after, Maloney again providing the try-making pass.

As the rain fell, Leeming, Luke Gale and Alex Mellor got Sutcliffe clear but his pass could only find touch after a clattering collision.

Maloney kicked a majestic 40/20, before he and Sam Tomkins combined to send Fouad Yaha in at the corner, with Mourgue converting from the touchline for his third goal.

On the Monday, the Dragons lost two players to two-match penalty notices, Joel Tomkins for a dangerous throw and Maloney for dangerous contact. Leeds' Martin got one match for the same offence, while Bodene Thompson received a three-match ban for a dangerous tackle.

On the same night, St Helens saw off the firm challenge of Wakefield, recording a 30-14 victory at Belle Vue. Hull KR-bound Lachlan Coote registered 18 points and proved the difference between the two sides but Wakefield gave as good as they got and were definitely not embarrassed against a St Helens side preparing for Wembley.

Saints led 14-0 after 25 minutes with Matty Ashurst, playing dummy-half and Tinirau Arona both off with concussion. Trinity coach Chris Chester claimed before the game he only had 17 fit men to choose from and when winger Liam Kay came off the bench to play dummy-half for the rest of the game it became obvious it was true.

Mark Percival was first over and was followed ten minutes later by a short-range stepping effort from Lewis Dodd, getting a start with Theo Fages the only first-choice absentee for Saints. Two Coote conversions and a penalty goal topped up the score.

When Saints knocked on from the resulting kick-off, Wakefield punished them as Lee Kershaw slid to the line. Wakefield had their tails up but an injudicious offload from Joe Westerman fell into the hands of Morgan Knowles, who ran 50 metres before feeding Percival. James Batchelor brought down the Saints centre but he held on too long and was sent to the sin bin for a professional foul.

Saints decided to run that penalty but took the two points barely seconds later when Trinity were found offside to make it 16-4. But Wakefield kept plugging away and on the stroke of half-time created space on the left for Innes Senior to just get the ball down. Mason Lino converted off the far post from out wide to bring Trinity back to 16-10.

Salford's Krisnan Inu tries to break free against Castleford

Wakefield received five penalties in succession early in the second forty minutes to continue where they left off in the first half and referee Ben Thaler had clearly had enough, as Percival was given a yellow card just seven minutes in.

The pressure had to tell eventually and finally the Saints' defence cracked on 50 minutes when Senior grabbed his second in an almost identical way to his first. Lino, however, couldn't convert, his attempt hitting the upright and bouncing out this time. But Wakefield were back to within two points.

Saints themselves earned a penalty after Eddie Battye was pulled up for a swinging arm and Coote duly obliged with another two-pointer to make it 18-14. And they dealt a killer blow when they stretched their lead with 15 minutes to go as Sione Mata'utia stepped past Lino and carried the ball 30 metres before offloading to Coote, who cantered over under the posts. The fullback himself converted and Saints led 24-14 and near the end Tommy Makinson finished well in the corner after good build-up play from Coote once more, who converted superbly to round off the scoring.

Mata'utia was to miss the following Saturday's Challenge Cup final after picking up two separate match penalty notices for a high tackle and for dangerous contact.

Two Sunday games remained, Wigan ending their five-game losing run with a hard-fought 16-12 home win over Huddersfield Giants, themselves now recording their fifth defeat on a row.

Both teams were without some key personnel, with Huddersfield probably suffering the most with at least nine first-teamers out.

The Warriors welcomed back prop forward Tony Clubb following his eight-match suspension for abusive language aimed at Hull FC's Andre Savelio back in April. The former England international returned in the front row, while Willie Isa and Ethan Havard were serving bans of their own.

Giants coach Ian Watson did a great piece of business and secured Nathan Peats and Nathaniel Peteru on season-long loan deals from bottom club Leigh Centurions. They both went into the squad, with Peats starting at hooker and Peteru on the bench, while there was almost a debut for Academy product Robson Stevens, who was selected on the bench but wasn't used.

The Giants raced ahead 12-0 thanks to tries from Chris McQueen and Leroy Cudjoe, converted by Oliver Russell but Liam Marshall scored just before half-time for Harry Smith to convert and drag Wigan into the game.

Nine minutes after the turnaround, Mitch Clark forced his way over before Wigan took the lead as Smith finished off a Liam Farrell break on 63 minutes and then converted.

With four minutes remaining, the Giants had their last chance to win the game when Ash Golding made a superb break down the left and passed to Louis Senior, who touched down in the corner. But the pass was forward.

On the same afternoon, Salford recorded their highest ever Super League points tally with a stunning 12-try, 70-18 destruction of a youthful Castleford Tigers at the Jungle.

The Tigers had five players on debut - Caelum Jordan, Jack Sadler, Cain Robb, Adam Rusling and Nathan Magee - as Daryl Powell explained he was not going to risk most of the players who would be playing at Wembley the following Saturday.

Morgan Escare and Rhys Williams both scored doubles as the Red Devils amassed 48 points in the second half.

Round 9, 10, 12

Covid-caused disruption was starting to raise great concern within the game.

With so many games being postponed as coronavirus infection rates soared and the situation expected to worsen after July 19th when most restrictions in the UK were to be lifted, it seemed highly unlikely that the final Super League standings would feature all twelve clubs playing 25 times.

The RFL had anticipated such a scenario and ruled that positions would be determined by win points percentage, with clubs required to complete 70 per cent of their fixtures (18 matches) to be eligible for the six-strong play-offs due to start on September 23rd.

Hull FC were forced to postpone Thursday's rescheduled Super League derby with Hull KR, after 11 of their top 25 squad players were ruled out by Covid-related issues. The first postponement had been due to problems in the Rovers camp

Following five successive postponements, Hull KR had played only ten games, with a month of inactivity after their 18-8 win at Wigan. Hull FC had so far played eleven times.

Three catch-up games went ahead on the Friday night, on the eve of the Cup Final.

In a round-10 game, Leeds suffered a second consecutive second-half collapse against Catalans, losing 27-18 at Stade Gilbert Brutus just seven days after an almost identical performance and result at Headingley, the Rhinos failing to score a single point after half-time in both fixtures.

The Dragons' halfback Arthur Mourgue played a pivotal role in a second-half recovery from a 16-point half-time deficit, scoring 14 points with five conversions and a try. Mourgue was drafted in to replace James Maloney, who picked up a two-match ban (along with Joel Tomkins) after the previous week's victory over Leeds.

Fierce and brilliant in the first half, the Rhinos were well worth their 16-point interval lead. Mourgue's early penalty put Catalans in front, before Tom Briscoe crossed twice for Leeds and Kruise Leeming added a try, with Luke Gale converting all three for their half-time lead of 18-2. But Catalans struck back after the break, with Sam Kasiano, Mourgue and Matt Whitley all touching down. Tom Davies' try and Sam Tomkins' field goal sealed the win for the hosts.

July

In Round 12, Salford won back-to-back Super League games for the first time in 2021 with a 24-14 victory over Wakefield Trinity, played at Warrington's Halliwell Jones Stadium because of pitch maintenance at the AJ Bell Stadium.

Both teams named 19-man squads, instead of 21, ahead of the game due to a host of suspensions, injuries and Covid-related isolation. And badly depleted Wakefield suffered a blow when in-form Joe Westerman had to withdraw at short notice on the morning of the game.

Wakefield had the best of the opening quarter, leading 12-0 before the Red Devils chased them down. A 70-metre Lee Kershaw break set up Innes Senior to score and Liam Kay's pass allowed Reece Lyne to go over to give Trinity a buffer after 20 minutes.

But Salford were level at the interval after Morgan Escare pounced on an error for a try before Krisnan Inu powered over.

The Red Devils continued their momentum, former Trinity forward Pauli Pauli causing mayhem, with Inu and Ken Sio each scoring in the right corner for a win that saw them leapfrog Wakefield into ninth in the Super League table

Trinity coach Chris Chester joined forces with chief executive Michael Carter in a blast at the RFL's disciplinary chiefs. The pair were frustrated by one-match bans for fullback Ryan Hampshire and centre Joe Arundel for dangerous contact during the 30-14 home defeat by St Helens. Saints forward Sione Mata'utia was also handed a controversial ban from the same game, which ruled him out of the Challenge Cup final at Wembley.

Wigan made it back-to-back Super League wins for the first time since May with a 14-12 round-9 win at Huddersfield.

The Warriors took the lead in the 32nd minute with Mitch Clark barging over from close range for his second try in as many games against the same opponents.

The second half was a much more entertaining affair, with youngster Will Pryce lighting up the stage with a fine individual try after Harry Smith's penalty had put Wigan eight points clear.

It looked like Wigan were going to finish strongly with a well-worked try involving Smith and Oliver Gildart, gamestar Liam Farrell crossing over and Smith converting for a 14-6 lead. But Huddersfield had the final say when Nathaniel Peteru crashed over, although it was too little, too late.

Challenge Cup Final

St Helens won their first Challenge Cup since 2008 with a masterful 26-12 victory over Castleford.

The official Met Office temperature at Wembley was 27 degrees Celsius as the Tigers looked well capable of building on a 12-6 half-time lead. But it was Saints who rose above the fiery heat to keep their cool, keeping Castleford scoreless after the interval.

After a quarter of an hour of St Helens dominance, one play lit the fuse for an epic Cup final. Starting inside their own half of the field, the Tigers needed something to shift the momentum after going 6-0 down. Paul McShane's quick cut-out pass gave them a small opening and once Gareth O'Brien had shifted the ball on, it was in the hands of Niall Evalds.

BETFRED CHALLENGE CUP FINAL

Saturday 17th July 2021

CASTLEFORD TIGERS 12 ST HELENS 26

TIGERS: 1 Niall Evalds; 2 Derrell Olpherts; 3 Peter Mata'utia; 4 Michael Shenton (C); 25 Jordan Turner; 6 Jake Trueman; 31 Gareth O'Brien; 15 George Griffin; 9 Paul McShane; 10 Grant Millington; 11 Oliver Holmes; 21 Jesse Sene-Lefao; 14 Nathan Massey. Subs (all used): 8 Liam Watts; 13 Adam Milner; 17 Alex Foster; 22 Daniel Smith.
Tries: Evalds (17), Trueman (25); **Goals:** O'Brien 2/2.
SAINTS: 1 Lachlan Coote; 2 Tommy Makinson; 3 Kevin Naiqama; 4 Mark Percival; 5 Regan Grace; 6 Jonny Lomax; 7 Theo Fages; 8 Alex Walmsley; 9 James Roby (C); 15 Louie McCarthy-Scarsbrook; 11 Joel Thompson; 20 Joe Batchelor; 13 Morgan Knowles. Subs (all used): 10 Matty Lees; 16 Kyle Amor; 17 Agnatius Paasi; 18 Jack Welsby.
Tries: Fages (10), Roby (42), Makinson (51), Amor (78);
Goals: Coote 5/7.
Rugby Leaguer & League Express Men of the Match:
Tigers: Niall Evalds; *Saints:* Lachlan Coote.
Penalty count: 4-6; **Half-time:** 12-6; **Referee:** Liam Moore;
Attendance: 40,000 *(at Wembley Stadium).*

Theo Fages celebrates with Kevin Naiqama and Tommy Makinson after opening the scoring in the Challenge Cup Final

The fullback waited for winger Regan Grace to commit himself before delivering for Peter Mata'utia to run into the space on the right. Then Evalds showed his pace and eye for an opportunity, supporting on the inside ready for the perfectly-weighted kick that would allow him to run clear and score.

That wonderful try was not the only reason why, for the first time in 16 years, the Lance Todd Trophy went to a player on the losing side in the Challenge Cup final. But it was man-of the-match Evalds who sparked the contest and he was always involved when Castleford were at their most threatening, as well as producing an exemplary performance at the back.

Evalds followed in some big footsteps as the eleventh losing player to claim or share the award, starting with Frank Whitcombe in 1948 and passing through Don Fox in 1968, through to the likes of Robbie Paul (1996) and most recently Kevin Sinfield (2005). He secured 18 votes, with St Helens skipper James Roby getting 13, Lachlan Coote five, Jonny Lomax three, and Tommy Makinson and Jesse Sene-Lefao one each. His St Helens counterpart Coote was also a star of the game, erasing the memory of his below-par show in Saints' defeat to Warrington two years earlier.

July

A Covid-reduced capacity crowd of 40,000 produced a fantastic atmosphere

When Lomax's neat grubber in the tenth minute wrong-footed Oliver Holmes and came back off the left post for Theo Fages to seize upon beneath the sticks, for Coote to goal, Saints looked in total control.

But seven minutes later, Evalds' try and Gareth O'Brien's conversion completely changed the direction of the game. Twenty-five minutes in, the Tigers took the lead as O'Brien's towering bomb towards the uprights was filched by Jake Truman amid a gaggle of competing players, the halfback delighted to spin and dot down after his impressive catch caught Saints flat-footed.

As temperatures climbed, Castleford continued to batter at the door, to no ultimate avail, even as the metronomic McShane guided their repeated knocks and, with only a six-point difference heading into the sheds, it felt as if momentum between the two had been duly checked.

Moments after the restart, however, controversy struck through video-referee Chris Kendall, after Roby had seized on a batted pass from Regan Grace on the left wing to dive over. Referee Liam Moore sent it upstairs as a try; contentious evidence that Mark Percival had both possibly knocked on and put the ball into touch in the build-up were not enough to rule it out conclusively and the try was duly given.

In short order, Saints regathered the lead too, Jack Welsby, who replaced Fages, who it emerged had played with a hairline fracture of the shoulder, after the break, cutting across broken play to work the overlap for Makinson on the right wing. Though Coote hooked his conversion wide, he atoned almost immediately with a superb tackle on a marauding Evalds before Grant Millington coughed up a crucial error for the Tigers.

From there on in, it became a case of Saints' shrewd game management and robust defensive exploits; a smart team effort to tip Derrell Olpherts into touch, a clear-eyed calmness when Evalds threatened further breaks. When Mata'utia was flagged for offside with a quarter-hour on the clock, there was no doubt from Roby that his kicker should go for goal.

As Castleford grew more desperate, Saints grew more expectant, their supporters sensing the shift of the tide. Another Saints penalty goal for exhausted infringements brought them extra breathing room, as both saw tired bodies drop to the floor with brutal frequency, sapped by the heat.

When Kyle Amor crashed through with two minutes on the clock, the Red and white section of the crowd exploded with joy.

Round 13, 15

Only three of the scheduled round-fifteen games went ahead, with another fixture very hastily re-arranged in the south of France.

Warrington fans were left still waiting for the debut of England halfback George Williams. Since he signed a three-and-a-half-year contract with the Wolves earlier in the month, the game at Hull KR on July 11th and now the Thursday fixture at Leigh had been called off.

With a number of players still unavailable following positive Covid tests, which led to the postponement of the Hull KR game, third-placed Warrington had a further positive test three days before the Leigh match, which took them to a total of nine players ruled out, one of whom was a close contact and therefore also required to isolate.

A club could apply for a postponement if they had seven or more of their 25 best-paid players ruled out as a result of Covid issues.

The two Wembley finalists also postponed their games. St Helens pulled out of their home game with with Hull KR, while Castleford couldn't fulfil their game at Catalans. But the round-13 fixture between the Dragons and Hull KR, postponed from July 5th, was quickly rearranged for the Saturday and it proved to be a thrilling game that Catalans, on the back of a nine-match winning run, edged 32-30.

Huddersfield's Leroy Cudjoe celebrates as he crosses against Hull FC

It was a first outing since the 18-8 win at Wigan on June 18th, over a month before, for Rovers, who had been hit by six Super League postponements for Covid-related issues.

With Jordan Abdull's kicking game highly effective, Rovers were 26-12 in front at half-time, only for the league leaders to hit back. The Robins' scrum-half, in his 100th Super League appearance, terrorised England duo Tom Davies and Sam Tomkins with a series of steepling kicks, dizzying the Dragons' defence with their height and precision. Abdull, Shaun Kenny-Dowall, Greg Minikin and Adam Quinlan all profited with tries, with Abdull kicking all the conversions plus a penalty goal for that half-time lead, Matt Whitley and Sam Tomkins getting the home tries.

After the break Abdull scored his second try on 48 minutes after Whitley got his second but that was the end of Rovers' scoring for the night as the Dragons clawed back to 30-all with Mickael Goudemand and Fouad Yaha tries.

Boom young gun Arthur Mourgue put the Dragons ahead for the first time in the game with a 70th minute penalty, his fifth goal from five attempts, as the humidity and temperature began to take its toll on Rovers and the league leaders hung on for yet another comeback.

The tenth win in a row for the Dragons was marred by the loss of captain Ben Garcia with a broken arm.

In the only remaining Thursday game, tenth-placed Huddersfield ended a seven-match losing run with a 40-26 home win over Hull FC, whose previous game was four weeks before when they beat the Giants at home 17-10.

Winger Jermaine McGillvary crossed four times as Leroy Cudjoe made his 300th club appearance and 18-year-old halfback halfback Will Pryce marked another mature display with a second-half finish his watching father Leon would have been proud of. Pryce was deputising for the injured Aidan Sezer, who had played his final game in claret and gold.

Pryce had made his Giants debut in the home Super League clash with Catalans, scoring his first try at senior level in the second of the back-to-back games against Wigan.

Giants coach Ian Watson defended Josh Jones, who was given a red card after he clashed with Hull's Andre Savelio. Watson claimed Savelio, who was also dismissed, was lining up a 'free shot' on teenager Robson Stevens and that Jones was acting as his 'protector'. On the Monday, Savelio was given a three-match penalty notice and Jones two games, reduced to one on appeal.

July

On the Friday night, Matt Prior marked his new contract extension through to 2023 by skippering Leeds in place of the omitted Luke Gale and scoring a late try as the Rhinos beat Salford 38-16, their first Super League win in three attempts.

The 33-year-old Gale was left out of coach Richard Agar's team and the club announced he had been stood down as captain 'for behaviours not aligned to team trademarks'. Gale had reportedly stormed out of a team meeting and apologised publicly. That week Leeds confirmed the signing of star Huddersfield halfback Aidan Sezer, on a two-year deal starting in 2022.

Salford's indiscipline proved their undoing. Debutant Tongan halfback Ata Hingano must have wondered what he had let himself in for at his new club. Brought on in the 49th minute, which saw Chris Atkin moved to hooker and knocking on with his first carry in the dummy-half role, by the time Hingano touched the ball, he had seen his fellow Tongan Tui Lolohea dispatched for persistent questioning of referee Ben Thaler and, within a minute, belligerent Seb Ikahihifo for looking to escalate an indiscretion. By the time they returned, the Rhinos had eased to a 32-4 lead, with two tries of note, from Gale's replacement Callum McLelland and Fijian prop King Vuniyayawa.

On the same night, Jackson Hastings produced an out-of-this world performance as Wigan Warriors recorded their third successive win, a 25-12 success over Wakefield.

Jake Bibby crossed for a brace of tries in the 13th and 39th minutes but they were both created by the brilliance of Hastings and the Australian-born Great Britain international then added a one-pointer as the hooter sounded.

Hastings continued to be a thorn in Wakefield's side as he took the line on at will and sent Bibby over for his hat-trick try with another great offload six minutes after the break.

Further tries from Joe Shorrocks and Liam Marshall put Wigan well in front at 25-0, though the final ten minutes saw Trinity register two tries through James Batchelor and Jay Pitts.

Round 16

Three more fixtures didn't take place in the last week of July - round 16 was a crammed-in midweek round - as the games between St Helens and Huddersfield, Salford and Hull KR and Leigh and Castleford were postponed.

Saints and Castleford were still both exceeding the minimum seven out of 25 senior squad players either testing positive or coming into close contact with people who had tested positive. Salford postponed not only their home game against Hull KR, but also the following Monday's trip to Wakefield.

Rovers had suffered more Covid-related call-offs than any other club, with the trip to Salford the seventh time they had had a match postponed and there were genuine fears within the club that they wouldn't play the minimum number of games to qualify for the play-offs, which they had every chance of doing.

The continuing postponement of matches in Super League were a significant factor in the decision of the Australian Rugby League Commission and the New Zealand Rugby League to withdraw from the World Cup, scheduled to be played in England in the autumn, leaving the competition in serious doubt.

On the Wednesday a Blake Austin field goal sealed Warrington's 21-8 home win over Wigan. Barely a month before, Wigan had been humbled at home by the Wolves, with Jake Mamo bagging a try hat-trick, two of which were over the length of the field.

And the same happened again this time around, although in different and perhaps controversial circumstances. In the 62nd minute, the pacy centre picked up a loose ball from an unfortunate incident in which Liam Marshall was knocked out by an accidental kick to the head from Josh Charnley. Mamo raced 80 metres to score the try that took the game away from Wigan, awarded by referee Robert Hicks without consultation with the video referee. At 20-8, the Wolves looked safe.

Leeds' Brad Dwyer jumps for joy after scoring against Hull FC

The Cherry and Whites came into the contest on the back of three straight wins and at times caused Warrington significant problems. But they were guilty of squandering chances in wet conditions. Although they dominated field position and possession in the first half, Warrington went in 8-6 up at half time.

Daryl Clark was the key to victory for Warrington, dictating the pace of the game through the middle, earning momentum back for his side on numerous occasions and setting up his side's opening try.

On the Thursday, Brad Dwyer and Richie Myler helped deliver a first victory at the freshly-rechristened MKM Stadium for Leeds Rhinos since 2017, as they ran in a three-try second-half salvo to sink Hull FC 22-12 on a breezy July night in front of almost 10,000 spectators.

The twosome, who were rejigged across the spine of Richard Agar's side after a distinctly bruising, mistake-ridden first stanza, injected the vital shot of adrenaline to the system for the Rhinos in the final quarter, as Hull were punished for their inability to convert prospects into points throughout the game.

Marc Sneyd's 250th career appearance ended in defeat and Hull were 22-8 down before Carlos Tuimavave's try and Sneyd's conversion two minutes from time made the scoreline more respectable.

On the same night, on a baking-hot evening in Perpignan, Catalans extended their club-record winning run to eleven games with a 40-20 victory over Wakefield Trinity and remained top of the table for the seventh successive week.

With two barnstorming tries from David Fifita, Trinity were in contention until the 72nd minute, before two tries by Fouad Yaha sealed the win for the league leaders. The return from suspension of James Maloney was key for the Dragons and the introduction on Sam Kasiano from the bench, he scored almost immediately, visibly lifted the Dragons.

BETFRED SUPER LEAGUE
Thursday 29th July

	P	W	D	L	F	A	Diff %	Win %
Catalans Dragons	15	14	0	1	459	246	186.59	93.33
St Helens	12	10	0	2	286	96	297.92	83.33
Warrington Wolves	14	10	1	3	429	221	194.12	75.00
Wigan Warriors	16	10	0	6	255	289	88.24	62.50
Hull FC	13	7	1	5	298	237	125.74	57.69
Hull Kingston Rovers	11	6	0	5	271	244	111.07	54.55
Leeds Rhinos	15	8	0	7	354	263	134.60	53.33
Castleford Tigers	14	6	0	8	251	354	70.90	42.86
Salford Red Devils	14	4	0	10	237	405	58.52	28.57
Huddersfield Giants	15	4	0	11	244	318	76.73	26.67
Wakefield Trinity	16	4	0	12	279	394	70.81	25.00
Leigh Centurions	13	0	0	13	212	508	41.73	0.00

AUGUST
Fixture frenzy

Round 17

With Super League trying to cram in fixtures, an almost full round was played on the first Sunday and Monday of August, Salford having already postponed their game at Wakefield.

On the Sunday, Wigan, with John Bateman returning from an ankle injury suffered in England's game against Combined Nations in June, bounced back from the defeat to Warrington by trouncing close neighbours Leigh at home by 50-6.

A frantic opening 15 minutes saw three tries and two red cards in what was a real blood and thunder local derby. The Warriors opened the scoring after just four minutes through Thomas Leuluai, before Liam Hood levelled moments later. Then Umyla Hanley went over in the corner from a neat Jackson Hastings pass, before chaos ensued.

Jack Ashworth, making his second debut for the Centurions, had only been on the field a matter of seconds before he was dismissed for throwing punches at Brad Singleton, with the Wigan man replying in kind and also getting his marching orders.

Leigh showed plenty of spirit but they were second best for the first 40 minutes and further tries from Liam Farrell, two, and Hanley put the Warriors 28-6 up at half-time.

The game was over as a contest at that point and, although Leigh fought until the end, they were clearly outclassed as Sam Halsall, his first in Super League start, Joe Shorrocks and Hastings all scored before Hanley completed his hat-trick.

Singleton was handed a three-match penalty notice and Ashworth two matches. Wigan's Oliver Partington and Wolves' Rob Butler, who was on Leigh debut on loan from Warrington, also received two-match bans for their part in the melee.

In the Sunday-night TV game from Headingley, George Williams finally made his Warrington debut. And what an impact he made, his last-minute field goal ending a rip-roaring, highly-entertaining clash against a Leeds side who thought they had won with five minutes left.

With the score at 26-20 heading into the 76th minute, Leeds' Tom Briscoe lost the ball. And, following a great run by Robbie Mulhern, Warrington's livewire hooker Danny Walker sniped through a gap to level the scores. Williams then sent the Wolves fans into raptures with a brilliant one-pointer to cap off a memorable debut and seal a 27-26 win.

It had been a topsy-turvy game throughout, with Harry Newman and Mike Cooper trading scores early on before Mikolaj Oledzki and Blake Austin did exactly the same as the clock approached the midway point in the first half. With the introduction of Brad Dwyer, the Rhinos were on the front foot and his try on the half-hour mark sent Leeds into the break 18-12 up.

Josh Charnley's try on 51 minutes levelled proceedings before the two sides exchanged penalties - with Jack Hughes sent to the sin bin for a late hit on Luke Gale - to make it 20-20.

Newman was able to register his second try of the evening on 70 minutes but Warrington again replied with four minutes left to leave the tie in the balance once more. It was to be Williams' and Warrington's night and the halfback duly obliged with

George Williams congratulated on a memorable Warrington debut, following victory over Leeds

a sensational field goal as the hooter sounded. Luke Gale later got a two-match penalty notice for contact with the referee.

Kevin Sinfield watched on before leaving his director of rugby role at the Rhinos. The 40-year-old, off to become defence coach at rugby union club Leicester Tigers, was due to depart at the end of the season.

On the Monday night, Huddersfield recorded back-to-back wins with a 34-16 success at Castleford. With 15 players unavailable, the Tigers relied on a number of Academy players alongside the evergreen Paul McShane and two loan players in Hull KR's Jimmy Keinhorst and Featherstone's Jake Sweeting, in their attempt to pick up their first home win since mid-April.

Huddersfield had their previous game against St Helens postponed but they flew out of the blocks when the in-form Leroy Cudjoe crossed early on. McShane did what he does best moments later, kicking through for himself before Cudjoe re-established the lead shortly after. It was Nathaniel Peteru's turn to crash over before half-time before Oliver Russell added a penalty to take the Giants into a 20-6 lead at the break.

Castleford never gave in and Brad Graham grabbed his first try for the club. But Luke Yates and Jermaine McGillvary put the icing on the cake late on, with Castleford skipper Michael Shenton leaving the field with a facial injury. Sweeting did manage to cross for the home side with minutes left. But the night belonged to Huddersfield.

St Helens took another step on the road to Old Trafford with an emphatic victory, this time a 42-10 away win over a Hull FC side looking void of confidence. The Airlie Birds were very much in the game until the hour mark but Saints registered four tries in the final 18 minutes to keep the pressure on Catalans at the top of the table.

Catalans registered their twelfth victory in a row, by 23-16, in difficult circumstances in East Hull. In front of a crowd of almost 6,500, Hull KR were rocking but the Dragons, who were buoyed by the excellent Sam Tomkins, held their nerve to come away with a priceless two points.

August

It was a game of attrition in the opening half-hour, with the Dragons breaking the deadlock in the 25th minute with a James Maloney penalty. But Jordan Abdull soon levelled proceedings with his own penalty before Romain Franco marked his debut with a try in the corner for the Catalans with time running out on the clock. Maloney converted before Abdull added a second penalty to cut the half-time lead to four points with Catalans leading 8-4.

It didn't take long for the Dragons to score again in the second half, with Samisoni Langi taking advantage of frail Rovers security under the high ball just three minutes in. But Adam Quinlan dummied his way through shortly after, with Abdull's conversion cutting the lead to four points once more.

The game, however, belonged to Tomkins and the Dragons and the tricky fullback weaved his way through for a try. Maloney's conversion and another penalty from the halfback meant Rovers needed two converted scores to even level the game. But the veteran Aussie's field goal made the result safe at 23-10.

Quinlan did cross again with two minutes remaining, as Catalans braved a last-minute fightback without their star man Tomkins, who had been sent to the sin bin for a professional foul.

* The World Cup, featuring men's, women's and wheelchair events, set to start in Newcastle on 23rd October, was postponed for a year after the withdrawal of Australia and New Zealand because of player welfare and safety concerns.

Round 18

Another game fell victim to Covid when the Sunday fixture between Warrington and Hull FC was postponed by the Airlie Birds early in the week.

League leaders Catalans' 12-match winning run came to an end at St Helens on the Saturday as a side full of young French reserves suffered a 34-12 defeat by the reigning champions.

It was disappointment for the TV audience to see a Dragons team lacking several star players take the field for what should have been the contest of the season so far and the hosts, cheered on by almost 8,000 fans on a wet afternoon, grabbed control of the game early on and did not look like losing after establishing an 18-0 advantage in even time.

The inexperienced Dragons dug in well after that shaky start and coach Steve McNamara was full of praise for debutants Cesar Rouge and Corentin Le Cam, plus fellow reserve players Joe Chan and Romain Franco, in only their second games for the first team. Catalans also lost Joel Tomkins early on with an elbow injury and Benjamin Jullien to a rib injury after a late tackle by Sione Mata'utia for which he was sin-binned.

For Saints, Lachlan Coote just pipped Lewis Dodd for the gamestar award with an assured performance in attack and defence and, though they remained second, they closed the percentage gap on the Dragons significantly.

The night before at Headingley, seventh-placed Leeds fell further behind the play-off places after a 32-18 defeat by Castleford, themselves reviving their top-six hopes.

After a disrupted pre and post-Wembley spell, the Tigers' scramble and metres gained out of defence by their tireless back three, led by the excellent Niall Evalds, were the platform for victory in an entertaining clash, best summed up by Castleford skipper Paul McShane, who twice somehow helped to prevent first Zane Tetevano and then Morgan Gannon getting across, when the game was in the balance.

The Rhinos, who had Robert Lui back but missed Matt Prior with Covid issues, had plenty of opportunities to have had more of an impact on the outcome.

The Tigers set a first-half platform with Greg Eden and Peter Mata'utia tries, while Lui's score for Leeds came with Mata'utia in the sin bin for dangerous contact on Ash Handley.

Leigh's Liam Hood gets to grips with Hull KR's Ben Crooks

The Rhinos skipper for the night, Handley, scored after the break to reduce the arrears to just two points. But Jordan Turner, Eden and Jimmy Keinhorst crossed to put the game to bed, despite Brad Dwyer's try in between.

Evalds' leap to palm back Danny Richardson's high kick, with Eden picking it off and weaving his way to the line to make it 26-12 with eight minutes to play proved the gamebreaker.

On the same Friday night, Wigan came out with a hard-fought 16-6 home win over Salford Red Devils in an occasionally volatile battle.

Wigan, the only team to have fulfilled all their fixtures, could have been out of sight in the opening 20 minutes as they dominated possession but they could only score one try through winger Sam Halsall as the Red Devils repelled the majority of their attacks.

Though Salford looked out of sorts at times after postponing their previous two games, the Warriors' inability to turn pressure into points allowed the Red Devils to grow in confidence and they levelled matters in the 25th minute with Joe Burgess crossing in the corner.

Morgan Smithies and Josh Johnson were both sin-binned for a small altercation and more ill-discipline from the Warriors on the hooter saw Harvey Livett kick a penalty to put the Red Devils 6-4 ahead at the break.

Wigan were the better team in the second half and dominated possession. Three penalties from Harry Smith saw the Warriors lead 10-6 and Sam Powell crashed over from close range to finally break Salford's spirit at a time where the Red Devils were down to twelve men, with Ata Hingano in the bin for a high tackle on gamestar Jackson Hastings.

August

Wigan welcomed back Jai Field for the first time since he tore his hamstring in round one against Leigh Centurions. He started in the halves alongside Smith, while Zak Hardaker returned from his neck injury to take a place on the bench, with Hastings remaining at fullback.

Dom Manfredi, who had brought forward his retirement, which was due at the end of the season following advice from a knee specialist, led the sides out.

On the Sunday evening Hull Kingston Rovers left it late with a 73rd-minute Ryan Hall try clinching a 34-28 victory over Leigh Centurions in a seesaw clash at Leigh Sports Village.

The Centurions took the lead in the first minute of the game through Junior Sa'u and when Dean Hadley had to leave the field four minutes later with a dislocated shoulder, the Robins looked to be in some danger of becoming Leigh's first victims of the season.

Leigh had a try claim by Joe Mellor ruled out for a knock-on before Rovers scored three tries in eight minutes from Kane Linnett, Greg Minikin and Shaun Kenny-Dowall, putting them 14-4 in front on 23 minutes. Star young gun Mikey Lewis was over almost immediately afterwards, stretching Rovers' lead to 14 points.

The Centurions needed to get back into the game and they did just before the break when Craig Mullen got over, converting his own try for 18-10.

Albert Vete scored the first try of the second half to put Rovers 14 points in front again but then shortly afterwards he was sin-binned for a high tackle on Matthew Foster. Seven minutes later they were down to eleven men when George Lawler was shown a yellow card for a similar offence.

Leigh took advantage by scoring three tries, two to Adam Sidlow and another to Sa'u, to take a 28-24 lead. But the Robins responded with Kenny-Dowall's second try, before Ryan Hall's late matchwinner inflicted Leigh's 15th successive defeat in Super League this season.

The Centurions did announce they had landed NRL duo Sam Stone and Jai Whitbread from Gold Coast Titans on immediate contracts through to the end of next season. And former Wigan, Hull KR and England second rower Joel Tomkins was to join them from Catalans for 2022.

Earlier that afternoon, Huddersfield put some daylight between the bottom three in the table with a 22-18 home win over 11th-placed Wakefield.

It was a classic see-saw game. After quarter of an hour it felt like there would only be one outcome. Wakefield blasted their way into an 18-0 lead, as Reece Lyne, Ryan Hampshire and Joe Westerman scored tries, all converted by Hampshire, to put them in what seemed total control.

Then, Oliver Russell left the field due to a head knock and didn't return, leaving teenager Will Pryce as the only recognised Giants halfback, with Sam Wood for support. Somehow, against the odds, they managed to pull off their third successive win.

The Giants revived their hopes when Louis Senior crossed in the corner before, on 37 minutes, the game's big moment arrived. Wakefield led by 14 points and looked to be in a real position of strength going into the interval. But when Innes Senior, on loan from the Giants for the season, was trapped in-goal, he inexplicably attempted to hurl the ball to Max Jowitt to prevent a drop-out.

Instead, the ball fell into the arms of Wood, who grounded and gave Pryce a simple conversion to reduce the gap to eight at half-time. It swung the momentum firmly in Huddersfield's favour and, after half-time, it only ever felt that one team would win.

Jermaine McGillvary's double continued their revival, though Pryce was unable to add the goal for the lead. However, Jake Wardle crossed to cap a remarkable turnaround for Huddersfield.

After the game, Trinity coach Chris Chester was scathing about his players' capitulation. On the Tuesday, after over five years at Belle Vue, Chester was sacked as head coach, with assistant Willie Poching taking over on an interim basis.

Round 19

Super League enjoyed a rare full round of fixtures as Hull KR kept their play-off pursuit alive in a dramatic, ultimately ill-tempered fashion, as three sin-bin offences in the final minute capped off a spirited 26-14 win over Wigan on a warm August night in east Hull.

Rovers pair Brad Takairangi (professional foul), Matt Parcell and Liam Farrell (fighting) all saw yellow inside the last sixty seconds as play boiled over into a melee that brought the curtain down on a potentially decisive result for both sides.

The Robins, with captain Shaun Kenny-Dowall outstanding, were forced to battle back after the Warriors swiftly tempered hopes of an early first-half blowout.

Wigan reduced Rovers' 16-point lead to 16-14 at the break with two tries by Liam Marshall and one from Jake Bibby. But the home side clinched it with second-half scores from Kane Linnett and Jez Litten.

Wigan were not helped by the early exit of talismanic hooker Sam Powell to a head injury and, roared on by a vocal home crowd, Rovers were shrewd enough to take advantage of their disarray almost immediately.

Albert Vete crashed over from short range. Rowan Milnes and Ethan Ryan tries quickly followed before Wigan clawed the scores back by the break.

The Linnett and Litten tries took Rovers clear, with the video-ref ruling out a try-effort by Jackson Hastings seven minutes from time and signalling the end of Wigan's chances.

The announcement before kick-off that club chairman Neil Hudgell had changed his mind and would retain ownership of Hull KR was met with a boisterous reception.

Rovers' win set up the following weekend's derby nicely, with Hull FC going into the eagerly-awaited clash at the MKM Stadium on the back of a 31-16 defeat by Catalans Dragons in France.

Ravaged by injuries, suspensions and the C-word, Hull had been expected to crumble to a Catalans' side that had seven senior players returning to duty following the previous week's defeat at St Helens.

But the Airlie Birds were in with a shout until ten minutes from the end of a steamy affair played in temperatures in the high thirties. Halfback Ben McNamara, son of Catalans coach Steve, produced a dazzling display of accurate goalkicking and composure with the ball. But a late second-half comeback by the Dragons sealed the home win.

The game looked like going to script after Tom Davies' try in the fourth minute. But just when Catalans seemed certain to score again, Sam Tomkins' pass was intercepted by Hull centre Carlos Tuimavave, who raced 90 metres to score and young McNamara added the conversion to put Hull ahead 6-4.

McNamara missed a penalty in the 24th minute but made amends two minutes later from the same spot as the Dragons were penalised for pushing at the play-the-ball.

But Davies scored his second in the right corner following good work from Tomkins and Dean Whare and this time Maloney was on target from the touchline to put the Dragons back in front at 10-8.

The introduction of giant prop Sam Kasiano from the bench on the half-hour put some fire in the Dragons' belly and when Tuimavave was sin-binned for a high tackle on the tallest player in the game, Corentin Le Cam, Hull were under the pump. But Kasiano didn't last long and had to return to the bench after just five minutes with a legacy of a recent knee injury.

Hull second-rower Jordan Lane burst through the Catalans' defence to put winger Bureta Faraimo in on the right, with McNamara adding a touchline conversion to make it 14-10 to the visitors at the interval.

Winger Fouad Yaha levelled the scores four minutes after the break with a try in the left corner following a break by Tomkins and Samisoni Langi, with Maloney putting Catalans ahead with the touchline conversion.

Greg Eden races away to seal a memorable Castleford win at St Helens

McNamara then levelled the scores again with a 58th-minute penalty. But the Dragons finally found their form, forcing Hull into a succession of goal-line drop-outs before Maloney landed a field goal to make it 17-16 with twelve minutes to go.

Tomkins put daylight between the teams a minute later when he climbed to steal the ball from Adam Swift and fall over the line for a try, Maloney's conversion making it 23-16.

Then French prop Julian Bousquet wrapped things up with a short-range burst to the posts, with Maloney adding the two points and a further penalty goal.

The win meant the Dragons moved further ahead at the top of the table as St Helens had gone down on the Thursday to a 20-10 defeat at home to Castleford, their first league win in St Helens for 31 years.

There was little sign of a dramatic end to come in the opening exchanges, with six penalties given by referee Ben Thaler in the first 13 minutes as neither side looked at their free-flowing or disciplined best. The Tigers had made six handling errors before the clock even struck the midway point in the half.

The Tigers edged the first half 6-4 as Greg Eden scored in the corner four minutes from half-time, Jack Welsby having opened the scoring after 20 minutes, Danny Richardson's conversion separating the teams.

Oliver Holmes' try in the 52nd minute, Richardson again on target, extended the Tigers' lead to 14-4 with over 25 minutes still to go.

The game had been simmering all night but it finally boiled over just after the hour mark when James Bentley gave Paul McShane some unwanted attention on the ground. Peter Mata'utia took exception, pushing Bentley and starting a fracas.

Thaler sent both Bentley and Mata'utia to the sin bin but that didn't calm things down and Tommy Makinson was red-carded two minutes later for a late, dangerous shot on Niall Evalds, who was left on the ground after passing the ball.

That fired the home side and, on the back of two penalties, a quick tap by Alex Walmsley saw the rampaging prop pick out a gap in the Castleford line and charge over. Coote converted to bring Saints back to within four points with just over ten minutes left and at this point they were constantly knocking at the Castleford door. Attack after attack came and, with time running out, Coote once more took the ball to the Tigers' line as the clock hit 78 minutes. But his pass to makeshift winger Kevin Naiqama only found the outstretched, grateful arms of Eden. Ninety-five metres later and the winger firmly etched the current Castleford side into folklore, confirming a famous victory. Richardson converted to make it 20-10 for a well-deserved win that edged the Tigers within sight of the play-off spots.

Makinson got three matches, reduced to two on appeal, for his late tackle.

Leeds replaced Hull FC in the top six as a result of their 46-10 hammering of Leigh at the Leigh Sports Village. Four tries in the last nine minutes added a gloss finish for the Rhinos as they ruthlessly took advantage of the Centurions in the closing stages to claim their first win in three games. Hooker Brad Dwyer was in great form around the ruck for Leeds, continually putting them on the front foot with smart running and distribution. Robert Lui's 71st minute try kick-started the late Rhinos' four-try rampage.

On the Friday, Salford staged a superb fightback to get another one over their former coach, on Ian Watson's first return to the AJ Bell Stadium, emerging 18-12 victors over Huddersfield.

The Red Devils had insisted pre-match that the evening was more about celebrating the career of club captain Lee Mossop, who had been forced into retirement through injury earlier in the week, than the presence of their previous boss.

But a first unrestricted home crowd in 17 months made no bones about the fact that they'd done the double over Watson, having also run out 9-8 victors at the John Smith's Stadium earlier in the season.

The Giants almost totally dominated the first half, despite losing Ricky Leutele to a head injury after ten minutes, with Will Pryce kicking an early penalty and converting Matty English's powerful try. But Salford cut the deficit to just two points when Krisnan Inu intercepted a flat Jack Cogger pass five minutes before half-time.

Sensing he didn't quite have the legs to go the length of the field, Inu released winger Rhys Williams to score from distance, as the Welshman was just about able to evade a covering Pryce.

Immediately after the restart, Tui Lolohea - expected to make the switch to join Huddersfield when his Salford contract expired at the end of the season - danced his way over the line to put the home side in front for the first time. Despite taking the lead, the Red Devils couldn't quite escape the discipline issues that had dogged them for much of the season and when two penalties were conceded in kickable range, Pryce stepped up to convert them and put the Giants back in front.

However, an error from the kick-off handed possession to the Red Devils in threatening range and after Kevin Brown was the surprise recipient of a crash ball close to the line and almost touched down, Andy Ackers stabbed a short kick through from dummy-half that Jack Ormondroyd was able to touch down acrobatically under the sticks.

The result all but ended the Giants' hopes of breaking into the end-of-season play-offs.

In the only Sunday game, Wakefield, with interim coach Willie Poching in charge for the first time, recorded a remarkable 28-22 home victory over Warrington.

With half an hour remaining, Trinity were 20-0 up. And then with 13 minutes left and Trinity leading 26-6, Warrington, who had earlier opened their scoring with a try from George Williams, which had all the hallmarks of a consolation, suddenly came to life.

First, Blake Austin dived over in the corner. Then on the following set, a long-range move was finished by Jake Mamo. Seconds later, Warrington scored again when another break from deep was finished by Josh Charnley. A game which looked to be petering out, with Wakefield leading 26-6, was now suddenly 26-22 - and Trinity had to show mettle, determination and grit to hang on.

There were further chances for Warrington after their three-try blitz. The pick came when the Wolves offloaded the ball on the last tackle but just as Ratchford looked to be in to give himself a simple conversion to put Warrington ahead, Yusuf Aydin and Matty Ashurst combined to deny him.

And then, with a minute remaining, Mason Lino, who kicked six goals from six attempts, finally ended any doubt over the result with a long-range penalty.

* The RFL announced that the 2022 Betfred Challenge Cup Final and AB Sundecks 1895 Cup Final would take place at the Tottenham Hotspur Stadium on Saturday, May 28th. The showpieces were expected to return to Wembley in 2023.

Round 20

Round twenty was labelled the 'Rivals Round' by Super League, with a number of derbies scheduled.

Alas, another highly anticipated clash, the Catalans' visit to Warrington on the Thursday night was postponed on the day of the game, when four members of the Dragons' essential staff tested positive for Covid-19, three of them on the morning of the game, shortly before the squad had been due to fly to England.

The game had been due to be broadcast by Sky Sports and the decision to postpone came too late to allow Sky to switch its broadcast operation. But fans were still left with two mouthwatering televised derbies, with Wigan taking on St Helens on the Friday and the Hull derby broadcast on the Saturday afternoon.

The Friday game turned out to be a disappointingly one-sided, niggly and sometimes nasty affair as Saints emerged 26-2 winners, with nineteen-year-old halfback Lewis Dodd, now first-choice scrum-half following the season-ending shoulder injury to Theo Fages, producing a polished performance. He scored a fine individual try when he stole the ball from Oliver Partington close to the Wigan line and was heavily involved in all the good things Saints produced.

Wigan's discipline left a lot to be desired as John Bateman was sent to the sin bin twice, while Willie Isa was put on report for a late hit on Welsby and seven minutes later shown a yellow card for a high tackle on Louie McCarthy-Scarsbrook.

Saints dominated the first half and deserved their 12-2 half-time lead thanks to tries from winger Regan Grace and Dodd. The only real fight the Warriors put up was through Bateman, when he lost his temper after being kicked by James Bentley, with both players sent to the sin bin to cool down.

St Helens were not at their fluent best, while the Warriors hardly looked like scoring at all. But Saints rubbed salt in their wounds with second-half tries from Mark Percival and Alex Walmsley.

Bentley was banned for one game and Bateman one game for using foul and abusive language towards referee Chris Kendall. But he successfully argued his comments were directed towards Saints forward McCarthy-Scarsbrook, while Isa got three matches for the hit on Welsby and one more for a high tackle on Percival.

Saturday afternoon's fare from the MKM Stadium in Hull was much better for the neutral, with a bumper, colourful crowd creating a superb atmosphere on a sunny afternoon.

Hull FC held on to a one-point margin in an excruciatingly exciting game, with three tries disallowed by the video referee Ben Thaler, to seal a 23-22 victory over Hull KR.

Manu Ma'u collared by Will Maher and Jez Litten during the Hull derby

Key returning players Marc Sneyd and Jake Connor showed a badly missed cutting edge and guile to see Hull through, ending a four-match losing run. And Jamie Shaul made his return to action in the 55th minute after having been out for ten months.

The game was won in the final play of the game. Sneyd potted a field goal with seven minutes to go to give Hull FC a 23-16 lead but Albert Vete's short-range try closed the gap to one point. Rovers lined up for a one-pointer to bring the scores level. But back-rower Jordan Lane found everything in his being to make sure he charged down Rowan Milnes' drop kick to keep the score at 23-22.

Two superbly worked tries on the wings had the scores level at 4-4 at quarter-time, first Connor's delayed long pass allowing Adam Swift into the corner, then Brad Takairangi's pass doing the same for Jimmy Keinhorst. The finishing skills of both wingers were spectacularly skilful.

Then Milnes instinctively chipped through Hull's defence and collected the ball to touch down to take Rovers 10-4 up going into the last ten minutes of the first half.

But two tries just before half-time put the Airlie Birds in the lead. Hull FC drew level with a move engineered by Sneyd, with Carlos Tuimavave moving the ball swiftly to Bureta Faraimo to score. Tuimavave then responded to his try being disallowed earlier in the half by dancing over line from a long pass by Josh Reynolds to put Hull up 16-10 at the break.

Rovers came out for the second half with a strong retort. Former Hull man Ben Crooks burst through the line to go over from a smart pass by Milnes, with the tryscorer converting his own try to bring the scores level. But Hull took the lead again when Faraimo got his second of the afternoon, assisted by Connor, and Sneyd converted a penalty after a high tackle by Crooks. Sneyd then scored the field goal that won a memorable derby.

Because of the percentage points system used in the table, the win put Hull FC back into the top six, their 14-all draw with Warrington in April - the only draw of the season - giving them a superior win percentage.

August

Leeds coach Richard Agar believed Rob Burrow inspired his team to the Thursday-night 18-12 Super League win over Huddersfield.

The club legend, cruelly struck by motor neurone disease, was the guest of honour and received a rousing reception when he appeared on the Emerald Headingley pitch before kick-off alongside his wife Lindsey.

After Callum McLelland fashioned the opening try on the quarter-hour, stepping on the outside of Oliver Wilson and drawing Ashton Golding perfectly to send Ash Handley over, Will Pryce pounced to level the scores. But in the lead-up to half-time, Robert Lui grubbered through, Luke Briscoe hacked on and Richie Myler won the race for the ball ahead of Golding, with Handley adding a fine touchline conversion.

Harry Newman had passed a head injury assessment in the first half to resume and he kicked two penalty goals after the break to extend the lead before Lui strolled in from a Kruise Leeming dart across the field.

Zane Tetevano was sin-binned in the final ten minutes for a late challenge on Oliver Russell to leave Leeds with twelve men for the late moments and the Giants might have levelled it up with late scores by Sam Wood and Owen Trout, with goal-kicking letting them down after three tries apiece, Pryce missing two conversion attempts and declining the last one in a desperate attempt to level in the last seconds.

On the Saturday, Castleford kept the play-offs in sight with a 23-18 home win over Wakefield - the Tigers' first victory in front of their faithful at the seventh time of asking. Since the fans' return to Wheldon Road in May, Daryl Powell's side had lost six on the bounce

In the first half, they looked exactly like the play-off contenders that three wins on the bounce meant they now were. With Danny Richardson pulling the strings, tries from Greg Eden, Oliver Holmes and Derrell Olpherts had them in a commanding lead.

Although Eden added another after the restart, the second half was an entirely different story. Wakefield upped their game considerably and tries from the wingers Tom Johnstone and Lee Kershaw gave them hope as they battled to the very end.

And on the Sunday, Leigh, after 16 defeats, at last broke their 2021 duck with a 32-22 home win over Salford.

Leigh, who had recent Aussie signing Sam Stone on debut in the centre, were more desperate than their opponents, forcing a number of errors from a frustrated Salford side, whose ill-discipline was their undoing, with Craig Mullen adding five penalty goals throughout a game that was finally decided in the final ten minutes with two late tries to the home side.

Centurions halfback Joe Mellor was the star of the show, scoring a brilliant individual try and was a constant thorn in Salford's side, stretching their defence on both sides of the field to eventually wear the Red Devils out. Liam Hood's try next to the posts a few minutes from time finally made the Leigh win a reality.

Round 21

With an August Bank Holiday Monday programme approaching, Super League tried to cram another round in on the preceding Wednesday and Thursday.

Wednesday's TV game saw Leeds record their first Super League win at the DW Stadium for eight years as the Warriors failed to score a try for the second game running, the Rhinos emerging 14-0 winners.

It was certainly a significant result for both sides, with Leeds up to fifth and now within sight of Wigan in fourth. Counting the second half at Hull KR, the Warriors had gone over 200 minutes without posting a four pointer.

The Rhinos spent over 20 minutes of the first half with twelve men as Zane Tetevano and Luke Briscoe were both shown yellow cards. But it was when the winger was off the field that the Rhinos hit the front, with Brad Dwyer collecting a kick from Kruise Leeming to score three minutes before half-time.

Salford's Sam Luckley and Ryan Lannon close down Catalans Dragons' Sam Kasiano

A fine try for Richie Myler following a great break from Rhyse Martin and a Martin penalty saw the Rhinos extend their lead to 14-0 and their defence handled everything Wigan could throw at them. Leeming was outstanding in the halfbacks, causing Wigan problems all night.

Tetevano got a three-match ban for a high tackle.

The next evening saw the rest of the round played, with Castleford's 23-12 win at the MKM Stadium and Wakefield's win at Hull KR seeing both Hull clubs drop out of the top six, Leeds and the Tigers replacing them.

It was a fourth win in a row for the gritty Tigers, who overcame the eighth-minute loss of Paul McShane to an abdomen injury. Halfback Danny Richardson steered them home though, Adam Milner epitomising Castleford's tough and committed display, coming off the bench after McShane's withdrawal to lead the charge to victory. Jordan Turner was another top performer and scored two first-half tries, both converted by Richardson, who also kicked a field goal after Adam Swift's converted try on 11 minutes.

At 13-6 down at half-time, Hull were certainly not out of it but Richardson kicked a penalty in the 57th minute on the back of a Milner break and then scored a try himself, squeezing in in the right corner after some fast hands.

However, Hull responded quickly. After winning the short kick-off, the home side worked the ball left, with Cameron Scott offloading out of the tackle to Jake Connor in support for a converted try to cut the gap to seven points. But Castleford put the game to bed with a scything Niall Evalds try five minutes from time.

Tensions boiled over in the closing seconds, with George Griffin and Scott Taylor both sin-binned for fighting

Over in east Hull, Wakefield halted Hull KR's momentum with a 25-18 win, after the Robins led 10-0 up to the half-hour mark on the back of Luis Johnson and George Lawler tries. Ben Crooks missed the second conversion attempt but Mason Lino kicked both of his following Jacob Miller and Ryan Hampshire tries for Trinity to lead 12-10 at half-time.

After the break Crooks kicked a penalty goal before Innes Senior and Jay Pitts tries took Wakefield clear. Crooks got a try back but Miller's 78th-minute field goal sealed it.

A first-half brace for Jake Mamo helped Warrington Wolves bounce back to winning ways with a 26-6 win at Huddersfield. The Wolves led 14-0 at the break thanks to Mamo's tries, both converted by Stefan Ratchford, who also added a penalty goal.

It was a tight second half but Mike Cooper added a third try, converted by Ratchford, with 12 minutes left before Jake Wardle's try, converted by Olly Russell, got the hosts on the scoresheet. Toby King's last-minute converted try completed the scoring as Warrington restored their 20-point advantage.

Rising star Jack Welsby touched down in both halves and created a try for Lachlan Coote in an eventually comfortable 42-12 win for St Helens over gutsy bottom club Leigh. Welsby was switched from centre to stand-off after the break to cover for Jonny Lomax, who was helped off the field with leg injury.

The final scoreline was harsh on a Leigh team that only trailed by six points going into the final quarter before Saints' late flurry. Keanan Brand had another terrific, brave performance at the back, Joe Mellor and Liam Hood never wavered in their creative efforts in the middle of the field and Matty Gee produced a huge effort before being forced to leave the action, shortly before Lomax, with a shoulder issue. Sione Mata'utia's 58th minute try sparked a late rush of Saints scores and took the game away from the Centurions.

Down the road in Salford, Catalans looked back to their best with a 42-14 win over the understrength Red Devils.

The French side controlled the game for most of it, though the end scoreline was harsh on Salford, who were rarely completely swamped and with Morgan Escare a firecracker against his old club, attacked with verve. But the Catalans' pack dominated their opponents with a controlled performance that allowed their talented backline to reap the rewards in a one-sided final quarter.

Sam Tomkins directed his team around the field with great assurance as sub Sam Kasiano's try on the stroke of half-time proved a sucker punch for Salford, 22-6 down at half-time. The Dragons were edging their way to a historic League Leaders title.

Round 22

So to Bank Holiday Monday, four days after the previous round of games, with all four teams battling for fifth and sixth positions being defeated.

Hull FC's season looked like tailing off badly when Salford gave them a 42-14 thrashing at the AJ Bell Stadium, winger Ken Sio finishing with four tries to his name.

The end result was as far away as possible in the first half, with the Red Devils leading just 12-8 at the break. Ligi Sao had put Hull ahead when he split the Salford defence open, with Marc Sneyd converting and then adding a penalty after Sio's first in the corner. Sio got his second just before half-time, grubbering brilliantly for himself to hand the Red Devils the lead for the first time.

When Danny Houghton crossed from a pinpoint Sneyd kick to put the Airlie Birds back in front on 49 minutes, there was little sign of what was to come.

However, Chris Atkin, Harvey Livett and Joe Burgess all crossed before Sio completed his hat-trick and then notched a fourth late on. It was five tries in 23 minutes for Salford as Krisnan Inu converted every try for seven out of seven.

Wakefield were in no mood to do neighbours Leeds a favour at Belle Vue as they registered a 20-13 win. With three wins in four games under interim head-coach Willie Poching, Trinity made their play-off hunting opponents lick their wounds following a dominant display, led by the likes of Jacob Miller and David Fifita.

The Rhinos crossed first after captain Matt Prior had been sent to the sin bin for a high tackle. Despite that, the ever-impressive Kruise Leeming dotted down before Kelepi Tanginoa levelled just after the half-hour mark.

Salford's Joe Burgess and Hull FC's Bureta Faraimo compete for a high ball

Brad Dwyer registered another effort before the break but Jordan Crowther once more levelled proceedings following the resumption.

It really was a game of attrition as both sides strived for good field position but Trinity had the upper hand for the majority of the second forty minutes. Miller put his side in the lead with a one-pointer but Robert Lui restored the deadlock shortly after before Ryan Hampshire edged Wakefield another point in front on 73 minutes.

And there was just enough time for Joe Arundel to cross for the hosts from a great offload by David Fifita to round off the scoring.

Hull KR were beaten 40-28 at Huddersfield, with Will Pryce converting six goals from seven attempts and scoring a special try as Huddersfield won for the first time in four matches.

The tone was set early at the John Smith's Stadium for the try-a-thon as the sides each scored two tries before the Giants opened up a 14-point lead shortly before half-time. Ricky Leutele was the first to extend that lead off a great looping pass from Oliver Russell before Sam Wood followed with his own effort. Greg Minikin's try right on the hooter gave Rovers hope of a second-half comeback, which was further boosted by Hall's superb catch of Mikey Lewis's pinpoint high kick following the resumption.

But with Pryce on fire, the Giants looked in control. The halfback converted his own try from Russell's grubber kick to restore the Giants' 12-point lead at 28-16. Pryce then added goals to tries from Joe Greenwood and Nathaniel Peteru to take his tally to 16 points, before Huddersfield then had to withstand some gutsy Rovers resilience as Kane Linnett and Matt Parcell went over in the closing minutes.

Wigan, suffering a points drought going into the game, clinically inflicted the Tigers' eighth home loss in nine games by 22-0. Led by Harry Smith and Jackson Hastings, the Warriors were the better team from the off and defended resolutely throughout.

August

It took 14 minutes for the Warriors to strike first as Hastings forced his way over for the club's first try in 217 minutes of play. Smith converted and the halfback had two opportunities to extend his side's lead with penalties but both went wide of the target.

Castleford's sloppiness on the Wigan line cost them as Jordan Turner dropped a long pass from Niall Evalds with the line at his mercy.

The Tigers' painful execution, Paul McShane was badly missed, didn't improve after the break as Liam Marshall gathered a wayward pass from Turner to canter over from 90 metres before Oliver Gildart finished well in the corner to make it 16-0. Brad Singleton put the cherry on top of the cake in the last minute as he ran a wonderful line and consolidated Wigan's position in fourth.

Castleford prop Liam Watts picked up a two-match ban for tripping.

St Helens came from behind to beat the Wolves on their own patch by 24-14 in a high-quality encounter. The Wolves had already beaten Saints in June but the latter were not to be denied again, despite Warrington holding a slender half-time lead.

Two tries in four minutes from Saints around the midway point in the first half, from Kevin Naiqama and Lewis Dodd, sent them 10-0 up but Ben Currie and George Williams responded in emphatic fashion.

And with Stefan Ratchford in fine form with the boot, the Wire racked up a 14-10 lead going into the break.

However, that was as good as it got for them as Saints registered another two tries after half-time through an unbelievable Mark Percival effort and then a fortunate James Bentley try from a conniving Jack Welsby kick through.

Warrington's Tom Lineham was sin-binned for a high tackle in the last ten minutes - he was banned for two games - before a mass brawl ended the contest, with Gareth Widdop and Bentley both being handed yellow cards for their role in the drama.

The defeat left the Wolves with barely a chance of catching St Helens in second spot, whilst looking over their shoulder at Wigan in fourth place.

Mike McMeeken and Fouad Yaha both scored hat-tricks as Super League leaders Catalans ran riot against struggling Leigh Centurions to win 64-0 in Perpignan.

The Dragons raced into a remarkable 28-0 lead after just 21 minutes and then a 40-0 half-time lead as the visitors just couldn't live with the pace and power of the home side.

McMeeken and Yaha both racked up their tries in the first forty minutes before Joel and Sam Tomkins combined to further extend the hosts' advantage early in the second half.

The victory was already complete but Tom Davies had just enough time to make it eleven tries for the night with five minutes left after Sam Tomkins had registered a double. James Maloney tagged on 24 points with a try and ten goals.

BETFRED SUPER LEAGUE
Monday 30th August

	P	W	D	L	F	A	Diff %	Win %
Catalans Dragons	20	18	0	2	631	326	193.56	90.00
St Helens	18	15	0	3	464	166	279.52	83.33
Warrington Wolves	18	12	1	5	518	305	169.84	69.44
Wigan Warriors	22	13	0	9	359	367	97.82	59.09
Leeds Rhinos	21	11	0	10	489	364	134.34	52.38
Castleford Tigers	20	10	0	10	365	468	77.99	50.00
Hull FC	18	8	1	9	373	397	93.95	47.22
Hull Kingston Rovers	17	8	0	9	415	397	104.53	47.06
Huddersfield Giants	21	7	0	14	370	442	83.71	33.33
Wakefield Trinity	21	7	0	14	388	492	78.86	33.33
Salford Red Devils	19	6	0	13	339	521	65.07	31.58
Leigh Centurions	19	1	0	18	300	766	39.16	5.26

SEPTEMBER
Kinda Magic

Round 23

Catalans Dragons made history by securing the League Leaders Shield on the big stage of Magic Weekend at Newcastle's St James's Park. And they did it by completing one of the most dramatic comebacks in League history, James Maloney kicking the field goal that sealed a 31-30 win over second-placed St Helens.

After looking completely dead and buried, the Dragons scored three converted tries in the final five minutes - from Dean Whare, Gil Dudson and Sam Kasiano - to draw level at 30-all, before Maloney kicked the winning one-pointer from over 40 metres, eight minutes into golden-point time.

Catalans had got off to a flyer, in the second Saturday game, when Sam Tomkins stepped over to open the scoring and two minutes later Tomkins was illegally tackled high by Mark Percival, whose yellow card reduced Saints to 12 men.

But, despite still being a body down, Lachlan Coote created the space for Tommy Makinson to score in the right corner on 14 minutes. On 20 minutes, within four minutes of returning to the fray, Percival then set up Coote for a second try, this one being successfully converted by the Australian fullback to put Saints 10-6 up.

Saints were in total control for almost the rest of the game. They strode clear just before the break when, in the space of three minutes, Sione Mata'utia got over for his first try, Coote converted, Catalans had prop Sam Kasiano sin-binned for dangerous contact and Coote added two more points when Maloney was penalised for a shoulder charge.

Having gone in 18-6 up at the interval, a second try for Mata'utia and then a fifth Saints try from Morgan Knowles, either side of a converted Julian Bousquet try, stretched the reigning Super League champions three converted scores clear at 30-12.

But Catalans had a sting in the tail, triggered by Whare in the 75th minute. Dudson got on the end of a nice to move to add another with a minute and a half left.

And Kasiano then completed the comeback as he held a high bomb to crash over the line by the posts, allowing Maloney to take the game to extra time with the third of his three successful late conversions.

The late drama continued into extra time. Samisoni Langi was stretchered off after a challenge by Agnatius Paasi and taken to hospital with Saints' Tongan forward in the sin bin.

Coote had first chance to win it but missed and, in the final minutes of golden-point extra time, Maloney's long low effort crept over to clinch a historic victory.

Paasi was banned for two games and Leeds-bound James Bentley had played his last game for Saints after suffering a back injury.

The game that followed, starting half an hour late, was also incredibly exciting as Leeds came late to beat Hull FC 25-24 in extra time, to cap Magic's most memorable day.

With the fifth and sixth finishing play-off spots in sight, the game was effectively a season's work on the line for both sides, and it took a first career field goal by Kruise Leeming in the 88th minute - after five missed in total between the two sides - to keep the

Catalans Dragons' Sam Tomkins beats St Helens' Morgan Knowles and Lachlan Coote at Magic Weekend

Rhinos on and Hull veering off their regular-season course, a third successive defeat and seventh in eight matches for Hull.

The ending was bizarre, with Rhyse Martin finding touch in the corner and as Hull brought play away from their own line, Manu Ma'u jumped to his feet so quickly to play the ball that Danny Houghton was not in position to pick it up.

He toed it ahead, Jack Broadbent snaffled it, King Vuniyayawa added extra metres, Brad Dwyer found Leeming - back in the halves after Robert Lui's early head-injury withdrawal - and he did the rest, rewarding the side that scored four tries to three.

Harry Newman was the gamestar, best seen in his shrugging off of Marc Sneyd and Ma'u for a fine solo try, defending with gusto and producing a mighty charge down in the first period of golden-point to deny a Sneyd field-goal attempt.

Hull's over-reliance on storming the middle, Tevita Satae again breaking the 200-metre mark, proved to be their undoing. With a ten-point lead in the second half, they weren't able to shut out the game.

Sneyd also missed a long-range field-goal attempt three minutes from normal time after Leeming and Broadbent tries brought the Rhinos level at 24-24, although Martin missed the second conversion from an angle he'd usually nail.

Only a magnificent tackle by Jamie Shaul prevented Ash Handley settling matters with a golden-point try from a Tom Briscoe charge, while Leeming was wide with a field-goal attempt on the back of the position. Richie Myler was the next to miss before Martin's one-point attempt hit the bar.

Hull couldn't get near enough to set up a decent position and Sneyd missed from half way but, after Hull's play-the-ball aberration, Leeming made no mistake.

In the Saturday opener, Castleford beat Salford 29-18 to keep them in the play-off mix. The loss at half-time of reigning Super League Man of Steel Paul McShane to an ankle injury took some of the gloss off the victory, which kept Daryl Powell's side's play-off bid on the boil. They started the game with stand-in halves in Peter Mata'utia and Jordan Turner but still managed to grind out the win.

Mata'utia kicked four from five goals and grabbed the final try to secure victory, which ensured the Tigers remained in sixth place with two matches to go.

Sunday's opener didn't provide edge-of-the-seat drama as Wakefield overcame an early Will Pryce try to dominate Huddersfield and record a 32-18 win.

Halves Mason Lino and Jacob Miller controlled matters in the middle of the field, with Lino also regularly the first in the kick-chase as part of an impressive defensive contribution. Joe Westerman - in his 300th Super League appearance - was as committed as ever at loose forward and back-rower Kelepi Tanginoa terrorised Huddersfield's right-side defence in the second half to continue the side's impressive run under their interim coach Wille Poching.

Barring Pryce's early salvo and a brief spell where they hinted at a comeback in the second half, it was a disappointing display from the Giants, despite big efforts from Olly Ashall-Bott and Sam Wood.

The 44th-minute sin-binning of Sam Hewitt for leading with the elbow was exploited by Wakefield as Tanginoa's converted try took them out to 20-6. The Giants fought back with Wood and Josh Jones tries but scores from Reece Lyne and Chris Green kept them at bay. Hewitt got a one-match ban.

Warrington beat Wigan 10-6 in the second Sunday game. The Warriors, who that week announced that head coach Adrian Lam would be leaving at the end of the season, managed just one try in 80 minutes and, painfully for the cherry and white, it was a former Wiganer in George Williams who made the telling blow against his old club.

Williams' first-half try was enough to snare victory for the Wolves, as they held on to third place on the Super League ladder.

Despite the impressive win at Castleford the previous Monday, Wigan's attack had been mis-firing, through no lack of effort and they again struggled to trouble Warrington's defence.

It took Warrington just 55 seconds to breach Wigan's line at a sun-soaked St James' Park. A disastrous bounce from a bomb launched by Gareth Widdop completely wrong footed the Warriors' defence and Josh Thewlis scooped up the ball to score.

Then, in the 26th minute, England star Williams powered over against his former club, after Widdop was hauled down inches from the try-line. Williams showed great speed and footwork to dance his way through for the four-pointer.

Stefan Ratchford added the goal and suddenly Warrington were in the driving seat. In the 37th minute, however, Jackson Hastings was held up over the try-line. Wigan then forced a drop-out as they inched closer to finally breaking their drought.

It happened right before half-time when Ethan Havard burst onto a great short ball from Sam Powell to crash through. Harry Smith added the goal and Wigan were back in the fight at 10-6 at the break.

Warrington came closest to scoring in the pointless second half as Jack Hughes crossed but his effort was chalked off by video referee Chris Kendall.

Hull KR kept their challenge for the play-offs alive in the final game, beating Leigh 44-6. It was a big defensive effort from the Centurions in the first half - they led 6-0 up to the half-hour mark - but in the end the energy they invested came back to bite them after the break and they were eventually beaten comfortably.

The Robins clicked into gear in the second half, showcasing the entertaining brand of rugby they'd played all year.

Hooker Matt Parcell did all the damage through the middle, scoring a try and carving up Leigh to lay the platform for Hull KR's dominance, as Brad Takairangi's try two minutes after half-time marked the start of Rovers second-half procession.

A total of 60,866 supporters attended the Magic Weekend, 35,104 on Saturday, and 25,762 on Sunday, around 4,000 higher than attended the event when it was held in Liverpool in 2019 and 4,000 down on the attendance in 2018, when it was last held in Newcastle. The Weekend was moved to September from its previous May scheduling, when it was originally intended to be staged in 2021.

Round 24

Three clubs were left with a chance of taking the last two play-off spots with one round to go with the percentage system employed for the second year running making it fiendishly difficult to decide on the permutations between Hull KR, Leeds and Castleford.

The Rhinos missed a chance to stay in fifth spot when they lost 40-6 at St Helens on the Friday night. The scoreline was a fair reflection on the contest as Alex Walmsley produced a front-rower's performance to rank alongside any in recent memory. The England prop provided a marauding first spell, trampling over Leeds defenders and powering over for a try. By the time he left the field on 32 minutes to a standing ovation, Kristian Woolf's side were 28-0 ahead.

Off the back of two-try Morgan Knowles and Walmsley's performance up front, young halfbacks Jack Welsby and Lewis Dodd again thrived, with James Roby having a field day around the ruck.

With accomplished finishers, such as Tommy Makinson and Regan Grace out wide, Saints had more than enough to account for an injury-hit but disappointing Leeds team, securing second place in the process.

Hull KR leapfrogged both Leeds, who were sixth and Castleford by beating the Tigers 26-19 at Craven Park.

Defeat would have ended Rovers' play-off hopes but they conjured a stirring comeback win, thanks to a two-try haul from Mikey Lewis and a kicking masterclass from Jordan Abdull.

Lewis scored twice and halfback partner Abdull kicked five goals and a vital 40/20, as the Robins fought back brilliantly in the second half to seal a crucial win.

The Tigers were missing hooker Paul McShane, who returned from an abdominal problem to start the Magic Weekend win over Salford - only to be forced off by an ankle injury. But they thought they had done enough when they led 19-12 after Niall Evalds' second try two minutes after half-time. And in the 52nd minute Evalds almost sped over again for his hat-trick but a quality cover tackle from Will Dagger cut him down short.

Matt Parcell's 55th-minute try from Brad Takairangi's knock down of a bomb near the line was contentious, though referee James Child awarded the try without sending it to the video referee. Abdull added the extras and suddenly the Tigers' lead was cut to a single point. Craven Park went up in cheers and then Abdull landed a brilliant 40/20.

There was more drama to come as Kane Linnett powered over from short range to snatch the lead back for his team. Abdull made no mistake and suddenly Hull KR were 24-19 ahead. The Robins were riding a wave of momentum, though the Tigers rallied to get back into the game, first forcing a goal-line drop-out and then Linnett was penalised for a ball steal. Adam Milner was then held up over the try-line but Hull KR would not be broken.

With both teams out on their feet, the home side held on grimly and Abdull added a final penalty goal to close out the game.

As chance would have it, Hull KR were due to play at Leeds in the final round. If Castleford could beat Warrington the night before, the loser at Headingley would be out. Hull KR's chances looked slimmer as Ryan Hall and Greg Minikin both picked up season-ending injuries.

Wigan clinched a fourth-placed finish and ended Hull's play-off hopes with a 10-0 triumph at the MKM Stadium on the Saturday. After a scoreless first half, Jake Bibby and Zak Hardaker scored tries and a second shutout in three matches indicated the Warriors' defence was in great shape for a Grand Final push.

The first try came in the 52nd minute as Jackson Hastings popped up a little kick and Bibby was sharper than Mitieli Vulikijapani to squeeze over in front of the travelling support. Hardaker was unable to convert but played the crucial role ten minutes later in their other score. The Warriors kept the ball alive out wide and shifted it inside to find

Catalans Dragons coach Steve McNamara and captain Benjamin Garcia show off the League Leaders' Shield

the fullback, who booted in behind a scattered Hull defence to set up a foot race with Jamie Shaul. It was neck-and-neck until the goal post intervened, pinging the ball into the grateful arms of the Wigan man to dive over.

The simple conversion made it 10-0; not necessarily game over but, with the ball in the hands of an increasingly reckless Hull side throwing wild passes and ambitious offloads, it would prove more than enough.

They did come close at times, with Shaul held out by impressive defence after combining with Carlos Tuimavave, and Vulikijapani having an effort ruled out for a forward Jake Connor pass.

All the remaining fixtures were played on the Saturday and there was a major upset in Perpignan where Huddersfield emerged 30-18 winners after the under-strength Catalans had shot into an 18-0 lead on the quarter-mark. Matt Whitley and Matthieu Laguerre scored the first two tries with Chris McQueen in the sin bin for a high tackle on Laguerre, Whitley getting his second after McQueen's return, James Maloney converting all three.

But by half-time Josh Jones and Louis Senior tries, both converted by Oliver Russell, had the Giants back in contention.

Russell was at the heart of early pressure from the Giants in the second half and it took ten minutes before scrum-half Jack Cogger struck in an angular run from 35 metres out, crossing on the right, with Russell levelling the scores with his conversion.

Fullback Olly Ashall-Bott then scored straight from the kick-off with a mesmerising 45-metre dash, shrugging off four defenders, with Russell again on target to silence the French crowd, putting Huddersfield ahead for the first time in the game at 24-18.

The killer blow was struck ten minutes from the end when prop Matty English forced his way between the posts for a try, giving Russell an easy shot at goal and putting the Giants twelve points in front. Huddersfield were full value for the victory.

September

The defeat didn't spoil the celebrations after the final whistle as the Dragons were presented with the League Leaders' Shield in front of their passionate fans.

Warrington Wolves, who had already clinched third place, needed extra time to thwart Salford as George Williams claimed a golden-point field goal for a 20-19 victory at the Halliwell Jones Stadium.

Winger Ken Sio scored two tries to take his league haul to 17 and stand-off Tui Lolohea one for Salford, who led with 20 minutes remaining then, after Williams kicked a one-pointer to put the home side 19-18 up, levelled thanks to Lolohea's field goal to force extra time.

The game had come to life inside the final ten minutes. Danny Addy was sent to the sin bin after a high tackle on Ellis Longstaff, before Gareth Widdop scored the resulting penalty to level the scores.

Salford were the first go at a field goal but Kristian Inu missed with his attempt. Warrington then came down the other end and Williams' 40-metre effort found the target to edge the Wolves ahead.

But that was not the end of the drama. With time running out, Salford continued throwing the ball around and eventually got the ball to Lolohea, whose deflected drop goal just got over to level the scores.

Warrington then thought they had won it with just five seconds left on the clock. Williams once again found his range but the referee gave a penalty to Salford after a player was taken out while trying to charge the attempt down, meaning the match went to golden point.

Salford did themselves a huge favour straight from the kick-off, getting the ball back after the kick-off bounced out. The Red Devils were able to see out the set but Inu once again could not find the target with his field-goal attempt.

Warrington made the most of this reprieve, as Williams' effort had enough on it to get over and win the game.

Leigh delivered a 26-18 home win over Wakefield for only their second victory of the season. They did it the hard way too, seeing a 10-0 lead evaporate, losing prop Nathan Mason at half-time to injury, overcoming an eight-point deficit and having two players sin-binned in a frantic last few minutes.

Ryan Brierley proved the difference, scoring a hat-trick and kicking three goals for a personal total of eighteen points.

Sam Stone's 68th-minute try that made the score 26-18 just gave Leigh enough breathing space for the frantic finale. There was a twist when Rob Butler was sin-binned with six minutes remaining for leading with his elbow. Wakefield didn't find touch from the penalty and the Centurions again went close.

Trinity then broke from deep, working the overlap for Innes Senior before Brierley tracked across and put him in touch with a diving tackle twenty metres from the line.

Another try saver from Brierley, this time on Reece Lyne, saw him sin-binned for slowing down the play-the-ball with a couple of minutes remaining. But Leigh weren't going to let this one slip.

Round 25

It was a simple target for Castleford when they played Warrington at home in the last regular-season round. With the only remaining rivals for the last play-off spots, Leeds and Hull KR, set to play each other the next night, a win would take the Tigers into the play-offs.

But it all went badly wrong as they fell to a 40-24 defeat after trailing 32-0 four minutes after half-time. The Wolves were on fire to dampen the spirits of the Tigers faithful who had come to say farewell to head coach Daryl Powell and stalwart players Michael Shenton, who was retiring and Grant Millington, returning to Australia after ten years at the club.

Salford's Andy Ackers gets a pass away as he is brought down against St Helens

Warrington, for whom fullback Matty Ashton scored a hat-trick and centre Jake Mamo a double, fought off a subsequent comeback by the home side that had the score at 32-24, with winger Josh Charnley in the sin bin for a tip tackle on Jordan Turner and then Mike Cooper sent off for a shoulder to the head of fellow prop Liam Watts. Cooper got a one-match penalty notice.

But the Wolves closed down the game superbly and Connor Wrench's try three minutes from time settled it.

The disappointing end to the Tigers' season didn't dampen the emotional scenes after the final whistle as the crowd showed their appreciation to the departees, who included Jesse Sene-Lefao, Alex Foster, Peter Mata'utia and the non-playing Oliver Holmes, the latter two set to join Powell at Warrington for 2022.

The Tigers' elimination meant that both Leeds and Hull KR would finish in the top six, though the result would decide who would have to visit fourth-placed Wigan or third-placed Warrington the following week. As it turned out a Robert Lui masterclass steered the Rhinos into fifth spot after an eventually comfortable 36-12 win.

Leeds looked best placed for a tilt at the top guns, more so with four forwards set to return from injury, as the Robins' casualty toll mounted, with Matt Parcell another major loss in the first half, the seasons of Ryan Hall and Greg Minikin both ended the previous week.

Lui's midfield solidity and creative difference in his final home game for the Rhinos before heading back to Australia was too much for the Robins. His partnership with Rhyse Martin was again hugely effective, whilst off the bench try scorers Tom Holroyd, in particular, and James Donaldson ensured the intensity went up to allow the Rhinos to complete the job.

Lui's opening try of the game, as he burst past George King and swept away Will Dagger for the opening solo score for Martin to land the first of six faultless conversions, was a beauty.

September

Winger Ash Handley best summed up the Rhinos' resolve going into knockout rugby. At fault for the opening Robins try, releasing the ball behind Tom Briscoe for Brad Takairangi to send in Mikey Lewis, he made two stunning try-saving tackles to prevent the luckless Ben Crooks crossing and again topped the metre-making tally with 180, the majority post-contact coming out of his own quarter.

The Rhinos led 24-6 at half-time courtesy of Lui's try and one each from Matt Prior, Tom Holroyd and Richie Myler, with Lewis scoring Rovers' only try.

Donaldson went over under the sticks for Leeds' fifth try of the evening and Handley did well at the corner to add their sixth from Myler's long pass before Will Dagger ran in a late second for the visitors.

Also on the Friday night, Wigan made a big statement of intent as they beat League Leaders Catalans at the DW Stadium by 12-8.

The defeat didn't affect league placings but the Dragons were hit by the 20th minute injury to Sam Tomkins who immediately left the field when he received a knock to his knee. It was a very tight game with James Maloney missing his two conversion attempts and Zak Hardaker hitting both.

The opening half was a bruising affair with defences on top for the large part. It took just short of half an hour for the first points to be scored but it was anything but dull.

Wigan's defence had improved week on week and they managed to keep the Dragons scoreless in the first half, to make it over 160 minutes without conceding a single point.

The opening try saw captain Willie Isa, back after a four-match suspension, pounce on a grubber kick from Jackson Hastings. Hardaker converted as the Warriors led 6-0 at the break.

It took 52 minutes until the Dragons breached Wigan's line, with Tom Davies crossing in the corner. Many thought the League Leaders would kick on and run away with it but Wigan extended their lead to eight points with a fine first try for the club for James McDonnell, recalled from loan at York, who burst through from 25 metres.

A scramble try from Matthieu Laguerre set up a tense finish but the Warriors hung on to become only the fourth side to beat Steve McNamara's men in the league.

Adrian Lam rested several key players. Liam Marshall, Brad Singleton and Morgan Smithies were excluded from the 21-man Wigan squad, while Sam Powell, Liam Farrell, John Bateman and Umyla Hanley were all left out of the 17-man squad selected for the game.

In the week, Catalans centre Samisoni Langi sent a personal apology to Wakefield Trinity for changing his mind after agreeing a deal to join the Yorkshire club for the next season.

A youthful St Helens side - with three debutants - suffered a 26-14 defeat at Salford on the Friday night.

Fullback Jon Bennison, who made a tryscoring debut, winger Shay Martyn, the son of St Helens legend Tommy Martyn, and back-rower Sam Royle were all selected in the starting line-up, helping St Helens to a 14-4 lead just two minutes before half-time, before former St Helens player Matty Costello pulled a try back for the Red Devils to make it 14-12 at half-time, with Salford scoring two converted tries in the second half to win the game.

Young centre Ben Davies also figured prominently and veteran Jonny Lomax returned to the team at stand-off and came through unscathed.

Bennison and Lomax tries gave Saints a flying start but Ken Sio and Costello pulled it back to 14-10 at the break.

The home side took control in the second period, with Chris Atkin, on his 200th career appearance, and Ellis Robson tries turning the score. Sio's second took the game away from Saints. It was handed to him on a plate by Atkin, who instead of touching down himself looked for Sio under the posts. It was his 19th of the season, making him Super League XXVI's top try-scorer.

Over at Wakefield on the same night, a new Super League record was set when Trinity halfback Mason Lino kicked his second goal of the night in a 44-12 hammering of Hull FC. It was his 36th consecutive successful conversion and passed Henry Paul's record of 35, set in 2001 while playing for Bradford Bulls. Canterbury winger Hazem El Masri set the same record for NRL in 2003.

Lino went on to extend the record to 37, four behind the all-competition record held by Liam Finn (Featherstone 2012) and Jamie Ellis (Hull KR 2017).

Trinity signed off their season in style with a first-half steamroller performance against a bruised Hull FC badly missing halves Marc Sneyd and Josh Reynolds.

Lino's efforts from the tee were only part of his best game in the red, white and blue, particularly across a rampant opening forty minutes that saw Trinity race into a 34-0 lead after Innes Senior opened the scoring in the third minute.

After the break, Hull worked a pair of consolation scores through Mitieli Vulikijapani and Jake Connor, the former off the latter's high kick, before bombing a few chances close to the line and allowing Wakefield to march downfield for the last word, first through a dive for the line by Kelepi Tanginoa for his second and lastly with a well-worked Liam Kay try down the right wing in the final minute.

David Fifita took on kicking duties for the former and promptly nailed a prop forward's conversion to raucous cheers. And even if he couldn't add a second after the final whistle, there was no disguising the grin on his or his teammates' faces.

One game remained for the Sunday, as Huddersfield secured ninth spot in the table - on points difference percentage from Wakefield - with a 42-24 win over relegated Leigh.

The Giants ended up coming from behind twice in what was a close first half. Back-to-back tries, from Owen Trout and Oliver Russell, just before the half-time hooter gave them the platform to pull away from the Centurions, who in true Leigh style had the final say with Brendan Elliot's spectacular last-minute try.

The highlight of an entertaining game was the try scored by Will Pryce in the 65th minute. Pryce took the ball at first receiver well in his own half, stepped through the line at speed and went 70 metres to score by the posts, rounding fullback Keanan Brand along the way.

BETFRED SUPER LEAGUE
Final table - Sunday 19th September

	P	W	D	L	F	A	Diff %	Win %
Catalans Dragons	23	19	0	4	688	398	172.86	82.61
St Helens	21	16	0	5	548	229	239.30	76.19
Warrington Wolves	21	15	1	5	588	354	166.10	73.81
Wigan Warriors	25	15	0	10	387	385	100.52	60.00
Leeds Rhinos	24	13	0	11	556	440	126.36	54.17
Hull Kingston Rovers	20	10	0	10	497	458	108.52	50.00
Castleford Tigers	23	11	0	12	437	552	79.17	47.83
Hull FC	21	8	1	12	409	476	85.92	40.48
Huddersfield Giants	24	9	0	15	460	516	89.15	37.50
Wakefield Trinity	24	9	0	15	482	548	87.96	37.50
Salford Red Devils	22	7	0	15	402	584	68.84	31.82
Leigh Centurions	22	2	0	20	356	870	40.92	9.09

The Eliminators

The story of the game as listed in League Express reflected perfectly how the first play-off on the Thursday night unfolded. It was only three lines long.

Fifth-placed Leeds went to fourth-placed Wigan and won through to the semi-finals with a dour 8-0 win at the DW Stadium. Adrian Lam's time as Warriors coach ended in disappointment as they were kept scoreless for the third time in 2021, the Rhinos keeping alive their hopes of a ninth Super League Grand Final win.

There was little or no adventure, just plenty of tough defence as the sides went in nil-nil at half-time. The second half saw Wigan huff and puff without creating many chances at all. The only try of the game came in the 51st minute when a moment of brilliance from Richie Myler saw Ash Handley cross. The conversion and a late penalty from Rhyse Martin saw the Rhinos home.

Leeds' Ash Handley looks for support at Wigan

Lam brought back Liam Marshall, Brad Singleton, Sam Powell, John Bateman, Liam Farrell and Morgan Smithies after they were rested for the round 25-win over Catalans. Tony Clubb, who had announced he would be retiring at the end of the season, was left out of the squad, while Kai Pearce-Paul, Joe Shorrocks and Ethan Havard were named on the bench.

Rhinos coach Richard Agar made a couple of changes from the team that beat Hull KR. Kruise Leeming was back in the halves with Richie Myler moving back to fullback. Brad Dwyer started at hooker, while prop forward Mikolaj Oledzki returned on the bench following foot surgery, despite originally being ruled out for the season. James Donaldson was promoted from the bench with Zane Tetevano also getting a starting place.

The Rhinos frustrated Zak Hardaker every time he got the ball, which led to a couple of confrontations with Matt Prior. He was halted by a massive hit from Robert Lui and then a two-man shot from Oledzki and Cameron Smith, which didn't improve his mood. Both sides were giving away unnecessary penalties as they were determined to keep their opponents pointless.

Leeds almost opened the scoring at the start of the second half with Dwyer darting from dummy-half but he was held inches short. Then seconds later it was Wigan who could have scored when Marshall came close to picking out a long ball for an interception. Had he caught it, no-one would have stopped him.

The Rhinos eventually made Wigan pay for some missed opportunities by going up to the other end of the field and opening the scoring. A high kick from Leeming was tapped back expertly by Myler to allow Handley to catch and go over. Martin converted and Leeds led 6-0.

Wigan had to throw caution to the wind in order to extend their season. Pearce-Paul was introduced to the action to see if he could do any damage with his offloads and he did manage to get one away to Harry Smith. But the halfback's kick towards the Rhinos' line was dealt with comfortably.

The Rhinos sealed victory with seven minutes remaining after Oliver Partington was penalised for reefing the ball. Martin slotted over the penalty to seal an 8-0 win.

It was a tame end to Wigan's season and one of the most unentertaining games of the year. They only had to wait two weeks to have their mood brightened when it was announced that former coach Shaun Wane would be returning to the club.

Hull KR's Mikey Lewis slides over to score a spectacular try against Warrington

The Friday night eliminator was a different animal to one the night before as Hull KR stunned Warrington at the Halliwell Jones Stadium, setting up a semi-final trip to Catalans with a 19-0 victory, arguably the biggest shock in Super League play-off history.

Sixth-placed Rovers, missing nine players who would all conceivably be in their first-choice seventeen, went to Warrington as 6/1 outsiders with some bookmakers. But they made those odds look ridiculous with a performance full of character, resilience and a sprinkling of class from their outstanding halfbacks Jordan Abdull and Mikey Lewis, who both scored tries.

The pair were supported by indefatigable hooker Jez Litten - who didn't have the luxury of being spelled by his usual partner in crime, the injured Matt Parcell - and they had Muizz Mustapha the pick of a terrific pack punching above its weight. The Robins - who finished eleventh in the previous two Super League seasons - also produced a series of remarkable last-ditch tackle efforts from across their committed team.

The Wolves were only without the suspended Mike Cooper, while Tom Lineham came in for Josh Charnley on the wing.

As expected, the home side dominated the opening exchanges. Twice they were handed early field position through Jimmy Keinhorst errors, only to come up with their own mistakes. Then Daryl Clark attacked the line and stretched out to score but lost the ball.

Rovers' best moment in the opening quarter of an hour saw Lewis's 40/20 attempt just stopped by Lineham and the Robins then lost Brad Takairangi temporality for a HIA assessment after an attempted big hit on Sitaleki Akauola went wrong.

After the vast majority of the game up to that point had been played in Robins territory, the visitors took the lead as Abdull dummied his way over in the corner on the last tackle. Abdull added the conversion from the left touchline for good measure.

September

Rovers were defensively excellent, catching Toby King on the last tackle, Abdull's tackle dislodging the ball from Jack Hughes, Shaun Kenny-Dowall stopping Jake Mamo. Even a sin bin for Albert Vete for a late hit on Gareth Widdop didn't help the Wolves, with Abdull kicking expertly in his absence, bar a missed field-goal attempt.

The first half, which had been full of mistakes for the most part, finished in thrilling fashion with the home side keeping the ball alive superbly to allow George Williams sight of the line, only for Mustapha and Will Dagger to combine brilliantly to stop him short as the hooter went. After the restart it was Litten and Keinhorst making the try-saving tackle on the England stand-off.

Then Rovers started to take the game away from their opponents. Lewis came up with his brilliant score, spotting Ratchford up in the line, chipping over and winning the race for an exhilarating try. Abdull added the straight-forward conversion, then pushed a penalty wide after a ball-steal on Vete but then made it 14-0 after a Ratchford high shot on the non-stop Mustapha.

Williams went close yet again, only for Litten and Matty Storton to haul him down short, before Rovers added the knock-out blow. Good hands from Abdull and Will Dagger gave Keinhorst enough space to finish out wide and although Abdull missed the difficult conversion, he completed the scoring with a late field goal to send the Rovers fans into raptures.

It was a sad ending for Wolves coach Steve Price after four years at the club which had been distinguished by a Challenge Cup victory over St Helens in 2019, a Grand Final defeat to Wigan in 2018 and a Challenge Cup defeat to the Catalans Dragons in the same year.

Semi-finals

Catalans made history by qualifying for their first Grand Final on an electric night at a sold-out Stade Gilbert Brutus, beating wildcards Hull KR by 28-10.

The Robins' progress to the penultimate game of the season was remarkable but their lengthy injury list finally caught up with them on a warm Perpignan late summer's evening. A herculean effort at centre from captain Shaun Kenny-Dowall and yet another towering bombing raid by Jordan Abdull weren't enough to defy a determined Dragons side.

A fearsome and ferocious return to form by Michael McIlorum was at the heart of the win. A rare eighty-minute stint from McIlorum was full of precise handling, clever timing at the ruck and astute game-management. But it was his defence that hit home with French supporters, brutally brilliant and effective in the middle of the pitch and clearly targeted at some of the bigger forwards in the Rovers' pack.

Rovers hurt Catalans at the very start of the match with a fumble from an Abdull high-ball by Arthur Mourgue, who was standing in for Sam Tomkins at fullback and a penalty for a high tackle by McIlorum. Then the young French star was penalised for a double-movement as he looked likely to score in the seventh minute.

It was left to Ben Garcia to open the scoring for the Dragons when he towed Rovers' winger Ben Crooks over the line after winning the fight for a high ball with Rovers' fullback Will Dagger in the ninth minute, James Maloney adding the conversion to make it 6-0.

A period of stalemate ensued between the two sides who had already fought three tight encounters this season but when giant substitute Sam Kasiano entered the fray, the Dragons went into overdrive.

First, winger Fouad Yaha was pulled back for a forward pass after he crossed the line on the left. Then Josh Drinkwater collected an interception and ran 80 metres to score in the 31st minute, Maloney making it 12-0 with a simple conversion.

Kasiano's destructive force up the middle of the pitch was taking its toll but it was

Catalans Dragons' Josh Drinkwater races away from Hull KR's Will Dagger

the brute force of another substitute forward that led to the next score. Rovers' hulking prop Albert Vete came off the bench to wreak some havoc of his own and a couple of powerful bursts led to centre Kenny-Dowall striding over the Dragons' line on the left, three minutes from the interval, too wide for Abdull to add the conversion.

At 12-4, Catalans still had work to do in the second half but a high kick from Maloney, fumbled by Dagger, was pounced upon by Mourgue in the first minute and the video referee agreed with official James Child that the young Frenchman had grounded correctly to make it 16-4, with Maloney wide with his conversion.

A series of penalties to Rovers had French fans howling but the return to the pitch of captain Garcia put Catalans back on the front foot. A blistering break by Mike McMeeken and Tom Davies on the right was switched to the left for Yaha to strike in the corner in the 61st minute, with Maloney missing the conversion from the touchline.

Joel Tomkins was pulled back by the video-referee for a knock-on over the line but when Josh Drinkwater stroked a grubber over the chalk, substitute Joe Chan was quick to pounce for his debut try, Maloney adding the conversion to make it 26-4 with eleven minutes left to play.

Rovers struck back with a try from winger Ryan Hall in the 74th minute, converted from the touchline by Abdull. But a penalty goal two minutes from the end by Maloney finished the game at 28-10, leaving French supporters singing long into the night after the fireworks faded, dreaming of a historic day at Old Trafford.

Richie Myler looks on as St Helens' Regan Grace heads for the Leeds tryline

On the Friday night, St Helens won the right to compete for their third successive Grand Final win with a convincing 36-8 home victory over Leeds.

Saints dominated the pace of the game almost from the off, making metres at will with the ball and restricting the Rhinos' progress up field.

Prop Alex Walmsley was again imperious in the middle, taking a lead that was followed by each of his teammates, especially hooker James Roby who thrived on the platform he and others laid.

Out wide Lachlan Coote overcame an early error to provide the perfect link between halfbacks and outside backs, where Mark Percival and Regan Grace both helped themselves to try doubles on the potent left side.

The result never looked in doubt from very early in the game, though the Rhinos deserved credit for somehow hanging into the contest beyond the hour mark, without ever looking like winning.

Robert Lui produced a wholly committed performance in his final game for the club before returning to Australia and Bodene Thompson was their best forward when he came off the bench. But they just couldn't deal with what St Helens offered on the night.

Kristian Woolf was able to welcome a host of key players back from the side that lost at Salford, while Richard Agar's only change was starting with Mikolaj Oledzki at prop, with Thompson on the bench.

Saints kicked off but the game could hardly have started worse for them, with Coote knocking on Lui's kick from the opening set. But for the vast majority of the remainder of the half - which yielded 14 penalties or set restarts - they dominated, playing the game at a speed that Leeds struggled to contain.

Grace opened the scoring, taking a smart cut-out pass from Coote to cross out wide, despite Richie Myler's efforts on the line. Coote missed the difficult conversion but added a penalty when Rhyse Martin was penalised for having a hand on the ball in the tackle.

The Rhinos were the first to be reduced to twelve men when Tom Briscoe was sin-binned for a high tackle on Coote, who duly converted the penalty.

Moments later, having earned his side a set restart, the rampaging Walmsley offloaded for evergreen skipper Roby to twist over from close range for his first try of the season.

Leeds somehow stayed in the contest and found a response before half-time, despite spluttering with the ball on several occasions.

It came after Saints had their own yellow card when Sione Mata'utia got ten minutes for a high shot on a falling Luke Briscoe.

A host of frantic sets saw them waste promising positions before the Rhinos' attack eventually clicked sufficiently for Myler to force his way to the line in the corner. Martin missed the conversion attempt from the touchline but his side would probably have been happy with a 14-4 interval scoreline on the overall balance of play.

Leeds' task became more difficult, though, within five minutes of the restart. James Donaldson was the next to be sent for ten minutes rest for a tackle on Coote that was again on a falling player.

Moments later Lui hit Grace with a tremendous shot but Saints players objected to Harry Newman and Zane Tetevano following through and a minor coming together ensued, which ended with a penalty for Saints.

They took full advantage, with Percival forcing his way over after Mata'utia shrewdly attacked the blindside from dummy-half. And it was effectively game over ten minutes later. Another smooth backline handling move saw Coote hit Kevin Naiqama on a superb line and the champions were now four scores ahead inside the final quarter.

Leeds refused to buckle completely. With Morgan Knowles completing a quartet of sin bins, good hands from Lui and Martin gave Luke Briscoe enough space to cross out wide. But it was Saints that finished with the flourish as scrum-half Lewis Dodd had hands in tries to Percival and Grace to complete their doubles.

SUPER LEAGUE GRAND FINAL
All Saints Day

Defending champions St Helens won their third Super League title in succession when they beat League Leaders Catalans by 12-10, with centre Kevin Naiqama, the scorer of both Saints tries, becoming the first Fijian to win the Harry Sunderland Trophy as man of the match.

Naiqama delivered the perfect farewell present for St Helens as he brought a close to his three-year stay at the club with a third consecutive Championship crown. Naiqama broke down in tears as he accepted the Trophy from Rob Burrow.

It was the thirteenth of 24 Grand Finals in which St Helens had played and their eighth victory, equalling Leeds Rhinos' record. And the third victory in a row also equalled the Rhinos' record from 2007 to 2009.

Naiqama was the third player in recent years to get a unanimous vote for the Harry Sunderland Trophy, following in the footsteps of Burrow himself in 2011 and Burrow's Leeds team-mate Danny McGuire in 2017. He did it without playing the full 80 minutes, although it was through no fault of his own. He needed a head assessment after being caught by winger Fouad Yaha's knee while crossing for the 66th-minute try, which set up teammate Lachlan Coote, another man-of-of-the-match contender along with Catalans duo Sam Tomkins and James Maloney, for what proved to be the winning conversion.

Saints were forced to fight tooth and nail for their latest triumph by the Dragons, who were gallant in defeat after weathering the early storm to serve up a pulsating encounter.

Steve McNamara's side, led from the back by the returning, newly-crowned Man of Steel Tomkins in the two sides' only combined change, had already delivered plenty of watershed moments since they escaped relegation in the Million Pound Game four years before. They only just came up short in a fine game, with Matt Whitley and skipper Ben Garcia particular heroes after playing on with broken hands.

The attendance was 45,177, at least higher than the very first Grand Final in 1998

BETFRED SUPER LEAGUE GRAND FINAL

Saturday 9th October 2021

CATALANS DRAGONS 10 ST HELENS 12

DRAGONS: 29 Sam Tomkins; 2 Tom Davies; 3 Samisoni Langi; 4 Dean Whare; 5 Fouad Yaha; 6 James Maloney; 7 Josh Drinkwater; 8 Gil Dudson; 9 Michael McIlorum; 10 Julian Bousquet; 11 Matt Whitley; 12 Mike McMeeken; 13 Benjamin Garcia (C). Subs (all used): 1 Arthur Mourgue; 17 Mickael Goudemand; 22 Joel Tomkins; 28 Sam Kasiano.
Try: McMeeken (50); **Goals:** Maloney 3/3.
On report: Yaha (66) - alleged use of the knee on Naiqama.
SAINTS: 1 Lachlan Coote; 2 Tommy Makinson; 3 Kevin Naiqama; 4 Mark Percival; 5 Regan Grace; 6 Jonny Lomax; 21 Lewis Dodd; 8 Alex Walmsley; 9 James Roby (C); 10 Matty Lees; 14 Sione Mata'utia; 20 Joe Batchelor; 13 Morgan Knowles. Subs: 15 Louie McCarthy-Scarsbrook; 16 Kyle Amor (not used); 17 Agnatius Paasi; 18 Jack Welsby.
Tries: Naiqama (13, 66); **Goals:** Coote 2/3.
Sin bin: Makinson (46) - high tackle on Yaha.
Rugby Leaguer & League Express Men of the Match:
Dragons: Josh Drinkwater; *Saints:* Kevin Naiqama.
Penalty count: 10-8; **Half-time:** 4-6; **Referee:** Liam Moore; **Attendance:** 45,177 (at Old Trafford, Manchester).

St Helens' Agnatius Paasi halted by Catalans Dragons' Joel Tomkins and Sam Kasiano

between Wigan and Leeds, which attracted 43,553 spectators. With Catalans having a week to organise travel for their fans amid the Covid constraints on travel, the low crowd was no surprise.

But by the time Jerusalem had been bellowed out, a fever-pitch mood had arisen inside the walls of Old Trafford.

That atmosphere spilled over almost immediately onto the pitch in an early incident waved away in back-play, where James Maloney and Sione Mata'utia came to blows in a scramble ignored by referee Liam Moore. Mata'utia was seen on the replay to have thrown a punch. No action was taken against him on the night but he took a one-match penalty notice with him into 2022.

Maloney, one of several faces bidding goodbye on either side, proved an astute marshal for the Dragons in his last match for them, bringing his own NRL Grand Final experience to bear when his side looked at risk of capsizing inside the first ten minutes of the match.

The veteran halfback successfully implemented an intelligent charge down to gain Catalans' first foothold, before he edged them into a lead with a penalty for offside at the play-the-ball, following their first serious incursion into opposition territory.

Harry Sunderland Trophy winner Kevin Naiqama shows his jubilation

Regardless, it took little time for Saints to reassert their control of the match, with Naiqama coming to the fore for the first time in arguably the play of the match, inside the opening quarter-hour, to notch up the first of his two tries.

Spun a pass by Coote out onto the right flank, he cut up Fouad Yaha and Samisoni Langi to dart to the line with excellent poise and control and then managed to ground the ball in-goal, despite serious attention from Sam Tomkins and Langi as they tried to hold him up over the line.

Coote, as dependably solid as ever in his final game before a move to Hull Kingston Rovers, failed to add the conversion but was able to correct his miss in short order after a swinging arm by Garcia on Jonny Lomax earned him a shot at the posts in kicking distance.

Yet having battered at the Dragons' door, Saints found themselves slowly pegged back by Catalans' grit and determination. Saints' discipline slipped, they suffered six-again calls and they ultimately conceded a penalty bang in front of the sticks, again for offside, which was an easy chance for Maloney to trim the gap to two points.

Louie McCarthy-Scarsbrook exchanged a spot of handbags with opposite number Sam Kasiano after a dangerous challenge saw him escape action too and then Saints came close to doubling their lead moments before the break, only for Dean Whare to pull off a superb try-saving tackle on Regan Grace.

Over-eager defence looked to have handed the Dragons a critical advantage shortly after the restart though, when Tommy Makinson made history as the first player to be sin-binned in a Grand Final following a wild high shot on Yaha as the latter dived for the corner. The winger got his marching orders for ten minutes but Catalans did not get the penalty try from video-referee James Child, which was one of the more contentious calls of the match.

The Dragons did exploit their one-man advantage though, with Mike McMeeken, after a Josh Drinkwater 40/20, catching the pat-back from Tom Davies off Drinkwater's high kick to dot down out wide. Maloney held his nerve to add the conversion for a four-point, 10-6 lead heading into the final quarter.

But cometh the hour, cometh the man, and Naiqama's second, with just over ten minutes on the clock, proved to be the crucial moment as he seized upon Lomax's low grubber to score, taking a nasty blow to the head in the process.

It proved to be Naiqama's final act, removed from the pitch as Coote - not long after being at the centre of another flashpoint after tipping a penalty back infield when replays showed he was in touch when he jumped off the ground - slotted the conversion to edge Saints back in front.

After that, it became a matter of whether the champions could survive the final desperate Catalans' rally. Time and again, they held their nerve, conceding goal-line drop-outs in back-to-back sets, and when Sam Tomkins knocked on just ten metres out, reaching for a pass, it all but signposted the end of the road for the Dragons' hopes.

SUPER LEAGUE AWARDS

STEVE PRESCOTT MAN OF STEEL
Sam Tomkins (Catalans Dragons)

YOUNG PLAYER OF THE YEAR
Jack Welsby (St Helens)

COACH OF THE YEAR
Steve McNamara (Catalans Dragons)

SUPER LEAGUE DREAM TEAM

			Previous selections
1	Sam Tomkins	Catalans Dragons	2009, 2010, 2011, 2012, 2013
2	Tom Davies	Catalans Dragons	Debut
3	Jack Welsby	St Helens	Debut
4	Mark Percival	St Helens	2017
5	Ken Sio	Salford Red Devils	Debut
6	Jonny Lomax	St Helens	2018, 2020
7	James Maloney	Catalans Dragons	Debut
8	Alex Walmsley	St Helens	2015, 2020
9	Kruise Leeming	Leeds Rhinos	Debut
10	Sam Kasiano	Catalans Dragons	Debut
11	Liam Farrell	Wigan Warriors	2015, 2019, 2020
12	Kane Linnett	Hull Kingston Rovers	Debut
13	Morgan Knowles	St Helens	2019, 2020

2
CHAMPIONSHIP, LEAGUE 1 & WOMEN 2021

CHAMPIONSHIP SEASON
Olympique gold medal

TOULOUSE OLYMPIQUE coupled up with Super League Grand Finalists Catalans Dragons to make it a terrific season for French Rugby League.

Sylvain Houles' slick promotion winners completed their campaign with a hundred per cent record following their Million Pound Game victory against Featherstone Rovers, an especially impressive achievement given its unprecedented nature as far as they were concerned.

That's because every regular-season game was played away from home.

Covid restrictions on travel to and from France meant part-time teams weren't required to travel to the Stade Ernest Wallon, the 18,000-capacity venue shared with the city's highly-successful rugby union club Stade Toulousain.

London Broncos, the division's only other full-time club, elected against crossing the Channel in April, so forfeiting the fixture, with Toulouse awarded a 24-0 win.

The 'home' games against Swinton and Widnes were both switched to the former's Heywood Road base in Sale while the other eight were cancelled.

That meant that before the play-off semi-final against Batley Bulldogs and big promotion showdown with Featherstone, which were both at the Stade Ernest Wallon, Olympique took to UK pitches 13 times, chalking up 13 victories and scoring an average of 52 points per game while conceding only 9.5.

They emulated Catalans by claiming the League Leaders' Shield.

FEATHERSTONE ROVERS had a fine year, but the prize they most wanted - a place in Super League - proved agonisingly elusive as they were beaten by Toulouse Olympique in France.

In 21 league games, Toulouse were the only team to get the better of James Webster's men, winning 23-6 at the Millennium Stadium in August, although the club were also docked two points after a breach of the game's Covid protocols.

That didn't stop Featherstone comfortably finishing second to Toulouse, with a win points percentage of 90.48. Rovers accrued 943 points in those 21 games, 78 of them coming in the final outing at home to Sheffield Eagles.

In that match, experienced and versatile back Craig Hall, who was named Championship Player of the Year, ran in five tries and kicked nine goals, taking his respective totals in league matches to 26 and 85, for 274 points, the highest in the division.

Winger Gareth Gale chalked up 27 league tries and Samoa international and former Canterbury Bulldogs and Cronulla Sharks halfback Fa'amanu Brown 15.

In all competitions, Featherstone played 28 times (as opposed to Toulouse's 15) and won on 25 occasions. Rovers reached the third round of the Challenge Cup, where they made Super League visitors Hull FC work for their success, and beat York City Knights to lift the 1895 Cup in the club's first visit to Wembley since 1983.

Featherstone's Craig Hall, Championship Player of the Year, makes a break against Bradford

HALIFAX PANTHERS, a second-tier side since relegation from Super League in 2003, fell short in the play-offs as they went down to Featherstone Rovers in the semi-finals.

But through their third-placed finish, the proud old club with a new addition to their name following a rebrand showed signs of both progress and potential in Simon Grix's first full season as coach following his appointment midway through 2019 and the early shutdown in 2020 due to the pandemic.

Halifax's form was patchy both at the start of the season, when despite kicking off the league campaign with a 47-14 home win over London Broncos, the next three games all brought losses, and the end, when they suffered five defeats in a seven-match sequence taking in two play-off ties.

But in the middle of the year came a nine-match winning run during which local rivals Batley Bulldogs and Bradford Bulls were both seen off. There were 13 league wins in all for a new-look side shorn of long-serving pair Scott Murrell and Steve Tyrer but boosted by the likes of centres Zack McComb and Greg Worthington, halves Liam Harris and Connor Robinson and props Dan Murray and Adam Tangata, who was snapped up from Wakefield Trinity during the season.

BATLEY BULLDOGS won a host of admirers - and Craig Lingard the Championship Coach of the Year award - after finishing fourth and toppling neighbours Bradford Bulls in the play-off eliminators to become the first side to make the trip to Toulouse Olympique in 2021.

The former long-serving Batley player and Keighley Cougars team chief was quick to praise his coaching and backroom staff, showing the unification and spirit which helped give the Bulldogs that all-important bite.

Batley's Luke Hooley crashes over for a try against Oldham

With the backing of chairman Kevin Nicholas and chief executive Paul Harrison, Lingard assembled a highly competitive squad on one of the division's lower budgets, with halfback Tom Gilmore, from Halifax, and ex-England Students representative back Elliot Hall, from Workington Town, particularly useful acquisitions.

Gilmore's fellow pivot Ben White, fullback Luke Hooley, winger Johnny Campbell and hooker Alistair Leak were also among the key performers in a side who, like Halifax Panthers, won 13 out of 21 league games, finishing below their West Yorkshire rivals on points scored percentage (561 for as opposed to 528, but 411 against as opposed to 354).

Batley, who twice chalked up four league wins on the spin, showed their resilience, and silenced their doubters, by bouncing back from three successive defeats in June and July to get back on track for what proved a pretty popular appearance in the play-offs.

BRADFORD BULLS achieved their highest league position since 2016, when they also finished fifth. But the club who were playing in Super League in 2014 and reached the following year's Million Pound Game fell at the first hurdle in the play-offs, so prolonging their absence from the top flight.

Part way through the campaign came a return to Odsal, the club's spiritual home which due to rising maintenance costs, had been vacated in September 2019 in favour of a groundshare at Dewsbury, eleven miles away.

In the first match back, Bradford beat York, one of twelve wins in 20 league outings for John Kear's side, who after being shaken by a heavy defeat at the hands of Sheffield Eagles in their opening game, responded by claiming seven successive wins.

That sequence was ended at Featherstone Rovers where the Bulls were nilled, and consistency proved hard to come by after that, with injuries in key positions not helping the cause and defeats in the final three games meaning Bradford failed to secure home advantage for their play-off eliminator (they were beaten 23-10 at Batley Bulldogs).

Kear admitted his side were too blunt in attack and not miserly enough in defence, with a record of 514 points scored to 501 conceded telling its own story.

WHITEHAVEN cast the signings net far wider than usual and uncovered a few gems as they encouragingly defied the odds for the second time in three years.

Two years earlier, in Gary Charlton's first season as coach, the Cumbrian club, with a mainly local side, gained automatic promotion from League 1.

This time, after a sluggish start which left them too close to the foot of the table for comfort, Charlton's charges swept to the play-offs by gaining eight wins in their last nine matches.

The mid-season addition of French halfback and former player Louis Jouffret, who had been at Avignon, proved a canny bit of business, as did the closed-season recruitment of Australian duo Lachlan Walmsley, a versatile back who scored 15 league tries, and Ryan King, a prop, along with Kiwi pivot Nikau Williams.

Having gained only two wins (and a draw) in their first ten league outings, Whitehaven won all but two of the next twelve, and gave Halifax a run for their money at the first stage of the play-offs, only to go down by four points.

That means there is plenty to build on for new coach Jonty Gorley, promoted from his role as assistant to Charlton, who has become director of rugby, although he will have to do without popular pair, skipper Marc Shackley and Papuan Jessie Joe Parker, who have both retired.

LONDON BRONCOS fans felt the fall-out from relegation from Super League in 2019 and the Covid-enforced curtailment of the 2020 campaign as the capital club parted company with coach Danny Ward. They later announced they would go part-time in 2022 and be coached by Jermaine Coleman as they missed out on the 2021 play-offs, finishing seventh. All that came against the backdrop of confirmation of another move, this time to AFC Wimbledon's new Plough Lane Stadium, which will be the tenth different venue used regularly since foundation as Fulham in 1980.

Ward, who guided the Broncos to Super League in his first season in charge in 2018, left in July, little more than a month after his assistant Jamie Langley joined the coaching staff at Sale Sharks. His side had won seven out of eleven league games played (the away fixture against Toulouse Olympique was forfeited after the Broncos elected not to travel to France as the issues posed by the pandemic continued) and occupied the sixth and final play-off place.

Former Coventry Bears coach Tom Tsang, who had stepped up from his role with the Broncos' Academy to replace Langley as Ward's assistant, took interim charge.

And while there were four wins out of eight under his command, with Abbas Miski and Gideon Boafo finishing with 18 and 15 league tries respectively, London lost out on that key sixth place on the final day of the regular season as they were beaten at York City Knights and Whitehaven won at Bradford Bulls.

WIDNES VIKINGS will look back on a frustrating year of what might have beens. And it's hard to escape the conclusion that they underachieved.

There was disruption ahead of pre-season when World Cup-winning head coach Tim Sheens unexpectedly resigned twelve months into a two-year contract as coach.

Former player Simon Finnigan was brought in on his own two-year deal after catching the eye at Newcastle Thunder and tasked with leading the former Super League club to the play-offs. Inconsistency, including a run of five straight losses, severely undermined that objective, although he did manage to guide his side to the third round of the Challenge Cup, where Salford Red Devils were too strong.

That meant Widnes made the semi-finals of the 1895 Cup, in which they were beaten finalists in 2019, and they gave hosts Featherstone Rovers a real test, only for hopes of a Wembley return to be ended by a 24-18 defeat.

That showed what the Vikings, for whom Deon Cross chalked up 17 league tries, were capable of, as did a double over Bradford Bulls and a victory over Halifax Panthers.

But after only one win and a draw in their first six league games, Finnigan and his players were always playing catch-up, and a late-season surge of four wins in five was too little, too late.

Championship Season

YORK CITY KNIGHTS were eager to build on their third-placed finish of 2019 and mark the move to their impressive new LNER Community Stadium by mounting a serious promotion challenge with a side bolstered by a number of experienced additions such as Ryan Atkins, Adam Cuthbertson and Danny Kirmond.

But, like Widnes, they ended up marooned in mid-table, in their case, after a dismal run of six successive defeats left them far closer to the bottom of the ladder than the top.

Coach James Ford, who certainly wasn't helped by a glut of injuries, made extensive use of a loan system which the governing body tailored to take account of Covid issues, and perhaps the up-and-down nature of the Knights' results reflected the difficulty he had in keeping a settled team.

Either side of that sextet of defeats, York managed sequences of four wins in five league games and five in seven, but the play-offs remained out of reach.

There was a run to the third round of the Challenge Cup which brought Wigan Warriors to the club's new home (a shame there could be no fans in attendance at that stage of the season).

Meanwhile, Ford's side made it to Wembley for an 1895 Cup Final meeting with Featherstone Rovers and, although beaten, played their part in making it a showdown worthy of the setting.

DEWSBURY RAMS, once again operating on a tight budget, once again retained second-tier status under Lee Greenwood, ultimately more comfortably than when relegation was previously a possibility two years earlier.

After opening with wins at home to Whitehaven and away to Widnes Vikings, there was only one (at Swinton) in the next seven games for a side boasting a veteran halfback combination of former England and Great Britain international Paul Sykes, who celebrated his 40th birthday during the season, and Ireland star Liam Finn, who was nearing 37 when he announced his retirement at the end of the campaign.

Victory at Oldham and a home draw against Sheffield Eagles brought some breathing space, but then a run of four straight losses, one of them at home to Swinton, set the alarm bells ringing for the Rams faithful.

But by completing doubles over Widnes and Oldham, winning at Sheffield and clinching a sweet derby success at Batley over the course of the last six games, Dewsbury hoisted themselves up to tenth with a final victory tally of eight from 21 league outings, thereby ensuring a 13th successive season at this level in 2022.

Greenwood pointed out how the problems created by Covid and the protocols made necessary had made life harder for all coaches.

NEWCASTLE THUNDER have ambitions of establishing themselves as a solid and sustainable Super League club, and took what they hope is another step on that journey by consolidating their freshly-earned Championship status.

The North-East club, last in the second tier in 2009, were elevated from League 1 through a bidding process to take the place of Leigh, who moved into Super League through the same method, in December 2020.

Newcastle were selected ahead of fellow applicants Rochdale Hornets, Workington Town, Barrow Raiders and Doncaster by an independent panel. That followed the departure of coach Simon Finnigan to Widnes Vikings, with ex-Ireland forward Eamon O'Carroll leaving his role as assistant coach at Catalans Dragons to come in and work alongside director of rugby Denis Betts at Kingston Park.

O'Carroll, with limited time to prepare for the new challenge, would be the first to admit it wasn't all plain-sailing, and while they drew their opening game at home to Widnes, his side managed only one win, over Sheffield Eagles, in their next six outings.

But Thunder warmed to their task, and as they introduced a hybrid part-time and full-time system (they will be entirely full-time in 2022) four victories in five boosted spirits and confidence.

Two further wins made it seven out of 20 and helped them to eleventh.

Sheffield's Rob Worrincy takes on York's Chris Clarkson and Ryan Atkins

SHEFFIELD EAGLES supremo Mark Aston's noted resilience was certainly put to the test as his side struggled through a campaign spent playing out of the Keepmoat Stadium at Doncaster due to ongoing building work at the Olympic Legacy Park in the steel city.

With one match postponed and two cancelled due to Covid issues in the camp, the club were affected more than any other in the division, and apart from at the end of the season, when there were five straight defeats leading to a final placing of twelfth, there was very little discernible pattern to results.

Having won their opening two league matches, at home to Bradford Bulls and away to York City Knights, there were only three more victories from the other 18 games played, while Sheffield were involved in three draws - at home to Whitehaven and Oldham and away to Dewsbury Rams.

Aston will be looking forward to getting back to OLP, but planning for a future without seasoned operators Matt James, Frankie Mariano, Scott Wheeldon and Rob Worrincy, who have all retired.

OLDHAM provided one of the stories of the season by persuading one the games's most successful coaches to come on board, but it was to no avail as the Roughyeds were relegated, two years after climbing out of League 1.

After defeats in four of the five league games his side were able to play in 2020, Matt Diskin brought in a number of new recruits to beef up the squad, and enjoyed on opening-round win at home to Swinton Lions.

Three games later, his team pulled off an impressive 16-12 home success over Halifax Panthers, but defeats in each of the next seven outings led to a parting of the ways.

Chairman Chris Hamilton took the bold step of bringing in ex-Leeds chief Brian McDermott to work with existing assistant coach Brendan Sheridan.

But the man who led the Rhinos to a World Club Challenge, four Super League titles and two Challenge Cups, then piloted Toronto Wolfpack to success over Featherstone Rovers in the 2019 Million Pound Game, couldn't stop the rot.

In his ten matches at the club, Oldham were only able to pick up one point, from a draw at Swinton, the only club they finished above and whose former coach Stuart Littler was handed the Roughyeds job soon after a difficult season was over.

Championship Season

SWINTON LIONS reached the third round of the Challenge Cup and in the 1895 Cup, were within a win of a first-ever trip to Wembley.

But defeats by Warrington Wolves and York City Knights respectively were accompanied by 19 in the league, and a basement finish.

While Stuart Littler enjoyed Challenge Cup wins over Newcastle Thunder and Oldham, the former Salford player, who had to deal with a number of injuries, just couldn't conjure one in the Championship.

After 14 losses, club and coach separated, with assistant Allan Coleman stepping up to take the reins.

With his first five matches yielding a victory at Dewsbury Rams and a draw at home to Oldham, the board had seen enough to hand the ex-Leigh Miners Rangers chief the reins on a permanent basis.

Swinton then won 34-28 at Sheffield Eagles in their penultimate match and while they accrued two wins and a draw like Oldham, they finished below the Roughyeds because they played one game more.

CHAMPIONSHIP AWARDS

PLAYER OF THE YEAR
Craig Hall (Featherstone Rovers)

YOUNG PLAYER OF THE YEAR
Tyler Dupree (Oldham)

COACH OF THE YEAR
Craig Lingard (Batley Bulldogs)

Championship Play-offs

The truncated three-week play-off system in Super League was adopted by the Championship for 2021, with all five games covered live by Sky Sports.

In the first week, the eliminators went to league position with the third and fourth placed teams winning through.

Surprise outfit Whitehaven had secured sixth spot with a last-round 36-22 win at Bradford, coupled with London Broncos' defeat at York City Knights and had the reward of a trip to third-placed Halifax, with a new nickname for the new season in the Panthers.

Halifax won it 24-20 but it was a spirited showing from the Cumbrians, who were never in front but created a sniff of victory when winger Andrew Bulman crossed for his second try with a minute left on the clock.

Veteran Scott Grix was the Panthers' key man at stand-off in his last game at the Shay before retiring at the end of the season and the club's reward was a semi-final berth at Featherstone.

Batley Bulldogs continued their dream season with another brilliant victory, beating Bradford Bulls 23-10 in a pulsating match at the Fox's Biscuits Stadium, earning them a crack at League Leaders Toulouse.

The first half saw the Bulldogs at their very best, playing down the slope and establishing a 16-0 lead with Ben Kaye getting the opening try and the excellent Tom Gilmore contributing the rest of the points and providing total control.

After the break they could have thrown it away with a succession of mistakes but that was when their team spirit came to the fore most, limiting the damage to two tries from Joe Brown and Jordan Lilley and producing some truly stunning goal-line defence before Elliot Hall spectacularly put the seal on their victory and Gilmore potted a field goal three minutes from time.

With all the play-off games played on Saturday, Toulouse Olympique were the first into the Championship Final, which the RFL chose to brand as 'the Million Pound Game', after an eventually comfortable 51-12 win over Batley. After a season of being on the road, Toulouse at last managed to stage a game at the Stade Ernest Wallon and astoundingly drew a crowd of almost seven thousand to the semi-final.

Batley were in the game at half-time, trailing only 16-12. But a brilliant second-half performance from old hands Mark Kheirallah and Johnathon Ford - near-decade-long veterans with Toulouse - took the game away from them.

Kheirallah's try, the second of two quick scores after the break, effectively pulled the rug out from under Batley and their hopes of a surprise.

In the second semi-final, Featherstone, whose only league defeat in 2021 was at the hands of Toulouse, beat Halifax by 42-10.

After a tense first half Rovers completely overwhelmed the shell-shocked Panthers, who were well in the game right up to the 52nd minute, at which point an eleven-minute purple patch yielded four consecutive touchdowns.

A frantic rush for airline tickets to Toulouse began.

Million Pound Game

Toulouse Olympique won promotion to Super League with a 34-12 win over Featherstone Rovers on a spectacular Sunday night at the Stade Ernest Wallon.

Sylvain Houles' men had to spend the whole season on the road because of Covid restrictions, or more aptly in the skies, but had been promoted unbeaten.

If they were going to be stopped by anyone this year, it was clear from early on that it would be Featherstone, and despite racing into a 16-0 lead they were made to work incredibly hard for victory.

Centre Mathieu Jussaume starred and scored two of their tries, but Harrison Hansen got the most important score to hold off a second-half fightback as Toulouse did enough.

Toulouse topped the table, the use of points percentages neutralising the fact not a single team travelled across the Channel over the course of the regular season as they won all 13 of the matches that did take place.

It was a more normal campaign for Featherstone, but they remained astonishingly consistent themselves, winning 20 of their 21 games with their only defeat coming at French hands.

Rovers needed a solid start but, after defending well in the first five minutes, they conceded in the sixth. After dropping the ball with their first good possession, Toulouse took advantage with Dom Peyroux offloading for Jussaume to go in.

The centre demonstrated brilliant footwork to step past two defenders and then managed to withstand an exceptional Kris Welham effort to eventually wriggle free and ground the ball, with Mark Kheirallah converting for a 6-0 lead.

Toulouse were now looking dominant going forward and when Remi Casty had the ball stripped from him by Connor Jones as he charged down the middle, Kheirallah happily added two points.

The visitors were not helping themselves and Brett Ferres' high tackle, following an Alex Walker error, allowed Kheirallah to add another two, before that was compounded by kicking out on the full.

This time they were made to pay with a try, Gigot seeing Latrell Schmaukel in space and smartly kicking early in the set for the winger to just about touch down in the corner.

Kheirallah couldn't convert from the touchline, but his tee was out again soon enough, Featherstone pulled for offside as they continued to struggle with the pace of the opposition and went down 16-0 as a result.

That's how it remained until half-time as Rovers began to get a small foothold, helped by some cheap penalties which put them in attacking positions for the first time. They failed to prise the door open but Toulouse had been warned that the contest was not over.

Toulouse's Mathieu Jussaume takes on Featherstone's Alex Walker and Kris Welham during the Million Pound Game

When the second half started in a similar vein and Fev got their first points, that was definitely the case. They were given a penalty with Johnathon Ford caught offside, and Dane Chisholm found Ferres running an irresistible line through the middle of the defence and under the sticks.

Craig Hall converted and the momentum was now all with Featherstone, their hosts stuck in defence and suddenly clinging on. Jy Hitchcox did exactly that to stop Hall from grounding in the corner, after Chisholm's 40/20, before Ferres was denied a second by the video referee as Hall's strip on Kheirallah was judged a knock-on.

It looked like it was game over when, against the run of play, Toulouse extended their lead. Casty found Eloi Pelissier and the hooker ducked under a challenge before finding Jussaume on his outside to score his second of the game.

But James Webster's side didn't know when they were beaten and hit back almost instantly, Dean Parata's short pass sending John Davies over. But they coughed up the ball straight after and a penalty allowed Kheirallah to make it 24-12.

At a two-score difference there was still hope, but that was finally extinguished with six minutes remaining. Ford slipped in Harrison Hansen, and Toulouse were in Super League, Lloyd White's sin-binning meaning nothing as Ford then waltzed in with the final action to cap it off perfectly.

A crowd of almost 10,000, including hundreds of Featherstone supporters, acclaimed the achievement of the Toulouse club.

MILLION POUND GAME

Sunday 10th October 2021

TOULOUSE OLYMPIQUE 34 FEATHERSTONE ROVERS 12

OLYMPIQUE: 1 Mark Kheirallah; 2 Jy Hitchcox; 4 Mathieu Jussaume; 3 Junior Vaivai; 21 Latrell Schaumkel; 6 Johnathon Ford; 31 Tony Gigot; 10 Harrison Hansen; 9 Lloyd White; 8 Remi Casty; 12 Dominique Peyroux; 16 Joe Bretherton; 13 Anthony Marion. Subs (all used): 14 Eloi Pelissier; 17 Joseph Paulo; 18 Mitch Garbutt; 23 Justin Sangare.
Tries: Jussaume (6, 65), Schaumkel (19), Hansen (74), Ford (80); **Goals:** Kheirallah 7/8, Casty 0/1.
Sin bin: White (79) - kicking out.
ROVERS: 36 Alex Walker; 1 Craig Hall; 4 Josh Hardcastle; 3 Kris Welham; 5 Gareth Gale; 7 Dane Chisholm; 9 Fa'amanu Brown; 8 Craig Kopczak; 14 Connor Jones; 13 James Lockwood; 11 Brett Ferres; 20 Frankie Halton; 19 Callum Field. Subs (all used): 15 John Davies; 16 Jack Bussey; 21 Dean Parata; 24 Dale Ferguson.
Tries: Ferres (52), Davies (68); **Goals:** Hall 2/2.
Rugby Leaguer & League Express Men of the Match:
Olympique: Mathieu Jussaume; *Rovers:* Brett Ferres.
Penalty count: 7-7; **Half-time:** 16-0;
Referee: Robert Hicks; **Attendance:** 9,235.

Featherstone celebrate their 1895 Cup Final victory over York

1895 Cup

Featherstone fought off the impact of Covid issues and a spirited York team to win 41-34 on their first Wembley appearance since 1983.

In 2021, the 1895 Cup was contested by 16 teams with Challenge Cup games doubling up before four teams, who qualified by reaching the third round of the Challenge Cup, played in the semi-finals. Rovers beat Widnes Vikings and the City Knights overcame Swinton to win through the Wembley curtain-raiser.

Covid threatened to deal the cruelest blow when numerous positive tests in the Rovers camp were announced two days beforehand and, though a clean follow-up round of testing brought a huge sigh of relief, Rovers still had to manage without a host of senior players and their head coach, James Webster, for the big occasion.

Happily, after a nervous week off the field - with the City Knights experiencing their own Covid scare and missing some big-hitters themselves - there was still plenty of drama left for the match itself.

1895 CUP - SEMI-FINALS

Sunday 6th June 2021

YORK CITY KNIGHTS 36 SWINTON LIONS 22

CITY KNIGHTS: 1 Matty Marsh; 2 Jason Bass; 3 Liam Salter; 4 Ryan Atkins; 5 Kieran Dixon; 37 Mikey Lewis; 29 Riley Dean; 10 Jack Teanby; 9 Will Jubb; 13 Adam Cuthbertson; 17 Danny Kirmond; 12 Sam Scott; 11 Chris Clarkson. Subs (all used): 14 Kriss Brining; 15 Jordan Baldwinson; 16 Marcus Stock; 19 James Green.
Tries: Salter (5), Stock (25), Atkins (37), Brining (43), Kirmond (54), Lewis (69); **Goals:** K Dixon 6/6.
LIONS: 22 Geronimo Doyle; 1 Mike Butt; 3 Mitch Cox; 11 Rhodri Lloyd; 25 Luis Roberts; 6 Martyn Ridyard; 7 Jack Hansen; 8 Sam Brooks; 9 Luke Waterworth; 40 Ronan Michael; 19 Deane Meadows; 12 Nick Gregson; 14 Billy Brickhill. Subs (all used): 15 Louis Brogan; 13 Will Hope; 16 Paddy Jones; 18 Cobi Green.
Tries: Butt (14, 58, 78), Michael (18); **Goals:** Ridyard 3/4.
Rugby Leaguer & League Express Men of the Match:
City Knights: Kriss Brining; *Lions:* Mike Butt.
Penalty count: 6-5; **Half-time:** 18-12; **Referee:** Tom Grant;
Attendance: 1,214.

FEATHERSTONE ROVERS 24 WIDNES VIKINGS 18

ROVERS: 1 Craig Hall; 5 Gareth Gale; 17 Thomas Minns; 20 Frankie Halton; 4 Josh Hardcastle; 6 Tom Holmes; 9 Fa'amanu Brown; 8 Craig Kopczak; 14 Connor Jones; 13 James Lockwood; 12 Brad Day; 31 Junior Moors; 27 Loui McConnell. Subs (all used): 21 Dean Parata; 15 John Davies; 19 Callum Field; 18 Luke Cooper.
Tries: Day (5, 8), Kopczak (12), Halton (38); **Goals:** Hall 4/5.
VIKINGS: 1 Jack Owens; 5 Deon Cross; 3 Jake Spedding; 4 Steve Tyrer; 2 Jayden Hatton; 6 Danny Craven; 17 Joe Lyons; 13 Kenny Baker; 28 Brad O'Neill; 10 Matt Cook; 11 Shane Grady; 12 Adam Lawton; 7 Matty Smith. Subs (all used): 8 Paul Clough; 24 Will Tilleke; 16 Owen Farnworth; 23 Lewis Else.
Tries: Tyrer (28), Lawton (33, 57); **Goals:** Tyrer 3/3.
Rugby Leaguer & League Express Men of the Match:
Rovers: Craig Kopczak; *Vikings:* Adam Lawton.
Penalty count: 4-11; **Half-time:** 22-12; **Referee:** Ben Thaler;
Attendance: 1,750.

Championship Season

Featherstone, led by assistant coach Paul March, led by a dozen points at the break after tries from Dane Chisholm, Craig Kopczak, Jacob Doyle and Fa'amanu Brown and three Craig Hall goals, with Ben Jones-Bishop and Marcus Stock replying for the City Knights.

And although York admirably hit back to level within eight minutes of the restart with tries from Kriss Brining and Jason Bass, Featherstone had the extra energy required to pull away as a penalty goal and quick tries from Doyle, James Harrison and Ray French Medal winner as man of the match Hall left too big a gap for York to close, despite late scores from Hull KR loanee Mikey Lewis and winger Perry Whiteley.

1895 CUP - FINAL

Saturday 17th July 2021

FEATHERSTONE ROVERS 41 YORK CITY KNIGHTS 34

ROVERS: 1 Craig Hall; 5 Gareth Gale; 4 Josh Hardcastle; 15 John Davies; 28 Jacob Doyle; 9 Fa'amanu Brown; 7 Dane Chisholm; 8 Craig Kopczak; 22 Jake Sweeting; 13 James Lockwood; 10 James Harrison; 11 Brett Ferres; 27 Loui McConnell. Subs (all used): 29 Harvey Spence; 18 Luke Cooper; 19 Callum Field; 23 Joe Summers.
Tries: Chisholm (7), Kopczak (21), Doyle (34, 54), Brown (36), Harrison (58), Hall (61); **Goals:** Hall 6/9; **Field goal:** Chisholm (77).
CITY KNIGHTS: 5 Kieran Dixon; 23 Ben Jones-Bishop; 30 Tyme Dow-Nikau; 2 Jason Bass; 22 Perry Whiteley; 37 Mikey Lewis; 28 Danny Washbrook; 8 Ronan Dixon; 9 Will Jubb; 10 Jack Teanby; 11 Chris Clarkson; 17 Danny Kirmond; 20 Tim Spears. Subs (all used): 14 Kriss Brining; 16 Marcus Stock; 13 Adam Cuthbertson; 12 Sam Scott.
Tries: Jones-Bishop (11), Stock (27), Brining (44), Bass (48), Lewis (72), Whiteley (79); **Goals:** K Dixon 4/5, Lewis 1/1.
Rugby Leaguer & League Express Men of the Match:
Rovers: Fa'amanu Brown; *City Knights:* Mikey Lewis.
Penalty count: 7-5; **Half-time:** 22-10; **Referee:** Robert Hicks.
(at Wembley Stadium)

LEAGUE 1 SEASON
Cumbrian revival

Right from the season kick-off **BARROW RAIDERS** more than lived up to their favourites tag in League 1.

Paul Crarey's men were keen to bounce straight back up to the Championship at the first attempt in 2020 and were looking good for it, beating both Doncaster and Coventry in the two league games they played before the pandemic shut the game down for over a year.

Barrow led the way in the downtime, finding new and innovative ways to bring additional funds into the club while games were still not allowed. That included hosting the area's largest beer garden on the pitch when restrictions allowed!

Healthy finances allowed the club to add some real experience to the side with former Super League stars Shaun Lunt, Ryan Shaw, Hakim Miloudi and Ben Harrison among the new signings, although Lunt later decided to retire from the game after a change in working hours prevented him from committing to training demands.

The top-level experience around the club saw the Raiders start like a house on fire - going nine games unbeaten at the start of the year.

But as with all clubs, Barrow had their fair share of disruption caused by Covid and had their round-12 Cumbrian derby against Workington postponed due to an outbreak of the virus. They were still down on numbers for the following game against Hunslet and Crarey showed his faith in some of the club's young up and coming players. They certainly did a job as Barrow ran out 40-10 winners.

Despite their early dominance, mounting pressure from those teams below them meant automatic promotion wasn't mathematically secured until the final day

The Barrow squad celebrate clinching automatic promotion to the Championship

of the season when West Wales Raiders made the long trip up to Furness. The visitors were down on numbers but wanted to do everything in their power to get the game on and Barrow wanted to earn promotion in style. So the Welsh side raided their local community game to find some extra bodies and even took a four from sides local to Barrow to fulfil a squad and get the game played.

It paid off for Barrow as Theerapol Ritson, who finished as the league's top try-scorer, crossed for a record-breaking seven tries as a place in the Championship was secured with a 76-0 victory.

WORKINGTON TOWN made sure all three Cumbrian sides would face each other in 2022 after becoming worthy winners of an exciting and entertaining play-off series.

A second-place finish in the league meant Chris Thorman's men just needed to beat Keighley Cougars in the qualifying semi-final to set up a home play-off final. They did that - just - with a Carl Forber golden-point penalty sealing a dramatic 18-16 win over Keighley Cougars.

Thankfully for all those involved at Derwent Park, the final was a much more straightforward game with Joe Brown, Conor Fitzsimmons, Carl Forber, Matty Henson, Marcus O'Brien and Brad Holroyd all crossing for tries in a relatively comfortable 36-12 win over Doncaster.

Forber's try in the promotion decider took him to within touching distance of another major milestone in what proved to be a memorable season for the 36-year-old. It was the 98th try of his career, meaning he will hit the century mark if he decided to go around again in 2022. If he had hit that landmark this year, it would have added to the achievement of scoring his 1,000th career goal, both including and not including field goals, 2,000 points for the club and making 300 appearances for Town.

When Thorman took over from Leon Pryce midway through the 2019 season he wanted the local community to be at the very centre of the club and, with many local players on the field as promotion was secured, Thorman fulfilled that aim.

The coach was also quick to dedicate the Final win to all the fans and volunteers who stuck by the club over the tumultuous 18 months that followed the shut-down of the league.

It is fair to say that **NORTH WALES CRUSADERS** were the surprise package of the year. While those involved at the club will have always fancied their chances of a real push for the top-six spots, very few outsiders would have expected them to finish third ahead of some of their more fancied league opponents.

They had lost some experienced heads at the end of 2019, with Jonny Walker, Alex Thompson and Stephen Wild all retiring and influential captain Kenny Baker joining Championship club Widnes Vikings. That all meant that had 2020 fully got going, it would have been a transitional year for Anthony Murray's squad.

Whilst many of the new faces were former Super League academy graduates looking to take the next step in their careers, Murray also went down the route of plucking some of the best players from the amateur ranks and giving them their first taste of professional sport. Murray seems to have found some more stars with both Gav Rodden and Jordy Gibson, in particular, impressing this year.

A key moment for the Crusaders came as early as round six when they went down 68-0 at home to Doncaster. Many harsh lessons were learnt that day but rather than lick their wounds, Crusaders dusted themselves down and resolved to make sure there was no repeat of that performance.

With the new mental resolve that gave them, the Crusaders lost just twice more in the 11 games that followed, a run which included wins against Barrow, Doncaster and Rochdale.

A young and experienced squad can only take you so far though and play-off games against Keighley and Doncaster proved a step too far for the Crusaders. A lack of big-game experience was evident as the Welsh side lost out in both.

Despite the play-off results, Murray had still done enough throughout the season to be named Coach of the Year.

As well as squad changes, another big difference in 2021 was the move away from Queensway Stadium in Wrexham to satisfy Covid protocols, as Zip World Stadium in Colwyn Bay became the club's new home. It proved a masterstroke. Old supporters made the move with them, while potential new supporters from a previously untapped area got on board.

KEIGHLEY COUGARS under Rhys Lovegrove seemed to be on the right path to bringing back the success of Cougarmania days.

After a fairly miserable 2019, when the club finished second bottom due to a 12-point deduction before the season, 2021 could hardly have gone much better for the Cougars.

One thing Lovegrove has always spoken passionately about is clubs producing their own players and developing them into future stars of the game. The fact that they had two of their own - Phoenix Laulu-Togaga'e and Charlie Graham - nominated for the Young Player of the Year award indicated they were starting to succeed with that. Laulu-Togaga'e signed for Super League side Hull KR for 2022, proving that the Cougars are getting the pathway right for these young stars.

Add to them the experience of the likes of Quentin Laulu-Togaga'e (Phoenix's dad), Scott Murrell and Jake Webster and the balance within the squad appeared just right.

The Cougars' biggest highlights of the season included the pre-season game against Bradford, when QLT and PLT made the rare feat of a father and son duo playing alongside each other. The Cougars were also the first side to defeat eventual champions Barrow Raiders.

The sides met for the second time in July and the Cougars put in a scintillating display to run out 40-12 winners.

Another memorable moment came ahead of their final home league match against North Wales Crusaders when the club unveiled a lasting memorial to one of the town's favourite sons.

The Captain Sir Tom Moore gate, at the Hard Royd Ings entrance at Cougar Park, pays tribute to former Army Officer Moore, who was born in Keighley. In 2020, at the age of 99, he raised over £30 million for NHS Charities and passed away in February 2021, two months before his 101st birthday.

Keighley's Phoenix Laulu-Togaga'e, League 1 Young Player of the Year, takes on the Doncaster defence

League 1 Season

DONCASTER once again suffered play-off heartache as their wait for a return to the Championship continued.

The South Yorkshire club were last in the second-tier in 2015 and will have thought they were in the best possible position to do that as they found themselves going into the end-of-season push in a much stronger position than in previous years.

In both 2018 and 2019, Doncaster found themselves short on numbers due to injuries and unavailability of dual registration players and it showed as they struggled to find any real form in the play-offs and crashed out in the semi-finals each time.

In 2021, however, they found themselves welcoming key players back to full fitness at the right time of the year and loan signings were committed until the end of the year. That showed in their form as they ended the regular season with wins over Hunslet, Coventry, Workington and Barrow plus a two-point defeat to Keighley as they enjoyed a run of five consecutive home games.

The experience of mid-season signing Ben Cockayne, who had come out of retirement to return to where his career began, came to the fore as his leadership skills proved vital at key moments in games.

That end-of-season momentum continued as they travelled to North Wales and Keighley in the play-offs and came out on top in both to finally make it to the final and 80 minutes away from their ultimate goal.

It proved to be a game too far though for Richard Horne's men, who went down 36-12 to Workington Town.

While London Skolars and West Wales Raiders faced a coaching change before the 2021 season kicked off, **HUNSLET** were the only team in League 1 this year to change their coach mid-season.

Defeat to Coventry Bears in early July signalled the end of Gary Thornton's four-year stint at the club, with the board deciding a change was needed to reinvigorate their season.

At the time Hunslet we're fifth in the league with four wins and a draw from nine games, so the decision came as a shock to many. But it proved to be a justified decision as under the stewardship of former Rochdale coach Alan Kilshaw, they went on to pick up five more wins and two draws in the final nine matches.

The way other results went saw them drop to sixth but they retained their spot in the play-off positions. However, the play-offs proved a game too far as they went down 31-10 to fifth-placed Doncaster in the first elimination game.

Kilshaw has already made some astute signing in his time at the club and already had designs on mounting a real challenge on the league in 2022. With a full pre-season with a squad of his own, there is no reason why this couldn't be possible.

ROCHDALE HORNETS started the year with so much promise but ultimately will have been disappointed not to deliver on most of it.

The 2020 season that never was started with real optimism for the Hornets. Despite all the upheaval that went on before it, with the club changing from fan-owned to private ownership and the delays that led to in terms of preparing a squad for the new campaign, they picked up two convincing wins in the Challenge Cup and then beat Keighley Cougars, a promotion rival, 29-14.

With the way that season had started and more time to strengthen a squad, hopes were high that the Hornets would mount a serious promotion bid when the game finally returned. So to not even make the play-offs will have felt like a hammer blow to all involved.

As with most things in 2021, Covid continued to play its part and unavailabilities through that as well as a series of unlucky injuries never gave the side a chance to gain any real consistency throughout the campaign. These unavailabilities also saw several players come in on short-term loans - again not that useful when trying to get some long-term cohesion in the side.

The unluckiest of the injuries came within weeks of announcing the signing of Rangi Chase in June. It was hoped that the former England International would be the catalyst the Hornets needed to propel them up the table but a broken arm sustained on his debut against North Wales Crusaders ruled the 35-year-old out until the final few games of the season.

In the brighter moments of the season, it was clear to see that all the necessary pieces were there for success. They'll just need to have a bit more luck on their side next year if it is all to slot together and lead the club back to the Championship.

They may have still finished eighth but 2021 was arguably **COVENTRY BEARS'** best season yet.

While this year's six wins from 17 games (35 per cent win ratio), may not be mathematically better than 2016's eight wins from 20 games (40 per cent), it was the manner of the more recent victories that was most impressive.

As well as beating the two teams that finished below them - West Wales twice and London Skolars away - the home fans at Butts Park Arena were given a real treat when the Bears overcame more established clubs in Rochdale Hornets, Hunslet and Keighley Cougars. All three games were close affairs, with the Bears doing just enough to hold out against much-fancied sides.

When the latter two happened in consecutive weeks in July, people started talking about the possibility of the Bears making the play-offs for the first time in their short history. But a few injuries to key men saw the year finish with a losing run of six games to end any hopes of a place in the top six.

It certainly made people sit up and take notice of the Bears and that was evident when fellow League 1 coaches named Richard Squires, in his first year in the role at any semi-professional level, as one of three nominees for League 1 Coach of the Year.

And away from the field, the Bears continued to build a presence for the game in the Midlands.

It will be all change at **LONDON SKOLARS** as 2021 signalled the end of Jermaine Coleman's six-and-a-half-year coaching spell with the club.

The former player and current Jamaica coach left the club to join London Broncos as they embark upon a new era as a part-time club.

The Skolars were perhaps hit harder than most by the pandemic, with their location often going against them. While other clubs across the league were able to take advantage of short-term loans for players from neighbouring clubs to get them through spells when they were down on numbers, it wasn't always possible for the Skolars. With only London Broncos in the immediate area they could only call on them for help but with the Championship side often also short on numbers themselves, very limited business could be done between the two.

That meant Coleman was often left selecting a side with players playing out of position or battling on through niggling injuries, which ordinarily would have been rested. Coleman himself even pulled his boots back on to play, which illustrated how much he needed the numbers to get through games.

That being said, the Skolars were just one of four clubs in the league - along with Keighley, Hunslet and West Wales - that fulfilled every game of the season with none falling victim to Covid and unavailabilities.

But all the disruption prevented the Skolars from fielding the same team in consecutive weeks for most of the season and the lack of consistency that caused could be seen on the field.

Wins against West Wales Raiders (twice) and Coventry Bears, as well pushing others close before narrowly losing out in the final quarter, shows the Skolars could compete. But they'll need a bigger squad and better luck next year if they are to climb up the table.

League 1 Season

In a season that started with so much promise following a couple of big-name signings, it proved to be a case of different year, same story for **WEST WALES RAIDERS**.

The Raiders hit the headlines with the close-season signings of former Albert Goldthorpe Medal winner and 2011 Man of Steel Rangi Chase and former British Lions union star Gavin Henson. Both were to be the catalysts that would help take the club forward and be competitive this year.

Sadly it didn't work out for either player with Rangi Chase requesting a release midway through the year and an injury and work commitments leaving Henson with just one appearance in the Challenge Cup against Widnes.

Having picked up a solitary win in 2019, it was just one point that prevented them from ending the year on zero in the points percentage column.

That draw came on August 7th when play-off chasing Doncaster took on an understrength Raiders side, who only had two fit substitutes on the bench. One of those was the returning Steve Parry, who hadn't played for the club in almost two years. He was thrown into the action early on and his experience seemed to spur the side on as they raced into an 18-4 half time lead.

Doncaster hit back though and when Tom Halliday crossed to level matters in the final minute, it looked as though it would end in heartbreak for the Raiders. But Matty Beharrell missed the conversion and the points were shared.

Coach Aaron Wood is gone and a new coaching team, which includes former Wigan Warriors star Ben Flower, will have their work cut out to transform the Raiders from also-rans.

LEAGUE 1 AWARDS

PLAYER OF THE YEAR
Rob Massam (North Wales Crusaders)

YOUNG PLAYER OF THE YEAR
Phoenix Laulu-Togaga'e
(Keighley Cougars)

COACH OF THE YEAR
Anthony Murray (North Wales Crusaders)

League 1 Play-offs

Barrow won automatic promotion to the Championship by finishing top of the ten-team table on percentage basis. The teams finishing second to sixth then entered a five-team play-off format system to decided the second promotion spot, with second-placed Workington Town beating fifth-placed Doncaster in the final at Derwent Park.

Doncaster kept their hopes of promotion from Betfred League 1 alive with a commanding 31-10 victory over Hunslet in the Elimination Play-off at the Keepmoat Stadium.

Hunslet scored first but their season was ended by a Doncaster side who shook off the early setback to dominate the contest and run in five tries, setting up a semi-final meeting against third-placed North Wales Crusaders, who were beaten 28-14 at home by Keighley Cougars in the Qualifying Final. Halfback Matty Beharrell played a starring role for the Dons, providing leadership and contributing 11 points with the boot.

Two late tries from former Italy international Brenden Santi helped Keighley edge an enthralling tie with North Wales Crusaders and book a straight shoot-out with Workington Town the next weekend for the chance to host the League 1 play-off final.

After the Cougars had established a healthy 14-0 lead in what was a real arm wrestle throughout, North Wales hit back to level the match at 14-14, setting up a grandstand finish.

Workington's Carl Forber is jubilant after scoring against Doncaster in the League 1 Play-off Final

Despite the home side looking the more likely to kick on with all the momentum in their favour, Keighley showed their big-game experience late on and Santi's two crash over plays saw them through.

North Wales got a second bite at the cherry at home to Doncaster the following Sunday and they produced another comeback that fell short. They turned around a 42-12 deficit on the hour mark to produce what would have been the comeback of all comebacks. But the Dons, with quality throughout their side, killed off the match to eliminate the Crusaders by 48-34.

Workington edged Keighley at Derwent Park in the Qualifying Semi-final, Carl Forber's penalty goal from under the sticks in golden-point extra time winning the tightest of games 18-16 and taking Town straight into the final, with home advantage guaranteed.

In the third week's Final Eliminator, there was drama to match as Doncaster scored on the final hooter to secure a Play-off Final place with a 28-26 win over Keighley at Cougar Park.

Trailing by four points as the hooter sounded, a Liam Johnson try was converted from the touchline by Jake Sweeting as the visitors booked a trip to west Cumbria.

With a big crowd and some fabulous Rugby League on display, it was just like the mid-1990s at Derwent Park as Workington secured promotion with a 36-12 victory over Doncaster.

Richard Horne's side fought valiantly but Town were magnificent. Conor

League 1 Season

Fitzsimmons and Rhys Clarke took them forward, Jamie Doran and Carl Forber pulled the strings, but it was Marcus O'Brien who deservedly took man-of-the-match honours with a wonderful all-round performance.

There were two key spells that went a long way to Town achieving their goal. First, when Dec O'Donnell received an early yellow card, which was followed by an immediate Doncaster try, Town regrouped, completed their sets, kicked brilliantly and scored a try of their own despite their numerical disadvantage.

And then early in the second half, Doncaster put together a number of strong sets, but Town stood firm and regained the initiative with Matty Henson's try. By the 70th minute, Doncaster were shot, and two late Town tries blew the scoreline out.

Town's win meant that all three professional clubs in Cumbria would play in the Championship in 2022.

PLAY-OFF FINAL

Sunday 10th October 2021

WORKINGTON TOWN 36 DONCASTER 12

TOWN: 2 Brad Holroyd; 5 Alex Young; 31 Joe Brown; 24 Ethan Bickerdike; 30 Zac Olstrom; 6 Jamie Doran; 7 Carl Forber; 25 Jake Lightowler; 9 Dec O'Donnell; 14 Marcus O'Brien; 8 Conor Fitzsimmons; 12 Caine Barnes; 13 Hanley Dawson. Subs (all used): 23 Matty Henson; 33 Rhys Clarke; 11 Perry Singleton; 17 Ryan Wilson.
Tries: J Brown (2), Fitzsimmons (14), Forber (32), Henson (48), O'Brien (70), Holroyd (75); **Goals:** Forber 6/6.
Sin bin: O'Donnell (5) - late challenge.
DONCASTER: 28 Misi Taulapapa; 18 Tom Halliday; 3 Sam Smeaton; 4 Jason Tali; 32 Ollie Greensmith; 36 Jake Sweeting; 7 Matty Beharrell; 30 Zach Braham; 6 Ben Cockayne; 10 Brandon Douglas; 23 Liam Johnson; 19 Aaron Ollett; 12 Brad Foster. Subs (all used): 22 Alex Holdstock; 1 Ben Johnston; 26 Ross Whitmore; 27 Aaron York.
Tries: L Johnson (6), Greensmith (40); **Goals:** Beharrell 2/2.
Rugby Leaguer & League Express Men of the Match:
Town: Marcus O'Brien; *Doncaster:* Jason Tali.
Penalty count: 5-7; **Half-time:** 18-12; **Referee:** Tom Grant; **Attendance:** 2,997.

WOMEN'S SUPER LEAGUE
Saints three up

After the entire 2020 season was wiped out due to the coronavirus pandemic, the Betfred Women's Super League came back with a bang and proved a real treat for long-term supporters and new fans alike.

More people than ever before were able to watch much of the action with games streamed weekly on OurLeague or Twitch and the Challenge Cup Final was shown live on the BBC. Sky Sports got in on the act too with live coverage of the League's Semi-Finals and Grand Final.

But it wasn't all plain sailing and, like most leagues in 2021, there were some bumps in the road along the way. Games were called off due to the ongoing pandemic but also, on occasion, because of a lack of available medical cover at grounds.

Unanticipated changes were also made mid-way through the year when the mid-season break was brought forward to give clubs a circuit breaker from the virus. That saw the final round of fixtures cancelled before the league split into two smaller leagues with all previous points total reset. The top-five teams went on to battle it out for the Super League title and the bottom five competed for the Shield. This was different to the original plan of a top-four/bottom-six split but everyone still played each other once more, with the top four then progressing to the semi-finals of the relevant competitions.

Despite all the upheaval, the players once again gave it their all to showcase the game in the best possible light and the 4,235 people that were in attendance at Emerald Headingley Stadium on Finals days certainly witnessed a treat as **ST HELENS** completed a historic treble.

Having already claimed the Challenge Cup with a 34-6 win over York in June and then the League Leaders Shield three months later, Saints made it a clean sweep with a 28-0 victory over reigning champions Leeds Rhinos.

Leah Burke crossed for two tries, with newly-crowned Woman of Steel Jodie Cunningham, Amy Hardcastle, Zoe Harris and Danielle Bush also crossing in another highly impressive display from the Saints.

Defence was the key to Saints' dominance. No team scored more than six points when up against Saints in the league, although in the Challenge Cup Leeds crossed for two tries in the 20-12 semi-final defeat to the eventual winners.

LEEDS RHINOS more than played their part in the final and the season as a whole. They were leading the table and unbeaten at the time of the split.

Having gone toe-to-toe with Saints all season, the Rhinos could have given themselves a shot at the League Leaders Shield when the two sides were due to meet at the start of September. But Leeds were hugely down on numbers and could not fulfil the match. As they did not meet the threshold of seven players being unavailable as a direct result of Covid, the Rhinos had to forfeit the match, handing a 24-0 win to St Helens, who never relinquished the two-point advantage that gave them.

Having won the League Leaders Shield and the Challenge Cup in 2018, followed by the Challenge Cup and the Super League title 12 months later, the Rhinos were disappointed not to end the year with some silverware. But under the leadership of head coach Lois Forsell, and with an exciting mix of experience and youth set to continue, the Rhinos will remain as one of the leading lights within the game.

Finals day also saw **HUDDERSFIELD GIANTS** celebrate their debut season in Super League by lifting the Shield with a 24-22 win over Featherstone Rovers. The Giants made huge progress throughout the season and eventually proved themselves as real competitors in the Shield.

An Erin Stott try in the third period of golden-point extra time in their semi-final against Warrington Wolves proved the Giants would never give up. They no doubt took a lot of confidence from that 30-26 win into the final against the much-fancied **FEATHERSTONE ROVERS**.

Rovers had been looking to send Andrea Dobson out on a high after the leading England appearance maker announced her retirement from the game.

It wasn't to be when they came up against the Giants, losing their only match of the Shield campaign. The challenge for the Rovers now will be how they can bridge the gap between themselves and the top four if they want to push forward and progress as a club.

Away from the finals, **YORK CITY KNIGHTS** got everyone talking this year after club owner Jon Flatman invested heavily to make sure his side could challenge the very best in the game.

It certainly worked. After bringing in former Castleford Tigers coach Lindsay Anfield, the club also recruited heavily when it came to players and brought in Rhiannon Marshall, Sinead Peach, Kelsey Gentles, Tamzin Renouf and Grace Field from the Tigers as well as Olivia Wood and Savannah Andrade from Bradford Bulls. That injection of experience proved vital as the City Knights went on to reach the Challenge Cup Final, as well as pushing Leeds Rhinos all the way in the League Semi-Final.

Those departures did hit **CASTLEFORD TIGERS** hard as they failed to build on their League Leaders Shield success of 2019. But despite that, they still finished in the top four, a big achievement for a side that in many weeks fielded a side with an average age of under 21 years. Their rebuilding process will only be aided by those young stars having an extra year of experience under their belt.

The same can be said for 2018 champions **WIGAN WARRIORS**, who again struggled to keep pace with the top four.

A change in coach, plus a big turnover of players since that inaugural win, has perhaps not seen the club develop as they would have liked. They may not have won a game after the leagues split but wins against Warrington Wolves, Bradford Bulls, Huddersfield Giants, Castleford Tigers and Featherstone Rovers in the opening five games of the season proved there is still potential in the Warriors ranks. The challenge now will be sustaining that for a full season - they failed to add any further victories to their tally.

Vicky Molyneux was Wigan's standout performer and shone enough to earn a recall to the England side for the first time since she was a teenager in 2007.

WARRINGTON WOLVES may have struggled against the teams in the top four, but against those teams of a similar standard they more than held their own in their debut Super League season.

WOMEN'S SUPER LEAGUE

	P	W	D	L	F	A	Diff %	Win %
Leeds Rhinos	7	7	0	0	364	38	957.89	100.00
St Helens	7	6	0	1	370	36	1027.78	85.71
Wigan Warriors	7	5	0	2	226	76	297.37	71.43
York City Knights	7	5	0	2	198	106	186.79	71.43
Castleford Tigers	6	4	0	2	166	96	172.92	66.67
Featherstone Rovers	8	3	0	5	152	308	49.35	37.50
Huddersfield Giants	7	2	0	5	104	288	36.11	28.57
Bradford Bulls	8	2	0	6	128	294	43.54	25.00
Warrington Wolves	8	2	0	6	150	334	44.91	25.00
Wakefield Trinity	7	0	0	7	50	332	15.06	0.00

WOMEN'S SUPER LEAGUE - PLAY-OFFS

	P	W	D	L	F	A	Diff	Pts
St Helens	4	4	0	0	158	6	152	8
Leeds Rhinos	4	3	0	1	70	44	26	6
York City Knights	4	2	0	2	52	66	-14	4
Castleford Tigers	4	1	0	3	36	112	-76	2
Wigan Warriors	4	0	0	4	22	110	-88	0

WOMEN'S SUPER LEAGUE - SHIELD

	P	W	D	L	F	A	Diff	Pts
Featherstone Rovers	4	4	0	0	130	36	94	8
Huddersfield Giants	4	3	0	1	152	52	100	6
Warrington Wolves	4	2	0	2	144	68	76	4
Bradford Bulls	4	1	0	3	66	90	-24	2
Wakefield Trinity	4	0	0	4	6	252	-246	0

They were aided along the way by the experience and leadership of Michelle Davis and picked up their first win of the season with a 44-8 win over fellow newcomers Huddersfield Giants.

BRADFORD BULLS perhaps saved their best performance until the end, beating Wakefield 46-6 in the final league game. Danielle Bose crossed for a hat-trick in her final game at Odsal Stadium after announcing she was bringing the curtain down on her 18-year career in the game.

Despite taking an early lead against Featherstone, the Bulls bowed out of the Shield at the semi-final stage, going down 30-12.

An already difficult season for **WAKEFIELD TRINITY** was made even harder when Liv Whitehead - arguably their best player - joined York City Knights after the league's split to try and fulfil her aim of breaking into the England set-up. On the field, Trinity were unable to find a win but, to their credit, they never gave up when scorelines were getting away from them.

Elsewhere, the newly-formed Super League South division eventually went the way of **CARDIFF DEMONS**, who scored in the dying moments to secure a 30-26 win over **THE ARMY**.

With just 10 seconds left on the clock, Ffion Lewis raced over to give Cardiff the lead for the first time. Her conversion sparked mass celebrations and handed the trophy to the Welsh side.

The competition started with two leagues with the Army, **LONDON BRONCOS** and **BEDFORD TIGERS** in the East division, with the West division made up of the Demons, **GOLDEN FERNS** and **CORNISH REBELS**. The top two from each league progressed to the semi-finals with the Army beating the Golden Ferns 110-0, while the Demons progressed to the final with a 38-20 win over the Broncos.

The pandemic caused the Championship and League 1 to temporarily revert to a community-led game. **LEIGH MINERS** took the Championship title with a 10-6 win at **BARROW** and were promoted to Super League, while **HULL KINGSTON ROVERS** beat **DEWSBURY MOOR** 28-16 to take the League 1 final.

2022 will see the arrival of at least one new club on the block, with **SALFORD RED DEVILS** already announcing they are to launch a Women's team.

Women's Super League

WOMEN'S SUPER LEAGUE GRAND FINAL

Sunday 10th October 2021

LEEDS RHINOS 0 ST HELENS 28

RHINOS: 1 Caitlin Beevers; 17 Tasha Gaines; 3 Sophie Robinson; 5 Fran Goldthorp; 13 Sophie Nuttall; 6 Hanna Butcher; 7 Courtney Winfield-Hill; 11 Aimee Staveley; 9 Kerea Bennett; 25 Zoe Hornby; 4 Chloe Kerrigan; 12 Elle Frain; 23 Orla McCallion. Subs (all used): 15 Danika Priim; 18 Sam Hulme; 20 Lucy Murray; 26 Beth Lockwood.
SAINTS: 24 Rachael Woosey; 21 Danielle Bush; 20 Carrie Roberts; 4 Amy Hardcastle; 5 Leah Burke; 15 Beth Stott; 6 Zoe Harris; 26 Isabelle Rudge; 9 Tara Jones; 13 Chantelle Crowl; 3 Naomi Williams; 12 Emily Rudge; 1 Jodie Cunningham. Subs (all used): 2 Rebecca Rotheram; 11 Philippa Birchall; 8 Victoria Whitfield; 19 Paige Travis.
Tries: Burke (21, 56), Cunningham (39), Hardcastle (58), Harris (66), Bush (71); **Goals:** Stott 2/6.
Sin bin: Cunningham (10) - delaying restart.
Rugby Leaguer & League Express Women of the Match:
Rhinos: Courtney Winfield-Hill; *Saints:* Zoe Harris.
Penalty count: 6-8; **Half-time:** 0-10; **Referee:** Aaron Moore; **Attendance:** 4,235 *(at Emerald Headingley)*.

WOMEN'S SUPER LEAGUE SEMI-FINALS
Sunday 26th September 2021
Leeds Rhinos 22 York City Knights 18
St Helens 58 Castleford Tigers 0

WOMEN'S SUPER LEAGUE SHIELD FINAL

Sunday 10th October 2021

FEATHERSTONE ROVERS 22 HUDDERSFIELD GIANTS 24

ROVERS: 6 Kath Hepworth; 18 Chloe Billington; 3 Brogan Kennedy; 31 Gabrielle Harrison; 30 Fran Copley; 13 Andrea Dobson; 27 Olivia Grace; 10 Brogan Churm; 14 Charley Blackburn; 8 Zoe Teece; 11 Jessica Hammond; 1 Hannah Watt; 23 Shanelle Mannion. Subs (all used): 22 Cairo Newby; 16 Jasmine Hazell; 26 Matilda Butler; 20 Grace Dyke.
Tries: Billington (13), Grace (35), Churm (44, 63); **Goals:** Hepworth 3/4.
GIANTS: 1 Philippa Curley; 5 Amelia Brown; 4 Erin Stott; 25 Ellie Thompson; 2 Annabel Loney; 27 Fran Townend; 6 Sade Rihari; 26 Charlotte Hawkins; 14 Isabella Sykes; 19 Jamie-Leigh Bellerby; 24 Olivia Rowe; 17 Isabel Northrop; 11 Emma Wilkinson. Subs (all used): 9 Bethan Oates; 16 Bridget Campbell; 13 Chloe Fairbank; 10 Rachel Barker.
Tries: Townend (7), Campbell (24), Brown (50, 55); **Goals:** Townend 4/4.
Rugby Leaguer & League Express Women of the Match:
Rovers: Andrea Dobson; *Giants:* Sade Rihari.
Penalty count: 3-5; **Half-time:** 10-12; **Referee:** Nick Bennett.
(at Emerald Headingley, Leeds).

WOMEN'S SUPER LEAGUE SHIELD SEMI-FINALS
Sunday 26th September 2021
Featherstone Rovers 30 Bradford Bulls 12
Huddersfield Giants 30 Warrington Wolves 26
(after golden point extra-time)

WOMEN'S CHALLENGE CUP FINAL

Saturday 5th June 2021

ST HELENS 34 YORK CITY KNIGHTS 6

SAINTS: 2 Rebecca Rotheram; 24 Rachael Woosey; 20 Carrie Roberts; 4 Amy Hardcastle; 21 Danielle Bush; 15 Beth Stott; 7 Faye Gaskin; 18 Dawn Akrigg; 9 Tara Jones; 13 Chantelle Crowl; 19 Paige Travis; 12 Emily Rudge; 1 Jodie Cunningham. Subs (all used): 26 Isabelle Rudge; 11 Philippa Birchall; 5 Leah Burke; 3 Naomi Williams.
Tries: Bush (15), Woosey (20, 54), E Rudge (33), Hardcastle (37), Roberts (58), Travis (68); **Goals:** Stott 3/7.
CITY KNIGHTS: 28 Emma Hardy; 23 Kelsey Gentles; 24 Tamzin Renouf; 25 Savannah Andrade; 3 Bettie Lambert; 22 Rhiannon Marshall; 7 Katie Langan; 26 Grace Field; 27 Sinead Peach; 13 Alisha Clayton; 21 Olivia Wood; 16 Daisy Sanderson; 1 Ellie Hendry. Subs (all used): 9 Elspeth Innes; 12 Lily Farrow; 4 Ashleigh Hyde; 18 Alex Stimpson.
Try: Peach (49); **Goals:** Marshall 1/1.
Rugby Leaguer & League Express Women of the Match:
Saints: Emily Rudge; *City Knights:* Rhiannon Marshall.
Penalty count: 3-3; **Half-time:** 20-0; **Referee:** Marcus Griffiths; **Attendance:** 1,000 *(at Leigh Sports Village)*.

WOMEN'S CHALLENGE CUP SEMI-FINALS
Saturday 22nd May 2021
Leeds Rhinos 12 St Helens 20
York City Knights 32 Castleford Tigers 4
(both at LNER Community Stadium, York)

3
SEASON DOWN UNDER

NRL
Mountain-men on top

Like the northern hemisphere, the Australian Rugby League season was badly affected by the lingering Covid-19 epidemic, which sporadically almost went away before occasionally raising its head again.

Reigning Premiers Melbourne Storm had to relocate to Queensland twice during the year and a July lockdown in Greater Sydney meant all the remaining clubs were relocated and played all their games, including the Finals, on grounds in Queensland.

That meant the 2021 Grand Final, which was contested by two Sydney clubs, was played at Suncorp Stadium for the first time in history and after concerns that a coronavirus outbreak was about to hit Brisbane at the time, a reduced capacity of 39,000 was enforced for the finale. It didn't stop thousands of South Sydney and Penrith fans flocking to Brisbane in their hordes to witness a compelling showdown as Clive Churchill Medalist Nathan Cleary booted the Panthers to their first NRL title since 2003.

The Penrith co-captain's superb kicking in general play, plus his three successful attempts from the tee, helped his side cling on to a thrilling 14-12 win.

South Sydney skipper Adam Reynolds missed the chance to be the hero in his final game for the Rabbitohs, slicing his late sideline conversion effort just wide, then mis-hitting a last-minute two-point field-goal bid.

Penrith winger Stephen Crichton had already claimed the winning moment, snaffling an intercept off Cody Walker for the decisive try late in the second half.

Walker had scored a memorable individual four-pointer to keep the Rabbitohs in touch 8-6 at the break, after Matt Burton opened the scoring for Penrith and Cleary's kicking performance controlled possession and territory from then on.

And although Alex Johnston's 30th try of the season gave Souths a late sniff, the boot of Broncos-bound Reynolds couldn't snatch a fairytale farewell for himself and departing coach Wayne Bennett.

The Panthers had lost just six games in the past two years - including the 2020 Grand Final to Melbourne and the 2021 Qualifying Final against Souths.

Penrith fullback Dylan Edwards spent the week in a surgical boot but shrugged off his foot issue with the assistance of pain-killing injections. Bulldogs-destined teammate Tevita Pangai Junior failed to overcome a knee injury and was replaced by front-rower Moses Leota on his return from a calf injury. South Sydney made no changes to the 17 that demolished Manly 36-16 the Friday before and were still without the suspended Latrell Mitchell.

After a thunderous start, a head injury assessment on Dane Gagai demanded an early Souths reshuffle. Benji Marshall entered the fray in the twelfth minute after Gagai copped a knock in a tackle on opposite number Paul Momirovski.

The Rabbitohs weathered three goal-line dropouts and one set restart before the dam wall eventually burst and the Panthers notched the first points. Jarome Luai's composed pass left exploited a poor defensive read by Souths centre Campbell Graham to send Burton over the stripe without a hand being laid on him.

Jai Arrow was the next Rabbitoh to go off for a HIA seconds after coming off the bench, courtesy of a Viliame Kikau high shot that was put on report. The resultant

Penrith Panthers celebrate their NRL Grand Final victory over South Sydney Rabbitohs

penalty placed the Bunnies on the front foot and Walker's surging solo run over the top of Cleary opened Souths' account.

Reynolds had forfeited the kicking tee to rookie fullback Blake Taaffe in the Preliminary Final due to a groin issue but the half's finely tuned boot made it 6-all.

Gagai and Arrow both returned to the field with a quarter of an hour left in the first half, just in time to see dummy-half Api Koroisau draw a penalty out of some tired Bunnies defenders. Cleary potted another two points to make it 8-6 at the break, a scoreline South Sydney should have been satisfied with, given Penrith's dominance of possession.

Reynolds' penalty goal erased Souths' arrears within five minutes of the restart, thanks to a Panthers shepherd in their own territory.

Moments after the Rabbitohs lost Arrow to a second head injury assessment, they almost lost parity on the scoreboard, only for referee Gerard Sutton to correctly reject Kikau's try claim for Cleary's forward pass.

Having dodged several more bullets, South Sydney were eventually breached by a flying Crichton. The speedy winger pounced on Walker's overly ambitious pass to streak 40 metres to score what turned out to be the decisive try. Cleary's conversion gave Penrith a six-point buffer with little over ten minutes remaining, prompting Bennett to re-inject Marshall for some inspiration off the interchange bench.

And, on their first meaningful second-half foray into the Panthers' end, Johnston beat Crichton into the left-hand corner - the result of a well executed passing move via Walker and Gagai.

Reynolds put the touchline conversion to the right of the target to leave the Rabbits trailing by two with four minutes to go. And, when his tough two-point field-goal shot fell short in the final minute, the Panthers had both hands on the NRL's ultimate prize.

It was a great finale to another difficult season for all the clubs. Here's how they all fared.

PENRITH PANTHERS (Premiers/2nd in table)
Top pointscorer: Nathan Cleary (231); Top tryscorer: Matt Burton (17)

The Panthers missed the minor premiership they won last year but managed to win their third Premiership, adding to those of 1991 and 2003. Halfback Nathan Cleary won the Clive Churchill medal as the player of the match in the thrilling win over South Sydney and finished runner-up for the Dally M, losing out to Manly's Tom Trbojevic.

Cleary, winger Brian To'o, centre Matt Burton, prop James Fisher-Harris and back-rowers Viliame Kikau and Isaah Yeo were all selected in the Dally M Team of the Year, which just about sums up the excellent season enjoyed by the men from the west of Sydney.

There was no doubting that the Panthers would be a serious force again when they recorded twelve straight wins at the start of the season, including a 56-12 victory over Grand Final opponents-to-be South Sydney. State of Origin put pay to that run when they lost 26-6 to Wests Tigers. Apisai Koroisau, To'o, Yeo, Jarome Luai, Liam Martin, Kurt Capewell and Cleary were all away on Origin duty and were missing again the following week when they lost by a point to Cronulla.

But they won nine of their next ten games before a surprise defeat to the Rabbitohs in the Qualifying Final, meaning their nail-biting eliminator win over the Eels the following week had them playing minor premiers Melbourne to get into the Grand Final. They won that 10-6, perfect preparation for the tight game to come in the season finale.

Burton and Brent Naden are heading for Canterbury Bulldogs and Capewell to the Broncos as coach Ivan Cleary evidently intends to again put faith in the renowned Panthers production line.

SOUTH SYDNEY RABBITOHS (Runners-up/3rd)
Top pointscorer: Adam Reynolds (260); Top tryscorer: Alex Johnston (30)

The Rabbitohs couldn't conjure up the perfect finish for coach Wayne Bennett or star halfback Adam Reynolds by winning the Premiership from third place but they enjoyed an excellent season.

The only blips were two defeats to the Panthers, the round 11 clash in Dubbo a real pasting, and a heavy defeat by Melbourne when they were well under strength. But they beat the Panthers and then in-form Manly to make the Grand Final and were two kicks away from taking the Premiership.

Bennett handed the head-coaching reins to his assistant Jason Demetriou before taking over as coach at the new Brisbane club, the Dolphins, who will enter the NRL in 2023.

Halfback Reynolds was instrumental in the Rabbitohs success and he was ably abetted by Cody Walker who was selected as Dally M five-eighth. The two together with fullback Latrell Mitchell and free-scoring winger Alex Johnston made their left-side attack at times look unstoppable. Veteran Benji Marshall played a smart cameo, usually off the bench. Cameron Murray and quicksilver hooker Damien Cook starred in the pack.

Johnston top-scored in the NRL with 30 tries, the most tries scored by a player in a season in the modern era.

Mitchell, on his day, provided the X factor for the Bunnies. But he missed four weeks with suspension mid-season for two offences in the win over Wests Tigers. And in the round 24, 54-12 win over the Roosters his season was ended when he was banned for six matches for a horrific-looking shoulder charge to Joseph Manu's head. That meant rookie Blake Taaffe was thrust into finals football before his time.

Reynolds is leaving for Brisbane, centre Dane Gagai going back to Newcastle and edge player Jaydn Su'A is Dragons-bound. Anthony Milford, along with Raiders' utility Siliva Havili, is incoming from Brisbane and will need to find consistency to supplement his brilliance if Souths can replicate their 2021 season.

MELBOURNE STORM (Minor Premiers)
Top pointscorer: Ryan Papenhuyzen (157); Top tryscorer: Josh Addo-Carr (23)

There was a big question mark hanging over the Storm at the start of 2021. Just how would they cope without captain Cameron Smith, who retired after the Grand Final win of 2020.

The answer turned out to be they could manage very well, despite the club again being forced to relocate to Queensland for much of the season due to Covid restrictions. Melbourne claimed the Minor Premiership, setting a number of club records with 21 wins and 815 points scored and equalled the league record for most consecutive victories, set by Eastern Suburbs in 1975, with 19 victories between rounds four and 23.

There were early doubts. They only won two out of their first three games, losing narrowly to both the Panthers and Eels. But after that they were back in the groove, their only other defeat, by Parramatta again, in round 24

Props Jesse Bromwich and Dale Finucane succeeded Smith in a co-captaincy role, as emerging players slotted seamlessly into the Storm system finely tuned by coach Craig Bellamy.

Fullback Ryan Papenhuyzen established himself as a true superstar and finished as the club's top scorer, even though he played in only 15 games because of injury, while winger Josh Addo-Carr's 23 tries included six scored in one game against the Rabbitohs.

Brandon Smith was a bundle of energy and beat off some stiff opposition to be named Dally M hooker of the year - centre Justin Olam forced his way into the imaginary team at centre - although Smith, along with stand-off Cameron Munster got into trouble with the NRL for some end-of-season off-field transgressions.

The Panthers proved just too good for Melbourne in the Preliminary Final, beating them 10-6, when they looked to set for back-to-back Premierships. And though there are some big losses in Addo-Carr, going to the Bulldogs, Cronulla-bound pair Finucane and Nicho Hynes and Brenko Lee, off to Brisbane, the Storm aren't standing still. Winger Xavier Coates has joined from Brisbane along with Canterbury's Nick Meaney and prop Josh King from Newcastle.

And master coach Bellamy will remain with Melbourne after turning down an offer from Cronulla Sharks to become their director of football.

MANLY SEA EAGLES (4th)
Top pointscorer: Reuben Garrick (334); Top tryscorer: Tom Trbojevic (28)

The Sea Eagles made fourth place thanks to their better points difference over the Roosters and might have finished even higher but for the injury absence of fullback Tom Trbojevic at the start of the year and for two short spells mid-season.

They lost their first four games but Tom Trbojevic proved unstoppable at the end of the regular season and finished with 28 tries in 18 games, a new club record, scoring five hat-tricks along the way. No surprise he was unveiled as the Dally M winner at the end of the year.

But Turbo Tommy wasn't the only big pointscorer at the Sea Eagles, winger Reuben Garrick amassing 334 points, the second highest points in a season, from 23 tries and 121 goals, just behind Hazem El Masri's NRL record of 342 in 2004.

Rookies Jason Saab and Josh Schuster also had strong seasons. Schuster established himself as a quality, ball playing back-rower while speedy winger Saab capped off a superb club debut season for Manly with 26 tries.

In the Finals, Melbourne found a way of keeping Tom Trbojevic quiet but Manly bounced back the next week, with captain Daly Cherry-Evans leading them to a big win over the Roosters, before Souths finished their season in the Preliminary Final.

There'll be little change in 2022 with Des Hasler still holding the coaching reins, St Helens-bound Curtis Sironen and centre Moses Suli to the Dragons the only departures and front-rower Ethan Bullemor from Brisbane the only arrival by the end of the season. Hasler will have to conjure some improvement to make the Sea Eagles into a premiership side - they didn't pick up a win against the other top-four clubs.

SYDNEY ROOSTERS (5th)
Top pointscorer: Adam Keighran (86); Top tryscorer: Daniel Tupou (15)

The Roosters were knocked out in the semi-finals for the second year running, although they took a harder route in 2021 from fifth in the ladder. But that was a bigger achievement under coach Trent Robinson, at the end of a season marred by injury to senior players.

The bare facts of the Roosters' results don't tell the story. In round one they hammered Manly 46-4 and at the end of the season were eliminated by the same opposition by a 42-6 scoreline. But by then the Roosters had lost almost all their star players to injury.

Halfbacks Sam Walker and Drew Hutchison only got their opportunities due to Luke Keary's season-ending ACL injury in round three and a short-term injury to Lachlan Lam. Matt Ikuvalu, Egan Butcher and Fletcher Baker started the season in reserve grade, while Ben Marschke started the year somewhere below reserve grade. Adam Keighran was in the 17 in round one but only because Sam Verrills was out injured.

In April, star hooker Jake Friend retired because of recurring injuries. In June captain Boyd Cordner also hung up his boots due to repeated concussions.

Joining Keary in the stands for the season were Lindsay Collins, Brett Morris, Joseph Suaalii and Billy Smith. Victor Radley and Angus Crichton spent lengthy stints on the sidelines through suspension.

Fullback James Tedesco took up the captaincy after both Cordner and Friend's shock retirements and led a team of previous unknowns into fifth place on the ladder.

Teenaged Leeds-born Walker, son of former Rhino Ben, was one of the biggest emerging players to burst onto the NRL scene, his wiry frame containing a huge talent that won more than one game for the Roosters. Top scorer Keighran, signed from the Warriors, started the season as bench hooker and finished it in the centre.

Prop Isaac Liu is off to the Titans for 2022 but utility Connor Watson is returning from the Knights and hard-hitting forward Renouf Atoni arrives from the Bulldogs, along with Kevin Naiqama from St Helens.

PARRAMATTA EELS (6th)
Top pointscorer: Mitchell Moses (146); Top tryscorer: Maika Sivo (17)

The Eels' 2021 season showed a similar pattern to previous years, looking like real contenders for the early part of the season before fading towards the end of the year and making their exit in the play-offs.

The Eels were in the top four until round 19 before losing narrowly to Canberra, then 28-0 to the Roosters, 40-12 to Souths and 56-10 to Manly.

However under-pressure coach Brad Arthur turned the tide, Parra beating minor premiers Melbourne for the second time in the season in Round 24 with a 22-10 upset. They beat the Knights in the Elimination Final before an 8-6 loss to eventual Premiers Penrith in a superb game.

The season-ending loss of boom hooker Reed Mahoney to a shoulder injury in the round-21 defeat by Souths made an Eels Premiership charge unlikely. Gamebreaking winger Maika Sivo joined him with a knee injury two weeks later.

Clint Gutherson, Dylan Brown and in particular Mitchell Moses had form slumps but re-found their mojo in the run-in. And in hindsight the Eels got the buy of the year from the Warriors in back-rower Isaiah Papali'i, selected at the end of the 2021 season as Dally M second-rower of the year.

Sam Walker shows his delight at kicking Sydney Roosters to a play-off triumph against Gold Coast Titans

And the Eels unearthed a real talent in centre Will Penisini, who after five NRL games, including two finals, looks set for a bright future in the NRL, while New Zealander Haze Dunster had a breakout season on the wing, confirmed by Blake Ferguson's release at the end of the season.

With no signings in the can by the end of the season, and Sivo set to miss the first half of the season, Arthur is evidently happy with the talent coming through at Bankwest Stadium.

NEWCASTLE KNIGHTS (7th)
Top pointscorer: Jake Clifford (78); Top tryscorer: Enari Tuala (13)

The Knights finished in seventh place for the second year running and were eliminated at the first stage of the finals, this year by the Eels.

Newcastle kicked off the year without their best player in Kalyn Ponga and then just as he returned, experienced halfback Mitchell Pearce was injured. Pearce played only 12 games and Ponga 15. Second-rower Lachlan Fitzgibbon played only ten games and boom centre Bradman Best missed eight, while Tyson Frizell and Daniel Saifiti also spent time on the sidelines

The Knights were close to full strength in their Elimination Final, so no excuses there.

Halfback Jake Clifford arrived at the club in mid-season. Clifford wasn't meant to start his two-year deal with the Knights until 2022 but coach Adam O'Brien got him to Newcastle in May, when Pearce was injured and former Hull KR and Wigan halfback Blake Green announced his retirement. Clifford was one of the Knights' best performers in the season run-in.

The Knights have a strong roster and there won't be too many changes to personnel.

Ponga is their main man but there is plenty of quality throughout, with captain hooker Jayden Brailey having a standout season along with the Saifiti brothers and Frizell, centre Enari Tuala their top try-scorer.

Utility Connor Watson is leaving to go back to the Roosters and front-rower Josh King will join Melbourne. But centre Dane Gagai will be back from South Sydney and St George Illawarra halfback Adam Clune is another recruit for 2022.

GOLD COAST TITANS (8th)

Top pointscorer: Jamal Fogarty (156); Top tryscorer: David Fifita (17)

The Titans made the finals in former St Helens coach Justin Holbrook's second season in charge, a second season of improvement.

They needed to win their last round game against the Warriors and rely on Cronulla and Canberra to lose. They both did and the Titans qualified in style with a 44-0 defeat of the Warriors. They came very close to beating the Roosters in Townsville in their Elimination Final and could have snatched victory in the closing seconds but for some heroic cover defence from the Tricolours.

Star fullback AJ Brimson suffered knee and jaw injuries, the latter ending his season in round 22. But his absence provided an opportunity for Jayden Campbell, son of 2001 Dally M winner Preston Campbell, to make a name for himself. The skinny 21-year-old more than held his own. He was so impressive in his seven games that Holbrook was said to be considering shifting Brimson to stand-off next season so Campbell can remain at fullback.

It seems an odd reflection to make on a back-rower who was the club's top tryscorer but David Fifita's season probably fell short. And he also led the Titans in linebreaks and the NRL in tackle busts, which illustrates the weight of expectation that lays on the shoulders of a very young man on a reputed $1.2 million salary.

In his first season at the Titans, back-rower Tino Fa'asuamaleaui had a fine season, along with prop Moeaki Fotuaika and former Widnes winger Corey Thompson.

The Titans started the season with Ash Taylor and Jamal Fogarty in the halves and ended it with Tyrone Peachey with Fogarty. Mitch Rein and Erin Clark interchanged at hooker.

Stalwart winger Anthony Don has retired and Peachey, Rein and Taylor have all been released while incoming are experienced Roosters prop Isaac Liu, hooker Aaron Booth from Melbourne and Warriors utility back Paul Turner.

CRONULLA SHARKS (9th)

Top pointscorer: Braydon Trindall (88); Top tryscorer: Will Kennedy, Connor Tracey (14)

The Sharks were in with a chance of making the play-offs right up to the final regular-season round but a 28-16 defeat by Melbourne Storm - who needed to win to secure the Minor Premiership - and a big win for Gold Coast scuppered their chances. Instead the Titans edged them into eighth on points difference.

Going close was an achievement in itself after the mid-April sacking of head coach John Morris, which coincided with the appointment of Roosters assistant Craig Fitzgibbon as head coach on a three-year contract from 2022. The Sharks lost five consecutive games after that, with assistant Josh Hannay taking over in the interim for the rest of the season, including a defeat by eventual wooden-spoonists Canterbury.

The Sharks' best result came in June when they beat the high-flying Panthers, who had walloped them 48-0 a month before, thanks to a late Shaun Johnson field goal. Johnson signed for his old club the Warriors for next season and was granted an early release from his contract in August so he could return home to New Zealand with his family. Josh Dugan announced his retirement less than an hour after Cronulla terminated the few months of his contract following a second breach of the NRL's biosecurity rules.

Prop Andrew Fifita had a bad year and was sorely missed, playing in only six NRL games, spending most of the year playing for Newtown Jets. And after he came back into the team he suffered a horrific life-threatening injury in the 16-14 defeat to Newcastle, being rushed to hospital and placed in an induced coma before doctors performed an operation to repair a fractured larynx.

Signings for 2022 include Storm duo Dale Finucane and Nicho Hynes as well as the Dragons' workaholic hooker/lock Cameron McInnes.

CANBERRA RAIDERS (10th)
Top pointscorer: Jarrod Croker (80); Top tryscorer: Jordan Rapana (12)

Not making the play-offs was a huge disappointment for the Raiders on the back of making the Grand Final in 2019 and going out in the Preliminary Final in 2020.

The missing link was John Bateman, who returned to Wigan at the end of the 2020 season with a year of his contract to go. Canberra badly missed his ability to create tries out of nothing. Then in mid-2021, the club released star halfback George Williams with immediate effect after he requested a release at the end of the season to allow him and his pregnant partner to return home. The club was left in a bad light as Williams tweeted: 'Instead of supporting me the club kicked me out the door.'

Injuries didn't help. The Raiders spent most of the season without captain Jarrod Croker and star fullback Charnze Nicoll-Klokstad. Centre Curtis Scott was stood down after round 12 following a charge of assault after a nightclub incident and then sacked in August before he had even faced the charges.

Josh Papali'i and Joseph Tapine were dropped after a five-match losing run in the early part of the season but responded by both showing great form towards the end. But a tendency to start well and then lose games in the second half developed and a last-round hammering by the Roosters ended their season.

Jamal Fogarty, released by the Titans, arrives to replace Williams, though the Raiders released Dunamis Lui, Siliva Havili and Caleb Aekins, as well as Williams and Scott, and Sia Soliola has retired. Prop Ryan James is off to Brisbane. Coach Ricky Stuart has a big job on his hands to get the Raiders back to play-off status.

ST GEORGE ILLAWARRA DRAGONS (11th)
Top pointscorer: Zac Lomax (86); Top tryscorer: Mikaele Ravalawa (14)

The Dragons' 2021 season, St George's centenary season, won't be remembered for what happened on the pitch but for a barbecue held by veteran prop Paul Vaughan.

After the first round of July, the Dragons were on the edge of the top-eight and had just beaten the Warriors in a round-16 clash on the Central Coast. Vaughan decided to hold a barbecue at his home south of Wollongong for him and his teammates the day after.

The gathering breached the NRL's own biosecurity rules as well as the NSW government's stay-at-home order to curb the spread of the Covid-19 Delta strain. Police broke it up after being alerted by local residents.

The NRL dished out $305,000 in fines and one-game suspensions for every player involved, bar Vaughan who got an eight-match ban, and NSW Police hit them all with a $1,000 fine.

Vaughan was sacked by the club and 12 players copped suspensions, which had to be rotated in order to get a team out every week. St George Illawarra lost all eight remaining games.

Injuries to skipper Ben Hunt, who wasn't at the barbecue, as well as centre Zac Lomax contributed to an ordinary first season at the helm for coach Anthony Griffin.

But there was a glimmer of good news with the unearthing of some brilliant young talent in Tyrell Sloan, Jayden Sullivan and Talatau Amone. The club has so much confidence in Sloan at fullback that Matt Dufty found himself edged out - he will be at the Bulldogs in 2022 - and Corey Norman is another not being retained.

Captain Cameron McInnes, who has headed for the Sharks in 2022, ruptured his ACL in pre-season training. Broncos hooker Andrew McCullough was brought in to cover at hooker.

Arrivals at the Dragons in 2022 are George Burgess, as he recovers from a serious hip injury, props Francis Molo from the Cowboys and Aaron Woods from Wests Tigers, Souths back-rower Jaydn Su'A, Manly centre Moses Suli and West Tigers' Moses Mbye.

NEW ZEALAND WARRIORS (12th)
Top pointscorer: Kodi Nikorima (100); Top tryscorer: Dallin Watene-Zelezniak, Reece Walsh (9)

Former Huddersfield and St Helens coach Nathan Brown didn't have a great first season at the Warriors. Injuries and Covid-enforced life away from home conspired to leave the New Zealand team four points off play-off contention and they ended the season with a 44-0 shellacking by the Titans.

Major signings Addin Fonua-Blake managed only 15 games and Ben Murdoch-Masila only 14 games. Mainstays Tohu Harris and Leeson Ah Mau also struggled with injury, along with Chanel Harris-Tavita, David Fusitu'a, Peta Hiku and Euan Aitken. Mid-season recruits Matt Lodge (suspensions) and Chad Townsend (shoulder) both missed big chunks of the season after their arrivals. Still, the Warriors were usually competitive, losing seven games by six points or less.

Roger Tuivasa-Sheck announced he would be moving to rugby union at the end of the season, but with the New Zealand/Australia Covid bubble under threat was allowed to head back home early. Ken Maumalo also left for Wests Tigers mid-season.

That allowed the highly talented teenager Reece Walsh to emerge as a future superstar. Walsh was signed on the three-year contract from Brisbane from 2022 but was allowed to join the Warriors early in the season. He starred in his first season of first grade, scoring nine tries and kicking 21 goals in 16 appearances

The 19-year-old fullback, who got himself into hot water with the NRL for an off-field misdemeanour post-season, would have earned his first Queensland State of Origin jersey in game two but a hamstring injury ruled him out. Young back-rower Josh Curran also emerged into a first-choice player.

Star halfback Shaun Johnson will be back from Cronulla in 2022 and should add sparkle amongst a side that has the potential to make the Finals and Ashley Taylor arrived after his release by the Titans. Dallin Watene-Zelezniak will join from the Bulldogs, though Townsend and Peta Hiku both headed to the Cowboys, Fusitu'a joined Leeds and Kane Evans was also released to move to Hull FC. A return to Mt Smart Stadium would help the Warriors cause but they were expected to be based in Redcliffe in Queensland at the start of 2022.

WESTS TIGERS (13th)
Top pointscorer: Adam Doueihi (174); Top tryscorer: Ken Maumalo (15)

Wests coach, former Wigan boss Michael Maguire's future at the joint venture was thought to be in doubt, despite him having two years to go on his contract, after a three-match losing run at the end of the regular season. The Sydney newspapers hammered the Tigers for yet another disappointing season - their 10th straight without making the Finals, finishing ninth, 11th and 13th under Maguire.

But, two weeks after the end of the regular season, the club's board announced that Maguire would be keeping his job. Having guided South Sydney to the Premiership in 2014 after his Wigan stint, he obviously still has the credentials. Another former Premiership-winning coach, Tim Sheens is joining the club as director of coaching to help turn their fortunes around.

The Tigers have some promising young talent, headed by boom fullback Daine Laurie, Adam Doueihi, Stefano Utoikamanu, Jake Simpkin and Shawn Blore, but have struggled to recruit big-name players. At the end of the season they were reported to have around $2 million in their salary cap to spend and had been linked with the likes of Tariq Sims and Adam Elliott.

Lebanon international Adam Doueihi found his role at five-eighth and was set to be joined by Jackson Hastings and Oliver Gildart from Wigan in 2022. Utility Tyrone Peachey has signed too after being released by the Titans. Moses Mbye headed out of the club to the Dragons.

Former Warrington and Salford star Ben Murdoch-Masila suffered an injury-hit season with New Zealand Warriors

Some of the more experience heads didn't hit the heights in 2021 James Tamou was hampered by injury and struggled for form, Joe Ofahengaue couldn't find consistency and the first-choice centre pairing of James Roberts and Joey Leilua never worked. The Tigers finished the season with back-rower Michael Chee-Kam and Tommy Talau in the centre and the 38-0 last-round loss to the bottom of the table Bulldogs was a real humiliation.

BRISBANE BRONCOS (14th)
Top pointscorer: Jamayne Isaako (124); Top tryscorer: Xavier Coates (11)

The Broncos didn't end up with the wooden spoon as they did in 2020 and finishing 14th is only a small improvement. But the back end of the season should give Broncos fans some hope for 2022. They got within six points of the Panthers in Round 19, hammered the Cowboys, lost to the Roosters by just one point in Round 21 and beat the Warriors a week later. In his first full season, coach Kevin Walters gradually restored some pride in the Broncos jersey.

The key to Brisbane's improvement was Payne Haas, who was Dally M front-rower of the year. The 21-year-old was again the Broncos' best player. His 20 appearances for the Broncos in 2021 produced 3,361 running metres (168 metres average from 15 hit-ups per game) and he collected a third consecutive Paul Morgan Medal as the Brisbane Broncos' Player of the Year.

Rookie of the Year went to Kobe Hetherington who made his NRL debut in the Round 11 upset win over the Sydney Roosters at the SCG. The 22-year-old Queenslander made 14 appearances and had cemented a starting position at lock by the end of the season.

Exiting are long-time servants captain Alex Glenn, who has retired, and Anthony Milford, heading for South Sydney. Brodie Croft never secured a halfback place and has joined Salford Red Devils for 2022.

Croft played only ten games in the halves as Walters could never settle on his preferred halfback pairing and went with eight different combinations.

An MCL injury to Kotoni Staggs, the brilliant Tongan centre, robbed the Broncos of some genuine star quality although 21-year-old English centre Herbie Farnworth came on leaps and bounds.

The Broncos' big recruitments are South Sydney's Adam Reynolds and Penrith's Kurt Capewell, along with new football manager Ben Ikin. Reynolds will be expected to solve the halfback problem and, with a host of eager youngsters around him, much more is expected to the Broncos in 2022.

NORTH QUEENSLAND COWBOYS (15th)

Top pointscorer: Valentine Holmes (126); Top tryscorer: Kyle Feldt (12)

Under new coach Todd Payten the Cowboys got off to a bad start, losing their first four games straight. But six wins out of their next eight games had them looking well capable of making the Finals.

After the bye round the Cowboys won only one more game out of 12 and only avoided the wooden spoon by one place as injuries hampered them badly. Star stand-off Michael Morgan had to call a day on his career after round two because of a recurring shoulder injury. Valentine Holmes suffered a shoulder injury in Origin and talisman Jason Taumalolo broke his hand three times, consequently missing ten games.

Payten had a plan to lighten Taumalolo's load by reducing his minutes but the Cowboys struggled without him on the field. Halfback Jake Clifford left in May to join Newcastle Knights and inexperienced youngster Tom Dearden was drafted in from the Broncos. He was just one of a host of younger players who were thrust into the NRL and around who the Cowboys hoped to build in the future.

Hamiso Tabuai-Fidow was hampered by injury but both he and Murray Taulagi were impressive in the backline. In the pack, Heilum Luki, Griffin Neame, Jeremiah Nanai and Ben Condon look to have big futures. Jake Granville showed his value coming off the bench while Scott Drinkwater was the club's most consistent performer.

Chad Townsend and Peta Hiku, from the Warriors, will join a young and promising roster and better things are expected in Townsville in 2022.

CANTERBURY BULLDOGS (16th)

Top pointscorer: Jake Averillo (82); Top tryscorer: Nick Meaney (10)

Three wins from 24 games was hardly a dream debut season for coach Trent Barrett. Poor defence, injuries, suspensions and off-field scandals dogged the Bulldogs all year, although they ended the season with a 38-0 victory against the West Tigers in Redcliffe.

Discipline was also a key weakness, the Bulldogs finishing as the most penalised team in the competition. The most amazing example of that was when playmaker Lachlan Lewis wrestled Cody Walker to the ground as the teams left the field for half-time during their round 18 game in Robina. Canterbury were leading 12-10 at the time, but Lewis's sin-binning effectively changed the momentum.

Halfback Kyle Flanagan's arrival from the Roosters didn't work out that well either, though he has two more years left on his contract.

Injury hit the Bulldogs throughout 2021. Nick Meaney suffered broken ribs, Adam Elliott fractured his cheekbone and Nick Cotric injured his toe in training. That thrust young players into first grade prematurely. Falakiko Manu, Bailey Biondi-Odo and Chris Patolo joined Brad Deitz, Jackson Topine and Aaron Schoupp to make their NRL debuts.

Lewis, out of contract at the end of the season, and Elliot, who had two years left on his high-earning contract, both had their contracts terminated at the end of the season for off-field misdemeanours.

Will Hopoate is off to St Helens and Dylan Napa has also been released. Dallin Watene-Zelezniak (Warriors) and Meaney (Storm) are other departees. Penrith's Matt Burton and Brent Naden, Melbourne flyer Josh Addo-Carr, St George Illawarra's electric fullback Matt Dufty and prop Paul Vaughan, plus Tevita Pangai Jr are all locked in, and the wily Phil Gould comes in as football manager. With top performers Jake Averillo, former St Helens prop Luke Thompson and Josh Jackson still at Belmore, optimism abounds at the Bulldogs.

NRL ROUND-UP

NRL PREMIERSHIP FINALS SERIES

QUALIFYING FINALS
Friday 10th September 2021
Melbourne Storm 40 .... Manly Sea Eagles 12
(at Sunshine Coast Stadium, Kawana Waters)
Saturday 11th September 2021
Penrith Panthers 10 ....South Sydney Rabbitohs 16
(at Queensland Country Bank Stadium, Townsville)

ELIMINATION FINALS
Saturday 11th September 2021
Sydney Roosters 25 ....Gold Coast Titans 24
(at Queensland Country Bank Stadium, Townsville)
Sunday 12th September 2021
Parramatta Eels 28...Newcastle Knights 20
(at Browne Park, Rockhampton)

SEMI-FINALS
Friday 17th September 2021
Manly Sea Eagles 42... Sydney Roosters 6
(at BB Print Stadium, Mackay)
Saturday 18th September 2021
Penrith Panthers 8..Parramatta Eels 6
(at BB Print Stadium, Mackay)

PRELIMINARY FINALS
Friday 24th September 2021
South Sydney Rabbitohs 36 ....Manly Sea Eagles 16
(at Suncorp Stadium, Brisbane)
Saturday 25th September 2021
Melbourne Storm 6..Penrith Panthers 10
(at Suncorp Stadium, Brisbane)

NRL GRAND FINAL

Sunday 3rd October 2021

PENRITH PANTHERS 14 SOUTH SYDNEY RABBITOHS 12

PANTHERS: 1 Dylan Edwards; 2 Stephen Crichton; 3 Paul Momirovski; 4 Matt Burton; 5 Brian To'o; 6 Jarome Luai; 7 Nathan Cleary (C); 8 Moses Leota; 9 Api Koroisau; 10 James Fisher-Harris; 12 Kurt Capewell; 17 Liam Martin; 13 Isaah Yeo. Subs (all used): 11 Viliame Kikau; 14 Tyrone May; 15 Scott Sorensen; 16 Spencer Leniu.
Tries: Burton (17), Crichton (67); **Goals:** Cleary 3/3.
RABBITOHS: 1 Blake Taaffe; 2 Alex Johnston; 3 Dane Gagai; 4 Campbell Graham; 5 Jaxson Paulo; 6 Cody Walker; 7 Adam Reynolds (C); 8 Mark Nicholls; 9 Damien Cook; 10 Tevita Tatola; 11 Keaon Koloamatangi; 12 Jaydn Su'A; 13 Cameron Murray. Subs (all used): 14 Benji Marshall; 15 Jacob Host; 16 Tom Burgess; 17 Jai Arrow.
Tries: Walker (21), Johnston (75); **Goals:** Reynolds 2/3.
Rugby Leaguer & League Express Men of the Match:
Panthers: Nathan Cleary; *Rabbitohs:* Cameron Murray.
Penalty count: 2-3; **Half-time:** 8-6; **Referee:** Gerard Sutton;
Attendance: 39,000 *(at Suncorp Stadium, Brisbane)*.

NRL PREMIERSHIP - FINAL TABLE

	P	W	D	L	F	A	D	Pts
Melbourne Storm	24	21	0	3	815	316	499	42
Penrith Panthers	24	21	0	3	676	286	390	42
South Sydney Rabbitohs	24	20	0	4	775	453	322	40
Manly Sea Eagles	24	16	0	8	744	492	252	32
Sydney Roosters	24	16	0	8	630	489	141	32
Parramatta Eels	24	15	0	9	566	457	109	30
Newcastle Knights	24	12	0	12	428	571	-143	24
Gold Coast Titans	24	10	0	14	580	583	-3	20
Cronulla Sharks	24	10	0	14	520	556	-36	20
Canberra Raiders	24	10	0	14	481	578	-97	20
St George Illawarra Dragons	24	8	0	16	474	616	-142	16
New Zealand Warriors	24	8	0	16	453	624	-171	16
Wests Tigers	24	8	0	16	500	714	-214	16
Brisbane Broncos	24	7	0	17	446	695	-249	14
North Queensland Cowboys	24	7	0	17	460	748	-288	14
Canterbury Bulldogs	24	3	0	21	340	710	-370	6

LEADING POINTSCORERS

Reuben Garrick	Manly Sea Eagles	334
Adam Reynolds	South Sydney Rabbitohs	260
Nathan Cleary	Penrith Panthers	231
Adam Doueihi	Wests Tigers	174
Ryan Papenhuyzen	Melbourne Storm	157

TOP TRYSCORERS

Alex Johnston	South Sydney Rabbitohs	30
Tom Trbojevic	Manly Sea Eagles	28
Jason Saab	Manly Sea Eagles	26
Reuben Garrick	Manly Sea Eagles	23
Josh Addo-Carr	Melbourne Storm	23

DALLY M AWARDS

Dally M Medal (Player of the Year):
Tom Trbojevic (Manly Sea Eagles)

Provan Summons Medal (People's choice):
Josh Morris (Sydney Roosters)

Coach of the Year:
Craig Bellamy (Melbourne Storm)

Captain of the Year:
James Tedesco (Sydney Roosters)

Rookie of the Year:
Sam Walker (Sydney Roosters)

* The NRLW (Women's Premiership) was cancelled due to Covid-19

STATE OF ORIGIN
Singing the Blues

New South Wales won their third Origin series out of the last four, after winning the opening two games by huge margins, before Queensland avoided the whitewash in game three.

Once again there was huge disruption as the Covid-19 epidemic caused the last-minute relocations of the first and last games.

The venue for game one, scheduled for 9th June, was originally the Melbourne Cricket Ground. But due to a spike in coronavirus cases which forced Victoria into a state-wide lockdown, it was moved at the end of May to Queensland Country Bank Stadium in Townsville.

Game two was played at Suncorp Stadium as programmed but the final clash, originally scheduled to be played at Stadium Australia (formerly ANZ Stadium) in Sydney, was moved a week before it was due to be played, to McDonald Jones Stadium in Newcastle, although the NSW government agreed to allow only a 75 per cent attendance.

However, on 10th July, four days before the scheduled game, the NSW government banned crowds of any size and the game was moved again, this time to Cbus Super Stadium on the Gold Coast. If the game had been a decider, there would have been uproar that all three games were staged in Queensland. But the series was done and dusted in favour of the Blues by then. Despite the chaos, all three games attracted capacity crowds

Game one was a humiliation for the Maroons as New South Wales hammered them 50-6, a record Blues triumph over Queensland and only two points shy of the Maroons' Origin record 52-6 scoreline in game three of 2015.

Blues coach Brad Fittler was criticised for selecting Canberra stand-off Jack Wighton and Parramatta fullback Clint Gutherson in the centres for the deciding game of the previous year's series, which the Blues lost 20-14 to a side unkindly dubbed the worst Queensland team in history.

But deploying Manly custodian Tom Trbojevic and South Sydney fullback Latrell Mitchell in the centres for the 2021 opener paid handsome dividends.

Neither man had played Origin since 2019 - Trbojevic due to injury, and Mitchell due to an apparent falling-out with Fittler - and they could hardly have produced a more explosive return to the interstate

STATE OF ORIGIN - GAME I

Wednesday 9th June 2021

QUEENSLAND 6 NEW SOUTH WALES 50

QUEENSLAND: 5 Valentine Holmes (North Queensland Cowboys); 2 Xavier Coates (Brisbane Broncos); 3 Kurt Capewell (Penrith Panthers); 4 Dane Gagai (South Sydney Rabbitohs); 18 Kyle Feldt (North Queensland Cowboys); 6 Cameron Munster (Melbourne Storm); 7 Daly Cherry-Evans (Manly Sea Eagles) (C); 8 Christian Welch (Melbourne Storm); 9 Harry Grant (Melbourne Storm); 10 Tino Fa'asuamaleaui (Gold Coast Titans); 11 Felise Kaufusi (Melbourne Storm); 12 David Fifita (Gold Coast Titans); 13 Jai Arrow (South Sydney Rabbitohs). Subs (all used): 14 AJ Brimson (Gold Coast Titans); 15 Jaydn Su'A (South Sydney Rabbitohs); 16 Moeaki Fotuaika (Gold Coast Titans); 17 Joe Ofahengaue (Wests Tigers).
Try: Capewell (35); **Goals:** Holmes 1/1.
NEW SOUTH WALES: 1 James Tedesco (Sydney Roosters) (C); 2 Brian To'o (Penrith Panthers); 3 Latrell Mitchell (South Sydney Rabbitohs); 4 Tom Trbojevic (Manly Sea Eagles); 5 Josh Addo-Carr (Melbourne Storm); 6 Jarome Luai (Penrith Panthers); 7 Nathan Cleary (Penrith Panthers); 8 Daniel Saifiti (Newcastle Knights); 9 Damien Cook (South Sydney Rabbitohs); 10 Jake Trbojevic (Manly Sea Eagles); 11 Cameron Murray (South Sydney Rabbitohs); 12 Tariq Sims (St George Illawarra Dragons); 13 Isaah Yeo (Penrith Panthers). Subs (all used): 14 Jack Wighton (Canberra Raiders); 15 Junior Paulo (Parramatta Eels); 16 Payne Haas (Brisbane Broncos); 17 Liam Martin (Penrith Panthers).
Tries: T Trbojevic (18, 59, 69), To'o (22, 27), Mitchell (49, 61), Saifiti (64); **Goals:** Cleary 8/8, Mitchell 1/1.
Rugby Leaguer & League Express Men of the Match:
Queensland: Moeaki Fotuaika; *New South Wales:* Tom Trbojevic.
Penalty count: 4-4; **Half-time:** 6-20; **Referee:** Gerard Sutton;
Attendance: 27,533 *(at Queensland Country Bank Stadium, Townsville).*

New South Wales' Tariq Sims looks for a way past Queensland's Felise Kaufusi during Origin I

arena, Trbojevic collecting a hat-trick and Mitchell a double as they ran amok.

With blood gushing from a wound under his right eye, Penrith halfback Nathan Cleary translated his red-hot NRL form into his best performance in a sky blue jersey. And Cleary's Panthers team-mates Jarome Luai and Brian To'o both enjoyed spectacular debuts, with powerful winger To'o scoring a brace of tries within five first-half minutes.

While the cross-border battles were traditionally won and lost with the physical exchanges in the middle, NSW's speedsters laid the foundation for victory. The warm tropical weather, combined with the ARL Commission's new rules designed to speed up the game, guaranteed a lightning quick contest that the Blues' superior backline could ruthlessly exploit.

To'o galloped for 233 running metres, Trbojevic 215, captain James Tedesco 212, Mitchell 167 and Josh Addo-Carr 101. Enforcers Daniel Saifiti and Payne Haas were the only NSW forwards to top 100 running metres, illustrating just how much heavy lifting the backs shouldered.

State of Origin

Queensland never really got into the contest. Star stand-off Cameron Munster and dynamic hooker Harry Grant both looked short of a run, having not played for the Storm since May 6th, and Munster was perhaps lucky to avoid suspension for a 55th-minute skirmish with Blues debutant Liam Martin.

Bench forward Moeaki Fotuaika, who replaced the concussed Christian Welch after 12 minutes, was one of the few Maroons to offer any resistance, although he copped a one-game ban for a first-half late shot on Mitchell.

The Townsville relocation gifted Queensland back-to-back matches on home turf for the first time in Origin's 42-year history, with game two scheduled for Brisbane's Suncorp Stadium on Sunday June 27th.

It did them no good. A one-sided 26-0 scoreline was a true reflection of the Blues' dominance, which they had established by half-time after the Maroons' pack tired themselves out in a breathless opening. The Blues came top in every department, their star-studded threequarter line playing as well if not better than in game one.

There were mitigating factors for the Maroons, with the last 24 hours of their preparation severely disrupted, first when Warriors teenager Reece Walsh, whose premature Origin debut was much anticipated, suffered a hamstring strain in the captain's run the day before, meaning Valentine Holmes had to play fullback again.

STATE OF ORIGIN - GAME II

Sunday 27th June 2021

QUEENSLAND 0 NEW SOUTH WALES 26

QUEENSLAND: 2 Valentine Holmes (North Queensland Cowboys); 5 Kyle Feldt (North Queensland Cowboys); 4 Dane Gagai (South Sydney Rabbitohs); 3 Kurt Capewell (Penrith Panthers); 20 Xavier Coates (Brisbane Broncos); 6 Cameron Munster (Melbourne Storm); 7 Daly Cherry-Evans (Manly Sea Eagles) (C); 8 Christian Welch (Melbourne Storm); 9 Andrew McCullough (St George Illawarra Dragons); 10 Josh Papalii (Canberra Raiders); 11 Jai Arrow (South Sydney Rabbitohs); 12 Felise Kaufusi (Melbourne Storm); 13 Tino Fa'asuamaleaui (Gold Coast Titans). Subs (all used): 14 Ben Hunt (St George Illawarra Dragons); 15 Moeaki Fotuaika (Gold Coast Titans); 16 David Fifita (Gold Coast Titans); 17 Francis Molo (North Queensland Cowboys).
NEW SOUTH WALES: 1 James Tedesco (Sydney Roosters) (C); 5 Josh Addo-Carr (Melbourne Storm); 4 Tom Trbojevic (Manly Sea Eagles); 3 Latrell Mitchell (South Sydney Rabbitohs); 2 Brian To'o (Penrith Panthers); 6 Jarome Luai (Penrith Panthers); 7 Nathan Cleary (Penrith Panthers); 8 Daniel Saifiti (Newcastle Knights); 9 Damien Cook (South Sydney Rabbitohs); 10 Junior Paulo (Parramatta Eels); 11 Cameron Murray (South Sydney Rabbitohs); 12 Tariq Sims (St George Illawarra Dragons); 13 Isaah Yeo (Penrith Panthers). Subs (all used): 14 Jack Wighton (Canberra Raiders); 15 Angus Crichton (Sydney Roosters); 16 Payne Haas (Brisbane Broncos); 17 Liam Martin (Penrith Panthers).
Tries: Addo-Carr (12, 70), Mitchell (25), T Trbojevic (33); **Goals:** Cleary 5/5.
Rugby Leaguer & League Express Men of the Match:
Queensland: Daly Cherry-Evans; *New South Wales:* James Tedesco.
Penalty count: 5-1; **Half-time:** 0-18; **Referee:** Gerard Sutton;
Attendance: 52,272 *(at Suncorp Stadium, Brisbane)*.

And hours before kick-off, Walsh's replacement, Cronulla's Ronaldo Mulitalo, was withdrawn by the Queensland Rugby League with a dispute brewing about the winger's eligibility to represent the state. Dropped Brisbane winger Xavier Coates was drafted in at the eleventh hour.

In other changes, St George Illawarra's Andrew McCullough came in at hooker for Harry Grant, who injured a hamstring in game one, with Dragons team-mate Ben Hunt on the bench after AJ Brimson was ruled out through a knee injury suffered in the Gold Coast's defeat by Cronulla.

Josh Papalii (suspension) returned in the front row, with Cowboys prop Francis Molo handed a debut from the bench.

In contrast, the Blues had a settled line-up, the only change was Jake Trbojevic being ruled out by a hip injury, meaning Junior Paulo started in the front row.

Queensland's strategy looked to be built on an offload game, with Christian Welch getting two away in the first seven minutes. But there were early warning signs that James Tedesco's speed and evasion was going to cause them big trouble.

NSW broke the deadlock in the 12th minute with a try that encapsulated the contest.

Latrell Mitchell stripped the ball from Kyle Feldt, on Queensland debut at the age of 29, as he returned a kick. From the play-the-ball, the ball was spun left and Tedesco put Josh Addo-Carr in for his ninth Origin try with a peach of a long cut-out ball. Nathan Cleary converted from wide out.

An 80-metre interception try from Mitchell came ten minutes after and, not long after that, Cameron Murray dropped Tom Trbojevic's try-making pass after the Manly superstar beat Kurt Capewell, not for the last time. But within three minutes it was 18-0 anyway.

Tedesco crabbed on his own '30', made an overlap via Cleary, Murray and Trbojevic, and Ado-Carr was away down the right, passing back inside to Trbojevic, who ran 30 metres to score.

Queensland needed to score first in the second half to have a chance of winning the game. But they didn't. Indeed the Blues were unlucky to not get a fourth try, five minutes after the turnaround. A stunning piece of speed from Ado-Carr looked to have created another try for Trbojevic on his inside, but referee Gerard Sutton had spotted that Murray had been in front of the play-the-ball.

The Maroons' only hope looked to be captain Daly Cherry-Evans and his pinpoint kicks to the corner and that nearly paid dividends, though Feldt couldn't hold the ball as he rose above To'o.

Before long Cleary was kicking an easy penalty goal at the other end after Tariq Sims was obstructed chasing a Cleary grubber into the in-goal.

Ben Hunt's introduction just before the break gave Queensland a bit more spark and they almost got a reward when Munster's lobbed pass sent Coates towards the left corner. But a huge tackle from Trbojevic somehow managed to stop Coates getting the ball down one-handed.

Gagai touched down Feldt's tap back from Munster's high kick to the corner, but the bunker ruled he had his elbow on the dead-ball line. Then To'o knocked on Hunt's spiralling bomb and on tackle three from the scrum McCullough was held up before Holmes grubbered dead.

With ten minutes to go it was all over. Damien Cook was held up, Jarome Luai's grubber trapped Feldt in goal and Feldt's drop-out went barely a yard before curling back into touch in goal. From the penalty Addo-Carr got his second try, cutting inside from Tedesco's one-handed flick. Cleary's fifth goal made it 26-0.

With some luck the Maroons would have scored a consolation to avoid the whitewash. Cherry-Evans' clever grubber was collected by Feldt, but he was forced to knock on by To'o. And, with a minute to go, Holmes, on the run, couldn't quite collect and hold Cherry-Evans' chip towards the Blues' posts.

The Maroons restored some pride on the Gold Coast two and a bit weeks later with a 20-18 win as Ben Hunt's two second-half tries helped deny New South Wales their first series clean sweep since 2000.

Hunt crossed twice inside seven minutes to swing the momentum of the final game.

The return of fit-again fullback Kalyn Ponga and the debut of 19-year-old speedster Hamiso Tabuai-Fidow energised the Maroons' back line, while the Blues sorely missed first-choice halves Cleary (shoulder) and Luai (knee) to injury.

NSW won the first two games by an aggregate score of 76-6, but stand-in playmakers Mitchell Moses and Jack Wighton failed to carry that form into Game Three.

Brad Fittler's men had the opportunity to square the score at 20-all with two minutes left, only for Latrell Mitchell's 50-metre penalty-goal attempt to fall metres short.

Maroons forward Jai Arrow's suspension for a Covid bubble breach and the last-minute change of venue stole the headlines in the build-up.

But under-siege Maroons coach Paul Green managed to overcome the turmoil to register his first Origin triumph as coach and avoid the ignominy of losing all three games in his first series in charge.

NSW fans directed their passion towards referee Gerard Sutton, who awarded ten set restarts and five penalties in a heavy-handed first half that tallied more infringements than points.

Sutton's first intervention in the fourth minute invited Holmes to kick a penalty goal that put Queensland ahead for the first time in the series. A superb solo run by the red-hot Latrell Mitchell secured his fourth try of the series and earned the Blues the lead on ten minutes. The South Sydney star also took the goal-kicking duties off injured sharp shooter Cleary, and he made no mistake with his first effort.

Seven minutes later, Tabuai-Fidow marked a dream debut with a try. A smart Munster run sent Tino Fa'asuamaleaui into space, and the towering forward found the teenage first-gamer.

After that initial flurry, the game settled into a slugfest punctuated by Sutton's whistle.

The Blues faced particular pressure leading into the break and, after ten minutes of repeat sets in their danger zone, they were lucky to both trail by two and have their full complement on the park, given their repeated infringements.

Holmes succumbed to a shoulder injury at half-time, and was replaced by substitute AJ Brimson on the Maroons' left edge.

But it was the Queenslanders' right-hand side defence that leaked the first try of the second half, when Moses and Wighton combined for their brightest moment of the match.

Taking the ball to the line, the Parramatta halfback threw it out the back to a hard-running Wighton, who busted through some stretched Queensland defence to put the Blues back in front.

A Cherry-Evans kick began the momentum shift, drawing a rare error out of Josh Addo-Carr, which was then compounded by back-to-back set restarts.

The pressure sapped the Blues' reserves of energy in defence, and halfback turned hooker Ben Hunt darted over from dummy-half in the 57th minute.

Cherry-Evans assumed the kicking tee off the sidelined Holmes and slotted the straightforward conversion to give Queensland a slender advantage.

Then, when Hunt bagged his brace on the other side of the hour mark, the scoreboard looked even friendlier to fans north of the Tweed River.

This time, Ponga pierced the NSW line down the left flank and, off the very next ruck, the Maroons spun the ball across the field, fraying the wall of blue jumpers and giving Hunt the space to steam onto a composed Kurt Capewell offload.

Munster's out-on-the-full kick opened the door for a Blues comeback, and they obliged with a razzle-dazzle team try that involved two Moses kicks and culminated in four points for debutant sub Api Koroisau.

With only two points splitting the sides, the Bunker rejected NSW's penalty-try claim for Munster blocking Liam Martin in pursuit of a dangerous kick.

But their best opportunity came with two minutes remaining, when Sutton penalised Christian Welch for flattening Moses after a kick on the halfway line.

Despite the distance, NSW elected to kick for goal, but Mitchell's tired legs couldn't make the distance, handing Queensland their consolation win.

Some consolation for Queensland but the Shield in NSW skipper James Tedesco's hands and the Wally Lewis Medal around Tom Trbojevic's neck after the final whistle was a reminder of the gulf in class in the 2021 Origin Series.

STATE OF ORIGIN - GAME III

Wednesday 14th July 2021

QUEENSLAND 20 NEW SOUTH WALES 18

QUEENSLAND: 1 Kalyn Ponga (Newcastle Knights); 2 Valentine Holmes (North Queensland Cowboys); 3 Dane Gagai (South Sydney Rabbitohs); 4 Hamiso Tabuai-Fidow (North Queensland Cowboys); 5 Xavier Coates (Brisbane Broncos); 6 Cameron Munster (Melbourne Storm); 7 Daly Cherry-Evans (Manly Sea Eagles) (C); 8 Christian Welch (Melbourne Storm); 9 Ben Hunt (St George Illawarra Dragons); 10 Josh Papalii (Canberra Raiders); 11 Kurt Capewell (Penrith Panthers); 12 Felise Kaufusi (Melbourne Storm); 15 Tino Fa'asuamaleaui (Gold Coast Titans). Subs (all used): 14 AJ Brimson (Gold Coast Titans); 16 Moeaki Fotuaika (Gold Coast Titans); 18 Francis Molo (North Queensland Cowboys); 20 Thomas Flegler (Brisbane Broncos). **Tries:** Tabuai-Fidow (18), Hunt (57, 64); **Goals:** Holmes 2/2, Cherry-Evans 2/2.
NEW SOUTH WALES: 1 James Tedesco (Sydney Roosters) (C); 2 Brian To'o (Penrith Panthers); 3 Latrell Mitchell (South Sydney Rabbitohs); 4 Tom Trbojevic (Manly Sea Eagles); 5 Josh Addo-Carr (Melbourne Storm); 6 Jack Wighton (Canberra Raiders); 7 Mitchell Moses (Parramatta Eels); 10 Junior Paulo (Parramatta Eels); 9 Damien Cook (South Sydney Rabbitohs); 18 Dale Finucane (Melbourne Storm); 11 Cameron Murray (South Sydney Rabbitohs); 12 Tariq Sims (St George Illawarra Dragons); 13 Isaah Yeo (Penrith Panthers). Subs (all used): 14 Api Koroisau (Penrith Panthers); 15 Angus Crichton (Sydney Roosters); 16 Payne Haas (Brisbane Broncos); 17 Liam Martin (Penrith Panthers).
Tries: Mitchell (11), Wighton (48), Koroisau (69); **Goals:** Mitchell 3/4.
Rugby Leaguer & League Express Men of the Match:
Queensland: Kalyn Ponga; *New South Wales:* James Tedesco.
Penalty count: 5-2; **Half-time:** 8-6; **Referee:** Gerard Sutton; **Attendance:** 26,307 (at Cbus Super Stadium, Robina).

Wally Lewis Medal (Man of the Series): Tom Trbojevic (New South Wales)

4
INTERNATIONAL YEAR

Internationals

England

With the end-of-season spectacular that was to be the 2021 World Cup postponed for a year after the withdrawal of the Australian and New Zealand Rugby Leagues, the amount of international League activity was much reduced.

England coach Shaun Wane had been appointed in February 2020 but the Covid Pandemic meant there was no international Rugby League that year, with an Ashes series cancelled and then Wane's World Cup target slipping away for another year.

There was at least one full Test match for England, who ran out 30-10 winners over France at the end of the season at Stade Gilbert Brutus in Perpignan, on the day that England should have been opening the World Cup against Samoa in Newcastle.

Despite defeat, it was a highly encouraging showing from the home side. Against opposition that had not defeated them for 40 years, a win for England was always the likely outcome and in the first quarter of the match, it was no contest. France were utterly off the pace and England ran rampant, building a 20-0 lead with ruthless aggression and four tries.

After that, France belatedly met the intensity required for a Test match and there was nothing between the two nations in a second half featuring two tries apiece.

Wane fielded eight debutants, with John Bateman captaining his country for the first time in the injury absence of Sam Tomkins. Bateman and Tommy Makinson each bagged a brace of tries and Liam Farrell the opener. Tom Davies got one of the other scores on his full debut, while there were also first caps for Niall Evalds, Jordan Abdull, Paul McShane, Morgan Knowles, Mikolaj Oledzki, Joe Philbin and Kruise Leeming.

France had a new team as well. They also fielded eight debutants in Mathieu Laguerre, Mathieu Jussaume, Arthur Mourgue, Jordan Dezaria, Paul Seguier, Maxime Puech and try-scoring duo Corentin Le Cam and Justin Sangare. Coach Laurent Frayssinous, in his first game in charge, could take plenty of positives.

But they started badly, right from the kick-off, as the French allowed the ball to bounce dead for a drop-out. And for the next 20 minutes, England ran amok.

Romain Navarrete caught Knowles high before Abdull's kick in-goal sparked a scramble and Bateman claimed a try. French referee Benjamin Casty sent the decision upstairs and Robert Hicks judged that Mark Kheirallah had grounded the ball before Bateman.

Not that it brought the home side any relief, as from the drop-out McShane slipped in Bateman's second-row partner Liam Farrell to hit and spin past Jussaume, with Abdull converting for his first England points.

France continued to be their own worst enemy as Kheirallah dropped an Abdull bomb, with Morgan Escare then knocking on. That gave England the chance to execute a wonderful try, which saw Jonny Lomax and Evalds combine to find Davies for a breathtaking airborne finish.

TEST MATCH

Saturday 23rd October 2021

FRANCE 10 ENGLAND 30

FRANCE: 1 Mark Kheirallah (Toulouse Olympique); 2 Morgan Escare (Salford Red Devils); 3 Matthieu Laguerre (Catalans Dragons); 4 Mathieu Jussaume (Toulouse Olympique); 5 Fouad Yaha (Catalans Dragons); 6 Arthur Mourgue (Catalans Dragons); 7 Tony Gigot (Toulouse Olympique) (C); 8 Romain Navarrete (Toulouse Olympique); 9 Anthony Marion (Toulouse Olympique); 10 Jordan Dezaria (Catalans Dragons); 11 Benjamin Jullien (Catalans Dragons); 12 Paul Seguier (Catalans Dragons); 13 Mickael Goudemand (Catalans Dragons). Subs (all used): 14 Eloi Pelissier (Toulouse Olympique); 15 Maxime Puech (Toulouse Olympique); 16 Justin Sangare (Toulouse Olympique); 17 Corentin Le Cam (Catalans Dragons).
Tries: Le Cam (46), Sangare (75); **Goals:** Kheirallah 1/2.
ENGLAND: 1 Niall Evalds (Castleford Tigers); 2 Tom Davies (Catalans Dragons); 3 Reece Lyne (Wakefield Trinity); 4 Zak Hardaker (Wigan Warriors); 5 Tommy Makinson (St Helens); 6 Jonny Lomax (St Helens); 7 Jordan Abdull (Hull Kingston Rovers); 8 Alex Walmsley (St Helens); 9 Paul McShane (Castleford Tigers); 10 Mike Cooper (Warrington Wolves); 11 John Bateman (Wigan Warriors) (C); 12 Liam Farrell (Wigan Warriors); 13 Morgan Knowles (St Helens). Subs (all used): 14 Ben Currie (Warrington Wolves); 15 Mikolaj Oledzki (Leeds Rhinos); 16 Joe Philbin (Warrington Wolves); 17 Kruise Leeming (Leeds Rhinos).
Tries: Farrell (4), Davies (10), Makinson (14, 72), Bateman (18, 78); **Goals:** Abdull 3/6.
Sin bin: Lomax (69) - professional foul.
Rugby Leaguer & League Express Men of the Match:
France: Corentin Le Cam; *England:* John Bateman.
Penalty count: 9-4; **Half-time:** 0-20; **Referee:** Benjamin Casty; **Attendance:** 5,500 *(at Stade Gilbert Brutus, Perpignan).*

England's Niall Evalds takes on France's Benjamin Jullien and Tony Gigot

Next it was Tony Gigot to invite England forward by booting the restart straight out of play and the chance was duly taken as Makinson was left free to score from Lomax's pass, with the French defence in disarray again.

And England's flawless opening quarter was completed by another excellent score, this time a true team effort. Lomax started things off by finding Reece Lyne, who did a one-two with his wide man Davies before finding Evalds. The fullback shifted the ball on to Bateman, who had only green grass ahead of him, to streak over.

As Abdull converted for a 20-point lead after as many minutes, it looked like it could be an easy day for England. But France were not minded to lie down any longer and sought to restore some pride.

They very nearly had something to take into the break after making a late push. Le Cam was halted by Oledzki following a Sangare offload and the crowd felt aggrieved when Lyne wasn't sin-binned following a tip-tackle on Mourgue.

France were energised after the break. After Eloi Pelissier's damaging run, giant interchange Le Cam did the rest, taking Mourgue's pass and dummying over. Kheirallah couldn't convert but they were finally in the contest and building up a real head of steam.

In the space of seven minutes, France had two decisions go against them at the hands of the video referee, with both on-field calls overturned, to the disgust of the home support.

First Gigot was denied after he picked the pocket of Philbin, following the interception of his own kick by Lyne. Gigot burst clear for the try amid confusion but it was eventually ruled that the Warrington forward had already been held on the floor.

Internationals

The second decision needed a good number of viewings before again going in favour of the English, who had been torn open. Seguier made a stunning break, complete with a big dummy past Evalds, before handing to Kheirallah at the line. But an obstruction in the build-up from Le Cam on Lomax meant it would mean nothing.

A break in the other direction should have seen France's hopes of a comeback extinguished. Lomax released Ben Currie and he sent Lyne away but with support either side he chose to look for Davies on the outside and Fouad Yaha was able to block.

The general direction of traffic was still towards England's line and they looked vulnerable again with eleven minutes left when Farrell prevented Kheirallah from chasing his own kick in-goal with a lazy arm. Bizarrely it was Lomax, not Farrell, sent to the sin bin.

France could not take advantage of the extra player, however, and four minutes later victory was secured with a second Makinson try. Farrell and Zak Hardaker combined to send him into the corner with an ease reminiscent of that opening quarter.

That meant that when France did go over for a second time it was too late with five minutes left. After Pelissier was held out, England's defence was left with a giant hole as Kheirallah's quick play-the-ball put the giant Sangare in.

But England finished on a bright note with the final try, when props Alex Walmsley and Mike Cooper both executed smart offloads for Bateman's second score. Abdull, having hit the post with his previous attempt, landed his third conversion to round things off.

* On the day when England should have been deep into their final preparations for their opening World Cup game against Brazil, England's women beat France in Perpignan by 40-4. Captain Emily Rudge, one of nine St Helens players in the squad, scored two tries on her record 24th England appearance.

England's men had another warm-up game earlier in the year when they met a Combined Nations All Stars side at Warrington.

A side made up of overseas players from Super League, plus Jermaine McGillvary and Jake Connor, both not selected for England, won a tight game 26-24. Jackson Hastings ran the show for the All Stars in the halves and McGillvary's stunning solo finish early in the second half was the standout try on a thoroughly entertaining night of international rugby

The All Stars deservedly led at half-time by two points. Connor was integral to the game's opening try, as his cut-out ball sent Salford's Ken Sio over for the first of two tries on the night.

However, Connor was caught out three minutes later as Liam Farrell marked his return to the international fold with a magnificent solo try, bursting through on halfway before outpacing Connor to touch down.

Eight minutes later, England moved ahead when Luke Gale's cute pass sent Farrell over for his second of the night and, at that stage, England looked to be in control.

However, the All Stars soon hit back. When Tom Davies was bundled into touch, it gave the All Stars prime attacking position, leading to Connor's ball sending Peter Mata'utia through to narrow the gap to two points.

INTERNATIONAL MATCH

Friday 25th June 2021

ENGLAND 24 COMBINED NATIONS ALL STARS 26

ENGLAND: 1 Sam Tomkins (Catalans Dragons) (C); 5 Tom Davies (Catalans Dragons); 3 Reece Lyne (Wakefield Trinity); 4 Ben Currie (Warrington Wolves); 2 Tommy Makinson (St Helens); 6 Stefan Ratchford (Warrington Wolves); 7 Luke Gale (Leeds Rhinos); 8 Morgan Knowles (St Helens); 9 Paul McShane (Castleford Tigers); 10 Mike Cooper (Warrington Wolves); 11 John Bateman (Wigan Warriors); 12 Liam Farrell (Wigan Warriors); 13 Joe Westerman (Wakefield Trinity). Subs (all used): 14 Ash Handley (Leeds Rhinos); 15 Daryl Clark (Warrington Wolves); 16 Mikolaj Oledzki (Leeds Rhinos); 17 Joe Philbin (Warrington Wolves).
Tries: Farrell (10, 18), Knowles (49), Davies (68); **Goals:** Ratchford 4/4.
COMBINED NATIONS ALL STARS: 1 Jake Connor (Hull FC); 2 Ken Sio (Salford Red Devils); 3 Peter Mata'utia (Castleford Tigers); 4 Ricky Leutele (Huddersfield Giants); 5 Jermaine McGillvary (Huddersfield Giants); 6 Jackson Hastings (Wigan Warriors) (C); 7 Aidan Sezer (Huddersfield Giants); 8 Matt Prior (Leeds Rhinos) (C); 9 Nathan Peats (Leigh Centurions); 10 Tevita Satae (Hull FC); 11 Kenny Edwards (Huddersfield Giants); 12 Kelepi Tanginoa (Wakefield Trinity); 13 Luke Yates (Huddersfield Giants). Subs (all used): 14 Kruise Leeming (Leeds Rhinos); 15 Pauli Pauli (Salford Red Devils); 16 Suaia Matagi (Castleford Tigers); 17 Andre Savelio (Hull FC).
Tries: Sio (7, 56), Mata'utia (24), McGillvary (46); **Goals:** Sezer 5/6.
Rugby Leaguer & League Express Men of the Match:
England: Morgan Knowles; *Combined Nations All Stars:* Jackson Hastings.
Penalty count: 8-3; **Half-time:** 12-14; **Referee:** James Child;
Attendance: 4,000 *(at Halliwell Jones Stadium, Warrington).*

Back-to-back penalties from Aidan Sezer then made it 14-12 at the interval and England encountered further problems in the run-up to the break, as John Bateman was withdrawn with an ankle injury and Ash Handley's night ended in disappointing fashion, with the Leeds winger suffering a head knock and failing his HIA.

Six minutes after half-time McGillvary's try got the All Stars two scores in front, before Morgan Knowles marked his 'international' debut with a great try.

It was Gale again who provided the killer pass, sending Knowles through a gap before the St Helens forward bounced off Connor to touch down under the posts.

Leeds' Kruise Leeming impressed from the bench for the All Stars and when he kicked a magnificent 40/20 with the hour mark approaching, it tipped the momentum back in the All Stars' favour. Four minutes later, they restored their eight-point lead when a kick from Hastings caused mayhem among the England defence. The ball bounced off Kenny Edwards' head into the arms of Sio, who touched down unmarked for his second.

But an England try with twelve minutes remaining set up a thrilling finish. Captain Sam Tomkins kept the ball alive well on the last tackle before Wakefield's Reece Lyne provided the killer pass for Davies to cross.

With Stefan Ratchford converting to reduce the gap to just two, England were filled with renewed hope and Daryl Clark was held up over the line in a desperate finish.

Other Internationals

Jamaica got on with their build-up for the World Cup with two games at the end of the season.

In the first they found England's young generation too hot to handle as the England Knights ran riot in a 56-4 win at the Mend-a-Hose Jungle, Castleford, in a game doubling as Jordan Turner's testimonial.

Try-doubles from Leeds' Jack Broadbent, Wolves' Matty Ashton and Aaron Smith from St Helens were among the highlights of a party-pooping performance from the Knights, with Huddersfield's Will Pryce the standout.

A week later Jamaica and Scotland delivered a rip-roaring international as an outstanding comeback from the Reggae Warriors saw honours finish even at 30-30 in the first-ever clash between the two nations.

Jamaica looked to be down and out when a ten-point lead was turned into a 30-10 deficit with five unanswered tries in 14 minutes either side of half-time.

Yet the side coached by Romeo Monteith and Jermaine Coleman recovered in style with four tries in the final hour, the last from Alex Brown levelling the scores, Izaac Farrell's conversion falling short.

Scotland's extra experience - although they had five debutants, with Kieran Buchanan, Lachlan Walmsley and Jack Teanby all earning their first caps from the start, as Rob Oakley and Charlie Emslie later joined them from the bench - made them favourites but, aside from a short spell, they lacked coherence in their first match in almost two years.

Leigh back-rower James Bell was their standout as coach Nathan Graham plotted Scotland's own World Cup campaign.

INTERNATIONAL MATCH

Friday 15th October 2021

ENGLAND KNIGHTS 56 JAMAICA 4

ENGLAND KNIGHTS: 1 Matty Ashton (Warrington Wolves); 2 Sam Halsall (Wigan Warriors); 3 Connor Wrench (Warrington Wolves); 4 Jack Broadbent (Leeds Rhinos); 5 Liam Marshall (Wigan Warriors); 6 Will Pryce (Huddersfield Giants); 7 Mikey Lewis (Hull Kingston Rovers); 8 George Lawler (Hull Kingston Rovers); 9 Danny Walker (Warrington Wolves) (C); 10 Matty English (Huddersfield Giants); 11 Kai Pearce-Paul (Wigan Warriors); 12 Ellis Longstaff (Warrington Wolves); 13 James McDonnell (Wigan Warriors). Subs (all used): 14 Aaron Smith (St Helens); 15 Morgan Gannon (Leeds Rhinos); 16 Tom Holroyd (Leeds Rhinos); 17 Matty Lees (St Helens).
Tries: Broadbent (14, 41), Walker (18), Pryce (35), Smith (40, 73), Longstaff (53), Ashton (56, 60), Wrench (78); **Goals:** Pryce 7/8, Lewis 1/2.
Sin bin: Lawler (29) - high tackle on Woodburn-Hall.
JAMAICA: 1 James Woodburn-Hall (Halifax Panthers); 2 Ben Jones-Bishop (York City Knights); 3 Joe Brown (Workington Town); 4 Jacob Ogden (London Broncos); 5 Greg Johnson (Batley Bulldogs); 6 Jordan Turner (Castleford Tigers) (C); 7 Jy-mel Coleman (Hunslet); 8 Ross Peltier (Doncaster); 9 Ashton Golding (Huddersfield Giants); 10 Michael Lawrence (Huddersfield Giants); 11 Danny Bravo (Doncaster); 12 Joel Farrell (Sheffield Eagles); 13 Keenen Tomlinson (Dewsbury Rams). Subs (all used): 14 Jon Magrin (Dewsbury Rams); 15 Jordan Andrade (Hunslet); 16 Kadeem Williams (Coventry Bears); 17 Mo Agoro (Keighley Cougars); 18 Abevia McDonald (London Skolars); 19 Alex Brown (Hunslet); 20 Chris Ball (London Skolars).
Try: Jones-Bishop (31); **Goals:** Coleman 0/1.
Rugby Leaguer & League Express Men of the Match:
England Knights: Will Pryce; *Jamaica:* Ashton Golding.
Penalty count: 5-3; **Half-time:** 24-4; **Referee:** James Child; **Attendance:** 2,250 (at Mend-a-Hose Jungle, Castleford).

Internationals

Scotland's Ryan Brierley brought to ground by Jamaica's Ashton Golding

JAMAICA: 1 Ben Jones-Bishop (York City Knights); 2 Mo Agoro (Keighley Cougars); 3 Joe Brown (Workington Town) (C); 4 Jacob Ogden (London Broncos); 5 Greg Johnson (Batley Bulldogs); 6 James Woodburn-Hall (Halifax Panthers); 7 Izaac Farrell (Sheffield Eagles); 8 Ross Peltier (Doncaster); 9 Jy-mel Coleman (Hunslet); 10 Michael Lawrence (Huddersfield Giants); 11 Keenen Tomlinson (Dewsbury Rams); 12 Joel Farrell (Sheffield Eagles); 13 Ashton Golding (Huddersfield Giants). Subs (all used): 14 Jordan Andrade (Hunslet); 15 Danny Bravo (Doncaster); 16 Jon Magrin (Dewsbury Rams); 17 Alex Brown (Hunslet).
Tries: Coleman (8), Jones-Bishop (14, 49), J Brown (59), Andrade (66), A Brown (76); **Goals:** I Farrell 3/6.
SCOTLAND: 6 Alex Walker (Featherstone Rovers); 4 Will Oakes (Dewsbury Rams); 3 Davey Dixon (Dewsbury Rams); 5 Kieran Buchanan (Batley Bulldogs); 2 Lachlan Walmsley (Whitehaven); 7 Ryan Brierley (Leigh Centurions); 1 Danny Addy (Salford Red Devils); 8 Jack Teanby (York City Knights); 9 Liam Hood (Leigh Centurions); 15 Sam Luckley (Salford Red Devils); 12 Ben Hellewell (Leigh Centurions); 11 Ben Kavanagh (Halifax Panthers); 13 James Bell (Leigh Centurions). Subs (all used): 10 Dale Ferguson (Featherstone Rovers) (C); 14 Rob Oakley (London Broncos); 16 Kieran Moran (Keighley Cougars); 17 Charlie Emslie (Barrow Raiders).
Tries: Emslie (28, 42), Dixon (31), Hellewell (37), Ferguson (40);
Goals: Walmsley 5/5.
Sin bin: Ferguson (75) - high tackle.
Rugby Leaguer & League Express Men of the Match:
Jamaica: Ben Jones-Bishop; *Scotland:* James Bell.
Penalty count: 9-9; **Half-time:** 10-24; **Referee:** James Jones.
(at Millennium Stadium, Featherstone).

WHEELCHAIR RUGBY LEAGUE

Celtic Cup
Saturday 12th June 2021
Scotland 32 Ireland 52
Ireland 16 Wales 96
Scotland 18 Wales 102
(all at Oriam, Scotland's Performance Sports Centre)
Other internationals
Saturday 26th June 2021
England 102 Wales 22
(at English Institute of Sport, Sheffield)
Saturday 16th October 2021
Wales 62 Ireland 48
(at Glyndwr University, Wrexham)

EUROPEAN CHAMPIONSHIP B

Sunday 3rd October 2021
Serbia 66 Russia 10
(at Paracin City Stadium, Paracin)
Wednesday 6th October 2021
Russia 18 Ukraine 96
(at FC Heroj Polet, Belgrade)
Saturday 9th October 2021
Ukraine 18 Serbia 54
(at FC Heroj Polet, Belgrade)

EUROPEAN CHAMPIONSHIP D

Thursday 14th October 2021
Malta 16 Czech Republic 40
Turkey 18 Netherlands 40
Sunday 17th October 2021
Final: Czech Republic 10 Netherlands 36
3rd place play-off: Turkey 36 Malta 12
(all at Huseyin Akar Tesisler Stadium, Bodrum)

England's Vicky Molyneux runs at France's Gaelle Alvherne and Cyndia Mansard

OTHER INTERNATIONALS

Sunday 6th June 2021
Bosnia & Herzegovina 4 Serbia 50
(at NK Rijeka Stadium, Vitez)
Sunday 13th June 2021
Brazil 8 Philippines 40
(at Kensington Oval, Sydney)
Saturday 19th June 2021
Bulgaria 16 Serbia 28
(at FC Trebich, Sofia)
Saturday 2nd October 2021
Germany 16 Netherlands 48
(at Dusseldorf Rugby Club)

WOMEN

Friday 25th June 2021
England 60 Wales 0
(at Halliwell Jones Stadium, Warrington)
Sunday 17th October 2021
Wales 24 Ireland 26
(at Stadiwm Zip World, Colwyn Bay)
Saturday 23rd October 2021
France 4 England 40
(at Stade Gilbert Brutus, Perpignan)

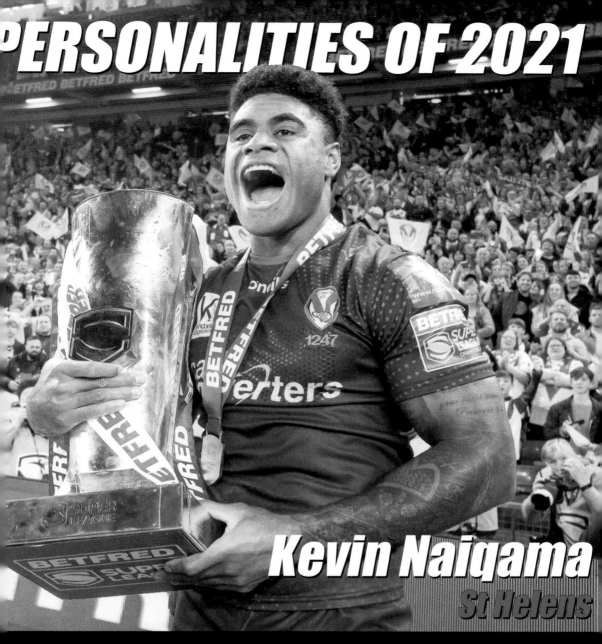

Kevin Naiqama
St Helens

cannot have been more successful spells in any
than that enjoyed by Kevin Naiqama at St Helens.
The Fijian centre's three seasons reaped three Super
e rings, along with in his Challenge Cup winners
l of 2021.

And he capped it all off with a man of the match
'mance in the 2021 Grand Final, becoming the first
to ever win the Harry Sunderland Trophy.
The awarding of the trophy pitchside by Rob Burrow
:he final whistle at Old Trafford was one of the great
onal moments of recent League history.
English fans got their first sighting of Naiqama in
)13 World Cup in a Fijian side that reached the semi-
oefore being knocked out by Australia at Wembley.
st represented Fiji in the Pacific Cup of 2009.
Naiqama made an immediate impression on his
at Saints for the 2019 season. In his very first game

in Super League, a 22-12 home win over Wigan, he took
less than two minutes to score his first try. And it was his
final try for St Helens that won the Grand Final, putting
them, with Lachlan Coote's conversion, into the 12-10
lead they managed to defend to the final whistle. He
sat out the rest of the game, failing a head assessment
after being caught by Fouad Yaha while crossing for the
66th-minute try. He had already claimed his first try after
13 minutes, showing great footwork to finish down the
Saints' right and then sheer determination to get the ball
down.

Naiqama scored 39 tries in 77 appearances for
Saints over one of the most glorious periods the club has
enjoyed and after the Grand Final was set to retire on his
return to Australia. But it was no big shock to see him
courted by NRL clubs on his arrival back in Sydney.

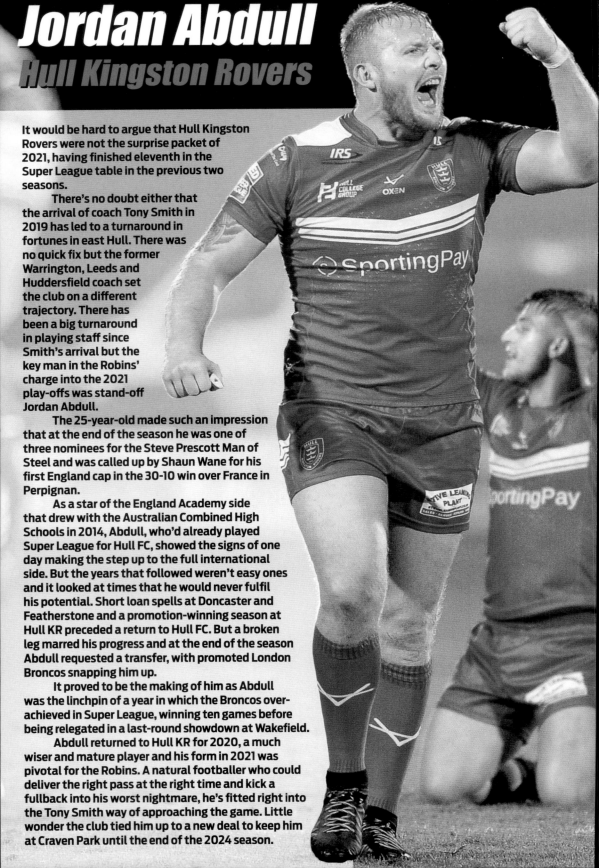

Jordan Abdull
Hull Kingston Rovers

It would be hard to argue that Hull Kingston Rovers were not the surprise packet of 2021, having finished eleventh in the Super League table in the previous two seasons.

There's no doubt either that the arrival of coach Tony Smith in 2019 has led to a turnaround in fortunes in east Hull. There was no quick fix but the former Warrington, Leeds and Huddersfield coach set the club on a different trajectory. There has been a big turnaround in playing staff since Smith's arrival but the key man in the Robins' charge into the 2021 play-offs was stand-off Jordan Abdull.

The 25-year-old made such an impression that at the end of the season he was one of three nominees for the Steve Prescott Man of Steel and was called up by Shaun Wane for his first England cap in the 30-10 win over France in Perpignan.

As a star of the England Academy side that drew with the Australian Combined High Schools in 2014, Abdull, who'd already played Super League for Hull FC, showed the signs of one day making the step up to the full international side. But the years that followed weren't easy ones and it looked at times that he would never fulfil his potential. Short loan spells at Doncaster and Featherstone and a promotion-winning season at Hull KR preceded a return to Hull FC. But a broken leg marred his progress and at the end of the season Abdull requested a transfer, with promoted London Broncos snapping him up.

It proved to be the making of him as Abdull was the linchpin of a year in which the Broncos over-achieved in Super League, winning ten games before being relegated in a last-round showdown at Wakefield.

Abdull returned to Hull KR for 2020, a much wiser and mature player and his form in 2021 was pivotal for the Robins. A natural footballer who could deliver the right pass at the right time and kick a fullback into his worst nightmare, he's fitted right into the Tony Smith way of approaching the game. Little wonder the club tied him up to a new deal to keep him at Craven Park until the end of the 2024 season.

Sam Tomkins
Catalans Dragons

It was the most important year in the relatively short history of Catalans Dragons, even bigger than the Challenge Cup winning season of 2018. In 2021 the Dragons showed true consistency throughout the season, discovering an ability to win games from seemingly hopeless situations.

The Dragons have made some high-profile signings since their elevation to Super League in 2006. But probably the most significant has been that of fullback Sam Tomkins, with 2021 the season when it paid its highest dividends. Tomkins led the Dragons in magnificent style as they secured the League Leaders Shield and went on to play their part in a tense and exciting Grand Final. A narrow two-point defeat to St Helens was by no means a disgrace. And he was named Steve Prescott Man of Steel at the end of the season, nine years after he first won the award when a Wigan player and eleven years after winning the Albert Goldthorpe Medal.

Sam Tomkins has been around a while - he made his Wigan debut in a 106-8 Challenge Cup win over Whitehaven in 2008 and scored five tries. He was a halfback then but gradually morphed into a fullback under coach Michael Maguire.

At the end of the Grand Final-winning 2013 season, having also played in the 2010 Champion Wigan team, Tomkins tried his arm in the NRL with New Zealand Warriors. He played 37 games in two seasons, although a knee injury hampered his impact, before returning to Wigan in 2016 for three seasons. His Catalans adventure began after the Warriors' 2018 Grand Final win over Warrington.

At the age of 32, Tomkins has matured into a consummate fullback and the experience and composure he showed in 2021 made him favourite to lead England into the delayed World Cup in 2022.

Sylvain Houlès
Toulouse Olympique

When Toulouse Olympique beat Featherstone Rovers in the Championship Grand Final at the Stade Ernest Vallon, in a showdown the RFL dubbed the 'Million Pound Game', it was the culmination of 15 years work by the southern French club to take up a place in Super League. And there was no-one who could take more satisfaction or a job well done than head coach Sylvain Houlès.

After a momentous evening at the ground Olympique now share with landlords Stade Toulousain, the city's highly successful rugby union side, the 40 year-old was almost speechless as around ten thousand French supporters celebrated in the stands.

Having taken up the coaching role at Toulouse in 2012, Houlès steadily built a side that was by 2021 full time and had gathered a side mixing French talent such as Remi Casty, Tony Gigot and Eloi Pelissier with Super League quality experience. It paid off big style.

Houlès came to England as a teenager in 2000, having already represented France on the wing, and spent five years with Huddersfield, London Broncos, Dewsbury

and Wakefield before returning to France as a player with Toulouse. His experience of Super League should stand him in good stead as he tries to maintain TO's place in the top tier in 2022.

In 2008, Toulouse lost out to Salford and the Crusaders for elevation to an expanded 14-team Super League. But instead of giving up the ghost, the club with big ambitions set a plan, which included a short spell in the Championship, from 2009 until 2011, before joining League 1 in 2016 and winning promotion at the end of that season. In 2019 they were within two games of Super League, losing to Featherstone in the Final Eliminator.

The 2020 season was wiped out after five rounds with Toulouse unbeaten and, considering the unfair funding allocation made to Leigh, it may have been a blessing in disguise when they were pipped by the Centurions in their bid to replace Toronto in Super League.

With two French clubs in the top tier in 2022, Super League's European claim will be all the more m

Jodie Cunningham
St Helens

Women's Rugby League took a major leap forward in 2021 with both the Women's Super League Grand Final and the Women's Challenge Cup Final enjoying live TV coverage, exposing the game to a whole new audience. Viewers will have been struck by the high quality of the top women's sides.

It was certainly a bumper year for St Helens, who swept the board honours-wise, winning both those finals as well as finishing League Leaders. And at the end of the season, their captain, Jodie Cunningham, was crowned the Woman of Steel at the Super League awards night.

Cunningham continues to be the face of women's Rugby League as she fulfils a role as an ambassador for the Rugby League World Cup.

Her involvement in the game has a long history, she made her first appearance for England when she was a sixth-form schoolgirl, having been a member of four-times Champion Schools winners Cardinal Newman High School in Warrington, encouraged to play the game by her long-time friend Emily Rudge, who is also a member of Saints' all-conquering side and was a nominee for the Woman of Steel.

Four cup final wins with Thatto Heath preceded the move to newly formed St Helens in 2018, at which time she was recovering from an anterior cruciate ligament injury suffered during the 2017 season. But Cunningham came back stronger, as did Saints, eliminated in 2019 at the semi-final stage by eventual champions Leeds.

After the 2020 season was cancelled, this year Saints got their revenge on Leeds in a 28-0 Grand Final win, Cunningham emerging from a spell in the sin bin for slowing down a re-start, to charge and swerve through the Rhinos defence on halfway and claim a sparkling solo try. It was a standout try of a very fine performance. And a record crowd of 4,235 was present at Headingley to witness it.

2021 SEASON
IN COLOUR

BETFRED CHALLENGE CUP

ROUND 3

LEFT: Leeds' Matt Prior gets to grips with St Helens' Kyle Amor

BELOW: Warrington's Greg Inglis feels the force of Catalans Dragons' Mike McMeeken

QUARTER FINALS

ABOVE: Wigan's Ethan Havard looks to close down Hull FC's Tevita Satae

RIGHT: Adam Milner and Derrell Olpherts celebrate Castleford's victory against Warrington

LEFT: St Helens' Regan Grace races away to score against Hull FC

SEMI-FINALS

BETFRED
CHALLENGE CUP

FINAL

BOVE: Tommy Makinson and Mark Percival lead the Helens celebrations following victory against Castleford in e Challenge Cup Final

GHT: Lance Todd Trophy winner Niall Evalds brings down chlan Coote

ELOW: James Roby dives over to score

TOP, INSET: Lee Gaskell kicks Huddersfield to victory against Leeds, despite the efforts of Luke Briscoe and Brad Dwyer

TOP: George King is distraught as Marc Sneyd celebrates landing the winning field goal in the Hull derby

ABOVE: Craig Mullen takes on Salford's Ken Sio during Leigh's first victory of the season

LEFT: St Helens' Morgan Knowles halted by Wigan's Willie Isa and Harry Smith

RIGHT: Sam Kasiano mobbed by teammates as his try forces extra-time during Catalans Dragons' thrilling comeback win against St Helens

BETFRED SUPER LEAGUE MAGIC WEEKEND

LEFT: Warrington's Gareth Widdop looks to escape from Wigan's Zak Hardaker

ABOVE: Kruise Leeming seals Leeds' golden point triumph against Hull FC

LEFT: Castleford's Derrell Olpherts swamped by the Salford defence

RIGHT: Wakefield's Eddie Battye loses the ball against Huddersfield

ABOVE: Hull Kingston Rovers' Ryan Hall ...vers over to score against Leigh

LEFT: James Maloney salutes the Catalans fans as the Dragons reach Old Trafford with victory against Hull Kingston Rovers

LEFT: St Helens' Mark Percival shows his delight at scoring against Leeds

LEFT: Tom Briscoe offloads as Leeds end Wigan's season

RIGHT: Albert Vete and Will Dagger celebrate Hull Kingston Rovers' memorable win against Warrington

Jodie Cunningham (Woman of Steel), Steve McNamara (Coach of the Year), Sam Tomkins (Man of Steel) and Jack Welsby (Young Player of the Year) show off their awards

![BETFRED SUPER LEAGUE GRAND FINAL]

ABOVE: James Roby and Alex Walmsley show off the Super League trophy following St Helens' third successive Grand Final win

RIGHT: Kevin Naiqama is presented with the Harry Sunderland Trophy by former multiple winner Rob Burrow

BELOW: Regan Grace feels the force of Sam Dudson, Arthur Mourgue and Mickael Goudemand

BELOW RIGHT: Mike McMeeken crashes over to score Catalans Dragons' try

LEFT: Ross Oakes takes on Lucas Walshaw as Batley battle past Bradford

ABOVE: Adam Tangata and Jacob Fairbank show their delight as Matt Garside goes over during Halifax's win against Whitehaven

ABOVE: Toulouse's Johnathon Ford on the charge during a big win against Batley

BETFRED CHAMPIONSHIP

ABOVE: Connor Jones races away for a try as Featherstone see off Halifax

BELOW: The champagne flows as Toulouse Olym celebrate Million Pound Game victory against Featherstone, and promotion to Super League

GAME WINNERS

CHAMPIONSHIP

BETFRED LEAGUE 1

ABOVE: Nathan Mossop lifts the League 1 trophy as Barrow Raiders earn automatic promotion to the Championship

[RI]GHT: Workington coach [Ch]ris Thorman is jubilant [fol]lowing Town's Play-off [fin]al win against Doncaster

ABOVE: Matty Beharrell holds off Dalton Desmond-Walker and Phoenix Laulu-Togaga'e to score as Doncaster edge Keighley in a play-off thriller

BELOW: Jacob Doyle motors across the Wembley turf for a try

ABOVE: Featherstone's Joe Summers, Loui McConnell and Harvey Spence with the 1895 Cup after victory against York

[B] Sundecks **1895 CUP**

[FI]NAL

GRAND FINAL

ABOVE: Penrith Panthers celebrate NRL Grand Final victory over South Sydney Rabbitohs

LEFT: Jaxson Paulo races away down the sideline

RIGHT: Blake Taaffe wrapped up by Jarome Luai and Api Koroisau

BELOW: New South Wales, 2021 State of Origin winners

LEFT: New South Wale Josh Addo- in action ag Queenslan during Orig

STATE OF ORIGIN

ABOVE: England Knights' Connor Wrench busts clear against Jamaica

RIGHT: England's John Bateman beats the challenge of France's Mark Kheirallah

BELOW: England's Sam Tomkins collared by Combined Nations All Stars' Andre Savelio

BELOW: Jamaica's Jy-mel Coleman crashes over to score against Scotland, despite the attentions of Ben Hellewell and James Bell

INTERNATIONALS

RIGHT: England's Amy Hardcastle breaks through against France

BELOW: England's Shona Hoyle looks for a way past Wales' Lowri Norkett

St Helens completed the domestic treble in 2021, winning the Super League Grand Final *(right)*, Challenge Cup Final *(below)* and League Leaders' Shield *(below right)*. Tara Jones and Jodie Cunningham are shown lifting the Shield

ABOVE: Huddersfield Giants, Super League Shield winners

6
STATISTICAL REVIEW

SUPER LEAGUE PLAYERS
1996-2021

Super League Players 1996-2021

PLAYER	CLUB	YEAR	APP	TRIES	GOALS	FG	PTS
Jordan Abdull	Hull KR	2020-21	25(1)	8	48	2	130
	London	2019	25(2)	10	1	0	42
	Hull	2014-16, 2018	32(20)	9	7	0	50
Carl Ablett	Leeds	2004,					
		2006-18	238(37)	63	0	0	252
	London	2005	3(2)	0	0	0	0
Darren Abram	Oldham	1996-97	25(2)	11	0	0	44
Mitch Achurch	Leeds	2013-16	25(50)	14	0	0	56
Andy Ackers	Salford	2020-21	17(8)	3	0	0	12
	Toronto	2020	5	1	0	0	4
Jamie Acton	Leigh	2017	11(4)	4	0	0	16
Brad Adams	Bradford	2014	1(1)	0	0	0	0
Darren Adams	Paris	1996	9(1)	1	0	0	4
Guy Adams	Huddersfield	1998	1(2)	0	0	0	0
Luke Adamson	Salford	2006-07,					
		2009-12	73(39)	11	1	0	46
Matt Adamson	Leeds	2002-04	54(8)	9	0	0	36
Phil Adamson	St Helens	1999	(1)	0	0	0	0
Toby Adamson	Salford	2010	(1)	0	0	0	0
Danny Addy	Salford	2021	6(4)	0	0	0	0
	Hull KR	2019	9(10)	2	0	0	8
	Bradford	2010-14	49(42)	13	7	0	66
Ade Adebisi	London	2004	(1)	0	0	0	0
Sadiq Adebiyi	London	2019	6(7)	3	0	0	12
Patrick Ah Van	Widnes	2012-18	99	73	56	0	404
	Bradford	2011	26	9	87	0	210
Jamie Ainscough	Wigan	2002-03	30(2)	18	0	0	72
Shaun Ainscough	Bradford	2011-12	27	15	0	0	60
	Wigan	2009-10	12	13	0	0	52
	Castleford	2010	7	4	0	0	16
Glen Air	London	1998-2001	57(13)	27	0	1	109
Paul Aiton	Catalans	2016-18	30(11)	3	0	0	12
	Leeds	2014-15	36(6)	2	0	0	8
	Wakefield	2012-13	43(2)	7	0	0	28
Makali Aizue	Hull KR	2007-09	18(32)	4	0	0	16
Sitaleki Akauola	Warrington	2018-21	12(48)	6	0	0	24
Darren Albert	St Helens	2002-05	105	77	0	0	308
Lucas Albert	Catalans	2015-20	35(10)	7	23	0	74
Wellington Albert	Leeds	2019	2(2)	0	0	0	0
	Widnes	2018	(11)	2	0	0	8
Paul Alcock	Widnes	2003, 2005	1(7)	1	0	0	4
Neil Alexander	Salford	1998	(1)	0	0	0	0
Malcolm Alker	Salford	1997-2002,					
		2004-07,					
		2009-10	271(2)	40	0	1	161
Danny Allan	Leeds	2008-09	2(5)	0	0	0	0
Chris Allen	Castleford	1996	(1)	0	0	0	0
Dave Allen	Widnes	2012-14	50(13)	5	0	0	20
	Wigan	2003, 2005	6(15)	2	0	0	8
Gavin Allen	London	1996	10	0	0	0	0
John Allen	Workington	1996	20(1)	6	0	0	24
Ray Allen	London	1996	5(3)	3	0	0	12
Mitch Allgood	Wakefield	2017	6(2)	0	0	0	0
	Hull KR	2015-16	27(2)	5	0	0	20
Richard Allwood	Gateshead	1999	(4)	0	0	0	0
Sean Allwood	Gateshead	1999	3(17)	1	0	0	4
David Alstead	Warrington	2000-02	23(10)	3	0	0	12
Luke Ambler	Harlequins	2011	5(17)	1	0	0	4
	Leeds	2010	1(8)	1	0	0	4
Asa Amone	Halifax	1996-97	32(7)	10	0	0	40
Kyle Amor	St Helens	2014-21	102(85)	18	0	0	72
	Wakefield	2011-13	51(23)	9	0	0	36
	Leeds	2010	(3)	0	0	0	0
Thibaut Ancely	Catalans	2011	(2)	0	0	0	0
Grant Anderson	Castleford	1996-97	15(6)	3	0	0	12
Louis Anderson	Catalans	2012-18	86(41)	32	0	0	128
	Warrington	2008-11	92	18	0	0	72
Paul Anderson	St Helens	2005-06	48(5)	7	1	0	30
	Bradford	1997-2004	74(104)	30	0	0	120
	Halifax	1996	5(1)	1	0	0	4
Paul Anderson	Sheffield	1999	3(7)	1	0	0	4
	St Helens	1996-98	2(28)	4	1	0	18
Scott Anderson	Wakefield	2014-16	25(18)	2	0	0	8
Vinnie Anderson	Salford	2011-12	33(3)	14	0	0	56
	Warrington	2007-10	57(19)	22	0	0	88
	St Helens	2005-06	28(14)	17	0	0	68
Phil Anderton	St Helens	2004	1	0	0	0	0
Chris Annakin	Wakefield	2013-19	7(62)	1	0	0	4
Eric Anselme	Leeds	2008	2(2)	2	0	0	8
	Halifax	1997	(2)	1	0	0	4
Mark Applegarth	Wakefield	2004-07	20(5)	3	0	0	12
Graham Appo	Warrington	2002-05	60(13)	35	80	0	300
	Huddersfield	2001	7	4	0	0	16
Guy Armitage	London	2019	(2)	0	0	0	0
Anthony Armour	London	2005	11(7)	1	0	0	4
Colin Armstrong	Workington	1996	11(2)	1	0	0	4
Tom Armstrong	Widnes	2017	11	1	0	0	4
	St Helens	2009-11	10(5)	9	0	0	36
Richard Armswood	Workington	1996	5(1)	1	0	0	4
Danny Arnold	Salford	2001-02	26(13)	13	0	0	52
	Huddersfield	1998-2000	55(7)	26	0	0	104
	Castleford	2000	(4)	0	0	0	0
	St Helens	1996-97	40(1)	33	0	0	132
Tinirau Arona	Wakefield	2016-21	89(41)	8	0	0	32
Joe Arundel	Wakefield	2015-21	88(11)	22	4	0	96
	Bradford	2014	9(3)	5	0	0	20
	Hull	2013-14	16	7	1	0	30
	Castleford	2008,					
		2010-12	35(4)	14	2	0	60
Craig Ashall	St Helens	2006	1	1	0	0	4
Olly Ashall-Bott	Huddersfield	2021	8(1)	2	0	0	8
	Wakefield	2021	2	1	0	0	4
	Salford	2020	3	1	0	0	4
	Widnes	2018	5	1	0	0	4
Nathan Ashe	St Helens	2011-13	6(4)	0	0	0	0
Chris Ashton	Wigan	2005-07	44(2)	25	2	0	104
Matty Ashton	Warrington	2020-21	12(7)	13	0	0	52
Matty Ashurst	Wakefield	2015-21	124(4)	20	0	0	80
	Salford	2012-14	65(7)	11	0	0	44
	St Helens	2009-11	12(39)	8	0	0	32
Jack Ashworth	Leigh	2021	1(4)	0	0	0	0
	Huddersfield	2021	2(2)	0	0	0	0
	St Helens	2015-16,					
		2018-20	6(37)	4	0	0	16
Roy Asotasi	Warrington	2014-15	16(37)	5	1	0	22
Connor Aspey	Salford	2020-21	(2)	0	0	0	0
Peter Aspinall	Huddersfield	2013	1(1)	0	0	0	0
Martin Aspinwall	Hull	2012	12(15)	0	0	0	0
	Castleford	2011	12(6)	2	0	0	8
	Huddersfield	2006-10	72(8)	22	0	0	88
	Wigan	2001-05	85(13)	27	0	0	108
Cory Aston	Castleford	2019	8	3	0	0	12
Mark Aston	Sheffield	1996-99	67(6)	6	243	6	516
Paul Atcheson	Widnes	2002-04	16(35)	4	0	0	16
	St Helens	1998-2000	58(4)	18	0	0	72
	Oldham	1996-97	40	21	0	0	84
Chris Atkin	Salford	2020-21	24(5)	7	3	1	35
	Hull KR	2018-19	28(20)	7	1	3	33
David Atkins	Huddersfield	2001	26(1)	4	0	0	16
Jordan Atkins	London	2014	13(1)	4	0	0	16
Ryan Atkins	Wakefield	2006-09,					
		2019-20	90(2)	47	0	0	188
	Warrington	2010-19	235(2)	139	0	0	556
Josh Atkinson	Castleford	2012	2	0	0	0	0
Brad Attwood	Halifax	2003	(3)	0	0	0	0
Blake Austin	Warrington	2019-21	57(2)	30	0	6	126
Yusuf Aydin	Wakefield	2020-21	2(11)	1	0	0	4
Warren Ayres	Salford	1999	2(9)	1	2	0	8
Jerome Azema	Paris	1997	(1)	0	0	0	0
Marcus Bai	Bradford	2006	24	9	0	0	36
	Leeds	2004-05	57	42	0	0	168
David Baildon	Hull	1998-99	26(2)	4	0	0	16
Jean-Philippe Baile	Catalans	2008-14	62(16)	23	0	0	92
Andy Bailey	Hull	2004-05	2(8)	1	0	0	4
Chris Bailey	Huddersfield	2014-15	17(17)	5	0	0	20
	London	2012-13	41	14	0	0	56
	Harlequins	2011	24	3	0	0	12
Connor Bailey	Wakefield	2020	3(2)	0	0	0	0
Julian Bailey	Huddersfield	2003-04	47	13	0	0	52
Phil Bailey	Wigan	2007-10	84(4)	13	0	0	52
Ricky Bailey	St Helens	2015, 2017	2	0	0	0	0
Ryan Bailey	Warrington	2016	1(11)	0	0	0	0
	Castleford	2015	3(2)	0	0	0	0
	Hull KR	2015	(1)	1	0	0	4
	Leeds	2002-14	171(102)	17	0	0	68
Jason Baitieri	Catalans	2011-21	136(89)	20	0	0	80
Simon Baldwin	Salford	2004-06	20(29)	3	0	0	12
	Sheffield	1999	7(15)	2	0	0	8
	Halifax	1996-98	41(15)	16	0	1	65
Jordan Baldwinson	Wakefield	2018	(4)	0	0	0	0
	Leeds	2013, 2016-17	4(9)	1	0	0	4
	Bradford	2014	2(4)	0	0	0	0
Rob Ball	Wigan	1998-2000	3(4)	0	0	0	0
Paul Ballard	Celtic	2009	2	0	0	0	0
	Widnes	2005	3(1)	2	0	0	8
Darren Bamford	Salford	2005	2(1)	0	0	0	0
Michael Banks	Bradford	1998	(1)	0	0	0	0
Steve Bannister	Harlequins	2007	(6)	0	0	0	0
	St Helens	2006-07	(3)	0	0	0	0
Frederic Banquet	Paris	1996	16(2)	7	4	0	36
Ben Barba	St Helens	2017-18	31	31	0	0	124
Lee Bardauskas	Castleford	1996-97	(2)	0	0	0	0

180

PLAYER	CLUB	YEAR	APP	TRIES	GOALS	FG	PTS
Harry Bardle	Hull KR	2019	(1)	0	0	0	0
Craig Barker	Workington	1996	(2)	0	0	0	0
Dwayne Barker	Harlequins	2008	5(5)	1	0	0	4
	London	2004	3	1	0	0	4
	Hull	2003	(1)	0	0	0	0
Mark Barlow	Wakefield	2002	(1)	0	0	0	0
Danny Barnes	Halifax	1999	2	0	0	0	0
Richie Barnett	Salford	2007	7	4	0	0	16
	Warrington	2006-07	26(10)	15	0	0	60
	Hull	2004-05	21(5)	21	0	0	84
	Widnes	2005	4	2	0	0	8
Richie Barnett	Hull	2003-04	31(1)	17	0	0	68
	London	2001-02	31(4)	13	0	0	52
David Barnhill	Leeds	2000	20(8)	5	0	0	20
Trent Barrett	Wigan	2007-08	53(1)	22	0	4	92
Paul Barrow	Warrington	1996-97	1(10)	1	0	0	4
Scott Barrow	St Helens	1997-2000	9(13)	1	0	0	4
Steve Barrow	London	2000	2	0	0	0	0
	Hull	1998-99	4(17)	1	0	0	4
	Wigan	1996	(8)	3	0	0	12
William Barthau	Catalans	2010, 2012-14	13(3)	2	15	0	38
Ben Barton	Huddersfield	1998	1(6)	1	0	0	4
Danny Barton	Salford	2001	1	0	0	0	0
Wayne Bartrim	Castleford	2002-03	41(2)	9	157	0	350
Greg Barwick	London	1996-97	30(4)	21	110	2	306
David Bastian	Halifax	1996	(2)	0	0	0	0
James Batchelor	Wakefield	2016-21	41(27)	10	13	0	66
Joe Batchelor	St Helens	2019-21	13(14)	3	0	0	12
Ashley Bateman	Celtic	2009	1	0	0	0	0
John Bateman	Wigan	2014-18, 2021	124(11)	32	0	0	128
	Bradford	2011-13	25(5)	7	0	0	28
David Bates	Castleford	2001-02	(4)	0	0	0	0
	Warrington	2001	1(2)	0	0	0	0
Sam Bates	Bradford	2014	(2)	0	0	0	0
Nathan Batty	Wakefield	2001	1(1)	0	0	0	0
Eddie Battye	Wakefield	2020-21	9(21)	1	0	0	4
	London	2019	19(10)	3	0	0	12
Andreas Bauer	Hull KR	2007	10(2)	5	0	0	20
Russell Bawden	London	1996-97, 2002-04	50(49)	15	0	0	60
Neil Baxter	Salford	2001	1	0	0	0	0
Neil Baynes	Salford	1999-2002, 2004	84(19)	10	0	0	40
	Wigan	1996-98	(10)	1	0	0	4
Chris Beasley	Celtic	2009	15(5)	2	0	0	8
Chris Beattie	Catalans	2006	22(5)	3	0	0	12
Richard Beaumont	Hull KR	2011-13	1(16)	1	0	0	4
Robbie Beazley	London	1997-99	48(15)	13	0	0	52
Robbie Beckett	Halifax	2002	27	15	0	0	60
Matty Beharrell	Hull KR	2013	1	0	0	0	0
Dean Bell	Leeds	1996	1	1	0	0	4
Ian Bell	Hull	2003	(1)	0	0	0	0
James Bell	Leigh	2021	16(2)	1	0	0	4
Mark Bell	Wigan	1998	22	12	0	0	48
Paul Bell	Leeds	2000	1	0	0	0	0
Steven Bell	Catalans	2009-10	43	14	0	0	56
Troy Bellamy	Paris	1997	5(10)	0	0	0	0
Adrian Belle	Huddersfield	1998	10(2)	0	0	0	0
	Oldham	1996	19	8	0	0	32
Lambert Belmas	Catalans	2017-21	3(13)	0	0	0	0
Jamie Benn	Castleford	1998, 2000	3(8)	1	15	0	34
Andy Bennett	Warrington	1996	6(5)	1	0	0	4
Mike Bennett	St Helens	2000-08	74(70)	15	0	0	60
Gavin Bennion	Salford	2018	1(1)	0	0	0	0
Jonathan Bennison	St Helens	2021	1	1	0	0	4
Andrew Bentley	Catalans	2007-10	9(15)	1	0	0	4
James Bentley	St Helens	2018-21	32(13)	9	0	0	36
John Bentley	Huddersfield	1999	13(4)	3	0	0	12
	Halifax	1996, 1998	22(3)	24	0	0	96
Kane Bentley	Catalans	2007-10	11(19)	5	0	0	20
Phil Bergman	Paris	1997	20(1)	14	0	0	56
Shaun Berrigan	Hull	2008-10	60(8)	12	0	0	48
Joe Berry	Huddersfield	1998-99	25(14)	3	0	0	12
David Berthezene	Salford	2007	9(1)	0	0	0	0
	Catalans	2006-07	5(14)	0	0	0	0
Colin Best	Hull	2003-04	57	34	0	0	136
Roger Best	London	1997-98	1(5)	1	0	0	4
Bob Beswick	Wigan	2004-05	5(14)	2	0	0	8
Monty Betham	Wakefield	2006	26	2	0	0	8
Mike Bethwaite	Workington	1996	17(3)	1	0	0	4
Denis Betts	Wigan	1998-2001	82(24)	33	0	0	132
Cliff Beverley	Salford	2004-05	47(1)	14	0	0	56
Kyle Bibb	Wakefield	2008-10	1(24)	0	0	0	0
	Harlequins	2010	(2)	0	0	0	0
	Hull KR	2009	(2)	0	0	0	0
Jake Bibby	Wigan	2020-21	44	18	0	0	72
	Salford	2016-19	65(3)	32	0	0	128
Adam Bibey	Widnes	2004	(1)	0	0	0	0
Ricky Bibey	Wakefield	2007-09	32(25)	1	0	0	4
	St Helens	2004	4(14)	0	0	0	0
	Wigan	2001-03	5(29)	0	0	0	0
Lewis Bienek	Castleford	2021	1(5)	0	0	0	0
	Hull	2018, 2020	(8)	0	0	0	0
Chris Birchall	Halifax	2002-03	24(22)	4	0	0	16
	Bradford	2000	(1)	0	0	0	0
Deon Bird	Castleford	2006	17(6)	5	0	0	20
	Widnes	2003-04	39(6)	9	0	0	36
	Wakefield	2002	10(1)	1	0	0	4
	Hull	2000-02	37(22)	20	0	0	80
	Gateshead	1999	19(3)	13	0	0	52
	Paris	1996-97	30	12	2	0	52
Greg Bird	Catalans	2009, 2017-19	68(6)	11	3	0	50
Mike Bishay	London	2013-14	7(11)	2	2	0	12
Nathan Blacklock	Hull	2005-06	44(3)	33	0	0	132
Ben Blackmore	Huddersfield	2013-14	3	4	0	0	16
	Castleford	2012	1	0	0	0	0
Richie Blackmore	Leeds	1997-2000	63	25	0	0	100
Anthony Blackwood	Crusaders	2010	1	0	0	0	0
	Celtic	2009	25	5	0	0	20
Jack Blagbrough	Huddersfield	2013	(1)	0	0	0	0
Cheyse Blair	Castleford	2019-21	36(4)	8	0	0	32
Maurice Blair	Hull KR	2015-16, 2018	62(3)	10	1	0	42
Luke Blake	Wakefield	2009	(2)	0	0	0	0
Matthew Blake	Wakefield	2003-04	1(5)	0	0	0	0
Steve Blakeley	Salford	1997-2002	103(5)	26	241	2	588
	Warrington	2000	4(3)	1	9	0	22
Richard Blakeway	Castleford	2002-04	1(14)	0	0	0	0
Damien Blanch	Catalans	2011-13	70	42	0	0	168
	Wakefield	2008-10	44(3)	31	0	0	124
	Castleford	2006	3(2)	0	0	0	0
Matt Blaymire	Wakefield	2007-11	96(3)	26	0	1	105
Ian Blease	Salford	1997	(1)	0	0	0	0
Jamie Bloem	Huddersfield	2003	18(4)	3	11	0	34
	Halifax	1998-2002	82(25)	25	100	2	302
Vea Bloomfield	Paris	1996	4(14)	3	0	0	12
Matty Blythe	Warrington	2007-12, 2017	30(28)	12	0	0	48
	Bradford	2013-14	24(6)	8	0	0	32
Ben Bolger	London	2012	2(7)	1	0	0	4
	Harlequins	2010-11	4(15)	0	0	0	0
Pascal Bomati	Paris	1996	17(1)	10	0	0	40
Simon Booth	Hull	1998-99	15(9)	2	0	0	8
	St Helens	1996-97	10(4)	1	0	0	4
Steve Booth	Huddersfield	1998-99	16(4)	2	3	0	14
Alan Boothroyd	Halifax	1997	2(3)	0	0	0	0
Thomas Bosc	Catalans	2006-17	199(21)	48	483	12	1170
John Boslem	Paris	1996	(5)	0	0	0	0
Liam Bostock	St Helens	2004	1	0	0	0	0
Liam Botham	Wigan	2005	5	0	0	0	0
	Leeds	2003-05	2(11)	4	0	0	16
	London	2004	6(2)	3	7	0	26
Frano Botica	Castleford	1996	21	5	84	2	190
Matthew Bottom	Leigh	2005	(1)	0	0	0	0
Hadj Boudebza	Paris	1996	(2)	0	0	0	0
John Boudebza	Hull KR	2015-16	13(17)	2	0	0	8
David Boughton	Huddersfield	1999	26(1)	4	0	0	16
Amir Bourouh	Wigan	2019-21	1(8)	0	0	0	0
Julian Bousquet	Catalans	2012-21	87(108)	20	0	0	80
David Bouveng	Halifax	1997-99	66(2)	19	0	0	76
Josh Bowden	Hull	2012-21	64(97)	13	0	0	52
Matt Bowen	Wigan	2014-15	43	21	31	0	146
Harry Bowes	Wakefield	2020-21	1(2)	0	0	0	0
Tony Bowes	Huddersfield	1998	3(2)	0	0	0	0
Radney Bowker	London	2004	3	1	0	0	4
	St Helens	2001	(1)	0	0	0	0
David Boyle	Bradford	1999-2000	36(13)	15	0	1	61
Ryan Boyle	Castleford	2006, 2008-09, 2013-16	12(60)	5	0	0	20
	Salford	2010-13	57(14)	3	0	0	12
Andy Bracek	Crusaders	2011	(2)	0	0	0	0
	Warrington	2005-08	7(49)	7	0	0	28
	St Helens	2004	(1)	0	0	0	0
David Bradbury	Hudds-Sheff	2000	21(2)	1	0	0	4
	Salford	1997-99	23(10)	6	0	0	24
	Oldham	1996-97	19(6)	9	0	0	36
John Braddish	St Helens	2001-02	1(1)	0	0	3	6
Graeme Bradley	Bradford	1996-98	62(1)	29	0	0	116
Nick Bradley-Qalilawa	Harlequins	2006	27	6	0	0	24
	London	2005	28	19	0	0	76

Super League Players 1996-2021

PLAYER	CLUB	YEAR	APP	TRIES	GOALS	FG	PTS
Darren Bradstreet	London	1999-2000	1(3)	0	0	0	0
Dominic Brambani	Castleford	2004	2(2)	0	0	0	0
Keanan Brand	Leigh	2021	12	1	0	0	4
	Warrington	2020	3	0	0	0	0
	Widnes	2018	1	0	0	0	0
Joe Bretherton	Wigan	2016-17	2(13)	1	0	0	4
Liam Bretherton	Wigan	1999	(5)	2	0	0	8
	Warrington	1997	(2)	0	0	0	0
Johnny Brewer	Halifax	1996	4(2)	2	0	0	8
Chris Bridge	Widnes	2016-17	28(1)	4	11	0	38
	Warrington	2005-15	186(17)	89	248	1	853
	Bradford	2003-04	2(14)	4	6	0	28
Danny Bridge	Bradford	2014	4(4)	0	0	0	0
	Warrington	2013	(2)	0	0	0	0
Ryan Brierley	Leigh	2021	17	10	29	0	98
	Hull KR	2020	10	3	8	0	28
	Huddersfield	2016-17	19(1)	6	2	0	28
Lee Briers	Warrington	1997-2013	365(12)	130	810	70	2210
	St Helens	1997	3	0	11	0	22
Carl Briggs	Salford	1999	8(5)	3	0	1	13
	Halifax	1996	5(3)	1	0	0	4
Kyle Briggs	Bradford	2011	6	4	0	0	16
	Harlequins	2011	3	0	0	0	0
Mike Briggs	Widnes	2002	1(2)	1	0	0	4
Kriss Brining	Salford	2017	2(20)	4	0	0	16
Luke Briscoe	Leeds	2014, 2016, 2018-21	47(9)	15	0	0	60
	Wakefield	2014	2	0	0	0	0
Shaun Briscoe	Widnes	2012-13	11(2)	4	0	0	16
	Hull KR	2008-11	92	27	0	0	108
	Hull	2004-07	83(9)	50	0	0	200
	Wigan	2002-03	23(5)	11	0	0	44
Tom Briscoe	Leeds	2014-21	158	64	0	0	256
	Hull	2008-13	131(3)	83	0	0	332
Darren Britt	St Helens	2002-03	41	3	0	0	12
Gary Broadbent	Salford	1997-2002	117(2)	22	0	0	88
Jack Broadbent	Leeds	2020-21	15(1)	9	0	0	36
Paul Broadbent	Wakefield	2002	16(5)	0	0	0	0
	Hull	2000-01	40(9)	3	0	0	12
	Halifax	1999	26(1)	2	0	0	8
	Sheffield	1996-98	63(1)	6	0	0	24
Robin Brochon	Catalans	2018-19, 2021	2(1)	0	0	0	0
Andrew Brocklehurst	Salford	2004-07	34(23)	5	0	0	20
	London	2004	12(6)	2	0	0	8
	Halifax	2001-03	37(8)	2	0	0	8
Justin Brooker	Wakefield	2001	25	9	0	0	36
	Bradford	2000	17(4)	11	0	0	44
Sam Brooks	Widnes	2016-17	1(3)	1	0	0	4
Danny Brough	Wakefield	2008-10, 2019-20	74(1)	16	247	9	567
	Huddersfield	2010-18	220(4)	45	721	20	1642
	Castleford	2006	10	1	31	2	68
	Hull	2005-06	25(12)	3	85	1	183
Jodie Broughton	Catalans	2016-19	48	34	0	0	136
	Huddersfield	2014-15	30	16	0	0	64
	Salford	2010-13	93	53	0	0	212
	Hull	2008-09	9(3)	6	0	0	24
Alex Brown	Hull KR	2013	16	9	0	0	36
	Huddersfield	2009	1	0	0	0	0
Darren Brown	Salford	1999-2001	47(9)	11	6	0	56
Gavin Brown	Leeds	1996-97	5(2)	1	2	0	8
Jack Brown	Hull	2019-21	1(17)	4	0	0	16
Kevin Brown	Salford	2020-21	18	6	1	0	26
	Warrington	2017-18	41(1)	9	0	0	36
	Widnes	2013-16	80	37	1	1	151
	Huddersfield	2006-12	156	43	0	1	173
	Wigan	2003-06	46(18)	27	0	0	108
Lee Brown	Hull	1999	(1)	0	0	0	0
Michael Brown	Huddersfield	2008	(1)	0	0	0	0
Michael Brown	London	1996	(2)	0	0	0	0
Mitch Brown	Warrington	2018	10(1)	2	0	0	8
	Leigh	2017	21	4	0	0	16
Todd Brown	Paris	1996	8(1)	2	0	0	8
Adrian Brunker	Wakefield	1999	17	6	0	0	24
Lamont Bryan	Harlequins	2008-11	9(22)	2	0	0	8
Justin Bryant	Paris	1996	4(1)	0	0	0	0
	London	1996	7(8)	1	0	0	4
Mark Bryant	London	2012-13	16(36)	3	1	0	14
	Crusaders	2010-11	42(8)	1	0	0	4
	Celtic	2009	23(3)	0	0	0	0
Austin Buchanan	Wakefield	2005-06	6	2	0	0	8
	London	2003	3(1)	2	0	0	8
Jack Buchanan	Widnes	2016-17	29(2)	2	0	0	8
Kieran Buchanan	Hull	2019-20	10(3)	3	0	0	12
Owen Buckley	Widnes	2018	4	3	0	0	12
Danny Buderus	Leeds	2009-11	57(14)	14	0	0	56
Neil Budworth	Celtic	2009	8(19)	0	0	0	0
	Harlequins	2006	2(19)	0	0	0	0
	London	2002-05	59(11)	4	1	0	18
Joe Bullock	Wigan	2019-21	27(27)	4	0	0	16
James Bunyan	Huddersfield	1998-99	8(7)	2	0	0	8
Andy Burgess	Salford	1997	3(12)	0	0	0	0
George Burgess	Wigan	2020	2(6)	1	0	0	4
Joe Burgess	Salford	2021	8	3	0	0	12
	Wigan	2013-15, 2017-20	115	91	0	0	364
Luke Burgess	Salford	2018	3(8)	0	0	0	0
	Catalans	2017	3(2)	0	0	0	0
	Leeds	2008-11	10(63)	6	0	0	24
	Harlequins	2007	(3)	0	0	0	0
Sam Burgess	Bradford	2006-09	46(34)	14	5	0	66
Tom Burgess	Bradford	2011-12	1(41)	3	0	0	12
Greg Burke	Salford	2018-21	28(34)	1	0	0	4
	Widnes	2016-18	22(12)	1	0	0	4
	Wigan	2013-14, 2016	13(26)	1	0	0	4
	Hull KR	2015	9(5)	0	0	0	0
	Bradford	2014	(1)	0	0	0	0
Joe Burke	Crusaders	2011	(1)	0	0	0	0
Mike Burnett	Harlequins	2011	16(4)	1	0	0	4
	Hull	2008-10	13(21)	3	0	0	12
Darren Burns	Warrington	2002-04	66(6)	19	0	0	76
Gary Burns	Oldham	1996	6	1	0	0	4
Paul Burns	Workington	1996	5(2)	1	0	0	4
Travis Burns	St Helens	2015-16	27(2)	4	28	0	72
	Hull KR	2013-14	46	8	81	2	196
Lachlan Burr	Leigh	2017	5(14)	1	0	0	4
Aidan Burrell	Hull	2021	(1)	0	0	0	0
Luther Burrell	Warrington	2019-20	2(6)	0	0	0	0
Rob Burrow	Leeds	2001-17	313(116)	168	131	5	939
Dean Busby	Warrington	1999-2002	34(34)	7	0	0	28
	Hull	1998	8(6)	0	0	0	0
	St Helens	1996-98	1(7)	0	0	0	0
Tom Bush	Leeds	2010	3(1)	1	0	0	4
Chester Butler	Huddersfield	2019	(1)	0	0	0	0
Rob Butler	Leigh	2021	3(3)	0	0	0	0
	Warrington	2021	(4)	0	0	0	0
	London	2019	17(7)	2	0	0	8
Ikram Butt	London	1996	5(1)	0	0	0	0
Reiss Butterworth	Huddersfield	2020	1(1)	0	0	0	0
Liam Byrne	Wigan	2019-21	8(40)	2	0	0	8
Shane Byrne	Huddersfield	1998-99	1(5)	0	0	0	0
Todd Byrne	Hull	2008-09	20	4	0	0	16
Didier Cabestany	Paris	1996-97	20(6)	2	0	0	8
Hep Cahill	Widnes	2012-18	106(13)	4	0	0	16
	Crusaders	2011	16	2	0	0	8
Joel Caine	Salford	2004	24	8	13	0	58
	London	2003	6	4	1	0	18
Mark Calderwood	Harlequins	2011	13	2	0	0	8
	Hull	2009-10	23	6	0	0	24
	Wigan	2006-08	64	23	0	0	92
	Leeds	2001-05	117(9)	88	0	0	352
Mike Callan	Warrington	2002	(4)	0	0	0	0
Matt Calland	Huddersfield	2003	2	0	0	0	0
	Hull	1999	1	0	0	0	0
	Bradford	1996-98	44(5)	24	0	0	96
Dean Callaway	London	1999-2000	26(24)	12	0	0	48
Laurent Cambres	Paris	1996	(1)	0	0	0	0
Chris Campbell	Warrington	2000	7(1)	2	0	0	8
Liam Campbell	Wakefield	2005	(1)	0	0	0	0
Logan Campbell	Hull	1998-99, 2001	70(13)	14	0	0	56
	Castleford	2000	14(2)	3	0	0	12
	Workington	1996	7(1)	1	0	0	4
Terry Campese	Hull KR	2015-16	19(1)	2	4	0	16
Blake Cannova	Widnes	2002	(1)	0	0	0	0
Phil Cantillon	Widnes	2002-03	27(21)	18	0	0	72
	Leeds	1997	(1)	0	0	0	0
Liam Carberry	Widnes	2014-15	2(5)	0	0	0	0
Damien Cardace	Catalans	2012, 2014-15	23	14	0	0	56
Daryl Cardiss	Warrington	2003-04	23(2)	3	4	0	20
	Halifax	1999-2003	91(8)	39	4	0	164
	Wigan	1996-98	12(6)	4	0	0	16
Dale Cardoza	Warrington	2002	5	1	0	0	4
	Halifax	2001	3	1	0	0	4
	Huddersfield	2000-01	20(9)	11	0	0	44
	Sheffield	1998-99	11(7)	3	0	0	12
Paul Carige	Salford	1999	24(1)	7	0	0	28
Dane Carlaw	Catalans	2008-10	58(15)	9	0	0	36
Keal Carlile	Hull KR	2012-15	6(28)	1	0	0	4
	Huddersfield	2009, 2011	2(1)	1	0	0	4
	Bradford	2008	(1)	0	0	0	0

PLAYER	CLUB	YEAR	APP	TRIES	GOALS	FG	PTS
Jim Carlton	Huddersfield	1999	3(11)	2	0	0	8
George Carmont	Wigan	2008-12	136	71	0	0	284
Brian Carney	Warrington	2009	4	2	0	0	8
	Wigan	2001-05	91(10)	42	1	0	170
	Hull	2000	13(3)	7	0	0	28
	Gateshead	1999	3(2)	2	0	0	8
Justin Carney	Hull KR	2018	14	3	0	0	12
	Salford	2016-17	28	12	0	0	48
	Castleford	2013-15	58	56	0	0	224
Martin Carney	Warrington	1997	(1)	0	0	0	0
Todd Carney	Hull KR	2018	(1)	0	0	0	0
	Salford	2017	9(5)	0	7	0	14
	Catalans	2015-16	32	9	4	1	45
Omari Caro	Hull KR	2013-14	21	20	0	0	80
	London	2012	11	4	0	0	16
Paul Carr	Sheffield	1996-98	45(5)	15	0	0	60
Bernard Carroll	London	1996	2(1)	1	0	0	4
Mark Carroll	London	1998	15(3)	1	0	0	4
Tonie Carroll	Leeds	2001-02	42(2)	30	0	0	120
Darren Carter	Workington	1996	10(3)	0	1	0	2
Steve Carter	Widnes	2002	14(7)	4	0	0	16
John Cartwright	Salford	1997	9	0	0	0	0
Garreth Carvell	Castleford	2014	1(4)	1	0	0	4
	Hull	2001-08, 2014	75(84)	22	0	0	88
	Warrington	2009-13	77(40)	13	0	0	52
	Leeds	1997-2000	(4)	0	0	0	0
	Gateshead	1999	4(4)	1	0	0	4
Garen Casey	Salford	1999	13(5)	3	23	0	58
Ray Cashmere	Salford	2009-11	63(3)	5	0	0	20
Mick Cassidy	Widnes	2005	24	0	0	0	0
	Wigan	1996-2004	184(36)	30	0	0	120
Remi Casty	Catalans	2006-13, 2015-20	207(97)	26	0	0	104
Ned Catic	Castleford	2008	7(7)	3	0	0	12
	Wakefield	2006-07	17(29)	4	0	0	16
Mason Caton-Brown							
	Wakefield	2017-19	34	27	0	0	108
	Salford	2014-16	28	10	0	0	40
	London	2013-14	19	15	0	0	60
Joe Cator	Hull	2020-21	18(6)	1	0	0	4
	Hull KR	2016, 2018	2(3)	0	0	0	0
Chris Causey	Warrington	1997-99	(18)	1	0	0	4
Jason Cayless	St Helens	2006-09	62(9)	7	0	0	28
Arnaud Cervello	Paris	1996	4	4	0	0	16
Marshall Chalk	Celtic	2009	13	4	0	0	16
Ed Chamberlain	Salford	2018-20	10(1)	3	21	0	54
	Widnes	2016-18	16(1)	2	7	0	22
Gary Chambers	Warrington	1996-2000	65(28)	2	0	0	8
Pierre Chamorin	Paris	1996-97	27(3)	8	3	0	38
Alex Chan	Catalans	2006-08	59(19)	11	0	0	44
Jason Chan	Hull KR	2014	5(1)	3	0	0	12
	Huddersfield	2012-14	46(12)	9	0	0	36
	Crusaders	2010-11	48(1)	10	0	0	40
	Celtic	2009	17(6)	3	0	0	12
Joe Chan	Catalans	2021	(6)	2	0	0	8
Joe Chandler	Leeds	2008	(1)	0	0	0	0
Michael Channing	Castleford	2013-15	27(2)	8	0	0	32
	London	2012-13	15(3)	2	0	0	8
Jay Chapelhow	Widnes	2016-18	23(15)	4	0	0	16
Ted Chapelhow	Widnes	2016-18	7(13)	0	0	0	0
Chris Chapman	Leeds	1999	(1)	0	0	0	0
Damien Chapman	London	1998	6(2)	3	4	1	21
David Chapman	Castleford	1996-98	24(6)	8	0	0	32
Jaymes Chapman	Halifax	2002-03	5(8)	1	0	0	4
Richard Chapman	Sheffield	1996	1	2	0	0	8
Chris Charles	Salford	2004-06	59(16)	6	140	0	304
	Castleford	2001	1(4)	1	0	0	4
Olivier Charles	Catalans	2007	2	2	0	0	8
Josh Charnley	Warrington	2018-21	85	49	0	0	196
	Wigan	2010-16	151(2)	141	77	0	718
	Hull KR	2010	5	5	0	0	20
Lewis Charnock	St Helens	2013, 2015	4(1)	2	6	0	20
Rangi Chase	Widnes	2017	6	0	0	0	0
	Castleford	2009-13, 2016-17	122(12)	39	0	3	159
	Salford	2014-15	37	10	13	2	68
Andy Cheetham	Huddersfield	1998-99	30	11	0	0	44
Kris Chesney	London	1998	1(2)	0	0	0	0
Chris Chester	Hull KR	2007-08	28(6)	4	0	0	16
	Hull	2002-06	67(25)	13	0	0	52
	Wigan	1999-2001	21(22)	5	0	0	20
	Halifax	1996-99	47(14)	16	15	1	95
Lee Chilton	Workington	1996	10(3)	6	0	0	24
Dane Chisholm	Hull KR	2015	1	0	0	0	0
Gary Christie	Bradford	1996-97	4(7)	1	0	0	4
James Clare	Castleford	2012-15, 2018-21	97(1)	49	0	0	196
Daryl Clark	Warrington	2015-21	150(15)	38	0	0	152
	Castleford	2011-14	34(51)	31	0	0	124
Dean Clark	Leeds	1996	11(2)	3	0	0	12
Des Clark	St Helens	1999	4	0	0	0	0
	Halifax	1998-99	35(13)	6	0	0	24
Jason Clark	Warrington	2019-21	24(34)	2	0	0	8
Mitch Clark	Wigan	2020-21	(16)	2	0	0	8
	Castleford	2018-19	(24)	3	0	0	12
Greg Clarke	Halifax	1997	1(1)	0	0	0	0
John Clarke	Oldham	1996-97	27(4)	5	0	0	20
Jon Clarke	Widnes	2012-14	59(1)	5	0	0	20
	Warrington	2001-11	217(25)	56	2	0	228
	London	2000-01	19(11)	2	0	0	8
	Wigan	1997-99	13(10)	3	0	0	12
Chris Clarkson	Castleford	2019	11(8)	4	0	0	16
	Hull KR	2016, 2018	38(2)	4	0	0	16
	Widnes	2015	17(1)	4	0	0	16
	Leeds	2010-14	61(39)	9	0	0	36
Adam Clay	Salford	2011	2	3	0	0	12
Ryan Clayton	Castleford	2004, 2008-10	36(24)	5	0	0	20
	Salford	2006	3(8)	2	0	0	8
	Huddersfield	2005	4(6)	0	0	0	0
	Halifax	2000, 2002-03	28(12)	6	0	0	24
Gavin Clinch	Salford	2004	21(1)	1	0	1	5
	Halifax	1998-99, 2001-02	88(2)	26	45	5	199
	Hudds-Sheff	2000	18(2)	5	0	1	21
	Wigan	1999	10(2)	4	12	0	40
Joel Clinton	Hull KR	2010-12	42(14)	2	0	0	8
John Clough	Salford	2004-06	1(16)	0	0	0	0
Paul Clough	Huddersfield	2017-20	35(43)	3	0	0	12
	Widnes	2014	4(8)	1	0	0	4
	St Helens	2005-13	53(113)	16	0	0	64
Tony Clubb	Wigan	2014-21	81(72)	20	0	0	80
	London	2012-13	24(8)	7	0	0	28
	Harlequins	2006-11	100(11)	29	0	0	116
Bradley Clyde	Leeds	2001	7(5)	1	0	0	4
Michael Coady	Leeds	2010	1	0	0	0	0
Evan Cochrane	London	1996	5(1)	1	0	0	4
Ben Cockayne	Hull KR	2007-11, 2014-16	125(30)	38	18	0	188
	Wakefield	2012-13	54	28	2	0	116
Jack Cogger	Huddersfield	2021	14(2)	1	0	0	4
Liam Colbon	Hull	2014	8	1	0	0	4
	London	2012-13	22	5	0	0	20
	Hull KR	2009-11	51	20	0	0	80
	Wigan	2004-05, 2007-08	37(14)	15	0	0	60
Anthony Colella	Huddersfield	2003	5(1)	2	0	0	8
Liam Coleman	Leigh	2005	1(4)	0	0	0	0
Andy Coley	Wigan	2008-11	100(10)	8	0	0	32
	Salford	2001-02, 2004-07	112(34)	34	0	0	136
Richard Colley	Bradford	2004	1	0	0	0	0
Steve Collins	Hull	2000	28	17	0	0	68
	Gateshead	1999	20(4)	13	0	0	52
Wayne Collins	Leeds	1997	21	3	0	0	12
Dean Collis	Wakefield	2012-15	64	28	0	0	112
Aurelien Cologni	Catalans	2006	4(1)	3	0	0	12
Gary Connolly	Widnes	2005	20	4	1	0	18
	Wigan	1996-2002, 2004	168(10)	70	5	0	290
	Leeds	2003-04	27	6	0	0	24
Jake Connor	Hull	2017-21	94(13)	30	75	3	273
	Huddersfield	2013-16	47(1)	21	2	0	88
Nathan Conroy	Bradford	2013-14	(4)	0	0	0	0
Matt Cook	Castleford	2008, 2015-20	22(88)	13	0	0	52
	London	2012-14	50(7)	8	0	0	32
	Hull KR	2010-11	9(16)	7	0	0	28
	Bradford	2005-09	11(52)	4	0	0	16
Mick Cook	Sheffield	1996	9(10)	2	0	0	8
Paul Cook	Huddersfield	1998-99	11(6)	2	13	0	34
	Bradford	1996-97	14(8)	7	38	1	105
Peter Cook	St Helens	2004	(1)	0	0	0	0
Paul Cooke	Wakefield	2010	16(1)	3	36	1	85
	Hull KR	2007-10	54(5)	8	76	2	186
	Hull	1999-2007	177(27)	32	333	4	798
Ben Cooper	Leigh	2005	25(1)	5	0	0	20
	Huddersfield	2000-01, 2003-04	28(12)	3	0	0	12

PLAYER	CLUB	YEAR	APP	TRIES	GOALS	FG	PTS
Mike Cooper	Warrington	2006-13,					
		2017-21	131(88)	18	0	0	72
	Castleford	2010	1(5)	2	0	0	8
Lachlan Coote	St Helens	2019-21	58	31	256	1	637
Ged Corcoran	Halifax	2003	1(11)	0	0	0	0
Wayne Corcoran	Halifax	2003	4(2)	0	0	0	0
Jamie Cording	Huddersfield	2011-13	4(21)	5	0	0	20
Josh Cordoba	Hull	2009	8	1	0	0	4
Mark Corvo	Salford	2002	7(5)	0	0	0	0
Matthew Costello	Salford	2021	9(1)	2	0	0	8
	St Helens	2018-20	22(2)	6	0	0	24
Neville Costigan	Hull KR	2014	24	3	0	0	12
Brandon Costin	Huddersfield	2001,					
		2003-04	69	42	93	3	357
	Bradford	2002	20(1)	8	0	0	32
Wes Cotton	London	1997-98	12	3	0	0	12
Phil Coussons	Salford	1997	7(2)	3	0	0	12
Alex Couttet	Paris	1997	1	0	0	0	0
Nick Couttet	Paris	1997	1	0	0	0	0
Jamie Coventry	Castleford	1996	1	0	0	0	0
Jimmy Cowan	Oldham	1996-97	2(8)	0	0	0	0
Will Cowell	Warrington	1998-2000	6(8)	1	0	0	4
Neil Cowie	Wigan	1996-2001	116(27)	10	0	1	41
Danny Cowling	Wakefield	2012-13	2	0	0	0	0
Jordan Cox	Warrington	2016	(16)	0	0	0	0
	Hull KR	2011-15	17(44)	4	0	0	16
	Huddersfield	2015	(2)	0	0	0	0
Mark Cox	London	2003	(3)	0	0	0	0
James Coyle	Wigan	2005	2(3)	1	0	0	4
Thomas Coyle	Wigan	2008	2(1)	0	0	0	0
Mathieu Cozza	Catalans	2021	(3)	0	0	0	0
Eorl Crabtree	Huddersfield	2001,					
		2003-16	180(167)	52	0	0	208
Andy Craig	Halifax	1999	13(7)	1	3	0	10
	Wigan	1996	5(5)	2	0	0	8
Owen Craigie	Widnes	2005	15	7	0	2	30
Scott Cram	London	1999-2002	65(7)	4	0	0	16
Danny Craven	Widnes	2012-15,					
		2017-18	53(17)	13	6	3	67
Steve Craven	Hull	1998-2003	53(42)	4	0	0	16
Nicky Crellin	Workington	1996	(2)	0	0	0	0
Jason Critchley	Wakefield	2000	7(1)	4	0	0	16
	Castleford	1997-98	27(3)	11	0	0	44
Jack Croft	Wakefield	2019-20	8	0	0	0	0
Jason Croker	Catalans	2007-09	56(2)	11	0	1	45
Martin Crompton	Salford	1998-2000	30(6)	11	6	2	58
	Oldham	1996-97	36(1)	16	0	3	67
Paul Crook	Widnes	2005	2(2)	0	5	1	11
Paul Crook	Oldham	1996	4(9)	0	3	0	6
Jason Crookes	Hull	2013-14	15(1)	5	0	0	20
	Bradford	2009-12	25(1)	7	0	0	28
Ben Crooks	Hull KR	2018-21	56	31	15	0	154
	Leigh	2017	19	6	0	0	24
	Castleford	2016	24(2)	5	1	0	22
	Hull	2012-14	42(3)	30	23	0	166
Lee Crooks	Castleford	1996-97	27(2)	2	14	0	36
Dominic Crosby	Leeds	2018	(2)	0	0	0	0
	Warrington	2017-18	(16)	0	0	0	0
	Wigan	2012-16	57(35)	6	0	0	24
Alan Cross	St Helens	1997	(2)	0	0	0	0
Ben Cross	Widnes	2012-13	27(1)	2	0	0	8
	Wigan	2011	(4)	0	0	0	0
	Leeds	2011	1(9)	0	0	0	0
Steve Crossley	Castleford	2015	(6)	0	0	0	0
	Bradford	2010-11	(9)	1	0	0	4
Garret Crossman	Hull KR	2008	8(18)	0	0	0	0
Steve Crouch	Castleford	2004	4(1)	2	0	0	8
Kevin Crouthers	Warrington	2001-03	12(1)	4	0	0	16
	London	2000	6(4)	1	0	0	4
	Wakefield	1999	4(4)	1	0	0	4
	Bradford	1997-98	3(9)	2	0	0	8
Jordan Crowther	Wakefield	2014-21	38(19)	3	0	0	12
Matt Crowther	Hull	2001-03	48	20	166	0	412
	Hudds-Sheff	2000	10(4)	5	22	0	64
	Sheffield	1996-99	43(4)	22	10	0	108
Heath Cruckshank	Halifax	2003	19(1)	0	0	0	0
	St Helens	2001	1(12)	0	0	0	0
Leroy Cudjoe	Huddersfield	2008-21	280(1)	107	57	1	543
Paul Cullen	Warrington	1996	19	3	0	0	12
Francis Cummins	Leeds	1996-2005	217(13)	120	26	2	534
James Cunningham							
	Huddersfield	2021	8(1)	0	0	0	0
	Toronto	2020	2(1)	0	0	0	0
	London	2014, 2019	34(8)	3	0	0	12
	Hull	2012, 2014-15	(9)	0	0	0	0
Keiron Cunningham							
	St Helens	1996-2010	357(24)	138	0	0	552
Liam Cunningham	Hull	2010	(1)	0	0	0	0
Ben Currie	Warrington	2012-21	146(31)	66	0	0	264
Andy Currier	Warrington	1996-97	(2)	1	0	0	4
Peter Cusack	Hull	2008-10	34(22)	3	0	0	12
Adam Cuthbertson	Leeds	2015-20	91(39)	30	0	0	120
Alrix Da Costa	Catalans	2016-21	34(34)	4	0	0	16
Will Dagger	Hull KR	2018-21	29(2)	3	12	0	36
	Warrington	2017	3	0	0	0	0
Joe Dakuitoga	Sheffield	1996	6(3)	0	0	0	0
Matty Dale	Hull	2006, 2008	(7)	1	0	0	4
	Wakefield	2008	1(1)	0	0	0	0
Brett Dallas	Wigan	2000-06	156	89	0	0	356
Mark Dalle Cort	Celtic	2009	23	4	0	0	16
Paul Darbyshire	Warrington	1997	(6)	0	0	0	0
James Davey	Wakefield	2009-11	3(14)	1	0	0	4
Maea David	Hull	1998	1	0	0	0	0
Alex Davidson	Salford	2011, 2013	(3)	0	0	0	0
Paul Davidson	Halifax	2001-03	22(30)	10	0	0	40
	London	2000	6(10)	4	0	0	16
	St Helens	1998-99	27(16)	7	0	0	28
	Oldham	1996-97	17(18)	14	0	1	57
Ben Davies	St Helens	2020-21	2	0	0	0	0
	Salford	2021	2(1)	1	0	0	4
Ben Davies	Castleford	2011, 2013	3(4)	2	0	0	8
	Widnes	2012-13	10(15)	3	0	0	12
	Wigan	2010	(5)	0	0	0	0
Gareth Davies	Warrington	1996-97	1(6)	0	0	0	0
Geraint Davies	Celtic	2009	(7)	0	0	0	0
John Davies	Castleford	2010-12	1(6)	1	0	0	4
Jordan Davies	Salford	2013	2(3)	0	0	0	0
Macauley Davies	Wigan	2016	(1)	0	0	0	0
Matthew Davies	London	2019	(1)	0	0	0	0
Olly Davies	St Helens	2016	(1)	0	0	0	0
Tom Davies	Catalans	2020-21	32	27	0	0	108
	Wigan	2017-19	57	27	0	0	108
Wes Davies	Wigan	1998-2001	22(22)	11	0	0	44
Brad Davis	Castleford	1997-2000,					
		2004, 2006	102(3)	31	43	10	220
	Wakefield	2001-03	51(12)	15	22	5	109
Matt Davis	Warrington	2019-21	15(27)	5	0	0	20
	London	2019	4	0	0	0	0
Sam Davis	London	2019	2(1)	0	0	0	0
Matty Dawson-Jones							
	Hull	2019	1	1	0	0	4
	Leigh	2017	23	12	0	0	48
	St Helens	2014-16	46(1)	15	0	0	60
	Huddersfield	2012-13	4	0	0	0	0
Brad Day	Castleford	2014	(1)	0	0	0	0
Matt Daylight	Hull	2000	17(1)	7	0	0	28
	Gateshead	1999	30	25	0	0	100
Michael De Vere	Huddersfield	2005-06	36	6	74	0	172
Paul Deacon	Wigan	2010-11	32(11)	4	14	0	44
	Bradford	1998-2009	258(43)	72	1029	23	2369
	Oldham	1997	(2)	0	0	0	0
Chris Dean	Widnes	2012-18	115(6)	23	0	0	92
	Wakefield	2011	20	8	0	0	32
	St Helens	2007-10	18(3)	9	0	0	36
Craig Dean	Halifax	1996-97	25(11)	12	1	1	51
Gareth Dean	London	2002	(4)	0	0	0	0
Riley Dean	Warrington	2019-21	2(1)	1	0	0	4
Yacine Dekkiche	Hudds-Sheff	2000	11(3)	3	0	0	12
Brett Delaney	Leeds	2010-18	151(30)	23	0	0	92
Jason Demetriou	Wakefield	2004-10	174(3)	50	2	0	204
	Widnes	2002-03	47(1)	15	1	0	62
Martin Dermott	Warrington	1997	1	0	0	0	0
David Despin	Paris	1996	(1)	0	0	0	0
Fabien Devecchi	Paris	1996-97	17(10)	2	0	0	8
Paul Devlin	Widnes	2002-04	32	16	0	0	64
Jordan Dezaria	Catalans	2016-17, 2021	6(7)	0	0	0	0
Stuart Dickens	Salford	2005	4(5)	0	4	0	8
Tyler Dickinson	Huddersfield	2016-18	(17)	1	0	0	4
Matt Diskin	Bradford	2011-14	64(16)	11	0	0	44
	Leeds	2001-10	195(37)	40	0	0	160
Andrew Dixon	Toronto	2020	1(1)	0	0	0	0
	Salford	2013-14	34(2)	8	0	0	32
	St Helens	2009-12	19(41)	12	0	0	48
Kieran Dixon	London	2012-14, 2019	76(1)	42	77	0	322
	Hull KR	2015-16	23(4)	21	9	0	102
Kirk Dixon	Castleford	2008-14	143(2)	63	267	0	786
	Hull	2004-06	13(4)	7	4	0	36
Paul Dixon	Sheffield	1996-97	5(9)	1	0	0	4
Nabil Djalout	Catalans	2017	1	0	0	0	0
Gareth Dobson	Castleford	1998-2000	(10)	0	0	0	0

Super League Players 1996-2021

PLAYER	CLUB	YEAR	APP	TRIES	GOALS	FG	PTS
Michael Dobson	Salford	2015-17	58(1)	14	77	1	211
	Hull KR	2008-13	142	51	500	11	1215
	Wigan	2006	14	5	61	0	142
	Catalans	2006	10	4	31	1	79
Michael Docherty	Hull	2000-01	(6)	0	0	0	0
Lewis Dodd	St Helens	2020-21	13(9)	6	5	0	34
Mitchell Dodds	Warrington	2016	(2)	0	0	0	0
Erjon Dollapi	London	2013-14	(18)	4	0	0	16
Sid Domic	Hull	2006-07	39(4)	15	0	0	60
	Wakefield	2004-05	48	30	0	0	120
	Warrington	2002-03	41(4)	17	0	0	68
Scott Donald	Leeds	2006-10	131	77	0	0	308
James Donaldson	Leeds	2019-21	13(47)	6	0	0	24
	Hull KR	2015-16, 2018	12(30)	4	0	0	16
	Bradford	2009-14	38(35)	4	0	0	16
Glen Donkin	Hull	2002-03	(10)	1	0	0	4
Stuart Donlan	Castleford	2008	20	8	0	0	32
	Huddersfield	2004-06	59(3)	15	0	0	60
	Halifax	2001-03	65(2)	22	0	0	88
Jason Donohue	Bradford	1996	(4)	0	0	0	0
Jeremy Donougher	Bradford	1996-99	40(21)	13	0	0	52
Justin Dooley	London	2000-01	37(18)	2	0	0	8
Dane Dorahy	Halifax	2003	20	7	45	0	118
	Wakefield	2000-01	16(2)	4	19	1	55
Jamie Doran	Wigan	2014	(2)	0	0	0	0
Luke Dorn	Castleford	2008, 2014-16	78(2)	60	0	0	240
	London	2005, 2012-13	58(8)	42	0	0	168
	Harlequins	2006, 2009-11	83(1)	57	0	0	228
	Salford	2007	19(8)	11	0	0	44
Eribe Doro	Warrington	2020-21	1(3)	1	0	0	4
Brandon Douglas	Castleford	2016	(1)	0	0	0	0
Luke Douglas	St Helens	2017-18	23(32)	5	0	0	20
Ewan Dowes	Hull	2003-11	169(51)	10	0	0	40
	Leeds	2001-03	1(9)	0	0	0	0
Jack Downs	Hull	2015-18	5(15)	1	0	0	4
Adam Doyle	Warrington	1998	9(3)	4	0	0	16
Rod Doyle	Sheffield	1997-99	52(10)	10	0	0	40
Brad Drew	Huddersfield	2005-07, 2010	78(13)	18	13	1	99
	Wakefield	2008-09	27(9)	7	14	1	57
Josh Drinkwater	Catalans	2018, 2020-21	54	13	53	0	158
	Hull KR	2019	29	4	6	0	28
	Leigh	2017	19	1	12	1	29
	London	2014	23(1)	5	54	0	128
Damien Driscoll	Salford	2001	23(1)	1	0	0	4
James Duckworth	London	2014	3	0	0	0	0
	Leeds	2013	2	1	0	0	4
Gil Dudson	Catalans	2021	17(2)	2	0	0	8
	Salford	2019-20	39(2)	2	0	0	8
	Widnes	2015-18	57(11)	1	0	0	4
	Wigan	2012-14	26(16)	2	0	0	8
	Crusaders	2011	3(7)	0	0	0	0
	Celtic	2009	(1)	0	0	0	0
Jason Duffy	Leigh	2005	3(1)	0	0	0	0
John Duffy	Leigh	2005	21	6	0	0	24
	Salford	2000	3(11)	0	1	1	3
	Warrington	1997-99	12(12)	0	0	0	0
Tony Duggan	Celtic	2009	4	3	0	0	12
Andrew Duncan	London	1997	2(4)	2	0	0	8
	Warrington	1997	(1)	0	0	0	0
Andrew Dunemann	Salford	2006	25	1	0	2	6
	Leeds	2003-05	76(4)	11	0	2	46
	Halifax	1999-2002	68	19	0	1	77
Matt Dunford	London	1997-98	18(20)	3	0	1	13
Vincent Duport	Catalans	2007-09, 2011-18	156(16)	75	0	0	300
Jamie Durbin	Widnes	2005	1	0	0	0	0
	Warrington	2003	(1)	0	0	0	0
Scott Dureau	Catalans	2011-15	88(1)	29	315	10	756
James Durkin	Paris	1997	(5)	0	0	0	0
Bernard Dwyer	Bradford	1996-2000	65(10)	14	0	0	56
Brad Dwyer	Leeds	2018-21	46(37)	22	0	1	89
	Warrington	2012-17	12(63)	11	0	0	44
	Huddersfield	2013	(6)	0	0	0	0
Luke Dyer	Crusaders	2010	23(1)	5	0	0	20
	Celtic	2009	21	6	0	0	24
	Hull KR	2007	26	13	0	0	52
	Castleford	2006	17(2)	5	0	0	20
Adam Dykes	Hull	2008	12	1	0	2	6
Jim Dymock	London	2001-04	94(1)	15	0	1	61
Leo Dynevor	London	1996	8(11)	5	7	0	34
Jason Eade	Paris	1997	9	4	0	0	16
Michael Eagar	Hull	2004-05	12	4	0	0	16
	Castleford	1999-2003	130(2)	60	0	0	240
	Warrington	1998	21	6	0	0	24
Kyle Eastmond	Leeds	2021	2	0	0	0	0
	St Helens	2007-11	46(20)	35	117	3	377
Greg Eastwood	Leeds	2010	5(12)	1	0	0	4
Barry Eaton	Widnes	2002	25	2	49	4	110
	Castleford	2000	1(4)	0	3	0	6
Josh Eaves	St Helens	2019-21	1(3)	1	0	0	4
	Leigh	2021	4(1)	0	0	0	0
	Wakefield	2021	(3)	0	0	0	0
Greg Ebrill	Salford	2002	15(6)	1	0	0	4
Cliff Eccles	Salford	1997-98	30(5)	1	0	0	4
Chris Eckersley	Warrington	1996	1	0	0	0	0
Greg Eden	Castleford	2011, 2017-21	83(1)	86	0	0	344
	Hull KR	2013-14	37	23	0	0	92
	Salford	2014	4	1	0	0	4
	Huddersfield	2012	24	8	0	0	32
Steve Edmed	Sheffield	1997	15(1)	0	0	0	0
Mark Edmondson	Salford	2007	10(2)	0	0	0	0
	St Helens	1999-2005	27(75)	10	0	0	40
Diccon Edwards	Castleford	1996-97	10(5)	1	0	0	4
Grant Edwards	Castleford	2006	(2)	0	0	0	0
Kenny Edwards	Huddersfield	2020-21	19(7)	2	0	0	8
	Catalans	2018-19	14(18)	10	0	0	40
Max Edwards	Harlequins	2010	1	0	0	0	0
Peter Edwards	Salford	1997-98	35(2)	4	0	0	16
Shaun Edwards	London	1997-2000	32(8)	16	1	0	66
	Bradford	1998	8(2)	4	0	0	16
	Wigan	1996	17(3)	12	1	0	50
Tuoyo Egodo	Castleford	2017-19	10(4)	11	0	0	44
Danny Ekis	Halifax	2001	(1)	0	0	0	0
Abi Ekoku	Bradford	1997-98	21(4)	6	0	0	24
	Halifax	1996	15(1)	5	0	0	20
Shane Elford	Huddersfield	2007-08	26(1)	7	0	0	28
Olivier Elima	Catalans	2008-10, 2013-16	99(35)	34	0	0	136
	Bradford	2011-12	37(3)	12	0	0	48
	Wakefield	2003-07	40(47)	13	0	0	52
	Castleford	2002	(1)	1	0	0	4
Abderazak Elkhalouki	Paris	1997	(1)	0	0	0	0
Brendan Elliot	Leigh	2021	10(1)	3	0	0	12
George Elliott	Leeds	2011	1	0	0	0	0
Andy Ellis	Wakefield	2012	10	0	0	0	0
	Harlequins	2010-11	26(11)	8	0	0	32
Gareth Ellis	Hull	2013-17, 2019-20	96(16)	19	0	0	76
	Leeds	2005-08	109	24	1	0	98
	Wakefield	1999-2004	86(17)	21	2	0	88
Jamie Ellis	Leigh	2021	4(4)	1	1	0	6
	Hull KR	2020	7	1	18	0	40
	Castleford	2012-14, 2018-19	58(8)	12	150	2	350
	Huddersfield	2015-16	37(3)	14	31	3	121
	Hull	2012	4(5)	1	0	0	4
	St Helens	2009	1(2)	0	1	0	2
Danny Ellison	Castleford	1998-99	7(16)	6	0	0	24
	Wigan	1996-97	15(1)	13	0	0	52
Andrew Emelio	Widnes	2005	22(2)	8	0	0	32
Jake Emmitt	Salford	2013	5(10)	0	0	0	0
	Castleford	2011-13	32(17)	0	0	0	0
	St Helens	2008-10	1(16)	1	0	0	4
Anthony England	Wakefield	2016-19	68(11)	2	0	0	8
	Warrington	2014-15	12(21)	3	0	0	12
Matty English	Huddersfield	2017-21	28(36)	7	0	0	28
Patrick Entat	Paris	1996	22	2	0	0	8
Jason Erba	Sheffield	1997	1(4)	0	0	0	0
Morgan Escare	Salford	2021	13	5	3	0	26
	Wakefield	2019	5	1	0	0	4
	Wigan	2017-19	23(22)	14	39	2	136
	Catalans	2013-16	83	58	1	2	236
Ryan Esders	Harlequins	2009-10	9(11)	3	0	0	12
	Hull KR	2009	(1)	0	0	0	0
Sonny Esslemont	Hull KR	2014-15	(5)	0	0	0	0
Niall Evalds	Castleford	2021	17	6	0	0	24
	Salford	2013-20	119(11)	88	0	0	352
Ben Evans	Warrington	2014-15	3(16)	2	0	0	8
	Bradford	2013	3(12)	1	0	0	4
James Evans	Castleford	2009-10	26(1)	13	0	0	52
	Bradford	2007-08	43(5)	20	0	0	80
	Wakefield	2006	6	3	0	0	12
	Huddersfield	2004-06	51	22	0	0	88
Paul Evans	Paris	1997	18	8	0	0	32

Super League Players 1996-2021

PLAYER	CLUB	YEAR	APP	TRIES	GOALS	FG	PTS
Rhys Evans	Leeds	2020	4(1)	1	0	0	4
	Warrington	2010-17	87(7)	37	0	0	148
Wayne Evans	London	2002	11(6)	2	0	0	8
Toby Everett	London	2014	(2)	0	0	0	0
Richie Eyres	Warrington	1997	2(5)	0	0	0	0
	Sheffield	1997	2(3)	0	0	0	0
Henry Fa'afili	Warrington	2004-07	90(1)	70	0	0	280
David Fa'alogo	Huddersfield	2010-12	38(16)	13	0	0	52
Sala Fa'alogo	Widnes	2004-05	8(15)	2	0	0	8
Richard Fa'aoso	Castleford	2006	10(15)	5	0	0	20
Maurie Fa'asavalu	St Helens	2004-10	5(137)	29	0	0	116
Bolouagi Fagborun	Huddersfield	2004-06	4(2)	1	0	0	4
Theo Fages	St Helens	2016-21	101(25)	34	0	2	138
	Salford	2013-15	57(5)	18	4	0	80
Esene Faimalo	Salford	1997-99	23(25)	2	0	0	8
	Leeds	1996	3(3)	0	0	0	0
Joe Faimalo	Salford	1998-2000	23(47)	7	0	0	28
	Oldham	1996-97	37(5)	7	0	0	28
Jacob Fairbank	Huddersfield	2011-15	12(3)	0	0	0	0
	Wakefield	2014	1(3)	0	0	0	0
	London	2013	4(1)	1	0	0	4
	Bradford	2013	(2)	0	0	0	0
Karl Fairbank	Bradford	1996	17(2)	4	0	0	16
David Fairleigh	St Helens	2001	26(1)	8	0	0	32
David Faiumu	Huddersfield	2008-14	38(108)	13	0	0	52
Jamal Fakir	Bradford	2014	5(8)	1	0	0	4
	Catalans	2006-14	55(100)	13	0	0	52
Jim Fallon	Leeds	1996	10	5	0	0	20
Beau Falloon	Leeds	2016	8(2)	0	0	0	0
Bureta Faraimo	Hull	2018-21	78(1)	37	4	0	156
Owen Farnworth	Widnes	2017-18	1(4)	0	0	0	0
Ben Farrar	London	2014	22	1	0	0	4
	Catalans	2011	13	3	0	0	12
Danny Farrar	Warrington	1998-2000	76	13	0	0	52
Andy Farrell	Wigan	1996-2004	230	77	1026	16	2376
Anthony Farrell	Widnes	2002-03	24(22)	4	1	0	18
	Leeds	1997-2001	99(23)	18	0	0	72
	Sheffield	1996	14(5)	5	0	0	20
Connor Farrell	Widnes	2016	3(9)	3	0	0	12
	Wigan	2014-15	1(8)	1	0	0	4
Craig Farrell	Hull	2000-01	1(3)	0	0	0	0
Izaac Farrell	Huddersfield	2019	2	0	4	0	8
Liam Farrell	Wigan	2010-21	212(50)	102	0	0	408
Brad Fash	Hull	2015, 2017-21	11(88)	2	0	0	8
Abraham Fatnowna							
	London	1997-98	7(2)	2	0	0	8
	Workington	1996	5	2	0	0	8
Sione Faumuina	Castleford	2009	18	1	0	0	4
	Hull	2005	3	1	0	0	4
Vince Fawcett	Wakefield	1999	13(1)	2	0	0	8
	Warrington	1998	4(7)	1	0	0	4
	Oldham	1997	5	3	0	0	12
Danny Fearon	Huddersfield	2001	(1)	0	0	0	0
	Halifax	1999-2000	5(6)	0	0	0	0
Chris Feather	Castleford	2009	1(23)	0	0	0	0
	Bradford	2007-08	7(20)	1	0	0	4
	Leeds	2003-04, 2006	16(35)	6	0	0	24
	Wakefield	2001-02, 2004-05	29(32)	9	0	0	36
Dom Feaunati	Leigh	2005	4	1	0	0	4
	St Helens	2004	10(7)	7	0	0	28
Adel Fellous	Hull	2008	1(2)	0	0	0	0
	Catalans	2006-07	16(22)	4	0	0	16
Luke Felsch	Hull	2000-01	46(6)	7	0	0	28
	Gateshead	1999	28(1)	2	0	0	8
Leon Felton	Warrington	2002	4(2)	0	0	0	0
	St Helens	2001	1(1)	0	0	0	0
Dale Ferguson	Huddersfield	2011-13, 2017-19	61(23)	16	0	0	64
	Bradford	2014	3(3)	0	0	0	0
	Hull KR	2013	3(1)	1	0	0	4
	Wakefield	2007-11	40(14)	12	0	0	48
Brett Ferres	Leeds	2016-20	52(16)	11	0	0	44
	Huddersfield	2012-15	72	27	0	0	108
	Castleford	2009-12	78(5)	26	0	0	104
	Wakefield	2007-08	36(2)	6	5	0	34
	Bradford	2005-06	18(17)	11	2	0	48
David Ferriol	Catalans	2007-12	72(55)	8	0	0	32
Jason Ferris	Leigh	2005	4	1	0	0	4
Callum Field	Wigan	2017-18	(8)	0	0	0	0
Jai Field	Wigan	2021	3(1)	0	0	0	0
Jamie Field	Wakefield	1999-2006	133(59)	19	0	0	76
	Huddersfield	1998	15(5)	0	0	0	0
	Leeds	1996-97	3(11)	0	0	0	0
Mark Field	Wakefield	2003-07	28(7)	3	0	0	12
Jamie Fielden	London	2003	(1)	0	0	0	0
	Huddersfield	1998-2000	4(8)	0	0	0	0
Stuart Fielden	Huddersfield	2013	8(1)	0	0	0	0
	Wigan	2006-12	105(24)	2	0	0	8
	Bradford	1998-2006	142(78)	41	0	0	164
David Fifita	Wakefield	2016-21	59(54)	23	1	0	94
Lafaele Filipo	Workington	1996	15(4)	3	0	0	12
Salesi Finau	Warrington	1996-97	16(15)	8	0	0	32
Brett Finch	Wigan	2011-12	49(3)	16	0	0	64
Vinny Finigan	Bradford	2010	4(1)	4	0	0	16
Liam Finn	Widnes	2018	1	0	0	0	0
	Wakefield	2004, 2016-18	71(4)	5	220	0	460
	Castleford	2014-15	45(2)	8	5	2	44
	Halifax	2002-03	16(5)	2	30	1	69
Lee Finnerty	Halifax	2003	18(2)	5	2	0	24
Phil Finney	Warrington	1998	1	0	0	0	0
Simon Finnigan	Widnes	2003-05, 2012	56(24)	21	0	0	84
	Huddersfield	2009-10	22(5)	6	0	0	24
	Bradford	2008	14(13)	8	0	0	32
	Salford	2006-07	50	17	0	0	68
Matt Firth	Halifax	2000-01	12(2)	0	0	0	0
Andy Fisher	Wakefield	1999-2000	31(8)	4	0	0	16
Ben Fisher	London	2013	8(12)	1	0	0	4
	Catalans	2012	9(5)	1	0	0	4
	Hull KR	2007-11	78(46)	18	0	0	72
Craig Fitzgibbon	Hull	2010-11	42(1)	9	8	0	52
Daniel Fitzhenry	Hull KR	2008-09	36(11)	14	0	0	56
Karl Fitzpatrick	Salford	2004-07, 2009-10	89(11)	33	2	0	136
Conor Fitzsimmons	Castleford	2016	(2)	0	0	0	0
Mark Flanagan	Salford	2016-20	62(27)	8	0	0	32
	St Helens	2012-15	40(39)	9	0	0	36
	Wigan	2009	3(7)	1	0	0	4
Chris Flannery	St Helens	2007-12	108(11)	32	0	0	128
Darren Fleary	Leigh	2005	24	1	0	0	4
	Huddersfield	2003-04	43(8)	4	0	0	16
	Leeds	1997-2002	98(9)	3	0	0	12
Dan Fleming	Castleford	2013-14, 2020	(16)	1	0	0	4
Greg Fleming	London	1999-2001	64(1)	40	2	0	164
Matty Fleming	London	2019	12(1)	6	0	0	24
	Leigh	2017	5	1	0	0	4
	St Helens	2015-17	17	7	0	0	28
Adam Fletcher	Castleford	2006, 2008	16(7)	11	0	0	44
Bryan Fletcher	Wigan	2006-07	47(2)	14	0	0	56
Richard Fletcher	Castleford	2006	13(5)	3	4	0	20
	Hull	1999-2004	11(56)	5	0	0	20
Greg Florimo	Halifax	2000	26	6	4	0	32
	Wigan	1999	18(2)	7	1	0	30
Ben Flower	Leigh	2021	2(2)	0	0	0	0
	Wigan	2012-20	131(37)	21	0	0	84
	Crusaders	2010-11	10(23)	2	0	0	8
	Celtic	2009	2(15)	0	0	0	0
Jason Flowers	Salford	2004	6(1)	0	0	0	0
	Halifax	2002	24(4)	4	0	0	16
	Castleford	1996-2001	119(19)	33	0	1	133
Stuart Flowers	Castleford	1996	(3)	0	0	0	0
Adrian Flynn	Castleford	1996-97	19(2)	10	0	0	40
Paddy Flynn	Castleford	2016	9(1)	6	0	0	24
	Widnes	2012-15	72	41	0	0	164
Wayne Flynn	Sheffield	1997	3(5)	0	0	0	0
Adam Fogerty	Warrington	1998	4	0	0	0	0
	St Helens	1996	13	1	0	0	4
Israel Folau	Catalans	2020	13	5	0	0	20
Mahe Fonua	Hull	2016-17, 2020-21	78(5)	39	0	0	156
Liam Foran	Salford	2013	10(3)	1	0	0	4
Carl Forber	Leigh	2005	4	1	0	0	4
	St Helens	2004	1(1)	0	6	0	12
Paul Forber	Salford	1997-98	19(12)	4	0	0	16
Byron Ford	Hull KR	2007	13	6	0	0	24
James Ford	Castleford	2009	3(5)	1	0	0	4
Mike Ford	Castleford	1997-98	25(12)	5	0	3	23
	Warrington	1996	3	0	0	0	0
Jim Forshaw	Salford	1999	(1)	0	0	0	0
Mike Forshaw	Warrington	2004	20(1)	5	0	0	20
	Bradford	1997-2003	162(7)	32	0	0	128
	Leeds	1996	11(3)	5	0	0	20
Carl Forster	Salford	2015-16	5(7)	1	0	0	4
	St Helens	2011-12, 2014	(4)	0	0	0	0
	London	2014	2(3)	0	0	0	0
Mark Forster	Warrington	1996-2000	102(1)	40	0	0	160
Liam Forsyth	Wigan	2017-18	11(2)	3	0	0	12

PLAYER	CLUB	YEAR	APP	TRIES	GOALS	FG	PTS
Alex Foster	Castleford	2017-21	40(18)	10	0	0	40
	London	2014	20	3	0	0	12
	Leeds	2013	(8)	1	0	0	4
David Foster	Halifax	2000-01	4(9)	0	0	0	0
Jamie Foster	Huddersfield	2016	3	2	5	0	18
	Bradford	2013-14	32	12	111	0	270
	Hull	2012	9	5	45	0	110
	St Helens	2010-12	44(3)	30	201	0	522
Matthew Foster	Leigh	2021	4(2)	0	0	0	0
	St Helens	2020	(1)	0	0	0	0
Peter Fox	Wakefield	2007, 2012-14	85	44	0	0	176
	Hull KR	2008-11	95	52	0	0	208
Matty Fozard	London	2019	7(16)	3	0	0	12
	St Helens	2014	1	0	0	0	0
Nick Fozzard	Castleford	2011	7(10)	0	0	0	0
	St Helens	2004-08, 2010	100(25)	7	0	0	28
	Hull KR	2009	18(4)	1	0	0	4
	Warrington	2002-03	43(11)	2	0	0	8
	Huddersfield	1998-2000	24(8)	2	0	0	8
	Leeds	1996-97	6(16)	3	0	0	12
David Fraisse	Workington	1996	8	0	0	0	0
Daniel Frame	Widnes	2002-05	100(6)	24	0	0	96
Romain Franco	Catalans	2021	3	1	0	0	4
Paul Franze	Castleford	2006	2(1)	0	0	0	0
Matt Frawley	Huddersfield	2019	19(2)	4	0	0	16
Laurent Frayssinous	Catalans	2006	14(2)	3	32	0	76
Bevan French	Wigan	2019-21	26(5)	24	0	0	96
Andrew Frew	Halifax	2003	17	5	0	0	20
	Wakefield	2002	21	8	0	0	32
	Huddersfield	2001	26	15	0	0	60
Dale Fritz	Castleford	1999-2003	120(4)	9	0	0	36
Gareth Frodsham	St Helens	2008-09	1(9)	0	0	0	0
Liam Fulton	Huddersfield	2009	12(3)	4	0	0	16
David Furner	Leeds	2003-04	45	8	23	0	78
	Wigan	2001-02	51(2)	21	13	0	110
David Furness	Castleford	1996	(1)	0	0	0	0
Matt Gafa	Harlequins	2006-09	81	26	16	0	136
Luke Gale	Leeds	2020-21	26	8	16	4	68
	Castleford	2015-18	100	32	402	15	947
	Bradford	2012-14	56(2)	13	108	4	272
	Harlequins	2009-11	56(12)	18	86	3	247
Ben Galea	Hull	2013	12(2)	3	0	0	12
	Hull KR	2008-12	115(2)	33	0	0	132
Danny Galea	Widnes	2014-15	38(4)	5	0	0	20
Tommy Gallagher	Hull KR	2007	1(7)	0	0	0	0
	Widnes	2004	(6)	0	0	0	0
	London	2003	1(9)	1	0	0	4
Keith Galloway	Leeds	2016-17	28(4)	1	0	0	4
Mark Gamson	Sheffield	1996	3	0	0	0	0
Jim Gannon	Hull KR	2007	7(16)	1	0	0	4
	Huddersfield	2003-06	79(14)	11	0	0	44
	Halifax	1999-2002	83(4)	14	0	0	56
Morgan Gannon	Leeds	2021	6(6)	1	0	0	4
Josh Ganson	Wigan	2017-18	1(6)	2	0	0	8
Mitch Garbutt	Hull KR	2019-20	5(22)	5	0	0	20
	Leeds	2015-18	36(25)	7	0	0	28
Steve Garces	Salford	2001	(1)	0	0	0	0
Benjamin Garcia	Catalans	2013-21	96(47)	25	0	0	100
Jean-Marc Garcia	Sheffield	1996-97	35(3)	22	0	0	88
Ade Gardner	Hull KR	2014	18	7	0	0	28
	St Helens	2002-13	236(12)	146	0	0	584
Matt Gardner	Harlequins	2009	6(3)	2	0	0	8
	Huddersfield	2006-07	22(3)	7	0	0	28
	Castleford	2004	1	1	0	0	4
Steve Gartland	Oldham	1996	1(1)	0	1	0	2
Daniel Gartner	Bradford	2001-03	74(1)	26	0	0	104
Dean Gaskell	Warrington	2002-06	58(1)	10	0	0	40
Lee Gaskell	Huddersfield	2017-21	89(1)	24	30	1	157
	Bradford	2014	21	5	0	0	20
	Salford	2013	17	8	2	0	36
	St Helens	2010-13	33(9)	14	12	1	81
George Gatis	Huddersfield	2008	5(5)	1	0	0	4
James Gavet	Huddersfield	2020-21	12(12)	4	0	0	16
Richard Gay	Castleford	1996-2002	94(16)	39	0	0	156
Andrew Gee	Warrington	2000-01	33(1)	4	0	0	16
Matty Gee	Leigh	2021	9(5)	4	0	0	16
	Hull KR	2020	6(5)	0	0	0	0
	London	2019	14(8)	5	0	0	20
	Salford	2015	(2)	0	0	0	0
Anthony Gelling	Leigh	2021	6	2	0	0	8
	Warrington	2020	11	6	0	0	24
	Wigan	2012-17	101(1)	52	0	0	208
Stanley Gene	Hull KR	2007-09	37(17)	9	0	0	36
	Bradford	2006	5(16)	8	0	0	32
	Huddersfield	2001, 2003-05	70(6)	27	0	0	108
	Hull	2000-01	5(23)	6	0	0	24
Steve Georgallis	Warrington	2001	5(1)	2	0	0	8
Luke George	Bradford	2014	9(1)	3	0	0	12
	Huddersfield	2012-13	28(2)	18	0	0	72
	Hull KR	2013	4	2	0	0	8
	Wakefield	2007-11	38(3)	24	0	0	96
Shaun Geritas	Warrington	1997	(5)	1	0	0	4
Alex Gerrard	Leigh	2021	5(9)	0	0	0	0
	Widnes	2012-18	48(40)	4	0	0	16
Anthony Gibbons	Leeds	1996	9(4)	2	0	1	9
David Gibbons	Leeds	1996	3(4)	2	0	0	8
Scott Gibbs	St Helens	1996	9	3	0	0	12
Ashley Gibson	Wakefield	2016-17	9	4	0	0	16
	Castleford	2014-15	27	9	0	0	36
	Salford	2010-13	77(4)	41	0	0	164
	Leeds	2005-09	25(7)	13	9	0	70
Damian Gibson	Castleford	2003-04	40(3)	5	0	0	20
	Salford	2002	28	3	0	0	12
	Halifax	1998-2001	104(1)	39	0	0	156
	Leeds	1997	18	3	0	0	12
Kurt Gidley	Warrington	2016-17	44	11	97	0	238
Matt Gidley	St Helens	2007-10	105	40	6	0	172
Tony Gigot	Wakefield	2020	6(1)	1	6	0	16
	Toronto	2020	2(1)	0	0	0	0
	Catalans	2010-11, 2015-19	117(13)	43	51	12	286
	London	2014	2	0	4	0	8
Ian Gildart	Oldham	1996-97	31(7)	0	0	0	0
Oliver Gildart	Wigan	2015-21	128(2)	58	0	0	232
	Salford	2015	3	1	0	0	4
Chris Giles	Widnes	2003-04	35	12	0	0	48
	St Helens	2002	(1)	0	0	0	0
Kieran Gill	Castleford	2017-18	4	4	0	0	16
Peter Gill	London	1996-99	75(6)	20	0	0	80
Carl Gillespie	Halifax	1996-99	47(36)	13	0	0	52
Michael Gillett	London	2001-02	23(21)	12	2	0	52
Simon Gillies	Warrington	1999	28	6	0	0	24
Tom Gilmore	Salford	2020	2	1	0	0	4
	Widnes	2012-18	38(1)	11	51	3	149
Lee Gilmour	Wakefield	2014	10(3)	2	0	0	8
	Castleford	2013	10(2)	0	0	0	0
	Huddersfield	2010-12	71(1)	17	0	0	68
	St Helens	2004-09	149(3)	41	0	0	164
	Bradford	2001-03	44(31)	20	0	0	80
	Wigan	1997-2000	44(39)	22	0	0	88
Marc Glanville	Leeds	1998-99	43(3)	5	0	0	20
Eddie Glaze	Castleford	1996	1	0	0	0	0
Paul Gleadhill	Leeds	1996	4	0	0	0	0
Ben Gledhill	Salford	2012-13	3(10)	1	0	0	4
	Wakefield	2010-11	(16)	0	0	0	0
Mark Gleeson	Warrington	2000-08	38(102)	12	0	0	48
Martin Gleeson	Salford	2013-14	26(1)	4	0	0	16
	Hull	2011	6	4	0	0	16
	Wigan	2009-11	46(1)	19	0	0	76
	Warrington	2005-09	110(1)	44	0	0	176
	St Helens	2002-04	56(1)	25	0	0	100
	Huddersfield	1999-2001	47(9)	18	0	0	72
Sean Gleeson	Hull KR	2013	6	0	0	0	0
	Salford	2011-12	35	14	0	0	56
	Wakefield	2007-10	67(6)	20	0	0	80
	Wigan	2005-06	3(3)	0	0	0	0
Jon Goddard	Hull KR	2007	20	2	0	0	8
	Castleford	2000-01	(2)	0	0	0	0
Richard Goddard	Castleford	1996-97	11(3)	2	10	0	28
Brad Godden	Leeds	1998-99	47	15	0	0	60
Pita Godinet	Wakefield	2014-15	18(19)	10	0	0	40
Wayne Godwin	Salford	2011-13, 2015	43(8)	6	0	0	24
	Bradford	2008-10	16(44)	9	0	0	36
	Hull	2007	3(13)	1	0	0	4
	Wigan	2005-06	9(38)	6	0	0	24
	Castleford	2001-04	30(33)	18	56	0	184
Jason Golden	London	2012	7(2)	1	0	0	4
	Harlequins	2009-11	34(12)	3	0	0	12
	Wakefield	2007-08	26(5)	1	0	0	4
Marvin Golden	Widnes	2003	4	1	0	0	4
	London	2001	17(2)	1	0	0	4
	Halifax	2000	20(2)	5	0	0	20
	Leeds	1996-99	43(11)	19	0	0	76
Ashton Golding	Huddersfield	2020-21	21	3	0	0	12
	Leeds	2014-18	42(9)	5	14	0	48

Super League Players 1996-2021

PLAYER	CLUB	YEAR	APP	TRIES	GOALS	FG	PTS
Brett Goldspink	Halifax	2000-02	64(5)	2	0	0	8
	Wigan	1999	6(16)	1	0	0	4
	St Helens	1998	19(4)	2	0	0	8
	Oldham	1997	13(2)	0	0	0	0
Lee Gomersall	Hull KR	2008	1	0	0	0	0
Bryson Goodwin	Warrington	2018-19	52	20	29	0	138
Luke Goodwin	London	1998	9(2)	3	1	1	15
	Oldham	1997	16(4)	10	17	2	76
Grant Gore	Widnes	2012-15	6(11)	1	0	0	4
Aaron Gorrell	Catalans	2007-08	23	6	14	0	52
Andy Gorski	Salford	2001-02	(2)	0	0	0	0
Cyrille Gossard	Catalans	2006-12	54(30)	5	0	0	20
Mickael Goudemand							
	Catalans	2018-21	20(35)	4	0	0	16
Bobbie Goulding	Salford	2001-02	31(1)	2	56	4	124
	Wakefield	2000	12	3	25	3	65
	Huddersfield	1998-99	27(1)	3	65	4	146
	St Helens	1996-98	42(2)	9	210	4	460
Bobbie Goulding (Jnr)							
	Wakefield	2013	1(2)	0	1	0	2
Darrell Goulding	Hull KR	2015	8	1	0	0	4
	Wigan	2005-14	129(24)	68	0	0	272
	Salford	2009	9	5	0	0	20
Mick Govin	Leigh	2005	5(6)	4	0	0	16
Craig Gower	London	2012-13	40	7	24	0	76
David Gower	Salford	2006-07	(16)	0	0	0	0
Regan Grace	St Helens	2017-21	120	71	0	0	284
Shane Grady	London	2013	5(4)	1	2	0	8
Brad Graham	Castleford	2020-21	3	1	0	0	4
James Graham	St Helens	2003-11,					
		2020	143(63)	48	0	0	192
Nathan Graham	Bradford	1996-98	17(28)	4	0	1	17
Nick Graham	Wigan	2003	13(1)	2	0	0	8
Dalton Grant	Crusaders	2011	(1)	0	0	0	0
Jon Grayshon	Harlequins	2007-09	10(32)	4	0	0	16
	Huddersfield	2003-06	7(43)	5	0	0	20
Blake Green	Wigan	2013-14	42(1)	15	0	0	60
	Hull KR	2011-12	35	14	0	0	56
Brett Green	Gateshead	1999	10(2)	0	0	0	0
Chris Green	Wakefield	2019-21	8(19)	1	0	0	4
	Hull	2012-19	33(92)	7	0	0	28
James Green	Castleford	2018	1(3)	0	0	0	0
	Leigh	2017	4(5)	0	0	0	0
	Hull KR	2012-16	8(64)	3	0	0	12
Toby Green	Huddersfield	2001	3(1)	1	0	0	4
Craig Greenhill	Castleford	2004	21(4)	1	0	0	4
	Hull	2002-03	56	3	2	0	16
Clint Greenshields	Catalans	2007-12	137	81	0	0	324
Ollie Greensmith	Wakefield	2021	1	0	0	0	0
Brandon Greenwood							
	Halifax	1996	1	0	0	0	0
Gareth Greenwood	Huddersfield	2003	(1)	0	0	0	0
	Halifax	2002	1	0	0	0	0
James Greenwood	Salford	2015,					
		2020-21	12(3)	2	0	0	8
	Hull KR	2015-16,					
		2018-19	29(23)	7	0	0	28
	Wigan	2013, 2015	(2)	0	0	0	0
	London	2014	10(5)	3	0	0	12
Joe Greenwood	Huddersfield	2021	14(4)	2	0	0	8
	Wigan	2018-20	23(16)	12	0	0	48
	St Helens	2012-17	40(28)	26	0	0	104
Lee Greenwood	Huddersfield	2005	7	3	0	0	12
	London	2004-05	30(2)	19	0	0	76
	Halifax	2000-03	38(2)	17	0	0	68
	Sheffield	1999	1(1)	0	0	0	0
Nick Gregson	Wigan	2016-17	5(9)	1	0	0	4
James Grehan	Castleford	2012	2(2)	0	0	0	0
Maxime Greseque	Wakefield	2007	2(1)	0	0	0	0
Mathieu Griffi	Catalans	2006-08	1(25)	0	0	0	0
Darrell Griffin	Salford	2013-15	31(27)	1	0	0	4
	Leeds	2012	8(19)	2	0	0	8
	Huddersfield	2007-11	65(60)	13	0	0	52
	Wakefield	2003-06	55(37)	9	3	0	42
George Griffin	Castleford	2020-21	25(2)	1	0	0	4
	Salford	2015-19	69(22)	16	0	0	64
	Wakefield	2015	5	0	0	0	0
	London	2014	(19)	1	0	0	4
	Hull KR	2012-13	11(7)	0	0	0	0
Josh Griffin	Hull	2017-21	93(5)	30	3	0	126
	Salford	2014-16	42	23	77	0	246
	Castleford	2012	20	13	1	0	54
	Wakefield	2011	17	5	21	0	62
	Huddersfield	2009	2	0	0	0	0
Jonathan Griffiths	Paris	1996	(4)	1	0	0	4
Andrew Grima	Workington	1996	2(9)	2	0	0	8
Tony Grimaldi	Hull	2000-01	56(1)	14	0	0	56
	Gateshead	1999	27(2)	10	0	0	40
Danny Grimley	Sheffield	1996	4(1)	1	0	0	4
Scott Grix	Huddersfield	2010-16,					
		2019	141(11)	53	32	0	276
	Wakefield	2008-09,					
		2017-18	81(3)	32	0	0	128
Simon Grix	Warrington	2006-14	133(25)	42	0	0	168
	Halifax	2003	2(4)	0	0	0	0
Brett Grogan	Gateshead	1999	14(7)	3	0	0	12
Brent Grose	Warrington	2003-07	134(1)	55	0	0	220
David Guasch	Catalans	2010	1	0	0	0	0
Joan Guasch	Catalans	2014-15	(6)	0	0	0	0
Renaud Guigue	Catalans	2006	14(4)	3	0	0	12
Jerome Guisset	Catalans	2006-10	102(23)	9	0	0	36
	Wigan	2005	20(2)	3	0	0	12
	Warrington	2000-04	59(65)	21	0	0	84
Awen Guttenbeil	Castleford	2008	19	0	0	0	0
Reece Guy	Oldham	1996	3(4)	0	0	0	0
Josh Guzdek	Hull KR	2013, 2015	2	1	0	0	4
Titus Gwaze	Wakefield	2019-20	(5)	0	0	0	0
Tom Haberecht	Castleford	2008	2(2)	1	0	0	4
Dean Hadley	Hull KR	2019-21	25(7)	4	0	0	16
	Hull	2013-16,					
		2018-19	55(26)	10	0	0	40
	Wakefield	2017	14(7)	2	0	0	8
Gareth Haggerty	Harlequins	2008-09	8(28)	6	0	0	24
	Salford	2004-07	1(93)	15	0	0	60
	Widnes	2002	1(2)	1	0	0	4
Kurt Haggerty	Widnes	2012	6(8)	2	0	0	8
Andy Haigh	St Helens	1996-98	20(16)	11	0	0	44
Scott Hale	St Helens	2011	(3)	1	0	0	4
Michael Haley	Leeds	2008	(1)	0	0	0	0
Carl Hall	Leeds	1996	7(2)	3	0	0	12
Corey Hall	Leeds	2020-21	1(2)	0	0	0	0
Craig Hall	Hull KR	2011-14,					
		2018-19	102(3)	51	65	2	336
	Wakefield	2015-16	35	14	30	0	116
	Hull	2007-10	59(9)	39	11	0	178
Glenn Hall	Bradford	2010	7(18)	2	0	0	8
Martin Hall	Halifax	1998	2(10)	0	0	0	0
	Hull	1999	7	0	0	0	0
	Castleford	1998	4	0	0	0	0
	Wigan	1996-97	31(5)	7	6	0	40
Ryan Hall	Hull KR	2021	20	16	0	0	64
	Leeds	2007-18	278(3)	196	0	0	784
Sam Hall	Castleford	2020-21	1(3)	0	0	0	0
Steve Hall	Widnes	2004	1	0	0	0	0
	London	2002-03	35(3)	10	0	0	40
	St Helens	1999-2001	36(22)	19	0	0	76
Graeme Hallas	Huddersfield	2001	1	0	0	0	0
	Hull	1998-99	30(10)	6	39	1	103
	Halifax	1996	11(4)	5	0	0	20
Sam Hallas	Leeds	2016	(2)	0	0	0	0
Macauley Hallett	Hull KR	2014	2	3	0	0	12
Dave Halley	Bradford	2007-10	63(12)	20	0	0	80
	Wakefield	2009	5	4	0	0	16
Danny Halliwell	Salford	2007	2(3)	0	0	0	0
	Leigh	2005	5	3	0	0	12
	Halifax	2000-03	17(8)	4	0	0	16
	Warrington	2002	9(1)	8	0	0	32
	Wakefield	2002	3	0	0	0	0
Colum Halpenny	Wakefield	2003-06	103(1)	36	0	0	144
	Halifax	2002	22	12	0	0	48
Sam Halsall	Wigan	2020-21	8	2	0	0	8
Jon Hamer	Bradford	1996	(1)	0	0	0	0
Andrew Hamilton	London	1997, 2003	1(20)	3	0	0	12
John Hamilton	St Helens	1998	3	0	0	0	0
Gabe Hamlin	Wigan	2018-19	6(18)	3	0	0	12
Karle Hammond	Halifax	2002	10(2)	2	14	0	36
	Salford	2001	2(3)	1	0	0	4
	London	1999-2000	47	23	2	3	99
	St Helens	1996-98	58(8)	28	0	4	116
Ryan Hampshire	Wakefield	2018-21	75(6)	27	122	3	355
	Leigh	2017	12(1)	3	0	0	12
	Castleford	2016	19(2)	8	0	0	32
	Wigan	2013-15	20(5)	8	24	0	80
Rhys Hanbury	Widnes	2012-18	153	71	99	1	483
	Crusaders	2010-11	26(1)	14	0	0	56
Anthony Hancock	Paris	1997	8(6)	1	0	0	4
Michael Hancock	Salford	2001-02	12(24)	7	0	0	28
Jordan Hand	Wakefield	2015	(2)	0	0	0	0
	St Helens	2013-14	(3)	0	0	0	0
Gareth Handford	Castleford	2001	7(2)	0	0	0	0
	Bradford	2000	1(1)	0	0	0	0

PLAYER	CLUB	YEAR	APP	TRIES	GOALS	FG	PTS
Paul Handforth	Castleford	2006	2(15)	2	1	0	10
	Wakefield	2000-04	17(44)	10	13	0	66
Ash Handley	Leeds	2014-21	123(3)	73	2	0	296
Paddy Handley	Leeds	1996	1(1)	2	0	0	8
Dean Hanger	Warrington	1999	7(11)	3	0	0	12
	Huddersfield	1998	20(1)	5	0	0	20
Chris Hankinson	Wigan	2018-20	18(4)	4	19	0	54
Umyla Hanley	Wigan	2020-21	9	4	0	0	16
Josh Hannay	Celtic	2009	17	2	24	0	56
Harrison Hansen	Widnes	2018	1	1	0	0	4
	Leigh	2017	19(2)	1	0	0	4
	Salford	2014-15	41(2)	7	0	0	28
	Wigan	2004-13	155(62)	39	0	0	156
Lee Hansen	Wigan	1997	10(5)	0	0	0	0
Shontayne Hape	Bradford	2003-08	123(2)	79	0	0	316
Lionel Harbin	Wakefield	2001	(1)	0	0	0	0
Zak Hardaker	Wigan	2019-21	64	20	175	2	432
	Castleford	2017	28	12	1	0	50
	Leeds	2011-16	135	57	43	1	315
Ian Hardman	Hull KR	2007	18	4	0	0	16
	St Helens	2003-07	32(11)	9	5	0	46
Jeff Hardy	Hudds-Sheff	2000	20(5)	6	0	1	25
	Sheffield	1999	22(4)	7	0	0	28
Spencer Hargrave	Castleford	1996-99	(6)	0	0	0	0
Bryn Hargreaves	Bradford	2011-12	45(5)	1	0	0	4
	St Helens	2007-10	53(44)	7	0	0	28
	Wigan	2004-06	16(12)	1	0	0	4
Lee Harland	Castleford	1996-2004	148(35)	20	0	0	80
Neil Harmon	Halifax	2003	13(3)	0	0	0	0
	Salford	2001	6(5)	0	0	0	0
	Bradford	1998-2000	15(13)	2	0	0	8
	Huddersfield	1998	12	1	0	0	4
	Leeds	1996	10	1	0	0	4
Ben Harris	Bradford	2005-07	70(4)	24	0	0	96
Iestyn Harris	Bradford	2004-08	109(11)	35	87	2	316
	Leeds	1997-2001	111(7)	57	490	6	1214
	Warrington	1996	16	4	63	2	144
Liam Harris	Hull	2018	9(2)	3	0	0	12
Ben Harrison	Wakefield	2016	3	0	0	0	0
	Warrington	2007-15	125(59)	14	0	0	56
James Harrison	Leeds	2020	2(2)	0	0	0	0
Karl Harrison	Hull	1999	26	2	0	0	8
	Halifax	1996-98	60(2)	2	0	0	8
Owen Harrison	Hull KR	2019-20	3(6)	0	0	0	0
Andrew Hart	London	2004	12(1)	2	0	0	8
Tim Hartley	Harlequins	2006	2	1	0	0	4
	Salford	2004-05	6(7)	5	0	0	20
Carlos Hassan	Bradford	1996	6(4)	2	0	0	8
Phil Hassan	Wakefield	2002	9(1)	0	0	0	0
	Halifax	2000-01	25(4)	3	0	0	12
	Salford	1998	15	2	0	0	8
	Leeds	1996-97	38(4)	12	0	0	48
James Hasson	Wakefield	2017	(4)	0	0	0	0
	Salford	2017	4(1)	0	0	0	0
Jackson Hastings	Wigan	2020-21	42	13	1	3	57
	Salford	2018-19	34	11	4	0	52
Tom Haughey	Castleford	2006	1(3)	1	0	0	4
	London	2003-04	10(8)	1	0	0	4
	Wakefield	2001-02	5(11)	0	0	0	0
Simon Haughton	Wigan	1996-2002	63(46)	32	0	0	128
Solomon Haumono							
	Harlequins	2006	10(9)	6	0	0	24
	London	2005	24(5)	8	0	0	32
Weller Hauraki	Hull KR	2019-20	34(4)	5	0	0	20
	Widnes	2018	7	0	0	0	0
	Salford	2015-18	45(12)	8	0	0	32
	Castleford	2013-14	50(2)	9	0	0	36
	Leeds	2011-12	18(17)	6	0	0	24
	Crusaders	2010	26(1)	11	0	0	44
Ethan Havard	Wigan	2019-21	13(20)	1	0	0	4
Richie Hawkyard	Bradford	2007	1(2)	1	0	0	4
Andy Hay	Widnes	2003-04	50(2)	7	0	0	28
	Leeds	1997-2002	112(27)	43	0	0	172
	Sheffield	1996-97	17(3)	5	0	0	20
Adam Hayes	Hudds-Sheff	2000	2(1)	0	0	0	0
Joey Hayes	Salford	1999	9	2	0	0	8
	St Helens	1996-98	11(6)	7	0	0	28
James Haynes	Hull KR	2009	1	0	0	0	0
Callum Hazzard	St Helens	2019	(1)	0	0	0	0
Mathew Head	Hull	2007	9(1)	1	0	1	5
Mitch Healey	Castleford	2001-03	68(1)	10	16	0	72
Daniel Heckenberg	Harlequins	2006-09	31(39)	4	0	0	16
Andrew Heffernan	Hull KR	2018	7	2	0	0	8
Chris Heil	Hull KR	2012-13	4	2	0	0	8
Ben Hellewell	Leigh	2021	22	4	0	0	16
	London	2019	2	0	0	0	0
Ricky Helliwell	Salford	1997-99	(2)	0	0	0	0
Tom Hemingway	Huddersfield	2005-09	7(7)	1	17	0	38
Bryan Henare	St Helens	2000-01	4(12)	1	0	0	4
Richard Henare	Warrington	1996-97	28(2)	24	0	0	96
Andrew Henderson							
	Castleford	2006, 2008	44(11)	4	0	0	16
Ian Henderson	Catalans	2011-15	118(9)	12	0	0	48
	Bradford	2005-07	33(37)	13	0	0	52
Kevin Henderson	Wakefield	2005-11	52(68)	9	0	0	36
	Leigh	2005	(1)	0	0	0	0
Adam Henry	Bradford	2014	23(1)	5	0	0	20
Mark Henry	Salford	2009-11	67	22	0	0	88
Brad Hepi	Castleford	1999, 2001	9(21)	3	0	0	12
	Salford	2000	3(5)	0	0	0	0
	Hull	1998	15(1)	3	0	0	12
Tyla Hepi	Castleford	2020-21	5(13)	0	0	0	0
	Hull KR	2013	(4)	0	0	0	0
Jon Hepworth	Castleford	2003-04	19(23)	7	8	0	44
	Leeds	2003	(1)	0	0	0	0
	London	2002	(2)	0	0	0	0
Marc Herbert	Bradford	2011	20	4	2	0	20
Aaron Heremaia	Widnes	2015-18	44(41)	7	0	0	28
	Hull	2012-14	27(37)	12	0	0	48
Maxime Herold	London	2014	(2)	0	0	0	0
Ian Herron	Hull	2000	9	1	17	0	38
	Gateshead	1999	25	4	105	0	226
Jason Hetherington							
	London	2001-02	37	9	0	0	36
Gareth Hewitt	Salford	1999	2(1)	0	0	0	0
Sam Hewitt	Huddersfield	2018-21	8(24)	1	0	0	4
Andrew Hick	Hull	2000	9(9)	1	0	0	4
	Gateshead	1999	12(5)	2	0	0	8
Jarrad Hickey	Wakefield	2011	(8)	2	0	0	8
Chris Hicks	Warrington	2008-10	72	56	119	0	462
Paul Hicks	Wakefield	1999	(1)	0	0	0	0
Darren Higgins	London	1998	5(6)	2	0	0	8
Iain Higgins	London	1997-98	1(7)	2	0	0	8
Liam Higgins	Wakefield	2011	4(12)	0	0	0	0
	Castleford	2008-10	42(32)	2	0	0	8
	Hull	2003-06	1(34)	0	0	0	0
Jack Higginson	Wigan	2016	2(1)	1	0	0	4
Micky Higham	Leigh	2017	11(1)	2	0	0	8
	Warrington	2009-15	73(78)	34	0	0	136
	Wigan	2006-08	61(28)	13	0	0	52
	St Helens	2001-05	43(56)	32	0	0	128
Chris Highton	Warrington	1997	1(1)	0	0	0	0
David Highton	London	2004-05	21(24)	2	0	0	8
	Salford	2002	4(5)	2	0	0	8
	Warrington	1998-2001	18(14)	2	0	0	8
Paul Highton	Salford	1998-2002, 2004-07	114(80)	14	0	0	56
	Halifax	1996-97	12(18)	2	0	0	8
Adam Higson	Leigh	2017	13	2	0	0	8
Peta Hiku	Warrington	2017	4	1	0	0	4
Andy Hill	Huddersfield	1999	(4)	0	0	0	0
	Castleford	1999	4(4)	0	0	0	0
Chris Hill	Warrington	2012-21	245(10)	28	0	0	112
	Leigh	2005	(1)	0	0	0	0
Danny Hill	Wigan	2006-07	1(10)	0	0	0	0
	Hull KR	2007	2	0	0	0	0
	Hull	2004-06	4(6)	0	0	0	0
Howard Hill	Oldham	1996-97	22(12)	4	0	0	16
John Hill	St Helens	2003	(1)	0	0	0	0
	Halifax	2003	1(2)	0	0	0	0
	Warrington	2001-02	(4)	0	0	0	0
Scott Hill	Harlequins	2007-08	41(2)	13	0	0	52
Mark Hilton	Warrington	1996-2000, 2002-06	141(40)	7	0	0	28
Ryan Hinchcliffe	Huddersfield	2016-18	70(11)	11	0	0	44
Daniel Hindmarsh	London	2019	(6)	0	0	0	0
Ian Hindmarsh	Catalans	2006	25	3	0	0	12
Ata Hingano	Salford	2021	3(2)	1	0	0	4
Keegan Hirst	Wakefield	2017-19	17(44)	1	0	0	4
Jy Hitchcox	Castleford	2016-18	25(1)	21	0	0	84
Brendan Hlad	Castleford	2008	(3)	0	0	0	0
Andy Hobson	Widnes	2004	5(13)	0	0	0	0
	Halifax	1998-2003	51(85)	8	0	0	32
Gareth Hock	Leigh	2017	12(1)	3	0	0	12
	Salford	2014-15	15(1)	4	0	0	16
	Widnes	2013	15(2)	9	1	0	38
	Wigan	2003-09, 2011-12	126(43)	38	0	0	152
Tommy Hodgkinson							
	St Helens	2006	(1)	0	0	0	0
Andy Hodgson	Wakefield	1999	14(2)	2	1	0	10
	Bradford	1997-98	8(2)	4	0	0	16

Super League Players 1996-2021

PLAYER	CLUB	YEAR	APP	TRIES	GOALS	FG	PTS
Bailey Hodgson	Castleford	2020	1	0	0	0	0
Brett Hodgson	Warrington	2011-13	66	33	268	1	669
	Huddersfield	2009-10	45	13	166	0	384
David Hodgson	Hull KR	2012-14	51	31	0	0	124
	Huddersfield	2008-11	84	59	0	0	236
	Salford	2005-07	81	30	47	0	214
	Wigan	2000-04	90(19)	43	0	0	172
	Halifax	1999	10(3)	5	0	0	20
Elliot Hodgson	Huddersfield	2009	1	0	0	0	0
Josh Hodgson	Hull KR	2010-14	98(29)	35	0	0	140
	Hull	2009	(2)	0	0	0	0
Ryan Hoffman	Wigan	2011	28(1)	11	0	0	44
Darren Hogg	London	1996	(1)	0	0	0	0
Michael Hogue	Paris	1997	5(7)	0	0	0	0
Lance Hohaia	St Helens	2012-15	67(9)	21	0	1	85
Chris Holden	Warrington	1996-97	2(1)	0	0	0	0
Daniel Holdsworth	Hull	2013	19	2	28	2	66
	Salford	2010-12	71	18	183	1	439
Stephen Holgate	Halifax	2000	1(10)	0	0	0	0
	Hull	1999	1	0	0	0	0
	Wigan	1997-98	11(26)	2	0	0	8
	Workington	1996	19	3	0	0	12
Stephen Holker	Hull KR	2015-16	(4)	0	0	0	0
Martyn Holland	Wakefield	2000-03	52(3)	6	0	0	24
Oliver Holmes	Castleford	2010-21	176(35)	42	0	0	168
Tim Holmes	Widnes	2004-05	15(4)	0	0	0	0
Tom Holmes	Huddersfield	2019-20	12(5)	0	0	0	0
	Castleford	2015-17	7(8)	3	0	0	12
Graham Holroyd	Huddersfield	2003	3(5)	0	0	0	0
	Salford	2000-02	40(11)	8	75	5	187
	Halifax	1999	24(2)	3	74	5	165
	Leeds	1996-98	40(26)	22	101	8	298
Tom Holroyd	Leeds	2018-21	7(20)	2	0	0	8
Dallas Hood	Wakefield	2003-04	18(9)	1	0	0	4
Liam Hood	Leigh	2017, 2021	24(8)	7	0	0	28
	Salford	2015	2(15)	0	0	0	0
	Leeds	2012	1(4)	3	0	0	12
Jacob Hookem	Hull	2021	(1)	0	0	0	0
Jason Hooper	St Helens	2003-07	89(6)	35	30	0	200
Will Hope	Salford	2013	1(2)	0	0	0	0
Lee Hopkins	Harlequins	2006-07	44(3)	11	0	0	44
	London	2005	29	6	0	0	24
Sam Hopkins	Leigh	2017	3(17)	6	0	0	24
Sean Hoppe	St Helens	1999-2002	69(16)	32	0	0	128
Graeme Horne	Hull KR	2012-16	81(18)	21	0	0	84
	Huddersfield	2010-11	23(17)	11	0	0	44
	Hull	2003-09	49(74)	24	0	0	96
Richard Horne	Hull	1999-2014	341(16)	115	12	6	490
Justin Horo	Wakefield	2018-19	22(14)	6	0	0	24
	Catalans	2016-17	34(1)	12	0	0	48
John Hough	Warrington	1996-97	9	2	0	0	8
Danny Houghton	Hull	2007-21	297(53)	43	0	0	172
Sylvain Houles	Wakefield	2003, 2005	8(1)	1	0	0	4
	London	2001-02	17(10)	11	0	0	44
	Hudds-Sheff	2000	5(2)	1	0	0	4
Chris Houston	Widnes	2016-18	58(1)	5	0	0	20
Harvey Howard	Wigan	2001-02	25(27)	1	0	0	4
	Bradford	1998	4(2)	1	0	0	4
	Leeds	1996	8	0	0	0	0
Kim Howard	London	1997	4(5)	0	0	0	0
Stuart Howarth	Wakefield	2011, 2015-16	30(5)	4	0	0	16
	Hull	2015	2(3)	0	0	0	0
	Salford	2012-14	25(12)	1	0	0	4
	St Helens	2013	14(1)	0	0	0	0
Stuart Howarth	Workington	1996	(2)	0	0	0	0
David Howell	London	2012-13	24	5	0	0	20
	Harlequins	2008-11	76	26	0	0	104
Phil Howlett	Bradford	1999	5(1)	2	0	0	8
Craig Huby	Wakefield	2017-19	25(26)	3	0	0	12
	Huddersfield	2015-16	37(2)	2	0	0	8
	Castleford	2003-04, 2006, 2008-14	130(57)	27	41	0	190
Ryan Hudson	Castleford	2002-04, 2009-12	138(12)	31	0	0	124
	Huddersfield	1998-99, 2007-08	51(22)	10	0	0	40
	Wakefield	2000-01	42(9)	11	0	1	45
Adam Hughes	Widnes	2002-05	89(2)	45	51	0	282
	Halifax	2001	8(8)	8	0	0	32
	Wakefield	1999-2000	43(3)	21	34	0	152
	Leeds	1996-97	4(5)	4	0	0	16
Ian Hughes	Sheffield	1996	9(8)	4	0	0	16
Jack Hughes	Warrington	2016-21	134(1)	19	0	0	76
	Huddersfield	2015	30(1)	5	0	0	20
	Wigan	2011-14	31(33)	9	0	0	36
Mark Hughes	Catalans	2006	23	9	0	0	36
Steffan Hughes	London	1999-2001	1(13)	1	0	0	4
David Hulme	Salford	1997-99	53(1)	5	0	0	20
	Leeds	1996	8(1)	2	0	0	8
Declan Hulme	Widnes	2013-15	5	2	0	0	8
Paul Hulme	Warrington	1996-97	23(1)	2	0	0	8
Gary Hulse	Widnes	2005	12(5)	2	0	0	8
	Warrington	2001-04	20(28)	8	0	1	33
Alan Hunte	Salford	2002	19(2)	9	0	0	36
	Warrington	1999-2001	83	49	0	0	196
	Hull	1998	21	7	0	0	28
	St Helens	1996-97	30(2)	28	0	0	112
Konrad Hurrell	Leeds	2019-21	47(5)	23	0	0	92
Alex Hurst	London	2013	8(2)	2	0	0	8
Kieran Hyde	Wakefield	2010-11	11	4	4	0	24
Nick Hyde	Paris	1997	5(5)	1	0	0	4
Chaz I'Anson	Hull KR	2007-10	17(13)	3	0	0	12
Sebastine Ikahihifo	Salford	2020-21	11(16)	0	0	0	0
	Huddersfield	2016-19	45(23)	1	0	0	4
Ryan Ince	Widnes	2016-18	19	11	0	0	44
Greg Inglis	Warrington	2021	2	2	0	0	8
Krisnan Inu	Salford	2019-21	43(3)	20	167	1	415
	Widnes	2018	14	6	21	0	66
	Catalans	2015-17	39	11	3	0	50
Mark Ioane	Leigh	2021	10(5)	2	0	0	8
	London	2019	1(14)	1	0	0	4
Andy Ireland	Hull	1998-99	22(15)	0	0	0	0
	Bradford	1996	1	0	0	0	0
Kevin Iro	St Helens	1999-2001	76	39	0	0	156
	Leeds	1996	16	9	0	0	36
Willie Isa	Wigan	2016-21	133(19)	14	0	0	56
	Widnes	2012-15	44(33)	3	0	0	12
	Castleford	2011	7(2)	6	0	0	24
Andrew Isherwood	Wigan	1998-99	(5)	0	0	0	0
Olu Iwenofu	London	2000-01	2(1)	0	0	0	0
Chico Jackson	Hull	1999	(4)	0	0	0	0
Lee Jackson	Hull	2001-02	37(9)	12	1	0	50
	Leeds	1999-2000	28(24)	7	0	0	28
Michael Jackson	Sheffield	1998-99	17(17)	2	0	0	8
	Halifax	1996-97	27(6)	11	0	0	44
Paul Jackson	Castleford	2003-04, 2010-12	44(30)	5	0	0	20
	Huddersfield	1998, 2005-09	50(73)	4	0	0	16
	Wakefield	1999-2002	57(42)	2	0	0	8
Rob Jackson	Leigh	2005	20(3)	5	0	0	20
	London	2002-04	26(14)	9	0	0	36
Wayne Jackson	Halifax	1996-97	17(5)	2	0	0	8
Aled James	Crusaders	2011	1	0	0	0	0
	Celtic	2009	3(3)	0	0	0	0
	Widnes	2003	1	0	0	0	0
Andy James	Halifax	1996	(4)	0	0	0	0
Jordan James	Wigan	2006, 2014	3(18)	4	0	0	16
	Salford	2012-13	1(40)	6	0	0	24
	Crusaders	2010-11	5(24)	3	0	0	12
	Celtic	2009	17(4)	1	0	0	4
Matt James	Wakefield	2012	(4)	0	0	0	0
	Harlequins	2010	(2)	0	0	0	0
	Bradford	2006-09	1(23)	0	0	0	0
Pascal Jampy	Catalans	2006	4(7)	0	0	0	0
	Paris	1996-97	3(2)	0	0	0	0
Adam Janowski	Harlequins	2008	(1)	0	0	0	0
Ben Jeffries	Bradford	2008-09, 2011-12	76(3)	20	0	0	80
	Wakefield	2003-07, 2010-11	151(10)	70	20	6	326
Mick Jenkins	Hull	2000	24	2	0	0	8
	Gateshead	1999	16	3	0	0	12
Ed Jennings	London	1998-99	1(2)	0	0	0	0
Rod Jensen	Huddersfield	2007-08	26(3)	13	0	0	52
Anthony Jerram	Warrington	2007	(2)	0	0	0	0
Lee Jewitt	Hull KR	2018-19	10(2)	0	0	0	0
	Castleford	2014-16	22(12)	0	0	0	0
	Salford	2007, 2009-13	32(62)	4	0	0	16
	Wigan	2005	(2)	0	0	0	0
Isaac John	Wakefield	2012	13	1	19	0	42
Andrew Johns	Warrington	2005	3	1	12	1	29
Matthew Johns	Wigan	2001	24	3	0	1	13
Andy Johnson	Salford	2004-05	8(26)	7	0	0	28
	Castleford	2002-03	32(16)	11	0	0	44
	London	2000-01	24(21)	12	0	0	48
	Huddersfield	1999	5	1	0	0	4
	Wigan	1996-99	24(20)	19	0	0	76
Bruce Johnson	Widnes	2004-05	(4)	0	0	0	0

PLAYER	CLUB	YEAR	APP	TRIES	GOALS	FG	PTS
Corey Johnson	Leeds	2019, 2021	(2)	0	0	0	0
Dallas Johnson	Catalans	2010	26	1	0	0	4
Greg Johnson	Salford	2014-19	86	36	1	0	146
	Wakefield	2011	12	2	0	0	8
Jack Johnson	Warrington	2015-17, 2019	17	5	0	0	20
	Widnes	2017	3	1	0	0	4
Jason Johnson	St Helens	1997-99	2	0	0	0	0
Josh Johnson	Salford	2019-21	10(15)	1	0	0	4
	Hull KR	2018	2(2)	0	0	0	0
	Huddersfield	2013-16	14(17)	0	0	0	0
Luis Johnson	Hull KR	2019, 2021	21(2)	1	0	0	4
	Warrington	2018-20	1(8)	0	0	0	0
Mark Johnson	Salford	1999-2000	22(9)	16	0	0	64
	Hull	1998	10(1)	4	0	0	16
	Workington	1996	12	4	0	0	16
Nick Johnson	Hull KR	2012	1	0	0	0	0
Nick Johnson	London	2003	(1)	0	0	0	0
Paul Johnson	Crusaders	2011	6(4)	0	0	0	0
	Wakefield	2010	12(3)	4	0	0	16
	Warrington	2007-09	37(9)	17	0	0	68
	Bradford	2004-06	46(8)	19	0	0	76
	Wigan	1996-2003	74(46)	54	0	0	216
Paul Johnson	Widnes	2014	5(11)	0	0	0	0
	Hull	2013	3(16)	0	0	0	0
	Wakefield	2011-12	25(21)	6	0	0	24
	St Helens	2010	(2)	0	0	0	0
Richard Johnson	Bradford	2008	(2)	0	0	0	0
Ben Johnston	Castleford	2012	2	0	0	0	0
Jordan Johnstone	Hull	2020-21	15(16)	1	0	0	4
	Widnes	2016-18	17(13)	1	0	0	4
Tom Johnstone	Wakefield	2015-21	96	74	0	0	296
Ben Jones	Harlequins	2010	(2)	0	0	0	0
Chris Jones	Leigh	2005	1(1)	0	0	0	0
Connor Jones	Salford	2020	7	1	0	0	4
Danny Jones	Halifax	2003	1	0	0	0	0
David Jones	Oldham	1997	14(1)	5	0	0	20
Josh Jones	Huddersfield	2021	22	3	0	0	12
	Hull	2020	7	0	0	0	0
	Salford	2016-19	92(4)	17	0	0	68
	St Helens	2012-15	88(9)	22	0	0	88
Mark Jones	Warrington	1996	8(11)	2	0	0	8
Phil Jones	Leigh	2005	16	8	31	0	94
	Wigan	1999-2001	14(7)	6	25	0	74
Stacey Jones	Catalans	2006-07	39	11	43	3	133
Stephen Jones	Huddersfield	2005	(1)	0	0	0	0
Stuart Jones	Castleford	2009-12	69(27)	14	0	0	56
	Huddersfield	2004-08	96(22)	17	0	0	68
	St Helens	2003	(18)	2	0	0	8
	Wigan	2002	5(3)	1	0	0	4
Ben Jones-Bishop	Wakefield	2016-20	110	61	0	0	244
	Salford	2015	17	12	0	0	48
	Leeds	2008-09, 2011-14	70(2)	46	0	0	184
	Harlequins	2010	17	10	0	0	40
Jamie Jones-Buchanan	Leeds	1999-2019	293(73)	70	1	0	282
Tim Jonkers	Wigan	2006	3(1)	0	0	0	0
	Salford	2004-06	5(11)	0	0	0	0
	St Helens	1999-2004	41(64)	12	0	0	48
Caelum Jordan	Castleford	2021	1	0	0	0	0
Darren Jordan	Wakefield	2003	(1)	0	0	0	0
Josh Jordan-Roberts	Leeds	2017	(1)	0	0	0	0
Phil Joseph	Salford	2016	(12)	0	0	0	0
	Widnes	2013-15	11(38)	1	0	0	4
	Bradford	2012	(6)	0	0	0	0
	Huddersfield	2004	7(6)	0	0	0	0
Max Jowitt	Wakefield	2014-21	74(2)	21	7	0	98
Warren Jowitt	Hull	2003	(2)	0	0	0	0
	Salford	2001-02	17(4)	2	0	0	8
	Wakefield	2000	19(3)	8	0	0	32
	Bradford	1996-99	13(25)	5	0	0	20
Chris Joynt	St Helens	1996-2004	201(14)	68	0	0	272
Benjamin Jullien	Catalans	2018-21	51(12)	14	0	0	56
	Warrington	2016-17	19(7)	4	0	0	16
Gregory Kacala	Paris	1996	7	1	0	0	4
Andy Kain	Castleford	2004, 2006	9(7)	3	10	0	32
Sam Kasiano	Catalans	2019-21	3(52)	10	0	0	40
Antonio Kaufusi	Huddersfield	2014	15(2)	1	0	0	4
	Bradford	2014	4	0	0	0	0
	London	2012-13	44(5)	5	0	0	20
Mal Kaufusi	London	2004	1(3)	0	0	0	0
Ben Kavanagh	Hull KR	2018	13(8)	0	0	0	0
	Wakefield	2015	6(3)	0	0	0	0
	Widnes	2012-15	18(33)	0	0	0	0
Liam Kay	Wakefield	2012-13, 2020-21	22(4)	13	0	0	52
	Toronto	2020	6	1	0	0	4
Ben Kaye	Harlequins	2009-10	2(13)	0	0	0	0
	Leeds	2008	2(2)	1	0	0	4
Elliot Kear	Salford	2020-21	12(1)	1	0	0	4
	London	2019	26	3	0	0	12
	Bradford	2012-14	53(2)	17	0	0	68
	Crusaders	2010-11	16(1)	4	0	0	16
	Celtic	2009	3	0	0	0	0
Brett Kearney	Bradford	2010-14	107	55	0	0	220
Stephen Kearney	Hull	2005	22(2)	5	0	0	20
Damon Keating	Wakefield	2002	7(17)	1	0	0	4
Kris Keating	Hull KR	2014	23	5	0	0	20
Shaun Keating	London	1996	1(3)	0	0	0	0
Mark Keenan	Workington	1996	3(4)	1	0	0	4
Jimmy Keinhorst	Hull KR	2019-21	27(7)	10	0	0	40
	Castleford	2021	(2)	1	0	0	4
	Leeds	2012-18	46(23)	25	0	0	100
	Widnes	2018	3	1	0	0	4
	Wakefield	2014	7	1	0	0	4
Albert Kelly	Hull	2017-20	63(2)	39	0	1	157
	Hull KR	2015-16	37	21	3	0	90
Tony Kemp	Wakefield	1999-2000	15(5)	2	0	1	9
	Leeds	1996-98	23(2)	5	0	2	22
Damien Kennedy	London	2003	5(11)	1	0	0	4
Ian Kenny	St Helens	2004	(1)	0	0	0	0
Sean Kenny	Salford	2016	(4)	0	0	0	0
Shaun Kenny-Dowall	Hull KR	2020-21	39	9	0	0	36
Jason Kent	Leigh	2005	23	1	0	0	4
Liam Kent	Hull	2012-13	1(5)	0	0	0	0
Shane Kenward	Wakefield	1999	28	6	0	0	24
	Salford	1998	1	0	0	0	0
Jason Keough	Paris	1997	2	1	0	0	4
Keiran Kerr	Widnes	2005	6	2	0	0	8
Lee Kershaw	Wakefield	2019-21	25	7	0	0	28
Martin Ketteridge	Halifax	1996	7(5)	0	0	0	0
Ronnie Kettlewell	Warrington	1996	(1)	0	0	0	0
Joe Keyes	Hull KR	2020-21	5(1)	1	6	0	16
	London	2014	7	5	0	0	20
Younes Khattabi	Catalans	2006-08	24(4)	10	0	0	40
Samy Kibula	Warrington	2020	(2)	0	0	0	0
	Wigan	2018	(1)	0	0	0	0
David Kidwell	Warrington	2001-02	14(12)	9	0	0	36
Ben Kilner	Wigan	2020	(1)	0	0	0	0
Andrew King	London	2003	23(1)	15	0	0	60
Dave King	Huddersfield	1998-99	11(17)	2	0	0	8
George King	Hull KR	2020-21	19(5)	1	0	0	4
	Wakefield	2019-20	8(19)	0	0	0	0
	Warrington	2014-18	12(68)	1	0	0	4
James King	Leigh	2005	5(7)	0	0	0	0
Kevin King	Wakefield	2005	8(1)	2	0	0	8
	Castleford	2004	(1)	0	0	0	0
Matt King	Warrington	2008-11	91	58	0	0	232
Paul King	Wakefield	2010-11	10(19)	0	0	1	1
	Hull	1999-2009	136(93)	20	0	1	81
Toby King	Warrington	2014-21	104(7)	37	0	0	148
Jon Luke Kirby	Huddersfield	2019	(3)	0	0	0	0
Andy Kirk	Wakefield	2005	6(3)	1	0	0	4
	Salford	2004	20	5	0	0	20
	Leeds	2001-02	4(4)	0	0	0	0
Ian Kirke	Wakefield	2015	2(2)	1	0	0	4
	Leeds	2006-14	52(132)	10	0	0	40
John Kirkpatrick	London	2004-05	18(1)	5	0	0	20
	St Helens	2001-03	10(11)	10	0	0	40
	Halifax	2003	4	1	0	0	4
Danny Kirmond	Wakefield	2010, 2012-20	147(15)	42	0	0	168
	Huddersfield	2008-11	18(31)	9	0	0	36
Wayne Kitchin	Workington	1996	11(6)	3	17	1	47
Sione Kite	Widnes	2012	6(8)	1	0	0	4
Ian Knott	Leigh	2005	8(1)	2	0	0	8
	Wakefield	2002-03	34(5)	7	79	0	186
	Warrington	1996-2001	68(41)	24	18	0	132
Matt Knowles	Wigan	1996	(3)	0	0	0	0
Michael Knowles	Castleford	2006	(1)	0	0	0	0
Morgan Knowles	St Helens	2016-21	87(48)	23	0	0	92
Phil Knowles	Salford	1997	1	0	0	0	0
Simon Knox	Halifax	1999	(6)	0	0	0	0
	Salford	1998	1(1)	0	0	0	0
	Bradford	1996-98	9(19)	7	0	0	28
Toa Kohe-Love	Warrington	1996-2001, 2005-06	166(3)	90	0	0	360
	Bradford	2004	1(1)	0	0	0	0
	Hull	2002-03	42	19	0	0	76

Super League Players 1996-2021

PLAYER	CLUB	YEAR	APP	TRIES	GOALS	FG	PTS
Paul Koloi	Wigan	1997	1(2)	1	0	0	4
Craig Kopczak	Wakefield	2019-20	25(15)	3	0	0	12
	Salford	2016-18	39(27)	11	0	0	44
	Huddersfield	2013-15	48(37)	6	0	0	24
	Bradford	2006-12	32(83)	10	0	0	40
Michael Korkidas	Wakefield	2003-06, 2009-11	133(36)	15	0	0	60
	Huddersfield	2009	4(1)	1	0	0	4
	Castleford	2008	15(6)	1	0	0	4
	Salford	2007	26(1)	1	0	0	4
Nick Kouparitsas	Harlequins	2011	2(13)	1	0	0	4
Olsi Krasniqi	London	2012-14, 2019	36(35)	3	0	0	12
	Salford	2015-17	8(29)	1	0	0	4
	Harlequins	2010-11	3(20)	1	0	0	4
David Krause	London	1996-97	22(1)	7	0	0	28
Ben Kusto	Huddersfield	2001	21(4)	9	0	1	37
Anthony Laffranchi	St Helens	2012-14	50(18)	19	0	0	76
Matthieu Laguerre	Catalans	2021	9	6	0	0	24
James Laithwaite	Warrington	2013-15	23(22)	1	0	0	4
	Hull KR	2012	1(2)	1	0	0	4
Adrian Lam	Wigan	2001-04	105(2)	40	1	9	171
Brock Lamb	London	2019	6	3	0	1	13
Callum Lancaster	Hull	2014-16	7	9	0	0	36
Jordan Lane	Hull	2018-21	38(23)	9	0	0	36
Mark Lane	Paris	1996	(2)	0	0	0	0
Allan Langer	Warrington	2000-01	47	13	4	0	60
Kevin Langer	London	1996	12(4)	2	0	0	8
Junior Langi	Salford	2005-06	27(7)	7	0	0	28
Samisoni Langi	Catalans	2018-21	80	19	0	0	76
	Leigh	2017	3	1	0	0	4
Chris Langley	Huddersfield	2000-01	18(1)	3	0	0	12
Gareth Langley	St Helens	2006	1	1	3	0	10
Jamie Langley	Hull KR	2014	6(5)	1	0	0	4
	Bradford	2002-13	182(57)	36	0	0	144
Ryan Lannon	Salford	2015-21	43(33)	6	0	0	24
	Hull KR	2019	1(5)	1	0	0	4
Kevin Larroyer	Castleford	2017	2(4)	0	0	0	0
	Hull KR	2014-16	34(13)	9	0	0	36
	Catalans	2012-13	9(10)	6	0	0	24
Andy Last	Hull	1999-2005	16(10)	4	0	0	16
Leilani Latu	Warrington	2020	3	1	0	0	4
Sam Latus	Hull KR	2010-13	34(3)	13	0	0	52
Epalahame Lauaki	Wigan	2012-13	14(16)	2	0	0	8
	Hull	2009-11	3(50)	4	0	0	16
Dale Laughton	Warrington	2002	15(1)	0	0	0	0
	Huddersfield	2000-01	36(2)	4	0	0	16
	Sheffield	1996-99	48(22)	5	0	0	20
Ali Lauitiiti	Wakefield	2012-15	46(31)	16	0	0	64
	Leeds	2004-11	64(117)	58	0	0	232
Quentin Laulu-Togaga'e	Castleford	2018	8(1)	6	0	0	24
Jason Laurence	Salford	1997	1	0	0	0	0
Graham Law	Wakefield	1999-2002	34(30)	6	40	0	104
Neil Law	Wakefield	1999-2002	83	39	0	0	156
	Sheffield	1998	1(1)	1	0	0	4
Dean Lawford	Widnes	2003-04	17(1)	5	2	4	28
	Halifax	2001	1(1)	0	0	0	0
	Leeds	1997-2000	15(8)	2	3	0	14
	Huddersfield	1999	6(1)	0	6	1	13
	Sheffield	1996	9(5)	2	1	1	11
George Lawler	Hull KR	2016, 2018-21	62(11)	5	0	0	20
Johnny Lawless	Halifax	2001-03	73(1)	10	0	0	40
	Hudds-Sheff	2000	19(6)	3	0	0	12
	Sheffield	1996-99	76(4)	11	0	0	44
Michael Lawrence	Huddersfield	2007-21	231(53)	47	0	0	188
Adam Lawton	Salford	2019	1(1)	0	0	0	0
	Widnes	2013-14	2(10)	5	0	0	20
Corentin Le Cam	Catalans	2021	3(1)	0	0	0	0
Charlie Leaeno	Wakefield	2010	7(3)	2	0	0	8
Mark Leafa	Castleford	2008	5(9)	1	0	0	4
	Leigh	2005	28	2	0	0	8
Leroy Leapai	London	1996	2	0	0	0	0
Jim Leatham	Hull	1998-99	20(18)	4	0	0	16
	Leeds	1997	(1)	0	0	0	0
Andy Leathem	Warrington	1999	2(8)	0	0	0	0
	St Helens	1996-98	20(1)	1	0	0	4
Danny Lee	Gateshead	1999	16(2)	0	0	0	0
Jason Lee	Halifax	2001	10(1)	2	0	0	8
Mark Lee	Salford	1997-2000	25(11)	1	0	4	8
Robert Lee	Hull	1999	4(3)	0	0	0	0
Tommy Lee	Hull KR	2018-19	24(6)	2	0	0	8
	St Helens	2017	9(9)	0	0	0	0
	Salford	2014-16	37(5)	4	0	0	16
	London	2013	16(4)	2	0	0	8
	Huddersfield	2012	11(7)	3	0	0	12
	Wakefield	2011	25	6	0	0	24
	Crusaders	2010	3(9)	0	0	0	0
	Hull	2005-09	44(27)	6	0	0	24
Kruise Leeming	Leeds	2020-21	32(4)	10	0	1	41
	Huddersfield	2013-19	49(67)	15	0	0	60
Matty Lees	St Helens	2017-21	33(41)	2	0	0	8
Matthew Leigh	Salford	2000	(6)	0	0	0	0
Chris Leikvoll	Warrington	2004-07	72(18)	4	0	0	16
Jim Lenihan	Huddersfield	1999	19(1)	10	0	0	40
Mark Lennon	Celtic	2009	10(3)	1	8	0	20
	Hull KR	2007	11(4)	5	7	0	34
	Castleford	2001-03	30(21)	10	21	0	82
Tevita Leo-Latu	Wakefield	2006-10	28(49)	10	0	0	40
Gary Lester	Hull	1998-99	46	17	0	0	68
Stuart Lester	Wigan	1997	1(3)	0	0	0	0
Heath L'Estrange	Bradford	2010-13	56(35)	7	0	0	28
Afi Leuila	Oldham	1996-97	17(3)	2	0	0	8
Kylie Leuluai	Leeds	2007-15	182(45)	20	0	0	80
Macgraff Leuluai	Widnes	2012-18	52(64)	5	0	0	20
Phil Leuluai	Salford	2007, 2009-10	7(47)	3	0	0	12
Thomas Leuluai	Wigan	2007-12, 2017-21	282(2)	64	0	1	257
	Harlequins	2006	15(2)	6	0	0	24
	London	2005	20	13	0	0	52
Ricky Leutele	Huddersfield	2021	13	5	0	0	20
	Toronto	2020	6	0	0	0	0
Mikey Lewis	Hull KR	2019-21	17(2)	10	2	0	44
Simon Lewis	Castleford	2001	4	3	0	0	12
Paul Leyland	St Helens	2006	1	0	0	0	0
Jon Liddell	Leeds	2001	1	0	0	0	0
Jason Lidden	Castleford	1997	15(1)	7	0	0	28
Jordan Lilley	Leeds	2015-18	21(11)	2	42	0	92
Danny Lima	Wakefield	2007	(3)	0	0	0	0
	Salford	2006	7(2)	0	0	0	0
	Warrington	2004-06	15(47)	9	0	0	36
	Catalans	2014-15	37(7)	3	1	0	14
Jeff Lima	Wigan	2011-12	24(29)	4	0	0	16
Tom Lineham	Warrington	2016-21	115	70	0	0	280
	Hull	2012-15	61(1)	50	0	0	200
Kane Linnett	Hull KR	2019-21	60(1)	23	0	0	92
Mason Lino	Wakefield	2021	23	5	75	1	171
Jez Litten	Hull KR	2019-21	12(21)	1	0	0	4
	Hull	2017-19	(17)	1	0	0	4
Harry Little	London	2013	2	0	0	0	0
Jack Littlejohn	Salford	2018	15(3)	3	1	0	14
Craig Littler	St Helens	2006	1	1	0	0	4
Stuart Littler	Salford	1998-2002, 2004-07, 2009-10	217(30)	65	0	0	260
Harvey Livett	Salford	2021	18	7	10	0	48
	Hull KR	2019-20	8(5)	3	0	0	12
	Warrington	2017-19	23(15)	13	21	0	94
Peter Livett	Workington	1996	3(1)	0	0	0	0
Rhodri Lloyd	Wigan	2012-13, 2015	3(4)	0	0	0	0
	Widnes	2014	(4)	0	0	0	0
	London	2013	2	0	0	0	0
Garry Lo	Castleford	2018	1	1	0	0	4
Kevin Locke	Wakefield	2015	3	0	0	0	0
	Salford	2014-15	13	6	11	0	46
Jack Logan	Leigh	2021	5	0	0	0	0
	Hull	2014-16, 2018-19, 2021	37(2)	16	0	0	64
Scott Logan	Wigan	2006	10(11)	0	0	0	0
	Hull	2001-03	27(20)	5	0	0	20
Jamahl Lolesi	Huddersfield	2007-10	75(9)	27	0	0	108
Filimone Lolohea	Harlequins	2006	3(6)	0	0	0	0
	London	2005	8(15)	0	0	0	0
Tui Lolohea	Salford	2019-21	50	17	29	1	127
	Leeds	2019	2	2	19	0	46
David Lomax	Huddersfield	2000-01	45(9)	4	0	0	16
	Paris	1997	19(2)	1	0	0	4
Jonny Lomax	St Helens	2009-21	237(2)	105	84	2	590
Dave Long	London	1999	(1)	0	0	0	0
Karl Long	London	2003	(1)	0	0	0	0
	Widnes	2002	4	1	0	0	4
Sean Long	Hull	2010-11	22	6	0	0	24
	St Helens	1997-2009	263(8)	126	826	20	2176
	Wigan	1996-97	1(5)	0	0	0	0
Davide Longo	Bradford	1996	1(3)	0	0	0	0
Ellis Longstaff	Warrington	2020-21	2(7)	0	0	0	0
Gary Lord	Oldham	1996-97	28(12)	3	0	0	12
Paul Loughlin	Huddersfield	1998-99	34(2)	4	4	0	24
	Bradford	1996-97	36(4)	15	8	0	76
Rhys Lovegrove	Hull KR	2007-14	75(74)	19	0	0	76
Karl Lovell	Hudds-Sheff	2000	14	5	0	0	20
	Sheffield	1999	22(4)	8	0	0	32
Will Lovell	London	2012-14, 2019	26(23)	5	0	0	20
James Lowes	Bradford	1996-2003	205	84	2	2	342

192

PLAYER	CLUB	YEAR	APP	TRIES	GOALS	FG	PTS
Laurent Lucchese	Paris	1996	13(5)	2	0	0	8
Sam Luckley	Salford	2021	(10)	0	0	0	0
Robert Lui	Leeds	2019-21	34	11	0	1	45
	Salford	2016-19	84(3)	26	33	0	170
Zebastian Luisi	Harlequins	2006-07	23(2)	4	0	0	16
	London	2004-05	21(1)	7	0	0	28
Keith Lulia	Bradford	2012-13	50	19	0	0	76
Shaun Lunt	Leeds	2012, 2019	15(10)	7	0	0	28
	Hull KR	2015-16, 2018-19	25(18)	11	0	0	44
	Huddersfield	2009-15	73(39)	60	0	0	240
Peter Lupton	Crusaders	2010-11	37(9)	10	0	0	40
	Celtic	2009	16(4)	4	0	0	16
	Castleford	2006, 2008	40	11	0	0	44
	Hull	2003-06	19(26)	10	3	0	46
	London	2000-02	10(15)	2	2	0	12
Darcy Lussick	Salford	2021	(4)	1	0	0	4
Joey Lussick	Salford	2019-20	27(21)	15	4	0	68
Andy Lynch	Castleford	1999-2004, 2014-17	157(54)	17	0	0	68
	Hull	2012-13	39(14)	3	0	0	12
	Bradford	2005-11	159(29)	46	0	0	184
Reece Lyne	Wakefield	2013-21	187(1)	57	0	0	228
	Hull	2010-11	11(1)	2	0	0	8
Jamie Lyon	St Helens	2005-06	54(1)	39	172	0	500
Iliess Macani	London	2013-14	12(3)	4	0	0	16
Duncan MacGillivray	Wakefield	2004-08	75(18)	6	0	0	24
Brad Mackay	Bradford	2000	24(2)	8	0	0	32
Graham Mackay	Hull	2002	27	18	24	0	120
	Bradford	2001	16(3)	12	1	0	50
	Leeds	2000	12(8)	10	2	0	44
Keiron Maddocks	Leigh	2005	1(3)	0	0	0	0
Steve Maden	Leigh	2005	23	9	0	0	36
	Warrington	2002	3	0	0	0	0
Mateaki Mafi	Warrington	1996-97	7(8)	7	0	0	28
Nathan Magee	Castleford	2021	(1)	0	0	0	0
Shaun Magennis	St Helens	2010-12	7(19)	3	0	0	12
Brendan Magnus	London	2000	3	1	0	0	4
Mark Maguire	London	1996-97	11(4)	7	13	0	54
Adam Maher	Hull	2000-03	88(4)	24	0	0	96
	Gateshead	1999	21(5)	3	0	0	12
Lee Maher	Leeds	1996	4(1)	0	0	0	0
Will Maher	Hull KR	2020-21	17(12)	0	0	0	0
	Castleford	2014-19	5(30)	1	0	0	4
Shaun Mahony	Paris	1997	5	0	0	0	0
Hutch Maiava	Hull	2007	(19)	1	0	0	4
David Maiden	Hull	2000-01	32(10)	11	0	0	44
	Gateshead	1999	5(16)	8	0	0	32
Craig Makin	Salford	1999-2001	24(20)	2	0	0	8
Tommy Makinson	St Helens	2011-21	233(5)	132	128	1	785
Brady Malam	Wigan	2000	5(20)	1	0	0	4
Dominic Maloney	Hull	2009	(7)	0	0	0	0
Francis Maloney	Castleford	1998-99, 2003-04	71(7)	24	33	3	165
	Salford	2001-02	45(1)	26	5	0	114
	Wakefield	2000	11	1	1	0	6
	Oldham	1996-97	39(2)	12	91	2	232
James Maloney	Catalans	2020-21	38	7	169	5	371
Jake Mamo	Warrington	2019-21	42(6)	27	0	0	108
	Huddersfield	2017-18	23	17	0	0	68
Dom Manfredi	Wigan	2013-16, 2018-21	73	55	0	0	220
	Salford	2014	1	2	0	0	8
George Mann	Warrington	1997	14(5)	1	0	0	4
	Leeds	1996	11(4)	2	0	0	8
Dane Manning	Leeds	2009	(1)	0	0	0	0
Josh Mantellato	Hull KR	2015-16	26	16	88	0	240
Misili Manu	Widnes	2005	1	0	0	0	0
Sika Manu	Hull	2016-19	90(4)	10	0	0	40
Willie Manu	St Helens	2013-14	35(11)	9	0	0	36
	Hull	2007-12	133(18)	33	0	0	132
	Castleford	2006	19(4)	9	0	0	36
Manase Manuokafoa	Widnes	2015-17	3(54)	3	0	0	12
	Bradford	2012-14	49(21)	3	0	0	12
Darren Mapp	Celtic	2009	9(2)	1	0	0	4
David March	Wakefield	1999-2007	164(23)	34	126	0	388
Paul March	Wakefield	1999-2001, 2007	42(31)	17	23	0	114
	Huddersfield	2003-06	71(19)	17	36	1	141
Nick Mardon	London	1997-98	14	2	0	0	8
Thibaut Margalet	Catalans	2013-18	1(22)	0	0	0	0
Remy Marginet	Catalans	2011	2	0	9	0	18
Antoni Maria	Catalans	2012-16, 2018-20	10(57)	0	0	0	0
	Hull KR	2019	2(3)	0	0	0	0
	Leigh	2017	2(6)	0	0	0	0
Frankie Mariano	Castleford	2014-16	14(21)	8	0	0	32
	Wakefield	2011-13	41(12)	20	0	0	80
	Hull KR	2010	(3)	0	0	0	0
Oliver Marns	Halifax	1996-2002	54(19)	23	0	0	92
Paul Marquet	Warrington	2002	23(2)	0	0	0	0
Callum Marriott	Salford	2011	(1)	0	0	0	0
Iain Marsh	Salford	1998-2001	1(4)	0	0	0	0
Lee Marsh	Salford	2001-02	3(4)	0	0	0	0
Matty Marsh	Hull KR	2015-16, 2018	18(4)	3	0	0	12
Stefan Marsh	Widnes	2012-18	122	56	21	0	266
	Wigan	2010-11	12	3	0	0	12
Liam Marshall	Wigan	2017-21	89	65	5	0	270
Richard Marshall	Leigh	2005	4(16)	0	0	0	0
	London	2002-03	33(11)	1	0	0	4
	Huddersfield	2000-01	35(14)	1	0	0	4
	Halifax	1996-99	38(34)	2	0	0	8
Brad Martin	Castleford	2020-21	5(4)	1	0	0	4
Charlie Martin	Castleford	2013	(6)	0	0	0	0
Jason Martin	Paris	1997	15(2)	3	0	0	12
Rhyse Martin	Leeds	2019-21	43(3)	7	166	0	360
Scott Martin	Salford	1997-99	32(18)	8	0	0	32
Tony Martin	Hull	2012	10	1	0	0	4
	Crusaders	2010-11	40(1)	14	1	0	58
	Wakefield	2008-09	33	10	33	0	106
	London	1996-97, 2001-03	97(1)	36	170	1	485
Ugo Martin	Catalans	2018	1	0	0	0	0
Mick Martindale	Halifax	1996	(4)	0	0	0	0
Sebastien Martins	Catalans	2006, 2009-11	(21)	2	0	0	8
Shay Martyn	St Helens	2021	1	0	3	0	6
Tommy Martyn	St Helens	1996-2003	125(20)	87	63	12	486
Dean Marwood	Workington	1996	9(6)	0	22	0	44
Martin Masella	Warrington	2001	10(14)	5	0	0	20
	Wakefield	2000	14(8)	4	0	0	16
	Leeds	1997-1999	59(5)	1	0	0	4
Colin Maskill	Castleford	1996	8	1	1	0	6
Mose Masoe	Hull KR	2018-19	28(18)	6	0	0	24
	St Helens	2014-15	17(39)	10	0	0	40
Keith Mason	Castleford	2006, 2013	11(6)	0	0	0	0
	Huddersfield	2006-12	118(14)	4	0	0	16
	St Helens	2003-05	33(23)	4	0	0	16
	Wakefield	2000-01	5(17)	0	0	0	0
Nathan Mason	Leigh	2021	4(4)	1	0	0	4
	London	2019	5(10)	1	0	0	4
	Huddersfield	2013, 2015-17	3(26)	3	0	0	12
Willie Mason	Catalans	2016	6(8)	1	0	0	4
	Hull KR	2011	6	1	0	0	4
Samy Masselot	Wakefield	2011	(1)	0	0	0	0
Nathan Massey	Castleford	2008-21	178(67)	10	0	0	40
Suaia Matagi	Castleford	2021	2(10)	0	0	0	0
	Huddersfield	2018-20	39(9)	3	0	0	12
Nesiasi Mataitonga	London	2014	11(1)	1	0	0	4
Peter Mata'utia	Castleford	2018-21	63	11	58	1	161
Sione Mata'utia	St Helens	2021	17(2)	5	0	0	20
Vila Matautia	St Helens	1996-2001	31(68)	9	0	0	36
Feleti Mateo	London	2005	4(10)	1	0	0	4
Barrie-Jon Mather	Castleford	1998, 2000-02	50(12)	21	0	0	84
Richard Mathers	Wakefield	2012-14	71	24	0	0	96
	Castleford	2011	21(1)	7	0	0	28
	Warrington	2002, 2009-10	42(3)	11	0	0	44
	Wigan	2008-09	23(1)	2	0	0	8
	Leeds	2002-06	85(2)	26	0	0	104
Jamie Mathiou	Leeds	1997-2001	31(82)	3	0	0	12
Masi Matongo	Hull	2015, 2017-20	16(38)	3	0	0	12
Terry Matterson	London	1996-98	46	15	90	6	246
Manu Ma'u	Hull	2020-21	28	4	0	0	16
Vic Mauro	Salford	2013	1(7)	1	0	0	4
Luke May	Harlequins	2009-10	(3)	0	0	0	0
Casey Mayberry	Halifax	2000	1(1)	0	0	0	0
Chris Maye	Halifax	2003	3(4)	0	0	0	0
Judah Mazive	Wakefield	2016	2	1	0	0	4
Joe Mbu	Harlequins	2006-09	33(20)	3	0	0	12
	London	2003-05	29(19)	4	0	0	16
Danny McAllister	Gateshead	1999	3(3)	1	0	0	4
	Sheffield	1996-97	33(7)	10	0	0	40
John McAtee	St Helens	1996	2(1)	0	0	0	0

PLAYER	CLUB	YEAR	APP	TRIES	GOALS	FG	PTS
Nathan McAvoy	Bradford	1998-2002, 2007	83(31)	46	0	0	184
	Wigan	2006	15(2)	5	0	0	20
	Salford	1997-98, 2004-05	57(4)	18	0	0	72
Tyrone McCarthy	Leigh	2021	8(3)	0	0	0	0
	Salford	2017-20	41(20)	8	2	0	36
	Hull KR	2015	20(1)	4	0	0	16
	Warrington	2009-13	12(24)	2	0	0	8
	Wakefield	2011	2(5)	1	0	0	4
Louie McCarthy-Scarsbrook	St Helens	2011-21	142(146)	56	0	0	224
	Harlequins	2006-10	41(50)	17	0	0	68
Dave McConnell	London	2003	(4)	0	0	0	0
	St Helens	2001-02	3(2)	4	0	0	16
Loui McConnell	Leeds	2020	(2)	0	0	0	0
Robbie McCormack	Wigan	1998	24	2	0	0	8
Josh McCrone	Toronto	2020	6	1	0	0	4
Steve McCurrie	Leigh	2005	7(3)	1	0	0	4
	Widnes	2002-04	55(22)	10	0	0	40
	Warrington	1998-2001	69(26)	31	0	0	124
Barrie McDermott	Leeds	1996-2005	163(69)	28	0	0	112
Brian McDermott	Bradford	1996-2002	138(32)	33	0	0	132
Ryan McDonald	Widnes	2002-03	6(4)	0	0	0	0
Wayne McDonald	Huddersfield	2005-06	11(23)	1	0	0	4
	Wigan	2005	(4)	0	0	0	0
	Leeds	2002-05	34(47)	14	0	0	56
	St Helens	2001	7(11)	4	0	0	16
	Hull	2000	5(8)	4	0	0	16
	Wakefield	1999	9(17)	8	0	0	32
James McDonnell	Wigan	2020-21	3	1	0	0	4
Shannon McDonnell							
	St Helens	2014-16	28	15	0	0	60
	Hull	2013	19	2	0	0	8
	Hull KR	2012	21	6	0	0	24
Craig McDowell	Huddersfield	2003	(1)	0	0	0	0
	Warrington	2002	(1)	0	0	0	0
	Bradford	2000	(1)	0	0	0	0
Wes McGibbon	Halifax	1999	1	0	0	0	0
Jermaine McGillvary							
	Huddersfield	2010-21	259(1)	181	0	0	724
Dean McGilvray	Salford	2009-10	14	4	0	0	16
	St Helens	2006-08	5(1)	1	0	0	4
Billy McGinty	Workington	1996	1	0	0	0	0
Ryan McGoldrick	Salford	2013	19(1)	3	0	1	13
	Hull	2012	8	1	0	0	4
	Castleford	2006, 2008-12	129(5)	24	11	0	118
Kevin McGuinness	Salford	2004-07	63(3)	11	0	0	44
Casey McGuire	Catalans	2007-10	87(4)	27	0	0	108
Danny McGuire	Hull KR	2018-19	36	9	1	3	41
	Leeds	2001-17	331(39)	238	0	6	958
Gary McGuirk	Workington	1996	(4)	0	0	0	0
Michael McIlorum	Catalans	2018-21	61(2)	6	0	0	24
	Wigan	2007-17	156(54)	22	0	0	88
Darnell McIntosh	Huddersfield	2017-21	91(1)	43	12	0	196
Richard McKell	Castleford	1997-98	22(7)	2	0	0	8
Chris McKenna	Bradford	2006-07	40(7)	7	0	0	28
	Leeds	2003-05	65(4)	18	0	0	72
Phil McKenzie	Workington	1996	4	0	0	0	0
Chris McKinney	Oldham	1996-97	4(9)	2	0	0	8
Wade McKinnon	Hull	2012	10	4	0	0	16
Callum McLelland	Leeds	2019-21	10(3)	1	0	0	4
Mark McLinden	Harlequins	2006-08	46(1)	20	0	1	81
	London	2005	22(3)	8	0	0	32
Mike McMeeken	Catalans	2021	23	10	0	0	40
	Castleford	2015-20	118(13)	30	0	0	120
	London	2012-14	25(9)	5	0	0	20
Shayne McMenemy							
	Hull	2003-07	80(8)	12	0	0	48
	Halifax	2001-03	63	11	0	0	44
Andy McNally	London	2004	5(3)	0	0	0	0
	Castleford	2001, 2003	2(5)	1	0	0	4
Gregg McNally	Leigh	2017	9	3	0	0	12
	Huddersfield	2011	1	0	6	0	12
Ben McNamara	Hull	2020-21	10(5)	1	4	0	12
Steve McNamara	Huddersfield	2001, 2003	41(9)	3	134	1	281
	Wakefield	2000	15(2)	2	32	0	72
	Bradford	1996-99	90(3)	14	348	7	759
Paul McNicholas	Hull	2004-05	28(12)	4	0	0	16
Neil McPherson	Salford	1997	(1)	0	0	0	0
Shannan McPherson							
	Salford	2012-14	20(11)	0	0	0	0
Chris McQueen	Huddersfield	2020-21	24(3)	6	0	0	24
Duncan McRae	London	1996	11(2)	3	0	1	13
Paul McShane	Castleford	2015-21	135(23)	22	50	1	189
	Wakefield	2014-15	39(9)	5	0	0	20
	Leeds	2009-13	17(38)	12	0	0	48
	Widnes	2012	6(5)	3	4	0	20
	Hull	2010	(4)	0	0	0	0
Derek McVey	St Helens	1996-97	28(4)	6	1	0	26
Dallas Mead	Warrington	1997	2	0	0	0	0
David Mead	Catalans	2018-20	51	23	0	0	92
James Meadows	London	2019	1	0	0	0	0
Robbie Mears	Leigh	2005	8(6)	0	0	0	0
	Leeds	2001	23	6	0	0	24
Paul Medley	Bradford	1996-98	6(35)	9	0	0	36
Francis Meli	Salford	2014	16	11	0	0	44
	St Helens	2006-13	194(1)	122	0	0	488
Vince Mellars	Wakefield	2012-13	21(5)	4	0	0	16
	Crusaders	2010-11	46	17	0	0	68
Chris Melling	London	2012-13	25(12)	5	2	0	24
	Harlequins	2007-11	100(11)	33	6	0	144
	Wigan	2004-05	8(2)	1	3	0	10
Alex Mellor	Leeds	2020-21	23(1)	4	0	0	16
	Huddersfield	2017-19	65(10)	19	0	0	76
	Bradford	2013-14	(10)	0	0	0	0
Joe Mellor	Leigh	2021	15	3	0	0	12
	Toronto	2020	2	0	0	0	0
	Widnes	2012-18	134(1)	46	0	1	185
	Wigan	2012	1(1)	1	0	0	4
	Harlequins	2011	(1)	0	0	0	0
Paul Mellor	Castleford	2003-04	36(3)	18	0	0	72
James Mendeika	London	2013	4(2)	2	0	0	8
Craig Menkins	Paris	1997	4(5)	0	0	0	0
Luke Menzies	Hull KR	2008	(1)	0	0	0	0
Steve Menzies	Catalans	2011-13	61(6)	30	0	0	120
	Bradford	2009-10	52(1)	24	1	0	98
Gary Mercer	Castleford	2002	(1)	0	0	0	0
	Leeds	1996-97, 2001	40(2)	9	0	0	36
	Warrington	2001	18	2	0	0	8
	Halifax	1998-2001	73(2)	16	0	0	64
Trent Merrin	Leeds	2019	27	4	0	0	16
Tony Mestrov	London	1996-97, 2001	59(8)	4	0	0	16
	Wigan	1998-2000	39(39)	3	0	0	12
Keiran Meyer	London	1996	4	1	0	0	4
Brad Meyers	Bradford	2005-06	40(11)	13	0	0	52
Ronan Michael	Huddersfield	2020	(1)	0	0	0	0
Steve Michaels	Hull	2015-17	68(1)	26	0	0	104
Gary Middlehurst	Widnes	2004	(2)	0	0	0	0
Simon Middleton	Castleford	1996-97	19(3)	8	0	0	32
Constantine Mika	Hull KR	2012-13	45(4)	9	0	0	36
Daryl Millard	Catalans	2011-14	91	38	1	0	154
	Wakefield	2010-11	21(1)	11	0	0	44
Shane Millard	Wigan	2007	19(6)	3	0	0	12
	Leeds	2006	6(21)	3	0	0	12
	Widnes	2003-05	69	23	0	0	92
	London	1998-2001	72(14)	11	0	0	46
Jack Miller	Huddersfield	2013	1	0	1	0	2
Jacob Miller	Wakefield	2015-21	154(3)	51	17	8	246
	Hull	2013-14	20	6	9	0	42
Grant Millington	Castleford	2012-21	155(75)	33	0	0	132
David Mills	Harlequins	2006-07, 2010	25(32)	2	0	0	8
	Hull KR	2008-09	20(11)	1	0	0	4
	Widnes	2002-05	17(77)	8	0	0	32
Lewis Mills	Celtic	2009	(4)	0	0	0	0
Adam Milner	Castleford	2010-21	163(92)	36	1	0	146
Lee Milner	Halifax	1999	(1)	0	0	0	0
Rowan Milnes	Hull KR	2020-21	12(2)	3	4	0	20
Hakim Miloudi	Toronto	2020	5(1)	1	0	0	4
	Hull	2018-19	13(2)	5	1	0	22
Elliot Minchella	Hull KR	2020-21	8(9)	3	0	0	12
	Leeds	2013-14	(6)	1	0	0	4
Mark Minichiello	Hull	2015-19	118(4)	20	0	0	80
Greg Minikin	Hull KR	2020-21	23	10	0	0	40
	Castleford	2016-19	89(2)	39	0	0	156
Thomas Minns	Hull KR	2016, 2018	24(1)	14	0	0	56
	London	2014	23	6	0	0	24
	Leeds	2013	2(1)	1	0	0	4
John Minto	London	1996	13	4	0	0	16
Lee Mitchell	Castleford	2012	13(10)	2	0	0	8
	Warrington	2007-11	8(27)	4	0	0	16
	Harlequins	2011	11(1)	1	0	0	4
Sam Moa	Catalans	2017-20	68(6)	6	0	0	24
	Hull	2009-12	29(44)	6	0	0	24
Martin Moana	Salford	2004	6(3)	1	0	0	4
	Halifax	1996-2001, 2003	126(22)	62	0	1	249
	Wakefield	2002	19(2)	10	0	0	40
	Huddersfield	2001	3(3)	2	0	0	8

PLAYER	CLUB	YEAR	APP	TRIES	GOALS	FG	PTS
Adam Mogg	Catalans	2007-10	74	19	0	1	77
Jon Molloy	Wakefield	2013-16	25(18)	5	0	0	20
	Huddersfield	2011-12	2(1)	0	0	0	0
Steve Molloy	Huddersfield	2000-01	26(20)	3	0	0	12
	Sheffield	1998-99	32(17)	3	0	0	12
Chris Molyneux	Huddersfield	2000-01	1(18)	0	0	0	0
	Sheffield	1999	1(2)	0	0	0	0
Joel Monaghan	Castleford	2016-17	29(3)	13	0	0	52
	Warrington	2011-15	127	125	2	0	504
Michael Monaghan	Warrington	2008-14	143(28)	31	0	4	128
Joel Moon	Leeds	2013-18	136(1)	61	0	0	244
	Salford	2012	17	9	0	0	36
Adrian Moore	Huddersfield	1998-99	1(4)	0	0	0	0
Brandon Moore	Huddersfield	2020	4	0	0	0	0
Danny Moore	London	2000	7	0	0	0	0
	Wigan	1998-99	49(3)	18	0	0	72
Gareth Moore	Wakefield	2011	5	1	14	1	33
Jason Moore	Workington	1996	(5)	0	0	0	0
Richard Moore	Wakefield	2007-10, 2014	52(57)	10	0	0	40
	Leeds	2012-13	3(27)	1	0	0	4
	Crusaders	2011	11(10)	1	0	0	4
	Leigh	2005	2(5)	0	0	0	0
	Bradford	2002-04	1(26)	0	0	0	0
	London	2002, 2004	5(9)	2	0	0	8
Scott Moore	Wakefield	2015-16	12(2)	2	0	0	8
	Castleford	2008, 2015	24(6)	2	0	0	8
	London	2014	26	3	0	0	12
	Huddersfield	2009, 2012	29(7)	9	0	0	36
	Widnes	2012	3(3)	0	0	0	0
	St Helens	2004-07, 2010-11	29(37)	9	0	0	36
Junior Moors	Castleford	2015-20	46(63)	18	0	0	72
Dennis Moran	Wigan	2005-06	39	17	1	1	71
	London	2001-04	107(2)	74	2	5	305
Kieran Moran	Hull KR	2016	(5)	0	0	0	0
Pat Moran	Warrington	2019	(1)	0	0	0	0
Ryan Morgan	London	2019	21	5	0	0	20
	St Helens	2017-18	46	22	0	0	88
Willie Morganson	Sheffield	1997-98	18(12)	5	3	0	26
Paul Moriarty	Halifax	1996	3(2)	0	0	0	0
Adrian Morley	Salford	2014-15	31(14)	2	0	0	8
	Warrington	2007-13	135(21)	8	0	0	32
	Bradford	2005	2(4)	0	0	0	0
	Leeds	1996-2000	95(14)	25	0	0	100
Chris Morley	Salford	1999	3(5)	0	0	0	0
	Warrington	1998	2(8)	0	0	0	0
	St Helens	1996-97	21(16)	4	0	0	16
Frazer Morris	Wakefield	2016	(1)	0	0	0	0
Glenn Morrison	Wakefield	2010-11	43(1)	9	0	0	36
	Bradford	2007-09	48(2)	19	0	0	76
Iain Morrison	Hull KR	2007	5(6)	1	0	0	4
	Huddersfield	2003-05	11(23)	0	0	0	0
	London	2001	(1)	0	0	0	0
Daniel Mortimer	Leigh	2017	3	0	0	0	0
Dale Morton	Wakefield	2009-11	22(3)	8	5	0	42
Gareth Morton	Hull KR	2007	7(4)	3	23	0	58
	Leeds	2001-02	1(1)	0	0	0	0
Kieren Moss	Hull KR	2018	2(1)	4	0	0	16
Lee Mossop	Salford	2017-21	68(3)	6	0	0	24
	Wigan	2008-13, 2015-16	80(65)	11	0	0	44
	Huddersfield	2009	1(4)	1	0	0	4
Aaron Moule	Salford	2006-07	45	17	0	0	68
	Widnes	2004-05	29	12	0	0	48
Bradley Moules	Wakefield	2016	(1)	0	0	0	0
Wilfred Moulinec	Paris	1996	1	0	0	0	0
Gregory Mounis	Catalans	2006-16	149(105)	27	19	0	146
Arthur Mourgue	Catalans	2018-21	12(17)	8	16	0	64
Mark Moxon	Huddersfield	1998-2001	20(5)	1	0	1	5
Robbie Mulhern	Warrington	2021	1(17)	0	0	0	0
	Hull KR	2016, 2018-20	43(27)	4	0	0	16
	Leeds	2014-15	(5)	0	0	0	0
Anthony Mullally	Toronto	2020	2(4)	0	0	0	0
	Leeds	2016-18	10(48)	9	0	0	36
	Wakefield	2015	(2)	0	0	0	0
	Huddersfield	2013-15	12(24)	5	0	0	20
	Bradford	2014	1(5)	0	0	0	0
	Widnes	2012	(9)	0	0	0	0
Jake Mullaney	Salford	2014	12	2	24	0	56
Craig Mullen	Leigh	2021	9(4)	1	13	0	30
	Wigan	2018	1(1)	0	0	0	0
Brett Mullins	Leeds	2001	5(3)	1	0	0	4
Damian Munro	Widnes	2002	8(2)	1	0	0	4
	Halifax	1996-97	9(6)	8	0	0	32
Matt Munro	Oldham	1996-97	26(5)	8	0	0	32
Ben Murdoch-Masila	Warrington	2018-20	23(35)	13	0	0	52
	Salford	2016-17	46(1)	15	0	0	60
Craig Murdock	Salford	2000	(2)	0	0	0	0
	Hull	1998-99	21(6)	8	0	2	34
	Wigan	1996-98	18(17)	14	0	0	56
Aaron Murphy	Huddersfield	2012-20	169(6)	71	0	0	284
	Wakefield	2008-11	57(2)	12	0	0	48
Jack Murphy	Wigan	2012, 2014	3	1	0	0	4
	Salford	2013	10	3	1	0	14
Jamie Murphy	Crusaders	2011	(2)	0	0	0	0
Jobe Murphy	Bradford	2013	(4)	0	0	0	0
Justin Murphy	Catalans	2006-08	59	49	0	0	196
	Widnes	2004	5	1	0	0	4
Daniel Murray	Hull KR	2019-20	15(8)	0	0	0	0
	Salford	2017-19	14(14)	2	0	0	8
Doc Murray	Warrington	1997	(2)	0	0	0	0
	Wigan	1997	6(2)	0	0	0	0
Scott Murrell	Hull KR	2007-12	114(24)	24	26	1	149
	Leeds	2005	(1)	0	0	0	0
	London	2004	3(3)	2	0	0	8
Muizz Mustapha	Hull KR	2021	1(9)	0	0	0	0
	Leeds	2020	(2)	0	0	0	0
David Mycoe	Sheffield	1996-97	12(13)	1	0	0	4
Richie Myler	Leeds	2018-21	75(4)	27	6	1	121
	Catalans	2016-17	40	21	2	0	88
	Warrington	2010-15	127(4)	69	1	1	279
	Salford	2009	18	11	0	0	44
Rob Myler	Oldham	1996-97	19(2)	6	0	0	24
Stephen Myler	Salford	2006	4(8)	1	15	0	34
	Widnes	2003-05	35(14)	8	74	0	180
Vinny Myler	Salford	2004	(4)	0	0	0	0
	Bradford	2003	(1)	0	0	0	0
Matt Nable	London	1997	2(2)	1	0	0	4
Kevin Naiqama	St Helens	2019-21	67	36	0	0	144
Brad Nairn	Workington	1996	14	4	0	0	16
Ben Nakubuwai	Salford	2018-19	7(28)	2	0	0	8
Frank Napoli	London	2000	14(6)	2	0	0	8
Carlo Napolitano	Salford	2000	(3)	1	0	0	4
Stephen Nash	Castleford	2012	3(4)	0	0	0	0
	Salford	2007, 2009	2(18)	1	0	0	4
	Widnes	2005	4(1)	0	0	0	0
Curtis Naughton	Leigh	2017	5	3	0	0	12
	Hull	2015-16	26	13	1	0	54
	Bradford	2013	1	0	0	0	0
Ratu Naulago	Hull	2019-20	30	20	0	0	80
Romain Navarrete	Wakefield	2020	3(7)	0	0	0	0
	Wigan	2017-19	36(20)	0	0	0	0
	Catalans	2016-17	1(12)	0	0	0	0
Jim Naylor	Halifax	2000	7(6)	2	0	0	8
Scott Naylor	Salford	1997-98, 2004	30(1)	9	0	0	36
	Bradford	1999-2003	127(1)	51	0	0	204
Adam Neal	Salford	2010-13	17(28)	0	0	0	0
Mike Neal	Salford	1998	(1)	0	0	0	0
	Oldham	1996-97	6(4)	3	0	0	12
Jonathan Neill	Huddersfield	1998-99	20(11)	0	0	0	0
	St Helens	1996	1	0	0	0	0
Chris Nero	Salford	2011-13	31(16)	7	0	0	28
	Bradford	2008-10	65(5)	24	0	0	96
	Huddersfield	2004-07	97(8)	38	0	0	152
Jason Netherton	Hull KR	2007-14	60(74)	4	0	0	16
	London	2003-04	6	0	0	0	0
	Halifax	2002	2(3)	0	0	0	0
	Leeds	2001	(3)	0	0	0	0
Kirk Netherton	Castleford	2009-10	5(23)	3	0	0	12
	Hull KR	2007-08	9(15)	2	0	0	8
Paul Newlove	Castleford	2004	5	1	0	0	4
	St Helens	1996-2003	162	106	0	0	424
Richard Newlove	Wakefield	2003	17(5)	8	0	0	32
Harry Newman	Leeds	2017-21	49	10	2	0	44
Clint Newton	Hull KR	2008-11	90(3)	37	0	0	148
Terry Newton	Wakefield	2010	(2)	0	0	0	0
	Bradford	2006-09	83(6)	26	0	0	104
	Wigan	2000-05	157(9)	62	0	0	248
	Leeds	1996-1999	55(14)	4	0	0	16
Gene Ngamu	Huddersfield	1999-2000	29(2)	9	67	0	170
Danny Nicklas	Hull	2010, 2012	2(8)	0	0	0	0
Sonny Nickle	St Helens	1999-2002	86(18)	14	0	0	56
	Bradford	1996-98	25(16)	9	0	0	36
Jason Nicol	Salford	2000-02	52(7)	11	0	0	44
Tawera Nikau	Warrington	2000-01	51	7	0	0	28
Tom Nisbet	Leigh	2021	1	0	0	0	0
	St Helens	2020	1	0	0	0	0
Rob Nolan	Hull	1998-99	20(11)	6	0	0	24

Super League Players 1996-2021

PLAYER	CLUB	YEAR	APP	TRIES	GOALS	FG	PTS
Paul Noone	Harlequins	2006	5(2)	0	0	0	0
	Warrington	2000-06	60(59)	12	20	0	88
Chris Norman	Halifax	2003	13(3)	2	0	0	8
Dan Norman	St Helens	2021	(1)	0	0	0	0
	Salford	2021	(3)	1	0	0	4
	Widnes	2018	(1)	0	0	0	0
Paul Norman	Oldham	1996	(1)	0	0	0	0
Andy Northey	St Helens	1996-97	8(17)	2	0	0	8
Danny Nutley	Castleford	2006	28	3	0	0	12
	Warrington	1998-2001	94(1)	3	0	0	12
Tony Nuttall	Oldham	1996-97	1(7)	0	0	0	0
Frank-Paul Nuuausala							
	Wigan	2016-18	34(8)	2	0	0	8
Levy Nzoungou	Hull	2019	(1)	0	0	0	0
	Salford	2018	(3)	0	0	0	0
Will Oakes	Hull KR	2016, 2018-19	12	5	0	0	20
Adam O'Brien	Huddersfield	2017-21	51(39)	16	0	0	64
	Bradford	2011-14	12(29)	6	0	0	24
Clinton O'Brien	Wakefield	2003	(2)	0	0	0	0
Gareth O'Brien	Castleford	2013, 2020-21	19	3	10	2	34
	Toronto	2020	4	1	2	0	8
	Salford	2016-18	49(3)	12	105	2	260
	Warrington	2011-15	48(3)	16	69	3	205
	St Helens	2013	7	0	25	0	50
	Widnes	2012	4	0	15	0	30
Sam Obst	Hull	2011	17(6)	6	0	0	24
	Wakefield	2005-11	100(28)	40	7	0	174
Jamie O'Callaghan	London	2012-14	44(2)	4	0	0	16
	Harlequins	2008-11	54(3)	12	0	0	48
Eamon O'Carroll	Widnes	2012-17	58(11)	3	0	0	12
	Hull	2012	1(9)	0	0	0	0
	Wigan	2006-11	2(59)	3	0	0	12
Jarrod O'Connor	Leeds	2020-21	8(7)	0	2	0	4
Matt O'Connor	Paris	1997	11(4)	1	26	2	58
Terry O'Connor	Widnes	2005	25	2	0	0	8
	Wigan	1996-2004	177(45)	9	0	0	36
Jarrod O'Doherty	Huddersfield	2003	26	3	0	0	12
David O'Donnell	Paris	1997	21	3	0	0	12
Luke O'Donnell	Huddersfield	2011-13	22(2)	2	0	0	8
Martin Offiah	Salford	2000-01	41	20	0	2	82
	London	1996-99	29(3)	21	0	0	84
	Wigan	1996	8	7	0	0	28
Jacob Ogden	London	2019	2	0	0	0	0
Mark O'Halloran	London	2004-05	34(3)	10	0	0	40
Ryan O'Hara	Hull KR	2012	8(7)	1	0	0	4
	Crusaders	2010-11	41(8)	3	0	0	12
	Celtic	2009	27	3	0	0	12
Hefin O'Hare	Huddersfield	2001, 2003-05	72(10)	27	0	0	108
Edwin Okanga-Ajwang							
	Salford	2013	2	0	0	0	0
Hitro Okesene	Hull	1998	21(1)	0	0	0	0
Anderson Okiwe	Sheffield	1997	1	0	0	0	0
Tom Olbison	Toronto	2020	3(3)	0	0	0	0
	Widnes	2017-18	18(22)	4	0	0	16
	Bradford	2009-14	55(26)	11	0	0	44
Michael Oldfield	Catalans	2014-15	41	28	0	0	112
Mikolaj Oledzki	Leeds	2017-21	40(31)	7	0	0	28
Jamie Olejnik	Paris	1997	11	8	0	0	32
Aaron Ollett	Hull KR	2013-15	5(16)	1	0	0	4
Kevin O'Loughlin	Halifax	1997-98	2(4)	0	0	0	0
	St Helens	1997	(3)	0	0	0	0
Sean O'Loughlin	Wigan	2002-20	371(32)	71	3	2	292
Derrell Olpherts	Castleford	2020-21	34	16	0	0	64
	Salford	2018-19	35	11	0	0	44
Mark O'Meley	Hull	2010-13	70(13)	13	0	0	52
Brad O'Neill	Wakefield	2021	1(7)	0	0	0	0
Jacques O'Neill	Castleford	2019-21	2(25)	3	0	0	12
Jules O'Neill	Widnes	2003-05	57(3)	14	158	7	379
	Wakefield	2005	10(2)	2	4	0	16
	Wigan	2002-03	29(1)	12	72	0	192
Julian O'Neill	Widnes	2002-05	57(39)	3	0	0	12
	Wakefield	2001	24(1)	2	0	0	8
	St Helens	1997-2000	95(8)	5	0	0	20
Mark O'Neill	Hull KR	2007	17	5	0	0	20
	Leeds	2006	1(8)	0	0	0	0
Steve O'Neill	Gateshead	1999	1(1)	0	0	0	0
Tom O'Reilly	Warrington	2001-02	8(6)	1	0	0	4
Matt Orford	Bradford	2010	12	3	31	2	76
Jack Ormondroyd	Salford	2020-21	16(8)	2	0	0	8
	Leeds	2017-18	3(9)	0	0	0	0
Gene Ormsby	Huddersfield	2016-17	8	4	0	0	16
	Warrington	2014-16	37	26	0	0	104
Chris Orr	Huddersfield	1998	19(3)	2	0	0	8
Danny Orr	Castleford	1997-2003, 2011-12	197(23)	75	308	3	919
	Harlequins	2007-10	90(4)	13	96	0	244
	Wigan	2004-06	66(2)	18	12	0	96
Gareth Owen	Salford	2010, 2012-13	4(32)	6	0	0	24
Nick Owen	Leigh	2005	8(1)	1	11	0	26
Richard Owen	Wakefield	2014-15	29(1)	9	0	0	36
	Castleford	2008-14	109(3)	57	0	0	228
Jack Owens	St Helens	2016-17	31	8	14	0	60
	Widnes	2012-15	53(1)	26	103	0	310
Agnatius Paasi	St Helens	2021	2(16)	0	0	0	0
Lopini Paea	Wakefield	2015	1(3)	0	0	0	0
	Catalans	2011-14	41(41)	9	0	0	36
Mickey Paea	Hull	2014-15, 2018-19	78(18)	9	0	0	36
	Hull KR	2012-13	34(17)	5	0	0	20
Liam Paisley	Wigan	2018-19	6(2)	2	0	0	8
Mathias Pala	Catalans	2011-15	28(1)	4	0	0	16
Iafeta Palea'aesina							
	Hull	2014-16	(47)	1	0	0	4
	Salford	2011-12	4(37)	3	0	0	12
	Wigan	2006-10	55(77)	16	0	0	64
Jason Palmada	Workington	1996	12	2	0	0	8
Junior Paramore	Castleford	1996	5(5)	3	0	0	12
Matt Parcell	Hull KR	2019-21	29(6)	13	0	0	52
	Leeds	2017-19	50(16)	27	0	0	108
Paul Parker	Hull	1999-2002	23(18)	9	0	0	36
Rob Parker	Castleford	2011	4(2)	2	0	0	8
	Salford	2009-11	23(14)	4	0	0	16
	Warrington	2006-08	10(56)	6	0	0	24
	Bradford	2000, 2002-05	19(76)	14	0	0	56
	London	2001	9	1	0	0	4
Wayne Parker	Halifax	1996-97	12(1)	0	0	0	0
Ian Parry	Warrington	2001	(1)	0	0	0	0
Jules Parry	Paris	1996	10(2)	0	0	0	0
Oliver Partington	Wigan	2018-21	52(14)	4	0	0	16
Regis Pastre-Courtine							
	Paris	1996	4(3)	4	0	0	16
Cory Paterson	Leigh	2017	13	2	0	0	8
	Salford	2015	14(1)	7	6	0	40
	Hull KR	2013	15	7	0	0	28
Andrew Patmore	Oldham	1996	8(5)	3	0	0	12
Larne Patrick	Castleford	2016-17	14(7)	1	0	0	4
	Huddersfield	2009-14, 2016	30(107)	30	0	0	120
	Wigan	2015	7(20)	4	0	0	16
Luke Patten	Salford	2011-12	53	16	0	0	64
Dec Patton	Salford	2021	6(4)	1	3	0	10
	Warrington	2015-20	69(18)	11	105	6	260
Henry Paul	Harlequins	2006-08	60(1)	8	94	2	222
	Bradford	1999-2001	81(5)	29	350	6	822
	Wigan	1996-98	60	37	23	0	194
Junior Paul	London	1996	3	1	0	0	4
Robbie Paul	Salford	2009	2(24)	2	0	0	8
	Huddersfield	2006-07	44(8)	7	0	0	28
	Bradford	1996-2005	198(31)	121	3	0	490
Pauli Pauli	Salford	2019-21	9(21)	4	0	0	16
	Wakefield	2018-19	14(30)	10	0	0	40
Joseph Paulo	St Helens	2019-20	6(25)	1	0	0	4
Jason Payne	Castleford	2006	1(1)	0	0	0	0
Lewis Peachey	Castleford	2019-21	1(10)	0	0	0	0
Danny Peacock	Bradford	1997-99	32(2)	15	0	0	60
Jamie Peacock	Leeds	2006-15	234(16)	24	0	0	96
	Bradford	1999-2005	163(25)	38	0	0	152
Kai Pearce-Paul	Wigan	2020-21	13(7)	0	0	0	0
Martin Pearson	Wakefield	2001	21(1)	3	60	3	135
	Halifax	1997-98, 2000	55(6)	24	181	0	458
	Sheffield	1999	17(6)	9	36	2	110
Nathan Peats	Huddersfield	2021	12	1	0	0	4
	Leigh	2021	2(8)	0	0	0	0
Jacques Pech	Paris	1996	16	0	0	0	0
Mike Pechey	Warrington	1998	6(3)	2	0	0	8
Bill Peden	London	2003	21(3)	7	0	0	28
Adam Peek	Crusaders	2010-11	5(22)	1	0	0	4
	Celtic	2009	5(12)	3	0	0	12
Eloi Pelissier	London	2019	7(6)	1	0	0	4
	Leigh	2017	4(16)	0	0	0	0
	Catalans	2011-16	38(104)	23	0	1	93
Dimitri Pelo	Catalans	2007-10	79	37	0	0	148
Sean Penkywicz	Huddersfield	2004-05	21(11)	7	0	0	28
	Halifax	2000-03	29(27)	8	0	0	32
Julian Penni	Salford	1998-99	4	0	0	0	0

PLAYER	CLUB	YEAR	APP	TRIES	GOALS	FG	PTS
Kevin Penny	Warrington	2006-09, 2014-17	83(1)	52	0	0	208
	Wakefield	2011	5	1	0	0	4
	Harlequins	2010	5	3	0	0	12
Lee Penny	Warrington	1996-2003	140(5)	54	0	0	216
Paul Penrice	Workington	1996	11(2)	2	0	0	8
Chris Percival	Widnes	2002-03	26	6	0	0	24
Mark Percival	St Helens	2013-21	163(2)	86	223	0	790
Apollo Perelini	St Helens	1996-2000	103(16)	27	0	0	108
Ugo Perez	Catalans	2015, 2017-18	2(5)	0	0	0	0
Mark Perrett	Halifax	1996-97	15(4)	4	0	0	16
Josh Perry	St Helens	2011-13	32(9)	2	0	0	8
Shane Perry	Catalans	2009	8(8)	1	0	0	4
Adam Peters	Paris	1997	16(3)	0	0	0	0
Dominic Peters	London	1998-2003	58(11)	12	0	0	48
Mike Peters	Warrington	2000	2(12)	1	0	0	4
	Halifax	2000	1	0	0	0	0
Willie Peters	Widnes	2004	9	3	0	2	14
	Wigan	2000	29	15	5	6	76
	Gateshead	1999	27	11	1	6	52
Dave Petersen	Hull KR	2012	2(2)	1	0	0	4
Matt Petersen	Wakefield	2008-09	14	3	0	0	12
Nathaniel Peteru	Huddersfield	2021	(12)	3	0	0	12
	Leigh	2021	2(8)	0	0	0	0
	Hull KR	2020	5(3)	0	0	0	0
	Leeds	2018-19	15(6)	0	0	0	0
Adrian Petrie	Workington	1996	(1)	0	0	0	0
Eddy Pettybourne	Wigan	2014	1(15)	0	0	0	0
Dominique Peyroux	St Helens	2016-20	88(25)	16	0	0	64
Cameron Phelps	Widnes	2012-15	66(1)	23	2	0	96
	Hull	2011	19	2	0	0	8
	Wigan	2008-10	43(1)	14	4	0	64
Joe Philbin	Warrington	2014-21	33(99)	10	0	0	40
Rowland Phillips	Workington	1996	22	1	0	0	4
Nathan Picchi	Leeds	1996	(1)	0	0	0	0
Ian Pickavance	Hull	1999	4(2)	2	0	0	8
	Huddersfield	1999	3(14)	0	0	0	0
	St Helens	1996-98	12(44)	6	0	0	24
James Pickering	Castleford	1999	1(19)	0	0	0	0
Steve Pickersgill	Widnes	2012-15	27(8)	1	0	0	4
	Warrington	2005-09	1(36)	0	0	0	0
Nick Pinkney	Salford	2000-02	64	29	0	0	116
	Halifax	1999	26(2)	13	0	0	52
	Sheffield	1997-98	33	10	0	0	40
Mikhail Piskunov	Paris	1996	1(1)	1	0	0	4
Darryl Pitt	London	1996	2(16)	4	0	1	17
Jay Pitts	Wakefield	2008-09, 2020-21	40(8)	8	0	0	32
	London	2019	27	7	0	0	28
	Bradford	2014	15(1)	3	0	0	12
	Hull	2012-14	18(30)	1	0	0	4
	Leeds	2009-12	10(15)	2	0	0	8
Andy Platt	Salford	1997-98	20(3)	1	0	0	4
Michael Platt	Salford	2001-02, 2014	4(1)	1	0	0	4
	Bradford	2007-13	121(6)	44	0	0	176
	Castleford	2006	26	7	0	0	28
Willie Poching	Leeds	2002-06	58(73)	44	0	0	176
	Wakefield	1999-2001	65(4)	20	0	0	80
Ben Pomeroy	Warrington	2017-18	3(7)	1	0	0	4
	Catalans	2014-15	44	10	0	0	40
Quentin Pongia	Wigan	2003-04	15(10)	0	0	0	0
Justin Poore	Hull KR	2014	7	0	0	0	0
	Wakefield	2013	23	1	0	0	4
Dan Potter	Widnes	2002-03	34(2)	6	0	0	24
	London	2001	1(3)	1	0	0	4
Craig Poucher	Hull	1999-2002	31(5)	5	0	0	20
Andy Powell	Wigan	2013	2(3)	1	0	0	4
Bryn Powell	Salford	2004	1(1)	0	0	0	0
Daio Powell	Sheffield	1999	13(1)	2	0	0	8
	Halifax	1997-98	30(3)	17	0	0	68
Daryl Powell	Leeds	1998-2000	49(30)	12	0	2	50
Sam Powell	Wigan	2012-21	160(50)	35	4	4	152
Karl Pratt	Bradford	2003-05	35(19)	18	0	0	72
	Leeds	1999-2002	62(12)	33	0	0	132
Paul Prescott	Wigan	2004-13	49(75)	4	0	0	16
Steve Prescott	Hull	1998-99, 2001-03	99	46	191	3	569
	Wakefield	2000	22(1)	3	13	0	38
	St Helens	1996-97	32	15	17	0	94
Lee Prest	Workington	1996	(1)	0	0	0	0
Gareth Price	Salford	2002	(2)	0	0	0	0
	London	2002	2(2)	3	0	0	12
	St Helens	1999	(11)	2	0	0	8
Gary Price	Wakefield	1999-2001	55(13)	11	0	0	44
Richard Price	Sheffield	1996	1(2)	0	0	0	0
Tony Priddle	Paris	1997	11(7)	3	0	0	12
Matt Prior	Leeds	2020-21	36	3	0	0	12
Frank Pritchard	Hull	2016	10(13)	4	0	0	16
Karl Pryce	Bradford	2003-06, 2012	47(19)	46	1	0	186
	Harlequins	2011	11(7)	12	0	0	48
	Wigan	2009-10	11(2)	12	0	0	48
Leon Pryce	Hull	2015-16	32(2)	8	0	0	32
	Catalans	2012-14	72(2)	15	0	0	60
	St Helens	2006-11	133(3)	64	0	0	256
	Bradford	1998-2005	159(29)	86	0	0	344
Waine Pryce	Wakefield	2007	10(2)	4	0	0	16
	Castleford	2000-06	97(12)	49	0	0	196
Will Pryce	Huddersfield	2021	9(4)	6	14	0	52
Tony Puletua	Hull KR	2015	7	0	0	0	0
	Salford	2014	16(9)	3	0	0	12
	St Helens	2009-13	108(18)	39	0	0	156
Andrew Purcell	Castleford	2000	15(5)	3	0	0	12
	Hull	1999	27	4	0	0	16
Rob Purdham	Harlequins	2006-11	112(3)	18	131	1	335
	London	2002-05	53(15)	16	2	1	69
Adrian Purtell	Bradford	2012-14	45(1)	16	0	0	64
Jason Qareqare	Castleford	2021	2(1)	1	0	0	4
Luke Quigley	Catalans	2007	16(1)	1	0	0	4
Adam Quinlan	Hull KR	2018-21	47	24	0	0	96
	St Helens	2015	11	6	0	0	24
Damien Quinn	Celtic	2009	20(1)	4	12	0	40
Scott Quinnell	Wigan	1996	6(3)	1	0	0	4
Florian Quintilla	Catalans	2008-09	1(4)	0	0	0	0
Lee Radford	Hull	1998, 2006-12	138(30)	23	1	0	94
	Bradford	1999-2005	79(65)	18	12	0	96
Kris Radlinski	Wigan	1996-2006	236(1)	134	1	0	538
Sebastien Raguin	Catalans	2007-12	103(22)	28	0	0	112
Adrian Rainey	Castleford	2002	4(7)	1	0	0	4
Andy Raleigh	Wakefield	2012-14	42(21)	9	0	0	36
	Huddersfield	2006-11	74(46)	13	0	0	52
Jean-Luc Ramondou	Paris	1996	1(1)	1	0	0	4
Chad Randall	London	2012-13	29(9)	4	0	0	16
	Harlequins	2006-11	141(2)	37	0	1	149
Craig Randall	Halifax	1999	8(11)	4	0	0	16
	Salford	1997-98	12(18)	4	0	0	16
Tyler Randell	Wakefield	2017-19	37(8)	9	1	0	38
Jordan Rankin	Castleford	2019-20	29(2)	10	19	0	78
	Huddersfield	2017-18	39	3	9	0	30
	Hull	2014-15	41(6)	20	43	0	166
Scott Ranson	Oldham	1996-97	19(2)	7	0	0	28
Aaron Raper	Castleford	1999-2001	48(4)	4	2	1	21
Sam Rapira	Huddersfield	2016-17	29(19)	3	0	0	12
Steve Rapira	Salford	2014	5(13)	0	0	0	0
Stefan Ratchford	Warrington	2012-21	231(11)	74	400	2	1098
	Salford	2007, 2009-11	65(5)	23	20	0	132
Mike Ratu	Hull KR	2010	5	1	0	0	4
	Leeds	2007, 2009	1(5)	1	0	0	4
Paul Rauhihi	Warrington	2006-09	67(20)	10	0	0	40
Ben Rauter	Wakefield	2001	15(6)	4	0	0	16
Nick Rawsthorne	Hull KR	2020	5	0	0	0	0
	Leigh	2017	1	1	0	0	4
	Hull	2017	3	2	2	0	12
Gareth Raynor	Bradford	2011	18	4	0	0	16
	Crusaders	2010	7	4	0	0	16
	Hull	2001-09	186	102	0	0	408
	Leeds	2000	(3)	0	0	0	0
Tony Rea	London	1996	22	4	0	0	16
Stuart Reardon	Crusaders	2011	25	11	0	0	44
	Bradford	2003-05, 2010	78(11)	37	0	0	148
	Warrington	2006-08	48	12	0	0	48
	Salford	2002	7(1)	3	0	0	12
Mark Reber	Wigan	1999-2000	9(9)	5	0	0	20
Alan Reddicliffe	Warrington	2001	1	0	0	0	0
Tahi Reihana	Bradford	1997-98	17(21)	0	0	0	0
Paul Reilly	Wakefield	2008	5(2)	1	0	0	4
	Huddersfield	1999-2001, 2003-07	150(8)	35	1	0	142
Robert Relf	Widnes	2002-04	68(2)	5	0	0	20
Steve Renouf	Wigan	2000-01	55	40	0	0	160
Steele Retchless	London	1998-2004	177(6)	13	0	0	52
Ben Reynolds	Leigh	2017, 2021	26	9	59	0	154
	Wakefield	2019	5	1	0	0	4
	Castleford	2013-14	1(3)	0	0	0	0
Josh Reynolds	Hull	2021	12	4	0	0	16
Scott Rhodes	Hull	2000	2	0	0	0	0
Phillipe Ricard	Paris	1996-97	2	0	0	0	0

PLAYER	CLUB	YEAR	APP	TRIES	GOALS	FG	PTS
Andy Rice	Huddersfield	2000-01	2(13)	1	0	0	4
Basil Richards	Huddersfield	1998-99	28(17)	1	0	0	4
Craig Richards	Oldham	1996	1	0	0	0	0
Greg Richards	London	2019	5(15)	0	0	0	0
	Leigh	2017	(1)	0	0	0	0
	St Helens	2013-17	19(49)	1	0	0	4
Pat Richards	Catalans	2016	19	9	69	0	174
	Wigan	2006-13	199	147	759	4	2110
Andy Richardson	Hudds-Sheff	2000	(2)	0	0	0	0
Danny Richardson	Castleford	2020-21	31	3	98	4	212
	St Helens	2017-19	52(2)	9	158	8	360
Sean Richardson	Widnes	2002	2(18)	1	0	0	4
	Wakefield	1999	5(1)	0	0	0	0
	Castleford	1996-97	3(8)	1	0	0	4
Mark Riddell	Wigan	2009-10	45(11)	5	2	0	24
Martyn Ridyard	Huddersfield	2017	7	1	26	0	56
	Leigh	2017	4	0	2	0	4
Neil Rigby	St Helens	2006	(1)	0	0	0	0
Shane Rigon	Bradford	2001	14(11)	12	0	0	48
Craig Rika	Halifax	1996	2	0	0	0	0
Chris Riley	Wakefield	2014-15	44	16	0	0	64
	Warrington	2005-14	146(10)	102	0	0	408
	Harlequins	2011	3	2	0	0	8
Glenn Riley	Warrington	2013-14	(15)	0	0	0	0
Peter Riley	Workington	1996	7(5)	0	0	0	0
Julien Rinaldi	London	2012	4(16)	1	0	0	4
	Wakefield	2002, 2010-11	27(9)	6	0	0	24
	Bradford	2009	(7)	1	0	0	4
	Harlequins	2007-08	4(43)	9	0	0	36
	Catalans	2006	16(6)	3	1	0	14
Dean Ripley	Castleford	2004	3(4)	1	0	0	4
Leroy Rivett	Warrington	2002	9	1	0	0	4
	Hudds-Sheff	2000	5(1)	1	0	0	4
	Leeds	1996-2000	39(15)	21	0	0	84
Nico Rizzelli	St Helens	2020	1	0	0	0	0
Jason Roach	Warrington	1998-99	29(7)	15	0	0	60
	Castleford	1997	7	4	0	0	16
Ben Roarty	Castleford	2006	11(6)	2	0	0	8
	Huddersfield	2003-04	52	5	0	0	20
Cain Robb	Castleford	2021	2	0	0	0	0
Amos Roberts	Wigan	2009-11	47(2)	27	5	0	118
Ben Roberts	Castleford	2015-19	60(15)	20	0	2	82
Luis Roberts	Salford	2020	2	0	0	0	0
Mark Roberts	Wigan	2003	(3)	0	0	0	0
Oliver Roberts	Salford	2020-21	13(7)	1	0	0	4
	Huddersfield	2016-19	40(43)	13	0	0	52
	Bradford	2013-14	(5)	0	0	0	0
Robert Roberts	Huddersfield	2001	(1)	0	0	0	0
	Halifax	2000	(3)	0	0	0	0
	Hull	1999	24(2)	4	13	4	46
Tyrone Roberts	Warrington	2018	28	5	32	1	85
Michael Robertson	London	2012-13	35	17	0	0	68
Stan Robin	Catalans	2015-16	5(2)	1	0	0	4
Chad Robinson	Harlequins	2009	13(1)	2	0	0	8
Connor Robinson	Hull KR	2014-15	(2)	0	0	0	0
Craig Robinson	Wakefield	2005	(1)	0	0	0	0
Jason Robinson	Wigan	1996-2000	126(1)	87	0	1	349
Jeremy Robinson	Paris	1997	10(3)	1	21	0	46
John Robinson	Widnes	2003-04	7	1	0	0	4
Luke Robinson	Huddersfield	2008-15	191(18)	45	4	0	188
	Salford	2005-07	79	28	10	2	134
	Wigan	2002-04	17(25)	9	6	1	49
	Castleford	2004	9	4	3	0	22
Will Robinson	Hull	2000	22	4	0	0	16
	Gateshead	1999	28	9	0	0	36
Ash Robson	Castleford	2015	3	1	0	0	4
Ellis Robson	Salford	2021	4(3)	1	0	0	4
	Warrington	2020-21	2(3)	0	0	0	0
James Roby	St Helens	2004-21	317(124)	101	1	1	407
Mike Roby	St Helens	2004	(1)	0	0	0	0
Colton Roche	Huddersfield	2018-19	1(7)	0	0	0	0
Carl Roden	Warrington	1997	1	0	0	0	0
Shane Rodney	London	2012-13	28	3	12	0	36
Matt Rodwell	Warrington	2002	10	3	0	0	12
Nathan Roebuck	Warrington	2020	1	1	0	0	4
Darren Rogers	Castleford	1999-2004	162(1)	81	0	0	324
	Salford	1997-98	42	16	0	0	64
Arthur Romano	Catalans	2017, 2019-20	17	3	0	0	12
Adam Rooks	Hull KR	2019	(4)	0	0	0	0
Jamie Rooney	Wakefield	2003-09	113(7)	60	321	21	903
	Castleford	2001	2(1)	0	6	0	12
Jonathan Roper	Castleford	2001	13	1	7	12	52
	Salford	2000	1(4)	1	3	0	10
	London	2000	4	0	0	0	0
	Warrington	1996-2000	75(8)	33	71	0	274

PLAYER	CLUB	YEAR	APP	TRIES	GOALS	FG	PTS
Scott Roskell	London	1996-97	30(2)	16	0	0	64
Steve Rosolen	London	1996-98	25(9)	10	0	0	40
Adam Ross	London	1996	(1)	0	0	0	0
Cesar Rouge	Catalans	2021	2	0	0	0	0
Paul Round	Castleford	1996	(3)	0	0	0	0
Steve Rowlands	Widnes	2004-05	18(3)	2	15	0	38
	St Helens	2003	(1)	0	0	0	0
Paul Rowley	Leigh	2005	15(7)	3	0	0	12
	Huddersfield	2001	24	3	0	0	12
	Halifax	1996-2000	107(3)	27	1	3	113
Nigel Roy	London	2001-04	100	39	0	0	156
Nicky Royle	Widnes	2004	13	7	0	0	28
Sam Royle	St Helens	2021	1	0	0	0	0
Shad Royston	Bradford	2011	17(1)	10	0	0	40
Chris Rudd	Warrington	1996-98	31(17)	10	16	0	72
Sean Rudder	Catalans	2006	22(1)	6	0	0	24
	Castleford	2004	9(3)	2	0	0	8
Charly Runciman	Widnes	2016-18	68	9	0	0	36
James Rushforth	Halifax	1997	(4)	0	0	0	0
Harry Rushton	Wigan	2020	1	0	0	0	0
Adam Rusling	Castleford	2021	(1)	0	0	0	0
Danny Russell	Huddersfield	1998-2000	50(13)	8	0	0	32
Ian Russell	Oldham	1997	1(3)	1	0	0	4
	Paris	1996	3	0	0	0	0
Matty Russell	Leigh	2021	12(1)	4	0	0	16
	Toronto	2020	6	2	0	0	8
	Warrington	2014-18	77(4)	22	0	0	88
	Hull	2012	6	0	0	0	0
	Wigan	2012	2	3	0	0	12
Oliver Russell	Huddersfield	2018-21	35(6)	4	87	4	194
Richard Russell	Castleford	1996-98	37(4)	2	0	0	8
Robert Russell	Salford	1998-99	2(1)	0	1	0	2
Sean Rutgerson	Salford	2004-06	60(9)	4	0	0	16
Chris Ryan	London	1998-99	44(3)	17	10	0	88
Ethan Ryan	Hull KR	2020-21	8	4	0	0	16
Matt Ryan	Wakefield	2014-15	28(12)	7	0	0	28
Sean Ryan	Castleford	2004	11(5)	2	0	0	8
	Hull	2002-03	53	8	0	0	32
Justin Ryder	Wakefield	2004	19(3)	11	0	0	44
Jason Ryles	Catalans	2009	19(2)	2	0	0	8
Setaimata Sa	Widnes	2016	7(5)	3	0	0	12
	Hull	2014-15	18(6)	6	0	0	24
	Catalans	2010-12	58(5)	21	0	0	84
Teddy Sadaoui	Catalans	2006	7	0	0	0	0
Jack Sadler	Castleford	2021	1	0	0	0	0
Liam Salter	Hull KR	2012-16, 2018	83(3)	17	0	0	68
Matt Salter	London	1997-99	14(34)	0	0	0	0
Ben Sammut	Hull	2000	20	4	67	0	150
	Gateshead	1999	26(2)	6	17	0	58
Jarrod Sammut	Wigan	2019	6(6)	2	0	0	8
	Wakefield	2014-15	19(1)	9	52	0	140
	Bradford	2012-13	35(3)	28	47	1	207
	Crusaders	2010-11	17(16)	17	0	0	68
Dean Sampson	Castleford	1996-2003	124(28)	24	0	0	96
Paul Sampson	London	2004	1(2)	1	0	0	4
	Wakefield	2000	17	8	0	0	32
Jack Sanderson	Castleford	2020	3	1	0	0	4
Lee Sanderson	London	2004	1(5)	1	7	0	18
Chris Sandow	Warrington	2015-16	27(1)	11	26	1	97
Jason Sands	Paris	1996-97	28	0	0	0	0
Ligi Sao	Hull	2020-21	31(5)	2	0	0	8
Mitchell Sargent	Castleford	2008-10	37(21)	6	0	0	24
Dan Sarginson	Salford	2020-21	21	3	0	0	12
	Wigan	2014-16, 2018-19	112(2)	30	0	0	120
	London	2012-13	35(1)	10	0	0	40
	Harlequins	2011	8	5	0	0	20
Matt Sarsfield	Salford	2016	2(2)	1	0	0	4
Tevita Satae	Hull	2019-21	18(20)	4	0	0	16
Junior Sa'u	Leigh	2021	15(1)	3	0	0	12
	Salford	2014-19	115	46	0	0	184
	Wakefield	2019	3	0	0	0	0
Andre Savelio	Hull	2019-21	26(8)	11	0	0	44
	Warrington	2017	3(14)	4	0	0	16
	Castleford	2016	6(1)	1	0	0	4
	St Helens	2014-16	12(25)	2	0	0	8
Lokeni Savelio	Halifax	2000	2(11)	0	0	0	0
	Salford	1997-98	18(20)	0	0	0	0
Tom Saxton	Salford	2007	5	0	0	0	0
	Wakefield	2006	9(6)	2	0	0	8
	Hull	2005	19(8)	3	0	0	12
	Castleford	2002-04	37(12)	11	0	0	44
Jonathan Scales	Halifax	2000	1	0	0	0	0
	Bradford	1996-98	46(4)	24	0	0	96
Andrew Schick	Castleford	1996-98	45(13)	10	0	0	40
Clinton Schifcofske	Crusaders	2010-11	44	5	115	0	250

PLAYER	CLUB	YEAR	APP	TRIES	GOALS	FG	PTS
Garry Schofield	Huddersfield	1998	(2)	0	0	0	0
Gary Schubert	Workington	1996	(1)	0	0	0	0
Matt Schultz	Hull	1998-99	23(9)	2	0	0	8
	Leeds	1996	2(4)	0	0	0	0
John Schuster	Halifax	1996-97	31	9	127	3	293
Cameron Scott	Hull	2018-21	21(6)	2	0	0	8
Nick Scruton	Hull KR	2018	7(10)	0	0	0	0
	Wakefield	2014-16	62(3)	9	0	0	36
	Bradford	2009-14	70(27)	5	0	0	20
	Leeds	2002, 2004-08	11(53)	3	0	0	12
	Hull	2004	2(16)	3	0	0	12
Danny Sculthorpe	Huddersfield	2009	5(8)	0	0	0	0
	Wakefield	2007-09	14(28)	1	0	0	4
	Castleford	2006	18(1)	4	0	1	17
	Wigan	2002-05	13(49)	7	0	0	28
Paul Sculthorpe	St Helens	1998-2008	223(4)	94	356	7	1095
	Warrington	1996-97	40	6	0	0	24
Mick Seaby	London	1997	3(2)	1	0	0	4
Danny Seal	Halifax	1996-99	8(17)	3	0	0	12
Matt Seers	Wakefield	2003	11(1)	2	0	0	8
James Segeyaro	Leeds	2016	3	1	0	0	4
Paul Seguier	Catalans	2016-17, 2020-21	2(23)	1	0	0	4
Anthony Seibold	London	1999-2000	33(19)	5	0	0	20
Jesse Sene-Lefao	Castleford	2017-21	72(30)	15	0	0	60
Innes Senior	Wakefield	2020-21	22	10	0	0	40
	Huddersfield	2018-19	25	8	0	0	32
Keith Senior	Leeds	1999-2011	319(2)	159	0	0	636
	Sheffield	1996-99	90(2)	40	0	0	160
Louis Senior	Huddersfield	2018-21	33	18	0	0	72
Fili Seru	Hull	1998-99	37(1)	13	0	0	52
Ava Seumanufagai	Leeds	2019-20	26(2)	3	0	0	12
Anthony Seuseu	Halifax	2003	1(11)	1	0	0	4
Jerry Seuseu	Wigan	2005-06	29(9)	1	0	0	4
Brett Seymour	Hull	2012-13	26(1)	7	0	0	28
Aidan Sezer	Huddersfield	2020-21	22(1)	9	60	2	158
Will Sharp	Hull	2011-12	27(8)	10	0	0	40
	Harlequins	2008-10	65(1)	19	0	0	76
Jamie Shaul	Hull	2013-21	166(1)	86	0	1	345
Darren Shaw	Salford	2002	5(9)	1	0	0	4
	London	1996, 2002	22(8)	3	0	0	12
	Castleford	2000-01	50(6)	1	0	0	4
	Sheffield	1998-99	51(1)	3	0	1	13
Mick Shaw	Halifax	1999	5	1	0	0	4
	Leeds	1996	12(2)	7	0	0	28
Ryan Shaw	Hull KR	2016, 2018-19	44(1)	19	125	0	326
	London	2013	2	1	2	0	8
Phil Shead	Paris	1996	3(2)	0	0	0	0
Richard Sheil	St Helens	1997	(1)	0	0	0	0
Kelly Shelford	Warrington	1996-97	25(3)	4	0	2	18
Kyle Shelford	Warrington	2020	(1)	0	0	0	0
	Wigan	2016	(1)	0	0	0	0
Michael Shenton	Castleford	2004, 2006, 2008-10, 2013-21	276(2)	111	0	0	444
	St Helens	2011-12	51	15	0	0	60
Ryan Sheridan	Castleford	2004	2	0	0	0	0
	Widnes	2003	14(3)	2	0	0	8
	Leeds	1997-2002	123(7)	46	0	1	185
	Sheffield	1996	9(3)	5	0	1	21
Louis Sheriff	Hull KR	2011-12	8	3	0	0	12
Rikki Sheriffe	Bradford	2009-10	51	14	0	0	56
	Harlequins	2006-08	35(1)	16	0	0	64
	Halifax	2003	6(1)	3	0	0	12
Ian Sherratt	Oldham	1996	5(3)	1	0	0	4
Brent Sherwin	Catalans	2010	12	1	0	1	5
	Castleford	2008-10	48(1)	4	0	3	19
Peter Shiels	St Helens	2001-02	44(3)	11	0	0	44
Gary Shillabeer	Huddersfield	1999	(2)	0	0	0	0
Mark Shipway	Salford	2004-05	30(12)	3	0	0	12
Jake Shorrocks	Wigan	2016-17, 2019-20	9(19)	2	8	0	24
	Salford	2018	10	0	1	0	2
Joe Shorrocks	Wigan	2019-21	8(24)	2	0	0	8
Ian Sibbit	Bradford	2011-12	11(7)	0	0	0	0
	Salford	2005-07, 2009-10	64(17)	11	0	0	44
	Warrington	1999-2001, 2003-04	63(18)	24	0	0	96
Mark Sibson	Huddersfield	1999	2	2	0	0	8
Adam Sidlow	Leigh	2021	10(1)	6	0	0	24
	Toronto	2020	3(3)	0	0	0	0
	Bradford	2013-14	20(22)	8	0	0	32
	Salford	2009-12	34(44)	14	0	0	56
Harry Siejka	Wakefield	2014	6(3)	1	0	0	4

PLAYER	CLUB	YEAR	APP	TRIES	GOALS	FG	PTS
Jordan Sigismeau	Catalans	2015-16	11	3	0	0	12
Josh Simm	St Helens	2019-21	11	3	0	0	12
	Leigh	2021	1	0	0	0	0
Jon Simms	St Helens	2002	(1)	0	0	0	0
Craig Simon	Hull	2000	23(2)	8	0	0	32
	Gateshead	1999	25(4)	6	0	0	24
Mickael Simon	Catalans	2010-14, 2017-20	55(76)	3	0	0	12
	Wakefield	2015-16	15(22)	3	0	0	12
Darren Simpson	Huddersfield	1998-99	17(1)	5	0	0	20
Jamie Simpson	Huddersfield	2011	8(1)	0	0	0	0
Jared Simpson	Huddersfield	2015-18	12	4	0	0	16
Robbie Simpson	London	1999	6(7)	0	0	0	0
Ashton Sims	Warrington	2015-17	69(11)	5	0	0	20
Korbin Sims	Hull KR	2021	5(8)	0	0	0	0
Kevin Sinfield	Leeds	1997-2015	425(29)	70	1566	31	3443
Matt Sing	Hull	2007-08	41	14	0	0	56
Wayne Sing	Paris	1997	18(1)	2	0	0	8
Brad Singleton	Wigan	2020-21	25(1)	3	0	0	12
	Toronto	2020	3(1)	1	0	0	4
	Leeds	2011-19	92(61)	17	0	0	68
	Wakefield	2013	(1)	0	0	0	0
Fata Sini	Salford	1997	22	7	0	0	28
Ken Sio	Salford	2019-21	48(1)	40	13	0	186
	Hull KR	2015-16	42	23	13	0	118
Michael Sio	Wakefield	2015-17	25(14)	6	0	0	24
John Skandalis	Huddersfield	2007-08	37(5)	4	0	0	16
Dylan Skee	Harlequins	2008-09	(3)	0	0	0	0
Ben Skerrett	Castleford	2003	(1)	0	0	0	0
Kelvin Skerrett	Halifax	1997-99	31(6)	2	0	0	8
	Wigan	1996	1(8)	0	0	0	0
Troy Slattery	Wakefield	2002-03	33(5)	4	0	0	16
	Huddersfield	1999	3	1	0	0	4
Mick Slicker	Huddersfield	2001, 2003-05	17(48)	2	0	0	8
	Sheffield	1999	(3)	1	0	0	4
	Halifax	1997	2(5)	0	0	0	0
Nick Slyney	London	2014	20(4)	3	0	0	12
Ian Smales	Castleford	1996-97	10(8)	5	0	0	20
Aaron Smith	St Helens	2018-21	13(24)	9	0	0	36
	Hull KR	2018	3(1)	0	0	0	0
Aaron Smith	Castleford	2006	(2)	0	0	0	0
	Bradford	2003-04	12(1)	3	0	0	12
Andy Smith	Harlequins	2007	6(3)	3	0	0	12
	Bradford	2004-06	9(9)	4	0	0	16
	Salford	2005	4	1	0	0	4
Byron Smith	Castleford	2004	(9)	0	0	0	0
	Halifax	2003	6(1)	0	0	0	0
Cameron Smith	Leeds	2016-21	21(46)	8	1	0	34
Chris Smith	Hull	2001-02	12	3	0	0	12
	St Helens	1998-2000	62(9)	26	0	0	104
	Castleford	1996-97	36(1)	12	0	0	48
Craig Smith	Wigan	2002-04	77(3)	10	0	0	40
Damien Smith	St Helens	1998	21(1)	8	0	0	32
Daniel Smith	Castleford	2019-21	21(23)	3	0	0	12
	Huddersfield	2015-18	9(38)	5	0	0	20
	Wakefield	2014-15	21(15)	6	0	0	24
Danny Smith	Paris	1996	10(2)	1	15	0	34
	London	1996	2(1)	1	0	0	4
Darren Smith	St Helens	2003	25(1)	14	0	0	56
Gary Smith	Castleford	2001	(1)	0	0	0	0
Harry Smith	Wigan	2019-21	29(13)	6	32	2	90
Hudson Smith	Bradford	2000	8(22)	2	0	0	8
	Salford	1999	23(2)	5	0	0	20
James Smith	Salford	2000	23(3)	6	0	0	24
Jamie Smith	Hull	1998-99	24(6)	6	12	0	48
	Workington	1996	5(3)	0	1	0	2
Jason Smith	Hull	2001-04	61(3)	17	0	1	69
Jeremy Smith	Wakefield	2011	9(1)	1	0	0	4
	Salford	2009-10	27(17)	2	0	0	8
Kris Smith	London	2001	(1)	0	0	0	0
	Halifax	2001	(1)	0	0	0	0
Lee Smith	Wakefield	2012-13, 2015	30(4)	16	54	2	174
	Leeds	2005-12	125(10)	60	34	1	309
Leigh Smith	Workington	1996	9	4	0	0	16
Mark Smith	Widnes	2005	12(15)	4	0	0	16
	Wigan	1999-2004	35(77)	8	0	0	32
Martyn Smith	Harlequins	2010	(2)	0	0	0	0
	Warrington	2019	4(1)	0	0	0	0
Matty Smith	Catalans	2019	16	0	0	1	1
	St Helens	2006-08, 2010, 2017-18	38(9)	5	10	4	44
	Wigan	2012-16	122(3)	17	279	25	651
	Salford	2010-12	67(4)	13	6	1	65
	Celtic	2009	15(1)	3	2	1	17

PLAYER	CLUB	YEAR	APP	TRIES	GOALS	FG	PTS
Michael Smith	Hull KR	2007	(3)	1	0	0	4
	Castleford	1998, 2001-04	86(33)	32	0	0	128
	Hull	1999	12(6)	3	0	0	12
Morgan Smith	London	2019	15(1)	1	1	2	8
	Warrington	2016-18	(18)	1	1	0	6
Paul Smith	Huddersfield	2004-06	52(17)	13	0	0	52
Paul Smith	Warrington	2001	(1)	0	0	0	0
	Castleford	1997-2000	6(37)	3	0	0	12
Paul Smith	London	1997	7(1)	2	0	0	8
Peter Smith	Oldham	1996	2	0	0	0	0
Richard Smith	Wakefield	2001	8(1)	1	0	0	4
	Salford	1997	(1)	1	0	0	4
Tim Smith	Wakefield	2012-15	79	11	0	0	44
	Salford	2014	12	2	7	0	22
	Wigan	2008-09	13(8)	2	0	0	8
Tony Smith	Hull	2001-03	43(5)	26	0	0	104
	Wigan	1997-2000	66(5)	46	0	0	184
	Castleford	1996-97	18(2)	10	0	0	40
Tony Smith	Workington	1996	9	1	0	0	4
Tyrone Smith	Harlequins	2006-07	49(3)	13	0	0	52
	London	2005	20(4)	11	0	0	44
Morgan Smithies	Wigan	2019-21	33(24)	1	0	0	4
Rob Smyth	Leigh	2005	15(1)	4	0	0	16
	Warrington	2000-03	65	35	20	0	180
	London	1998-2000	32(2)	9	15	0	66
	Wigan	1996	11(5)	16	0	0	64
Marc Sneyd	Hull	2015-21	161	19	558	33	1225
	Castleford	2014	25(1)	6	100	2	226
	Salford	2010-13	33(12)	4	61	3	141
Steve Snitch	Castleford	2010-12	38(18)	10	0	0	40
	Wakefield	2002-05, 2009	33(55)	9	0	0	36
	Huddersfield	2006-08	24(35)	12	0	0	48
Bright Sodje	Wakefield	2000	15	4	0	0	16
	Sheffield	1996-99	54	34	0	0	136
Iosia Soliola	St Helens	2010-14	83(24)	27	0	0	108
David Solomona	Warrington	2010-12	8(49)	16	1	0	66
	Bradford	2007-09	44(9)	19	0	0	76
	Wakefield	2004-06	73(3)	26	0	0	104
Denny Solomona	Castleford	2015-16	42	58	0	0	232
	London	2014	19(1)	8	0	0	32
Alfred Songoro	Wakefield	1999	8(5)	4	0	0	16
Romain Sort	Paris	1997	(1)	0	0	0	0
Paul Southern	Salford	1997-2002	79(33)	6	13	0	50
	St Helens	2002	1(1)	0	0	0	0
Steve Southern	Wakefield	2012	7(8)	3	0	0	12
Cain Southernwood	Bradford	2010	2	0	0	0	0
Roy Southernwood	Wakefield	1999	1	0	0	0	0
	Halifax	1996	2	0	0	0	0
Jason Southwell	Huddersfield	2004	(1)	0	0	0	0
Waisale Sovatabua	Salford	2001-03	44(3)	19	0	0	76
	Hudds-Sheff	2000	23(1)	8	0	0	32
	Sheffield	1996-99	56(17)	19	0	1	77
Jamie Soward	London	2013	6(1)	4	21	0	58
Yusef Sozi	London	2000-01	(5)	0	0	0	0
Scott Spaven	Hull KR	2010	(2)	0	0	0	0
Andy Speak	Castleford	2001	4(4)	0	0	0	0
	Wakefield	2000	6(5)	2	0	0	8
	Leeds	1999	4	1	0	0	4
Dom Speakman	St Helens	2013	(1)	0	0	0	0
Tim Spears	Castleford	2003	(3)	0	0	0	0
Jake Spedding	St Helens	2016-18	3(1)	0	0	0	0
Ady Spencer	London	1996-99	8(36)	5	0	0	20
Jack Spencer	Salford	2009-11	(7)	0	0	0	0
Tom Spencer	Leigh	2021	(1)	0	0	0	0
	Wigan	2012-13	(7)	0	0	0	0
Rob Spicer	Wakefield	2002-05	28(18)	4	0	0	16
Russ Spiers	Wakefield	2011	(2)	0	0	0	0
Gadwin Springer	Toronto	2020	4(1)	0	0	0	0
	Castleford	2015-18	15(41)	3	0	0	12
	Catalans	2014-15	(3)	1	0	0	4
Stuart Spruce	Widnes	2002-03	45(4)	19	0	0	76
	Bradford	1996-2001	107(2)	57	0	0	228
Lee St Hilaire	Castleford	1997	4(2)	0	0	0	0
Marcus St Hilaire	Bradford	2006-07	34(1)	12	0	0	48
	Huddersfield	2003-05	72(2)	30	0	0	120
	Leeds	1996-2002	59(33)	31	0	0	124
Cyril Stacul	Catalans	2007-12	61(1)	18	0	0	72
Dylan Stainton	Workington	1996	2(3)	0	0	0	0
Mark Stamper	Workington	1996	(1)	0	0	0	0
John Stankevitch	Widnes	2005	17(5)	0	0	0	0
	St Helens	2000-04	74(40)	25	0	0	100
Gareth Stanley	Bradford	2000	1	1	0	0	4
Craig Stapleton	Salford	2009	24	2	0	0	8
	Leigh	2005	27(1)	4	0	0	16
Graham Steadman	Castleford	1996-97	11(17)	5	0	0	20
Jon Steel	Hull KR	2007-08	18	6	0	0	24
Jamie Stenhouse	Warrington	2000-01	9(3)	3	0	0	12
Gareth Stephens	Sheffield	1997-99	23(6)	2	0	0	8
David Stephenson	Hull	1998	11(7)	3	0	0	12
	Oldham	1997	10(8)	2	0	0	8
Francis Stephenson	London	2002-05	42(34)	5	0	0	20
	Wigan	2001	2(9)	0	0	0	0
	Wakefield	1999-2000	50(1)	6	0	0	24
Paul Sterling	Leeds	1997-2000	79(12)	50	0	0	200
Paul Stevens	Oldham	1996	2(1)	0	0	0	0
	London	1996	(1)	0	0	0	0
Robson Stevens	Huddersfield	2021	(2)	0	0	0	0
Warren Stevens	Leigh	2005	4(14)	1	0	0	4
	Warrington	1996-99, 2002-05	17(66)	1	0	0	4
	Salford	2001	(8)	0	0	0	0
Anthony Stewart	Harlequins	2006	4	0	0	0	0
	Salford	2004-06	51(2)	15	0	0	60
	St Helens	1997-2003	93(23)	44	0	0	176
Glenn Stewart	Leigh	2017	15	0	0	0	0
	Catalans	2016	28	3	0	0	12
Sam Stone	Leigh	2021	5	2	0	0	8
Troy Stone	Widnes	2002	18(6)	1	0	0	4
	Huddersfield	2001	12(1)	1	0	0	4
Matthew Storton	Hull KR	2020-21	14(15)	1	0	0	4
James Stosic	Wakefield	2009	8(10)	1	0	0	4
Lynton Stott	Wakefield	1999	21	4	6	1	29
	Sheffield	1996-98	40(4)	15	0	0	60
Mitchell Stringer	Salford	2005-06	12(4)	0	0	0	0
	London	2004-05	10(19)	0	0	0	0
Graham Strutton	London	1996	9(1)	2	0	0	8
Matt Sturm	Leigh	2005	8(19)	3	0	0	12
	Warrington	2002-04	1(18)	0	0	0	0
	Huddersfield	1998-99	46	8	0	0	32
Anthony Sullivan	St Helens	1996-2001	137(2)	105	0	0	420
Michael Sullivan	Warrington	2006-07	21(16)	8	1	0	34
Phil Sumner	Warrington	1996	(5)	0	0	0	0
Alex Sutcliffe	Leeds	2017, 2019-21	10(5)	2	0	0	8
Liam Sutcliffe	Leeds	2013-21	134(32)	52	168	3	547
	Bradford	2014	3(1)	1	0	0	4
Ryan Sutton	Wigan	2014-18	38(65)	10	0	0	40
Simon Svabic	Salford	1998-2000	13(5)	3	19	0	50
Luke Swain	Salford	2009-10	54	3	0	0	12
Richard Swain	Hull	2004-07	89	5	0	0	20
Anthony Swann	Warrington	2001	3	1	0	0	4
Logan Swann	Warrington	2005-06	49(1)	17	0	0	68
	Bradford	2004	25	6	0	0	24
Willie Swann	Warrington	1996-97	25(2)	6	0	0	24
Jake Sweeting	Castleford	2021	(1)	1	0	0	4
Adam Swift	Hull	2020-21	22	16	0	0	64
	St Helens	2012-19	120	80	0	0	320
Nathan Sykes	Castleford	1996-2004	158(52)	3	0	0	12
Paul Sykes	Wakefield	2012-14	59(1)	12	135	6	324
	Bradford	1999-2002, 2008-12	99(4)	35	64	2	270
	Harlequins	2006-07	31(2)	15	47	1	155
	London	2001-05	95(1)	26	219	3	545
Wayne Sykes	London	1999	(2)	0	0	0	0
Tom Symonds	Huddersfield	2016-18	6(1)	3	0	0	12
Ukuma Ta'ai	Huddersfield	2013-20	118(63)	43	0	0	172
Semi Tadulala	Wakefield	2004-07, 2011	92	37	0	0	148
	Bradford	2008-09	49	30	0	0	120
Whetu Taewa	Sheffield	1997-98	33(7)	8	0	0	32
Zeb Taia	St Helens	2017-20	96(3)	22	0	0	88
	Catalans	2013-15	75	35	0	0	140
Alan Tait	Leeds	1996	3(3)	1	0	0	4
Brad Takairangi	Hull KR	2021	19	2	0	0	8
Fetuli Talanoa	Hull	2014-18	115(1)	54	0	0	216
Willie Talau	Salford	2009-10	22	4	0	0	16
	St Helens	2003-08	130(1)	50	0	0	200
Ian Talbot	Wakefield	1999	9(5)	2	31	0	70
	Wigan	1997	3	1	0	0	4
Albert Talipeau	Wakefield	2004	2(3)	0	0	0	0
Gael Tallec	Halifax	2000	5(19)	3	0	0	12
	Castleford	1998-99	19(21)	3	0	0	12
	Wigan	1996-97	8(12)	3	0	0	12
Joe Tamani	Bradford	1996	11(3)	4	0	0	16
Ryan Tandy	Hull KR	2007	8(4)	2	0	0	8
Adam Tangata	Wakefield	2019-21	2(15)	1	0	0	4
Andrew Tangata-Toa	Huddersfield	1999	15	2	0	0	8

PLAYER	CLUB	YEAR	APP	TRIES	GOALS	FG	PTS
David Tangata-Toa	Celtic	2009	1(18)	4	0	0	16
	Hull KR	2007	(17)	3	0	0	12
Kelepi Tanginoa	Wakefield	2019-21	48(6)	13	0	0	52
Jordan Tansey	Huddersfield	2016	2	1	1	0	6
	Wakefield	2015	4	1	0	0	4
	Castleford	2013-15	44(1)	15	0	0	60
	Crusaders	2011	14(4)	5	0	0	20
	Hull	2009-10	30	9	0	0	36
	Leeds	2006-08	18(32)	19	3	0	82
Lama Tasi	Warrington	2019	9(8)	0	0	0	0
	Salford	2014-15, 2017-18	55(26)	4	0	0	16
	St Helens	2016	9(8)	0	0	0	0
Kris Tassell	Wakefield	2002	24	10	0	0	40
	Salford	2000-01	35(10)	12	0	0	48
Will Tate	Hull KR	2020-21	4(3)	1	0	0	4
Shem Tatupu	Wigan	1996	(3)	0	0	0	0
Tony Tatupu	Wakefield	2000-01	20	2	0	0	8
	Warrington	1997	21(1)	6	0	0	24
Taulima Tautai	Wigan	2015-19	7(111)	4	0	0	16
	Wakefield	2013-14	6(19)	2	0	0	8
Dave Taylor	Catalans	2016	20(4)	8	0	0	32
Elijah Taylor	Salford	2021	11(2)	0	0	0	0
James Taylor	Leigh	2005	(4)	0	0	0	0
Joe Taylor	Paris	1997	9(5)	2	0	0	8
Lawrence Taylor	Sheffield	1996	(1)	0	0	0	0
Scott Taylor	Hull	2016-21	112(14)	16	0	0	64
	Salford	2015	23	5	0	0	20
	Wigan	2013-14	18(29)	6	0	0	24
	Hull KR	2009-12	21(29)	8	0	0	32
Frederic Teixido	Sheffield	1999	(4)	0	0	0	0
	Paris	1996-97	2(3)	1	0	0	4
Lionel Teixido	Catalans	2006-07	11(13)	3	0	0	12
Karl Temata	London	2005, 2012	1(8)	1	0	0	4
	Harlequins	2006-11	94(22)	7	0	0	28
Jason Temu	Hull	1998	13(2)	1	0	0	4
	Oldham	1996-97	25(3)	1	0	0	4
Paul Terry	London	1997	(1)	0	0	0	0
Zane Tetevano	Leeds	2021	13	1	0	0	4
Anthony Thackeray							
	Castleford	2008	3(6)	0	0	0	0
	Hull	2007	2	0	0	0	0
Jamie Thackray	Crusaders	2010	1(16)	2	0	0	8
	Hull	2005-06, 2008-09	37(45)	6	0	0	24
	Leeds	2006-07	5(27)	7	0	0	28
	Castleford	2003-04	7(11)	3	0	0	12
	Halifax	2000-02	10(38)	3	0	0	12
Adam Thaler	Castleford	2002	(1)	0	0	0	0
Josh Thewlis	Warrington	2019-21	18	5	0	0	20
Gareth Thomas	Crusaders	2010-11	27(1)	6	0	0	24
Giles Thomas	London	1997-99	1(2)	0	0	0	0
Oscar Thomas	London	2014	4(2)	0	1	0	2
Rob Thomas	Harlequins	2011	(2)	0	0	0	0
Steve Thomas	London	2004	4(2)	0	0	0	0
	Warrington	2001	2	0	0	0	0
Alex Thompson	Warrington	2009	(1)	1	0	0	4
Alex Thompson	Sheffield	1997	4(11)	0	0	0	0
Bobby Thompson	Salford	1999	28	5	2	0	24
Bodene Thompson	Leeds	2020-21	23(5)	2	0	0	8
	Toronto	2020	4(1)	1	0	0	4
	Warrington	2018	7	0	0	0	0
Corey Thompson	Widnes	2016-17	48	36	9	0	162
David Thompson	Leigh	2017	1	0	0	0	0
	Hull KR	2016	1	0	0	0	0
Joel Thompson	St Helens	2021	13(2)	1	0	0	4
Jordan Thompson	Leigh	2021	13(5)	1	0	0	4
	Hull	2014-17, 2019	27(81)	12	0	0	48
	Leeds	2018	1	0	0	0	0
	Castleford	2009-13	47(24)	25	0	0	100
Luke Thompson	St Helens	2013-20	100(54)	28	0	0	112
Sam Thompson	Harlequins	2009	(2)	0	0	0	0
	St Helens	2008	(5)	0	0	0	0
Chris Thorman	Hull	2009	19(2)	1	0	0	4
	Huddersfield	2000-01, 2005-08	126(20)	51	320	3	847
	London	2003	26(1)	7	81	1	191
	Sheffield	1999	5(13)	2	8	1	25
Tony Thorniley	Warrington	1997	(5)	0	0	0	0
Andy Thornley	Salford	2009	(1)	1	0	0	4
Iain Thornley	Leigh	2021	19	3	0	0	12
	Catalans	2017-18	31(1)	7	0	0	28
	Hull KR	2016	21	10	0	0	40
	Wigan	2012-14	40	25	0	0	100
Danny Tickle	Hull KR	2018	14(3)	4	20	0	56
	Leigh	2017	10(13)	4	0	0	16
	Castleford	2016	6(3)	0	1	0	2
	Widnes	2014-15	33(1)	3	88	0	188
	Hull	2007-13	159(5)	45	528	1	1237
	Wigan	2002-06	94(36)	34	200	2	538
	Halifax	2000-02	25(17)	10	91	2	224
Kris Tickle	Warrington	2001	(1)	0	0	0	0
Lewis Tierney	Leigh	2021	8	2	0	0	8
	Catalans	2017-20	52	15	0	0	60
	Wigan	2013-17	35	17	0	0	68
James Tilley	St Helens	2013-14	(3)	0	0	0	0
Dane Tilse	Hull KR	2015-16	29(1)	1	0	0	4
John Timu	London	1998-2000	57(3)	11	0	0	44
Liam Tindall	Leeds	2020-21	3(1)	1	0	0	4
Kerrod Tindall	London	1997	2(2)	0	0	0	0
Tulsen Tollett	London	1996-2001	105(5)	38	49	1	251
Joel Tomkins	Catalans	2020-21	17(6)	5	0	0	20
	Hull KR	2018-19	27	7	0	0	28
	Wigan	2005-11, 2014-18	161(51)	60	0	0	240
Logan Tomkins	Salford	2014-19	85(31)	6	0	0	24
	Wigan	2012-15	9(32)	1	0	0	4
Sam Tomkins	Catalans	2019-21	56	24	79	2	256
	Wigan	2009-13, 2016-18	177(6)	129	125	7	773
Glen Tomlinson	Wakefield	1999-2000	41(5)	8	0	0	32
	Hull	1998	5	1	0	0	4
	Bradford	1996-97	27(13)	12	0	0	48
Willie Tonga	Leigh	2017	3	0	0	0	0
	Catalans	2015	18	6	0	0	24
Ryan Tongia	Wakefield	2011	4	2	0	0	8
Ian Tonks	Castleford	1996-2001	32(50)	11	13	0	70
Tony Tonks	Huddersfield	2012	(1)	0	0	0	0
Motu Tony	Wakefield	2011-12	7(3)	1	0	0	4
	Hull	2005-09	76(20)	25	0	0	100
	Castleford	2004	8(1)	1	0	0	4
Mark Tookey	Harlequins	2006	12(14)	1	0	0	4
	London	2005	13(14)	5	0	0	20
	Castleford	2004	2(8)	1	0	0	4
Clinton Toopi	Leeds	2006-08	40(3)	9	0	0	36
David Tootill	Harlequins	2008	(4)	0	0	0	0
Paul Topping	Oldham	1996-97	23(10)	1	19	0	42
Patrick Torreilles	Paris	1996	9(1)	1	25	0	54
Albert Torrens	Huddersfield	2006	7	5	0	0	20
Mat Toshack	London	1998-2004	120(21)	24	0	0	96
Julien Touxagas	Catalans	2006-11	14(45)	4	0	0	16
Darren Treacy	Salford	2002	24(1)	6	1	0	26
Dean Treister	Hull	2003	16(1)	3	0	0	12
Rocky Trimarchi	Crusaders	2010	16(8)	0	0	0	0
Steve Trindall	London	2003-05	40(20)	3	0	0	12
Shane Tronc	Wakefield	2010	8(3)	2	0	0	8
Kyle Trout	Hull KR	2019-20	1(14)	0	0	0	0
	Wakefield	2012-15	6(17)	3	0	0	12
Owen Trout	Huddersfield	2020-21	9(12)	3	0	0	12
	Leeds	2019	1(1)	0	0	0	0
George Truelove	Wakefield	2002	2	1	0	0	4
	London	2000	5	1	0	0	4
Jake Trueman	Castleford	2017-21	76(2)	22	0	1	89
Va'aiga Tuigamala	Wigan	1996	21	10	3	0	46
Fereti Tuilagi	St Helens	1999-2000	43(15)	21	0	0	84
	Halifax	1996-98	55(3)	27	0	0	108
Carlos Tuimavave	Hull	2016-21	121(6)	42	0	0	168
Evarn Tuimavave	Hull KR	2013	11(12)	2	0	0	8
Sateki Tuipulotu	Leeds	1996	6(3)	1	2	0	8
Anthony Tupou	Wakefield	2016	12(9)	4	0	0	16
Bill Tupou	Wakefield	2015-21	109(3)	38	0	0	152
Tame Tupou	Bradford	2007-08	10(7)	8	0	0	32
Jansin Turgut	Salford	2019	8(2)	1	0	0	4
	Hull	2015-18	10(18)	3	0	0	12
Neil Turley	Leigh	2005	6(3)	2	20	1	49
Calum Turner	Castleford	2018-20	7(6)	4	10	0	36
Darren Turner	Huddersfield	2000-01, 2003-04	42(13)	13	0	0	52
	Sheffield	1996-99	41(29)	15	0	0	60
Ian Turner	Paris	1996	1(1)	1	0	0	4
Jordan Turner	Castleford	2021	15(1)	13	0	1	53
	Huddersfield	2017-20	66(2)	10	0	1	41
	St Helens	2013-16	106(14)	44	13	3	205
	Hull	2010-12	62(5)	28	0	0	112
	Salford	2006-07, 2009	22(10)	4	1	0	18
Chris Tuson	Hull	2014	10(1)	0	0	0	0
	Wigan	2008, 2010-13	24(49)	13	0	0	52
	Castleford	2010	3(5)	0	0	0	0

Super League Players 1996-2021

PLAYER	CLUB	YEAR	APP	TRIES	GOALS	FG	PTS
Gregory Tutard	Paris	1996	1(1)	0	0	0	0
Brendon Tuuta	Warrington	1998	18(2)	4	0	0	16
	Castleford	1996-97	41(1)	3	0	0	12
Steve Tyrer	Salford	2010	20	6	9	0	42
	Celtic	2009	8	2	5	0	18
	St Helens	2006-08	17(3)	12	42	0	132
Bobby Tyson-Wilson	Hull	2015	(1)	0	0	0	0
Harry Tyson-Wilson	Hull	2014	(1)	0	0	0	0
Akuila Uate	Huddersfield	2019	12	5	0	0	20
Wayne Ulugia	Hull KR	2014	3	1	0	0	4
Mike Umaga	Halifax	1996-97	38(1)	16	5	0	74
Kava Utoikamanu	Paris	1996	6(3)	0	0	0	0
Frederic Vaccari	Catalans	2010-11, 2013-14	50	26	0	0	104
David Vaealiki	Wigan	2005-07	67(1)	17	0	0	68
Joe Vagana	Bradford	2001-08	176(44)	17	0	0	68
Nigel Vagana	Warrington	1997	20	17	0	0	68
Tevita Vaikona	Bradford	1998-2004	145(2)	89	0	0	356
Lesley Vainikolo	Bradford	2002-07	132(4)	136	1	0	546
Junior Vaivai	Hull KR	2018-19	22(1)	8	0	0	32
Eric Van Brussell	Paris	1996	2	0	0	0	0
Jace Van Dijk	Celtic	2009	19	1	1	0	6
Richard Varkulis	Warrington	2004	4(1)	3	0	0	12
Marcus Vassilakopoulos	Sheffield	1997-99	15(11)	3	10	2	34
	Leeds	1996-97	1(3)	0	0	0	0
Manu Vatuvei	Salford	2017	7	5	0	0	20
Atelea Vea	Leigh	2017	19(1)	5	0	0	20
	St Helens	2015-16	19(17)	10	0	0	40
	London	2014	19(3)	2	0	0	8
Josh Veivers	Salford	2012	5	2	0	0	8
	Wakefield	2011	10(2)	2	22	0	52
Phil Veivers	Huddersfield	1998	7(6)	1	0	0	4
	St Helens	1996	(1)	1	0	0	4
Michael Vella	Hull KR	2007-11	111(5)	13	0	0	52
Bruno Verges	Catalans	2006	25	6	0	0	24
Eric Vergniol	Paris	1996	14(1)	6	0	0	24
Albert Vete	Hull KR	2021	5(10)	4	0	0	16
Gray Viane	Salford	2007	9	2	0	0	8
	Castleford	2006	20(7)	14	0	0	56
	Widnes	2005	20	13	0	0	52
	St Helens	2004	4	1	0	0	4
Joe Vickery	Leeds	2013	9	1	0	0	4
Daniel Vidot	Salford	2016	5(1)	5	0	0	20
Adrian Vowles	Castleford	1997-2001, 2003	125(1)	29	1	1	119
	Wakefield	2002-03	24(3)	6	1	0	26
	Leeds	2002	14(3)	2	0	0	8
Mitieli Vulikijapani	Hull	2021	4(2)	3	0	0	12
King Vuniyayawa	Leeds	2021	3(12)	1	0	0	4
Michael Wainwright	Castleford	2008-10	70	22	0	0	88
	Wakefield	2004-05	21(10)	8	0	0	32
Mike Wainwright	Salford	2000-02, 2007	75(3)	9	0	0	36
	Warrington	1996-99, 2003-07	168(14)	23	0	0	92
Shannon Wakeman	Huddersfield	2017-18	16(13)	3	0	0	12
Adam Walker	Salford	2019	9(14)	4	0	0	16
	Wakefield	2017	5(1)	0	0	0	0
	St Helens	2017	(9)	1	0	0	4
	Hull KR	2013-16	60(27)	6	0	0	24
	Huddersfield	2010-12	1(5)	0	0	0	0
Alex Walker	Wakefield	2020-21	8	1	0	0	4
	London	2014, 2019	28	6	0	0	24
Anthony Walker	Wakefield	2015-17	1(11)	1	0	0	4
	St Helens	2013-14	9(7)	2	0	0	8
Ben Walker	Leeds	2002	23(1)	8	100	0	232
Brad Walker	Wakefield	2020-21	11(5)	0	0	0	0
	Widnes	2016-18	3(5)	0	0	0	0
Chev Walker	Bradford	2011-14	44(22)	5	0	0	20
	Hull KR	2008-09	24(7)	5	0	0	20
	Leeds	1999-2006	142(19)	77	0	0	308
Chris Walker	Catalans	2010	11	6	2	0	28
Danny Walker	Warrington	2019-21	14(26)	7	0	0	28
	Widnes	2017-18	3(16)	2	0	0	8
Jack Walker	Leeds	2017-20	52(14)	18	0	0	72
Jonathan Walker	Hull KR	2014	2(6)	0	0	0	0
	Castleford	2010-13	17(31)	4	0	0	16
Jonny Walker	Wigan	2010	(1)	0	0	0	0
Marcus Walker	Hull	2021	1	0	0	0	0
Matt Walker	Huddersfield	2001	3(6)	0	0	0	0
Anthony Wall	Paris	1997	9	3	3	0	18
Blake Wallace	Leigh	2021	2	0	0	0	0
	Toronto	2020	5(1)	0	7	0	14
Jon Wallace	London	2014	4(12)	0	0	0	0
Mark Wallace	Workington	1996	14(1)	3	0	0	12
Elliot Wallis	Hull KR	2018	4	2	0	0	8
Alex Walmsley	St Helens	2013-21	133(73)	40	0	0	160
Adam Walne	Huddersfield	2018-20	4(9)	0	0	0	0
	Salford	2012-17	15(50)	2	0	0	8
Jordan Walne	Hull KR	2018	(6)	0	0	0	0
	Salford	2013-17	20(32)	3	0	0	12
Joe Walsh	Huddersfield	2009	1(1)	1	0	0	4
	Harlequins	2007-08	1(4)	0	0	0	0
Liam Walsh	Widnes	2017	1	0	0	0	0
Luke Walsh	Catalans	2017-18	23	2	71	4	154
	St Helens	2014-16	56(2)	14	188	9	441
Lucas Walshaw	Wakefield	2011-14	15(6)	3	0	0	12
Josh Walters	Leeds	2014-18	15(36)	9	0	0	36
Kerrod Walters	Gateshead	1999	10(12)	2	1	0	10
Kevin Walters	Warrington	2001	1	0	0	0	0
Sam Walters	Leeds	2020-21	8(3)	2	0	0	8
Jason Walton	Wakefield	2016	7(8)	0	0	0	0
	Salford	2009, 2014-15	7(19)	1	0	0	4
Barry Ward	St Helens	2002-03	20(30)	4	0	0	16
Danny Ward	Harlequins	2008-11	89(7)	4	0	0	16
	Hull KR	2007	11(9)	0	0	0	0
	Castleford	2006	18(7)	2	0	0	8
	Leeds	1999-2005	70(48)	9	0	1	37
Robbie Ward	Leeds	2014-15	5(3)	1	0	0	4
Stevie Ward	Leeds	2012-20	86(29)	19	0	0	76
Joe Wardill	Hull KR	2016, 2018	6(2)	1	0	0	4
Jake Wardle	Huddersfield	2018-21	55	18	6	0	84
Joe Wardle	Huddersfield	2011-16, 2019-21	152(2)	65	0	0	260
	Castleford	2018	15(2)	1	0	0	4
	Bradford	2010	1(1)	0	0	0	0
Phil Waring	Salford	1997-99	6(8)	2	0	0	8
Brett Warton	London	1999-2001	49(7)	14	133	0	322
Kyle Warren	Castleford	2002	13(14)	3	0	0	12
Danny Washbrook	Hull	2005-11, 2016-19	136(71)	19	0	0	76
	Wakefield	2012-15	93(8)	12	0	0	48
Adam Watene	Wakefield	2006-08	45(8)	5	0	0	20
	Bradford	2006	(4)	0	0	0	0
Frank Watene	Wakefield	1999-2001	24(37)	6	0	0	24
Trent Waterhouse	Warrington	2012-14	65(5)	15	0	0	60
Luke Waterworth	Wigan	2016	1	0	0	0	0
Kallum Watkins	Salford	2020-21	12	2	0	0	8
	Leeds	2008-19	215(7)	110	85	0	610
Dave Watson	Sheffield	1998-99	41(4)	4	0	0	16
Ian Watson	Salford	1997, 2002	24(17)	8	3	5	43
	Workington	1996	4(1)	1	15	0	34
Kris Watson	Warrington	1996	11(2)	2	0	0	8
Anthony Watts	Widnes	2012	(1)	0	0	0	0
Brad Watts	Widnes	2005	6	3	0	0	12
Liam Watts	Castleford	2018-21	68(9)	7	0	0	28
	Hull	2012-18	116(19)	9	0	0	36
	Hull KR	2008, 2010-12	31(26)	6	0	0	24
Michael Watts	Warrington	2002	3	0	0	0	0
Brent Webb	Catalans	2013-14	10	2	0	0	8
	Leeds	2007-12	137(1)	73	0	0	292
Jason Webber	Salford	2000	25(1)	10	0	0	40
Ian Webster	St Helens	2006	1	0	0	0	0
Jake Webster	Castleford	2013-18	103(12)	45	0	0	180
	Hull KR	2008-12	95(1)	34	7	0	150
James Webster	Hull	2008	1	0	0	0	0
	Hull KR	2007-08	36	2	0	2	10
Pat Weisner	Hull KR	2007	(2)	0	0	0	0
	Harlequins	2006	10(6)	3	0	0	12
Taylor Welch	Warrington	2008	1	0	0	0	0
Kris Welham	Salford	2017-20	85(1)	27	0	0	108
	Hull KR	2007-15	164(2)	90	1	0	362
Paul Wellens	St Helens	1998-2015	399(40)	199	34	1	865
Calvin Wellington	St Helens	2016	1	0	0	0	0
Jack Wells	Salford	2021	5(5)	1	0	0	4
	Wigan	2016-17, 2020	5(12)	1	0	0	4
	Toronto	2020	(2)	1	0	0	4
Jon Wells	Harlequins	2006-09	66	10	0	0	40
	London	2004-05	42(2)	19	0	0	76
	Wakefield	2003	22(1)	1	0	0	4
	Castleford	1996-2002	114(14)	49	0	0	196
Jack Welsby	St Helens	2018-21	40(9)	25	0	1	101
Dwayne West	St Helens	2000-02	8(16)	6	0	0	24
	Wigan	1999	1(1)	0	0	0	0

PLAYER	CLUB	YEAR	APP	TRIES	GOALS	FG	PTS
Joe Westerman	Wakefield	2020-21	31	6	0	0	24
	Hull	2011-15, 2018-19	135(13)	36	52	1	249
	Warrington	2016-17	45(1)	12	0	0	48
	Castleford	2008-10	68(7)	29	151	0	418
Craig Weston	Widnes	2002, 2004	23(9)	2	1	2	12
	Huddersfield	1998-99	46(1)	15	15	0	90
Dayne Weston	Leigh	2017	6(5)	1	0	0	4
Ben Westwood	Warrington	2002-19	363(29)	112	64	0	576
	Wakefield	1999-2002	31(7)	8	1	0	34
Michael Weyman	Hull KR	2014	22(1)	7	0	0	28
Andrew Whalley	Workington	1996	(2)	0	0	0	0
Dean Whare	Catalans	2021	22	4	0	0	16
Paul Whatuira	Huddersfield	2008-10	59	23	0	0	92
Scott Wheeldon	Castleford	2014-15	14(23)	5	0	0	20
	London	2012-13	27(4)	3	0	0	12
	Hull KR	2009-12	30(42)	4	0	0	16
	Hull	2006-08	2(60)	4	0	0	16
Gary Wheeler	Toronto	2020	(2)	2	0	0	8
	Warrington	2015-16	6(4)	4	0	0	16
	St Helens	2008-14	48(10)	17	13	0	94
Matt Whitaker	Castleford	2006	8(2)	0	0	0	0
	Widnes	2004-05	10(20)	9	0	0	36
	Huddersfield	2003-04	3(14)	0	0	0	0
Jai Whitbread	Leigh	2021	2(2)	1	0	0	4
Ben White	Leeds	2014	1	0	0	0	0
David White	Wakefield	2000	(1)	0	0	0	0
Josh White	Salford	1998	18(3)	5	5	1	31
	London	1997	14(2)	8	0	1	33
Lloyd White	Widnes	2012-18	72(43)	27	24	1	157
	Crusaders	2010-11	13(11)	8	0	0	32
	Celtic	2009	6	1	0	0	4
Paul White	Salford	2009	1	1	0	0	4
	Wakefield	2006-07	24(12)	12	0	0	48
	Huddersfield	2003-05	11(32)	17	16	0	100
Elliott Whitehead	Catalans	2013-15	64(1)	30	0	0	120
	Bradford	2009-13	90(10)	30	0	0	120
Harvey Whiteley	Leeds	2017, 2020	(3)	0	0	0	0
Richard Whiting	Hull	2004-15	163(72)	69	19	2	316
Matt Whitley	Catalans	2019-21	49(4)	20	0	0	80
	Widnes	2015-18	50(27)	13	0	0	52
Emmerson Whittel	Bradford	2014	(1)	0	0	0	0
Danny Whittle	Warrington	1998	(2)	0	0	0	0
David Whittle	St Helens	2002	1(2)	0	0	0	0
	Warrington	2001	1(2)	0	0	0	0
Jon Whittle	Wakefield	2006	8(2)	3	0	0	12
	Widnes	2005	13	2	0	0	8
	Wigan	2003	1	0	0	0	0
Joel Wicks	London	2013-14	3(10)	0	0	0	0
Dean Widders	Castleford	2009-11	25(32)	23	0	0	92
Gareth Widdop	Warrington	2020-21	31	15	32	1	125
Stephen Wild	Salford	2011-13	71	4	0	0	16
	Huddersfield	2006-10	116(2)	33	0	0	132
	Wigan	2001-05	67(20)	24	0	0	96
Sam Wilde	Widnes	2017-18	14(7)	2	0	0	8
	Warrington	2015-16	3(15)	1	0	0	4
Matty Wildie	Leigh	2021	2(9)	0	0	0	0
	Wakefield	2010-14	13(26)	3	0	0	12
Brayden Wiliame	Catalans	2017-19	64	25	0	0	100
Oliver Wilkes	Wakefield	2008-09, 2012-13	55(47)	10	0	0	40
	Harlequins	2010-11	39(13)	4	0	0	16
	Wigan	2006	1(5)	0	0	0	0
	Leigh	2005	13(1)	1	0	0	4
	Huddersfield	2000-01	1(6)	0	0	0	0
	Sheffield	1998	(1)	0	0	0	0
Jon Wilkin	Toronto	2020	5	1	0	0	4
	St Helens	2003-18	350(30)	78	0	2	314
Alex Wilkinson	Hull	2003-04	11(4)	1	0	0	4
	Huddersfield	2003	8	4	0	0	16
	London	2002	5(1)	0	0	0	0
	Bradford	2000-01	3(3)	1	0	0	4
Bart Williams	London	1998	5(3)	1	0	0	4
Connor Williams	Salford	2016	(1)	0	0	0	0
Daley Williams	Salford	2006-07	9(2)	4	0	0	16
Danny Williams	Harlequins	2006	9(13)	4	0	0	16
	London	2005	1(16)	0	0	0	0
Danny Williams	Bradford	2014	7	2	0	0	8
	Salford	2011-14	54	31	0	0	124
	Leeds	2006, 2008	13(2)	7	0	0	28
	Hull	2008	3	0	0	0	0
Dave Williams	Harlequins	2008-11	1(17)	0	0	0	0
Desi Williams	Wigan	2004	2	0	0	0	0
George Williams	Warrington	2021	8	3	0	3	15
	Wigan	2013-19	149(13)	55	56	1	333
Jonny Williams	London	2004	(4)	0	0	0	0
Lee Williams	Crusaders	2011	1(7)	0	0	0	0
Rhys Williams	Salford	2013, 2020-21	39	11	0	0	44
	London	2019	29	13	0	0	52
	Warrington	2010-13	23(1)	15	0	0	60
	Castleford	2012	8	4	0	0	16
	Crusaders	2011	6	3	0	0	12
Sam Williams	Wakefield	2017	17(5)	4	26	0	68
	Catalans	2014	11(1)	4	21	0	58
Sonny Bill Williams	Toronto	2020	4(1)	0	0	0	0
Luke Williamson	Harlequins	2009-10	39	6	0	0	24
John Wilshere	Salford	2006-07, 2009	72(2)	32	142	0	412
	Leigh	2005	26	8	6	0	44
	Warrington	2004	5	2	0	0	8
Craig Wilson	Hull	2000	2(16)	1	0	1	5
	Gateshead	1999	17(11)	5	0	1	21
George Wilson	Paris	1996	7(2)	3	0	0	12
John Wilson	Catalans	2006-08	69	23	0	0	92
Oliver Wilson	Huddersfield	2019-21	11(18)	0	0	0	0
Richard Wilson	Hull	1998-99	(13)	0	0	0	0
Scott Wilson	Warrington	1998-99	23(2)	6	0	0	24
Johan Windley	Hull	1999	2(2)	1	0	0	4
Jake Wingfield	St Helens	2020-21	2(6)	0	0	0	0
Paul Wingfield	Warrington	1997	5(3)	6	1	0	26
Frank Winterstein	Widnes	2012-13	37(9)	16	0	0	64
	Crusaders	2010-11	26(19)	4	0	0	16
	Wakefield	2009	(5)	0	0	0	0
Lincoln Withers	Hull KR	2012-13	18(22)	10	0	0	40
	Crusaders	2010-11	47	4	0	0	16
	Celtic	2009	21	6	0	0	24
Michael Withers	Wigan	2007	6(1)	1	0	0	4
	Bradford	1999-2006	156(6)	94	15	4	410
Michael Witt	London	2012-13	37	10	89	1	219
	Crusaders	2010-11	39	13	47	4	150
Jeff Wittenberg	Huddersfield	1998	18(1)	1	0	0	4
	Bradford	1997	8(9)	4	0	0	16
Josh Wood	Wakefield	2020-21	7(6)	1	0	0	4
	Salford	2015-19	19(17)	2	0	0	8
Kyle Wood	Wakefield	2012-13, 2017-21	62(93)	26	0	0	104
	Huddersfield	2011, 2013-16	39(33)	7	0	0	28
	Castleford	2010	1(4)	0	0	0	0
Martin Wood	Sheffield	1997-98	24(11)	4	18	2	54
Mikey Wood	Huddersfield	2016-17	1(1)	0	0	0	0
Nathan Wood	Warrington	2002-05	90	38	0	3	155
	Wakefield	2002	11	2	0	0	8
Paul Wood	Warrington	2000-14	138(171)	40	0	0	160
Phil Wood	Widnes	2004	2(1)	0	0	0	0
Sam Wood	Bradford	2013-14	7(1)	0	0	0	0
Sam Wood	Huddersfield	2016-18, 2020-21	39(9)	13	4	0	60
James Woodburn-Hall	London	2013-14	9(4)	2	0	0	8
Darren Woods	Widnes	2005	(1)	0	0	0	0
David Woods	Halifax	2002	18(2)	8	0	0	32
Josh Woods	Wigan	2017-18	10(1)	1	4	1	13
Simon Worrall	Leeds	2008-09	5(16)	1	0	0	4
Michael Worrincy	Bradford	2009-10	12(34)	12	0	0	48
	Harlequins	2006-08	20(12)	10	0	0	40
Rob Worrincy	Castleford	2004	1	0	0	0	0
Greg Worthington	Toronto	2020	(1)	0	0	0	0
James Worthington	Wigan	2017	1	2	0	0	8
Troy Wozniak	Widnes	2004	13(7)	1	0	0	4
Matthew Wray	Wakefield	2002-03	13(3)	2	0	0	8
Connor Wrench	Warrington	2020-21	7(1)	2	0	0	8
David Wrench	Wakefield	2002-06	28(52)	6	0	0	24
	Leeds	1999-2001	7(17)	0	0	0	0
Callum Wright	Wigan	2014	(2)	0	0	0	0
Craig Wright	Castleford	2000	1(9)	0	0	0	0
Nigel Wright	Huddersfield	1999	4(6)	1	0	0	4
	Wigan	1996-97	5(5)	2	0	1	9
Ricky Wright	Sheffield	1997-99	2(13)	0	0	0	0
Vincent Wulf	Paris	1996	13(4)	4	0	0	16
Connor Wynne	Hull	2019-21	11(4)	5	0	0	20
Andrew Wynyard	London	1999-2000	34(6)	4	0	0	16
Bagdad Yaha	Paris	1996	4(4)	2	4	0	16
Fouad Yaha	Catalans	2015-21	105	67	0	0	268
Malakai Yasa	Sheffield	1996	1(3)	0	0	0	0
Andy Yates	Wakefield	2016	(7)	0	0	0	0
	Leeds	2015	(9)	1	0	0	4
Luke Yates	Huddersfield	2021	18	2	0	0	8
	Salford	2020	12(5)	3	0	0	12
	London	2019	28	2	0	0	8
Kirk Yeaman	Hull	2001-16, 2018	322(18)	159	0	0	636
Dominic Young	Huddersfield	2019-20	2	0	0	0	0

Super League Players 1996-2021

PLAYER	CLUB	YEAR	APP	TRIES	GOALS	FG	PTS
Grant Young	London	1998-99	22(2)	2	0	0	8
Nick Youngquest	Castleford	2011-12	37	28	0	0	112
	Crusaders	2010	26(1)	9	0	0	36
Ronel Zenon	Paris	1996	(4)	0	0	0	0
Nick Zisti	Bradford	1999	6(1)	0	0	0	0
Freddie Zitter	Catalans	2006	1	0	0	0	0

NEW FACES - Players making their Super League debuts in 2021

PLAYER	CLUB	DEBUT vs	ROUND	DATE
James Bell	Leigh	Castleford (a)	3	16/4/21
Jonathan Bennison	St Helens	Salford (a)	25	17/9/21
Aidan Burrell	Hull FC	Huddersfield (h)	11	25/6/21
Joe Chan	Catalans	Hull KR (a)	17	2/8/21
		(club debut: Warrington (h), CCQF, 7/5/21)		
Jack Cogger	Huddersfield	Hull FC (a)	1	28/3/21
Mathieu Cozza	Catalans	Salford (a)	21	26/8/21
Brendan Elliot	Leigh	Huddersfield (h)	7	23/5/21
Jai Field	Wigan	Leigh (a)	1	26/3/21
Romain Franco	Catalans	Hull KR (a)	17	2/8/21
Morgan Gannon	Leeds	Wigan (h)	3	15/4/21
		(club debut: St Helens (a), CC3, 10/4/21)		
Ollie Greensmith	Wakefield	Salford (a)	12	16/7/21
Ata Hingano	Salford	Leeds (a)	15	23/7/21
Jacob Hookem	Hull FC	Wakefield (a)	25	17/9/21
Greg Inglis	Warrington	Hull KR (h)	5	1/5/21
Caelum Jordan	Castleford	Salford (h)	14	11/7/21
Matthieu Laguerre	Catalans	Hull KR (a)	1	27/3/21
Corentin Le Cam	Catalans	St Helens (a)	18	7/8/21
Mason Lino	Wakefield	Leeds (h)	1	27/3/21
Sam Luckley	Salford	Warrington (h)	8	27/5/21
Darcy Lussick	Salford	Catalans (a)	3	17/4/21
		(club debut: Widnes (h), CC3, 10/4/21)		
Nathan Magee	Castleford	Salford (h)	14	11/7/21
Shay Martyn	St Helens	Salford (a)	25	17/9/21
Sione Mata'utia	St Helens	Salford (h)	1	26/3/21
Brad O'Neill	Wigan	Wakefield (a)	11	24/6/21
Agnatius Paasi	St Helens	Salford (h)	1	26/3/21
Nathan Peats	Leigh	Castleford (a)	3	16/4/21
		(club debut: Huddersfield (h), CC3, 11/4/21)		
Will Pryce	Huddersfield	Catalans (h)	12	1/7/21
Jason Qareqare	Castleford	Hull FC (h)	9	10/6/21
Josh Reynolds	Hull FC	Huddersfield (h)	1	28/3/21
Cain Robb	Castleford	Salford (h)	14	11/7/21
Cesar Rouge	Catalans	St Helens (a)	18	7/8/21
Sam Royle	St Helens	Salford (a)	25	17/9/21
Adam Rusling	Castleford	Salford (h)	14	11/7/21
Jack Sadler	Castleford	Salford (h)	14	11/7/21
Korbin Sims	Hull KR	Catalans (a)	1	27/3/21
Robson Stevens	Huddersfield	Wigan (h)	9	16/7/21
Sam Stone	Leigh	Salford (h)	20	22/8/21
Jake Sweeting	Castleford	Huddersfield (h)	17	2/8/21
Brad Takairangi	Hull KR	Leeds (h)	4	23/4/21
Elijah Taylor	Salford	St Helens (a)	1	26/3/21
Zane Tetevano	Leeds	Wakefield (a)	1	27/3/21
Joel Thompson	St Helens	Salford (h)	1	26/3/21
Albert Vete	Hull KR	Catalans (a)	1	27/3/21
Mitieli Vulikijapani	Hull FC	Leigh (a)	10	19/6/21
King Vuniyayawa	Leeds	Hull KR (a)	4	23/4/21
		(club debut: St Helens (a), CC3, 10/4/21)		
Marcus Walker	Hull FC	Catalans (a)	19	13/8/21
Dean Whare	Catalans	Hull KR (h)	1	27/3/21
Jai Whitbread	Leigh	Catalans (a)	22	30/8/21

*All totals in 'Super League Players 1996-2021' include play-off games &
Super League Super 8s from 2015-2018. Super 8s (Qualifiers) not included.*

Toronto Wolfpack games from 2020 season also included.

OLD FACES - Players making their Super League debuts for new clubs in 2021

PLAYER	CLUB	DEBUT vs	ROUND	DATE
Danny Addy	Salford	St Helens (a)	1	26/3/21
Olly Ashall-Bott	Wakefield	Catalans (h)	5	30/4/21
Olly Ashall-Bott	Huddersfield	Hull FC (a)	11	25/6/21
Jack Ashworth	Huddersfield	Hull KR (a)	3	16/4/21
(club debut: Leigh (a), CC3, 11/4/21)				
Jack Ashworth	Leigh	Wigan (a) (D2)	17	1/8/21
John Bateman	Wigan	Leigh (a) (D2)	1	26/3/21
Lewis Bienek	Castleford	Leigh (h)	3	16/4/21
Keanan Brand	Leigh	Wigan (h)	1	26/3/21
Ryan Brierley	Leigh	Wigan (h) (D3)	1	26/3/21
Robin Brochon	Catalans	Huddersfield (h) (D2)	24	11/9/21
Joe Burgess	Salford	Hull KR (a)	9	11/6/21
Rob Butler	Warrington	Leigh (h)	2	2/4/21
Rob Butler	Leigh	Wigan (a)	17	1/8/21
Matthew Costello	Salford	Catalans (a)	3	17/4/21
(club debut: Widnes (h), CC3, 10/4/21)				
James Cunningham	Huddersfield	Hull FC (a)	1	28/3/21
Ben Davies	Salford	Hull KR (a)	9	11/6/21
Jordan Dezaria	Catalans	Wakefield (a) (D2)	5	30/4/21
Gil Dudson	Catalans	Huddersfield (a)	2	3/4/21
Kyle Eastmond	Leeds	Wigan (h)	3	15/4/21
Josh Eaves	Leigh	Wigan (h) (D2)	1	26/3/21
Josh Eaves	Wakefield	Catalans (h)	5	30/4/21
Jamie Ellis	Leigh	Wigan (h) (D2)	6	17/5/21
Morgan Escare	Salford	Catalans (a)	3	17/4/21
(club debut: Widnes (h), CC3, 10/4/21)				
Niall Evalds	Castleford	Warrington (h)	1	28/3/21
Ben Flower	Leigh	Castleford (a)	3	16/4/21
(club debut: Huddersfield (h), CC3, 11/4/21)				
Matthew Foster	Leigh	Wigan (h)	1	26/3/21
Matty Gee	Leigh	Wigan (h)	1	26/3/21
Anthony Gelling	Leigh	Salford (a)	4	23/4/21
Alex Gerrard	Leigh	Warrington (a)	2	2/4/21
(club debut: Dewsbury (a), Ch1, 31/1/20)				
Joe Greenwood	Huddersfield	Hull FC (a)	1	28/3/21
Ryan Hall	Hull KR	Catalans (a)	1	27/3/21
Ben Hellewell	Leigh	Wigan (h)	1	26/3/21
(club debut: Dewsbury (a), Ch1, 31/1/20)				
Liam Hood	Leigh	Wigan (h)	1	26/3/21
(club debut: Halifax (a), Ch6, 13/3/16; second debut: Swinton (a), Ch6, 10/3/19)				
Mark Ioane	Leigh	Wigan (h)	1	26/3/21
(club debut: Sheffield (h), Ch2, 8/2/20)				
Corey Johnson	Leeds	St Helens (a) (D2)	24	10/9/21
Luis Johnson	Hull KR	Huddersfield (h)	3	16/4/21
(club debut: Castleford (h) (D2), CC3, 9/4/21)				
Josh Jones	Huddersfield	Hull FC (a)	1	28/3/21
Jimmy Keinhorst	Castleford	Huddersfield (h)	17	2/8/21
Ricky Leutele	Huddersfield	Hull FC (a)	1	28/3/21
Harvey Livett	Salford	St Helens (a)	1	26/3/21
Jack Logan	Hull FC	Huddersfield (h) (D2)	11	25/6/21
Jack Logan	Leigh	Hull KR (h)	18	8/8/21
Nathan Mason	Leigh	Wigan (h)	1	26/3/21
(club debut: Toronto (h), Ch1, 4/2/18; second debut: Dewsbury (a), Ch1, 31/1/20)				
Suaia Matagi	Castleford	Warrington (a)	7	22/5/21
Tyrone McCarthy	Leigh	Warrington (a) (D2)	2	2/4/21
Mike McMeeken	Catalans	Hull KR (h)	1	27/3/21
Joe Mellor	Leigh	Wigan (h)	1	26/3/21
Robbie Mulhern	Warrington	Castleford (a)	1	28/3/21
Craig Mullen	Leigh	Castleford (a)	3	16/4/21
(club debut: Batley (h), CC4, 21/2/20)				
Muizz Mustapha	Hull KR	St Helens (h)	2	1/4/21
Tom Nisbet	Leigh	Catalans (a)	22	30/8/21
Dan Norman	St Helens	Salford (a)	25	17/9/21
(club debut: Hull FC, CCSF, 5/6/21)				
Dan Norman	Salford	Castleford (a)	14	11/7/21
Dec Patton	Salford	St Helens (a)	1	26/3/21
Nathan Peats	Huddersfield	Wigan (a)	14	11/7/21
Nathaniel Peteru	Leigh	Wigan (h)	1	26/3/21
Nathaniel Peteru	Huddersfield	Wigan (a)	14	11/7/21
Ben Reynolds	Leigh	Warrington (a) (D3)	2	2/4/21
Ellis Robson	Salford	Wigan (a)	18	6/8/21
Matty Russell	Leigh	Wigan (h) (D2)	1	26/3/21
Junior Sa'u	Leigh	St Helens (h)	5	30/4/21
(club debut: Batley (h), Ch22, 21/7/19)				
Adam Sidlow	Leigh	Wigan (h)	1	26/3/21
Josh Simm	Leigh	Castleford (a) (D2)	3	16/4/21
Tom Spencer	Leigh	Catalans (a)	22	30/8/21
(club debut: Sheffield (a), NRC2, 19/2/12; second debut: Featherstone (a), Ch1, 3/2/13; third debut: Toulouse (h), Ch1, 3/2/19)				
Jordan Thompson	Leigh	Wigan (h)	1	26/3/21
(club debut: Toronto (h), Ch1, 4/2/18; second debut: Bradford (h), Ch17, 16/6/19)				
Iain Thornley	Leigh	Wigan (h)	1	26/3/21
(club debut: Halifax (h), Ch20, 31/7/13; second debut: Toulouse (h), Ch1, 3/2/19)				
Lewis Tierney	Leigh	Wigan (h)	1	26/3/21
Jordan Turner	Castleford	Warrington (a)	1	28/3/21
Blake Wallace	Leigh	Wigan (h)	1	26/3/21
Jack Wells	Salford	St Helens (a)	1	26/3/21
Matty Wildie	Leigh	Warrington (a)	2	2/4/21
(club debut: Dewsbury (a), Ch1, 31/1/20)				
George Williams	Warrington	Leeds (a)	17	1/8/21
Luke Yates	Huddersfield	Hull FC (a)	1	28/3/21

SUPER LEAGUE XXVI
Club by Club

23rd November 2020 - Oliver Holmes signs new one-year contract.

23rd November 2020 - Paul McShane named Steve Prescott Man of Steel.

24th November 2020 - Hull FC prop Lewis Bienek signs on one-year deal.

25th November 2020 - Huddersfield Giants prop Suaia Matagi joins on one-year loan deal.

27th November 2020 - Huddersfield Giants centre Jordan Turner signs on one-year contract.

6th December 2020 - prop Daniel Smith signs new one-year contract.

9th December 2020 - James Clare signs new one-year contract.

11th December 2020 - Mike McMeeken leaves for Catalans Dragons.

18th February 2021 - Sosaia Feki ruptures Achilles tendon in pre-season training.

14th March 2021 - 30-20 win at Hull KR in Adam Milner Testimonial.

18th March 2021 - head coach Daryl Powell to leave Tigers at end of 2021 season.

28th March 2021 - 21-12 win over Warrington in season opener at Headingley.

2nd April 2021 - 18-10 round-two win over Leeds at St Helens.

8th April 2021 - Jon Wells to step down as director of rugby at end of May.

9th April 2021 - Gareth O'Brien golden-point field goal in 99th minute seals 33-32 Challenge Cup third-round win at Hull KR.

16th April 2021 - 52-16 round-three victory over Leigh on return to Jungle.

22nd April 2021 - 22-16 defeat at Wigan ends 100 per cent start. Tyla Hepi banned for two matches for dangerous contact.

27th April 2021 - Lee Radford to become head coach at end of season on two-year contract.

8th May 2021 - Gareth O'Brien golden-point field goal secures 19-18 Challenge Cup quarter-final win over Salford at Headingley.

12th May 2021 - fullback Niall Evalds signs new two-year contract extension to end of 2023, with extra-year option in favour of club.

14th May 2021 - prop Nathan Massey agrees two-year contract extension.

16th May 2021 - prop Daniel Smith signs two-year contract extension to end of 2023.

17th May 2021 - fans return for 26-22 home defeat by Hull KR.

17th May 2021 - depleted side suffers 38-14 away defeat to Warrington.

17th May 2021 - utility Jordan Turner signs two-year contract extension to end of 2023.

26th May 2021 - club triggers one-year extension of George Griffin contract to end of 2022 season.

28th May 2021 - crushing 60-6 home defeat by Leeds.

5th June 2021 - 35-20 win over Warrington at Leigh earns trip to Wembley.

KEY DATES

9th June 2021 - Oliver Holmes and Peter Mata'utia to join Warrington at end of season.

10th June 2021 - 17-year-old Jason Qareqare scores in first minute of debut in 30-12 home defeat by Hull FC.

20th June 2021 - utility forward Jacques O'Neill signs new two-year deal to end of 2023 season.

22nd June 2021 - Joe Westerman signs from Wakefield on two-year deal from 2022 season.

28th June 2021 - home fixture with St Helens scheduled for Wednesday (June 30th) cancelled with Tigers unable to field 17-man squad. St Helens awarded 24-0 victory.

1st July 2021 - Jake Mamo signs from Warrington from 2022 season on three-year deal.

2nd July 2021 - hooker Paul McShane signs three-year contract extension to end of 2025 season.

5th July 2021 - Tigers awarded 24-0 win from fixture against Huddersfield (scheduled for July 6th) with Giants unable to field 17-man squad.

11th July 2021 - shadow team with five debutants loses at home 70-18 to Salford.

17th July 2021 - Niall Evalds wins Lance Todd Trophy in 26-12 Wembley defeat to St Helens.

21st July 2021 - round-15 game at Catalans (Saturday 24th July) postponed due to Covid issues in Tigers camp.

25th July 2021 - round-16 game at Leigh (scheduled 29th July) postponed.

31st July 2021 - Jimmy Keinhorst joins from Hull KR on short-term loan.

2nd August 2021 - youthful side including on-loan Jake Sweeting from Featherstone falls to 34-16 home defeat by Huddersfield.

5th August 2021 - Bureta Fairamo signs from Hull FC on two-year contract from 2022.

6th August 2021 - Greg Eden scores double in 32-18 win at Leeds.

11th August 2021 - Jake Trueman undergoes surgery for persistent back injury and is out for season.

12th August 2021 - 20-10 win at St Helens is first for 30 years. Greg Eden scores another double.

16th August 2021 - Adam Milner signs two-year contract extension to end of 2023.

24th August 2021 - Tigers fined £35,000 (£15,000 suspended for two years) for failing to fulfil fixture against St Helens and breaching Covid protocols on return coach journey from Challenge Cup Final

26th August 2021 - Jordan Turner scores try double in 23-12 victory at Hull FC.

27th August 2021 - Grant Millington to retire at end of season.

30th August 2021 - 22-0 home defeat to Wigan ends winning run at four games.

4th September 2021 - 29-18 Magic Weekend win over Salford in Newcastle.

8th September 2021 - forward Jesse Sene-Lefao to leave at end of season after five years at Tigers.

11th September 2021 - Oliver Holmes suffers season-ending whiplash injury in 26-19 defeat at Hull KR.

14th September 2021 - captain Michael Shenton to retire at end of season

13th September 2021 - utility Alex Foster to leave at end of season.

16th September 2021 - 40-20 home defeat by Warrington, after trailing 26-0 at half-time, ends play-off chances. Paul McShane plays 300th career game.

19th September 2021 - Huddersfield back-rower Kenny Edwards joins on one-year loan deal for 2022.

21st September 2021 - Leeds Rhinos second row/centre Alex Sutcliffe joins on two-year contract.

25th September 2021 - forward Tyla Hepi signs new contract to end of 2023.

2nd October 2021 - front-rowers Brad Martin and Sam Hall sign new one-year contracts.

2nd October 2021 - Andy Last appointed assistant coach.

5th October 2021 - Hull KR back-rower George Lawler joins on two-year contract.

7th October 2021 - forward Lewis Peachey signs new contract to end of 2022.

10th October 2021 - on-loan Huddersfield prop Suaia Matagi signs permanent two-year contract.

11th October 2021 - Leeds halfback Callum McLelland re-joins on two-year contract, with option of two further seasons.

13th October 2021 - released Hull FC outside back Mahe Fonua joins on initial one-year deal.

CLUB RECORDS

Highest score:
106-0 v Rochdale, 9/9/2007
Highest score against:
12-76 v Leeds, 14/8/2009
Record attendance:
25,449 v Hunslet, 9/3/35

MATCH RECORDS

Tries:
5 Derek Foster v Hunslet, 10/11/72
John Joyner v Millom, 16/9/73
Steve Fenton v Dewsbury, 27/1/78
Ian French v Hunslet, 9/2/86
St John Ellis v Whitehaven, 10/12/89
Greg Eden v Warrington, 11/6/2017
Goals: 17 Sammy Lloyd v Millom, 16/9/73
Points: 43 Sammy Lloyd v Millom, 16/9/73

SEASON RECORDS

Tries: 42 Denny Solomona 2016
Goals: 158 Sammy Lloyd 1976-77
Points: 355 Luke Gale 2017

CAREER RECORDS

Tries: 206 Alan Hardisty 1958-71
Goals: 875 Albert Lunn 1951-63
Points: 1,870 Albert Lunn 1951-63
Appearances: 613 John Joyner 1973-92

CASTLEFORD TIGERS

DATE	FIXTURE	RESULT	SCORERS	LGE	ATT
28/3/21	Warrington (h) ●	W21-12	t:Holmes,Evalds,Turner(2) g:O'Brien,McShane fg:McShane	3rd	BCD
2/4/21	Leeds (a) ●●	W10-18	t:Holmes,Evalds,Turner g:Richardson(3)	4th	BCD
9/4/21	Hull KR (a) (CCR3)	W32-33		N/A	BCD
		(aet)	t:Trueman,Olpherts(2),McShane(2),Turner g:Richardson(4) fg:O'Brien		
16/4/21	Leigh (h)	W52-16	t:Watts,Smith,Olpherts(2),Eden,Evalds,Shenton,Turner,Trueman		BCD
			g:O'Brien(2),McShane(6)		
22/4/21	Wigan (a)	L22-12	t:Olpherts(2) g:McShane(2)	3rd	BCD
30/4/21	Salford (a)	W18-28	t:Eden,Watts,Blair,Trueman g:Richardson(6)	4th	BCD
8/5/21	Salford (h) (CCQF) ●	W19-18		3rd	BCD
		(aet)	t:Smith,Mata'utia,Shenton g:Richardson(2),O'Brien fg:O'Brien	N/A	BCD
17/5/21	Hull KR (h)	L22-26	t:Clare,Shenton,Olpherts g:Richardson(5)	4th	3,600
22/5/21	Warrington (a)	L38-14	t:Trueman,Turner(2) g:Richardson	6th	4,000
28/5/21	Leeds (h)	L6-60	t:Turner g:Richardson	7th	4,000
5/6/21	Warrington (CCSF) ●●●	W35-20	t:O'Brien,Turner(3),Sene-Lefao,McShane g:O'Brien(5) fg:McShane	N/A	-
10/6/21	Hull FC (h)	L12-30	t:Qareqare,Holmes g:Richardson(2)	7th	4,000
16/6/21	Wakefield (a)	W12-18	t:Griffin,Turner,Shenton,Mata'utia g:Richardson	7th	2,262
24/6/21	Catalans Dragons (h)	L6-16	t:Olpherts g:Richardson	7th	4,000
11/7/21	Salford (h)	L18-70	t:Millington,Martin,Foster g:Richardson(3)	8th	3,900
17/7/21	St Helens (CCF) ●●●●	L12-26	t:Evalds,Trueman g:O'Brien(2)	N/A	40,000
2/8/21	Huddersfield (h)	L16-34	t:McShane,Graham,Sweeting g:McShane(2)	8th	5,126
6/8/21	Leeds (a)	W18-32	t:Eden(2),Mata'utia,Turner,Keinhorst g:Richardson(6)	8th	10,838
12/8/21	St Helens (a)	W10-20	t:Eden(2),Holmes g:Richardson(4)	8th	7,050
21/8/21	Wakefield (h)	W23-18	t:Eden(2),Holmes,Olpherts g:Richardson(3) fg:Richardson	8th	4,987
26/8/21	Hull FC (a)	W12-23	t:Turner(2),Richardson,Evalds g:Richardson(3) fg:Richardson	6th	8,121
30/8/21	Wigan (h)	L0-22		6th	4,729
4/9/21	Salford (MW) ●●●●●	W29-18	t:McShane,Smith,Holmes,Turner,Mata'utia g:Mata'utia(4) fg:Turner	6th	-
11/9/21	Hull KR (a)	L26-19	t:Evalds(2),Olpherts g:Richardson(3) fg:Richardson	7th	6,840
16/9/21	Warrington (h)	L24-40	t:Mata'utia(2),Turner,Millington g:Richardson(4)	7th	5,126

● Played at Emerald Headingley, Leeds ●● Played at Totally Wicked Stadium, St Helens ●●● Played at Leigh Sports Village
●●●● Played at Wembley Stadium ●●●●● Played at St James' Park, Newcastle

Catalans Dragons (a) (R15) and Leigh (a) (R16) games were postponed, and not rearranged

St Helens (h) (R12) game ruled a 24-0 defeat after being unable to field a team

Huddersfield (a) (R13) game ruled a 24-0 victory after the Giants were unable to field a team

		APP		TRIES		GOALS		FG		PTS	
	D.O.B.	ALL	SL	ALL	SL	ALL	SL	ALL	SL	ALL	SL
Lewis Bienek	11/4/98	1(5)	1(5)	0	0	0	0	0	0	0	0
Cheyse Blair	18/1/92	9(3)	8(3)	1	1	0	0	0	0	4	4
James Clare	13/4/91	7(1)	7	1	1	0	0	0	0	4	4
Greg Eden	14/11/90	8(1)	8(1)	8	8	0	0	0	0	32	32
Niall Evalds	26/8/93	20	17	7	6	0	0	0	0	28	24
Alex Foster	25/9/93	6(7)	6(5)	1	1	0	0	0	0	4	4
Brad Graham	1/9/01	2	2	1	1	0	0	0	0	4	4
George Griffin	26/6/92	15(2)	12(2)	1	1	0	0	0	0	4	4
Sam Hall	8/5/02	1(2)	1(2)	0	0	0	0	0	0	0	0
Tyla Hepi	15/6/93	2(9)	2(9)	0	0	0	0	0	0	0	0
Oliver Holmes	7/8/92	19(1)	15(1)	6	6	0	0	0	0	24	24
Caelum Jordan	16/9/02	1	1	0	0	0	0	0	0	0	0
Jimmy Keinhorst	14/7/90	(2)	(2)	1	1	0	0	0	0	4	4
Nathan Magee	5/6/03	(1)	(1)	0	0	0	0	0	0	0	0
Brad Martin	6/2/01	5(4)	5(3)	1	1	0	0	0	0	4	4
Nathan Massey	11/7/89	21(1)	17(1)	0	0	0	0	0	0	0	0
Peter Mata'utia	2/11/90	21	17	6	5	4	4	0	0	32	28
Suaia Matagi	23/3/88	3(10)	2(10)	0	0	0	0	0	0	0	0
Paul McShane	19/11/89	20(1)	16(1)	5	2	11	11	2	1	44	31
Grant Millington	1/11/86	12(2)	9(2)	2	2	0	0	0	0	8	8
Adam Milner	19/12/91	10(9)	8(7)	0	0	0	0	0	0	0	0
Gareth O'Brien	31/10/91	12(1)	9	1	0	11	3	2	0	28	6
Jacques O'Neill	8/5/99	1(5)	1(4)	0	0	0	0	0	0	0	0
Derrell Olpherts	7/1/92	24	20	10	8	0	0	0	0	40	32
Lewis Peachey	25/3/01	1(6)	1(6)	0	0	0	0	0	0	0	0
Jason Qareqare	26/1/04	2(1)	2(1)	1	1	0	0	0	0	4	4
Danny Richardson	2/9/96	18	16	1	1	52	46	3	3	111	99
Cain Robb	5/1/03	2	2	0	0	0	0	0	0	0	0
Adam Rusling	25/5/03	(1)	(1)	0	0	0	0	0	0	0	0
Jack Sadler	28/9/02	1	1	0	0	0	0	0	0	0	0
Jesse Sene-Lefao	8/12/89	16(3)	14(2)	1	0	0	0	0	0	4	0
Michael Shenton	22/7/86	19	15	4	3	0	0	0	0	16	12
Daniel Smith	20/3/93	10(8)	10(5)	3	2	0	0	0	0	12	8
Jake Sweeting	15/12/99	(1)	(1)	1	1	0	0	0	0	4	4
Jake Trueman	16/2/99	11	7	5	3	0	0	0	0	20	12
Jordan Turner	9/1/89	19(1)	15(1)	17	13	0	0	1	1	69	53
Liam Watts	8/7/90	6(12)	6(8)	2	2	0	0	0	0	8	8

Jordan Turner

'SL' totals include Super League games only; 'All' totals also include Challenge Cup

30th November 2020 - captain Remi Casty not offered new deal after 14 seasons at Dragons.

9th December 2020 - back-rower Matt Whitley signs new two-year contract.

11th December 2020 - forward Mike McMeeken signs from Castleford on two-year contract.

16th December 2020 - Salford prop Gil Dudson joins on two-year deal.

21st December 2020 - halfback Arthur Mourgue signs new three-year contract. Lewis Tierney leaves for Leigh.

5th February 2021 - Benjamin Garcia appointed club captain.

8th February 2021 - centre Dean Whare signs from Penrith on two-year contract.

21st February 2021 - winger Fouad Yaha signs new two-year contract.

1st March 2021 - Dragons return to training.

5th March 2021 - Jason Baitieri signs new one-year contract.

13th March 2021 - 40-28 win over Toulouse Olympique in pre-season warm-up.

27th March 2021 - James Maloney golden-point field goal secures 29-28 round-one win over Hull KR at Headingley.

3rd April 2021 - 20-10 win over Huddersfield at St Helens.

8th April 2021 - forward Jordan Dezaria signs full-time contract.

10th April 2021 - comfortable 26-6 Challenge Cup third-round victory over Wakefield at St Helens.

17th April 2021 - Fouad Yaha scores hat-trick in 42-6 home round-three home win over Salford.

24th April 2021 - 24-8 home defeat to Warrington ends 100 per cent start.

30th April 2021 - Tom Davies scores hat-trick in 38-18 win at Wakefield. Paul Seguier suffers knee injury.

4th May 2021 - Jordan Dezaria suspended for one game for dangerous throw.

7th May 2021 - 16-6 Challenge Cup quarter-final defeat to Warrington. Gil Dudson gets one-match penalty notice for dangerous contact.

22nd May 2021 - Sam Tomkins and Samisoni Langi injured in warm up before 20-16 home win over undefeated St Helens. Alrix Da Costa suffers knee injury.

29th May 2021 - 48-0 home win over Wigan ends last hundred per cent record.

1st June 2021 - Joel Tomkins banned for four games for punching.

12th June 2021 - 36-30 win at Leigh moves Dragons to top of table.

15th June 2021 - home fixture with Leeds, scheduled for Saturday June 19th, postponed after further positive Covid-19 tests in Rhinos squad.

24th June 2021 - home game with Hull KR, scheduled for Monday July 5, postponed due to positive cases of Covid-19 at Hull KR.

KEY DATES

28th June 2021 - club reaches agreement with Israel Folau who is released from contract with immediate effect.

1st July 2021 - 50-12 win at Huddersfield. Gil Dudson and Sam Kasiano get one-match bans for dangerous tackles.

3rd July 2021 - Benjamin Garcia signs new three-year contract to end of 2024 season.

7th July 2021 - Sam Kasiano appeal against one-match ban successful.

7th July 2021 - winger Tom Davies signs new three-year contract to end of 2024 season.

11th July 2021 - fullback Sam Tomkins activates one-year contract extension to end of 2022, initially signing three-year contract with option of further year.

12th July 2021 - James Maloney (dangerous contact) and Joel Tomkins (dangerous throw) both get two-match penalty notices.

16th July 2021 - 27-18 home win over Leeds after trailing 18-2 at half-time.

20th July 2021 - prop Lambert Belmas released at end of contract.

21st July 2021 - round-15 home game with Castleford (Saturday 24th July) postponed due to Covid issues in Tigers camp. Previously postponed game with Hull KR re-arranged.

24th July 2021 - 70th-minute Arthur Mourgue penalty secures 32-20 home win over Hull KR. Ben Garcia breaks arm.

29th July 2021 - two late Fouad Yaha tries secure 40-20 home win over Wakefield.

30th July 2021 - prop Mickael Goudemand signs new two-year contract to end of 2023 season.

2nd August 2021 - hard-fought 23-16 victory at Hull KR is twelfth consecutive win. Romain France scores on debut.

7th August 2021 - winning run ends at 12 games as weakened side suffers 34-12 loss at St Helens. Second-rower Corentin Le Cam and halfback Cesar Rouge make debuts.

9th August 2021 - hooker Alrix Da Costa signs new one-year contract to end of 2022 season.

10th August 2021 - centre Arthur Romano signs new one-year contract to end of 2022 season.

15th August 2021 - Sam Kasiano signs new one-year contract to end of 2022 season.

16th August 2021 - James Maloney to retire at end of season.

19th August 2021 - match at Warrington postponed as essential staff test positive for Covid-19 shortly before squad were due to fly to England.

21st August 2021 - utility Benjamin Jullien signs new one-year contract

22nd August 2021 - prop Paul Seguier signs new one-year contract.

26th August 2021 - Benjamin Jullien scores twice in 42-14 win at Salford. Prop Matthieu Cozza makes debut.

30th August 2021 - Mike McMeeken and Fouad Yaha score hat-tricks in 64-0 home win over Leigh.

4th September 2021 - James Maloney field goal in golden point seals 31-30 Magic Weekend win over St Helens in Newcastle and secures League Leaders' Shield.

11th September 2021 - 30-18 home defeat by Huddersfield after leading 18-0. League Leaders Trophy presented after final whistle.

17th September 2021 - 12-8 last-round defeat at Wigan.

24th September 2021 - hooker Michael McIlorum signs new one-year contract.

30th September 2021 - 28-10 home semi-final win over Hull KR earns place in Grand Final.

4th October 2021 - Sam Tomkins wins Man of Steel, Steve McNamara named coach of the year.

9th October 2021 - 12-10 Grand Final defeat by St Helens.

11th October 2021 - Michael McIlorum gets one-game ban for tripping.

19th October 2021 - centre Samisoni Langi signs one-year contract extension.

CLUB RECORDS

Highest score: 92-8 v York, 12/5/2013
Highest score against:
0-62 v Hull FC, 12/5/2017
Record attendance: 31,555 v Wigan,
18/5/2019 *(Barcelona)*
11,856 v Wigan, 2/7/2016
(Stade Gilbert Brutus)

MATCH RECORDS

Tries:
4 Justin Murphy v Warrington, 13/9/2008
Damien Cardace v Widnes, 31/3/2012
Kevin Larroyer v York, 12/5/2013
Jodie Broughton v St Helens, 14/4/2016
Fouad Yaha v Salford, 21/7/2018
David Mead v Huddersfield, 29/9/2018
Fouad Yaha v Leeds, 2/7/2019
Brayden Wiliame v Doncaster, 11/5/2019
Goals:
11 Thomas Bosc v Featherstone, 31/3/2007
Thomas Bosc v Batley, 29/5/2010
Scott Dureau v Widnes, 31/3/2012
Points:
26 Thomas Bosc v Featherstone, 31/3/2007

SEASON RECORDS

Tries: 29 Morgan Escare 2014
Goals: 134 Scott Dureau 2012
Points: 319 Scott Dureau 2012

CAREER RECORDS

Tries: 87 Vincent Duport
2007-2009; 2011-2018
Goals:
579 *(inc 14fg)* Thomas Bosc 2006-2017
Points: 1,380 Thomas Bosc 2006-2017
Appearances:
337 Remi Casty 2006-2013; 2015-2020

CATALANS DRAGONS

DATE	FIXTURE	RESULT	SCORERS	LGE	ATT
27/3/21	Hull KR (h) ●	W29-28 *(aet)*	t:Yaha(2),Whitley,Laguerre,Garcia g:Maloney(4) fg:Maloney	6th	BCD
3/4/21	Huddersfield (a) ●●	W10-20	t:Whitley,Garcia,McMeeken g:Maloney(3),S Tomkins	5th	BCD
10/4/21	Wakefield (h) (CCR3) ●●	W26-6	t:S Tomkins,Drinkwater,Davies,Dudson g:Maloney(5)	N/A	BCD
17/4/21	Salford (h)	W42-6	t:Garcia,Langi,Drinkwater,Yaha(3),Davies g:Maloney(7)	4th	BCD
24/4/21	Warrington (h)	L8-24	t:Maloney g:Maloney(2)	5th	BCD
30/4/21	Wakefield (a)	W18-38	t:Davies(3),McMeeken,Whare(2),Langi g:Maloney(5)	4th	BCD
7/5/21	Warrington (h) (CCQF) ●	L6-16	t:McMeeken g:Maloney	N/A	BCD
17/5/21	Hull FC (a)	W10-27	t:Kasiano,McMeeken,Davies(2) g:Maloney(4),Mourgue fg:Maloney	3rd	5,527
22/5/21	St Helens (h)	W20-16	t:Maloney,Whare,Jullien g:Maloney(4)	3rd	1,000
29/5/21	Wigan (h)	W48-0	t:McIlorum,S Tomkins(2),Mourgue,Drinkwater(2),McMeeken,Laguerre g:Maloney(8)	2nd	1,000
12/6/21	Leigh (a)	W30-36	t:Drinkwater,Maloney,Langi,Davies,Jullien,Mourgue g:Maloney(6)	1st	1,840
24/6/21	Castleford (a)	W6-16	t:Yaha,Langi,Laguerre g:Maloney(2)	1st	4,000
1/7/21	Huddersfield (a)	W12-50	t:Jullien,McMeeken,Langi,Garcia,Mourgue,S Tomkins,Maloney,Davies g:Maloney(9)	1st	1,904
9/7/21	Leeds (a)	W18-26	t:Mourgue,Whitley,McMeeken,Yaha g:Maloney(2),Mourgue(3)	1st	4,000
16/7/21	Leeds (h)	W27-18	t:Kasiano,Mourgue,Whitley,Davies g:Mourgue(5) fg:S Tomkins	1st	4,800
24/7/21	Hull KR (h)	W32-30	t:Whitley(2),S Tomkins,Goudemand,Yaha g:Mourgue(6)	1st	5,586
29/7/21	Wakefield (h)	W40-20	t:S Tomkins,Da Costa,Kasiano,Dudson,Yaha(2) g:Maloney(8)	1st	6,267
2/8/21	Hull KR (a)	W16-23	t:Franco,Langi,S Tomkins g:Maloney(5) fg:Maloney	1st	6,347
7/8/21	St Helens (a)	L34-12	t:Laguerre,Goudemand g:Maloney(2)	1st	7,758
13/8/21	Hull FC (h)	W31-16	t:Davies(2),Yaha,S Tomkins,Bousquet g:Maloney(5) fg:Maloney	1st	7,129
26/8/21	Salford (a)	W14-42	t:Jullien(2),Goudemand,Kasiano,Davies,Chan,Langi g:Maloney(7)	1st	2,742
30/8/21	Leigh (h)	W64-0	t:McMeeken(3),Yaha(3),Maloney,J Tomkins,S Tomkins(2),Davies g:Maloney(10)	1st	6,512
4/9/21	St Helens (MW) ●●●	W31-30 *(aet)*	t:S Tomkins,Bousquet,Whare,Dudson,Kasiano g:Maloney(5) fg:Maloney	1st	-
11/9/21	Huddersfield (h)	L18-30	t:Whitley(2),Laguerre g:Maloney(3)	1st	7,318
17/9/21	Wigan (a)	L12-8	t:Davies,Laguerre	1st	12,852
30/9/21	Hull KR (h) (SF)	W28-10	t:Garcia,Drinkwater,Mourgue,Yaha,Chan g:Maloney(4)	N/A	11,530
9/10/21	St Helens (GF) ●●●●	L10-12	t:McMeeken g:Maloney(3)	N/A	45,177

● *Played at Emerald Headingley, Leeds*
●● *Played at Totally Wicked Stadium, St Helens*
●●● *Played at St James' Park, Newcastle*
●●●● *Played at Old Trafford, Manchester*

Castleford (h) (R15) and Warrington (a) (R20) games were postponed, and not rearranged

		APP		TRIES		GOALS		FG		PTS	
	D.O.B.	ALL	SL	ALL	SL	ALL	SL	ALL	SL	ALL	SL
Jason Baitieri	2/7/89	1(12)	1(10)	0	0	0	0	0	0	0	0
Lambert Belmas	11/8/97	(2)	(2)	0	0	0	0	0	0	0	0
Julian Bousquet	18/7/91	23	21	2	2	0	0	0	0	8	8
Robin Brochon	21/9/00	(1)	(1)	0	0	0	0	0	0	0	0
Joe Chan	10/3/02	(7)	(6)	2	2	0	0	0	0	8	8
Mathieu Cozza	12/4/00	(3)	(3)	0	0	0	0	0	0	0	0
Alrix Da Costa	2/10/97	11(3)	10(2)	1	1	0	0	0	0	4	4
Tom Davies	11/1/97	24	22	15	14	0	0	0	0	60	56
Jordan Dezaria	6/11/96	3(5)	3(5)	0	0	0	0	0	0	0	0
Josh Drinkwater	15/6/92	25	23	6	5	0	0	0	0	24	20
Gil Dudson	16/6/90	19(2)	17(2)	3	2	0	0	0	0	12	8
Romain Franco	5/6/98	3	3	1	1	0	0	0	0	4	4
Benjamin Garcia	5/4/93	17(1)	15(1)	5	5	0	0	0	0	20	20
Mickael Goudemand	9/3/96	13(8)	13(8)	3	3	0	0	0	0	12	12
Benjamin Jullien	1/3/95	11(2)	11(2)	5	5	0	0	0	0	20	20
Sam Kasiano	21/9/90	(22)	(20)	5	5	0	0	0	0	20	20
Matthieu Laguerre	3/2/99	9	9	6	6	0	0	0	0	24	24
Samisoni Langi	11/6/93	23	21	7	7	0	0	0	0	28	28
Corentin Le Cam	8/6/99	3(1)	3(1)	0	0	0	0	0	0	0	0
James Maloney	15/6/86	25	23	5	5	114	108	5	5	253	241
Michael McIlorum	10/1/88	13(2)	12(2)	1	1	0	0	0	0	4	4
Mike McMeeken	10/5/94	25	23	11	10	0	0	0	0	44	40
Arthur Mourgue	2/5/99	8(16)	8(15)	6	6	15	15	0	0	54	54
Cesar Rouge	3/10/02	2	2	0	0	0	0	0	0	0	0
Paul Seguier	8/9/97	1(13)	1(12)	0	0	0	0	0	0	0	0
Joel Tomkins	21/3/87	8(6)	7(6)	1	1	0	0	0	0	4	4
Sam Tomkins	23/3/89	22	20	11	10	1	1	1	1	47	43
Dean Whare	22/1/90	24	22	4	4	0	0	0	0	16	16
Matt Whitley	20/1/96	14(2)	13(2)	8	8	0	0	0	0	32	32
Fouad Yaha	19/8/96	22	22	15	15	0	0	0	0	60	60

Fouad Yaha

'SL' totals include regular season & play-offs; 'All' totals also include Challenge Cup

25th November 2020 - Suaia Matagi joins Castleford on season-long loan.

26th November 2020 - Jordan Turner signs for Castleford. Hooker Reiss Butterworth leaves by mutual consent.

30th November 2020 - back-rower Jack Ashworth joins on two-year deal from St Helens.

1st December 2020 - England Academy hooker George Roby signs from Warrington on two-year deal.

7th December 2020 - halfback Jack Cogger signs from Canterbury Bulldogs on two-year contract.

10th December 2020 - second row Joe Greenwood signs from Wigan on two-year contract.

16th December 2020 - halfback Tom Holmes leaves for Featherstone. Winger Innes Senior returns to Wakefield on season-long loan.

29th December 2020 - former Toronto Wolfpack centre Ricky Leutele signs on one-year deal.

29th December 2020 - GB international Josh Jones signs from Hull FC on one-year contract for undisclosed fee.

29th December 2020 - prop Luke Yates joins from Salford on two-year deal.

18th January 2021 - fullback Ashton Golding has surgery on training shoulder injury.

21st January 2021 - Giants training facility closed following positive Covid-19 tests.

24th January 2021 - 23-year-old fullback Olly Ashall-Bott joins from London Broncos on ten-month deal.

13th February 2021 - prop Sam Hewitt goes to Halifax on season-loan.

14th March 2021 - 22-16 win over Leeds Rhinos in home pre-season warm-up.

21st March 2021 - Michael Lawrence appointed club captain.

28th March 2021 - team captain Aidan Sezer misses 22-10 round-one defeat by Hull FC at Headingley with groin strain. Ricky Leutele suffers broken hand.

3rd April 2021 - Michael Lawrence makes 300th career appearance in 20-10 defeat to Catalans at St Helens.

11th April 2021 - Jermaine McGillvary scores hat-trick in 36-18 Challenge Cup third round win at Leigh.

16th April 2021 - Aidan Sezer returns for 25-24 defeat at Hull KR.

22nd April 2021 - 18-10 round-four defeat by St Helens on return to John Smith's Stadium.

26th April 2021 - Olly Ashall-Bott joins Wakefield on loan.

28th April 2021 - prop Ronan Michael joins Whitehaven on loan. Hooker George Roby joins North Wales Crusaders on loan.

2nd May 2021 - Ricky Leutele returns from hand injury as last-second Lee Gaskell field goal secures 14-13 home win over Leeds to get off the mark.

7th May 2021 - 23-18 defeat to St Helens at Headingley means Challenge Cup quarter-final exit.

KEY DATES

17th May 2021 - Lee Gaskell scores try-brace in 26-20 win at Warrington.

23rd May 2021 - Ricky Leutele scores try-double in 44-6 win at Leigh.

30th May 2021 - Lee Gaskell, linked with move to Salford, misses 38-12 defeat at Wakefield.

8th June 2021 - round-9 home game with Wigan, scheduled for the Friday night (June 11) postponed after seven Huddersfield players test positive for Covid-19.

14th June 2021 - Giants return to training.

18th June 2021 - Chris Atkin field goal means 9-8 home defeat to 12-man Salford.

25th June 2021 - five players away on Combined Nations All Stars duty for spirited 17-10 defeat at Hull FC.

28th June 2021 - Lee Gaskell to join Wakefield at end of season.

1st July 2021 - injury-hit side falls to 50-12 home defeat by table-toppers Catalans. Will Pryce makes debut off bench.

4th July 2021 - home fixture with Castleford (scheduled for July 6th) postponed, with Giants unable to field 17-man squad. Tigers awarded 24-0 win.

7th July 2021 - Kenny Edwards banned for 10 games after being found guilty of making inappropriate contact with backside of Dragons' prop Sam Kasiano.

9th July 2021 - hooker Nathan Peats and prop Nathan Peteru join from Leigh on season-long loan. Jack Ashworth heads other way.

11th July 2021 - Nathan Peats and Nathaniel Peteru make debuts in 16-12 defeat at Wigan.

16th July 2021 - 14-12 home defeat by Wigan.

21st July 2021 - prop James Gavet to leave club.

22nd July 2021 - Jermaine McGillvary scores four tries in 40-26 home win over Hull FC.

2nd August 2021 - Leroy Cudjoe scores try-double in 34-16 win at Castleford.

8th August 2021 - 22-18 home win over Wakefield after trailing 18-0 on 13 minutes.

13th August 2021 - Ricky Leutele and Jack Cogger return from injury in 18-12 defeat at Salford.

19th August 2021 - 18-12 defeat at Leeds.

24th August 2021 - Giants fined £30,000 (£15,000 suspended for two years) for failing to fulfil fixture against Castleford on 4th July.

26th August 2021 - 26-6 home defeat to Warrington.

30th August 2021 - 40-28 home win over Hull KR ends three-match losing run.

1st September 2021 - prop Luke Yates signs new three-year contract to end of 2024.

5th September 2021 - 32-18 Magic Weekend defeat by Wakefield in Newcastle.

7th September 2021 - Leroy Cudjoe signs one-year contract extension for 2022.

9th September 2021 - forward Josh Jones signs new three-year contract.

10th September 2021 - international prop Chris Hill signs from Warrington on two-year contract.

11th September 2021 - 30-18 win at League Leaders Catalans after trailing 18-0.

15th September 2021 - prop Nathan Mason returns from Leigh on one-year deal for 2022 season.

18th September 2021 - prop Sebastine Ikahihifo returns after two seasons on loan at Salford.

19th September 2021 - 42-24 last-round home win over Leigh confirms ninth-placed finish.

21st September 2021 - Tui Lolohea signs from Salford on two-year contract.

22nd September 2021 - prop Matty English extends contract to end of 2023 season.

29th September 2021 - New Zealand hooker Danny Levi joins from Brisbane Broncos on two-year deal.

7th October 2021 - winger Louis Senior sign new 12-month contract.

14th October 2021 - French international halfback Theo Fages signs from St Helens on three-year deal.

23rd October 2021 - Innes Senior returns from season loan at Wakefield and signs new one-year contract.

CLUB RECORDS
Highest score: 142-4 v Blackpool, 26/11/94 **Highest score against:** 12-94 v Castleford, 18/9/88 **Record attendance:** 32,912 v Wigan, 4/3/50 (Fartown) 15,629 v Leeds, 10/2/2008 (McAlpine/Galpharm/ John Smith's Stadium)

MATCH RECORDS
Tries: 10 Lionel Cooper v Keighley, 17/11/51 **Goals:** 18 Major Holland v Swinton Park, 28/2/1914 **Points:** 39 Major Holland v Swinton Park, 28/2/1914

SEASON RECORDS
Tries: 80 Albert Rosenfeld 1913-14 **Goals:** 156 (inc 2fg) Danny Brough 2013 **Points:** 346 Danny Brough 2013

CAREER RECORDS
Tries: 420 Lionel Cooper 1947-55 **Goals:** 958 Frank Dyson 1949-63 **Points:** 2,072 Frank Dyson 1949-63 **Appearances:** 485 Douglas Clark 1909-29

HUDDERSFIELD GIANTS

DATE	FIXTURE	RESULT	SCORERS	LGE	ATT
28/3/21	Hull FC (a) ●	L22-10	t:Leutele,Gavet g:Russell	11th	BCD
3/4/21	Catalans Dragons (h) ●●	L10-20	t:McQueen,Wood g:Jake Wardle	9th	BCD
11/4/21	Leigh (a) (CCR3)	W18-36	t:Edwards,Wood(2),McGillvary(3),Gaskell g:Jake Wardle(4)	N/A	BCD
16/4/21	Hull KR (a)	L25-24	t:McGillvary,McIntosh(2),Jake Wardle,McQueen g:Sezer(2)	9th	BCD
22/4/21	St Helens (h)	L10-18	t:McQueen,McGillvary g:Sezer	10th	BCD
2/5/21	Leeds (h)	W14-13	t:Sezer(2) g:Sezer(2) fg:Sezer,Gaskell	8th	BCD
7/5/21	St Helens (a) (CCQF) ●	L23-18	t:Lawrence,McIntosh(2) g:Sezer(3)	N/A	BCD
17/5/21	Warrington (a)	W20-26	t:Gaskell,McGillvary,Edwards g:Sezer(5)	8th	4,000
23/5/21	Leigh (a)	W6-44	t:Leutele(2),Edwards,Jake Wardle,O'Brien,McGillvary,Lawrence g:Sezer(8)	7th	2,008
30/5/21	Wakefield (a)	L38-12	t:Gavet,Jake Wardle g:Sezer(2)	9th	4,000
18/6/21	Salford (a)	L8-9	t:Joe Wardle g:Sezer(2)	9th	2,352
25/6/21	Hull FC (a)	L17-10	t:Ashall-Bott g:Russell(3)	10th	5,527
1/7/21	Catalans Dragons (h)	L12-50	t:Golding,Jake Wardle g:Russell(2)	10th	1,904
11/7/21	Wigan (a)	L16-12	t:McQueen,Cudjoe g:Russell(2)	11th	4,439
16/7/21	Wigan (h)	L12-14	t:Pryce,Peteru g:Russell(2)	11th	3,139
22/7/21	Hull FC (h)	W40-26	t:McGillvary(4),Peats,Yates,Pryce,Cudjoe g:Russell(4)	10th	3,699
2/8/21	Castleford (a)	W16-34	t:Cudjoe(2),Peteru,Yates,McGillvary g:Russell(7)	9th	5,126
8/8/21	Wakefield (h)	W22-18	t:Senior,Wood,McGillvary(2),Jake Wardle g:Pryce	9th	3,964
13/8/21	Salford (a)	L18-12	t:English g:Pryce(4)	9th	3,066
19/8/21	Leeds (a)	L18-12	t:Pryce,Wood,Trout	9th	11,110
26/8/21	Warrington (h)	L6-26	t:Jake Wardle g:Russell	9th	4,017
30/8/21	Hull KR (h)	W40-28	t:Russell,Jones,Leutele,Wood,Pryce,Greenwood,Peteru g:Pryce(6)	9th	3,652
5/9/21	Wakefield (MW) ●●●	L18-32	t:Pryce,Wood,Jones g:Pryce(3)	10th	-
11/9/21	Catalans Dragons (a)	W18-30	t:Jones,Senior,Cogger,Ashall-Bott,English g:Russell(5)	9th	7,318
19/9/21	Leigh (h)	W42-24	t:Senior(2),Cudjoe,Trout,Russell,Greenwood,Pryce,Leutele g:Russell(5)	9th	3,867

● *Played at Emerald Headingley, Leeds*
●● *Played at Totally Wicked Stadium, St Helens*
●●● *Played at St James' Park, Newcastle*

St Helens (a) (R16) game was postponed, and not rearranged

Castleford (h) (R13) game ruled a 24-0 defeat after being unable to field a team

		APP		TRIES		GOALS		FG		PTS	
	D.O.B.	ALL	SL	ALL	SL	ALL	SL	ALL	SL	ALL	SL
Olly Ashall-Bott	24/11/97	8(1)	8(1)	2	2	0	0	0	0	8	8
Jack Ashworth	3/7/95	3(2)	2(2)	0	0	0	0	0	0	0	0
Jack Cogger	5/8/97	16(2)	14(2)	1	1	0	0	0	0	4	4
Leroy Cudjoe	7/4/88	20	19	5	5	0	0	0	0	20	20
James Cunningham	3/4/94	10(1)	8(1)	0	0	0	0	0	0	0	0
Kenny Edwards	13/9/89	10(2)	8(2)	3	2	0	0	0	0	12	8
Matty English	14/11/97	2(17)	2(15)	2	2	0	0	0	0	8	8
Lee Gaskell	28/10/90	10(1)	8(1)	3	2	0	0	1	1	13	9
James Gavet	19/10/89	9	9	2	2	0	0	0	0	8	8
Ashton Golding	4/9/96	10	10	1	1	0	0	0	0	4	4
Joe Greenwood	2/4/93	15(4)	14(4)	2	2	0	0	0	0	8	8
Sam Hewitt	29/4/99	(11)	(11)	0	0	0	0	0	0	0	0
Josh Jones	12/5/93	24	22	3	3	0	0	0	0	12	12
Michael Lawrence	12/4/90	9(5)	8(4)	2	1	0	0	0	0	8	4
Ricky Leutele	10/4/90	14	13	5	5	0	0	0	0	20	20
Jermaine McGillvary	16/5/88	17(1)	15(1)	14	11	0	0	0	0	56	44
Darnell McIntosh	5/7/97	11	9	4	2	0	0	0	0	16	8
Chris McQueen	8/3/87	17(3)	15(3)	4	4	0	0	0	0	16	16
Adam O'Brien	11/7/93	1(10)	1(8)	1	1	0	0	0	0	4	4
Nathan Peats	5/10/90	12	12	1	1	0	0	0	0	4	4
Nathaniel Peteru	1/1/92	(12)	(12)	3	3	0	0	0	0	12	12
Will Pryce	5/12/02	9(4)	9(4)	6	6	14	14	0	0	52	52
Oliver Russell	21/9/98	12(2)	12(2)	2	2	32	32	0	0	72	72
Louis Senior	30/5/00	10	10	4	4	0	0	0	0	16	16
Aidan Sezer	24/6/91	7(1)	6(1)	2	2	25	22	1	1	59	53
Robson Stevens	4/4/02	(2)	(2)	0	0	0	0	0	0	0	0
Owen Trout	15/10/99	9(8)	9(6)	2	2	0	0	0	0	8	8
Jake Wardle	18/11/98	18	17	6	6	5	1	0	0	34	26
Joe Wardle	22/9/91	1(1)	1(1)	1	1	0	0	0	0	4	4
Oliver Wilson	22/3/99	9(3)	9(3)	0	0	0	0	0	0	0	0
Sam Wood	11/6/97	12(5)	11(4)	7	5	0	0	0	0	28	20
Luke Yates	6/3/95	20	18	2	2	0	0	0	0	8	8

Josh Jones

'SL' totals include Super League games only; 'All' totals also include Challenge Cup

25th November 2020 - Brett Hodgson appointed head coach.

6th December 2020 - halfback Josh Reynolds signs from Wests Tigers on two-year deal with option for third year.

21st December 2020 - coach Andy Last leaves for assistant coach role at Wakefield.

24th December 2020 - back-rower Josh Jones signs for Huddersfield for undisclosed fee.

6th March 2021 - Danny Houghton, Marc Sneyd and Scott Taylor appointed co-captains.

11th March 2021 - 28-22 friendly win at York in first ever game at LNER Community Stadium.

28th March 2021 - Josh Griffin scores try on 100th Hull appearance in 22-10 round-one win over Huddersfield at Headingley.

3rd April 2021 - comprehensive 35-4 round-two victory over Salford at St Helens.

10th April 2021 - 34-14 Challenge Cup round-three win at Featherstone.

16th April 2021 - Fijian British Army threequarter Mitieli Vulikijapani signs on one-year deal with club option for further year.

18th April 2021 - late try by Warrington's Jake Mamo forces extra-time which remains deadlocked at 14-14 on return to KCOM Stadium. Danny Houghton makes 85 tackles.

21st April 2021 - Connor Wynne joins York on loan.

23rd April 2021 - late Carlos Tuimavave try secures 20-14 home win over Wakefield. Bureta Fairamo banned for two games for late high tackle.

29th April 2021 - Zak Hardaker penalty 15 minutes from end decides tight game at Wigan, by 16-14.

3rd May 2021 - Jake Connor banned for one game for high tackle on Zak Hardaker. Brad Fash gets one game for dangerous contact.

8th May 2021 - 20-10 Challenge Cup quarter-final win over Wigan.

18th May 2021 - fans return for first time for 27-10 home defeat to Catalans.

23rd May 2021 - Josh Griffin stars in 18-12 win at rainy Leeds.

28th May 2021 - 34-16 round-8 defeat at St Helens.

5th June 2021 - 33-18 Challenge Cup semi-final defeat to St Helens at Leigh. Josh Griffin ruptures Achilles.

10th June 2021 - Mahe Fonua stars in convincing 30-12 win at Castleford.

17th June 2021 - prop Tevita Satae signs two-year contract extension to end of 2023.

KEY DATES

19th June 2021 - Andre Savelio scores hat-trick in 64-22 win at Leigh.

22nd June 2021 - Jack Logan re-joins on four-week loan deal from Batley Bulldogs.

24th June 2021 - fixture at Hull KR scheduled for 1st July postponed until Thursday 15th July because of Covid outbreak in Rovers camp.

25th June 2021 - stadium renamed MKM Stadium after deal with building supplies company.

25th June 2021 - 17-10 home win over Huddersfield by team missing ten first-team players due to injuries and international call-ups. Jake Connor injures knee while playing for Combined Nations All Stars.

30th June 2021 - home fixture against Salford, scheduled for Monday 5th July, postponed due to Covid outbreak in Red Devils camp.

10th July 2021 - home match against Leigh (Sunday 11th July) postponed as another player tests positive.

11th July 2021 - in-form winger Adam Swift signs two-year contract extension to end of 2023 season.

12th July 2021 - home derby (scheduled Thursday July 15th) postponed for second time because of Covid in FC camp.

22nd July 2021 - 40-26 defeat at Huddersfield in first game for almost a month.

28th July 2021 - prop Brad Fash signs two-year contract extension to end of 2023.

29th July 2021 - 22-12 defeat at home to Leeds.

5th August 2021 - utility back Darnell McIntosh signs from Huddersfield for 2022 season on three-year contract. Bureta Fairamo to join Castleford.

6th August 2021 - prop Joe Cator signs new two-year contract.

7th August 2021 - fixture (scheduled Sunday 7th August) at Warrington postponed after Covid outbreak at Hull FC.

13th August 2021 - 31-16 defeat at Catalans. Academy pair Marcus Walker, starting at centre, and Jacob Hookem, from the bench, make debuts.

16th August 2021 - Jake Connor signs two-year contract extension to end of 2023.

21st August 2021 - Jamie Shaul back from ACL injury sustained in October and Jake Connor back after two months out as Marc Sneyd field goal seals thrilling 23-22 home derby win.

25th August 2021 - Joe Cator (Achilles) and Josh Reynolds (knee) set for surgery after derby injuries and out for season.

26th August 2021 - 23-12 home defeat to Castleford.

30th August 2021 - 42-14 defeat at Salford.

4th September 2021 - Kruise Leeming field goal in golden-point extra time means 25-24 Magic Weekend defeat by Leeds.

11th September 2021 - 10-0 home defeat by Wigan ends play-off chances.

17th September 2021 - 44-12 last-round defeat at Wakefield confirms eighth-placed finish.

24th September 2021 - centre Josh Griffin signs new contract to end of 2023 season.

26th September 2021 - prop Jack Brown and halfback Ben McNamara sign new two-year contracts, fullback Connor Wynne signs for 12 months with option for another year.

1st October 2021 - hooker Joe Lovodua joins from South Sydney on one-year deal.

3rd October 2021 - forward Andre Savelio signs new two-year deal to end of 2023 season.

9th October 2021 - winger Mahe Fonua, contracted to end of 2022, released after financial agreement.

CLUB RECORDS
Highest score: 88-0 v Sheffield, 2/3/2003
Highest score against: 10-80 v Warrington, 30/8/2018
Record attendance: 28,798 v Leeds, 7/3/36 *(The Boulevard)* 23,004 v Hull KR, 2/9/2007 *(KC/KCOM/MKM Stadium)*

MATCH RECORDS
Tries: 7 Clive Sullivan v Doncaster, 15/4/68
Goals: 14 Jim Kennedy v Rochdale, 7/4/1921 Sammy Lloyd v Oldham, 10/9/78 Matt Crowther v Sheffield, 2/3/2003
Points: 36 Jim Kennedy v Keighley, 29/1/1921

SEASON RECORDS
Tries: 52 Jack Harrison 1914-15
Goals: 170 Sammy Lloyd 1978-79
Points: 369 Sammy Lloyd 1978-79

CAREER RECORDS
Tries: 250 Clive Sullivan 1961-74; 1981-85
Goals: 687 Joe Oliver 1928-37; 1943-45
Points: 1,842 Joe Oliver 1928-37; 1943-45
Appearances: 500 Edward Rogers 1906-25

HULL F.C.

HULL F.C.

DATE	FIXTURE	RESULT	SCORERS	LGE	ATT
28/3/21	Huddersfield (h) ●	W22-10	t:Connor,Griffin,Reynolds g:Sneyd(5)	2nd	BCD
3/4/21	Salford (a) ●●	W4-35	t:Savelio,Reynolds(2),Griffin,Scott g:Sneyd(5),Connor(2) fg:Connor	2nd	BCD
10/4/21	Featherstone (a) (CCR3)	W14-34	t:Faraimo,Tuimavave(2),Griffin(2),Johnstone g:Connor(5)	N/A	BCD
18/4/21	Warrington (h)	D14-14			BCD
		(aet)	t:Connor,Tuimavave g:Sneyd(3)	5th	
23/4/21	Wakefield (h)	W20-14	t:Savelio,Swift,Tuimavave g:Sneyd(4)	3rd	BCD
29/4/21	Wigan (a)	L16-14	t:Swift,Fonua g:Sneyd(3)	5th	BCD
8/5/21	Wigan (h) (CCQF) ●	W20-10	t:Satae(2),Swift g:Sneyd(4)	N/A	BCD
17/5/21	Catalans Dragons (h)	L10-27	t:Fonua,Reynolds g:Sneyd	6th	5,527
23/5/21	Leeds (a)	W12-18	t:Swift(2),Griffin g:Sneyd(3)	5th	4,000
28/5/21	St Helens (a)	L34-16	t:Swift,Fonua(2) g:Sneyd(2)	5th	4,000
5/6/21	St Helens (CCSF) ●●●	L18-33	t:Fonua,Houghton,Scott g:Sneyd(3)	N/A	-
10/6/21	Castleford (h)	W12-30	t:Swift(2),Fonua(2),Connor g:Sneyd(4),Connor	5th	4,000
19/6/21	Leigh (a)	W22-64	t:Connor,Swift(2),Ma'u,Faraimo,Fonua,Savelio(3),Wynne,Brown,Satae g:Sneyd(8)	5th	2,338
25/6/21	Huddersfield (h)	W17-10	t:Fonua,Logan,Wynne g:Sneyd(2) fg:Sneyd	5th	5,527
22/7/21	Huddersfield (a)	L40-26	t:Tuimavave,Vulikijapani(2),Lane,Satae g:Sneyd(3)	5th	3,699
29/7/21	Leeds (h)	L12-22	t:Swift,Tuimavave g:Sneyd(2)	5th	9,356
2/8/21	St Helens (a)	L10-42	t:Swift,Faraimo g:Sneyd	5th	7,038
13/8/21	Catalans Dragons (a)	L31-16	t:Tuimavave,Faraimo g:McNamara(4)	7th	7,129
21/8/21	Hull KR (h)	W23-22	t:Swift,Faraimo(2),Tuimavave g:Sneyd(3) fg:Sneyd	6th	13,709
26/8/21	Castleford (h)	L12-23	t:Swift,Connor g:Sneyd(2)	8th	8,121
30/8/21	Salford (a)	L42-14	t:Sao,Houghton g:Sneyd(3)	7th	3,297
4/9/21	Leeds (MW) ●●●●	L24-25		8th	-
		(aet)	t:Houghton,Tuimavave,Connor g:Sneyd(6)	8th	
11/9/21	Wigan (h)	L0-10		8th	10,043
17/9/21	Wakefield (a)	L44-12	t:Vulikijapani,Lane g:Connor(2)	8th	4,039

● Played at Emerald Headingley, Leeds
●● Played at Totally Wicked Stadium, St Helens
●●● Played at Leigh Sports Village
●●●● Played at St James' Park, Newcastle

Hull KR (a) (R12), Salford (h) (R13), Leigh (h) (R14) and Warrington (a) (R18) games were postponed, and not rearranged

	D.O.B.	APP		TRIES		GOALS		FG		PTS	
		ALL	SL	ALL	SL	ALL	SL	ALL	SL	ALL	SL
Josh Bowden	14/1/92	(13)	(11)	0	0	0	0	0	0	0	0
Jack Brown	25/6/00	(10)	(8)	1	1	0	0	0	0	4	4
Aidan Burrell	3/8/03	(1)	(1)	0	0	0	0	0	0	0	0
Joe Cator	15/6/98	9(6)	9(4)	0	0	0	0	0	0	0	0
Jake Connor	18/10/94	18	16	6	6	10	5	1	1	45	35
Bureta Faraimo	16/7/90	15(1)	14(1)	6	5	0	0	0	0	24	20
Brad Fash	24/1/96	4(18)	4(16)	0	0	0	0	0	0	0	0
Mahe Fonua	24/12/92	17(2)	14(2)	9	8	0	0	0	0	36	32
Josh Griffin	9/5/90	11	8	5	3	0	0	0	0	20	12
Jacob Hookem	4/10/02	(1)	(1)	0	0	0	0	0	0	0	0
Danny Houghton	25/9/88	20	17	3	2	0	0	0	0	12	8
Jordan Johnstone	24/5/97	6(12)	5(11)	1	0	0	0	0	0	4	0
Jordan Lane	20/10/97	20(2)	17(2)	2	2	0	0	0	0	8	8
Jack Logan	8/9/95	1	1	1	1	0	0	0	0	4	4
Manu Ma'u	24/8/88	20	17	1	1	0	0	0	0	4	4
Ben McNamara	18/12/01	9(3)	8(3)	0	0	4	4	0	0	8	8
Josh Reynolds	13/4/89	14	12	4	4	0	0	0	0	16	16
Ligi Sao	11/10/92	22	20	1	1	0	0	0	0	4	4
Tevita Satae	22/10/92	18(3)	15(3)	4	2	0	0	0	0	16	8
Andre Savelio	21/3/95	19	16	5	5	0	0	0	0	20	20
Cameron Scott	7/10/99	11(8)	10(6)	2	1	0	0	0	0	8	4
Jamie Shaul	1/7/92	3(1)	3(1)	0	0	0	0	0	0	0	0
Marc Sneyd	9/2/91	21	19	0	0	67	60	2	2	136	122
Adam Swift	20/2/93	19	17	14	13	0	0	0	0	56	52
Scott Taylor	27/2/91	5(4)	4(4)	0	0	0	0	0	0	0	0
Carlos Tuimavave	10/1/92	20	17	9	7	0	0	0	0	36	28
Mitieli Vulikijapani	27/6/94	4(2)	4(2)	3	3	0	0	0	0	12	12
Marcus Walker	12/8/02	1	1	0	0	0	0	0	0	0	0
Connor Wynne	15/1/01	5(4)	5(3)	2	2	0	0	0	0	8	8

Adam Swift

'SL' totals include Super League games only; 'All' totals also include Challenge Cup

5th November 2020 - Will Oakes signs permanent deal with Dewsbury.

6th November 2020 - Kyle Trout, Dan Murray, Nathaniel Peteru, Harvey Livett and Weller Hauraki not offered new contracts.

10th December 2020 - second-rower Luis Johnson joins on one year deal from Warrington. Prop Robbie Mulhern signs for Warrington.

16th December 2020 - utility Brad Takairangi joins from Parramatta on two-year deal.

25th February 2021 - Nick Rawsthorne joins Championship side Halifax Panthers.

8th March 2021 - Shaun Kenny-Dowall appointed team captain.

27th March 2021 - James Maloney golden-point field goal means 29-28 round-one defeat to Catalans after come back from 28-4 to level at full time. Ryan Hall scores hat-trick on debut.

2nd April 2021 - 25-0 defeat at St Helens in round-two Easter programme dedicated to Mose Masoe.

2nd April 2021 - Elliot Minchella out for season with ACL injury sustained in defeat at St Helens.

9th April 2021 - golden-point Gareth O'Brien field goal in fourth period of extra-time means 33-22 Challenge Cup third-round home defeat to Castleford.

14th April 2021 - Joe Keyes joins York on loan.

16th April 2021 - late Jordan Abdull field goal seals first win of season, 25-24 over Huddersfield at home.

17th April 2021 - Elliot Wallis departs the club with immediate effect by mutual consent.

21st April 2021 - hooker Jez Litten signs new four-year contract until end of 2025.

23rd April 2021 - Kane Linnett scores hat-trick in commanding home 26-6 victory over Leeds.

1st May 2021 - 50-26 defeat at Warrington after being level with 20 minutes to go.

11th May 2021 - Jordan Abdull signs three-year contract extension to end of 2024.

12th May 2021 - Mikey Lewis joins York on month's loan.

12th May 2021 - winger Ethan Ryan, struggling with recurrent wrist injury, signs two-year contract extension to end of 2023.

17th May 2021 - last-minute Jordan Abdull try seals comeback 26-22 win at Castleford.

23rd May 2021 - Korbin Sims sent off for high tackle in 28-12 defeat at win-less Wakefield. Sims found not guilty

30th May 2021 - fans return to Craven Park after 441 days as Ryan Hall scores hat-trick in 40-16 home win over Leigh and Rovers move into top six.

11th June 2021 - comprehensive 40-4 home victory over Salford cements top-sic spot.

16th June 2021 - captain Shaun Kenny-Dowall signs one-year contract extension to end of 2022.

16th June 2021 - Kane Linnett signs one-year extension, with option to extend.

KEY DATES

18th June 2021 - 18-8 win at Wigan.

21st June 2021 - fixture at St Helens scheduled for Friday June 25th postponed. Five Rovers players test positive for Covid-19, nine others forced to isolate.

22nd June 2021 - back-rower Luis Johnson signs two-year contract extension.

24th June 2021 - next two fixtures against Catalans (July 5th) and Hull FC (July 1st) postponed because of ongoing Covid-19 issues at Rovers.

30th June 2021 - Matt Parcell signs contract extension until end of 2022.

4th July 2021 - utility forward Frankie Halton signed from Featherstone on two-year contract from 2022 season.

7th July 2021 - fullback Lachlan Coote signs from St Helens on two-year deal from 2022.

10th July 2021 - home Warrington fixture (scheduled for Sunday 11th July) postponed because of Covid issues in Wolves camp.

12th July 2021 - away derby (scheduled for Thursday July 15th) postponed for second time because of Covid in FC camp.

13th July 2021 - Huddersfield utility back Sam Wood signs for 2022 season on 12-month deal. Prop Tom Garratt signs from Dewsbury on two-year deal.

21st July 2021 - fixture at St Helens postponed due to Covid in Saints camp. Previously postponed game at Catalans to be played.

25th July 2021 - late Arthur Mourgue penalty means 32-30 defeat at Catalans.

27th July 2021 - Salford postpone following Thursday fixture.

2nd August 2021 - 23-16 home defeat to table-toppers Catalans.

8th August 2021 - late Ryan Hall try secures 34-28 home win over win-less Leigh.

10th August 2021 - 18-year-old fullback Phoenix Laulu-Togaga'e joins from Keighley until end of 2023. He rejoins Cougars on loan until end of season.

12th August 2021 - Rowan Milnes signs new three-year contract extension.

15th August 2021 - Neil Hudgell reverses decision to sell club.

16th August 2021 - prop Matty Storton signs new two-year contract extension.

18th August 2021 - 26-14 home win over Wigan after leading 16-0. Winger Ethan Ryan fractures scaphoid (wrist) and out for season.

21st August 2021 - late Marc Sneyd field goal means 23-22 defeat at Hull FC.

26th August 2021 - 25-18 home defeat to Wakefield after leading 10-0 means Robins drop out of top six.

30th August 2021 - 40-28 defeat at Huddersfield.

5th September 2021 - 44-6 Magic Weekend win over Leigh in Newcastle.

6th September 2021 - centre Greg Minikin to leave for Warrington at end of season.

8th September 2021 - prop Greg Richards signs from Championship side London Broncos for 2022 on one-year deal.

11th September 2021 - 26-19 home win over Castleford keeps play-off hopes alive with one game to go as Mose Masoe says farewell.

14th September 2021 - fullback Will Dagger signs two-year contract extension.

16th September 2021 - centre Greg Minikin out with cruciate ligament knee injury suffered in Castleford win.

16th September 2021 - Ryan Hall signs contract to end of 2022.

17th September 2021 - 36-12 last-round defeat at Leeds means sixth-placed finish.

22nd September 2021 - prop Will Maher signs one-year contract extension to end of 2022 season.

24th September 2021 - shock 19-0 victory at third-placed Warrington sets up semi-final at Catalans.

30th September 2021 - 28-10 semi-final defeat at Catalans.

5th October 2021 - back-rower George Lawler moves to Castleford.

21st October 2021 - prop George King signs new three-year contract to end of 2025.

CLUB RECORDS
Highest score: 100-6 v Nottingham City, 19/8/90 **Highest score against:** 6-84 v Wigan, 1/4/2013 **Record attendance:** 27,670 v Hull FC, 3/4/53 *(Boothferry Park)* 12,100 v Hull FC, 1/2/2019 *(Craven Park)*

MATCH RECORDS
Tries: 11 George West v Brooklands Rovers, 4/3/1905 **Goals:** 14 Alf Carmichael v Merthyr, 8/10/1910 Mike Fletcher v Whitehaven, 18/3/90 Colin Armstrong v Nottingham City, 19/8/90 Damien Couturier v Halifax, 23/4/2006 **Points:** 53 George West v Brooklands Rovers, 4/3/1905

SEASON RECORDS
Tries: 45 Gary Prohm 1984-85 **Goals:** 199 Mike Fletcher 1989-90 **Points:** 450 Mike Fletcher 1989-90

CAREER RECORDS
Tries: 207 Roger Millward 1966-80 **Goals:** 1,268 Mike Fletcher 1987-98 **Points:** 2,760 Mike Fletcher 1987-98 **Appearances:** 489 Mike Smith 1975-91

HULL KINGSTON ROVERS

DATE	FIXTURE	RESULT	SCORERS	LGE	ATT
27/3/21	Catalans Dragons (a) ●	L29-28 *(aet)*	t:Hall(3),Lewis,King g:Abdull(4)	7th	BCD
1/4/21	St Helens (h) ●●	L0-25		8th	BCD
9/4/21	Castleford (h) (CCR3)	L32-33 *(aet)*	t:Ryan,Quinlan,Vete,Parcell,Kenny-Dowall,Abdull g:Abdull(2),Lewis(2)	N/A	BCD
16/4/21	Huddersfield (h)	W25-24	t:Crooks(2),Lewis,Linnett g:Abdull(4) fg:Abdull	8th	BCD
23/4/21	Leeds (h)	W26-6	t:Hall,Parcell,Linnett(3) g:Abdull(3)	7th	BCD
1/5/21	Warrington (a)	L50-26	t:Kenny-Dowall,Hall(2),Abdull,Linnett g:Abdull(3)	7th	BCD
17/5/21	Castleford (a)	W22-26	t:Crooks(2),Parcell,Hall,Abdull g:Abdull(3)	7th	3,600
23/5/21	Wakefield (a)	L28-12	t:Quinlan,Crooks g:Milnes,Abdull	8th	4,000
30/5/21	Leigh (h)	W40-16	t:Linnett(2),Hall(3),Minikin,Milnes,Hadley g:Abdull(4)	6th	4,000
11/6/21	Salford (h)	W40-4	t:Lawler,Crooks,Takairangi,Kenny-Dowall,Parcell,Hall,Linnett g:Abdull(5),Milnes	6th	4,000
18/6/21	Wigan (a)	W8-18	t:Crooks,Hall,Quinlan g:Crooks(3)	6th	5,018
24/7/21	Catalans Dragons (a)	L32-30	t:Abdull(2),Kenny-Dowall,Minikin,Quinlan g:Abdull(5)	6th	5,586
2/8/21	Catalans Dragons (h)	L16-23	t:Quinlan(2) g:Abdull(4)	7th	6,347
8/8/21	Leigh (a)	W28-34	t:Linnett,Minikin,Kenny-Dowall(2),Lewis,Vete,Hall g:Crooks(3)	5th	2,941
13/8/21	Wigan (h)	W26-14	t:Vete,Milnes,Ryan,Linnett,Litten g:Crooks(3)	5th	6,230
21/8/21	Hull FC (a)	L23-22	t:Keinhorst,Milnes,Crooks,Vete g:Crooks(3)	5th	13,709
26/8/21	Wakefield (h)	L18-25	t:Johnson,Lawler,Crooks g:Crooks(3)	7th	6,439
30/8/21	Huddersfield (a)	L40-28	t:Lewis,Linnett(2),Minikin,Hall,Parcell g:Milnes(2)	8th	3,652
5/9/21	Leigh (MW) ●●●	W44-6	t:Crooks,Vete,Takairangi,Parcell,Hall,Keinhorst,Storton,Keyes g:Keyes(6)	7th	-
11/9/21	Castleford (h)	W26-19	t:Lewis(2),Parcell,Linnett g:Abdull(5)	5th	6,840
17/9/21	Leeds (a)	L36-12	t:Lewis,Dagger g:Abdull(2)	6th	13,106
24/9/21	Warrington (a) (E)	W0-19	t:Abdull,Lewis,Keinhorst g:Abdull(3) fg:Abdull	N/A	6,252
30/9/21	Catalans Dragons (a) (SF)	L28-10	t:Kenny-Dowall,Hall g:Abdull	N/A	11,530

● *Played at Emerald Headingley, Leeds*
●● *Played at Totally Wicked Stadium*
●●● *Played at St James' Park, Newcastle*

St Helens (h) (R11), Hull FC (h) (R12), Warrington (h) (R14), St Helens (a) (R15) and Salford (a) (R16) games were postponed, and not rearranged

		APP		TRIES		GOALS		FG		PTS	
	D.O.B.	ALL	SL	ALL	SL	ALL	SL	ALL	SL	ALL	SL
Jordan Abdull	5/2/96	16	15	6	5	49	47	2	2	124	116
Ben Crooks	15/6/93	19	19	10	10	15	15	0	0	70	70
Will Dagger	21/2/99	5	5	1	1	0	0	0	0	4	4
Dean Hadley	5/8/92	11(3)	11(3)	1	1	0	0	0	0	4	4
Ryan Hall	27/11/87	21	20	16	16	0	0	0	0	64	64
Luis Johnson	20/2/99	18(2)	17(2)	1	1	0	0	0	0	4	4
Jimmy Keinhorst	14/7/90	4(5)	4(4)	3	3	0	0	0	0	12	12
Shaun Kenny-Dowall	23/1/88	23	22	7	6	0	0	0	0	28	24
Joe Keyes	17/9/95	1	1	1	1	6	6	0	0	16	16
George King	24/2/95	18(3)	17(3)	1	1	0	0	0	0	4	4
George Lawler	1/9/95	15(3)	14(3)	2	2	0	0	0	0	8	8
Mikey Lewis	4/7/01	13	12	8	8	2	0	0	0	36	32
Kane Linnett	11/1/89	23	22	13	13	0	0	0	0	52	52
Jez Litten	10/3/98	6(17)	6(16)	1	1	0	0	0	0	4	4
Will Maher	4/11/95	11(6)	11(6)	0	0	0	0	0	0	0	0
Rowan Milnes	1/9/97	10(1)	10(1)	3	3	4	4	0	0	20	20
Elliot Minchella	28/1/96	(2)	(2)	0	0	0	0	0	0	0	0
Greg Minikin	29/3/95	14	13	4	4	0	0	0	0	16	16
Muizz Mustapha	3/4/00	1(10)	1(9)	0	0	0	0	0	0	0	0
Matt Parcell	30/10/92	17(4)	16(4)	7	6	0	0	0	0	28	24
Adam Quinlan	13/11/92	13	12	6	5	0	0	0	0	24	20
Ethan Ryan	12/5/96	5	4	2	1	0	0	0	0	8	4
Korbin Sims	2/1/92	6(8)	5(8)	0	0	0	0	0	0	0	0
Matthew Storton	10/3/99	5(14)	5(14)	1	1	0	0	0	0	4	4
Brad Takairangi	14/6/89	19	19	2	2	0	0	0	0	8	8
Will Tate	20/12/01	(3)	(3)	0	0	0	0	0	0	0	0
Albert Vete	24/1/93	5(11)	5(10)	5	4	0	0	0	0	20	16

'SL' totals include regular season & play-offs; 'All' totals also include Challenge Cup

Jordan Abdull

26th December 2020 - New Zealand international forward Zane Tetevano signs from Penrith Panthers on three-year marquee deal.

27th December 2020 - prop Ava Seumanufagai granted release to return home to Australia for family reasons because of global pandemic.

31st December 2020 - Rob Burrow awarded MBE in New Year Honours list for services to Rugby League and Motor Neurone Disease community.

5th January 2021 - Stevie Ward announces retirement, aged 27, because of concussion issues.

16th January 2021 - Fijian international forward King Vuniyayawa joins from NZ Warriors on one-year contract.

21st January 2021 - training ground closed following positive Covid-19 tests on six players and one staff member.

11th February 2021 - Jack Broadbent signs new two-year contract to end of 2022

12th February 2021 - Liam Sutcliffe signs new three-year contract to end of 2024 season.

2nd March 2021 - Robert Lui out for eight weeks with quad tear suffered in training. Jack Walker to miss entire season with foot injury despite off-season surgery.

3rd March 2021 - dual-code international Kyle Eastmond joins on two-year contract.

23rd March 2021 - utility forward James Donaldson signs new two-year contract extension to end of 2023.

25th March 2021 - hooker Kruise Leeming signs contract extension to end of 2024.

27th March 2021 - youngster Jack Broadbent stars in 28-22 round-one comeback win over Wakefield in 'away' game at Headingley.

2nd April 2021 - Brad Dwyer makes 200th career appearance in 18-10 round-two defeat by Castleford at St Helens.

10th April 2021 - Zane Tetevano dismissed for late tackle as under-strength side loses 26-18 at St Helens in third round of Challenge Cup. King Vuniyayawa and 17-year-old Morgan Gannon make debuts.

13th April 2021 - Zane Tetevano suspended for four games.

15th April 2021 - Kyle Eastmond makes debut in 19-6 home defeat to Wigan.

21st April 2021 - winger Ash Handley signs one-year contract extension to end of 2024.

23rd April 2021 - forward Sam Walters, 20, signs one-year contract extension to end of 2023.

23rd April 2021 - 26-6 round-four defeat at Hull KR. Richie Myler banned for two games for questioning referee's decision.

2nd May 2021 - last-second Lee Gaskell field goal means 14-13 defeat at Huddersfield.

14th May 2021 - Luke Gale returns as Rhyse Martin golden-point penalty secures 15-13 home win over Wakefield.

17th May 2021 - Kyle Eastmond announces immediate retirement after two games into two-year contract.

KEY DATES

23rd May 2021 - Zane Tetevano, Bodene Thompson, James Donaldson and Richie Myler back for 18-12 defeat by Hull FC as fans return to Headingley.

28th May 2021 - 60-6 win at Castleford after trailing 6-0.

9th June 2021 - round-9 home game with St Helens postponed after Covid outbreak in Leeds camp.

11th June 2021 - Kevin Sinfield awarded OBE in Queen's birthday honours list.

17th June 2021 - director of rugby Kevin Sinfield OBE to leave at end of season to join Leicester rugby union club.

18th June 2021 - St Helens back-rower James Bentley signs on two-year contract from 2022 season.

27th June 2021 - 38-12 bad-tempered win at Salford. Bodene Thompson sent off. Thompson and Alex Mellor (contact with referee) banned for one match each, Luke Gale two for punching.

1st July 2021 - Robert Lui returns and Jack Broadbent gets four tries on right wing in 48-18 home win over Leigh.

5th July 2021 - despite two yellow cards in last ten minutes, 26-16 victory at in-form Warrington is fourth successive win.

9th July 2021 - 26-18 defeat to Catalans after leading 18-8 at half-time ends winning run at four matches.

13th July 2021 - Bodene Thompson (dangerous tackle) and Rhyse Martin (late hit) handed three and one-game bans respectively by RFL Match Review Panel.

16th July 2021 - Liam Sutcliffe plays 200th career game in 27-18 defeat at Catalans. Harry Newman returns from broken leg suffered previous September.

19th July 2021 - Halfback Aidan Sezer signs from Huddersfield on two-year contract from 2022.

23rd July 2021 - prop Matt Prior agrees new two-year contract to end of 2023 season.

23rd July 2021 - 38-16 home win over Salford in front of first unrestricted crowd.

26th July 2021 - Luke Gale stood down as captain after bust up in team meeting.

1st August 2021 - last minute George Williams field goal means 27-26 home defeat to Warrington. Prop Mikolaj Oledzki suffers season-ending foot injury. Director of Rugby Kevin Sinfield OBE departs club after game.

3rd August 2021 - Luke Gale banned for two games for contact with match official. Matt Prior appointed captain.

4th August 2021 - Blake Austin signs from Warrington for 2022 season on one-year contract.

6th August 2021 - 32-18 home defeat to Castleford.

12th August 2021 - Liam Sutcliffe's season ends after knee surgery on long-standing injury.

16th August 2021 - Rhyse Martin banned for one game for dangerous contact in 46-10 win at Leigh.

25th August 2021 - Tom Briscoe plays 350th career game in 14-0 win at Wigan. Zane Tetevano suspended for three matches for high tackle.

30th August 2021 - Matt Prior sin-binned twice in 20-13 defeat at Wakefield,

3rd September 2021 - back-rower Rhyse Martin signs new one-year deal to end of 2022 season.

4th September 2021 - Kruise Leeming field goal in golden-point time seals 25-24 Magic Weekend win over Hull FC in Newcastle.

10th September 2021 - 40-6 defeat at St Helens puts top-six finish in balance.

17th September 2021 - 36-12 last-round home win over Hull KR secures fifth placed finish.

21st September 2021 - Alex Sutcliffe signs for Castleford.

23rd September 2021 - Ash Handley scores only try of game in 8-0 win at fourth-placed Wigan.

1st October 2021 - 36-8 defeat at second-placed St Helens ends season.

9th October 2021 - prop King Vuniyayawa joins Salford.

18th October 2021 - winger David Fusitu'a joins from NZ Warriors on two-year contract.

CLUB RECORDS		
Highest score:		
106-10 v Swinton, 11/2/2001		
Highest score against:		
6-74 v Wigan, 20/5/92		
Record attendance:		
40,175 v Bradford, 21/5/47		

MATCH RECORDS		
Tries:		
8 Fred Webster v Coventry, 12/4/1913		
Eric Harris v Bradford, 14/9/31		
Goals:		
17 Iestyn Harris v Swinton, 11/2/2001		
Points:		
42 Iestyn Harris v Huddersfield, 16/7/99		

SEASON RECORDS		
Tries: 63 Eric Harris 1935-36		
Goals: 173 *(inc 5fg)* Kevin Sinfield 2012		
Points: 431 Lewis Jones 1956-57		

CAREER RECORDS		
Tries: 391 Eric Harris 1930-39		
Goals:		
1,831 *(inc 39fg)* Kevin Sinfield 1997-2015		
Points: 3,967 Kevin Sinfield 1997-2015		
Appearances: 625 John Holmes 1968-89		

LEEDS RHINOS

DATE	FIXTURE	RESULT	SCORERS	LGE	ATT
27/3/21	Wakefield (a) ●	W22-28	t:L Briscoe,A Sutcliffe,Dwyer,Myler,Broadbent g:Martin(4)	4th	BCD
2/4/21	Castleford (h) ●●	L10-18	t:L Briscoe,Prior g:Martin	7th	BCD
10/4/21	St Helens (a) (CCR3)	L26-18	t:Oledzki,Dwyer(2) g:Martin(3)	N/A	BCD
15/4/21	Wigan (h)	L6-19	t:Mellor g:Martin	7th	BCD
23/4/21	Hull KR (a)	L26-6	t:Dwyer g:Handley	8th	BCD
2/5/21	Huddersfield (a)	L14-13	t:Thompson,Handley g:Martin(2) fg:L Sutcliffe	9th	BCD
14/5/21	Wakefield (h)	W15-13 (aet)	t:Martin,Hurrell g:Martin(3) fg:Gale	9th	BCD
23/5/21	Hull FC (h)	L12-18	t:L Sutcliffe,T Briscoe g:Martin(2)	9th	4,000
28/5/21	Castleford (a)	W6-60	t:T Briscoe(2),Broadbent,Leeming(2),Myler,L Briscoe,Hurrell,Dwyer,Gannon,Gale g:Martin(8)	8th	4,000
27/6/21	Salford (a)	W12-38	t:Broadbent(2),T Briscoe,Myler(2),Leeming,Gale g:Martin(5)	8th	2,219
1/7/21	Leigh (h)	W48-18	t:Donaldson,Broadbent(4),Leeming,L Sutcliffe,Walters,Holroyd g:Martin(6)	7th	4,000
5/7/21	Warrington (a)	W16-22	t:Lui,Mellor,Handley g:Martin(5)	7th	4,000
9/7/21	Catalans Dragons (h)	L18-26	t:Martin,Thompson,L Sutcliffe g:Martin(3)	7th	4,000
16/7/21	Catalans Dragons (a)	L27-18	t:T Briscoe(2),Leeming g:Gale(3)	7th	4,800
23/7/21	Salford (h)	W38-16	t:Newman,Leeming(2),McLelland,Vuniyayawa,Prior g:Martin(7)	7th	10,515
29/7/21	Hull FC (a)	W12-22	t:Dwyer,Myler,Smith g:Martin(5)	7th	9,356
1/8/21	Warrington (h)	L26-27	t:Newman(2),Oledzki,Dwyer g:Martin(5)	6th	9,196
6/8/21	Castleford (h)	L18-32	t:Lui,Handley,Dwyer g:Martin(3)	7th	10,838
13/8/21	Leigh (a)	W10-46	t:Tetevano,T Briscoe(2),Smith,Lui,Dwyer,Handley,Leeming g:Martin(7)	6th	2,818
19/8/21	Huddersfield (h)	W18-12	t:Handley,Myler,Lui g:Handley,Newman(2)	7th	11,110
25/8/21	Wigan (a)	W0-14	t:Dwyer,Myler g:Martin(3)	5th	11,390
30/8/21	Wakefield (a)	L20-13	t:Leeming,Dwyer g:Martin(2) fg:Lui	5th	5,420
4/9/21	Hull FC (MW) ●●●	W24-25 (aet)	t:Martin,Newman,Leeming,Broadbent g:Martin(4) fg:Leeming	5th	-
10/9/21	St Helens (a)	L40-6	t:Dwyer g:Martin	6th	12,568
17/9/21	Hull KR (a)	W36-12	t:Lui,Prior,Holroyd,Myler,Donaldson,Handley g:Martin(6)	5th	13,106
23/9/21	Wigan (a) (E)	W0-8	t:Handley g:Martin(2)	N/A	7,396
1/10/21	St Helens (a) (SF)	L36-8	t:Myler,L Briscoe	N/A	11,688

● *Played at Emerald Headingley*
●● *Played at Totally Wicked Stadium, St Helens*
●●● *Played at St James' Park, Newcastle*

St Helens (h) (R9) game was postponed, and not rearranged

		APP		TRIES		GOALS		FG		PTS	
	D.O.B.	ALL	SL	ALL	SL	ALL	SL	ALL	SL	ALL	SL
Luke Briscoe	11/3/94	21(4)	20(4)	4	4	0	0	0	0	16	16
Tom Briscoe	19/3/90	27	26	8	8	0	0	0	0	32	32
Jack Broadbent	1/11/01	13(1)	12(1)	9	9	0	0	0	0	36	36
James Donaldson	14/9/91	10(14)	9(14)	2	2	0	0	0	0	8	8
Brad Dwyer	28/4/93	12(15)	12(14)	12	10	0	0	0	0	48	40
Kyle Eastmond	17/7/89	2	2	0	0	0	0	0	0	0	0
Luke Gale	22/6/88	11	11	2	2	3	3	1	1	15	15
Morgan Gannon	2/12/03	6(7)	6(6)	1	1	0	0	0	0	4	4
Corey Hall	7/8/02	1	1	0	0	0	0	0	0	0	0
Ash Handley	16/2/96	18	18	7	7	2	2	0	0	32	32
Tom Holroyd	9/2/01	4(12)	4(12)	2	2	0	0	0	0	8	8
Konrad Hurrell	5/8/91	13(4)	13(4)	2	2	0	0	0	0	8	8
Corey Johnson	16/11/00	(1)	(1)	0	0	0	0	0	0	0	0
Kruise Leeming	7/9/95	25(1)	24(1)	10	10	0	0	1	1	41	41
Robert Lui	23/2/90	11	11	5	5	0	0	1	1	21	21
Rhyse Martin	1/3/93	24(1)	23(1)	3	3	88	85	0	0	188	182
Callum McLelland	16/9/99	3(2)	3(2)	1	1	0	0	0	0	4	4
Alex Mellor	24/9/94	15	14	2	2	0	0	0	0	8	8
Richie Myler	21/5/90	20	20	9	9	0	0	0	0	36	36
Harry Newman	19/2/00	14	14	4	4	2	2	0	0	20	20
Jarrod O'Connor	20/7/01	6(6)	6(5)	0	0	0	0	0	0	0	0
Mikolaj Oledzki	8/11/98	15(1)	14(1)	2	1	0	0	0	0	8	4
Matt Prior	27/5/87	24	23	3	3	0	0	0	0	12	12
Cameron Smith	7/11/98	4(14)	3(14)	2	2	0	0	0	0	8	8
Alex Sutcliffe	21/1/99	5(1)	4(1)	1	1	0	0	0	0	4	4
Liam Sutcliffe	25/11/94	13	13	3	3	0	0	1	1	13	13
Zane Tetevano	4/11/90	14	13	1	1	0	0	0	0	4	4
Bodene Thompson	1/8/88	12(5)	12(5)	2	2	0	0	0	0	8	8
Liam Tindall	27/9/01	(1)	(1)	0	0	0	0	0	0	0	0
King Vuniyayawa	13/3/95	3(13)	3(12)	1	1	0	0	0	0	4	4
Sam Walters	25/12/00	5(3)	4(3)	1	1	0	0	0	0	4	4

Rhyse Martin

'SL' totals include regular season & play-offs; 'All' totals also include Challenge Cup

10th August 2020 - prop Adam Walker and vice captain hooker Liam Hood re-sign for 2021.

20th August 2020 - props Alex Gerrard, Tom Spencer and Nathan Mason sign new contracts for 2021.

2nd September 2020 - Ian Thornley, Ben Hellewell and Jordan Thompson sign new contracts for 2021.

5th September 2020 - Jamie Ellis returns from Hull KR and ex-Toronto halfback Blake Wallace signs, both on one-year contracts.

7th September 2020 - Ryan Shaw signs new one-year contract. Martyn Ridyard joins Swinton.

14th September 2020 - Mattie Wildie and Junior Sa'u sign new one-year contracts.

24th September 2020 - prop Mark Ioane signs new one-year contract.

5th October 2020 - second-rower Matty Gee signs from Hull KR for 2021 season.

30th October 2020 - Ryan Brierley returns from Hull KR for 2021 season.

6th November 2020 - Kiwi forward Nathaniel Peteru signs from Hull KR for 2021 season.

7th November 2020 - ex-Toronto outside back Matty Russell signs on one-year contract.

10th November 2020 - ex-Toronto halfback Joe Mellor signs on undisclosed contract.

17th November 2020 - on-loan outside-back Craig Mullen signs permanent deal for 2021. Adam Walker leaves club with immediate effect.

20th November 2020 - ex-Toronto prop Adam Sidlow joins on one-year deal.

30th November 2020 - Welsh international prop Ben Flower joins from Wigan on one-year deal.

14th December 2020 - Leigh Centurions application for Super League 2021 succeeds.

18th December 2020 - centre Keanan Brand joins from Warrington on season-long loan.

25th December 2020 - winger Lewis Tierney signs from Catalans for 2021.

7th January 2021 - Kurt Haggerty joins as assistant coach.

14th January 2021 - Garreth Carvell appointed new head of rugby.

5th February 2021 - backrower Tyrone McCarthy joins on one-year contract.

17th February 2021 - utility back Brendan Elliot signs for 2021 from Manly.

10th March 2021 - hooker Liam Hood appointed team captain.

13th March 2021 - 25-24 win at St Helens in Tommy Makinson testimonial.

17th March 2021 - St Helens' Josh Eaves and Matty Foster and Nathan Roebuck and Tom Burnett from Warrington all join on loan.

22nd March 2021 - former Origin hooker Nathan Peats signs for 2021 season.

26th March 2021 - 20-18 round-one defeat by Wigan at Headingley after leading 18-0.

KEY DATES

1st April 2021 - Ben Reynolds re-joins club after agreeing transfer fee with Toulouse Olympique.

2nd April 2021 - 44-12 defeat by Warrington at St Helens.

11th April 2021 - 36-18 home Challenge Cup third round defeat by Huddersfield.

12th April 2021 - former Wigan and Warrington centre Anthony Gelling signs for 2021.

16th April 2021 - 52-16 defeat at Castleford.

23rd April 2021 - 34-8 defeat at Salford after leading 8-6 at half-time.

30th April 2021 - Ben Flower suffers hamstring injury in 22-12 home defeat to St Helens.

17th May 2021 - fans return for 30-16 home defeat to Wigan after leading 10-0.

23rd May 2021 - Brendan Elliot makes debut in 44-6 home defeat by Huddersfield.

30th May 2021 - 40-16 defeat at Hull KR is eighth on a row.

2nd June 2021 - head of rugby Garreth Carvell leaves with immediate effect by mutual agreement.

2nd June 2021 - head coach John Duffy leaves with immediate effect by mutual agreement. Assistant Kurt Haggerty takes interim charge.

6th June 2021 - 30-20 battling defeat at Wakefield.

7th June 2021 - Anthony Gelling leaves to return to New Zealand.

12th June 2021 - battling 36-30 home defeat by top-of-the-table Catalans.

19th June 2021 - 64-22 home defeat by Hull FC.

24th June 2021 - 44-18 defeat at Warrington.

1st July 2021 - 48-18 defeat at Leeds.

8th July 2021 - prop Rob Butler joins on loan from Warrington.

10th July 2021 - away fixture at Hull FC (Sunday 11th July) postponed due to Covid issues at Hull FC.

10th July 2021 - Jack Ashworth joins on season-long loan from Huddersfield with Nathan Peats and Nathaniel Peteru going the other way.

19th July 2021 - home game against Warrington (scheduled for Thursday July 22) postponed by Wolves under the Covid Fixture Protocols.

1st August 2021 - 50-6 defeat at Wigan.

2nd August 2021 - forwards Sam Stone and Jai Whitbread sign from Gold Coast Titans on contracts through to the end of 2022.

3rd August 2021 - Joe Mellor extends contract to end of 2022.

6th August 2021 - Joel Tomkins signs one-year contract for 2022.

8th August 2021 - late Ryan Hall try means 34-28 defeat at Hull KR.

13th August 2021 - 46-10 home defeat to Leeds.

22nd August 2021 - round-20, 32-22 home win over Salford is first of season.

26th August 2021 - 42-12 defeat at St Helens.

30th August 2021 - 64-0 defeat at Catalans.

31st August 2021 - prop Adam Sidlow signs one-year contract extension.

1st September 2021 - Ben Reynolds signs two-year contract extension.

5th September 2021 - 44-6 Magic Weekend defeat by Hull KR in Newcastle.

12th September 2021 - Ryan Brierley scores hat-trick in 26-18 home win over Wakefield.

15th September 2021 - prop Nathan Mason signs for Huddersfield for 2022 season.

19th September 2021 - 42-24 last-round defeat at Huddersfield.

19th September 2021 - Ryan Brierley leaves for Salford.

23rd September 2021 - back-rower James Bell leaves for St Helens.

28th September 2021 - former Wakefield and Hull KR coach Chris Chester appointed head of rugby.

CLUB RECORDS

Highest score: 92-2 v Keighley, 30/4/86
Highest score against:
4-94 v Workington, 26/2/95
Record attendance:
31,326 v St Helens, 14/3/53 *(Hilton Park)*;
10,556 v Batley, 17/9/2016
(Leigh Sports Village)

MATCH RECORDS

Tries: 6 Jack Wood v York, 4/10/47;
Neil Turley v Workington, 31/1/2001
Goals: 15 Mick Stacey v Doncaster, 28/3/76
Points: 42 Neil Turley v Chorley, 4/4/2004

SEASON RECORDS

Tries: 55 Neil Turley 2001
Goals: 187 Neil Turley 2004
Points: 468 Neil Turley 2004

CAREER RECORDS

Tries: 189 Mick Martyn 1954-67
Goals: 1,043 Jimmy Ledgard 1948-58
Points:
2,492 John Woods 1976-85; 1990-92
Appearances: 503 Albert Worrall 1920-38

LEIGH CENTURIONS

DATE	FIXTURE	RESULT	SCORERS	LGE	ATT
26/3/21	Wigan (h) ●	L18-20	t:Hood,Thornley,Hellewell g:Brierley(3)	8th	BCD
2/4/21	Warrington (a) ●●	L44-12	t:Sidlow,Brierley g:Reynolds(2)	10th	BCD
11/4/21	Huddersfield (h) (CCR3)	L18-36	t:Thompson(2),Peats g:Reynolds(3)	N/A	BCD
16/4/21	Castleford (a)	L52-16	t:Thompson,Reynolds,Brierley g:Reynolds(2)	10th	BCD
23/4/21	Salford (a)	L34-8	t:Russell,Thornley	12th	BCD
30/4/21	St Helens (h)	L12-22	t:Russell,Gelling g:Reynolds(2)	12th	BCD
17/5/21	Wigan (h)	L16-30	t:Gelling,Mason,Ellis g:Reynolds(2)	12th	1,702
23/5/21	Huddersfield (h)	L6-44	t:Tierney g:Reynolds	12th	2,008
30/5/21	Hull KR (a)	L40-16	t:Hellewell(2),Brierley g:Reynolds(2)	12th	4,000
6/6/21	Wakefield (a)	L30-20	t:Mellor(2),Tierney g:Brierley(4)	12th	4,000
12/6/21	Catalans Dragons (h)	L30-36	t:Reynolds,Elliot,Gee,Hellewell,Brierley g:Brierley(5)	12th	1,840
19/6/21	Hull FC (h)	L22-64	t:Bell,Reynolds,Brierley(2) g:Brierley(3)	12th	2,338
24/6/21	Warrington (a)	L44-18	t:Hood,Sa'u,Ioane g:Brierley(3)	12th	4,000
1/7/21	Leeds (h)	L48-18	t:Russell,Ioane,Brierley g:Brierley(3)	12th	4,000
1/8/21	Wigan (a)	L50-6	t:Hood g:Ellis	12th	9,206
8/8/21	Hull KR (h)	L28-34	t:Sa'u(2),Mullen,Sidlow(2) g:Mullen(4)	12th	2,941
13/8/21	Leeds (h)	L10-46	t:Gee(2) g:Mullen	12th	2,818
22/8/21	Salford (h)	W32-22	t:Mellor,Brand,Hood,Sidlow g:Mullen(8)	12th	3,304
26/8/21	St Helens (a)	L42-12	t:Gee,Sidlow g:Brierley(2)	12th	8,221
30/8/21	Catalans Dragons (a)	L64-0		12th	6,512
5/9/21	Hull KR (MW) ●●●	L44-6	t:Russell g:Brierley	12th	-
12/9/21	Wakefield (h)	W26-18	t:Sidlow,Brierley(3),Stone g:Brierley(3)	12th	2,905
19/9/21	Huddersfield (a)	L42-24	t:Whitbread,Thornley,Elliot(2),Stone g:Brierley(2)	12th	3,867

● *Played at Emerald Headingley, Leeds*
●● *Played at Totally Wicked Stadium, St Helens*
●●● *Played at St James' Park, Newcastle*

Hull FC (a) (R14), Warrington (h) (R15) and Castleford (h) (R16) games were postponed, and not rearranged

		APP		TRIES		GOALS		FG		PTS	
	D.O.B.	ALL	SL	ALL	SL	ALL	SL	ALL	SL	ALL	SL
Jack Ashworth	3/7/95	1(4)	1(4)	0	0	0	0	0	0	0	0
James Bell	2/5/94	16(2)	16(2)	1	1	0	0	0	0	4	4
Keanan Brand	8/1/99	13	12	1	1	0	0	0	0	4	4
Ryan Brierley	12/3/92	18	17	10	10	29	29	0	0	98	98
Rob Butler	15/5/98	3(3)	3(3)	0	0	0	0	0	0	0	0
Josh Eaves	20/10/97	4(1)	4(1)	0	0	0	0	0	0	0	0
Brendan Elliot	1/1/94	10(1)	10(1)	3	3	0	0	0	0	12	12
Jamie Ellis	4/10/89	4(4)	4(4)	1	1	1	1	0	0	6	6
Ben Flower	19/10/87	3(2)	2(2)	0	0	0	0	0	0	0	0
Matthew Foster	25/6/01	4(2)	4(2)	0	0	0	0	0	0	0	0
Matty Gee	12/12/94	10(5)	9(5)	4	4	0	0	0	0	16	16
Anthony Gelling	18/10/90	6	6	2	2	0	0	0	0	8	8
Alex Gerrard	5/11/91	5(9)	5(9)	0	0	0	0	0	0	0	0
Ben Hellewell	30/1/92	23	22	4	4	0	0	0	0	16	16
Liam Hood	6/1/92	17(3)	16(3)	4	4	0	0	0	0	16	16
Mark Ioane	3/2/90	10(6)	10(5)	2	2	0	0	0	0	8	8
Jack Logan	8/9/95	5	5	0	0	0	0	0	0	0	0
Nathan Mason	8/9/93	4(4)	4(4)	1	1	0	0	0	0	4	4
Tyrone McCarthy	21/4/88	9(3)	8(3)	0	0	0	0	0	0	0	0
Joe Mellor	28/11/90	15	15	3	3	0	0	0	0	12	12
Craig Mullen	15/1/98	10(4)	9(4)	1	1	13	13	0	0	30	30
Tom Nisbet	8/10/99	1	1	0	0	0	0	0	0	0	0
Nathan Peats	5/10/90	2(9)	2(8)	1	0	0	0	0	0	4	0
Nathaniel Peteru	1/1/92	2(9)	2(8)	0	0	0	0	0	0	0	0
Ben Reynolds	15/1/94	11	10	3	3	14	11	0	0	40	34
Matty Russell	6/6/93	12(1)	12(1)	4	4	0	0	0	0	16	16
Junior Sa'u	18/4/87	15(1)	15(1)	3	3	0	0	0	0	12	12
Adam Sidlow	25/10/87	11(1)	10(1)	6	6	0	0	0	0	24	24
Josh Simm	27/2/01	1	1	0	0	0	0	0	0	0	0
Tom Spencer	2/1/91	(1)	(1)	0	0	0	0	0	0	0	0
Sam Stone	4/8/97	5	5	2	2	0	0	0	0	8	8
Jordan Thompson	4/9/91	13(6)	13(5)	3	1	0	0	0	0	12	4
Iain Thornley	11/9/91	20	19	3	3	0	0	0	0	12	12
Lewis Tierney	20/10/94	9	8	2	2	0	0	0	0	8	8
Blake Wallace	18/6/92	3	2	0	0	0	0	0	0	0	0
Jai Whitbread	16/1/98	2(2)	2(2)	1	1	0	0	0	0	4	4
Matty Wildie	25/10/90	2(9)	2(9)	0	0	0	0	0	0	0	0

'SL' totals include Super League games only; 'All' totals also include Challenge Cup

Ryan Brierley

1st December 2020 - St Helens assistant Richard Marshall appointed head coach.

2rd December 2020 - prop Greg Burke signs two-year contract extension.

4th December 2020 - winger Joe Burgess signs from Wigan on two-year deal.

6th December 2020 - Scotland international forward Sam Luckley joins from Ottawa Aces on one-year contract.

9th December 2020 - Matt Costello signs from St Helens on three-year contract.

10th December 2020 - Danny Orr joins as assistant coach.

10th December 2020 - forward Jack Wells signs from Wigan.

11th December 2020 - Harvey Livett signs from Hull KR on two-year contract.

18th December 2020 - Red Devils fined ⊛£15,000, half suspended, for failing to fulfil fixture against Warrington on Friday October 30th.

19th December 2020 - Danny Addy signs from Leigh on three-year contract.

25th December 2020 - Krisnan Inu signs new contract for 2021.

28th December 2020 - Ed Chamberlain signs two-year contract extension and joins London Broncos on season-long loan.

29th December 2020 - New Zealand international forward Elijah Taylor signs two-year contract

1st January 2021 - former Toronto prop Darcy Lussick joins on one-year contract.

8th January 2021 - Paul Rowley appointed Head of Rugby Development, Talent and Pathways.

13th January 2021 - Josh Johnson and Ryan Lannon both sign two-year contract extensions.

22nd January 2021 - Declan Patton signs from Warrington on one-year contract.

14th March 2021 - 20-6 home win over Wigan in pre-season friendly.

26th March 2021 - 29-6 round-one defeat by St Helens at Headingley.

3rd April 2021 - 35-4 round-two defeat to Hull FC at St Helens.

10th April 2021 - debutants Morgan Escare and Matt Costello both score two tries in 68-4 Challenge Cup third round win over Widnes.

17th April 2021 - 42-6 round-three defeat at Catalans.

23rd April 2021 - 34-8 round-four home win over Leigh, after trailing at the break, is first of season.

8th May 2021 - golden-point field goal from former Red Devil Gareth O'Brien means 19-18 defeat to Castleford in Challenge Cup quarter-final.

13th May 2021 - Elliot Kear to join Bradford to progress part-time career.

17th May 2021 - Andy Ackers sidelined with head knock after two minutes of 28-0 round-six defeat at St Helens.

KEY DATES

22nd May 2021 - Jackson Hastings field goal gives Wigan 17-16 win at AJ Bell Stadium.

27th May 2021 - 62-18 home defeat by Warrington.

9th June 2021 - Kristian Inu fined four weeks' salary and suspended for social media postings on Jarryd Hayne sexual assault conviction made on 6th May, for which he apologises.

11th June 2021 - Pauli Pauli sent off near end of 40-4 defeat at Hull KR.

15th June 2021 - Tongan halfback Ata Hingano signs until end of season, with option to extend for two years.

18th June 2021 - Chris Atkin field goal secures 9-8 win at Huddersfield.

27th June 2021 - Lee Mossop sent off for punching in 38-12 home defeat by Leeds. Mossop gets two-match ban.

30th June 2021 - Wakefield (scheduled July 1st) and Hull FC (July 5th) games postponed due to on-going Covid problems in Red Devils camp.

6th July 2021 - Chris Atkin signs two-year contract extension with option for third year.

11th July 2021 - 70-18 win at Castleford is third of season.

16th July 2021 - Krisnan Inu scores double in 24-14 rescheduled Round 12 'home' win over Wakefield at Halliwell Jones Stadium

27th July 2021 - positive Covid tests in camp means home game against Hull KR (Thursday 29th July) and fixture at Wakefield (Monday August 2nd) both postponed.

6th August 2021 - 16-6 defeat at Wigan.

7th August 2021 - winger Rhys Williams extends contract until end of 2023 season.

9th August 2021 - captain Lee Mossop forced to retire with immediate effect on medical orders after eleven reconstruction operations on his shoulders.

9th August 2021 - Brisbane halfback Brodie Croft joins for 2022 on two-year deal.

13th August 2021 - Lee Mossop gets send off from crowd before 18-12 home win over Huddersfield.

18th August 2021 - Wigan hooker Amir Bourouh signs on two-year deal, with option of further year.

22nd August 2021 - 32-22 defeat at previously win-less Leigh.

24th August 2021 - Red Devils fined £25,000 (£12,500 suspended for one year) for breaches of Covid protocols which led to postponements of fixtures against Wakefield (1st July) and Hull FC (5th July).

26th August 2021 - 42-14 home defeat to Catalans.

30th August 2021 - Ken Sio scores four tries in 42-14 home win over Hull FC.

4th September 2021 - 29-18 Magic Weekend defeat by Castleford in Newcastle.

11th September 2021 - two late George Williams field goals means 20-19 defeat at Warrington.

16th September 2021 - prop James Greenwood signs two-year contract extension with option of third year.

17th September 2021 - Ken Sio scores double in 26-14 last-round home defeat of St Helens.

18th September 2021 - prop Sebastine Ikahihifo returns to Huddersfield after two seasons on loan.

19th September 2021 - utility back Ryan Brierley signs from Leigh Centurions on two-year contract.

21st September 2021 - prop Jack Ormondroyd signs new two-year deal to end of 2023. Tui Lolohea leaves for Huddersfield.

22nd September 2021 - head coach Richard Marshall leaves by mutual consent after one season in charge.

23rd September 2021 - winger Ken Sio signs new two-year contract.

9th October 2021 - Leeds prop King Vuniyayawa joins on two-year contract.

13th October 2021 - prop Sam Luckley signs contract extension to end of 2022.

16th October 2021 - back-rower Shane Wright signs from North Queensland Cowboys on two-year deal.

23rd October 2021 - Tonga international prop Sitaleki Akauola signs from Warrington on two-year contract.

CLUB RECORDS

Highest score:
100-12 v Gateshead, 23/3/2003
Highest score against:
16-96 v Bradford, 25/6/2000
Record attendance:
26,470 v Warrington, 13/2/37
(The Willows)
7,102 v Wakefield, 16/2/2014
(AJ Bell Stadium)

MATCH RECORDS

Tries:
6 Frank Miles v Lees, 5/3/1898
Ernest Bone v Goole, 29/3/1902
Jack Hilton v Leigh, 7/10/39
Goals:
14 Steve Blakeley v Gateshead, 23/3/2003
Points:
39 Jim Lomas v Liverpool City, 2/2/1907

SEASON RECORDS

Tries: 46 Keith Fielding 1973-74
Goals: 221 David Watkins 1972-73
Points: 493 David Watkins 1972-73

CAREER RECORDS

Tries: 297 Maurice Richards 1969-83
Goals: 1,241 David Watkins 1967-79
Points: 2,907 David Watkins 1967-79
Appearances:
498 Maurice Richards 1969-83

SALFORD RED DEVILS

DATE	FIXTURE	RESULT	SCORERS	LGE	ATT
26/3/21	St Helens (a) ●	L29-6	t:Sio g:Inu	12th	BCD
3/4/21	Hull FC (h) ●●	L4-35	t:Sio	12th	BCD
10/4/21	Widnes (h) (CCR3)	W68-4	t:Escare(2),Costello(2),Lolohea,Patton,Ackers,Ikahihifo,Watkins, Ormondroyd,Williams,Atkin g:Inu(10)	N/A	BCD
17/4/21	Catalans Dragons (a)	L42-6	t:Livett g:Escare	12th	BCD
23/4/21	Leigh (h)	W34-8	t:Greenwood,Brown(2),Sio,Atkin,Livett g:Inu(5)	9th	BCD
30/4/21	Castleford (h)	L18-28	t:Brown,Ackers,Lolohea g:Livett(2),Brown	10th	BCD
8/5/21	Castleford (a) (CCQF) ●	L19-18		N/A	BCD
		(aet)	t:Livett(2),Mossop g:Livett(3)		
17/5/21	St Helens (a)	L28-0		10th	4,000
22/5/21	Wigan (h)	L16-17	t:Livett,Wells g:Livett(4)	11th	2,033
27/5/21	Warrington (h)	L18-62	t:Sio,Livett,Lussick g:Livett(3)	11th	2,306
11/6/21	Hull KR (a)	L40-4	t:Sio	11th	4,000
18/6/21	Huddersfield (a)	W8-9	t:Ackers g:Patton(2) fg:Atkin	11th	2,352
27/6/21	Leeds (h)	L12-38	t:Atkin,Escare g:Atkin,Patton	11th	2,219
11/7/21	Castleford (a)	W18-70	t:Ormondroyd,Roberts,Escare(2),Williams(2),Sio,Patton,Costello,Atkin, Norman,Davies g:Inu(11)	10th	3,900
16/7/21	Wakefield (h) ●●●	W24-14	t:Escare,Inu(2),Sio g:Inu(4)	9th	1,323
23/7/21	Leeds (a)	L38-16	t:Sio,Lolohea,Inu g:Inu(2)	9th	10,515
6/8/21	Wigan (a)	L16-6	t:Burgess g:Livett	10th	9,431
13/8/21	Huddersfield (h)	W18-12	t:Williams,Lolohea,Ormondroyd g:Inu(3)	10th	3,066
22/8/21	Leigh (a)	L32-22	t:Williams,Livett,Sio(2) g:Inu(3)	10th	3,304
26/8/21	Catalans Dragons (h)	L14-42	t:Livett,Sarginson,Escare g:Inu	11th	2,742
30/8/21	Hull FC (h)	W42-14	t:Sio(4),Atkin,Livett,Burgess g:Inu(7)	11th	3,297
4/9/21	Castleford (MW) ●●●●	L29-18	t:Sio,Burgess,Hingano g:Inu(3)	11th	-
11/9/21	Warrington (a)	L20-19			
		(aet)	t:Sio(2),Lolohea g:Escare(2),Inu fg:Lolohea	11th	7,351
17/9/21	St Helens (h)	W26-14	t:Sio(2),Costello,Atkin,Robson g:Atkin(2),Inu	11th	5,130

● Played at Emerald Headingley, Leeds
●● Played at Totally Wicked Stadium, St Helens
●●● Played at Halliwell Jones Stadium, Warrington
●●●● Played at St James' Park, Newcastle

Hull FC (a) (R13), Hull KR (h) (R16) and Wakefield (a) (R17) games were postponed, and not rearranged

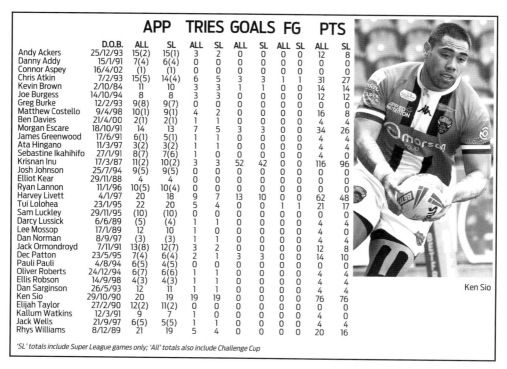

		APP		TRIES		GOALS		FG		PTS	
	D.O.B.	ALL	SL	ALL	SL	ALL	SL	ALL	SL	ALL	SL
Andy Ackers	25/12/93	15(2)	15(1)	3	2	0	0	0	0	12	8
Danny Addy	15/1/91	7(4)	6(4)	0	0	0	0	0	0	0	0
Connor Aspey	16/4/02	(1)	(1)	0	0	0	0	0	0	0	0
Chris Atkin	7/2/93	15(5)	14(4)	6	5	3	3	1	1	31	27
Kevin Brown	2/10/84	11	10	3	3	1	1	0	0	14	14
Joe Burgess	14/10/94	8	8	3	3	0	0	0	0	12	12
Greg Burke	12/2/93	9(8)	9(7)	0	0	0	0	0	0	0	0
Matthew Costello	9/4/98	10(1)	9(1)	4	2	0	0	0	0	16	8
Ben Davies	21/4/00	2(1)	2(1)	1	1	0	0	0	0	4	4
Morgan Escare	18/10/91	14	13	7	5	3	3	0	0	34	26
James Greenwood	17/6/91	6(1)	5(1)	1	1	0	0	0	0	4	4
Ata Hingano	11/3/97	3(2)	3(2)	1	1	0	0	0	0	4	4
Sebastine Ikahihifo	27/1/91	8(7)	7(6)	1	0	0	0	0	0	4	0
Krisnan Inu	17/3/87	11(2)	10(2)	3	3	52	42	0	0	116	96
Josh Johnson	25/7/94	9(5)	9(5)	0	0	0	0	0	0	0	0
Elliot Kear	29/11/88	4	4	0	0	0	0	0	0	0	0
Ryan Lannon	11/1/96	10(5)	10(4)	0	0	0	0	0	0	0	0
Harvey Livett	4/1/97	20	18	9	7	13	10	0	0	62	48
Tui Lolohea	23/1/95	22	20	5	4	0	0	1	1	21	17
Sam Luckley	29/11/95	(10)	(10)	0	0	0	0	0	0	0	0
Darcy Lussick	6/6/89	(5)	(4)	1	1	0	0	0	0	4	4
Lee Mossop	17/1/89	12	10	1	0	0	0	0	0	4	0
Dan Norman	8/9/97	(3)	(3)	1	1	0	0	0	0	4	4
Jack Ormondroyd	7/11/91	13(8)	12(7)	3	2	0	0	0	0	12	8
Dec Patton	23/5/95	7(4)	6(4)	2	1	3	3	0	0	14	10
Pauli Pauli	4/8/94	6(5)	4(5)	0	0	0	0	0	0	0	0
Oliver Roberts	24/12/94	6(7)	6(6)	1	1	0	0	0	0	4	4
Ellis Robson	14/9/98	4(3)	4(3)	1	1	0	0	0	0	4	4
Dan Sarginson	26/5/93	12	11	1	1	0	0	0	0	4	4
Ken Sio	29/10/90	20	19	19	19	0	0	0	0	76	76
Elijah Taylor	27/2/90	12(2)	11(2)	0	0	0	0	0	0	0	0
Kallum Watkins	12/3/91	9	7	1	0	0	0	0	0	4	0
Jack Wells	21/9/97	6(5)	5(5)	1	1	0	0	0	0	4	4
Rhys Williams	8/12/89	21	19	5	4	0	0	0	0	20	16

Ken Sio

'SL' totals include Super League games only; 'All' totals also include Challenge Cup

30th November 2020 - Jack Ashworth signs for Huddersfield.

1st December 2020 - assistant Richard Marshall appointed head coach at Salford.

3rd December 2020 - former Widnes prop Dan Norman joins on two-year deal from London Broncos.

4th December 2020 - youngsters Josh Eaves, Tom Nisbet, Nico Rizzelli and Sam Royle sign extended one-year contracts.

9th December 2020 - Matt Costello joins Salford.

15th January 2021 - squad return for pre-season training.

13th March 2021 - Tommy Makinson scores two tries in his testimonial match, a 25-24 defeat by Leigh.

26th March 2021 - 29-6 round-one victory over Salford at Headingley.

30th March 2021 - centre Josh Simm signs one year contract extension to end of 2022 season.

30th March 2021 - 19-year-old forward Jake Wingfield signs two-year extension to end of 2023.

31st March 2021 - Alex Walmsley signs contract extension to end of 2024 season. Matty Foster breaks jaw playing for Leigh and returns to Saints along with Josh Eaves.

1st April 2021 - Regan Grace scores double in 25-0 home win over Hull KR in round two.

8th April 2021 - Jonny Lomax signs two-year extension to end of 2024 season.

10th April 2021 - hard-fought 26-18 home Challenge Cup third-round win over weakened Leeds. Matty Lees injures ankle and requires surgery.

16th April 2021 - Tommy Makinson injures foot in 34-6 home round-three win over Wakefield after drawing 0-0 at half-time.

22nd April 2021 - Mark Percival back for 18-10 round-four win at Huddersfield.

30th April 2021 - James Bentley stretchered off with broken leg near end of 22-12 win at Leigh.

4th May 2021 - winger Regan Grace extends contract for further year to end of 2022 season.

7th May 2021 - Regan Grace hat-trick in hard-fought 23-18 Challenge Cup quarter-final win over Huddersfield at Headingley. Tommy Makinson returns but suffers recurrence of foot injury after three minutes.

17th May 2021 - 28-0 home win over Salford as fans return.

22nd May 2021 - hundred per cent record ended with 20-16 defeat at Catalans.

28th May 2021 - Jack Welsby scores hat-trick on wing in 34-16 home defeat of Hull FC.

5th June 2021 - Tommy Makinson returns but Mark Percival misses 38-18 Challenge Cup semi-final win over Hull FC at Leigh.

5th June 2021 - St Helens win Women's Challenge Cup with 34-6 win over York at Leigh.

8th June 2021 - Jack Welsby signs three-year contract extension to end of 2024 season.

9th June 2021 - Friday (11th June) round-9 game at Leeds postponed because of Covid outbreak in Rhinos camp.

17th June 2021 - 6-2 home defeat to Warrington.

18th June 2021 - James Bentley to move to Leeds at end of season.

KEY DATES

21st June 2021 - fixture at Hull KR (Friday June 25th) postponed due to Covid outbreak in Rovers camp.

22nd June 2021 - back-rower Joel Thompson to retire at end of 2021 season, halfway into two-year contract.

28th June 2021 - Tommy Makinson extends current contract by further two years until end of 2024 season.

28th June 2021 - fixture at Castleford scheduled for Wednesday night (June 30th) cancelled, with Castleford unable to field 17-man squad. Saints awarded 24-0 victory.

7th July 2021 - Lachlan Coote to join Hull KR at end of season.

13th July 2021 - Sione Mata'utia handed two-match ban for two separate offences in 30-14 win at Wakefield. Reduced to one match on appeal.

17th July 2021 - 26-12 win over Castleford secures first Challenge Cup since 2008. Theo Fages breaks shoulder and out for season.

21st July 2021 - home game against Hull KR (scheduled for Friday 23rd July) postponed with positive Covid tests in Saints camp.

25th July 2021 - round-16 game with Huddersfield (Wednesday 28th July) postponed.

29th July 2021 - head coach Kristian Woolf extends contract into third season until end of 2022.

2nd August 2021 - Jack Welsby scores hat-trick in 42-10 win at Hull FC.

5th August 2021 - centre Kevin Naiqama to leave at end of 2021 season and return home to Australia.

7th August 2021 - 34-12 home win over weakened top of the table Catalans.

9th August 2021 - 29-year-old Tongan International Will Hopoate signs two-year deal from 2022 with option for third year

12th August 2021 - Tommy Makinson sent off in 67th minute of 20-10 home defeat by Castleford for late high tackle.

16th August 2021 - Tommy Makinson banned for three games, reduced to two on appeal.

19th August 2021 - captain James Roby agrees one-year-contract extension for 2022.

20th August 2021 - dominant 26-2 away win over Wigan.

23rd August 2021 - James Bentley handed one-match ban for 'striking, kicking, making light contact' with Wigan's John Bateman.

24th August 2021 - Joe Batchelor signs new two-year deal until end of 2023 season.

24th August 2021 - Saints fined £5,000, £1,000 suspended until end of season, for breaches of Covid protocols leading to postponement of post-Wembley fixtures against Hull KR and Huddersfield in July.

1st September 2021 - Louie McCarthy-Scarsbrook signs 12-month contract extension for 2022 season.

2nd September 2021 - 28-year-old second rower Curtis Sironen signs from Manly on two-year deal from 2022, with option for third year.

4th September 2021 - James Maloney field goal in golden-point time means 31-30 Magic Weekend win defeat by Catalans in Newcastle and concedes League Leaders title.

6th September 2021 - Agnatius Paasi gets two-match penalty notice for high tackle on Samisoni Langi.

15th September 2021 - former Salford hooker Joey Lussick signs from Parramatta Eels on three-year contract from 2022.

10th September 2021 - Morgan Knowles scores twice as 40-6 home win over Leeds secures second-placed finish.

17th September 2021 - youthful side suffers 26-14 last-round home defeat at Salford. Jonathan Bennison, Shay Martyn and Sam Royle make debuts.

21st September 2021 - prop Kyle Amor signs one-year contract extension.

23rd September 2021 - back-rower James Bell signs from Leigh on two-year contract from 2022.

28th September 2021 - 19-year-old utility back Daniel Hill signs from Widnes on two-year contract.

1st October 2021 - 36-8 home win over Leeds earns place in third successive Grand Final.

9th October 2021 - two-try Kevin Naiqama wins Harry Sunderland Trophy in 12-10 third successive Grand Final win over Catalans.

10th October 2021 - 28-0 win over Leeds at Headingley secures Women's Grand Final win.

11th October 2021 - Sione Mata'utia gets one-game ban for punch to Dragons halfback James Maloney.

22nd October 2021 - Tongan international centre Konrad Hurrell signs from Leeds on one-year contract.

ST HELENS

DATE	FIXTURE	RESULT	SCORERS	LGE	ATT
26/3/21	Salford (h) ●	W29-6	t:Makinson,Grace,Percival,Naiqama,Walmsley g:Makinson(4) fg:Welsby	1st	BCD
1/4/21	Hull KR (a) ●●	W0-25	t:Grace(2),Welsby,Smith g:Makinson(4) fg:Fages	1st	BCD
10/4/21	Leeds (h) (CCR3)	W26-18	t:Makinson(2),Grace(2) g:Makinson(3)	N/A	BCD
16/4/21	Wakefield (h)	W34-6	t:Naiqama(2),Bentley,Welsby,Grace(2) g:Makinson(4),Dodd	1st	BCD
22/4/21	Huddersfield (a)	W10-18	t:Fages,Percival,Lomax g:Coote(3)	1st	BCD
30/4/21	Leigh (a)	W12-22	t:Mata'utia,Coote,Welsby,Naiqama g:Coote(3)	1st	BCD
7/5/21	Huddersfield (h) (CCQF) ●	W23-18	t:Grace(3),Percival g:Coote(3) fg:Fages	N/A	BCD
17/5/21	Salford (h)	W28-0	t:Walmsley,Fages,Naiqama,McCarthy-Scarsbrook,Grace g:Coote(4)	1st	4,000
22/5/21	Catalans Dragons (a)	L20-16	t:Percival(2),Grace g:Coote(2)	2nd	1,000
28/5/21	Hull FC (h)	W34-16	t:Welsby(3),Coote,Knowles,Batchelor g:Coote(5)	1st	4,000
5/6/21	Hull FC (CCSF) ●●●	W18-33	t:Grace(2),Fages,Welsby,Coote g:Coote(6) fg:Fages	N/A	-
17/6/21	Warrington (h)	L2-6	g:Coote	2nd	4,000
4/7/21	Wigan (h)	W24-6	t:Grace,Coote,Percival g:Coote(6)	2nd	4,000
9/7/21	Wakefield (a)	W14-30	t:Percival,Dodd,Coote,Makinson g:Coote(7)	2nd	4,000
17/7/21	Castleford (CCF) ●●●●	W12-26	t:Fages,Roby,Makinson,Amor g:Coote(5)	N/A	40,000
2/8/21	Hull FC (h)	W10-42	t:Thompson,Makinson,Welsby(3),Amor,Naiqama g:Coote(7)	2nd	7,038
7/8/21	Catalans Dragons (h)	W34-12	t:Makinson,Dodd,Grace,Batchelor,Coote g:Coote(7)	2nd	7,758
12/8/21	Castleford (h)	L10-20	t:Welsby,Walmsley g:Coote	2nd	7,050
20/8/21	Wigan (a)	W2-26	t:Grace,Dodd,Percival,Walmsley g:Coote(4),Dodd	2nd	16,319
26/8/21	Leigh (h)	W42-12	t:Grace,Welsby(2),Mata'utia,Coote,Batchelor,Dodd g:Coote(7)	2nd	8,221
30/8/21	Warrington (a)	W14-24	t:Naiqama,Dodd,Percival,Bentley g:Coote(4)	2nd	10,006
4/9/21	Catalans Dragons (MW) ●●●●●	L31-30 (aet)	t:Makinson,Coote,Mata'utia(2),Knowles g:Coote(5)	2nd	-
10/9/21	Leeds (h)	W40-6	t:Grace,Welsby,Knowles(2),Makinson,Walmsley,Mata'utia g:Coote(6)	2nd	12,568
17/9/21	Salford (a)	L26-14	t:Bennison,Lomax g:Martyn(3)	2nd	5,130
1/10/21	Leeds (h) (SF)	W36-8	t:Grace(2),Roby,Percival(2),Naiqama g:Coote(6)	N/A	11,688
9/10/21	Catalans Dragons (GF) ●●●●●●	W10-12	t:Naiqama(2) g:Coote(2)	N/A	45,177

● Played at Emerald Headingley, Leeds
●● Played at Totally Wicked Stadium
●●● Played at Leigh Sports Village
●●●● Played at Wembley Stadium
●●●●● Played at St James' Park, Newcastle
●●●●●● Played at Old Trafford, Manchester

Leeds (a) (R9), Hull KR (a) (R11), Hull KR (h) (R15) and Huddersfield (h) (R16) games were postponed, and not rearranged

Castleford (a) (R12) game ruled a 24-0 victory after the Tigers were unable to field a team

		APP		TRIES		GOALS		FG		PTS	
	D.O.B.	ALL	SL	ALL	SL	ALL	SL	ALL	SL	ALL	SL
Kyle Amor	26/5/87	2(21)	2(17)	2	1	0	0	0	0	8	4
Joe Batchelor	28/10/94	12(10)	10(9)	3	3	0	0	0	0	12	12
Jonathan Bennison	1/12/02	1	1	1	1	0	0	0	0	4	4
James Bentley	19/10/97	9(1)	8(1)	2	2	0	0	0	0	8	8
Lachlan Coote	6/4/90	23	19	8	7	94	80	0	0	220	188
Ben Davies	21/4/00	1	1	0	0	0	0	0	0	0	0
Lewis Dodd	27/1/02	12(9)	12(7)	5	5	2	2	0	0	24	24
Josh Eaves	20/10/97	(1)	(1)	0	0	0	0	0	0	0	0
Theo Fages	23/8/94	14	10	4	2	0	0	3	1	19	9
Regan Grace	12/12/96	23	19	21	14	0	0	0	0	84	56
Morgan Knowles	5/11/96	17	15	4	4	0	0	0	0	16	16
Matty Lees	4/2/98	12(3)	11(2)	0	0	0	0	0	0	0	0
Jonny Lomax	4/9/90	23	19	2	2	0	0	0	0	8	8
Tommy Makinson	10/10/91	18	14	9	6	17	12	0	0	70	48
Shay Martyn	15/11/02	1	1	0	0	3	3	0	0	6	6
Sione Mata'utia	25/6/96	20(2)	17(2)	5	5	0	0	0	0	20	20
Louie McCarthy-Scarsbrook	14/1/86	12(10)	9(9)	1	1	0	0	0	0	4	4
Kevin Naiqama	4/2/89	25	21	10	10	0	0	0	0	40	40
Dan Norman	8/9/97	(2)	(1)	0	0	0	0	0	0	0	0
Agnatius Paasi	30/11/91	2(19)	2(16)	0	0	0	0	0	0	0	0
Mark Percival	29/5/94	19	17	11	10	0	0	0	0	44	40
James Roby	22/11/85	24(1)	20(1)	2	1	0	0	0	0	8	4
Sam Royle	12/2/00	1	1	0	0	0	0	0	0	0	0
Josh Simm	27/2/01	4	4	0	0	0	0	0	0	0	0
Aaron Smith	12/10/96	2(7)	2(6)	1	1	0	0	0	0	4	4
Joel Thompson	24/8/88	17(2)	13(2)	1	1	0	0	0	0	4	4
Alex Walmsley	10/4/90	24(1)	20(1)	5	5	0	0	0	0	20	20
Jack Welsby	17/3/01	18(8)	16(6)	14	13	0	0	1	1	57	53
Jake Wingfield	1/8/01	2(5)	2(5)	0	0	0	0	0	0	0	0

Jack Welsby

'SL' totals include regular season & play-offs; 'All' totals also include Challenge Cup

25th November 2020 - 26-year-old Samoa stand-off Mason Lino signs from Newcastle Knights on three-year deal.

17th December 2020 - Huddersfield winger Innes Senior extends loan deal for 2021 campaign.

21st December 2020 - Hull coach Andy Last joins as assistant to Chris Chester.

21st December 2020 - Jay Pitts signs new contract to end of 2022.

3rd January 2021 - Tony Gigot leaves club by mutual consent.

9th January 2021 - three players fined for breaking Covid rules on New Year's Eve.

24th January 2021 - prop Eddie Battye joins on permanent three-year deal from London Broncos.

13th March 2021 - 30-10 home pre-season friendly win over Dewsbury.

27th March 2021 - 28-22 round-one 'home' defeat by Leeds at Headingley after leading 18-6.

1st April 2021 - 34-6 defeat in round two at Wigan after being level 6-6 at break. Tom Johnstone fails HIA before half-time.

10th April 2021 - 26-6 Challenge Cup round-three defeat by Catalans Dragons. Tom Johnstone misses second half with head knock. Kelepi Tanginoa banned for one game for high tackle.

16th April 2021 - Jacob Miller suffers knee injury in 34-6 round-three defeat at St Helens after drawing 0-0 at half-time.

23rd April 2021 - late Carlos Tuimavave try means 20-14 defeat Hull FC. Max Jowitt fails HIA in first half.

26th April 2021 - fullback Olly Ashall-Bott and hooker Josh Eaves join on loan from Huddersfield and St Helens.

1st May 2021 - Olly Ashall-Bott and Josh Eaves make debuts in 38-18 defeat to Catalans on return to Belle Vue.

14th May 2021 - controversial golden-point penalty under sticks means 15-13 defeat at Leeds.

23rd May 2021 - Jacob Miller returns, along with fans, and Bill Tupou stars as 28-12 home win over Hull KR ends losing start to season at six games.

30th May 2021 - 38-12 home win over Huddersfield after leading 30-0 at half-time.

5th June 2021 - late Liam Kay and Mason Lino tries secure 30-20 home win over win-less Leigh in brought-forward round-13 game.

11th June 2021 - 38-18 defeat at Warrington ends winning run at three games.

KEY DATES

17th June 2021 - Tom Johnstone returns from long concussion lay-off as Bill Tupou suffers season-ending injury in 18-12 home defeat to Castleford.

23rd June 2021 - Matty Ashurst signs new two-year contract to end of 2023.

24th June 2021 - Tom Johnstone suffers knee cartilage damage and Jordan Crowther knee injury in 14-6 Wednesday night home win over Wigan.

28th June 2021 - Lee Gaskell signs from Huddersfield on two-year deal from 2022.

30th June 2021 - fixture at Salford scheduled for 1st July postponed because of Covid outbreak at Red Devils.

2nd July 2021 - Max Jowitt signs new contract until end of 2023 season,

5th July 2021 - Jordan Crowther signs new contract until end of 2023 season.

9th July 2021 - Innes Senior scores try-double in 30-14 home defeat by St Helens as fit squad down to 17 men.

13th July 2021 - Joe Arundel and Ryan Hampshire get one-match penalty notices for dangerous contact.

16th July 2021 - 24-14 away defeat to Salford at Warrington.

23rd July 2021 - 25-12 defeat at Wigan. Jay Pitts gets two-match penalty notice for dangerous contact.

27th July 2021 - positive Covid tests in Salford camp means home fixture with Red Devils (Monday August 2nd) postponed.

29th July 2021 - David Fifita scores try-double in 40-20 Thursday-night defeat at Catalans.

8th August 2021 - 22-18 defeat at Huddersfield after leading 18-0.

10th August 2021 - head coach Chris Chester sacked. Willie Poching takes over as interim.

15th August 2021 - 28-22 home win over Warrington ends five-game losing run.

16th August 2021 - Reece Lyne (to end of 2025) and Brad Walker (one year) sign new contracts.

16th August 2021 - Leigh hooker Liam Hood (two years) and Warrington winger Tom Lineham (three years) sign for 2022.

21st August 2021 - 23-18 defeat at Castleford.

26th August 2021 - Jacob Miller field goal seals 25-18 win at Hull KR after trailing 10-0.

30th August 2021 - 20-13 home Bank Holiday win over Leeds.

5th September 2021 - 32-18 Magic Weekend win over Huddersfield in Newcastle. Concussion ends Tom Johnstone's season.

12th September 2021 - 26-18 defeat at Leigh ends winning run at three games.

17th September 2021 - Mason Lino sets Super League record with 37th consecutive successful conversion as 44-12 last-round home defeat of Hull FC confirms tenth-placed finish.

22nd September 2021 - interim boss Willie Poching appointed head coach.

29th September 2021 - Francis Cummins and Mark Applegarth appointed assistant coaches. Andy Last leaves for Castleford.

30th September 2021 - centre Joe Arundel leaves after six years.

8th October 2021 - back-rower James Batchelor signs new one-year contract.

11th October 2021 - Kyle Wood leaves for Halifax, Josh Wood for Barrow and Chris Green for Leigh.

15th October 2021 - forward Sadiq Adebiyi joins from London Broncos on one-year deal.

18th October 2021 - winger Lee Kershaw signs new two-year contract. On-loan Innes Senior goes back to parent club Huddersfield.

CLUB RECORDS
Highest score: 90-12 v Highfield, 27/10/92 **Highest score against:** 0-86 v Castleford, 17/4/95 **Record attendance:** 30,676 v Huddersfield, 26/2/1921

MATCH RECORDS
Tries: 7 Fred Smith v Keighley, 25/4/59 Keith Slater v Hunslet, 6/2/71 **Goals:** 13 Mark Conway v Highfield, 27/10/92 **Points:** 36 Jamie Rooney v Chorley, 27/2/2004

SEASON RECORDS
Tries: 38 Fred Smith 1959-60 David Smith 1973-74 **Goals:** 163 Neil Fox 1961-62 **Points:** 407 Neil Fox 1961-62

CAREER RECORDS
Tries: 272 Neil Fox 1956-74 **Goals:** 1,836 Neil Fox 1956-74 **Points:** 4,488 Neil Fox 1956-74 **Appearances:** 605 Harry Wilkinson 1930-49

WAKEFIELD TRINITY

DATE	FIXTURE	RESULT	SCORERS	LGE	ATT
27/3/21	Leeds (h) ●	L22-28	t:Johnstone(2),Senior,Ashurst g:Lino(3)	9th	BCD
1/4/21	Wigan (a) ●●	L34-6	t:Fifita g:Lino	11th	BCD
10/4/21	Catalans Dragons (a) (CCR3) ●●	L26-6	t:Lino g:Lino	N/A	BCD
16/4/21	St Helens (a)	L34-6	t:Pitts g:Lino	11th	BCD
23/4/21	Hull FC (a)	L20-14	t:Kershaw,Batchelor,Lino g:Lino	11th	BCD
30/4/21	Catalans Dragons (h)	L18-38	t:Ashall-Bott,Jowitt,Lyne g:Lino(3)	11th	BCD
14/5/21	Leeds (a)	L15-13 (aet)	t:Kay,Lino g:Lino(2) fg:Lino	11th	BCD
23/5/21	Hull KR (h)	W28-12	t:Kay(2),Arona,Miller g:Lino(6)	10th	4,000
30/5/21	Huddersfield (h)	W38-12	t:Kay(2),Tanginoa,Pitts,Westerman,Tupou,Lino g:Lino(5)	10th	4,000
6/6/21	Leigh (h)	W30-20	t:Pitts,Batchelor,Westerman,Kay,Lino g:Lino(5)	10th	4,000
11/6/21	Warrington (a)	L38-18	t:Fifita,Arundel,Kershaw g:Lino(3)	10th	4,000
16/6/21	Castleford (h)	L12-18	t:Miller(2) g:Lino(2)	10th	2,262
24/6/21	Wigan (h)	W14-6	t:Hampshire,Ashurst g:Lino(3)	9th	2,262
9/7/21	St Helens (h)	L14-30	t:Kershaw,Senior(2) g:Lino	9th	4,000
16/7/21	Salford (a) ●●●	L24-14	t:Senior,Lyne g:Lino(3)	10th	1,323
23/7/21	Wigan (a)	L25-12	t:Batchelor,Pitts g:Lino(2)	11th	5,555
29/7/21	Catalans Dragons (a)	L40-20	t:Aydin,Fifita(2) g:Lino(4)	11th	6,267
8/8/21	Huddersfield (a)	L22-18	t:Lyne,Hampshire,Westerman g:Hampshire(3)	11th	3,964
15/8/21	Warrington (h)	W28-22	t:Johnstone,Fifita,Lino,Kershaw g:Lino(6)	11th	3,445
21/8/21	Castleford (a)	L23-18	t:Arona,Johnstone,Kershaw g:Lino(3)	11th	4,987
26/8/21	Hull KR (a)	W18-25	t:Miller,Hampshire,Senior,Pitts g:Lino(4) fg:Miller	10th	6,439
30/8/21	Leeds (h)	W20-13	t:Tanginoa,Crowther,Arundel g:Lino(3) fg:Miller,Hampshire	10th	5,420
5/9/21	Huddersfield (MW) ●●●●	W18-32	t:Johnstone,Hampshire,Tanginoa,Lyne,Green g:Lino(6)	9th	-
12/9/21	Leigh (a)	L26-18	t:Lyne,Tanginoa,Fifita g:Lino(3)	10th	2,905
17/9/21	Hull FC (h)	W44-12	t:Senior,Batchelor,Tanginoa(2),Miller,Fifita,Hampshire,Kay g:Lino(5),Fifita	10th	4,039

● Played at Emerald Headingley
●● Played at Totally Wicked Stadium, St Helens
●●● Played at Halliwell Jones Stadium, Warrington
●●●● Played at St James' Park, Newcastle

Salford (h) (R17) game was postponed, and not rearranged

		APP		TRIES		GOALS		FG		PTS	
	D.O.B.	ALL	SL	ALL	SL	ALL	SL	ALL	SL	ALL	SL
Tinirau Arona	8/5/89	16(5)	16(4)	2	2	0	0	0	0	8	8
Joe Arundel	22/8/91	15(2)	15(2)	2	2	0	0	0	0	8	8
Olly Ashall-Bott	24/11/97	2	2	1	1	0	0	0	0	4	4
Matty Ashurst	1/11/89	16	15	2	2	0	0	0	0	8	8
Yusuf Aydin	13/9/00	1(9)	1(9)	1	1	0	0	0	0	4	4
James Batchelor	9/4/98	9(12)	9(11)	4	4	0	0	0	0	16	16
Eddie Battye	24/7/91	7(15)	7(15)	0	0	0	0	0	0	0	0
Harry Bowes	7/9/01	(1)	(1)	0	0	0	0	0	0	0	0
Jordan Crowther	19/2/97	9(3)	9(2)	1	1	0	0	0	0	4	4
Josh Eaves	20/10/97	(3)	(3)	0	0	0	0	0	0	0	0
David Fifita	28/6/89	9(16)	8(16)	7	7	1	1	0	0	30	30
Chris Green	3/1/90	5(10)	5(9)	1	1	0	0	0	0	4	4
Ollie Greensmith	3/12/99	1	1	0	0	0	0	0	0	0	0
Ryan Hampshire	29/12/94	12(1)	12(1)	5	5	3	3	1	1	27	27
Tom Johnstone	13/8/95	11	10	5	5	0	0	0	0	20	20
Max Jowitt	6/5/97	14	13	1	1	0	0	0	0	4	4
Liam Kay	17/12/91	15(4)	15(4)	7	7	0	0	0	0	28	28
Lee Kershaw	2/5/99	19	19	5	5	0	0	0	0	20	20
Mason Lino	4/2/94	24	23	6	5	76	75	1	1	177	171
Reece Lyne	2/12/92	20	19	5	5	0	0	0	0	20	20
Jacob Miller	22/8/92	21	20	5	5	0	0	2	2	22	22
Jay Pitts	9/12/89	20	19	5	5	0	0	0	0	20	20
Innes Senior	30/5/00	16	15	6	6	0	0	0	0	24	24
Adam Tangata	17/3/91	(1)	(1)	0	0	0	0	0	0	0	0
Kelepi Tanginoa	1/3/94	21(1)	20(1)	6	6	0	0	0	0	24	24
Bill Tupou	2/7/90	9	8	1	1	0	0	0	0	4	4
Alex Walker	4/9/95	1	1	0	0	0	0	0	0	0	0
Brad Walker	30/1/98	10(3)	10(3)	0	0	0	0	0	0	0	0
Joe Westerman	15/11/89	17	16	3	3	0	0	0	0	12	12
Josh Wood	15/11/95	2(2)	1(2)	0	0	0	0	0	0	0	0
Kyle Wood	18/6/89	3(12)	3(12)	0	0	0	0	0	0	0	0

Mason Lino

'SL' totals include Super League games only; 'All' totals also include Challenge Cup

23rd November 2020 - Ben Currie (to November 2023), Jason Clark (2021) and Matt Davis (November 2022) sign new contracts.

24th November 2020 - prop Rob Butler signs from London Broncos on two-year contract.

30th November 2020 - Anthony Gelling released from final year of contract by mutual consent.

10th December 2020 - prop Robbie Mulhern signs from Hull KR on two-year deal. Second-rower Luis Johnson joins Hull KR.

18th December 2020 - centre Keanan Brand joins Leigh on season loan.

20th December 2020 - prop Samy Kibula joins Newcastle Thunder on 12-month loan.

12th January 2021 - squad returns for pre-season training.

24th January 2021 - Joe Philbin signs contract extension to end of 2024.

10th February 2021 - prop Leilani Latu released from contract by mutual agreement.

16th February 2021 - Jack Hughes appointed team captain.

16th February 2021 - coach Steve Price to leave club at end of 2021 season.

25th February 2021 - Riley Dean joins York on season's loan.

19th March 2021 - 34-12 home win over Leigh in Chris Hill testimonial.

28th March 2021 - 21-12 round-one defeat by Castleford at Headingley.

2nd April 2021 - Gareth Widdop stars in 44-12 round-two Good Friday win over Leigh at St Helens.

6th April 2021 - Daryl Powell appointed head coach from 2022 on three-year contract.

11th April 2021 - 32-8 Challenge Cup third-round win at Swinton. Tom Lineham banned for three games for late hit.

18th April 2021 - last-second Jake Mamo try forces extra-time which remains deadlocked at 14-14 in round-three game at Hull FC.

20th April 2021 - assistant coaches Lee Briers and Andrew Henderson to leave at end of season.

24th April 2021 - 24-8 win in Perpignan ends Catalans' 100 per cent start.

1st May 2021 - Greg Inglis scores on debut in 50-26 home win over Hull KR.

6th May 2021 - Connor Wrench and Ellis Longstaff join Newcastle Thunder on loan.

7th May 2021 - Daryl Clark scores two tries in 16-6 Challenge Cup quarter-final win over Catalans at Headingley.

9th May 2021 - Eribe Doro banned for two months, with one month suspended, for breaching RFL betting code.

17th May 2021 - fans return for 26-20 home defeat to Huddersfield. Greg Inglis tears hamstring.

KEY DATES

22nd May 2021 - Gareth Widdop scores hat-trick in 38-14 home win over Castleford.

27th May 2021 - Toby King signs contract extension to end of 2025.

27th May 2021 - Gareth Widdop stars and scores try-double in 62-18 win at Salford.

5th June 2021 - 35-20 defeat to Castleford in Challenge Cup semi-final.

11th June 2021 - Josh Charnley scores hat-trick in 38-18 home win over Wakefield.

15th June 2021 - Castleford pair Oliver Holmes (three-years until November 2024) and Peter Mata'utia two-year contract until end 2023) sign for 2022 season.

17th June 2021 - Ben Currie scores only try in 6-2 win at St Helens.

24th June 2021 - side featuring six academy graduate records 44-18 home win over Leigh.

29th June 2021 - hooker Danny Waker signs one-year contract extension until end of 2022.

30th July 2021 - Jake Mamo scores opportunistic hat-trick in 40-14 away win over Wigan.

1st July 2021 - Jake Mamo to join Castleford at end of season.

2nd July 2021 - Greg Inglis retires as player and released from playing contract with immediate effect.

5th July 2021 - 22-16 home defeat by Leeds ends winning run at six games.

9th July 2021 - England international halfback George Williams signs on three-and-a-half year deal.

10th July 2021 - away fixture at Hull KR (scheduled for Sunday 11th July) postponed because of Covid issues in Wolves camp.

15th July 2021 - Josh Thewlis (three years), Ellis Longstaff, Connor Wrench (both two), Riley Dean, Eribe Doro and Jacob Gannon (all 12 months) sign contract extensions.

19th July 2021 - game at Leigh (Thursday July 22nd) postponed with Covid problems in Wolves camp.

28th July 2021 - 21-8 home win over Wigan in front of unrestricted attendance.

1st August 2021 - last-minute field goal from debutant George Williams seals 27-26 win at Leeds.

4th August 2021 - Blake Austin to move to Leeds at end of season.

4th August 2021 - forward James Harrison signs from Featherstone Rovers on a two-year contract until November 2023.

7th August 2021 - Hull FC postpone Sunday game (8th August) because of Covid issues.

15th August 2021 - late comeback from 26-6 deficit at Wakefield ends in 28-22 defeat.

16th August 2021 - winger Tom Lineham signs for Wakefield from 2022.

19th August 2021 - home game with table-toppers Catalans postponed on morning of match due to Covid issues at Dragons.

26th August 2021 - Jake Mamo scores two first-half tries in 26-6 away win at Huddersfield.

30th August 2021 - 24-14 home defeat to St Helens after tight contest.

5th September 2021 - 10-6 Magic Weekend win over Wigan in Newcastle.

6th September 2021 - Hull Kingston Rovers centre Greg Minikin signs one-year deal for 2022 season.

10th September 2021 - Chris Hill signs for Huddersfield for 2022 season.

11th September 2021 - George Williams kicks two late field goals as 20-19 home win over Salford secures third-placed finish.

16th September 2021 - Matty Ashton scores hat-trick in 40-20 last-round win at Castleford, after leading 32-0. Mike Cooper sent off for high tackle.

20th September 2021 - Mike Cooper gets one-match penalty notice.

24th September 2021 - shock 19-0 home defeat by sixth-placed Hull KR ends season.

6th October 2021 - Wigan Warriors prop Joe Bullock signs on three-year deal.

CLUB RECORDS

Highest score:
112-0 v Swinton, 20/5/2011
Highest score against:
12-84 v Bradford, 9/9/2001
Record attendance:
34,404 v Wigan, 22/1/49 *(Wilderspool)*
15,008 v Widnes, 25/3/2016
(Halliwell Jones Stadium)

MATCH RECORDS

Tries:
7 Brian Bevan v Leigh, 29/3/48
Brian Bevan v Bramley, 22/4/53
Goals:
16 Lee Briers v Swinton, 20/5/2011
Points:
44 Lee Briers v Swinton, 20/5/2011

SEASON RECORDS

Tries: 66 Brian Bevan 1952-53
Goals: 170 Steve Hesford 1978-79
Points: 363 Harry Bath 1952-53

CAREER RECORDS

Tries: 740 Brian Bevan 1945-62
Goals: 1,159 Steve Hesford 1975-85
Points: 2,586 Lee Briers 1997-2013
Appearances: 620 Brian Bevan 1945-62

WARRINGTON WOLVES

DATE	FIXTURE	RESULT	SCORERS	LGE	ATT
28/3/21	Castleford (a) ●	L21-12	t:King,D Clark,Austin	10th	BCD
2/4/21	Leigh (h) ●●	W44-12	t:Lineham(2),King(2),Mamo,Widdop(2),Currie g:Ratchford(6)	6th	BCD
11/4/21	Swinton (a) (CCR3)	W8-32	t:King(2),Lineham,Austin,Ashton,Walker g:Ratchford(4)	N/A	BCD
18/4/21	Hull FC (a)	D14-14			BCD
		(aet)	t:Hill,Mamo g:Ratchford(2),Widdop	6th	BCD
24/4/21	Catalans Dragons (a)	W8-24	t:Currie,King,Mamo,Widdop g:Ratchford(4)	6th	BCD
1/5/21	Hull KR (h)	W50-26	t:King,Currie(2),Inglis,D Clark,Mamo,Charnley(2),Walker g:Ratchford(7)	6th	BCD
7/5/21	Catalans Dragons (a) (CCQF) ●	W6-16	t:D Clark(2) g:Widdop(4)	N/A	BCD
17/5/21	Huddersfield (h)	L20-26	t:Inglis,D Clark,Thewlis g:Widdop(4)	5th	4,000
22/5/21	Castleford (h)	W38-14	t:Charnley,King(2),Widdop(3),D Clark g:Ratchford(5)	4th	4,000
27/5/21	Salford (a)	W18-62	t:Ratchford,Walker,King(2),Mamo(2),Widdop(2),Hill,Currie g:Ratchford(11)	4th	2,306
5/6/21	Castleford (CCSF) ●●●	L35-20	t:Currie,Mamo,King,Charnley g:Widdop(2)	N/A	-
11/6/21	Wakefield (h)	W38-18	t:Widdop,Currie,Mamo,Charnley(3) g:Widdop(7)	4th	4,000
17/6/21	St Helens (a)	W2-6	t:Currie g:Widdop	4th	4,000
24/6/21	Leigh (a)	W44-18	t:Austin,Davis,Widdop,Charnley,Walker,Doro,Lineham g:Widdop(8)	3rd	4,000
30/6/21	Wigan (a)	W14-40	t:Wrench,Mamo(3),Davis,Hughes,Currie g:Ratchford(6)	3rd	5,537
5/7/21	Leeds (h)	L16-22	t:Walker,Charnley(2) g:Ratchford(2)	3rd	4,000
28/7/21	Wigan (h)	W21-8	t:Austin,Thewlis,Mamo g:Ratchford(4) fg:Austin	3rd	8,014
1/8/21	Leeds (a)	W26-27	t:Cooper,Austin,Charnley,Walker g:Ratchford(5) fg:Williams	3rd	9,196
15/8/21	Wakefield (a)	L28-22	t:Williams,Austin,Mamo,Charnley g:Ratchford(3)	3rd	3,445
26/8/21	Huddersfield (a)	W6-26	t:Mamo(2),Cooper,King g:Ratchford(5)	3rd	4,017
30/8/21	St Helens (h)	L14-24	t:Currie,Williams g:Ratchford(3)	3rd	10,006
5/9/21	Wigan (MW) ●●●●	W10-6	t:Thewlis,Williams g:Ratchford	3rd	-
11/9/21	Salford (h)	W20-19			
		(aet)	t:Ashton,Davis,Charnley g:Widdop(3) fg:Williams(2)	3rd	7,351
16/9/21	Castleford (a)	W24-40	t:Ashton(3),Mamo(2),Wrench g:Ratchford(7),Widdop	3rd	5,126
24/9/21	Hull KR (h) (E)	L0-19		N/A	6,252

● *Played at Emerald Headingley, Leeds*
●● *Played at Totally Wicked Stadium, St Helens*
●●● *Played at Leigh Sports Village*
●●●● *Played at St James' Park, Newcastle*

Hull KR (a) (R14), Leigh (a) (R15), Hull FC (h) (R18) and Catalans Dragons (h) (R20) games were postponed, and not rearranged

		APP		TRIES		GOALS		FG		PTS	
	D.O.B.	ALL	SL	ALL	SL	ALL	SL	ALL	SL	ALL	SL
Sitaleki Akauola	7/4/92	3(13)	3(11)	0	0	0	0	0	0	0	0
Matty Ashton	28/7/98	5(4)	4(4)	5	4	0	0	0	0	20	16
Blake Austin	1/2/91	17(2)	14(2)	6	5	0	0	1	1	25	21
Rob Butler	15/5/98	(5)	(4)	0	0	0	0	0	0	0	0
Josh Charnley	26/6/91	22	19	13	12	0	0	0	0	52	48
Daryl Clark	10/2/93	17(2)	14(2)	6	4	0	0	0	0	24	16
Jason Clark	28/6/89	5(12)	3(12)	0	0	0	0	0	0	0	0
Mike Cooper	15/9/88	19	17	2	2	0	0	0	0	8	8
Ben Currie	15/7/94	24	21	10	9	0	0	0	0	40	36
Matt Davis	5/7/96	11(8)	10(6)	3	3	0	0	0	0	12	12
Riley Dean	10/8/01	(1)	(1)	0	0	0	0	0	0	0	0
Eribe Doro	26/3/01	1(1)	1(1)	1	1	0	0	0	0	4	4
Chris Hill	3/11/87	24	21	2	2	0	0	0	0	8	8
Jack Hughes	4/1/92	22	20	1	1	0	0	0	0	4	4
Greg Inglis	15/1/87	3	2	2	2	0	0	0	0	8	8
Toby King	9/7/96	22	19	13	10	0	0	0	0	52	40
Tom Lineham	21/9/91	15	13	4	3	0	0	0	0	16	12
Ellis Longstaff	5/7/02	1(6)	1(6)	0	0	0	0	0	0	0	0
Jake Mamo	6/6/94	23	20	17	16	0	0	0	0	68	64
Robbie Mulhern	18/10/94	1(20)	1(17)	0	0	0	0	0	0	0	0
Joe Philbin	16/11/94	12(9)	11(7)	0	0	0	0	0	0	0	0
Stefan Ratchford	19/7/88	22(1)	20(1)	1	1	75	71	0	0	154	146
Ellis Robson	14/9/98	1(1)	(1)	0	0	0	0	0	0	0	0
Josh Thewlis	30/4/02	15	14	3	3	0	0	0	0	12	12
Danny Walker	29/6/99	6(11)	6(9)	6	5	0	0	0	0	24	20
Gareth Widdop	12/3/89	20	18	10	10	31	25	0	0	102	90
George Williams	31/10/94	8	8	3	3	0	0	3	3	15	15
Connor Wrench	4/10/01	6(1)	6(1)	2	2	0	0	0	0	8	8

'SL' totals include regular season & play-offs; 'All' totals also include Challenge Cup

Ben Currie

1st December 2020 - Ben Flower leaves for Leigh.

2nd December 2020 - coach Adrian Lam signs new contract for 2021 season.

4th December 2020 - Joe Burgess and Jack Wells leave to join Salford.

7th December 2020 - Thomas Leuluai signs new contract for 2021.

10th December 2020 - second-rower Joe Greenwood leaves to join Huddersfield.

21st December 2020 - Jake Shorrocks and Josh Woods leave the club.

31st December 2020 - Chris Hankinson joins London Broncos on year-long loan.

9th January 2021 - prop Romain Navarrete joins London Broncos.

28th January 2021 - hooker Amir Bourouh joins Halifax on season-long loan.

3rd February 2021 - George Burgess leaves by mutual consent because of hip injury.

8th February 2021 - Robin Park training ground closed for ten days following positive Covid-19 tests.

26th March 2021 - Jake Bibby try-double spearheads comeback from 18-0 to win 20-18 in round-one opener against Leigh at Headingley.

1st April 2021 - second-half Jake Bibby hat-trick in 34-6 win over Wakefield at St Helens.

9th April 2021 - Sam Halsall and Umyla Hanley score first senior tries in 26-0 Challenge Cup third round win at York.

15th April 2021 - Liam Farrell try-double in 19-6 round-three win at Leeds.

18th April 2021 - 21-year-old halfback Harry Smith signs new four-year contract to end of 2024.

19th April 2021 - Jackson Hastings to leave for NRL Wests Tigers at end of season.

22nd April 2021 - Bevan French scores two tries on the wing in his first game of season, 22-12 home win over unbeaten Castleford.

29th April 2021 - Zak Hardaker penalty 15 minutes from end edges 16-14 home win over Hull FC.

5th May 2021 - prop Tony Clubb banned by RFL for eight games and fined two weeks' wages by club for 'ethnically offensive' abuse against Andre Savelio.

8th May 2021 - 20-12 defeat by Hull FC at Headingley means Challenge Cup quarter-final exit.

17th May 2021 - Jake Bibby double in 30-16 win at Leigh.

22nd May 2021 - late Jackson Hastings field goal seals 17-16 win at Salford. Bevan French suffers season-ending hamstring injury.

KEY DATES

28th May 2021 - Oliver Gildart, yet to appear in 2021, to join NRL Wests Tigers at end of season. Prop forward Ben Kilner leaves by mutual consent and retires from game.

29th May 2021 - 48-0 hammering at Catalans ends hundred per cent record. Zak Hardaker sent off for head butt and banned for two games.

8th June 2021 - round-9 fixture at Huddersfield (Friday 11th June) postponed due to Covid outbreak in Giants camp.

18th June 2021 - 18-8 home defeat by Hull KR.

18th June 2021 - George Williams not returning to Wigan after Canberra departure.

21st June 2021 - Brad Singleton banned for two games for head-butting.

24th June 2021 - Brad O'Neill makes debut in 14-6 defeat at Wakefield.

25th June 2021 - John Bateman sprains ankle in England game against Combined All Stars.

27th June 2021 - Dom Manfredi to retire at the end of 2021 season due to knee injury.

30th June 2021 - 40-14 home round-12 defeat at home to Warrington.

4th July 2021 - 24-6 defeat at rain-soaked St Helens.

11th July 2021 - losing run ended at five matches with 16-12 home win over Huddersfield.

12th July 2021 - Jackson Hastings handed one-match suspension for 'other contrary behaviour', contact with elbow while shrugging off tackler.

16th July 2021 - 14-12 win at Huddersfield in re-arranged round-nine game.

19th July 2021 - Lebanese international London Broncos winger Abbas Miski and NRL prop forwards Patrick Mago (Souths) and Kaide Ellis (St George Illawarra) all sign two-year contracts from 2022 with option of third year.

23rd July 2021 - Jake Bibby hat-trick in 25-12 home win over Wakefield.

1st August 2021 - Umyla Hanley scores hat-trick in 50-6 home win over Leigh. Thomas Leuluai tears hamstring and is out for season.

4th August 2021 - Dom Manfredi retires with immediate effect.

6th August 2021 - Zak Hardaker back from neck injury in 16-6 round-18 home win over Salford.

13th August 2021 - Sam Powell suffers head knock in second minute of 26-14 defeat at Hull KR.

18th August 2021 - hooker Amir Bourouh to join Salford at end of season.

20th August 2021 - 26-2 home defeat by St Helens in fiery derby.

23rd August 2021 - Willie Isa gets a three-match ban for striking and one more for 'other contrary behaviour'. John Bateman gets one game for questioning official's decision, revoked on appeal.

25th August 2021 - 14-0 home defeat to Leeds.

30th August 2021 - hard earned 22-0 win at Castleford ends losing run at three matches.

31st August 2021 - head coach Adrian Lam to leave at end of 2021 season after three years in charge.

5th September 2021 - 10-6 Magic Weekend defeat by Warrington in Newcastle.

11th September 2021 - 10-0 win at Hull FC secures fourth-placed finish.

17th September 2021 - 12-8 last-round home win over League Leaders Catalans.

22nd September 2021 - prop forward Tony Clubb to retire at end of season.

23rd September 2021 - 8-0 home defeat by fifth-placed Leeds ends season.

5th October 2021 - former coach Shaun Wane returns in leadership role, with Matty Peet new head coach and Sean O'Loughlin and Lee Briers as assistants.

6th October 2021 - prop Joe Bullock moves to Warrington Wolves.

CLUB RECORDS
Highest score: 116-0 v Flimby & Fothergill, 14/2/25 **Highest score against:** 0-75 v St Helens, 26/6/2005 **Record attendance:** 47,747 v St Helens, 27/3/59 *(Central Park)* 25,004 v St Helens, 25/3/2005 *(JJB/DW Stadium)*

MATCH RECORDS
Tries: 10 Martin Offiah v Leeds, 10/5/92 Shaun Edwards v Swinton, 29/9/92 **Goals:** 22 Jim Sullivan v Flimby & Fothergill, 14/2/25 **Points:** 44 Jim Sullivan v Flimby & Fothergill, 14/2/25

SEASON RECORDS
Tries: 62 Johnny Ring 1925-26 **Goals:** 186 Frano Botica 1994-95 **Points:** 462 Pat Richards 2010

CAREER RECORDS
Tries: 478 Billy Boston 1953-68 **Goals:** 2,317 Jim Sullivan 1921-46 **Points:** 4,883 Jim Sullivan 1921-46 **Appearances:** 774 Jim Sullivan 1921-46

WIGAN WARRIORS

DATE	FIXTURE	RESULT	SCORERS	LGE	ATT
26/3/21	Leigh (a) ●	W18-20	t:Bibby(2),Hardaker,Bullock g:Hardaker(2)	5th	BCD
1/4/21	Wakefield (h) ●●	W34-6	t:Partington,Bibby(3),Hardaker,Bateman g:Hardaker(5)	3rd	BCD
9/4/21	York (a) (CCR3)	W0-26	t:Hardaker,Smith,Halsall,Hanley,Clubb g:Hardaker(3)	N/A	BCD
15/4/21	Leeds (a)	W6-19	t:Farrell(2),Hardaker,Hastings g:Hardaker fg:Hardaker	2nd	BCD
22/4/21	Castleford (h)	W22-12	t:Hardaker,French(2),Powell g:Hardaker(3)	2nd	BCD
29/4/21	Hull FC (h)	W16-14	t:Hastings,Farrell,Bibby g:Hardaker(2)	2nd	BCD
8/5/21	Hull FC (a) (CCQF) ●	L20-10	t:Bibby,Manfredi g:Smith	N/A	BCD
17/5/21	Leigh (a)	W16-30	t:Smith,Manfredi,French,Farrell,Bibby(2) g:Smith(3)	2nd	1,702
22/5/21	Salford (h)	W16-17	t:Singleton(2),Farrell g:Smith(2) fg:Hastings	1st	2,033
29/5/21	Catalans Dragons (a)	L48-0		3rd	1,000
18/6/21	Hull KR (h)	L8-18	t:Gildart(2)	3rd	5,018
24/6/21	Wakefield (a)	L14-6	t:Hanley g:Smith	4th	2,262
30/6/21	Warrington (h)	L14-40	t:Powell,Isa,Gildart g:Smith	5th	5,537
4/7/21	St Helens (a)	L24-6	t:Farrell g:Smith	6th	4,000
11/7/21	Huddersfield (h)	W16-12	t:Marshall,Clark,Smith g:Smith(2)	5th	4,439
16/7/21	Huddersfield (a)	W12-14	t:Clark,Farrell g:Smith(3)	5th	3,139
23/7/21	Wakefield (h)	W25-12	t:Bibby(3),Shorrocks,Marshall g:Smith(2) fg:Hastings	4th	5,555
28/7/21	Warrington (a)	L21-8	t:Marshall(2)	4th	8,014
1/8/21	Leigh (h)	W50-6	t:Leuluai,Hanley(3),Farrell(2),Halsall,Shorrocks,Hastings g:Smith(7)	4th	9,206
6/8/21	Salford (h)	W16-6	t:Halsall,Powell g:Smith(4)	4th	9,431
13/8/21	Hull KR (a)	L26-14	t:Bibby,Marshall(2) g:Smith	4th	6,230
20/8/21	St Helens (h)	L2-26	g:Smith	4th	16,319
25/8/21	Leeds (h)	L0-14		4th	11,390
30/8/21	Castleford (a)	W0-22	t:Hastings,Marshall,Gildart,Singleton g:Smith(2),Hastings	4th	4,729
5/9/21	Warrington (MW) ●●●	L10-6	t:Havard g:Smith	4th	-
11/9/21	Hull FC (a)	W0-10	t:Bibby,Hardaker g:Hardaker	4th	10,043
17/9/21	Catalans Dragons (h)	W12-8	t:Isa,McDonnell g:Hardaker(2)	4th	12,852
23/9/21	Leeds (h) (E)	L0-8		N/A	7,396

● *Played at Emerald Headingley, Leeds*
●● *Played at Totally Wicked Stadium, St Helens*
●●● *Played at St James' Park, Newcastle*

	APP		TRIES		GOALS		FG		PTS	
	D.O.B.	ALL	SL	ALL	SL	ALL	SL	ALL	SL	ALL	SL

	D.O.B.	ALL	SL	ALL	SL	ALL	SL	ALL	SL	ALL	SL
John Bateman	30/9/93	16(3)	14(3)	1	1	0	0	0	0	4	4
Jake Bibby	17/6/96	28	26	14	13	0	0	0	0	56	52
Amir Bourouh	5/1/01	(5)	(5)	0	0	0	0	0	0	0	0
Joe Bullock	27/11/92	8(12)	7(11)	1	1	0	0	0	0	4	4
Liam Byrne	18/8/99	1(24)	(23)	0	0	0	0	0	0	0	0
Mitch Clark	13/3/93	(8)	(8)	2	2	0	0	0	0	8	8
Tony Clubb	12/6/87	10(1)	10	1	0	0	0	0	0	4	0
Liam Farrell	2/7/90	24	23	9	9	0	0	0	0	36	36
Jai Field	6/9/97	3(1)	3(1)	0	0	0	0	0	0	0	0
Bevan French	4/1/96	5	4	3	3	0	0	0	0	12	12
Oliver Gildart	6/8/96	14	14	4	4	0	0	0	0	16	16
Sam Halsall	18/8/01	8	7	3	2	0	0	0	0	12	8
Umyla Hanley	5/3/02	9	8	5	4	0	0	0	0	20	16
Zak Hardaker	17/10/91	18(1)	16(1)	6	5	19	16	1	1	63	53
Jackson Hastings	14/1/96	25	23	4	4	1	1	2	2	20	20
Ethan Havard	26/10/00	8(17)	8(15)	1	1	0	0	0	0	4	4
Willie Isa	1/1/89	20	18	2	2	0	0	0	0	8	8
Thomas Leuluai	22/6/85	13	13	1	1	0	0	0	0	4	4
Dom Manfredi	1/10/93	3(1)	3	2	1	0	0	0	0	8	4
Liam Marshall	9/5/96	16	16	7	7	0	0	0	0	28	28
James McDonnell	12/1/00	2	2	1	1	0	0	0	0	4	4
Brad O'Neill	22/7/02	1(7)	1(7)	0	0	0	0	0	0	0	0
Oliver Partington	3/9/98	24(1)	22(1)	1	1	0	0	0	0	4	4
Kai Pearce-Paul	19/2/01	13(6)	13(6)	0	0	0	0	0	0	0	0
Sam Powell	3/7/92	22(1)	20(1)	3	3	0	0	0	0	12	12
Joe Shorrocks	25/11/99	8(20)	8(18)	2	2	0	0	0	0	8	8
Brad Singleton	29/10/92	22	20	3	3	0	0	0	0	12	12
Harry Smith	25/1/00	25(3)	23(3)	3	2	32	31	0	0	76	70
Morgan Smithies	7/11/00	18(1)	16(1)	0	0	0	0	0	0	0	0

Jake Bibby

'SL' totals include regular season & play-offs; 'All' totals also include Challenge Cup

SUPER LEAGUE XXVI
Round by Round

ROUND 1

Friday 26th March 2021

ST HELENS 29 SALFORD RED DEVILS 6

SAINTS: 18 Jack Welsby; 2 Tommy Makinson; 3 Kevin Naiqama; 4 Mark Percival; 5 Regan Grace; 6 Jonny Lomax; 7 Theo Fages; 8 Alex Walmsley; 9 James Roby (C); 10 Matty Lees; 11 Joel Thompson (D); 12 James Bentley; 14 Sione Mata'utia (D). Subs (all used): 15 Louie McCarthy-Scarsbrook; 16 Kyle Amor; 17 Agnatius Paasi (D); 19 Aaron Smith.
Tries: Makinson (2), Grace (34), Percival (60), Naiqama (72), Walmsley (76); **Goals:** Makinson 4/6; **Field goal:** Welsby (40).
RED DEVILS: 23 Dan Sarginson; 2 Ken Sio; 3 Kallum Watkins; 19 Elliot Kear; 4 Krisnan Inu; 6 Tui Lolohea; 7 Kevin Brown; 8 Lee Mossop (C); 14 Danny Addy (D); 10 Sebastine Ikahihifo; 20 Harvey Livett (D); 11 Ryan Lannon; 13 Elijah Taylor (D). Subs (all used): 12 Pauli Pauli; 25 Jack Ormondroyd; 26 Jack Wells (D); 29 Dec Patton (D).
Try: Sio (55); **Goals:** Inu 1/1.
Rugby Leaguer & League Express Men of the Match: *Saints:* Jonny Lomax; *Red Devils:* Elijah Taylor.
Penalty count: 7-8; **Half-time:** 13-0;
Referee: Liam Moore. *(at Emerald Headingley, Leeds).*

LEIGH CENTURIONS 18 WIGAN WARRIORS 20

CENTURIONS: 1 Ryan Brierley (D3); 5 Lewis Tierney (D); 24 Keanan Brand (D); 3 Iain Thornley; 2 Matty Russell (D2); 6 Blake Wallace (D); 7 Joe Mellor (D); 20 Adam Sidlow (D); 9 Liam Hood (C); 10 Mark Ioane; 18 Matty Gee (D); 11 Ben Hellewell; 12 Jordan Thompson. Subs (all used): 16 Nathaniel Peteru (D); 27 Josh Eaves (D2); 19 Nathan Mason; 28 Matthew Foster (D).
Tries: Hood (5), Thornley (24), Hellewell (27);
Goals: Brierley 3/3.
WARRIORS: 3 Zak Hardaker; 6 Jai Field (D); 11 Willie Isa; 22 Jake Bibby; 30 Umyla Hanley; 7 Thomas Leuluai (C); 20 Harry Smith; 8 Brad Singleton; 9 Sam Powell; 10 Joe Bullock; 13 John Bateman (D2); 12 Liam Farrell; 14 Oliver Partington. Subs (all used): 21 Ethan Havard; 19 Liam Byrne; 25 Joe Shorrocks; 15 Morgan Smithies.
Tries: Bibby (37, 66), Hardaker (39), Bullock (63);
Goals: Hardaker 2/4.
Rugby Leaguer & League Express Men of the Match: *Centurions:* Liam Hood; *Warriors:* Sam Powell.
Penalty count: 4-3; **Half-time:** 18-8;
Referee: Ben Thaler. *(at Emerald Headingley, Leeds).*

Saturday 27th March 2021

WAKEFIELD TRINITY 22 LEEDS RHINOS 28

TRINITY: 21 Alex Walker; 18 Innes Senior; 4 Reece Lyne; 3 Bill Tupou; 2 Tom Johnstone; 6 Jacob Miller (C); 7 Mason Lino (D); 8 David Fifita; 19 Jordan Crowther; 10 Tinirau Arona; 11 Matty Ashurst; 12 Kelepi Tanginoa; 13 Joe Westerman. Subs (all used): 23 Josh Wood; 16 James Batchelor; 17 Chris Green; 22 Adam Tangata.
Tries: Johnstone (9, 55), Senior (16), Ashurst (20);
Goals: Lino 3/4.
RHINOS: 16 Richie Myler; 2 Tom Briscoe; 27 Jack Broadbent; 21 Alex Sutcliffe; 24 Luke Briscoe; 15 Liam Sutcliffe; 7 Luke Gale (C); 8 Mikolaj Oledzki; 9 Kruise Leeming; 10 Matt Prior; 11 Alex Mellor; 12 Rhyse Martin; 13 Zane Tetevano (D). Subs (all used): 14 Brad Dwyer; 20 Bodene Thompson; 25 James Donaldson; 17 Cameron Smith.
Tries: L Briscoe (5), A Sutcliffe (26), Dwyer (34), Myler (37), Broadbent (60); **Goals:** Martin 4/6.
Rugby Leaguer & League Express Men of the Match: *Trinity:* Tom Johnstone; *Rhinos:* Richie Myler.
Penalty count: 2-2; **Half-time:** 16-22;
Referee: Scott Mikalauskas. *(at Emerald Headingley).*

CATALANS DRAGONS 29
HULL KINGSTON ROVERS 28
(after golden point extra-time)

DRAGONS: 29 Sam Tomkins; 2 Tom Davies; 4 Dean Whare (D); 20 Matthieu Laguerre (D); 5 Fouad Yaha; 6 James Maloney; 7 Josh Drinkwater; 10 Julian Bousquet; 14 Alrix Da Costa; 17 Mickael Goudemand; 11 Matt Whitley; 12 Mike McMeeken (D); 13 Benjamin Garcia (C). Subs (all used): 1 Arthur Mourgue; 16 Paul Seguier; 24 Jason Baitieri; 28 Sam Kasiano.
Tries: Yaha (4, 50), Whitley (15), Laguerre (39), Garcia (44);
Goals: Maloney 4/5; **Field goal:** Maloney (82).
Sin bin: Bousquet (67) - fighting.
ROVERS: 1 Adam Quinlan; 2 Ben Crooks; 3 Greg Minikin; 4 Shaun Kenny-Dowall (C); 5 Ryan Hall (D); 7 Jordan Abdull; 20 Mikey Lewis; 16 George King; 14 Jez Litten; 10 Korbin Sims (D); 13 Dean Hadley; 12 Kane Linnett; 15 George Lawler. Subs (all used): 8 Albert Vete (D); 9 Matt Parcell; 17 Elliot Minchella; 18 Matthew Storton.
Tries: Hall (26, 57, 72), Lewis (55), King (77);
Goals: Abdull 4/5.
Rugby Leaguer & League Express Men of the Match: *Dragons:* Sam Tomkins; *Rovers:* Ryan Hall.
Penalty count: 2-7; **Half-time:** 18-4;
Referee: James Child. *(at Emerald Headingley, Leeds).*

Sunday 28th March 2021

HULL FC 22 HUDDERSFIELD GIANTS 10

HULL FC: 1 Jake Connor; 5 Mahe Fonua; 3 Carlos Tuimavave; 4 Josh Griffin; 21 Adam Swift; 6 Josh Reynolds (D); 7 Marc Sneyd (C); 10 Tevita Satae; 9 Danny Houghton; 13 Ligi Sao; 11 Andre Savelio; 12 Manu Ma'u; 16 Jordan Lane. Subs (all used): 8 Scott Taylor; 15 Joe Cator; 22 Josh Bowden; 24 Cameron Scott.
Tries: Connor (16), Griffin (21), Reynolds (60);
Goals: Sneyd 5/5.
GIANTS: 6 Lee Gaskell; 2 Jermaine McGillvary; 21 Leroy Cudjoe (C); 4 Ricky Leutele (D); 5 Darnell McIntosh; 16 Jack Cogger (D); 23 Oliver Russell; 8 Luke Yates (D); 19 James Cunningham (D); 22 James Gavet; 17 Chris McQueen; 15 Joe Greenwood (D); 13 Josh Jones (D). Subs (all used): 9 Adam O'Brien; 11 Kenny Edwards; 14 Matty English; 20 Oliver Wilson.
Tries: Leutele (69), Gavet (79); **Goals:** Russell 1/2.
Sin bin: Edwards (49) - professional foul.
Rugby Leaguer & League Express Men of the Match: *Hull FC:* Jake Connor; *Giants:* James Gavet.
Penalty count: 6-5; **Half-time:** 12-0;
Referee: Robert Hicks. *(at Emerald Headingley, Leeds).*

CASTLEFORD TIGERS 21 WARRINGTON WOLVES 12

TIGERS: 1 Niall Evalds (D); 2 Derrell Olpherts; 3 Peter Mata'utia; 4 Michael Shenton (C); 25 Jordan Turner (D); 6 Jake Trueman; 31 Gareth O'Brien; 10 Grant Millington; 9 Paul McShane; 15 George Griffin; 11 Oliver Holmes; 12 Cheyse Blair; 14 Nathan Massey. Subs (all used): 8 Liam Watts; 13 Adam Milner; 18 Jacques O'Neill; 22 Daniel Smith.
Tries: Holmes (5), Evalds (29), Turner (39, 57);
Goals: O'Brien 1/1, Mata'utia 0/2, McShane 1/1;
Field goal: McShane (71).
WOLVES: 1 Stefan Ratchford; 2 Tom Lineham; 27 Connor Wrench; 4 Toby King; 5 Josh Charnley; 6 Blake Austin; 7 Gareth Widdop; 8 Chris Hill; 16 Danny Walker; 10 Mike Cooper; 11 Ben Currie; 12 Jack Hughes (C); 13 Joe Philbin. Subs (all used): 9 Daryl Clark; 14 Jason Clark; 17 Matty Ashton; 19 Robbie Mulhern (D).
Tries: King (7), D Clark (50), Austin (74);
Goals: Ratchford 0/2, Widdop 0/1.
Rugby Leaguer & League Express Men of the Match: *Tigers:* Paul McShane; *Wolves:* Robbie Mulhern.
Penalty count: 4-4; **Half-time:** 14-4;
Referee: Chris Kendall. *(at Emerald Headingley, Leeds).*

ROUND 2

Thursday 1st April 2021

WIGAN WARRIORS 34 WAKEFIELD TRINITY 6

WARRIORS: 3 Zak Hardaker; 22 Jake Bibby; 11 Willie Isa; 12 Liam Farrell; 30 Umyla Hanley; 7 Thomas Leuluai (C); 31 Jackson Hastings; 8 Brad Singleton; 9 Sam Powell; 10 Joe Bullock; 13 John Bateman; 15 Morgan Smithies; 14 Oliver Partington. Subs (all used): 19 Liam Byrne; 20 Harry Smith; 21 Ethan Havard; 25 Joe Shorrocks.
Tries: Partington (24), Bibby (47, 60, 77), Hardaker (56), Bateman (69); **Goals:** Hardaker 5/6.
TRINITY: 29 Ryan Hampshire; 18 Innes Senior; 4 Reece Lyne; 3 Bill Tupou; 2 Tom Johnstone; 6 Jacob Miller (C); 7 Mason Lino; 8 David Fifita; 19 Jordan Crowther; 10 Tinirau Arona; 11 Matty Ashurst; 14 Jay Pitts; 13 Joe Westerman. Subs (all used): 12 Kelepi Tanginoa; 16 James Batchelor; 17 Chris Green; 23 Josh Wood.
Try: Fifita (21); **Goals:** Lino 1/1.
Rugby Leaguer & League Express Men of the Match: *Warriors:* Zak Hardaker; *Trinity:* David Fifita.
Penalty count: 4-3; **Half-time:** 6-6;
Referee: Scott Mikalauskas.
(at Totally Wicked Stadium, St Helens).

HULL KINGSTON ROVERS 0 ST HELENS 25

ROVERS: 1 Adam Quinlan; 2 Ben Crooks; 3 Greg Minikin; 4 Shaun Kenny-Dowall (C); 5 Ryan Hall; 20 Mikey Lewis; 7 Jordan Abdull; 16 George King; 14 Jez Litten; 10 Korbin Sims; 12 Kane Linnett; 13 Dean Hadley; 15 George Lawler. Subs (all used): 9 Matt Parcell; 17 Elliot Minchella; 18 Matthew Storton; 28 Muizz Mustapha (D).
Sin bin: Lawler (61) - interference.
SAINTS: 18 Jack Welsby; 2 Tommy Makinson; 3 Kevin Naiqama; 22 Josh Simm; 5 Regan Grace; 6 Jonny Lomax; 7 Theo Fages; 8 Alex Walmsley; 9 James Roby (C); 10 Matty Lees; 11 Joel Thompson; 12 James Bentley; 14 Sione Mata'utia. Subs (all used): 15 Louie McCarthy-Scarsbrook; 16 Kyle Amor; 19 Aaron Smith; 20 Joe Batchelor.
Tries: Grace (3, 71), Welsby (8), Smith (62);
Goals: Makinson 4/5; **Field goal:** Fages (55).
Rugby Leaguer & League Express Men of the Match: *Rovers:* Matt Parcell; *Saints:* Theo Fages.
Penalty count: 7-5; **Half-time:** 0-10;
Referee: Robert Hicks. *(at Totally Wicked Stadium).*

Friday 2nd April 2021

WARRINGTON WOLVES 44 LEIGH CENTURIONS 12

WOLVES: 1 Stefan Ratchford; 2 Tom Lineham; 18 Jake Mamo; 4 Toby King; 5 Josh Charnley; 6 Blake Austin; 7 Gareth Widdop; 8 Chris Hill; 9 Daryl Clark; 10 Mike Cooper; 11 Ben Currie; 12 Jack Hughes (C); 13 Joe Philbin. Subs (all used): 14 Jason Clark; 16 Danny Walker; 19 Robbie Mulhern; 21 Rob Butler (D).
Tries: Lineham (10, 69), King (23, 63), Mamo (25), Widdop (37, 74), Currie (53); **Goals:** Ratchford 6/8.
CENTURIONS: 1 Ryan Brierley; 2 Matty Russell; 3 Iain Thornley; 24 Keanan Brand; 5 Lewis Tierney; 6 Blake Wallace; 30 Ben Reynolds (D3); 10 Mark Ioane; 9 Liam Hood (C); 20 Adam Sidlow; 11 Ben Hellewell; 18 Matty Gee; 12 Jordan Thompson. Subs (all used): 14 Matty Wildie; 15 Alex Gerrard; 16 Nathaniel Peteru; 21 Tyrone McCarthy (D2).
Tries: Sidlow (58), Brierley (78); **Goals:** Reynolds 2/2.
Rugby Leaguer & League Express Men of the Match: *Wolves:* Gareth Widdop; *Centurions:* Mark Ioane.
Penalty count: 4-4; **Half-time:** 22-0;
Referee: James Child.
(at Totally Wicked Stadium, St Helens).

LEEDS RHINOS 10 CASTLEFORD TIGERS 18

RHINOS: 27 Jack Broadbent; 2 Tom Briscoe; 28 Corey Hall; 21 Alex Sutcliffe; 24 Luke Briscoe; 15 Liam Sutcliffe; 7 Luke Gale (C); 8 Mikolaj Oledzki; 9 Kruise Leeming; 10 Matt Prior; 11 Alex Mellor; 12 Rhyse Martin; 13 Zane Tetevano. Subs (all used): 14 Brad Dwyer; 17 Cameron Smith; 20 Bodene Thompson; 25 James Donaldson.
Tries: L Briscoe (29), Prior (61); **Goals:** Martin 1/2.
TIGERS: 1 Niall Evalds; 2 Derrell Olpherts; 3 Peter Mata'utia; 4 Michael Shenton (C); 25 Jordan Turner; 6 Jake Trueman; 7 Danny Richardson; 8 Liam Watts; 9 Paul McShane; 10 Grant Millington; 11 Oliver Holmes; 12 Cheyse Blair; 14 Nathan Massey. Subs (all used): 13 Adam Milner; 19 Tyla Hepi; 21 Jesse Sene-Lefao; 22 Daniel Smith.
Tries: Holmes (12), Evalds (23), Turner (71);
Goals: Richardson 3/3.
Rugby Leaguer & League Express Men of the Match: *Rhinos:* Jack Broadbent; *Tigers:* Oliver Holmes.
Penalty count: 6-5; **Half-time:** 4-12;
Referee: Liam Moore.
(at Totally Wicked Stadium, St Helens).

Saturday 3rd April 2021

SALFORD RED DEVILS 4 HULL FC 35

RED DEVILS: 23 Dan Sarginson; 2 Ken Sio; 3 Kallum Watkins; 19 Elliot Kear; 22 Rhys Williams; 6 Tui Lolohea; 7 Kevin Brown; 8 Lee Mossop (C); 9 Andy Ackers; 10 Sebastine Ikahihifo; 20 Harvey Livett; 11 Ryan Lannon; 13 Elijah Taylor. Subs (all used): 17 Josh Johnson; 26 Jack Wells; 25 Jack Ormondroyd; 29 Dec Patton.
Try: Sio (58); **Goals:** Lolohea 0/1.
Sin bin: Lannon (26) - late challenge on Sneyd.
HULL FC: 1 Jake Connor; 5 Mahe Fonua; 3 Carlos Tuimavave; 4 Josh Griffin; 21 Adam Swift; 6 Josh Reynolds; 7 Marc Sneyd; 13 Ligi Sao; 9 Danny Houghton; 10 Tevita Satae; 11 Andre Savelio; 12 Manu Ma'u; 16 Jordan Lane. Subs (all used): 8 Scott Taylor (C); 15 Joe Cator; 17 Brad Fash; 24 Cameron Scott.
Tries: Savelio (20), Reynolds (39, 45), Griffin (49), Scott (76); **Goals:** Sneyd 5/5, Connor 2/2;
Field goal: Connor (73).
Rugby Leaguer & League Express Men of the Match: *Red Devils:* Elijah Taylor; *Hull FC:* Jake Connor.
Penalty count: 3-7; **Half-time:** 0-14;
Referee: Chris Kendall.
(at Totally Wicked Stadium, St Helens).

HUDDERSFIELD GIANTS 10 CATALANS DRAGONS 20

GIANTS: 5 Darnell McIntosh; 2 Jermaine McGillvary; 21 Leroy Cudjoe; 3 Jake Wardle; 27 Sam Wood; 6 Lee Gaskell; 16 Jack Cogger; 8 Luke Yates; 19 James Cunningham; 22 James Gavet; 17 Chris McQueen; 15 Joe Greenwood; 13 Josh Jones. Subs (all used): 9 Adam O'Brien; 11 Kenny Edwards; 10 Michael Lawrence (C); 14 Matty English.
Tries: McQueen (12), Wood (58); **Goals:** Jake Wardle 1/2.
Dismissal: Greenwood (76) - high tackle on Langi.

DRAGONS: 29 Sam Tomkins; 2 Tom Davies; 4 Dean Whare; 3 Samisoni Langi; 5 Fouad Yaha; 6 James Maloney; 7 Josh Drinkwater; 10 Julian Bousquet; 14 Alrix Da Costa; 8 Gil Dudson (D); 12 Mike McMeeken; 11 Matt Whitley; 13 Benjamin Garcia (C). Subs (all used): 1 Arthur Mourgue; 16 Paul Seguier; 24 Jason Baitieri; 28 Sam Kasiano.
Tries: Whitley (5), Garcia (32), McMeeken (39);
Goals: Maloney 3/3, S Tomkins 1/1.
Sin bin: Maloney (26) - dangerous contact.
Rugby Leaguer & League Express Men of the Match:
Giants: Jack Cogger; *Dragons:* Sam Tomkins.
Penalty count: 3-5; **Half-time:** 6-20;
Referee: Ben Thaler. *(at Totally Wicked Stadium, St Helens).*

ROUND 3

Thursday 15th April 2021

LEEDS RHINOS 6 WIGAN WARRIORS 19

RHINOS: 27 Jack Broadbent; 2 Tom Briscoe; 11 Alex Mellor; 21 Alex Sutcliffe; 24 Luke Briscoe; 12 Rhyse Martin; 33 Kyle Eastmond (D); 8 Mikolaj Oledzki; 9 Kruise Leeming; 10 Matt Prior (C); 25 James Donaldson; 22 Sam Walters; 17 Cameron Smith. Subs: 14 Brad Dwyer; 26 Jarrod O'Connor; 28 Corey Hall (not used); 31 Morgan Gannon.
Try: Mellor (45); **Goals:** Martin 1/1.
WARRIORS: 3 Zak Hardaker; 22 Jake Bibby; 11 Willie Isa; 12 Liam Farrell; 30 Umyla Hanley; 7 Thomas Leuluai (C); 31 Jackson Hastings; 8 Brad Singleton; 9 Sam Powell; 17 Tony Clubb; 13 John Bateman; 15 Morgan Smithies; 14 Oliver Partington. Subs (all used): 10 Joe Bullock; 20 Harry Smith; 21 Ethan Havard; 25 Joe Shorrocks.
Tries: Farrell (18, 72), Hardaker (33), Hastings (59);
Goals: Hardaker 1/4; **Field goal:** Hardaker (79).
Rugby Leaguer & League Express Men of the Match:
Rhinos: Mikolaj Oledzki; *Warriors:* Zak Hardaker.
Penalty count: 6-6; **Half-time:** 0-8;
Referee: Chris Kendall.

Friday 16th April 2021

CASTLEFORD TIGERS 52 LEIGH CENTURIONS 16

TIGERS: 1 Niall Evalds; 2 Derrell Olpherts; 3 Peter Mata'utia; 4 Michael Shenton (C); 23 Greg Eden; 6 Jake Trueman; 31 Gareth O'Brien; 8 Liam Watts; 9 Paul McShane; 22 Daniel Smith; 11 Oliver Holmes; 21 Jesse Sene-Lefao; 14 Nathan Massey. Subs (all used): 10 Grant Millington; 13 Adam Milner; 25 Jordan Turner; 26 Lewis Bienek (D).
Tries: Watts (5), Smith (15), Olpherts (20, 58), Eden (27), Evalds (30), Shenton (40), Turner (45), Trueman (61);
Goals: O'Brien 2/2, McShane 6/7.
Sin bin: Sene-Lefao (55) - late challenge on McCarthy.
CENTURIONS: 1 Ryan Brierley; 2 Matty Russell; 31 Josh Simm (D2); 22 Craig Mullen; 5 Lewis Tierney; 30 Ben Reynolds; 7 Joe Mellor; 20 Adam Sidlow; 9 Liam Hood (C); 16 Nathaniel Peteru; 11 Ben Hellewell; 12 Jordan Thompson; 21 Tyrone McCarthy. Subs (all used): 8 Ben Flower; 13 James Bell (D); 15 Alex Gerrard; 26 Nathan Peats.
Tries: Thompson (50), Reynolds (65), Brierley (76);
Goals: Reynolds 2/3.
Rugby Leaguer & League Express Men of the Match:
Tigers: Paul McShane; *Centurions:* Ben Reynolds.
Penalty count: 5-10; **Half-time:** 34-0;
Referee: Marcus Griffiths.

ST HELENS 34 WAKEFIELD TRINITY 6

SAINTS: 1 Lachlan Coote; 2 Tommy Makinson; 3 Kevin Naiqama; 18 Jack Welsby; 5 Regan Grace; 6 Jonny Lomax; 7 Theo Fages; 8 Alex Walmsley; 9 James Roby (C); 17 Agnatius Paasi; 11 Joel Thompson; 12 James Bentley; 20 Joe Batchelor. Subs (all used): 15 Louie McCarthy-Scarsbrook; 16 Kyle Amor; 21 Lewis Dodd; 23 Jake Wingfield.
Tries: Naiqama (42, 70), Bentley (46), Welsby (52), Grace (63, 73); **Goals:** Makinson 4/4, Dodd 1/2.
Sin bin: Bentley (17) - dissent.
TRINITY: 29 Ryan Hampshire; 27 Lee Kershaw; 4 Reece Lyne; 20 Joe Arundel; 18 Innes Senior; 6 Jacob Miller (C); 7 Mason Lino; 8 David Fifita; 19 Jordan Crowther; 10 Tinirau Arona; 16 James Batchelor; 14 Jay Pitts; 13 Joe Westerman. Subs (all used): 9 Kyle Wood; 15 Eddie Battye; 25 Brad Walker; 17 Chris Green.
Try: Pitts (75); **Goals:** Lino 1/1.
Rugby Leaguer & League Express Men of the Match:
Saints: Jack Welsby; *Trinity:* Joe Westerman.
Penalty count: 9-7; **Half-time:** 0-0; **Referee:** James Child.

HULL KINGSTON ROVERS 25 HUDDERSFIELD GIANTS 24

ROVERS: 1 Adam Quinlan; 23 Ethan Ryan; 2 Ben Crooks; 4 Shaun Kenny-Dowall (C); 5 Ryan Hall; 7 Jordan Abdull; 20 Mikey Lewis; 10 Korbin Sims; 9 Matt Parcell; 16 George King; 12 Kane Linnett; 27 Luis Johnson; 15 George Lawler. Subs (all used): 8 Albert Vete; 13 Dean Hadley; 14 Jez Litten; 28 Muizz Mustapha.
Tries: Crooks (1, 24), Lewis (26), Linnett (69);
Goals: Abdull 4/5; **Field goal:** Abdull (77).
GIANTS: 5 Darnell McIntosh; 2 Jermaine McGillvary; 3 Jake Wardle; 21 Leroy Cudjoe; 27 Sam Wood; 16 Jack Cogger; 7 Aidan Sezer (C); 8 Luke Yates; 19 James Cunningham; 10 Michael Lawrence; 11 Kenny Edwards; 17 Chris McQueen; 13 Josh Jones. Subs (all used): 14 Matty English; 9 Adam O'Brien; 6 Lee Gaskell; 18 Jack Ashworth.
Tries: McGillvary (34), McIntosh (54, 73), Jake Wardle (60), McQueen (66); **Goals:** Sezer 2/5.
Rugby Leaguer & League Express Men of the Match:
Rovers: Matt Parcell; *Giants:* Kenny Edwards.
Penalty count: 5-4; **Half-time:** 18-4; **Referee:** Liam Moore.

Saturday 17th April 2021

CATALANS DRAGONS 42 SALFORD RED DEVILS 6

DRAGONS: 29 Sam Tomkins; 2 Tom Davies; 3 Samisoni Langi; 4 Dean Whare; 5 Fouad Yaha; 6 James Maloney; 7 Josh Drinkwater; 8 Gil Dudson; 14 Alrix Da Costa; 10 Julian Bousquet; 11 Matt Whitley; 12 Mike McMeeken; 13 Benjamin Garcia (C). Subs (all used): 9 Michael McIlorum; 16 Paul Seguier; 24 Jason Baitieri; 28 Sam Kasiano.
Tries: Garcia (12), Langi (16), Drinkwater (29), Yaha (43, 61, 70), Davies (49); **Goals:** Maloney 7/8.
RED DEVILS: 1 Morgan Escare; 2 Ken Sio; 3 Kallum Watkins; 24 Matthew Costello; 22 Rhys Williams; 6 Tui Lolohea; 7 Kevin Brown; 8 Lee Mossop (C); 29 Dec Patton; 25 Jack Ormondroyd; 20 Harvey Livett; 12 Pauli Pauli; 13 Elijah Taylor. Subs (all used): 9 Andy Ackers; 10 Sebastine Ikahihifo; 26 Jack Wells; 28 Darcy Lussick.
Try: Livett (53); **Goals:** Escare 1/1.
Rugby Leaguer & League Express Men of the Match:
Dragons: James Maloney; *Red Devils:* Harvey Livett.
Penalty count: 4-3; **Half-time:** 20-0; **Referee:** Ben Thaler.

Sunday 18th April 2021

HULL FC 14 WARRINGTON WOLVES 14
(after golden point extra-time)

HULL FC: 1 Jake Connor; 2 Bureta Faraimo; 3 Carlos Tuimavave; 4 Josh Griffin; 21 Adam Swift; 19 Ben McNamara; 7 Marc Sneyd (C); 8 Scott Taylor; 9 Danny Houghton; 10 Tevita Satae; 11 Andre Savelio; 16 Jordan Lane; 15 Joe Cator. Subs: 17 Brad Fash; 20 Jack Brown; 22 Josh Bowden; 24 Cameron Scott (not used).
Tries: Connor (56), Tuimavave (69); **Goals:** Sneyd 3/3.
WOLVES: 1 Stefan Ratchford; 23 Josh Thewlis; 18 Jake Mamo; 4 Toby King; 5 Josh Charnley; 6 Blake Austin; 7 Gareth Widdop; 8 Chris Hill; 9 Daryl Clark; 10 Mike Cooper; 11 Ben Currie; 12 Jack Hughes (C); 15 Matt Davis. Subs (all used): 13 Joe Philbin; 14 Jason Clark; 16 Danny Walker; 19 Robbie Mulhern.
Tries: Hill (61), Mamo (80);
Goals: Ratchford 2/2, Widdop 1/1.
Rugby Leaguer & League Express Men of the Match:
Hull FC: Jordan Lane; *Wolves:* Daryl Clark.
Penalty count: 6-4; **Half-time:** 2-2; **Referee:** Robert Hicks.

ROUND 4

Thursday 22nd April 2021

WIGAN WARRIORS 22 CASTLEFORD TIGERS 12

WARRIORS: 3 Zak Hardaker; 22 Jake Bibby; 11 Willie Isa; 12 Liam Farrell (C); 1 Bevan French; 20 Harry Smith; 31 Jackson Hastings; 8 Brad Singleton; 9 Sam Powell; 17 Tony Clubb; 13 John Bateman; 15 Morgan Smithies; 14 Oliver Partington. Subs (all used): 10 Joe Bullock; 19 Liam Byrne; 21 Ethan Havard; 25 Joe Shorrocks.
Tries: Hardaker (25), French (37, 52), Powell (76);
Goals: Hardaker 3/4.
TIGERS: 1 Niall Evalds; 2 Derrell Olpherts; 3 Peter Mata'utia; 4 Michael Shenton (C); 23 Greg Eden; 25 Jordan Turner; 6 Jake Trueman; 19 Tyla Hepi; 9 Paul McShane; 8 Liam Watts; 11 Oliver Holmes; 12 Cheyse Blair; 14 Nathan Massey. Subs (all used): 10 Grant Millington; 13 Adam Milner; 26 Lewis Bienek; 28 Brad Martin.
Tries: Olpherts (15, 47); **Goals:** McShane 2/3.
Rugby Leaguer & League Express Men of the Match:
Warriors: Bevan French; *Tigers:* Derrell Olpherts.
Penalty count: 7-7; **Half-time:** 12-8; **Referee:** Chris Kendall.

HUDDERSFIELD GIANTS 10 ST HELENS 18

GIANTS: 6 Lee Gaskell; 2 Jermaine McGillvary; 27 Sam Wood; 17 Chris McQueen; 5 Darnell McIntosh; 16 Jack Cogger; 7 Aidan Sezer (C); 18 Jack Ashworth; 19 James Cunningham; 22 James Gavet; 8 Luke Yates; 11 Kenny Edwards; 13 Josh Jones. Subs (all used): 9 Adam O'Brien; 10 Michael Lawrence; 14 Matty English; 20 Oliver Wilson.
Tries: McQueen (46), McGillvary (72); **Goals:** Sezer 1/2.
SAINTS: 1 Lachlan Coote; 3 Kevin Naiqama; 18 Jack Welsby; 4 Mark Percival; 5 Regan Grace; 6 Jonny Lomax; 7 Theo Fages; 8 Alex Walmsley; 9 James Roby (C); 15 Louie McCarthy-Scarsbrook; 11 Joel Thompson; 12 James Bentley; 14 Sione Mata'utia. Subs (all used): 16 Kyle Amor; 17 Agnatius Paasi; 21 Lewis Dodd; 23 Jake Wingfield.
Tries: Fages (5), Percival (37), Lomax (63);
Goals: Coote 3/3.
Rugby Leaguer & League Express Men of the Match:
Giants: Luke Yates; *Saints:* Jonny Lomax.
Penalty count: 5-3; **Half-time:** 0-12; **Referee:** Robert Hicks.

Friday 23rd April 2021

HULL KINGSTON ROVERS 26 LEEDS RHINOS 6

ROVERS: 1 Adam Quinlan; 23 Ethan Ryan; 11 Brad Takairangi (D); 4 Shaun Kenny-Dowall (C); 5 Ryan Hall; 25 Rowan Milnes; 7 Jordan Abdull; 8 Albert Vete; 9 Matt Parcell; 16 George King; 12 Kane Linnett; 27 Luis Johnson; 15 George Lawler. Subs (all used): 13 Dean Hadley; 14 Jez Litten; 18 Matthew Storton; 28 Muizz Mustapha.
Tries: Hall (12), Parcell (17), Linnett (26, 49, 69);
Goals: Abdull 3/6.
RHINOS: 5 Ash Handley; 2 Tom Briscoe; 21 Alex Sutcliffe; 4 Konrad Hurrell; 24 Luke Briscoe; 16 Richie Myler; 33 Kyle Eastmond; 8 Mikolaj Oledzki; 9 Kruise Leeming; 10 Matt Prior (C); 11 Alex Mellor; 12 Rhyse Martin; 25 James Donaldson. Subs (all used): 14 Brad Dwyer; 19 King Vuniyayawa; 20 Bodene Thompson; 27 Jack Broadbent.
Try: Dwyer (29); **Goals:** Handley 1/1.
Sin bin: Myler (67) - dissent.
Rugby Leaguer & League Express Men of the Match:
Rovers: Kane Linnett; *Rhinos:* Alex Mellor.
Penalty count: 11-5; **Half-time:** 16-6;
Referee: Marcus Griffiths.

SALFORD RED DEVILS 34 LEIGH CENTURIONS 8

RED DEVILS: 19 Elliot Kear; 2 Ken Sio; 4 Krisnan Inu; 24 Matthew Costello; 22 Rhys Williams; 6 Tui Lolohea; 7 Kevin Brown; 8 Lee Mossop (C); 29 Dec Patton; 10 Sebastine Ikahihifo; 20 Harvey Livett; 15 Oliver Roberts; 26 Jack Wells. Subs (all used): 21 James Greenwood; 28 Darcy Lussick; 18 Chris Atkin; 16 Greg Burke.
Tries: Greenwood (21), Brown (49, 69), Sio (62), Atkin (72), Livett (79); **Goals:** Inu 5/6.
CENTURIONS: 22 Craig Mullen; 2 Matty Russell; 32 Anthony Gelling (D); 3 Iain Thornley; 24 Keanan Brand; 30 Ben Reynolds; 1 Ryan Brierley; 21 Tyrone McCarthy; 9 Liam Hood (C); 8 Ben Flower; 11 Ben Hellewell; 12 Jordan Thompson; 13 James Bell. Subs (all used): 26 Nathan Peats; 10 Mark Ioane; 15 Alex Gerrard; 18 Matty Gee.
Tries: Russell (6), Thornley (29); **Goals:** Reynolds 0/2.
Rugby Leaguer & League Express Men of the Match:
Red Devils: Kevin Brown; *Centurions:* Iain Thornley.
Penalty count: 3-8; **Half-time:** 6-8; **Referee:** James Child.

HULL FC 20 WAKEFIELD TRINITY 14

HULL FC: 1 Jake Connor; 2 Bureta Faraimo; 3 Carlos Tuimavave; 4 Josh Griffin; 21 Adam Swift; 19 Ben McNamara; 7 Marc Sneyd (C); 8 Scott Taylor; 9 Danny Houghton; 13 Ligi Sao; 11 Andre Savelio; 16 Jordan Lane; 15 Joe Cator. Subs (all used): 10 Tevita Satae; 14 Jordan Johnstone; 17 Brad Fash; 22 Josh Bowden.
Tries: Savelio (11), Swift (45), Tuimavave (74);
Goals: Sneyd 4/4.
Sin bin: Faraimo (40) - late challenge on Jowitt.
TRINITY: 1 Max Jowitt; 27 Lee Kershaw; 4 Reece Lyne; 20 Joe Arundel; 5 Liam Kay; 7 Mason Lino; 29 Ryan Hampshire; 8 David Fifita; 9 Kyle Wood; 12 Kelepi Tanginoa; 14 Jay Pitts; 16 James Batchelor; 13 Joe Westerman. Subs (all used): 10 Tinirau Arona (C); 15 Eddie Battye; 17 Chris Green; 19 Jordan Crowther.
Tries: Kershaw (37), Batchelor (50), Lino (68);
Goals: Lino 1/3.
Rugby Leaguer & League Express Men of the Match:
Hull FC: Jake Connor; *Trinity:* Joe Westerman.
Penalty count: 1-4; **Half-time:** 8-6; **Referee:** Ben Thaler.

Saturday 24th April 2021

CATALANS DRAGONS 8 WARRINGTON WOLVES 24

DRAGONS: 29 Sam Tomkins; 2 Tom Davies; 3 Samisoni Langi; 4 Dean Whare; 5 Fouad Yaha; 6 James Maloney; 7 Josh Drinkwater; 8 Gil Dudson; 14 Alrix Da Costa; 10 Julian Bousquet; 11 Matt Whitley; 12 Mike McMeeken; 13 Benjamin Garcia (C). Subs (all used): 9 Michael McIlorum; 16 Paul Seguier; 24 Jason Baitieri; 28 Sam Kasiano.
Try: Maloney (26); **Goals:** Maloney 2/2.
WOLVES: 17 Matty Ashton; 23 Josh Thewlis; 18 Jake Mamo; 4 Toby King; 5 Josh Charnley; 1 Stefan Ratchford; 7 Gareth Widdop; 8 Chris Hill; 9 Daryl Clark; 10 Mike Cooper; 11 Ben Currie; 12 Jack Hughes (C); 15 Matt Davis. Subs (all used): 13 Joe Philbin; 14 Jason Clark; 16 Danny Walker; 19 Robbie Mulhern.

Tries: Currie (33), King (38), Mamo (43), Widdop (66);
Goals: Ratchford 4/4.
Rugby Leaguer & League Express Men of the Match:
Dragons: Sam Tomkins; *Wolves:* Gareth Widdop.
Penalty count: 4-7; **Half-time:** 8-12; **Referee:** Liam Moore.

ROUND 5

Thursday 29th April 2021

WIGAN WARRIORS 16 HULL FC 14

WARRIORS: 3 Zak Hardaker; 22 Jake Bibby; 11 Willie Isa; 12 Liam Farrell; 1 Bevan French; 20 Harry Smith; 31 Jackson Hastings; 8 Brad Singleton; 9 Sam Powell (C); 17 Tony Clubb; 13 John Bateman; 15 Morgan Smithies; 14 Oliver Partington. Subs (all used): 10 Joe Bullock; 19 Liam Byrne; 21 Ethan Havard; 25 Joe Shorrocks.
Tries: Hastings (10), Farrell (38), Bibby (59);
Goals: Hardaker 2/4.
On report: Clubb (34) - alleged racist remark to Savelio.
HULL FC: 1 Jake Connor; 5 Mahe Fonua; 3 Carlos Tuimavave; 4 Josh Griffin; 21 Adam Swift; 19 Ben McNamara; 7 Marc Sneyd; 8 Scott Taylor; 9 Danny Houghton (C); 13 Ligi Sao; 11 Andre Savelio; 16 Jordan Lane; 15 Joe Cator. Subs (all used): 10 Tevita Satae; 14 Jordan Johnstone; 17 Brad Fash; 24 Cameron Scott.
Tries: Swift (18), Fonua (47); **Goals:** Sneyd 3/4.
Sin bin: Connor (32) - high tackle on Hardaker.
Rugby Leaguer & League Express Men of the Match:
Warriors: Jackson Hastings; *Hull FC:* Marc Sneyd.
Penalty count: 5-4; **Half-time:** 10-8; **Referee:** James Child.

Friday 30th April 2021

LEIGH CENTURIONS 12 ST HELENS 22

CENTURIONS: 1 Ryan Brierley; 2 Matty Russell; 3 Iain Thornley; 32 Anthony Gelling; 4 Junior Sa'u; 30 Ben Reynolds; 14 Matty Wildie; 8 Ben Flower; 26 Nathan Peats; 19 Nathan Mason; 11 Ben Hellewell; 12 Jordan Thompson; 21 Tyrone McCarthy. Subs (all used): 9 Liam Hood (C); 13 James Bell; 15 Alex Gerrard; 16 Nathaniel Peteru.
Tries: Russell (35), Gelling (47); **Goals:** Reynolds 2/2.
SAINTS: 1 Lachlan Coote; 3 Kevin Naiqama; 18 Jack Welsby; 4 Mark Percival; 5 Regan Grace; 6 Jonny Lomax; 7 Theo Fages; 8 Alex Walmsley; 9 James Roby (C); 15 Louie McCarthy-Scarsbrook; 14 Sione Mata'utia; 12 James Bentley; 23 Jake Wingfield. Subs (all used): 16 Kyle Amor; 17 Agnatius Paasi; 20 Joe Batchelor; 21 Lewis Dodd.
Tries: Mata'utia (19), Coote (42), Welsby (45), Naiqama (59); **Goals:** Coote 3/4.
Sin bin: Fages (34) - repeated team offences.
Rugby Leaguer & League Express Men of the Match:
Centurions: Liam Hood; *Saints:* Jonny Lomax.
Penalty count: 10-8; **Half-time:** 6-6;
Referee: Marcus Griffiths.

WAKEFIELD TRINITY 18 CATALANS DRAGONS 38

TRINITY: 28 Olly Ashall-Bott (D); 27 Lee Kershaw; 4 Reece Lyne; 3 Bill Tupou; 5 Liam Kay; 1 Max Jowitt; 7 Mason Lino; 17 Chris Green; 9 Kyle Wood; 12 Kelepi Tanginoa; 14 Jay Pitts; 16 James Batchelor; 13 Joe Westerman. Subs (all used): 8 David Fifita; 10 Tinirau Arona (C); 15 Eddie Battye; 30 Josh Eaves (D).
Tries: Ashall-Bott (12), Jowitt (28), Lyne (47);
Goals: Lino 3/3.
DRAGONS: 29 Sam Tomkins; 2 Tom Davies; 3 Samisoni Langi; 4 Dean Whare; 5 Fouad Yaha; 6 James Maloney; 7 Josh Drinkwater; 8 Gil Dudson; 9 Michael McIlorum; 10 Julian Bousquet; 16 Paul Seguier; 12 Mike McMeeken; 13 Benjamin Garcia (C). Subs (all used): 1 Arthur Mourgue; 22 Joel Tomkins; 24 Jason Baitieri; 30 Jordan Dezaria (D2).
Tries: Davies (9, 23, 76), McMeeken (20), Whare (35, 68), Langi (78); **Goals:** Maloney 5/7.
Rugby Leaguer & League Express Men of the Match:
Trinity: Joe Westerman; *Dragons:* Tom Davies.
Penalty count: 8-4; **Half-time:** 12-20;
Referee: Chris Kendall.

SALFORD RED DEVILS 18 CASTLEFORD TIGERS 28

RED DEVILS: 19 Elliot Kear; 2 Ken Sio; 3 Kallum Watkins; 20 Harvey Livett; 22 Rhys Williams; 6 Tui Lolohea; 7 Kevin Brown; 8 Lee Mossop (C); 9 Andy Ackers; 10 Sebastine Ikahihifo; 21 James Greenwood; 15 Oliver Roberts; 14 Danny Addy. Subs (all used): 25 Jack Ormondroyd; 18 Chris Atkin; 16 Greg Burke; 17 Josh Johnson.
Tries: Brown (12), Ackers (15), Lolohea (72);
Goals: Livett 2/2, Brown 1/1.
Sin bin: Mossop (68) - late challenge on Richardson.
TIGERS: 1 Niall Evalds; 2 Derrell Olpherts; 3 Peter Mata'utia; 4 Michael Shenton (C); 23 Greg Eden; 6 Jake Trueman; 7 Danny Richardson; 14 Nathan Massey; 9 Paul McShane; 10 Grant Millington; 11 Oliver Holmes; 21 Jesse Sene-Lefao; 13 Adam Milner. Subs (all used): 8 Liam Watts; 12 Cheyse Blair; 27 Lewis Peachey; 28 Brad Martin.
Tries: Eden (7), Watts (21), Blair (42), Trueman (61);
Goals: Richardson 6/7.
Rugby Leaguer & League Express Men of the Match:
Red Devils: Kevin Brown; *Tigers:* Paul McShane.
Penalty count: 4-9; **Half-time:** 12-14;
Referee: Robert Hicks.

Saturday 1st May 2021

WARRINGTON WOLVES 50 HULL KINGSTON ROVERS 26

WOLVES: 17 Matty Ashton; 18 Jake Mamo; 3 Greg Inglis (D); 4 Toby King; 5 Josh Charnley; 1 Stefan Ratchford; 7 Gareth Widdop; 8 Chris Hill; 9 Daryl Clark; 10 Mike Cooper; 11 Ben Currie; 12 Jack Hughes (C); 15 Matt Davis. Subs (all used): 13 Joe Philbin; 14 Jason Clark; 16 Danny Walker; 20 Sitaleki Akauola.
Tries: King (10), Currie (17, 44), Inglis (51), D Clark (63), Mamo (69), Charnley (73, 80), Walker (79);
Goals: Ratchford 7/9.
ROVERS: 1 Adam Quinlan; 23 Ethan Ryan; 11 Brad Takairangi; 4 Shaun Kenny-Dowall (C); 5 Ryan Hall; 25 Rowan Milnes; 7 Jordan Abdull; 15 George Lawler; 9 Matt Parcell; 16 George King; 12 Kane Linnett; 27 Luis Johnson; 13 Dean Hadley. Subs (all used): 10 Korbin Sims; 14 Jez Litten; 18 Matthew Storton; 28 Muizz Mustapha.
Tries: Kenny-Dowall (4), Hall (25, 59), Abdull (38), Linnett (76); **Goals:** Abdull 3/6.
Sin bin: Johnson (79) - professional foul.
Rugby Leaguer & League Express Men of the Match:
Wolves: Toby King; *Rovers:* Jordan Abdull.
Penalty count: 4-2; **Half-time:** 12-18;
Referee: Scott Mikalauskas.

Sunday 2nd May 2021

HUDDERSFIELD GIANTS 14 LEEDS RHINOS 13

GIANTS: 6 Lee Gaskell; 2 Jermaine McGillvary; 4 Ricky Leutele; 17 Chris McQueen; 5 Darnell McIntosh; 16 Jack Cogger; 7 Aidan Sezer (C); 8 Luke Yates; 19 James Cunningham; 22 James Gavet; 13 Josh Jones; 11 Kenny Edwards; 15 Joe Greenwood. Subs: 9 Adam O'Brien; 14 Matty English; 10 Michael Lawrence; 27 Sam Wood (not used).
Tries: Sezer (33, 41); **Goals:** Sezer 2/3;
Field goals: Sezer (75), Gaskell (80).
RHINOS: 27 Jack Broadbent; 2 Tom Briscoe; 4 Konrad Hurrell; 11 Alex Mellor; 5 Ash Handley; 15 Liam Sutcliffe; 9 Kruise Leeming; 8 Mikolaj Oledzki; 14 Brad Dwyer; 10 Matt Prior (C); 22 Sam Walters; 20 Bodene Thompson; 26 Jarrod O'Connor. Subs (all used): 12 Rhyse Martin; 19 King Vuniyayawa; 24 Luke Briscoe; 25 James Donaldson.
Tries: Thompson (16), Handley (57);
Goals: L Sutcliffe 0/1, Martin 2/2; **Field goal:** L Sutcliffe (74).
Rugby Leaguer & League Express Men of the Match:
Giants: Aidan Sezer; *Rhinos:* Mikolaj Oledzki.
Penalty count: 9-8; **Half-time:** 6-4; **Referee:** Liam Moore.

ROUND 6

Friday 14th May 2021

LEEDS RHINOS 15 WAKEFIELD TRINITY 13
(after golden point extra-time)

RHINOS: 27 Jack Broadbent; 24 Luke Briscoe; 4 Konrad Hurrell; 2 Tom Briscoe; 5 Ash Handley; 15 Liam Sutcliffe; 7 Luke Gale (C); 8 Mikolaj Oledzki; 14 Brad Dwyer; 10 Matt Prior; 11 Alex Mellor; 12 Rhyse Martin; 26 Jarrod O'Connor. Subs (all used): 9 Kruise Leeming; 19 King Vuniyayawa; 22 Sam Walters; 31 Morgan Gannon.
Tries: Martin (33), Hurrell (54); **Goals:** Martin 3/3;
Field goal: Gale (75).
TRINITY: 28 Olly Ashall-Bott; 27 Lee Kershaw; 4 Reece Lyne; 20 Joe Arundel; 5 Liam Kay; 1 Max Jowitt; 7 Mason Lino; 10 Tinirau Arona (C); 19 Jordan Crowther; 12 Kelepi Tanginoa; 11 Matty Ashurst; 14 Jay Pitts; 13 Joe Westerman. Subs (all used): 8 David Fifita; 15 Eddie Battye; 17 Chris Green; 30 Josh Eaves.
Tries: Kay (18), Lino (22); **Goals:** Lino 2/4;
Field goal: Lino (78).
Rugby Leaguer & League Express Men of the Match:
Rhinos: Jarrod O'Connor; *Trinity:* Joe Westerman.
Penalty count: 6-8; **Half time:** 6-10;
Referee: Robert Hicks.

Monday 17th May 2021

CASTLEFORD TIGERS 22 HULL KINGSTON ROVERS 26

TIGERS: 1 Niall Evalds; 2 Derrell Olpherts; 3 Peter Mata'utia; 4 Michael Shenton (C); 20 James Clare; 6 Jake Trueman; 7 Danny Richardson; 14 Nathan Massey; 13 Adam Milner; 15 George Griffin; 11 Oliver Holmes; 25 Jordan Turner; 28 Brad Martin. Subs (all used): 9 Paul McShane; 21 Jesse Sene-Lefao; 22 Daniel Smith; 27 Lewis Peachey.
Tries: Clare (3), Shenton (16), Olpherts (38);
Goals: Richardson 5/5.
ROVERS: 1 Adam Quinlan; 2 Ben Crooks; 11 Brad Takairangi; 4 Shaun Kenny-Dowall (C); 5 Ryan Hall; 25 Rowan Milnes; 7 Jordan Abdull; 15 George Lawler; 9 Matt Parcell; 16 George King; 12 Kane Linnett; 27 Luis Johnson; 13 Dean Hadley. Subs (all used): 10 Korbin Sims; 14 Jez Litten; 18 Matthew Storton; 26 Will Maher.
Tries: Crooks (23, 56), Parcell (28), Hall (48), Abdull (78);
Goals: Abdull 3/5.
Sin bin: Sims (71) - professional foul.
Rugby Leaguer & League Express Men of the Match:
Tigers: Paul McShane; *Rovers:* Jordan Abdull.
Penalty count: 11-4; **Half-time:** 20-12;
Referee: Marcus Griffiths; **Attendance:** 3,600.

HULL FC 10 CATALANS DRAGONS 27

HULL FC: 1 Jake Connor; 5 Mahe Fonua; 3 Carlos Tuimavave; 4 Josh Griffin; 21 Adam Swift; 6 Josh Reynolds; 7 Marc Sneyd (C); 10 Tevita Satae; 9 Danny Houghton; 13 Ligi Sao; 11 Andre Savelio; 12 Manu Ma'u; 16 Jordan Lane. Subs (all used): 14 Jordan Johnstone; 15 Joe Cator; 17 Brad Fash; 24 Cameron Scott.
Tries: Fonua (17), Reynolds (41); **Goals:** Sneyd 1/2.
Sin bin: Tuimavave (21) - professional foul;
Satae (71) - high tackle.
DRAGONS: 29 Sam Tomkins; 2 Tom Davies; 3 Samisoni Langi; 4 Dean Whare; 5 Fouad Yaha; 6 James Maloney; 7 Josh Drinkwater; 22 Joel Tomkins; 9 Michael McIlorum; 10 Julian Bousquet; 15 Benjamin Jullien; 12 Mike McMeeken; 13 Benjamin Garcia (C). Subs (all used): 1 Arthur Mourgue; 17 Mickael Goudemand; 24 Jason Baitieri; 28 Sam Kasiano.
Tries: Kasiano (55), McMeeken (69), Davies (75, 78);
Goals: Maloney 4/5, Mourgue 1/1; **Field goal:** Maloney (72).
Sin bin: Maloney (13) - professional foul.
Rugby Leaguer & League Express Men of the Match:
Hull FC: Tevita Satae; *Dragons:* Sam Tomkins.
Penalty count: 6-8; **Half-time:** 4-4;
Referee: Chris Kendall; **Attendance:** 5,527.

LEIGH CENTURIONS 16 WIGAN WARRIORS 30

CENTURIONS: 1 Ryan Brierley; 32 Anthony Gelling; 3 Iain Thornley; 4 Junior Sa'u; 5 Lewis Tierney; 30 Ben Reynolds; 14 Matty Wildie; 10 Mark Ioane; 9 Liam Hood (C); 19 Nathan Mason; 11 Ben Hellewell; 12 Jordan Thompson; 13 James Bell. Subs (all used): 16 Nathaniel Peteru; 17 Jamie Ellis (D2); 21 Tyrone McCarthy; 26 Nathan Peats.
Tries: Gelling (13), Mason (20), Ellis (38);
Goals: Reynolds 2/3.
WARRIORS: 1 Bevan French; 2 Dom Manfredi; 11 Willie Isa; 22 Jake Bibby; 3 Zak Hardaker; 31 Jackson Hastings; 20 Harry Smith; 8 Brad Singleton; 9 Sam Powell; 14 Oliver Partington; 12 Liam Farrell (C); 13 John Bateman; 15 Morgan Smithies. Subs (all used): 19 Liam Byrne; 23 Mitch Clark; 21 Ethan Havard; 25 Joe Shorrocks.
Tries: Smith (26), Manfredi (31), French (36), Farrell (47), Bibby (57, 60); **Goals:** Smith 3/6.
Rugby Leaguer & League Express Men of the Match:
Centurions: Liam Hood; *Warriors:* Bevan French.
Penalty count: 10-11; **Half-time:** 16-16;
Referee: Ben Thaler; **Attendance:** 1,702.

ST HELENS 28 SALFORD RED DEVILS 0

SAINTS: 1 Lachlan Coote; 3 Kevin Naiqama; 4 Mark Percival; 18 Jack Welsby; 5 Regan Grace; 6 Jonny Lomax; 7 Theo Fages; 8 Alex Walmsley; 9 James Roby (C); 15 Louie McCarthy-Scarsbrook; 11 Joel Thompson; 14 Sione Mata'utia; 13 Morgan Knowles. Subs (all used): 16 Kyle Amor; 17 Agnatius Paasi; 19 Aaron Smith; 20 Joe Batchelor.
Tries: Walmsley (24), Fages (43), Naiqama (60), McCarthy-Scarsbrook (67), Grace (79); **Goals:** Coote 4/5.
RED DEVILS: 23 Dan Sarginson; 2 Ken Sio; 3 Kallum Watkins; 24 Matthew Costello; 22 Rhys Williams; 6 Tui Lolohea; 7 Kevin Brown; 8 Lee Mossop (C); 9 Andy Ackers; 16 Greg Burke; 21 James Greenwood; 11 Ryan Lannon; 13 Elijah Taylor. Subs (all used): 10 Sebastine Ikahihifo; 12 Pauli Pauli; 18 Chris Atkin; 25 Jack Ormondroyd.
Rugby Leaguer & League Express Men of the Match:
Saints: Theo Fages; *Red Devils:* Chris Atkin.
Penalty count: 6-8; **Half-time:** 6-0;
Referee: Liam Moore; **Attendance:** 4,000.

WARRINGTON WOLVES 20 HUDDERSFIELD GIANTS 26

WOLVES: 1 Stefan Ratchford; 23 Josh Thewlis; 3 Greg Inglis; 18 Jake Mamo; 5 Josh Charnley; 6 Blake Austin; 7 Gareth Widdop; 8 Chris Hill; 9 Daryl Clark; 10 Mike Cooper (C); 11 Ben Currie; 4 Toby King; 14 Jason Clark. Subs (all used): 13 Joe Philbin; 15 Matt Davis; 19 Robbie Mulhern; 20 Sitaleki Akauola.

Tries: Inglis (43), D Clark (50), Thewlis (59);
Goals: Widdop 4/4.
GIANTS: 6 Lee Gaskell; 2 Jermaine McGillvary; 3 Jake Wardle; 4 Ricky Leutele; 5 Darnell McIntosh; 7 Aidan Sezer (C); 16 Jack Cogger; 10 Michael Lawrence; 19 James Cunningham; 15 Joe Greenwood; 11 Kenny Edwards; 13 Josh Jones; 8 Luke Yates. Subs (all used): 9 Adam O'Brien; 14 Matty English; 17 Chris McQueen; 25 Owen Trout.
Tries: Gaskell (4, 11), McGillvary (34), Edwards (67);
Goals: Sezer 5/6.
Rugby Leaguer & League Express Men of the Match:
Wolves: Daryl Clark; *Giants:* Lee Gaskell.
Penalty count: 7-7; **Half-time:** 0-20;
Referee: James Child; **Attendance:** 4,000.

ROUND 7

Saturday 22nd May 2021

SALFORD RED DEVILS 16 WIGAN WARRIORS 17

RED DEVILS: 1 Morgan Escare; 2 Ken Sio; 3 Kallum Watkins (C); 20 Harvey Livett; 22 Rhys Williams; 6 Tui Lolohea; 29 Dec Patton; 10 Sebastine Ikahihifo; 14 Danny Addy; 16 Greg Burke; 11 Ryan Lannon; 12 Pauli Pauli; 13 Elijah Taylor. Subs (all used): 18 Chris Atkin; 25 Jack Ormondroyd; 26 Jack Wells; 28 Darcy Lussick.
Tries: Livett (10), Wells (24); **Goals:** Livett 4/5.
WARRIORS: 1 Bevan French; 2 Dom Manfredi; 25 Joe Shorrocks; 22 Jake Bibby; 3 Zak Hardaker; 20 Harry Smith; 31 Jackson Hastings; 8 Brad Singleton; 9 Sam Powell; 21 Ethan Havard; 13 John Bateman; 12 Liam Farrell (C); 14 Oliver Partington. Subs (all used): 10 Joe Bullock; 19 Liam Byrne; 23 Mitch Clark; 27 Kai Pearce-Paul.
Tries: Singleton (19, 65), Farrell (34); **Goals:** Smith 2/3;
Field goal: Hastings (77).
Rugby Leaguer & League Express Men of the Match:
Red Devils: Morgan Escare; *Warriors:* Liam Farrell.
Penalty count: 10-5; **Half-time:** 14-10;
Referee: James Child; **Attendance:** 2,033.

WARRINGTON WOLVES 38 CASTLEFORD TIGERS 14

WOLVES: 1 Stefan Ratchford; 23 Josh Thewlis; 18 Jake Mamo; 4 Toby King; 5 Josh Charnley; 6 Blake Austin; 7 Gareth Widdop; 8 Chris Hill; 9 Daryl Clark; 10 Mike Cooper; 11 Ben Currie; 12 Jack Hughes (C); 13 Joe Philbin. Subs (all used): 14 Jason Clark; 15 Matt Davis; 19 Robbie Mulhern; 21 Rob Butler.
Tries: Charnley (10), King (13, 67), Widdop (23, 61, 63), D Clark (74); **Goals:** Ratchford 5/8.
TIGERS: 20 James Clare; 2 Derrell Olpherts; 21 Jesse Sene-Lefao; 4 Michael Shenton (C); 25 Jordan Turner; 6 Jake Trueman; 7 Danny Richardson; 14 Nathan Massey; 9 Paul McShane; 22 Daniel Smith; 15 George Griffin; 28 Brad Martin; 13 Adam Milner. Subs (all used): 19 Tyla Hepi; 24 Suaia Matagi (D); 26 Lewis Bienek; 27 Lewis Peachey.
Tries: Trueman (2), Turner (18, 78); **Goals:** Richardson 1/3.
Rugby Leaguer & League Express Men of the Match:
Wolves: Gareth Widdop; *Tigers:* Jake Trueman.
Penalty count: 6-3; **Half-time:** 16-10;
Referee: Chris Kendall; **Attendance:** 4,000.

CATALANS DRAGONS 20 ST HELENS 16

DRAGONS: 1 Arthur Mourgue; 2 Tom Davies; 20 Matthieu Laguerre; 4 Dean Whare; 5 Fouad Yaha; 6 James Maloney; 7 Josh Drinkwater; 8 Gil Dudson; 9 Michael McIlorum; 10 Julian Bousquet; 15 Benjamin Jullien; 12 Mike McMeeken; 13 Benjamin Garcia (C). Subs (all used): 14 Alrix Da Costa; 17 Mickael Goudemand; 22 Joel Tomkins; 28 Sam Kasiano.
Tries: Maloney (24), Whare (42), Jullien (57);
Goals: Maloney 4/4.
SAINTS: 1 Lachlan Coote; 3 Kevin Naiqama; 4 Mark Percival; 18 Jack Welsby; 5 Regan Grace; 6 Jonny Lomax; 7 Theo Fages; 17 Agnatius Paasi; 9 James Roby (C); 15 Louie McCarthy-Scarsbrook; 14 Sione Mata'utia; 11 Joel Thompson; 13 Morgan Knowles. Subs (all used): 8 Alex Walmsley; 16 Kyle Amor; 20 Joe Batchelor; 21 Lewis Dodd.
Tries: Percival (50, 70), Grace (75); **Goals:** Coote 2/4.
Rugby Leaguer & League Express Men of the Match:
Dragons: James Maloney; *Saints:* Mark Percival.
Penalty count: 6-7; **Half-time:** 8-2;
Referee: Robert Hicks; **Attendance:** 1,000.

Sunday 23rd May 2021

LEIGH CENTURIONS 6 HUDDERSFIELD GIANTS 44

CENTURIONS: 25 Brendan Elliot (D); 2 Matty Russell; 3 Iain Thornley; 32 Anthony Gelling; 5 Lewis Tierney; 30 Ben Reynolds; 17 Jamie Ellis; 20 Adam Sidlow; 26 Nathan Peats; 10 Mark Ioane; 11 Ben Hellewell; 12 Jordan Thompson; 13 James Bell. Subs (all used): 4 Junior Sa'u; 14 Matty Wildie; 16 Nathaniel Peteru; 21 Tyrone McCarthy (C).
Try: Tierney (15); **Goals:** Reynolds 1/2.
Sin bin: Bell (61) - high tackle on O'Brien.
GIANTS: 6 Lee Gaskell; 2 Jermaine McGillvary; 3 Jake Wardle; 4 Ricky Leutele; 5 Darnell McIntosh; 7 Aidan Sezer (C); 16 Jack Cogger; 10 Michael Lawrence; 19 James Cunningham; 15 Joe Greenwood; 11 Kenny Edwards; 13 Josh Jones; 8 Luke Yates. Subs (all used): 9 Adam O'Brien; 14 Matty English; 17 Chris McQueen; 25 Owen Trout.
Tries: Leutele (27, 79), Edwards (49), Jake Wardle (58), O'Brien (66), McGillvary (73), Lawrence (80);
Goals: Sezer 8/9.
Rugby Leaguer & League Express Men of the Match:
Centurions: Brendan Elliot; *Giants:* Ricky Leutele.
Penalty count: 5-8; **Half-time:** 6-10;
Referee: Scott Mikalauskas; **Attendance:** 2,008.

WAKEFIELD TRINITY 28 HULL KINGSTON ROVERS 12

TRINITY: 1 Max Jowitt; 27 Lee Kershaw; 4 Reece Lyne; 3 Bill Tupou; 5 Liam Kay; 6 Jacob Miller (C); 7 Mason Lino; 12 Kelepi Tanginoa; 25 Brad Walker; 10 Tinirau Arona; 14 Jay Pitts; 11 Matty Ashurst; 13 Joe Westerman. Subs (all used): 8 David Fifita; 15 Eddie Battye; 16 James Batchelor; 30 Josh Eaves.
Tries: Kay (14, 37), Arona (43), Miller (77); **Goals:** Lino 6/6.
ROVERS: 1 Adam Quinlan; 2 Ben Crooks; 11 Brad Takairangi; 4 Shaun Kenny-Dowall (C); 5 Ryan Hall; 25 Rowan Milnes; 7 Jordan Abdull; 10 Korbin Sims; 9 Matt Parcell; 15 George Lawler; 12 Kane Linnett; 27 Luis Johnson; 28 Muizz Mustapha. Subs (all used): 13 Dean Hadley; 14 Jez Litten; 18 Matthew Storton; 26 Will Maher.
Tries: Quinlan (55), Crooks (67);
Goals: Milnes 1/1, Abdull 1/1.
Dismissal: Sims (70) - high tackle on Jowitt.
Rugby Leaguer & League Express Men of the Match:
Trinity: Bill Tupou; *Rovers:* Jez Litten.
Penalty count: 8-3; **Half-time:** 16-0;
Referee: Liam Moore; **Attendance:** 4,000.

LEEDS RHINOS 12 HULL FC 18

RHINOS: 16 Richie Myler; 24 Luke Briscoe; 4 Konrad Hurrell; 2 Tom Briscoe; 5 Ash Handley; 15 Liam Sutcliffe; 7 Luke Gale (C); 8 Mikolaj Oledzki; 9 Kruise Leeming; 10 Matt Prior; 11 Alex Mellor; 12 Rhyse Martin; 13 Zane Tetevano. Subs (all used): 14 Brad Dwyer; 19 King Vuniyayawa; 25 James Donaldson; 31 Morgan Gannon.
Tries: L Sutcliffe (10), T Briscoe (77); **Goals:** Martin 2/3.
HULL FC: 1 Jake Connor; 5 Mahe Fonua; 3 Carlos Tuimavave; 4 Josh Griffin; 21 Adam Swift; 6 Josh Reynolds; 7 Marc Sneyd; 13 Ligi Sao; 9 Danny Houghton (C); 10 Tevita Satae; 11 Andre Savelio; 12 Manu Ma'u; 15 Joe Cator. Subs (all used): 2 Bureta Faraimo; 14 Jordan Johnstone; 16 Jordan Lane; 17 Brad Fash.
Tries: Swift (20, 31), Griffin (38); **Goals:** Sneyd 3/3.
Rugby Leaguer & League Express Men of the Match:
Rhinos: Konrad Hurrell; *Hull FC:* Josh Griffin.
Penalty count: 9-5; **Half-time:** 8-18;
Referee: Marcus Griffiths; **Attendance:** 4,000.

ROUND 8

Thursday 27th May 2021

SALFORD RED DEVILS 18 WARRINGTON WOLVES 62

RED DEVILS: 1 Morgan Escare; 2 Ken Sio; 3 Kallum Watkins (C); 20 Harvey Livett; 22 Rhys Williams; 6 Tui Lolohea; 18 Chris Atkin; 25 Jack Ormondroyd; 13 Elijah Taylor; 10 Sebastine Ikahihifo; 11 Ryan Lannon; 15 Oliver Roberts; 16 Greg Burke. Subs (all used): 26 Jack Wells; 27 Sam Luckley (D); 28 Darcy Lussick; 29 Dec Patton.
Tries: Sio (22), Livett (33), Lussick (49); **Goals:** Livett 3/3.
Sin bin: Escare (52) - high tackle; Lussick (58) - high tackle.
WOLVES: 1 Stefan Ratchford; 2 Tom Lineham; 18 Jake Mamo; 4 Toby King; 5 Josh Charnley; 6 Blake Austin; 7 Gareth Widdop; 8 Chris Hill; 16 Danny Walker; 13 Joe Philbin; 11 Ben Currie; 12 Jack Hughes (C); 15 Matt Davis. Subs: 9 Daryl Clark (not used); 14 Jason Clark; 19 Robbie Mulhern; 20 Sitaleki Akauola.
Tries: Ratchford (2), Walker (7), King (11, 60), Mamo (39, 53), Widdop (42, 78), Hill (64), Currie (69);
Goals: Ratchford 11/11.
Rugby Leaguer & League Express Men of the Match:
Red Devils: Harvey Livett; *Wolves:* Gareth Widdop.
Penalty count: 1-5; **Half-time:** 12-26;
Referee: Scott Mikalauskas; **Attendance:** 2,306.

Friday 28th May 2021

CASTLEFORD TIGERS 6 LEEDS RHINOS 60

TIGERS: 23 Greg Eden; 2 Derrell Olpherts; 3 Peter Mata'utia; 12 Cheyse Blair; 20 James Clare; 25 Jordan Turner; 7 Danny Richardson; 8 Liam Watts; 9 Paul McShane (C); 22 Daniel Smith; 21 Jesse Sene-Lefao; 15 George Griffin; 18 Jacques O'Neill. Subs (all used): 19 Tyla Hepi; 24 Suaia Matagi; 27 Lewis Peachey; 28 Brad Martin.
Try: Turner (2); **Goals:** Richardson 1/1.
RHINOS: 16 Richie Myler; 24 Luke Briscoe; 4 Konrad Hurrell; 27 Jack Broadbent; 2 Tom Briscoe; 15 Liam Sutcliffe; 7 Luke Gale (C); 8 Mikolaj Oledzki; 9 Kruise Leeming; 10 Matt Prior; 11 Alex Mellor; 12 Rhyse Martin; 13 Zane Tetevano. Subs (all used): 14 Brad Dwyer; 19 King Vuniyayawa; 25 James Donaldson; 31 Morgan Gannon.
Tries: T Briscoe (6, 75), Broadbent (11), Leeming (19, 32), Myler (25), L Briscoe (29), Hurrell (48), Dwyer (64), Gannon (68), Gale (78); **Goals:** Martin 8/11.
Rugby Leaguer & League Express Men of the Match:
Tigers: Paul McShane; *Rhinos:* Kruise Leeming.
Penalty count: 4-4; **Half-time:** 6-32;
Referee: Liam Moore; **Attendance:** 4,000.

ST HELENS 34 HULL FC 16

SAINTS: 1 Lachlan Coote; 3 Kevin Naiqama; 22 Josh Simm; 4 Mark Percival; 18 Jack Welsby; 6 Jonny Lomax; 7 Theo Fages; 8 Alex Walmsley; 9 James Roby (C); 15 Louie McCarthy-Scarsbrook; 11 Joel Thompson; 14 Sione Mata'utia; 13 Morgan Knowles. Subs (all used): 16 Kyle Amor; 17 Agnatius Paasi; 20 Joe Batchelor; 21 Lewis Dodd.
Tries: Welsby (2, 35, 45), Coote (7), Knowles (17), Batchelor (67); **Goals:** Coote 5/7.
HULL FC: 1 Jake Connor; 5 Mahe Fonua; 3 Carlos Tuimavave; 4 Josh Griffin; 21 Adam Swift; 6 Josh Reynolds; 7 Marc Sneyd; 13 Ligi Sao; 9 Danny Houghton (C); 10 Tevita Satae; 16 Jordan Lane; 12 Manu Ma'u; 15 Joe Cator. Subs (all used): 14 Jordan Johnstone; 17 Brad Fash; 20 Jack Brown; 22 Josh Bowden.
Tries: Swift (10), Fonua (59, 80); **Goals:** Sneyd 2/3.
Rugby Leaguer & League Express Men of the Match:
Saints: Jonny Lomax; *Hull FC:* Brad Fash.
Penalty count: 4-5; **Half-time:** 22-4;
Referee: Chris Kendall; **Attendance:** 4,000.

Saturday 29th May 2021

CATALANS DRAGONS 48 WIGAN WARRIORS 0

DRAGONS: 29 Sam Tomkins; 2 Tom Davies; 3 Samisoni Langi; 4 Dean Whare; 20 Matthieu Laguerre; 6 James Maloney; 7 Josh Drinkwater; 8 Gil Dudson; 9 Michael McIlorum; 10 Julian Bousquet; 15 Benjamin Jullien; 12 Mike McMeeken; 13 Benjamin Garcia (C). Subs (all used): 1 Arthur Mourgue; 17 Mickael Goudemand; 22 Joel Tomkins; 28 Sam Kasiano.
Tries: McIlorum (6), S Tomkins (18, 39), Mourgue (52), Drinkwater (55, 59), McMeeken (62), Laguerre (74);
Goals: Maloney 8/10.
Sin bin: J Tomkins (78) - punching Hardaker.
WARRIORS: 3 Zak Hardaker; 2 Dom Manfredi; 22 Jake Bibby; 12 Liam Farrell; 30 Umyla Hanley; 7 Thomas Leuluai (C); 31 Jackson Hastings; 8 Brad Singleton; 9 Sam Powell; 21 Ethan Havard; 13 John Bateman; 15 Morgan Smithies; 14 Oliver Partington. Subs (all used): 10 Joe Bullock; 19 Liam Byrne; 20 Harry Smith; 25 Joe Shorrocks.
Dismissal: Hardaker (78) - use of the head on S Tomkins.
Rugby Leaguer & League Express Men of the Match:
Dragons: Josh Drinkwater; *Warriors:* Jackson Hastings.
Penalty count: 11-6; **Half-time:** 16-0;
Referee: James Child; **Attendance:** 1,000.

Sunday 30th May 2021

HULL KINGSTON ROVERS 40 LEIGH CENTURIONS 16

ROVERS: 1 Adam Quinlan; 3 Greg Minikin; 11 Brad Takairangi; 4 Shaun Kenny-Dowall (C); 5 Ryan Hall; 25 Rowan Milnes; 7 Jordan Abdull; 15 George Lawler; 9 Matt Parcell; 26 Will Maher; 12 Kane Linnett; 27 Luis Johnson; 13 Dean Hadley. Subs (all used): 10 Korbin Sims; 18 Matthew Storton; 14 Jez Litten; 33 Jimmy Keinhorst.
Tries: Linnett (3, 28), Hall (8, 68, 77), Minikin (14), Milnes (51), Hadley (62); **Goals:** Abdull 4/8.
CENTURIONS: 1 Ryan Brierley; 5 Lewis Tierney; 3 Iain Thornley; 4 Junior Sa'u; 32 Anthony Gelling; 30 Ben Reynolds; 17 Jamie Ellis; 21 Tyrone McCarthy; 9 Liam Hood (C); 10 Mark Ioane; 11 Ben Hellewell; 12 Jordan Thompson; 13 James Bell. Subs (all used): 26 Nathan Peats; 18 Matty Gee; 25 Brendan Elliot; 14 Matty Wildie.
Tries: Hellewell (11, 73), Brierley (19); **Goals:** Reynolds 2/3.
Rugby Leaguer & League Express Men of the Match:
Rovers: Jordan Abdull; *Centurions:* James Bell.
Penalty count: 10-12; **Half time:** 18-12;
Referee: Marcus Griffiths; **Attendance:** 4,000.

WAKEFIELD TRINITY 38 HUDDERSFIELD GIANTS 12

TRINITY: 1 Max Jowitt; 27 Lee Kershaw; 4 Reece Lyne; 3 Bill Tupou; 5 Liam Kay; 6 Jacob Miller (C); 7 Mason Lino; 12 Kelepi Tanginoa; 25 Brad Walker; 10 Tinirau Arona; 14 Jay Pitts; 11 Matty Ashurst; 13 Joe Westerman. Subs (all used): 8 David Fifita; 9 Kyle Wood; 15 Eddie Battye; 16 James Batchelor.
Tries: Kay (5, 65), Tanginoa (20), Pitts (30), Westerman (33), Tupou (39), Lino (73);
Goals: Lino 5/6, Jowitt 0/1.
Sin bin: Miller (16) - high tackle on Sezer.

GIANTS: 5 Darnell McIntosh; 2 Jermaine McGillvary; 3 Jake Wardle; 4 Ricky Leutele; 21 Leroy Cudjoe; 7 Aidan Sezer (C); 16 Jack Cogger; 15 Joe Greenwood; 19 James Cunningham; 22 James Gavet; 11 Kenny Edwards; 13 Josh Jones; 10 Michael Lawrence. Subs (all used): 9 Adam O'Brien; 14 Matty English; 17 Chris McQueen; 25 Owen Trout.
Tries: Gavet (77), Jake Wardle (79); **Goals:** Sezer 2/2.
Rugby Leaguer & League Express Men of the Match: *Trinity:* Joe Westerman; *Giants:* Michael Lawrence.
Penalty count: 4-9; **Half-time:** 30-0;
Referee: Robert Hicks; **Attendance:** 4,000.

ROUND 13

Sunday 6th June 2021

WAKEFIELD TRINITY 30 LEIGH CENTURIONS 20

TRINITY: 1 Max Jowitt; 27 Lee Kershaw; 4 Reece Lyne; 3 Bill Tupou; 5 Liam Kay; 6 Jacob Miller (C); 7 Mason Lino; 10 Tinirau Arona; 25 Brad Walker; 12 Kelepi Tanginoa; 14 Jay Pitts; 16 James Batchelor; 13 Joe Westerman. Subs (all used): 8 David Fifita; 9 Kyle Wood; 15 Eddie Battye; 20 Joe Arundel.
Tries: Pitts (35), Batchelor (38), Westerman (50), Kay (71), Lino (78); **Goals:** Lino 5/5.
CENTURIONS: 25 Brendan Elliot; 5 Lewis Tierney; 4 Junior Sa'u; 3 Iain Thornley; 32 Anthony Gelling; 1 Ryan Brierley; 7 Joe Mellor; 10 Mark Ioane; 9 Liam Hood (C); 21 Tyrone McCarthy; 11 Ben Hellewell; 18 Matty Gee; 13 James Bell. Subs (all used): 14 Matty Wildie; 26 Nathan Peats; 22 Craig Mullen; 17 Jamie Ellis.
Tries: Mellor (7, 54), Tierney (65); **Goals:** Brierley 4/4.
Rugby Leaguer & League Express Men of the Match: *Trinity:* Joe Westerman; *Centurions:* Joe Mellor.
Penalty count: 4-3; **Half-time:** 12-8;
Referee: Scott Mikalauskas; **Attendance:** 4,000.

ROUND 9

Thursday 10th June 2021

CASTLEFORD TIGERS 12 HULL FC 30

TIGERS: 3 Peter Mata'utia; 2 Derrell Olpherts; 17 Alex Foster; 4 Michael Shenton (C); 33 Jason Qareqare (D); 9 Paul McShane; 7 Danny Richardson; 28 Brad Martin; 13 Adam Milner; 15 George Griffin; 11 Oliver Holmes; 21 Jesse Sene-Lefao; 14 Nathan Massey. Subs (all used): 8 Liam Watts; 18 Jacques O'Neill; 19 Tyla Hepi; 27 Lewis Peachey.
Tries: Qareqare (1), Holmes (77); **Goals:** Richardson 2/3.
HULL FC: 1 Jake Connor; 2 Bureta Faraimo; 3 Carlos Tuimavave; 5 Mahe Fonua; 21 Adam Swift; 6 Josh Reynolds; 7 Marc Sneyd (C); 13 Ligi Sao; 9 Danny Houghton; 10 Tevita Satae; 11 Andre Savelio; 12 Manu Ma'u; 16 Jordan Lane. Subs (all used): 14 Jordan Johnstone; 17 Brad Fash; 22 Josh Bowden; 24 Cameron Scott.
Tries: Swift (14, 43), Fonua (40, 55), Connor (73);
Goals: Sneyd 4/4, Connor 1/1.
Sin bin: Sneyd (70) - persistent offending.
Rugby Leaguer & League Express Men of the Match: *Tigers:* Paul McShane; *Hull FC:* Jake Connor.
Penalty count: 7-5; **Half-time:** 6-12;
Referee: Robert Hicks; **Attendance:** 4,000.

Friday 11th June 2021

HULL KINGSTON ROVERS 40 SALFORD RED DEVILS 4

ROVERS: 1 Adam Quinlan; 2 Ben Crooks; 11 Brad Takairangi; 4 Shaun Kenny-Dowall (C); 5 Ryan Hall; 25 Rowan Milnes; 7 Jordan Abdull; 15 George Lawler; 9 Matt Parcell; 26 Will Maher; 12 Kane Linnett; 27 Luis Johnson; 13 Dean Hadley. Subs (all used): 10 Korbin Sims; 14 Jez Litten; 16 George King; 18 Matthew Storton.
Tries: Lawler (20), Crooks (23), Takairangi (35), Kenny-Dowall (62), Parcell (66), Hall (69), Linnett (80);
Goals: Abdull 5/7, Milnes 1/1.
Sin bin: Quinlan (51) - professional foul.
RED DEVILS: 1 Morgan Escare; 5 Joe Burgess (D); 2 Ken Sio; 31 Ben Davies (D); 22 Rhys Williams; 6 Tui Lolohea; 18 Chris Atkin; 8 Lee Mossop (C); 9 Andy Ackers; 26 Jack Wells; 20 Harvey Livett; 12 Pauli Pauli; 13 Elijah Taylor. Subs (all used): 10 Sebastine Ikahihifo; 16 Greg Burke; 27 Sam Luckley; 29 Dec Patton.
Try: Sio (6); **Goals:** Sio 0/1.
Dismissal: Pauli (80) - late challenge on Abdull.
Sin bin: Atkin (18) - dissent.
Rugby Leaguer & League Express Men of the Match: *Rovers:* Shaun Kenny-Dowall; *Red Devils:* Sebastine Ikahihifo.
Penalty count: 10-5; **Half-time:** 16-4;
Referee: Chris Kendall; **Attendance:** 4,000.

WARRINGTON WOLVES 38 WAKEFIELD TRINITY 18

WOLVES: 1 Stefan Ratchford; 2 Tom Lineham; 18 Jake Mamo; 4 Toby King; 5 Josh Charnley; 6 Blake Austin; 7 Gareth Widdop; 8 Chris Hill; 9 Daryl Clark; 10 Mike Cooper; 11 Ben Currie; 12 Jack Hughes (C); 13 Joe Philbin. Subs (all used): 15 Matt Davis; 16 Danny Walker; 19 Robbie Mulhern; 20 Sitaleki Akauola.
Tries: Widdop (8), Currie (15), Mamo (44), Charnley (49, 70, 74); **Goals:** Widdop 7/7.
TRINITY: 1 Max Jowitt; 27 Lee Kershaw; 4 Reece Lyne; 3 Bill Tupou; 5 Liam Kay; 6 Jacob Miller (C); 7 Mason Lino; 15 Eddie Battye; 25 Brad Walker; 10 Tinirau Arona; 14 Jay Pitts; 20 Joe Arundel; 13 Joe Westerman. Subs (all used): 8 David Fifita; 9 Kyle Wood; 16 James Batchelor; 26 Yusuf Aydin.
Tries: Fifita (26), Arundel (53), Kershaw (79);
Goals: Lino 3/3.
Rugby Leaguer & League Express Men of the Match: *Wolves:* Gareth Widdop; *Trinity:* Joe Westerman.
Penalty count: 5-5; **Half-time:** 14-6;
Referee: Marcus Griffiths; **Attendance:** 4,000.

Saturday 12th June 2021

LEIGH CENTURIONS 30 CATALANS DRAGONS 36

CENTURIONS: 1 Ryan Brierley; 25 Brendan Elliot; 4 Junior Sa'u; 3 Iain Thornley; 5 Lewis Tierney; 30 Ben Reynolds; 7 Joe Mellor; 21 Tyrone McCarthy; 9 Liam Hood (C); 10 Mark Ioane; 11 Ben Hellewell; 18 Matty Gee; 13 James Bell. Subs (all used): 14 Matty Wildie; 16 Nathaniel Peteru; 19 Nathan Mason; 26 Nathan Peats.
Tries: Reynolds (2), Elliot (15), Gee (24), Hellewell (73), Brierley (75); **Goals:** Brierley 5/5.
DRAGONS: 29 Sam Tomkins; 2 Tom Davies; 3 Samisoni Langi; 4 Dean Whare; 5 Fouad Yaha; 6 James Maloney; 7 Josh Drinkwater; 17 Mickael Goudemand; 9 Michael McIlorum; 10 Julian Bousquet; 15 Benjamin Jullien; 12 Mike McMeeken; 13 Benjamin Garcia (C). Subs (all used): 1 Arthur Mourgue; 16 Paul Seguier; 18 Lambert Belmas; 24 Jason Baitieri.
Tries: Drinkwater (10), Maloney (30), Langi (48), Davies (51), Jullien (54), Mourgue (58); **Goals:** Maloney 6/7.
Rugby Leaguer & League Express Men of the Match: *Centurions:* Ryan Brierley; *Dragons:* Benjamin Jullien.
Penalty count: 5-4; **Half-time:** 18-12;
Referee: Tom Grant; **Attendance:** 1,840.

ROUND 10

Wednesday 16th June 2021

WAKEFIELD TRINITY 12 CASTLEFORD TIGERS 18

TRINITY: 1 Max Jowitt; 27 Lee Kershaw; 4 Reece Lyne; 3 Bill Tupou; 2 Tom Johnstone; 6 Jacob Miller (C); 7 Mason Lino; 10 Tinirau Arona; 25 Brad Walker; 12 Kelepi Tanginoa; 14 Jay Pitts; 11 Matty Ashurst; 13 Joe Westerman. Subs (all used): 8 David Fifita; 9 Kyle Wood; 15 Eddie Battye; 20 Joe Arundel.
Tries: Miller (25, 69); **Goals:** Lino 2/2.
TIGERS: 1 Niall Evalds; 2 Derrell Olpherts; 4 Michael Shenton (C); 3 Peter Mata'utia; 25 Jordan Turner; 31 Gareth O'Brien; 7 Danny Richardson; 15 George Griffin; 9 Paul McShane; 24 Suaia Matagi; 11 Oliver Holmes; 21 Jesse Sene-Lefao; 14 Nathan Massey. Subs (all used): 8 Liam Watts; 17 Alex Foster; 22 Daniel Smith; 33 Jason Qareqare.
Tries: Griffin (21), Turner (35), Shenton (50), Mata'utia (60); **Goals:** Richardson 1/4.
Rugby Leaguer & League Express Men of the Match: *Trinity:* Jacob Miller; *Tigers:* Peter Mata'utia.
Penalty count: 6-7; **Half-time:** 6-10;
Referee: Liam Moore; **Attendance:** 2,262.

Thursday 17th June 2021

ST HELENS 2 WARRINGTON WOLVES 6

SAINTS: 1 Lachlan Coote; 2 Tommy Makinson; 3 Kevin Naiqama; 18 Jack Welsby; 5 Regan Grace; 6 Jonny Lomax; 7 Theo Fages; 8 Alex Walmsley; 9 James Roby (C); 15 Louie McCarthy-Scarsbrook; 11 Joel Thompson; 14 Sione Mata'utia; 13 Morgan Knowles. Subs (all used): 16 Kyle Amor; 17 Agnatius Paasi; 20 Joe Batchelor; 21 Lewis Dodd.
Goals: Coote 1/1.
WOLVES: 1 Stefan Ratchford; 2 Tom Lineham; 18 Jake Mamo; 4 Toby King; 5 Josh Charnley; 6 Blake Austin; 7 Gareth Widdop; 8 Chris Hill; 9 Daryl Clark; 10 Mike Cooper; 11 Ben Currie; 12 Jack Hughes (C); 13 Joe Philbin. Subs (all used): 16 Danny Walker; 15 Matt Davis; 19 Robbie Mulhern; 20 Sitaleki Akauola.
Try: Currie (23); **Goals:** Widdop 1/2.
Rugby Leaguer & League Express Men of the Match: *Saints:* Alex Walmsley; *Wolves:* Stefan Ratchford.
Penalty count: 6-3; **Half-time:** 2-6;
Referee: Chris Kendall; **Attendance:** 4,000.

Friday 18th June 2021

HUDDERSFIELD GIANTS 8 SALFORD RED DEVILS 9

GIANTS: 1 Ashton Golding; 2 Jermaine McGillvary; 4 Ricky Leutele; 3 Jake Wardle; 21 Leroy Cudjoe; 16 Jack Cogger; 6 Lee Gaskell; 8 Luke Yates; 9 Adam O'Brien; 20 Oliver Wilson; 11 Kenny Edwards; 15 Joe Greenwood; 13 Josh Jones. Subs (all used): 7 Aidan Sezer (C); 12 Joe Wardle; 10 Michael Lawrence; 25 Owen Trout.
Try: Joe Wardle (48); **Goals:** Sezer 2/2.
RED DEVILS: 23 Dan Sarginson; 2 Ken Sio; 5 Joe Burgess; 31 Ben Davies; 22 Rhys Williams; 18 Chris Atkin; 29 Dec Patton; 10 Sebastine Ikahihifo; 9 Andy Ackers (C); 26 Jack Wells; 20 Harvey Livett; 21 James Greenwood; 13 Elijah Taylor. Subs (all used): 15 Oliver Roberts; 16 Greg Burke; 17 Josh Johnson; 25 Jack Ormondroyd.
Try: Ackers (10); **Goals:** Patton 2/2; **Field goal:** Atkin (78).
Dismissal: Greenwood (33) - high tackle on O'Brien.
Rugby Leaguer & League Express Men of the Match: *Giants:* Kenny Edwards; *Red Devils:* Chris Atkin.
Penalty count: 4-4; **Half-time:** 2-8;
Referee: Scott Mikalauskas; **Attendance:** 2,352.

WIGAN WARRIORS 8 HULL KINGSTON ROVERS 18

WARRIORS: 31 Jackson Hastings; 22 Jake Bibby; 11 Willie Isa; 4 Oliver Gildart; 5 Liam Marshall; 7 Thomas Leuluai (C); 20 Harry Smith; 8 Brad Singleton; 9 Sam Powell; 10 Joe Bullock; 13 John Bateman; 12 Liam Farrell; 14 Oliver Partington. Subs (all used): 19 Liam Byrne; 21 Ethan Havard; 25 Joe Shorrocks; 27 Kai Pearce-Paul.
Tries: Gildart (67, 70); **Goals:** Smith 0/2.
ROVERS: 1 Adam Quinlan; 2 Ben Crooks; 3 Greg Minikin; 4 Shaun Kenny-Dowall (C); 5 Ryan Hall; 11 Brad Takairangi; 20 Mikey Lewis; 15 George Lawler; 9 Matt Parcell; 26 Will Maher; 12 Kane Linnett; 27 Luis Johnson; 13 Dean Hadley. Subs (all used): 8 Albert Vete; 14 Jez Litten; 16 George King; 18 Matthew Storton.
Tries: Crooks (38), Hall (62), Quinlan (75);
Goals: Crooks 3/3.
Sin bin: King (31) - persistent offending.
Rugby Leaguer & League Express Men of the Match: *Warriors:* Kai Pearce-Paul; *Rovers:* Brad Takairangi.
Penalty count: 7-1; **Half-time:** 0-6;
Referee: Robert Hicks; **Attendance:** 5,018.

Saturday 19th June 2021

LEIGH CENTURIONS 22 HULL FC 64

CENTURIONS: 1 Ryan Brierley; 4 Junior Sa'u; 3 Iain Thornley; 11 Ben Hellewell; 22 Craig Mullen; 30 Ben Reynolds; 7 Joe Mellor; 19 Nathan Mason; 9 Liam Hood (C); 10 Mark Ioane; 21 Tyrone McCarthy; 18 Matty Gee; 13 James Bell. Subs (all used): 26 Nathan Peats; 16 Nathaniel Peteru; 14 Matty Wildie; 2 Matty Russell.
Tries: Bell (6), Reynolds (45), Brierley (57, 76);
Goals: Brierley 3/4.
HULL FC: 1 Jake Connor; 2 Bureta Faraimo; 5 Mahe Fonua; 23 Connor Wynne; 21 Adam Swift; 6 Josh Reynolds; 7 Marc Sneyd; 13 Ligi Sao; 9 Danny Houghton (C); 10 Tevita Satae; 11 Andre Savelio; 12 Manu Ma'u; 16 Jordan Lane. Subs (all used): 14 Jordan Johnstone; 17 Brad Fash; 20 Jack Brown; 27 Mitieli Vulikijapani (D).
Tries: Connor (2), Swift (13, 34), Ma'u (17), Faraimo (24), Fonua (28), Savelio (38, 53, 69), Wynne (41), Brown (50), Satae (63); **Goals:** Sneyd 8/12.
Rugby Leaguer & League Express Men of the Match: *Centurions:* Ryan Brierley; *Hull FC:* Tevita Satae.
Penalty count: 6-3; **Half-time:** 6-34;
Referee: James Child; **Attendance:** 2,338.

ROUND 11

Thursday 24th June 2021

CASTLEFORD TIGERS 6 CATALANS DRAGONS 16

TIGERS: 1 Niall Evalds; 2 Derrell Olpherts; 20 James Clare; 4 Michael Shenton (C); 30 Brad Graham; 8 Liam Watts; 7 Danny Richardson; 22 Daniel Smith; 13 Adam Milner; 15 George Griffin; 11 Oliver Holmes; 17 Alex Foster; 14 Nathan Massey. Subs (all used): 18 Jacques O'Neill; 19 Tyla Hepi; 26 Lewis Bienek; 29 Sam Hall.
Try: Olpherts (74); **Goals:** Richardson 1/1.
DRAGONS: 1 Arthur Mourgue; 20 Matthieu Laguerre; 4 Dean Whare; 3 Samisoni Langi; 5 Fouad Yaha; 6 James Maloney; 7 Josh Drinkwater; 8 Gil Dudson; 14 Alrix Da Costa; 10 Julian Bousquet (C); 15 Benjamin Jullien; 12 Mike McMeeken; 17 Mickael Goudemand. Subs (all used): 11 Matt Whitley; 18 Lambert Belmas; 24 Jason Baitieri; 28 Sam Kasiano.
Tries: Yaha (7), Langi (20), Laguerre (54);
Goals: Maloney 2/4.
Rugby Leaguer & League Express Men of the Match: *Tigers:* Liam Watts; *Dragons:* Josh Drinkwater.
Penalty count: 5-6; **Half-time:** 0-8;
Referee: Chris Kendall; **Attendance:** 4,000.

WAKEFIELD TRINITY 14 WIGAN WARRIORS 6

TRINITY: 1 Max Jowitt; 27 Lee Kershaw; 20 Joe Arundel; 18 Innes Senior; 2 Tom Johnstone; 29 Ryan Hampshire; 7 Mason Lino; 10 Tinirau Arona (C); 25 Brad Walker; 15 Eddie Battye; 14 Jay Pitts; 11 Matty Ashurst; 19 Jordan Crowther. Subs (all used): 8 David Fifita; 9 Kyle Wood; 16 James Batchelor; 26 Yusuf Aydin.
Tries: Hampshire (17), Ashurst (40); **Goals:** Lino 3/3.
WARRIORS: 5 Liam Marshall; 22 Jake Bibby; 11 Willie Isa; 29 James McDonnell; 30 Umyla Hanley; 20 Harry Smith; 7 Thomas Leuluai (C); 10 Joe Bullock; 9 Sam Powell; 21 Ethan Havard; 15 Morgan Smithies; 27 Kai Pearce-Paul; 14 Oliver Partington. Subs (all used): 19 Liam Byrne; 23 Mitch Clark; 34 Brad O'Neill (D); 25 Joe Shorrocks.
Try: Hanley (62); **Goals:** Smith 1/1.
Rugby Leaguer & League Express Men of the Match:
Trinity: Ryan Hampshire; *Warriors:* Ethan Havard.
Penalty count: 6-7; **Half-time:** 12-0;
Referee: Tom Grant; **Attendance:** 2,262.

WARRINGTON WOLVES 44 LEIGH CENTURIONS 18

WOLVES: 23 Josh Thewlis; 2 Tom Lineham; 18 Jake Mamo; 27 Connor Wrench; 5 Josh Charnley; 6 Blake Austin; 7 Gareth Widdop; 8 Chris Hill; 16 Danny Walker; 20 Sitaleki Akauola; 26 Ellis Longstaff; 12 Jack Hughes (C); 15 Matt Davis. Subs (all used): 21 Rob Butler; 24 Riley Dean; 25 Eribe Doro; 22 Ellis Robson.
Tries: Austin (9), Davis (15), Widdop (49), Charnley (53), Walker (64), Doro (70), Lineham (75);
Goals: Widdop 8/9.
CENTURIONS: 1 Ryan Brierley; 2 Matty Russell; 3 Iain Thornley; 4 Junior Sa'u; 22 Craig Mullen; 30 Ben Reynolds; 7 Joe Mellor; 10 Mark Ioane; 9 Liam Hood (C); 21 Tyrone McCarthy; 11 Ben Hellewell; 18 Matty Gee; 13 James Bell. Subs (all used): 12 Jordan Thompson; 14 Matty Wildie; 16 Nathaniel Peteru; 19 Nathan Mason.
Tries: Hood (45), Sa'u (58), Ioane (78); **Goals:** Brierley 3/3.
Rugby Leaguer & League Express Men of the Match:
Wolves: Danny Walker; *Centurions:* Liam Hood.
Penalty count: 5-10; **Half-time:** 14-0;
Referee: Jack Smith; **Attendance:** 4,000.

Friday 25th June 2021

HULL FC 17 HUDDERSFIELD GIANTS 10

HULL FC: 23 Connor Wynne; 2 Bureta Faraimo; 5 Mahe Fonua; 30 Jack Logan (D2); 27 Mitieli Vulikijapani; 6 Josh Reynolds; 7 Marc Sneyd (C); 13 Ligi Sao; 14 Jordan Johnstone; 17 Brad Fash; 12 Manu Ma'u; 24 Cameron Scott; 15 Joe Cator. Subs: 19 Ben McNamara; 20 Jack Brown; 31 Aidan Burrell (D); 32 Marcus Walker (not used).
Tries: Fonua (49), Logan (54), Wynne (61);
Goals: Sneyd 2/4; **Field goal:** Sneyd (76).
GIANTS: 31 Olly Ashall-Bott (D); 24 Louis Senior; 21 Leroy Cudjoe (C); 27 Sam Wood; 5 Darnell McIntosh; 6 Lee Gaskell; 23 Oliver Russell; 22 James Gavet; 1 Ashton Golding; 18 Jack Ashworth; 13 Josh Jones; 15 Joe Greenwood; 25 Owen Trout. Subs (all used): 14 Matty English; 19 James Cunningham; 28 Sam Hewitt; 20 Oliver Wilson.
Try: Ashall-Bott (8); **Goals:** Russell 3/3.
Sin bin: Russell (40) - high tackle on Wynne.
Rugby Leaguer & League Express Men of the Match:
Hull FC: Mitieli Vulikijapani; *Giants:* Olly Ashall-Bott.
Penalty count: 7-7; **Half-time:** 0-10;
Referee: Liam Moore; **Attendance:** 5,527.

Sunday 27th June 2021

SALFORD RED DEVILS 12 LEEDS RHINOS 38

RED DEVILS: 6 Tui Lolohea; 1 Morgan Escare; 5 Joe Burgess; 24 Matthew Costello; 22 Rhys Williams; 29 Dec Patton; 18 Chris Atkin; 8 Lee Mossop (C); 9 Andy Ackers; 26 Jack Wells; 20 Harvey Livett; 15 Oliver Roberts; 13 Elijah Taylor. Subs (all used): 25 Jack Ormondroyd; 17 Josh Johnson; 11 Ryan Lannon; 27 Sam Luckley.
Tries: Atkin (28), Escare (73); **Goals:** Atkin 1/1, Patton 1/2.
Dismissal: Mossop (16) - fighting.
Sin bin: Wells (20) - dangerous challenge; Lannon (43) - fighting.
RHINOS: 16 Richie Myler; 24 Luke Briscoe; 4 Konrad Hurrell; 2 Tom Briscoe; 27 Jack Broadbent; 9 Kruise Leeming; 7 Luke Gale (C); 8 Mikolaj Oledzki; 14 Brad Dwyer; 10 Matt Prior; 11 Alex Mellor; 12 Rhyse Martin; 20 Bodene Thompson. Subs (all used): 18 Tom Holroyd; 19 King Vuniyayawa; 25 James Donaldson; 31 Morgan Gannon.
Tries: Broadbent (18, 45), T Briscoe (22), Myler (37, 39), Leeming (56), Gale (64); **Goals:** Martin 5/7.
Dismissal: Thompson (16) - fighting.
Sin bin: Gale (43) - fighting.
Rugby Leaguer & League Express Men of the Match:
Red Devils: Chris Atkin; *Rhinos:* Richie Myler.
Penalty count: 8-2; **Half-time:** 8-22;
Referee: Robert Hicks; **Attendance:** 2,219.

ROUND 12

Wednesday 30th June 2021

WIGAN WARRIORS 14 WARRINGTON WOLVES 40

WARRIORS: 31 Jackson Hastings; 22 Jake Bibby; 11 Willie Isa; 4 Oliver Gildart; 5 Liam Marshall; 7 Thomas Leuluai (C); 20 Harry Smith; 21 Ethan Havard; 9 Sam Powell; 14 Oliver Partington; 27 Kai Pearce-Paul; 12 Liam Farrell; 15 Morgan Smithies. Subs (all used): 10 Joe Bullock; 19 Liam Byrne; 25 Joe Shorrocks; 34 Brad O'Neill.
Tries: Powell (34), Isa (50), Gildart (58); **Goals:** Smith 1/3.
WOLVES: 23 Josh Thewlis; 2 Tom Lineham; 18 Jake Mamo; 27 Connor Wrench; 5 Josh Charnley; 6 Blake Austin; 1 Stefan Ratchford; 8 Chris Hill; 9 Daryl Clark; 10 Mike Cooper; 11 Ben Currie; 12 Jack Hughes (C); 15 Matt Davis. Subs (all used): 13 Joe Philbin; 14 Jason Clark; 16 Danny Walker; 19 Robbie Mulhern.
Tries: Wrench (7), Mamo (15, 43, 76), Davis (22), Hughes (63), Currie (73); **Goals:** Ratchford 6/7.
Rugby Leaguer & League Express Men of the Match:
Warriors: Jackson Hastings; *Wolves:* Jake Mamo.
Penalty count: 4-3; **Half-time:** 6-18;
Referee: Robert Hicks; **Attendance:** 5,537.

CASTLEFORD TIGERS 0 ST HELENS 24
(win awarded to St Helens after Castleford not able to field a team)

Thursday 1st July 2021

HUDDERSFIELD GIANTS 12 CATALANS DRAGONS 50

GIANTS: 31 Olly Ashall-Bott; 2 Jermaine McGillvary; 4 Ricky Leutele; 3 Jake Wardle; 21 Leroy Cudjoe (C); 27 Sam Wood; 23 Oliver Russell; 22 James Gavet; 1 Ashton Golding; 8 Luke Yates; 11 Kenny Edwards; 13 Josh Jones; 25 Owen Trout. Subs (all used): 15 Joe Greenwood; 18 Jack Ashworth; 28 Sam Hewitt; 32 Will Pryce (D).
Tries: Golding (46), Jake Wardle (69); **Goals:** Russell 2/2.
DRAGONS: 29 Sam Tomkins; 2 Tom Davies; 3 Samisoni Langi; 4 Dean Whare; 5 Fouad Yaha; 6 James Maloney; 7 Josh Drinkwater; 8 Gil Dudson; 13 Benjamin Garcia (C); 10 Julian Bousquet; 15 Benjamin Jullien; 12 Mike McMeeken; 17 Mickael Goudemand. Subs (all used): 1 Arthur Mourgue; 11 Matt Whitley; 24 Jason Baitieri; 28 Sam Kasiano.
Tries: Jullien (19), McMeeken (29), Langi (36), Garcia (48), Mourgue (54), S Tomkins (58), Maloney (62), Davies (78); **Goals:** Maloney 9/9.
Sin bin: Baitieri (44) - professional foul; Drinkwater (73) - dissent; Dudson (75) - professional foul.
Rugby Leaguer & League Express Men of the Match:
Giants: Jake Wardle; *Dragons:* Sam Tomkins.
Penalty count: 13-6; **Half-time:** 0-20;
Referee: Ben Thaler; **Attendance:** 1,904.

LEEDS RHINOS 48 LEIGH CENTURIONS 18

RHINOS: 15 Liam Sutcliffe; 24 Luke Briscoe; 12 Rhyse Martin; 2 Tom Briscoe; 27 Jack Broadbent; 6 Robert Lui; 9 Kruise Leeming; 8 Mikolaj Oledzki; 14 Brad Dwyer; 18 Tom Holroyd; 25 James Donaldson; 31 Morgan Gannon; 10 Matt Prior (C). Subs (all used): 19 King Vuniyayawa; 22 Sam Walters; 26 Jarrod O'Connor; 29 Liam Tindall.
Tries: Donaldson (16), Broadbent (20, 24, 58, 74), Leeming (28), L Sutcliffe (37), Walters (61), Holroyd (76);
Goals: Martin 6/9.
CENTURIONS: 22 Craig Mullen; 2 Matty Russell; 3 Iain Thornley; 4 Junior Sa'u; 24 Keanan Brand; 1 Ryan Brierley; 7 Joe Mellor; 16 Nathaniel Peteru; 9 Liam Hood (C); 12 Jordan Thompson; 11 Ben Hellewell; 18 Matty Gee; 13 James Bell. Subs (all used): 10 Mark Ioane; 14 Matty Wildie; 15 Alex Gerrard; 26 Nathan Peats.
Tries: Russell (2), Ioane (48), Brierley (67);
Goals: Brierley 3/3.
Sin bin: Bell (13) - dangerous challenge on Oledzki.
Rugby Leaguer & League Express Men of the Match:
Rhinos: Matt Prior; *Centurions:* Matty Russell.
Penalty count: 10-4; **Half-time:** 24-6;
Referee: Aaron Moore; **Attendance:** 4,000.

ROUND 13

Sunday 4th July 2021

ST HELENS 24 WIGAN WARRIORS 6

SAINTS: 1 Lachlan Coote; 2 Tommy Makinson; 3 Kevin Naiqama; 4 Mark Percival; 5 Regan Grace; 6 Jonny Lomax; 7 Theo Fages; 8 Alex Walmsley; 9 James Roby (C); 15 Louie McCarthy-Scarsbrook; 14 Sione Mata'utia; 20 Joe Batchelor; 13 Morgan Knowles. Subs (all used): 16 Kyle Amor; 17 Agnatius Paasi; 18 Jack Welsby; 21 Lewis Dodd.
Tries: Grace (14), Coote (24), Percival (49);
Goals: Coote 6/7.
WARRIORS: 31 Jackson Hastings; 22 Jake Bibby; 11 Willie Isa; 4 Oliver Gildart; 5 Liam Marshall; 7 Thomas Leuluai (C); 20 Harry Smith; 8 Brad Singleton; 9 Sam Powell; 10 Joe Bullock; 27 Kai Pearce-Paul; 12 Liam Farrell; 21 Ethan Havard. Subs (all used): 14 Oliver Partington; 19 Liam Byrne; 25 Joe Shorrocks; 34 Brad O'Neill.
Try: Farrell (55); **Goals:** Smith 1/1.
Sin bin: Pearce-Paul (40) - shoulder charge on Coote; Isa (44) - dangerous challenge on Welsby.
On report: Isa (36) - alleged off-the-ball challenge on Percival.
Rugby Leaguer & League Express Men of the Match:
Saints: Lachlan Coote; *Warriors:* Liam Farrell.
Penalty count: 12-11; **Half-time:** 18-0;
Referee: James Child; **Attendance:** 4,000.

Monday 5th July 2021

WARRINGTON WOLVES 16 LEEDS RHINOS 22

WOLVES: 23 Josh Thewlis; 2 Tom Lineham; 18 Jake Mamo; 4 Toby King; 5 Josh Charnley; 6 Blake Austin; 1 Stefan Ratchford; 8 Chris Hill; 16 Danny Walker; 10 Mike Cooper; 11 Ben Currie; 12 Jack Hughes (C); 15 Matt Davis. Subs (all used): 9 Daryl Clark; 13 Joe Philbin; 20 Sitaleki Akauola; 21 Rob Butler.
Tries: Walker (15), Charnley (71, 79); **Goals:** Ratchford 2/3.
RHINOS: 15 Liam Sutcliffe; 5 Ash Handley; 2 Tom Briscoe; 27 Jack Broadbent; 24 Luke Briscoe; 6 Robert Lui; 9 Kruise Leeming; 8 Mikolaj Oledzki; 14 Brad Dwyer; 10 Matt Prior (C); 11 Alex Mellor; 12 Rhyse Martin; 20 Bodene Thompson. Subs (all used): 4 Konrad Hurrell; 18 Tom Holroyd; 25 James Donaldson; 26 Jarrod O'Connor.
Tries: Lui (7), Mellor (24), Handley (31); **Goals:** Martin 5/5.
Sin bin: L Sutcliffe (70) - high tackle on Thewlis; Lui (76) - professional foul.
Rugby Leaguer & League Express Men of the Match:
Wolves: Mike Cooper; *Rhinos:* Matt Prior.
Penalty count: 9-7; **Half-time:** 6-20;
Referee: Liam Moore; **Attendance:** 4,000.

Tuesday 6th July 2021

HUDDERSFIELD GIANTS 0 CASTLEFORD TIGERS 24
(win awarded to Castleford after Huddersfield not able to field a team)

ROUND 14

Friday 9th July 2021

LEEDS RHINOS 18 CATALANS DRAGONS 26

RHINOS: 16 Richie Myler; 24 Luke Briscoe; 4 Konrad Hurrell; 15 Liam Sutcliffe; 2 Tom Briscoe; 9 Kruise Leeming; 7 Luke Gale (C); 10 Matt Prior; 14 Brad Dwyer; 18 Tom Holroyd; 11 Alex Mellor; 12 Rhyse Martin; 20 Bodene Thompson. Subs (all used): 17 Cameron Smith; 19 King Vuniyayawa; 25 James Donaldson; 26 Jarrod O'Connor.
Tries: Martin (14), Thompson (22), L Sutcliffe (38);
Goals: Martin 3/3.
DRAGONS: 29 Sam Tomkins; 2 Tom Davies; 3 Samisoni Langi; 4 Dean Whare; 5 Fouad Yaha; 6 James Maloney; 1 Arthur Mourgue; 10 Julian Bousquet; 13 Benjamin Garcia (C); 22 Joel Tomkins; 11 Matt Whitley; 12 Mike McMeeken; 17 Mickael Goudemand. Subs (all used): 14 Alrix Da Costa; 16 Paul Seguier; 24 Jason Baitieri; 28 Sam Kasiano.
Tries: Mourgue (10), Whitley (51), McMeeken (56), Yaha (63); **Goals:** Maloney 2/2, Mourgue 3/3.
Sin bin: Kasiano (34) - high tackle on L Briscoe.
Rugby Leaguer & League Express Men of the Match:
Rhinos: Rhyse Martin; *Dragons:* James Maloney.
Penalty count: 7-8; **Half time:** 18-8;
Referee: James Child; **Attendance:** 4,000.

WAKEFIELD TRINITY 14 ST HELENS 30

TRINITY: 29 Ryan Hampshire; 27 Lee Kershaw; 4 Reece Lyne; 20 Joe Arundel; 18 Innes Senior; 6 Jacob Miller (C); 7 Mason Lino; 10 Tinirau Arona; 16 James Batchelor; 12 Kelepi Tanginoa; 14 Jay Pitts; 11 Matty Ashurst; 13 Joe Westerman. Subs (all used): 5 Liam Kay; 8 David Fifita; 15 Eddie Battye; 26 Yusuf Aydin.
Tries: Kershaw (27), Senior (39, 50); **Goals:** Lino 1/3.
Sin bin: Batchelor (34) - professional foul.
SAINTS: 1 Lachlan Coote; 2 Tommy Makinson; 3 Kevin Naiqama; 4 Mark Percival; 5 Regan Grace; 21 Lewis Dodd; 6 Jonny Lomax; 8 Alex Walmsley; 9 James Roby (C); 16 Kyle Amor; 14 Sione Mata'utia; 20 Joe Batchelor; 13 Morgan Knowles. Subs (all used): 10 Matty Lees; 11 Joel Thompson; 17 Agnatius Paasi; 18 Jack Welsby.
Tries: Percival (13), Dodd (24), Coote (65), Makinson (79);
Goals: Coote 7/7.
Sin bin: Percival (47) - persistent offending.
Rugby Leaguer & League Express Men of the Match:
Trinity: Reece Lyne; *Saints:* Lachlan Coote.
Penalty count: 13-6; **Half-time:** 10-16;
Referee: Ben Thaler; **Attendance:** 4,000.

Sunday 11th July 2021

CASTLEFORD TIGERS 18 SALFORD RED DEVILS 70

TIGERS: 33 Jason Qareqare; 34 Caelum Jordan (D); 12 Cheyse Blair; 17 Alex Foster; 20 James Clare; 35 Jack Sadler (D); 7 Danny Richardson; 19 Tyla Hepi; 32 Cain Robb (D); 10 Grant Millington (C); 21 Jesse Sene-Lefao; 28 Brad Martin; 26 Lewis Bienek. Subs (all used): 27 Lewis Peachey; 29 Sam Hall; 36 Adam Rusling (D); 37 Nathan Magee (D).
Tries: Millington (7), Martin (42), Foster (71);
Goals: Richardson 3/3.
RED DEVILS: 1 Morgan Escare; 2 Ken Sio; 4 Krisnan Inu; 24 Matthew Costello; 22 Rhys Williams; 29 Dec Patton; 18 Chris Atkin; 17 Josh Johnson; 9 Andy Ackers; 25 Jack Ormondroyd; 20 Harvey Livett; 11 Ryan Lannon; 16 Greg Burke (C). Subs (all used): 12 Pauli Pauli; 15 Oliver Roberts; 31 Ben Davies; 32 Dan Norman (D).
Tries: Ormondroyd (14), Roberts (27), Escare (31, 53), Williams (37, 79), Sio (48), Patton (57), Costello (59), Atkin (64), Norman (75), Davies (77); **Goals:** Inu 11/12.
Rugby Leaguer & League Express Men of the Match: *Tigers:* Grant Millington; *Red Devils:* Krisnan Inu.
Penalty count: 5-4; **Half-time:** 6-22;
Referee: Tom Grant; **Attendance:** 3,900.

WIGAN WARRIORS 16 HUDDERSFIELD GIANTS 12

WARRIORS: 31 Jackson Hastings; 30 Umyla Hanley; 22 Jake Bibby; 4 Oliver Gildart; 5 Liam Marshall; 7 Thomas Leuluai (C); 20 Harry Smith; 8 Brad Singleton; 9 Sam Powell; 17 Tony Clubb; 27 Kai Pearce-Paul; 12 Liam Farrell; 10 Joe Bullock. Subs (all used): 19 Liam Byrne; 23 Mitch Clark; 25 Joe Shorrocks; 34 Brad O'Neill.
Tries: Marshall (38), Clark (49), Smith (63);
Goals: Smith 2/3.
GIANTS: 1 Ashton Golding; 31 Olly Ashall-Bott; 3 Jake Wardle; 21 Leroy Cudjoe (C); 24 Louis Senior; 27 Sam Wood; 23 Oliver Russell; 8 Luke Yates; 35 Nathan Peats (D); 22 James Gavet; 13 Josh Jones; 17 Chris McQueen; 15 Joe Greenwood. Subs: 28 Sam Hewitt; 32 Will Pryce; 33 Robson Stevens (not used); 34 Nathaniel Peteru (D).
Tries: McQueen (9), Cudjoe (13); **Goals:** Russell 2/2.
Rugby Leaguer & League Express Men of the Match: *Warriors:* Harry Smith; *Giants:* Ashton Golding.
Penalty count: 5-3; **Half-time:** 6-12;
Referee: Marcus Griffiths; **Attendance:** 4,439.

ROUND 10

Friday 16th July 2021

CATALANS DRAGONS 27 LEEDS RHINOS 18

DRAGONS: 29 Sam Tomkins; 2 Tom Davies; 4 Dean Whare; 3 Samisoni Langi; 5 Fouad Yaha; 1 Arthur Mourgue; 7 Josh Drinkwater; 8 Gil Dudson; 14 Alrix Da Costa; 17 Mickael Goudemand; 11 Matt Whitley; 12 Mike McMeeken; 13 Benjamin Garcia (C). Subs (all used): 15 Benjamin Jullien; 16 Paul Seguier; 28 Sam Kasiano; 30 Jordan Dezaria.
Tries: Kasiano (43), Mourgue (48), Whitley (53), Davies (61); **Goals:** Mourgue 5/6;
Field goal: S Tomkins (72).
RHINOS: 16 Richie Myler; 24 Luke Briscoe; 4 Konrad Hurrell; 3 Harry Newman; 2 Tom Briscoe; 15 Liam Sutcliffe; 7 Luke Gale (C); 10 Matt Prior; 9 Kruise Leeming; 18 Tom Holroyd; 11 Alex Mellor; 22 Sam Walters; 17 Cameron Smith. Subs (all used): 14 Brad Dwyer; 23 Callum McLelland; 25 James Donaldson; 26 Jarrod O'Connor.
Tries: T Briscoe (13, 36), Leeming (39); **Goals:** Gale 3/3.
Rugby Leaguer & League Express Men of the Match: *Dragons:* Sam Tomkins; *Rhinos:* Luke Gale.
Penalty count: 13-7; **Half-time:** 2-18;
Referee: Ben Thaler; **Attendance:** 4,800.

ROUND 12

Friday 16th July 2021

SALFORD RED DEVILS 24 WAKEFIELD TRINITY 14

RED DEVILS: 1 Morgan Escare; 2 Ken Sio; 4 Krisnan Inu; 24 Matthew Costello; 22 Rhys Williams; 6 Tui Lolohea; 18 Chris Atkin; 17 Josh Johnson; 9 Andy Ackers; 25 Jack Ormondroyd; 20 Harvey Livett; 11 Ryan Lannon; 16 Greg Burke (C). Subs (all used): 10 Sebastine Ikahihifo; 12 Pauli Pauli; 15 Oliver Roberts; 27 Sam Luckley.
Tries: Escare (22), Inu (34, 64), Sio (72); **Goals:** Inu 4/5.
TRINITY: 5 Liam Kay; 27 Lee Kershaw; 4 Reece Lyne; 32 Ollie Greensmith (D); 18 Innes Senior; 6 Jacob Miller (C); 7 Mason Lino; 10 Tinirau Arona; 25 Brad Walker; 12 Kelepi Tanginoa; 11 Matty Ashurst; 14 Jay Pitts; 16 James Batchelor. Subs (all used): 8 David Fifita; 15 Eddie Battye; 26 Yusuf Aydin; 33 Harry Bowes.
Tries: Senior (9), Lyne (16); **Goals:** Lino 3/3.
Rugby Leaguer & League Express Men of the Match: *Red Devils:* Pauli Pauli; *Trinity:* Kelepi Tanginoa.
Penalty count: 3-4; **Half-time:** 12-12;
Referee: Gareth Hewer; **Attendance:** 1,323
(at Halliwell Jones Stadium, Warrington).

ROUND 9

Friday 16th July 2021

HUDDERSFIELD GIANTS 12 WIGAN WARRIORS 14

GIANTS: 1 Ashton Golding; 24 Louis Senior; 27 Sam Wood; 3 Jake Wardle; 21 Leroy Cudjoe (C); 32 Will Pryce; 23 Oliver Russell; 22 James Gavet; 35 Nathan Peats; 20 Oliver Wilson; 13 Josh Jones; 8 Luke Yates; 17 Chris McQueen. Subs (all used): 2 Jermaine McGillvary; 28 Sam Hewitt; 33 Robson Stevens (D); 34 Nathaniel Peteru.
Tries: Pryce (60), Peteru (74); **Goals:** Russell 2/2.
WARRIORS: 30 Umyla Hanley; 28 Sam Halsall; 22 Jake Bibby; 4 Oliver Gildart; 5 Liam Marshall; 7 Thomas Leuluai (C); 20 Harry Smith; 8 Brad Singleton; 34 Brad O'Neill; 17 Tony Clubb; 27 Kai Pearce-Paul; 12 Liam Farrell; 14 Oliver Partington. Subs (all used): 21 Ethan Havard; 23 Mitch Clark; 25 Joe Shorrocks; 33 Amir Bourouh.
Tries: Clark (32), Farrell (70); **Goals:** Smith 3/3.
Rugby Leaguer & League Express Men of the Match: *Giants:* Will Pryce; *Warriors:* Liam Farrell.
Penalty count: 4-6; **Half-time:** 0-6;
Referee: Scott Mikalauskas; **Attendance:** 3,139.

ROUND 15

Thursday 22nd July 2021

HUDDERSFIELD GIANTS 40 HULL FC 26

GIANTS: 1 Ashton Golding; 2 Jermaine McGillvary; 21 Leroy Cudjoe (C); 3 Jake Wardle; 24 Louis Senior; 23 Oliver Russell; 32 Will Pryce; 20 Oliver Wilson; 35 Nathan Peats; 8 Luke Yates; 17 Chris McQueen; 13 Josh Jones; 25 Owen Trout. Subs (all used): 28 Sam Hewitt; 27 Sam Wood; 33 Robson Stevens; 34 Nathaniel Peteru.
Tries: McGillvary (8, 39, 49, 65), Peats (11), Yates (31), Pryce (34), Cudjoe (73); **Goals:** Russell 4/8.
Dismissal: Jones (80) - fighting.
HULL FC: 21 Adam Swift; 27 Mitieli Vulikijapani; 3 Carlos Tuimavave; 5 Mahe Fonua; 24 Cameron Scott; 19 Ben McNamara; 7 Marc Sneyd; 10 Tevita Satae; 9 Danny Houghton (C); 13 Ligi Sao; 16 Jordan Lane; 11 Andre Savelio; 17 Brad Fash. Subs: 14 Jordan Johnstone; 20 Jack Brown; 22 Josh Bowden; 31 Aidan Burrell (not used).
Tries: Tuimavave (4), Vulikijapani (17, 59), Lane (27), Satae (78); **Goals:** Sneyd 3/5.
Dismissal: Savelio (80) - fighting.
Sin bin: Sao (56) - high tackle.
Rugby Leaguer & League Express Men of the Match: *Giants:* Jermaine McGillvary; *Hull FC:* Ben McNamara.
Penalty count: 4-4; **Half-time:** 22-16;
Referee: Chris Kendall; **Attendance:** 3,699.

Friday 23rd July 2021

LEEDS RHINOS 38 SALFORD RED DEVILS 16

RHINOS: 16 Richie Myler; 2 Tom Briscoe; 4 Konrad Hurrell; 3 Harry Newman; 5 Ash Handley; 15 Liam Sutcliffe; 23 Callum McLelland; 10 Matt Prior (C); 9 Kruise Leeming; 19 King Vuniyayawa; 11 Alex Mellor; 12 Rhyse Martin; 26 Jarrod O'Connor. Subs (all used): 14 Brad Dwyer; 17 Cameron Smith; 24 Luke Briscoe; 25 James Donaldson.
Tries: Newman (7), Leeming (9, 31), McLelland (54), Vuniyayawa (57), Prior (76); **Goals:** Martin 7/7.
Sin bin: Myler (77) - dissent.
RED DEVILS: 1 Morgan Escare; 2 Ken Sio; 4 Krisnan Inu; 20 Harvey Livett; 22 Rhys Williams; 6 Tui Lolohea; 18 Chris Atkin; 8 Lee Mossop (C); 9 Andy Ackers; 25 Jack Ormondroyd; 26 Jack Wells; 12 Pauli Pauli; 11 Ryan Lannon. Subs (all used): 10 Sebastine Ikahihifo; 15 Oliver Roberts; 27 Sam Luckley; 33 Ata Hingano (D).
Tries: Sio (47), Lolohea (62), Inu (77); **Goals:** Inu 2/3.
Sin bin: Lolohea (50) - dissent; Ikahihifo (51) - fighting.
Rugby Leaguer & League Express Men of the Match: *Rhinos:* Kruise Leeming; *Red Devils:* Ken Sio.
Penalty count: 10-9; **Half-time:** 20-0;
Referee: Ben Thaler; **Attendance:** 10,515.

WIGAN WARRIORS 25 WAKEFIELD TRINITY 12

WARRIORS: 31 Jackson Hastings; 22 Jake Bibby; 11 Willie Isa; 4 Oliver Gildart; 5 Liam Marshall; 7 Thomas Leuluai (C); 20 Harry Smith; 8 Brad Singleton; 9 Sam Powell; 17 Tony Clubb; 27 Kai Pearce-Paul; 12 Liam Farrell; 14 Oliver Partington. Subs (all used): 21 Ethan Havard; 23 Mitch Clark; 25 Joe Shorrocks; 34 Brad O'Neill.
Tries: Bibby (13, 39, 46), Shorrocks (49), Marshall (56);
Goals: Smith 2/5; **Field goal:** Hastings (40).
TRINITY: 29 Ryan Hampshire; 27 Lee Kershaw; 4 Reece Lyne; 20 Joe Arundel; 18 Innes Senior; 6 Jacob Miller (C); 7 Mason Lino; 8 David Fifita; 25 Brad Walker; 12 Kelepi Tanginoa; 11 Matty Ashurst; 14 Jay Pitts; 15 Eddie Battye. Subs (all used): 5 Liam Kay; 16 James Batchelor; 17 Chris Green; 26 Yusuf Aydin.
Tries: Batchelor (70), Pitts (75); **Goals:** Lino 2/2.
Rugby Leaguer & League Express Men of the Match: *Warriors:* Jackson Hastings; *Trinity:* James Batchelor.
Penalty count: 6-9; **Half-time:** 9-0;
Referee: Tom Grant; **Attendance:** 5,555.

ROUND 13

Saturday 24th July 2021

CATALANS DRAGONS 32
HULL KINGSTON ROVERS 30

DRAGONS: 29 Sam Tomkins; 2 Tom Davies; 3 Samisoni Langi; 4 Dean Whare; 5 Fouad Yaha; 1 Arthur Mourgue; 7 Josh Drinkwater; 8 Gil Dudson; 14 Alrix Da Costa; 10 Julian Bousquet; 11 Matt Whitley; 12 Mike McMeeken; 13 Benjamin Garcia (C). Subs (all used): 15 Benjamin Jullien; 16 Paul Seguier; 17 Mickael Goudemand; 28 Sam Kasiano.
Tries: Whitley (10, 43), S Tomkins (25), Goudemand (51), Yaha (66); **Goals:** Mourgue 6/6.
ROVERS: 1 Adam Quinlan; 2 Ben Crooks; 3 Greg Minikin; 4 Shaun Kenny-Dowall (C); 5 Ryan Hall; 11 Brad Takairangi; 7 Jordan Abdull; 15 George Lawler; 14 Jez Litten; 26 Will Maher; 27 Luis Johnson; 12 Kane Linnett; 13 Dean Hadley. Subs (all used): 8 Albert Vete; 9 Matt Parcell; 10 Korbin Sims; 16 George King.
Tries: Abdull (5, 48), Kenny-Dowall (20), Minikin (35), Quinlan (38); **Goals:** Abdull 5/6.
Rugby Leaguer & League Express Men of the Match: *Dragons:* Matt Whitley; *Rovers:* Jordan Abdull.
Penalty count: 13-7; **Half-time:** 12-26;
Referee: James Child; **Attendance:** 5,586.

ROUND 16

Wednesday 28th July 2021

WARRINGTON WOLVES 21 WIGAN WARRIORS 8

WOLVES: 23 Josh Thewlis; 5 Josh Charnley; 18 Jake Mamo; 4 Toby King; 20 Sitaleki Akauola; 6 Blake Austin; 1 Stefan Ratchford; 8 Chris Hill; 9 Daryl Clark; 10 Mike Cooper; 11 Ben Currie; 12 Jack Hughes (C); 14 Jason Clark. Subs (all used): 13 Joe Philbin; 15 Matt Davis; 19 Robbie Mulhern; 27 Connor Wrench.
Tries: Austin (18), Thewlis (39), Mamo (62);
Goals: Ratchford 4/4; **Field goal:** Austin (77).
Sin bin: Mamo (69) - fighting.
WARRIORS: 31 Jackson Hastings; 22 Jake Bibby; 11 Willie Isa; 4 Oliver Gildart; 5 Liam Marshall; 7 Thomas Leuluai (C); 20 Harry Smith; 8 Brad Singleton; 9 Sam Powell; 17 Tony Clubb; 27 Kai Pearce-Paul; 12 Liam Farrell; 14 Oliver Partington. Subs (all used): 19 Liam Byrne; 21 Ethan Havard; 25 Joe Shorrocks; 33 Amir Bourouh.
Tries: Marshall (15, 24); **Goals:** Smith 0/2.
Sin bin: Partington (69) - fighting.
Rugby Leaguer & League Express Men of the Match: *Wolves:* Daryl Clark; *Warriors:* Jackson Hastings.
Penalty count: 4-5; **Half-time:** 12-8;
Referee: Robert Hicks; **Attendance:** 8,014.

Thursday 29th July 2021

CATALANS DRAGONS 40 WAKEFIELD TRINITY 20

DRAGONS: 29 Sam Tomkins (C); 2 Tom Davies; 3 Samisoni Langi; 4 Dean Whare; 5 Fouad Yaha; 6 James Maloney; 7 Josh Drinkwater; 8 Gil Dudson; 14 Alrix Da Costa; 10 Julian Bousquet; 11 Matt Whitley; 15 Benjamin Jullien; 22 Joel Tomkins. Subs (all used): 1 Arthur Mourgue; 16 Paul Seguier; 17 Mickael Goudemand; 28 Sam Kasiano.
Tries: S Tomkins (5), Da Costa (28), Kasiano (30), Dudson (65), Yaha (72, 79); **Goals:** Maloney 8/8.
TRINITY: 1 Max Jowitt; 18 Innes Senior; 4 Reece Lyne; 20 Joe Arundel; 5 Liam Kay; 6 Jacob Miller (C); 7 Mason Lino; 8 David Fifita; 9 Kyle Wood; 10 Tinirau Arona; 11 Matty Ashurst; 12 Kelepi Tanginoa; 26 Yusuf Aydin. Subs (all used): 15 Eddie Battye; 17 Chris Green; 25 Brad Walker; 29 Ryan Hampshire.
Tries: Aydin (9), Fifita (20, 68); **Goals:** Lino 4/4.
Rugby Leaguer & League Express Men of the Match: *Dragons:* James Maloney; *Trinity:* Mason Lino.
Penalty count: 8-4; **Half-time:** 20-12;
Referee: Marcus Griffiths; **Attendance:** 6,267.

HULL FC 12 LEEDS RHINOS 22

HULL FC: 23 Connor Wynne; 21 Adam Swift; 3 Carlos Tuimavave; 5 Mahe Fonua; 2 Bureta Faraimo; 6 Josh Reynolds; 7 Marc Sneyd; 13 Ligi Sao; 9 Danny Houghton (C); 10 Tevita Satae; 16 Jordan Lane; 12 Manu Ma'u; 15 Joe Cator. Subs (all used): 14 Jordan Johnstone; 17 Brad Fash; 22 Josh Bowden; 24 Cameron Scott.
Tries: Swift (26), Tuimavave (78); **Goals:** Sneyd 2/3.
Sin bin: Johnstone (58) - late challenge;
Reynolds (70) - fighting.
RHINOS: 16 Richie Myler; 2 Tom Briscoe; 4 Konrad Hurrell; 3 Harry Newman; 5 Ash Handley; 23 Callum McLelland; 7 Luke Gale; 8 Mikolaj Oledzki; 9 Kruise Leeming; 10 Matt Prior (C); 11 Alex Mellor; 12 Rhyse Martin; 13 Zane Tetevano. Subs (all used): 14 Brad Dwyer; 17 Cameron Smith; 19 King Vuniyayawa; 25 James Donaldson.
Tries: Dwyer (58), Myler (65), Smith (69);
Goals: Martin 5/5.
Sin bin: Myler (70) - fighting.
Rugby Leaguer & League Express Men of the Match:
Hull FC: Danny Houghton; *Rhinos:* Brad Dwyer.
Penalty count: 5-6; **Half-time:** 6-4;
Referee: Liam Moore; **Attendance:** 9,356.

ROUND 17

Sunday 1st August 2021

WIGAN WARRIORS 50 LEIGH CENTURIONS 6

WARRIORS: 31 Jackson Hastings; 28 Sam Halsall; 11 Willie Isa; 22 Jake Bibby; 30 Umyla Hanley; 7 Thomas Leuluai (C); 20 Harry Smith; 8 Brad Singleton; 9 Sam Powell; 14 Oliver Partington; 27 Kai Pearce-Paul; 12 Liam Farrell; 25 Joe Shorrocks. Subs (all used): 13 John Bateman; 19 Liam Byrne; 23 Mitch Clark; 33 Amir Bourouh.
Tries: Leuluai (4), Hanley (12, 38, 78), Farrell (27, 40), Halsall (54), Shorrocks (62), Hastings (67);
Goals: Smith 7/9.
Dismissal: Singleton (15) - fighting.
CENTURIONS: 25 Brendan Elliot; 22 Craig Mullen; 4 Junior Sa'u; 3 Iain Thornley; 24 Keanan Brand; 7 Joe Mellor; 17 Jamie Ellis; 33 Rob Butler (D); 9 Liam Hood (C); 10 Mark Ioane; 11 Ben Hellewell; 18 Matty Gee; 12 Jordan Thompson. Subs (all used): 14 Matty Wildie; 15 Alex Gerrard; 20 Adam Sidlow; 34 Jack Ashworth (D2).
Try: Hood (10); **Goals:** Ellis 1/1.
Dismissal: Ashworth (15) - fighting.
Rugby Leaguer & League Express Men of the Match:
Warriors: Joe Shorrocks; *Centurions:* Liam Hood.
Penalty count: 6-8; **Half-time:** 28-6;
Referee: Scott Mikalauskas; **Attendance:** 9,206.

LEEDS RHINOS 26 WARRINGTON WOLVES 27

RHINOS: 16 Richie Myler; 2 Tom Briscoe; 4 Konrad Hurrell; 3 Harry Newman; 5 Ash Handley; 15 Liam Sutcliffe; 7 Luke Gale; 8 Mikolaj Oledzki; 14 Brad Dwyer; 10 Matt Prior (C); 25 James Donaldson; 12 Rhyse Martin; 13 Zane Tetevano. Subs: 17 Cameron Smith; 18 Tom Holroyd; 19 King Vuniyayawa (not used); 24 Luke Briscoe.
Tries: Newman (8, 70), Oledzki (17), Dwyer (29);
Goals: Martin 5/5.
WOLVES: 1 Stefan Ratchford; 5 Josh Charnley; 18 Jake Mamo; 4 Toby King; 2 Tom Lineham; 6 Blake Austin; 31 George Williams (D); 8 Chris Hill; 9 Daryl Clark; 10 Mike Cooper; 11 Ben Currie; 12 Jack Hughes (C); 15 Matt Davis. Subs (all used): 16 Danny Walker; 19 Robbie Mulhern; 20 Sitaleki Akauola; 26 Ellis Longstaff.
Tries: Cooper (11), Austin (19), Charnley (51), Walker (76);
Goals: Ratchford 5/5; **Field goal:** Williams (80).
Sin bin: Hughes (67) - late challenge on Gale.
Rugby Leaguer & League Express Men of the Match:
Rhinos: Brad Dwyer; *Wolves:* George Williams.
Penalty count: 7-6; **Half-time:** 18-12;
Referee: Chris Kendall; **Attendance:** 9,196.

Monday 2nd August 2021

CASTLEFORD TIGERS 16 HUDDERSFIELD GIANTS 34

TIGERS: 1 Niall Evalds; 2 Derrell Olpherts; 12 Cheyse Blair; 4 Michael Shenton (C); 30 Brad Graham; 22 Daniel Smith; 32 Cain Robb; 14 Nathan Massey; 9 Paul McShane; 29 Sam Hall; 28 Brad Martin; 27 Lewis Peachey; 17 Alex Foster. Subs (all used): 24 Suaia Matagi; 26 Lewis Bienek; 38 Jimmy Keinhorst (D); 39 Jake Sweeting (D).
Tries: McShane (15), Graham (48), Sweeting (78);
Goals: McShane 2/3.
GIANTS: 1 Ashton Golding; 2 Jermaine McGillvary; 3 Jake Wardle; 21 Leroy Cudjoe (C); 24 Louis Senior; 32 Will Pryce; 23 Oliver Russell; 25 Owen Trout; 35 Nathan Peats; 20 Oliver Wilson; 27 Sam Wood; 17 Chris McQueen; 8 Luke Yates. Subs (all used): 14 Matty English; 28 Sam Hewitt; 31 Olly Ashall-Bott; 34 Nathaniel Peteru.
Tries: Cudjoe (9, 23), Peteru (28), Yates (70), McGillvary (76); **Goals:** Russell 7/7.
Rugby Leaguer & League Express Men of the Match:
Tigers: Paul McShane; *Giants:* Leroy Cudjoe.
Penalty count: 4-6; **Half-time:** 6-20;
Referee: Tom Grant; **Attendance:** 5,126.

HULL FC 10 ST HELENS 42

HULL FC: 23 Connor Wynne; 2 Bureta Faraimo; 24 Cameron Scott; 5 Mahe Fonua; 21 Adam Swift; 6 Josh Reynolds; 7 Marc Sneyd (C); 10 Tevita Satae; 14 Jordan Johnstone; 13 Ligi Sao; 12 Manu Ma'u; 16 Jordan Lane; 15 Joe Cator. Subs (all used): 17 Brad Fash; 19 Ben McNamara; 20 Jack Brown; 27 Mitieli Vulikijapani.
Tries: Swift (36), Faraimo (45); **Goals:** Sneyd 1/2.
Sin bin: Sao (72) - high tackle on Coote.
SAINTS: 1 Lachlan Coote; 2 Tommy Makinson; 3 Kevin Naiqama; 4 Mark Percival; 18 Jack Welsby; 6 Jonny Lomax; 21 Lewis Dodd; 8 Alex Walmsley; 9 James Roby (C); 15 Louie McCarthy-Scarsbrook; 11 Joel Thompson; 20 Joe Batchelor; 13 Morgan Knowles. Subs (all used): 10 Matty Lees; 14 Sione Mata'utia; 16 Kyle Amor; 19 Aaron Smith.
Tries: Thompson (4), Makinson (14), Welsby (23, 74, 80), Amor (62), Naiqama (67); **Goals:** Coote 7/10.
Rugby Leaguer & League Express Men of the Match:
Hull FC: Brad Fash; *Saints:* Jack Welsby.
Penalty count: 7-7; **Half-time:** 4-16;
Referee: James Child; **Attendance:** 7,038.

HULL KINGSTON ROVERS 16 CATALANS DRAGONS 23

ROVERS: 1 Adam Quinlan; 2 Ben Crooks; 3 Greg Minikin; 4 Shaun Kenny-Dowall (C); 5 Ryan Hall; 11 Brad Takairangi; 7 Jordan Abdull; 16 George King; 9 Matt Parcell; 26 Will Maher; 12 Kane Linnett; 27 Luis Johnson; 13 Dean Hadley. Subs (all used): 8 Albert Vete; 14 Jez Litten; 15 George Lawler; 18 Matthew Storton.
Tries: Quinlan (53, 78); **Goals:** Abdull 4/4.
DRAGONS: 29 Sam Tomkins (C); 32 Romain Franco (D); 4 Dean Whare; 3 Samisoni Langi; 5 Fouad Yaha; 6 James Maloney; 7 Josh Drinkwater; 17 Mickael Goudemand; 14 Alrix Da Costa; 8 Gil Dudson; 15 Benjamin Jullien; 12 Mike McMeeken; 22 Joel Tomkins. Subs (all used): 1 Arthur Mourgue; 16 Paul Seguier; 27 Joe Chan; 28 Sam Kasiano.
Tries: Franco (39), Langi (42), S Tomkins (68);
Goals: Maloney 5/5; **Field goal:** Maloney (77).
Sin bin: S Tomkins (79) - professional foul.
Rugby Leaguer & League Express Men of the Match:
Rovers: Adam Quinlan; *Dragons:* Sam Tomkins.
Penalty count: 7-7; **Half-time:** 4-8;
Referee: Robert Hicks; **Attendance:** 6,347.

ROUND 18

Friday 6th August 2021

LEEDS RHINOS 18 CASTLEFORD TIGERS 32

RHINOS: 16 Richie Myler; 2 Tom Briscoe; 4 Konrad Hurrell; 3 Harry Newman; 5 Ash Handley (C); 15 Liam Sutcliffe; 6 Robert Lui; 19 King Vuniyayawa; 9 Kruise Leeming; 20 Bodene Thompson; 25 James Donaldson; 12 Rhyse Martin; 13 Zane Tetevano. Subs (all used): 17 Cameron Smith; 18 Tom Holroyd; 14 Brad Dwyer; 31 Morgan Gannon.
Tries: Lui (31), Handley (48), Dwyer (76); **Goals:** Martin 3/3.
TIGERS: 1 Niall Evalds; 2 Derrell Olpherts; 3 Peter Mata'utia; 25 Jordan Turner; 23 Greg Eden; 31 Gareth O'Brien; 7 Danny Richardson; 22 Daniel Smith; 9 Paul McShane (C); 10 Grant Millington; 11 Oliver Holmes; 21 Jesse Sene-Lefao; 13 Adam Milner. Subs (all used): 14 Nathan Massey; 17 Alex Foster; 24 Suaia Matagi; 38 Jimmy Keinhorst.
Tries: Eden (14, 72), Mata'utia (22), Turner (58), Keinhorst (79); **Goals:** Richardson 6/6.
Sin bin: Mata'utia (28) - dangerous challenge on Handley.
Rugby Leaguer & League Express Men of the Match:
Rhinos: Robert Lui; *Tigers:* Niall Evalds.
Penalty count: 9-3; **Half time:** 6-14;
Referee: Ben Thaler; **Attendance:** 10,838.

WIGAN WARRIORS 16 SALFORD RED DEVILS 6

WARRIORS: 31 Jackson Hastings; 28 Sam Halsall; 11 Willie Isa; 22 Jake Bibby; 5 Liam Marshall; 6 Jai Field; 20 Harry Smith; 17 Tony Clubb; 9 Sam Powell (C); 21 Ethan Havard; 27 Kai Pearce-Paul; 15 Morgan Smithies; 25 Joe Shorrocks. Subs (all used): 3 Zak Hardaker; 10 Joe Bullock; 13 John Bateman; 19 Liam Byrne.
Tries: Halsall (14), Powell (68); **Goals:** Smith 4/5.
Sin bin: Smithies (32) - fighting.
RED DEVILS: 6 Tui Lolohea; 22 Rhys Williams; 24 Matthew Costello; 23 Dan Sarginson; 5 Joe Burgess; 18 Chris Atkin; 7 Kevin Brown; 8 Lee Mossop (C); 9 Andy Ackers; 25 Jack Ormondroyd; 20 Harvey Livett; 13 Elijah Taylor; 14 Danny Addy. Subs (all used): 12 Pauli Pauli; 17 Josh Johnson; 33 Ata Hingano; 35 Ellis Robson (D).
Try: Burgess (25); **Goals:** Livett 1/2.
Sin bin: Johnson (32) - fighting;
Hingano (63) - high tackle on Hastings.
Rugby Leaguer & League Express Men of the Match:
Warriors: Jackson Hastings; *Red Devils:* Joe Burgess.
Penalty count: 10-6; **Half-time:** 4-6;
Referee: Tom Grant; **Attendance:** 9,431.

Saturday 7th August 2021

ST HELENS 34 CATALANS DRAGONS 12

SAINTS: 1 Lachlan Coote; 2 Tommy Makinson; 3 Kevin Naiqama; 4 Mark Percival; 5 Regan Grace; 6 Jonny Lomax; 21 Lewis Dodd; 8 Alex Walmsley; 9 James Roby (C); 15 Louie McCarthy-Scarsbrook; 11 Joel Thompson; 20 Joe Batchelor; 13 Morgan Knowles. Subs (all used): 14 Sione Mata'utia; 16 Kyle Amor; 17 Agnatius Paasi; 18 Jack Welsby.
Tries: Makinson (4), Dodd (8), Grace (17), Batchelor (51), Coote (70); **Goals:** Coote 7/7.
Sin bin: Mata'utia (53) - late challenge on Jullien.
DRAGONS: 1 Arthur Mourgue; 32 Romain Franco; 20 Matthieu Laguerre; 4 Dean Whare; 5 Fouad Yaha; 6 James Maloney (C); 31 Cesar Rouge (D); 8 Gil Dudson; 14 Alrix Da Costa; 17 Mickael Goudemand; 15 Benjamin Jullien; 12 Mike McMeeken; 22 Joel Tomkins. Subs (all used): 16 Paul Seguier; 21 Corentin Le Cam (D); 27 Joe Chan; 30 Jordan Dezaria.
Tries: Laguerre (22), Goudemand (55); **Goals:** Maloney 2/2.
Sin bin: Chan (35) - late challenge on Mata'utia.
Rugby Leaguer & League Express Men of the Match:
Saints: Lachlan Coote; *Dragons:* Matthieu Laguerre.
Penalty count: 5-8; **Half-time:** 20-6;
Referee: Liam Moore; **Attendance:** 7,758.

Sunday 8th August 2021

HUDDERSFIELD GIANTS 22 WAKEFIELD TRINITY 18

GIANTS: 31 Olly Ashall-Bott; 2 Jermaine McGillvary; 3 Jake Wardle; 21 Leroy Cudjoe (C); 24 Louis Senior; 23 Oliver Russell; 32 Will Pryce; 8 Luke Yates; 35 Nathan Peats; 20 Oliver Wilson; 13 Josh Jones; 17 Chris McQueen; 25 Owen Trout. Subs (all used): 15 Joe Greenwood; 27 Sam Wood; 28 Sam Hewitt; 34 Nathaniel Peteru.
Tries: Senior (18), Wood (37), McGillvary (49, 61), Jake Wardle (70); **Goals:** Russell 0/1, Pryce 1/4.
Sin bin: Russell (1) - professional foul.
TRINITY: 1 Max Jowitt; 18 Innes Senior; 4 Reece Lyne; 20 Joe Arundel; 2 Tom Johnstone; 6 Jacob Miller (C); 29 Ryan Hampshire; 8 David Fifita; 5 Liam Kay; 17 Chris Green; 11 Matty Ashurst; 12 Kelepi Tanginoa; 13 Joe Westerman. Subs (all used): 9 Kyle Wood; 10 Tinirau Arona; 15 Eddie Battye; 16 James Batchelor.
Tries: Lyne (3), Hampshire (5), Westerman (14);
Goals: Hampshire 3/3.
Rugby Leaguer & League Express Men of the Match:
Giants: Will Pryce; *Trinity:* Reece Lyne.
Penalty count: 6-4; **Half-time:** 10-18;
Referee: James Child; **Attendance:** 3,964.

LEIGH CENTURIONS 28 HULL KINGSTON ROVERS 34

CENTURIONS: 24 Keanan Brand; 2 Matty Russell; 3 Iain Thornley; 35 Jack Logan (D); 4 Junior Sa'u; 22 Craig Mullen; 7 Joe Mellor; 20 Adam Sidlow; 27 Josh Eaves; 15 Alex Gerrard; 11 Ben Hellewell; 28 Matthew Foster; 13 James Bell. Subs (all used): 9 Liam Hood (C); 10 Mark Ioane; 12 Jordan Thompson; 18 Matty Gee.
Tries: Sa'u (1, 59), Mullen (37), Sidlow (52, 64);
Goals: Mullen 4/5.
ROVERS: 2 Ben Crooks; 3 Greg Minikin; 11 Brad Takairangi; 4 Shaun Kenny-Dowall (C); 5 Ryan Hall; 20 Mikey Lewis; 25 Rowan Milnes; 16 George King; 9 Matt Parcell; 26 Will Maher; 12 Kane Linnett; 13 Dean Hadley; 10 Korbin Sims. Subs (all used): 8 Albert Vete; 14 Jez Litten; 15 George Lawler; 18 Matthew Storton.
Tries: Linnett (16), Minikin (19), Kenny-Dowall (23, 66), Lewis (32), Vete (45), Hall (73); **Goals:** Crooks 3/7.
Sin bin: Vete (51) - high tackle; Lawler (58) - high tackle.
Rugby Leaguer & League Express Men of the Match:
Centurions: Junior Sa'u; *Rovers:* Mikey Lewis.
Penalty count: 5-3; **Half-time:** 10-18;
Referee: Chris Kendall; **Attendance:** 2,941.

ROUND 19

Thursday 12th August 2021

ST HELENS 10 CASTLEFORD TIGERS 20

SAINTS: 1 Lachlan Coote; 2 Tommy Makinson; 3 Kevin Naiqama; 4 Mark Percival; 18 Jack Welsby; 6 Jonny Lomax; 21 Lewis Dodd; 8 Alex Walmsley; 9 James Roby (C); 10 Matty Lees; 11 Joel Thompson; 20 Joe Batchelor; 14 Sione Mata'utia. Subs (all used): 12 James Bentley; 15 Louie McCarthy-Scarsbrook; 16 Kyle Amor; 17 Agnatius Paasi.
Tries: Welsby (20), Walmsley (68); **Goals:** Coote 1/2.

Dismissal: Makinson (65) - late challenge on Evalds.
Sin bin: Bentley (63) - dangerous challenge on McShane.
TIGERS: 1 Niall Evalds; 2 Derrell Olpherts; 3 Peter Mata'utia; 25 Jordan Turner; 23 Greg Eden; 31 Gareth O'Brien; 7 Danny Richardson; 24 Suaia Matagi; 9 Paul McShane (C); 10 Grant Millington; 11 Oliver Holmes; 21 Jesse Sene-Lefao; 22 Daniel Smith. Subs (all used): 8 Liam Watts; 12 Cheyse Blair; 15 George Griffin; 19 Tyla Hepi.
Tries: Eden (36, 79), Holmes (52); **Goals:** Richardson 4/4.
Sin bin: Mata'utia (63) - retaliation.
Rugby Leaguer & League Express Men of the Match: *Saints:* Alex Walmsley; *Tigers:* Paul McShane.
Penalty count: 10-12; **Half-time:** 4-6;
Referee: Ben Thaler; **Attendance:** 7,050.

Friday 13th August 2021

CATALANS DRAGONS 31 HULL FC 16

DRAGONS: 29 Sam Tomkins (C); 2 Tom Davies; 3 Samisoni Langi; 4 Dean Whare; 5 Fouad Yaha; 6 James Maloney; 7 Josh Drinkwater; 8 Gil Dudson; 9 Michael Mcllorum; 10 Julian Bousquet; 21 Corentin Le Cam; 12 Mike McMeeken; 17 Mickael Goudemand. Subs (all used): 1 Arthur Mourgue; 27 Joe Chan; 28 Sam Kasiano; 30 Jordan Dezaria.
Tries: Davies (5, 24), Yaha (44), S Tomkins (70), Bousquet (73); **Goals:** Maloney 5/6;
Field goal: Maloney (68).
HULL FC: 21 Adam Swift; 2 Bureta Faraimo; 32 Marcus Walker (D); 3 Carlos Tuimavave; 24 Cameron Scott; 6 Josh Reynolds; 19 Ben McNamara; 17 Brad Fash; 9 Danny Houghton (C); 13 Ligi Sao; 12 Manu Ma'u; 16 Jordan Lane; 15 Joe Cator. Subs: 8 Scott Taylor; 20 Jack Brown; 22 Josh Bowden; 33 Jacob Hookem (not used).
Tries: Tuimavave (15), Faraimo (35); **Goals:** McNamara 4/5.
Sin bin: Tuimavave (33) - high tackle on Le Cam.
Rugby Leaguer & League Express Men of the Match: *Dragons:* James Maloney; *Hull FC:* Ben McNamara.
Penalty count: 8-5; **Half-time:** 10-14;
Referee: James Child; **Attendance:** 7,129.

SALFORD RED DEVILS 18 HUDDERSFIELD GIANTS 12

RED DEVILS: 6 Tui Lolohea; 22 Rhys Williams; 4 Krisnan Inu; 24 Matthew Costello; 5 Joe Burgess; 18 Chris Atkin; 7 Kevin Brown (C); 17 Josh Johnson; 9 Andy Ackers; 25 Jack Ormondroyd; 20 Harvey Livett; 21 James Greenwood; 16 Greg Burke. Subs (all used): 27 Sam Luckley; 32 Dan Norman; 14 Danny Addy; 35 Ellis Robson.
Tries: Williams (36), Lolohea (42), Ormondroyd (57);
Goals: Inu 3/4.
Sin bin: Burke (79) - fighting.
GIANTS: 1 Ashton Golding; 4 Ricky Leutele; 3 Jake Wardle; 21 Leroy Cudjoe (C); 24 Louis Senior; 16 Jack Cogger; 32 Will Pryce; 25 Owen Trout; 35 Nathan Peats; 20 Oliver Wilson; 15 Joe Greenwood; 13 Josh Jones; 8 Luke Yates. Subs (all used): 14 Matty English; 27 Sam Wood; 28 Sam Hewitt; 34 Nathaniel Peteru.
Try: English (23); **Goals:** Pryce 4/4.
Sin bin: Cudjoe (79) - fighting.
Rugby Leaguer & League Express Men of the Match: *Red Devils:* Harvey Livett; *Giants:* Will Pryce.
Penalty count: 5-8; **Half-time:** 6-8;
Referee: Chris Kendall; **Attendance:** 3,066.

HULL KINGSTON ROVERS 26 WIGAN WARRIORS 14

ROVERS: 2 Ben Crooks; 23 Ethan Ryan; 3 Greg Minikin; 4 Shaun Kenny-Dowall (C); 5 Ryan Hall; 11 Brad Takairangi; 25 Rowan Milnes; 8 Albert Vete; 9 Matt Parcell; 16 George King; 12 Kane Linnett; 27 Luis Johnson; 15 George Lawler. Subs (all used): 10 Korbin Sims; 14 Jez Litten; 18 Matthew Storton; 26 Will Maher.
Tries: Vete (6), Milnes (11), Ryan (17), Linnett (56), Litten (59); **Goals:** Crooks 3/5.
Sin bin: Takairangi (80) - professional foul; Parcell (80) - fighting.
WARRIORS: 3 Zak Hardaker; 22 Jake Bibby; 11 Willie Isa; 4 Oliver Gildart; 5 Liam Marshall; 20 Harry Smith; 31 Jackson Hastings; 17 Tony Clubb; 9 Sam Powell (C); 21 Ethan Havard; 12 Liam Farrell; 27 Kai Pearce-Paul; 15 Morgan Smithies. Subs (all used): 6 Jai Field; 10 Joe Bullock; 19 Liam Byrne; 25 Joe Shorrocks.
Tries: Bibby (24), Marshall (28, 38); **Goals:** Smith 1/3.
Sin bin: Farrell (80) - fighting.
Rugby Leaguer & League Express Men of the Match: *Rovers:* Shaun Kenny-Dowall; *Warriors:* Harry Smith.
Penalty count: 5-6; **Half-time:** 16-14;
Referee: Liam Moore; **Attendance:** 6,230.

LEIGH CENTURIONS 10 LEEDS RHINOS 46

CENTURIONS: 24 Keanan Brand; 2 Matty Russell; 3 Iain Thornley; 35 Jack Logan; 4 Junior Sa'u; 22 Craig Mullen; 7 Joe Mellor (C); 12 Jordan Thompson; 27 Josh Eaves; 15 Alex Gerrard; 11 Ben Hellewell; 28 Matthew Foster; 13 James Bell. Subs (all used): 8 Ben Flower; 10 Mark Ioane; 17 Jamie Ellis; 18 Matty Gee.
Tries: Gee (25, 56); **Goals:** Mullen 1/2.
RHINOS: 16 Richie Myler; 2 Tom Briscoe; 3 Harry Newman; 4 Konrad Hurrell; 5 Ash Handley (C); 6 Robert Lui; 7 Luke Gale; 20 Bodene Thompson; 9 Kruise Leeming; 13 Zane Tetevano; 31 Morgan Gannon; 12 Rhyse Martin; 26 Jarrod O'Connor. Subs (all used): 14 Brad Dwyer; 17 Cameron Smith; 18 Tom Holroyd; 24 Luke Briscoe.
Tries: Tetevano (10), T Briscoe (19, 45), Smith (48), Lui (71), Dwyer (73), Handley (78), Leeming (80);
Goals: Martin 7/9.
On report:
Tetevano (28) - alleged dangerous challenge on Russell.
Rugby Leaguer & League Express Men of the Match: *Centurions:* James Bell; *Rhinos:* Brad Dwyer.
Penalty count: 7-7; **Half-time:** 6-10;
Referee: Robert Hicks; **Attendance:** 2,818.

Sunday 15th August 2021

WAKEFIELD TRINITY 28 WARRINGTON WOLVES 22

TRINITY: 1 Max Jowitt; 27 Lee Kershaw; 20 Joe Arundel; 18 Innes Senior; 2 Tom Johnstone; 6 Jacob Miller (C); 7 Mason Lino; 10 Tinirau Arona; 25 Brad Walker; 12 Kelepi Tanginoa; 14 Jay Pitts; 11 Matty Ashurst; 13 Joe Westerman. Subs (all used): 8 David Fifita; 5 Liam Kay; 15 Eddie Battye; 26 Yusuf Aydin.
Tries: Johnstone (11), Fifita (23), Lino (48), Kershaw (62);
Goals: Lino 6/6.
WOLVES: 1 Stefan Ratchford; 2 Tom Lineham; 18 Jake Mamo; 27 Connor Wrench; 5 Josh Charnley; 7 Gareth Widdop; 31 George Williams; 8 Chris Hill; 16 Danny Walker; 10 Mike Cooper (C); 11 Ben Currie; 4 Toby King; 15 Matt Davis. Subs: 6 Blake Austin; 20 Sitaleki Akauola; 17 Matty Ashton; 30 Morgan Burgess (not used).
Tries: Williams (57), Austin (67), Mamo (70), Charnley (72);
Goals: Ratchford 3/4.
Rugby Leaguer & League Express Men of the Match: *Trinity:* Jacob Miller; *Wolves:* Danny Walker.
Penalty count: 7-5; **Half-time:** 12-0;
Referee: Marcus Griffiths; **Attendance:** 3,445.

ROUND 20

Thursday 19th August 2021

LEEDS RHINOS 18 HUDDERSFIELD GIANTS 12

RHINOS: 16 Richie Myler; 24 Luke Briscoe; 3 Harry Newman; 2 Tom Briscoe; 5 Ash Handley (C); 23 Callum McLelland; 6 Robert Lui; 13 Zane Tetevano; 9 Kruise Leeming; 20 Bodene Thompson; 25 James Donaldson; 26 Jarrod O'Connor; 31 Morgan Gannon. Subs (all used): 14 Brad Dwyer; 18 Tom Holroyd; 19 King Vuniyayawa; 22 Sam Walters.
Tries: Handley (16), Myler (35), Lui (59);
Goals: Handley 1/2, Newman 2/3.
Sin bin: Tetevano (72) - late challenge on Russell.
GIANTS: 1 Ashton Golding; 21 Leroy Cudjoe (C); 3 Jake Wardle; 27 Sam Wood; 24 Louis Senior; 16 Jack Cogger; 32 Will Pryce; 25 Owen Trout; 35 Nathan Peats; 20 Oliver Wilson; 13 Josh Jones; 15 Joe Greenwood; 8 Luke Yates. Subs (all used): 14 Matty English; 23 Oliver Russell; 28 Sam Hewitt; 34 Nathaniel Peteru.
Tries: Pryce (24), Wood (73), Trout (79);
Goals: Pryce 0/2 *(last conversion attempt not taken)*.
Rugby Leaguer & League Express Men of the Match: *Rhinos:* Kruise Leeming; *Giants:* Owen Trout.
Penalty count: 7-8; **Half time:** 10-4;
Referee: Ben Thaler; **Attendance:** 11,110.

Friday 20th August 2021

WIGAN WARRIORS 2 ST HELENS 26

WARRIORS: 3 Zak Hardaker; 22 Jake Bibby; 11 Willie Isa; 4 Oliver Gildart; 5 Liam Marshall; 20 Harry Smith; 31 Jackson Hastings; 21 Ethan Havard; 25 Joe Shorrocks; 14 Oliver Partington; 12 Liam Farrell (C); 27 Kai Pearce-Paul; 15 Morgan Smithies. Subs (all used): 10 Joe Bullock; 13 John Bateman; 19 Liam Byrne; 33 Amir Bourouh.
Goals: Smith 1/1.
Sin bin: Bateman (16) - retaliation, (51) - dissent; Isa (62) - high tackle on McCarthy-Scarsbrook.
On report: Isa (55) - alleged late challenge on Welsby.
SAINTS: 1 Lachlan Coote; 5 Regan Grace; 3 Kevin Naiqama; 4 Mark Percival; 18 Jack Welsby; 6 Jonny Lomax; 21 Lewis Dodd; 8 Alex Walmsley; 9 James Roby (C); 10 Matty Lees; 11 Joel Thompson; 12 James Bentley; 13 Morgan Knowles. Subs (all used): 15 Louie McCarthy-Scarsbrook; 17 Agnatius Paasi; 19 Aaron Smith; 20 Joe Batchelor.
Tries: Grace (9), Dodd (20), Percival (63), Walmsley (80);
Goals: Coote 4/6, Dodd 1/1.
Sin bin: Bentley (16) - kicking Bateman.
Rugby Leaguer & League Express Men of the Match: *Warriors:* Oliver Gildart; *Saints:* Lewis Dodd.
Penalty count: 4-9; **Half-time:** 2-12;
Referee: Chris Kendall; **Attendance:** 16,319.

Saturday 21st August 2021

HULL FC 23 HULL KINGSTON ROVERS 22

HULL FC: 1 Jake Connor; 21 Adam Swift; 24 Cameron Scott; 3 Carlos Tuimavave; 2 Bureta Faraimo; 6 Josh Reynolds; 7 Marc Sneyd; 13 Ligi Sao; 9 Danny Houghton (C); 17 Brad Fash; 12 Manu Ma'u; 11 Andre Savelio; 16 Jordan Lane. Subs (all used): 8 Scott Taylor; 15 Joe Cator; 20 Jack Brown; 29 Jamie Shaul.
Tries: Swift (3), Faraimo (35, 49), Tuimavave (39);
Goals: Sneyd 3/5; **Field goal:** Sneyd (74).
ROVERS: 2 Ben Crooks; 33 Jimmy Keinhorst; 3 Greg Minikin; 4 Shaun Kenny-Dowall (C); 5 Ryan Hall; 11 Brad Takairangi; 25 Rowan Milnes; 8 Albert Vete; 9 Matt Parcell; 16 George King; 12 Kane Linnett; 27 Luis Johnson; 15 George Lawler. Subs (all used): 10 Korbin Sims; 14 Jez Litten; 18 Matthew Storton; 26 Will Maher.
Tries: Keinhorst (19), Milnes (31), Crooks (45), Vete (75);
Goals: Crooks 3/4.
Rugby Leaguer & League Express Men of the Match: *Hull FC:* Jake Connor; *Rovers:* Rowan Milnes.
Penalty count: 5-2; **Half-time:** 16-10;
Referee: Liam Moore; **Attendance:** 13,709.

CASTLEFORD TIGERS 23 WAKEFIELD TRINITY 18

TIGERS: 1 Niall Evalds; 2 Derrell Olpherts; 3 Peter Mata'utia; 25 Jordan Turner; 23 Greg Eden; 31 Gareth O'Brien; 7 Danny Richardson; 15 George Griffin; 9 Paul McShane (C); 10 Grant Millington; 11 Oliver Holmes; 21 Jesse Sene-Lefao; 14 Nathan Massey. Subs (all used): 8 Liam Watts; 12 Cheyse Blair; 19 Tyla Hepi; 24 Suaia Matagi.
Tries: Eden (8, 47), Holmes (11), Olpherts (33);
Goals: Richardson 3/4, O'Brien 0/1;
Field goal: Richardson (40).
Sin bin: Richardson (27) - fighting.
TRINITY: 1 Max Jowitt; 27 Lee Kershaw; 20 Joe Arundel; 18 Innes Senior; 2 Tom Johnstone; 6 Jacob Miller (C); 7 Mason Lino; 8 David Fifita; 25 Brad Walker; 10 Tinirau Arona; 11 Matty Ashurst; 14 Jay Pitts; 12 Kelepi Tanginoa. Subs (all used): 5 Liam Kay; 15 Eddie Battye; 16 James Batchelor; 17 Chris Green.
Tries: Arona (15), Johnstone (61), Kershaw (75);
Goals: Lino 3/3.
Sin bin: Lino (27) - fighting.
Rugby Leaguer & League Express Men of the Match: *Tigers:* Danny Richardson; *Trinity:* Lee Kershaw.
Penalty count: 7-7; **Half-time:** 19-6;
Referee: James Child; **Attendance:** 4,987.

Sunday 22nd August 2021

LEIGH CENTURIONS 32 SALFORD RED DEVILS 22

CENTURIONS: 24 Keanan Brand; 25 Brendan Elliot; 36 Sam Stone (D); 3 Iain Thornley; 22 Craig Mullen; 13 James Bell; 7 Joe Mellor; 34 Jack Ashworth; 27 Josh Eaves; 20 Adam Sidlow; 11 Ben Hellewell; 28 Matthew Foster; 15 Alex Gerrard. Subs (all used): 9 Liam Hood (C); 33 Rob Butler; 10 Mark Ioane; 18 Matty Gee.
Tries: Mellor (19), Brand (23), Hood (74), Sidlow (77);
Goals: Mullen 8/9.
RED DEVILS: 6 Tui Lolohea; 2 Ken Sio; 4 Krisnan Inu; 23 Dan Sarginson; 22 Rhys Williams; 33 Ata Hingano; 7 Kevin Brown (C); 17 Josh Johnson; 9 Andy Ackers; 25 Jack Ormondroyd; 20 Harvey Livett; 21 James Greenwood; 14 Danny Addy. Subs (all used): 11 Ryan Lannon; 13 Elijah Taylor; 16 Greg Burke; 32 Dan Norman.
Tries: Williams (2), Livett (30), Sio (46, 80); **Goals:** Inu 3/5.
Rugby Leaguer & League Express Men of the Match: *Centurions:* Joe Mellor; *Red Devils:* Tui Lolohea.
Penalty count: 11-5; **Half-time:** 14-10;
Referee: Marcus Griffiths; **Attendance:** 3,304.

ROUND 21

Wednesday 25th August 2021

WIGAN WARRIORS 0 LEEDS RHINOS 14

WARRIORS: 6 Jai Field; 22 Jake Bibby; 3 Zak Hardaker; 4 Oliver Gildart; 5 Liam Marshall; 20 Harry Smith; 31 Jackson Hastings; 8 Brad Singleton; 25 Joe Shorrocks; 14 Oliver Partington; 12 Liam Farrell (C); 13 John Bateman; 15 Morgan Smithies. Subs (all used): 19 Liam Byrne; 21 Ethan Havard; 27 Kai Pearce-Paul; 33 Amir Bourouh.
RHINOS: 16 Richie Myler; 24 Luke Briscoe; 3 Harry Newman; 2 Tom Briscoe; 5 Ash Handley; 6 Robert Lui; 9 Kruise Leeming; 20 Bodene Thompson; 14 Brad Dwyer; 10 Matt Prior (C); 31 Morgan Gannon; 12 Rhyse Martin; 13 Zane Tetevano. Subs (all used): 17 Cameron Smith; 18 Tom Holroyd; 19 King Vuniyayawa; 25 James Donaldson.
Tries: Dwyer (37), Myler (46); **Goals:** Martin 3/3.
Sin bin: Tetevano (22) - high tackle on Farrell; L Briscoe (31) - professional foul.

Rugby Leaguer & League Express Men of the Match: *Warriors:* Jackson Hastings; *Rhinos:* Kruise Leeming.
Penalty count: 8-7; **Half-time:** 0-6;
Referee: Robert Hicks; **Attendance:** 11,390.

Thursday 26th August 2021

SALFORD RED DEVILS 14 CATALANS DRAGONS 42

RED DEVILS: 1 Morgan Escare; 2 Ken Sio; 4 Krisnan Inu; 23 Dan Sarginson; 22 Rhys Williams; 6 Tui Lolohea; 18 Chris Atkin; 25 Jack Ormondroyd; 9 Andy Ackers; 17 Josh Johnson; 20 Harvey Livett; 11 Ryan Lannon; 16 Greg Burke (C). Subs (all used): 14 Danny Addy; 15 Oliver Roberts; 27 Sam Luckley; 35 Ellis Robson.
Tries: Livett (37), Sarginson (43), Escare (72); **Goals:** Inu 1/3.
DRAGONS: 29 Sam Tomkins (C); 2 Tom Davies; 20 Matthieu Laguerre; 3 Samisoni Langi; 5 Fouad Yaha; 6 James Maloney; 7 Josh Drinkwater; 10 Julian Bousquet; 9 Michael McIlorum; 30 Jordan Dezaria; 15 Benjamin Jullien; 12 Mike McMeeken; 17 Mickael Goudemand. Subs (all used): 1 Arthur Mourgue; 23 Mathieu Cozza (D); 27 Joe Chan; 28 Sam Kasiano.
Tries: Jullien (10, 26), Goudemand (29), Kasiano (39), Davies (57), Chan (66), Langi (79); **Goals:** Maloney 7/8.
Sin bin: McIlorum (46) - high tackle on Lannon.
Rugby Leaguer & League Express Men of the Match: *Red Devils:* Morgan Escare; *Dragons:* Sam Tomkins.
Penalty count: 8-7; **Half-time:** 6-22;
Referee: Liam Moore; **Attendance:** 2,742.

HUDDERSFIELD GIANTS 6 WARRINGTON WOLVES 26

GIANTS: 1 Ashton Golding; 2 Jermaine McGillvary; 3 Jake Wardle; 4 Ricky Leutele; 21 Leroy Cudjoe (C); 32 Will Pryce; 16 Jack Cogger; 15 Joe Greenwood; 35 Nathan Peats; 25 Owen Trout; 13 Josh Jones; 17 Chris McQueen; 8 Luke Yates. Subs (all used): 14 Matty English; 23 Oliver Russell; 27 Sam Wood; 34 Nathaniel Peteru.
Try: Jake Wardle (72); **Goals:** Russell 1/1.
Sin bin: McQueen (39) - professional foul.
WOLVES: 1 Stefan Ratchford; 2 Tom Lineham; 18 Jake Mamo; 4 Toby King; 23 Josh Thewlis; 31 George Williams; 7 Gareth Widdop; 8 Chris Hill; 9 Daryl Clark; 10 Mike Cooper; 11 Ben Currie; 12 Jack Hughes (C); 13 Joe Philbin. Subs (all used): 15 Matt Davis; 17 Matty Ashton; 19 Robbie Mulhern; 20 Sitaleki Akauola.
Tries: Mamo (17, 28), Cooper (68), King (78);
Goals: Ratchford 5/5.
Rugby Leaguer & League Express Men of the Match: *Giants:* Luke Yates; *Wolves:* Jake Mamo.
Penalty count: 5-6; **Half-time:** 0-14;
Referee: James Child; **Attendance:** 4,017.

HULL FC 12 CASTLEFORD TIGERS 23

HULL FC: 1 Jake Connor; 21 Adam Swift; 24 Cameron Scott; 3 Carlos Tuimavave; 2 Bureta Faraimo; 19 Ben McNamara; 7 Marc Sneyd (C); 13 Ligi Sao; 9 Danny Houghton; 8 Scott Taylor; 12 Manu Ma'u; 11 Andre Savelio; 16 Jordan Lane. Subs (all used): 5 Mahe Fonua; 10 Tevita Satae; 14 Jordan Johnstone; 17 Brad Fash.
Tries: Swift (11), Connor (63); **Goals:** Sneyd 2/2.
Sin bin: Taylor (79) - fighting.
TIGERS: 1 Niall Evalds; 2 Derrell Olpherts; 3 Peter Mata'utia; 25 Jordan Turner; 23 Greg Eden; 7 Danny Richardson; 31 Gareth O'Brien; 15 George Griffin; 9 Paul McShane (C); 22 Daniel Smith; 17 Alex Foster; 12 Cheyse Blair; 14 Nathan Massey. Subs (all used): 8 Liam Watts; 11 Oliver Holmes; 13 Adam Milner; 24 Suaia Matagi.
Tries: Turner (3, 37), Richardson (60), Evalds (75);
Goals: Richardson 3/5; **Field goal:** Richardson (30).
Sin bin: Watts (26) - trip on Lane; Griffin (79) - fighting.
Rugby Leaguer & League Express Men of the Match: *Hull FC:* Manu Ma'u; *Tigers:* Adam Milner.
Penalty count: 7-5; **Half-time:** 6-13;
Referee: Ben Thaler; **Attendance:** 8,121.

HULL KINGSTON ROVERS 18 WAKEFIELD TRINITY 25

ROVERS: 2 Ben Crooks; 33 Jimmy Keinhorst; 3 Greg Minikin; 4 Shaun Kenny-Dowall (C); 5 Ryan Hall; 11 Brad Takairangi; 20 Mikey Lewis; 8 Albert Vete; 9 Matt Parcell; 16 George King; 12 Kane Linnett; 27 Luis Johnson; 13 Dean Hadley. Subs (all used): 14 Jez Litten; 15 George Lawler; 26 Will Maher; 28 Muizz Mustapha.
Tries: Johnson (4), Lawler (24), Crooks (62);
Goals: Crooks 3/4.
TRINITY: 29 Ryan Hampshire; 27 Lee Kershaw; 18 Innes Senior; 16 James Batchelor; 2 Tom Johnstone; 6 Jacob Miller (C); 7 Mason Lino; 12 Kelepi Tanginoa; 5 Liam Kay; 13 Joe Westerman; 14 Jay Pitts; 11 Matty Ashurst; 19 Jordan Crowther. Subs (all used): 8 David Fifita; 9 Kyle Wood; 15 Eddie Battye; 26 Yusuf Aydin.
Tries: Miller (30), Hampshire (37), Senior (54), Pitts (56);
Goals: Lino 4/4; **Field goal:** Miller (78).

Rugby Leaguer & League Express Men of the Match: *Rovers:* Matt Parcell; *Trinity:* Kelepi Tanginoa.
Penalty count: 14-4; **Half-time:** 10-12;
Referee: Marcus Griffiths; **Attendance:** 6,439.

ST HELENS 42 LEIGH CENTURIONS 12

SAINTS: 1 Lachlan Coote; 3 Kevin Naiqama; 22 Josh Simm; 18 Jack Welsby; 5 Regan Grace; 6 Jonny Lomax; 21 Lewis Dodd; 8 Alex Walmsley; 19 Aaron Smith; 10 Matty Lees; 14 Sione Mata'utia; 20 Joe Batchelor; 13 Morgan Knowles. Subs (all used): 9 James Roby (C); 16 Kyle Amor; 17 Agnatius Paasi; 23 Jake Wingfield.
Tries: Grace (4), Welsby (30, 47), Mata'utia (59), Coote (65), Batchelor (72), Dodd (77); **Goals:** Coote 7/8.
CENTURIONS: 24 Keanan Brand; 25 Brendan Elliot; 36 Sam Stone; 4 Junior Sa'u; 2 Matty Russell; 1 Ryan Brierley; 7 Joe Mellor; 20 Adam Sidlow; 9 Liam Hood (C); 15 Alex Gerrard; 11 Ben Hellewell; 18 Matty Gee; 13 James Bell. Subs (all used): 12 Jordan Thompson; 22 Craig Mullen; 33 Rob Butler; 34 Jack Ashworth.
Tries: Gee (25), Sidlow (55); **Goals:** Brierley 2/2.
Rugby Leaguer & League Express Men of the Match: *Saints:* Jack Welsby; *Centurions:* Keanan Brand.
Penalty count: 5-3; **Half-time:** 12-6;
Referee: Tom Grant; **Attendance:** 8,221.

ROUND 22

Monday 30th August 2021

SALFORD RED DEVILS 42 HULL FC 14

RED DEVILS: 1 Morgan Escare; 2 Ken Sio; 4 Krisnan Inu; 23 Dan Sarginson; 5 Joe Burgess; 6 Tui Lolohea; 33 Ata Hingano; 25 Jack Ormondroyd; 18 Chris Atkin; 17 Josh Johnson; 20 Harvey Livett; 35 Ellis Robson; 16 Greg Burke (C). Subs (all used): 27 Sam Luckley; 15 Oliver Roberts; 11 Ryan Lannon; 14 Danny Addy.
Tries: Sio (13, 36, 72, 79), Atkin (58), Livett (67), Burgess (70); **Goals:** Inu 7/7.
HULL FC: 1 Jake Connor; 21 Adam Swift; 24 Cameron Scott; 23 Connor Wynne; 2 Bureta Faraimo; 19 Ben McNamara; 7 Marc Sneyd (C); 13 Ligi Sao; 9 Danny Houghton; 10 Tevita Satae; 12 Manu Ma'u; 11 Andre Savelio; 16 Jordan Lane. Subs (all used): 5 Mahe Fonua; 14 Jordan Johnstone; 17 Brad Fash; 22 Josh Bowden.
Tries: Sao (4), Houghton (49); **Goals:** Sneyd 3/3.
Rugby Leaguer & League Express Men of the Match: *Red Devils:* Ken Sio; *Hull FC:* Jordan Lane.
Penalty count: 6-4; **Half-time:** 12-8;
Referee: Scott Mikalauskas; **Attendance:** 3,297.

WAKEFIELD TRINITY 20 LEEDS RHINOS 13

TRINITY: 29 Ryan Hampshire; 27 Lee Kershaw; 20 Joe Arundel; 18 Innes Senior; 2 Tom Johnstone; 6 Jacob Miller (C); 7 Mason Lino; 15 Eddie Battye; 5 Liam Kay; 17 Chris Green; 14 Jay Pitts; 12 Kelepi Tanginoa; 19 Jordan Crowther. Subs (all used): 8 David Fifita; 9 Kyle Wood; 16 James Batchelor; 26 Yusuf Aydin.
Tries: Tanginoa (32), Crowther (53), Arundel (79);
Goals: Lino 3/3; **Field goals:** Miller (69), Hampshire (74).
Sin bin: Green (65) - fighting.
RHINOS: 16 Richie Myler; 24 Luke Briscoe; 3 Harry Newman; 2 Tom Briscoe; 5 Ash Handley; 6 Robert Lui; 9 Kruise Leeming; 10 Matt Prior (C); 14 Brad Dwyer; 20 Bodene Thompson; 12 Rhyse Martin; 25 James Donaldson; 13 Zane Tetevano. Subs (all used): 19 King Vuniyayawa; 23 Callum McLelland; 18 Tom Holroyd; 17 Cameron Smith.
Tries: Leeming (15), Dwyer (37); **Goals:** Martin 2/2;
Field goal: Lui (72).
Sin bin: Prior (5) - high tackle, (65) - fighting.
Rugby Leaguer & League Express Men of the Match: *Trinity:* Jacob Miller; *Rhinos:* Kruise Leeming.
Penalty count: 7-3; **Half-time:** 6-12;
Referee: Chris Kendall; **Attendance:** 5,420.

CASTLEFORD TIGERS 0 WIGAN WARRIORS 22

TIGERS: 1 Niall Evalds; 2 Derrell Olpherts; 3 Peter Mata'utia; 4 Michael Shenton (C); 25 Jordan Turner; 31 Gareth O'Brien; 7 Danny Richardson; 8 Liam Watts; 13 Adam Milner; 10 Grant Millington; 11 Oliver Holmes; 21 Jesse Sene-Lefao; 14 Nathan Massey. Subs (all used): 15 George Griffin; 17 Alex Foster; 23 Greg Eden; 24 Suaia Matagi.
Sin bin: Sene-Lefao (40) - high tackle.
WARRIORS: 3 Zak Hardaker; 28 Sam Halsall; 22 Jake Bibby; 4 Oliver Gildart; 5 Liam Marshall; 20 Harry Smith; 31 Jackson Hastings; 8 Brad Singleton; 25 Joe Shorrocks; 14 Oliver Partington; 12 Liam Farrell (C); 13 John Bateman; 15 Morgan Smithies. Subs (all used): 10 Joe Bullock; 19 Liam Byrne; 27 Kai Pearce-Paul; 34 Brad O'Neill.
Tries: Hastings (14), Marshall (60), Gildart (68), Singleton (80); **Goals:** Smith 2/4, Hastings 1/2.
Sin bin: Byrne (41) - dangerous challenge.

Rugby Leaguer & League Express Men of the Match: *Tigers:* Suaia Matagi; *Warriors:* Harry Smith.
Penalty count: 11-8; **Half-time:** 0-6;
Referee: James Child; **Attendance:** 4,729.

CATALANS DRAGONS 64 LEIGH CENTURIONS 0

DRAGONS: 29 Sam Tomkins (C); 2 Tom Davies; 20 Matthieu Laguerre; 3 Samisoni Langi; 5 Fouad Yaha; 6 James Maloney; 7 Josh Drinkwater; 10 Julian Bousquet; 9 Michael McIlorum; 30 Jordan Dezaria; 21 Corentin Le Cam; 12 Mike McMeeken; 17 Mickael Goudemand. Subs (all used): 1 Arthur Mourgue; 22 Joel Tomkins; 23 Mathieu Cozza; 27 Joe Chan.
Tries: McMeeken (2, 11, 36), Yaha (6, 21, 33), Maloney (17), J Tomkins (51), S Tomkins (59, 62), Davies (75);
Goals: Maloney 10/11.
CENTURIONS: 24 Keanan Brand; 25 Brendan Elliot; 4 Junior Sa'u; 35 Jack Logan; 38 Tom Nisbet (D); 1 Ryan Brierley; 7 Joe Mellor (C); 19 Nathan Mason; 27 Josh Eaves; 33 Rob Butler; 11 Ben Hellewell; 28 Matthew Foster; 12 Jordan Thompson. Subs (all used): 15 Alex Gerrard; 22 Craig Mullen; 23 Tom Spencer; 37 Jai Whitbread (D).
Rugby Leaguer & League Express Men of the Match: *Dragons:* Mike McMeeken; *Centurions:* Ryan Brierley.
Penalty count: 7-5; **Half-time:** 40-0;
Referee: Aaron Moore; **Attendance:** 6,512.

HUDDERSFIELD GIANTS 40
HULL KINGSTON ROVERS 28

GIANTS: 31 Olly Ashall-Bott; 21 Leroy Cudjoe; 3 Jake Wardle; 4 Ricky Leutele; 27 Sam Wood; 32 Will Pryce; 23 Oliver Russell; 10 Michael Lawrence (C); 35 Nathan Peats; 15 Joe Greenwood; 13 Josh Jones; 17 Chris McQueen; 8 Luke Yates. Subs (all used): 14 Matty English; 16 Jack Cogger; 28 Sam Hewitt; 34 Nathaniel Peteru.
Tries: Russell (16), Jones (20), Leutele (33), Wood (37), Pryce (54), Greenwood (65), Peteru (74);
Goals: Pryce 6/7.
ROVERS: 2 Ben Crooks; 3 Greg Minikin; 11 Brad Takairangi; 4 Shaun Kenny-Dowall (C); 5 Ryan Hall; 20 Mikey Lewis; 25 Rowan Milnes; 8 Albert Vete; 14 Jez Litten; 16 George King; 12 Kane Linnett; 27 Luis Johnson; 15 George Lawler. Subs (all used): 9 Matt Parcell; 18 Matthew Storton; 26 Will Maher; 28 Muizz Mustapha.
Tries: Lewis (6), Linnett (29, 69), Minikin (39), Hall (47), Parcell (78); **Goals:** Milnes 2/6.
Rugby Leaguer & League Express Men of the Match: *Giants:* Will Pryce; *Rovers:* Rowan Milnes.
Penalty count: 5-9; **Half-time:** 22-12;
Referee: Robert Hicks; **Attendance:** 3,652.

WARRINGTON WOLVES 14 ST HELENS 24

WOLVES: 1 Stefan Ratchford; 2 Tom Lineham; 18 Jake Mamo; 4 Toby King; 23 Josh Thewlis; 31 George Williams; 7 Gareth Widdop; 8 Chris Hill; 9 Daryl Clark; 13 Joe Philbin; 11 Ben Currie; 12 Jack Hughes (C); 14 Jason Clark. Subs (all used): 16 Danny Walker; 19 Robbie Mulhern; 20 Sitaleki Akauola; 26 Ellis Longstaff.
Tries: Currie (33), Williams (37); **Goals:** Ratchford 3/4.
Sin bin: Lineham (74) - high tackle; Widdop (80) - fighting.
SAINTS: 1 Lachlan Coote; 2 Tommy Makinson; 3 Kevin Naiqama; 4 Mark Percival; 5 Regan Grace; 18 Jack Welsby; 21 Lewis Dodd; 8 Alex Walmsley; 9 James Roby (C); 10 Matty Lees; 14 Sione Mata'utia; 12 James Bentley; 13 Morgan Knowles. Subs: 15 Louie McCarthy-Scarsbrook; 17 Agnatius Paasi; 20 Joe Batchelor; 23 Jake Wingfield (not used).
Tries: Naiqama (16), Dodd (20), Percival (49), Bentley (58);
Goals: Coote 4/5.
Sin bin: Bentley (80) - fighting.
Rugby Leaguer & League Express Men of the Match: *Wolves:* George Williams; *Saints:* Lewis Dodd.
Penalty count: 5-9; **Half-time:** 14-10;
Referee: Liam Moore; **Attendance:** 10,006.

ROUND 23 - MAGIC WEEKEND

Saturday 4th September 2021

CASTLEFORD TIGERS 29 SALFORD RED DEVILS 18

TIGERS: 1 Niall Evalds; 2 Derrell Olpherts; 12 Cheyse Blair; 4 Michael Shenton (C); 20 James Clare; 25 Jordan Turner; 3 Peter Mata'utia; 15 George Griffin; 9 Paul McShane; 22 Daniel Smith; 11 Oliver Holmes; 21 Jesse Sene-Lefao; 14 Nathan Massey. Subs (all used): 13 Adam Milner; 17 Alex Foster; 19 Tyla Hepi; 24 Suaia Matagi.
Tries: McShane (8), Smith (18), Holmes (38), Turner (50), Mata'utia (73); **Goals:** Mata'utia 4/5;
Field goal: Turner (80).
RED DEVILS: 1 Morgan Escare; 2 Ken Sio; 4 Krisnan Inu; 23 Dan Sarginson; 5 Joe Burgess; 6 Tui Lolohea; 33 Ata Hingano; 17 Josh Johnson; 18 Chris Atkin; 16 Greg Burke; 15 Oliver Roberts; 35 Ellis Robson; 7 Kevin Brown (C). Subs (all used): 11 Ryan Lannon; 14 Danny Addy; 24 Matthew Costello; 27 Sam Luckley.
Tries: Sio (14), Burgess (25), Hingano (57); **Goals:** Inu 3/3.

Rugby Leaguer & League Express Men of the Match:
Tigers: Peter Mata'utia; *Red Devils:* Tui Lolohea.
Penalty count: 4-8; **Half-time:** 16-12;
Referee: Chris Kendall.

CATALANS DRAGONS 31 ST HELENS 30
(after golden point extra-time)

DRAGONS: 29 Sam Tomkins (C); 2 Tom Davies; 3 Samisoni Langi; 4 Dean Whare; 5 Fouad Yaha; 6 James Maloney; 7 Josh Drinkwater; 30 Jordan Dezaria; 9 Michael McIlorum; 10 Julian Bousquet; 11 Matt Whitley; 12 Mike McMeeken; 17 Mickael Goudemand. Subs (all used): 1 Arthur Mourgue; 8 Gil Dudson; 22 Joel Tomkins; 28 Sam Kasiano.
Tries: S Tomkins (3), Bousquet (57), Whare (76), Dudson (78), Kasiano (80); **Goals:** Maloney 5/5;
Field goal: Maloney (88).
Sin bin: Kasiano (38) - dangerous contact on Bentley.
SAINTS: 1 Lachlan Coote; 2 Tommy Makinson; 3 Kevin Naiqama; 4 Mark Percival; 5 Regan Grace; 18 Jack Welsby; 21 Lewis Dodd; 8 Alex Walmsley; 9 James Roby (C); 10 Matty Lees; 14 Sione Mata'utia; 12 James Bentley; 13 Morgan Knowles. Subs (all used): 16 Kyle Amor; 17 Agnatius Paasi; 20 Joe Batchelor; 23 Jake Wingfield.
Tries: Makinson (13), Coote (19), Mata'utia (35, 47), Knowles (69); **Goals:** Coote 5/6.
Sin bin: Percival (6) - high tackle on S Tomkins; Paasi (84) - high tackle on Langi.
Rugby Leaguer & League Express Men of the Match:
Dragons: Sam Tomkins; *Saints:* Sione Mata'utia.
Penalty count: 5-5; **Half-time:** 6-18; **Referee:** Liam Moore.

HULL FC 24 LEEDS RHINOS 25
(after golden point extra-time)

HULL FC: 29 Jamie Shaul; 2 Bureta Faraimo; 3 Carlos Tuimavave; 24 Cameron Scott; 5 Mahe Fonua; 1 Jake Connor; 7 Marc Sneyd (C); 13 Ligi Sao; 9 Danny Houghton; 10 Tevita Satae; 11 Andre Savelio; 12 Manu Ma'u; 14 Jordan Johnstone. Subs: 22 Josh Bowden; 17 Brad Fash; 23 Connor Wynne; 19 Ben McNamara (not used).
Tries: Houghton (10), Tuimavave (19), Connor (48);
Goals: Sneyd 6/6.
RHINOS: 27 Jack Broadbent; 24 Luke Briscoe; 3 Harry Newman; 2 Tom Briscoe; 5 Ash Handley; 6 Robert Lui; 16 Richie Myler; 19 King Vuniyayawa; 9 Kruise Leeming; 10 Matt Prior (C); 31 Morgan Gannon; 12 Rhyse Martin; 20 Bodene Thompson. Subs (all used): 14 Brad Dwyer; 17 Cameron Smith; 18 Tom Holroyd; 25 James Donaldson.
Tries: Martin (4), Newman (25), Leeming (53), Broadbent (71); **Goals:** Martin 4/5;
Field goal: Leeming (88).
Rugby Leaguer & League Express Men of the Match:
Hull FC: Carlos Tuimavave; *Rhinos:* Harry Newman.
Penalty count: 4-7; **Half time:** 16-14;
Referee: Robert Hicks.

Attendance: 35,104 *(at St James' Park, Newcastle)*.

Sunday 5th September 2021

HUDDERSFIELD GIANTS 18 WAKEFIELD TRINITY 32

GIANTS: 31 Olly Ashall-Bott; 21 Leroy Cudjoe; 3 Jake Wardle; 4 Ricky Leutele; 27 Sam Wood; 32 Will Pryce; 23 Oliver Russell; 25 Owen Trout; 35 Nathan Peats; 15 Joe Greenwood; 13 Josh Jones; 17 Chris McQueen; 10 Michael Lawrence (C). Subs (all used): 14 Matty English; 16 Jack Cogger; 28 Sam Hewitt; 34 Nathaniel Peteru.
Tries: Pryce (2), Wood (62), Jones (74); **Goals:** Pryce 3/3.
Sin bin: Hewitt (44) - leading with the arm.
TRINITY: 29 Ryan Hampshire; 27 Lee Kershaw; 4 Reece Lyne; 20 Joe Arundel; 2 Tom Johnstone; 6 Jacob Miller (C); 7 Mason Lino; 17 Chris Green; 5 Liam Kay; 15 Eddie Battye; 14 Jay Pitts; 12 Kelepi Tanginoa; 13 Joe Westerman. Subs (all used): 9 Kyle Wood; 8 David Fifita; 16 James Batchelor; 19 Jordan Crowther.
Tries: Johnstone (10), Hampshire (14), Tanginoa (46), Lyne (68), Green (77); **Goals:** Lino 6/6.
Rugby Leaguer & League Express Men of the Match:
Giants: Olly Ashall-Bott; *Trinity:* Mason Lino.
Penalty count: 4-6; **Half-time:** 6-14; **Referee:** Ben Thaler.

WARRINGTON WOLVES 10 WIGAN WARRIORS 6

WOLVES: 1 Stefan Ratchford; 5 Josh Charnley; 18 Jake Mamo; 4 Toby King; 23 Josh Thewlis; 31 George Williams; 7 Gareth Widdop; 8 Chris Hill; 16 Danny Walker; 10 Mike Cooper; 11 Ben Currie; 12 Jack Hughes (C); 13 Joe Philbin. Subs (all used): 14 Jason Clark; 26 Ellis Longstaff; 19 Robbie Mulhern; 20 Sitaleki Akauola.
Tries: Thewlis (1), Williams (26); **Goals:** Ratchford 1/2.
WARRIORS: 3 Zak Hardaker; 28 Sam Halsall; 22 Jake Bibby; 12 Liam Farrell (C); 5 Liam Marshall; 20 Harry Smith; 31 Jackson Hastings; 8 Brad Singleton; 25 Joe Shorrocks; 14 Oliver Partington; 13 John Bateman; 27 Kai Pearce-Paul; 15 Morgan Smithies. Subs (all used): 19 Liam Byrne; 21 Ethan Havard; 10 Joe Bullock; 9 Sam Powell.
Try: Havard (39); **Goals:** Smith 1/1.
Rugby Leaguer & League Express Men of the Match:
Wolves: Mike Cooper; *Warriors:* Jackson Hastings.
Penalty count: 4-2; **Half-time:** 10-6; **Referee:** James Child.

HULL KINGSTON ROVERS 44 LEIGH CENTURIONS 6

ROVERS: 19 Will Dagger; 2 Ben Crooks; 3 Greg Minikin; 4 Shaun Kenny-Dowall (C); 5 Ryan Hall; 20 Mikey Lewis; 24 Joe Keyes; 16 George King; 9 Matt Parcell; 26 Will Maher; 11 Brad Takairangi; 12 Kane Linnett; 18 Matthew Storton. Subs (all used): 8 Albert Vete; 14 Jez Litten; 27 Luis Johnson; 33 Jimmy Keinhorst.
Tries: Crooks (30), Vete (34), Takairangi (43), Parcell (47), Hall (54), Keinhorst (68), Storton (74), Keyes (77);
Goals: Keyes 6/8.
CENTURIONS: 24 Keanan Brand; 2 Matty Russell; 3 Iain Thornley; 4 Junior Sa'u; 25 Brendan Elliot; 1 Ryan Brierley; 7 Joe Mellor; 15 Alex Gerrard; 9 Liam Hood (C); 20 Adam Sidlow; 11 Ben Hellewell; 36 Sam Stone; 13 James Bell. Subs (all used): 12 Jordan Thompson; 22 Craig Mullen; 28 Matthew Foster; 37 Jai Whitbread.
Try: Russell (23); **Goals:** Brierley 1/1.
Rugby Leaguer & League Express Men of the Match:
Rovers: Matt Parcell; *Centurions:* Liam Hood.
Penalty count: 10-7; **Half-time:** 10-6;
Referee: Marcus Griffiths.

Attendance: 25,762 *(at St James' Park, Newcastle)*.

ROUND 24

Friday 10th September 2021

ST HELENS 40 LEEDS RHINOS 6

SAINTS: 1 Lachlan Coote; 2 Tommy Makinson; 3 Kevin Naiqama; 4 Mark Percival; 5 Regan Grace; 18 Jack Welsby; 21 Lewis Dodd; 8 Alex Walmsley; 9 James Roby (C); 10 Matty Lees; 14 Sione Mata'utia; 20 Joe Batchelor; 13 Morgan Knowles. Subs (all used): 11 Joel Thompson; 16 Kyle Amor; 19 Aaron Smith; 23 Jake Wingfield.
Tries: Grace (3), Welsby (17), Knowles (20, 74), Makinson (23), Walmsley (32), Mata'utia (45);
Goals: Coote 6/7.
RHINOS: 27 Jack Broadbent; 24 Luke Briscoe; 3 Harry Newman; 2 Tom Briscoe; 5 Ash Handley; 9 Kruise Leeming; 16 Richie Myler; 18 Tom Holroyd; 14 Brad Dwyer; 10 Matt Prior (C); 22 Sam Walters; 12 Rhyse Martin; 26 Jarrod O'Connor. Subs (all used): 17 Cameron Smith; 21 Alex Sutcliffe; 20 Bodene Thompson; 32 Corey Johnson (D2).
Try: Dwyer (36); **Goals:** Martin 1/1.
Rugby Leaguer & League Express Men of the Match:
Saints: Alex Walmsley; *Rhinos:* Richie Myler.
Penalty count: 3-5; **Half-time:** 28-6;
Referee: Chris Kendall; **Attendance:** 12,568.

Saturday 11th September 2021

HULL FC 0 WIGAN WARRIORS 10

HULL FC: 29 Jamie Shaul; 27 Mitieli Vulikijapani; 3 Carlos Tuimavave; 5 Mahe Fonua; 2 Bureta Faraimo; 1 Jake Connor; 7 Marc Sneyd (C); 10 Tevita Satae; 14 Jordan Johnstone; 13 Ligi Sao; 11 Andre Savelio; 24 Cameron Scott; 12 Manu Ma'u. Subs (all used): 16 Jordan Lane; 17 Brad Fash; 19 Ben McNamara; 23 Connor Wynne.
WARRIORS: 3 Zak Hardaker; 28 Sam Halsall; 22 Jake Bibby; 4 Oliver Gildart; 5 Liam Marshall; 20 Harry Smith; 31 Jackson Hastings; 14 Oliver Partington; 9 Sam Powell; 8 Brad Singleton; 12 Liam Farrell (C); 13 John Bateman; 15 Morgan Smithies. Subs (all used): 19 Liam Byrne; 21 Ethan Havard; 27 Kai Pearce-Paul; 25 Joe Shorrocks.
Tries: Bibby (52), Hardaker (62); **Goals:** Hardaker 1/2.
Rugby Leaguer & League Express Men of the Match:
Hull FC: Jordan Johnstone; *Warriors:* Zak Hardaker.
Penalty count: 3-5; **Half-time:** 0-0;
Referee: Liam Moore; **Attendance:** 10,043.

WARRINGTON WOLVES 20 SALFORD RED DEVILS 19
(after golden point extra-time)

WOLVES: 17 Matty Ashton; 23 Josh Thewlis; 27 Connor Wrench; 4 Toby King; 5 Josh Charnley; 31 George Williams; 7 Gareth Widdop; 25 Eribe Doro; 15 Matt Davis; 19 Robbie Mulhern; 11 Ben Currie; 6 Blake Austin; 12 Jack Hughes (C). Subs: 1 Stefan Ratchford; 14 Jason Clark; 26 Ellis Longstaff; 32 Tom Whitehead (not used).
Tries: Ashton (15), Davis (28), Charnley (31);
Goals: Widdop 3/4; **Field goals:** Williams (78, 84).
RED DEVILS: 1 Morgan Escare; 2 Ken Sio; 5 Joe Burgess; 23 Dan Sarginson; 22 Rhys Williams; 6 Tui Lolohea; 18 Chris Atkin (C); 25 Jack Ormondroyd; 9 Andy Ackers; 17 Josh Johnson; 11 Ryan Lannon; 35 Ellis Robson; 14 Danny Addy. Subs (all used): 4 Krisnan Inu; 13 Elijah Taylor; 16 Greg Burke; 27 Sam Luckley.
Tries: Sio (8, 39), Lolohea (59); **Goals:** Escare 2/2, Inu 1/1;
Field goal: Lolohea (79).
Sin bin: Addy (74) - high tackle on Longstaff.
Rugby Leaguer & League Express Men of the Match:
Wolves: Ben Currie; *Red Devils:* Tui Lolohea.
Penalty count: 6-5; **Half-time:** 16-12;
Referee: Scott Mikalauskas; **Attendance:** 7,351.

CATALANS DRAGONS 18 HUDDERSFIELD GIANTS 30

DRAGONS: 1 Arthur Mourgue; 2 Tom Davies; 20 Matthieu Laguerre; 11 Matt Whitley; 32 Romain Franco; 6 James Maloney; 7 Josh Drinkwater; 8 Gil Dudson; 31 Cesar Rouge; 17 Mickael Goudemand; 15 Benjamin Jullien; 21 Corentin Le Cam; 24 Jason Baitieri (C). Subs (all used): 16 Paul Seguier; 23 Mathieu Cozza; 30 Jordan Dezaria; 35 Robin Brochon (D2).
Tries: Whitley (12, 22), Laguerre (17); **Goals:** Maloney 3/3.
GIANTS: 31 Olly Ashall-Bott; 21 Leroy Cudjoe; 3 Jake Wardle; 4 Ricky Leutele; 24 Louis Senior; 23 Oliver Russell; 16 Jack Cogger; 20 Oliver Wilson; 35 Nathan Peats; 14 Matty English; 13 Josh Jones; 17 Chris McQueen; 10 Michael Lawrence (C). Subs (all used): 15 Joe Greenwood; 25 Owen Trout; 32 Will Pryce; 34 Nathaniel Peteru.
Tries: Jones (29), Senior (38), Cogger (51), Ashall-Bott (54), English (70); **Goals:** Russell 5/5.
Sin bin: McQueen (11) - high tackle on Laguerre.
Rugby Leaguer & League Express Men of the Match:
Dragons: James Maloney; *Giants:* Olly Ashall-Bott.
Penalty count: 5-5; **Half-time:** 18-12;
Referee: Tom Grant; **Attendance:** 7,318.

HULL KINGSTON ROVERS 26 CASTLEFORD TIGERS 19

ROVERS: 19 Will Dagger; 2 Ben Crooks; 3 Greg Minikin; 4 Shaun Kenny-Dowall (C); 5 Ryan Hall; 20 Mikey Lewis; 7 Jordan Abdull; 16 George King; 9 Matt Parcell; 26 Will Maher; 12 Kane Linnett; 11 Brad Takairangi; 18 Matthew Storton. Subs (all used): 8 Albert Vete; 14 Jez Litten; 27 Luis Johnson; 33 Jimmy Keinhorst.
Tries: Lewis (5, 27), Parcell (55), Linnett (58);
Goals: Abdull 5/5.
TIGERS: 1 Niall Evalds; 20 James Clare; 3 Peter Mata'utia; 4 Michael Shenton (C); 2 Derrell Olpherts; 25 Jordan Turner; 7 Danny Richardson; 15 George Griffin; 13 Adam Milner; 22 Daniel Smith; 11 Oliver Holmes; 21 Jesse Sene-Lefao; 14 Nathan Massey. Subs (all used): 17 Alex Foster; 18 Jacques O'Neill; 19 Tyla Hepi; 24 Suaia Matagi.
Tries: Evalds (12, 42), Olpherts (20);
Goals: Richardson 3/3; **Field goal:** Richardson (38).
Rugby Leaguer & League Express Men of the Match:
Rovers: Jordan Abdull; *Tigers:* Niall Evalds.
Penalty count: 7-5; **Half-time:** 12-13;
Referee: James Child; **Attendance:** 6,840.

Sunday 12th September 2021

LEIGH CENTURIONS 26 WAKEFIELD TRINITY 18

CENTURIONS: 1 Ryan Brierley; 25 Brendan Elliot; 3 Iain Thornley; 11 Ben Hellewell; 35 Jack Logan; 13 James Bell; 7 Joe Mellor; 20 Adam Sidlow; 9 Liam Hood (C); 33 Rob Butler; 36 Sam Stone; 12 Jordan Thompson; 37 Jai Whitbread. Subs (all used): 15 Alex Gerrard; 17 Jamie Ellis; 19 Nathan Mason; 34 Jack Ashworth.
Tries: Sidlow (10), Brierley (14, 42, 57), Stone (68);
Goals: Brierley 3/5.
Sin bin: Butler (74) - use of the elbow; Brierley (78) - professional foul.
TRINITY: 29 Ryan Hampshire; 27 Lee Kershaw; 4 Reece Lyne; 20 Joe Arundel; 18 Innes Senior; 6 Jacob Miller (C); 7 Mason Lino; 17 Chris Green; 5 Liam Kay; 15 Eddie Battye; 16 James Batchelor; 12 Kelepi Tanginoa; 19 Jordan Crowther. Subs (all used): 8 David Fifita; 9 Kyle Wood; 10 Tinirau Arona; 25 Brad Walker.
Tries: Lyne (20), Tanginoa (23), Fifita (33); **Goals:** Lino 3/3.
Rugby Leaguer & League Express Men of the Match:
Centurions: Ryan Brierley; *Trinity:* Mason Lino.
Penalty count: 4-6; **Half-time:** 10-18;
Referee: Robert Hicks; **Attendance:** 2,905.

ROUND 25

Thursday 16th September 2021

CASTLEFORD TIGERS 24 WARRINGTON WOLVES 40

TIGERS: 1 Niall Evalds; 2 Derrell Olpherts; 3 Peter Mata'utia; 4 Michael Shenton (C); 25 Jordan Turner; 31 Gareth O'Brien; 7 Danny Richardson; 15 George Griffin; 9 Paul McShane; 10 Grant Millington; 17 Alex Foster; 21 Jesse Sene-Lefao; 14 Nathan Massey. Subs (all used): 8 Liam Watts; 13 Adam Milner; 22 Daniel Smith; 24 Suaia Matagi.
Tries: Mata'utia (53, 56), Turner (59), Millington (63);
Goals: Richardson 4/4.
WOLVES: 17 Matty Ashton; 23 Josh Thewlis; 27 Connor Wrench; 18 Jake Mamo; 5 Josh Charnley; 31 George Williams; 7 Gareth Widdop; 8 Chris Hill; 1 Stefan Ratchford; 10 Mike Cooper; 11 Ben Currie; 12 Jack Hughes (C); 13 Joe Philbin. Subs (all used): 6 Blake Austin; 14 Jason Clark; 19 Robbie Mulhern; 26 Ellis Longstaff.

Tries: Ashton (6, 26, 44), Mamo (8, 32), Wrench (77);
Goals: Ratchford 7/7, Widdop 1/1.
Dismissal: Cooper (66) - shoulder to the head of Watts.
Sin bin: Charnley (58) - dangerous challenge on Turner.
Rugby Leaguer & League Express Men of the Match:
Tigers: Adam Milner; *Wolves:* Matty Ashton.
Penalty count: 5-8; **Half-time:** 0-26;
Referee: Liam Moore; **Attendance:** 5,126.

Friday 17th September 2021

LEEDS RHINOS 36 HULL KINGSTON ROVERS 12

RHINOS: 27 Jack Broadbent; 24 Luke Briscoe; 3 Harry Newman; 2 Tom Briscoe; 5 Ash Handley; 6 Robert Lui; 16 Richie Myler; 20 Bodene Thompson; 9 Kruise Leeming; 10 Matt Prior (C); 31 Morgan Gannon; 12 Rhyse Martin; 17 Cameron Smith. Subs (all used): 4 Konrad Hurrell; 14 Brad Dwyer; 18 Tom Holroyd; 25 James Donaldson.
Tries: Lui (13), Prior (29), Holroyd (35), Myler (40), Donaldson (46), Handley (63); **Goals:** Martin 6/6.
ROVERS: 19 Will Dagger; 2 Ben Crooks; 11 Brad Takairangi; 4 Shaun Kenny-Dowall (C); 33 Jimmy Keinhorst; 20 Mikey Lewis; 7 Jordan Abdull; 16 George King; 9 Matt Parcell; 26 Will Maher; 12 Kane Linnett; 27 Luis Johnson; 18 Matthew Storton. Subs (all used): 10 Korbin Sims; 14 Jez Litten; 28 Muizz Mustapha; 30 Will Tate.
Tries: Lewis (17), Dagger (75); **Goals:** Abdull (2).
Rugby Leaguer & League Express Men of the Match:
Rhinos: Robert Lui; *Rovers:* Matthew Storton.
Penalty count: 7-6; **Half time:** 24-6;
Referee: Chris Kendall; **Attendance:** 13,106.

SALFORD RED DEVILS 26 ST HELENS 14

RED DEVILS: 1 Morgan Escare; 2 Ken Sio; 24 Matthew Costello; 23 Dan Sarginson; 22 Rhys Williams; 6 Tui Lolohea; 18 Chris Atkin (C); 25 Jack Ormondroyd; 9 Andy Ackers; 17 Josh Johnson; 15 Oliver Roberts; 35 Ellis Robson; 13 Elijah Taylor. Subs (all used): 4 Krisnan Inu; 10 Sebastine Ikahihifo; 16 Greg Burke; 30 Connor Aspey.
Tries: Sio (13, 54), Costello (40), Atkin (43), Robson (48); **Goals:** Escare 0/1, Atkin 2/2, Inu 1/2.
SAINTS: 31 Jonathan Bennison (D); 32 Shay Martyn (D); 29 Ben Davies; 22 Josh Simm; 5 Regan Grace; 6 Jonny Lomax (C); 21 Lewis Dodd; 16 Kyle Amor; 19 Aaron Smith; 10 Matty Lees; 11 Joel Thompson; 30 Sam Royle (D); 23 Jake Wingfield. Subs (all used): 15 Louie McCarthy-Scarsbrook; 18 Jack Welsby; 24 Josh Eaves; 25 Dan Norman.
Tries: Bennison (5), Lomax (17); **Goals:** Martyn 3/3.
Rugby Leaguer & League Express Men of the Match:
Red Devils: Andy Ackers; *Saints:* Ben Davies.
Penalty count: 5-7; **Half-time:** 10-14;
Referee: Marcus Griffiths; **Attendance:** 5,130.

WAKEFIELD TRINITY 44 HULL FC 12

TRINITY: 29 Ryan Hampshire; 18 Innes Senior; 4 Reece Lyne; 20 Joe Arundel; 5 Liam Kay; 6 Jacob Miller (C); 7 Mason Lino; 15 Eddie Battye; 23 Josh Wood; 10 Tinirau Arona; 12 Kelepi Tanginoa; 16 James Batchelor; 19 Jordan Crowther. Subs (all used): 8 David Fifita; 9 Kyle Wood; 17 Chris Green; 26 Yusuf Aydin.
Tries: Senior (3), Batchelor (13), Tanginoa (21, 75), Miller (25), Fifita (28), Hampshire (31), Kay (80);
Goals: Lino 5/6, Fifita 1/2.
HULL FC: 29 Jamie Shaul; 2 Bureta Faraimo; 3 Carlos Tuimavave; 24 Cameron Scott; 27 Mitieli Vulikijapani; 1 Jake Connor; 19 Ben McNamara; 10 Tevita Satae; 14 Jordan Johnstone; 13 Ligi Sao; 11 Andre Savelio; 12 Manu Ma'u (C); 16 Jordan Lane. Subs (all used): 17 Brad Fash; 22 Josh Bowden; 23 Connor Wynne; 33 Jacob Hookem (D).
Tries: Vulikijapani (60), Lane (68); **Goals:** Connor 2/2.
Rugby Leaguer & League Express Men of the Match:
Trinity: Mason Lino; *Hull FC:* Manu Ma'u.
Penalty count: 6-6; **Half-time:** 34-0;
Referee: Robert Hicks; **Attendance:** 4,039.

WIGAN WARRIORS 12 CATALANS DRAGONS 8

WARRIORS: 3 Zak Hardaker; 22 Jake Bibby; 11 Willie Isa (C); 4 Oliver Gildart; 28 Sam Halsall; 31 Harry Smith; 31 Jackson Hastings; 10 Joe Bullock; 25 Joe Shorrocks; 17 Tony Clubb; 27 Kai Pearce-Paul; 29 James McDonnell; 14 Oliver Partington. Subs (all used): 19 Liam Byrne; 21 Ethan Havard; 23 Mitch Clark; 34 Brad O'Neill.
Tries: Isa (27), McDonnell (62); **Goals:** Hardaker 2/2.
DRAGONS: 29 Sam Tomkins; 2 Tom Davies; 3 Samisoni Langi; 4 Dean Whare; 20 Matthieu Laguerre; 6 James Maloney; 7 Josh Drinkwater; 8 Gil Dudson; 9 Michael McIlorum; 10 Julian Bousquet; 11 Matt Whitley; 12 Mike McMeeken; 22 Joel Tomkins. Subs (all used): 1 Arthur Mourgue; 13 Benjamin Garcia (C); 17 Mickael Goudemand; 28 Sam Kasiano.
Tries: Davies (53), Laguerre (72); **Goals:** Maloney 0/2.
Sin bin: Kasiano (77) - dissent.

Hull KR's Will Dagger beats Warrington's Gareth Widdop to a high ball

Rugby Leaguer & League Express Men of the Match:
Warriors: Willie Isa; *Dragons:* Sam Kasiano.
Penalty count: 3-4; **Half-time:** 6-0;
Referee: James Child; **Attendance:** 12,852.

Sunday 19th September 2021

HUDDERSFIELD GIANTS 42 LEIGH CENTURIONS 24

GIANTS: 31 Olly Ashall-Bott; 2 Jermaine McGillvary; 21 Leroy Cudjoe; 4 Ricky Leutele; 24 Louis Senior; 16 Jack Cogger; 23 Oliver Russell; 20 Oliver Wilson; 35 Nathan Peats; 14 Matty English; 13 Josh Jones; 17 Chris McQueen; 10 Michael Lawrence (C). Subs (all used): 15 Joe Greenwood; 25 Owen Trout; 34 Nathaniel Peteru; 32 Will Pryce.
Tries: Senior (4, 48), Cudjoe (18), Trout (37), Russell (40), Greenwood (57), Pryce (65), Leutele (71); **Goals:** Russell 5/7, Pryce 0/1.
Sin bin: Peteru (77) - kicking out.
CENTURIONS: 24 Keanan Brand; 25 Brendan Elliot; 4 Junior Sa'u; 3 Iain Thornley; 35 Jack Logan; 1 Ryan Brierley; 17 Jamie Ellis; 20 Adam Sidlow; 9 Liam Hood (C); 37 Jai Whitbread; 36 Sam Stone; 11 Ben Hellewell; 13 James Bell. Subs (all used): 12 Jordan Thompson; 15 Alex Gerrard; 33 Rob Butler; 34 Jack Ashworth.
Tries: Whitbread (14), Thornley (29), Elliot (61, 80), Stone (68); **Goals:** Brierley 2/4, Hood 0/1.
Sin bin: Ashworth (56) - high tackle on Cogger.
Rugby Leaguer & League Express Men of the Match:
Giants: Leroy Cudjoe; *Centurions:* James Bell.
Penalty count: 5-6; **Half-time:** 22-12;
Referee: Tom Grant; **Attendance:** 3,867.

POSTPONED GAMES
(all subsequently not rearranged)

ROUND 9
Leeds Rhinos v St Helens

ROUND 11
Hull Kingston Rovers v St Helens

ROUND 12
Hull Kingston Rovers v Hull FC

ROUND 13
Hull FC v Salford Red Devils

ROUND 14
Hull FC v Leigh Centurions
Hull Kingston Rovers v Warrington Wolves

ROUND 15
Catalans Dragons v Castleford Tigers
Leigh Centurions v Warrington Wolves
St Helens v Hull Kingston Rovers

ROUND 16
Leigh Centurions v Castleford Tigers
Salford Red Devils v Hull Kingston Rovers
St Helens v Huddersfield Giants

ROUND 17
Wakefield Trinity v Salford Red Devils

ROUND 18
Warrington Wolves v Hull FC

ROUND 20
Warrington Wolves v Catalans Dragons

(Cancelled/awarded games shown with relevant round on earlier pages)

THE ELIMINATORS

Thursday 23rd September 2021

WIGAN WARRIORS 0 LEEDS RHINOS 8

WARRIORS: 3 Zak Hardaker; 22 Jake Bibby; 11 Willie Isa; 4 Oliver Gildart; 5 Liam Marshall; 20 Harry Smith; 31 Jackson Hastings; 8 Brad Singleton; 9 Sam Powell; 14 Oliver Partington; 13 John Bateman; 12 Liam Farrell (C); 15 Morgan Smithies. Subs (all used): 19 Liam Byrne; 21 Ethan Havard; 25 Joe Shorrocks; 27 Kai Pearce-Paul.

St Helens' Kevin Naiqama takes on Catalan Dragons' Fouad Yaha during the Super League Grand Final

RHINOS: 16 Richie Myler; 24 Luke Briscoe; 3 Harry Newman; 2 Tom Briscoe; 5 Ash Handley; 6 Robert Lui; 9 Kruise Leeming; 20 Bodene Thompson; 14 Brad Dwyer; 10 Matt Prior (C); 25 James Donaldson; 12 Rhyse Martin; 13 Zane Tetevano. Subs (all used): 4 Konrad Hurrell; 8 Mikolaj Oledzki; 17 Cameron Smith; 18 Tom Holroyd.
Try: Handley (51); **Goals:** Martin 2/2.
Rugby Leaguer & League Express Men of the Match: *Warriors:* Morgan Smithies; *Rhinos:* Ash Handley.
Penalty count: 4-6; **Half-time:** 0-0;
Referee: Robert Hicks; **Attendance:** 7,396.

Friday 24th September 2021

WARRINGTON WOLVES 0
HULL KINGSTON ROVERS 19

WOLVES: 1 Stefan Ratchford; 2 Tom Lineham; 18 Jake Mamo; 4 Toby King; 23 Josh Thewlis; 31 George Williams; 7 Gareth Widdop; 8 Chris Hill; 9 Daryl Clark; 20 Sitaleki Akauola; 11 Ben Currie; 12 Jack Hughes (C); 13 Joe Philbin. Subs (all used): 14 Jason Clark; 17 Matty Ashton; 19 Robbie Mulhern; 26 Ellis Longstaff.
On report: Hill (8) - alleged dangerous contact on Lewis.
ROVERS: 19 Will Dagger; 2 Ben Crooks; 11 Brad Takairangi; 4 Shaun Kenny-Dowall (C); 33 Jimmy Keinhorst; 20 Mikey Lewis; 7 Jordan Abdull; 16 George King; 14 Jez Litten; 26 Will Maher; 12 Kane Linnett; 27 Luis Johnson; 18 Matthew Storton. Subs (all used): 8 Albert Vete; 25 Rowan Milnes; 28 Muizz Mustapha; 30 Will Tate.
Tries: Abdull (16), Lewis (47), Keinhorst (68);
Goals: Abdull 3/5; **Field goal:** Abdull (72).
Sin bin: Vete (31) - late challenge on Widdop.
Rugby Leaguer & League Express Men of the Match: *Wolves:* Ellis Longstaff; *Rovers:* Jordan Abdull.
Penalty count: 6-6; **Half-time:** 0-6;
Referee: Liam Moore; **Attendance:** 6,252.

SEMI-FINALS

Thursday 30th September 2021

CATALANS DRAGONS 28 HULL KINGSTON ROVERS 10

DRAGONS: 1 Arthur Mourgue; 2 Tom Davies; 3 Samisoni Langi; 4 Dean Whare; 5 Fouad Yaha; 6 James Maloney; 7 Josh Drinkwater; 22 Joel Tomkins; 9 Michael McIlorum; 10 Julian Bousquet; 11 Matt Whitley; 12 Mike McMeeken; 13 Benjamin Garcia (C). Subs (all used): 8 Gil Dudson; 17 Mickael Goudemand; 27 Joe Chan; 28 Sam Kasiano.
Tries: Garcia (8), Drinkwater (31), Mourgue (41), Yaha (59), Chan (68); **Goals:** Maloney 4/6.
ROVERS: 19 Will Dagger; 2 Ben Crooks; 11 Brad Takairangi; 4 Shaun Kenny-Dowall (C); 5 Ryan Hall; 20 Mikey Lewis; 7 Jordan Abdull; 16 George King; 14 Jez Litten; 26 Will Maher; 27 Luis Johnson; 12 Kane Linnett; 18 Matthew Storton. Subs (all used): 8 Albert Vete; 28 Muizz Mustapha; 30 Will Tate; 33 Jimmy Keinhorst.
Tries: Kenny-Dowall (36), Hall (74); **Goals:** Abdull 1/2.
Rugby Leaguer & League Express Men of the Match: *Dragons:* Michael McIlorum; *Rovers:* Shaun Kenny-Dowall.
Penalty count: 7-6; **Half-time:** 12-4;
Referee: James Child; **Attendance:** 11,530.

Friday 1st October 2021

ST HELENS 36 LEEDS RHINOS 8

SAINTS: 1 Lachlan Coote; 2 Tommy Makinson; 3 Kevin Naiqama; 4 Mark Percival; 5 Regan Grace; 6 Jonny Lomax; 21 Lewis Dodd; 8 Alex Walmsley; 9 James Roby (C); 10 Matty Lees; 14 Sione Mata'utia; 20 Joe Batchelor; 13 Morgan Knowles. Subs (all used): 15 Louie McCarthy-Scarsbrook; 16 Kyle Amor; 17 Agnatius Paasi; 18 Jack Welsby.
Tries: Grace (5, 77), Roby (23), Percival (50, 72), Naiqama (60); **Goals:** Coote 6/8.
Sin bin: Mata'utia (30) - high tackle on L Briscoe; Knowles (67) - late challenge.

RHINOS: 16 Richie Myler; 24 Luke Briscoe; 3 Harry Newman; 2 Tom Briscoe; 5 Ash Handley; 9 Kruise Leeming; 6 Robert Lui; 8 Mikolaj Oledzki; 14 Brad Dwyer; 10 Matt Prior (C); 25 James Donaldson; 12 Rhyse Martin; 13 Zane Tetevano. Subs (all used): 4 Konrad Hurrell; 17 Cameron Smith; 18 Tom Holroyd; 20 Bodene Thompson.
Tries: Myler (38), L Briscoe (67); **Goals:** Martin 0/2.
Sin bin: T Briscoe (21) - high tackle on Coote; Donaldson (45) - high tackle on Coote.
Rugby Leaguer & League Express Men of the Match: *Saints:* Alex Walmsley; *Rhinos:* Robert Lui.
Penalty count: 5-5; **Half-time:** 16-4;
Referee: Chris Kendall; **Attendance:** 11,688.

GRAND FINAL

Saturday 9th October 2021

CATALANS DRAGONS 10 ST HELENS 12

DRAGONS: 29 Sam Tomkins; 2 Tom Davies; 3 Samisoni Langi; 4 Dean Whare; 5 Fouad Yaha; 6 James Maloney; 10 Julian Bousquet; 11 Matt Whitley; 12 Mike McMeeken; 13 Benjamin Garcia (C). Subs (all used): 1 Arthur Mourgue; 17 Mickael Goudemand; 22 Joel Tomkins; 28 Sam Kasiano.
Try: McMeeken (50); **Goals:** Maloney 3/3.
On report: Yaha (66) - alleged use of the knee on Naiqama.
SAINTS: 1 Lachlan Coote; 2 Tommy Makinson; 3 Kevin Naiqama; 4 Mark Percival; 5 Regan Grace; 6 Jonny Lomax; 21 Lewis Dodd; 8 Alex Walmsley; 9 James Roby (C); 10 Matty Lees; 14 Sione Mata'utia; 20 Joe Batchelor; 13 Morgan Knowles. Subs: 15 Louie McCarthy-Scarsbrook; 16 Kyle Amor (not used); 17 Agnatius Paasi; 18 Jack Welsby.
Tries: Naiqama (13, 66); **Goals:** Coote 2/3.
Sin bin: Makinson (46) - high tackle on Yaha.
Rugby Leaguer & League Express Men of the Match: *Dragons:* Josh Drinkwater; *Saints:* Kevin Naiqama.
Penalty count: 10-8; **Half-time:** 4-6;
Referee: Liam Moore; **Attendance:** 45,177
(at Old Trafford, Manchester).

SUPER LEAGUE RECORDS *1996-2021*

PLAYER RECORDS

COMPETITION
Includes play-off games & Super League Super 8s (2015-2018)

TRIES
Danny McGuire (Hull Kingston Rovers/Leeds Rhinos)
(2001-2019) 247

GOALS
Kevin Sinfield (Leeds Rhinos) (1997-2015) 1,566

FIELD GOALS
Lee Briers (Warrington Wolves/St Helens) (1997-2013) 70

POINTS
Kevin Sinfield (Leeds Rhinos) (1997-2015) 3,443

APPEARANCES
Kevin Sinfield (Leeds Rhinos) (1997-2015) 454

SEASON
Includes play-off games & Super League Super 8s (2015-2018)
(Play-offs in brackets)

TRIES
Denny Solomona (Castleford Tigers) (2016) 40 (-)

GOALS
Henry Paul (Bradford Bulls) (2001) 178 (13)

FIELD GOALS
Lee Briers (Warrington Wolves) (2002) 11 (-)

POINTS
Pat Richards (Wigan Warriors) (2010) 434 (46)

MATCH RECORDS

Includes play-off games & Super League Super 8s (2015-2018)

TRIES
Lesley Vainikolo (Bradford Bulls) 6
(v Hull FC (h), 2/9/05)

GOALS
Henry Paul (Bradford Bulls) 14
(v Salford City Reds (h), 25/6/00)

FIELD GOALS
Lee Briers (Warrington Wolves) 5
(v Halifax Blue Sox (a), 25/5/02)

POINTS
Iestyn Harris (Leeds Rhinos) 42
(v Huddersfield Giants (h), 16/7/99)

TEAM RECORDS

Includes play-off games & Super League Super 8s (2015-2018)

HIGHEST SCORE
Bradford Bulls 96 Salford City Reds 16 (25/6/00)

WIDEST MARGIN
Leeds Rhinos 86 Huddersfield Giants 6 (16/7/99)
Bradford Bulls 96 Salford City Reds 16 (25/6/00)
Warrington Wolves 80 Wakefield Trinity Wildcats 0 (11/4/15)

ATTENDANCE RECORDS

GRAND FINAL
73,512 Leeds Rhinos v Wigan Warriors (10/10/15)

PLAY-OFFS
21,790 Wigan Warriors v St Helens (3/10/03)

REGULAR SEASON *(includes Super League Super 8s (2015-2018)*
31,555 Catalans Dragons v Wigan Warriors (18/5/19)
(at Camp Nou, Barcelona)

CHAMPIONSHIP 2021
Club by Club

BATLEY BULLDOGS

DATE	FIXTURE	RESULT	SCORERS	LGE	ATT
20/3/21	Halifax (a) (CCR1)	W6-19	t:Logan,Broughton,Kaye g:Morton(3) fg:White	N/A	BCD
27/3/21	Featherstone (a) (CCR2)	L30-22	t:Morton,Hall,Hooley,Campbell g:Morton(3)	N/A	BCD
2/4/21	Featherstone (a)	L28-18	t:Hall,Walshaw,Logan g:Gilmore(3)	10th	BCD
17/4/21	Oldham (h)	W48-10	t:Tonks,Hooley,Broughton,Logan,White(2),Campbell(2),Hall g:Gilmore(3),Hooley(3)	6th	BCD
24/4/21	Widnes (h)	W48-16	t:Campbell(2),Tonks,Ward,White,Morton,Hooley,Broughton,Manning g:Morton(6)	3rd	BCD
2/5/21	Newcastle (a)	W16-28	t:Hall,Morton,Leak(2),Gilmore g:Gilmore(4)	3rd	BCD
7/5/21	Sheffield (a)	W18-30	t:Hooley(2),Gilmore,Manning,Campbell,Hall g:Gilmore(2),Morton	3rd	BCD
15/5/21	London Broncos (h)	L6-40	t:Hall g:Morton	4th	BCD
30/5/21	Swinton (h)	W26-12	t:Kaye,Brown,Broughton,Leak g:Morton(5)	4th	930
13/6/21	Whitehaven (a)	W20-24	t:Hooley,Ward,Hall,Lillycrop g:Hooley(4)	4th	632
20/6/21	York (a)	W20-22	t:Hooley,Broughton(2),Walshaw g:Hooley(3)	3rd	1,486
27/6/21	Halifax (h)	L12-22	t:Lillycrop g:Hooley(4)	3rd	1,193
4/7/21	Bradford (a)	L30-16	t:White,Hall,Walshaw g:Hooley(2)	5th	2,831
11/7/21	Toulouse (h)	L12-32	t:Johnson,Gledhill g:Hooley(2)	6th	782
15/7/21	Dewsbury (a)	W10-38	t:Edwards(2),Campbell,Blagbrough,Manning,Leak(2) g:Hooley(5)	6th	1,021
25/7/21	Newcastle (h)	W42-12	t:Blagbrough,Kaye,Flynn,Walshaw,Buchanan,Edwards,White g:Gilmore(7)	5th	932
1/8/21	Widnes (a)	W16-34	t:Buchanan,Hall(2),Leak,Manning,Edwards g:Gilmore(5)	4th	1,258
8/8/21	Featherstone (h)	L13-28	t:Gledhill,Johnson g:Gilmore(2) fg:Gilmore	5th	1,259
15/8/21	Swinton (a)	W6-38	t:Campbell(2),Senior,Leak(3),Johnson g:Gilmore(5)	5th	842
22/8/21	Sheffield (h)	W56-12	t:Johnson(3),Morton,Walshaw(2),Hooley(2),Flynn,Campbell g:Hooley(2),Gilmore(6)	5th	859
5/9/21	Whitehaven (h)	L14-22	t:Johnson,White g:Gilmore(3)	5th	922
12/9/21	Dewsbury (h)	L24-31	t:White,Senior,Buchanan,Broughton g:Gilmore(4)	5th	1,532
19/9/21	Halifax (a)	W10-12	t:Walshaw,Campbell g:Gilmore(2)	4th	2,216
25/9/21	Bradford (h) (E)	W23-10	t:Kaye,Gilmore,Hall g:Gilmore(5) fg:Gilmore	N/A	2,005
2/10/21	Toulouse (a) (SF)	L51-12	t:Manning,Johnson g:Gilmore(2)	N/A	6,871

Toulouse (a) (R19) game was cancelled

		APP		TRIES		GOALS		FG		PTS	
	D.O.B.	ALL	Ch	ALL	Ch	ALL	Ch	ALL	Ch	ALL	Ch
Jack Blagbrough	18/1/94	19(5)	18(4)	2	2	0	0	0	0	8	8
Anthony Bowman	18/3/92	1(1)	1(1)	0	0	0	0	0	0	0	0
Jodie Broughton	9/1/88	13(1)	12(1)	7	6	0	0	0	0	28	24
James Brown	6/5/88	6(8)	6(8)	1	1	0	0	0	0	4	4
Kieran Buchanan	26/1/98	20	18	3	3	0	0	0	0	12	12
Oli Burton	15/3/02	3(1)	3(1)	0	0	0	0	0	0	0	0
Johnny Campbell	17/7/87	21	20	11	10	0	0	0	0	44	40
Levi Edwards	25/12/03	5	5	4	4	0	0	0	0	16	16
Toby Everett	22/12/95	19(1)	17(1)	0	0	0	0	0	0	0	0
Oli Field	3/9/02	1	1	0	0	0	0	0	0	0	0
Nyle Flynn	27/7/97	14(5)	14(4)	2	2	0	0	0	0	8	8
Tom Gilmore	2/2/94	24	22	3	3	53	53	2	2	120	120
Adam Gledhill	15/2/93	11(1)	10(1)	2	2	0	0	0	0	8	8
Elliot Hall	6/7/97	9(10)	7(10)	11	10	0	0	0	0	44	40
Luke Hooley	1/8/98	19	17	9	8	25	25	0	0	86	82
Aiden Ineson	16/9/97	(1)	(1)	0	0	0	0	0	0	0	0
Greg Johnson	20/2/90	9	9	8	8	0	0	0	0	32	32
Ben Kaye	19/12/88	16	14	4	3	0	0	0	0	16	12
Alistair Leak	5/4/92	6(17)	6(15)	9	9	0	0	0	0	36	36
Tom Lillycrop	29/11/91	1(15)	(14)	2	2	0	0	0	0	8	8
Jack Logan	8/9/95	8	6	3	2	0	0	0	0	12	8
Dane Manning	15/4/89	23	23	5	5	0	0	0	0	20	20
Dale Morton	31/10/90	18(3)	16(3)	4	3	19	13	0	0	54	38
George Senior	29/8/99	6(5)	6(4)	2	2	0	0	0	0	8	8
Josh Tonks	14/8/91	8	7	2	2	0	0	0	0	8	8
Lucas Walshaw	4/8/92	20(2)	18(2)	7	7	0	0	0	0	28	28
Michael Ward	10/2/91	(23)	(21)	2	2	0	0	0	0	8	8
Ben White	27/10/94	25	23	7	7	0	0	1	0	29	28

'Ch' totals include regular season & play-offs; 'All' totals also include Challenge Cup

Tom Gilmore

CLUB RECORDS
MATCH RECORDS

Highest score: 100-4 v Gateshead, 17/3/2010 **Highest score against:** 9-78 v Wakefield, 26/8/67 **Record attendance:** 23,989 v Leeds, 14/3/25
Tries: 5 Joe Oakland v Bramley, 19/12/1908; Tommy Brannan v Swinton, 17/1/1920; Jim Wale v Bramley, 4/12/26; Jim Wale v Cottingham, 12/2/27;
Tommy Oldroyd v Highfield, 6/3/94; Ben Feehan v Halifax, 10/8/2008; Jermaine McGillvary v Whitehaven, 24/5/2009
Goals: 16 Gareth Moore v Gateshead, 17/3/2010 **Points:** 40 Gareth Moore v Gateshead, 17/3/2010

SEASON RECORDS
CAREER RECORDS

Tries: 30 Johnny Campbell 2010 **Goals:** 144 Barry Eaton 2004 **Points:** 308 Richard Price 1997
Tries: 142 Craig Lingard 1998-2008 **Goals:** 463 Wharton 'Wattie' Davies 1897-1912 **Points:** 1,297 Wharton 'Wattie' Davies 1897-1912
Appearances: 421 Wharton 'Wattie' Davies 1897-1912

BRADFORD BULLS

DATE	FIXTURE	RESULT	SCORERS	LGE	ATT
21/3/21	Featherstone (a) (CCR1)	L41-16	t:Hamlett(2),Scurr g:Brough(2)	N/A	BCD
4/4/21	Sheffield (a)	L50-12	t:Rooks,Brown g:Brough(2)	14th	BCD
18/4/21	Halifax (h) ●	W27-26	t:Lilley,Fleming,Pickersgill,Foggin-Johnston g:Brough(5) fg:Lilley	9th	BCD
25/4/21	Dewsbury (h) ●	W35-14	t:England,Oakes,Brown(2),Brough g:Brough(7) fg:Flanagan	6th	BCD
2/5/21	Whitehaven (a)	W22-30	t:Crossley(2),Brown,Pickersgill,Scurr g:Brough(5)	4th	BCD
9/5/21	Swinton (a)	W22-23	t:Doyle,Foggin-Johnston,Brown,Pickersgill g:Brough(3) fg:Lilley	4th	BCD
23/5/21	London Broncos (a) ●●	W8-33	t:Murphy,Doyle,Pickersgill,Robson(2) g:Brough(4),Lilley(2) fg:Brough	3rd	533
30/5/21	York (h)	W37-18	t:Brown(2),Lilley,Golding,Oakes g:Brough(8) fg:Brough	3rd	3,742
6/6/21	Newcastle (h)	W31-12	t:Lilley,Robson,Walker,Crossley,Doyle g:Brough(4),Lilley fg:Brough	3rd	3,562
13/6/21	Featherstone (a)	L44-0		3rd	1,700
27/6/21	Widnes (h)	L12-25	t:Walker,Scurr g:Lilley(2)	4th	3,153
4/7/21	Batley (h)	W30-16	t:Doyle,Brown,England,Burton,B Evans g:Keyes(5)	3rd	2,831
11/7/21	Oldham (a)	W22-54	t:Foggin-Johnston,Keyes(3),Pickersgill(2),Brown,R Evans,England g:Keyes(9)	3rd	650
25/7/21	Featherstone (h)	L30-36	t:B Evans,Foggin-Johnston,Pickersgill,R Evans,Flanagan g:Keyes(4),Flanagan	4th	3,708
1/8/21	Halifax (a)	L24-21	t:Pickersgill,Doyle,England,Brown g:Hallas(2) fg:Flanagan	5th	2,696
14/8/21	Newcastle (a)	W12-36	t:Crossley,Foggin-Johnston(2),Rooks,Flanagan(2) g:Lilley(6)	4th	1,168
22/8/21	Swinton (h)	W30-26	t:Pickersgill,Oakes,Flanagan(2),Foggin-Johnston g:Lilley(5)	4th	2,819
29/8/21	York (a)	W18-36	t:Lilley,B Evans,R Evans(3),Foggin-Johnston g:Brough(6)	4th	2,841
5/9/21	Toulouse (a) ●	L6-60	t:Flanagan g:Lilley	4th	2,445
12/9/21	Widnes (a)	L10-9	t:Lilley g:Lilley(2) fg:Brough	4th	1,725
19/9/21	Whitehaven (h)	L22-36	t:B Evans(2),Murphy,Foggin-Johnston g:Brough(2),Hallas	5th	5,340
25/9/21	Batley (a) (E)	L23-10	t:Brown,Lilley g:Brough	N/A	2,005

● Played at Tetley's Stadium, Dewsbury
●● Played at Trailfinders Sports Ground, Ealing

Sheffield (h) (R16) game was postponed, and not rearranged

Toulouse (a) (R10) game was cancelled

		APP		TRIES		GOALS		FG		PTS	
	D.O.B.	ALL	Ch	ALL	Ch	ALL	Ch	ALL	Ch	ALL	Ch
Jordan Baldwinson	10/11/94	(1)	(1)	0	0	0	0	0	0	0	0
Danny Brough	15/1/83	13	12	2	2	49	47	5	5	111	107
Joe Brown	14/1/92	21	20	10	10	0	0	0	0	40	40
Joe Burton	15/3/02	2(5)	2(5)	1	1	0	0	0	0	4	4
Steve Crossley	28/11/89	21	20	4	4	0	0	0	0	16	16
Matty Dawson-Jones	2/10/90	2	2	0	0	0	0	0	0	0	0
Thomas Doyle	29/6/99	20	19	5	5	0	0	0	0	20	20
Brad England	20/11/94	14(4)	14(3)	4	4	0	0	0	0	16	16
Ben Evans	30/10/92	16(3)	16(3)	5	5	0	0	0	0	20	20
Rhys Evans	30/10/92	22	21	5	5	0	0	0	0	20	20
George Flanagan	8/10/86	(12)	(11)	6	6	1	1	1	1	27	27
Dan Fleming	8/7/92	10(8)	9(8)	1	1	0	0	0	0	4	4
David Foggin-Johnston	19/8/96	15(1)	15(1)	9	9	0	0	0	0	36	36
Brad Gallagher	28/2/00	7	6	0	0	0	0	0	0	0	0
Ashton Golding	4/9/96	1(1)	1(1)	1	1	0	0	0	0	4	4
Sam Hallas	18/10/96	14	13	0	0	3	3	0	0	6	6
Reece Hamlett	26/4/01	7	6	2	0	0	0	0	0	8	0
Bradley Ho	16/12/00	(2)	(2)	0	0	0	0	0	0	0	0
Billy Jowitt	7/4/01	2(2)	2(2)	0	0	0	0	0	0	0	0
Elliot Kear	29/11/88	3	3	0	0	0	0	0	0	0	0
Joe Keyes	17/9/95	3	3	3	3	18	18	0	0	48	48
Jordan Lilley	4/9/96	18	18	6	6	19	19	2	2	64	64
Masi Matongo	15/5/96	(1)	(1)	0	0	0	0	0	0	0	0
Aaron Murphy	26/11/88	17	17	2	2	0	0	0	0	8	8
Eldon Myers	27/6/95	(2)	(2)	0	0	0	0	0	0	0	0
Levy Nzoungou	22/1/98	3(1)	3(1)	0	0	0	0	0	0	0	0
Ethan O'Hanlon	19/5/01	(1)	(1)	0	0	0	0	0	0	0	0
Ross Oakes	12/10/96	22	21	3	3	0	0	0	0	12	12
Brandon Pickersgill	29/3/97	19	18	9	9	0	0	0	0	36	36
Ellis Robson	14/9/98	(4)	(4)	3	3	0	0	0	0	12	12
Adam Rooks	15/1/99	6(8)	5(8)	2	2	0	0	0	0	8	8
Jack Sanderson	18/3/98	2	1	0	0	0	0	0	0	0	0
Ebon Scurr	11/5/00	(16)	(15)	3	2	0	0	0	0	12	8
Mitieli Vulikijapani	27/6/94	2	2	0	0	0	0	0	0	0	0
Anthony Walker	28/12/91	3(15)	3(14)	2	2	0	0	0	0	8	8
Oliver Wilson	22/3/99	1(1)	1(1)	0	0	0	0	0	0	0	0

Joe Brown

'Ch' totals include regular season & play-offs; 'All' totals also include Challenge Cup

CLUB RECORDS MATCH RECORDS	**Highest score:** 124-0 v West Wales, 6/5/2018 **Highest score against:** 6-84 v Wigan, 21/4/2014 **Record attendance:** 69,429 v Huddersfield, 14/3/53 **Tries:** 6 Eric Batten v Leeds, 15/9/45; Trevor Foster v Wakefield, 10/4/48; Steve McGowan v Barrow, 8/11/92; Lesley Vainikolo v Hull, 2/9/2005 **Goals:** 20 Dane Chisholm v West Wales, 6/5/2018 **Points:** 48 Dane Chisholm v West Wales, 6/5/2018
SEASON RECORDS CAREER RECORDS	**Tries:** 63 Jack McLean 1951-52 **Goals:** 213 *(inc 5fg)* Henry Paul 2001 **Points:** 457 Henry Paul 2001 **Tries:** 261 Jack McLean 1950-56 **Goals:** 1,165 *(inc 25fg)* Paul Deacon 1998-2009 **Points:** 2,605 Paul Deacon 1998-2009 **Appearances:** 588 Keith Mumby 1973-90; 1992-93

DEWSBURY RAMS

DATE	FIXTURE	RESULT	SCORERS	LGE	ATT
20/3/21	Whitehaven (a) (CCR1)	L23-16	t:Morris,Ryder,Fleming g:Sykes(2)	N/A	BCD
3/4/21	Whitehaven (h)	W17-8	t:Day,Fleming(2) g:Sykes(2) fg:Finn	4th	BCD
17/4/21	Widnes (a)	W14-22	t:Martin,Oakes,Gabriel(2) g:Sykes(3)	4th	BCD
25/4/21	Bradford (a) ●	L35-14	t:Gabriel(2),Ryder g:Sykes	5th	BCD
2/5/21	York (h)	L20-30	t:Fleming,Gabriel,Hall g:Sykes(4)	7th	BCD
9/5/21	Halifax (h)	L0-36		10th	BCD
17/5/21	Swinton (a)	W18-20	t:Gabriel,Knowles,Tomlinson g:Sykes(4)	8th	416
30/5/21	London Broncos (a) ●●	L30-10	t:Wood,Gabriel g:Sykes	10th	280
13/6/21	Toulouse (h)	L12-56	t:Smith,Oakes g:Knowles,Sykes	10th	418
20/6/21	Featherstone (h)	L24-68	t:Liu,Garratt,Butterworth,Carr g:Finn(4)	11th	792
27/6/21	Oldham (a)	W4-18	t:Dixon,Gabriel,Oakes g:Sykes(3)	8th	600
4/7/21	Sheffield (h)	D18-18	t:Speakman,Knowles(2) g:Sykes(3)	9th	549
11/7/21	Newcastle (a)	L24-12	t:Carr,Dixon g:Knowles(2)	10th	789
15/7/21	Batley (h)	L10-38	t:Gabriel,Oakes g:Sykes	11th	1,021
1/8/21	Swinton (h)	L18-22	t:Fleming,Magrin,Day g:Sykes(3)	12th	616
8/8/21	Whitehaven (a)	L20-18	t:Gabriel,Schofield,Dixon g:Sykes(3)	12th	730
15/8/21	Widnes (h)	W23-22	t:Fleming,Beckett,Ferguson g:Dean(5) fg:Dean	12th	726
22/8/21	Featherstone (a)	L64-6	t:Gabriel g:Sykes	12th	2,115
29/8/21	Newcastle (h)	L22-43	t:Fleming,Magrin,Sykes,Garratt g:Sykes(3)	12th	540
5/9/21	Sheffield (a)	W20-24	t:Smith,Tomlinson,Schofield,Gabriel g:Finn(4)	12th	432
12/9/21	Batley (a)	W24-31	t:Ryder,Finn,Gabriel,Garratt,Schofield g:Sykes(5) fg:Sykes	11th	1,532
19/9/21	Oldham (h)	W21-14	t:Carr,Ryder(2),Knowles g:Sykes(2) fg:Sykes	10th	827

● Played at Tetley's Stadium
●● Played at Trailfinders Sports Ground, Ealing

Toulouse (a) (R14) game was cancelled

		APP		TRIES		GOALS		FG		PTS	
	D.O.B.	ALL	Ch	ALL	Ch	ALL	Ch	ALL	Ch	ALL	Ch
Chris Annakin	30/1/91	12(5)	12(5)	0	0	0	0	0	0	0	0
Jimmy Beckett	29/8/99	10(2)	10(2)	1	1	0	0	0	0	4	4
Reiss Butterworth	7/12/98	12(3)	11(3)	1	1	0	0	0	0	4	4
Lewis Carr	11/8/00	13	12	3	3	0	0	0	0	12	12
Connor Davies	17/1/97	(1)	(1)	0	0	0	0	0	0	0	0
Rhys Davies	9/6/96	(1)	(1)	0	0	0	0	0	0	0	0
Sam Day	12/6/94	7(9)	7(8)	2	2	0	0	0	0	8	8
Riley Dean	10/8/01	4(1)	4(1)	0	0	5	5	1	1	11	11
Davey Dixon	31/5/97	10	10	3	3	0	0	0	0	12	12
Sonny Esslemont	29/12/93	3	3	0	0	0	0	0	0	0	0
Dale Ferguson	13/4/88	(1)	(1)	1	1	0	0	0	0	4	4
Liam Finn	2/11/83	15(1)	14(1)	1	1	8	8	1	1	21	21
Matty Fleming	13/1/96	18	17	7	6	0	0	0	0	28	24
Matthew Fletcher	15/2/00	(2)	(2)	0	0	0	0	0	0	0	0
Andy Gabriel	21/12/93	21	20	13	13	0	0	0	0	52	52
Tom Garratt	25/10/94	19(1)	18(1)	3	3	0	0	0	0	12	12
Jamie Greenwood	27/10/98	(1)	(1)	0	0	0	0	0	0	0	0
Aaron Hall	19/2/93	4(10)	3(10)	1	1	0	0	0	0	4	4
Dan Hawksworth	30/3/93	1(4)	1(4)	0	0	0	0	0	0	0	0
Jon Luke Kirby	23/9/98	1	1	0	0	0	0	0	0	0	0
Michael Knowles	2/5/87	18	17	4	4	3	3	0	0	22	22
Bayley Liu	3/8/96	4(3)	4(3)	1	1	0	0	0	0	4	4
Jon Magrin	8/10/94	10(7)	10(6)	2	2	0	0	0	0	8	8
Joe Martin	28/3/95	14(3)	13(3)	1	1	0	0	0	0	4	4
Zack McComb	9/9/95	2	2	0	0	0	0	0	0	0	0
Frazer Morris	22/2/97	4(1)	3(1)	1	0	0	0	0	0	4	0
Will Oakes	27/2/99	13(1)	13	4	4	0	0	0	0	16	16
Adam Ryder	20/10/89	10	9	5	4	0	0	0	0	20	16
Jordan Schofield	23/9/00	1(6)	1(6)	3	3	0	0	0	0	12	12
Connor Scott	27/5/93	(1)	0	0	0	0	0	0	0	0	0
Alex Smith	17/8/97	6(2)	6(2)	2	2	0	0	0	0	8	8
Dom Speakman	22/3/94	4(7)	4(7)	1	1	0	0	0	0	4	4
Robson Stevens	4/4/02	2(8)	2(8)	0	0	0	0	0	0	0	0
Robbie Storey	21/10/99	5(2)	5(2)	0	0	0	0	0	0	0	0
Paul Sykes	11/8/81	18	17	1	1	42	40	2	2	90	86
James Thornton	30/9/95	4(2)	4(2)	0	0	0	0	0	0	0	0
Keenen Tomlinson	22/5/97	11(1)	10(1)	2	2	0	0	0	0	8	8
Jason Walton	13/6/90	7(1)	7(1)	0	0	0	0	0	0	0	0
Dane Windrow	9/6/02	2	2	0	0	0	0	0	0	0	0
Sam Wood	11/6/97	1	1	1	1	0	0	0	0	4	4

'Ch' totals include Championship games only; 'All' totals also include Challenge Cup

Andy Gabriel

CLUB RECORDS
MATCH RECORDS
SEASON RECORDS
CAREER RECORDS

Highest score: 90-5 v Blackpool, 4/4/93 **Highest score against:** 0-82 v Widnes, 30/11/86
Record attendance: 26,584 v Halifax, 30/10/1920 *(Crown Flatt)*; 4,068 v Bradford, 6/4/2015 *(Tetley's Stadium)*
Tries: 8 Dai Thomas v Liverpool, 13/4/1907
Goals: 13 Greg Pearce v Blackpool Borough, 4/4/93; Francis Maloney v Hunslet, 25/3/2007 **Points:** 32 Les Holliday v Barrow, 11/9/94
Tries: 40 Dai Thomas 1906-07 **Goals:** 169 Barry Eaton 2000 **Points:** 394 Barry Eaton 2000
Tries: 144 Joe Lyman 1913-31 **Goals:** 863 Nigel Stephenson 1967-78; 1984-86 **Points:** 2,082 Nigel Stephenson 1967-78; 1984-86
Appearances: 454 Joe Lyman 1913-31

FEATHERSTONE ROVERS

DATE	FIXTURE	RESULT	SCORERS	LGE	ATT
21/3/21	Bradford (h) (CCR1)	W41-16	t:Jones,Minns,Blackmore,Harrison(2),Parata,Hall g:Hall(6) fg:Hall	N/A	BCD
27/3/21	Batley (h) (CCR2)	W30-22	t:Day,Blackmore,Brown,Welham,Harrison,Parata g:Hall(3)	N/A	BCD
2/4/21	Batley (h)	W28-18	t:Kopczak,Welham,Halton,Brown,Gale,Moors g:Hall,Chisholm	5th	BCD
10/4/21	Hull FC (h) (CCR3)	L14-34	t:Hardcastle,Ferres,Blackmore g:Chisholm	N/A	BCD
18/4/21	Swinton (a)	W6-36	t:Gale,Holmes,Minns,Day,Davies,Blackmore(2) g:Brown(4)	3rd	BCD
25/4/21	Whitehaven (h)	W48-14	t:Ferres,Jones,Bussey,Kopczak,Brown,Moors,Hardcastle,Gale,Hall g:Brown(6)	1st	BCD
9/5/21	York (a)	W12-16	t:Gale(2),Hall g:Brown(2)	2nd	BCD
17/5/21	Oldham (h)	W68-0	t:Chisholm,Hall(2),Bussey(2),Day,Minns,Hardcastle,Holmes,Brown,Jones,Gale g:Chisholm(10)	2nd	
23/5/21	Sheffield (a)	W18-50	t:Doyle,Gale(2),Bussey,Lockwood(2),Field,Brown,Hall g:Chisholm(7)	2nd	1,670
30/5/21	Halifax (a)	W8-16	t:Brown,Hall,Gale g:Chisholm(2)	2nd	620
6/6/21	Widnes (h) (1895CSF)	W24-18	t:Day(2),Kopczak,Halton g:Hall(4)	N/A	882
13/6/21	Bradford (h)	W44-0	t:Jones,Hall,Gale,Dagger,Minns,Holmes,Parata,Field g:Hall(6)	2nd	1,750
20/6/21	Dewsbury (a)	W24-68	t:Kopczak,Parata(4),Hall(3),Gale(2),Cooper g:Hall(12)	2nd	792
26/6/21	Newcastle (a)	W68-12	t:Gale(6),Jones,Whiteley,Hardcastle(2),Hall,Parata,Holmes g:Hall(8)	2nd	1,750
3/7/21	London Broncos (h)	W63-14	t:Hall(3),Dagger,Chisholm,Moors,Parata(2),Gale,Brown(2) g:Hall(9) fg:Chisholm	2nd	1,750
11/7/21	Widnes (a)	W10-32	t:Brown(3),Jones,Gale g:Chisholm(6)	2nd	947
17/7/21	York (1895CF) ●	W41-34	t:Chisholm,Kopczak,Doyle(2),Brown,Harrison,Hall g:Hall(6) fg:Chisholm	N/A	-
25/7/21	Bradford (a)	W30-36	t:Doyle,Brown(2),Harrison(2),Chisholm g:Hall(6)	2nd	3,708
1/8/21	Toulouse (a)	L6-23	t:Gale g:Hall	2nd	4,021
8/8/21	Batley (a)	W13-28	t:Chisholm,Brown,Blackmore,Walker,Halton g:Hall(4)	2nd	1,259
14/8/21	York (h)	W44-14	t:Blackmore,Harrison,Walker(2),Hall g:Hall(6)	2nd	2,183
22/8/21	Dewsbury (h)	W64-6	t:Springer,Blackmore(2),Field,Hall(3),Walker,Cooper,Davies,Jones g:Hall(10)	2nd	2,115
29/8/21	Oldham (a)	W10-48	t:Parata(2),Ferres(2),Welham,Kopczak(2),Walker(2) g:Chisholm(4),Ferres(2)	2nd	1,158
5/9/21	Halifax (h)	W54-22	t:Welham,Chisholm(2),Gale(2),Blackmore(2),Jones,Ferres,Brown g:Hall(7)	2nd	3,063
12/9/21	London Broncos (a) ●●	W28-48	t:Gale(2),Jones(3),Field,Walker,Holmes,Halton g:Hall(6)	2nd	555
19/9/21	Sheffield (h)	W78-10	t:Hall(5),Brown,Halton(3),Ferres(2),Bussey,Gale(2),Hardcastle g:Hall(9)	2nd	1,750
2/10/21	Halifax (h) (SF)	W42-10	t:Halton,Kopczak,Ferres,Hardcastle,Jones(2),Welham g:Hall(7)	N/A	2,084
10/10/21	Toulouse (a) (MPG)	L34-12	t:Ferres,Davies g:Hall(2)	N/A	9,235

● Played at Wembley Stadium
●● Played at Trailfinders Sports Ground, Ealing

Toulouse (a) (R4) game was postponed, and not rearranged

	D.O.B.	APP ALL	APP Ch	TRIES ALL	TRIES Ch	GOALS ALL	GOALS Ch	FG ALL	FG Ch	PTS ALL	PTS Ch
Jimmy Beckett	29/8/99	(2)	(2)	0	0	0	0	0	0	0	0
Ben Blackmore	19/2/93	11	8	11	8	0	0	0	0	44	32
Fa'amanu Brown	24/12/94	26(1)	22	17	15	12	12	0	0	92	84
Jack Bussey	17/8/92	9(3)	7(3)	5	5	0	0	0	0	20	20
Dane Chisholm	4/7/90	18(2)	14(2)	7	6	31	30	2	1	92	85
Luke Cooper	28/7/94	(18)	(14)	2	2	0	0	0	0	8	8
Will Dagger	21/2/99	5	5	2	2	0	0	0	0	8	8
John Davies	8/1/91	4(19)	3(18)	3	3	0	0	0	0	12	12
Brad Day	23/9/94	12	8	5	2	0	0	0	0	20	8
Jacob Doyle	12/3/01	3	2	4	2	0	0	0	0	16	8
Dale Ferguson	13/4/88	(4)	(3)	0	0	0	0	0	0	0	0
Brett Ferres	17/4/86	16(1)	14	9	8	2	2	0	0	40	36
Callum Field	7/10/97	10(12)	10(9)	4	4	0	0	0	0	16	16
Gareth Gale	5/6/93	26	21	27	27	0	0	0	0	108	108
Craig Hall	21/2/88	26	21	28	26	113	94	1	0	339	292
Frankie Halton	18/6/96	21(2)	17(2)	8	7	0	0	0	0	32	28
Josh Hardcastle	28/8/92	22(1)	17(1)	7	6	0	0	0	0	28	24
James Harrison	15/6/96	7(5)	5(3)	7	3	0	0	0	0	28	12
Tom Holmes	2/3/96	16(2)	14(2)	5	5	0	0	0	0	20	20
Connor Jones	26/1/96	19(4)	16(4)	13	12	0	0	0	0	52	48
Craig Kopczak	20/12/86	21(1)	17(1)	8	6	0	0	0	0	32	24
James Lockwood	21/3/86	24	20	2	2	0	0	0	0	8	8
Darcy Lussick	6/6/89	2	2	0	0	0	0	0	0	0	0
Loui McConnell	21/11/99	8(1)	5(1)	0	0	0	0	0	0	0	0
Thomas Minns	4/9/94	10	8	4	3	0	0	0	0	16	12
Junior Moors	30/7/86	11(7)	10(5)	3	3	0	0	0	0	12	12
Dean Parata	4/10/91	7(15)	6(12)	12	10	0	0	0	0	48	40
Harvey Spence	14/9/00	1(3)	1(2)	0	0	0	0	0	0	0	0
Gadwin Springer	4/4/93	1(6)	1(6)	1	1	0	0	0	0	4	4
Joe Summers	7/11/99	(2)	(1)	0	0	0	0	0	0	0	0
Jake Sweeting	15/12/99	1(1)	(1)	0	0	0	0	0	0	0	0
Alex Walker	4/9/95	9	9	7	7	0	0	0	0	28	28
Kris Welham	12/5/87	16	14	5	4	0	0	0	0	20	16
Perry Whiteley	22/2/93	2	2	1	1	0	0	0	0	4	4

Gareth Gale

'Ch' totals include regular season & play-offs; 'All' totals also include Challenge Cup & 1895 Cup

CLUB RECORDS MATCH RECORDS
Highest score: 96-0 v Castleford Lock Lane, 8/2/2004 **Highest score against:** 14-80 v Bradford, 3/4/2005 **Record attendance:** 17,531 v St Helens, 21/3/59
Tries: 6 Mike Smith v Doncaster, 14/4/68; Chris Bibb v Keighley, 17/9/89; Brad Dwyer v Rochdale, 1/7/2018; Gareth Gale v Newcastle, 26/6/2021
Goals: 13 Mark Knapper v Keighley, 17/9/89; Liam Finn v Hunslet Old Boys, 25/3/2012; Liam Finn v Swinton, 12/8/2012
Points: 40 Martin Pearson v Whitehaven, 26/11/95

SEASON RECORDS CAREER RECORDS
Tries: 48 Paul Newlove 1992-93 **Goals:** 183 *(inc 2fg)* Liam Finn 2012 **Points:** 436 Liam Finn 2012
Tries: 162 Don Fox 1953-66 **Goals:** 1,210 Steve Quinn 1975-88 **Points:** 2,654 Steve Quinn 1975-88 **Appearances:** 440 Jim Denton 1921-34

HALIFAX PANTHERS

DATE	FIXTURE	RESULT	SCORERS	LGE	ATT
20/3/21	Batley (h) (CCR1)	L6-19	t:Garside g:Robinson	N/A	BCD
2/4/21	London Broncos (h)	W47-14	t:Morris,Harris,Barber(2),McComb,Grix,Fairbank,McGrath g:Robinson(6),Harris fg:Robinson	3rd	BCD
18/4/21	Bradford (a) ●	L27-26	t:Saltonstall,Grix,Springer,Larroyer g:Robinson(5)	5th	BCD
25/4/21	Toulouse (h)	L34-44	t:Saltonstall(3),McComb,Woodburn-Hall,Barber g:Robinson(5)	9th	BCD
1/5/21	Oldham (a)	L16-12	t:McGrath,Woodburn-Hall g:Robinson(2)	12th	BCD
9/5/21	Dewsbury (a)	W0-36	t:Barber(2),Moore,Rawsthorne,Morris g:Robinson(8)	7th	BCD
23/5/21	Newcastle (a)	W0-32	t:Woodburn-Hall(2),Rawsthorne,Barber,Bourouh g:Robinson(6)	6th	604
30/5/21	Featherstone (h)	L8-16	t:Tangata g:Robinson,Harris	8th	882
6/6/21	Sheffield (h)	W46-12	t:Rawsthorne(2),Kavanagh,Woodburn-Hall,Hewitt(2),Larroyer(2),Murray g:Rawsthorne(4),Harris	6th	734
13/6/21	York (h)	W30-6	t:Kavanagh,Garside,Rawsthorne,Moore,Saltonstall,Tangata g:Harris(3)	6th	828
20/6/21	Swinton (a)	W4-34	t:Grix(2),McGrath,Kavanagh,Bourouh g:Harris(5)	6th	520
27/6/21	Batley (a)	W12-22	t:Harris(3),Woodburn-Hall g:Harris(3)	6th	1,193
4/7/21	Widnes (h)	W17-16	t:Morris,Saltonstall(2) g:Harris(2) fg:Harris	4th	1,232
11/7/21	Whitehaven (h)	W14-4	t:Curtis Davies,Garside g:Harris(3)	4th	877
25/7/21	Sheffield (h) ●●	W28-40	t:Fairbank(2),Tangata(3),McGrath,Harris g:Harris(6)	3rd	775
1/8/21	Bradford (h)	W24-21	t:Woodburn-Hall,Worthington,Saltonstall(2),Harris g:Harris(2)	3rd	2,696
8/8/21	Newcastle (h)	W14-12	t:McComb,Tibbs,Curtis Davies g:Barber	3rd	1,541
22/8/21	Widnes (a)	L25-6	t:Barber g:Woodburn-Hall	3rd	1,252
29/8/21	Swinton (h)	W48-12	t:Moore(2),Saltonstall,Kavanagh,Harris,Garside,Tibbs,Grix,McComb g:Robinson(6)	3rd	1,663
5/9/21	Featherstone (a)	L54-22	t:McComb,Garside,Barber,Woodburn-Hall g:Robinson(3)	3rd	3,063
12/9/21	Whitehaven (a)	L19-6	t:Grix g:Barber	3rd	1,258
19/9/21	Batley (h)	L10-12	t:Saltonstall,McGrath g:Robinson	3rd	2,216
25/9/21	Whitehaven (h) (E)	W24-20	t:McGrath,Garside(2),Woodburn-Hall g:Harris(2),Woodburn-Hall,Robinson	N/A	1,289
2/10/21	Featherstone (a) (SF)	L42-10	t:McGrath,Harris g:Robinson	N/A	2,084

● *Played at Tetley's Stadium, Dewsbury*
●● *Played at Mobile Rocket Stadium, Wakefield*

Toulouse (a) (R17) game was cancelled

		APP		TRIES		GOALS		FG		PTS	
	D.O.B.	ALL	Ch	ALL	Ch	ALL	Ch	ALL	Ch	ALL	Ch
Ed Barber	26/4/90	12(5)	11(5)	8	8	2	2	0	0	36	36
Amir Bourouh	5/1/01	(10)	(10)	2	2	0	0	0	0	8	8
Paul Brearley	5/2/92	2(1)	2(1)	0	0	0	0	0	0	0	0
Will Calcott	16/12/97	8(4)	7(4)	0	0	0	0	0	0	0	0
Connor Davies	17/1/97	(7)	(6)	0	0	0	0	0	0	0	0
Curtis Davies	17/1/97	(9)	(8)	2	2	0	0	0	0	8	8
Jacob Fairbank	4/3/90	13(7)	13(6)	3	3	0	0	0	0	12	12
Matt Garside	1/10/90	21	20	7	6	0	0	0	0	28	24
Scott Grix	1/5/84	19	18	6	6	0	0	0	0	24	24
Liam Harris	20/4/97	21	20	8	8	29	29	1	1	91	91
Sam Hewitt	29/4/99	6(1)	6(1)	2	2	0	0	0	0	8	8
Ben Kavanagh	4/3/88	17(2)	17(2)	4	4	0	0	0	0	16	16
Kevin Larroyer	19/6/89	6(14)	5(14)	3	3	0	0	0	0	12	12
Zack McComb	9/9/95	18	18	5	5	0	0	0	0	20	20
Conor McGrath	14/8/96	13	12	8	8	0	0	0	0	32	32
Brandon Moore	27/7/96	24	23	4	4	0	0	0	0	16	16
Elliot Morris	4/1/96	4(15)	4(15)	3	3	0	0	0	0	12	12
Daniel Murray	21/3/96	21(2)	20(2)	1	1	0	0	0	0	4	4
Nick Rawsthorne	30/9/95	11	10	5	5	4	4	0	0	28	28
Connor Robinson	23/10/94	11(3)	10(3)	0	0	46	45	1	1	93	91
Oliver Russell	21/9/98	(1)	(1)	0	0	0	0	0	0	0	0
James Saltonstall	27/9/93	21	20	11	11	0	0	0	0	44	44
Gadwin Springer	4/4/93	6(5)	6(4)	1	1	0	0	0	0	4	4
Adam Tangata	17/3/91	14(5)	14(5)	5	5	0	0	0	0	20	20
Ben Tibbs	3/11/00	1(3)	1(3)	2	2	0	0	0	0	8	8
James Woodburn-Hall	2/2/95	21(1)	20(1)	9	9	2	2	0	0	40	40
Greg Worthington	17/7/90	22	22	1	1	0	0	0	0	4	4

'Ch' totals include regular season & play-offs; 'All' totals also include Challenge Cup

Brandon Moore

CLUB RECORDS	
	Highest score: 94-4 v Myton, 25/3/2012 **Highest score against:** 6-88 v Hull KR, 23/4/2006
MATCH RECORDS	**Record attendance:** 29,153 v Wigan, 21/3/59 *(Thrum Hall)*; 9,827 v Bradford, 12/3/2000 *(The Shay)*
	Tries: 8 Keith Williams v Dewsbury, 9/11/57 **Goals:** 14 Bruce Burton v Hunslet, 27/8/72
	Points: 32 John Schuster v Doncaster, 9/10/94; Steve Tyrer v Whitehaven, 7/2/2016
SEASON RECORDS	**Tries:** 48 Johnny Freeman 1956-57 **Goals:** 156 Graham Holroyd 2008 **Points:** 362 John Schuster 1994-95
CAREER RECORDS	**Tries:** 290 Johnny Freeman 1954-67 **Goals:** 1,028 Ronnie James 1961-71 **Points:** 2,191 Ronnie James 1961-71 **Appearances:** 482 Stan Kielty 1946-58

252

LONDON BRONCOS

DATE	FIXTURE	RESULT	SCORERS	LGE	ATT
20/3/21	Keighley (h) (CCR1) ●	W24-10	t:Boafo,Jones,Davis,Navarrete g:Hankinson(4)	N/A	BCD
28/3/21	York (h) (CCR2) ●	L2-14	g:Chamberlain	N/A	BCD
2/4/21	Halifax (a)	L47-14	t:Miski(2),Egodo g:Fozard	12th	BCD
24/4/21	Oldham (h) ●	W38-24	t:Egodo(3),Sammut(2),Hindmarsh,Walters g:Hankinson(5)	12th	BCD
1/5/21	Sheffield (a)	D20-20	t:Egodo,Miski(3) g:Hankinson,Sammut	11th	BCD
9/5/21	Newcastle (h) ●	W50-30	t:Fozard,Hankinson,Miski(2),Boafo(2),Richards,Sammut g:Hankinson(8),Sammut	6th	BCD
15/5/21	Batley (a)	W6-40	t:Walters,Hankinson(2),Miski,Curran,Jones,Boafo g:Hankinson(6)	5th	BCD
23/5/21	Bradford (h) ●●	L8-33	t:Curran g:Hankinson(2)	7th	533
30/5/21	Dewsbury (h) ●●	W30-10	t:Walters(2),Fozard,Aston,Meadows g:Hankinson(5)	5th	280
13/6/21	Widnes (a)	W22-24	t:Miski,Curran,Navarrete,Gwaze g:Hankinson(4)	5th	1,211
20/6/21	Whitehaven (h) ●●	W46-12	t:Hankinson(2),Meadows,Hodson,Gwaze,Curran,Aston,Sammut g:Hankinson(7)	5th	250
27/6/21	Swinton (h) ●●	W38-24	t:Boafo(3),Miski(2),Lovell,Sammut g:Hankinson(5)	5th	240
3/7/21	Featherstone (a)	L63-14	t:Hankinson,Sammut,Miski g:Hankinson	6th	1,750
11/7/21	York (h) ●●	W50-22	t:Lovell(2),Hodson,Hankinson(2),Leyland,Miski,Jones g:Hankinson(9)	5th	312
1/8/21	Oldham (a)	W20-30	t:Walters,Miski(2),Sammut,Jones g:Hankinson(5)	6th	948
8/8/21	Toulouse (h) ●●	L6-66	t:Egodo g:Hankinson	6th	500
15/8/21	Whitehaven (a)	L32-18	t:Miski,Hodson,Curran g:Hankinson(3)	6th	792
29/8/21	Sheffield (h) ●●	W42-12	t:Boafo(3),Ogden,Fozard,Walters,Hankinson,Miski g:Hankinson(5)	6th	350
5/9/21	Swinton (a)	W32-34	t:Richards,Moran,Miski,Adebiyi,Boafo(2) g:Hankinson(5)	6th	542
12/9/21	Featherstone (h) ●●	L28-48	t:Boafo(4),Hodson g:Hankinson(4)	6th	555
19/9/21	York (a)	L32-22	t:Richards,Hankinson,Jones,Gwaze g:Hankinson(3)	7th	2,782

● *Played at The Rock, Roehampton*
●● *Played at Trailfinders Sports Ground, Ealing*

Newcastle (a) (R18) game was postponed, and not rearranged

Widnes (h) (R14) game was cancelled

Toulouse (a) (R2) game ruled a 24-0 defeat due to refusal to travel

		APP		TRIES		GOALS		FG		PTS	
	D.O.B.	ALL	Ch	ALL	Ch	ALL	Ch	ALL	Ch	ALL	Ch
Sadiq Adebiyi	8/1/97	1(2)	1(2)	1	1	0	0	0	0	4	4
Cory Aston	1/3/95	7	6	2	2	0	0	0	0	8	8
Will Blakemore	20/9/98	1(2)	1(2)	0	0	0	0	0	0	0	0
Gideon Boafo	10/2/99	9(4)	7(4)	16	15	0	0	0	0	64	60
Ed Chamberlain	8/2/96	7	5	0	0	1	0	0	0	2	0
Rhys Curran	7/7/97	13	12	5	5	0	0	0	0	20	20
Sam Davis	11/11/98	5(4)	3(4)	1	0	0	0	0	0	4	0
Tuoyo Egodo	16/2/97	8(1)	8(1)	6	6	0	0	0	0	24	24
Matty Fozard	3/3/95	13	13	3	3	1	1	0	0	14	14
Titus Gwaze	8/6/99	6(14)	6(12)	3	3	0	0	0	0	12	12
Chris Hankinson	30/11/93	19	18	10	10	83	79	0	0	206	198
Dan Hindmarsh	8/8/98	10(10)	9(10)	1	1	0	0	0	0	4	4
Josh Hodson	15/6/00	15(2)	14(1)	4	4	0	0	0	0	16	16
Rian Horsman	4/4/01	6(2)	5(2)	0	0	0	0	0	0	0	0
Jacob Jones	15/2/99	14(6)	12(6)	5	4	0	0	0	0	20	16
Olsi Krasniqi	26/6/92	3	1	0	0	0	0	0	0	0	0
Paulos Latu	23/11/90	(2)	0	0	0	0	0	0	0	0	0
Oliver Leyland	17/5/01	7(2)	6(2)	1	1	0	0	0	0	4	4
Will Lovell	10/5/93	19	17	3	3	0	0	0	0	12	12
James Meadows	15/6/99	19	18	2	2	0	0	0	0	8	8
Abbas Miski	25/7/95	21	19	18	18	0	0	0	0	72	72
Pat Moran	2/4/98	9(3)	9(3)	1	1	0	0	0	0	4	4
Romain Navarrete	30/6/94	8(3)	6(3)	2	1	0	0	0	0	8	4
Rob Oakley	8/11/99	2(5)	2(5)	0	0	0	0	0	0	0	0
Jacob Ogden	23/1/98	4(4)	4(4)	1	1	0	0	0	0	4	4
Greg Richards	12/7/95	17(3)	17(1)	3	3	0	0	0	0	12	12
Jarrod Sammut	15/2/87	9(4)	9(4)	7	7	2	2	0	0	32	32
Josh Walters	23/12/94	18	16	6	6	0	0	0	0	24	24
Jordan Williams	4/6/97	3(9)	3(8)	0	0	0	0	0	0	0	0

'Ch' totals include Championship games only; 'All' totals also include Challenge Cup

Abbas Miski

CLUB RECORDS	**Highest score:** 82-0 v Highfield, 12/11/95; 82-2 v Barrow, 20/5/2006 **Highest score against:** 6-82 v Warrington, 20/3/2011; 10-82 v Warrington, 8/6/2013
MATCH RECORDS	**Record attendance:** 15,013 v Wakefield, 15/2/81 *(Craven Cottage)*; 3,051 v Leeds, 1/9/2019 *(Trailfinders Sports Ground)*
	Tries: 5 Martin Offiah v Whitehaven, 14/3/99; Sean Morris v Batley, 13/9/2015
SEASON RECORDS	**Goals:** 13 Rob Purdham v Barrow, 20/5/2006 **Points:** 34 Rob Purdham v Barrow, 20/5/2006; Jarrod Sammut v Sheffield, 13/5/2018
CAREER RECORDS	**Tries:** 43 Mark Johnson 1993-94 **Goals:** 159 John Gallagher 1993-94 **Points:** 384 John Gallagher 1993-94
	Tries: 109 Luke Dorn 2005-2006; 2009-2013 **Goals:** 309 Steve Diamond 1981-84 **Points:** 772 Paul Sykes 2001-2007
	Appearances: 202 Steele Retchless 1998-2004

NEWCASTLE THUNDER

DATE	FIXTURE	RESULT	SCORERS	LGE	ATT
21/3/21	Swinton (a) (CCR1)	L28-16	t:Ta'ai,Tyrer,S Wilde g:Wright(2)	N/A	BCD
4/4/21	Widnes (h)	D30-30	t:Gill(2),S Wilde,Ta'ai,Bailey,Johnson g:Wright(3)	7th	BCD
18/4/21	Whitehaven (a)	L29-20	t:Gill,Johnson,S Wilde,Clegg g:J Woods(2)	10th	BCD
25/4/21	Sheffield (h)	W24-16	t:Johnson,Oakley,J Chapelhow,Ta'ai g:J Woods(4)	7th	BCD
2/5/21	Batley (h)	L16-28	t:Gill(2),Shorrocks g:J Woods(2)	10th	BCD
9/5/21	London Broncos (a) ●	L50-30	t:Gill(2),Wrench,Simons,N Wilde g:J Woods(5)	12th	BCD
23/5/21	Halifax (h)	L0-32		13th	604
6/6/21	Bradford (a)	L31-12	t:Dean,Gill g:Dean(2)	13th	3,562
13/6/21	Swinton (a)	W30-36	t:Ta'ai,Beswick,Wright(2),Bailey,Turner g:J Woods(5),Wright	11th	455
20/6/21	Oldham (h)	W40-6	t:Johnson(2),Ta'ai,Halsall,Beswick,Shorrocks,J Woods g:J Woods(6)	10th	1,087
26/6/21	Featherstone (a)	L68-12	t:Gill,Beswick g:J Woods(2)	11th	1,750
4/7/21	York (a)	W26-28	t:Shorrocks,Harrison,Simons,Clegg(2) g:J Woods(4)	8th	1,497
11/7/21	Dewsbury (h)	W24-12	t:Johnson,Bailey,Ta'ai,Clegg,Gill g:J Woods(2)	7th	789
25/7/21	Batley (a)	L42-12	t:Ta'ai,McAvoy g:J Woods(2)	8th	932
1/8/21	Whitehaven (h)	L14-20	t:Ta'ai,Gill g:J Woods(3)	10th	1,647
8/8/21	Halifax (a)	L14-12	t:Johnson,T Chapelhow g:Wright(2)	11th	1,541
14/8/21	Bradford (h)	L12-36	t:Johnson,Gill g:J Woods(2)	11th	1,168
29/8/21	Dewsbury (a)	W22-43	t:Turner,Johnson(3),Shorrocks,J Woods,T Chapelhow,Wright g:J Woods(5) fg:J Woods	9th	540
3/9/21	York (h)	L16-29	t:Clegg,Johnson,Gill g:J Woods(2)	10th	1,115
12/9/21	Oldham (a)	W24-38	t:J Woods,Ta'ai,Bailey,Gill,Nokes,Donaghy(2) g:J Woods(5)	10th	723
18/9/21	Toulouse (h)	L12-82	t:Roebuck(2) g:J Woods(2)	11th	428

● Played at The Rock, Roehampton

London Broncos (h) (R18) game was postponed, and not rearranged

Toulouse (a) (R8) game was cancelled

		APP		TRIES		GOALS		FG		PTS	
	D.O.B.	ALL	Ch	ALL	Ch	ALL	Ch	ALL	Ch	ALL	Ch
Jake Anderson	21/11/02	(4)	(4)	0	0	0	0	0	0	0	0
Connor Aspey	16/4/02	1	1	0	0	0	0	0	0	0	0
Connor Bailey	10/10/00	16(2)	15(2)	4	4	0	0	0	0	16	16
Bob Beswick	8/12/84	12	12	3	3	0	0	0	0	12	12
Harry Bowes	7/9/01	(1)	(1)	0	0	0	0	0	0	0	0
Joe Brown	24/4/87	2	2	0	0	0	0	0	0	0	0
Jay Chapelhow	21/9/95	2(14)	2(13)	1	1	0	0	0	0	4	4
Ted Chapelhow	21/9/95	15(4)	15(3)	2	2	0	0	0	0	8	8
Mitch Clark	13/3/93	(2)	(2)	0	0	0	0	0	0	0	0
Alex Clegg	9/7/99	19	19	5	5	0	0	0	0	20	20
Reece Dean	30/11/96	6(4)	6(4)	1	1	2	2	0	0	8	8
Alex Donaghy	22/9/01	7(2)	7(2)	2	2	0	0	0	0	8	8
Kieran Gill	4/12/95	15	15	14	14	0	0	0	0	56	56
Sam Halsall	18/8/01	6	6	1	1	0	0	0	0	4	4
Owen Harrison	10/4/99	2(6)	2(6)	1	1	0	0	0	0	4	4
Evan Hodgson	14/9/98	(3)	(2)	0	0	0	0	0	0	0	0
Kieran Hudson	13/6/00	(3)	(3)	0	0	0	0	0	0	0	0
Jack Johnson	25/4/96	18	17	12	12	0	0	0	0	48	48
Ellis Longstaff	5/7/02	1(1)	1(1)	0	0	0	0	0	0	0	0
Liam McAvoy	24/9/93	7(6)	7(6)	1	1	0	0	0	0	4	4
Matty Nicholson	18/7/03	1	1	0	0	0	0	0	0	0	0
Isaac Nokes	14/11/01	3(2)	3(2)	1	1	0	0	0	0	4	4
Cole Oakley	25/10/00	3(7)	3(6)	1	1	0	0	0	0	4	4
Nathan Roebuck	2/10/99	1	1	2	2	0	0	0	0	8	8
Jake Shorrocks	26/10/95	17	16	4	4	0	0	0	0	16	16
Evan Simons	11/10/91	10(9)	9(9)	2	2	0	0	0	0	8	8
Tom Spencer	2/1/91	(3)	(3)	0	0	0	0	0	0	0	0
Ukuma Ta'ai	17/1/87	14(4)	13(4)	9	8	0	0	0	0	36	32
Kyle Trout	1/3/91	6(2)	6(2)	0	0	0	0	0	0	0	0
Calum Turner	29/4/99	12	11	2	2	0	0	0	0	8	8
Cian Tyrer	3/2/01	4	3	1	0	0	0	0	0	4	0
Nathan Wilde	29/12/99	17(1)	16(1)	1	1	0	0	0	0	4	4
Sam Wilde	8/9/95	11(2)	10(2)	3	2	0	0	0	0	12	8
Todd Wilkinson	8/8/02	(1)	(1)	0	0	0	0	0	0	0	0
Mikey Wood	18/4/96	8	7	0	0	0	0	0	0	0	0
Josh Woods	13/12/97	18	17	3	3	53	53	1	1	119	119
Connor Wrench	4/10/01	1(1)	1(1)	1	1	0	0	0	0	4	4
Matthew Wright	30/1/91	14	13	3	3	8	6	0	0	28	24
Lewis Young	1/7/95	4	3	0	0	0	0	0	0	0	0

Josh Woods

'Ch' totals include Championship games only; 'All' totals also include Challenge Cup

CLUB RECORDS Highest score: 98-6 v West Wales, 23/9/2018 Highest score against: 0-132 v Blackpool Panthers, 16/5/2010
Record attendance: 6,631 v Bradford, 16/5/99 *(Gateshead International Stadium)*; 4,137 v Bradford, 18/5/2018 *(Kingston Park)*
MATCH RECORDS Tries: 5 Andy Walker v London Skolars, 22/6/2003 Goals: 12 Rhys Clarke v Coventry, 18/8/2019 Points: 28 Benn Hardcastle v Oxford, 18/6/2017
SEASON RECORDS Tries: 28 Kieran Gill 2019 Goals: 129 *(inc 1fg)* Dan Russell 2008 Points: 293 Dan Russell 2008
CAREER RECORDS Tries: 74 Kevin Neighbour 2001-2006; 2008-2010 Goals: 283 *(inc 8fg)* Benn Hardcastle 2013-2017 Points: 682 Benn Hardcastle 2013-2017
Appearances: 234 Joe Brown 2005-2006; 2010-2021

OLDHAM

DATE	FIXTURE	RESULT	SCORERS	LGE	ATT
20/3/21	Barrow (h) (CCR1)	W20-6	t:Charnock,Langtree,Brierley g:D Abram(4)	N/A	BCD
28/3/21	Swinton (a) (CCR2)	L23-14	t:Langtree,Dupree,Heaton g:D Abram	N/A	BCD
2/4/21	Swinton (h)	W28-20	t:Roberts,Ince,Heaton(2),Dupree g:D Abram(4)	6th	BCD
17/4/21	Batley (a)	L48-10	t:Charnock,Brierley g:D Abram	8th	BCD
24/4/21	London Broncos (a) ●	L38-24	t:Nelmes,Bibby,Langtree,Hewitt g:Green(4)	11th	BCD
1/5/21	Halifax (h)	W16-12	t:Brierley,Reilly,Croft g:Green(2)	8th	BCD
8/5/21	Whitehaven (h)	L4-36	t:Green	11th	BCD
17/5/21	Featherstone (a)	L68-0		11th	1,670
23/5/21	York (a)	L34-6	t:Pick g:D Abram	12th	1,000
30/5/21	Widnes (h)	L18-40	t:Senior,Brierley,Langtree g:D Abram(3)	13th	600
12/6/21	Sheffield (h)	L28-32	t:Roberts,D Abram,Reilly,Kirk,Brierley g:D Abram(4)	13th	475
20/6/21	Newcastle (a)	L40-6	t:Kirk g:D Abram	13th	1,087
27/6/21	Dewsbury (h)	L4-18	t:Dupree	13th	600
11/7/21	Bradford (h)	L22-54	t:Holcroft,Reilly,D Abram,Dupree g:D Abram(3)	13th	650
25/7/21	Whitehaven (h)	L28-24	t:Hewitt,D Abram,Dupree,Nelmes g:D Abram(4)	13th	920
1/8/21	London Broncos (h)	L20-30	t:Ince,Dupree,Reilly g:D Abram(4)	13th	948
8/8/21	Swinton (a)	D22-22	t:Dupree(2),Roby,Barran g:D Abram(3)	13th	1,527
15/8/21	Sheffield (a)	L25-18	t:Langtree,Reilly,Dupree g:D Abram(3)	13th	372
22/8/21	Toulouse (h)	L6-34	t:Reilly g:D Abram	13th	743
29/8/21	Featherstone (h)	L10-48	t:Hartley,Bridge g:D Abram	13th	1,158
5/9/21	Widnes (a)	L62-4	t:Holcroft	13th	1,088
12/9/21	Newcastle (h)	L24-38	t:Charnock,D Abram,Dupree,Roberts(2) g:D Abram(2)	13th	723
19/9/21	Dewsbury (a)	L21-14	t:D Abram,Bridge g:D Abram(3)	13th	827

● Played at The Rock, Roehampton

Toulouse (a) (R12) game was cancelled

		APP		TRIES		GOALS		FG		PTS	
	D.O.B.	ALL	Ch	ALL	Ch	ALL	Ch	ALL	Ch	ALL	Ch
Dan Abram	11/11/95	20	18	5	5	43	38	0	0	106	96
Jamie Abram	6/6/00	1(6)	1(6)	0	0	0	0	0	0	0	0
James Barran	26/10/98	9(1)	7(1)	1	1	0	0	0	0	4	4
Liam Bent	11/10/97	19(4)	17(4)	0	0	0	0	0	0	0	0
Jack Bibby	14/10/01	(2)	(2)	1	1	0	0	0	0	4	4
Danny Bridge	4/1/93	14(3)	12(3)	2	2	0	0	0	0	8	8
Tommy Brierley	8/9/96	19(1)	17(1)	5	4	0	0	0	0	20	16
Lewis Charnock	2/9/94	18(3)	16(3)	3	2	0	0	0	0	12	8
Jack Croft	21/12/00	2	2	1	1	0	0	0	0	4	4
Tyler Dupree	8/2/00	6(12)	6(10)	10	9	0	0	0	0	40	36
Matthew Fletcher	15/2/00	1(7)	1(7)	0	0	0	0	0	0	0	0
Callum Green	27/9/99	5(2)	5(1)	1	1	6	6	0	0	16	16
Dec Gregory	18/1/97	2(13)	2(12)	0	0	0	0	0	0	0	0
Joe Hartley	2/5/98	6	6	1	1	0	0	0	0	4	4
Ben Heaton	12/3/90	5	3	3	2	0	0	0	0	12	8
Dave Hewitt	4/11/95	13	13	2	2	0	0	0	0	8	8
Ben Holcroft	24/11/00	13	13	2	2	0	0	0	0	8	8
John Hutchings	1/1/99	1	1	0	0	0	0	0	0	0	0
Ryan Ince	16/9/96	20	18	2	2	0	0	0	0	8	8
Brad Jinks	19/12/00	1(2)	1(2)	0	0	0	0	0	0	0	0
Phil Joy	4/9/91	6	6	0	0	0	0	0	0	0	0
Liam Kirk	26/3/97	15(1)	13(1)	2	2	0	0	0	0	8	8
Danny Langtree	18/2/91	22(1)	20(1)	5	3	0	0	0	0	20	12
Luke Nelmes	7/6/93	11(10)	10(10)	2	2	0	0	0	0	8	8
Tom Nisbet	8/10/99	1	1	0	0	0	0	0	0	0	0
Gareth Owen	3/7/92	18	16	0	0	0	0	0	0	0	0
Shaun Pick	21/9/93	6(9)	6(7)	1	1	0	0	0	0	4	4
Martyn Reilly	5/1/96	10(11)	9(10)	6	6	0	0	0	0	24	24
Max Roberts	8/9/00	23	21	4	4	0	0	0	0	16	16
Lloyd Roby	3/1/99	1(1)	1(1)	1	1	0	0	0	0	4	4
Fenton Rogers	4/8/03	(1)	(1)	0	0	0	0	0	0	0	0
Louis Senior	30/5/00	1	1	1	1	0	0	0	0	4	4
Harvey Spence	14/9/00	5	5	0	0	0	0	0	0	0	0
Jack Spencer	21/12/90	5(2)	5(1)	0	0	0	0	0	0	0	0

'Ch' totals include Championship games only; 'All' totals also include Challenge Cup

CLUB RECORDS

MATCH RECORDS

SEASON RECORDS
CAREER RECORDS

Highest score: 102-6 v West Wales, 8/7/2018 **Highest score against:** 0-84 v Widnes, 25/7/99
Record attendance: 28,000 v Huddersfield, 24/2/1912 *(Watersheddings)*; 2,394 v Warrington, 7/5/2016 *(Bower Fold)*
Tries: 7 James Miller v Barry, 31/10/1908 **Goals:** 14 Bernard Ganley v Liverpool City, 4/4/59
Points: 34 Andy Ballard v London Skolars, 2/5/2009; Chris Baines v Hunslet, 20/9/2009; Lewis Palfrey v Hemel, 9/8/2015
Tries: 49 Reg Farrar 1921-22 **Goals:** 200 Bernard Ganley 1957-58 **Points:** 412 Bernard Ganley 1957-58
Tries: 174 Alan Davies 1950-61 **Goals:** 1,358 Bernard Ganley 1951-61 **Points:** 2,761 Bernard Ganley 1951-61 **Appearances:** 627 Joe Ferguson 1899-1923

Tyler Dupree

SHEFFIELD EAGLES

DATE	FIXTURE	RESULT	SCORERS		LGE	ATT
19/3/21	York (h) (CCR1)	L6-30	t:G Burns g:I Farrell		N/A	BCD
4/4/21	Bradford (h)	W50-12	t:Brown(2),Guzdek,Glover(2),J Farrell,I Farrell,Thackeray(2),Millar			
			g:I Farrell(4),Glover		1st	BCD
18/4/21	York (a)	W14-20	t:Thackeray(2),Dickinson g:I Farrell(4)		2nd	BCD
25/4/21	Newcastle (a)	L24-16	t:Glover,J Farrell,Render g:I Farrell(2)		4th	BCD
1/5/21	London Broncos (h)	D20-20	t:Glover,I Farrell,Brown g:I Farrell(4)		5th	BCD
7/5/21	Batley (h)	L18-30	t:Worrincy(2),Bull g:I Farrell(3)		5th	BCD
23/5/21	Featherstone (h)	L18-50	t:Knowles,B Tyson-Wilson,I Farrell g:I Farrell(3)		9th	620
30/5/21	Whitehaven (h)	D25-25	t:G Burns,Knowles,I Farrell,Thackeray g:I Farrell(4) fg:Thackeray		9th	343
6/6/21	Halifax (a)	L46-12	t:Broadbent,Millar g:I Farrell(2)		10th	734
12/6/21	Oldham (a)	W28-32	t:Glover(2),Worrincy(3),Brown g:I Farrell(4)		8th	475
20/6/21	Widnes (a)	L30-20	t:Millar,Glover(2),Corion g:I Farrell,Glover		9th	984
27/6/21	Toulouse (h) ●	L6-54	t:Davies g:H Tyson-Wilson		10th	319
4/7/21	Dewsbury (a)	D18-18	t:Corion,Thackeray,Brown g:I Farrell(3)		10th	549
11/7/21	Swinton (a)	W22-30	t:Millar(3),Davies(2) g:I Farrell(5)		9th	501
25/7/21	Halifax (h) ●	L28-40	t:Millar(3),Thackeray,Brown g:I Farrell(4)		9th	775
15/8/21	Oldham (h)	W25-18	t:James,Davies,Millar,Guzdek g:Guzdek(4) fg:H Tyson-Wilson		8th	372
22/8/21	Batley (a)	L56-12	t:Davey,Davies g:Guzdek(2)		9th	859
29/8/21	London Broncos (a) ●●	L42-12	t:Johnson,Broadbent g:Guzdek(2)		10th	350
5/9/21	Dewsbury (a)	L20-24	t:Dickinson,Thackeray,Worrincy g:I Farrell(4)		11th	432
12/9/21	Swinton (h)	L28-34	t:Dickinson,J Farrell(2),Worrincy,Butterworth g:I Farrell(4)		12th	430
19/9/21	Featherstone (a)	L78-10	t:Johnson,Worrincy g:Guzdek		12th	1,750

Home games played at Keepmoat Stadium, Doncaster (unless stated)

● *Played at Mobile Rocket Stadium, Wakefield*
●● *Played at Trailfinders Sports Ground, Ealing*

York (h) (R15) and Bradford (a) (R16) games were postponed, and not rearranged

		APP		TRIES		GOALS		FG		PTS	
	D.O.B.	ALL	Ch	ALL	Ch	ALL	Ch	ALL	Ch	ALL	Ch
Mike Adlard	27/6/97	2	2	0	0	0	0	0	0	0	0
Chris Ball	1/3/00	(2)	(2)	0	0	0	0	0	0	0	0
Connor Bower	18/1/97	11(1)	11(1)	0	0	0	0	0	0	0	0
Blake Broadbent	11/12/98	(12)	(11)	2	2	0	0	0	0	8	8
Aaron Brown	27/7/92	21	20	6	6	0	0	0	0	24	24
Jordan Bull	14/12/99	1(2)	1(2)	1	1	0	0	0	0	4	4
Greg Burns	25/3/95	11(7)	10(7)	2	1	0	0	0	0	8	4
Paddy Burns	15/3/98	2(10)	2(9)	0	0	0	0	0	0	0	0
Olly Butterworth	12/1/98	1	1	1	1	0	0	0	0	4	4
Max Clarke	1/1/00	1	1	0	0	0	0	0	0	0	0
Travis Corion	27/3/01	4(1)	4(1)	2	2	0	0	0	0	8	8
James Davey	21/8/89	8(10)	8(10)	1	1	0	0	0	0	4	4
Olly Davies	30/11/95	21	20	5	5	0	0	0	0	20	20
Tyler Dickinson	18/8/96	8(12)	8(11)	3	3	0	0	0	0	12	12
Izaac Farrell	30/1/98	16	15	4	4	52	51	0	0	120	118
Joel Farrell	15/3/94	11	10	4	4	0	0	0	0	16	16
James Glover	2/12/93	18	17	8	8	2	2	0	0	36	36
Josh Guzdek	22/4/95	16	15	2	2	9	9	0	0	26	26
Evan Hodgson	14/9/98	6(5)	6(5)	0	0	0	0	0	0	0	0
Matt James	26/3/87	16(1)	15(1)	1	1	0	0	0	0	4	4
Ryan Johnson	3/8/00	12(1)	11(1)	2	2	0	0	0	0	8	8
Brad Knowles	31/7/93	11(5)	10(5)	2	2	0	0	0	0	8	8
Frankie Mariano	10/5/87	2(2)	2(2)	0	0	0	0	0	0	0	0
Ryan Millar	12/5/94	19	18	10	10	0	0	0	0	40	40
Jack Render	4/7/99	1	1	1	1	0	0	0	0	4	4
Anthony Thackeray	19/2/86	16	15	8	8	0	0	1	1	33	33
Bobby Tyson-Wilson	6/11/94	1(3)	1(3)	1	1	0	0	0	0	4	4
Harry Tyson-Wilson	29/12/96	5(2)	5(2)	0	0	1	1	1	1	3	3
Robbie Ward	27/10/95	2(1)	2	0	0	0	0	0	0	0	0
Scott Wheeldon	23/2/86	10(6)	10(6)	0	0	0	0	0	0	0	0
Rob Worrincy	9/7/85	20	19	8	8	0	0	0	0	32	32

Olly Davies

'Ch' totals include Championship games only; 'All' totals also include Challenge Cup

CLUB RECORDS	**Highest score:** 112-6 v Leigh East, 7/4/2013 **Highest score against:** 0-88 v Hull, 2/3/2003
	Record attendance: 10,603 v Bradford, 16/8/97 *(Don Valley Stadium)*; 1,711 v Bradford, 15/2/2019 *(Olympic Legacy Park)*
MATCH RECORDS	**Tries:** 5 Daryl Powell v Mansfield, 2/1/89; Menzie Yere v Leigh East, 7/4/2013; Quentin Laulu-Togaga'e v Rochdale, 7/9/2014; Garry Lo v Rochdale, 4/6/2017
	Goals: 14 Dominic Brambani v Leigh East, 7/4/2013 **Points:** 32 Roy Rafferty v Fulham, 21/9/86
SEASON RECORDS	**Tries:** 46 Menzie Yere 2013 **Goals:** 169 *(inc 1fg)* Dominic Brambani 2013 **Points:** 361 Dominic Brambani 2013
CAREER RECORDS	**Tries:** 196 Menzie Yere 2009-2020 **Goals:** 986 Mark Aston 1986-2004 **Points:** 2,142 Mark Aston 1986-2004 **Appearances:** 389 Mark Aston 1986-2004

SWINTON LIONS

DATE	FIXTURE	RESULT	SCORERS	LGE	ATT
21/3/21	Newcastle (h) (CCR1)	W28-16	t:Lloyd,Butt(2),Hansen,Doyle g:Ridyard(4)	N/A	BCD
28/3/21	Oldham (h) (CCR2)	W23-14	t:Grant,Hope,Ridyard,Meadows g:Ridyard(3) fg:Ridyard	N/A	BCD
2/4/21	Oldham (a)	L28-20	t:Butt,Waterworth,Lloyd,Hansen g:Ridyard(2)	9th	BCD
11/4/21	Warrington (h) (CCR3)	L8-32	t:Roberts g:Ridyard(2)	N/A	BCD
18/4/21	Featherstone (h)	L6-36	t:Cox g:Ridyard	13th	BCD
25/4/21	York (h)	L16-64	t:Roberts,Butt,Brogan g:Hansen(2)	14th	BCD
2/5/21	Widnes (a)	L46-10	t:Rizzelli,Butt g:Hansen	14th	BCD
9/5/21	Bradford (h)	L22-23	t:Rizzelli,Roberts,Lloyd,Hansen g:Ridyard(3)	14th	BCD
17/5/21	Dewsbury (h)	L18-20	t:Cox,Brickhill(2) g:Ridyard(3)	14th	416
22/5/21	Toulouse (a) ●	L66-18	t:Gregson,Hansen,Cox g:Ridyard(3)	14th	186
30/5/21	Batley (a)	L26-12	t:Cox,Brooks g:Ridyard(2)	14th	930
6/6/21	York (a) (1895CSF)	L36-22	t:Butt(3),Michael g:Ridyard(3)	N/A	1,214
13/6/21	Newcastle (h)	L30-36	t:Hope(2),Cox,Gregson,Hansen g:Ridyard(5)	14th	455
20/6/21	Halifax (h)	L4-34	t:Roberts	14th	520
27/6/21	London Broncos (a) ●●	L38-24	t:Lloyd,Green,Butt,Roberts g:Ridyard(4)	14th	240
4/7/21	Whitehaven (a)	L36-22	t:Meadows,Nash,Cox,Doyle g:Ridyard(3)	14th	746
11/7/21	Sheffield (h)	L22-30	t:Lloyd,Buckley,Heyes,Hansen g:Ridyard(3)	14th	501
25/7/21	York (h)	L46-10	t:Heyes,Meadows g:Hansen	14th	1,344
1/8/21	Dewsbury (a)	W18-22	t:Buckley,Brogan,Cox,Hansen g:Hansen(3)	14th	616
8/8/21	Oldham (h)	D22-22	t:Hatton(2),Butt,Meadows g:Ridyard(2),Gregson	14th	1,527
15/8/21	Batley (h)	L6-38	t:Roberts g:Ridyard	14th	842
22/8/21	Bradford (a)	L30-26	t:Roberts(2),Heyes,Lloyd,Ridyard g:Gregson,Ridyard(2)	14th	2,819
29/8/21	Halifax (a)	L48-12	t:Lloyd,Hope g:Ridyard(2)	14th	1,663
5/9/21	London Broncos (h)	L32-34	t:Hansen,Hatton,Ridyard,Butt,Heyes,Roberts g:Ridyard(4)	14th	542
12/9/21	Sheffield (a)	W28-34	t:Roberts,Gregson,Hamlett,Cox,Doyle,Hatton g:Ridyard(5)	14th	430
19/9/21	Widnes (h)	L16-26	t:Doyle,Cox,Hamlett g:Ridyard(2)	14th	1,358

● *Played at Heywood Road*
●● *Played at Trailfinders Sports Ground, Ealing*

		APP		TRIES		GOALS		FG		PTS	
	D.O.B.	ALL	Ch	ALL	Ch	ALL	Ch	ALL	Ch	ALL	Ch
Billy Brickhill	30/4/97	10(9)	9(8)	2	2	0	0	0	0	8	8
Louis Brogan	6/5/00	15(7)	13(5)	2	2	0	0	0	0	8	8
Sam Brooks	29/9/93	15(3)	12(3)	1	1	0	0	0	0	4	4
Jordan Brown	30/9/00	1(7)	1(6)	0	0	0	0	0	0	0	0
Tayler Brown	16/10/99	(9)	(7)	0	0	0	0	0	0	0	0
Owen Buckley	15/11/98	4	4	2	2	0	0	0	0	8	8
Mike Butt	6/5/95	23	19	11	6	0	0	0	0	44	24
Dan Clare	24/10/00	1	1	0	0	0	0	0	0	0	0
Mitch Cox	15/11/93	26	22	9	9	0	0	0	0	36	36
Geronimo Doyle	6/1/97	21	19	4	3	0	0	0	0	16	12
Liam Forsyth	23/3/96	1	0	0	0	0	0	0	0	0	0
Sam Grant	24/3/99	2(1)	1(1)	1	0	0	0	0	0	4	0
Cobi Green	4/3/99	7(6)	7(4)	1	1	0	0	0	0	4	4
Nick Gregson	17/12/95	21(1)	17(1)	3	3	2	2	0	0	16	16
Reece Hamlett	26/4/01	5	5	2	2	0	0	0	0	8	8
Jack Hansen	12/1/97	24	20	8	7	7	7	0	0	46	42
Lewis Hatton	14/1/97	10	8	4	4	0	0	0	0	16	16
Ben Heyes	5/10/98	6(3)	6(3)	4	4	0	0	0	0	16	16
Will Hope	2/6/93	20(2)	17(1)	4	3	0	0	0	0	16	12
Dom Horn	13/3/95	(1)	(1)	0	0	0	0	0	0	0	0
Paddy Jones	7/2/97	2(17)	2(14)	0	0	0	0	0	0	0	0
Richard Lepori	22/10/91	5	2	0	0	0	0	0	0	0	0
Rhodri Lloyd	22/7/93	25	21	7	6	0	0	0	0	28	24
Sam Luckley	29/11/95	3(1)	3(1)	0	0	0	0	0	0	0	0
Deane Meadows	11/5/94	9(10)	7(8)	4	3	0	0	0	0	16	12
Ronan Michael	3/7/00	4(7)	3(7)	1	0	0	0	0	0	4	0
Paul Nash	16/4/00	1(14)	1(12)	1	1	0	0	0	0	4	4
Martyn Ridyard	25/7/86	23	19	3	2	59	47	1	0	131	102
Nico Rizzelli	28/3/00	3	3	2	2	0	0	0	0	8	8
Luis Roberts	24/3/02	20	17	10	9	0	0	0	0	40	36
Tom Spencer	2/1/91	6(6)	6(6)	0	0	0	0	0	0	0	0
Luke Waterworth	20/6/96	25	21	1	1	0	0	0	0	4	4

Mitch Cox

'Ch' totals include Championship games only; 'All' totals also include Challenge Cup & 1895 Cup

CLUB RECORDS		
	Highest score: 96-4 v Oxford, 12/7/2015 **Highest score against:** 0-112 v Warrington, 20/5/2011	
	Record attendance: 26,891 v Wigan, 12/2/64 *(Station Road)*; 2,155 v Toulouse, 28/4/2018 *(Heywood Road)*	
MATCH RECORDS	**Tries:** 6 Mark Riley v Prescot, 11/8/96 **Goals:** 14 Ian Mort v Oxford, 12/7/2015 **Points:** 48 Ian Mort v Oxford, 12/7/2015	
SEASON RECORDS	**Tries:** 42 John Stopford 1963-64 **Goals:** 128 Albert Blan 1960-61 **Points:** 338 Ian Mort 2011	
CAREER RECORDS	**Tries:** 197 Frank Evans 1921-31 **Goals:** 970 Ken Gowers 1954-73 **Points:** 2,105 Ken Gowers 1954-73 **Appearances:** 601 Ken Gowers 1954-73	

TOULOUSE OLYMPIQUE

DATE	FIXTURE	RESULT	SCORERS	LGE	ATT
3/4/21	York (a)	W6-21	t:Peyroux,Garbutt,Bretherton g:Marion(4) fg:White	2nd	BCD
25/4/21	Halifax (a)	W34-44	t:Vaivai(2),Bretherton,White(2),Dixon,Casty g:Marion(8)	2nd	BCD
9/5/21	Widnes (h) ●	W70-0	t:White,Jussaume,Sangare,Dixon(3),Hitchcox,Garbutt,Flovie,Pelissier(3), Schaumkel g:Marion(9)	1st	BCD
16/5/21	Whitehaven (a)	W0-66	t:Jussaume(2),White,Dixon,Marion(2),Pelissier,Vaivai(2),Peyroux,Hitchcox, Flovie(2) g:Marion(7)	1st	BCD
22/5/21	Swinton (h) ●	W66-18	t:Casty,Marion,Jussaume,Schaumkel(3),Bretherton,Garbutt,Pelissier, Kheirallah,Peyroux,Ford g:Kheirallah(9)	1st	186
13/6/21	Dewsbury (a)	W12-56	t:Jussaume(2),Hitchcox(3),Pelissier(2),Garbutt,Sangare,Pezet g:Kheirallah(8)	1st	418
27/6/21	Sheffield (a) ●●	W6-54	t:Vaivai,Kheirallah,Bergal(2),Jussaume(2),Pelissier,Hansen,Armitage,Marion g:Kheirallah(7)	1st	319
11/7/21	Batley (a)	W12-32	t:Hansen,Schaumkel,Sangare,Vaivai(2),Jussaume g:Kheirallah(4)	1st	782
1/8/21	Featherstone (a)	W6-23	t:Peyroux(2),Sangare,Casty g:Kheirallah(3) fg:Gigot	1st	4,021
8/8/21	London Broncos (a) ●●●	W6-66	t:Marion,Vaivai(3),Peyroux(2),Schaumkel,Ford(2),Bretherton,Gigot g:Kheirallah(11)	1st	500
22/8/21	Oldham (a)	W6-34	t:Vaivai,Sangare,Pelissier(2),Peyroux,Garbutt g:Kheirallah(5)	1st	743
5/9/21	Bradford (a) ●●●●	W6-60	t:Armitage(2),Hitchcox,Bergal,Navarrete,Sangare(2),Bretherton,Casty, Kheirallah(2) g:Kheirallah(8)	1st	2,445
18/9/21	Newcastle (a)	W12-82	t:Hitchcox(4),Bretherton(2),Peyroux,Jussaume(2),Sangare(2),Paulo, Navarrete,Kheirallah,Marion g:Kheirallah(11)	1st	428
2/10/21	Batley (h) (SF)	W51-12	t:Casty,Gigot,Bretherton,Vaivai(2),Kheirallah,Sangare,Jussaume,Garbutt g:Kheirallah(7) fg:Gigot	N/A	6,871
10/10/21	Featherstone (h) (MPG)	W34-12	t:Jussaume(2),Schaumkel,Hansen,Ford g:Kheirallah(7)	N/A	9,235

● *Played at Heywood Road, Sale*
●● *Played at Mobile Rocket Stadium, Wakefield*
●●● *Played at Trailfinders Sports Ground, Ealing*
●●●● *Played at Tetley's Stadium, Dewsbury*

Featherstone (h) (R4) game was postponed, and not rearranged

Newcastle (h) (R8), Bradford (h) (R10), Oldham (h) (R12), Dewsbury (h) (R14), Halifax (h) (R17), Batley (h) (R19) and York (h) (R21) games were cancelled

London Broncos (h) (R2) game ruled a 24-0 victory due to London's refusal to travel

		APP		TRIES		GOALS		FG		PTS	
	D.O.B.	ALL	Ch	ALL	Ch	ALL	Ch	ALL	Ch	ALL	Ch
Lucas Albert	4/7/98	(1)	(1)	0	0	0	0	0	0	0	0
Guy Armitage	29/11/91	2	2	3	3	0	0	0	0	12	12
Ilias Bergal	6/4/96	8	8	3	3	0	0	0	0	12	12
Clement Boyer	27/7/94	1	1	0	0	0	0	0	0	0	0
Joe Bretherton	5/10/95	11	11	8	8	0	0	0	0	32	32
Remi Casty	5/2/85	12(1)	12(1)	5	5	0	0	0	0	20	20
Andrew Dixon	28/2/90	9	9	5	5	0	0	0	0	20	20
Jordan Flovie	15/9/97	2	2	3	3	0	0	0	0	12	12
Johnathon Ford	17/8/89	15	15	4	4	0	0	0	0	16	16
Mitch Garbutt	18/4/89	(13)	(13)	6	6	0	0	0	0	24	24
Maxime Garcia	15/1/98	(5)	(5)	0	0	0	0	0	0	0	0
Tony Gigot	27/12/90	11	11	2	2	0	0	2	2	10	10
Harrison Hansen	26/10/85	13	13	3	3	0	0	0	0	12	12
Jy Hitchcox	18/8/89	10	10	10	10	0	0	0	0	40	40
Mathieu Jussaume	17/5/99	15	15	14	14	0	0	0	0	56	56
Mark Kheirallah	15/2/90	12	12	6	6	80	80	0	0	184	184
Ben Laguerre	13/9/01	1	1	0	0	0	0	0	0	0	0
Anthony Marion	12/1/94	13	13	6	6	28	28	0	0	80	80
Romain Navarrete	30/6/94	(4)	(4)	2	2	0	0	0	0	8	8
Joseph Paulo	2/1/88	4(7)	4(7)	1	1	0	0	0	0	4	4
Eloi Pelissier	18/6/91	3(11)	3(11)	10	10	0	0	0	0	40	40
Dominique Peyroux	21/1/89	11	11	9	9	0	0	0	0	36	36
Hugo Pezet	20/10/00	(3)	(3)	1	1	0	0	0	0	4	4
Maxime Puech	16/3/94	4(2)	4(2)	0	0	0	0	0	0	0	0
Hugo Salabio	27/7/00	(2)	(2)	0	0	0	0	0	0	0	0
Justin Sangare	7/3/98	2(11)	2(11)	10	10	0	0	0	0	40	40
Latrell Schaumkel	22/7/94	11	11	7	7	0	0	0	0	28	28
Junior Vaivai	18/1/90	14	14	13	13	0	0	0	0	52	52
Lloyd White	9/8/88	11	11	4	4	0	0	1	1	17	17

'Ch' totals include regular season & play-offs

Mathieu Jussaume

CLUB RECORDS	**Highest score:** 84-6 v Keighley, 18/6/2016 **Highest score against:** 10-90 v Featherstone, 3/7/2011 **Record attendance:** 9,235 v Featherstone, 10/10/2021
MATCH RECORDS	**Tries:** 6 Ilias Bergal v Rochdale, 13/7/2019 **Goals:** 12 Mark Kheirallah v Keighley, 18/6/2016 **Points:** 40 Mark Kheirallah v Keighley, 18/6/2016
SEASON RECORDS	**Tries:** 36 Kuni Minga 2016 **Goals:** 171 Mark Kheirallah 2016 **Points:** 466 Mark Kheirallah 2016
CAREER RECORDS	**Tries:** 98 Mark Kheirallah 2016-2021 **Goals:** 650 (inc 1fg) Mark Kheirallah 2016-2021 **Points:** 1,691 Mark Kheirallah 2016-2021 **Appearances:** 129 Mark Kheirallah 2016-2021

● *Records only include seasons when the club competed in the British game (2009-2011 & 2016-2021)*

WHITEHAVEN

DATE	FIXTURE	RESULT	SCORERS	LGE	ATT
20/3/21	Dewsbury (h) (CCR1)	W23-16	t:Walmsley,Taylor,Shackley,McNally g:Walmsley(3) fg:McNally	N/A	BCD
28/3/21	Widnes (a) (CCR2)	L34-10	t:C Phillips,Croston g:Walmsley	N/A	BCD
3/4/21	Dewsbury (a)	L17-8	t:Walmsley,Mossop	11th	BCD
18/4/21	Newcastle (h)	W29-20	t:Bulman(2),Holliday,Dixon,Walmsley g:Walmsley(3),Holliday fg:Williams	7th	BCD
25/4/21	Featherstone (a)	L48-14	t:Dixon,Worthington,Purewal g:Walmsley	10th	BCD
2/5/21	Bradford (h)	L22-30	t:Bulman,Parker,Mossop,Roden g:Walmsley(3)	13th	BCD
8/5/21	Oldham (a)	W4-36	t:Cooper,Parker,C Phillips(4) g:Walmsley(6)	9th	BCD
16/5/21	Toulouse (h)	L0-66		10th	BCD
23/5/21	Widnes (a)	L44-6	t:Bradley g:Walmsley	11th	1,043
30/5/21	Sheffield (a)	D25-25	t:Holliday,Walmsley,McNally,Bradley g:Walmsley(4) fg:McNally	11th	343
13/6/21	Batley (h)	L20-24	t:Taylor,Walmsley,Dixon,Bulman g:Walmsley(2)	12th	632
20/6/21	London Broncos (a) ●	L46-12	t:Wilkinson,Cooper g:Walmsley(2)	12th	250
27/6/21	York (h)	W37-12	t:Newton,Holliday(2),Dixon,Walmsley,Bulman g:Walmsley(6) fg:Williams	12th	601
4/7/21	Swinton (h)	W36-22	t:Williams,Holliday(2),Walmsley(2),Dixon g:Walmsley(5),Holliday	11th	746
11/7/21	Halifax (a)	L14-4	g:Walmsley(2)	11th	877
25/7/21	Oldham (h)	W28-24	t:Bulman,C Phillips(2),Jouffret,Wilkinson g:Jouffret(4)	11th	920
1/8/21	Newcastle (a)	W14-20	t:Walmsley,Dixon,Bulman g:Walmsley(4)	10th	1,647
8/8/21	Dewsbury (h)	W20-18	t:Jouffret,Bulman(2) g:Walmsley(2)	7th	730
15/8/21	London Broncos (h)	W32-18	t:Wilkinson,Cooper,Bulman,Williams,Walmsley g:Walmsley(6)	7th	792
22/8/21	York (h)	L30-12	t:Walmsley,Bradley g:Walmsley(2)	7th	1,460
29/8/21	Widnes (h)	W64-6	t:Dixon,Newton(2),Bulman(2),Aiye,Walmsley,King,Bradley,Jouffret,C Phillips g:Walmsley(10)	7th	951
5/9/21	Batley (a)	W14-22	t:Walmsley(2),Dixon,Jouffret g:Walmsley(3)	7th	922
12/9/21	Halifax (h)	W19-6	t:Walmsley,Mossop,King g:Walmsley(3) fg:McNally	7th	1,258
19/9/21	Bradford (a)	W22-36	t:Walker,Jouffret(2),McNally,Taylor,Walmsley g:Walmsley(6)	6th	5,340
25/9/21	Halifax (a) (E)	L24-20	t:Cooper,Bulman(2),King g:Jouffret(2)	N/A	1,289

● *Played at Trailfinders Sports Ground, Ealing*

		APP		TRIES		GOALS		FG		PTS	
	D.O.B.	ALL	Ch	ALL	Ch	ALL	Ch	ALL	Ch	ALL	Ch
Dion Aiye	6/11/87	(14)	(13)	1	1	0	0	0	0	4	4
Jake Bradley	29/4/01	3(11)	3(11)	4	4	0	0	0	0	16	16
Andrew Bulman	4/10/99	18	16	14	14	0	0	0	0	56	56
Liam Cooper	28/7/94	16(7)	15(6)	4	4	0	0	0	0	16	16
Sean Croston	1/11/99	5	4	1	0	0	0	0	0	4	0
Andrew Dawson	12/3/89	8(12)	7(12)	0	0	0	0	0	0	0	0
Karl Dixon	13/9/93	21	19	8	8	0	0	0	0	32	32
Ellis Gillam	6/10/97	17(1)	15(1)	0	0	0	0	0	0	0	0
Guy Graham	29/8/98	11(2)	11(2)	0	0	0	0	0	0	0	0
Connor Holliday	9/6/95	15(1)	14	6	6	2	2	0	0	28	28
Louis Jouffret	24/5/95	11	11	6	6	6	6	0	0	36	36
Ethan Kelly	31/12/94	1(3)	1(2)	0	0	0	0	0	0	0	0
Ryan King	28/6/97	4(6)	4(6)	3	3	0	0	0	0	12	12
Gregg McNally	2/1/91	14	13	3	2	0	0	3	2	15	10
Ronan Michael	3/7/00	(4)	(4)	0	0	0	0	0	0	0	0
Jason Mossop	12/9/85	20	19	3	3	0	0	0	0	12	12
James Newton	20/12/91	15(5)	14(5)	3	3	0	0	0	0	12	12
Karl Olstrom	21/9/91	(3)	(3)	0	0	0	0	0	0	0	0
Jessie Joe Parker	22/8/85	13(1)	12(1)	2	2	0	0	0	0	8	8
Brett Phillips	25/10/88	2	1	0	0	0	0	0	0	0	0
Callum Phillips	19/2/92	5(7)	4(6)	8	7	0	0	0	0	32	28
Aaron Purewal	2/2/98	1	1	1	1	0	0	0	0	4	4
Glenn Riley	29/1/92	3(1)	2(1)	0	0	0	0	0	0	0	0
Aiden Roden	4/6/00	6(1)	6(1)	1	1	0	0	0	0	4	4
Marc Shackley	14/1/89	7	6	1	0	0	0	0	0	4	0
Chris Taylor	25/10/93	19(1)	18(1)	3	2	0	0	0	0	12	8
Oscar Thomas	3/1/94	1(9)	1(8)	0	0	0	0	0	0	0	0
Andy Thornley	1/3/89	5(3)	5(2)	0	0	0	0	0	0	0	0
Tom Walker	25/12/94	10(4)	10(3)	1	1	0	0	0	0	4	4
Lachlan Walmsley	12/6/98	23	21	16	15	75	71	0	0	214	202
Tom Wilkinson	19/4/96	21	20	3	3	0	0	0	0	12	12
Nikau Williams	11/11/99	24	22	3	3	0	0	2	2	14	14
James Worthington	21/5/99	4	3	1	1	0	0	0	0	4	4
Dean Zammit	11/12/92	2(4)	1(4)	0	0	0	0	0	0	0	0

Lachlan Walmsley

'Ch' totals include regular season & play-offs; 'All' totals also include Challenge Cup

CLUB RECORDS
MATCH RECORDS

Highest score: 86-6 v Highfield, 25/1/95 **Highest score against:** 8-106 v Wigan, 12/5/2008 **Record attendance:** 18,500 v Wakefield, 19/3/60
Tries: 6 Vince Gribbin v Doncaster, 18/11/84; Andrew Bulman v Wigan St Patricks, 10/3/2019
Goals: 13 Lee Anderson v Highfield, 25/1/95 **Points:** 32 Mick Nanyn v Batley, 22/8/2004

SEASON RECORDS
CAREER RECORDS

Tries: 34 Mike Pechey 1994-95 **Goals:** 141 John McKeown 1956-57 **Points:** 398 Mick Nanyn 2004
Tries: 239 Craig Calvert 2004-2017 **Goals:** 1,050 John McKeown 1948-61 **Points:** 2,133 John McKeown 1948-61 **Appearances:** 417 John McKeown 1948-61

WIDNES VIKINGS

WIDNES VIKINGS

DATE	FIXTURE	RESULT	SCORERS	LGE	ATT
21/3/21	West Wales (a) (CCR1)	W4-58	t:Grady,Tyrer(3),Cross,Owens(3),Spedding(2),Lawton g:Owens(7)	N/A	BCD
28/3/21	Whitehaven (h) (CCR2)	W34-10	t:Tyrer,Craven,Else(2),Owens,Tilleke g:Owens(5)	N/A	BCD
4/4/21	Newcastle (a)	D30-30	t:Cross(2),Cook,Grady,Owens g:Owens(5)	7th	BCD
10/4/21	Salford (a) (CCR3)	L68-4	t:Hill	N/A	BCD
17/4/21	Dewsbury (h)	L14-22	t:Smith,Roby,Tyrer g:Tyrer	11th	BCD
24/4/21	Batley (a)	L48-16	t:Doro,Baker,Buckley g:Tyrer(2)	13th	BCD
2/5/21	Swinton (h)	W46-10	t:Cross(2),Baker,B O'Neill,Tyrer,Robson,Grady,Lawton g:Tyrer(7)	9th	BCD
9/5/21	Toulouse (a) ●	L70-0		13th	BCD
16/5/21	York (h)	L14-35	t:Lawton,Cross g:Tyrer(3)	13th	BCD
23/5/21	Whitehaven (h)	W44-6	t:B O'Neill,Lawton(2),Craven(2),Tilleke,Owens g:Tyrer(8)	10th	1,043
30/5/21	Oldham (a)	W18-40	t:Hatton,Tyrer,Cross(2),Owens(2),Spedding g:Tyrer(6)	7th	600
6/6/21	Featherstone (a) (1895CSF)	L24-18	t:Tyrer,Lawton(2) g:Tyrer(3)	N/A	1,750
13/6/21	London Broncos (h)	L22-24	t:Craven,Cross,Lawton,Edge g:Tyrer(3)	9th	1,211
20/6/21	Sheffield (h)	W30-20	t:Grady,Lyons,Craven,Lawton(2) g:Tyrer(5)	7th	984
27/6/21	Bradford (a)	W12-25	t:Else,Cross,Hatton,Lawton g:Tyrer(4) fg:Smith	7th	3,153
4/7/21	Halifax (a)	L17-16	t:Owens,Hatton g:Tyrer(4)	7th	1,232
11/7/21	Featherstone (h)	L10-32	t:Baker,Cross g:Tyrer	8th	947
1/8/21	Batley (h)	L16-34	t:Cross(2),Craven g:Owens(2)	8th	1,258
8/8/21	York (a)	L34-20	t:Owens,Cross,Lyons,Tyrer g:Owens(2)	10th	1,386
15/8/21	Dewsbury (a)	L23-22	t:Tyrer,Cross,Edge,Baker g:Owens(3)	10th	726
22/8/21	Halifax (h)	W25-6	t:Craven,Brookes,Tyrer,Baker g:Owens(4) fg:Craven	10th	1,252
29/8/21	Whitehaven (a)	L64-6	t:Roby g:Owens	11th	951
5/9/21	Oldham (h)	W62-4	t:Lawton(2),Brookes(2),Grady,Cross(2),Aspey,Baker,Craven,Tyrer g:Owens(9)	9th	1,088
12/9/21	Bradford (h)	W10-9	t:Owens g:Owens(3)	8th	1,725
19/9/21	Swinton (a)	W16-26	t:Lawton,Cross,Tyrer,Hatton,Hulme g:Owens(3)	8th	1,358

● Played at Heywood Road, Sale

London Broncos (a) (R14) game was cancelled

		APP		TRIES		GOALS		FG		PTS	
	D.O.B.	ALL	Ch	ALL	Ch	ALL	Ch	ALL	Ch	ALL	Ch
Connor Aspey	16/4/02	(2)	(2)	1	1	0	0	0	0	4	4
Kenny Baker	1/3/92	21(2)	18(2)	6	6	0	0	0	0	24	24
Ollie Brookes	19/6/01	5(1)	5(1)	3	3	0	0	0	0	12	12
Owen Buckley	15/11/98	5	2	1	1	0	0	0	0	4	4
Paul Clough	27/9/87	7(12)	6(10)	0	0	0	0	0	0	0	0
Matt Cook	14/11/86	5(6)	4(5)	1	1	0	0	0	0	4	4
Danny Craven	21/11/91	22	18	8	7	0	0	1	1	33	29
Deon Cross	30/7/96	25	21	18	17	0	0	0	0	72	68
Eribe Doro	26/3/01	3	3	1	1	0	0	0	0	4	4
Connor Dwyer	29/12/93	1(3)	(2)	0	0	0	0	0	0	0	0
Joe Edge	22/2/00	7(5)	7(5)	2	2	0	0	0	0	8	8
Lewis Else	30/3/00	7(8)	6(5)	3	1	0	0	0	0	12	4
Owen Farnworth	11/2/99	9(6)	7(5)	0	0	0	0	0	0	0	0
Shane Grady	13/12/89	21	18	5	4	0	0	0	0	20	16
Jayden Hatton	23/9/99	15	14	4	4	0	0	0	0	16	16
Daniel Hill	15/7/02	2(4)	1(4)	1	0	0	0	0	0	4	0
Lewis Hulme	1/7/94	7(2)	7(2)	1	1	0	0	0	0	4	4
Lee Jewitt	14/2/87	2	1	0	0	0	0	0	0	0	0
Adam Lawton	13/6/93	20(5)	16(5)	14	11	0	0	0	0	56	44
Joe Lyons	16/10/97	22(2)	19(1)	2	2	0	0	0	0	8	8
Brad O'Neill	22/7/02	8(1)	7(1)	2	2	0	0	0	0	8	8
Calum O'Neill	12/8/00	1(2)	(2)	0	0	0	0	0	0	0	0
Jack Owens	3/6/94	24	20	11	7	44	32	0	0	132	92
Ellis Robson	14/9/98	4	4	1	1	0	0	0	0	4	4
Lloyd Roby	3/1/99	10	9	2	2	0	0	0	0	8	8
Aiden Roden	4/6/00	2(4)	2(4)	0	0	0	0	0	0	0	0
Matty Smith	23/7/87	23	19	1	1	0	0	1	1	5	5
Jake Spedding	26/9/96	13(1)	9(1)	3	1	0	0	0	0	12	4
Will Tilleke	18/11/99	5(20)	5(16)	2	1	0	0	0	0	8	4
Steve Tyrer	16/3/89	24	20	13	8	47	44	0	0	146	120
Josh Wilde	4/1/01	5(5)	5(2)	0	0	0	0	0	0	0	0

'Ch' totals include Championship games only; 'All' totals also include Challenge Cup & 1895 Cup

Deon Cross

CLUB RECORDS	**Highest score:** 90-4 v Doncaster, 10/6/2007; 90-0 v Coventry, 21/4/2018 **Highest score against:** 6-76 v Catalans Dragons, 31/3/2012
	Record attendance: 24,205 v St Helens, 16/2/61
MATCH RECORDS	**Tries:** 7 Phil Cantillon v York, 18/2/2001 **Goals:** 14 Mark Hewitt v Oldham, 25/7/99; Tim Hartley v Saddleworth, 7/3/2009
	Points: 38 Gavin Dodd v Doncaster, 10/6/2007
SEASON RECORDS	**Tries:** 58 Martin Offiah 1988-89 **Goals:** 161 Mick Nanyn 2007 **Points:** 434 Mick Nanyn 2007
CAREER RECORDS	**Tries:** 234 Mal Aspey 1964-80 **Goals:** 1,083 Ray Dutton 1966-78 **Points:** 2,195 Ray Dutton 1966-78 **Appearances:** 591 Keith Elwell 1970-86

YORK CITY KNIGHTS

DATE	FIXTURE	RESULT	SCORERS	LGE	ATT
19/3/21	Sheffield (a) (CCR1)	W6-30	t:Whiteley(2),Brining,Jones-Bishop,Atkins g:K Dixon(5)	N/A	BCD
28/3/21	London Broncos (a) (CCR2) ●	W2-14	t:Porter,Salter g:K Dixon(3)	N/A	BCD
3/4/21	Toulouse (h)	L6-21	t:Jones-Bishop g:K Dixon	N/A	BCD
9/4/21	Wigan (h) (CCR3)	L0-26		13th	BCD
18/4/21	Sheffield (h)	L14-20	t:Jubb,K Dixon,Salter g:K Dixon	12th	BCD
25/4/21	Swinton (a)	W16-64	t:K Dixon,R Dixon(2),Marsh(4),Wynne,Dean(2),Atkins g:K Dixon(10)	8th	BCD
2/5/21	Dewsbury (a)	W20-30	t:Atkins,Stock,K Dixon,Marsh(2) g:K Dixon(5)	6th	BCD
9/5/21	Featherstone (h)	L12-16	t:Marsh,Salter g:K Dixon(2)	8th	BCD
16/5/21	Widnes (a)	W14-35	t:Scott,Jones-Bishop,Washbrook,Lewis(2) g:K Dixon(7) fg:Dean	6th	BCD
23/5/21	Oldham (h)	W34-6	t:Jubb(2),K Dixon,Dean,Marsh,Clarkson g:K Dixon(5)	5th	1,000
30/5/21	Bradford (a)	L37-18	t:K Dixon,Atkins,Clarkson g:K Dixon(3)	6th	3,742
6/6/21	Swinton (h) (1895CSF)	W36-22	t:Salter,Stock,Atkins,Brining,Kirmond,Lewis g:K Dixon(6)	N/A	1,214
13/6/21	Halifax (a)	L30-6	t:Marsh g:K Dixon	7th	828
20/6/21	Batley (h)	L20-22	t:Jones-Bishop,K Dixon(2) g:K Dixon(4)	8th	1,486
27/6/21	Whitehaven (a)	L37-12	t:Baldwinson,K Dixon g:K Dixon(2)	9th	601
4/7/21	Newcastle (h)	L26-28	t:Atkins,Clarkson,Scott,Whiteley g:K Dixon(5)	12th	1,497
11/7/21	London Broncos (a) ●●	L50-22	t:Whiteley,K Dixon,Jubb,Atkins g:K Dixon(3)	12th	312
17/7/21	Featherstone (1895CF) ●●●	L41-34	t:Jones-Bishop,Stock,Brining,Bass,Lewis,Whiteley g:K Dixon(4),Lewis	N/A	-
25/7/21	Swinton (a)	W46-10	t:Clarkson,R Dixon,K Dixon(2),Kirmond,Marsh(2),Dow-Nikau g:K Dixon(7)	11th	1,344
8/8/21	Widnes (h)	W34-20	t:O'Hagan(3),Dow-Nikau(2),Teanby g:Marsh(5)	8th	1,386
14/8/21	Featherstone (a)	L44-14	t:Jones-Bishop(2),Marsh g:Johnson	9th	2,183
22/8/21	Whitehaven (h)	W30-12	t:Teanby,Jones-Bishop,Stock,Whiteley,Scott g:Marsh(5)	8th	1,460
29/8/21	Bradford (h)	L18-36	t:Atkins,Green,Kirmond g:K Dixon(3)	8th	2,841
3/9/21	Newcastle (a)	W16-29	t:Clarkson,Jones-Bishop,McGowan(2),Whiteley g:Harrison(4) fg:Marsh	8th	1,115
19/9/21	London Broncos (h)	W32-22	t:Clarkson,Bass,Kirmond,Marsh,Dow-Nikau,Washbrook g:Harrison(3),Green	9th	2,782

● Played at The Rock, Roehampton   ●● Played at Trailfinders Sports Ground, Ealing   ●●● Played at Wembley Stadium

Sheffield (a) (R15) game was postponed, and not rearranged; Toulouse (a) (R21) game was cancelled

APP   TRIES GOALS FG   PTS

	D.O.B.	ALL	Ch	ALL	Ch	ALL	Ch	ALL	Ch	ALL	Ch
Ryan Atkins	7/10/85	19	16	8	6	0	0	0	0	32	24
Yusuf Aydin	13/9/00	3	3	0	0	0	0	0	0	0	0
Jordan Baldwinson	10/11/94	9(8)	7(7)	1	1	0	0	0	0	4	4
Daniel Barcoe	5/7/00	(2)	0	0	0	0	0	0	0	0	0
Jason Bass	10/5/96	10(2)	6(2)	2	1	0	0	0	0	8	4
Kriss Brining	16/11/93	(8)	(5)	3	0	0	0	0	0	12	0
Chris Clarkson	7/4/90	22	18	6	6	0	0	0	0	24	24
Adam Cuthbertson	24/2/85	4(11)	2(9)	0	0	0	0	0	0	0	0
Riley Dean	10/8/01	9	8	3	3	0	0	1	1	13	13
Kieran Dixon	22/8/92	20	15	11	11	77	59	0	0	198	162
Ronan Dixon	25/7/97	11(2)	9(2)	3	3	0	0	0	0	12	12
Tyme Dow-Nikau	25/6/92	12	9	4	4	0	0	0	0	16	16
Jamie Ellis	4/10/89	2	2	0	0	0	0	0	0	0	0
Jacob Gannon	18/3/02	(2)	(2)	0	0	0	0	0	0	0	0
James Green	29/11/90	6(11)	5(8)	1	1	1	1	0	0	6	6
Corey Hall	7/8/02	3	3	0	0	0	0	0	0	0	0
Myles Harrison	11/8/03	3	2	0	0	7	7	0	0	14	14
Tyla Hepi	15/6/93	(2)	(2)	0	0	0	0	0	0	0	0
Corey Johnson	16/11/00	5(2)	5(2)	0	0	1	1	0	0	2	2
Ben Jones-Bishop	24/8/88	19	17	9	7	0	0	0	0	36	28
Will Jubb	17/9/96	21(2)	16(2)	4	4	0	0	0	0	16	16
Joe Keyes	17/9/95	1	1	0	0	0	0	0	0	0	0
Danny Kirmond	11/11/85	16(2)	12(2)	4	3	0	0	0	0	16	12
Mikey Lewis	4/7/01	6	4	4	2	1	0	0	0	18	8
Matty Marsh	21/4/95	22	18	13	13	10	10	1	1	73	73
James McDonnell	12/1/00	7	7	0	0	0	0	0	0	0	0
Aidan McGowan	12/3/02	2(1)	2(1)	2	2	0	0	0	0	8	8
Brendan O'Hagan	30/10/98	8	6	3	3	0	0	0	0	12	12
Lewis Peachey	25/3/01	1(1)	1(1)	0	0	0	0	0	0	0	0
Joe Porter	26/1/93	3(6)	2(4)	1	0	0	0	0	0	4	0
Liam Salter	14/6/93	18	15	4	2	0	0	0	0	16	8
Sam Scott	5/6/90	15(3)	13(2)	3	3	0	0	0	0	12	12
Tim Spears	27/7/84	9(6)	6(6)	0	0	0	0	0	0	0	0
Marcus Stock	1/5/96	2(19)	2(15)	4	2	0	0	0	0	16	8
Jake Sweeting	15/12/99	1	1	0	0	0	0	0	0	0	0
Jack Teanby	14/5/96	15	12	2	2	0	0	0	0	8	8
AJ Towse	19/8/03	1(1)	1	0	0	0	0	0	0	0	0
Toby Warren	5/9/03	2	2	0	0	0	0	0	0	0	0
Danny Washbrook	18/9/85	7(8)	4(8)	2	2	0	0	0	0	8	8
Perry Whiteley	22/2/93	9	6	7	4	0	0	0	0	28	16
Connor Wynne	15/1/01	2	2	1	1	0	0	0	0	4	4

Matty Marsh

'Ch' totals include Championship games only; 'All' totals also include Challenge Cup & 1895 Cup

CLUB RECORDS	Highest score: 144-0 v West Wales, 29/4/2018 Highest score against: 0-98 v Rochdale, 8/4/2001
MATCH RECORDS	Record attendance: 14,689 v Swinton, 10/2/34 *(Clarence Street)*; 2,841 v Bradford, 29/8/2021 *(LNER Community Stadium)*
	Tries: 7 Brad Davis v Highfield, 17/9/95; Kieren Moss v West Wales, 29/4/2018
	Goals: 21 Connor Robinson v West Wales, 11/8/2018 Points: 56 Chris Thorman v Northumbria University, 6/3/2011
SEASON RECORDS	Tries: 35 John Crossley 1980-81 Goals: 186 *(inc 4fg)* Connor Robinson 2018 Points: 420 Connor Robinson 2018
CAREER RECORDS	Tries: 167 Peter Foster 1955-67 Goals: 1,060 Vic Yorke 1954-67 Points: 2,159 Vic Yorke 1954-67 Appearances: 449 Willie Hargreaves 1952-65

ROUND 1

Friday 2nd April 2021

HALIFAX PANTHERS 47 LONDON BRONCOS 14

PANTHERS: 1 Scott Grix; 5 James Saltonstall; 12 Ed Barber; 21 Zack McComb; 19 Conor McGrath; 7 Connor Robinson; 6 Liam Harris; 8 Elliot Morris; 9 Brandon Moore; 10 Daniel Murray; 26 Sam Hewitt; 11 Matt Garside; 14 Kevin Larroyer. Subs (all used): 15 Gadwin Springer; 13 Jacob Fairbank; 20 Curtis Davies; 27 Paul Brearley.
Tries: Morris (4), Harris (18), Barber (25, 41), McComb (55), Grix (61), Fairbank (68), McGrath (77);
Goals: Robinson 6/7, Harris 1/1; **Field goal:** Robinson (80).
Sin bin: Fairbank (39) - fighting.
BRONCOS: 5 Ed Chamberlain; 17 Abbas Miski; 23 Josh Hodson; 4 Will Lovell; 2 Tuoyo Egodo; 1 James Meadows; 21 Rian Horsman; 15 Romain Navarrete; 9 Matty Fozard; 8 Olsi Krasniqi; 13 Josh Walters; 25 Jacob Jones; 24 Will Blakemore. Subs (all used): 16 Dan Hindmarsh; 28 Titus Gwaze; 10 Greg Richards; 19 Jacob Ogden.
Tries: Miski (29, 47), Egodo (74);
Goals: Chamberlain 0/2, Fozard 1/1.
Sin bin: Miski (17) - delaying restart; Richards (39) - fighting.
Rugby Leaguer & League Express Men of the Match:
Panthers: Liam Harris; *Broncos:* Will Lovell.
Penalty count: 8-6; **Half-time:** 18-4;
Referee: Gareth Hewer.

OLDHAM 28 SWINTON LIONS 20

OLDHAM: 1 Dan Abram; 27 Ben Holcroft; 3 Ben Heaton; 24 Max Roberts; 5 Ryan Ince; 6 Lewis Charnock; 7 Dave Hewitt; 17 Liam Kirk; 9 Gareth Owen; 13 Martyn Reilly; 21 Shaun Pick; 25 Danny Bridge; 12 Liam Bent. Subs (all used): 10 Jack Spencer; 11 Danny Langtree; 16 Tyler Dupree; 30 Dec Gregory.
Tries: Roberts (5), Ince (15), Heaton (47, 68), Dupree (50);
Goals: D Abram 4/6.
Sin bin: Heaton (9) - professional foul.
LIONS: 22 Geronimo Doyle; 2 Richard Lepori; 3 Mitch Cox; 11 Rhodri Lloyd; 1 Mike Butt; 6 Martyn Ridyard; 7 Jack Hansen; 15 Louis Brogan; 9 Luke Waterworth; 8 Sam Brooks; 19 Deane Meadows; 12 Nick Gregson; 13 Will Hope. Subs (all used): 14 Billy Brickhill; 16 Paddy Jones; 20 Tayler Brown; 39 Tom Spencer.
Tries: Butt (11), Waterworth (22), Lloyd (30), Hansen (33, pen); **Goals:** Ridyard 2/4.
Dismissal: Spencer (65) - punching.
Rugby Leaguer & League Express Men of the Match:
Oldham: Gareth Owen; *Lions:* Geronimo Doyle.
Penalty count: 9-6; **Half-time:** 10-20;
Referee: Cameron Worsley.

FEATHERSTONE ROVERS 28 BATLEY BULLDOGS 18

ROVERS: 1 Craig Hall; 5 Gareth Gale; 4 Josh Hardcastle; 3 Kris Welham; 2 Ben Blackmore; 9 Fa'amanu Brown; 7 Dane Chisholm; 8 Craig Kopczak; 14 Connor Jones; 13 James Lockwood; 20 Frankie Halton; 12 Brad Day; 16 Jack Bussey. Subs (all used): 21 Dean Parata; 31 Junior Moors; 10 James Harrison; 18 Luke Cooper.
Tries: Kopczak (16), Welham (19), Halton (31), Brown (39), Gale (47), Moors (64); **Goals:** Hall 1/5, Chisholm 1/1.
BULLDOGS: 14 Elliot Hall; 5 Johnny Campbell; 23 Jack Logan; 3 Kieran Buchanan; 21 Jodie Broughton; 6 Ben White; 7 Tom Gilmore; 8 Adam Gledhill; 9 Alistair Leak; 13 James Brown; 11 Dane Manning; 12 Lucas Walshaw; 17 Josh Tonks. Subs (all used): 26 Nyle Flynn; 10 Toby Everett; 16 Michael Ward; 15 Jack Blagbrough.
Tries: Hall (23), Walshaw (59), Logan (70);
Goals: Gilmore 3/3.
Rugby Leaguer & League Express Men of the Match:
Rovers: Craig Kopczak; *Bulldogs:* Dane Manning.
Penalty count: 5-7; **Half-time:** 18-6; **Referee:** Jack Smith.

Saturday 3rd April 2021

YORK CITY KNIGHTS 6 TOULOUSE OLYMPIQUE 21

CITY KNIGHTS: 1 Matty Marsh; 23 Ben Jones-Bishop; 30 Tyme Dow-Nikau; 4 Ryan Atkins; 5 Kieran Dixon; 29 Riley Dean; 6 Brendan O'Hagan; 15 Jordan Baldwinson; 9 Will Jubb; 10 Jack Teanby; 3 Liam Salter; 17 Danny Kirmond; 20 Tim Spears. Subs (all used): 19 James Green; 21 Joe Porter; 28 Danny Washbrook; 13 Adam Cuthbertson.
Try: Jones-Bishop (13); **Goals:** K Dixon 1/1.
OLYMPIQUE: 1 Mark Kheirallah; 20 Ilias Bergal; 4 Mathieu Jussaume; 3 Junior Vaivai; 21 Latrell Schaumkel; 6 Johnathon Ford; 13 Anthony Marion; 16 Joe Bretherton; 9 Lloyd White; 10 Harrison Hansen; 11 Andrew Dixon; 12 Dominique Peyroux; 17 Joseph Paulo. Subs (all used): 14 Eloi Pelissier; 15 Maxime Puech; 8 Remi Casty; 18 Mitch Garbutt.
Tries: Peyroux (19), Garbutt (48), Bretherton (58);
Goals: Marion 4/6; **Field goal:** White (80).
Rugby Leaguer & League Express Men of the Match:
City Knights: Tyme Dow-Nikau; *Olympique:* Andrew Dixon.
Penalty count: 3-8; **Half-time:** 6-8; **Referee:** Tom Grant.

DEWSBURY RAMS 17 WHITEHAVEN 8

RAMS: 1 Joe Martin; 2 Andy Gabriel; 3 Adam Ryder; 4 Matty Fleming; 5 Will Oakes; 6 Paul Sykes; 7 Liam Finn; 8 Frazer Morris; 9 Reiss Butterworth; 10 Tom Garratt; 15 Keenen Tomlinson; 12 Michael Knowles; 13 Chris Annakin. Subs (all used): 14 Sam Day; 11 Jason Walton; 23 Jon Magrin; 20 Aaron Hall.
Tries: Day (37), Fleming (49, 53); **Goals:** Sykes 2/3;
Field goal: Finn (74).
WHITEHAVEN: 1 Gregg McNally; 2 Lachlan Walmsley; 3 Chris Taylor; 23 Jason Mossop; 25 James Worthington; 6 Karl Dixon; 7 Nikau Williams; 8 Marc Shackley; 18 James Newton; 27 Andrew Dawson; 11 Brett Phillips; 19 Ellis Gillam; 16 Tom Wilkinson. Subs (all used): 12 Liam Cooper; 32 Aiden Roden; 33 Andy Thornley; 17 Tom Walker.
Tries: Walmsley (13), Mossop (75); **Goals:** Walmsley 0/2.
Rugby Leaguer & League Express Men of the Match:
Rams: Sam Day; *Whitehaven:* Lachlan Walmsley.
Penalty count: 5-8; **Half-time:** 6-4; **Referee:** Aaron Moore.

Sunday 4th April 2021

SHEFFIELD EAGLES 50 BRADFORD BULLS 12

EAGLES: 1 Josh Guzdek; 2 Rob Worrincy; 24 Ryan Johnson; 4 James Glover; 5 Ryan Millar; 22 Izaac Farrell; 7 Anthony Thackeray; 11 Brad Knowles; 14 Greg Burns; 10 Matt James; 15 Olly Davies; 12 Joel Farrell; 13 Aaron Brown. Subs (all used): 9 James Davey; 18 Tyler Dickinson; 19 Blake Broadbent; 20 Paddy Burns.
Tries: Brown (4, 24), Guzdek (10), Glover (33, 40), J Farrell (37), I Farrell (47), Thackeray (63, 66), Millar (75);
Goals: I Farrell 4/9, Glover 1/1.
Sin bin: J Farrell (71) - fighting; I Farrell (73) - late challenge.
BULLS: 2 Joe Brown; 22 Reece Hamlett; 3 Rhys Evans; 4 Ross Oakes; 25 Jack Sanderson; 1 Brandon Pickersgill; 6 Danny Brough; 15 Dan Fleming; 9 Thomas Doyle; 10 Steve Crossley; 11 Adam Rooks; 16 Brad Gallagher; 12 Aaron Murphy. Subs (all used): 24 Ben Evans; 27 Billy Jowitt; 17 Levy Nzoungou; 18 Ebon Scurr.
Tries: Rooks (56), Brown (58); **Goals:** Brough 2/2.
Sin bin: Brough (71) - fighting.
Rugby Leaguer & League Express Men of the Match:
Eagles: Anthony Thackeray; *Bulls:* Billy Jowitt.
Penalty count: 7-6; **Half-time:** 28-0; **Referee:** James Vella.

NEWCASTLE THUNDER 30 WIDNES VIKINGS 30

THUNDER: 5 Calum Turner; 2 Jack Johnson; 3 Matthew Wright; 4 Kieran Gill; 18 Alex Clegg; 6 Jake Shorrocks; 7 Josh Woods; 8 Nathan Wilde; 33 Connor Aspey; 10 Mikey Wood; 11 Ukuma Ta'ai; 12 Sam Wilde; 13 Liam McAvoy. Subs (all used): 14 Evan Simons; 15 Ted Chapelhow; 16 Jay Chapelhow; 17 Connor Bailey.
Tries: Gill (2, 78), S Wilde (21), Ta'ai (30), Bailey (70), Johnson (76); **Goals:** Wright 3/6.
Sin bin: N Wilde (70) - fighting.
VIKINGS: 1 Jack Owens; 5 Deon Cross; 3 Jake Spedding; 4 Steve Tyrer; 20 Owen Buckley; 6 Danny Craven; 7 Matty Smith; 10 Matt Cook; 23 Lewis Else; 27 Eribe Doro; 11 Shane Grady; 12 Adam Lawton; 8 Paul Clough. Subs: 17 Joe Lyons; 18 Lloyd Roby (not used); 22 Josh Wilde; 24 Will Tilleke.
Tries: Cross (10, 24), Cook (14), Grady (34), Owens (39);
Goals: Owens 5/6.
Sin bin: Doro (70) - fighting.
Rugby Leaguer & League Express Men of the Match:
Thunder: Kieran Gill; *Vikings:* Jack Owens.
Penalty count: 6-7; **Half-time:** 16-30;
Referee: Marcus Griffiths.

ROUND 2

Saturday 17th April 2021

BATLEY BULLDOGS 48 OLDHAM 10

BULLDOGS: 1 Luke Hooley; 5 Johnny Campbell; 22 Dale Morton; 23 Jack Logan; 21 Jodie Broughton; 6 Ben White; 7 Tom Gilmore; 8 Adam Gledhill; 9 Alistair Leak; 10 Toby Everett; 3 Kieran Buchanan; 11 Dane Manning; 17 Josh Tonks. Subs (all used): 13 James Brown; 14 Elliot Hall; 15 Jack Blagbrough; 26 Nyle Flynn.
Tries: Tonks (7), Hooley (10), Broughton (32), Logan (35), White (40, 79), Campbell (45, 57), Hall (61);
Goals: Gilmore 3/5, Hooley 3/5.
OLDHAM: 1 Dan Abram; 2 Tommy Brierley; 3 Ben Heaton; 24 Max Roberts; 5 Ryan Ince; 6 Lewis Charnock; 7 Dave Hewitt; 10 Jack Spencer; 9 Gareth Owen; 15 Luke Nelmes; 11 Danny Langtree; 25 Danny Bridge; 12 Liam Bent. Subs (all used): 16 Tyler Dupree; 19 Matthew Fletcher; 23 Callum Green; 30 Dec Gregory.
Tries: Charnock (18), Brierley (72);
Goals: D Abram 1/1, Green 0/1.
Rugby Leaguer & League Express Men of the Match:
Bulldogs: Josh Tonks; *Oldham:* Dec Gregory.
Penalty count: 8-4; **Half-time:** 28-6;
Referee: James Vella.

WIDNES VIKINGS 14 DEWSBURY RAMS 22

VIKINGS: 1 Jack Owens; 2 Jayden Hatton; 4 Steve Tyrer; 18 Lloyd Roby; 5 Deon Cross; 6 Danny Craven; 7 Matty Smith; 8 Paul Clough; 23 Lewis Else; 14 Lee Jewitt; 11 Shane Grady; 12 Adam Lawton; 27 Eribe Doro. Subs (all used): 13 Kenny Baker; 15 Connor Dwyer; 24 Will Tilleke; 28 Brad O'Neill.
Tries: Smith (21), Roby (39), Tyrer (76);
Goals: Owens 0/1, Tyrer 1/2.
Sin bin: Craven (80) - dissent.
RAMS: 1 Joe Martin; 2 Andy Gabriel; 3 Adam Ryder; 15 Keenen Tomlinson; 5 Will Oakes; 6 Paul Sykes; 7 Liam Finn; 8 Frazer Morris; 9 Reiss Butterworth; 10 Tom Garratt; 11 Jason Walton; 12 Michael Knowles; 13 Chris Annakin. Subs (all used): 14 Sam Day; - Jimmy Beckett; 20 Aaron Hall; 26 Bayley Liu.
Tries: Martin (15), Oakes (34), Gabriel (42, 50);
Goals: Sykes 3/5.
Rugby Leaguer & League Express Men of the Match:
Vikings: Steve Tyrer; *Rams:* Andy Gabriel.
Penalty count: 7-7; **Half-time:** 8-12;
Referee: Cameron Worsley.

TOULOUSE OLYMPIQUE 24 LONDON BRONCOS 0
(win awarded to Toulouse due to London's refusal to travel)

Sunday 18th April 2021

SWINTON LIONS 6 FEATHERSTONE ROVERS 36

LIONS: 22 Geronimo Doyle; 1 Mike Butt; 3 Mitch Cox; 25 Luis Roberts; 2 Richard Lepori; 6 Martyn Ridyard; 7 Jack Hansen; 15 Louis Brogan; 9 Luke Waterworth; 8 Sam Brooks; 11 Rhodri Lloyd; 13 Will Hope; 39 Tom Spencer. Subs (all used): 5 Sam Grant; 18 Cobi Green; 16 Paddy Jones; 26 Jordan Brown.
Try: Cox (64); **Goals:** Ridyard 1/1.
ROVERS: 1 Craig Hall; 2 Ben Blackmore; 3 Kris Welham; 17 Thomas Minns; 5 Gareth Gale; 6 Tom Holmes; 9 Fa'amanu Brown; 8 Craig Kopczak; 14 Connor Jones; 13 James Lockwood; 12 Brad Day; 11 Brett Ferres; 16 Jack Bussey. Subs (all used): 21 Dean Parata; 31 Junior Moors; 15 John Davies; 20 Frankie Halton.
Tries: Gale (5), Holmes (15), Minns (17), Day (34), Davies (37), Blackmore (56, 79); **Goals:** Brown 4/7.
Rugby Leaguer & League Express Men of the Match:
Lions: Luis Roberts; *Rovers:* Tom Holmes.
Penalty count: 4-4; **Half-time:** 0-26;
Referee: Aaron Moore.

WHITEHAVEN 29 NEWCASTLE THUNDER 20

WHITEHAVEN: 2 Lachlan Walmsley; 5 Andrew Bulman; 3 Chris Taylor; 4 Jessie Joe Parker; 23 Jason Mossop; 6 Karl Dixon; 7 Nikau Williams; 27 Andrew Dawson; 32 Aiden Roden; 17 Tom Walker; 15 Connor Holliday; 19 Ellis Gillam; 16 Tom Wilkinson. Subs (all used): 12 Liam Cooper; 18 James Newton; 29 Dean Zammit; 28 Karl Olstrom.
Tries: Bulman (12, 35), Holliday (18), Dixon (54), Walmsley (74); **Goals:** Walmsley 3/5, Holliday 1/1;
Field goal: Williams (78).
THUNDER: 1 Lewis Young; 2 Jack Johnson; 5 Calum Turner; 4 Kieran Gill; 18 Alex Clegg; 6 Jake Shorrocks; 7 Josh Woods; 8 Nathan Wilde; 14 Evan Simons; 10 Mikey Wood; 20 Cole Oakley; 12 Sam Wilde; 13 Liam McAvoy. Subs (all used): 19 Evan Hodgson; 15 Ted Chapelhow; 16 Jay Chapelhow; 21 Reece Dean.
Tries: Gill (29), Johnson (61), S Wilde (67), Clegg (79);
Goals: J Woods 2/4.
Rugby Leaguer & League Express Men of the Match:
Whitehaven: Karl Dixon; *Thunder:* Sam Wilde.
Penalty count: 6-4; **Half-time:** 18-6; **Referee:** Jack Smith.

BRADFORD BULLS 27 HALIFAX PANTHERS 26

BULLS: 1 Brandon Pickersgill; 2 Joe Brown; 3 Rhys Evans; 4 Ross Oakes; 19 David Foggin-Johnston; 6 Danny Brough; 7 Jordan Lilley; 17 Levy Nzoungou; 9 Thomas Doyle; 10 Steve Crossley; 11 Adam Rooks; 12 Aaron Murphy; 24 Ben Evans. Subs (all used): 27 Billy Jowitt; 18 Ebon Scurr; 15 Dan Fleming; 20 Brad England.
Tries: Lilley (26), Fleming (35), Pickersgill (44), Foggin-Johnston (52); **Goals:** Brough 5/6;
Field goal: Lilley (77).
Sin bin: Rooks (15) - late challenge on Larroyer; Fleming (38) - fighting.
PANTHERS: 1 Scott Grix; 2 Nick Rawsthorne; 3 Greg Worthington; 21 Zack McComb; 5 James Saltonstall; 6 Liam Harris; 7 Connor Robinson; 8 Elliot Morris; 9 Brandon Moore; 10 Daniel Murray; 11 Matt Garside; 27 Paul Brearley; 14 Kevin Larroyer. Subs (all used): 22 Amir Bourouh; 15 Gadwin Springer; 16 Will Calcott; 12 Ed Barber.

Tries: Saltonstall (7), Grix (20), Springer (59), Larroyer (65); **Goals:** Robinson 5/5.
Sin bin: Saltonstall (32) - trip on Foggin-Johnston; Springer (38) - high tackle on Lilley.
Rugby Leaguer & League Express Men of the Match: *Bulls:* Jordan Lilley; *Panthers:* Amir Bourouh.
Penalty count: 8-12; **Half-time:** 12-14; **Referee:** Tom Grant. *(at Tetley's Stadium, Dewsbury).*

YORK CITY KNIGHTS 14 SHEFFIELD EAGLES 20

CITY KNIGHTS: 1 Matty Marsh; 23 Ben Jones-Bishop; 3 Liam Salter; 4 Ryan Atkins; 5 Kieran Dixon; 6 Brendan O'Hagan; 36 Joe Keyes; 8 Ronan Dixon; 9 Will Jubb; 41 Yusuf Aydin; 21 Joe Porter; 12 Sam Scott; 16 Marcus Stock. Subs (all used): 13 Adam Cuthbertson; 19 James Green; 28 Danny Washbrook; 39 Lewis Peachey.
Tries: Jubb (29), K Dixon (44), Salter (75); **Goals:** K Dixon 1/3.
EAGLES: 29 Mike Adlard; 2 Rob Worrincy; 1 Josh Guzdek; 4 James Glover; 5 Ryan Millar; 22 Izaac Farrell; 7 Anthony Thackeray; 8 Scott Wheeldon; 14 Greg Burns; 10 Matt James; 15 Olly Davies; 12 Joel Farrell; 13 Aaron Brown. Subs (all used): 9 James Davey; 17 Frankie Mariano; 18 Tyler Dickinson; 20 Paddy Burns.
Tries: Thackeray (6, 35), Dickinson (40); **Goals:** I Farrell 4/4.
Rugby Leaguer & League Express Men of the Match: *City Knights:* Adam Cuthbertson; *Eagles:* Anthony Thackeray.
Penalty count: 7-5; **Half-time:** 6-18; **Referee:** Gareth Hewer.

ROUND 3

Saturday 24th April 2021

LONDON BRONCOS 38 OLDHAM 24

BRONCOS: 1 James Meadows; 2 Tuoyo Egodo; 23 Josh Hodson; 3 Chris Hankinson; 17 Abbas Miski; 7 Jarrod Sammut; 6 Cory Aston; 15 Romain Navarrete; 9 Matty Fozard; 18 Jordan Williams; 4 Will Lovell; 13 Josh Walters; 10 Greg Richards. Subs (all used): 28 Titus Gwaze; 16 Dan Hindmarsh; 14 Sam Davis; 20 Gideon Boafo.
Tries: Egodo (10, 45, 71), Sammut (19, 49), Hindmarsh (34), Walters (79); **Goals:** Hankinson 5/5, Sammut 0/2.
OLDHAM: 23 Callum Green; 2 Tommy Brierley; 28 Joe Hartley; 24 Max Roberts; 27 Ben Holcroft; 6 Lewis Charnock; 7 Dave Hewitt; 10 Jack Spencer; 9 Gareth Owen; 15 Luke Nelmes; 12 Liam Bent; 11 Danny Langtree; 19 Matthew Fletcher. Subs (all used): 30 Dec Gregory; 16 Tyler Dupree; 34 Jack Bibby; 26 James Barran.
Tries: Nelmes (22), Bibby (63), Langtree (74), Hewitt (76); **Goals:** Green 4/4.
Rugby Leaguer & League Express Men of the Match: *Broncos:* Abbas Miski; *Oldham:* Callum Green.
Penalty count: 3-6; **Half-time:** 18-6; **Referee:** Michael Mannifield. *(at The Rock, Roehampton).*

BATLEY BULLDOGS 48 WIDNES VIKINGS 16

BULLDOGS: 1 Luke Hooley; 5 Johnny Campbell; 22 Dale Morton; 23 Jack Logan; 21 Jodie Broughton; 6 Ben White; 7 Tom Gilmore; 8 Adam Gledhill; 24 Ben Kaye; 15 Jack Blagbrough; 3 Kieran Buchanan; 11 Dane Manning; 17 Josh Tonks. Subs (all used): 14 Elliot Hall; 9 Alistair Leak; 13 James Brown; 16 Michael Ward.
Tries: Campbell (20, 60), Tonks (25), Ward (46), White (53), Morton (56), Hooley (58), Broughton (64), Manning (79); **Goals:** Morton 6/10.
VIKINGS: 17 Joe Lyons; 5 Deon Cross; 18 Lloyd Roby; 4 Steve Tyrer; 20 Owen Buckley; 6 Danny Craven; 7 Matty Smith; 8 Paul Clough; 28 Brad O'Neill; 13 Kenny Baker; 11 Shane Grady; 29 Ellis Robson; 27 Eribe Doro. Subs (all used): 23 Lewis Else; 12 Adam Lawton; 16 Owen Farnworth; 24 Will Tilleke.
Tries: Doro (6), Baker (10), Buckley (40); **Goals:** Tyrer 2/4.
Rugby Leaguer & League Express Men of the Match: *Bulldogs:* Alistair Leak; *Vikings:* Kenny Baker.
Penalty count: 8-7; **Half-time:** 10-16; **Referee:** Gareth Hewer.

Sunday 25th April 2021

SWINTON LIONS 16 YORK CITY KNIGHTS 64

LIONS: 22 Geronimo Doyle; 1 Mike Butt; 3 Mitch Cox; 25 Luis Roberts; 5 Sam Grant; 6 Martyn Ridyard; 7 Jack Hansen; 8 Sam Brooks; 9 Luke Waterworth; 15 Louis Brogan; 11 Rhodri Lloyd; 12 Nick Gregson; 13 Will Hope. Subs (all used): 39 Tom Spencer; 16 Paddy Jones; 38 Sam Luckley; 24 Paul Nash.
Tries: Roberts (41), Butt (70), Brogan (72); **Goals:** Hansen 2/3.
Sin bin: Hope (54) - dangerous challenge; Gregson (58) - shoulder charge.
CITY KNIGHTS: 42 Connor Wynne; 23 Ben Jones-Bishop; 3 Liam Salter; 4 Ryan Atkins; 5 Kieran Dixon; 1 Matty Marsh; 29 Riley Dean; 8 Ronan Dixon; 9 Will Jubb; 41 Yusuf Aydin; 17 Danny Kirmond; 39 Lewis Peachey; 11 Chris Clarkson. Subs (all used): 28 Danny Washbrook; 15 Jordan Baldwinson; 16 Marcus Stock; 13 Adam Cuthbertson.
Tries: K Dixon (3), R Dixon (6, 19), Marsh (15, 30, 52, 80), Wynne (26), Dean (45, 59), Atkins (56); **Goals:** K Dixon 10/11.
Rugby Leaguer & League Express Men of the Match: *Lions:* Jack Hansen; *City Knights:* Matty Marsh.
Penalty count: 2-3; **Half-time:** 0-34; **Referee:** Matt Rossleigh.

FEATHERSTONE ROVERS 48 WHITEHAVEN 14

ROVERS: 1 Craig Hall; 2 Ben Blackmore; 17 Thomas Minns; 3 Kris Welham; 5 Gareth Gale; 6 Tom Holmes; 9 Fa'amanu Brown; 31 Junior Moors; 14 Connor Jones; 13 James Lockwood; 11 Brett Ferres; 12 Brad Day; 16 Jack Bussey. Subs (all used): 21 Dean Parata; 4 Josh Hardcastle; 15 John Davies; 8 Craig Kopczak.
Tries: Ferres (7), Jones (10), Bussey (30), Kopczak (51), Brown (59), Moors (63), Hardcastle (65), Gale (75), Hall (76); **Goals:** Brown 6/9.
WHITEHAVEN: 2 Lachlan Walmsley; 25 James Worthington; 30 Sean Croston; 4 Jessie Joe Parker; 34 Aaron Purewal; 6 Karl Dixon; 7 Nikau Williams; 21 Glenn Riley; 32 Aiden Roden; 29 Dean Zammit; 19 Ellis Gillam; 15 Connor Holliday; 16 Tom Wilkinson. Subs (all used): 18 James Newton; 24 Ethan Kelly; 3 Chris Taylor; 35 Guy Graham.
Tries: Dixon (14), Worthington (42), Purewal (54); **Goals:** Walmsley 1/2, Holliday 0/1.
Rugby Leaguer & League Express Men of the Match: *Rovers:* Tom Holmes; *Whitehaven:* Lachlan Walmsley.
Penalty count: 5-6; **Half-time:** 16-6; **Referee:** Aaron Moore.

HALIFAX PANTHERS 34 TOULOUSE OLYMPIQUE 44

PANTHERS: 4 James Woodburn-Hall; 2 Nick Rawsthorne; 3 Greg Worthington; 21 Zack McComb; 5 James Saltonstall; 6 Liam Harris; 7 Connor Robinson; 8 Elliot Morris; 9 Brandon Moore; 10 Daniel Murray; 12 Ed Barber; 27 Paul Brearley; 17 Ben Kavanagh. Subs (all used): 13 Jacob Fairbank; 22 Amir Bourouh; 26 Sam Hewitt; 25 Adam Tangata.
Tries: Saltonstall (38, 40, 76), McComb (49), Woodburn-Hall (52), Barber (62); **Goals:** Robinson 5/6.
Sin bin: Bourouh (55) - late challenge.
OLYMPIQUE: 21 Latrell Schaumkel; 20 Ilias Bergal; 4 Mathieu Jussaume; 3 Junior Vaivai; 30 Ben Laguerre; 6 Johnathon Ford; 13 Anthony Marion; 15 Maxime Puech; 9 Lloyd White; 25 Clement Boyer; 11 Andrew Dixon; 16 Joe Bretherton; 8 Remi Casty. Subs (all used): 14 Eloi Pelissier; 18 Mitch Garbutt; 23 Justin Sangare; 27 Maxime Garcia.
Tries: Vaivai (10, 29), Bretherton (12), White (18, 19), Dixon (23), Casty (56); **Goals:** Marion 8/9.
Sin bin: Sangare (36) - trip; Schaumkel (47) - holding down.
Rugby Leaguer & League Express Men of the Match: *Panthers:* James Saltonstall; *Olympique:* Remi Casty.
Penalty count: 10-12; **Half-time:** 10-34; **Referee:** Jack Smith.

NEWCASTLE THUNDER 24 SHEFFIELD EAGLES 16

THUNDER: 27 Alex Donaghy; 2 Jack Johnson; 23 Joe Brown; 29 Isaac Nokes; 18 Alex Clegg; 6 Jake Shorrocks; 7 Josh Woods; 15 Ted Chapelhow; 9 Bob Beswick; 10 Mikey Wood; 20 Cole Oakley; 12 Sam Wilde; 8 Nathan Wilde. Subs (all used): 16 Jay Chapelhow; 11 Ukuma Ta'ai; 14 Evan Simons; 21 Reece Dean.
Tries: Johnson (9), Oakley (44), J Chapelhow (57), Ta'ai (78); **Goals:** J Woods 4/4.
Sin bin: Brown (70) - professional foul.
EAGLES: 29 Mike Adlard; 28 Jack Render; 1 Josh Guzdek; 4 James Glover; 5 Ryan Millar; 22 Izaac Farrell; 7 Anthony Thackeray; 8 Scott Wheeldon; 14 Greg Burns; 10 Matt James; 15 Olly Davies; 12 Joel Farrell; 13 Aaron Brown. Subs (all used): 9 James Davey; 11 Brad Knowles; 18 Tyler Dickinson; 19 Blake Broadbent.
Tries: Glover (23), J Farrell (40), Render (76); **Goals:** I Farrell 2/3.
Rugby Leaguer & League Express Men of the Match: *Thunder:* Jack Johnson; *Eagles:* Anthony Thackeray.
Penalty count: 6-6; **Half-time:** 6-12; **Referee:** James Vella.

BRADFORD BULLS 35 DEWSBURY RAMS 14

BULLS: 1 Brandon Pickersgill; 2 Joe Brown; 3 Rhys Evans; 4 Ross Oakes; 19 David Foggin-Johnston; 6 Danny Brough; 7 Jordan Lilley; 17 Levy Nzoungou; 9 Thomas Doyle; 10 Steve Crossley; 20 Brad England; 12 Aaron Murphy; 24 Ben Evans. Subs (all used): 11 Adam Rooks; 15 Dan Fleming; 18 Ebon Scurr; 23 Anthony Walker.
Tries: England (8), Oakes (21), Brown (35, 78), Brough (39); **Goals:** Brough 7/7; **Field goal:** Brough (67).
RAMS: 1 Joe Martin; 2 Andy Gabriel; 3 Adam Ryder; 15 Keenen Tomlinson; 5 Will Oakes; 6 Paul Sykes; 7 Liam Finn; 8 Frazer Morris; 9 Reiss Butterworth; 10 Tom Garratt; 11 Jason Walton; 12 Michael Knowles; 13 Chris Annakin. Subs (all used): 14 Sam Day; 20 Aaron Hall; 23 Jon Magrin; 26 Bayley Liu.
Tries: Gabriel (31, 44), Ryder (73); **Goals:** Sykes 1/3.
Rugby Leaguer & League Express Men of the Match: *Bulls:* Danny Brough; *Rams:* Andy Gabriel.
Penalty count: 8-6; **Half-time:** 28-6; **Referee:** Scott Mikalauskas. *(at Tetley's Stadium).*

ROUND 4

Saturday 1st May 2021

OLDHAM 16 HALIFAX PANTHERS 12

OLDHAM: 23 Callum Green; 2 Tommy Brierley; 29 Jack Croft; 24 Max Roberts; 27 Ben Holcroft; 6 Lewis Charnock; 7 Dave Hewitt; 17 Liam Kirk; 9 Gareth Owen; 15 Luke Nelmes; 11 Danny Langtree; 12 Liam Bent; 10 Jack Spencer. Subs (all used): 13 Martyn Reilly; 19 Matthew Fletcher; 30 Dec Gregory; 34 Jack Bibby.
Tries: Brierley (22), Reilly (44), Croft (76); **Goals:** Green 2/3.
PANTHERS: 4 James Woodburn-Hall; 2 Nick Rawsthorne; 3 Greg Worthington; 12 Ed Barber; 19 Conor McGrath; 6 Liam Harris; 7 Connor Robinson; 16 Will Calcott; 9 Brandon Moore; 25 Adam Tangata; 11 Matt Garside; 26 Sam Hewitt; 14 Kevin Larroyer. Subs: 17 Ben Kavanagh; 15 Gadwin Springer; 22 Amir Bourouh; 24 Ben Tibbs (not used).
Tries: McGrath (18), Woodburn-Hall (38); **Goals:** Robinson 2/2.
Rugby Leaguer & League Express Men of the Match: *Oldham:* Jack Croft; *Panthers:* James Woodburn-Hall.
Penalty count: 6-6; **Half-time:** 4-12; **Referee:** Gareth Hewer.

SHEFFIELD EAGLES 20 LONDON BRONCOS 20

EAGLES: 1 Josh Guzdek; 2 Rob Worrincy; 24 Ryan Johnson; 4 James Glover; 5 Ryan Millar; 22 Izaac Farrell; 7 Anthony Thackeray; 8 Scott Wheeldon; 14 Greg Burns; 10 Matt James; 15 Olly Davies; 17 Frankie Mariano; 13 Aaron Brown. Subs (all used): 9 James Davey; 18 Tyler Dickinson; 11 Brad Knowles; 20 Paddy Burns.
Tries: Glover (13), I Farrell (26), Brown (78); **Goals:** I Farrell 4/4.
BRONCOS: 5 Ed Chamberlain; 2 Tuoyo Egodo; 4 Will Lovell; 3 Chris Hankinson; 17 Abbas Miski; 7 Jarrod Sammut; 6 Cory Aston; 15 Romain Navarrete; 9 Matty Fozard; 12 Rhys Curran; 25 Jacob Jones; 13 Josh Walters; 10 Greg Richards. Subs: 28 Titus Gwaze; 16 Dan Hindmarsh; 14 Sam Davis (not used); 20 Gideon Boafo.
Tries: Egodo (21), Miski (34, 62, 73); **Goals:** Hankinson 1/3, Sammut 1/2.
Rugby Leaguer & League Express Men of the Match: *Eagles:* James Glover; *Broncos:* Abbas Miski.
Penalty count: 6-6; **Half-time:** 12-8; **Referee:** Ben Thaler.

Sunday 2nd May 2021

NEWCASTLE THUNDER 16 BATLEY BULLDOGS 28

THUNDER: 27 Alex Donaghy; 2 Jack Johnson; 4 Kieran Gill; 23 Joe Brown; 18 Alex Clegg; 6 Jake Shorrocks; 7 Josh Woods; 8 Nathan Wilde; 9 Bob Beswick; 10 Mikey Wood; 17 Connor Bailey; 12 Sam Wilde; 14 Evan Simons. Subs (all used): 15 Ted Chapelhow; 11 Ukuma Ta'ai; 19 Evan Hodgson; 21 Reece Dean.
Tries: Gill (27, 68), Shorrocks (72); **Goals:** J Woods 2/3.
BULLDOGS: 14 Elliot Hall; 5 Johnny Campbell; 22 Dale Morton; 23 Jack Logan; 21 Jodie Broughton; 6 Ben White; 7 Tom Gilmore; 8 Adam Gledhill; 24 Ben Kaye; 15 Jack Blagbrough; 3 Kieran Buchanan; 11 Dane Manning; 17 Josh Tonks. Subs (all used): 9 Alistair Leak; 12 Lucas Walshaw; 16 Michael Ward; 19 Tom Lillycrop.
Tries: Hall (7), Morton (30), Leak (45, 55), Gilmore (77); **Goals:** Gilmore 4/5.
Rugby Leaguer & League Express Men of the Match: *Thunder:* Josh Woods; *Bulldogs:* Alistair Leak.
Penalty count: 7-7; **Half-time:** 6-10; **Referee:** Aaron Moore.

WHITEHAVEN 22 BRADFORD BULLS 30

WHITEHAVEN: 2 Lachlan Walmsley; 5 Andrew Bulman; 3 Chris Taylor; 23 Jason Mossop; 4 Jessie Joe Parker; 6 Karl Dixon; 7 Nikau Williams; 17 Tom Walker; 32 Aiden Roden; 27 Andrew Dawson; 15 Connor Holliday; 19 Ellis Gillam; 16 Tom Wilkinson. Subs (all used): 12 Liam Cooper; 18 James Newton; 28 Karl Olstrom; 36 Ronan Michael.
Tries: Bulman (11), Parker (42), Mossop (77), Roden (80); **Goals:** Walmsley 3/5.
BULLS: 1 Brandon Pickersgill; 2 Joe Brown; 3 Rhys Evans; 4 Ross Oakes; 19 David Foggin-Johnston; 6 Danny Brough; 7 Jordan Lilley; 17 Levy Nzoungou; 9 Thomas Doyle; 10

Steve Crossley; 20 Brad England; 12 Aaron Murphy; 24 Ben Evans. Subs (all used): 23 Anthony Walker; 18 Ebon Scurr; 15 Dan Fleming; 11 Adam Rooks.
Tries: Crossley (17, 64), Brown (20), Pickersgill (30), Scurr (52); **Goals:** Brough 5/5.
Sin bin: Nzoungou (56) - dangerous contact on Cooper.
Rugby Leaguer & League Express Men of the Match: *Whitehaven:* Aiden Roden; *Bulls:* Ebon Scurr.
Penalty count: 10-7; **Half-time:** 6-18;
Referee: James Vella.

WIDNES VIKINGS 46 SWINTON LIONS 10

VIKINGS: 1 Jack Owens; 2 Jayden Hatton; 4 Steve Tyrer; 19 Joe Edge; 5 Deon Cross; 17 Joe Lyons; 7 Matty Smith; 16 Owen Farnworth; 28 Brad O'Neill; 13 Kenny Baker; 11 Shane Grady; 29 Ellis Robson; 8 Paul Clough. Subs (all used): 12 Adam Lawton; 21 Calum O'Neill; 23 Lewis Else; 24 Will Tilleke.
Tries: Cross (28, 69), Baker (34), B O'Neill (37), Tyrer (44), Robson (47), Grady (60), Lawton (65);
Goals: Tyrer 7/8.
LIONS: 22 Geronimo Doyle; 1 Mike Butt; 3 Mitch Cox; 25 Luis Roberts; 37 Nico Rizzelli; 12 Nick Gregson; 7 Jack Hansen; 15 Louis Brogan; 24 Paul Nash; 38 Sam Luckley; 11 Rhodri Lloyd; 19 Deane Meadows; 13 Will Hope. Subs (all used): 14 Billy Brickhill; 8 Sam Brooks; 39 Tom Spencer; 18 Cobi Green.
Tries: Rizzelli (53), Butt (76); **Goals:** Hansen 1/2.
Sin bin: Lloyd (79) - high tackle.
Rugby Leaguer & League Express Men of the Match: *Vikings:* Brad O'Neill; *Lions:* Jack Hansen.
Penalty count: 7-6; **Half-time:** 18-0; **Referee:** Jack Smith.

DEWSBURY RAMS 20 YORK CITY KNIGHTS 30

RAMS: 1 Joe Martin; 2 Andy Gabriel; 3 Adam Ryder; 4 Matty Fleming; 5 Will Oakes; 6 Paul Sykes; 7 Liam Finn; 31 Jimmy Beckett; 9 Reiss Butterworth; 10 Tom Garratt; 11 Jason Walton; 39 Dane Windrow; 13 Chris Annakin. Subs (all used): 23 Jon Magrin; 15 Keenen Tomlinson; 20 Aaron Hall; 14 Sam Day.
Tries: Fleming (17), Gabriel (27), Hall (51); **Goals:** Sykes 4/4.
CITY KNIGHTS: 42 Connor Wynne; 23 Ben Jones-Bishop; 3 Liam Salter; 4 Ryan Atkins; 5 Kieran Dixon; 1 Matty Marsh; 29 Riley Dean; 8 Ronan Dixon; 9 Will Jubb; 41 Yusuf Aydin; 11 Chris Clarkson; 17 Danny Kirmond; 15 Jordan Baldwinson. Subs (all used): 28 Danny Washbrook; 16 Marcus Stock; 13 Adam Cuthbertson; 19 James Green.
Tries: Atkins (20), Stock (33), K Dixon (42), Marsh (59, 78);
Goals: K Dixon 5/6.
Rugby Leaguer & League Express Men of the Match: *Rams:* Tom Garratt; *City Knights:* Danny Washbrook.
Penalty count: 5-7; **Half-time:** 14-14; **Referee:** Tom Grant.

ROUND 5

Friday 7th May 2021

SHEFFIELD EAGLES 18 BATLEY BULLDOGS 30

EAGLES: 1 Josh Guzdek; 2 Rob Worrincy; 24 Ryan Johnson; 4 James Glover; 5 Ryan Millar; 22 Izaac Farrell; 7 Anthony Thackeray; 8 Scott Wheeldon; 14 Greg Burns; 10 Matt James; 15 Olly Davies; 17 Frankie Mariano; 13 Aaron Brown. Subs (all used): 9 James Davey; 11 Brad Knowles; 18 Tyler Dickinson; 25 Jordan Bull.
Tries: Worrincy (23, 41), Bull (56); **Goals:** I Farrell 3/3.
BULLDOGS: 1 Luke Hooley; 5 Johnny Campbell; 22 Dale Morton; 23 Jack Logan; 21 Jodie Broughton; 6 Ben White; 7 Tom Gilmore; 8 Adam Gledhill; 24 Ben Kaye; 15 Jack Blagbrough; 3 Kieran Buchanan; 11 Dane Manning; 12 Lucas Walshaw. Subs (all used): 9 Alistair Leak; 14 Elliot Hall; 16 Michael Ward; 19 Tom Lillycrop.
Tries: Hooley (13, 62), Gilmore (28), Manning (68), Campbell (74), Hall (79); **Goals:** Gilmore 2/5, Morton 1/1.
Rugby Leaguer & League Express Men of the Match: *Eagles:* Rob Worrincy; *Bulldogs:* Dane Manning.
Penalty count: 6-4; **Half-time:** 6-10;
Referee: Gareth Hewer.

Saturday 8th May 2021

OLDHAM 4 WHITEHAVEN 36

OLDHAM: 23 Callum Green; 2 Tommy Brierley; 29 Jack Croft; 24 Max Roberts; 27 Ben Holcroft; 6 Lewis Charnock; 1 Dan Abram; 17 Liam Kirk; 9 Gareth Owen; 15 Luke Nelmes; 11 Danny Langtree; 12 Liam Bent; 10 Jack Spencer. Subs (all used): 13 Martyn Reilly; 30 Dec Gregory; 25 Danny Bridge; 21 Shaun Pick.
Try: Green (29); **Goals:** D Abram 0/1.
WHITEHAVEN: 2 Lachlan Walmsley; 5 Andrew Bulman; 3 Chris Taylor; 23 Jason Mossop; 4 Jessie Joe Parker; 6 Karl Dixon; 7 Nikau Williams; 17 Tom Walker; 32 Aiden Roden; 27 Andrew Dawson; 19 Ellis Gillam; 12 Liam Cooper; 16 Tom Wilkinson. Subs (all used): 9 Callum Phillips; 28 Karl Olstrom; 33 Ronan Michael; 20 Jake Bradley.
Tries: Cooper (39), Parker (42), C Phillips (47, 60, 72, 75);
Goals: Walmsley 6/6.
Rugby Leaguer & League Express Men of the Match: *Oldham:* Liam Bent; *Whitehaven:* Callum Phillips.
Penalty count: 4-5; **Half-time:** 4-6;
Referee: Scott Mikalauskas.

Sunday 9th May 2021

SWINTON LIONS 22 BRADFORD BULLS 23

LIONS: 22 Geronimo Doyle; 1 Mike Butt; 3 Mitch Cox; 37 Nico Rizzelli; 25 Luis Roberts; 6 Martyn Ridyard; 7 Jack Hansen; 15 Louis Brogan; 9 Luke Waterworth; 38 Sam Luckley; 11 Rhodri Lloyd; 19 Deane Meadows; 13 Will Hope. Subs (all used): 24 Paul Nash; 14 Billy Brickhill; 8 Sam Brooks; 39 Tom Spencer.
Tries: Rizzelli (7), Roberts (40), Lloyd (68), Hansen (71);
Goals: Ridyard 3/4.
Sin bin: Waterworth (58) - holding down.
BULLS: 1 Brandon Pickersgill; 2 Joe Brown; 3 Rhys Evans; 4 Ross Oakes; 19 David Foggin-Johnston; 6 Danny Brough; 7 Jordan Lilley; 24 Ben Evans; 9 Thomas Doyle; 10 Steve Crossley; 16 Brad Gallagher; 12 Aaron Murphy; 15 Dan Fleming. Subs (all used): 34 Joe Burton; 18 Ebon Scurr; 11 Adam Rooks; 23 Anthony Walker.
Tries: Doyle (19), Foggin-Johnston (26), Brough (35), Pickersgill (49); **Goals:** Brough 3/4; **Field goal:** Lilley (61).
Rugby Leaguer & League Express Men of the Match: *Lions:* Mike Butt; *Bulls:* Brandon Pickersgill.
Penalty count: 7-6; **Half-time:** 10-18;
Referee: Marcus Griffiths.

LONDON BRONCOS 50 NEWCASTLE THUNDER 30

BRONCOS: 22 Oliver Leyland; 17 Abbas Miski; 3 Chris Hankinson; 4 Will Lovell; 20 Gideon Boafo; 1 James Meadows; 7 Jarrod Sammut; 16 Dan Hindmarsh; 9 Matty Fozard; 10 Greg Richards; 12 Rhys Curran; 25 Jacob Jones; 13 Josh Walters. Subs (all used): 14 Sam Davis; 18 Jordan Williams; 19 Jacob Ogden; 28 Titus Gwaze.
Tries: Fozard (8), Hankinson (33), Miski (37, 80), Boafo (43, 52), Richards (66), Sammut (72);
Goals: Hankinson 8/8, Sammut 1/1.
Sin bin: Curran (17) - late challenge on J Woods; Gwaze (56) - high tackle.
THUNDER: 1 Lewis Young; 18 Alex Clegg; - Connor Wrench; 4 Kieran Gill; 28 Cian Tyrer; 7 Josh Woods; 6 Jake Shorrocks; 15 Ted Chapelhow; 9 Bob Beswick; 10 Mikey Wood; 17 Connor Bailey; 12 Sam Wilde; 8 Nathan Wilde. Subs (all used): - Ellis Longstaff; 14 Evan Simons; 16 Jay Chapelhow; 20 Cole Oakley.
Tries: Gill (2, 75), Wrench (18), Simons (22), N Wilde (63);
Goals: J Woods 5/5.
Rugby Leaguer & League Express Men of the Match: *Broncos:* Gideon Boafo; *Thunder:* Kieran Gill.
Penalty count: 7-6; **Half-time:** 18-18; **Referee:** Jack Smith.
(at The Rock, Roehampton).

TOULOUSE OLYMPIQUE 70 WIDNES VIKINGS 0

OLYMPIQUE: 21 Latrell Schaumkel; 2 Jy Hitchcox; 4 Mathieu Jussaume; 3 Junior Vaivai; 30 Jordan Flovie; 6 Johnathon Ford; 13 Anthony Marion; 23 Justin Sangare; 9 Lloyd White; 10 Harrison Hansen; 11 Andrew Dixon; 16 Joe Bretherton; 8 Remi Casty. Subs (all used): 14 Eloi Pelissier; 18 Mitch Garbutt; 27 Maxime Garcia; 28 Hugo Salabio.
Tries: White (8), Jussaume (11), Sangare (20), Dixon (25, 37, 71), Hitchcox (40), Garbutt (44), Flovie (52), Pelissier (55, 67, 78), Schaumkel (62);
Goals: Marion 9/13.
VIKINGS: 1 Jack Owens; 5 Deon Cross; 19 Joe Edge; 4 Steve Tyrer; 2 Jayden Hatton; 17 Joe Lyons; 7 Matty Smith; 16 Owen Farnworth; 28 Brad O'Neill; 13 Kenny Baker; 11 Shane Grady; 29 Ellis Robson; 8 Paul Clough. Subs (all used): 24 Will Tilleke; 12 Adam Lawton; 21 Calum O'Neill; 23 Lewis Else.
Sin bin: Lawton (58) - high tackle.
On report: Edge (61) - alleged eye gouge on Sangare.
Rugby Leaguer & League Express Men of the Match: *Olympique:* Latrell Schaumkel; *Vikings:* Jack Owens.
Penalty count: 11-5; **Half-time:** 30-0; **Referee:** Tom Grant.
(at Heywood Road, Sale).

DEWSBURY RAMS 0 HALIFAX PANTHERS 36

RAMS: 1 Joe Martin; 2 Andy Gabriel; 3 Adam Ryder; 4 Matty Fleming; 5 Will Oakes; 6 Paul Sykes; 7 Liam Finn; 31 Jimmy Beckett; 9 Reiss Butterworth; 10 Tom Garratt; 11 Jason Walton; 39 Dane Windrow; 13 Chris Annakin. Subs (all used): 19 Jamie Greenwood; 8 Frazer Morris; 23 Jon Magrin; 20 Aaron Hall.
Sin bin: Annakin (75) - fighting.
PANTHERS: 4 James Woodburn-Hall; 19 Conor McGrath; 12 Ed Barber; 3 Greg Worthington; 2 Nick Rawsthorne; 6 Liam Harris; 7 Connor Robinson; 25 Adam Tangata; 9 Brandon Moore; 10 Daniel Murray; 26 Sam Hewitt; 11 Matt Garside; 13 Jacob Fairbank. Subs (all used): 22 Amir Bourouh; 14 Kevin Larroyer; 17 Ben Kavanagh; 8 Elliot Morris.
Tries: Barber (13, 35), Moore (46), Rawsthorne (60), Morris (67); **Goals:** Robinson 8/8.
Rugby Leaguer & League Express Men of the Match: *Rams:* Jason Walton; *Panthers:* Liam Harris.
Penalty count: 4-7; **Half-time:** 0-16;
Referee: Aaron Moore.

YORK CITY KNIGHTS 12 FEATHERSTONE ROVERS 16

CITY KNIGHTS: 5 Kieran Dixon; 23 Ben Jones-Bishop; 3 Liam Salter; 4 Ryan Atkins; 2 Jason Bass; 1 Matty Marsh; 29 Riley Dean; 8 Ronan Dixon; 11 Chris Clarkson; 15 Jordan Baldwinson; 17 Danny Kirmond; 12 Sam Scott; 20 Tim Spears. Subs (all used): 9 Will Jubb; 21 Joe Porter; 16 Marcus Stock; 19 James Green.
Tries: Marsh (6), Salter (28); **Goals:** K Dixon 2/2.
ROVERS: 7 Dane Chisholm; 1 Craig Hall; 17 Thomas Minns; 4 Josh Hardcastle; 5 Gareth Gale; 6 Tom Holmes; 9 Fa'amanu Brown; 13 James Lockwood; 14 Connor Jones; 8 Craig Kopczak; 12 Brad Day; 31 Junior Moors; 16 Jack Bussey. Subs (all used): 21 Dean Parata; 15 John Davies; 20 Frankie Halton; 18 Luke Cooper.
Tries: Gale (12, 58), Hall (76); **Goals:** Brown 2/5.
Sin bin: Davies (28) - dangerous challenge.
Rugby Leaguer & League Express Men of the Match: *City Knights:* Kieran Dixon; *Rovers:* Dane Chisholm.
Penalty count: 6-6; **Half-time:** 12-6;
Referee: Chris Kendall.

ROUND 6

Saturday 15th May 2021

BATLEY BULLDOGS 6 LONDON BRONCOS 40

BULLDOGS: 14 Elliot Hall; 5 Johnny Campbell; 22 Dale Morton; 3 Kieran Buchanan; 21 Jodie Broughton; 6 Ben White; 1 Luke Hooley; 10 Toby Everett; 24 Ben Kaye; 15 Jack Blagbrough; 12 Lucas Walshaw; 11 Dane Manning; 17 Josh Tonks. Subs (all used): 19 Tom Lillycrop; 9 Alistair Leak; 16 Michael Ward; 13 James Brown.
Try: Hall (37); **Goals:** Morton 1/2.
BRONCOS: 5 Ed Chamberlain; 20 Gideon Boafo; 3 Chris Hankinson; 4 Will Lovell; 17 Abbas Miski; 7 Jarrod Sammut; 1 James Meadows; 15 Romain Navarrete; 9 Matty Fozard; 10 Greg Richards; 12 Rhys Curran; 13 Josh Walters; 16 Dan Hindmarsh. Subs (all used): 28 Titus Gwaze; 18 Jordan Williams; 14 Sam Davis; 25 Jacob Jones.
Tries: Walters (16), Hankinson (20, 58), Miski (24), Curran (43), Jones (49), Boafo (70); **Goals:** Hankinson 6/7.
Rugby Leaguer & League Express Men of the Match: *Bulldogs:* Alistair Leak; *Broncos:* James Meadows.
Penalty count: 4-3; **Half-time:** 6-18; **Referee:** Tom Grant.

Sunday 16th May 2021

WHITEHAVEN 0 TOULOUSE OLYMPIQUE 66

WHITEHAVEN: 31 Oscar Thomas; 25 James Worthington; 4 Jessie Joe Parker; 23 Jason Mossop; 30 Sean Croston; 9 Callum Phillips; 7 Nikau Williams; 21 Glenn Riley; 32 Aiden Roden; 24 Ethan Kelly; 15 Connor Holliday; 12 Liam Cooper; 20 Jake Bradley. Subs (all used): 18 James Newton; 29 Dean Zammit; 33 Ronan Michael; 35 Guy Graham.
OLYMPIQUE: 21 Latrell Schaumkel; 2 Jy Hitchcox; 4 Mathieu Jussaume; 3 Junior Vaivai; 30 Jordan Flovie; 6 Johnathon Ford; 13 Anthony Marion; 16 Joe Bretherton; 9 Lloyd White; 10 Harrison Hansen; 11 Andrew Dixon; 12 Dominique Peyroux; 8 Remi Casty. Subs (all used): 14 Eloi Pelissier; 18 Mitch Garbutt; 27 Maxime Garcia; 28 Hugo Salabio.
Tries: Jussaume (17, 78), White (19), Dixon (28), Marion (36, 65), Pelissier (39), Vaivai (47, 51), Peyroux (54), Hitchcox (58), Flovie (71, 76); **Goals:** Marion 7/13.
Sin bin: Peyroux (4) - late challenge.
Rugby Leaguer & League Express Men of the Match: *Whitehaven:* Jake Bradley; *Olympique:* Johnathon Ford.
Penalty count: 9-7; **Half-time:** 0-26; **Referee:** Jack Smith.

WIDNES VIKINGS 14 YORK CITY KNIGHTS 35

VIKINGS: 1 Jack Owens; 2 Jayden Hatton; 4 Steve Tyrer; 3 Jake Spedding; 5 Deon Cross; 6 Danny Craven; 17 Joe Lyons; 10 Matt Cook; 28 Brad O'Neill; 13 Kenny Baker; 11 Shane Grady; 29 Ellis Robson; 7 Matty Smith. Subs (all used): 12 Adam Lawton; 19 Joe Edge; 24 Will Tilleke; 25 Daniel Hill.
Tries: Lawton (25), Cross (34); **Goals:** Tyrer 3/3.
CITY KNIGHTS: 37 Mikey Lewis; 23 Ben Jones-Bishop; 3 Liam Salter; 4 Ryan Atkins; 5 Kieran Dixon; 1 Matty Marsh; 29 Riley Dean; 19 James Green; 9 Will Jubb; 16

Championship 2021 - Round by Round

Marcus Stock; 39 James McDonnell; 12 Sam Scott; 11 Chris Clarkson. Subs (all used): 28 Danny Washbrook; 15 Jordan Baldwinson; 13 Adam Cuthbertson; 21 Joe Porter.
Tries: Scott (6), Jones-Bishop (45), Washbrook (58), Lewis (66, 80); **Goals:** K Dixon 7/7; **Field goal:** Dean (79).
Rugby League & League Express Men of the Match: *Vikings:* Jack Owens; *City Knights:* Mikey Lewis.
Penalty count: 7-11; **Half-time:** 14-8;
Referee: Gareth Hewer.

Monday 17th May 2021

SWINTON LIONS 18 DEWSBURY RAMS 20

LIONS: 22 Geronimo Doyle; 25 Luis Roberts; 3 Mitch Cox; 37 Nico Rizzelli; 1 Mike Butt; 6 Martyn Ridyard; 7 Jack Hansen; 8 Sam Brooks; 9 Luke Waterworth; 38 Sam Luckley; 11 Rhodri Lloyd; 19 Deane Meadows; 13 Will Hope. Subs (all used): 14 Billy Brickhill; 15 Louis Brogan; 16 Paddy Jones; 39 Tom Spencer.
Tries: Cox (51), Brickhill (74, 76); **Goals:** Ridyard 3/3.
Sin bin: Jones (29) - late challenge on Hall.
RAMS: 4 Matty Fleming; 2 Andy Gabriel; 3 Adam Ryder; 33 Zack McComb; 5 Will Oakes; 6 Paul Sykes; 7 Liam Finn; 39 Jon Luke Kirby; 14 Sam Day; 10 Tom Garratt; 11 Jason Walton; 12 Michael Knowles; 15 Keenen Tomlinson. Subs (all used): 1 Joe Martin; 9 Reiss Butterworth; 20 Aaron Hall; 13 Chris Annakin.
Tries: Gabriel (3), Knowles (16), Tomlinson (18);
Goals: Sykes 4/6.
Rugby League & League Express Men of the Match: *Lions:* Martyn Ridyard; *Rams:* Zack McComb.
Penalty count: 7-7; **Half-time:** 0-16;
Referee: Cameron Worsley; **Attendance:** 416.

FEATHERSTONE ROVERS 68 OLDHAM 0

ROVERS: 7 Dane Chisholm; 1 Craig Hall; 4 Josh Hardcastle; 17 Thomas Minns; 5 Gareth Gale; 6 Tom Holmes; 9 Fa'amanu Brown; 8 Craig Kopczak; 21 Dean Parata; 13 James Lockwood; 12 Brad Day; 31 Junior Moors; 16 Jack Bussey. Subs (all used): 14 Connor Jones; 15 John Davies; 18 Luke Cooper; 19 Callum Field.
Tries: Chisholm (2), Hall (9, 32), Bussey (13, 16), Day (37), Minns (39), Hardcastle (50), Holmes (55), Brown (62), Jones (72), Gale (76); **Goals:** Chisholm 10/12.
OLDHAM: 23 Callum Green; 31 John Hutchings; 28 Joe Hartley; 24 Max Roberts; 5 Ryan Ince; 1 Dan Abram; 7 Dave Hewitt; 13 Martyn Reilly; 9 Gareth Owen; 15 Luke Nelmes; 12 Liam Bent; 11 Danny Langtree; 10 Jack Spencer. Subs (all used): 30 Dec Gregory; 21 Shaun Pick; 19 Matthew Fletcher; 2 Tommy Brierley.
Sin bin: Roberts (8) - dissent.
Rugby League & League Express Men of the Match: *Rovers:* Dane Chisholm; *Oldham:* Martyn Reilly.
Penalty count: 6-6; **Half-time:** 40-0;
Referee: James Vella; **Attendance:** 1,670.

ROUND 7

Saturday 22nd May 2021

TOULOUSE OLYMPIQUE 66 SWINTON LIONS 18

OLYMPIQUE: 1 Mark Kheirallah; 2 Jy Hitchcox; 4 Mathieu Jussaume; 3 Junior Vaivai; 21 Latrell Schaumkel; 6 Johnathon Ford; 31 Tony Gigot; 8 Remi Casty; 9 Lloyd White; 10 Harrison Hansen; 16 Joe Bretherton; 12 Dominique Peyroux; 13 Anthony Marion. Subs (all used): 14 Eloi Pelissier; 18 Mitch Garbutt; 23 Justin Sangare; 27 Maxime Garcia.
Tries: Casty (3), Marion (6), Jussaume (18), Schaumkel (20, 63, 69), Bretherton (39), Garbutt (46), Pelissier (53), Kheirallah (56), Peyroux (77), Ford (78);
Goals: Kheirallah 9/12.
LIONS: 22 Geronimo Doyle; 1 Mike Butt; 3 Mitch Cox; 11 Rhodri Lloyd; 25 Luis Roberts; 6 Martyn Ridyard; 7 Jack Hansen; 8 Sam Brooks; 9 Luke Waterworth; 26 Jordan Brown; 19 Deane Meadows; 12 Nick Gregson; 14 Billy Brickhill. Subs (all used): 16 Paddy Jones; 21 Ben Heyes; 24 Paul Nash; 20 Tayler Brown.
Tries: Gregson (11), Hansen (13), Cox (25);
Goals: Ridyard 3/3.
Sin bin: Lloyd (52) - holding down.
Rugby League & League Express Men of the Match: *Olympique:* Tony Gigot; *Lions:* Nick Gregson.
Penalty count: 8-7; **Half-time:** 24-18;
Referee: Jack Smith; **Attendance:** 186 *(at Heywood Road)*.

Sunday 23rd May 2021

LONDON BRONCOS 8 BRADFORD BULLS 33

BRONCOS: 5 Ed Chamberlain; 2 Tuoyo Egodo; 4 Will Lovell; 3 Chris Hankinson; 17 Abbas Miski; 6 Cory Aston; 1 James Meadows; 15 Romain Navarrete; 9 Matty Fozard; 10 Greg Richards; 12 Rhys Curran; 13 Josh Walters; 16 Dan Hindmarsh. Subs (all used): 25 Jacob Jones; 18 Jordan Williams; 14 Sam Davis; 28 Titus Gwaze.
Try: Curran (6); **Goals:** Hankinson 2/2.
Sin bin: Navarrete (60) - high tackle; Richards (65) - fighting.
BULLS: 1 Brandon Pickersgill; 2 Joe Brown; 3 Rhys Evans; 4 Ross Oakes; 36 Mitieli Vulikijapani; 6 Danny Brough; 7 Jordan Lilley; 15 Dan Fleming; 9 Thomas Doyle; 10 Steve Crossley; 20 Brad England; 12 Aaron Murphy; 24 Ben Evans. Subs (all used): 18 Ebon Scurr; 34 Joe Burton; 35 Ellis Robson; 23 Anthony Walker.
Tries: Murphy (13), Doyle (25), Pickersgill (27), Robson (61, 71); **Goals:** Brough 4/4, Lilley 2/2;
Field goal: Brough (39).
Sin bin: Fleming (65) - fighting; Pickersgill (72) - repeated team offences.
Rugby League & League Express Men of the Match: *Broncos:* Sam Davis; *Bulls:* Danny Brough.
Penalty count: 8-9; **Half-time:** 8-19;
Referee: James Vella; **Attendance:** 533 *(at Trailfinders Sports Ground, Ealing)*.

NEWCASTLE THUNDER 0 HALIFAX PANTHERS 32

THUNDER: 1 Lewis Young; 2 Jack Johnson; 3 Matthew Wright; 4 Kieran Gill; 18 Alex Clegg; 6 Jake Shorrocks; 21 Reece Dean; 8 Nathan Wilde; 9 Bob Beswick; 10 Mikey Wood; - Ellis Longstaff; 12 Sam Wilde; 13 Liam McAvoy. Subs (all used): 11 Ukuma Ta'ai; 16 Jay Chapelhow; 17 Connor Bailey; 34 Connor Wrench.
PANTHERS: 4 James Woodburn-Hall; 2 Nick Rawsthorne; 3 Greg Worthington; 12 Ed Barber; 5 James Saltonstall; 6 Liam Harris; 7 Connor Robinson; 15 Gadwin Springer; 9 Brandon Moore; 25 Adam Tangata; 11 Matt Garside; 26 Sam Hewitt; 13 Jacob Fairbank. Subs (all used): 22 Amir Bourouh; 14 Kevin Larroyer; 10 Daniel Murray; 8 Elliot Morris.
Tries: Woodburn-Hall (12, 33), Rawsthorne (24), Barber (41), Bourouh (54); **Goals:** Robinson 6/7.
Rugby League & League Express Men of the Match: *Thunder:* Jack Johnson; *Panthers:* Brandon Moore.
Penalty count: 5-3; **Half-time:** 0-22;
Referee: Gareth Hewer; **Attendance:** 604.

WIDNES VIKINGS 44 WHITEHAVEN 6

VIKINGS: 1 Jack Owens; 2 Jayden Hatton; 4 Steve Tyrer; 3 Jake Spedding; 5 Deon Cross; 6 Danny Craven; 17 Joe Lyons; 10 Matt Cook; 28 Brad O'Neill; 13 Kenny Baker; 11 Shane Grady; 12 Adam Lawton; 7 Matty Smith. Subs (all used): 8 Paul Clough; 15 Connor Dwyer; 16 Owen Farnworth; 24 Will Tilleke.
Tries: B O'Neill (19), Lawton (37, 74), Craven (45, 47), Tilleke (57), Owens (66); **Goals:** Tyrer 8/8.
WHITEHAVEN: 1 Gregg McNally; 2 Lachlan Walmsley; 3 Chris Taylor; 23 Jason Mossop; 4 Jessie Joe Parker; 6 Karl Dixon; 7 Nikau Williams; 17 Tom Walker; 32 Aiden Roden; 27 Andrew Dawson; 19 Ellis Gillam; 12 Liam Cooper; 16 Tom Wilkinson. Subs (all used): 20 Jake Bradley; - Ronan Michael; 18 James Newton; 31 Oscar Thomas.
Try: Bradley (53); **Goals:** Walmsley 1/1.
Rugby League & League Express Men of the Match: *Vikings:* Danny Craven; *Whitehaven:* Jake Bradley.
Penalty count: 7-10; **Half-time:** 14-0;
Referee: John McMullen; **Attendance:** 1,043.

YORK CITY KNIGHTS 34 OLDHAM 6

CITY KNIGHTS: 37 Mikey Lewis; 23 Ben Jones-Bishop; 30 Tyme Dow-Nikau; 4 Ryan Atkins; 5 Kieran Dixon; 1 Matty Marsh; 29 Riley Dean; 19 James Green; 9 Will Jubb; 15 Jordan Baldwinson; 39 James McDonnell; 12 Sam Scott; 11 Chris Clarkson. Subs (all used): 14 Kriss Brining; 16 Marcus Stock; 13 Adam Cuthbertson; 8 Ronan Dixon.
Tries: Jubb (17, 76), K Dixon (54), Dean (59), Marsh (61), Clarkson (68); **Goals:** K Dixon 5/6.
OLDHAM: 29 Tom Nisbet; 2 Tommy Brierley; 25 Danny Bridge; 24 Max Roberts; 5 Ryan Ince; 1 Dan Abram; 7 Dave Hewitt; 17 Liam Kirk; 30 Dec Gregory; 15 Luke Nelmes; 21 Shaun Pick; 11 Danny Langtree; 12 Liam Bent. Subs (all used): 33 Jamie Abram; 13 Martyn Reilly; 19 Matthew Fletcher; 16 Tyler Dupree.
Try: Pick (13); **Goals:** D Abram 1/1.
Dismissal: Nisbet (37) - high tackle on Dow-Nikau.
Rugby League & League Express Men of the Match: *City Knights:* Sam Scott; *Oldham:* Dec Gregory.
Penalty count: 6-3; **Half-time:** 6-6;
Referee: Nick Bennett; **Attendance:** 1,000.

SHEFFIELD EAGLES 18 FEATHERSTONE ROVERS 50

EAGLES: 1 Josh Guzdek; 2 Rob Worrincy; 24 Ryan Johnson; 4 James Glover; 27 Travis Corion; 22 Izaac Farrell; 13 Aaron Brown; 8 Scott Wheeldon; 9 James Davey; 10 Matt James; 11 Brad Knowles; 15 Olly Davies; 20 Paddy Burns. Subs (all used): 23 Harry Tyson-Wilson; 31 Bobby Tyson-Wilson; 18 Tyler Dickinson; 25 Jordan Bull.
Tries: Knowles (22), B Tyson-Wilson (30), I Farrell (71);
Goals: I Farrell 3/3.
ROVERS: 7 Dane Chisholm; 5 Gareth Gale; 1 Craig Hall; 17 Thomas Minns; 28 Jacob Doyle; 9 Fa'amanu Brown; 6 Tom Holmes; 8 Craig Kopczak; 14 Connor Jones; 13 James Lockwood; 20 Frankie Halton; 12 Brad Day; 16 Jack Bussey. Subs (all used): 21 Dean Parata; 15 John Davies; 19 Callum Field; 27 Loui McConnell.
Tries: Doyle (6), Gale (9, 37), Bussey (17), Lockwood (27, 57), Field (34), Brown (45), Hall (65); **Goals:** Chisholm 7/9.
Rugby League & League Express Men of the Match: *Eagles:* Bobby Tyson-Wilson; *Rovers:* Jack Bussey.
Penalty count: 6-3; **Half-time:** 12-32;
Referee: Aaron Moore; **Attendance:** 620.

ROUND 8

Sunday 30th May 2021

BATLEY BULLDOGS 26 SWINTON LIONS 12

BULLDOGS: 1 Luke Hooley; 5 Johnny Campbell; 22 Dale Morton; 3 Kieran Buchanan; 21 Jodie Broughton; 6 Ben White; 7 Tom Gilmore; 8 Adam Gledhill; 24 Ben Kaye; 15 Jack Blagbrough; 17 Josh Tonks; 11 Dane Manning; 13 James Brown. Subs (all used): 9 Alistair Leak; 12 Lucas Walshaw; 14 Elliot Hall; 19 Tom Lillycrop.
Tries: Kaye (24), Brown (41), Broughton (72), Leak (78);
Goals: Morton 5/5.
LIONS: 22 Geronimo Doyle; 1 Mike Butt; 3 Mitch Cox; 39 Reece Hamlett; 25 Luis Roberts; 6 Martyn Ridyard; 7 Jack Hansen; 8 Sam Brooks; 9 Luke Waterworth; 40 Ronan Michael; 11 Rhodri Lloyd; 12 Nick Gregson; 14 Billy Brickhill. Subs (all used): 16 Paddy Jones; 20 Tayler Brown; 19 Deane Meadows; 18 Cobi Green.
Tries: Cox (1), Brooks (13); **Goals:** Ridyard 2/3.
Sin bin: Waterworth (65) - dissent.
Rugby League & League Express Men of the Match: *Bulldogs:* Dale Morton; *Lions:* Geronimo Doyle.
Penalty count: 8-6; **Half-time:** 6-10;
Referee: Gareth Hewer; **Attendance:** 930.

BRADFORD BULLS 37 YORK CITY KNIGHTS 18

BULLS: 1 Brandon Pickersgill; 2 Joe Brown; 3 Rhys Evans; 4 Ross Oakes; 36 Mitieli Vulikijapani; 6 Danny Brough; 7 Jordan Lilley; 15 Dan Fleming; 9 Thomas Doyle; 10 Steve Crossley; 20 Brad England; 12 Aaron Murphy; 24 Ben Evans. Subs (all used): 18 Ebon Scurr; 35 Ellis Robson; 37 Oliver Wilson; 38 Ashton Golding.
Tries: Brown (5, 73), Lilley (24), Golding (38), Oakes (47);
Goals: Brough 8/8; **Field goal:** Brough (52).
CITY KNIGHTS: 37 Mikey Lewis; 23 Ben Jones-Bishop; 3 Liam Salter; 4 Ryan Atkins; 5 Kieran Dixon; 1 Matty Marsh; 6 Brendan O'Hagan; 10 Jack Teanby; 9 Will Jubb; 15 Jordan Baldwinson; 12 Sam Scott; 17 Danny Kirmond; 11 Chris Clarkson. Subs (all used): 14 Kriss Brining; 19 James Green; 16 Marcus Stock; 13 Adam Cuthbertson.
Tries: K Dixon (10), Atkins (33), Clarkson (62);
Goals: K Dixon 3/3.
Rugby League & League Express Men of the Match: *Bulls:* Danny Brough; *City Knights:* Mikey Lewis.
Penalty count: 10-7; **Half-time:** 24-12;
Referee: Ben Thaler; **Attendance:** 3,742.

HALIFAX PANTHERS 8 FEATHERSTONE ROVERS 16

PANTHERS: 4 James Woodburn-Hall; 5 James Saltonstall; 12 Ed Barber; 3 Greg Worthington; 2 Nick Rawsthorne; 6 Liam Harris; 7 Connor Robinson; 15 Gadwin Springer; 9 Brandon Moore; 25 Adam Tangata; 11 Matt Garside; 26 Sam Hewitt; 13 Jacob Fairbank. Subs (all used): 28 Oliver Russell; 14 Kevin Larroyer; 10 Daniel Murray; 8 Elliot Morris.
Try: Tangata (58); **Goals:** Robinson 1/1, Harris 1/1.
ROVERS: 7 Dane Chisholm; 5 Gareth Gale; 17 Thomas Minns; 20 Frankie Halton; 1 Craig Hall; 6 Tom Holmes; 9 Fa'amanu Brown; 8 Craig Kopczak; 21 Dean Parata; 13 James Lockwood; 12 Brad Day; 31 Junior Moors; 27 Loui McConnell. Subs (all used): 14 Connor Jones; 15 John Davies; 19 Callum Field; 26 Jimmy Beckett.
Tries: Brown (33), Hall (42), Gale (51); **Goals:** Chisholm 2/3.
Sin bin: Davies (59) - late challenge on Russell.
Rugby League & League Express Men of the Match: *Panthers:* Connor Robinson; *Rovers:* Gareth Gale.
Penalty count: 4-11; **Half-time:** 2-6;
Referee: Tom Grant; **Attendance:** 882.

LONDON BRONCOS 30 DEWSBURY RAMS 10

BRONCOS: 1 James Meadows; 23 Josh Hodson; 4 Will Lovell; 3 Chris Hankinson; 17 Abbas Miski; 6 Cory Aston; 9 Matty Fozard; 10 Greg Richards; 14 Sam Davis; 28 Titus Gwaze; 12 Rhys Curran; 13 Josh Walters; 25 Jacob Jones. Subs (all used): 18 Jordan Williams; 16 Dan Hindmarsh; 15 Romain Navarrete; 7 Jarrod Sammut.
Tries: Walters (3, 40), Fozard (9), Aston (45), Meadows (66); **Goals:** Hankinson 5/5.

York's Matty Marsh and Ben Jones-Bishop can't prevent Bradford's Joe Brown from scoring

RAMS: 4 Matty Fleming; 2 Andy Gabriel; 3 Adam Ryder; 33 Zack McComb; 5 Will Oakes; 6 Paul Sykes; 7 Liam Finn; 10 Tom Garratt; 14 Sam Day; 23 Jon Magrin; 11 Jason Walton; 12 Michael Knowles; 39 Sam Wood. Subs (all used): 9 Reiss Butterworth; 1 Joe Martin; 13 Chris Annakin; 20 Aaron Hall.
Tries: Wood (20), Gabriel (60); **Goals:** Sykes 1/2.
Rugby Leaguer & League Express Men of the Match: *Broncos:* Matty Fozard; *Rams:* Liam Finn.
Penalty count: 4-4; **Half-time:** 18-6;
Referee: Aaron Moore; **Attendance:** 280
(at Trailfinders Sports Ground, Ealing).

OLDHAM 18 WIDNES VIKINGS 40

OLDHAM: 1 Dan Abram; 2 Tommy Brierley; 35 Louis Senior; 24 Max Roberts; 5 Ryan Ince; 6 Lewis Charnock; 7 Dave Hewitt; 17 Liam Kirk; 9 Gareth Owen; 15 Luke Nelmes; 11 Danny Langtree; 25 Danny Bridge; 12 Liam Bent. Subs (all used): 13 Martyn Reilly; 30 Dec Gregory; 21 Shaun Pick; 16 Tyler Dupree.
Tries: Senior (40), Brierley (58), Langtree (80);
Goals: D Abram 3/3.
VIKINGS: 1 Jack Owens; 2 Jayden Hatton; 4 Steve Tyrer; 3 Jake Spedding; 5 Deon Cross; 6 Danny Craven; 17 Joe Lyons; 10 Matt Cook; 28 Brad O'Neill; 13 Kenny Baker; 11 Shane Grady; 12 Adam Lawton; 7 Matty Smith. Subs (all used): 8 Paul Clough; 16 Owen Farnworth; 24 Will Tilleke; 23 Lewis Else.
Tries: Hatton (7), Tyrer (19), Cross (22, 49), Owens (34, 45), Spedding (62); **Goals:** Tyrer 6/7.
Rugby Leaguer & League Express Men of the Match: *Oldham:* Dec Gregory; *Vikings:* Danny Craven.
Penalty count: 7-7; **Half-time:** 6-22;
Referee: Jack Smith; **Attendance:** 600.

SHEFFIELD EAGLES 25 WHITEHAVEN 25

EAGLES: 1 Josh Guzdek; 2 Rob Worrincy; 3 Connor Bower; 4 James Glover; 5 Ryan Millar; 22 Izaac Farrell; 7 Anthony Thackeray; 8 Scott Wheeldon; 14 Greg Burns; 10 Matt James; 11 Brad Knowles; 15 Olly Davies; 13 Aaron Brown. Subs (all used): 9 James Davey; 19 Blake Broadbent; 18 Tyler Dickinson; 31 Bobby Tyson-Wilson.
Tries: G Burns (9), Knowles (12), I Farrell (67), Thackeray (71); **Goals:** I Farrell 4/4.
Field goal: Thackeray (80).
WHITEHAVEN: 1 Gregg McNally; 4 Jessie Joe Parker; 3 Chris Taylor; 23 Jason Mossop; 2 Lachlan Walmsley; 6 Karl Dixon; 7 Nikau Williams; 17 Tom Walker; 18 James Newton;

12 Liam Cooper; 19 Ellis Gillam; 15 Connor Holliday; 16 Tom Wilkinson. Subs (all used): 13 Dion Aiye; 20 Jake Bradley; 27 Andrew Dawson; 31 Oscar Thomas.
Tries: Holliday (1), Walmsley (32), McNally (34), Bradley (57); **Goals:** Walmsley 4/4;
Field goal: McNally (39).
Rugby Leaguer & League Express Men of the Match: *Eagles:* Greg Burns; *Whitehaven:* Gregg McNally.
Penalty count: 10-2; **Half-time:** 12-19;
Referee: Cameron Worsley; **Attendance:** 343.

ROUND 6

Sunday 6th June 2021

HALIFAX PANTHERS 46 SHEFFIELD EAGLES 12

PANTHERS: 4 James Woodburn-Hall; 2 Nick Rawsthorne; 3 Greg Worthington; 12 Ed Barber; 5 James Saltonstall; 6 Liam Harris; 1 Scott Grix; 15 Gadwin Springer; 9 Brandon Moore; 10 Daniel Murray; 17 Ben Kavanagh; 26 Sam Hewitt; 13 Jacob Fairbank. Subs (all used): 14 Kevin Larroyer; 8 Elliot Morris; 22 Amir Bourouh; 16 Will Calcott.
Tries: Rawsthorne (10, 76), Kavanagh (16), Woodburn-Hall (24), Hewitt (27, 53), Larroyer (45, 74), Murray (55); **Goals:** Rawsthorne 4/8, Harris 1/1.
EAGLES: 24 Ryan Johnson; 2 Rob Worrincy; 3 Connor Bower; 4 James Glover; 5 Ryan Millar; 22 Izaac Farrell; 7 Anthony Thackeray; 8 Scott Wheeldon; 14 Greg Burns; 10 Matt James; 11 Brad Knowles; 15 Olly Davies; 13 Aaron Brown. Subs (all used): 9 James Davey; 19 Blake Broadbent; 26 Chris Ball; 18 Tyler Dickinson.
Tries: Broadbent (34), Millar (62); **Goals:** I Farrell 2/2.
Dismissal: Wheeldon (70) - late challenge on Larroyer.
Rugby Leaguer & League Express Men of the Match: *Panthers:* James Woodburn-Hall; *Eagles:* Rob Worrincy.
Penalty count: 5-6; **Half-time:** 20-6;
Referee: Robert Hicks; **Attendance:** 734.

BRADFORD BULLS 31 NEWCASTLE THUNDER 12

BULLS: 1 Brandon Pickersgill; 38 Ashton Golding; 3 Rhys Evans; 4 Ross Oakes; 2 Joe Brown; 6 Danny Brough; 7 Jordan Lilley; 37 Oliver Wilson; 9 Thomas Doyle; 10 Steve Crossley; 20 Brad England; 16 Brad Gallagher; 13 Sam Hallas. Subs (all used): 19 David Foggin-Johnston; 35 Ellis Robson; 18 Ebon Scurr; 23 Anthony Walker.
Tries: Lilley (3), Robson (41), Walker (45), Crossley (71), Doyle (79); **Goals:** Brough 4/4, Lilley 1/1;
Field goal: Brough (62).

THUNDER: 5 Calum Turner; 2 Jack Johnson; 18 Alex Clegg; 3 Matthew Wright; 33 Sam Halsall; 6 Jake Shorrocks; 21 Reece Dean; 8 Nathan Wilde; 9 Bob Beswick; 10 Mikey Wood; 4 Kieran Gill; 17 Connor Bailey; 13 Liam McAvoy. Subs (all used): 11 Ukuma Ta'ai; 36 Owen Harrison; 14 Evan Simons; 20 Cole Oakley.
Tries: Dean (14), Gill (52); **Goals:** Dean 2/2.
Rugby Leaguer & League Express Men of the Match: *Bulls:* Anthony Walker; *Thunder:* Bob Beswick.
Penalty count: 5-7; **Half-time:** 6-6;
Referee: James Child; **Attendance:** 3,562.

ROUND 9

Saturday 12th June 2021

OLDHAM 28 SHEFFIELD EAGLES 32

OLDHAM: 1 Dan Abram; 2 Tommy Brierley; 25 Danny Bridge; 24 Max Roberts; 5 Ryan Ince; 6 Lewis Charnock; 7 Dave Hewitt; 8 Phil Joy; 9 Gareth Owen; 17 Liam Kirk; 12 Liam Bent; 11 Danny Langtree; 13 Martyn Reilly. Subs (all used): 30 Dec Gregory; 19 Matthew Fletcher; 16 Tyler Dupree; 15 Luke Nelmes.
Tries: Roberts (25), D Abram (53), Reilly (66), Kirk (71), Brierley (77); **Goals:** D Abram 4/6.
EAGLES: 24 Ryan Johnson; 2 Rob Worrincy; 3 Connor Bower; 4 James Glover; 5 Ryan Millar; 22 Izaac Farrell; 7 Anthony Thackeray; 8 Scott Wheeldon; 14 Greg Burns; 18 Tyler Dickinson; 32 Evan Hodgson; 15 Olly Davies; 13 Aaron Brown. Subs (all used): 9 James Davey; 19 Blake Broadbent; 20 Paddy Burns; 10 Matt James.
Tries: Glover (17, 40), Worrincy (22, 58, 61), Brown (55); **Goals:** I Farrell 4/6.
Dismissal: Dickinson (67) - high tackle on Charnock.
Rugby Leaguer & League Express Men of the Match: *Oldham:* Martyn Reilly; *Eagles:* Rob Worrincy.
Penalty count: 8-4; **Half-time:** 6-14;
Referee: Michael Mannifield; **Attendance:** 475.

Sunday 13th June 2021

DEWSBURY RAMS 12 TOULOUSE OLYMPIQUE 56

RAMS: 4 Matty Fleming; 27 Lewis Carr; 26 Bayley Liu; 5 Will Oakes; 18 Davey Dixon; 6 Paul Sykes; 30 Alex Smith; 23 Jon Magrin; 14 Sam Day; 10 Tom Garratt; 11 Jason Walton; 12 Michael Knowles; 13 Chris Annakin. Subs (all used): 9 Reiss Butterworth; 39 Dan Hawksworth; 20 Aaron Hall; 29 Rhys Davies.

267

Championship 2021 - Round by Round

Tries: Smith (46), Oakes (79); **Goals:** Knowles 1/1, Sykes 1/1.
Sin bin: Sykes (37) - holding down;
Hawksworth (44) - high tackle.
OLYMPIQUE: 1 Mark Kheirallah; 2 Jy Hitchcox; 4 Mathieu Jussaume; 3 Junior Vaivai; 20 Ilias Bergal; 6 Johnathon Ford; 31 Tony Gigot; 8 Remi Casty; 14 Eloi Pelissier; 15 Maxime Puech; 10 Harrison Hansen; 17 Joseph Paulo; 13 Anthony Marion. Subs (all used): 18 Mitch Garbutt; 23 Justin Sangare; 26 Hugo Pezet; 27 Maxime Garcia.
Tries: Jussaume (4, 62), Hitchcox (8, 72, 77), Pelissier (16, 66), Garbutt (31), Sangare (52), Pezet (75);
Goals: Kheirallah 8/11.
Rugby Leaguer & League Express Men of the Match: *Rams:* Will Oakes; *Olympique:* Tony Gigot.
Penalty count: 6-6; **Half-time:** 0-22;
Referee: Ben Thaler; **Attendance:** 418.

FEATHERSTONE ROVERS 44 BRADFORD BULLS 0

ROVERS: 32 Will Dagger; 1 Craig Hall; 17 Thomas Minns; 4 Josh Hardcastle; 5 Gareth Gale; 6 Tom Holmes; 9 Fa'amanu Brown; 8 Craig Kopczak; 14 Connor Jones; 13 James Lockwood; 12 Brad Day; 20 Frankie Halton; 33 Darcy Lussick. Subs (all used): 15 John Davies; 19 Callum Field; 21 Dean Parata; 31 Junior Moors.
Tries: Jones (14), Hall (17), Gale (22), Dagger (34), Minns (37), Holmes (66), Parata (73), Field (76);
Goals: Hall 6/8.
BULLS: 2 Joe Brown; 22 Reece Hamlett; 4 Ross Oakes; 3 Rhys Evans; 19 David Foggin-Johnston; 1 Brandon Pickersgill; 7 Jordan Lilley; 10 Steve Crossley; 9 Thomas Doyle; 24 Ben Evans; 16 Brad Gallagher; 20 Brad England; 13 Sam Hallas. Subs (all used): 18 Ebon Scurr; 23 Anthony Walker; 34 Joe Burton; 35 Ellis Robson.
Rugby Leaguer & League Express Men of the Match: *Rovers:* Connor Jones; *Bulls:* Brandon Pickersgill.
Penalty count: 5-6; **Half-time:** 26-0;
Referee: Aaron Moore; **Attendance:** 1,700.

HALIFAX PANTHERS 30 YORK CITY KNIGHTS 6

PANTHERS: 4 James Woodburn-Hall; 2 Nick Rawsthorne; 3 Greg Worthington; 21 Zack McComb; 5 James Saltonstall; 6 Liam Harris; 1 Scott Grix; 15 Gadwin Springer; 9 Brandon Moore; 10 Daniel Murray; 17 Ben Kavanagh; 11 Matt Garside; 25 Adam Tangata. Subs (all used): 8 Elliot Morris; 13 Jacob Fairbank; 14 Kevin Larroyer; 22 Amir Bourouh.
Tries: Kavanagh (7), Garside (15), Rawsthorne (50), Moore (53), Saltonstall (56), Tangata (76);
Goals: Harris 3/6.
Sin bin: Bourouh (78) - fighting.
CITY KNIGHTS: 1 Matty Marsh; 23 Ben Jones-Bishop; 3 Liam Salter; 4 Ryan Atkins; 5 Kieran Dixon; 6 Brendan O'Hagan; 29 Riley Dean; 15 Jordan Baldwinson; 9 Will Jubb; 10 Jack Teanby; 21 Joe Porter; 12 Sam Scott; 11 Chris Clarkson. Subs (all used): 14 Kriss Brining; 20 Tim Spears; 16 Marcus Stock; 19 James Green.
Try: Marsh (43); **Goals:** K Dixon 1/1.
Sin bin: Baldwinson (78) - fighting.
Rugby Leaguer & League Express Men of the Match: *Panthers:* Scott Grix; *City Knights:* Matty Marsh.
Penalty count: 6-4; **Half-time:** 10-0;
Referee: Gareth Hewer; **Attendance:** 828.

SWINTON LIONS 30 NEWCASTLE THUNDER 36

LIONS: 21 Ben Heyes; 25 Luis Roberts; 11 Rhodri Lloyd; 3 Mitch Cox; 1 Mike Butt; 6 Martyn Ridyard; 7 Jack Hansen; 13 Will Hope; 9 Luke Waterworth; 8 Sam Brooks; 19 Deane Meadows; 12 Nick Gregson; 14 Billy Brickhill. Subs (all used): 16 Paddy Jones; 15 Louis Brogan; 39 Dom Horn; 24 Paul Nash.
Tries: Hope (32, 58), Cox (35), Gregson (37), Hansen (50);
Goals: Ridyard 5/5.
Sin bin: Waterworth (55) - fighting.
THUNDER: 5 Calum Turner; 2 Jack Johnson; 33 Sam Halsall; 3 Matthew Wright; 18 Alex Clegg; 7 Josh Woods; 6 Jake Shorrocks; 15 Ted Chapelhow; 9 Bob Beswick; 8 Nathan Wilde; 11 Ukuma Ta'ai; 17 Connor Bailey; 13 Liam McAvoy. Subs (all used): 16 Jay Chapelhow; 37 Mitch Clark; 36 Owen Harrison; 14 Evan Simons.
Tries: Ta'ai (8), Beswick (10), Wright (15, 46), Bailey (24), Turner (27); **Goals:** J Woods 5/6, Wright 1/1.
Sin bin: J Chapelhow (55) - fighting.
Rugby Leaguer & League Express Men of the Match: *Lions:* Will Hope; *Thunder:* Bob Beswick.
Penalty count: 9-5; **Half-time:** 18-30;
Referee: John McMullen; **Attendance:** 455.

WHITEHAVEN 20 BATLEY BULLDOGS 24

WHITEHAVEN: 1 Gregg McNally; 5 Andrew Bulman; 3 Chris Taylor; 23 Jason Mossop; 2 Lachlan Walmsley; 6 Karl Dixon; 7 Nikau Williams; 17 Tom Walker; 9 Callum Phillips; 12 Liam Cooper; 15 Connor Holliday; 19 Ellis Gillam; 16 Tom Wilkinson. Subs (all used): 13 Dion Aiye; 20 Jake Bradley; 27 Andrew Dawson; 31 Oscar Thomas.
Tries: Taylor (5), Walmsley (33), Dixon (38), Bulman (64);
Goals: Walmsley 2/4.
BULLDOGS: 1 Luke Hooley; 5 Johnny Campbell; 18 George Senior; 12 Lucas Walshaw; 14 Elliot Hall; 6 Ben White; 7 Tom Gilmore; 8 Adam Gledhill; 9 Alistair Leak; 10 Toby Everett; 25 Anthony Bowman; 11 Dane Manning; 15 Jack Blagbrough. Subs (all used): 16 Michael Ward; 19 Tom Lillycrop; 26 Nyle Flynn; 27 Aiden Ineson.
Tries: Hooley (8), Ward (46), Hall (50), Lillycrop (56);
Goals: Hooley 4/4.
Sin bin: Everett (21) - late challenge on Wilkinson.
Rugby Leaguer & League Express Men of the Match: *Whitehaven:* Lachlan Walmsley; *Bulldogs:* Michael Ward.
Penalty count: 9-6; **Half-time:** 16-6;
Referee: Nick Bennett; **Attendance:** 632.

WIDNES VIKINGS 22 LONDON BRONCOS 24

VIKINGS: 1 Jack Owens; 2 Jayden Hatton; 4 Steve Tyrer; 19 Joe Edge; 5 Deon Cross; 6 Danny Craven; 17 Joe Lyons; 16 Owen Farnworth; 23 Lewis Else; 13 Kenny Baker; 11 Shane Grady; 12 Adam Lawton; 7 Matty Smith. Subs (all used): 8 Paul Clough; 10 Matt Cook; 22 Josh Wilde; 24 Will Tilleke.
Tries: Craven (5), Cross (38), Lawton (55), Edge (70);
Goals: Tyrer 3/5.
Sin bin: Craven (10) - professional foul.
BRONCOS: 1 James Meadows; 23 Josh Hodson; 4 Will Lovell; 3 Chris Hankinson; 17 Abbas Miski; 6 Cory Aston; 9 Matty Fozard; 31 Pat Moran; 14 Sam Davis; 28 Titus Gwaze; 12 Rhys Curran; 25 Jacob Jones; 18 Jordan Williams. Subs (all used): 15 Romain Navarrete; 16 Dan Hindmarsh; 20 Gideon Boafo; 7 Jarrod Sammut.
Tries: Miski (11), Curran (44), Navarrete (67), Gwaze (77);
Goals: Hankinson 4/4.
Rugby Leaguer & League Express Men of the Match: *Vikings:* Adam Lawton; *Broncos:* Jarrod Sammut.
Penalty count: 5-7; **Half-time:** 14-6;
Referee: Liam Staveley; **Attendance:** 1,211.

ROUND 10

Sunday 20th June 2021

DEWSBURY RAMS 24 FEATHERSTONE ROVERS 68

RAMS: 4 Matty Fleming; 2 Andy Gabriel; 26 Bayley Liu; 18 Davey Dixon; 27 Lewis Carr; 30 Alex Smith; 7 Liam Finn; 23 Jon Magrin; 9 Reiss Butterworth; 20 Aaron Hall; 10 Tom Garratt; 12 Michael Knowles; 13 Chris Annakin. Subs: 33 Dom Speakman; 6 Paul Sykes (not used); 39 Dan Hawksworth; 31 Robson Stevens.
Tries: Liu (22), Garratt (57), Butterworth (71), Carr (80);
Goals: Finn 4/4.
Sin bin: Fleming (46) - holding down.
ROVERS: 32 Will Dagger; 5 Gareth Gale; 4 Josh Hardcastle; 1 Craig Hall; 34 Perry Whiteley; 9 Fa'amanu Brown; 6 Tom Holmes; 8 Craig Kopczak; 21 Dean Parata; 33 Darcy Lussick; 31 Junior Moors; 20 Frankie Halton; 27 Loui McConnell. Subs (all used): 29 Harvey Spence; 15 John Davies; 18 Luke Cooper; 19 Callum Field.
Tries: Kopczak (4), Parata (29, 60, 67, 78), Hall (37, 52, 65), Gale (43, 50), Cooper (47); **Goals:** Hall 12/13.
Rugby Leaguer & League Express Men of the Match: *Rams:* Tom Garratt; *Rovers:* Dean Parata.
Penalty count: 7-9; **Half-time:** 6-20;
Referee: Michael Mannifield; **Attendance:** 792.

LONDON BRONCOS 46 WHITEHAVEN 12

BRONCOS: 1 James Meadows; 23 Josh Hodson; 4 Will Lovell; 3 Chris Hankinson; 17 Abbas Miski; 6 Cory Aston; 7 Jarrod Sammut; 31 Pat Moran; 14 Sam Davis; 28 Titus Gwaze; 12 Rhys Curran; 25 Jacob Jones; 10 Greg Richards. Subs (all used): 15 Romain Navarrete; 16 Dan Hindmarsh; 20 Gideon Boafo; 26 Rob Oakley.
Tries: Hankinson (30, 72), Meadows (44), Hodson (46), Gwaze (53), Curran (57), Aston (63), Sammut (65);
Goals: Hankinson 7/9.
WHITEHAVEN: 2 Lachlan Walmsley; 5 Andrew Bulman; 3 Chris Taylor; 23 Jason Mossop; 4 Jessie Joe Parker; 6 Karl Dixon; 7 Nikau Williams; 27 Andrew Dawson; 18 James Newton; 35 Guy Graham; 12 Liam Cooper; 19 Ellis Gillam; 16 Tom Wilkinson. Subs (all used): 13 Dion Aiye; 24 Ethan Kelly; 31 Oscar Thomas; 20 Jake Bradley.
Tries: Wilkinson (20), Cooper (24); **Goals:** Walmsley 2/2.
Rugby Leaguer & League Express Men of the Match: *Broncos:* Chris Hankinson; *Whitehaven:* Liam Cooper.
Penalty count: 9-4; **Half-time:** 4-12;
Referee: Jack Smith; **Attendance:** 250
(at Trailfinders Sports Ground, Ealing).

NEWCASTLE THUNDER 40 OLDHAM 6

THUNDER: 5 Calum Turner; 2 Jack Johnson; 33 Sam Halsall; 3 Matthew Wright; 18 Alex Clegg; 6 Jake Shorrocks; 7 Josh Woods; 15 Ted Chapelhow; 9 Bob Beswick; 8 Nathan Wilde; 11 Ukuma Ta'ai; 17 Connor Bailey; 13 Liam McAvoy. Subs (all used): 14 Evan Simons; 16 Jay Chapelhow; 37 Mitch Clark; 36 Owen Harrison.
Tries: Johnson (8, 22), Ta'ai (46), Halsall (49), Beswick (52), Shorrocks (56), J Woods (72); **Goals:** J Woods 6/7.
OLDHAM: 1 Dan Abram; 2 Tommy Brierley; 3 Ben Heaton; 24 Max Roberts; 5 Ryan Ince; 6 Lewis Charnock; 26 James Barran; 17 Liam Kirk; 30 Dec Gregory; 8 Phil Joy; 12 Liam Bent; 11 Danny Langtree; 13 Martyn Reilly. Subs (all used): 33 Jamie Abram; 21 Shaun Pick; 15 Luke Nelmes; 19 Matthew Fletcher.
Try: Kirk (70); **Goals:** D Abram 1/1.
Rugby Leaguer & League Express Men of the Match: *Thunder:* Josh Woods; *Oldham:* Liam Kirk.
Penalty count: 6-4; **Half-time:** 12-0;
Referee: Aaron Moore; **Attendance:** 1,087.

SWINTON LIONS 4 HALIFAX PANTHERS 34

LIONS: 1 Mike Butt; 28 Dan Clare; 3 Mitch Cox; 11 Rhodri Lloyd; 25 Luis Roberts; 6 Martyn Ridyard; 7 Jack Hansen; 8 Sam Brooks; 9 Luke Waterworth; 39 Tom Spencer; 13 Will Hope; 12 Nick Gregson; 14 Billy Brickhill. Subs (all used): 15 Louis Brogan; 26 Jordan Brown; 16 Paddy Jones; 19 Deane Meadows.
Try: Roberts (56); **Goals:** Ridyard 0/1.
Sin bin: Spencer (75) - obstruction.
PANTHERS: 4 James Woodburn-Hall; 2 Nick Rawsthorne; 3 Greg Worthington; 21 Zack McComb; 19 Conor McGrath; 6 Liam Harris; 1 Scott Grix; 15 Gadwin Springer; 9 Brandon Moore; 10 Daniel Murray; 17 Ben Kavanagh; 11 Matt Garside; 25 Adam Tangata. Subs (all used): 22 Amir Bourouh; 14 Kevin Larroyer; 16 Will Calcott; 8 Elliot Morris.
Tries: Grix (16, 29), McGrath (32, 38), Kavanagh (52), Bourouh (61); **Goals:** Harris 5/6.
Rugby Leaguer & League Express Men of the Match: *Lions:* Nick Gregson; *Panthers:* Liam Harris.
Penalty count: 6-6; **Half-time:** 0-22;
Referee: Nick Bennett; **Attendance:** 520.

WIDNES VIKINGS 30 SHEFFIELD EAGLES 20

VIKINGS: 1 Jack Owens; 5 Deon Cross; 19 Joe Edge; 4 Steve Tyrer; 2 Jayden Hatton; 6 Danny Craven; 17 Joe Lyons; 11 Shane Grady; 28 Brad O'Neill; 13 Kenny Baker; 12 Adam Lawton; 22 Josh Wilde; 7 Matty Smith. Subs (all used): 8 Paul Clough; 24 Will Tilleke; 23 Lewis Else; 26 Ollie Brookes.
Tries: Grady (16), Lyons (36), Craven (49), Lawton (56, 59);
Goals: Tyrer 5/5.
Dismissal: Lawton (80) - off-the-ball challenge on Davies.
EAGLES: 5 Ryan Millar; 27 Travis Corion; 3 Connor Bower; 4 James Glover; 2 Rob Worrincy; 22 Izaac Farrell; 7 Anthony Thackeray; 31 Bobby Tyson-Wilson; 16 Robbie Ward; 10 Matt James; 32 Evan Hodgson; 15 Olly Davies; 13 Aaron Brown. Subs (all used): 18 Tyler Dickinson; 19 Blake Broadbent; 20 Paddy Burns; 23 Harry Tyson-Wilson.
Tries: Millar (30), Glover (45, 69), Corion (80);
Goals: I Farrell 1/2, Glover 1/2.
Rugby Leaguer & League Express Men of the Match: *Vikings:* Matty Smith; *Eagles:* James Glover.
Penalty count: 5-7; **Half-time:** 12-6;
Referee: Ben Thaler; **Attendance:** 984.

YORK CITY KNIGHTS 20 BATLEY BULLDOGS 22

CITY KNIGHTS: 1 Matty Marsh; 23 Ben Jones-Bishop; 3 Liam Salter; 4 Ryan Atkins; 5 Kieran Dixon; 28 Danny Washbrook; 39 Jamie Ellis; 13 Adam Cuthbertson; 36 Jake Sweeting; 10 Jack Teanby; 11 Chris Clarkson; 12 Sam Scott; 20 Tim Spears. Subs (all used): 2 Jason Bass; 15 Jordan Baldwinson; 16 Marcus Stock; 38 Tyla Hepi.
Tries: Jones-Bishop (52), K Dixon (56, 59);
Goals: K Dixon 4/4.
Sin bin: Jones-Bishop (63) - professional foul.
BULLDOGS: 1 Luke Hooley; 5 Johnny Campbell; 12 Lucas Walshaw; 23 Jack Logan; 21 Jodie Broughton; 6 Ben White; 7 Tom Gilmore; 10 Toby Everett; 24 Ben Kaye; 15 Jack Blagbrough; 11 Dane Manning; 3 Kieran Buchanan; 26 Nyle Flynn. Subs (all used): 14 Elliot Hall; 9 Alistair Leak; 19 Tom Lillycrop; 16 Michael Ward.
Tries: Hooley (18), Broughton (29, 63), Walshaw (74);
Goals: Hooley 3/4.
Rugby Leaguer & League Express Men of the Match: *City Knights:* Danny Washbrook; *Bulldogs:* Luke Hooley.
Penalty count: 3-3; **Half-time:** 0-10;
Referee: Tom Grant; **Attendance:** 1,486.

ROUND 11

Saturday 26th June 2021

FEATHERSTONE ROVERS 68 NEWCASTLE THUNDER 12

ROVERS: 32 Will Dagger; 5 Gareth Gale; 4 Josh Hardcastle; 1 Craig Hall; 34 Perry Whiteley; 6 Tom Holmes; 9 Fa'amanu Brown; 10 James Harrison; 14 Connor Jones;

13 James Lockwood; 31 Junior Moors; 20 Frankie Halton; 27 Loui McConnell. Subs (all used): 21 Dean Parata; 15 John Davies; 19 Callum Field; 18 Luke Cooper.
Tries: Gale (10, 24, 29, 40, 49, 78), Jones (14), Whiteley (22), Hardcastle (32, 58), Hall (34), Parata (56), Holmes (74); **Goals:** Hall 8/13.
THUNDER: 5 Calum Turner; 28 Cian Tyrer; 33 Sam Halsall; 4 Kieran Gill; 18 Alex Clegg; 21 Reece Dean; 7 Josh Woods; 15 Ted Chapelhow; 9 Bob Beswick; 8 Nathan Wilde; 36 Owen Harrison; 12 Sam Wilde; 14 Evan Simons. Subs (all used): 10 Kyle Trout; 16 Jay Chapelhow; 30 Jake Anderson; 29 Isaac Nokes.
Tries: Gill (42), Beswick (65); **Goals:** J Woods 2/2.
Rugby Leaguer & League Express Men of the Match: *Rovers:* Junior Moors; *Thunder:* Josh Woods.
Penalty count: 7-5; **Half-time:** 42-0;
Referee: Nick Bennett; **Attendance:** 1,750.

Sunday 27th June 2021

BATLEY BULLDOGS 12 HALIFAX PANTHERS 22

BULLDOGS: 1 Luke Hooley; 14 Elliot Hall; 22 Dale Morton; 3 Kieran Buchanan; 21 Jodie Broughton; 6 Ben White; 7 Tom Gilmore; 10 Toby Everett; 24 Ben Kaye; 15 Jack Blagbrough; 11 Dane Manning; 12 Lucas Walshaw; 26 Nyle Flynn. Subs (all used): 9 Alistair Leak; 18 George Senior; 16 Michael Ward; 19 Tom Lillycrop.
Try: Lillycrop (29); **Goals:** Hooley 4/4.
PANTHERS: 4 James Woodburn-Hall; 5 James Saltonstall; 3 Greg Worthington; 21 Zack McComb; 19 Conor McGrath; 6 Liam Harris; 1 Scott Grix; 15 Gadwin Springer; 9 Brandon Moore; 10 Daniel Murray; 11 Matt Garside; 17 Ben Kavanagh; 25 Adam Tangata. Subs (all used): 22 Amir Bourouh; 14 Kevin Larroyer; 16 Will Calcott; 8 Elliot Morris.
Tries: Harris (19, 71, 79), Woodburn-Hall (64); **Goals:** Harris 3/4.
Sin bin: Bourouh (37) - late challenge on Gilmore.
Rugby Leaguer & League Express Men of the Match: *Bulldogs:* Luke Hooley; *Panthers:* Liam Harris.
Penalty count: 6-10; **Half-time:** 10-6;
Referee: Ben Thaler; **Attendance:** 1,193.

BRADFORD BULLS 12 WIDNES VIKINGS 25

BULLS: 1 Brandon Pickersgill; 34 Joe Burton; 3 Rhys Evans; 4 Ross Oakes; 2 Joe Brown; 27 Billy Jowitt; 7 Jordan Lilley; 10 Steve Crossley; 13 Sam Hallas; 15 Dan Fleming; 12 Aaron Murphy; 16 Brad Gallagher; 24 Ben Evans. Subs (all used): 23 Anthony Walker; 18 Ebon Scurr; 20 Brad England; 11 Adam Rooks.
Tries: Walker (31), Scurr (43); **Goals:** Lilley 2/2.
VIKINGS: 1 Jack Owens; 5 Deon Cross; 18 Lloyd Roby; 4 Steve Tyrer; 2 Jayden Hatton; 6 Danny Craven; 17 Joe Lyons; 8 Paul Clough; 23 Lewis Else; 13 Kenny Baker; 22 Josh Wilde; 12 Adam Lawton; 7 Matty Smith. Subs: 10 Matt Cook; 24 Will Tilleke; 26 Ollie Brookes (not used); 20 Owen Buckley (not used).
Tries: Else (8), Cross (27), Hatton (37), Lawton (47); **Goals:** Tyrer 4/4; **Field goal:** Smith (39).
Rugby Leaguer & League Express Men of the Match: *Bulls:* Anthony Walker; *Vikings:* Jayden Hatton.
Penalty count: 10-8; **Half-time:** 6-19;
Referee: Scott Mikalauskas; **Attendance:** 3,153.

LONDON BRONCOS 38 SWINTON LIONS 24

BRONCOS: 17 Abbas Miski; 23 Josh Hodson; 4 Will Lovell; 3 Chris Hankinson; 20 Gideon Boafo; 1 James Meadows; 7 Jarrod Sammut; 10 Greg Richards; 26 Rob Oakley; 31 Pat Moran; 25 Jacob Jones; 12 Rhys Curran; 16 Dan Hindmarsh. Subs: 24 Will Blakemore; 28 Titus Gwaze; 22 Oliver Leyland (not used); 18 Jordan Williams.
Tries: Boafo (13, 17, 55), Miski (31, 57), Lovell (70), Sammut (75); **Goals:** Hankinson 5/7.
LIONS: 7 Jack Hansen; 1 Mike Butt; 3 Mitch Cox; 11 Rhodri Lloyd; 25 Luis Roberts; 6 Martyn Ridyard; 18 Cobi Green; 8 Sam Brooks; 9 Luke Waterworth; 39 Tom Spencer; 13 Will Hope; 12 Nick Gregson; 14 Billy Brickhill. Subs (all used): 20 Tayler Brown; 16 Paddy Jones; 19 Deane Meadows; 24 Paul Nash.
Tries: Lloyd (5), Green (34), Butt (37), Roberts (45); **Goals:** Ridyard 4/4.
Rugby Leaguer & League Express Men of the Match: *Broncos:* Gideon Boafo; *Lions:* Martyn Ridyard.
Penalty count: 2-3; **Half-time:** 18-18;
Referee: Michael Smaill; **Attendance:** 240
(at Trailfinders Sports Ground, Ealing).

OLDHAM 4 DEWSBURY RAMS 18

OLDHAM: 23 Callum Green; 2 Tommy Brierley; 5 Ryan Ince; 24 Max Roberts; 27 Ben Holcroft; 9 Gareth Owen; 26 James Barran; 17 Liam Kirk; 6 Lewis Charnock; 15 Luke Nelmes; 11 Danny Langtree; 12 Liam Bent; 13 Martyn Reilly. Subs (all used): 19 Matthew Fletcher; 30 Dec Gregory; 21 Shaun Pick; 16 Tyler Dupree.
Try: Dupree (59); **Goals:** Green 0/1.
RAMS: 4 Matty Fleming; 2 Andy Gabriel; 5 Will Oakes; 18 Davey Dixon; 27 Lewis Carr; 6 Paul Sykes; 7 Liam Finn; 23 Jon Magrin; 9 Reiss Butterworth; 32 Jimmy Beckett; 26 Bayley Liu; 12 Michael Knowles; 13 Chris Annakin. Subs (all used): 33 Dom Speakman; 1 Joe Martin; 20 Aaron Hall; 31 Robson Stevens.
Tries: Dixon (9), Gabriel (13), Oakes (62); **Goals:** Sykes 3/3.
Rugby Leaguer & League Express Men of the Match: *Oldham:* Tyler Dupree; *Rams:* Will Oakes.
Penalty count: 4-6; **Half-time:** 0-12;
Referee: Matt Rossleigh; **Attendance:** 600.

SHEFFIELD EAGLES 6 TOULOUSE OLYMPIQUE 54

EAGLES: 5 Ryan Millar; 2 Rob Worrincy; 25 Jordan Bull; 30 Max Clarke; 27 Travis Corion; 23 Harry Tyson-Wilson; 7 Anthony Thackeray; 18 Tyler Dickinson; 16 Robbie Ward; 10 Matt James; 32 Evan Hodgson; 15 Olly Davies; 13 Aaron Brown. Subs (all used): 14 Greg Burns; 19 Blake Broadbent; 20 Paddy Burns; 26 Chris Ball.
Try: Davies (80); **Goals:** H Tyson-Wilson 1/1.
OLYMPIQUE: 1 Mark Kheirallah; 24 Guy Armitage; 4 Mathieu Jussaume; 3 Junior Vaivai; 20 Ilias Bergal; 6 Johnathon Ford; 31 Tony Gigot; 8 Remi Casty; 14 Eloi Pelissier; 15 Maxime Puech; 11 Andrew Dixon; 10 Harrison Hansen; 13 Anthony Marion. Subs (all used): 17 Joseph Paulo; 18 Mitch Garbutt; 23 Justin Sangare; 26 Hugo Pezet.
Tries: Vaivai (3), Kheirallah (12), Bergal (26, 77), Jussaume (31, 46), Pelissier (37), Hansen (59), Armitage (64), Marion (75); **Goals:** Kheirallah 7/10.
Rugby Leaguer & League Express Men of the Match: *Eagles:* Ryan Millar; *Olympique:* Eloi Pelissier.
Penalty count: 5-2; **Half-time:** 0-26;
Referee: Gareth Hewer; **Attendance:** 319
(at Mobile Rocket Stadium, Wakefield).

WHITEHAVEN 37 YORK CITY KNIGHTS 12

WHITEHAVEN: 2 Lachlan Walmsley; 4 Jessie Joe Parker; 30 Sean Croston; 23 Jason Mossop; 5 Andrew Bulman; 6 Karl Dixon; 7 Nikau Williams; 27 Andrew Dawson; 18 James Newton; 35 Guy Graham; 15 Connor Holliday; 19 Ellis Gillam; 16 Tom Wilkinson. Subs (all used): 12 Liam Cooper; 20 Jake Bradley; 29 Dean Zammit; 31 Oscar Thomas.
Tries: Newton (17), Holliday (23, 68), Dixon (26), Walmsley (38), Bulman (63); **Goals:** Walmsley 6/7; **Field goal:** Williams (80).
CITY KNIGHTS: 1 Matty Marsh; 23 Ben Jones-Bishop; 3 Liam Salter; 2 Jason Bass; 5 Kieran Dixon; 39 Jamie Ellis; 28 Danny Washbrook; 13 Adam Cuthbertson; 11 Chris Clarkson; 10 Jack Teanby; 17 Danny Kirmond; 12 Sam Scott; 20 Tim Spears. Subs (all used): 9 Will Jubb; 15 Jordan Baldwinson; 16 Marcus Stock; 38 Tyla Hepi.
Tries: Baldwinson (44), K Dixon (77); **Goals:** K Dixon 2/2.
Rugby Leaguer & League Express Men of the Match: *Whitehaven:* Guy Graham; *City Knights:* Jack Teanby.
Penalty count: 9-5; **Half-time:** 24-0;
Referee: Michael Mannifield; **Attendance:** 601.

ROUND 12

Saturday 3rd July 2021

FEATHERSTONE ROVERS 63 LONDON BRONCOS 14

ROVERS: 32 Will Dagger; 5 Gareth Gale; 4 Josh Hardcastle; 17 Thomas Minns; 1 Craig Hall; 7 Dane Chisholm; 9 Fa'amanu Brown; 8 Craig Kopczak; 14 Connor Jones; 10 James Harrison; 11 Brett Ferres; 31 Junior Moors; 16 Jack Bussey. Subs (all used): 21 Dean Parata; 15 John Davies; 19 Callum Field; 18 Luke Cooper.
Tries: Hall (6, 27, 33), Dagger (14), Chisholm (22), Moors (25), Parata (40, 49), Gale (45), Brown (52, 74); **Goals:** Hall 9/11; **Field goal:** Chisholm (38).
BRONCOS: 17 Abbas Miski; 23 Josh Hodson; 4 Will Lovell; 3 Chris Hankinson; 20 Gideon Boafo; 1 James Meadows; 7 Jarrod Sammut; 15 Romain Navarrete; 25 Jacob Jones; 10 Greg Richards; 13 Josh Walters; 18 Jordan Williams; 28 Titus Gwaze. Subs (all used): 31 Pat Moran; 16 Dan Hindmarsh; 26 Rob Oakley; 22 Oliver Leyland.
Tries: Hankinson (18), Sammut (30), Miski (76); **Goals:** Hankinson 1/3.
Sin bin: Gwaze (23) - dangerous challenge on Bussey.
Rugby Leaguer & League Express Men of the Match: *Rovers:* Craig Hall; *Broncos:* Jarrod Sammut.
Penalty count: 5-2; **Half-time:** 41-10;
Referee: Scott Mikalauskas; **Attendance:** 1,750.

Sunday 4th July 2021

BRADFORD BULLS 30 BATLEY BULLDOGS 16

BULLS: 1 Brandon Pickersgill; 34 Joe Burton; 3 Rhys Evans; 4 Ross Oakes; 2 Joe Brown; 39 Joe Keyes; 7 Jordan Lilley; 10 Steve Crossley; 9 Thomas Doyle; 15 Dan Fleming; 12 Aaron Murphy; 20 Brad England; 13 Sam Hallas. Subs (all used): 14 George Flanagan; 23 Anthony Walker; 24 Ben Evans; 11 Adam Rooks.
Tries: Doyle (25), Brown (29), England (32), Burton (37), B Evans (56); **Goals:** Keyes 5/6.
BULLDOGS: 1 Luke Hooley; 22 Dale Morton; 12 Lucas Walshaw; 3 Kieran Buchanan; 21 Jodie Broughton; 6 Ben White; 7 Tom Gilmore; 15 Jack Blagbrough; - Oli Burton; 10 Toby Everett; 11 Dane Manning; 26 Nyle Flynn; 13 James Brown. Subs (all used): 14 Elliot Hall; 18 George Senior; 16 Michael Ward; 19 Tom Lillycrop.
Tries: White (51), Hall (67), Walshaw (75); **Goals:** Hooley 2/3.
Rugby Leaguer & League Express Men of the Match: *Bulls:* Joe Keyes; *Bulldogs:* Luke Hooley.
Penalty count: 8-4; **Half-time:** 24-0;
Referee: Aaron Moore; **Attendance:** 2,831.

DEWSBURY RAMS 18 SHEFFIELD EAGLES 18

RAMS: 1 Joe Martin; 2 Andy Gabriel; 18 Davey Dixon; 5 Will Oakes; 27 Lewis Carr; 6 Paul Sykes; 7 Liam Finn; 23 Jon Magrin; 33 Dom Speakman; 32 Jimmy Beckett; 10 Tom Garratt; 12 Michael Knowles; 13 Chris Annakin. Subs (all used): 30 Alex Smith; 31 Robson Stevens; 34 Robbie Storey; 39 Dan Hawksworth.
Tries: Speakman (11), Knowles (14, 32); **Goals:** Sykes 3/3.
Sin bin: Finn (79) - fighting.
EAGLES: 5 Ryan Millar; 2 Rob Worrincy; 3 Connor Bower; 4 James Glover; 27 Travis Corion; 22 Izaac Farrell; 7 Anthony Thackeray; 18 Tyler Dickinson; 14 Greg Burns; 10 Matt James; 15 Olly Davies; 12 Joel Farrell; 13 Aaron Brown. Subs (all used): 9 James Davey; 32 Evan Hodgson; 20 Paddy Burns; 11 Brad Knowles.
Tries: Corion (19), Thackeray (59), Brown (61); **Goals:** Glover 0/1, I Farrell 3/3.
Sin bin: I Farrell (17) - high tackle; J Farrell (79) - fighting.
Rugby Leaguer & League Express Men of the Match: *Rams:* Dom Speakman; *Eagles:* Olly Davies.
Penalty count: 6-10; **Half-time:** 18-4;
Referee: Matt Rossleigh; **Attendance:** 549.

HALIFAX PANTHERS 17 WIDNES VIKINGS 16

PANTHERS: 4 James Woodburn-Hall; 2 Nick Rawsthorne; 3 Greg Worthington; 21 Zack McComb; 5 James Saltonstall; 6 Liam Harris; 1 Scott Grix; 16 Will Calcott; 9 Brandon Moore; 10 Daniel Murray; 17 Ben Kavanagh; 11 Matt Garside; 25 Adam Tangata. Subs (all used): 8 Elliot Morris; 15 Gadwin Springer; 22 Amir Bourouh; 13 Jacob Fairbank.
Tries: Morris (30), Saltonstall (59, 66); **Goals:** Harris 2/3; **Field goal:** Harris (79).
VIKINGS: 1 Jack Owens; 5 Deon Cross; 18 Lloyd Roby; 4 Steve Tyrer; 2 Jayden Hatton; 6 Danny Craven; 17 Joe Lyons; 13 Kenny Baker; 23 Lewis Else; 11 Shane Grady; 12 Adam Lawton; 22 Josh Wilde; 7 Matty Smith. Subs (all used): 10 Matt Cook; 24 Will Tilleke; 30 Lewis Hulme; 25 Daniel Hill.
Tries: Owens (6), Hatton (15); **Goals:** Tyrer 4/4.
Rugby Leaguer & League Express Men of the Match: *Panthers:* James Saltonstall; *Vikings:* Jack Owens.
Penalty count: 9-7; **Half-time:** 6-16;
Referee: Michael Mannifield; **Attendance:** 1,232.

WHITEHAVEN 36 SWINTON LIONS 22

WHITEHAVEN: 32 Louis Jouffret; 2 Lachlan Walmsley; 3 Chris Taylor; 23 Jason Mossop; 4 Jessie Joe Parker; 6 Karl Dixon; 7 Nikau Williams; 8 Marc Shackley; 18 James Newton; 35 Guy Graham; 15 Connor Holliday; 19 Ellis Gillam; 16 Tom Wilkinson. Subs (all used): 12 Liam Cooper; 13 Dion Aiye; 27 Andrew Dawson; 31 Oscar Thomas.
Tries: Williams (10), Holliday (23, 73), Walmsley (34, 64), Dixon (67); **Goals:** Walmsley 5/6, Holliday 1/1.
Sin bin: Walmsley (9) - fighting.
LIONS: 7 Jack Hansen; 25 Luis Roberts; 11 Rhodri Lloyd; 3 Mitch Cox; 22 Geronimo Doyle; 6 Martyn Ridyard; 18 Cobi Green; 39 Tom Spencer; 9 Luke Waterworth; 19 Deane Meadows; 13 Will Hope; 12 Nick Gregson; 14 Billy Brickhill. Subs (all used): 20 Tayler Brown; 21 Ben Heyes; 24 Paul Nash; 26 Jordan Brown.
Tries: Meadows (6), Nash (42), Cox (44), Doyle (51); **Goals:** Ridyard 3/4.
Sin bin: Lloyd (9) - fighting; Green (27) - professional foul.
Rugby Leaguer & League Express Men of the Match: *Whitehaven:* Lachlan Walmsley; *Lions:* Tayler Brown.
Penalty count: 8-9; **Half-time:** 18-6;
Referee: John McMullen; **Attendance:** 746.

YORK CITY KNIGHTS 26 NEWCASTLE THUNDER 28

CITY KNIGHTS: 5 Kieran Dixon; 22 Perry Whiteley; 3 Liam Salter; 4 Ryan Atkins; 2 Jason Bass; 23 Ben Jones-Bishop; 11 Chris Clarkson; 19 James Green; 9 Will Jubb; 10 Jack Teanby; 12 Sam Scott; 17 Danny Kirmond; 20 Tim Spears. Subs (all used): 28 Danny Washbrook; 16 Marcus Stock; 21 Joe Porter; 8 Ronan Dixon.
Tries: Atkins (52), Clarkson (56), Scott (63), Whiteley (76); **Goals:** K Dixon 5/5.

THUNDER: 27 Alex Donaghy; 2 Jack Johnson; 33 Sam Halsall; 3 Matthew Wright; 18 Alex Clegg; 6 Jake Shorrocks; 7 Josh Woods; 15 Ted Chapelhow; 14 Evan Simons; 8 Nathan Wilde; 17 Connor Bailey; 11 Ukuma Ta'ai; 10 Kyle Trout. Subs (all used): 16 Jay Chapelhow; 36 Owen Harrison; 30 Jake Anderson; 20 Cole Oakley.
Tries: Shorrocks (14), Harrison (39), Simons (43), Clegg (44, 69); **Goals:** J Woods 4/5.
Rugby Leaguer & League Express Men of the Match: *City Knights:* Kieran Dixon; *Thunder:* Alex Clegg.
Penalty count: 2-5; **Half-time:** 2-12;
Referee: Nick Bennett; **Attendance:** 1,497.

ROUND 13

Sunday 11th July 2021

BATLEY BULLDOGS 12 TOULOUSE OLYMPIQUE 32

BULLDOGS: 1 Luke Hooley; 22 Dale Morton; 12 Lucas Walshaw; 30 Levi Edwards; 29 Greg Johnson; 6 Ben White; 7 Tom Gilmore; 8 Adam Gledhill; 9 Alistair Leak; 10 Toby Everett; 32 Oli Field; 11 Dane Manning; 13 James Brown. Subs (all used): 31 Oli Burton; 16 Michael Ward; 19 Tom Lillycrop; 26 Nyle Flynn.
Tries: Johnson (10), Gledhill (20); **Goals:** Hooley 2/2.
OLYMPIQUE: 1 Mark Kheirallah; 20 Ilias Bergal; 4 Mathieu Jussaume; 3 Junior Vaivai; 21 Latrell Schaumkel; 6 Johnathon Ford; 31 Tony Gigot; 8 Remi Casty; 13 Anthony Marion; 10 Harrison Hansen; 11 Andrew Dixon; 12 Dominique Peyroux; 16 Joe Bretherton. Subs (all used): 14 Eloi Pelissier; 18 Mitch Garbutt; 17 Joseph Paulo; 23 Justin Sangare.
Tries: Hansen (4), Schaumkel (30), Sangare (35), Vaivai (51, 56), Jussaume (72); **Goals:** Kheirallah 4/6.
Rugby Leaguer & League Express Men of the Match: *Bulldogs:* Luke Hooley; *Olympique:* Johnathon Ford.
Penalty count: 7-8; **Half-time:** 12-16;
Referee: Scott Mikalauskas; **Attendance:** 782.

HALIFAX PANTHERS 14 WHITEHAVEN 4

PANTHERS: 4 James Woodburn-Hall; 5 James Saltonstall; 3 Greg Worthington; 21 Zack McComb; 19 Conor McGrath; 6 Liam Harris; 1 Scott Grix; 16 Will Calcott; 9 Brandon Moore; 10 Daniel Murray; 17 Ben Kavanagh; 11 Matt Garside; 25 Adam Tangata. Subs (all used): 20 Curtis Davies; 14 Kevin Larroyer; 13 Jacob Fairbank; 8 Elliot Morris.
Tries: Curtis Davies (39), Garside (72); **Goals:** Harris 3/3.
Sin bin: Larroyer (33) - punching.
WHITEHAVEN: 2 Lachlan Walmsley; 30 Sean Croston; 3 Chris Taylor; 23 Jason Mossop; 4 Jessie Joe Parker; 32 Louis Jouffret; 7 Nikau Williams; 8 Marc Shackley; 18 James Newton; 35 Guy Graham; 19 Ellis Gillam; 15 Connor Holliday; 12 Liam Cooper. Subs (all used): 26 Ryan King; 21 Glenn Riley; 31 Oscar Thomas; 29 Dean Zammit.
Goals: Walmsley 2/2.
Rugby Leaguer & League Express Men of the Match: *Panthers:* Brandon Moore; *Whitehaven:* Ryan King.
Penalty count: 6-6; **Half-time:** 6-4;
Referee: Matt Rossleigh; **Attendance:** 877.

LONDON BRONCOS 50 YORK CITY KNIGHTS 22

BRONCOS: 22 Oliver Leyland; 2 Tuoyo Egodo; 23 Josh Hodson; 3 Chris Hankinson; 17 Abbas Miski; 1 James Meadows; 7 Jarrod Sammut; 31 Pat Moran; 26 Rob Oakley; 10 Greg Richards; 4 Will Lovell; 13 Josh Walters; 16 Dan Hindmarsh. Subs (all used): 25 Jacob Jones; 28 Titus Gwaze; 19 Jacob Ogden; 24 Will Blakemore.
Tries: Lovell (7, 46), Hodson (16), Hankinson (20, 53), Leyland (57), Miski (60), Jones (72); **Goals:** Hankinson 9/9.
CITY KNIGHTS: 5 Kieran Dixon; 2 Jason Bass; 3 Liam Salter; 4 Ryan Atkins; 27 Perry Whiteley; 29 Riley Dean; 28 Danny Washbrook; 8 Ronan Dixon; 9 Will Jubb; 10 Jack Teanby; 17 Danny Kirmond; 12 Sam Scott; 11 Chris Clarkson. Subs (all used): 36 Corey Johnson; 20 Tim Spears; 16 Marcus Stock; 15 Jordan Baldwinson.
Tries: Whiteley (29), K Dixon (32), Jubb (68), Atkins (78); **Goals:** K Dixon 3/4.
Rugby Leaguer & League Express Men of the Match: *Broncos:* Chris Hankinson; *City Knights:* Danny Washbrook.
Penalty count: 4-5; **Half-time:** 20-10;
Referee: John McMullen; **Attendance:** 312
(at Trailfinders Sports Ground, Ealing).

NEWCASTLE THUNDER 24 DEWSBURY RAMS 12

THUNDER: 27 Alex Donaghy; 2 Jack Johnson; 3 Matthew Wright; 4 Kieran Gill; 18 Alex Clegg; 21 Reece Dean; 7 Josh Woods; 15 Ted Chapelhow; 14 Evan Simons; 8 Nathan Wilde; 17 Connor Bailey; 11 Ukuma Ta'ai; 10 Kyle Trout. Subs (all used): 16 Jay Chapelhow; 36 Owen Harrison; 30 Jake Anderson; 29 Isaac Nokes.
Tries: Johnson (3), Bailey (27), Ta'ai (42), Clegg (47), Gill (62); **Goals:** J Woods 2/6.
RAMS: 4 Matty Fleming; 2 Andy Gabriel; 18 Davey Dixon; 5 Will Oakes; 27 Lewis Carr; 30 Alex Smith; 1 Joe Martin; 39 Dan Hawksworth; 33 Dom Speakman; 20 Aaron Hall; 34 Robbie Storey; 12 Michael Knowles; 25 James Thornton. Subs (all used): 7 Liam Finn; 13 Chris Annakin; 23 Jon Magrin; 10 Tom Garratt.
Tries: Carr (7), Dixon (67); **Goals:** Knowles 2/3.
Rugby Leaguer & League Express Men of the Match: *Thunder:* Evan Simons; *Rams:* Davey Dixon.
Penalty count: 5-6; **Half-time:** 10-6;
Referee: Jack Smith; **Attendance:** 789.

OLDHAM 22 BRADFORD BULLS 54

OLDHAM: 1 Dan Abram; 28 Joe Hartley; 5 Ryan Ince; 24 Max Roberts; 27 Ben Holcroft; 6 Lewis Charnock; 26 James Barran; 17 Liam Kirk; 9 Gareth Owen; 13 Martyn Reilly; 11 Danny Langtree; 21 Shaun Pick; 12 Liam Bent. Subs (all used): 16 Tyler Dupree; 15 Luke Nelmes; 33 Jamie Abram; 25 Danny Bridge.
Tries: Holcroft (55), Reilly (62), D Abram (76), Dupree (79); **Goals:** D Abram 3/4.
BULLS: 1 Brandon Pickersgill; 22 Reece Hamlett; 3 Rhys Evans; 4 Ross Oakes; 19 David Foggin-Johnston; 2 Joe Brown; 39 Joe Keyes; 10 Steve Crossley; 9 Thomas Doyle; 15 Dan Fleming; 12 Aaron Murphy; 20 Brad England; 24 Ben Evans. Subs (all used): 14 George Flanagan; 23 Anthony Walker; 18 Ebon Scurr; 11 Adam Rooks.
Tries: Foggin-Johnston (3), Keyes (16, 29, 47), Pickersgill (24, 70), Brown (51), R Evans (67), England (73); **Goals:** Keyes 9/10.
Sin bin: Doyle (78) - high tackle.
Rugby Leaguer & League Express Men of the Match: *Oldham:* Tyler Dupree; *Bulls:* Joe Keyes.
Penalty count: 10-7; **Half-time:** 0-26;
Referee: Brad Milligan; **Attendance:** 650.

SWINTON LIONS 22 SHEFFIELD EAGLES 30

LIONS: 7 Jack Hansen; 38 Owen Buckley; 11 Rhodri Lloyd; 3 Mitch Cox; 22 Geronimo Doyle; 6 Martyn Ridyard; 18 Cobi Green; 39 Tom Spencer; 9 Luke Waterworth; 15 Louis Brogan; 13 Will Hope; 12 Nick Gregson; 14 Billy Brickhill. Subs (all used): 21 Ben Heyes; 24 Paul Nash; 20 Tayler Brown; 19 Deane Meadows.
Tries: Lloyd (5), Buckley (16), Heyes (72), Hansen (80); **Goals:** Ridyard 3/4.
EAGLES: 1 Josh Guzdek; 2 Rob Worrincy; 3 Connor Bower; 24 Ryan Johnson; 5 Ryan Millar; 22 Izaac Farrell; 7 Anthony Thackeray; 18 Tyler Dickinson; 9 James Davey; 11 Brad Knowles; 15 Olly Davies; 12 Joel Farrell; 13 Aaron Brown. Subs (all used): 27 Travis Corion; 14 Greg Burns; 32 Evan Hodgson; 8 Scott Wheeldon.
Tries: Millar (13, 58, 66), Davies (31, 38); **Goals:** I Farrell 5/6.
Rugby Leaguer & League Express Men of the Match: *Lions:* Cobi Green; *Eagles:* Anthony Thackeray.
Penalty count: 5-5; **Half-time:** 10-18;
Referee: Tom Crashley; **Attendance:** 501.

WIDNES VIKINGS 10 FEATHERSTONE ROVERS 32

VIKINGS: 1 Jack Owens; 2 Jayden Hatton; 4 Steve Tyrer; 18 Lloyd Roby; 5 Deon Cross; 6 Danny Craven; 17 Joe Lyons; 11 Shane Grady; 30 Lewis Hulme; 13 Kenny Baker; 22 Josh Wilde; 12 Adam Lawton; 7 Matty Smith. Subs: 10 Matt Cook; 24 Will Tilleke; 25 Daniel Hill; 26 Ollie Brookes (not used).
Tries: Baker (50), Cross (53); **Goals:** Tyrer 1/2.
ROVERS: 32 Will Dagger; 5 Gareth Gale; 4 Josh Hardcastle; 15 John Davies; 29 Harvey Spence; 9 Fa'amanu Brown; 7 Dane Chisholm; 8 Craig Kopczak; 14 Connor Jones; 10 James Harrison; 31 Junior Moors; 11 Brett Ferres; 27 Loui McConnell. Subs (all used): 22 Jake Sweeting; 19 Callum Field; 18 Luke Cooper; 26 Jimmy Beckett.
Tries: Brown (15, 65, 71), Jones (34), Gale (77); **Goals:** Chisholm 6/6.
Rugby Leaguer & League Express Men of the Match: *Vikings:* Kenny Baker; *Rovers:* Fa'amanu Brown.
Penalty count: 6-4; **Half-time:** 0-14;
Referee: Aaron Moore; **Attendance:** 947.

ROUND 7

Thursday 15th July 2021

DEWSBURY RAMS 10 BATLEY BULLDOGS 38

RAMS: 1 Joe Martin; 2 Andy Gabriel; 4 Matty Fleming; 5 Will Oakes; 27 Lewis Carr; 6 Paul Sykes; 7 Liam Finn; 23 Jon Magrin; 14 Sam Day; 10 Tom Garratt; 15 Keenen Tomlinson; 12 Michael Knowles; 25 James Thornton. Subs (all used): 13 Chris Annakin; 32 Connor Davies; 33 Dom Speakman; 39 Dan Hawksworth.
Tries: Gabriel (20), Oakes (42); **Goals:** Sykes 1/2.
BULLDOGS: 1 Luke Hooley; 5 Johnny Campbell; 12 Lucas Walshaw; 30 Levi Edwards; 29 Greg Johnson; 6 Ben White; 7 Tom Gilmore; 8 Adam Gledhill; 9 Alistair Leak; 10 Toby Everett; 3 Kieran Buchanan; 11 Dane Manning; 26 Nyle Flynn. Subs (all used): 14 Elliot Hall; 15 Jack Blagbrough; 16 Michael Ward; 22 Dale Morton.
Tries: Edwards (11, 78), Campbell (37), Blagbrough (46), Manning (48), Leak (62, 73); **Goals:** Hooley 5/7.
Rugby Leaguer & League Express Men of the Match: *Rams:* Tom Garratt; *Bulldogs:* Alistair Leak.
Penalty count: 4-5; **Half-time:** 6-10;
Referee: Michael Mannifield; **Attendance:** 1,021.

ROUND 14

Sunday 25th July 2021

SHEFFIELD EAGLES 28 HALIFAX PANTHERS 40

EAGLES: 1 Josh Guzdek; 2 Rob Worrincy; 24 Ryan Johnson; 3 Connor Bower; 5 Ryan Millar; 22 Izaac Farrell; 7 Anthony Thackeray; 11 Brad Knowles; 9 James Davey; 10 Matt James; 15 Olly Davies; 12 Joel Farrell; 13 Aaron Brown. Subs: 23 Harry Tyson-Wilson (not used); 18 Tyler Dickinson; 8 Scott Wheeldon; 32 Evan Hodgson.
Tries: Millar (13, 47, 71), Thackeray (34), Brown (61); **Goals:** I Farrell 4/5.
PANTHERS: 4 James Woodburn-Hall; 19 Conor McGrath; 3 Greg Worthington; 21 Zack McComb; 5 James Saltonstall; 6 Liam Harris; 1 Scott Grix; 14 Kevin Larroyer; 9 Brandon Moore; 10 Daniel Murray; 11 Matt Garside; 17 Ben Kavanagh; 13 Jacob Fairbank. Subs (all used): 20 Curtis Davies; 25 Adam Tangata; 8 Elliot Morris; 12 Ed Barber.
Tries: Fairbank (20, 55), Tangata (28, 66, 69), McGrath (38), Harris (79); **Goals:** Harris 6/8.
Rugby Leaguer & League Express Men of the Match: *Eagles:* Ryan Millar; *Panthers:* Adam Tangata.
Penalty count: 3-6; **Half-time:** 12-16;
Referee: Brad Milligan; **Attendance:** 775
(at Mobile Rocket Stadium, Wakefield).

BATLEY BULLDOGS 42 NEWCASTLE THUNDER 12

BULLDOGS: 14 Elliot Hall; 5 Johnny Campbell; 12 Lucas Walshaw; 30 Levi Edwards; 29 Greg Johnson; 6 Ben White; 7 Tom Gilmore; 15 Jack Blagbrough; 24 Ben Kaye; 10 Toby Everett; 11 Dane Manning; 3 Kieran Buchanan; 26 Nyle Flynn. Subs (all used): 9 Alistair Leak; 16 Michael Ward; 13 James Brown; 22 Dale Morton.
Tries: Blagbrough (3), Kaye (6), Flynn (21), Walshaw (27), Buchanan (47), Edwards (57), White (78); **Goals:** Gilmore 7/7, Morton 0/1.
THUNDER: 27 Alex Donaghy; 2 Jack Johnson; 3 Matthew Wright; 4 Kieran Gill; 18 Alex Clegg; 21 Reece Dean; 7 Josh Woods; 15 Ted Chapelhow; 17 Connor Bailey; 16 Jay Chapelhow; 20 Cole Oakley; 11 Ukuma Ta'ai; 36 Owen Harrison. Subs (all used): 12 Sam Wilde; 13 Liam McAvoy; 26 Kieran Hudson; 32 Todd Wilkinson.
Tries: Ta'ai (33), McAvoy (44); **Goals:** J Woods 2/2.
Sin bin: Dean (27) - professional foul; Hudson (77) - professional foul.
Rugby Leaguer & League Express Men of the Match: *Bulldogs:* Nyle Flynn; *Thunder:* Ukuma Ta'ai.
Penalty count: 10-5; **Half-time:** 24-6;
Referee: Marcus Griffiths; **Attendance:** 932.

BRADFORD BULLS 30 FEATHERSTONE ROVERS 36

BULLS: 1 Brandon Pickersgill; 22 Reece Hamlett; 3 Rhys Evans; 4 Ross Oakes; 19 David Foggin-Johnston; 2 Joe Brown; 39 Joe Keyes; 10 Steve Crossley; 13 Sam Hallas; 15 Dan Fleming; 16 Brad Gallagher; 20 Brad England; 24 Ben Evans. Subs (all used): 14 George Flanagan; 11 Adam Rooks; 18 Ebon Scurr; 23 Anthony Walker.
Tries: B Evans (4), Foggin-Johnston (31), Pickersgill (35), R Evans (68), Flanagan (75); **Goals:** Keyes 4/6, Flanagan 1/1.
ROVERS: 1 Craig Hall; 5 Gareth Gale; 3 Kris Welham; 4 Josh Hardcastle; 28 Jacob Doyle; 15 John Davies; 7 Dane Chisholm; 10 James Harrison; 9 Fa'amanu Brown; 13 James Lockwood; 11 Brett Ferres; 20 Frankie Halton; 27 Loui McConnell. Subs (all used): 18 Luke Cooper; 19 Callum Field; 23 Joe Summers; 29 Harvey Spence.
Tries: Doyle (22), Brown (25, 59), Harrison (45, 49), Chisholm (78); **Goals:** Hall 6/7.
Sin bin: Gale (73) - professional foul.
Rugby Leaguer & League Express Men of the Match: *Bulls:* Ben Evans; *Rovers:* James Harrison.
Penalty count: 7-6; **Half-time:** 20-14;
Referee: Michael Mannifield; **Attendance:** 3,708.

WHITEHAVEN 28 OLDHAM 24

WHITEHAVEN: 1 Gregg McNally; 4 Jessie Joe Parker; 3 Chris Taylor; 23 Jason Mossop; 5 Andrew Bulman; 6 Karl Dixon; 32 Louis Jouffret; 8 Marc Shackley; 9 Callum

Phillips; 17 Tom Walker; 15 Connor Holliday; 19 Ellis Gillam; 16 Tom Wilkinson. Subs (all used): 12 Liam Cooper; 13 Dion Aiye; 26 Ryan King; 27 Andrew Dawson.
Tries: Bulman (19), C Phillips (23, 29), Jouffret (56), Wilkinson (61); **Goals:** Jouffret 4/5.
Sin bin: King (78) - fighting.
OLDHAM: 1 Dan Abram; 2 Tommy Brierley; 5 Ryan Ince; 24 Max Roberts; 27 Ben Holcroft; 6 Lewis Charnock; 7 Dave Hewitt; 17 Liam Kirk; 26 James Barran; 13 Martyn Reilly; 11 Danny Langtree; 25 Danny Bridge; 12 Liam Bent. Subs (all used): 15 Luke Nelmes; 16 Tyler Dupree; 21 Shaun Pick; 33 Jamie Abram.
Tries: Hewitt (14), D Abram (34), Dupree (41), Nelmes (48); **Goals:** D Abram 4/4.
Sin bin: Dupree (78) - fighting.
Rugby Leaguer & League Express Men of the Match: *Whitehaven:* Tom Wilkinson; *Oldham:* Max Roberts.
Penalty count: 4-4; **Half-time:** 16-12;
Referee: Aaron Moore; **Attendance:** 920.

YORK CITY KNIGHTS 46 SWINTON LIONS 10

CITY KNIGHTS: 2 Jason Bass; 22 Perry Whiteley; 42 Corey Hall; 30 Tyme Dow-Nikau; 5 Kieran Dixon; 37 Mikey Lewis; 1 Matty Marsh; 10 Jack Teanby; 9 Will Jubb; 8 Ronan Dixon; 17 Danny Kirmond; 11 Chris Clarkson; 20 Tim Spears. Subs (all used): 36 Corey Johnson; 16 Marcus Stock; 13 Adam Cuthbertson; 12 Sam Scott.
Tries: Clarkson (2), R Dixon (7), K Dixon (10, 70), Kirmond (33), Marsh (61, 68), Dow-Nikau (73);
Goals: K Dixon 7/8.
LIONS: 22 Geronimo Doyle; 38 Owen Buckley; 3 Mitch Cox; 25 Luis Roberts; 21 Ben Heyes; 18 Cobi Green; 7 Jack Hansen; 39 Tom Spencer; 9 Luke Waterworth; 40 Ronan Michael; 13 Will Hope; 12 Nick Gregson; 15 Louis Brogan. Subs (all used): 26 Jordan Brown; 16 Paddy Jones; 19 Deane Meadows; 24 Paul Nash.
Tries: Heyes (23), Meadows (52); **Goals:** Hansen 1/2.
Rugby Leaguer & League Express Men of the Match: *City Knights:* Matty Marsh; *Lions:* Owen Buckley.
Penalty count: 7-4; **Half-time:** 22-4;
Referee: Scott Mikalauskas; **Attendance:** 1,344.

ROUND 15

Sunday 1st August 2021

DEWSBURY RAMS 18 SWINTON LIONS 22

RAMS: 4 Matty Fleming; 2 Andy Gabriel; 34 Robbie Storey; 18 Davey Dixon; 27 Lewis Carr; 6 Paul Sykes; 1 Joe Martin; 23 Jon Magrin; 33 Dom Speakman; 10 Tom Garratt; 35 Sonny Esslemont; 12 Michael Knowles; 13 Chris Annakin. Subs (all used): 14 Sam Day; 20 Aaron Hall; 25 James Thornton; 32 Jimmy Beckett.
Tries: Fleming (18), Magrin (27), Day (42); **Goals:** Sykes 3/3.
Sin bin: Sykes (49) - late challenge on Hatton.
LIONS: 22 Geronimo Doyle; 38 Owen Buckley; 11 Rhodri Lloyd; 3 Mitch Cox; 1 Mike Butt; 7 Jack Hansen; 18 Cobi Green; 16 Paddy Jones; 9 Luke Waterworth; 10 Lewis Hatton; 15 Louis Brogan; 12 Nick Gregson; 13 Will Hope. Subs (all used): 19 Deane Meadows; 40 Ronan Michael; 39 Tom Spencer; 24 Paul Nash.
Tries: Buckley (4), Brogan (52), Cox (55), Hansen (80);
Goals: Hansen 3/5.
Sin bin: Lloyd (47) - late challenge on Day.
Rugby Leaguer & League Express Men of the Match: *Rams:* Jon Magrin; *Lions:* Jack Hansen.
Penalty count: 6-7; **Half-time:** 12-4;
Referee: Michael Smaill; **Attendance:** 616.

FEATHERSTONE ROVERS 6 TOULOUSE OLYMPIQUE 23

ROVERS: 1 Craig Hall; 5 Gareth Gale; 4 Josh Hardcastle; 15 John Davies; 3 Kris Welham; 6 Tom Holmes; 9 Fa'amanu Brown; 8 Craig Kopczak; 14 Connor Jones; 13 James Lockwood; 11 Brett Ferres; 20 Frankie Halton; 19 Callum Field. Subs (all used): 10 James Harrison; 18 Luke Cooper; 21 Dean Parata; 31 Junior Moors.
Try: Gale (55); **Goals:** Hall 1/1.
OLYMPIQUE: 1 Mark Kheirallah; 21 Latrell Schaumkel; 4 Mathieu Jussaume; 3 Junior Vaivai; 2 Jy Hitchcox; 6 Johnathon Ford; 31 Tony Gigot; 8 Remi Casty; 9 Lloyd White; 10 Harrison Hansen; 11 Andrew Dixon; 12 Dominique Peyroux; 13 Anthony Marion. Subs (all used): 14 Eloi Pelissier; 17 Joseph Paulo; 18 Mitch Garbutt; 23 Justin Sangare.
Tries: Peyroux (17, 60), Sangare (48), Casty (75);
Goals: Kheirallah 3/4; **Field goal:** Gigot (72).
Rugby Leaguer & League Express Men of the Match: *Rovers:* James Harrison; *Olympique:* Tony Gigot.
Penalty count: 6-2; **Half-time:** 0-6;
Referee: Jack Smith; **Attendance:** 4,021.

HALIFAX PANTHERS 24 BRADFORD BULLS 21

PANTHERS: 4 James Woodburn-Hall; 21 Zack McComb; 3 Greg Worthington; 12 Ed Barber; 5 James Saltonstall; 6 Liam Harris; 1 Scott Grix; 25 Adam Tangata; 9 Brandon Moore; 10 Daniel Murray; 11 Matt Garside; 17 Ben Kavanagh; 13 Jacob Fairbank. Subs (all used): 20 Curtis Davies; 8 Elliot Morris; 14 Kevin Larroyer; 18 Connor Davies.
Tries: Woodburn-Hall (2), Worthington (16), Saltonstall (23, 77), Harris (69); **Goals:** Harris 2/5.
BULLS: 1 Brandon Pickersgill; 22 Reece Hamlett; 3 Rhys Evans; 4 Ross Oakes; 19 David Foggin-Johnston; 2 Joe Brown; 7 Jordan Lilley; 23 Anthony Walker; 9 Thomas Doyle; 10 Steve Crossley; 20 Brad England; 12 Aaron Murphy; 13 Sam Hallas. Subs (all used): 14 George Flanagan; - Jordan Baldwinson; 11 Adam Rooks; 18 Ebon Scurr.
Tries: Pickersgill (11), Doyle (38), England (42), Brown (55);
Goals: Hallas 2/4; **Field goal:** Flanagan (73).
Rugby Leaguer & League Express Men of the Match: *Panthers:* James Saltonstall; *Bulls:* Jordan Lilley.
Penalty count: 7-6; **Half-time:** 14-10;
Referee: Aaron Moore; **Attendance:** 2,696.

NEWCASTLE THUNDER 14 WHITEHAVEN 20

THUNDER: 27 Alex Donaghy; 2 Jack Johnson; 4 Kieran Gill; 3 Matthew Wright; 18 Alex Clegg; 6 Jake Shorrocks; 7 Josh Woods; 15 Ted Chapelhow; 14 Evan Simons; 16 Jay Chapelhow; 11 Ukuma Ta'ai; 17 Connor Bailey; 12 Sam Wilde. Subs (all used): 13 Liam McAvoy; 20 Cole Oakley; 26 Kieran Hudson; 19 Harry Bowes.
Tries: Ta'ai (11), Gill (15); **Goals:** J Woods 3/3.
WHITEHAVEN: 1 Gregg McNally; 5 Andrew Bulman; 3 Chris Taylor; 6 Karl Dixon; 2 Lachlan Walmsley; 32 Louis Jouffret; 7 Nikau Williams; 17 Tom Walker; 18 James Newton; 35 Guy Graham; 15 Connor Holliday; 19 Ellis Gillam; 16 Tom Wilkinson. Subs (all used): 9 Callum Phillips; 27 Andrew Dawson; 20 Jake Bradley; 26 Ryan King.
Tries: Walmsley (28), Dixon (48), Bulman (59);
Goals: Walmsley 4/5.
Rugby Leaguer & League Express Men of the Match: *Thunder:* Josh Woods; *Whitehaven:* Connor Holliday.
Penalty count: 6-9; **Half-time:** 14-6;
Referee: Brad Milligan; **Attendance:** 1,647.

OLDHAM 20 LONDON BRONCOS 30

OLDHAM: 1 Dan Abram; 2 Tommy Brierley; 5 Ryan Ince; 24 Max Roberts; 27 Ben Holcroft; 26 James Barran; 7 Dave Hewitt; 17 Liam Kirk; 6 Lewis Charnock; 13 Martyn Reilly; 11 Danny Langtree; 25 Danny Bridge; 12 Liam Bent. Subs (all used): 16 Tyler Dupree; 15 Luke Nelmes; 33 Jamie Abram; 21 Shaun Pick.
Tries: Ince (20), Dupree (45), Reilly (65);
Goals: D Abram 4/4.
BRONCOS: 22 Oliver Leyland; 2 Tuoyo Egodo; 23 Josh Hodson; 19 Jacob Ogden; 17 Abbas Miski; 3 Chris Hankinson; 1 James Meadows; 31 Pat Moran; 25 Jacob Jones; 10 Greg Richards; 4 Will Lovell; 12 Rhys Curran; 13 Josh Walters. Subs (all used): 16 Dan Hindmarsh; 21 Rian Horsman; 18 Jordan Williams; 7 Jarrod Sammut.
Tries: Walters (35), Miski (53, 70), Sammut (75), Jones (78);
Goals: Hankinson 5/6.
Rugby Leaguer & League Express Men of the Match: *Oldham:* Danny Langtree; *Broncos:* Abbas Miski.
Penalty count: 6-9; **Half-time:** 8-6;
Referee: Craig Smith; **Attendance:** 948.

WIDNES VIKINGS 16 BATLEY BULLDOGS 34

VIKINGS: 1 Jack Owens; 2 Jayden Hatton; 4 Steve Tyrer; 3 Jake Spedding; 5 Deon Cross; 6 Danny Craven; 17 Joe Lyons; 11 Shane Grady; 31 Aiden Roden; 13 Kenny Baker; 22 Josh Wilde; 12 Adam Lawton; 7 Matty Smith. Subs (all used): 8 Paul Clough; 16 Owen Farnworth; 24 Will Tilleke; 30 Lewis Hulme.
Tries: Cross (26, 48), Craven (36); **Goals:** Owens 2/3.
BULLDOGS: 14 Elliot Hall; 5 Johnny Campbell; 12 Lucas Walshaw; 30 Levi Edwards; 22 Dale Morton; 6 Ben White; 7 Tom Gilmore; 10 Toby Everett; 24 Ben Kaye; 15 Jack Blagbrough; 3 Kieran Buchanan; 11 Dane Manning; 26 Nyle Flynn. Subs (all used): 9 Alistair Leak; 13 James Brown; 16 Michael Ward; 18 George Senior.
Tries: Buchanan (12), Hall (55, 69), Leak (60), Manning (66), Edwards (74); **Goals:** Gilmore 5/6.
Rugby Leaguer & League Express Men of the Match: *Vikings:* Deon Cross; *Bulldogs:* Alistair Leak.
Penalty count: 4-6; **Half-time:** 10-6;
Referee: Nick Bennett; **Attendance:** 1,258.

ROUND 16

Sunday 8th August 2021

BATLEY BULLDOGS 13 FEATHERSTONE ROVERS 28

BULLDOGS: 5 Johnny Campbell; 22 Dale Morton; 12 Lucas Walshaw; 30 Levi Edwards; 29 Greg Johnson; 6 Ben White; 7 Tom Gilmore; 8 Adam Gledhill; 24 Ben Kaye; 10 Toby Everett; 18 George Senior; 11 Dane Manning; 26 Nyle Flynn. Subs: 9 Alistair Leak; 16 Michael Ward; 15 Jack Blagbrough; 32 Joe Chandler (not used).
Tries: Gledhill (25), Johnson (30); **Goals:** Gilmore 2/2;
Field goal: Gilmore (39).
ROVERS: 36 Alex Walker; 1 Craig Hall; 3 Kris Welham; 4 Josh Hardcastle; 2 Ben Blackmore; 9 Fa'amanu Brown; 7 Dane Chisholm; 20 Frankie Halton; 14 Connor Jones; 13 James Lockwood; 31 Junior Moors; 11 Brett Ferres; 19 Callum Field. Subs (all used): 21 Dean Parata; 15 John Davies; 10 James Harrison; 35 Gadwin Springer.
Tries: Chisholm (11), Brown (15), Blackmore (42), Walker (56), Halton (62); **Goals:** Hall 4/5.
Rugby Leaguer & League Express Men of the Match: *Bulldogs:* Tom Gilmore; *Rovers:* Fa'amanu Brown.
Penalty count: 2-6; **Half-time:** 13-12;
Referee: Aaron Moore; **Attendance:** 1,259.

HALIFAX PANTHERS 14 NEWCASTLE THUNDER 12

PANTHERS: 4 James Woodburn-Hall; 21 Zack McComb; 3 Greg Worthington; 12 Ed Barber; 5 James Saltonstall; 6 Liam Harris; 1 Scott Grix; 16 Will Calcott; 9 Brandon Moore; 10 Daniel Murray; 17 Ben Kavanagh; 14 Kevin Larroyer; 13 Jacob Fairbank. Subs (all used): 20 Curtis Davies; 25 Adam Tangata; 18 Connor Davies; 24 Ben Tibbs.
Tries: McComb (20), Tibbs (26), Curtis Davies (37);
Goals: Harris 0/2, Barber 1/2.
Sin bin: Tangata (55) - late challenge on Shorrocks.
THUNDER: 5 Calum Turner; 2 Jack Johnson; 3 Matthew Wright; 4 Kieran Gill; 18 Alex Clegg; 6 Jake Shorrocks; 17 Connor Bailey; 8 Nathan Wilde; 14 Evan Simons; 15 Ted Chapelhow; 11 Ukuma Ta'ai; 12 Sam Wilde; 13 Liam McAvoy. Subs (all used): 10 Kyle Trout; 36 Owen Harrison; 16 Jay Chapelhow; 20 Cole Oakley.
Tries: Johnson (57), T Chapelhow (74); **Goals:** Wright 2/2.
Rugby Leaguer & League Express Men of the Match: *Panthers:* James Saltonstall; *Thunder:* Ted Chapelhow.
Penalty count: 3-7; **Half-time:** 12-0;
Referee: Jack Smith; **Attendance:** 1,541.

LONDON BRONCOS 6 TOULOUSE OLYMPIQUE 66

BRONCOS: 22 Oliver Leyland; 2 Tuoyo Egodo; 23 Josh Hodson; 3 Chris Hankinson; 17 Abbas Miski; 1 James Meadows; 7 Jarrod Sammut; 31 Pat Moran; 25 Jacob Jones; 10 Greg Richards; 12 Rhys Curran; 4 Will Lovell; 13 Josh Walters. Subs (all used): 16 Dan Hindmarsh; 21 Rian Horsman; 28 Titus Gwaze; 19 Jacob Ogden.
Try: Egodo (60); **Goals:** Hankinson 1/1.
OLYMPIQUE: 1 Mark Kheirallah; 2 Jy Hitchcox; 4 Mathieu Jussaume; 3 Junior Vaivai; 21 Latrell Schaumkel; 6 Johnathon Ford; 31 Tony Gigot; 16 Joe Bretherton; 9 Lloyd White; 15 Maxime Puech; 11 Andrew Dixon; 12 Dominique Peyroux; 13 Anthony Marion. Subs (all used): 14 Eloi Pelissier; 28 Romain Navarrete; 23 Justin Sangare; 17 Joseph Paulo.
Tries: Marion (1), Vaivai (16, 26, 40), Peyroux (18, 22), Schaumkel (45), Ford (51, 57), Bretherton (66), Gigot (74);
Goals: Kheirallah 11/11.
Rugby Leaguer & League Express Men of the Match: *Broncos:* Titus Gwaze; *Olympique:* Johnathon Ford.
Penalty count: 6-4; **Half-time:** 0-36;
Referee: Scott Mikalauskas; **Attendance:** 500
(at Trailfinders Sports Ground, Ealing).

SWINTON LIONS 22 OLDHAM 22

LIONS: 22 Geronimo Doyle; 37 Owen Buckley; 3 Mitch Cox; 11 Rhodri Lloyd; 1 Mike Butt; 6 Martyn Ridyard; 7 Jack Hansen; 16 Paddy Jones; 9 Luke Waterworth; 10 Lewis Hatton; 12 Nick Gregson; 15 Louis Brogan; 13 Will Hope. Subs (all used): 8 Sam Brooks; 40 Ronan Michael; 24 Paul Nash; 19 Deane Meadows.
Tries: Hatton (44, 53), Butt (61), Meadows (78);
Goals: Ridyard 2/3, Gregson 1/1.
OLDHAM: 1 Dan Abram; 2 Tommy Brierley; 28 Joe Hartley; 24 Max Roberts; 5 Ryan Ince; 6 Lewis Charnock; 26 James Barran; 16 Tyler Dupree; 33 Jamie Abram; 17 Liam Kirk; 11 Danny Langtree; 21 Shaun Pick; 25 Danny Bridge. Subs (all used): 29 Lloyd Roby; 13 Martyn Reilly; 12 Liam Bent; 15 Luke Nelmes.
Tries: Dupree (19, 27), Roby (48), Barran (67);
Goals: D Abram 3/4.
Sin bin: Dupree (76) - shoulder charge.
Rugby Leaguer & League Express Men of the Match: *Lions:* Lewis Hatton; *Oldham:* Lewis Charnock.
Penalty count: 9-8; **Half-time:** 0-12;
Referee: Gareth Hewer; **Attendance:** 1,527.

WHITEHAVEN 20 DEWSBURY RAMS 18

WHITEHAVEN: 1 Gregg McNally; 5 Andrew Bulman; 3 Chris Taylor; 23 Jason Mossop; 2 Lachlan Walmsley; 32 Louis Jouffret; 7 Nikau Williams; 17 Tom Walker; 18 James Newton; 35 Guy Graham; 15 Connor Holliday; 12 Liam Cooper; 16 Tom Wilkinson. Subs (all used): 9 Callum Phillips; 13 Dion Aiye; 19 Ellis Gillam; 27 Andrew Dawson.
Tries: Jouffret (12), Williams (20), Bulman (24, 33);
Goals: Walmsley 2/5.

No way through the Widnes defence for Dewsbury's Sonny Esslemont

RAMS: 4 Matty Fleming; 2 Andy Gabriel; 18 Davey Dixon; 34 Robbie Storey; 27 Lewis Carr; 6 Paul Sykes; 1 Joe Martin; 13 Chris Annakin; 9 Reiss Butterworth; 32 Jimmy Beckett; 35 Sonny Esslemont; 12 Michael Knowles; 25 James Thornton. Subs (all used): 14 Sam Day; - Riley Dean; 24 Jordan Schofield; 31 Robson Stevens.
Tries: Gabriel (56), Schofield (61), Dixon (73);
Goals: Sykes 3/3.
Sin bin: Annakin (30) - dissent.
Rugby Leaguer & League Express Men of the Match: *Whitehaven:* Louis Jouffret; *Rams:* Chris Annakin.
Penalty count: 7-6; **Half-time:** 18-0;
Referee: John McMullen; **Attendance:** 730.

YORK CITY KNIGHTS 34 WIDNES VIKINGS 20

CITY KNIGHTS: 1 Matty Marsh; 22 Perry Whiteley; 30 Tyme Dow-Nikau; 42 Corey Hall; 23 Ben Jones-Bishop; 6 Brendan O'Hagan; 36 Corey Johnson; 8 Ronan Dixon; 9 Will Jubb; 10 Jack Teanby; 17 Danny Kirmond; 39 James McDonnell; 11 Chris Clarkson. Subs (all used): 12 Sam Scott; 14 Kriss Brining; 15 Jordan Baldwinson; 20 Tim Spears.
Tries: O'Hagan (15, 26, 58), Dow-Nikau (43, 46), Teanby (75); **Goals:** Marsh 5/6.
VIKINGS: 1 Jack Owens; 5 Deon Cross; 3 Jake Spedding; 4 Steve Tyrer; 2 Jayden Hatton; 6 Danny Craven; 17 Joe Lyons; 13 Kenny Baker; 30 Lewis Hulme; 24 Will Tilleke; 11 Shane Grady; 12 Adam Lawton; 7 Matty Smith. Subs: 16 Owen Farnworth; 19 Joe Edge; 26 Ollie Brookes (not used); 31 Aiden Roden.
Tries: Owens (9), Cross (20), Lyons (32), Tyrer (36);
Goals: Owens 2/4.
Rugby Leaguer & League Express Men of the Match: *City Knights:* Brendan O'Hagan; *Vikings:* Kenny Baker.
Penalty count: 3-4; **Half-time:** 12-20;
Referee: Nick Bennett; **Attendance:** 1,386.

ROUND 17

Saturday 14th August 2021

NEWCASTLE THUNDER 12 BRADFORD BULLS 36

THUNDER: 5 Calum Turner; 2 Jack Johnson; 4 Kieran Gill; 33 Sam Halsall; 18 Alex Clegg; 3 Matthew Wright; 7 Josh Woods; 8 Nathan Wilde; 9 Bob Beswick; 15 Ted Chapelhow; 11 Ukuma Ta'ai; 38 Matty Nicholson; 17 Connor Bailey. Subs (all used): 12 Sam Wilde; 13 Liam McAvoy; 14 Evan Simons; 30 Jake Anderson.

Tries: Johnson (37), Gill (39); **Goals:** J Woods 2/2.
Sin bin: Wright (67) - high tackle.
BULLS: 1 Brandon Pickersgill; 22 Reece Hamlett; 3 Rhys Evans; 4 Ross Oakley; 19 David Foggin-Johnston; 2 Joe Brown; 7 Jordan Lilley; 23 Anthony Walker; 9 Thomas Doyle; 10 Steve Crossley; 11 Adam Rooks; 12 Aaron Murphy; 13 Sam Hallas. Subs (all used): 14 George Flanagan; 18 Ebon Scurr; 24 Ben Evans; 34 Joe Burton.
Tries: Crossley (5), Foggin-Johnston (33, 51), Rooks (42), Flanagan (61, 68); **Goals:** Lilley 6/7.
Rugby Leaguer & League Express Men of the Match: *Thunder:* Josh Woods; *Bulls:* Jordan Lilley.
Penalty count: 8-3; **Half-time:** 12-14;
Referee: Nick Bennett; **Attendance:** 1,168.

FEATHERSTONE ROVERS 44 YORK CITY KNIGHTS 14

ROVERS: 36 Alex Walker; 2 Ben Blackmore; 4 Josh Hardcastle; 3 Kris Welham; 1 Craig Hall; 7 Dane Chisholm; 9 Fa'amanu Brown; 10 James Harrison; 14 Connor Jones; 13 James Lockwood; 11 Brett Ferres; 20 Frankie Halton; 19 Callum Field. Subs (all used): 21 Dean Parata; 15 John Davies; 18 Luke Cooper; 35 Gadwin Springer.
Tries: Blackmore (12), Harrison (19), Walker (40, 44), Hall (47, 56, 62, 71); **Goals:** Hall 6/8.
Sin bin: Chisholm (23) - high tackle on O'Hagan.
CITY KNIGHTS: 1 Matty Marsh; 42 Corey Hall; 30 Tyme Dow-Nikau; 4 Ryan Atkins; 23 Ben Jones-Bishop; 6 Brendan O'Hagan; 36 Corey Johnson; 8 Ronan Dixon; 9 Will Jubb; 10 Jack Teanby; 12 Sam Scott; 39 James McDonnell; 11 Chris Clarkson. Subs (all used): 14 Kriss Brining; 20 Tim Spears; 15 Jordan Baldwinson; 13 Adam Cuthbertson.
Tries: Chisholm (2, 6), Marsh (32);
Goals: Marsh 0/2, Johnson 1/1.
Rugby Leaguer & League Express Men of the Match: *Rovers:* Craig Hall; *City Knights:* Brendan O'Hagan.
Penalty count: 8-9; **Half-time:** 18-14;
Referee: Matt Rossleigh; **Attendance:** 2,183.

Sunday 15th August 2021

DEWSBURY RAMS 23 WIDNES VIKINGS 22

RAMS: 1 Joe Martin; 2 Andy Gabriel; 18 Davey Dixon; 4 Matty Fleming; 27 Lewis Carr; 30 Alex Smith; 36 Riley Dean; 31 Robson Stevens; 9 Reiss Butterworth; 32 Jimmy Beckett; 35 Sonny Esslemont; 12 Tom Garratt; 13 Chris Annakin. Subs (all used): 33 Dom Speakman; 24 Jordan Schofield; - Dale Ferguson; 25 James Thornton.

Tries: Fleming (5), Beckett (15), Ferguson (35);
Goals: Dean 5/5; **Field goal:** Dean (39).
Sin bin: Annakin (11) - dangerous challenge.
VIKINGS: 1 Jack Owens; 5 Deon Cross; 3 Jake Spedding; 4 Steve Tyrer; 26 Ollie Brookes; 6 Danny Craven; 17 Joe Lyons; 24 Will Tilleke; 30 Lewis Hulme; 16 Owen Farnworth; 11 Shane Grady; 19 Joe Edge; 7 Matty Smith. Subs (all used): 13 Kenny Baker; 25 Daniel Hill; 12 Adam Lawton; 31 Aiden Roden.
Tries: Tyrer (20), Cross (48), Edge (62), Baker (67);
Goals: Owens 3/4.
Rugby Leaguer & League Express Men of the Match: *Rams:* Dale Ferguson; *Vikings:* Jack Owens.
Penalty count: 6-7; **Half-time:** 19-6;
Referee: Tom Grant; **Attendance:** 726.

SHEFFIELD EAGLES 25 OLDHAM 18

EAGLES: 1 Josh Guzdek; 2 Rob Worrincy; 3 Connor Bower; 4 James Glover; 5 Ryan Millar; 13 Aaron Brown; 23 Harry Tyson-Wilson; 18 Tyler Dickinson; 9 James Davey; 11 Brad Knowles; 15 Olly Davies; 32 Evan Hodgson; 10 Matt James. Subs (all used): 14 Greg Burns; 8 Scott Wheeldon; 24 Ryan Johnson; 20 Paddy Burns.
Tries: James (21), Davies (27), Millar (44), Guzdek (55); **Goals:** Guzdek 4/4; **Field goal:** H Tyson-Wilson (76).
OLDHAM: 1 Dan Abram; 2 Tommy Brierley; 29 Lloyd Roby; 24 Max Roberts; 5 Ryan Ince; 6 Lewis Charnock; 26 James Barran; 16 Tyler Dupree; 9 Gareth Owen; 8 Phil Joy; 11 Danny Langtree; 21 Shaun Pick; 15 Luke Nelmes. Subs (all used): 33 Brad Jinks; 13 Martyn Reilly; 35 Fenton Rogers; 12 Liam Bent.
Tries: Langtree (18), Reilly (37), Dupree (62);
Goals: D Abram 3/3.
Sin bin: Rogers (47) - high tackle on Dickinson.
Rugby Leaguer & League Express Men of the Match: *Eagles:* James Glover; *Oldham:* Martyn Reilly.
Penalty count: 8-4; **Half-time:** 12-12;
Referee: Aaron Moore; **Attendance:** 372.

SWINTON LIONS 6 BATLEY BULLDOGS 38

LIONS: 22 Geronimo Doyle; 1 Mike Butt; 11 Rhodri Lloyd; 25 Luis Roberts; 21 Ben Heyes; 6 Martyn Ridyard; 18 Cobi Green; 40 Ronan Michael; 9 Luke Waterworth; 10 Lewis Hatton; 3 Mitch Cox; 12 Nick Gregson; 15 Louis Brogan. Subs (all used): 14 Billy Brickhill; 16 Paddy Jones; 26 Jordan Brown; 20 Tayler Brown.
Try: Roberts (9); **Goals:** Ridyard 1/1.

BULLDOGS: 5 Johnny Campbell; 22 Dale Morton; 12 Lucas Walshaw; 18 George Senior; 29 Greg Johnson; 6 Ben White; 7 Tom Gilmore; 10 Toby Everett; 24 Ben Kaye; 15 Jack Blagbrough; 17 Josh Tonks; 11 Dane Manning; 26 Nyle Flynn. Subs (all used): 9 Alistair Leak; 16 Michael Ward; 19 Tom Lillycrop; 25 Anthony Bowman.
Tries: Campbell (28, 40), Senior (35), Leak (42, 52, 75), Johnson (64); **Goals:** Gilmore 5/7.
Rugby Leaguer & League Express Men of the Match: *Lions:* Mike Butt; *Bulldogs:* Alistair Leak.
Penalty count: 6-3; **Half-time:** 6-16;
Referee: Scott Mikalauskas; **Attendance:** 842.

WHITEHAVEN 32 LONDON BRONCOS 18

WHITEHAVEN: 1 Gregg McNally; 5 Andrew Bulman; 3 Chris Taylor; 23 Jason Mossop; 2 Lachlan Walmsley; 6 Karl Dixon; 7 Nikau Williams; 8 Marc Shackley; 18 James Newton; 17 Tom Walker; 19 Ellis Gillam; 12 Liam Cooper; 16 Tom Wilkinson. Subs (all used): 9 Callum Phillips; 13 Dion Aiye; 26 Ryan King; 27 Andrew Dawson.
Tries: Wilkinson (10), Cooper (35), Bulman (46), Williams (54), Walmsley (64); **Goals:** Walmsley 6/6.
BRONCOS: 22 Oliver Leyland; 17 Abbas Miski; 3 Chris Hankinson; 23 Josh Hodson; 19 Jacob Ogden; 1 James Meadows; 21 Ryan Horsman; 10 Greg Richards; 9 Matty Fozard; 28 Titus Gwaze; 12 Rhys Curran; 13 Josh Walters; 16 Dan Hindmarsh. Subs (all used): 26 Rob Oakley; 25 Jacob Jones; 31 Pat Moran; 18 Jordan Williams.
Tries: Miski (5), Hodson (18), Curran (24);
Goals: Hankinson 3/3.
Rugby Leaguer & League Express Men of the Match: *Whitehaven:* Ryan King; *Broncos:* Chris Hankinson.
Penalty count: 7-8; **Half-time:** 12-18;
Referee: Jack Smith; **Attendance:** 792.

ROUND 18

Sunday 22nd August 2021

BATLEY BULLDOGS 56 SHEFFIELD EAGLES 12

BULLDOGS: 1 Luke Hooley; 5 Johnny Campbell; 18 George Senior; 22 Dale Morton; 29 Greg Johnson; 6 Ben White; 7 Tom Gilmore; 10 Toby Everett; 24 Ben Kaye; 15 Jack Blagbrough; 12 Lucas Walshaw; 11 Dane Manning; 26 Nyle Flynn. Subs (all used): 9 Alistair Leak; 16 Michael Ward; 13 James Brown; 19 Tom Lillycrop.
Tries: Johnson (10, 16, 74), Morton (33), Walshaw (38, 55), Hooley (49, 57), Flynn (71), Campbell (77);
Goals: Hooley 2/4, Gilmore 6/6.
EAGLES: 1 Josh Guzdek; 2 Rob Worrincy; 3 Connor Bower; 4 James Glover; 5 Ryan Millar; 13 Aaron Brown; 23 Harry Tyson-Wilson; 8 Scott Wheeldon; 9 James Davey; 11 Brad Knowles; 15 Olly Davies; 32 Evan Hodgson; 20 Paddy Burns. Subs (all used): 14 Greg Burns; 19 Blake Broadbent; 17 Frankie Mariano; 31 Bobby Tyson-Wilson.
Tries: Davey (27), Davies (61); **Goals:** Guzdek 2/2.
Rugby Leaguer & League Express Men of the Match: *Bulldogs:* Greg Johnson; *Eagles:* Rob Worrincy.
Penalty count: 9-5; **Half-time:** 20-6;
Referee: Brad Milligan; **Attendance:** 859.

BRADFORD BULLS 30 SWINTON LIONS 26

BULLS: 1 Brandon Pickersgill; 5 Matty Dawson-Jones; 3 Rhys Evans; 4 Ross Oakes; 19 David Foggin-Johnston; 2 Joe Brown; 7 Jordan Lilley; 23 Anthony Walker; 9 Thomas Doyle; 24 Ben Evans; 11 Adam Rooks; 12 Aaron Murphy; 13 Sam Hallas. Subs (all used): 14 George Flanagan; 20 Brad England; 15 Dan Fleming; 28 Bradley Ho.
Tries: Pickersgill (15), Oakes (23), Flanagan (52, 55), Foggin-Johnston (66); **Goals:** Lilley 5/5.
LIONS: 22 Geronimo Doyle; 25 Luis Roberts; 11 Rhodri Lloyd; 1 Mike Butt; 21 Ben Heyes; 6 Martyn Ridyard; 7 Jack Hansen; 8 Sam Brooks; 9 Luke Waterworth; 10 Lewis Hatton; 3 Mitch Cox; 12 Nick Gregson; 15 Louis Brogan. Subs (all used): 14 Billy Brickhill; 40 Ronan Michael; 16 Paddy Jones; 18 Cobi Green.
Tries: Roberts (26, 59), Heyes (29), Lloyd (70), Ridyard (77);
Goals: Hansen 0/1, Gregson 1/1, Ridyard 2/3.
Rugby Leaguer & League Express Men of the Match: *Bulls:* George Flanagan; *Lions:* Rhodri Lloyd.
Penalty count: 9-7; **Half-time:** 12-10;
Referee: Matt Rossleigh; **Attendance:** 2,819.

FEATHERSTONE ROVERS 64 DEWSBURY RAMS 6

ROVERS: 36 Alex Walker; 2 Ben Blackmore; 3 Kris Welham; 1 Craig Hall; 5 Gareth Gale; 6 Tom Holmes; 9 Fa'amanu Brown; 35 Gadwin Springer; 21 Dean Parata; 13 James Lockwood; 11 Brett Ferres; 20 Frankie Halton; 19 Callum Field. Subs (all used): 14 Connor Jones; 15 John Davies; 18 Luke Cooper; 24 Dale Ferguson.
Tries: Springer (3), Blackmore (8, 70), Field (18), Hall (21, 28, 80), Walker (26), Cooper (60), Davies (75), Jones (78); **Goals:** Hall 10/11.
RAMS: 6 Paul Sykes; 2 Andy Gabriel; 34 Robbie Storey; 5 Will Oakes; 27 Lewis Carr; 30 Alex Smith; 36 Riley Dean; 20 Aaron Hall; 9 Reiss Butterworth; 24 Jordan Schofield; 10 Tom Garratt; 15 Keenen Tomlinson; 25 James Thornton. Subs (all used): 14 Sam Day; 38 Matthew Fletcher; 13 Chris Annakin; 31 Robson Stevens.
Try: Gabriel (37); **Goals:** Sykes 1/1.
Sin bin: Smith (70) - holding down.
Rugby Leaguer & League Express Men of the Match: *Rovers:* Craig Hall; *Rams:* Robson Stevens.
Penalty count: 6-5; **Half-time:** 36-6;
Referee: Scott Mikalauskas; **Attendance:** 2,115.

OLDHAM 6 TOULOUSE OLYMPIQUE 34

OLDHAM: 1 Dan Abram; 2 Tommy Brierley; 5 Ryan Ince; 24 Max Roberts; 27 Ben Holcroft; 22 Harvey Spence; 7 Dave Hewitt; 8 Phil Joy; 9 Gareth Owen; 16 Tyler Dupree; 11 Danny Langtree; 21 Shaun Pick; 25 Danny Bridge. Subs (all used): 6 Lewis Charnock; 12 Liam Bent; 13 Martyn Reilly; 15 Luke Nelmes.
Try: Reilly (40); **Goals:** D Abram 1/1.
OLYMPIQUE: 1 Mark Kheirallah; 20 Ilias Bergal; 4 Mathieu Jussaume; 3 Junior Vaivai; 21 Latrell Schaumkel; 6 Johnathon Ford; 31 Tony Gigot; 23 Justin Sangare; 14 Eloi Pelissier; 10 Harrison Hansen; 11 Andrew Dixon; 12 Dominique Peyroux; 17 Joseph Paulo. Subs (all used): 15 Maxime Puech; 18 Mitch Garbutt; 26 Hugo Pezet; 28 Romain Navarrete.
Tries: Vaivai (15), Sangare (19), Pelissier (28, 52), Peyroux (32), Garbutt (48); **Goals:** Kheirallah 5/6.
Rugby Leaguer & League Express Men of the Match: *Oldham:* Max Roberts; *Olympique:* Eloi Pelissier.
Penalty count: 10-3; **Half-time:** 6-22;
Referee: Jack Smith; **Attendance:** 743.

WIDNES VIKINGS 25 HALIFAX PANTHERS 6

VIKINGS: 25 Daniel Hill; 26 Ollie Brookes; 4 Steve Tyrer; 3 Jake Spedding; 5 Deon Cross; 6 Danny Craven; 17 Joe Lyons; 24 Will Tilleke; 30 Lewis Hulme; 13 Kenny Baker; 11 Shane Grady; 12 Adam Lawton; 1 Jack Owens. Subs: 8 Paul Clough; 18 Lloyd Roby (not used); 19 Joe Edge; 31 Aiden Roden.
Tries: Craven (5), Brookes (39), Tyrer (49), Baker (80);
Goals: Owens 4/5; **Field goal:** Craven (77).
PANTHERS: 4 James Woodburn-Hall; 21 Zack McComb; 3 Greg Worthington; 12 Ed Barber; 5 James Saltonstall; 6 Liam Harris; 1 Scott Grix; 16 Will Calcott; 9 Brandon Moore; 10 Daniel Murray; 11 Matt Garside; 17 Ben Kavanagh; 8 Elliot Morris. Subs (all used): 13 Jacob Fairbank; 18 Connor Davies; 20 Curtis Davies; 24 Ben Tibbs.
Try: Barber (20); **Goals:** Woodburn-Hall 1/2.
Rugby Leaguer & League Express Men of the Match: *Vikings:* Steve Tyrer; *Panthers:* Greg Worthington.
Penalty count: 4-8; **Half-time:** 10-6;
Referee: Tom Grant; **Attendance:** 1,252.

YORK CITY KNIGHTS 30 WHITEHAVEN 12

CITY KNIGHTS: 23 Ben Jones-Bishop; 22 Perry Whiteley; 30 Tyme Dow-Nikau; 4 Ryan Atkins; 3 Liam Salter; 1 Matty Marsh; 36 Corey Johnson; 8 Ronan Dixon; 9 Will Jubb; 10 Jack Teanby; 12 Sam Scott; 39 James McDonnell; 11 Chris Clarkson. Subs (all used): 16 Marcus Stock; 17 Danny Kirmond; 19 James Green; 28 Danny Washbrook.
Tries: Teanby (3), Jones-Bishop (14), Stock (42), Whiteley (58), Scott (62); **Goals:** Marsh 5/5.
WHITEHAVEN: 1 Gregg McNally; 2 Lachlan Walmsley; 23 Jason Mossop; 6 Karl Dixon; 5 Andrew Bulman; 32 Louis Jouffret; 7 Nikau Williams; 8 Marc Shackley; 18 James Newton; 35 Guy Graham; 15 Connor Holliday; 12 Liam Cooper; 20 Jake Bradley. Subs (all used): 13 Dion Aiye; 26 Ryan King; 31 Oscar Thomas; 33 Andy Thornley.
Tries: Walmsley (20), Bradley (78); **Goals:** Walmsley 2/2.
Rugby Leaguer & League Express Men of the Match: *City Knights:* Tyme Dow-Nikau; *Whitehaven:* Jake Bradley.
Penalty count: 4-3; **Half-time:** 12-6;
Referee: Aaron Moore; **Attendance:** 1,460.

ROUND 19

Sunday 29th August 2021

DEWSBURY RAMS 22 NEWCASTLE THUNDER 43

RAMS: 1 Joe Martin; 2 Andy Gabriel; 6 Paul Sykes; 15 Keenen Tomlinson; 4 Matty Fleming; 30 Alex Smith; 36 Riley Dean; 31 Robson Stevens; 33 Dom Speakman; 32 Jimmy Beckett; 10 Tom Garratt; 12 Michael Knowles; 9 Reiss Butterworth. Subs (all used): 14 Sam Day; 34 Robbie Storey; 24 Jordan Schofield; 23 Jon Magrin.
Tries: Fleming (6), Magrin (57), Sykes (75), Garratt (79);
Goals: Sykes 3/4.
THUNDER: 5 Calum Turner; 2 Jack Johnson; 3 Matthew Wright; 4 Kieran Gill; 18 Alex Clegg; 6 Jake Shorrocks; 7 Josh Woods; 15 Ted Chapelhow; 9 Bob Beswick; 10 Kyle Trout; 12 Sam Wilde; 17 Connor Bailey; 11 Ukuma Ta'ai. Subs (all used): 16 Jay Chapelhow; 14 Evan Simons; 13 Liam McAvoy; 27 Alex Donaghy.
Tries: Turner (16), Johnson (21, 24, 46), Shorrocks (27), J Woods (64), T Chapelhow (71), Wright (80);
Goals: J Woods 5/8; **Field goal:** J Woods (40).
Rugby Leaguer & League Express Men of the Match: *Rams:* Tom Garratt; *Thunder:* Jack Johnson.
Penalty count: 4-5; **Half-time:** 4-21;
Referee: Gareth Hewer; **Attendance:** 540.

HALIFAX PANTHERS 48 SWINTON LIONS 12

PANTHERS: 1 Scott Grix; 24 Ben Tibbs; 3 Greg Worthington; 21 Zack McComb; 5 James Saltonstall; 6 Liam Harris; 7 Connor Robinson; 10 Daniel Murray; 9 Brandon Moore; 16 Will Calcott; 11 Matt Garside; 17 Ben Kavanagh; 13 Jacob Fairbank. Subs (all used): 4 James Woodburn-Hall; 12 Ed Barber; 20 Curtis Davies; 25 Adam Tangata.
Tries: Moore (8, 13), Saltonstall (17), Kavanagh (27), Harris (39), Garside (61), Tibbs (76), Grix (77), McComb (80); **Goals:** Robinson 6/9.
LIONS: 7 Jack Hansen; 22 Geronimo Doyle; 1 Mike Butt; 39 Reece Hamlett; 25 Luis Roberts; 6 Martyn Ridyard; 18 Cobi Green; 13 Will Hope; 9 Luke Waterworth; 10 Lewis Hatton; 11 Rhodri Lloyd; 3 Mitch Cox; 15 Louis Brogan. Subs (all used): 14 Billy Brickhill; 16 Paddy Jones; 24 Paul Nash; 40 Ronan Michael.
Tries: Lloyd (44), Hope (57); **Goals:** Ridyard 2/2.
Rugby Leaguer & League Express Men of the Match: *Panthers:* Scott Grix; *Lions:* Rhodri Lloyd.
Penalty count: 3-7; **Half-time:** 26-0;
Referee: Nick Bennett; **Attendance:** 1,663.

LONDON BRONCOS 42 SHEFFIELD EAGLES 12

BRONCOS: 3 Chris Hankinson; 20 Gideon Boafo; 19 Jacob Ogden; 4 Will Lovell; 17 Abbas Miski; 1 James Meadows; 21 Rian Horsman; 10 Greg Richards; 9 Matty Fozard; 31 Pat Moran; 12 Rhys Curran; 13 Josh Walters; 16 Dan Hindmarsh. Subs (all used): 25 Jacob Jones; 26 Rob Oakley; 23 Josh Hodson; 28 Titus Gwaze.
Tries: Boafo (4, 25, 32), Ogden (47), Fozard (50), Walters (57), Hankinson (73), Miski (77);
Goals: Hankinson 5/8.
Sin bin: Gwaze (45) - fighting.
EAGLES: 1 Josh Guzdek; 2 Rob Worrincy; 3 Connor Bower; 5 Ryan Millar; 24 Ryan Johnson; 4 James Glover; 23 Harry Tyson-Wilson; 18 Tyler Dickinson; 9 James Davey; 10 Matt James; 15 Olly Davies; 12 Joel Farrell; 13 Aaron Brown. Subs (all used): 8 Scott Wheeldon; 14 Greg Burns; 19 Blake Broadbent; 20 Paddy Burns.
Tries: Johnson (19), Broadbent (35); **Goals:** Guzdek 2/2.
Sin bin: J Farrell (45) - fighting.
Rugby Leaguer & League Express Men of the Match: *Broncos:* Rian Horsman; *Eagles:* Harry Tyson-Wilson.
Penalty count: 2-4; **Half-time:** 14-12;
Referee: Cameron Worsley; **Attendance:** 350
(at Trailfinders Sports Ground, Ealing).

OLDHAM 10 FEATHERSTONE ROVERS 48

OLDHAM: 1 Dan Abram; 5 Ryan Ince; 28 Joe Hartley; 24 Max Roberts; 27 Ben Holcroft; 22 Harvey Spence; 7 Dave Hewitt; 8 Phil Joy; 9 Gareth Owen; 16 Tyler Dupree; 11 Danny Langtree; 25 Danny Bridge; 12 Liam Bent. Subs (all used): 6 Lewis Charnock; 13 Martyn Reilly; 15 Luke Nelmes; 30 Dec Gregory.
Tries: Hartley (21), Bridge (40); **Goals:** D Abram 1/2.
ROVERS: 36 Alex Walker; 5 Gareth Gale; 3 Kris Welham; 4 Josh Hardcastle; 2 Ben Blackmore; 6 Tom Holmes; 7 Dane Chisholm; 8 Craig Kopczak; 21 Dean Parata; 13 James Lockwood; 11 Brett Ferres; 20 Frankie Halton; 19 Callum Field. Subs (all used): 14 Connor Jones; 18 Luke Cooper; 24 Dale Ferguson; 35 Gadwin Springer.
Tries: Parata (5, 48), Ferres (9, 60), Welham (11), Kopczak (14, 36), Walker (41, 76);
Goals: Chisholm 4/7, Ferres 2/2.
Sin bin: Chisholm (34) - kicking out.
Rugby Leaguer & League Express Men of the Match: *Oldham:* Tyler Dupree; *Rovers:* Craig Kopczak.
Penalty count: 8-5; **Half-time:** 10-26;
Referee: Michael Smaill; **Attendance:** 1,158.

WHITEHAVEN 64 WIDNES VIKINGS 6

WHITEHAVEN: 1 Gregg McNally; 5 Andrew Bulman; 3 Chris Taylor; 6 Karl Dixon; 2 Lachlan Walmsley; 32 Louis Jouffret; 7 Nikau Williams; 33 Andy Thornley; 18 James Newton; 35 Guy Graham; 12 Liam Cooper; 26 Ryan King; 16 Tom Wilkinson. Subs (all used): 9 Callum Phillips; 13 Dion Aiye; 20 Jake Bradley; 27 Andrew Dawson.
Tries: Dixon (5), Newton (7, 74), Bulman (11, 55), Aiye (34), Walmsley (39), King (47), Bradley (52), Jouffret (67), C Phillips (77); **Goals:** Walmsley 10/11.

VIKINGS: 1 Jack Owens; 5 Deon Cross; 3 Jake Spedding; 18 Lloyd Roby; 26 Ollie Brookes; 6 Danny Craven; 17 Joe Lyons; 13 Kenny Baker; 31 Aiden Roden; 24 Will Tilleke; 19 Joe Edge; 12 Adam Lawton; 16 Owen Farnworth. Subs (only three named): 32 Connor Aspey; 8 Paul Clough; 20 Owen Buckley (not used).
Try: Roby (59); **Goals:** Owens 1/1.
Rugby Leaguer & League Express Men of the Match: *Whitehaven:* Louis Jouffret; *Vikings:* Paul Clough.
Penalty count: 4-4; **Half-time:** 28-0;
Referee: Brad Milligan; **Attendance:** 951.

YORK CITY KNIGHTS 18 BRADFORD BULLS 36

CITY KNIGHTS: 42 Aidan McGowan; 23 Ben Jones-Bishop; 30 Tyme Dow-Nikau; 4 Ryan Atkins; 5 Kieran Dixon; 1 Matty Marsh; 36 Corey Johnson; 15 Jordan Baldwinson; 9 Will Jubb; 17 Danny Kirmond; 39 James McDonnell; 3 Liam Salter; 11 Chris Clarkson. Subs (all used): 16 Marcus Stock; 19 James Green; 2 Jason Bass; 37 Jacob Gannon.
Tries: Atkins (19), Green (47), Kirmond (54);
Goals: K Dixon 3/3.
Sin bin: McDonnell (51) - professional foul.
BULLS: 1 Brandon Pickersgill; 5 Matty Dawson-Jones; 3 Rhys Evans; 4 Ross Oakes; 19 David Foggin-Johnston; 6 Danny Brough; 7 Jordan Lilley; 24 Ben Evans; 9 Thomas Doyle; 10 Steve Crossley; 20 Brad England; 12 Aaron Murphy; 13 Sam Hallas. Subs (all used): 15 Dan Fleming; 14 George Flanagan; 23 Anthony Walker; 41 Masi Matongo.
Tries: Lilley (11), B Evans (17), R Evans (28, 43, 73), Foggin-Johnston (71); **Goals:** Brough 6/8.
Sin bin: Fleming (77) - late challenge.
Rugby Leaguer & League Express Men of the Match: *City Knights:* Matty Marsh; *Bulls:* Danny Brough.
Penalty count: 6-6; **Half time:** 6-20;
Referee: Jack Smith; **Attendance:** 2,841.

ROUND 20

Friday 3rd September 2021

NEWCASTLE THUNDER 16 YORK CITY KNIGHTS 29

THUNDER: 5 Calum Turner; 2 Jack Johnson; 3 Matthew Wright; 4 Kieran Gill; 18 Alex Clegg; 6 Jake Shorrocks; 7 Josh Woods; 15 Ted Chapelhow; 9 Bob Beswick; 10 Kyle Trout; 11 Ukuma Ta'ai; 17 Connor Bailey; 14 Evan Simons. Subs (all used): 26 Tom Spencer; 8 Nathan Wilde; 13 Liam McAvoy; 27 Alex Donaghy.
Tries: Clegg (20), Johnson (35), Gill (48);
Goals: J Woods 2/3.
CITY KNIGHTS: 26 Myles Harrison; 23 Ben Jones-Bishop; 30 Tyme Dow-Nikau; 3 Liam Salter; 22 Perry Whiteley; 1 Matty Marsh; 36 Corey Johnson; 19 James Green; 28 Danny Washbrook; 17 Danny Kirmond; 39 James McDonnell; 27 Toby Warren; 11 Chris Clarkson. Subs (all used): 42 Aidan McGowan; 37 Jacob Gannon; 16 Marcus Stock; 20 Tim Spears.
Tries: Clarkson (4), Jones-Bishop (15), McGowan (26, 28), Whiteley (58); **Goals:** Harrison 4/5; **Field goal:** Marsh (73).
Rugby Leaguer & League Express Men of the Match: *Thunder:* Jack Johnson; *City Knights:* Myles Harrison.
Penalty count: 6-2; **Half-time:** 10-24;
Referee: Aaron Moore; **Attendance:** 1,115.

Sunday 5th September 2021

BATLEY BULLDOGS 14 WHITEHAVEN 22

BULLDOGS: 1 Luke Hooley; 5 Johnny Campbell; 22 Dale Morton; 18 George Senior; 29 Greg Johnson; 6 Ben White; 7 Tom Gilmore; 10 Toby Everett; 24 Ben Kaye; 15 Jack Blagbrough; 3 Kieran Buchanan; 11 Dane Manning; 26 Nyle Flynn. Subs (all used): 9 Alistair Leak; 16 Michael Ward; 13 James Brown; 19 Tom Lillycrop.
Tries: Johnson (6), White (34);
Goals: Hooley 0/1, Gilmore 3/3.
Sin bin: Hooley (70) - fighting.
WHITEHAVEN: 1 Gregg McNally; 2 Lachlan Walmsley; 3 Chris Taylor; 6 Karl Dixon; 5 Andrew Bulman; 32 Louis Jouffret; 7 Nikau Williams; 33 Andy Thornley; 18 James Newton; 20 Jake Bradley; 15 Connor Holliday; 12 Liam Cooper; 16 Tom Wilkinson. Subs (all used): 13 Dion Aiye; 27 Andrew Dawson; 26 Ryan King; 9 Callum Phillips.
Tries: Walmsley (12, 37), Dixon (73), Jouffret (79);
Goals: Walmsley 3/6.
Sin bin: McNally (70) - fighting.
Rugby Leaguer & League Express Men of the Match: *Bulldogs:* Dane Manning; *Whitehaven:* Louis Jouffret.
Penalty count: 6-7; **Half-time:** 10-8;
Referee: Michael Mannifield; **Attendance:** 922.

BRADFORD BULLS 6 TOULOUSE OLYMPIQUE 60

BULLS: 1 Brandon Pickersgill; 2 Joe Brown; 3 Rhys Evans; 4 Ross Oakes; 19 David Foggin-Johnston; 7 Jordan Lilley; 27 Billy Jowitt; 24 Ben Evans; 9 Thomas Doyle; 10 Steve Crossley; 20 Brad England; 13 Sam Hallas; 15 Dan Fleming. Subs (all used): 34 Joe Burton; 14 George Flanagan; 28 Bradley Ho; 31 Ethan O'Hanlon.
Try: Flanagan (56); **Goals:** Lilley 1/1.
Sin bin: Hallas (49) - fighting.
OLYMPIQUE: 1 Mark Kheirallah; 20 Ilias Bergal; 4 Mathieu Jussaume; 24 Guy Armitage; 2 Jy Hitchcox; 6 Johnathon Ford; 31 Tony Gigot; 8 Remi Casty; 9 Lloyd White; 10 Harrison Hansen; 12 Dominique Peyroux; 16 Joe Bretherton; 17 Joseph Paulo. Subs (all used): 14 Eloi Pelissier; 18 Mitch Garbutt; 23 Justin Sangare; 28 Romain Navarrete.
Tries: Armitage (3, 11), Hitchcox (28), Bergal (32), Navarrete (38), Sangare (44, 47), Bretherton (61), Casty (65), Kheirallah (72, 77);
Goals: Kheirallah 8/9, Gigot 0/2.
Sin bin: Bergal (49) - fighting;
Kheirallah (59) - dangerous challenge.
Rugby Leaguer & League Express Men of the Match: *Bulls:* David Foggin-Johnston; *Olympique:* Tony Gigot.
Penalty count: 13-8; **Half-time:** 0-30;
Referee: Gareth Hewer; **Attendance:** 2,445
(at Tetley's Stadium, Dewsbury).

FEATHERSTONE ROVERS 54 HALIFAX PANTHERS 22

ROVERS: 36 Alex Walker; 2 Ben Blackmore; 3 Kris Welham; 1 Craig Hall; 5 Gareth Gale; 7 Dane Chisholm; 9 Fa'amanu Brown; 8 Craig Kopczak; 14 Connor Jones; 13 James Lockwood; 11 Brett Ferres; 20 Frankie Halton; 19 Callum Field. Subs (all used): 6 Tom Holmes; 15 John Davies; 31 Junior Moors; 35 Gadwin Springer.
Tries: Welham (6), Chisholm (15, 40), Gale (30, 62), Blackmore (34, 57), Jones (42), Ferres (76), Brown (80);
Goals: Hall 7/11.
PANTHERS: 1 Scott Grix; 19 Conor McGrath; 3 Greg Worthington; 21 Zack McComb; 5 James Saltonstall; 4 James Woodburn-Hall; 7 Connor Robinson; 10 Daniel Murray; 9 Brandon Moore; 16 Will Calcott; 17 Ben Kavanagh; 11 Matt Garside; 13 Jacob Fairbank. Subs (all used): 20 Curtis Davies; 25 Adam Tangata; 14 Kevin Larroyer; 12 Ed Barber.
Tries: McComb (12), Garside (49), Barber (60), Woodburn-Hall (65); **Goals:** Robinson 3/4, Grix 0/1.
Rugby Leaguer & League Express Men of the Match: *Rovers:* Gareth Gale; *Panthers:* James Woodburn-Hall.
Penalty count: 6-9; **Half-time:** 24-8;
Referee: Cameron Worsley; **Attendance:** 3,063.

SHEFFIELD EAGLES 20 DEWSBURY RAMS 24

EAGLES: 1 Josh Guzdek; 2 Rob Worrincy; 3 Connor Bower; 4 James Glover; 5 Ryan Millar; 22 Izaac Farrell; 7 Anthony Thackeray; 18 Tyler Dickinson; 9 James Davey; 11 Brad Knowles; 12 Joel Farrell; 15 Olly Davies; 13 Aaron Brown. Subs (all used): 8 Scott Wheeldon; 14 Greg Burns; 19 Blake Broadbent; 32 Evan Hodgson.
Tries: Dickinson (24), Thackeray (33), Worrincy (79);
Goals: I Farrell 4/4.
RAMS: 1 Joe Martin; 2 Andy Gabriel; 4 Matty Fleming; 26 Bayley Liu; 34 Robbie Storey; 36 Riley Dean; 7 Liam Finn; 32 Jimmy Beckett; 14 Sam Day; 10 Tom Garratt; 15 Keenen Tomlinson; 12 Michael Knowles; 23 Jon Magrin. Subs (all used): 33 Dom Speakman; 30 Alex Smith; 31 Robson Stevens; 24 Jordan Schofield.
Tries: Smith (7), Tomlinson (47), Schofield (58), Gabriel (74); **Goals:** Finn 4/5.
Rugby Leaguer & League Express Men of the Match: *Eagles:* Tyler Dickinson; *Rams:* Matty Fleming.
Penalty count: 8-10; **Half-time:** 14-6;
Referee: James Vella; **Attendance:** 432.

SWINTON LIONS 32 LONDON BRONCOS 34

LIONS: 22 Geronimo Doyle; 21 Ben Heyes; 1 Mike Butt; 39 Reece Hamlett; 25 Luis Roberts; 6 Martyn Ridyard; 7 Jack Hansen; 8 Sam Brooks; 9 Luke Waterworth; 10 Lewis Hatton; 11 Rhodri Lloyd; 3 Mitch Cox; 14 Billy Brickhill. Subs (all used): 12 Nick Gregson; 15 Louis Brogan; 13 Will Hope; 40 Ronan Michael.
Tries: Hansen (4), Hatton (10), Ridyard (26), Butt (57), Heyes (66), Roberts (77); **Goals:** Ridyard 4/6.
BRONCOS: 3 Chris Hankinson; 17 Abbas Miski; 23 Josh Hodson; 4 Will Lovell; 20 Gideon Boafo; 1 James Meadows; 21 Rian Horsman; 10 Greg Richards; 9 Matty Fozard; 31 Pat Moran; 13 Josh Walters; 25 Jacob Jones; 16 Dan Hindmarsh. Subs (all used): 28 Titus Gwaze; 11 Sadiq Adebiyi; 18 Jordan Williams; 2 Tuoyo Egodo.
Tries: Richards (16), Moran (19), Miski (29), Adebiyi (32), Boafo (35, 51); **Goals:** Hankinson 5/6.
Rugby Leaguer & League Express Men of the Match: *Lions:* Luke Waterworth; *Broncos:* Rian Horsman.
Penalty count: 6-5; **Half-time:** 16-28;
Referee: Craig Smith; **Attendance:** 542.

WIDNES VIKINGS 62 OLDHAM 4

VIKINGS: 1 Jack Owens; 26 Ollie Brookes; 4 Steve Tyrer; 18 Lloyd Roby; 5 Deon Cross; 6 Danny Craven; 17 Joe Lyons; 16 Owen Farnworth; 30 Lewis Hulme; 13 Kenny Baker; 11 Shane Grady; 12 Adam Lawton; 7 Matty Smith. Subs (all used): 8 Paul Clough; 19 Joe Edge; 24 Will Tilleke; 32 Connor Aspey.
Tries: Lawton (2, 40), Brookes (4, 30), Grady (15), Cross (21, 76), Aspey (48), Baker (62), Craven (67), Tyrer (80); **Goals:** Owens 9/11.
OLDHAM: 1 Dan Abram; 2 Tommy Brierley; 28 Joe Hartley; 5 Ryan Ince; 27 Ben Holcroft; 22 Harvey Spence; 7 Dave Hewitt; 15 Luke Nelmes; 9 Gareth Owen; 8 Phil Joy; 11 Danny Langtree; 24 Max Roberts; 13 Martyn Reilly. Subs (all used): 30 Dec Gregory; 6 Lewis Charnock; 25 Danny Bridge; 12 Liam Bent.
Try: Holcroft (36); **Goals:** D Abram 0/1.
Rugby Leaguer & League Express Men of the Match: *Vikings:* Ollie Brookes; *Oldham:* Dan Abram.
Penalty count: 1-3; **Half-time:** 32-4;
Referee: Matt Rossleigh; **Attendance:** 1,088.

ROUND 21

Sunday 12th September 2021

BATLEY BULLDOGS 24 DEWSBURY RAMS 31

BULLDOGS: 1 Luke Hooley; 5 Johnny Campbell; 12 Lucas Walshaw; 18 George Senior; 21 Jodie Broughton; 6 Ben White; 7 Tom Gilmore; 10 Toby Everett; 31 Oli Burton; 15 Jack Blagbrough; 3 Kieran Buchanan; 11 Dane Manning; 26 Nyle Flynn. Subs (all used): 9 Alistair Leak; 16 Michael Ward; 13 James Brown; 22 Dale Morton.
Tries: White (7), Senior (32), Buchanan (34), Broughton (75); **Goals:** Gilmore 4/4.
RAMS: 4 Matty Fleming; 2 Andy Gabriel; 3 Adam Ryder; 18 Davey Dixon; 27 Lewis Carr; 6 Paul Sykes; 7 Liam Finn; 32 Jimmy Beckett; 14 Sam Day; 10 Tom Garratt; 15 Keenen Tomlinson; 12 Michael Knowles; 23 Jon Magrin. Subs (all used): 33 Dom Speakman; 31 Robson Stevens; 24 Jordan Schofield; 26 Bayley Liu.
Tries: Ryder (20), Finn (22), Gabriel (38), Garratt (46), Schofield (67); **Goals:** Sykes 5/5; **Field goal:** Sykes (40).
Dismissal: Day (60) - headbutt.
Sin bin: Magrin (29) - dangerous challenge.
Rugby Leaguer & League Express Men of the Match: *Bulldogs:* Tom Gilmore; *Rams:* Liam Finn.
Penalty count: 7-9; **Half-time:** 18-19;
Referee: Ben Thaler; **Attendance:** 1,532.

LONDON BRONCOS 28 FEATHERSTONE ROVERS 48

BRONCOS: 3 Chris Hankinson; 17 Abbas Miski; 19 Jacob Ogden; 23 Josh Hodson; 20 Gideon Boafo; 1 James Meadows; 21 Rian Horsman; 10 Greg Richards; 9 Matty Fozard; 31 Pat Moran; 13 Josh Walters; 25 Jacob Jones; 16 Dan Hindmarsh. Subs (all used): 26 Rob Oakley; 11 Sadiq Adebiyi; 28 Titus Gwaze; 22 Oliver Leyland.
Tries: Boafo (25, 52, 60, 78), Hodson (46);
Goals: Hankinson 4/5.
ROVERS: 36 Alex Walker; 5 Gareth Gale; 4 Josh Hardcastle; 3 Kris Welham; 1 Craig Hall; 9 Fa'amanu Brown; 7 Dane Chisholm; 8 Craig Kopczak; 14 Connor Jones; 13 James Lockwood; 31 Junior Moors; 20 Frankie Halton; 19 Callum Field. Subs (all used): 15 John Davies; 6 Tom Holmes; 18 Luke Cooper; 35 Gadwin Springer.
Tries: Gale (1, 55), Jones (7, 20, 75), Field (15), Walker (30), Holmes (48), Halton (50); **Goals:** Hall 6/9.
Rugby Leaguer & League Express Men of the Match: *Broncos:* Gideon Boafo; *Rovers:* Connor Jones.
Penalty count: 6-4; **Half-time:** 4-28;
Referee: Nick Bennett; **Attendance:** 555
(at Trailfinders Sports Ground, Ealing).

OLDHAM 24 NEWCASTLE THUNDER 38

OLDHAM: 2 Tommy Brierley; 1 Dan Abram; 5 Ryan Ince; 24 Max Roberts; 27 Ben Holcroft; 22 Harvey Spence; 6 Lewis Charnock; 25 Danny Bridge; 9 Gareth Owen; 16 Tyler Dupree; 11 Danny Langtree; 12 Liam Bent; 35 Brad Jinks. Subs (all used): 13 Martyn Reilly; 15 Luke Nelmes; 17 Liam Kirk; 30 Dec Gregory.
Tries: Charnock (2), D Abram (62), Dupree (64), Roberts (67, 75); **Goals:** D Abram 2/4, Charnock 0/1.
THUNDER: 27 Alex Donaghy; 18 Alex Clegg; 29 Isaac Nokes; 4 Kieran Gill; 2 Jack Johnson; 6 Jake Shorrocks; 7 Josh Woods; 15 Ted Chapelhow; 14 Evan Simons; 8 Nathan Wilde; 17 Connor Bailey; 11 Ukuma Ta'ai; 10 Kyle Trout. Subs (all used): 16 Jay Chapelhow; 21 Reece Dean; 26 Kieran Hudson; 36 Tom Spencer.
Tries: J Woods (25), Ta'ai (33), Bailey (44), Gill (47), Nokes (49), Donaghy (54, 58); **Goals:** J Woods 5/7.
Rugby Leaguer & League Express Men of the Match: *Oldham:* Ryan Ince; *Thunder:* Josh Woods.
Penalty count: 6-4; **Half-time:** 6-12;
Referee: Jack Smith; **Attendance:** 723.

WHITEHAVEN 19 HALIFAX PANTHERS 6

WHITEHAVEN: 1 Gregg McNally; 5 Andrew Bulman; 23 Jason Mossop; 6 Karl Dixon; 2 Lachlan Walmsley; 32 Louis Jouffret; 7 Nikau Williams; 33 Andy Thornley; 9 Callum Phillips; 35 Guy Graham; 26 Ryan King; 12 Liam Cooper; 16 Tom Wilkinson. Subs (all used): 4 Jessie Joe Parker; 13 Dion Aiye; 20 Jake Bradley; 27 Andrew Dawson.
Tries: Walmsley (4), Mossop (22), King (51);
Goals: Walmsley 3/3; **Field goal:** McNally (73).
PANTHERS: 5 James Saltonstall; 19 Conor McGrath; 12 Ed Barber; 3 Greg Worthington; 21 Zack McComb; 1 Scott Grix; 4 James Woodburn-Hall; 25 Adam Tangata; 9 Brandon Moore; 10 Daniel Murray; 17 Ben Kavanagh; 11 Matt Garside; 13 Jacob Fairbank. Subs (all used): 7 Connor Robinson; 18 Connor Davies; 8 Elliot Morris; 14 Kevin Larroyer.
Try: Grix (13); **Goals:** Barber 1/1.
Rugby Leaguer & League Express Men of the Match:
Whitehaven: Dion Aiye; *Panthers:* Zack McComb.
Penalty count: 7-5; **Half-time:** 12-6;
Referee: Aaron Moore; **Attendance:** 1,258.

WIDNES VIKINGS 10 BRADFORD BULLS 9

VIKINGS: 1 Jack Owens; 26 Ollie Brookes; 4 Steve Tyrer; 18 Lloyd Roby; 5 Deon Cross; 6 Danny Craven; 17 Joe Lyons; 16 Owen Farnworth; 30 Lewis Hulme; 13 Kenny Baker; 11 Shane Grady; 12 Adam Lawton; 7 Matty Smith. Subs: 8 Paul Clough; 19 Joe Edge; 24 Will Tilleke; 32 Connor Aspey (not used).
Try: Owens (16); **Goals:** Owens 3/3.
BULLS: 53 Elliot Kear; 2 Joe Brown; 3 Rhys Evans; 4 Ross Oakes; 19 David Foggin-Johnston; 6 Danny Brough; 7 Jordan Lilley; 24 Ben Evans; 9 Thomas Doyle; 10 Steve Crossley; 20 Brad England; 12 Aaron Murphy; 13 Sam Hallas. Subs (all used): 14 George Flanagan; 15 Dan Fleming; 23 Anthony Walker; 43 Eldon Myers.
Try: Lilley (50); **Goals:** Lilley 2/2; **Field goal:** Brough (77).
Rugby Leaguer & League Express Men of the Match:
Vikings: Jack Owens; *Bulls:* Steve Crossley.
Penalty count: 4-7; **Half-time:** 6-0;
Referee: Marcus Griffiths; **Attendance:** 1,725.

SHEFFIELD EAGLES 28 SWINTON LIONS 34

EAGLES: 1 Josh Guzdek; 2 Rob Worrincy; 24 Ryan Johnson; 4 James Glover; 33 Olly Butterworth; 22 Izaac Farrell; 7 Anthony Thackeray; 18 Tyler Dickinson; 9 James Davey; 10 Matt James; 15 Olly Davies; 12 Joel Farrell; 13 Aaron Brown. Subs (all used): 8 Scott Wheeldon; 14 Greg Burns; 11 Brad Knowles; 32 Evan Hodgson.
Tries: Dickinson (15), J Farrell (26, 80), Worrincy (30), Butterworth (47); **Goals:** I Farrell 4/5.
LIONS: 22 Geronimo Doyle; 39 Reece Hamlett; 1 Mike Butt; 11 Rhodri Lloyd; 25 Luis Roberts; 6 Martyn Ridyard; 7 Jack Hansen; 8 Sam Brooks; 9 Luke Waterworth; 10 Lewis Hatton; 12 Nick Gregson; 3 Mitch Cox; 13 Will Hope. Subs (all used): 15 Louis Brogan; 14 Billy Brickhill; 16 Paddy Jones; 40 Ronan Michael.
Tries: Roberts (5), Gregson (10), Hamlett (52), Cox (63), Doyle (69), Hatton (74); **Goals:** Ridyard 5/6.
Rugby Leaguer & League Express Men of the Match:
Eagles: Greg Burns; *Lions:* Mike Butt.
Penalty count: 4-5; **Half-time:** 16-10;
Referee: Gareth Hewer; **Attendance:** 430.

ROUND 22

Saturday 18th September 2021

NEWCASTLE THUNDER 12 TOULOUSE OLYMPIQUE 82

THUNDER: 21 Reece Dean; 28 Cian Tyrer; 5 Calum Turner; 29 Isaac Nokes; - Nathan Roebuck; 6 Jake Shorrocks; 7 Josh Woods; 15 Ted Chapelhow; 9 Bob Beswick; 10 Kyle Trout; 11 Ukuma Ta'ai; 17 Connor Bailey; 8 Nathan Wilde. Subs (all used): 36 Tom Spencer; 14 Evan Simons; 13 Liam McAvoy; 20 Cole Oakley.
Tries: Roebuck (7, 54); **Goals:** J Woods 2/2.
OLYMPIQUE: 1 Mark Kheirallah; 20 Ilias Bergal; 4 Mathieu Jussaume; 3 Junior Vaivai; 2 Jy Hitchcox; 6 Johnathon Ford; 31 Tony Gigot; 8 Remi Casty; 9 Lloyd White; 10 Harrison Hansen; 16 Joe Bretherton; 12 Dominique Peyroux; 13 Anthony Marion. Subs (all used): 7 Lucas Albert; 17 Joseph Paulo; 23 Justin Sangare; 28 Romain Navarrete.
Tries: Hitchcox (3, 26, 40, 74), Bretherton (10, 48), Peyroux (17), Jussaume (22, 67), Sangare (31, 45), Paulo (41), Navarrete (60), Kheirallah (62), Marion (70); **Goals:** Kheirallah 11/15.
Rugby Leaguer & League Express Men of the Match:
Thunder: Josh Woods; *Olympique:* Jy Hitchcox.
Penalty count: 6-2; **Half-time:** 6-36;
Referee: Cameron Worsley; **Attendance:** 428.

Sunday 19th September 2021

BRADFORD BULLS 22 WHITEHAVEN 36

BULLS: 53 Elliot Kear; 2 Joe Brown; 3 Rhys Evans; 4 Ross Oakes; 19 David Foggin-Johnston; 6 Danny Brough; 7 Jordan Lilley; 24 Ben Evans; 9 Thomas Doyle; 10 Steve Crossley; 20 Brad England; 12 Aaron Murphy; 13 Sam Hallas. Subs (all used): 14 George Flanagan; 15 Dan Fleming; 23 Anthony Walker; 43 Eldon Myers.
Tries: B Evans (5, 74), Murphy (10), Foggin-Johnston (29); **Goals:** Brough 2/3, Hallas 1/1.
WHITEHAVEN: 1 Gregg McNally; 5 Andrew Bulman; 3 Chris Taylor; 23 Jason Mossop; 2 Lachlan Walmsley; 32 Louis Jouffret; 7 Nikau Williams; 33 Andy Thornley; 18 James Newton; 35 Guy Graham; 26 Ryan King; 12 Liam Cooper; 16 Tom Wilkinson. Subs (all used): 13 Dion Aiye; 17 Tom Walker; 20 Jake Bradley; 27 Andrew Dawson.
Tries: Walker (38), Jouffret (39, 49), McNally (41), Taylor (54), Walmsley (63); **Goals:** Walmsley 6/7.
Rugby Leaguer & League Express Men of the Match:
Bulls: Steve Crossley; *Whitehaven:* Dion Aiye.
Penalty count: 5-7; **Half-time:** 16-12;
Referee: Aaron Moore; **Attendance:** 5,340.

DEWSBURY RAMS 21 OLDHAM 14

RAMS: 4 Matty Fleming; 2 Andy Gabriel; 3 Adam Ryder; 18 Davey Dixon; 27 Lewis Carr; 6 Paul Sykes; 7 Liam Finn; 32 Jimmy Beckett; 14 Sam Day; 10 Tom Garratt; 15 Keenen Tomlinson; 12 Michael Knowles; 23 Jon Magrin. Subs (all used): 24 Jordan Schofield; 31 Robson Stevens; 33 Dom Speakman; 38 Matthew Fletcher.
Tries: Carr (10), Ryder (17, 73), Knowles (80);
Goals: Sykes 2/4; **Field goal:** Sykes (76).
Sin bin: Speakman (79) - fighting.
OLDHAM: 2 Tommy Brierley; 27 Ben Holcroft; 24 Max Roberts; 5 Ryan Ince; 1 Dan Abram; 6 Lewis Charnock; 22 Harvey Spence; 16 Tyler Dupree; 9 Gareth Owen; 17 Liam Kirk; 11 Danny Langtree; 12 Liam Bent; 25 Danny Bridge. Subs (all used): 13 Martyn Reilly; 15 Luke Nelmes; 33 Jamie Abram; 35 Brad Jinks.
Tries: D Abram (23), Bridge (38); **Goals:** D Abram 3/3.
Sin bin: Charnock (79) - fighting.
Rugby Leaguer & League Express Men of the Match:
Rams: Adam Ryder; *Oldham:* Luke Nelmes.
Penalty count: 4-2; **Half-time:** 8-12;
Referee: Matt Rossleigh; **Attendance:** 827.

FEATHERSTONE ROVERS 78 SHEFFIELD EAGLES 10

ROVERS: 36 Alex Walker; 5 Gareth Gale; 4 Josh Hardcastle; 1 Craig Hall; 3 Kris Welham; 9 Fa'amanu Brown; 6 Tom Holmes; 8 Craig Kopczak; 21 Dean Parata; 13 James Lockwood; 11 Brett Ferres; 20 Frankie Halton; 19 Callum Field. Subs (all used): 7 Dane Chisholm; 15 John Davies; 16 Jack Bussey; 35 Gadwin Springer.
Tries: Hall (2, 24, 51, 57, 65), Brown (19), Halton (22, 26, 32), Ferres (43, 69), Bussey (47), Gale (49, 77), Hardcastle (55); **Goals:** Hall 9/15.
EAGLES: 1 Josh Guzdek; 2 Rob Worrincy; 24 Ryan Johnson; 4 James Glover; 5 Ryan Millar; 13 Aaron Brown; 23 Harry Tyson-Wilson; 8 Scott Wheeldon; 14 Greg Burns; 11 Brad Knowles; 15 Olly Davies; 12 Joel Farrell; 32 Evan Hodgson. Subs (all used): 3 Connor Bower; 9 James Davey; 19 Blake Broadbent; 18 Tyler Dickinson.
Tries: Johnson (14), Worrincy (80);
Goals: Guzdek 1/1, Wheeldon 0/1.
Rugby Leaguer & League Express Men of the Match:
Rovers: Craig Hall; *Eagles:* Scott Wheeldon.
Penalty count: 4-6; **Half-time:** 32-6;
Referee: Brad Milligan; **Attendance:** 1,750.

HALIFAX PANTHERS 10 BATLEY BULLDOGS 12

PANTHERS: 4 James Woodburn-Hall; 5 James Saltonstall; 3 Greg Worthington; 21 Zack McComb; 19 Conor McGrath; 1 Scott Grix; 7 Connor Robinson; 25 Adam Tangata; 9 Brandon Moore; 10 Daniel Murray; 11 Matt Garside; 17 Ben Kavanagh; 13 Jacob Fairbank. Subs (all used): 12 Ed Barber; 8 Elliot Morris; 14 Kevin Larroyer; 18 Connor Davies.
Tries: Saltonstall (9), McGrath (45); **Goals:** Robinson 1/2.
BULLDOGS: 1 Luke Hooley; 5 Johnny Campbell; 22 Dale Morton; 3 Kieran Buchanan; 21 Jodie Broughton; 6 Ben White; 7 Tom Gilmore; 15 Jack Blagbrough; 31 Oli Burton; 10 Toby Everett; 11 Dane Manning; 12 Lucas Walshaw; 26 Nyle Flynn. Subs (all used): 14 Elliot Kaufman; 18 George Senior; 16 Michael Ward; 19 Tom Lillycrop.
Tries: Walshaw (27), Campbell (40); **Goals:** Gilmore 2/2.
Rugby Leaguer & League Express Men of the Match:
Panthers: Conor McGrath; *Bulldogs:* Tom Gilmore.
Penalty count: 4-6; **Half-time:** 4-12;
Referee: Jack Smith; **Attendance:** 2,216.

SWINTON LIONS 16 WIDNES VIKINGS 26

LIONS: 22 Geronimo Doyle; 21 Ben Heyes; 11 Rhodri Lloyd; 1 Mike Butt; 39 Reece Hamlett; 6 Martyn Ridyard; 12 Nick Gregson; 14 Billy Brickhill; 9 Luke Waterworth; 10 Lewis Hatton; 3 Mitch Cox; 13 Will Hope; 15 Louis Brogan. Subs (all used): 24 Paul Nash; 19 Deane Meadows; 40 Ronan Michael; 26 Jordan Brown.
Tries: Doyle (23), Cox (47), Hamlett (77);
Goals: Ridyard 2/3.
VIKINGS: 1 Jack Owens; 5 Deon Cross; 18 Lloyd Roby; 4 Steve Tyrer; 2 Jayden Hatton; 23 Lewis Else; 17 Joe Lyons; 13 Kenny Baker; 30 Lewis Hulme; 24 Will Tilleke; 19 Joe Edge; 12 Adam Lawton; 7 Matty Smith. Subs (all used): 10 Matt Cook; 31 Aiden Roden; 8 Paul Clough; 3 Jake Spedding.
Tries: Lawton (27), Cross (31), Tyrer (39), Hatton (53), Hulme (55); **Goals:** Owens 3/5.
Rugby Leaguer & League Express Men of the Match:
Lions: Geronimo Doyle; *Vikings:* Joe Lyons.
Penalty count: 7-4; **Half-time:** 4-14;
Referee: Gareth Hewer; **Attendance:** 1,358.

YORK CITY KNIGHTS 32 LONDON BRONCOS 22

CITY KNIGHTS: 26 Myles Harrison; 25 AJ Towse; 30 Tyme Dow-Nikau; 4 Ryan Atkins; 2 Jason Bass; 1 Matty Marsh; 42 Aidan McGowan; 15 James Green; 9 Will Jubb; 10 Jack Teanby; 12 Sam Scott; 27 Toby Warren; 11 Chris Clarkson. Subs (all used): 28 Danny Washbrook; 16 Marcus Stock; 20 Tim Spears; 17 Danny Kirmond.
Tries: Clarkson (14), Bass (19), Kirmond (34), Marsh (43), Dow-Nikau (54), Washbrook (59);
Goals: Harrison 3/6, Green 1/1.
BRONCOS: 3 Chris Hankinson; 17 Abbas Miski; 5 Ed Chamberlain; 23 Josh Hodson; 2 Tuoyo Egodo; 22 Oliver Leyland; 1 James Meadows; 10 Greg Richards; 9 Matty Fozard; 28 Titus Gwaze; 4 Will Lovell; 11 Sadiq Adebiyi; 13 Josh Walters. Subs (all used): 16 Dan Hindmarsh; 31 Pat Moran; 25 Jacob Jones; 7 Jarrod Sammut.
Tries: Richards (11), Hankinson (67), Jones (71), Gwaze (78); **Goals:** Hankinson 3/4.
Sin bin: Sammut (80) - fighting.
Rugby Leaguer & League Express Men of the Match:
City Knights: Matty Marsh; *Broncos:* Titus Gwaze.
Penalty count: 4-6; **Half-time:** 14-6;
Referee: Scott Mikalauskas; **Attendance:** 2,782.

POSTPONED GAMES
(all subsequently not rearranged)

ROUND 4
Toulouse Olympique v Featherstone Rovers

ROUND 15
Sheffield Eagles v York City Knights

ROUND 16
Bradford Bulls v Sheffield Eagles

ROUND 18
Newcastle Thunder v London Broncos

CANCELLED GAMES

ROUND 8
Toulouse Olympique v Newcastle Thunder

ROUND 10
Toulouse Olympique v Bradford Bulls

ROUND 12
Toulouse Olympique v Oldham

ROUND 14
London Broncos v Widnes Vikings
Toulouse Olympique v Dewsbury Rams

ROUND 17
Toulouse Olympique v Halifax Panthers

ROUND 19
Toulouse Olympique v Batley Bulldogs

ROUND 21
Toulouse Olympique v York City Knights

(Awarded game shown with relevant round on earlier page)

Toulouse's Johnathon Ford dives past Featherstone's Alex Walker to score in the Million Pound Game

THE ELIMINATORS

Saturday 25th September 2021

BATLEY BULLDOGS 23 BRADFORD BULLS 10

BULLDOGS: 1 Luke Hooley; 5 Johnny Campbell; 22 Dale Morton; 3 Kieran Buchanan; 29 Greg Johnson; 6 Ben White; 7 Tom Gilmore; 13 James Brown; 24 Ben Kaye; 15 Jack Blagbrough; 12 Lucas Walshaw; 11 Dane Manning; 26 Nyle Flynn. Subs (all used): 9 Alistair Leak; 14 Elliot Hall; 16 Michael Ward; 19 Tom Lillycrop.
Tries: Kaye (16), Gilmore (36), Hall (73);
Goals: Gilmore 5/5; **Field goal:** Gilmore (77).
BULLS: 53 Elliot Kear; 2 Joe Brown; 3 Rhys Evans; 4 Ross Oakes; 19 David Foggin-Johnston; 6 Danny Brough; 7 Jordan Lilley; 24 Ben Evans; 9 Thomas Doyle; 10 Steve Crossley; 11 Adam Rooks; 12 Aaron Murphy; 13 Sam Hallas. Subs (all used): 14 George Flanagan; 15 Dan Fleming; 18 Ebon Scurr; 23 Anthony Walker.
Tries: Brown (54), Lilley (64); **Goals:** Brough 1/2.
Rugby Leaguer & League Express Men of the Match:
Bulldogs: Tom Gilmore; *Bulls:* Ross Oakes.
Penalty count: 4-4; **Half-time:** 16-0;
Referee: James Child; **Attendance:** 2,005.

HALIFAX PANTHERS 24 WHITEHAVEN 20

PANTHERS: 4 James Woodburn-Hall; 5 James Saltonstall; 3 Greg Worthington; 21 Zack McComb; 19 Conor McGrath; 1 Scott Grix; 6 Liam Harris; 25 Adam Tangata; 9 Brandon Moore; 10 Daniel Murray; 11 Matt Garside; 17 Ben Kavanagh; 13 Jacob Fairbank. Subs (all used): 7 Connor Robinson; 8 Elliot Morris; 14 Kevin Larroyer; 18 Connor Davies.
Tries: McGrath (10, 39), Woodburn-Hall (31);
Goals: Harris 2/3, Woodburn-Hall 1/1, Robinson 1/1.
WHITEHAVEN: 2 Lachlan Walmsley; 5 Andrew Bulman; 3 Chris Taylor; 6 Karl Dixon; 23 Jason Mossop; 32 Louis Jouffret; 7 Nikau Williams; 33 Andy Thornley; 18 James Newton; 35 Guy Graham; 26 Ryan King; 12 Liam Cooper; 16 Tom Wilkinson. Subs (all used): 13 Dion Aiye; 17 Tom Walker; 20 Jake Bradley; 27 Andrew Dawson.
Tries: Cooper (22), Bulman (44, 79), King (53);
Goals: Jouffret 2/2, Walmsley 0/2.

Rugby Leaguer & League Express Men of the Match:
Panthers: Scott Grix; *Whitehaven:* Louis Jouffret.
Penalty count: 2-2; **Half-time:** 22-6;
Referee: Chris Kendall; **Attendance:** 1,289.

SEMI-FINALS

Saturday 2nd October 2021

TOULOUSE OLYMPIQUE 51 BATLEY BULLDOGS 12

OLYMPIQUE: 1 Mark Kheirallah; 2 Jy Hitchcox; 3 Junior Vaivai; 4 Mathieu Jussaume; 21 Latrell Schaumkel; 31 Tony Gigot; 6 Johnathon Ford; 8 Remi Casty; 9 Lloyd White; 10 Harrison Hansen; 16 Joe Bretherton; 12 Dominique Peyroux; 13 Anthony Marion. Subs (all used): 14 Eloi Pelissier; 17 Joseph Paulo; 18 Mitch Garbutt; 23 Justin Sangare.
Tries: Casty (10), Gigot (15), Bretherton (21), Vaivai (42, 79), Kheirallah (45), Sangare (52), Jussaume (58), Garbutt (66);
Goals: Kheirallah 7/9; **Field goal:** Gigot (78).
BULLDOGS: 1 Luke Hooley; 5 Johnny Campbell; 12 Lucas Walshaw; 3 Kieran Buchanan; 29 Greg Johnson; 6 Ben White; 7 Tom Gilmore; 15 Jack Blagbrough; 9 Alistair Leak; 10 Toby Everett; 11 Dane Manning; 26 Nyle Flynn; 13 James Brown. Subs (all used): 8 Adam Gledhill; 14 Elliot Hall; 16 Michael Ward; 21 Jodie Broughton.
Tries: Manning (17), Johnson (28); **Goals:** Gilmore 2/2.
Rugby Leaguer & League Express Men of the Match:
Olympique: Mark Kheirallah; *Bulldogs:* Tom Gilmore.
Penalty count: 8-4; **Half-time:** 16-12;
Referee: Liam Moore; **Attendance:** 6,871.

FEATHERSTONE ROVERS 42 HALIFAX PANTHERS 10

ROVERS: 36 Alex Walker; 5 Gareth Gale; 4 Josh Hardcastle; 3 Kris Welham; 1 Craig Hall; 6 Tom Holmes; 9 Fa'amanu Brown; 8 Craig Kopczak; 14 Connor Jones; 13 James Lockwood; 11 Brett Ferres; 20 Frankie Halton; 19 Callum Field. Subs (all used): 7 Dane Chisholm; 15 John Davies; 16 Jack Bussey; 18 Luke Cooper.
Tries: Halton (6), Kopczak (20), Ferres (52), Hardcastle (55), Jones (57, 70), Welham (63);
Goals: Hall 7/8.

Sin bin: Holmes (10) - late challenge; Cooper (73) - late challenge.
PANTHERS: 4 James Woodburn-Hall; 19 Conor McGrath; 21 Zack McComb; 3 Greg Worthington; 5 James Saltonstall; 6 Liam Harris; 1 Scott Grix; 25 Adam Tangata; 9 Brandon Moore; 10 Daniel Murray; 17 Ben Kavanagh; 11 Matt Garside; 13 Jacob Fairbank. Subs (all used): 7 Connor Robinson; 8 Elliot Morris; 14 Kevin Larroyer; 24 Ben Tibbs.
Tries: McGrath (11), Harris (67);
Goals: Harris 0/1, Robinson 1/1.
Sin bin: Tibbs (76) - kicking the ball away.
Rugby Leaguer & League Express Men of the Match:
Rovers: Frankie Halton; *Panthers:* Scott Grix.
Penalty count: 5-7; **Half-time:** 14-4;
Referee: Robert Hicks; **Attendance:** 2,084.

MILLION POUND GAME

Sunday 10th October 2021

TOULOUSE OLYMPIQUE 34 FEATHERSTONE ROVERS 12

OLYMPIQUE: 1 Mark Kheirallah; 2 Jy Hitchcox; 4 Mathieu Jussaume; 3 Junior Vaivai; 21 Latrell Schaumkel; 6 Johnathon Ford; 31 Tony Gigot; 10 Harrison Hansen; 9 Lloyd White; 8 Remi Casty; 12 Dominique Peyroux; 16 Joe Bretherton; 13 Anthony Marion. Subs (all used): 14 Eloi Pelissier; 17 Joseph Paulo; 18 Mitch Garbutt; 23 Justin Sangare.
Tries: Jussaume (6, 65), Schaumkel (19), Hansen (74), Ford (80); **Goals:** Kheirallah 7/8, Casty 0/1.
Sin bin: White (79) - kicking out.
ROVERS: 36 Alex Walker; 1 Craig Hall; 4 Josh Hardcastle; 3 Kris Welham; 5 Gareth Gale; 7 Dane Chisholm; 9 Fa'amanu Brown; 8 Craig Kopczak; 14 Connor Jones; 13 James Lockwood; 11 Brett Ferres; 20 Frankie Halton; 19 Callum Field. Subs (all used): 15 John Davies; 16 Jack Bussey; 21 Dean Parata; 24 Dale Ferguson.
Tries: Ferres (52), Davies (68); **Goals:** Hall 2/2.
Rugby Leaguer & League Express Men of the Match:
Olympique: Mathieu Jussaume; *Rovers:* Brett Ferres.
Penalty count: 7-7; **Half-time:** 16-0;
Referee: Robert Hicks; **Attendance:** 9,235.

LEAGUE 1 2021
Club by Club

BARROW RAIDERS

DATE	FIXTURE	RESULT	SCORERS	LGE	ATT
20/3/21	Oldham (a) (CCR1)	L20-6	t:Shaw g:Shaw	N/A	BCD
9/5/21	Coventry (a)	W20-38	t:Mossop,Carter(2),Tyson,Forster,S Toal,A Walne g:Carter(5)	3rd	BCD
16/5/21	Keighley (h)	W40-18	t:Cresswell,Stack(2),Miloudi,Dallimore,Harrison g:Carter(5),Dallimore(3)	2nd	BCD
23/5/21	Hunslet (a)	W6-29	t:Carter,Dallimore,Ritson(2),Johnston g:Dallimore(4) fg:Dallimore	2nd	452
30/5/21	North Wales (h)	W44-8	t:A Walne,Tyson(2),Ritson,Carter,Stack,S Toal,Cresswell g:Carter(6)	1st	1,915
5/6/21	West Wales (a)	W10-60	t:Mossop(2),Ritson(3),Terrill,Morrow,Duffy,Hulme,Stack,Tyson g:Johnston(5),Ritson(3)	1st	BCD
12/6/21	Rochdale (h)	W40-4	t:Ritson(3),Stack,Bustin,Forster g:Dallimore(8)	1st	1,758
19/6/21	London Skolars (a)	W14-24	t:Carter,Cresswell,Swarbrick,Ritson g:Dallimore(4)	1st	391
27/6/21	Workington (h)	D24-24	t:Dallimore,A Walne,Dowsett g:Dallimore(6)	1st	3,146
4/7/21	Doncaster (h)	W31-6	t:Dallimore,Stack,Johnston(2),J Walne g:Dallimore(2),Shaw(3) fg:Johnston	1st	2,005
11/7/21	Keighley (a)	L40-12	t:Stack g:Dallimore(4)	1st	572
25/7/21	Coventry (h)	W40-12	t:Hulme,Mossop,Shaw,Bustin,Swarbrick,Forster(2) g:Dallimore(6)	1st	1,862
8/8/21	Hunslet (h)	W40-10	t:Johnston(2),Ritson(4),Cresswell g:Shaw(6)	1st	1,918
15/8/21	North Wales (a)	L23-10	t:Tyson,Bustin g:Dallimore	2nd	727
22/8/21	Doncaster (a)	L26-18	t:Tyson,S Toal g:Dallimore(5)	2nd	1,019
29/8/21	London Skolars (h)	W38-24	t:Miloudi,Cresswell,Dallimore,D Toal,Duffy,Hulme,Morrow g:Dallimore(5)	1st	1,486
5/9/21	Rochdale (h)	W30-32	t:Cresswell,Ritson,Carter,Hulme g:Shaw(8)	1st	1,064
11/9/21	West Wales (h)	W76-0	t:Cresswell,Ritson(7),Bustin,Stack(2),Emslie,Hulme,S Toal g:Shaw(10)	1st	1,922

Workington (a) (R12) game was postponed, and not rearranged

		APP		TRIES		GOALS		FG		PTS	
	D.O.B.	ALL	L1	ALL	L1	ALL	L1	ALL	L1	ALL	L1
Callum Bustin	12/8/97	2(14)	2(13)	4	4	0	0	0	0	16	16
Jake Carter	24/11/98	13(2)	13(1)	6	6	16	16	0	0	56	56
Bradd Crellin	2/7/89	3(3)	3(3)	0	0	0	0	0	0	0	0
Luke Cresswell	5/5/95	15	15	7	7	0	0	0	0	28	28
Jamie Dallimore	20/8/88	12	11	5	5	48	48	1	1	117	117
Sam Dowsett	2/11/92	2(9)	2(9)	1	1	0	0	0	0	4	4
Ryan Duffy	13/5/93	(13)	(12)	2	2	0	0	0	0	8	8
Jake Emmitt	4/10/88	4(1)	4(1)	0	0	0	0	0	0	0	0
Charlie Emslie	30/10/00	5(3)	5(3)	1	1	0	0	0	0	4	4
Carl Forster	4/6/92	18	17	4	4	0	0	0	0	16	16
Ben Harrison	24/2/88	5	4	1	1	0	0	0	0	4	4
Tom Hopkins	21/12/92	13	13	0	0	0	0	0	0	0	0
Declan Hulme	14/1/93	7(3)	6(3)	5	5	0	0	0	0	20	20
Ryan Johnston	16/3/98	10(4)	9(4)	5	5	5	5	1	1	31	31
Carl McBain	30/9/89	(5)	(5)	0	0	0	0	0	0	0	0
Hakim Miloudi	26/6/93	8	8	2	2	0	0	0	0	8	8
Danny Morrow	30/4/90	8(2)	8(2)	2	2	0	0	0	0	8	8
Nathan Mossop	21/2/88	15(2)	15(2)	4	4	0	0	0	0	16	16
Theerapol Ritson	7/1/96	15	14	22	22	3	3	0	0	94	94
Ryan Shaw	27/2/92	9	8	2	1	28	27	0	0	64	58
Jarrad Stack	13/2/88	15	14	9	9	0	0	0	0	36	36
Harry Swarbrick	12/2/97	4(1)	3(1)	2	2	0	0	0	0	8	8
Connor Terrill	3/7/01	5	5	1	1	0	0	0	0	4	4
Dan Toal	22/9/89	1(9)	1(8)	1	1	0	0	0	0	4	4
Shane Toal	11/11/95	16	15	4	4	0	0	0	0	16	16
Mark Tyson	31/5/90	10(1)	9(1)	6	6	0	0	0	0	24	24
Adam Walne	3/10/90	12	11	3	3	0	0	0	0	12	12
Jordan Walne	28/12/92	5	4	1	1	0	0	0	0	4	4
Gary Wheeler	30/9/89	2	2	0	0	0	0	0	0	0	0

Theerapol Ritson

'L1' totals include League 1 games only; 'All' totals also include Challenge Cup

CLUB RECORDS	**Highest score:** 138-0 v Nottingham City, 27/11/94 **Highest score against:** 0-90 v Leeds, 11/2/90 **Record attendance:** 21,651 v Salford, 15/4/38
MATCH RECORDS	**Tries:** 7 Theerapol Ritson v West Wales, 11/9/2021 **Goals:** 17 Darren Carter v Nottingham City, 27/11/94 **Points:** 42 Darren Carter v Nottingham City, 27/11/94
SEASON RECORDS	**Tries:** 50 Jim Lewthwaite 1956-57 **Goals:** 135 Joe Ball 1956-57 **Points:** 323 Jamie Rooney 2010
CAREER RECORDS	**Tries:** 352 Jim Lewthwaite 1943-57 **Goals:** 1,099 *(inc 63fg)* Darren Holt 1998-2002; 2004-2009; 2012
	Points: 2,403 Darren Holt 1998-2002; 2004-2009; 2012 **Appearances:** 500 Jim Lewthwaite 1943-57

COVENTRY BEARS

DATE	FIXTURE	RESULT	SCORERS	LGE	ATT
9/5/21	Barrow (h)	L20-38	t:Hill(2),Bowring,L Welham g:Coates(2)	8th	BCD
15/5/21	West Wales (a)	W10-36	t:Ryan(2),Towse,L Welham,Hill,Sherratt g:Coates(6)	5th	BCD
23/5/21	London Skolars (h)	L26-44	t:L Welham,Sherratt,Scott,Coates(2) g:Scott(3)	6th	210
30/5/21	Rochdale (h)	W38-30	t:Scott(2),Williams,L Welham,Hill,Kaufman,M Welham g:Coates(5)	7th	232
6/6/21	North Wales (a)	L36-12	t:Scott,Townsend g:Coates(2)	7th	BCD
13/6/21	Workington (h)	L12-30	t:Sherratt,Ho g:Coates(2)	7th	198
27/6/21	Doncaster (h)	L16-34	t:Rance,Scott(2) g:Coates(2)	8th	275
4/7/21	Hunslet (h)	W46-44	t:Wallis,Dawson(3),L Welham,Cullimore,Scott,Sherratt g:Coates(7)	8th	255
16/7/21	Keighley (h)	W24-18	t:Coates,L Welham,Hamilton,Bowring g:Coates(4)	8th	387
25/7/21	Barrow (a)	L40-12	t:Coates,L Welham g:Coates(2)	8th	1,862
31/7/21	London Skolars (a)	W12-14	t:L Welham,Scott g:Coates(3)	8th	190
8/8/21	North Wales (h)	L16-32	t:Freeman,Hudson,Kaufman g:Coates(2)	8th	378
15/8/21	Keighley (a)	L46-18	t:Freeman,Coates,Clavering g:Coates(2),Scott	8th	1,028
22/8/21	West Wales (h)	W50-18	t:Freeman,Rance(2),Sherratt,Hudson,Hill(2),L Welham,M Welham,Scott g:Coates(5)	8th	280
29/8/21	Hunslet (a)	L32-30	t:Ryan,Freeman,Bowring,M Welham,Coates g:Coates(5)	8th	353
5/9/21	Doncaster (a)	L18-13	t:Coates,Williams g:Coates(2) fg:Coates	8th	1,138
12/9/21	Rochdale (a)	L50-22	t:Bull,Scott,Coates,Cullimore g:Coates(3)	8th	693

Workington (a) (R10) game was postponed, and not rearranged

		APP		TRIES		GOALS		FG		PTS	
	D.O.B.	ALL	L1	ALL	L1	ALL	L1	ALL	L1	ALL	L1
Stefanos Bastas	22/12/93	(3)	(3)	0	0	0	0	0	0	0	0
Delaine Bedward	28/6/01	(3)	(3)	0	0	0	0	0	0	0	0
Sam Bowring	1/7/91	12(1)	12(1)	3	3	0	0	0	0	12	12
Will Budd	19/6/00	4(5)	4(5)	0	0	0	0	0	0	0	0
Jordan Bull	14/12/99	1	1	1	1	0	0	0	0	4	4
Jed Charlton	14/1/99	8	8	0	0	0	0	0	0	0	0
Brad Clavering	14/3/98	10	10	1	1	0	0	0	0	4	4
Dan Coates	30/8/99	17	17	8	8	54	54	1	1	141	141
Chris Cullimore	13/2/93	16	16	2	2	0	0	0	0	8	8
Jack Dawson	12/1/93	11(3)	11(3)	3	3	0	0	0	0	12	12
Josh Dunne	27/1/00	5(3)	5(3)	0	0	0	0	0	0	0	0
Hayden Freeman	20/8/97	7(1)	7(1)	4	4	0	0	0	0	16	16
Darius Hamilton	2/12/91	(5)	(5)	1	1	0	0	0	0	4	4
Nathan Hill	13/7/97	16	16	6	6	0	0	0	0	24	24
Bradley Ho	16/12/00	4(7)	4(7)	1	1	0	0	0	0	4	4
Kieran Hudson	13/6/00	(2)	(2)	2	2	0	0	0	0	8	8
Harry Kaufman	20/12/91	2(6)	2(6)	2	2	0	0	0	0	8	8
Ryan Langton	16/4/96	3(11)	3(11)	0	0	0	0	0	0	0	0
Jordan Paga	23/5/01	(1)	(1)	0	0	0	0	0	0	0	0
Reece Rance	17/7/93	17	17	3	3	0	0	0	0	12	12
Peter Ryan	25/2/95	13(1)	13(1)	3	3	0	0	0	0	12	12
Dave Scott	8/6/93	17	17	10	10	4	4	0	0	48	48
Brad Sheridan	24/3/94	1(1)	1(1)	0	0	0	0	0	0	0	0
Kieran Sherratt	15/11/95	15	15	5	5	0	0	0	0	20	20
Connor Terrill	3/7/01	(1)	(1)	0	0	0	0	0	0	0	0
Elliot Townsend	21/1/96	2(6)	2(6)	1	1	0	0	0	0	4	4
AJ Towse	19/8/03	2	2	1	1	0	0	0	0	4	4
Elliot Wallis	10/5/00	6	6	1	1	0	0	0	0	4	4
Liam Welham	11/11/88	16	16	9	9	0	0	0	0	36	36
Matt Welham	1/2/93	11	11	3	3	0	0	0	0	12	12
Kadeem Williams	23/3/95	4	4	2	2	0	0	0	0	8	8
Elliott Windley	9/7/99	1(8)	1(8)	0	0	0	0	0	0	0	0

Dave Scott

CLUB RECORDS	**Highest score:** 64-6 v West Wales, 25/7/2018 **Highest score against:** 6-98 v Keighley, 6/5/2018 **Record attendance:** 1,465 v Bradford, 30/6/2018
MATCH RECORDS	**Tries:** 3 *(11 players)* **Goals:** 8 Connor Robinson v Hemel, 19/4/2015; Ben Stead v West Wales, 25/7/2018 **Points:** 22 Dan Parker v London Skolars, 7/6/2015
SEASON RECORDS	**Tries:** 17 Elliot Hall 2019 **Goals:** 61 Ben Stead 2018 **Points:** 141 Dan Coates 2021
CAREER RECORDS	**Tries:** 41 Hayden Freeman 2016-2021 **Goals:** 61 Ben Stead 2018 **Points:** 164 Hayden Freeman 2016-2021 **Appearances:** 106 Chris Barratt 2015-2019

DONCASTER

DATE	FIXTURE	RESULT	SCORERS	LGE	ATT
9/5/21	Keighley (a)	L44-18	t:Cross,L Johnson,Beharrell g:Boas(2),Beharrell	9th	BCD
16/5/21	Rochdale (h)	W30-22	t:Douglas,Tali,Greensmith(2),Smeaton g:Beharrell(5)	8th	BCD
23/5/21	West Wales (h)	W62-24	t:Beharrell,Halliday(2),Tali,Smeaton,Peltier,Douglas,York(2),Greensmith, Holdstock g:Beharrell(9)	4th	784
30/5/21	Workington (a)	W24-26	t:Peltier,Beharrell,Halliday,Holdstock g:Beharrell(5)	3rd	942
6/6/21	London Skolars (h)	W46-12	t:Tali,Beharrell(2),L Johnson,Bravo,Greensmith,Smeaton,B Johnston g:Beharrell(7)	3rd	882
13/6/21	North Wales (a)	W0-68	t:Taulapapa(2),Doherty(2),Greensmith(3),L Johnson,B Johnston,Smeaton, Foster(2),Holdstock g:Beharrell(3),Doherty(5)	2nd	BCD
20/6/21	Hunslet (a)	D18-18	t:L Johnson,York,Beharrell g:Beharrell(3)	3rd	527
27/6/21	Coventry (a)	W16-34	t:Taulapapa,York,Beharrell(2),Douglas,Halliday g:Beharrell(5)	2nd	275
4/7/21	Barrow (a)	L31-6	t:Foster g:Beharrell	3rd	2,005
16/7/21	London Skolars (a)	D16-16	t:Smeaton,Doherty,Howe g:Beharrell(2)	3rd	575
1/8/21	Hunslet (h)	L24-46	t:Ward,Tali,York(2) g:Beharrell(4)	3rd	1,179
7/8/21	West Wales (a)	D24-24	t:York,Sweeting,Bravo,Dixon,Halliday g:Beharrell(2)	3rd	180
15/8/21	Rochdale (a)	L44-8	t:Tali(2)	4th	882
22/8/21	Barrow (h)	W26-18	t:Beharrell,Tindall,McConnell,Tali g:Beharrell(3),Sweeting(2)	4th	1,019
29/8/21	Workington (h)	W22-12	t:York,Halliday(2),Tindall,L Johnson g:Sweeting	4th	948
5/9/21	Coventry (h)	W18-13	t:Tali(2),L Johnson g:Sweeting(3)	3rd	1,138
12/9/21	Keighley (h)	L26-28	t:Foster,Halliday,Sweeting(2) g:Sweeting(5)	5th	738
19/9/21	Hunslet (h) (EPO)	W31-10	t:Smeaton,Douglas(2),L Johnson,Sweeting g:Beharrell(5) fg:Beharrell	N/A	547
26/9/21	North Wales (a) (ESF)	W34-48	t:Tindall,Ollett,Peltier,Douglas,Cockayne,Tali,Beharrell,Sweeting g:Beharrell(8)	N/A	432
3/10/21	Keighley (a) (PF)	W26-28	t:Holdstock,Beharrell,L Johnson(2),Tali g:Beharrell(2),Sweeting(2)	N/A	1,128
10/10/21	Workington (a) (POF)	L36-12	t:L Johnson,Greensmith g:Beharrell(2)	N/A	2,997

North Wales (h) (R11) game was postponed, and not rearranged

		APP		TRIES		GOALS		FG		PTS	
	D.O.B.	ALL	L1	ALL	L1	ALL	L1	ALL	L1	ALL	L1
Matty Beharrell	29/3/94	17	17	11	11	67	67	1	1	179	179
Watson Boas	8/11/94	5	5	0	0	2	2	0	0	4	4
Ryan Boyle	17/10/87	10(2)	10(2)	0	0	0	0	0	0	0	0
Zach Braham	14/1/95	8(1)	8(1)	0	0	0	0	0	0	0	0
Danny Bravo	25/10/90	5(4)	5(4)	2	2	0	0	0	0	8	8
Jordan Bull	14/12/99	1	1	0	0	0	0	0	0	0	0
Ben Cockayne	20/7/83	7(2)	7(2)	1	1	0	0	0	0	4	4
Kieran Cross	18/2/95	1	1	1	1	0	0	0	0	4	4
Ryan Dixon	11/8/93	(2)	(2)	1	1	0	0	0	0	4	4
Sam Doherty	14/11/93	6	6	3	3	5	5	0	0	22	22
Brandon Douglas	17/8/97	11(2)	11(2)	6	6	0	0	0	0	24	24
Joe Fella	31/1/00	(1)	(1)	0	0	0	0	0	0	0	0
Brad Foster	28/8/95	15(1)	15(1)	4	4	0	0	0	0	16	16
Ollie Greensmith	3/12/99	16	16	8	8	0	0	0	0	32	32
Tom Halliday	2/2/97	17	17	8	8	0	0	0	0	32	32
Alex Holdstock	16/6/01	7(11)	7(11)	4	4	0	0	0	0	16	16
Ben Howe	17/1/01	2(1)	2(1)	1	1	0	0	0	0	4	4
Liam Johnson	12/5/97	15(3)	15(3)	10	10	0	0	0	0	40	40
Ben Johnston	8/3/92	9(6)	9(6)	2	2	0	0	0	0	8	8
Loui McConnell	21/11/99	(4)	(4)	1	1	0	0	0	0	4	4
Anesu Mudoti	19/1/01	4(6)	4(6)	0	0	0	0	0	0	0	0
Aaron Ollett	19/11/92	17(3)	17(3)	1	1	0	0	0	0	4	4
Ross Peltier	24/4/92	1(14)	1(14)	3	3	0	0	0	0	12	12
Sam Smeaton	26/10/88	20	20	6	6	0	0	0	0	24	24
Russ Spiers	28/4/91	1	1	0	0	0	0	0	0	0	0
Jake Sweeting	15/12/99	9(1)	9(1)	5	5	13	13	0	0	46	46
Jason Tali	7/7/89	19	19	11	11	0	0	0	0	44	44
Misi Taulapapa	25/1/82	12	12	3	3	0	0	0	0	12	12
Liam Tindall	27/9/01	8	8	3	3	0	0	0	0	12	12
Bobby Tyson-Wilson	6/11/94	(1)	(1)	0	0	0	0	0	0	0	0
Harry Tyson-Wilson	29/12/96	2	2	0	0	0	0	0	0	0	0
Robbie Ward	27/10/95	1	1	1	1	0	0	0	0	4	4
Ross Whitmore	9/2/00	12(8)	12(8)	0	0	0	0	0	0	0	0
Brandan Wilkinson	7/9/97	6(1)	6(1)	0	0	0	0	0	0	0	0
Aaron York	7/4/99	9(10)	9(10)	8	8	0	0	0	0	32	32

'L1' totals include regular season & play-offs

Matty Beharrell

CLUB RECORDS	**Highest score:** 102-6 v West Wales, 15/7/2018 **Highest score against:** 4-90 v Widnes, 10/6/2007
MATCH RECORDS	**Record attendance:** 10,000 v Bradford, 16/2/52 *(York Road)*; 6,528 v Castleford, 12/4/2007 *(Keepmoat Stadium)* **Tries:** 6 Kane Epati v Oldham, 30/7/2006; Lee Waterman v Sharlston, 24/3/2012 **Goals:** 15 Liam Harris v West Wales, 15/7/2018 **Points:** 38 Liam Harris v West Wales, 15/7/2018
SEASON RECORDS	**Tries:** 36 Lee Waterman 2012 **Goals:** 129 Jonny Woodcock 2002 **Points:** 306 Jonny Woodcock 2002
CAREER RECORDS	**Tries:** 112 Mark Roache 1985-97 **Goals:** 850 David Noble 1976-77; 1980-89; 1992 **Points:** 1,751 David Noble 1976-77; 1980-89; 1992 **Appearances:** 327 Audley Pennant 1980-83; 1985-97

HUNSLET

DATE	FIXTURE	RESULT	SCORERS	LGE	ATT
9/5/21	Workington (h)	L16-28	t:Andrade,Conroy,Chrimes g:Brambani(2)	6th	BCD
15/5/21	North Wales (a)	W18-26	t:Ashton,Jones,Hartley(2) g:Brambani(5)	7th	BCD
23/5/21	Barrow (h)	L6-29	t:Ashton g:Brambani	9th	452
30/5/21	Keighley (a)	L40-0		9th	683
6/6/21	Rochdale (h)	W36-22	t:A Brown(2),Rowe(2),McClean,Ashton g:Brambani(3),Coleman(3)	9th	483
12/6/21	London Skolars (a)	W10-62	t:Ashton(2),Gibbons(2),Halafihi(3),S Brown,Jones(2),Chrimes,Rowe g:Gibbons(7)	5th	370
20/6/21	Doncaster (h)	D18-18	t:Chrimes,Wood,Gibbons g:Gibbons(3)	5th	527
26/6/21	West Wales (a)	W12-38	t:Cooke,Ashton,Straugheir(2),S Brown,Andrade,Young g:Brambani(5)	5th	204
4/7/21	Coventry (a)	L46-44	t:Halafihi,Chrimes(3),A Brown(2),Hey,Young g:Brambani(6)	5th	255
11/7/21	North Wales (h)	L24-34	t:Andrade,Halafihi,Young,Chrimes g:Brambani(4)	7th	404
25/7/21	Keighley (h)	D20-20	t:Andrade(2),Halafihi g:Coleman(4)	7th	714
1/8/21	Doncaster (a)	W24-46	t:Wood,Chrimes(2),Cooke,Gibbons,Halafihi,Reittie,Andrade g:Gibbons(7)	6th	1,179
8/8/21	Barrow (a)	L40-10	t:Hartley,Young g:Gibbons	7th	1,918
15/8/21	London Skolars (h)	W38-10	t:Reittie,Chrimes,Straugheir,Coleman,Young,Andrade g:Coleman(7)	7th	435
22/8/21	Rochdale (a)	D34-34	t:Kidd,McClean,Coleman(2),Hartley,Young g:Coleman(5)	7th	822
29/8/21	Coventry (h)	W32-30	t:Kidd,Chapman-Smith,Coleman,Young,Straugheir,Halafihi g:Brambani(4)	6th	353
5/9/21	West Wales (h)	W82-6	t:Brambani,Hartley(3),Halafihi,Straugheir,Chrimes(3),Chapman-Smith, Whiteley(2),Young,Wray,Andrade g:Brambani(11)	6th	474
12/9/21	Workington (a)	W14-32	t:Wood,Rowe,Straugheir,Chapman-Smith,Young g:Brambani(6)	6th	1,397
19/9/21	Doncaster (a) (EPO)	L31-10	t:Reittie,Chrimes g:Brambani	N/A	547

		APP		TRIES		GOALS		FG		PTS	
	D.O.B.	ALL	L1	ALL	L1	ALL	L1	ALL	L1	ALL	L1
Jordan Andrade	24/1/92	2(16)	2(16)	8	8	0	0	0	0	32	32
Tom Ashton	20/6/92	8	8	6	6	0	0	0	0	24	24
AJ Boardman	11/11/89	1(1)	1(1)	0	0	0	0	0	0	0	0
Zach Braham	14/1/95	3	3	0	0	0	0	0	0	0	0
Dom Brambani	10/5/85	13	13	1	1	48	48	0	0	100	100
Alex Brown	28/8/87	7	7	4	4	0	0	0	0	16	16
Simon Brown	23/6/89	10	10	2	2	0	0	0	0	8	8
Reece Chapman-Smith	8/11/98	8	8	3	3	0	0	0	0	12	12
Matty Chrimes	2/11/97	16	16	14	14	0	0	0	0	56	56
Jy-mel Coleman	13/10/88	8(1)	8(1)	4	4	19	19	0	0	54	54
Nathan Conroy	6/3/95	4(9)	4(9)	1	1	0	0	0	0	4	4
Will Cooke	22/12/96	8	8	2	2	0	0	0	0	8	8
Liam Copland	5/6/93	1	1	0	0	0	0	0	0	0	0
Curtis Davies	17/1/97	1	1	0	0	0	0	0	0	0	0
Dave Gibbons	27/11/01	7(2)	7(2)	4	4	18	18	0	0	52	52
Vila Halafihi	24/1/94	14(1)	14(1)	9	9	0	0	0	0	36	36
Harvey Hallas	14/11/97	3(10)	3(10)	0	0	0	0	0	0	0	0
Kiedan Hartley	3/7/00	8	8	7	7	0	0	0	0	28	28
Brad Hey	4/9/94	12	12	1	1	0	0	0	0	4	4
Sion Jones	16/12/97	1(5)	1(5)	3	3	0	0	0	0	12	12
Aaron Jones-Bishop	18/1/90	3	3	0	0	0	0	0	0	0	0
Harry Kidd	12/6/95	14	14	2	2	0	0	0	0	8	8
Joe McClean	10/8/89	5(5)	5(5)	2	2	0	0	0	0	8	8
Frazer Morris	22/2/97	3(3)	3(3)	0	0	0	0	0	0	0	0
Wayne Reittie	21/1/88	16	16	3	3	0	0	0	0	12	12
Alex Rowe	11/3/85	11(7)	11(7)	4	4	0	0	0	0	16	16
George Senior	29/8/99	4	4	0	0	0	0	0	0	0	0
Duane Straugheir	29/9/89	14	14	6	6	0	0	0	0	24	24
Joe Summers	7/11/99	1(4)	1(4)	0	0	0	0	0	0	0	0
Jake Sweeting	15/12/99	1	1	0	0	0	0	0	0	0	0
Ben Tibbs	3/11/00	1	1	0	0	0	0	0	0	0	0
Niall Walker	21/4/97	3	3	0	0	0	0	0	0	0	0
Jimmy Watson	9/9/91	2	2	0	0	0	0	0	0	0	0
Harvey Whiteley	26/9/98	2(4)	2(4)	2	2	0	0	0	0	8	8
Mikey Wood	18/4/96	14	14	3	3	0	0	0	0	12	12
Lewis Wray	6/5/98	6(8)	6(8)	1	1	0	0	0	0	4	4
Lewis Young	1/7/95	12	12	9	9	0	0	0	0	36	36

'L1' totals include regular season & play-offs

Matty Chrimes

CLUB RECORDS	
MATCH RECORDS	**Highest score:** 86-0 v West Wales, 27/5/2018; 86-6 v West Wales, 4/8/2018 **Highest score against:** 0-82 v Bradford, 2/3/2003
	Record attendance: 24,700 v Wigan, 15/3/24 *(Parkside)*; 2,454 v Wakefield, 13/4/98 *(South Leeds Stadium)*
	Tries: 7 George Dennis v Bradford, 20/1/34 **Goals:** 13 Joe Sanderson v West Wales, 27/5/2018; Joe Sanderson v West Wales, 4/8/2018
SEASON RECORDS	**Points:** 30 Simon Wilson v Highfield, 21/1/96; Joe Sanderson v West Wales, 27/5/2018
CAREER RECORDS	**Tries:** 34 Alan Snowden 1956-57 **Goals:** 181 Billy Langton 1958-59 **Points:** 380 Billy Langton 1958-59
	Tries: 154 Fred Williamson 1943-55 **Goals:** 1,044 Billy Langton 1955-66 **Points:** 2,202 Billy Langton 1955-66 **Appearances:** 579 Geoff Gunney 1951-73

KEIGHLEY COUGARS

DATE	FIXTURE	RESULT	SCORERS	LGE	ATT
20/3/21	London Broncos (a) (CCR1) ●	L24-10	t:Agoro,Santi g:Miller	N/A	BCD
9/5/21	Doncaster (h)	W44-18	t:Q Laulu-Togaga'e,Graham(2),Levy,Seeley,Coventry,Santi,Miller g:Miller(6)	2nd	BCD
16/5/21	Barrow (a)	L40-18	t:Santi,Webster,Murrell g:Miller(3)	6th	BCD
23/5/21	Rochdale (h)	L36-43	t:Seeley,Murrell,Webster,Levy,Graham,Miller g:Miller(6)	5th	700
30/5/21	Hunslet (h)	W40-0	t:Moran,Miller,Graham(2),Santi(3) g:Miller(6)	4th	683
6/6/21	Workington (a)	L34-20	t:Slingsby(2),Santi,Prell g:Miller(2)	4th	942
13/6/21	West Wales (h)	W70-12	t:Webster,Parker(3),Prell(2),Miller(2),Slingsby,Q Laulu-Togaga'e(2),Levy,Darley g:Miller(9)	4th	463
27/6/21	London Skolars (h)	W34-22	t:Slingsby,Q Laulu-Togaga'e,Miller,Santi(2) g:Miller(7)	4th	548
4/7/21	North Wales (a)	L34-28	t:Graham,Levy(2),Murrell,Santi g:Miller(4)	4th	437
11/7/21	Barrow (h)	W40-12	t:Levy,Agoro,Q Laulu-Togaga'e,Miller,Graham,Santi g:Miller(8)	4th	572
16/7/21	Coventry (a)	L24-18	t:Graham,P Laulu-Togaga'e(2),Agoro g:Miller	4th	387
25/7/21	Hunslet (a)	D20-20	t:Parker,Prell,Graham,Desmond-Walker g:Miller(2)	4th	714
1/8/21	Rochdale (a)	W20-42	t:Prell(2),Slingsby,Agoro(2),Levy,Stead g:Miller(7)	5th	891
8/8/21	Workington (h)	L18-22	t:Agoro,Slingsby,Mika g:Miller(3)	5th	774
15/8/21	Coventry (h)	W46-18	t:Graham,Parker(2),Agoro(3),Miller,Wright g:Miller(7)	6th	1,028
21/8/21	London Skolars (a)	W14-34	t:Levy,Bailey,Arnold,Prell(2),Wright g:Miller(5)	5th	228
28/8/21	West Wales (a)	W12-42	t:Miller(3),Slingsby,Q Laulu-Togaga'e,Webster,Lynam,P Laulu-Togaga'e g:Miller(5)	5th	267
5/9/21	North Wales (h)	W34-14	t:Murrell,Webster,Prell,Q Laulu-Togaga'e,Stephenson,Parker g:Miller(5)	5th	1,327
12/9/21	Doncaster (a)	W26-28	t:Webster(2),Mika,Prell,P Laulu-Togaga'e g:Miller(4)	4th	738
18/9/21	North Wales (a) (QPO)	W14-28	t:Webster,Miller,Santi(2) g:Miller(6)	N/A	488
26/9/21	Workington (a) (QSF)	L18-16 (aet)	t:Miller,Graham,Kesik g:Miller(2)	N/A	1,221
3/10/21	Doncaster (h) (PF)	L26-28	t:Miller,P Laulu-Togaga'e,Murrell,Graham g:Miller(5)	N/A	1,128

● Played at The Rock, Roehampton

		APP		TRIES		GOALS		FG		PTS	
	D.O.B.	ALL	L1	ALL	L1	ALL	L1	ALL	L1	ALL	L1
Mo Agoro	29/1/93	13(1)	12(1)	9	8	0	0	0	0	36	32
Jack Arnold	23/9/97	3(5)	3(4)	1	1	0	0	0	0	4	4
Matthew Bailey	1/12/91	7(12)	6(12)	1	1	0	0	0	0	4	4
Zach Braham	14/1/95	2	2	0	0	0	0	0	0	0	0
Jack Coventry	5/3/94	8(6)	8(5)	1	1	0	0	0	0	4	4
Bobby Darbyshire	30/6/01	1(1)	1(1)	0	0	0	0	0	0	0	0
Spencer Darley	25/9/98	2(2)	2(2)	1	1	0	0	0	0	4	4
Dalton Desmond-Walker	25/4/93	3(9)	3(9)	1	1	0	0	0	0	4	4
James Feather	15/4/84	3(4)	3(4)	0	0	0	0	0	0	0	0
Billy Gaylor	30/4/97	12(3)	11(3)	0	0	0	0	0	0	0	0
Charlie Graham	14/5/00	18(1)	17(1)	12	12	0	0	0	0	48	48
Dan Hawksworth	30/3/93	(1)	(1)	0	0	0	0	0	0	0	0
Kyle Kesik	3/6/89	17(4)	17(3)	1	1	0	0	0	0	4	4
Phoenix Laulu-Togaga'e	16/4/03	10(2)	10(2)	5	5	0	0	0	0	20	20
Quentin Laulu-Togaga'e	1/12/84	12	12	7	7	0	0	0	0	28	28
Aaron Levy	19/12/95	17(4)	17(3)	8	8	0	0	0	0	32	32
Josh Lynam	16/2/93	5(2)	4(2)	1	1	0	0	0	0	4	4
Robert Matamosi	23/2/97	3	2	0	0	0	0	0	0	0	0
Con Mika	14/9/89	7(2)	7(2)	2	2	0	0	0	0	8	8
Jack Miller	28/11/94	22	21	14	14	104	103	0	0	264	262
Kieran Moran	2/11/96	5(6)	4(6)	1	1	0	0	0	0	4	4
Jason Muranka	4/8/89	2(2)	2(2)	0	0	0	0	0	0	0	0
Scott Murrell	5/9/85	19	19	5	5	0	0	0	0	20	20
Dan Parker	11/3/93	14(5)	13(5)	7	7	0	0	0	0	28	28
Taylor Prell	3/7/96	18	17	10	10	0	0	0	0	40	40
Morgan Robinson	1/10/98	1	1	0	0	0	0	0	0	0	0
Brenden Santi	5/8/93	18	17	13	12	0	0	0	0	52	48
Aidan Scully	16/5/92	1	1	0	0	0	0	0	0	0	0
Alfie Seeley	30/12/96	5(1)	5(1)	2	2	0	0	0	0	8	8
Josh Slingsby	28/12/00	10	10	7	7	0	0	0	0	28	28
Ben Stead	13/10/92	5(1)	4(1)	1	1	0	0	0	0	4	4
Alix Stephenson	19/4/99	6	6	1	1	0	0	0	0	4	4
Jake Webster	29/10/83	13	13	8	8	0	0	0	0	32	32
Ryan Wright	28/10/91	4(12)	3(12)	2	2	0	0	0	0	8	8

'L1' totals include regular season & play-offs; 'All' totals also include Challenge Cup

CLUB RECORDS	
MATCH RECORDS	**Highest score:** 112-6 v West Wales, 15/9/2018 **Highest score against:** 2-92 v Leigh, 30/4/86 **Record attendance:** 14,500 v Halifax, 3/3/51
	Tries: 6 Jason Critchley v Widnes, 18/8/96
	Goals: 15 John Wasyliw v Nottingham City, 1/11/92; Martyn Wood v Lancashire Lynx, 1/5/2000 **Points:** 36 John Wasyliw v Nottingham City, 1/11/92
SEASON RECORDS	**Tries:** 45 Nick Pinkney 1994-95 **Goals:** 187 John Wasyliw 1992-93 **Points:** 490 John Wasyliw 1992-93
CAREER RECORDS	**Tries:** 155 Sam Stacey 1904-20 **Goals:** 967 Brian Jefferson 1965-77 **Points:** 2,116 Brian Jefferson 1965-77
	Appearances: 372 Hartley Tempest 1902-15; David McGoun 1925-38

Jack Miller

LONDON SKOLARS

DATE	FIXTURE	RESULT	SCORERS	LGE	ATT
8/5/21	North Wales (h)	L24-44	t:M Greenhalgh,Pearce-Paul,Oakley(2) g:Caro,Thorman(3)	7th	BCD
16/5/21	Workington (a)	L50-16	t:Pearce-Paul,Carter,Thomas g:Thorman(2)	9th	BCD
23/5/21	Coventry (a)	W26-44	t:Latu,Wilkinson,J Greenhalgh,Varela(2),Juma,M Greenhalgh,Caro g:Thorman(6)	8th	210
29/5/21	West Wales (a)	W10-52	t:Caro(5),Tyas,Thomas,Gale,Jy-mel Coleman g:Thorman(5),Caro(3)	6th	BCD
6/6/21	Doncaster (a)	L46-12	t:Wilkinson,Juma g:Thorman(2)	6th	882
12/6/21	Hunslet (h)	L10-62	t:Juma,Johnson g:Thorman	8th	370
19/6/21	Barrow (h)	L14-24	t:Hammond,Carter,Bryan g:Thorman	9th	391
27/6/21	Keighley (a)	L34-22	t:Firth,Juma(2),Grant g:Caro,Thorman(2)	9th	548
4/7/21	Rochdale (a)	L22-4	g:Thomas(2)	9th	1,171
16/7/21	Doncaster (h)	D16-16	t:Thomas,Small g:Thorman(4)	9th	575
24/7/21	West Wales (h)	W46-30	t:Latu(3),Bryan(2),Singleton,Thomas,J Greenhalgh g:Thorman(7)	9th	196
31/7/21	Coventry (h)	L12-14	t:Juma(2) g:Thorman(2)	9th	190
7/8/21	Rochdale (h)	L34-38	t:Lloyd-Jones,Clarke,M Greenhalgh,Firth,Bryan,Juma g:Thorman(5)	9th	208
15/8/21	Hunslet (a)	L38-10	t:Bryan,Juma g:Thorman	9th	435
21/8/21	Keighley (h)	L14-34	t:Yates,Latu g:Thorman(3)	9th	228
29/8/21	Barrow (a)	L38-24	t:M Greenhalgh,Small(2),Latu g:Thorman(4)	9th	1,486
4/9/21	Workington (h)	L18-35	t:Juma,Latu,Sykes g:Thorman(3)	9th	241
11/9/21	North Wales (a)	L44-0		9th	560

		APP		TRIES		GOALS		FG		PTS	
	D.O.B.	ALL	L1	ALL	L1	ALL	L1	ALL	L1	ALL	L1
Chris Ball	1/3/00	9	9	0	0	0	0	0	0	0	0
Mike Bishay	8/2/93	5	5	0	0	0	0	0	0	0	0
Will Blakemore	20/9/98	3(1)	3(1)	0	0	0	0	0	0	0	0
Lamont Bryan	12/4/88	5(4)	5(4)	5	5	0	0	0	0	20	20
Ryan Cane	17/1/97	(1)	(1)	0	0	0	0	0	0	0	0
Omari Caro	7/3/91	8	8	6	6	5	5	0	0	34	34
Errol Carter	22/1/96	6	6	2	2	0	0	0	0	8	8
Max Clarke	1/1/00	3	3	1	1	0	0	0	0	4	4
Jermaine Coleman	17/6/82	4	4	0	0	0	0	0	0	0	0
Jy-mel Coleman	13/10/88	2	2	1	1	0	0	0	0	4	4
Alex Davidson	1/11/92	(2)	(2)	0	0	0	0	0	0	0	0
Tom Firth	14/3/99	3(8)	3(8)	2	2	0	0	0	0	8	8
Christian Gale	28/12/99	10(7)	10(7)	1	1	0	0	0	0	4	4
Dalton Grant	21/4/90	7	7	1	1	0	0	0	0	4	4
Judd Greenhalgh	16/1/93	3(12)	3(12)	2	2	0	0	0	0	8	8
Mike Greenhalgh	8/6/94	17	17	4	4	0	0	0	0	16	16
Charles Hammond	1/2/97	2(1)	2(1)	1	1	0	0	0	0	4	4
Marcus Hockey	30/10/97	(1)	(1)	0	0	0	0	0	0	0	0
Greg Johnson	20/2/90	3	3	1	1	0	0	0	0	4	4
Lameck Juma	6/12/90	12	12	10	10	0	0	0	0	40	40
Paulos Latu	23/11/90	12(1)	12(1)	7	7	0	0	0	0	28	28
Oliver Leyland	17/5/01	4	4	0	0	0	0	0	0	0	0
Malikhi Lloyd-Jones	29/8/94	4(10)	4(10)	1	1	0	0	0	0	4	4
Iliess Macani	6/12/93	10	10	0	0	0	0	0	0	0	0
Eddie Mbaraga	9/9/87	2(4)	2(4)	0	0	0	0	0	0	0	0
Abevia McDonald	6/7/92	4	4	0	0	0	0	0	0	0	0
Rob Oakley	8/11/99	1(1)	1(1)	2	2	0	0	0	0	8	8
Jacob Ogden	23/1/98	1	1	0	0	0	0	0	0	0	0
Kameron Pearce-Paul	28/2/97	9	9	2	2	0	0	0	0	8	8
Matt Ross	2/9/92	7(5)	7(5)	0	0	0	0	0	0	0	0
Louis Sheriff	6/9/92	2	2	0	0	0	0	0	0	0	0
Louis Singleton	29/9/91	4(4)	4(4)	1	1	0	0	0	0	4	4
Aaron Small	28/10/91	11	11	3	3	0	0	0	0	12	12
Michael Sykes	10/12/86	(4)	(4)	1	1	0	0	0	0	4	4
Jacob Thomas	9/10/93	16	16	4	4	2	2	0	0	20	20
Neil Thorman	4/6/84	14(4)	14(4)	0	0	51	51	0	0	102	102
James Tyas	12/11/91	6(1)	6(1)	1	1	0	0	0	0	4	4
Jonah Varela	29/7/01	9	9	2	2	0	0	0	0	8	8
Adam Vrahnos	1/10/92	7	7	0	0	0	0	0	0	0	0
Richard Wilkinson	26/10/93	2	2	2	2	0	0	0	0	8	8
Jordan Williams	4/6/97	2	2	0	0	0	0	0	0	0	0
Jerome Yates	31/10/97	5	5	1	1	0	0	0	0	4	4

Lameck Juma

CLUB RECORDS	
MATCH RECORDS	**Highest score:** 76-8 v West Wales, 7/4/2018; 76-6 v Hemel, 8/9/2018 **Highest score against:** 4-98 v Sheffield, 3/8/2003
	Record attendance: 1,524 v Toronto, 4/3/2017
SEASON RECORDS	**Tries:** 5 Mark Cantoni v Gateshead, 27/6/2004; Omari Caro v West Wales, 29/5/2021
	Goals: 12 Neil Thorman v West Wales, 7/4/2018 **Points:** 28 Dylan Skee v South Wales, 29/7/2012
CAREER RECORDS	**Tries:** 20 Mark Cantoni 2004; James Anthony 2013 **Goals:** 100 Dylan Skee 2013 **Points:** 248 Dylan Skee 2013
	Tries: 57 Austen Aggrey 2004-2012 **Goals:** 230 *(inc 1fg)* Dylan Skee 2011-2013 **Points:** 579 Dylan Skee 2011-2013 **Appearances:** 198 Gareth Honor 2003-2011

NORTH WALES CRUSADERS

DATE	FIXTURE	RESULT	SCORERS	LGE	ATT
8/5/21	London Skolars (a)	W24-44	t:Ah Van(3),Gibson(2),Smith,Massam,Hurst g:Billsborough(6)	4th	BCD
15/5/21	Hunslet (h)	L18-26	t:Brown,Eckley,Rodden g:Billsborough(3)	4th	BCD
23/5/21	Workington (h)	L16-44	t:Gibson,Massam,Rodden g:Johnson(2)	7th	BCD
30/5/21	Barrow (a)	L44-8	t:Massam,Dow-Nikau	8th	1,915
6/6/21	Coventry (h)	W36-12	t:Dow-Nikau(2),Massam(3),Johnson,Morris g:Johnson(4)	8th	BCD
13/6/21	Doncaster (h)	L0-68		9th	BCD
19/6/21	West Wales (a)	W10-60	t:Dow-Nikau(2),Massam(3),Reid(2),Aspey(2),Billsborough,Brown,Ah Van g:Billsborough(6)	6th	285
27/6/21	Rochdale (a)	L38-28	t:Rodden,Massam(2),Aspey,Barratt g:Johnson(4)	7th	1,389
4/7/21	Keighley (h)	W34-28	t:Billsborough,Rodden,Johnson(2),Massam,Ah Van g:Johnson(5)	7th	437
11/7/21	Hunslet (a)	W24-34	t:Brennan,Rodden(2),Johnson,Reid,Ah Van g:Johnson(5)	6th	404
1/8/21	West Wales (h)	W72-4	t:Race(2),Morris,Massam(2),Ah Van,Thompson,Gibson,Rodden,Hazzard,Berry,Reid(2) g:Johnson(10)	4th	610
8/8/21	Coventry (a)	W16-32	t:Massam,Ashall,Gibson(2),Rodden,Johnson g:Johnson(4)	4th	378
15/8/21	Barrow (h)	W23-10	t:Eckley,Johnson,Massam(2) g:Johnson(3) fg:Race	3rd	727
22/8/21	Workington (a)	W18-40	t:Morris,Thompson,Eckley,Ah Van,Massam,Reid,Race g:Johnson(6)	3rd	1,457
29/8/21	Rochdale (h)	W36-10	t:Eckley,Johnson(2),Ah Van,Reid,Gibson g:Johnson(6)	3rd	617
5/9/21	Keighley (a)	L34-14	t:Rodden,Brennan g:Johnson(3)	4th	1,327
11/9/21	London Skolars (h)	W44-0	t:Massam(4),Rodden,Johnson,Eccleston,Ah Van g:Johnson(6)	3rd	560
18/9/21	Keighley (h) (QPO)	L14-28	t:Billsborough,Ah Van g:Johnson(3)	N/A	488
26/9/21	Doncaster (h) (ESF)	L34-48	t:Hazzard,Brennan,Gibson,Morris,Johnson,Rodden g:Johnson(5)	N/A	432

Doncaster (a) (R11) game was postponed, and not rearranged

		APP		TRIES		GOALS		FG		PTS	
	D.O.B.	ALL	L1	ALL	L1	ALL	L1	ALL	L1	ALL	L1
Patrick Ah Van	17/3/88	18	18	11	11	0	0	0	0	44	44
Karl Ashall	3/11/89	18	18	1	1	0	0	0	0	4	4
Connor Aspey	16/4/02	(2)	(2)	3	3	0	0	0	0	12	12
Andy Ball	24/7/91	(7)	(7)	0	0	0	0	0	0	0	0
Chris Barratt	7/2/93	18	18	1	1	0	0	0	0	4	4
Cameron Berry	7/8/01	(2)	(2)	1	1	0	0	0	0	4	4
Brad Billsborough	4/8/98	11(2)	11(2)	3	3	15	15	0	0	42	42
Brad Brennan	18/1/93	6(12)	6(12)	3	3	0	0	0	0	12	12
Cam Brown	17/9/98	1(1)	1(1)	2	2	0	0	0	0	8	8
Brad Calland	20/4/01	(3)	(3)	0	0	0	0	0	0	0	0
Jack Cottington	7/4/98	(7)	(7)	0	0	0	0	0	0	0	0
Rhys Davies	9/6/96	(1)	(1)	0	0	0	0	0	0	0	0
Tyme Dow-Nikau	25/6/92	4	4	5	5	0	0	0	0	20	20
Dave Eccleston	12/9/96	7	7	1	1	0	0	0	0	4	4
Alex Eckley	25/8/99	17	17	4	4	0	0	0	0	16	16
Jordy Gibson	11/6/92	19	19	8	8	0	0	0	0	32	32
Callum Hazzard	9/1/99	4(11)	4(11)	2	2	0	0	0	0	8	8
Jack Holmes	5/1/94	8(3)	8(3)	0	0	0	0	0	0	0	0
Jack Houghton	10/1/97	(5)	(5)	0	0	0	0	0	0	0	0
Earl Hurst	21/4/89	2	2	1	1	0	0	0	0	4	4
Elliott Jenkins	6/2/99	3	3	0	0	0	0	0	0	0	0
Tommy Johnson	19/4/91	16	16	10	10	66	66	0	0	172	172
Ethan Kelly	31/12/94	(7)	(7)	0	0	0	0	0	0	0	0
Rob Massam	29/11/87	18	18	22	22	0	0	0	0	88	88
Dante Morley-Samuels	22/11/98	2	2	0	0	0	0	0	0	0	0
Ben Morris	1/8/97	16	16	4	4	0	0	0	0	16	16
Ethan O'Hanlon	19/5/01	(5)	(5)	0	0	0	0	0	0	0	0
Matthew Race	26/3/01	5	5	3	3	0	0	1	1	13	13
Matt Reid	16/9/92	13	13	7	7	0	0	0	0	28	28
George Roby	3/5/02	(2)	(2)	0	0	0	0	0	0	0	0
Gav Rodden	20/12/96	19	19	11	11	0	0	0	0	44	44
Joe Sanderson	17/3/97	3	3	0	0	0	0	0	0	0	0
Jono Smith	12/11/88	4	4	1	1	0	0	0	0	4	4
Connor Terrill	3/7/01	(1)	(1)	0	0	0	0	0	0	0	0
Warren Thompson	24/2/90	14	14	2	2	0	0	0	0	8	8
James Thornton	30/9/95	1(4)	1(4)	0	0	0	0	0	0	0	0

'L1' totals include regular season & play-offs

Rob Massam

CLUB RECORDS	**Highest score:** 82-6 v West Hull, 6/4/2013 **Highest score against:** 4-98 v Wigan, 15/4/2012
MATCH RECORDS	**Record attendance:** 1,562 v South Wales, 1/9/2013 *(Racecourse Ground)*; 727 v Barrow, 15/8/2021 *(Stadiwm Zip World)* **Tries:** 5 Rob Massam v Rochdale, 30/6/2013; Jono Smith v Hemel, 16/5/2015 **Goals:** 11 Tommy Johnson v West Hull, 6/4/2013; Ian Mort v Hemel, 16/5/2015; Ben Stead v West Wales, 19/4/2019 **Points:** 30 Tommy Johnson v West Hull, 6/4/2013
SEASON RECORDS	**Tries:** 29 Rob Massam 2015 **Goals:** 109 Tommy Johnson 2015 **Points:** 266 Tommy Johnson 2015
CAREER RECORDS	**Tries:** 144 Rob Massam 2012-2016; 2019-2021 **Goals:** 630 Tommy Johnson 2012-2018, 2020-2021 **Points:** 1,524 Tommy Johnson 2012-2018, 2020-2021 **Appearances:** 186 Tommy Johnson 2012-2018, 2020-2021

ROCHDALE HORNETS

DATE	FIXTURE	RESULT	SCORERS	LGE	ATT
9/5/21	West Wales (h)	W40-16	t:Bennion,Penkywicz(4),Yates,L Sheridan g:Freeman(6)	1st	BCD
16/5/21	Doncaster (a)	L30-22	t:Ainscough,Baker,Fowden,Higginson g:Freeman(3)	3rd	BCD
23/5/21	Keighley (a)	W36-43	t:Galbraith,Forshaw,Bennion,Ainscough(2),Fairclough,Jordan-Roberts,Moimoi g:Jordan-Roberts(5) fg:Fairclough	3rd	700
30/5/21	Coventry (a)	L38-30	t:Fowden,Fairclough,Ainscough,Moimoi,Marriott g:Jordan-Roberts(5)	5th	232
6/6/21	Hunslet (a)	L36-22	t:Penkywicz,D Sheridan,L Sheridan(2) g:Jordan-Roberts(3)	5th	483
12/6/21	Barrow (a)	L40-4	t:Nixon	6th	1,758
20/6/21	Workington (a)	L34-28	t:L Sheridan,Fowden,Ainscough,Moores,Moimoi g:Jordan-Roberts(3),Syme	8th	942
27/6/21	North Wales (h)	W38-28	t:L Sheridan,Nixon,Yates(2),Fowden,Moimoi(2) g:Jordan-Roberts(3),Baker(2)	6th	1,389
4/7/21	London Skolars (h)	W22-4	t:Robinson,L Sheridan(2),Whur g:Jordan-Roberts,Baker(2)	6th	1,171
10/7/21	West Wales (a)	W18-30	t:Penkywicz,Freeman,Fowden,Moimoi,Marriott,Nixon g:Baker(3)	5th	318
1/8/21	Keighley (h)	L20-42	t:Tate(2),Taira,Nixon g:Jordan-Roberts(2)	7th	891
7/8/21	London Skolars (a)	W34-38	t:Brearley(2),Nixon,Syme,Ashton,Fowden,Littlewood g:Dean(5)	6th	208
15/8/21	Doncaster (h)	W44-8	t:Robinson,Tyrer(2),Syme(2),Jordan-Roberts,Bennion,L Sheridan g:Dean(6)	5th	882
22/8/21	Hunslet (h)	D34-34	t:Penkywicz,Jordan-Roberts,Ainscough,L Sheridan,Taira,Syme g:Dean(2),Jordan-Roberts,Fairclough(2)	6th	822
29/8/21	North Wales (a)	L36-10	t:Chase,L Sheridan g:Jordan-Roberts	7th	617
5/9/21	Barrow (h)	L30-32	t:Nixon,Moores,Moimoi,Marriott(2) g:Jordan-Roberts,Syme(4)	7th	1,064
12/9/21	Coventry (h)	W50-22	t:Calland(2),Bennion(2),Moimoi,Penkywicz,Robinson,Nixon(2),Ashton g:Syme(4),Penkywicz	7th	693

Workington (h) (R11) game was postponed, and not rearranged

	D.O.B.	APP		TRIES		GOALS		FG		PTS	
		ALL	L1	ALL	L1	ALL	L1	ALL	L1	ALL	L1
Shaun Ainscough	27/11/89	11	11	6	6	0	0	0	0	24	24
Tom Ashton	20/6/92	5	5	2	2	0	0	0	0	8	8
Zac Baker	1/3/92	11	11	1	1	7	7	0	0	18	18
Gavin Bennion	31/12/93	9(1)	9(1)	5	5	0	0	0	0	20	20
Dale Bloomfield	24/10/87	3	3	0	0	0	0	0	0	0	0
Paul Brearley	5/2/92	7	7	2	2	0	0	0	0	8	8
Ben Calland	24/9/96	10	10	2	2	0	0	0	0	8	8
Rangi Chase	11/4/86	4	4	1	1	0	0	0	0	4	4
Jimmy Connaughton	28/3/98	6(1)	6(1)	0	0	0	0	0	0	0	0
Reece Dean	30/11/96	4	4	0	0	13	13	0	0	26	26
Rob Fairclough	10/9/97	7	7	2	2	2	2	1	1	13	13
Ryan Forshaw	23/9/00	4	4	1	1	0	0	0	0	4	4
Ben Forster	27/12/00	2(9)	2(9)	0	0	0	0	0	0	0	0
Luke Fowden	1/9/96	1(14)	1(14)	6	6	0	0	0	0	24	24
Sam Freeman	3/4/99	5	5	1	1	9	9	0	0	22	22
Lewis Galbraith	1/2/95	3	3	1	1	0	0	0	0	4	4
Myles Harrison	11/8/03	(1)	(1)	0	0	0	0	0	0	0	0
Adam Hesketh	27/11/93	4(1)	4(1)	0	0	0	0	0	0	0	0
Jack Higginson	4/4/97	2	2	1	1	0	0	0	0	4	4
Kenny Hughes	30/3/90	(1)	(1)	0	0	0	0	0	0	0	0
Josh Jordan-Roberts	26/8/98	16(1)	16(1)	3	3	25	25	0	0	62	62
Luke Littlewood	7/11/00	(1)	(1)	1	1	0	0	0	0	4	4
Callum Marriott	30/5/93	10(1)	10(1)	4	4	0	0	0	0	16	16
Fuifui Moimoi	26/9/79	3(9)	3(9)	8	8	0	0	0	0	32	32
Ben Moores	6/12/93	10(2)	10(2)	2	2	0	0	0	0	8	8
Dan Nixon	27/7/02	10	10	8	8	0	0	0	0	32	32
Cole Oakley	25/10/00	2	2	0	0	0	0	0	0	0	0
Callum Ogden	26/4/97	3(3)	3(3)	0	0	0	0	0	0	0	0
Sean Penkywicz	18/5/82	8(8)	8(8)	8	8	1	1	0	0	34	34
Lee Registe	17/3/98	(2)	(2)	0	0	0	0	0	0	0	0
Shaun Robinson	13/7/89	7	7	3	3	0	0	0	0	12	12
Declan Sheridan	24/2/97	2(2)	2(2)	1	1	0	0	0	0	4	4
Lewis Sheridan	14/1/94	9(4)	9(4)	10	10	0	0	0	0	40	40
Jordan Syme	14/11/96	16	16	4	4	9	9	0	0	34	34
Joe Taira	30/3/89	7(3)	7(3)	2	2	0	0	0	0	8	8
Will Tate	20/12/01	2	2	2	2	0	0	0	0	8	8
AJ Towse	19/8/03	1	1	0	0	0	0	0	0	0	0
Cian Tyrer	3/2/01	6	6	2	2	0	0	0	0	8	8
Tyler Walton	20/12/00	1(1)	1(1)	0	0	0	0	0	0	0	0
Toby Warren	5/9/03	1	1	0	0	0	0	0	0	0	0
Liam Whalley	27/4/93	(1)	(1)	0	0	0	0	0	0	0	0
Tom Whur	15/11/01	(2)	(2)	1	1	0	0	0	0	4	4
Danny Yates	28/5/94	9	9	3	3	0	0	0	0	12	12

Lewis Sheridan

CLUB RECORDS

Highest score: 120-4 v Illingworth, 13/3/2005 **Highest score against:** 0-106 v Castleford, 9/9/2007

MATCH RECORDS

Record attendance: 26,664 v Oldham, 25/3/22 *(Athletic Grounds)*; 8,061 v Oldham, 26/12/89 *(Spotland)*

Tries: 5 Jack Corsi v Barrow, 31/12/1921; Jack Corsi v Broughton Moor, 25/2/22; Jack Williams v St Helens, 4/4/33; Norman Brelsford v Whitehaven, 3/9/73; Marlon Billy v York, 8/4/2001 **Goals:** 18 Lee Birdseye v Illingworth, 13/3/2005 **Points:** 44 Lee Birdseye v Illingworth, 13/3/2005

SEASON RECORDS

Tries: 31 Marlon Billy 2001 **Goals:** 150 Martin Strett 1994-95 **Points:** 350 Mick Nanyn 2003

CAREER RECORDS

Tries: 103 Jack Williams 1931-37 **Goals:** 741 Walter Gowers 1922-36

Points: 1,497 Walter Gowers 1922-36; Paul Crook 2010-2016 **Appearances:** 456 Walter Gowers 1922-36

WEST WALES RAIDERS

DATE	FIXTURE	RESULT	SCORERS	LGE	ATT
21/3/21	Widnes (h) (CCR1)	L4-58	t:Naulusala	N/A	BCD
9/5/21	Rochdale (a)	L40-16	t:Webb,M Evans,Connor g:Ramsey(2)	10th	BCD
15/5/21	Coventry (h)	L10-36	t:Webb,D Phillips g:Ramsey	10th	BCD
23/5/21	Doncaster (a)	L62-24	t:Burke,Holden,Chase,Herron g:Ramsey(4)	10th	784
29/5/21	London Skolars (h)	L10-52	t:Webb,Stroud g:Ramsey	10th	BCD
5/6/21	Barrow (h)	L10-60	t:Murphy(2) g:Ramsey	10th	BCD
13/6/21	Keighley (a)	L70-12	t:Murphy,Herron g:Ramsey(2)	10th	463
19/6/21	North Wales (h)	L10-60	t:D Evans(2) g:Murphy	10th	285
26/6/21	Hunslet (h)	L12-38	t:Cowburn,Bodman g:Ramsey(2)	10th	204
4/7/21	Workington (a)	L66-0		10th	942
10/7/21	Rochdale (h)	L18-30	t:Merrett,Murphy,D Phillips g:Ramsey(3)	10th	318
24/7/21	London Skolars (a)	L46-30	t:Murphy(4),Ramsey,Coleman g:Ramsey(3)	10th	196
1/8/21	North Wales (a)	L72-4	t:Kaye	10th	610
7/8/21	Doncaster (h)	D24-24	t:Merrett,Parry(2),D Phillips g:Ramsey(4)	10th	180
14/8/21	Workington (h)	L22-36	t:Pope,Parry,Murphy(2) g:Ramsey(3)	10th	239
22/8/21	Coventry (a)	L50-18	t:Cowburn,Uren,Coleman,D Evans g:Ramsey	10th	280
28/8/21	Keighley (h)	L12-42	t:Ramsey,Cowburn g:Ramsey,Tennant	10th	267
5/9/21	Hunslet (a)	L82-6	t:M Evans g:M Morgan	10th	474
11/9/21	Barrow (a)	L76-0		10th	1,922

		APP		TRIES		GOALS		FG		PTS	
	D.O.B.	ALL	L1	ALL	L1	ALL	L1	ALL	L1	ALL	L1
Morgan Allen	12/3/90	3(3)	2(3)	0	0	0	0	0	0	0	0
Ewan Badham	29/11/01	7(3)	7(3)	0	0	0	0	0	0	0	0
Ieuan Badham	29/11/01	1(5)	1(5)	0	0	0	0	0	0	0	0
Julius Banks	21/11/98	(1)	(1)	0	0	0	0	0	0	0	0
Ashley Bateman	11/2/01	18(1)	18	0	0	0	0	0	0	0	0
Charley Bodman	7/12/01	12(2)	12(2)	1	1	0	0	0	0	4	4
Eparama Boginsoko	23/6/95	(2)	(1)	0	0	0	0	0	0	0	0
Paul Bolger	6/10/95	2(3)	2(3)	0	0	0	0	0	0	0	0
Harry Boots	15/12/96	(9)	(9)	0	0	0	0	0	0	0	0
Joe Burke	18/5/90	16	15	1	1	0	0	0	0	4	4
Rangi Chase	11/4/86	4	3	1	1	0	0	0	0	4	4
Aedan Coleman	2/3/98	8	8	2	2	0	0	0	0	8	8
Mike Connor	27/3/94	4(1)	3(1)	1	1	0	0	0	0	4	4
Phil Cowburn	15/10/90	8	7	3	3	0	0	0	0	12	12
Rhys Davies	9/6/96	3	3	0	0	0	0	0	0	0	0
Dai Evans	30/7/92	6	6	3	3	0	0	0	0	12	12
Morgan Evans	23/3/92	14	13	2	2	0	0	0	0	8	8
Leon Hayes	3/4/04	(1)	(1)	0	0	0	0	0	0	0	0
Gavin Henson	1/2/82	1	0	0	0	0	0	0	0	0	0
Sam Herron	13/12/93	6(7)	6(6)	2	2	0	0	0	0	8	8
Alex Hicken	4/3/88	(3)	(3)	0	0	0	0	0	0	0	0
Michael Holden	29/5/00	16	16	1	1	0	0	0	0	4	4
Ben Jackson	27/8/92	1	1	0	0	0	0	0	0	0	0
Rowland Kaye	27/8/99	6	6	1	1	0	0	0	0	4	4
Jamie Laing	6/2/89	2	2	0	0	0	0	0	0	0	0
Craig Lewis	15/10/86	2(1)	2(1)	0	0	0	0	0	0	0	0
Jordan Liney	5/5/98	(1)	(1)	0	0	0	0	0	0	0	0
Joe McClean	10/8/89	1	1	0	0	0	0	0	0	0	0
Callum Merrett	27/9/97	4	4	2	2	0	0	0	0	8	8
Kian Monaghan	2/2/01	1	1	0	0	0	0	0	0	0	0
Matthew Morgan	17/1/01	1	1	0	0	1	1	0	0	2	2
Tom Morgan	18/10/89	4(1)	3(1)	0	0	0	0	0	0	0	0
Darrel Moyle	8/11/90	(1)	(1)	0	0	0	0	0	0	0	0
Callum Mulkeen	10/12/90	17	17	0	0	0	0	0	0	0	0
Jamie Murphy	29/12/89	9	8	10	10	1	1	0	0	42	42
Emosi Nadaubale	6/11/92	2	1	0	0	0	0	0	0	0	0
Uraia Naulusala	8/10/94	3	2	1	0	0	0	0	0	4	0
Steve Parry	19/10/88	1(1)	1(1)	3	3	0	0	0	0	12	12
Dafydd Phillips	10/8/95	8(5)	7(5)	3	3	0	0	0	0	12	12
Osian Phillips	2/5/94	5	5	0	0	0	0	0	0	0	0
Alan Pope	1/4/85	4(2)	4(2)	1	1	0	0	0	0	4	4
Will Ramsey	21/4/99	15	15	2	2	28	28	0	0	64	64
Connor Saunders	31/5/97	1	1	0	0	0	0	0	0	0	0
Ryan Shallish	25/2/93	3(2)	3(2)	0	0	0	0	0	0	0	0
Fraser Stroud	12/4/99	13(2)	13(1)	1	1	0	0	0	0	4	4
Shaun Tennant	25/7/93	1(2)	1(2)	0	0	1	1	0	0	2	2
Jack Torkington	10/5/96	(1)	(1)	0	0	0	0	0	0	0	0
Jack Uren	3/1/98	5(4)	5(4)	1	1	0	0	0	0	4	4
Louis Watson	30/10/00	1	1	0	0	0	0	0	0	0	0
Marcus Webb	11/1/97	8	7	3	3	0	0	0	0	12	12

Morgan Evans

'L1' totals include League 1 games only; 'All' totals also include Challenge Cup

CLUB RECORDS	**Highest score:** 44-16 v Coventry, 20/7/2019 **Highest score against:** 0-144 v York, 29/4/2018 **Record attendance:** 826 v Bradford, 9/9/2018
MATCH RECORDS	**Tries:** 4 Jamie Murphy v London Skolars, 24/7/2021 **Goals:** 6 Phil Cowburn v Coventry, 20/7/2019 **Points:** 16 Jamie Murphy v London Skolars, 24/7/2021
SEASON RECORDS	**Tries:** 10 Jamie Murphy 2021 **Goals:** 28 Will Ramsey 2021 **Points:** 64 Will Ramsey 2021
CAREER RECORDS	**Tries:** 16 Steve Parry 2018-2019; 2021 **Goals:** 28 Will Ramsey 2021 **Points:** 84 Phil Cowburn 2018-2021
	Appearances: 45 Archie Snook 2018-2020; Rowland Kaye 2018-2021

WORKINGTON TOWN

DATE	FIXTURE	RESULT	SCORERS	LGE	ATT
9/5/21	Hunslet (a)	W16-28	t:Doran,Henson(2),O'Donnell(2) g:Forber(4)	5th	BCD
16/5/21	London Skolars (h)	W50-16	t:Lightowler,Young(2),Henson,Holroyd(3),O'Donnell,Fitzsimmons g:Forber(7)	1st	BCD
23/5/21	North Wales (a)	W16-44	t:Dawson,Holroyd,Henson(2),Wellington,Bickerdike,L Brown,Young g:Forber(6)	1st	BCD
30/5/21	Doncaster (a)	L24-26	t:Scholey,Henson,Young,Barnes,J Brown g:Forber(2)	2nd	942
6/6/21	Keighley (h)	W34-20	t:Moore,Holroyd(2),Lightowler,Barnes,Henson g:Forber(5)	2nd	942
13/6/21	Coventry (a)	W12-30	t:Dawson,Bickerdike,Holroyd,Forber g:Forber(5)	3rd	198
20/6/21	Rochdale (h)	W34-28	t:O'Donnell,Doran,Moore,Holroyd,Fitzsimmons,Forber g:Forber(5)	2nd	942
27/6/21	Barrow (a)	D24-24	t:Doran,Henson,Marwood,Holroyd g:Forber(4)	3rd	3,146
4/7/21	West Wales (h)	W66-0	t:Barnes,Henson,Bickerdike(2),Clarke,Moore(2),Dawson,O'Donnell, Marwood(2),J Brown g:Forber(9)	2nd	942
8/8/21	Keighley (a)	W18-22	t:J Brown,Dawson,Moore,Holroyd g:Forber(3)	2nd	774
14/8/21	West Wales (a)	W22-36	t:Wellington,Forber(3),Postlethwaite,Holroyd g:Forber(6)	1st	239
22/8/21	North Wales (h)	L18-40	t:Olstrom,O'Brien,Wellington g:Forber(3)	1st	1,457
29/8/21	Doncaster (a)	L22-12	t:Holroyd,Dawson g:Forber(2)	2nd	948
4/9/21	London Skolars (a)	W18-35	t:Clarke,Holroyd(2),Fitzsimmons,Henson,Doran g:Forber(5) fg:Holroyd	2nd	241
12/9/21	Hunslet (h)	L14-32	t:Holroyd,J Brown(2) g:Forber	2nd	1,397
26/9/21	Keighley (h) (QSF)	W18-16 (aet)	t:Barnes(2),Holroyd g:Forber(3)	N/A	1,221
10/10/21	Doncaster (h) (POF)	W36-12	t:J Brown,Fitzsimmons,Forber,Henson,O'Brien,Holroyd g:Forber(6)	N/A	2,997

Coventry (h) (R10), Rochdale (a) (R11) and Barrow (h) (R12) games were postponed, and not rearranged

		APP		TRIES		GOALS		FG		PTS	
	D.O.B.	ALL	L1	ALL	L1	ALL	L1	ALL	L1	ALL	L1
Caine Barnes	22/2/99	15(1)	15(1)	5	5	0	0	0	0	20	20
Ethan Bickerdike	15/2/01	10	10	4	4	0	0	0	0	16	16
Joe Brown	24/4/87	15	15	6	6	0	0	0	0	24	24
Lewis Brown	29/11/98	(3)	(3)	1	1	0	0	0	0	4	4
Rhys Clarke	12/3/91	3(14)	3(14)	2	2	0	0	0	0	8	8
Tom Curwen	15/8/89	(1)	(1)	0	0	0	0	0	0	0	0
Hanley Dawson	25/5/96	13(3)	13(3)	5	5	0	0	0	0	20	20
Jamie Doran	8/12/94	17	17	4	4	0	0	0	0	16	16
Gabe Fell	12/9/95	7	7	0	0	0	0	0	0	0	0
Conor Fitzsimmons	7/5/98	17	17	4	4	0	0	0	0	16	16
Carl Forber	17/3/85	17	17	6	6	76	76	0	0	176	176
Johnny Goulding	7/10/88	(1)	(1)	0	0	0	0	0	0	0	0
Matty Henson	31/10/94	4(12)	4(12)	11	11	0	0	0	0	44	44
Brad Holroyd	15/4/00	17	17	18	18	0	0	1	1	73	73
John Hutchings	1/1/99	1(2)	1(2)	0	0	0	0	0	0	0	0
Jake Lightowler	22/2/99	7(4)	7(4)	2	2	0	0	0	0	8	8
Blain Marwood	23/1/98	(4)	(4)	3	3	0	0	0	0	12	12
Jake Moore	6/9/96	11(2)	11(2)	5	5	0	0	0	0	20	20
Marcus O'Brien	13/7/93	11	11	2	2	0	0	0	0	8	8
Dec O'Donnell	7/9/98	12(1)	12(1)	5	5	0	0	0	0	20	20
Jordan O'Leary	8/10/97	(2)	(2)	0	0	0	0	0	0	0	0
Zac Olstrom	11/3/00	5	5	1	1	0	0	0	0	4	4
Lee Postlethwaite	22/8/94	3	3	1	1	0	0	0	0	4	4
Adam Ramsden	27/8/91	(1)	(1)	0	0	0	0	0	0	0	0
Stevie Scholey	7/1/96	3(2)	3(2)	1	1	0	0	0	0	4	4
Perry Singleton	5/1/94	3(5)	3(5)	0	0	0	0	0	0	0	0
Jordan Thomson	23/1/93	2(1)	2(1)	0	0	0	0	0	0	0	0
David Weetman	24/5/98	3	3	0	0	0	0	0	0	0	0
Calvin Wellington	10/12/95	12	12	3	3	0	0	0	0	12	12
Ryan Wilson	24/7/91	(8)	(8)	0	0	0	0	0	0	0	0
Alex Young	6/4/99	13	13	4	4	0	0	0	0	16	16

Brad Holroyd

'L1' totals include regular season & play-offs

CLUB RECORDS **MATCH RECORDS**	**Highest score:** 94-4 v Leigh, 26/2/95 **Highest score against:** 0-92 v Bradford, 14/2/99 **Record attendance:** 17,741 v Wigan, 3/3/65 **Tries:** 7 Ike Southward v Blackpool, 17/9/55 **Goals:** 14 Darren Holt v Gateshead, 12/6/2011 **Points:** 42 Dean Marwood v Highfield, 1/11/92; Dean Marwood v Leigh, 26/2/95
SEASON RECORDS **CAREER RECORDS**	**Tries:** 49 Johnny Lawrenson 1951-52 **Goals:** 186 Lyn Hopkins 1981-82 **Points:** 438 Lyn Hopkins 1981-82 **Tries:** 274 Ike Southward 1952-68 **Goals:** 890 *(inc 5fg)* Carl Forber 2007-2009; 2012-2021 **Points:** 2,027 Carl Forber 2007-2009; 2012-2021 **Appearances:** 419 Paul Charlton 1961-69; 1975-80

LEAGUE 1 2021
Round by Round

ROUND 1

Saturday 8th May 2021

LONDON SKOLARS 24
NORTH WALES CRUSADERS 44

SKOLARS: 1 Omari Caro; 2 Jonah Varela; 4 Lameck Juma; 3 Kameron Pearce-Paul; 5 Errol Carter; 6 Jacob Thomas; 7 Mike Bishay; 8 Eddie Mbaraga; 9 Tom Firth; 10 James Tyas; 11 Adam Vrahnos; 12 Mike Greenhalgh; 13 Christian Gale. Subs (all used): 25 Neil Thorman; 17 Rob Oakley; 18 Lamont Bryan; 15 Malikhi Lloyd-Jones.
Tries: M Greenhalgh (11), Pearce-Paul (62), Oakley (68, 77);
Goals: Caro 1/1, Thorman 3/3.
Sin bin: Caro (32) - high tackle on Gibson.
CRUSADERS: 2 Jack Holmes; 15 Patrick Ah Van; 3 Ben Morris; 4 Earl Hurst; 5 Rob Massam; 6 Brad Billsborough; 7 Jordy Gibson; 8 Chris Barratt; 9 Karl Ashall; 10 Warren Thompson; 11 Gav Rodden; 13 Jono Smith; 12 Alex Eckley. Subs (all used): 14 George Roby; 17 Callum Hazzard; 16 Brad Brennan; 18 Jack Cottington.
Tries: Ah Van (24, 45, 65), Gibson (32, 40), Smith (52), Massam (55), Hurst (80);
Goals: Billsborough 6/8, Gibson 0/1.
Rugby Leaguer & League Express Men of the Match: *Skolars:* Neil Thorman; *Crusaders:* Jordy Gibson.
Penalty count: 11-6; **Half-time:** 6-20;
Referee: James Vella.

Sunday 9th May 2021

HUNSLET 16 WORKINGTON TOWN 28

HUNSLET: 24 Jake Sweeting; 2 Kiedan Hartley; 5 Matty Chrimes; 4 Tom Ashton; 19 Liam Copland; 6 Simon Brown; 7 Dom Brambani; 8 Jordan Andrade; 9 Vila Halafihi; 10 Harry Kidd; 11 Brad Hey; 18 AJ Boardman; 13 Harvey Hallas. Subs (all used): 14 Nathan Conroy; 15 Alex Rowe; 21 Joe McClean; 16 Sion Jones.
Tries: Andrade (15), Conroy (34), Chrimes (72);
Goals: Brambani 2/3.
TOWN: 1 Gabe Fell; 2 Brad Holroyd; 24 Ethan Bickerdike; 4 Calvin Wellington; 5 Alex Young; 6 Jamie Doran; 7 Carl Forber; 8 Conor Fitzsimmons; 9 Dec O'Donnell; 25 Jake Lightowler; 16 Jake Moore; 12 Caine Barnes; 13 Hanley Dawson. Subs (all used): 23 Matty Henson; 15 Tom Curwen; 33 Rhys Clarke; 20 Lewis Brown.
Tries: Doran (11), Henson (30, 76), O'Donnell (43, 46);
Goals: Forber 4/5.
Sin bin: Holroyd (70) - holding down.
Rugby Leaguer & League Express Men of the Match: *Hunslet:* Jordan Andrade; *Town:* Jamie Doran.
Penalty count: 9-3; **Half-time:** 12-12;
Referee: Cameron Worsley.

COVENTRY BEARS 20 BARROW RAIDERS 38

BEARS: 1 Nathan Hill; 2 Hayden Freeman; 3 Liam Welham; 4 Matt Welham; 23 Reece Rance; 6 Dave Scott; 7 Dan Coates; 8 Peter Ryan; 9 Chris Cullimore; 19 Bradley Ho; 11 Jed Charlton; 14 Elliot Townsend; 12 Kieran Sherratt. Subs (all used): 18 Jordan Paga; 25 Jack Dawson; 16 Sam Bowring; 22 Josh Dunne.
Tries: Hill (20, 30), Bowring (25), L Welham (53);
Goals: Coates 2/4.
Sin bin: Hill (65) - holding down.
RAIDERS: 1 Luke Cresswell; 2 Theerapol Ritson; 3 Declan Hulme; 4 Mark Tyson; 5 Shane Toal; 14 Jake Carter; 7 Ryan Johnston; 10 Carl Forster; 9 Nathan Mossop; 17 Adam Walne; 16 Tom Hopkins; 12 Jarrad Stack; 20 Ben Harrison. Subs (all used): 27 Harry Swarbrick; 15 Dan Toal; 8 Ryan Duffy; 25 Callum Bustin.
Tries: Mossop (6), Carter (10, 46), Tyson (14), Forster (28), S Toal (68), A Walne (78); **Goals:** Carter 5/7.
Rugby Leaguer & League Express Men of the Match: *Bears:* Nathan Hill; *Raiders:* Jake Carter.
Penalty count: 8-6; **Half-time:** 14-24;
Referee: Matt Rossleigh.

KEIGHLEY COUGARS 44 DONCASTER 18

COUGARS: 1 Quentin Laulu-Togaga'e; 2 Mo Agoro; 3 Jake Webster; 31 Charlie Graham; 21 Alfie Seeley; 15 Scott Murrell; 7 Jack Miller; 29 Zach Braham; 14 Ryan Wright; 20 Brenden Santi; 28 Josh Lynam; 12 Dan Parker; 24 Kieran Moran. Subs (all used): 8 Jack Coventry; 9 Kyle Kesik; 13 Aaron Levy; 27 Jack Arnold.
Tries: Q Laulu-Togaga'e (4), Graham (28, 78), Levy (39), Seeley (51), Coventry (55), Santi (64), Miller (74);
Goals: Miller 6/8.
Sin bin: Webster (50) - fighting.
DONCASTER: 1 Ben Johnston; 28 Misi Taulapapa; 3 Sam Smeaton; 4 Jason Tali; 18 Tom Halliday; 24 Watson Boas; 7 Matty Beharrell; 8 Russ Spiers; 9 Kieran Cross; 10 Brandon Douglas; 23 Liam Johnson; 19 Aaron Ollett; 27 Aaron York. Subs (all used): 15 Ryan Boyle; 17 Ross Peltier; 21 Ryan Dixon; 26 Ross Whitmore.
Tries: Cross (18), L Johnson (21), Beharrell (45);
Goals: Boas 2/2, Beharrell 1/1.
Sin bin: Beharrell (9) - dangerous challenge; B Johnston (50) - fighting.
Rugby Leaguer & League Express Men of the Match: *Cougars:* Kyle Kesik; *Doncaster:* Brandon Douglas.
Penalty count: 12-12; **Half-time:** 18-12;
Referee: John McMullen.

ROCHDALE HORNETS 40 WEST WALES RAIDERS 16

HORNETS: 1 Sam Freeman; 2 Shaun Ainscough; 3 Ben Calland; 12 Jordan Syme; 4 Jack Higginson; 7 Rob Fairclough; 15 Danny Yates; 10 Gavin Bennion; 21 Ben Moores; 16 Adam Hesketh; 11 Josh Jordan-Roberts; 8 Callum Marriott; 20 Zac Baker. Subs (all used): 17 Fuifui Moimoi; 13 Joe Taira; 9 Sean Penkywicz; 6 Lewis Sheridan.
Tries: Bennion (4), Penkywicz (32, 43, 47, 57), Yates (45), L Sheridan (73); **Goals:** Freeman 6/7.
RAIDERS: 31 Will Ramsey; 22 Michael Holden; 25 Jamie Laing; 4 Marcus Webb; 5 Dai Evans; 23 Fraser Stroud; 6 Rangi Chase; 8 Tom Morgan; 15 Ashley Bateman; 13 Morgan Evans; 11 Mike Connor; 30 Callum Mulkeen; 12 Joe Burke. Subs (all used): 9 Dafydd Phillips; 27 Morgan Allen; 34 Ewan Badham; 28 Eparama Boginsoko.
Tries: Webb (26), M Evans (54), Connor (79);
Goals: Ramsey 2/3.
Rugby Leaguer & League Express Men of the Match: *Hornets:* Sean Penkywicz; *Raiders:* Will Ramsey.
Penalty count: 7-13; **Half-time:** 12-4;
Referee: Michael Mannifield.

ROUND 2

Saturday 15th May 2021

NORTH WALES CRUSADERS 18 HUNSLET 26

CRUSADERS: 1 Jack Holmes; 15 Patrick Ah Van; 3 Cam Brown; 4 Earl Hurst; 5 Rob Massam; 6 Brad Billsborough; 7 Jordy Gibson; 8 Chris Barratt; 9 Karl Ashall; 10 Warren Thompson; 11 Gav Rodden; 13 Jono Smith; 12 Alex Eckley. Subs (all used): 14 George Roby; 17 Callum Hazzard; 16 Brad Brennan; 18 Jack Cottington.
Tries: Brown (10), Eckley (21), Rodden (47);
Goals: Billsborough 3/3.
Dismissal: Roby (77) - high tackle.
HUNSLET: 2 Kiedan Hartley; 25 Wayne Reittie; 24 George Senior; 4 Tom Ashton; 5 Matty Chrimes; 6 Simon Brown; 7 Dom Brambani; 8 Jordan Andrade; 9 Vila Halafihi; 10 Harry Kidd; 11 Brad Hey; 12 Duane Straugheir; 17 Lewis Wray. Subs (all used): 14 Nathan Conroy; 13 Harvey Hallas; 15 Alex Rowe; 16 Sion Jones.
Tries: Ashton (4), Jones (29), Hartley (34, 67);
Goals: Brambani 5/5.
Sin bin: Hartley (74) - shoulder charge.
Rugby Leaguer & League Express Men of the Match: *Crusaders:* Cam Brown; *Hunslet:* Tom Ashton.
Penalty count: 6-7; **Half-time:** 12-18;
Referee: Matt Rossleigh.

WEST WALES RAIDERS 10 COVENTRY BEARS 36

RAIDERS: 31 Will Ramsey; 22 Michael Holden; 4 Marcus Webb; 5 Dai Evans; 2 Uraia Naulusala; 23 Fraser Stroud; 6 Rangi Chase; 8 Tom Morgan; 15 Ashley Bateman; 13 Morgan Evans; 17 Rhys Davies; 30 Callum Mulkeen; 12 Joe Burke. Subs (all used): 9 Dafydd Phillips; 27 Morgan Allen; 11 Mike Connor; 16 Sam Herron.
Tries: Webb (24), D Phillips (44); **Goals:** Ramsey 1/2.
BEARS: 1 Nathan Hill; 2 AJ Towse; 25 Jack Dawson; 4 Liam Welham; 23 Reece Rance; 7 Dan Coates; 6 Dave Scott; 8 Peter Ryan; 9 Chris Cullimore; 19 Bradley Ho; 11 Jed Charlton; 16 Sam Bowring; 12 Kieran Sherratt. Subs (all used): 10 Stefanos Bastas; 14 Elliot Townsend; 21 Josh Dunne; 13 Ryan Langton.
Tries: Ryan (4, 19), Towse (34), L Welham (39), Hill (71), Sherratt (80); **Goals:** Coates 6/7.
Rugby Leaguer & League Express Men of the Match: *Raiders:* Michael Holden; *Bears:* Peter Ryan.
Penalty count: 6-7; **Half-time:** 4-22;
Referee: Liam Staveley.

Sunday 16th May 2021

WORKINGTON TOWN 50 LONDON SKOLARS 16

TOWN: 1 Gabe Fell; 2 Brad Holroyd; 24 Ethan Bickerdike; 4 Calvin Wellington; 5 Alex Young; 6 Jamie Doran; 7 Carl Forber; 8 Conor Fitzsimmons; 9 Dec O'Donnell; 25 Jake Lightowler; 16 Jake Moore; 12 Caine Barnes; 14 Marcus O'Brien. Subs (all used): 23 Matty Henson; 33 Rhys Clarke; 21 Adam Ramsden; 20 Lewis Brown.
Tries: Lightowler (18), Young (28, 67), Henson (32), Holroyd (35, 48, 64), O'Donnell (42), Fitzsimmons (57);
Goals: Forber 7/9.
SKOLARS: 1 Louis Sheriff; 2 Errol Carter; 3 Jonah Varela; 4 Kameron Pearce-Paul; 5 Omari Caro; 6 Jacob Thomas; 7 Mike Bishay; 8 Christian Gale; 9 Neil Thorman; 10 James Tyas; 11 Adam Vrahnos; 12 Eddie Mbaraga; 13 Rob Oakley. Subs (all used): 14 Malikhi Lloyd-Jones; 15 Charles Hammond; 16 Marcus Hockey; 17 Louis Singleton.
Tries: Pearce-Paul (6), Carter (39), Thomas (73);
Goals: Thorman 2/2, Caro 0/1.
Rugby Leaguer & League Express Men of the Match: *Town:* Jamie Doran; *Skolars:* Eddie Mbaraga.
Penalty count: 5-3; **Half-time:** 22-10;
Referee: John McMullen.

BARROW RAIDERS 40 KEIGHLEY COUGARS 18

RAIDERS: 1 Luke Cresswell; 5 Shane Toal; 32 Hakim Miloudi; 4 Mark Tyson; 2 Theerapol Ritson; 6 Jamie Dallimore; 14 Jake Carter; 17 Adam Walne; 9 Nathan Mossop; 10 Carl Forster; 16 Tom Hopkins; 12 Jarrad Stack; 20 Ben Harrison. Subs (all used): 7 Ryan Johnston; 8 Ryan Duffy; 15 Dan Toal; 25 Callum Bustin.
Tries: Cresswell (7), Stack (13, 68), Miloudi (24), Dallimore (38), Harrison (78);
Goals: Carter 5/6, Dallimore 3/3.
Sin bin: Dallimore (48) - high tackle on Webster.
COUGARS: 1 Quentin Laulu-Togaga'e; 4 Taylor Prell; 3 Jake Webster; 31 Charlie Graham; 21 Alfie Seeley; 15 Scott Murrell; 7 Jack Miller; 29 Zach Braham; 14 Ryan Wright; 20 Brenden Santi; 28 Josh Lynam; 12 Dan Parker; 24 Kieran Moran. Subs (all used): 8 Jack Coventry; 9 Kyle Kesik; 13 Aaron Levy; 27 Jack Arnold.
Tries: Santi (33), Webster (46), Murrell (52);
Goals: Miller 3/3.
Rugby Leaguer & League Express Men of the Match: *Raiders:* Ben Harrison; *Cougars:* Brenden Santi.
Penalty count: 10-8; **Half-time:** 24-6;
Referee: Michael Mannifield.

DONCASTER 30 ROCHDALE HORNETS 22

DONCASTER: 28 Misi Taulapapa; 32 Ollie Greensmith; 3 Sam Smeaton; 4 Jason Tali; 5 Sam Doherty; 24 Watson Boas; 7 Matty Beharrell; 15 Ryan Boyle; 26 Ross Whitmore; 10 Brandon Douglas; 23 Liam Johnson; 19 Aaron Ollett; 16 Brandan Wilkinson. Subs (all used): 1 Ben Johnston; 29 Anesu Mudoti; 17 Ross Peltier; 27 Aaron York.
Tries: Douglas (5), Tali (10), Greensmith (37, 61), Smeaton (48); **Goals:** Beharrell 5/5.
HORNETS: 6 Lewis Sheridan; 2 Shaun Ainscough; 3 Ben Calland; 4 Jack Higginson; 1 Sam Freeman; 7 Rob Fairclough; 29 Ryan Forshaw; 10 Gavin Bennion; 19 Callum Ogden; 16 Adam Hesketh; 11 Josh Jordan-Roberts; 12 Jordan Syme; 20 Zac Baker. Subs (all used): 9 Sean Penkywicz; 13 Joe Taira; 26 Liam Whalley; 18 Luke Fowden.
Tries: Ainscough (39), Baker (54), Fowden (58), Higginson (72); **Goals:** Freeman 3/4.
Rugby Leaguer & League Express Men of the Match: *Doncaster:* Sam Smeaton; *Hornets:* Zac Baker.
Penalty count: 5-5; **Half-time:** 18-4;
Referee: Nick Bennett.

ROUND 3

Sunday 23rd May 2021

DONCASTER 62 WEST WALES RAIDERS 24

DONCASTER: 28 Misi Taulapapa; 18 Tom Halliday; 3 Sam Smeaton; 4 Jason Tali; 32 Ollie Greensmith; 24 Watson Boas; 7 Matty Beharrell; 29 Anesu Mudoti; 26 Ross Whitmore; 10 Brandon Douglas; 23 Liam Johnson; 19 Aaron Ollett; 16 Brandan Wilkinson. Subs (all used): 1 Ben Johnston; 22 Alex Holdstock; 17 Ross Peltier; 27 Aaron York.
Tries: Beharrell (9), Halliday (13, 60), Tali (30), Smeaton (39), Peltier (48), Douglas (55), York (71, 80), Greensmith (75), Holdstock (77); **Goals:** Beharrell 9/11.
RAIDERS: 31 Will Ramsey; 22 Michael Holden; 1 Phil Cowburn; 5 Dai Evans; 4 Marcus Webb; 23 Fraser Stroud; 6 Rangi Chase; 13 Morgan Evans; 15 Ashley Bateman; 27 Morgan Allen; 30 Callum Mulkeen; 17 Rhys Davies; 12 Joe Burke. Subs (all used): 8 Tom Morgan; 34 Ewan Badham; 32 Ieuan Badham; 16 Sam Herron.
Tries: Burke (4), Holden (23), Chase (43), Herron (68);
Goals: Ramsey 4/4.
Sin bin: Webb (28) - professional foul.
Rugby Leaguer & League Express Men of the Match: *Doncaster:* Matty Beharrell; *Raiders:* Rangi Chase.
Penalty count: 8-4; **Half-time:** 22-12;
Referee: Cameron Worsley; **Attendance:** 784.

NORTH WALES CRUSADERS 16
WORKINGTON TOWN 44

CRUSADERS: 1 Tommy Johnson; 15 Patrick Ah Van; 3 Jack Holmes; 4 Dante Morley-Samuels; 5 Rob Massam; 6 Elliott Jenkins; 7 Jordy Gibson; 8 Chris Barratt; 9 Brad

Billsborough; 10 Warren Thompson; 11 Gav Rodden; 13 Jono Smith; 12 Alex Eckley. Subs (all used): 14 Andy Ball; 17 Callum Hazzard; 16 Brad Brennan; 18 Jack Cottington.
Tries: Gibson (11), Massam (26), Rodden (47);
Goals: Johnson 2/3.
Sin bin: Barratt (69) - late challenge.
TOWN: 24 Ethan Bickerdike; 2 Brad Holroyd; 31 Joe Brown; 4 Calvin Wellington; 5 Alex Young; 6 Jamie Doran; 7 Carl Forber; 8 Conor Fitzsimmons; 9 Dec O'Donnell; 33 Rhys Clarke; 14 Marcus O'Brien; 12 Caine Barnes; 13 Hanley Dawson. Subs (all used): 23 Matty Henson; 11 Perry Singleton; 10 Stevie Scholey; 20 Lewis Brown.
Tries: Dawson (17), Holroyd (23), Henson (29, 56), Wellington (40), Bickerdike (59), L Brown (70), Young (73);
Goals: Forber 6/8.
Sin bin: Doran (46) - shoulder charge on Jenkins.
Rugby Leaguer & League Express Men of the Match:
Crusaders: Jono Smith; *Town:* Jamie Doran.
Penalty count: 4-7; **Half-time:** 10-24;
Referee: Tom Crashley;
Attendance: N/A *(behind closed doors)*.

COVENTRY BEARS 26 LONDON SKOLARS 44

BEARS: 1 Nathan Hill; 2 AJ Towse; 3 Matt Welham; 4 Liam Welham; 23 Reece Rance; 6 Dan Coates; 7 Dave Scott; 8 Peter Ryan; 9 Chris Cullimore; 19 Bradley Ho; 11 Jed Charlton; 16 Sam Bowring; 12 Kieran Sherratt. Subs (all used): 10 Stefanos Bastas; 25 Jack Dawson; 21 Josh Dunne; 13 Ryan Langton.
Tries: L Welham (2), Sherratt (20), Scott (23), Coates (30, 61); **Goals:** Scott 3/5.
SKOLARS: 1 Richard Wilkinson; 2 Lameck Juma; 4 Louis Sheriff; 3 Jonah Varela; 5 Omari Caro; 21 Jy-mel Coleman; 6 Jacob Thomas; 15 Malikhi Lloyd-Jones; 9 Neil Thorman; 10 James Tyas; 12 Mike Greenhalgh; 11 Paulos Latu; 13 Christian Gale. Subs (all used): 8 Eddie Mbaraga; 14 Louis Singleton; 22 Judd Greenhalgh; 17 Will Blakemore.
Tries: Latu (12), Wilkinson (13), J Greenhalgh (39), Varela (58, 73), Juma (66), M Greenhalgh (69), Caro (76);
Goals: Thorman 6/8.
Rugby Leaguer & League Express Men of the Match:
Bears: Dave Scott; *Skolars:* Jonah Varela.
Penalty count: 9-9; **Half-time:** 20-18;
Referee: Liam Staveley; **Attendance:** 210.

HUNSLET 6 BARROW RAIDERS 29

HUNSLET: 2 Kiedan Hartley; 25 Wayne Reittie; 24 George Senior; 4 Tom Ashton; 20 Niall Walker; 6 Simon Brown; 7 Dom Brambani; 15 Alex Rowe; 9 Vila Halafihi; 10 Harry Kidd; 11 Brad Hey; 12 Duane Straugheir; 17 Lewis Wray. Subs (all used): 14 Nathan Conroy; 8 Jordan Andrade; 21 Joe McClean; 13 Harvey Hallas.
Try: Ashton (33); **Goals:** Brambani 1/1.
RAIDERS: 1 Luke Cresswell; 2 Theerapol Ritson; 32 Hakim Miloudi; 3 Declan Hulme; 5 Shane Toal; 6 Jamie Dallimore; 14 Jake Carter; 10 Carl Forster; 9 Nathan Mossop; 17 Adam Walne; 16 Tom Hopkins; 12 Jarrad Stack; 20 Ben Harrison. Subs (all used): 7 Ryan Johnston; 15 Dan Toal; 11 Danny Morrow; 25 Callum Bustin.
Tries: Carter (37), Dallimore (59), Ritson (63, 75), Johnston (66); **Goals:** Dallimore 4/5;
Field goal: Dallimore (79).
Rugby Leaguer & League Express Men of the Match:
Hunslet: Harry Kidd; *Raiders:* Theerapol Ritson.
Penalty count: 3-5; **Half-time:** 6-6;
Referee: Michael Smaill; **Attendance:** 452.

KEIGHLEY COUGARS 36 ROCHDALE HORNETS 43

COUGARS: 25 Ben Stead; 4 Taylor Prell; 3 Jake Webster; 31 Charlie Graham; 21 Alfie Seeley; 15 Scott Murrell; 7 Jack Miller; 23 Matthew Bailey; 19 Billy Gaylor; 20 Brenden Santi; 11 Jason Muranka; 27 Jack Arnold; 13 Aaron Levy. Subs (all used): 8 Jack Coventry; 9 Kyle Kesik; 17 Dan Hawksworth; 18 Spencer Darley.
Tries: Seeley (19), Murrell (26), Webster (60), Levy (69), Graham (71), Miller (74); **Goals:** Miller 6/7.
HORNETS: 1 Sam Freeman; 2 Shaun Ainscough; 12 Jordan Syme; 30 Lewis Galbraith; 5 Dale Bloomfield; 29 Ryan Forshaw; 7 Rob Fairclough; 17 Fuifui Moimoi; 9 Sean Penkywicz; 13 Joe Taira; 8 Callum Marriott; 11 Josh Jordan-Roberts; 20 Zac Baker. Subs (all used): 10 Gavin Bennion; 14 Declan Sheridan; 16 Adam Hesketh; 18 Luke Fowden.
Tries: Galbraith (11), Forshaw (15), Bennion (31), Ainscough (36, 76), Fairclough (45), Jordan-Roberts (55), Moimoi (64); **Goals:** Jordan-Roberts 5/8;
Field goal: Fairclough (40).
Rugby Leaguer & League Express Men of the Match:
Cougars: Charlie Graham; *Hornets:* Rob Fairclough.
Penalty count: 3-10; **Half-time:** 12-21;
Referee: Kevin Moore; **Attendance:** 700.

ROUND 4

Saturday 29th May 2021

WEST WALES RAIDERS 10 LONDON SKOLARS 52

RAIDERS: 4 Marcus Webb; 20 Ryan Shallish; 30 Callum Mulkeen; 25 Jamie Laing; 22 Michael Holden; 31 Will Ramsey; 23 Fraser Stroud; 8 Tom Morgan; 15 Ashley Bateman; 13 Morgan Evans; 11 Mike Connor; 17 Rhys Davies; 12 Joe Burke. Subs (all used): 9 Dafydd Phillips; 34 Ewan Badham; 32 Ieuan Badham; 27 Morgan Allen.
Tries: Webb (40), Stroud (49); **Goals:** Ramsey 1/2.
SKOLARS: 6 Jacob Thomas; 2 Omari Caro; 3 Jonah Varela; 4 Lameck Juma; 25 Errol Carter; 21 Jy-mel Coleman; 7 Mike Bishay; 8 Christian Gale; 9 Neil Thorman; 10 James Tyas; 18 Paulos Latu; 12 Mike Greenhalgh; 13 Will Blakemore. Subs (all used): 14 Tom Firth; 15 Eddie Mbaraga; 17 Malikhi Lloyd-Jones; 19 Judd Greenhalgh.
Tries: Caro (4, 10, 18, 43, 58), Tyas (25), Thomas (62), Gale (68), Jy-mel Coleman (80);
Goals: Thorman 5/5, Caro 3/3, Bishay 0/1.
Rugby Leaguer & League Express Men of the Match:
Raiders: Marcus Webb; *Skolars:* Omari Caro.
Penalty count: 6-7; **Half-time:** 6-24;
Referee: Tom Crashley;
Attendance: N/A *(behind closed doors)*.

Sunday 30th May 2021

WORKINGTON TOWN 24 DONCASTER 26

TOWN: 1 Gabe Fell; 2 Brad Holroyd; 31 Joe Brown; 4 Calvin Wellington; 5 Alex Young; 6 Jamie Doran; 7 Carl Forber; 8 Conor Fitzsimmons; 9 Dec O'Donnell; 14 Marcus O'Brien; 12 Caine Barnes; 11 Perry Singleton; 13 Hanley Dawson. Subs (all used): 10 Stevie Scholey; 16 Jake Moore; 33 Rhys Clarke; 23 Matty Henson.
Tries: Scholey (43), Henson (47), Young (55), Barnes (70), J Brown (78); **Goals:** Forber 2/5.
DONCASTER: 28 Misi Taulapapa; 18 Tom Halliday; 3 Sam Smeaton; 4 Jason Tali; 32 Ollie Greensmith; 24 Watson Boas; 7 Matty Beharrell; 29 Anesu Mudoti; 26 Ross Whitmore; 16 Brandan Wilkinson; 12 Brad Foster; 19 Aaron Ollett; 27 Aaron York. Subs (all used): 1 Ben Johnston; 17 Ross Peltier; 25 Joe Fella; 22 Alex Holdstock.
Tries: Peltier (14), Beharrell (19), Halliday (34), Holdstock (59); **Goals:** Beharrell 5/6.
Sin bin: Foster (2) - professional foul;
Halliday (8) - shoulder charge.
Rugby Leaguer & League Express Men of the Match:
Town: Caine Barnes; *Doncaster:* Jason Tali.
Penalty count: 5-3; **Half-time:** 0-16;
Referee: Michael Mannifield; **Attendance:** 942.

BARROW RAIDERS 44 NORTH WALES CRUSADERS 8

RAIDERS: 1 Luke Cresswell; 5 Shane Toal; 3 Declan Hulme; 4 Mark Tyson; 2 Theerapol Ritson; 14 Jake Carter; 7 Ryan Johnston; 10 Carl Forster; 9 Nathan Mossop; 17 Adam Walne; 16 Tom Hopkins; 12 Jarrad Stack; 20 Ben Harrison. Subs (all used): 39 Sam Dowsett; 15 Dan Toal; 11 Danny Morrow; 25 Callum Bustin.
Tries: A Walne (4), Tyson (29, 57), Ritson (33), Carter (38), Stack (47), S Toal (64), Cresswell (70);
Goals: Carter 6/8.
CRUSADERS: 1 Tommy Johnson; 15 Patrick Ah Van; 3 Tyme Dow-Nikau; 4 Jack Holmes; 5 Rob Massam; 7 Jordy Gibson; 6 Joe Sanderson; 8 Chris Barratt; 9 Karl Ashall; 10 Warren Thompson; 11 Gav Rodden; 13 Jono Smith; 12 Alex Eckley. Subs (all used): 14 Brad Billsborough; 18 Jack Cottington; 16 Brad Brennan; 17 Callum Hazzard.
Tries: Massam (76), Dow-Nikau (80); **Goals:** Johnson 0/2.
Rugby Leaguer & League Express Men of the Match:
Raiders: Jake Carter; *Crusaders:* Alex Eckley.
Penalty count: 4-7; **Half-time** 24-0;
Referee: Kevin Moore; **Attendance:** 1,915.

COVENTRY BEARS 38 ROCHDALE HORNETS 30

BEARS: 1 Nathan Hill; 20 Kadeem Williams; 3 Matt Welham; 4 Liam Welham; 23 Reece Rance; 6 Dan Coates; 7 Dave Scott; 8 Peter Ryan; 9 Chris Cullimore; 15 Will Budd; 11 Jack Dawson; 16 Sam Bowring; 12 Kieran Sherratt. Subs (all used): 14 Elliot Townsend; 21 Harry Kaufman; 19 Bradley Ho; 13 Ryan Langton.
Tries: Scott (8, 75), Williams (23), L Welham (30), Hill (42), Kaufman (62), M Welham (68); **Goals:** Coates 5/7.
HORNETS: 15 Danny Yates; 2 Shaun Ainscough; 6 Lewis Sheridan; 30 Lewis Galbraith; 5 Dale Bloomfield; 29 Ryan Forshaw; 7 Rob Fairclough; 16 Adam Hesketh; 19 Callum Ogden; 18 Luke Fowden; 12 Jordan Syme; 8 Callum Marriott; 11 Josh Jordan-Roberts. Subs (all used): 14 Declan Sheridan; 17 Fuifui Moimoi; 13 Joe Taira; 23 Lee Registe.
Tries: Fowden (15), Fairclough (18), Ainscough (30), Moimoi (36), Marriott (53); **Goals:** Jordan-Roberts 5/5.
Sin bin: Forshaw (62) - dangerous challenge.
Rugby Leaguer & League Express Men of the Match:
Bears: Dave Scott; *Hornets:* Josh Jordan-Roberts.
Penalty count: 8-8; **Half-time:** 16-24;
Referee: Andrew Sweet; **Attendance:** 232.

KEIGHLEY COUGARS 40 HUNSLET 0

COUGARS: 25 Ben Stead; 34 Josh Slingsby; 4 Taylor Prell; 31 Charlie Graham; 21 Alfie Seeley; 15 Scott Murrell; 7 Jack Miller; 23 Matthew Bailey; 9 Kyle Kesik; 27 Jack Arnold; 3 Jake Webster; 20 Brenden Santi; 13 Aaron Levy. Subs (all used): 10 Dalton Desmond-Walker; 12 Dan Parker; 24 Kieran Moran; 26 Bobby Darbyshire.
Tries: Moran (51), Miller (56), Graham (58, 72), Santi (64, 77, 79); **Goals:** Miller 6/7.
HUNSLET: 5 Matty Chrimes; 26 Wayne Reittie; 3 Ben Tibbs; 4 Tom Ashton; 23 Aaron Jones-Bishop; 24 Dave Gibbons; 7 Dom Brambani; 15 Alex Rowe; 25 Curtis Davies; 10 Harry Kidd; 11 Brad Hey; 16 George Senior; 17 Lewis Wray. Subs (all used): 8 Jordan Andrade; 13 Harvey Hallas; 14 Nathan Conroy; 18 AJ Boardman.
Sin bin: Rowe (74) - dangerous challenge.
Rugby Leaguer & League Express Men of the Match:
Cougars: Brenden Santi; *Hunslet:* Matty Chrimes.
Penalty count: 11-6; **Half-time:** 0-0;
Referee: Nick Bennett; **Attendance:** 683.

ROUND 5

Saturday 5th June 2021

WEST WALES RAIDERS 10 BARROW RAIDERS 60

WEST WALES: 31 Will Ramsey; 4 Marcus Webb; 3 Emosi Nadaubale; 15 Ashley Bateman; 22 Michael Holden; 33 Jamie Murphy; 23 Fraser Stroud; 34 Ewan Badham; 9 Dafydd Phillips; 16 Sam Herron; 18 Charley Bodman; 11 Mike Connor; 12 Joe Burke. Subs: 32 Ieuan Badham; 19 Alan Pope; 20 Ryan Shallish; 30 Callum Mulkeen (not used).
Tries: Murphy (18, 70); **Goals:** Ramsey 1/2.
Sin bin: E Badham (22) - high tackle;
I Badham (68) - fighting.
BARROW: 2 Theerapol Ritson; 27 Harry Swarbrick; 3 Declan Hulme; 12 Jarrad Stack; 5 Shane Toal; 4 Mark Tyson; 7 Ryan Johnston; 25 Callum Bustin; 9 Nathan Mossop; 10 Carl Forster; 16 Tom Hopkins; 11 Danny Morrow; 19 Connor Terrill. Subs (all used): 8 Ryan Duffy; 15 Dan Toal; 22 Carl McBain; 39 Sam Dowsett.
Tries: Mossop (7, 58), Ritson (12, 60, 75), Terrill (23), Morrow (26), Duffy (30), Hulme (39), Stack (42), Tyson (53); **Goals:** Johnston 5/7, Ritson 3/4.
Sin bin: D Toal (68) - fighting.
Rugby Leaguer & League Express Men of the Match:
West Wales: Jamie Murphy; *Barrow:* Theerapol Ritson.
Penalty count: 7-3; **Half-time:** 4-34;
Referee: Andrew Sweet;
Attendance: N/A *(behind closed doors)*.

Sunday 6th June 2021

WORKINGTON TOWN 34 KEIGHLEY COUGARS 20

TOWN: 24 Ethan Bickerdike; 2 Brad Holroyd; 31 Joe Brown; 4 Calvin Wellington; 5 Alex Young; 6 Jamie Doran; 7 Carl Forber; 8 Conor Fitzsimmons; 9 Dec O'Donnell; 10 Stevie Scholey; 16 Jake Moore; 12 Caine Barnes; 13 Hanley Dawson. Subs (all used): 23 Matty Henson; 33 Rhys Clarke; 18 Jordan Thomson; 25 Jake Lightowler.
Tries: Moore (12), Holroyd (15, 45), Lightowler (35), Barnes (71), Henson (77); **Goals:** Forber 5/6.
COUGARS: 1 Quentin Laulu-Togaga'e; 34 Josh Slingsby; 4 Taylor Prell; 31 Charlie Graham; 21 Alfie Seeley; 9 Kyle Kesik; 7 Jack Miller; 23 Matthew Bailey; 26 Bobby Darbyshire; 27 Jack Arnold; 3 Jake Webster; 20 Brenden Santi; 13 Aaron Levy. Subs (all used): 10 Dalton Desmond-Walker; 12 Dan Parker; 14 Ryan Wright; 24 Kieran Moran.
Tries: Slingsby (5, 24), Santi (21), Prell (49);
Goals: Miller 2/4.
Rugby Leaguer & League Express Men of the Match:
Town: Jamie Doran; *Cougars:* Quentin Laulu-Togaga'e.
Penalty count: 7-5; **Half-time:** 18-16;
Referee: Gareth Hewer; **Attendance:** 942.

NORTH WALES CRUSADERS 36 COVENTRY BEARS 12

CRUSADERS: 1 Tommy Johnson; 15 Patrick Ah Van; 3 Tyme Dow-Nikau; 4 Jack Holmes; 5 Rob Massam; 6 Joe Sanderson; 7 Jordy Gibson; 17 Callum Hazzard; 9 Karl Ashall; 10 Warren Thompson; 11 Gav Rodden; 18 Ben Morris; 12 Alex Eckley. Subs (all used): 14 Brad Billsborough; 13 Brad Calland; 16 Brad Brennan; 8 James Thornton.
Tries: Dow-Nikau (7, 58), Massam (18, 63, 80), Johnson (38), Morris (44); **Goals:** Johnson 4/7.
BEARS: 1 Nathan Hill; 23 Reece Rance; 16 Sam Bowring; 4 Liam Welham; 20 Kadeem Williams; 6 Dave Scott; 7 Dan

Coates; 8 Peter Ryan; 9 Chris Cullimore; 15 Will Budd; 11 Jed Charlton; 25 Jack Dawson; 12 Kieran Sherratt. Subs (all used): 14 Elliot Townsend; 19 Bradley Ho; 21 Harry Kaufman; 13 Ryan Langton.
Tries: Scott (53), Townsend (68); **Goals:** Coates 2/2.
Rugby Leaguer & League Express Men of the Match: *Crusaders:* Tyme Dow-Nikau; *Bears:* Elliot Townsend.
Penalty count: 8-7; **Half-time:** 16-0;
Referee: Cameron Worsley;
Attendance: N/A *(behind closed doors)*.

DONCASTER 46 LONDON SKOLARS 12

DONCASTER: 28 Misi Taulapapa; 18 Tom Halliday; 3 Sam Smeaton; 4 Jason Tali; 32 Ollie Greensmith; 1 Ben Johnston; 7 Matty Beharrell; 29 Anesu Mudoti; 24 Watson Boas; 15 Ryan Boyle; 23 Liam Johnson; 11 Danny Bravo; 12 Brad Foster. Subs (all used): 16 Brandan Wilkinson; 17 Ross Peltier; 22 Alex Holdstock; 26 Ross Whitmore.
Tries: Tali (29), Beharrell (34, 78), L Johnson (45), Bravo (51), Greensmith (56), Smeaton (60), B Johnston (69); **Goals:** Beharrell 7/8.
SKOLARS: 1 Richard Wilkinson; 2 Greg Johnson; 3 Jonah Varela; 4 Kameron Pearce-Paul; 25 Errol Carter; 6 Oliver Leyland; 7 Mike Bishay; 8 Christian Gale; 9 Neil Thorman; 10 James Tyas; 12 Mike Greenhalgh; 11 Lameck Juma; 13 Will Blakemore. Subs (all used): 14 Tom Firth; 15 Malikhi Lloyd-Jones; 21 Judd Greenhalgh; 22 Eddie Mbaraga.
Tries: Wilkinson (8), Juma (23); **Goals:** Thorman 2/2.
Rugby Leaguer & League Express Men of the Match: *Doncaster:* Matty Beharrell; *Skolars:* Christian Gale.
Penalty count: 8-5; **Half-time:** 12-12;
Referee: John McMullen; **Attendance:** 882.

HUNSLET 36 ROCHDALE HORNETS 22

HUNSLET: 1 Jimmy Watson; 26 Wayne Reittie; 5 Matty Chrimes; 4 Tom Ashton; 18 Alex Brown; 22 Jy-mel Coleman; 7 Dom Brambani; 15 Alex Rowe; 14 Nathan Conroy; 27 Zach Braham; 11 Brad Hey; 16 George Senior; 17 Lewis Wray. Subs (all used): 24 Dave Gibbons; 8 Jordan Andrade; 21 Joe McClean; 13 Harvey Hallas.
Tries: A Brown (10, 47), Rowe (15, 59), McClean (30), Ashton (80); **Goals:** Brambani 3/3, Coleman 3/4.
HORNETS: 6 Lewis Sheridan; 27 Dan Nixon; 12 Jordan Syme; 30 Lewis Galbraith; 14 Declan Sheridan; 29 Ryan Forshaw; 15 Danny Yates; 16 Adam Hesketh; 9 Sean Penkywicz; 17 Fuifui Moimoi; 11 Josh Jordan-Roberts; 8 Callum Marriott; 20 Zac Baker. Subs (all used): 19 Callum Ogden; 24 Ben Forster; 22 Jimmy Connaughton; 18 Luke Fowden.
Tries: Penkywicz (19), D Sheridan (40), L Sheridan (51, 68); **Goals:** Jordan-Roberts 3/4.
Sin bin: Moimoi (24) - late challenge.
Rugby Leaguer & League Express Men of the Match: *Hunslet:* Zach Braham; *Hornets:* Lewis Sheridan.
Penalty count: 9-4; **Half-time:** 18-10;
Referee: Aaron Moore; **Attendance:** 483.

ROUND 6

Saturday 12th June 2021

BARROW RAIDERS 40 ROCHDALE HORNETS 4

RAIDERS: 1 Luke Cresswell; 5 Shane Toal; 3 Declan Hulme; 4 Mark Tyson; 2 Theerapol Ritson; 6 Jamie Dallimore; 7 Ryan Johnston; 17 Adam Walne; 9 Nathan Mossop; 10 Carl Forster; 11 Danny Morrow; 12 Jarrad Stack; 16 Tom Hopkins. Subs (all used): 18 Bradd Crellin; 8 Ryan Duffy; 15 Dan Toal; 25 Callum Bustin.
Tries: Ritson (37, 59, 62), Stack (42), Bustin (52), Forster (71); **Goals:** Dallimore 8/8.
Sin bin: Crellin (76) - late challenge.
HORNETS: 6 Lewis Sheridan; 2 Shaun Ainscough; 12 Jordan Syme; 27 Dan Nixon; 5 Dale Bloomfield; 15 Danny Yates; 9 Sean Penkywicz; 8 Callum Marriott; 21 Ben Moores; 17 Fuifui Moimoi; 40 Paul Brearley; 11 Josh Jordan-Roberts; 20 Zac Baker. Subs (all used): 38 Tyler Walton; 19 Callum Ogden; 18 Luke Fowden; 24 Ben Forster.
Try: Nixon (20); **Goals:** Jordan-Roberts 0/1.
Sin bin: Brearley (47) - professional foul; Baker (50) - late challenge.
Rugby Leaguer & League Express Men of the Match: *Raiders:* Theerapol Ritson; *Hornets:* Paul Brearley.
Penalty count: 12-6; **Half-time** 8-4;
Referee: Cameron Worsley; **Attendance** 1,758.

LONDON SKOLARS 10 HUNSLET 62

SKOLARS: 1 Jacob Thomas; 25 Dalton Grant; 4 Kameron Pearce-Paul; 3 Jonah Varela; 5 Greg Johnson; 6 Oliver Leyland; 7 Mike Bishay; 8 Judd Greenhalgh; 9 Neil Thorman; 10 James Tyas; 19 Paulos Latu; 12 Lameck Juma; 21 Mike Greenhalgh. Subs (all used): - Tom Firth; 13 Christian Gale; - Eddie Mbaraga; 15 Malikhi Lloyd-Jones.
Tries: Juma (6), Johnson (61); **Goals:** Thorman 1/2.
Sin bin: M Greenhalgh (75) - fighting.
HUNSLET: 1 Jimmy Watson; 20 Niall Walker; 5 Matty Chrimes; 4 Tom Ashton; 13 Alex Brown; 6 Simon Brown; 24 Dave Gibbons; 27 Zach Braham; 9 Vila Halafihi; 15 Alex Rowe; 11 Brad Hey; 12 Duane Straugheir; 16 Mikey Wood. Subs (all used): 14 Nathan Conroy; 26 Sion Jones; 21 Joe McClean; 17 Lewis Wray.
Tries: Ashton (9, 11), Gibbons (15, 27), Halafihi (25, 30, 69), S Brown (40), Jones (42, 48), Chrimes (72), Rowe (80); **Goals:** S Brown 0/2, Gibbons 7/10.
Rugby Leaguer & League Express Men of the Match: *Skolars:* Lameck Juma; *Hunslet:* Zach Braham.
Penalty count: 4-7; **Half-time:** 6-36;
Referee: Kevin Moore; **Attendance:** 370.

Sunday 13th June 2021

COVENTRY BEARS 12 WORKINGTON TOWN 30

BEARS: 3 Matt Welham; 25 Jack Dawson; 12 Kieran Sherratt; 16 Sam Bowring; 23 Reece Rance; 7 Dan Coates; 6 Dave Scott; 8 Peter Ryan; 9 Chris Cullimore; 15 Josh Dunne; 11 Jed Charlton; 14 Elliot Townsend; 19 Bradley Ho. Subs (all used): 18 Elliott Windley; 22 Stefanos Bastas; 21 Harry Kaufman; 10 Darius Hamilton.
Tries: Sherratt (16), Ho (79); **Goals:** Coates 2/2.
Sin bin: Cullimore (8) - late challenge.
TOWN: 24 Ethan Bickerdike; 2 Brad Holroyd; 31 Joe Brown; 4 Calvin Wellington; 5 Alex Young; 6 Jamie Doran; 7 Carl Forber; 8 Conor Fitzsimmons; 9 Dec O'Donnell; 10 Stevie Scholey; 16 Jake Moore; 12 Caine Barnes; 13 Hanley Dawson. Subs (all used): 23 Matty Henson; 33 Rhys Clarke; 17 Johnny Goulding; 25 Jake Lightowler.
Tries: Dawson (3), Bickerdike (19), Holroyd (54, 60), Forber (75); **Goals:** Forber 5/5.
Rugby Leaguer & League Express Men of the Match: *Bears:* Kieran Sherratt; *Town:* Brad Holroyd.
Penalty count: 7-5; **Half-time:** 6-12;
Referee: Tom Crashley; **Attendance:** 198.

KEIGHLEY COUGARS 70 WEST WALES RAIDERS 12

COUGARS: 1 Quentin Laulu-Togaga'e; 34 Josh Slingsby; 3 Jake Webster; 4 Taylor Prell; 5 Robert Matamosi; 15 Scott Murrell; 7 Jack Miller; 23 Matthew Bailey; 14 Ryan Wright; 18 Spencer Darley; 13 Aaron Levy; 12 Dan Parker; 9 Kyle Kesik. Subs (all used): 8 Jack Coventry; 10 Dalton Desmond-Walker; 24 Kieran Moran; 33 Phoenix Laulu-Togaga'e.
Tries: Webster (3), Parker (14, 56, 59), Prell (17, 51), Miller (23, 68), Slingsby (28), Q Laulu-Togaga'e (31, 76), Levy (65), Darley (79); **Goals:** Miller 9/13.
Sin bin: Moran (64) - fighting.
RAIDERS: 31 Will Ramsey; 4 Marcus Webb; 20 Ryan Shallish; 2 Uraia Naulusala; 22 Michael Holden; 23 Fraser Stroud; 33 Jamie Murphy; 13 Morgan Evans; 9 Dafydd Phillips; 34 Ewan Badham; 30 Callum Mulkeen; 12 Joe Burke; 15 Ashley Bateman. Subs (all used): 16 Sam Herron; 18 Charley Bodman; 26 Alex Hicken; 32 Ieuan Badham.
Tries: Murphy (36), Herron (45); **Goals:** Ramsey 2/2.
Dismissal: E Badham (64) - fighting.
Rugby Leaguer & League Express Men of the Match: *Cougars:* Kyle Kesik; *Raiders:* Michael Holden.
Penalty count: 3-2; **Half-time:** 34-6;
Referee: Matt Rossleigh; **Attendance:** 463.

NORTH WALES CRUSADERS 0 DONCASTER 68

CRUSADERS: 1 Tommy Johnson; 15 Patrick Ah Van; 3 Tyme Dow-Nikau; 4 Jack Holmes; 5 Rob Massam; 6 Elliott Jenkins; 7 Joe Sanderson; 16 Brad Brennan; 9 Karl Ashall; 13 Chris Barratt; 11 Gav Rodden; 12 Ben Morris; 10 Jordy Gibson. Subs (all used): 14 Andy Ball; 17 Brad Calland; 18 Jack Cottington; 8 James Thornton.
Sin bin: Dow-Nikau (44) - late challenge.
DONCASTER: 28 Misi Taulapapa; 5 Sam Doherty; 3 Sam Smeaton; 4 Jason Tali; 32 Ollie Greensmith; 1 Ben Johnston; 7 Matty Beharrell; 15 Ryan Boyle; 26 Ross Whitmore; 16 Brandan Wilkinson; 23 Liam Johnson; 11 Danny Bravo; 12 Brad Foster. Subs (all used): 27 Aaron York; 17 Ross Peltier; 19 Aaron Ollett; 22 Alex Holdstock.
Tries: Taulapapa (4, 22), Doherty (9, 45), Greensmith (15, 58, 79), L Johnson (18), B Johnston (29), Smeaton (39), Foster (58, 77), Holdstock (73);
Goals: Beharrell 3/8, Doherty 5/5.
Rugby Leaguer & League Express Men of the Match: *Crusaders:* Jordy Gibson; *Doncaster:* Misi Taulapapa.
Penalty count: 3-6; **Half-time:** 0-34;
Referee: James Vella;
Attendance: N/A *(behind closed doors)*.

ROUND 7

Saturday 19th June 2021

WEST WALES RAIDERS 10
NORTH WALES CRUSADERS 60

RAIDERS: 22 Michael Holden; 16 Sam Herron; 5 Dai Evans; 20 Ryan Shallish; 21 Aedan Coleman; 23 Fraser Stroud; 33 Jamie Murphy; 13 Morgan Evans; 15 Ashley Bateman; 27 Morgan Allen; 30 Callum Mulkeen; 18 Charley Bodman; 12 Joe Burke. Subs: 26 Alex Hicken; 10 Harry Boots; 31 Will Ramsey (not used); 28 Eparama Boginsoko (not used).
Tries: D Evans (60, 77); **Goals:** Murphy 1/2.
CRUSADERS: 1 Elliott Jenkins; 15 Patrick Ah Van; 3 Tyme Dow-Nikau; 4 Matt Reid; 5 Rob Massam; 6 Brad Billsborough; 7 Jordy Gibson; 16 Brad Brennan; 9 Karl Ashall; 10 James Thornton; 11 Gav Rodden; 12 Ben Morris; 13 Chris Barratt. Subs (all used): 14 Connor Aspey; 19 Cam Brown; 8 Ethan O'Hanlon; 17 Jack Cottington.
Tries: Dow-Nikau (9, 48), Massam (12, 21, 70), Reid (36, 45), Aspey (52, 56), Billsborough (64), Brown (73), Ah Van (80); **Goals:** Billsborough 6/12.
Rugby Leaguer & League Express Men of the Match: *Raiders:* Dai Evans; *Crusaders:* Rob Massam.
Penalty count: 0-3; **Half-time:** 0-20;
Referee: Matt Rossleigh; **Attendance:** 285.

LONDON SKOLARS 14 BARROW RAIDERS 24

SKOLARS: 1 Iliess Macani; 5 Charles Hammond; 4 Kameron Pearce-Paul; 3 Aaron Small; 25 Errol Carter; 7 Jermaine Coleman; 6 Jacob Thomas; 18 Matt Ross; 9 Tom Firth; 15 Malikhi Lloyd-Jones; 19 Paulos Latu; 11 Lameck Juma; 13 Mike Greenhalgh. Subs (all used): 23 Neil Thorman; 22 Lamont Bryan; 8 Judd Greenhalgh; 21 James Tyas.
Tries: Hammond (40), Carter (56) Bryan (75);
Goals: Thorman 1/3.
Dismissal: M Greenhalgh (31) - high tackle.
RAIDERS: 1 Luke Cresswell; 27 Harry Swarbrick; 5 Shane Toal; 16 Tom Hopkins; 2 Theerapol Ritson; 6 Jamie Dallimore; 14 Jake Carter; 10 Carl Forster; 9 Nathan Mossop; 17 Adam Walne; 31 Charlie Emslie; 11 Danny Morrow; 18 Bradd Crellin. Subs (all used): 7 Ryan Johnston; 22 Carl McBain; 25 Callum Bustin; 8 Ryan Duffy.
Tries: Carter (20), Cresswell (26), Swarbrick (32), Ritson (69); **Goals:** Dallimore 4/4.
Sin bin: A Walne (49) - late challenge.
Rugby Leaguer & League Express Men of the Match: *Skolars:* Jacob Thomas; *Raiders:* Harry Swarbrick.
Penalty count: 11-9; **Half-time:** 6-18;
Referee: James Vella; **Attendance:** 391.

Sunday 20th June 2021

WORKINGTON TOWN 34 ROCHDALE HORNETS 28

TOWN: 1 Gabe Fell; 2 Brad Holroyd; 31 Joe Brown; 4 Calvin Wellington; 5 Alex Young; 6 Jamie Doran; 7 Carl Forber; 8 Conor Fitzsimmons; 9 Dec O'Donnell; 10 Stevie Scholey; 16 Jake Moore; 12 Caine Barnes; 14 Marcus O'Brien. Subs (all used): 23 Matty Henson; 33 Rhys Clarke; 13 Hanley Dawson; 25 Jake Lightowler.
Tries: O'Donnell (18), Doran (46), Moore (52), Holroyd (64), Fitzsimmons (70), Forber (80); **Goals:** Forber 5/6.
HORNETS: 6 Lewis Sheridan; 2 Shaun Ainscough; 3 Ben Calland; 27 Dan Nixon; 1 Sam Freeman; 15 Danny Yates; 9 Sean Penkywicz; 22 Jimmy Connaughton; 21 Ben Moores; 38 Tyler Walton; 12 Jordan Syme; 39 Cole Oakley; 11 Josh Jordan-Roberts. Subs (all used): 24 Ben Forster; 19 Callum Ogden; 17 Fuifui Moimoi; 18 Luke Fowden.
Tries: L Sheridan (13), Fowden (37), Ainscough (43), Moores (57), Moimoi (73);
Goals: Jordan-Roberts 3/4, Syme 1/2.
Rugby Leaguer & League Express Men of the Match: *Town:* Jamie Doran; *Hornets:* Danny Yates.
Penalty count: 4-5; **Half-time:** 6-14;
Referee: Craig Smith; **Attendance:** 942.

HUNSLET 18 DONCASTER 18

HUNSLET: 25 Lewis Young; 1 Wayne Reittie; 5 Matty Chrimes; 4 Tom Ashton; 18 Alex Brown; 6 Simon Brown; 24 Dave Gibbons; 27 Zach Braham; 14 Nathan Conroy; 15 Alex Rowe; 11 Brad Hey; 12 Duane Straugheir; 16 Mikey Wood. Subs (all used): 26 Sion Jones; 8 Jordan Andrade; 21 Joe McClean; 13 Harvey Hallas.
Tries: Chrimes (52), Wood (65), Gibbons (71);
Goals: Gibbons 3/4.
DONCASTER: 28 Misi Taulapapa; 5 Sam Doherty; 3 Sam Smeaton; 4 Jason Tali; 32 Ollie Greensmith; 1 Ben Johnston; 7 Matty Beharrell; 10 Brandon Douglas; 26 Ross Whitmore; 15 Ryan Boyle; 23 Liam Johnson; 19 Aaron Ollett; 12 Brad Foster. Subs (all used): 11 Danny Bravo; 17 Ross Peltier; 22 Alex Holdstock; 27 Aaron York.
Tries: L Johnson (48), York (60), Beharrell (78);
Goals: Beharrell 3/3.
Sin bin: Peltier (76) - late challenge.
Rugby Leaguer & League Express Men of the Match: *Hunslet:* Dave Gibbons; *Doncaster:* Matty Beharrell.
Penalty count: 8-5; **Half-time:** 0-0;
Referee: Liam Staveley; **Attendance:** 527.

ROUND 8

Saturday 26th June 2021

WEST WALES RAIDERS 12 HUNSLET 38

RAIDERS: 31 Will Ramsey; 22 Michael Holden; 15 Ashley Bateman; 1 Phil Cowburn; 21 Aedan Coleman; 23 Fraser Stroud; 33 Jamie Murphy; 13 Morgan Evans; 9 Dafydd Phillips; 34 Ewan Badham; 30 Callum Mulkeen; 18 Charley Bodman; 12 Joe Burke. Subs: 16 Sam Herron; 32 Ieuan Badham (not used); 10 Harry Boots; 24 Jordan Liney.
Tries: Cowburn (58), Bodman (75); **Goals:** Ramsey 2/2.
HUNSLET: 25 Lewis Young; 2 Wayne Reittie; 3 Will Cooke; 4 Tom Ashton; 22 Niall Walker; 6 Simon Brown; 7 Dom Brambani; 15 Alex Rowe; 9 Vila Halafihi; 26 Sion Jones; 11 Brad Hey; 12 Duane Straugheir; 16 Mikey Wood. Subs (all used): 24 Dave Gibbons; 8 Jordan Andrade; 17 Lewis Wray; 13 Harvey Hallas.
Tries: Cooke (5), Ashton (10), Straugheir (28, 33), S Brown (36), Andrade (50), Young (66);
Goals: Brambani 5/7.
Rugby Leaguer & League Express Men of the Match: *Raiders:* Morgan Evans; *Hunslet:* Dom Brambani.
Penalty count: 5-5; **Half-time:** 0-26;
Referee: Craig Smith; **Attendance:** 204.

Sunday 27th June 2021

BARROW RAIDERS 24 WORKINGTON TOWN 24

RAIDERS: 1 Luke Cresswell; 2 Theerapol Ritson; 16 Tom Hopkins; 14 Jake Carter; 5 Shane Toal; 6 Jamie Dallimore; 7 Ryan Johnston; 10 Carl Forster; 9 Nathan Mossop; 25 Callum Bustin; 11 Danny Morrow; 18 Bradd Crellin; 17 Adam Walne. Subs (all used): 39 Sam Dowsett; 22 Carl McBain; 31 Charlie Emslie; 8 Ryan Duffy.
Tries: Dallimore (12), A Walne (22), Dowsett (24);
Goals: Dallimore 6/7.
Sin bin: A Walne (71) - high tackle.
TOWN: 1 Gabe Fell; 2 Brad Holroyd; 31 Joe Brown; 4 Calvin Wellington; 5 Alex Young; 6 Jamie Doran; 7 Carl Forber; 8 Conor Fitzsimmons; 9 Dec O'Donnell; 25 Jake Lightowler; 16 Jake Moore; 12 Caine Barnes; 14 Marcus O'Brien. Subs (all used): 23 Matty Henson; 33 Rhys Clarke; 13 Hanley Dawson; 22 Blain Marwood.
Tries: Doran (7), Henson (53), Marwood (64), Holroyd (70);
Goals: Forber 4/5.
Sin bin: Barnes (20) - late challenge.
Rugby Leaguer & League Express Men of the Match: *Raiders:* Charlie Emslie; *Town:* Jamie Doran.
Penalty count: 10-13; **Half-time:** 20-6;
Referee: Tom Crashley; **Attendance:** 3,146.

COVENTRY BEARS 16 DONCASTER 34

BEARS: 1 Nathan Hill; 2 Elliot Wallis; 3 Matt Welham; 4 Liam Welham; 23 Reece Rance; 7 Dan Coates; 6 Dave Scott; 14 Josh Dunne; 18 Elliott Windley; 22 Brad Clavering; 11 Jed Charlton; 16 Sam Bowring; 12 Kieran Sherratt. Subs (all used): 21 Harry Kaufman; 25 Jack Dawson; 19 Bradley Ho; 13 Ryan Langton.
Tries: Rance (2), Scott (18, 28); **Goals:** Coates 2/3.
DONCASTER: 28 Misi Taulapapa; 18 Tom Halliday; 3 Sam Smeaton; 4 Jason Tali; 32 Ollie Greensmith; 1 Ben Johnston; 7 Matty Beharrell; 15 Ryan Boyle; 19 Aaron Ollett; 16 Brandan Wilkinson; 23 Liam Johnson; 11 Danny Bravo; 12 Brad Foster. Subs (all used): 10 Brandon Douglas; 22 Alex Holdstock; 20 Ben Howe; 27 Aaron York.
Tries: Taulapapa (22), York (39), Beharrell (43, 62), Douglas (73), Halliday (79); **Goals:** Beharrell 5/6.
Rugby Leaguer & League Express Men of the Match: *Bears:* Dave Scott; *Doncaster:* Matty Beharrell.
Penalty count: 8-7; **Half-time:** 16-12;
Referee: Kevin Moore; **Attendance:** 275.

KEIGHLEY COUGARS 34 LONDON SKOLARS 22

COUGARS: 1 Quentin Laulu-Togaga'e; 2 Mo Agoro; 4 Taylor Prell; 32 Aidan Scully; 34 Josh Slingsby; 15 Scott Murrell; 7 Jack Miller; 20 Brenden Santi; 9 Kyle Kesik; 12 Dan Parker; 3 Jake Webster; 30 Morgan Robinson; 13 Aaron Levy. Subs: 19 Billy Gaylor (not used); 21 Alfie Seeley; 25 Ben Stead; 33 Phoenix Laulu-Togaga'e.
Tries: Slingsby (10), Q Laulu-Togaga'e (18), Miller (33), Santi (50, 61); **Goals:** Miller 7/8.
SKOLARS: 1 Iliess Macani; 25 Errol Carter; 2 Omari Caro; 4 Dalton Grant; 5 Greg Johnson; 6 Jacob Thomas; 7 Jermaine Coleman; 15 Malikhi Lloyd-Jones; 9 Tom Firth; 18 Matt Ross; 12 Lameck Juma; 11 Kameron Pearce-Paul; 13 Mike Greenhalgh. Subs (all used): 8 Judd Greenhalgh; 10 Lamont Bryan; 19 Christian Gale; 23 Neil Thorman.
Tries: Firth (6), Juma (29, 77), Grant (69);
Goals: Caro 1/1, Thorman 2/3.
Sin bin:
M Greenhalgh (79) - late challenge on P Laulu-Togaga'e.
Rugby Leaguer & League Express Men of the Match: *Cougars:* Brenden Santi; *Skolars:* Iliess Macani.
Penalty count: 10-3; **Half-time:** 16-12;
Referee: Brad Milligan; **Attendance:** 548.

ROCHDALE HORNETS 38 NORTH WALES CRUSADERS 28

HORNETS: 6 Lewis Sheridan; 2 Shaun Ainscough; 3 Ben Calland; 12 Jordan Syme; 27 Dan Nixon; 33 Rangi Chase; 15 Danny Yates; 11 Josh Jordan-Roberts; 21 Ben Moores; 8 Callum Marriott; 40 Cole Oakley; 39 Paul Brearley; 20 Zac Baker. Subs (all used): 9 Sean Penkywicz; 17 Fuifui Moimoi; 18 Luke Fowden; 24 Ben Forster.
Tries: L Sheridan (4), Nixon (11), Yates (21, 68), Fowden (27), Moimoi (63, 74);
Goals: Jordan-Roberts 3/4, Baker 2/3.
CRUSADERS: 1 Tommy Johnson; 15 Patrick Ah Van; 3 Ben Morris; 4 Matt Reid; 5 Rob Massam; 6 Brad Billsborough; 7 Jordy Gibson; 16 Brad Brennan; 9 Karl Ashall; 10 Callum Hazzard; 11 Gav Rodden; 12 Alex Eckley; 13 Chris Barratt. Subs (all used): 14 Connor Aspey; 17 James Thornton; 18 Jack Cottington; 8 Ethan O'Hanlon.
Tries: Rodden (19), Massam (37, 76), Aspey (40), Barratt (70); **Goals:** Johnson 4/5.
Rugby Leaguer & League Express Men of the Match: *Hornets:* Fuifui Moimoi; *Crusaders:* Matt Reid.
Penalty count: 3-7; **Half-time:** 20-18;
Referee: James Vella; **Attendance:** 1,389.

ROUND 9

Sunday 4th July 2021

WORKINGTON TOWN 66 WEST WALES RAIDERS 0

TOWN: 2 Brad Holroyd; 31 Joe Brown; 12 Caine Barnes; 16 Jake Moore; 24 Ethan Bickerdike; 6 Jamie Doran; 7 Carl Forber; 33 Rhys Clarke; 23 Matty Henson; 14 Marcus O'Brien; 8 Conor Fitzsimmons; 18 Jordan Thomson; 13 Hanley Dawson. Subs (all used): 22 Blain Marwood; 9 Dec O'Donnell; 19 Jordan O'Leary; 32 Johnny Goulding (not used).
Tries: Barnes (1), Henson (4), Bickerdike (16, 35), Clarke (20), Moore (29, 47), Dawson (42), O'Donnell (44), Marwood (68, 74), J Brown (71); **Goals:** Forber 9/12.
RAIDERS: 31 Will Ramsey; 4 Marcus Webb; 21 Aedan Coleman; 30 Callum Mulkeen; 22 Michael Holden; 23 Fraser Stroud; 33 Jamie Murphy; 12 Joe Burke; 9 Dafydd Phillips; 34 Ewan Badham; 18 Charley Bodman; 13 Morgan Evans; 15 Ashley Bateman. Subs (all used): 32 Ieuan Badham; 25 Jack Uren; 16 Sam Herron; 10 Harry Boots.
Rugby Leaguer & League Express Men of the Match: *Town:* Caine Barnes; *Raiders:* Morgan Evans.
Penalty count: 6-5; **Half-time:** 34-0;
Referee: Luke Bland; **Attendance:** 942.

NORTH WALES CRUSADERS 34 KEIGHLEY COUGARS 28

CRUSADERS: 1 Tommy Johnson; 15 Patrick Ah Van; 14 Jack Holmes; 4 Matt Reid; 5 Rob Massam; 6 Brad Billsborough; 7 Jordy Gibson; 12 Alex Eckley; 9 Karl Ashall; 10 Warren Thompson; 11 Gav Rodden; 3 Ben Morris; 13 Chris Barratt. Subs: 18 Brad Calland; 16 Ethan O'Hanlon; 17 James Thornton; - Dante Morley-Samuels (not used).
Tries: Billsborough (6), Rodden (9), Johnson (14, 23), Massam (17), Ah Van (78); **Goals:** Johnson 5/8.
COUGARS: 1 Quentin Laulu-Togaga'e; 2 Mo Agoro; 4 Taylor Prell; 31 Charlie Graham; 33 Phoenix Laulu-Togaga'e; 15 Scott Murrell; 7 Jack Miller; 23 Matthew Bailey; 9 Kyle Kesik; 18 Spencer Darley; 13 Aaron Levy; 20 Brenden Santi; 12 Dan Parker. Subs (all used): 8 Jack Coventry; 11 Jason Muranka; 14 Ryan Wright; 19 Billy Gaylor.
Tries: Graham (36), Levy (40, 42), Murrell (50), Santi (56);
Goals: Miller 4/5.
Rugby Leaguer & League Express Men of the Match: *Crusaders:* Karl Ashall; *Cougars:* Scott Murrell.
Penalty count: 6-2; **Half-time:** 26-12;
Referee: Michael Smaill; **Attendance:** 437.

BARROW RAIDERS 31 DONCASTER 6

RAIDERS: 1 Luke Cresswell; 5 Shane Toal; 12 Jarrad Stack; 16 Tom Hopkins; 26 Ryan Shaw; 6 Jamie Dallimore; 7 Ryan Johnston; 10 Carl Forster; 39 Sam Dowsett; 17 Adam Walne; 11 Danny Morrow; 31 Charlie Emslie; 13 Jordan Walne. Subs (all used): 8 Ryan Duffy; 9 Nathan Mossop; 18 Bradd Crellin; 25 Callum Bustin.
Tries: Dallimore (29), Stack (35), Johnston (49, 79), J Walne (75); **Goals:** Dallimore 2/2, Shaw 3/3;
Field goal: Johnston (56).
Dismissal: Dallimore (39) - high tackle on Bravo.
DONCASTER: 28 Misi Taulapapa; 3 Sam Smeaton; 11 Danny Bravo; 4 Jason Tali; 18 Tom Halliday; 1 Ben Johnston; 7 Matty Beharrell; 10 Brandon Douglas; 26 Ross Whitmore; 16 Brandan Wilkinson; 23 Liam Johnson; 19 Aaron Ollett; 12 Brad Foster. Subs (all used): 17 Ross Peltier; 22 Alex Holdstock; 27 Aaron York; 29 Anesu Mudoti.
Try: Foster (60); **Goals:** Beharrell 1/1.
Rugby Leaguer & League Express Men of the Match: *Raiders:* Jarrad Stack; *Doncaster:* Matty Beharrell.
Penalty count: 5-4; **Half-time:** 12-0;
Referee: Craig Smith; **Attendance:** 2,005.

COVENTRY BEARS 46 HUNSLET 44

BEARS: 1 Nathan Hill; 2 Elliot Wallis; 4 Liam Welham; 3 Matt Welham; 23 Reece Rance; 6 Dave Scott; 7 Dan Coates; 8 Josh Dunne; 9 Chris Cullimore; 22 Brad Clavering; 11 Jed Charlton; 25 Jack Dawson; 12 Kieran Sherratt. Subs (all used): 13 Ryan Langton; 19 Bradley Ho; 15 Will Budd; 17 Elliot Townsend.
Tries: Wallis (4), Dawson (20, 59, 65), L Welham (49), Cullimore (53), Scott (63), Sherratt (79); **Goals:** Coates 7/8.
HUNSLET: 25 Lewis Young; 20 Wayne Reittie; 3 Will Cooke; 5 Matty Chrimes; 27 Alex Brown; 6 Simon Brown; 7 Dom Brambani; 15 Alex Rowe; 9 Vila Halafihi; 10 Harry Kidd; 11 Brad Hey; 12 Duane Straugheir; 16 Mikey Wood. Subs (all used): 14 Nathan Conroy; 8 Jordan Andrade; 26 Sion Jones; 17 Lewis Wray.
Tries: Halafihi (10), Chrimes (14, 53, 65), A Brown (26, 33), Hey (38), Young (43); **Goals:** Brambani 6/8.
Rugby Leaguer & League Express Men of the Match: *Bears:* Jack Dawson; *Hunslet:* Matty Chrimes.
Penalty count: 10-9; **Half-time:** 10-28;
Referee: Brad Milligan; **Attendance:** 255.

ROCHDALE HORNETS 22 LONDON SKOLARS 4

HORNETS: 6 Lewis Sheridan; 27 Dan Nixon; 24 Ben Forster; 39 Will Tate; 36 Shaun Robinson; 21 Ben Moores; 15 Danny Yates; 22 Jimmy Connaughton; 19 Callum Ogden; 8 Callum Marriott; 31 Paul Brearley; 11 Josh Jordan-Roberts; 20 Zac Baker. Subs (all used): 9 Sean Penkywicz; 17 Fuifui Moimoi; 18 Luke Fowden; 37 Tom Whur.
Tries: Robinson (19), L Sheridan (51, 79), Whur (73);
Goals: Jordan-Roberts 1/2, Baker 2/2.
Sin bin: Baker (44) - late challenge.
SKOLARS: 1 Iliess Macani; 2 Charles Hammond; 3 Aaron Small; 4 Dalton Grant; 5 Jerome Yates; 6 Jacob Thomas; 7 Jermaine Coleman; 18 Matt Ross; 9 Neil Thorman; 15 Malikhi Lloyd-Jones; 21 Lamont Bryan; 12 Mike Greenhalgh; 13 Christian Gale. Subs (all used): 14 Tom Firth; 22 Michael Sykes; 10 Judd Greenhalgh; 17 Louis Singleton.
Goals: Thomas 2/2.
Rugby Leaguer & League Express Men of the Match: *Hornets:* Lewis Sheridan; *Skolars:* Iliess Macani.
Penalty count: 8-6; **Half-time:** 4-2;
Referee: Andrew Sweet; **Attendance:** 1,171.

ROUND 10

Saturday 10th July 2021

WEST WALES RAIDERS 18 ROCHDALE HORNETS 30

RAIDERS: 31 Will Ramsey; 21 Aedan Coleman; 33 Jamie Murphy; 15 Ashley Bateman; 22 Michael Holden; 7 Callum Merrett; 23 Fraser Stroud; 34 Ewan Badham; 9 Dafydd Phillips; 32 Ieuan Badham; 30 Callum Mulkeen; 18 Charley Bodman; 12 Joe Burke. Subs (all used): 16 Sam Herron; 10 Harry Boots; 20 Ryan Shallish; 25 Jack Uren.
Tries: Merrett (38), Murphy (43), D Phillips (70);
Goals: Ramsey 3/3.
Sin bin: I Badham (16) - high tackle.
HORNETS: 1 Sam Freeman; 2 Shaun Ainscough; 12 Jordan Syme; 24 Ben Forster; 27 Dan Nixon; 15 Danny Yates; 9 Sean Penkywicz; 22 Jimmy Connaughton; 21 Ben Moores; 13 Joe Taira; 8 Callum Marriott; 11 Josh Jordan-Roberts; 20 Zac Baker. Subs (all used): 25 Kenny Hughes; 17 Fuifui Moimoi; 23 Lee Registe; 18 Luke Fowden.
Tries: Penkywicz (9), Freeman (17), Fowden (30), Moimoi (60), Marriott (66), Nixon (79);
Goals: Jordan-Roberts 0/2, Baker 3/4.
Dismissal: Marriott (74) - high tackle.
Rugby Leaguer & League Express Men of the Match: *Raiders:* Ashley Bateman; *Hornets:* Fuifui Moimoi.
Penalty count: 9-9; **Half-time:** 6-14;
Referee: James Jones; **Attendance:** 318.

Sunday 11th July 2021

HUNSLET 24 NORTH WALES CRUSADERS 34

HUNSLET: 25 Lewis Young; 1 Wayne Reittie; 5 Matty Chrimes; 3 Will Cooke; 27 Alex Brown; 24 Dave Gibbons; 7 Dom Brambani; 10 Harry Kidd; 9 Vila Halafihi; 15 Alex Rowe; 11 Brad Hey; 12 Duane Straugheir; 16 Mikey Wood. Subs (all used): 22 Jy-mel Coleman; 8 Jordan Andrade; 17 Lewis Wray; 13 Harvey Hallas.
Tries: Andrade (47), Halafihi (55), Young (68), Chrimes (75); **Goals:** Brambani 4/4.

CRUSADERS: 1 Tommy Johnson; 15 Patrick Ah Van; 3 Ben Morris; 4 Matt Reid; 5 Rob Massam; 6 Brad Billsborough; 7 Jordy Gibson; 16 Brad Brennan; 9 Karl Ashall; 10 Warren Thompson; 11 Gav Rodden; 12 Alex Eckley; 13 Chris Barratt. Subs (all used): 14 Andy Ball; 8 Ethan Kelly; 18 Brian O'Hanlon; 17 Connor Terrill.
Tries: Brennan (8), Rodden (18, 42), Johnson (24), Reid (40), Ah Van (80); Goals: Johnson 5/7.
Rugby Leaguer & League Express Men of the Match: *Hunslet:* Vila Halafihi; *Crusaders:* Tommy Johnson.
Penalty count: 7-7; Half-time: 0-26.
Referee: Kevin Moore; Attendance: 404.

KEIGHLEY COUGARS 40 BARROW RAIDERS 12

COUGARS: 1 Quentin Laulu-Togaga'e; 2 Mo Agoro; 4 Taylor Prell; 31 Charlie Graham; 33 Phoenix Laulu-Togaga'e; 15 Scott Murrell; 7 Jack Miller; 20 Brenden Santi; 9 Kyle Kesik; 8 Jack Coventry; 13 Aaron Levy; 12 Dan Parker; 19 Billy Gaylor. Subs (all used): 10 Dalton Desmond-Walker; 14 Ryan Wright; 23 Matthew Bailey; 24 Kieran Moran.
Tries: Levy (19), Agoro (40), Q Laulu-Togaga'e (50), Miller (56), Graham (63), Santi (69); Goals: Miller 8/8.
Sin bin: Wright (61) - late challenge on Dallimore.
RAIDERS: 14 Jake Carter; 5 Shane Toal; 12 Jarrad Stack; 29 Gary Wheeler; 26 Ryan Shaw; 6 Jamie Dallimore; 7 Ryan Johnston; 10 Carl Forster; 39 Sam Dowsett; 17 Adam Walne; 31 Charlie Emslie; 16 Tom Hopkins; 13 Jordan Walne. Subs (all used): 8 Ryan Duffy; 9 Nathan Mossop; 18 Bradd Crellin; 25 Callum Bustin.
Try: Stack (78); Goals: Dallimore 4/4.
On report: Dallimore (80) - alleged bite.
Rugby Leaguer & League Express Men of the Match: *Cougars:* Dalton Desmond-Walker; *Raiders:* Charlie Emslie.
Penalty count: 4-9; Half-time: 16-6.
Referee: Nick Bennett; Attendance: 572.

Friday 16th July 2021

LONDON SKOLARS 16 DONCASTER 16

SKOLARS: 1 Iliess Macani; 2 Omari Caro; 4 Dalton Grant; 3 Aaron Small; 5 Jerome Yates; 11 Abevia McDonald; 6 Jacob Thomas; 18 Matt Ross; 9 Neil Thorman; 21 Lamont Bryan; 12 Chris Ball; 15 Paulos Latu; 19 Mike Greenhalgh. Subs (all used): 14 Louis Singleton; 8 Judd Greenhalgh; 10 Alex Davidson; 13 Christian Gale.
Tries: Thomas (16), Small (32); Goals: Thorman 4/5.
DONCASTER: 20 Ben Howe; 5 Sam Doherty; 3 Sam Smeaton; 28 Misi Taulapapa; 18 Tom Halliday; 1 Ben Johnston; 7 Matty Beharrell; 10 Brandon Douglas; 26 Ross Whitmore; 15 Ryan Boyle; 12 Brad Foster; 27 Aaron York; 22 Alex Holdstock. Subs (all used): 23 Liam Johnson; 29 Anesu Mudoti; 19 Aaron Ollett; 17 Ross Peltier.
Tries: Smeaton (8), Doherty (52), Howe (62); Goals: Beharrell 2/3.
Rugby Leaguer & League Express Men of the Match: *Skolars:* Jacob Thomas; *Doncaster:* Sam Smeaton.
Penalty count: 5-6; Half-time: 12-6.
Referee: Matt Rossleigh; Attendance: 575.

ROUND 7

Friday 16th July 2021

COVENTRY BEARS 24 KEIGHLEY COUGARS 18

BEARS: 1 Nathan Hill; 2 Elliot Wallis; 3 Matt Welham; 4 Liam Welham; 23 Reece Rance; 6 Dave Scott; 7 Dan Coates; 22 Brad Clavering; 9 Chris Cullimore; 8 Josh Dunne; 11 Jed Charlton; 16 Sam Bowring; 13 Ryan Langton. Subs (all used): 19 Bradley Ho; 15 Will Budd; 20 Darius Hamilton; 18 Elliott Windley.
Tries: Coates (7), L Welham (17), Hamilton (55), Bowring (58); Goals: Coates 4/6.
COUGARS: 1 Quentin Laulu-Togaga'e; 2 Mo Agoro; 12 Dan Parker; 31 Charlie Graham; 33 Phoenix Laulu-Togaga'e; 15 Scott Murrell; 7 Jack Miller; 24 Kieran Moran; 9 Kyle Kesik; 8 Jack Coventry; 11 Jason Muranka; 35 Con Mika; 13 Aaron Levy. Subs (all used): 10 Dalton Desmond-Walker; 19 Billy Gaylor; 14 Ryan Wright; 23 Matthew Bailey.
Tries: Graham (21), P Laulu-Togaga'e (40, 45), Agoro (80); Goals: Miller 1/4.
Rugby Leaguer & League Express Men of the Match: *Bears:* Brad Clavering; *Cougars:* Charlie Graham.
Penalty count: 6-6; Half-time: 16-8.
Referee: Kevin Moore; Attendance: 387.

ROUND 11

Saturday 24th July 2021

LONDON SKOLARS 46 WEST WALES RAIDERS 30

SKOLARS: 2 Omari Caro; 5 Abevia McDonald; 4 Dalton Grant; 3 Aaron Small; 1 Jerome Yates; 25 Louis Singleton;

North Wales' Chris Barratt makes a break against Hunslet

6 Jacob Thomas; 18 Matt Ross; 9 Neil Thorman; 21 Lamont Bryan; 12 Chris Ball; 15 Paulos Latu; 24 Mike Greenhalgh. Subs (all used): 22 Michael Sykes; 13 Judd Greenhalgh; 8 Alex Davidson; 19 Christian Gale.
Tries: Latu (5, 8, 77), Bryan (10, 18), Singleton (15), Thomas (50), J Greenhalgh (59); Goals: Thorman 7/9.
RAIDERS: 33 Jamie Murphy; 22 Michael Holden; 15 Ashley Bateman; 17 Rowland Kaye; 21 Aedan Coleman; 31 Will Ramsey; 7 Callum Merrett; 16 Sam Herron; 9 Dafydd Phillips; 34 Ewan Badham; 30 Callum Mulkeen; 18 Charley Bodman; 12 Joe Burke. Subs (all used): 25 Jack Uren; 10 Harry Boots; 28 Paul Bolger; 23 Fraser Stroud.
Tries: Murphy (20, 42, 46, 72), Ramsey (27), Coleman (35); Goals: Ramsey 3/6.
Rugby Leaguer & League Express Men of the Match: *Skolars:* Paulos Latu; *Raiders:* Jamie Murphy.
Penalty count: 7-9; Half-time: 28-14.
Referee: James Jones; Attendance: 196.

Sunday 25th July 2021

BARROW RAIDERS 40 COVENTRY BEARS 12

RAIDERS: 1 Luke Cresswell; 27 Harry Swarbrick; 3 Declan Hulme; 4 Mark Tyson; 26 Ryan Shaw; 6 Jamie Dallimore; 14 Jake Carter; 10 Carl Forster; 9 Nathan Mossop; 19 Connor Terrill; 16 Tom Hopkins; 11 Danny Morrow; 13 Jordan Walne. Subs (all used): 39 Sam Dowsett; 22 Carl McBain; 25 Callum Bustin; 8 Ryan Duffy.
Tries: Hulme (9), Mossop (12), Shaw (15), Bustin (32), Swarbrick (65), Forster (70, 79); Goals: Dallimore 6/7.
BEARS: 1 Nathan Hill; 2 Elliot Wallis; 3 Matt Welham; 4 Liam Welham; 23 Reece Rance; 7 Dan Coates; 6 Dave Scott; 10 Josh Dunne; 9 Chris Cullimore; 22 Brad Clavering; 16 Sam Bowring; 25 Jack Dawson; 13 Ryan Langton. Subs (all used): 18 Elliott Windley; 8 Peter Ryan; 14 Elliot Townsend; 21 Harry Kaufman.
Tries: Coates (25), L Welham (47); Goals: Coates 2/2.
Rugby Leaguer & League Express Men of the Match: *Raiders:* Jamie Dallimore; *Bears:* Dan Coates.
Penalty count: 5-6; Half-time: 24-12.
Referee: Michael Smaill; Attendance: 1,862.

HUNSLET 20 KEIGHLEY COUGARS 20

HUNSLET: 20 Reece Chapman-Smith; 27 Wayne Reittie;

3 Will Cooke; 5 Matty Chrimes; 26 Alex Brown; 22 Jy-mel Coleman; 7 Dave Gibbons; 10 Alex Rowe; 9 Vila Halafihi; 15 Harry Kidd; 11 Brad Hey; 12 Harvey Hallas; 16 Mikey Wood. Subs (all used): 25 Frazer Morris; 8 Jordan Andrade; 17 Lewis Wray; 14 Nathan Conroy.
Tries: Andrade (30, 38), Halafihi (44); Goals: Coleman 4/5.
COUGARS: 7 Jack Miller; 2 Mo Agoro; 4 Taylor Prell; 31 Charlie Graham; 34 Josh Slingsby; 19 Billy Gaylor; 15 Scott Murrell; 8 Jack Coventry; 9 Kyle Kesik; 10 Dalton Desmond-Walker; 13 Aaron Levy; 12 Dan Parker; 23 Matthew Bailey. Subs (all used): 14 Ryan Wright; 18 Spencer Darley; 24 Kieran Moran; 36 James Feather.
Tries: Parker (5), Prell (13), Graham (77), Desmond-Walker (79); Goals: Miller 2/4.
Rugby Leaguer & League Express Men of the Match: *Hunslet:* Jordan Andrade; *Cougars:* Scott Murrell.
Penalty count: 8-5; Half-time: 12-10.
Referee: Craig Smith; Attendance: 714.

ROUND 12

Saturday 31st July 2021

LONDON SKOLARS 12 COVENTRY BEARS 14

SKOLARS: 7 Iliess Macani; 16 Max Clarke; 3 Aaron Small; 20 Kameron Pearce-Paul; 5 Lameck Juma; 6 Jacob Thomas; 2 Omari Caro; 10 Lamont Bryan; 9 Neil Thorman; 18 Matt Ross; 21 Paulos Latu; 12 Chris Ball; 13 Mike Greenhalgh. Subs: 8 Judd Greenhalgh; 15 Malikhi Lloyd-Jones; 14 Louis Singleton (not used); 19 Christian Gale.
Tries: Juma (5, 57); Goals: Thorman 2/4.
Sin bin: Small (78) - late challenge.
BEARS: 1 Nathan Hill; 2 Elliot Wallis; 25 Jack Dawson; 20 Kadeem Williams; 23 Reece Rance; 7 Dan Coates; 6 Dave Scott; 8 Peter Ryan; 9 Chris Cullimore; 22 Brad Clavering; 4 Liam Welham; 12 Kieran Sherratt; 13 Ryan Langton. Subs (all used): 14 Elliot Townsend; 18 Elliott Windley; 5 Hayden Freeman; 15 Will Budd.
Tries: L Welham (23), Scott (42); Goals: Coates 3/4.
Sin bin: Ryan (75) - dangerous challenge.
Rugby Leaguer & League Express Men of the Match: *Skolars:* Jacob Thomas; *Bears:* Dan Coates.
Penalty count: 8-10; Half-time: 8-6.
Referee: Liam Rush; Attendance: 190.

293

Sunday 1st August 2021

DONCASTER 24 HUNSLET 46

DONCASTER: 1 Ben Johnston; 5 Sam Doherty; 32 Jordan Bull; 4 Jason Tali; 18 Tom Halliday; - Harry Tyson-Wilson; 7 Matty Beharrell; 15 Ryan Boyle; - Robbie Ward; 29 Anesu Mudoti; 23 Liam Johnson; 27 Aaron York; 12 Brad Foster. Subs (all used): 19 Aaron Ollett; 17 Ross Peltier; 13 Bobby Tyson-Wilson; 26 Ross Whitmore.
Tries: Ward (37), Tali (51), York (59, 67);
Goals: Beharrell 4/4.
Sin bin: Beharrell (77) - dissent.
HUNSLET: 25 Lewis Young; 18 Kiedan Hartley; 3 Will Cooke; 5 Matty Chrimes; 20 Wayne Reittie; 24 Dave Gibbons; 14 Nathan Conroy; 15 Alex Rowe; 9 Vila Halafihi; 10 Harry Kidd; 13 Harvey Hallas; 17 Lewis Wray; 16 Mikey Wood. Subs (all used): 8 Jordan Andrade; 26 Frazer Morris; 19 Harvey Whiteley; 28 Joe Summers.
Tries: Wood (25), Chrimes (34, 40), Cooke (46), Gibbons (55), Halafihi (69), Reittie (75), Andrade (78);
Goals: Gibbons 7/9.
Rugby Leaguer & League Express Men of the Match: *Doncaster:* Harry Tyson-Wilson; *Hunslet:* Vila Halafihi.
Penalty count: 4-2; **Half-time:** 6-16;
Referee: Matt Rossleigh; **Attendance:** 1,179.

NORTH WALES CRUSADERS 72
WEST WALES RAIDERS 4

CRUSADERS: 1 Tommy Johnson; 15 Patrick Ah Van; 3 Ben Morris; 4 Matt Reid; 5 Rob Massam; 6 Matthew Race; 7 Jordy Gibson; 16 Brad Brennan; 9 Karl Ashall; 10 Warren Thompson; 11 Gav Rodden; 12 Alex Eckley; 13 Chris Barratt. Subs (all used): 8 Ethan Kelly; 18 Ethan O'Hanlon; 17 Callum Hazzard; 14 Cameron Berry.
Tries: Race (7, 56), Morris (10), Massam (15, 35), Ah Van (26), Thompson (31), Gibson (38), Rodden (40), Hazzard (47), Berry (53), Reid (61, 69);
Goals: Johnson 10/13.
RAIDERS: 15 Ashley Bateman; 21 Aedan Coleman; 17 Rowland Kaye; 18 Charley Bodman; 22 Michael Holden; 7 Callum Merrett; 31 Will Ramsey; 34 Ewan Badham; 25 Jack Uren; 16 Sam Herron; 13 Morgan Evans; 30 Callum Mulkeen; 12 Joe Burke. Subs: 28 Paul Bolger; 26 Alex Hicken; 19 Alan Pope; 32 Ieuan Badham (not used).
Try: Kaye (80); **Goals:** Ramsey 0/1.
Rugby Leaguer & League Express Men of the Match: *Crusaders:* Matt Reid; *Raiders:* Morgan Evans.
Penalty count: 4-2; **Half-time:** 46-0;
Referee: James Vella; **Attendance:** 610.

ROCHDALE HORNETS 20 KEIGHLEY COUGARS 42

HORNETS: 6 Lewis Sheridan; 27 Dan Nixon; 3 Ben Calland; 39 Will Tate; 32 Shaun Robinson; 40 Reece Dean; 15 Danny Yates; 10 Gavin Bennion; 21 Ben Moores; 13 Joe Taira; 31 Paul Brearley; 11 Josh Jordan-Roberts; 12 Jordan Syme. Subs (all used): 9 Sean Penkywicz; 37 Tom Whur; 18 Luke Fowden; 24 Ben Forster.
Tries: Tate (15, 42), Taira (51), Nixon (75);
Goals: Jordan-Roberts 2/4.
COUGARS: 25 Ben Stead; 2 Mo Agoro; 4 Taylor Prell; 31 Charlie Graham; 34 Josh Slingsby; 15 Scott Murrell; 7 Jack Miller; 8 Jack Coventry; 9 Kyle Kesik; 20 Brenden Santi; 13 Aaron Levy; 12 Dan Parker; 19 Billy Gaylor. Subs (all used): 10 Dalton Desmond-Walker; 14 Ryan Wright; 23 Matthew Bailey; 35 Con Mika.
Tries: Prell (1, 34), Slingsby (29), Agoro (39, 44), Levy (59), Stead (67); **Goals:** Miller 7/8.
Rugby Leaguer & League Express Men of the Match: *Hornets:* Reece Dean; *Cougars:* Taylor Prell.
Penalty count: 8-12; **Half-time:** 6-22;
Referee: James Jones; **Attendance:** 891.

ROUND 13

Saturday 7th August 2021

WEST WALES RAIDERS 24 DONCASTER 24

RAIDERS: 25 Jack Uren; 22 Michael Holden; 15 Ashley Bateman; 18 Charley Bodman; 17 Rowland Kaye; 31 Will Ramsey; 7 Callum Merrett; 13 Morgan Evans; 9 Dafydd Phillips; 16 Sam Herron; 12 Joe McClean; 19 Alan Pope; 30 Callum Mulkeen. Subs: 24 Steve Parry; 28 Paul Bolger; 21 Aedan Coleman (not used); 23 Fraser Stroud (not used).
Tries: Merrett (3), Parry (8, 34), D Phillips (52);
Goals: Ramsey 4/5.
DONCASTER: 31 Liam Tindall; 5 Sam Doherty; 3 Sam Smeaton; 19 Aaron Ollett; 18 Tom Halliday; 14 Harry Tyson-Wilson; 7 Matty Beharrell; 15 Ryan Boyle; 26 Ross Whitmore; 22 Alex Holdstock; 23 Liam Johnson; 27 Aaron York; 12 Brad Foster. Subs (all used): - Zach Braham; 11 Danny Bravo; 21 Ryan Dixon; 32 Jake Sweeting.
Tries: York (22), Sweeting (45), Bravo (47), Dixon (50), Halliday (79); **Goals:** Beharrell 2/5.
Rugby Leaguer & League Express Men of the Match: *Raiders:* Steve Parry; *Doncaster:* Aaron York.
Penalty count: 8-6; **Half-time:** 18-4;
Referee: Liam Rush; **Attendance:** 180.

LONDON SKOLARS 34 ROCHDALE HORNETS 38

SKOLARS: 7 Iliess Macani; 16 Max Clarke; 3 Aaron Small; 24 Kameron Pearce-Paul; 5 Lameck Juma; 6 Jacob Thomas; 11 Jermaine Coleman; 10 Lamont Bryan; 9 Neil Thorman; 18 Matt Ross; 21 Paulos Latu; 12 Chris Ball; 13 Mike Greenhalgh. Subs (all used): 19 Judd Greenhalgh; 15 Malikhi Lloyd-Jones; 14 Tom Firth; 20 Christian Gale.
Tries: Lloyd-Jones (26), Clarke (32), M Greenhalgh (43), Firth (52), Bryan (67), Juma (78); **Goals:** Thorman 5/7.
Dismissal: Pearce-Paul (20) - dangerous challenge.
Sin bin: Small (18) - fighting.
HORNETS: 29 Cian Tyrer; 26 AJ Towse; 27 Dan Nixon; 8 Tom Ashton; 2 Shaun Ainscough; 31 Paul Brearley; 40 Reece Dean; 10 Gavin Bennion; 9 Sean Penkywicz; 22 Jimmy Connaughton; 11 Josh Jordan-Roberts; 16 Toby Warren; 12 Jordan Syme. Subs (all used): 28 Luke Littlewood; 18 Luke Fowden; 25 Myles Harrison; 24 Ben Forster.
Tries: Brearley (2, 31), Nixon (5), Syme (12), Ashton (49), Fowden (57), Littlewood (76); **Goals:** Dean 5/7.
Sin bin: Penkywicz (18) - fighting.
Rugby Leaguer & League Express Men of the Match: *Skolars:* Lameck Juma; *Hornets:* Paul Brearley.
Penalty count: 9-7; **Half-time:** 14-24;
Referee: James Vella; **Attendance:** 208.

Sunday 8th August 2021

BARROW RAIDERS 40 HUNSLET 10

RAIDERS: 1 Luke Cresswell; 26 Ryan Shaw; 32 Hakim Miloudi; 4 Mark Tyson; 2 Theerapol Ritson; 14 Jake Carter; 7 Ryan Johnston; 19 Connor Terrill; 9 Nathan Mossop; 10 Carl Forster; 31 Charlie Emslie; 12 Jarrad Stack; 18 Bradd Crellin. Subs (all used): 39 Sam Dowsett; 23 Jake Emmitt; 15 Dan Toal; 22 Carl McBain.
Tries: Johnston (9, 44), Ritson (16, 56, 63, 74), Cresswell (35); **Goals:** Shaw 6/10.
HUNSLET: 2 Kiedan Hartley; 20 Wayne Reittie; 5 Matty Chrimes; 6 Reece Chapman-Smith; 27 Alex Brown; 25 Lewis Young; 24 Dave Gibbons; 15 Alex Rowe; 9 Vila Halafihi; 10 Harry Kidd; 28 Joe Summers; 12 Duane Straugheir; 16 Mikey Wood. Subs (all used): 14 Nathan Conroy; 26 Frazer Morris; 17 Lewis Wray; 8 Jordan Andrade.
Tries: Hartley (47), Young (53); **Goals:** Gibbons 1/2.
Sin bin: Chapman-Smith (45) - dissent; Kidd (69) - dissent.
Rugby Leaguer & League Express Men of the Match: *Raiders:* Theerapol Ritson; *Hunslet:* Vila Halafihi.
Penalty count: 8-3; **Half-time:** 14-0;
Referee: Michael Mannifield; **Attendance:** 1,918.

COVENTRY BEARS 16 NORTH WALES CRUSADERS 32

BEARS: 1 Nathan Hill; 2 Elliot Wallis; 3 Hayden Freeman; 4 Liam Welham; 23 Reece Rance; 6 Dave Scott; 7 Dan Coates; 22 Brad Clavering; 9 Chris Cullimore; 8 Peter Ryan; 11 Jack Dawson; 16 Kieran Sherratt; 13 Harry Kaufman. Subs (all used): 15 Will Budd; 19 Bradley Ho; 10 Kieran Hudson; 18 Elliott Windley.
Tries: Freeman (5), Hudson (52), Kaufman (58);
Goals: Coates 2/3.
CRUSADERS: 1 Tommy Johnson; 15 Patrick Ah Van; 3 Ben Morris; 4 Matt Reid; 5 Rob Massam; 7 Jordy Gibson; 6 Matthew Race; 10 Brad Brennan; 9 Karl Ashall; 18 Warren Thompson; 11 Gav Rodden; 12 Alex Eckley; 13 Chris Barratt. Subs (all used): 14 Cameron Berry; 17 Callum Hazzard; 19 Jack Holmes; 8 Ethan Kelly.
Tries: Massam (1), Ashall (12), Gibson (18, 23), Rodden (64), Johnson (79); **Goals:** Johnson 4/6.
Rugby Leaguer & League Express Men of the Match: *Bears:* Harry Kaufman; *Crusaders:* Tommy Johnson.
Penalty count: 8-9; **Half-time:** 4-22;
Referee: Craig Smith; **Attendance:** 378.

KEIGHLEY COUGARS 18 WORKINGTON TOWN 22

COUGARS: 25 Ben Stead; 2 Mo Agoro; 4 Taylor Prell; 31 Charlie Graham; 34 Josh Slingsby; 15 Scott Murrell; 7 Jack Miller; 24 Kieran Moran; 9 Kyle Kesik; 20 Brenden Santi; 13 Aaron Levy; 12 Dan Parker; 19 Billy Gaylor. Subs (all used): 10 Dalton Desmond-Walker; 14 Ryan Wright; 23 Matthew Bailey; 35 Con Mika.
Tries: Agoro (4), Slingsby (19), Mika (64); **Goals:** Miller 3/4.
On report:
Parker (80) - alleged dangerous contact on Wilson.
TOWN: 2 Brad Holroyd; 28 Lee Postlethwaite; 31 Joe Brown; 4 Calvin Wellington; 5 Alex Young; 6 Jamie Doran; 7 Carl Forber; 8 Conor Fitzsimmons; 9 Dec O'Donnell; 14 Marcus O'Brien; 16 Jake Moore; 18 Jordan Thomson; 13 Hanley Dawson. Subs (all used): 11 Perry Singleton; 17 Ryan Wilson; 23 Matty Henson; 33 Rhys Clarke.
Tries: J Brown (38), Dawson (51), Moore (56), Holroyd (73);
Goals: Forber 3/4.
Rugby Leaguer & League Express Men of the Match: *Cougars:* Billy Gaylor; *Town:* Jamie Doran.
Penalty count: 10-8; **Half-time:** 10-6;
Referee: Michael Smaill; **Attendance:** 774.

ROUND 14

Saturday 14th August 2021

WEST WALES RAIDERS 22 WORKINGTON TOWN 36

RAIDERS: 1 Phil Cowburn; 21 Aedan Coleman; 15 Ashley Bateman; 5 Dai Evans; 22 Michael Holden; 31 Will Ramsey; 33 Jamie Murphy; 19 Alan Pope; 24 Steve Parry; 29 Osian Phillips; 18 Charley Bodman; 2 Craig Lewis; 30 Callum Mulkeen. Subs (all used): 9 Dafydd Phillips; 10 Harry Boots; 20 Shaun Tennant; 25 Jack Uren.
Tries: Pope (11), Parry (22), Murphy (30, 55);
Goals: Ramsey 3/4.
TOWN: 2 Brad Holroyd; 28 Lee Postlethwaite; 31 Joe Brown; 4 Calvin Wellington; 30 Zac Olstrom; 6 Jamie Doran; 7 Carl Forber; 8 Conor Fitzsimmons; 9 Dec O'Donnell; 36 David Weetman; 16 Jake Moore; 12 Caine Barnes; 13 Hanley Dawson. Subs (all used): 23 Matty Henson; 33 Rhys Clarke; 11 Perry Singleton; 17 Ryan Wilson.
Tries: Wellington (3), Forber (14, 28, 75), Postlethwaite (24), Holroyd (59); **Goals:** Forber 6/7.
Rugby Leaguer & League Express Men of the Match: *Raiders:* Jamie Murphy; *Town:* Carl Forber.
Penalty count: 8-10; **Half-time:** 16-22;
Referee: Kevin Moore; **Attendance:** 239.

Sunday 15th August 2021

NORTH WALES CRUSADERS 23 BARROW RAIDERS 10

CRUSADERS: 1 Tommy Johnson; 15 Patrick Ah Van; 3 Dave Eccleston; 4 Matt Reid; 5 Rob Massam; 6 Matthew Race; 7 Jordy Gibson; 10 Callum Hazzard; 9 Karl Ashall; 8 Chris Barratt; 11 Ben Morris; 12 Gav Rodden; 13 Alex Eckley. Subs (all used): 14 Andy Ball; 16 Ethan Kelly; 18 Jack Houghton; 17 Brad Brennan.
Tries: Eckley (9), Johnson (57), Massam (65, 73);
Goals: Johnson 3/6; **Field goal:** Race (77).
RAIDERS: 1 Luke Cresswell; 2 Theerapol Ritson; 32 Hakim Miloudi; 4 Mark Tyson; 5 Shane Toal; 6 Jamie Dallimore; 14 Jake Carter; 17 Adam Walne; 9 Nathan Mossop; 10 Carl Forster; 31 Charlie Emslie; 12 Jarrad Stack; 23 Jake Emmitt. Subs (all used): 7 Ryan Johnston; 15 Dan Toal; 25 Callum Bustin; 8 Ryan Duffy.
Tries: Tyson (25), Bustin (34); **Goals:** Dallimore 1/2.
Rugby Leaguer & League Express Men of the Match: *Crusaders:* Alex Eckley; *Raiders:* Nathan Mossop.
Penalty count: 8-6; **Half-time:** 8-10;
Referee: Michael Smaill; **Attendance:** 727.

HUNSLET 38 LONDON SKOLARS 10

HUNSLET: 25 Lewis Young; 20 Wayne Reittie; 5 Matty Chrimes; 1 Reece Chapman-Smith; 2 Kiedan Hartley; 22 Jy-mel Coleman; 14 Nathan Conroy; 26 Frazer Morris; 9 Vila Halafihi; 10 Harry Kidd; 21 Joe McClean; 12 Duane Straugheir; 16 Mikey Wood. Subs (all used): 19 Harvey Whiteley; 8 Jordan Andrade; 15 Alex Rowe; 13 Harvey Hallas.
Tries: Reittie (8), Chrimes (24), Straugheir (29), Coleman (56), Young (64), Andrade (76);
Goals: Coleman 7/7.
Sin bin: Morris (62) - dangerous challenge on Bryan.
SKOLARS: 1 Iliess Macani; 23 Max Clarke; 3 Aaron Small; 4 Kameron Pearce-Paul; 5 Lameck Juma; 6 Jacob Thomas; 7 Neil Thorman; 19 Judd Greenhalgh; 14 Louis Singleton; 10 Christian Gale; 11 Adam Vrahnos; 12 Chris Ball; 13 Mike Greenhalgh. Subs (all used): 21 Lamont Bryan; 15 Paulos Latu; 18 Matt Ross; 9 Tom Firth.
Tries: Bryan (44), Juma (51); **Goals:** Thorman 1/2.
Sin bin: Vrahnos (39) - high tackle on Coleman; Small (72) - dissent.
Rugby Leaguer & League Express Men of the Match: *Hunslet:* Jy-mel Coleman; *Skolars:* Lameck Juma.
Penalty count: 7-5; **Half-time:** 20-0;
Referee: Cameron Worsley; **Attendance:** 435.

KEIGHLEY COUGARS 46 COVENTRY BEARS 18

COUGARS: 33 Phoenix Laulu-Togaga'e; 2 Mo Agoro; 4 Taylor Prell; 31 Charlie Graham; 34 Josh Slingsby; 15 Scott Murrell; 7 Jack Miller; 12 Dan Parker; 9 Kyle Kesik; 20 Brenden Santi; 35 Con Mika; 13 Aaron Levy; 19 Billy Gaylor. Subs (all used): 10 Dalton Desmond-Walker; 14 Ryan Wright; 23 Matthew Bailey; 24 Kieran Moran.
Tries: Graham (1), Parker (4, 14), Agoro (10, 18, 28), Miller (34), Wright (78); **Goals:** Miller 7/8.
Sin bin: Prell (68) - retaliation.

BEARS: 1 Nathan Hill; 5 Hayden Freeman; 3 Matt Welham; 4 Liam Welham; 23 Reece Rance; 7 Dan Coates; 6 Dave Scott; 8 Peter Ryan; 9 Chris Cullimore; 22 Brad Clavering; 16 Sam Bowring; 12 Kieran Sherratt; 21 Harry Kaufman. Subs (all used): 10 Connor Terrill; 13 Ryan Langton; 15 Will Budd; 19 Darius Hamilton.
Tries: Freeman (23), Coates (40), Clavering (44);
Goals: Coates 2/2, Scott 1/1.
Rugby Leaguer & League Express Men of the Match:
Cougars: Mo Agoro; *Bears:* Dave Scott.
Penalty count: 9-5; **Half-time:** 40-12;
Referee: Liam Staveley; **Attendance:** 1,028.

ROCHDALE HORNETS 44 DONCASTER 8

HORNETS: 29 Cian Tyrer; 14 Declan Sheridan; 3 Ben Calland; 37 Tom Ashton; 32 Shaun Robinson; 40 Reece Dean; 7 Rob Fairclough; 10 Gavin Bennion; 9 Sean Penkywicz; 22 Jimmy Connaughton; 11 Josh Jordan-Roberts; 12 Jordan Syme; 31 Paul Brearley. Subs (all used): 6 Lewis Sheridan; 21 Ben Moores; 24 Ben Forster; 18 Luke Fowden.
Tries: Robinson (4), Tyrer (7, 70), Syme (38, 78), Jordan-Roberts (61), Bennion (73), L Sheridan (76);
Goals: Dean 6/9.
DONCASTER: 6 Ben Cockayne; 31 Liam Tindall; 3 Sam Smeaton; 4 Jason Tali; 32 Ollie Greensmith; 20 Ben Howe; 36 Jake Sweeting; 15 Ryan Boyle; 26 Ross Whitmore; 30 Zach Braham; 19 Aaron Ollett; 11 Danny Bravo; 23 Liam Johnson. Subs (all used): 22 Alex Holdstock; 29 Anesu Mudoti; 17 Ross Peltier; 27 Aaron York.
Tries: Tali (24, 79); **Goals:** Sweeting 0/2.
Sin bin: Peltier (35) - punching;
Cockayne (67) - late challenge on Dean.
Rugby Leaguer & League Express Men of the Match:
Hornets: Rob Fairclough; *Doncaster:* Jason Tali.
Penalty count: 6-8; **Half-time:** 14-4;
Referee: James Jones; **Attendance:** 882.

ROUND 15

Saturday 21st August 2021

LONDON SKOLARS 14 KEIGHLEY COUGARS 34

SKOLARS: 1 Jonah Varela; 2 Abevia McDonald; 3 Aaron Small; 19 Paulos Latu; 5 Jerome Yates; 6 Iliess Macani; 7 Neil Thorman; 10 Mike Greenhalgh; 14 Louis Singleton; 15 Jordan Williams; 11 Jacob Ogden; 24 Chris Ball; 13 Adam Vrahnos. Subs (all used): 21 Judd Greenhalgh; 18 Matt Ross; 9 Tom Firth; 20 Christian Gale.
Tries: Yates (10), Latu (75); **Goals:** Thorman 3/4.
Sin bin: Ogden (29) - late challenge on Kesik;
M Greenhalgh (80) - retaliation.
COUGARS: 33 Phoenix Laulu-Togaga'e; 5 Robert Matamosi; 4 Taylor Prell; 31 Charlie Graham; 34 Josh Slingsby; 9 Kyle Kesik; 7 Jack Miller; 8 Jack Coventry; 36 James Feather; 20 Brenden Santi; 12 Dan Parker; 13 Aaron Levy; 19 Billy Gaylor. Subs: 1 Quentin Laulu-Togaga'e (not used); 14 Ryan Wright; 23 Matthew Bailey; 27 Jack Arnold.
Tries: Levy (6), Bailey (30), Arnold (38), Prell (40, 65), Wright (44); **Goals:** Miller 5/6.
Rugby Leaguer & League Express Men of the Match:
Skolars: Paulos Latu; *Cougars:* Kyle Kesik.
Penalty count: 5-4; **Half-time:** 10-22;
Referee: Luke Bland; **Attendance:** 228.

Sunday 22nd August 2021

WORKINGTON TOWN 18
NORTH WALES CRUSADERS 40

TOWN: 2 Brad Holroyd; 28 Lee Postlethwaite; 31 Joe Brown; 4 Calvin Wellington; 30 Zac Olstrom; 6 Jamie Doran; 7 Carl Forber; 8 Conor Fitzsimmons; 14 Marcus O'Brien; 25 Jake Lightowler; 16 Jake Moore; 11 Perry Singleton; 13 Hanley Dawson. Subs (all used): 22 Blain Marwood; 33 Rhys Clarke; 17 Ryan Wilson; 12 Caine Barnes.
Tries: Olstrom (21), O'Brien (36), Wellington (79);
Goals: Forber 3/3.
CRUSADERS: 1 Tommy Johnson; 15 Patrick Ah Van; 3 Dave Eccleston; 4 Matt Reid; 5 Rob Massam; 6 Matthew Race; 7 Jordy Gibson; 13 Chris Barratt; 9 Karl Ashall; 10 Warren Thompson; 12 Gav Rodden; 11 Ben Morris; 18 Alex Eckley. Subs (all used): 14 Andy Ball; 17 Callum Hazzard; 8 Ethan Kelly; 16 Brad Brennan.
Tries: Morris (2), Thompson (9), Eckley (28), Ah Van (44), Massam (62), Reid (67), Race (71);
Goals: Johnson 6/8.
Rugby Leaguer & League Express Men of the Match:
Town: Brad Holroyd; *Crusaders:* Tommy Johnson.
Penalty count: 4-8; **Half-time:** 12-18;
Referee: Craig Smith; **Attendance:** 1,457.

COVENTRY BEARS 50 WEST WALES RAIDERS 18

BEARS: 3 Matt Welham; 5 Hayden Freeman; 1 Nathan Hill; 4 Liam Welham; 23 Reece Rance; 6 Dave Scott; 7 Dan Coates; 22 Brad Clavering; 9 Chris Cullimore; 8 Peter Ryan; 25 Jack Dawson; 16 Sam Bowring; 12 Kieran Sherratt. Subs (all used): 10 Kieran Hudson; 13 Ryan Langton; 18 Brad Sheridan; 20 Delaine Bedward.
Tries: Freeman (4), Rance (14, 70), Sherratt (31), Hudson (44), Hill (49, 54), L Welham (62), M Welham (64), Scott (66); **Goals:** Coates 5/10.
RAIDERS: 1 Phil Cowburn; 19 Alan Pope; 15 Ashley Bateman; 21 Aedan Coleman; 5 Dai Evans; 31 Will Ramsey; 23 Fraser Stroud; 29 Osian Phillips; 25 Jack Uren; 16 Sam Herron; 13 Morgan Evans; 30 Callum Mulkeen; 12 Joe Burke. Subs (all used): 18 Charley Bodman; 2 Craig Lewis; 20 Shaun Tennant; 10 Harry Boots.
Tries: Cowburn (9), Uren (27), Coleman (40), D Evans (76);
Goals: Ramsey 1/4.
Sin bin: D Evans (57) - dissent.
Rugby Leaguer & League Express Men of the Match:
Bears: Liam Welham; *Raiders:* Callum Mulkeen.
Penalty count: 6-3; **Half-time:** 14-14;
Referee: Michael Smaill; **Attendance:** 280.

DONCASTER 26 BARROW RAIDERS 18

DONCASTER: 35 Liam Tindall; 18 Tom Halliday; 3 Sam Smeaton; 4 Jason Tali; 32 Ollie Greensmith; 36 Jake Sweeting; 7 Matty Beharrell; 15 Ryan Boyle; 26 Ross Whitmore; 30 Zach Braham; 27 Aaron York; 19 Aaron Ollett; 22 Alex Holdstock. Subs (all used): 6 Ben Cockayne; 34 Loui McConnell; 29 Anesu Mudoti; 17 Ross Peltier.
Tries: Beharrell (4), Tindall (42), McConnell (70), Tali (80);
Goals: Beharrell 3/4, Sweeting 2/2.
RAIDERS: 1 Luke Cresswell; 2 Theerapol Ritson; 32 Hakim Miloudi; 26 Ryan Shaw; 5 Shane Toal; 6 Jamie Dallimore; 14 Jake Carter; 17 Adam Walne; 9 Nathan Mossop; 10 Carl Forster; 11 Danny Morrow; 12 Jarrad Stack; 23 Jake Emmitt. Subs (all used): 39 Sam Dowsett; 4 Mark Tyson; 25 Callum Bustin; 8 Ryan Duffy.
Tries: Tyson (24), S Toal (76); **Goals:** Dallimore 5/6.
Sin bin: Dowsett (55) - high tackle; Dallimore (79) - dissent.
Rugby Leaguer & League Express Men of the Match:
Doncaster: Matty Beharrell; *Raiders:* Jamie Dallimore.
Penalty count: 10-12; **Half-time:** 6-10;
Referee: Kevin Moore; **Attendance:** 1,019.

ROCHDALE HORNETS 34 HUNSLET 34

HORNETS: 29 Cian Tyrer; 2 Shaun Ainscough; 3 Ben Calland; 13 Joe Taira; 32 Shaun Robinson; 40 Reece Dean; 7 Rob Fairclough; 22 Jimmy Connaughton; 9 Sean Penkywicz; 8 Callum Marriott; 11 Josh Jordan-Roberts; 12 Jordan Syme; 10 Gavin Bennion. Subs (all used): 21 Ben Moores; 6 Lewis Sheridan; 24 Ben Forster; 18 Luke Fowden.
Tries: Penkywicz (18), Jordan-Roberts (25), Ainscough (38), L Sheridan (69), Taira (74), Syme (75);
Goals: Dean 2/3, Jordan-Roberts 1/2, Fairclough 2/2.
Sin bin: Fairclough (15) - fighting, (79) - holding down.
HUNSLET: 25 Lewis Young; 20 Wayne Reittie; 23 Aaron Jones-Bishop; 1 Reece Chapman-Smith; 2 Kiedan Hartley; 22 Jy-mel Coleman; 7 Dom Brambani; 26 Frazer Morris; 9 Vila Halafihi; 10 Harry Kidd; 21 Joe McClean; 12 Duane Straugheir; 16 Mikey Wood. Subs (all used): 14 Nathan Conroy; 15 Alex Rowe; 8 Jordan Andrade; 28 Joe Summers.
Tries: Kidd (4), McClean (21), Coleman (33, 56), Hartley (61), Young (66); **Goals:** Coleman 5/8.
Sin bin: Jones-Bishop (15) - fighting;
Halafihi (25) - high tackle; Young (73) - holding down.
Rugby Leaguer & League Express Men of the Match:
Hornets: Rob Fairclough; *Hunslet:* Jy-mel Coleman.
Penalty count: 9-8; **Half time:** 16-18;
Referee: Liam Rush; **Attendance:** 822.

ROUND 16

Saturday 28th August 2021

WEST WALES RAIDERS 12 KEIGHLEY COUGARS 42

RAIDERS: 1 Phil Cowburn; 19 Alan Pope; 15 Ashley Bateman; 17 Rowland Kaye; 20 Shaun Tennant; 23 Fraser Stroud; 31 Will Ramsey; 12 Joe Burke; 25 Jack Uren; 27 Osian Phillips; 18 Charley Bodman; 2 Craig Lewis; 30 Callum Mulkeen. Subs (only three named): 9 Dafydd Phillips; 10 Harry Boots; 16 Sam Herron (not used).
Tries: Ramsey (24), Cowburn (63);
Goals: Ramsey 1/1, Tennant 1/1.
Sin bin: Bateman (74) - dissent.
COUGARS: 1 Quentin Laulu-Togaga'e; 34 Josh Slingsby; 3 Jake Webster; 22 Alix Stephenson; 33 Phoenix Laulu-Togaga'e; 15 Scott Murrell; 7 Jack Miller; 8 Jack Coventry; 9 Kyle Kesik; 10 Dalton Desmond-Walker; 35 Con Mika; 13 Aaron Levy; 19 Billy Gaylor. Subs (all used): 11 Jason Muranka; 23 Matthew Bailey; 28 Josh Lynam; 36 James Feather.
Tries: Miller (4, 48, 75), Slingsby (14), Q Laulu-Togaga'e (30), Webster (34), Lynam (51), P Laulu-Togaga'e (56); **Goals:** Miller 5/8.
Rugby Leaguer & League Express Men of the Match:
Raiders: Shaun Tennant; *Cougars:* Jack Miller.
Penalty count: 7-5; **Half-time:** 6-20;
Referee: James Jones; **Attendance:** 267.

Sunday 29th August 2021

BARROW RAIDERS 38 LONDON SKOLARS 24

RAIDERS: 1 Luke Cresswell; 2 Theerapol Ritson; 32 Hakim Miloudi; 26 Ryan Shaw; 5 Shane Toal; 6 Jamie Dallimore; 29 Gary Wheeler; 19 Connor Terrill; 9 Nathan Mossop; 10 Carl Forster; 11 Danny Morrow; 12 Jarrad Stack; 15 Dan Toal. Subs (all used): 3 Declan Hulme; 8 Ryan Duffy; 14 Jake Carter; 39 Sam Dowsett.
Tries: Miloudi (4), Cresswell (12), Dallimore (17), D Toal (26), Duffy (34), Hulme (57), Morrow (73);
Goals: Dallimore 5/7.
SKOLARS: 1 Iliess Macani; 5 Abevia McDonald; 21 Paulos Latu; 3 Aaron Small; 2 Jerome Yates; 6 Jacob Thomas; 7 Oliver Leyland; 10 Mike Greenhalgh; 9 Louis Singleton; 8 Christian Gale; 24 Adam Vrahnos; 11 Chris Ball; 13 Will Blakemore. Subs (all used): 15 Malikhi Lloyd-Jones; 18 Matt Ross; 22 Michael Sykes; 23 Neil Thorman.
Tries: M Greenhalgh (41), Small (54, 68), Latu (65);
Goals: Thorman 4/4.
Rugby Leaguer & League Express Men of the Match:
Raiders: Jarrad Stack; *Skolars:* Paulos Latu.
Penalty count: 7-6; **Half-time:** 28-0;
Referee: Liam Rush; **Attendance:** 1,486.

NORTH WALES CRUSADERS 36
ROCHDALE HORNETS 10

CRUSADERS: 1 Tommy Johnson; 15 Patrick Ah Van; 3 Dave Eccleston; 4 Matt Reid; 5 Rob Massam; 6 Matthew Race; 7 Jordy Gibson; 10 Callum Hazzard; 9 Karl Ashall; 13 Chris Barratt; 17 Ben Morris; 11 Gav Rodden; 12 Alex Eckley. Subs (all used): 8 Ethan Kelly; 14 Andy Ball; 16 Brad Brennan; 18 Jack Houghton.
Tries: Eckley (27), Johnson (29, 79), Ah Van (38), Reid (46), Gibson (60); **Goals:** Johnson 6/7.
HORNETS: 29 Cian Tyrer; 2 Shaun Ainscough; 3 Ben Calland; 37 Tom Ashton; 32 Shaun Robinson; 33 Rangi Chase; 7 Rob Fairclough; 10 Gavin Bennion; 21 Ben Moores; 13 Joe Taira; 11 Josh Jordan-Roberts; 12 Jordan Syme; 20 Zac Baker. Subs (all used): 6 Lewis Sheridan; 9 Sean Penkywicz; 17 Fuifui Moimoi; 24 Ben Forster.
Tries: Chase (13), L Sheridan (53);
Goals: Jordan-Roberts 1/2.
Dismissal: Robinson (20) - high tackle on Ah Van.
Sin bin: Chase (80) - high tackle.
Rugby Leaguer & League Express Men of the Match:
Crusaders: Tommy Johnson; *Hornets:* Sean Penkywicz.
Penalty count: 14-5; **Half-time:** 20-4;
Referee: Michael Mannifield; **Attendance:** 617.

DONCASTER 22 WORKINGTON TOWN 12

DONCASTER: 35 Liam Tindall; 18 Tom Halliday; 3 Sam Smeaton; 4 Jason Tali; 32 Ollie Greensmith; 1 Ben Johnston; 36 Jake Sweeting; 22 Alex Holdstock; 26 Ross Whitmore; 30 Zach Braham; 19 Aaron Ollett; 27 Aaron York; 12 Brad Foster. Subs (all used): 6 Ben Cockayne; 34 Loui McConnell; 29 Anesu Mudoti; 23 Liam Johnson.
Tries: York (6), Halliday (20, 24), Tindall (56), L Johnson (76); **Goals:** Sweeting 1/5.
TOWN: 2 Brad Holroyd; 19 John Hutchings; 31 Joe Brown; 4 Calvin Wellington; 5 Alex Young; 6 Jamie Doran; 7 Carl Forber; 8 Conor Fitzsimmons; 23 Matty Henson; 32 David Weetman; 11 Perry Singleton; 12 Caine Barnes; 14 Marcus O'Brien. Subs (all used): 13 Hanley Dawson; 33 Rhys Clarke; 16 Jake Moore; 17 Ryan Wilson.
Tries: Holroyd (33), Dawson (43); **Goals:** Forber 2/2.
Rugby Leaguer & League Express Men of the Match:
Doncaster: Liam Tindall; *Town:* Conor Fitzsimmons.
Penalty count: 5-4; **Half-time:** 14-6;
Referee: Craig Smith; **Attendance:** 948.

HUNSLET 32 COVENTRY BEARS 30

HUNSLET: 25 Lewis Young; 20 Wayne Reittie; 23 Aaron Jones-Bishop; 5 Matty Chrimes; 1 Reece Chapman-Smith; 6 Simon Brown; 7 Dom Brambani; 16 Mikey Wood; 9 Vila Halafihi; 10 Harry Kidd; 21 Joe McClean; 12 Duane Straugheir; 22 Jy-mel Coleman. Subs (all used): 19 Harvey Whiteley; 8 Jordan Andrade; 15 Alex Rowe; 13 Harvey Hallas.
Tries: Kidd (9), Chapman-Smith (12), Coleman (22), Young (31), Straugheir (38), Halafihi (60);
Goals: Brambani 4/6.
BEARS: 3 Matt Welham; 5 Hayden Freeman; 1 Nathan Hill; 4 Liam Welham; 23 Reece Rance; 7 Dan Coates; 6 Dave Scott; 22 Brad Clavering; 9 Chris Cullimore; 8 Peter Ryan; 25 Jack Dawson; 16 Sam Bowring; 12 Kieran Sherratt. Subs (all used): 13 Ryan Langton; 18 Elliott Windley; 21 Harry Kaufman; 19 Bradley Ho.

Tries: Ryan (19), Freeman (45), Bowring (58), M Welham (62), Coates (66); Goals: Coates 5/5.
Rugby Leaguer & League Express Men of the Match: Hunslet: Dom Brambani; Bears: Dan Coates.
Penalty count: 5-7; Half-time: 26-6;
Referee: James Vella; Attendance: 353.

ROUND 17

Saturday 4th September 2021

LONDON SKOLARS 18 WORKINGTON TOWN 35

SKOLARS: 1 Jonah Varela; 2 Dalton Grant; 3 Aaron Small; 19 Paulos Latu; 5 Lameck Juma; 6 Jacob Thomas; 7 Oliver Leyland; 12 Judd Greenhalgh; 9 Neil Thorman; 10 Christian Gale; 20 Adam Vrahnos; 11 Chris Ball; 21 Mike Greenhalgh. Subs (all used): 25 Ryan Cane; 15 Malikhi Lloyd-Jones; 18 Matt Ross; 22 Michael Sykes.
Tries: Juma (42), Latu (50), Sykes (68);
Goals: Thorman 3/4.
Sin bin: Sykes (60) - dangerous contact.
TOWN: 1 Gabe Fell; 2 Brad Holroyd; 31 Joe Brown; 24 Ethan Bickerdike; 5 Alex Young; 6 Jamie Doran; 7 Carl Forber; 32 David Weetman; 23 Matty Henson; 33 Rhys Clarke; 8 Conor Fitzsimmons; 12 Caine Barnes; 13 Hanley Dawson. Subs (all used): 22 Blain Marwood; 17 Ryan Wilson; 25 Jake Lightowler; 19 John Hutchings.
Tries: Clarke (14), Holroyd (21, 38), Fitzsimmons (54), Henson (60), Doran (75); Goals: Forber 5/7.
Field goal: Holroyd (73).
Rugby Leaguer & League Express Men of the Match: Skolars: Paulos Latu; Town: Brad Holroyd.
Penalty count: 7-6; Half-time: 0-18;
Referee: Andrew Sweet; Attendance: 241.

Sunday 5th September 2021

DONCASTER 18 COVENTRY BEARS 13

DONCASTER: 35 Liam Tindall; 18 Tom Halliday; 3 Sam Smeaton; 4 Jason Tali; 32 Ollie Greensmith; 6 Ben Cockayne; 36 Jake Sweeting; 30 Zach Braham; 26 Ross Whitmore; 22 Alex Holdstock; 19 Aaron Ollett; 27 Aaron York; 12 Brad Foster. Subs (all used): 17 Ross Peltier; 34 Loui McConnell; 10 Brandon Douglas; 23 Liam Johnson.
Tries: Tali (11, 30), L Johnson (65); Goals: Sweeting 3/3.
BEARS: 1 Nathan Hill; 5 Hayden Freeman; 4 Liam Welham; 3 Kadeem Williams; 23 Reece Rance; 7 Dan Coates; 6 Dave Scott; 8 Peter Ryan; 9 Chris Cullimore; 15 Will Budd; 16 Sam Bowring; 25 Jack Dawson; 12 Kieran Sherratt. Subs (all used): 10 Darius Hamilton; 18 Elliott Windley; 13 Ryan Langton; 20 Delaine Bedward.
Tries: Coates (18), Williams (25); Goals: Coates 2/2.
Field goal: Coates (37).
Rugby Leaguer & League Express Men of the Match: Doncaster: Jason Tali; Bears: Dan Coates.
Penalty count: 4-4; Half-time: 12-13;
Referee: Kevin Moore; Attendance: 1,138.

HUNSLET 82 WEST WALES RAIDERS 6

HUNSLET: 25 Lewis Young; 2 Kiedan Hartley; 3 Will Cooke; 5 Matty Chrimes; 1 Reece Chapman-Smith; 6 Simon Brown; 7 Dom Brambani; 16 Mikey Wood; 9 Vila Halafihi; 27 Frazer Morris; 21 Joe McClean; 12 Duane Straugheir; 26 Jy-mel Coleman. Subs (all used): 19 Harvey Whiteley; 8 Jordan Andrade; 17 Lewis Wray; 13 Harvey Hallas.
Tries: Brambani (3), Hartley (7, 46, 61), Halafihi (13), Straugheir (16), Chrimes (25, 30, 79), Chapman-Smith (43), Whiteley (55, 68), Young (58), Wray (63), Andrade (78);
Goals: Brambani 11/15.
RAIDERS: 1 Phil Cowburn; 22 Michael Holden; 4 Matthew Morgan; 23 Fraser Stroud; 17 Rowland Kaye; 13 Morgan Evans; 25 Jack Uren; 18 Charley Bodman; 15 Ashley Bateman; 27 Osian Phillips; 28 Paul Bolger; 30 Callum Mulkeen; 12 Joe Burke. Sub (used, only one named): 10 Harry Boots.
Try: M Evans (19); Goals: M Morgan 1/1.
Rugby Leaguer & League Express Men of the Match: Hunslet: Harvey Whiteley; Raiders: Ashley Bateman.
Penalty count: 3-1; Half-time: 32-6;
Referee: Luke Bland; Attendance: 474.

KEIGHLEY COUGARS 34 NORTH WALES CRUSADERS 14

COUGARS: 1 Quentin Laulu-Togaga'e; 4 Taylor Prell; 3 Jake Webster; 22 Alix Stephenson; 33 Phoenix Laulu-Togaga'e; 15 Scott Murrell; 7 Jack Miller; 8 Jack Coventry; 36 James Feather; 20 Brenden Santi; 35 Con Mika; 13 Aaron Levy; 19 Billy Gaylor. Subs (all used): 12 Dan Parker; 14 Ryan Wright; 23 Matthew Bailey; 31 Charlie Graham.
Tries: Murrell (34), Webster (52), Prell (58), Q Laulu-Togaga'e (62), Stephenson (68), Parker (79);
Goals: Miller 5/6.

CRUSADERS: 1 Tommy Johnson; 2 Dave Eccleston; 3 Jack Holmes; 15 Matt Reid; 5 Rob Massam; 6 Brad Billsborough; 7 Jordy Gibson; 13 Chris Barratt; 9 Karl Ashall; 10 Warren Thompson; 17 Ben Morris; 11 Gav Rodden; 12 Alex Eckley. Subs (all used): 8 Ethan Kelly; 14 Andy Ball; 16 Brad Brennan; 18 Callum Hazzard.
Tries: Rodden (24), Brennan (44); Goals: Johnson 3/3.
Rugby Leaguer & League Express Men of the Match: Cougars: Con Mika; Crusaders: Gav Rodden.
Penalty count: 4-7; Half-time: 6-8;
Referee: Liam Staveley; Attendance: 1,327.

ROCHDALE HORNETS 30 BARROW RAIDERS 32

HORNETS: 29 Cian Tyrer; 27 Dan Nixon; 3 Ben Calland; 37 Tom Ashton; 32 Shaun Robinson; 6 Lewis Sheridan; 33 Rangi Chase; 13 Joe Taira; 21 Ben Moores; 10 Gavin Bennion; 11 Josh Jordan-Roberts; 12 Jordan Syme; 20 Zac Baker. Subs (all used): 9 Sean Penkywicz; 8 Callum Marriott; 17 Fuifui Moimoi; 18 Luke Fowden.
Tries: Nixon (11), Moores (27), Moimoi (38), Marriott (60, 69); Goals: Jordan-Roberts 1/3, Syme 4/4.
Dismissal: Taira (18) - high tackle on Hopkins.
Sin bin: Fowden (54) - obstruction.
RAIDERS: 1 Luke Cresswell; 2 Theerapol Ritson; 32 Hakim Miloudi; 26 Ryan Shaw; 5 Shane Toal; 14 Jake Carter; 7 Ryan Johnston; 10 Carl Forster; 9 Nathan Mossop; 19 Connor Terrill; 16 Tom Hopkins; 12 Jarrad Stack; 23 Jake Emmitt. Subs (all used): 39 Sam Dowsett; 31 Charlie Emslie; 3 Declan Hulme; 25 Callum Bustin.
Tries: Cresswell (21), Ritson (40), Carter (48), Hulme (79); Goals: Shaw 8/8.
Sin bin: Dowsett (32) - high tackle on L Sheridan.
Rugby Leaguer & League Express Men of the Match: Hornets: Ben Moores; Raiders: Carl Forster.
Penalty count: 7-9; Half-time: 18-16;
Referee: James Jones; Attendance: 1,064.

ROUND 18

Saturday 11th September 2021

NORTH WALES CRUSADERS 44 LONDON SKOLARS 0

CRUSADERS: 1 Tommy Johnson; 15 Patrick Ah Van; 4 Dave Eccleston; 3 Matt Reid; 5 Rob Massam; 6 Brad Billsborough; 7 Jordy Gibson; 10 Warren Thompson; 9 Karl Ashall; 13 Chris Barratt; 17 Ben Morris; 11 Gav Rodden; 12 Alex Eckley. Subs (all used): 14 Jack Houghton; 8 Rhys Davies; 18 Callum Hazzard; 16 Brad Brennan.
Tries: Massam (8, 20, 52, 80), Rodden (31), Johnson (46), Eccleston (65), Ah Van (77); Goals: Johnson 6/8.
SKOLARS: 1 Jonah Varela; 2 Dalton Grant; 3 Aaron Small; 19 Paulos Latu; 5 Lameck Juma; 6 Jacob Thomas; 7 Iliess Macani; 8 Mike Greenhalgh; 9 Neil Thorman; 10 Christian Gale; 12 Jordan Williams; 11 Chris Ball; 13 Adam Vrahnos. Subs (all used): 14 Tom Firth; 15 Malikhi Lloyd-Jones; 18 Matt Ross; 21 Judd Greenhalgh.
Rugby Leaguer & League Express Men of the Match: Crusaders: Tommy Johnson; Skolars: Chris Ball.
Penalty count: 6-2; Half-time: 18-0;
Referee: Brad Milligan; Attendance: 560.

BARROW RAIDERS 76 WEST WALES RAIDERS 0

BARROW: 1 Luke Cresswell; 2 Theerapol Ritson; 32 Hakim Miloudi; 26 Ryan Shaw; 5 Shane Toal; 4 Mark Tyson; 14 Jake Carter; 13 Jordan Walne; 9 Nathan Mossop; 10 Carl Forster; 16 Tom Hopkins; 12 Jarrad Stack; 23 Jake Emmitt. Subs (all used): 39 Sam Dowsett; 31 Charlie Emslie; 3 Declan Hulme; 25 Callum Bustin.
Tries: Cresswell (9), Ritson (11, 27, 39, 44, 62, 67), Bustin (23), Stack (32, 47), Emslie (57), Hulme (59), S Toal (79); Goals: Shaw 10/14.
WEST WALES: 1 Phil Cowburn; 22 Michael Holden; 30 Callum Mulkeen; 23 Ben Jackson; 20 Louis Watson; 12 Kian Monaghan; 15 Ashley Bateman; 27 Osian Phillips; 9 Connor Saunders; 28 Paul Bolger; 18 Charley Bodman; 17 Rowland Kaye; 13 Morgan Evans. Subs (all used): 16 Jack Torkington; 32 Julius Banks; 8 Darrel Moyle; 34 Leon Hayes.
Rugby Leaguer & League Express Men of the Match: Barrow: Theerapol Ritson; West Wales: Charley Bodman.
Penalty count: 3-3; Half-time: 34-0;
Referee: John McMullen; Attendance: 1,922.

Sunday 12th September 2021

WORKINGTON TOWN 14 HUNSLET 32

TOWN: 1 Gabe Fell; 2 Brad Holroyd; 31 Joe Brown; 24 Ethan Bickerdike; 30 Zac Olstrom; 6 Jamie Doran; 7 Carl Forber; 8 Conor Fitzsimmons; 23 Matty Henson; 25 Jake Lightowler; 16 Jake Moore; 12 Caine Barnes; 13 Hanley Dawson. Subs (all used): - John Hutchings; 33 Rhys Clarke; 17 Ryan Wilson; 19 Jordan O'Leary.
Tries: Holroyd (7), J Brown (23, 39); Goals: Forber 1/3.
Sin bin: Fell (19) - professional foul.

HUNSLET: 25 Lewis Young; 20 Wayne Reittie; 3 Will Cooke; 5 Matty Chrimes; 1 Reece Chapman-Smith; 6 Simon Brown; 7 Dom Brambani; 29 Mikey Wood; 33 Harvey Whiteley; 10 Harry Kidd; 21 Joe McClean; 12 Duane Straugheir; 22 Jy-mel Coleman. Subs (all used): 8 Jordan Andrade; 17 Lewis Wray; 15 Alex Rowe; 34 Joe Summers.
Tries: Wood (19), Rowe (33), Straugheir (43), Chapman-Smith (55), Young (70); Goals: Brambani 6/7.
Sin bin: Brown (6) - high tackle on Fitzsimmons.
Rugby Leaguer & League Express Men of the Match: Town: Jamie Doran; Hunslet: Dom Brambani.
Penalty count: 2-10; Half-time: 14-12;
Referee: Tom Crashley; Attendance: 1,397.

DONCASTER 26 KEIGHLEY COUGARS 28

DONCASTER: 35 Liam Tindall; 18 Tom Halliday; 3 Sam Smeaton; 4 Jason Tali; 32 Ollie Greensmith; 6 Ben Cockayne; 36 Jake Sweeting; 30 Zach Braham; 19 Aaron Ollett; 10 Brandon Douglas; 27 Aaron York; 12 Brad Foster; 22 Alex Holdstock. Subs (all used): 17 Ross Peltier; 34 Loui McConnell; 15 Ryan Boyle; 26 Ross Whitmore.
Tries: Foster (3), Halliday (6), Sweeting (58, 60);
Goals: Sweeting 5/5.
Dismissal: Cockayne (16) - headbutt.
COUGARS: 2 Quentin Laulu-Togaga'e; 22 Alix Stephenson; 4 Taylor Prell; 31 Charlie Graham; 33 Phoenix Laulu-Togaga'e; 15 Scott Murrell; 7 Jack Miller; 8 Jack Coventry; 9 Kyle Kesik; 20 Brenden Santi; 35 Con Mika; 3 Jake Webster; 13 Aaron Levy. Subs (all used): 2 Mo Agoro; 12 Dan Parker; 14 Ryan Wright; 23 Matthew Bailey.
Tries: Webster (22, 67), Mika (27), Prell (69), P Laulu-Togaga'e (77); Goals: Miller 4/5.
Rugby Leaguer & League Express Men of the Match: Doncaster: Jake Sweeting; Cougars: Jake Webster.
Penalty count: 8-4; Half-time: 14-12;
Referee: Michael Mannifield; Attendance: 738.

ROCHDALE HORNETS 50 COVENTRY BEARS 22

HORNETS: 38 Cian Tyrer; 27 Dan Nixon; 3 Ben Calland; 34 Tom Ashton; 32 Shaun Robinson; 31 Paul Brearley; 33 Rangi Chase; 10 Gavin Bennion; 21 Ben Moores; 13 Joe Taira; 8 Callum Marriott; 12 Jordan Syme; 20 Zac Baker. Subs (all used): 9 Sean Penkywicz; 11 Josh Jordan-Roberts; 18 Luke Fowden; 17 Fuifui Moimoi.
Tries: Calland (6, 11), Bennion (15, 21), Moimoi (38), Penkywicz (51), Robinson (54), Nixon (71, 72), Ashton (75); Goals: Syme 4/9, Penkywicz 1/1.
BEARS: 6 Dave Scott; 5 Hayden Freeman; 1 Nathan Hill; 4 Liam Welham; 23 Reece Rance; 7 Dan Coates; 17 Brad Sheridan; 8 Peter Ryan; 9 Chris Cullimore; 15 Will Budd; 16 Jordan Bull; 12 Kieran Sherratt; 22 Brad Clavering. Subs (all used): 10 Darius Hamilton; 18 Elliott Windley; 13 Ryan Langton; 20 Delaine Bedward.
Tries: Bull (30), Scott (56), Coates (57), Cullimore (59); Goals: Coates 3/4.
Rugby Leaguer & League Express Men of the Match: Hornets: Gavin Bennion; Bears: Dave Scott.
Penalty count: 5-6; Half-time: 26-6;
Referee: Michael Smaill; Attendance: 693.

POSTPONED GAMES

(all subsequently not rearranged)

ROUND 10

Workington Town v Coventry Bears

ROUND 11

Doncaster v North Wales Crusaders
Rochdale Hornets v Workington Town

ROUND 12

Workington Town v Barrow Raiders

QUALIFYING PLAY-OFF

Saturday 18th September 2021

NORTH WALES CRUSADERS 14 KEIGHLEY COUGARS 28

CRUSADERS: 1 Tommy Johnson; 15 Patrick Ah Van; 4 Dave Eccleston; 3 Matt Reid; 5 Rob Massam; 6 Brad Billsborough; 7 Jordy Gibson; 10 Warren Thompson; 9 Karl Ashall; 13 Chris Barratt; 17 Ben Morris; 12 Alex Eckley. Subs (all used): 18 Jack Houghton; 14 Jack Holmes; 8 Callum Hazzard; 16 Brad Brennan.
Tries: Billsborough (40), Ah Van (47); Goals: Johnson 3/3.
COUGARS: 1 Quentin Laulu-Togaga'e; 2 Mo Agoro; 4 Taylor Prell; 31 Charlie Graham; 22 Alix Stephenson; 15 Scott Murrell; 7 Jack Miller; 28 Josh Lynam; 9 Kyle Kesik; 20 Brenden Santi; 3 Jake Webster; 35 Con Mika; 19 Billy Gaylor. Subs (all used): 10 Dalton Desmond-Walker; 23 Matthew Bailey; 27 Jack Arnold; 36 James Feather.

Workington's Marcus O'Brien crashes over the Doncaster tryline during the League 1 Play-off Final

Tries: Webster (18), Miller (27), Santi (69, 73);
Goals: Miller 6/6.
Sin bin: Arnold (44) - dangerous contact.
Rugby Leaguer & League Express Men of the Match:
Crusaders: Tommy Johnson; *Cougars:* Brenden Santi.
Penalty count: 4-7; **Half-time:** 6-14;
Referee: Michael Smaill; **Attendance:** 488.

ELIMINATION PLAY-OFF

Sunday 19th September 2021

DONCASTER 31 HUNSLET 10

DONCASTER: 35 Liam Tindall; 18 Tom Halliday; 3 Sam Smeaton; 4 Jason Tali; 32 Ollie Greensmith; 36 Jake Sweeting; 7 Matty Beharrell; 30 Zach Braham; 6 Ben Cockayne; 10 Brandon Douglas; 23 Liam Johnson; 19 Aaron Ollett; 12 Brad Foster. Subs (all used): 11 Danny Bravo; 27 Aaron York; 22 Alex Holdstock; 26 Ross Whitmore.
Tries: Smeaton (13), Douglas (20, 75), L Johnson (40), Sweeting (73); **Goals:** Beharrell 5/5;
Field goal: Beharrell (67).
HUNSLET: 25 Lewis Young; 20 Wayne Reittie; 3 Will Cooke; 5 Matty Chrimes; 1 Reece Chapman-Smith; 26 Jy-mel Coleman; 7 Dom Brambani; 17 Lewis Wray; 19 Harvey Whiteley; 10 Harry Kidd; 11 Brad Hey; 12 Duane Straugheir; 16 Mikey Wood. Subs (all used): 9 Vila Halafihi; 15 Alex Rowe; 8 Jordan Andrade; 28 Joe Summers.
Tries: Reittie (5), Chrimes (77); **Goals:** Brambani 1/2.
Rugby Leaguer & League Express Men of the Match:
Doncaster: Matty Beharrell; *Hunslet:* Brad Hey.
Penalty count: 5-4; **Half-time:** 18-6;
Referee: Nick Bennett; **Attendance:** 547.

QUALIFYING SEMI-FINAL

Sunday 26th September 2021

WORKINGTON TOWN 18 KEIGHLEY COUGARS 16
(after golden point extra-time)

TOWN: 2 Brad Holroyd; 30 Zac Olstrom; 31 Joe Brown; 24 Ethan Bickerdike; 5 Alex Young; 6 Jamie Doran; 7 Carl Forber; 14 Marcus O'Brien; 9 Dec O'Donnell; 25 Jake Lightowler; 12 Caine Barnes; 8 Conor Fitzsimmons; 13 Hanley Dawson. Subs (all used): 11 Perry Singleton; 17 Ryan Wilson; 23 Matty Henson; 33 Rhys Clarke.

Tries: Barnes (3, 27), Holroyd (16); **Goals:** Forber 3/4.
COUGARS: 22 Alix Stephenson; 2 Mo Agoro; 4 Taylor Prell; 31 Charlie Graham; 33 Phoenix Laulu-Togaga'e; 15 Scott Murrell; 7 Jack Miller; 28 Josh Lynam; 9 Kyle Kesik; 20 Brenden Santi; 3 Jake Webster; 13 Aaron Levy; 19 Billy Gaylor. Subs (all used): 12 Dan Parker; 14 Ryan Wright; 23 Matthew Bailey; 36 James Feather.
Tries: Miller (6), Graham (48), Kesik (79); **Goals:** Miller 2/3.
Rugby Leaguer & League Express Men of the Match:
Town: Caine Barnes; *Cougars:* Jack Miller.
Penalty count: 8-7; **Half-time:** 16-6;
Referee: Marcus Griffiths; **Attendance:** 1,221.

ELIMINATION SEMI-FINAL

Sunday 26th September 2021

NORTH WALES CRUSADERS 34 DONCASTER 48

CRUSADERS: 1 Tommy Johnson; 15 Patrick Ah Van; 4 Dave Eccleston; 3 Matt Reid; 5 Dante Morley-Samuels; 6 Brad Billsborough; 7 Jordy Gibson; 10 Warren Thompson; 9 Karl Ashall; 13 Chris Barratt; 17 Ben Morris; 11 Gav Rodden; 12 Alex Eckley. Subs (all used): 18 Jack Houghton; 14 Jack Holmes; 8 Callum Hazzard; 16 Brad Brennan.
Tries: Hazzard (39), Brennan (44), Gibson (61), Morris (64), Johnson (67), Rodden (73); **Goals:** Johnson 5/6.
DONCASTER: 35 Liam Tindall; 18 Tom Halliday; 3 Sam Smeaton; 4 Jason Tali; 32 Ollie Greensmith; 36 Jake Sweeting; 7 Matty Beharrell; 10 Brandon Douglas; 6 Ben Cockayne; 30 Zach Braham; 23 Liam Johnson; 19 Aaron Ollett; 12 Brad Foster. Subs (all used): 11 Danny Bravo; 22 Alex Holdstock; 1 Ben Johnston; 26 Ross Whitmore.
Tries: Tindall (5), Ollett (8), Peltier (14), Douglas (24), Cockayne (33), Tali (56), Beharrell (58), Sweeting (79);
Goals: Beharrell 8/8.
Rugby Leaguer & League Express Men of the Match:
Crusaders: Patrick Ah Van; *Doncaster:* Jason Tali.
Penalty count: 2-2; **Half-time:** 6-30;
Referee: Tom Grant; **Attendance:** 432.

PRELIMINARY FINAL

Sunday 3rd October 2021

KEIGHLEY COUGARS 26 DONCASTER 28

COUGARS: 33 Phoenix Laulu-Togaga'e; 2 Mo Agoro; 3

Jake Webster; 31 Charlie Graham; 22 Alix Stephenson; 15 Scott Murrell; 7 Jack Miller; 20 Brenden Santi; 36 James Feather; 10 Dalton Desmond-Walker; 35 Con Mika; 12 Dan Parker; 9 Kyle Kesik. Subs (all used): 13 Aaron Levy; 19 Billy Gaylor; 23 Matthew Bailey; 28 Josh Lynam.
Tries: Miller (8), P Laulu-Togaga'e (12), Murrell (47), Graham (56); **Goals:** Miller 5/5.
DONCASTER: 28 Misi Taulapapa; 18 Tom Halliday; 3 Sam Smeaton; 4 Jason Tali; 32 Ollie Greensmith; 36 Jake Sweeting; 7 Matty Beharrell; 10 Brandon Douglas; 6 Ben Cockayne; 30 Zach Braham; 23 Liam Johnson; 19 Aaron Ollett; 22 Alex Holdstock. Subs (all used): 1 Ben Johnston; 12 Brad Foster; 26 Ross Whitmore; 27 Aaron York.
Tries: Holdstock (18), Beharrell (24), L Johnson (63, 80), Tali (75); **Goals:** Beharrell 2/2, Sweeting 2/3.
Rugby Leaguer & League Express Men of the Match:
Cougars: Charlie Graham; *Doncaster:* Jake Sweeting.
Penalty count: 5-8; **Half-time:** 14-12;
Referee: Tom Grant; **Attendance:** 1,128.

PLAY-OFF FINAL

Sunday 10th October 2021

WORKINGTON TOWN 36 DONCASTER 12

TOWN: 2 Brad Holroyd; 5 Alex Young; 31 Joe Brown; 24 Ethan Bickerdike; 30 Zac Olstrom; 6 Jamie Doran; 7 Carl Forber; 25 Jake Lightowler; 9 Dec O'Donnell; 14 Marcus O'Brien; 8 Conor Fitzsimmons; 12 Caine Barnes; 13 Hanley Dawson. Subs (all used): 23 Matty Henson; 33 Rhys Clarke; 11 Perry Singleton; 17 Ryan Wilson.
Tries: J Brown (2), Fitzsimmons (14), Forber (32), Henson (48), O'Brien (70), Holroyd (75); **Goals:** Forber 6/6.
Sin bin: O'Donnell (5) - late challenge.
DONCASTER: 28 Misi Taulapapa; 18 Tom Halliday; 3 Sam Smeaton; 4 Jason Tali; 32 Ollie Greensmith; 36 Jake Sweeting; 7 Matty Beharrell; 30 Zach Braham; 6 Ben Cockayne; 10 Brandon Douglas; 23 Liam Johnson; 19 Aaron Ollett; 12 Brad Foster. Subs (all used): 22 Alex Holdstock; 1 Ben Johnston; 26 Ross Whitmore; 27 Aaron York.
Tries: L Johnson (6), Greensmith (40); **Goals:** Beharrell 2/2.
Rugby Leaguer & League Express Men of the Match:
Town: Marcus O'Brien; *Doncaster:* Jason Tali.
Penalty count: 5-7; **Half-time:** 18-12;
Referee: Tom Grant; **Attendance:** 2,997.

CHALLENGE CUP 2021
Round by Round

ROUND 1

Friday 19th March 2021

SHEFFIELD EAGLES 6 YORK CITY KNIGHTS 30

EAGLES: 1 Josh Guzdek; 2 Rob Worrincy; 24 Ryan Johnson; 4 James Glover; 5 Ryan Millar; 22 Izaac Farrell; 7 Anthony Thackeray; 11 Brad Knowles; 14 Greg Burns; 10 Matt James; 15 Olly Davies; 12 Joel Farrell; 13 Aaron Brown. Subs (all used): 16 Robbie Ward; 18 Tyler Dickinson; 19 Blake Broadbent; 20 Paddy Burns.
Try: G Burns (16); **Goals:** I Farrell 1/1.
CITY KNIGHTS: 23 Ben Jones-Bishop; 22 Perry Whiteley; 2 Jason Bass; 4 Ryan Atkins; 5 Kieran Dixon; 6 Brendan O'Hagan; 1 Matty Marsh; 15 Jordan Baldwinson; 9 Will Jubb; 10 Jack Teanby; 11 Chris Clarkson; 17 Danny Kirmond; 28 Danny Washbrook. Subs (all used): 14 Kriss Brining; 21 Joe Porter; 16 Marcus Stock; 19 James Green.
Tries: Whiteley (4, 60), Brining (33), Jones-Bishop (35), Atkins (80); **Goals:** K Dixon 5/6.
Rugby Leaguer & League Express Men of the Match:
Eagles: Rob Worrincy; *City Knights:* Brendan O'Hagan.
Penalty count: 5-7; **Half-time:** 6-20; **Referee:** Tom Grant.

Saturday 20th March 2021

OLDHAM 20 BARROW RAIDERS 6

OLDHAM: 1 Dan Abram; 2 Tommy Brierley; 3 Ben Heaton; 24 Max Roberts; 5 Ryan Ince; 6 Lewis Charnock; 26 James Barran; 15 Luke Nelmes; 9 Gareth Owen; 17 Liam Kirk; 11 Danny Langtree; 25 Danny Bridge; 12 Liam Bent. Subs (all used): 13 Martyn Reilly; 16 Tyler Dupree; 21 Shaun Pick; 30 Dec Gregory.
Tries: Charnock (23), Langtree (31), Brierley (43);
Goals: D Abram 4/4.
Sin bin: Pick (38) - late challenge.
RAIDERS: 2 Theerapol Ritson; 5 Shane Toal; 3 Declan Hulme; 4 Mark Tyson; 26 Ryan Shaw; 6 Jamie Dallimore; 7 Ryan Johnston; 17 Adam Walne; 31 Harry Swarbrick; 10 Carl Forster; 12 Jarrad Stack; 13 Jordan Walne; 20 Ben Harrison. Subs (all used): 8 Ryan Duffy; 14 Jake Carter; 15 Dan Toal; 25 Callum Bustin.
Try: Shaw (40); **Goals:** Shaw 1/1.
Rugby Leaguer & League Express Men of the Match:
Oldham: Danny Langtree; *Raiders:* Ben Harrison.
Penalty count: 10-7; **Half-time:** 12-6;
Referee: Marcus Griffiths.

LONDON BRONCOS 24 KEIGHLEY COUGARS 10

BRONCOS: 5 Ed Chamberlain; 20 Gideon Boafo; 4 Will Lovell; 3 Chris Hankinson; 17 Abbas Miski; 1 James Meadows; 6 Cory Aston; 15 Romain Navarrete; 14 Sam Davis; 8 Olsi Krasniqi; 12 Rhys Curran; 25 Jacob Jones; 13 Josh Walters. Subs (all used): 10 Greg Richards; 28 Titus Gwaze; 30 Paulos Latu; 23 Josh Hodson.
Tries: Boafo (3), Jones (17), Davis (52), Navarrete (65);
Goals: Hankinson 4/4.
Sin bin: Miski (36) - fighting; Latu (38) - late challenge.
COUGARS: 25 Ben Stead; 2 Mo Agoro; 4 Taylor Prell; 31 Charlie Graham; 5 Robert Matamosi; 19 Billy Gaylor; 7 Jack Miller; 23 Matthew Bailey; 14 Ryan Wright; 20 Brenden Santi; 28 Josh Lynam; 12 Dan Parker; 24 Kieran Moran. Subs (all used): 8 Jack Coventry; 9 Kyle Kesik; 13 Aaron Levy; 27 Jack Arnold.
Tries: Agoro (67), Santi (80); **Goals:** Miller 1/2.
Sin bin: Matamosi (36) - dangerous challenge.
Rugby Leaguer & League Express Men of the Match:
Broncos: Gideon Boafo; *Cougars:* Jack Miller.
Penalty count: 9-8; **Half-time:** 12-0;
Referee: Robert Hicks. *(at The Rock, Roehampton)*.

WHITEHAVEN 23 DEWSBURY RAMS 16

WHITEHAVEN: 1 Gregg McNally; 2 Lachlan Walmsley; 3 Chris Taylor; 23 Jason Mossop; 5 Andrew Bulman; 6 Karl Dixon; 7 Nikau Williams; 8 Marc Shackley; 18 James Newton; 27 Andrew Dawson; 11 Brett Phillips; 19 Ellis Gillam; 12 Liam Cooper. Subs (all used): 9 Callum Phillips; 17 Tom Walker; 13 Dion Aiye; 15 Connor Holliday.
Tries: Walmsley (18), Taylor (30), Shackley (58), McNally (69); **Goals:** Walmsley 3/4;
Field goal: McNally (75).
Dismissal:
C Phillips (34) - dangerous challenge on Knowles.
RAMS: 1 Joe Martin; 2 Andy Gabriel; 3 Adam Ryder; 4 Matty Fleming; 27 Lewis Carr; 6 Paul Sykes; 7 Liam Finn; 20 Aaron Hall; 9 Reiss Butterworth; 10 Tom Garratt; 15 Keenen Tomlinson; 12 Michael Knowles; 8 Frazer Morris. Subs (all used): 14 Sam Day; 5 Will Oakes; 23 Jon Magrin; 16 Connor Scott.
Tries: Morris (8), Ryder (36), Fleming (60);
Goals: Sykes 2/3.
Rugby Leaguer & League Express Men of the Match:
Whitehaven: Lachlan Walmsley; *Rams:* Reiss Butterworth.
Penalty count: 5-3; **Half-time:** 10-10;
Referee: James Child.

HALIFAX PANTHERS 6 BATLEY BULLDOGS 19

PANTHERS: 1 Scott Grix; 19 Conor McGrath; 2 Nick Rawsthorne; 4 James Woodburn-Hall; 5 James Saltonstall; 6 Liam Harris; 7 Connor Robinson; 16 Will Calcott; 9 Brandon Moore; 10 Daniel Murray; 11 Matt Garside; 12 Ed Barber; 14 Kevin Larroyer. Subs (all used): 20 Curtis Davies; 15 Gadwin Springer; 13 Jacob Fairbank; 18 Connor Davies.
Try: Garside (52); **Goals:** Robinson 1/1.
BULLDOGS: 1 Luke Hooley; 14 Elliot Hall; 22 Dale Morton; 23 Jack Logan; 21 Jodie Broughton; 6 Ben White; 7 Tom Gilmore; 8 Adam Gledhill; 24 Ben Kaye; 10 Toby Everett; 3 Kieran Buchanan; 12 Lucas Walshaw; 17 Josh Tonks. Subs (all used): 9 Alistair Leak; 16 Michael Ward; 15 Jack Blagbrough; 19 Tom Lillycrop.
Tries: Logan (31), Broughton (50), Kaye (67);
Goals: Morton 3/4; **Field goal:** White (67).
Rugby Leaguer & League Express Men of the Match:
Panthers: Gadwin Springer; *Bulldogs:* Josh Tonks.
Penalty count: 2-5; **Half-time:** 0-8; **Referee:** Ben Thaler.

Sunday 21st March 2021

WEST WALES RAIDERS 4 WIDNES VIKINGS 58

RAIDERS: 1 Phil Cowburn; 2 Uraia Naulusala; 33 Jamie Murphy; 4 Marcus Webb; 3 Emosi Nadaubale; 6 Gavin Henson; 7 Rangi Chase; 8 Tom Morgan; 9 Dafydd Phillips; 27 Morgan Allen; 11 Mike Connor; 12 Joe Burke; 13 Morgan Evans. Subs (all used): 15 Ashley Bateman; 28 Eparama Boginsoko; 16 Sam Herron; 23 Fraser Stroud.
Try: Naulusala (12); **Goals:** Henson 0/1.
Dismissal: Murphy (20) - dangerous challenge on Buckley.
VIKINGS: 1 Jack Owens; 20 Owen Buckley; 3 Jake Spedding; 4 Steve Tyrer; 5 Deon Cross; 6 Danny Craven; 7 Matty Smith; 16 Owen Farnworth; 17 Joe Lyons; 13 Kenny Baker; 11 Shane Grady; 12 Adam Lawton; 21 Calum O'Neill. Subs (all used): 23 Lewis Else; 15 Connor Dwyer; 22 Josh Wilde; 24 Will Tilleke.
Tries: Grady (16), Tyrer (23, 56, 72), Cross (27), Owens (30, 41, 78), Spedding (38, 63), Lawton (75);
Goals: Owens 7/11.
Sin bin: Craven (11) - high tackle;
Tilleke (45) - dangerous contact.
Rugby Leaguer & League Express Men of the Match:
Raiders: Rangi Chase; *Vikings:* Steve Tyrer.
Penalty count: 5-8; **Half-time:** 4-28; **Referee:** Liam Moore.

FEATHERSTONE ROVERS 41 BRADFORD BULLS 16

ROVERS: 1 Craig Hall; 5 Gareth Gale; 4 Josh Hardcastle; 17 Thomas Minns; 2 Ben Blackmore; 9 Fa'amanu Brown; 7 Dane Chisholm; 8 Craig Kopczak; 14 Connor Jones; 13 James Lockwood; 20 Frankie Halton; 12 Brad Day; 16 Jack Bussey. Subs (all used): 21 Dean Parata; 10 James Harrison; 18 Luke Cooper; 24 Dale Ferguson.
Tries: Jones (22), Minns (26), Blackmore (34), Harrison (37, 58), Parata (61), Hall (65); **Goals:** Hall 6/7;
Field goal: Hall (79).
Sin bin: Gale (76) - late challenge.
BULLS: 2 Joe Brown; 22 Reece Hamlett; 3 Rhys Evans; 4 Ross Oakes; 25 Jack Sanderson; 1 Brandon Pickersgill; 6 Danny Brough; 15 Dan Fleming; 9 Thomas Doyle; 10 Steve Crossley; 11 Adam Rooks; 16 Brad Gallagher; 13 Sam Hallas. Subs (all used): 14 George Flanagan; 18 Ebon Scurr; 20 Brad England; 23 Anthony Walker.
Tries: Hamlett (10, 48), Scurr (56); **Goals:** Brough 2/3.
Rugby Leaguer & League Express Men of the Match:
Rovers: Craig Hall; *Bulls:* Reece Hamlett.
Penalty count: 5-6; **Half-time:** 24-6;
Referee: Chris Kendall.

SWINTON LIONS 28 NEWCASTLE THUNDER 16

LIONS: 22 Geronimo Doyle; 2 Richard Lepori; 3 Mitch Cox; 4 Liam Forsyth; 1 Mike Butt; 6 Martyn Ridyard; 7 Jack Hansen; 8 Sam Brooks; 9 Luke Waterworth; 10 Lewis Hatton; 11 Rhodri Lloyd; 12 Nick Gregson; 13 Will Hope. Subs (all used): 15 Louis Brogan; 16 Paddy Jones; 24 Paul Nash; 19 Deane Meadows.
Tries: Lloyd (12), Butt (31, 40), Hansen (64), Doyle (78);
Goals: Ridyard 4/5.
THUNDER: 1 Lewis Young; 2 Jack Johnson; 3 Matthew Wright; 5 Calum Turner; 28 Cian Tyrer; 6 Jake Shorrocks; 7 Josh Woods; 8 Nathan Wilde; 14 Evan Simons; 10 Mikey Wood; 11 Ukuma Ta'ai; 12 Sam Wilde; 17 Connor Bailey. Subs (all used): 15 Ted Chapelhow; 16 Jay Chapelhow; 19 Evan Hodgson; 20 Cole Oakley.
Tries: Ta'ai (58), Tyrer (68), S Wilde (74); **Goals:** Wright 2/3.
Rugby Leaguer & League Express Men of the Match:
Lions: Martyn Ridyard; *Thunder:* Evan Simons.
Penalty count: 3-1; **Half-time:** 16-0;
Referee: Scott Mikalauskas.

ROUND 2

Saturday 27th March 2021

FEATHERSTONE ROVERS 30 BATLEY BULLDOGS 22

ROVERS: 1 Craig Hall; 5 Gareth Gale; 4 Josh Hardcastle; 3 Kris Welham; 2 Ben Blackmore; 9 Fa'amanu Brown; 7 Dane Chisholm; 8 Craig Kopczak; 14 Connor Jones; 13 James Lockwood; 20 Frankie Halton; 12 Brad Day; 16 Jack Bussey. Subs (all used): 21 Dean Parata; 31 Junior Moors; 10 James Harrison; 11 Brett Ferres.
Tries: Day (11), Blackmore (15), Brown (18), Welham (20), Harrison (66), Parata (68); **Goals:** Hall 3/6.
BULLDOGS: 1 Luke Hooley; 14 Elliot Hall; 22 Dale Morton; 23 Jack Logan; 5 Johnny Campbell; 6 Ben White; 7 Tom Gilmore; 19 Tom Lillycrop; 24 Ben Kaye; 10 Toby Everett; 3 Kieran Buchanan; 12 Lucas Walshaw; 15 Jack Blagbrough. Subs (all used): 9 Alistair Leak; 16 Michael Ward; 18 George Senior; 26 Nyle Flynn.
Tries: Morton (8), Hall (31), Hooley (50), Campbell (58);
Goals: Morton 3/5.
Rugby Leaguer & League Express Men of the Match:
Rovers: James Harrison; *Bulldogs:* Tom Gilmore.
Penalty count: 4-5; **Half-time:** 18-12;
Referee: Gareth Hewer.

Sunday 28th March 2021

SWINTON LIONS 23 OLDHAM 14

LIONS: 1 Mike Butt; 2 Richard Lepori; 3 Mitch Cox; 5 Sam Grant; 25 Luis Roberts; 6 Martyn Ridyard; 7 Jack Hansen; 15 Louis Brogan; 9 Luke Waterworth; 10 Lewis Hatton; 11 Rhodri Lloyd; 12 Nick Gregson; 13 Will Hope. Subs (all used): 24 Paul Nash; 20 Tayler Brown; 14 Billy Brickhill; 19 Deane Meadows.
Tries: Grant (5), Hope (43), Ridyard (50), Meadows (56);
Goals: Ridyard 3/4; **Field goal:** Ridyard (72).
OLDHAM: 1 Dan Abram; 2 Tommy Brierley; 3 Ben Heaton; 24 Max Roberts; 5 Ryan Ince; 6 Lewis Charnock; 26 James Barran; 17 Liam Kirk; 9 Gareth Owen; 13 Martyn Reilly; 25 Danny Bridge; 11 Danny Langtree; 12 Liam Bent. Subs (all used): 16 Tyler Dupree; 10 Jack Spencer; 21 Shaun Pick; 23 Callum Green.
Tries: Langtree (23), Dupree (47), Heaton (76);
Goals: D Abram 1/3.
Rugby Leaguer & League Express Men of the Match:
Lions: Nick Gregson; *Oldham:* Danny Langtree.
Penalty count: 6-7; **Half-time:** 6-4; **Referee:** Tom Grant.

LONDON BRONCOS 2 YORK CITY KNIGHTS 14

BRONCOS: 5 Ed Chamberlain; 20 Gideon Boafo; 4 Will Lovell; 23 Josh Hodson; 17 Abbas Miski; 22 Oliver Leyland; 21 Rian Horsman; 15 Romain Navarrete; 14 Sam Davis; 8 Olsi Krasniqi; 13 Josh Walters; 25 Jacob Jones; 16 Dan Hindmarsh. Subs (all used): 10 Greg Richards; 28 Titus Gwaze; 30 Paulos Latu; 18 Jordan Williams.
Goals: Chamberlain 1/1.
Sin bin: Jones (33) - high tackle.
CITY KNIGHTS: 5 Kieran Dixon; 30 Tyme Dow-Nikau; 3 Liam Salter; 4 Ryan Atkins; 2 Jason Bass; 6 Brendan O'Hagan; 1 Matty Marsh; 8 Ronan Dixon; 9 Will Jubb; 15 Jordan Baldwinson; 11 Chris Clarkson; 17 Danny Kirmond; 20 Tim Spears. Subs (all used): 24 Daniel Barcoe; 21 Joe Porter; 13 Adam Cuthbertson; 19 James Green.
Tries: Porter (42), Salter (77); **Goals:** K Dixon 3/3.
Rugby Leaguer & League Express Men of the Match:
Broncos: Sam Davis; *City Knights:* Brendan O'Hagan.
Penalty count: 11-10; **Half-time:** 2-0;
Referee: Marcus Griffiths. *(at The Rock, Roehampton)*.

WIDNES VIKINGS 34 WHITEHAVEN 10

VIKINGS: 1 Jack Owens; 5 Deon Cross; 3 Jake Spedding; 4 Steve Tyrer; 20 Owen Buckley; 6 Danny Craven; 7 Matty Smith; 16 Owen Farnworth; 17 Joe Lyons; 8 Paul Clough; 15 Connor Dwyer; 12 Adam Lawton; 13 Kenny Baker. Subs (all used): 23 Lewis Else; 10 Matt Cook; 24 Will Tilleke; 22 Josh Wilde.
Tries: Tyrer (16), Craven (34), Else (40, 70), Owens (43), Tilleke (67); **Goals:** Owens 5/6.
WHITEHAVEN: 2 Lachlan Walmsley; 25 James Worthington; 30 Sean Croston; 4 Jessie Joe Parker; 5 Andrew Bulman; 6 Karl Dixon; 7 Nikau Williams; 21 Glenn Riley; 9 Callum Phillips; 29 Dean Zammit; 15 Connor Holliday; 19 Ellis Gillam; 16 Tom Wilkinson. Subs (all used): 12 Liam Cooper; 24 Ethan Kelly; 31 Oscar Thomas; 33 Andy Thornley.
Tries: C Phillips (8), Croston (80);
Goals: Walmsley 1/1, Holliday 0/1.
On report: Walmsley (27) - alleged biting.
Rugby Leaguer & League Express Men of the Match:
Vikings: Lewis Else; *Whitehaven:* Callum Phillips.
Penalty count: 8-9; **Half-time:** 16-6; **Referee:** Jack Smith.

ROUND 3

Friday 9th April 2021

HULL KINGSTON ROVERS 32 CASTLEFORD TIGERS 33
(after golden point extra-time)

ROVERS: 1 Adam Quinlan; 23 Ethan Ryan; 3 Greg Minikin; 4 Shaun Kenny-Dowall (C); 5 Ryan Hall; 7 Jordan Abdull; 20 Mikey Lewis; 10 Korbin Sims; 9 Matt Parcell; 16 George King; 12 Kane Linnett; 27 Luis Johnson (D2); 15 George Lawler. Subs (all used): 8 Albert Vete; 14 Jez Litten; 28 Muizz Mustapha; 33 Jimmy Keinhorst.
Tries: Ryan (8), Quinlan (28), Vete (31), Parcell (35), Kenny-Dowall (59), Abdull (62);
Goals: Abdull 2/4, Lewis 2/2.
TIGERS: 31 Gareth O'Brien; 2 Derrell Olpherts; 3 Peter Mata'utia; 4 Michael Shenton (C); 25 Jordan Turner; 7 Danny Richardson; 6 Jake Trueman; 15 George Griffin; 9 Paul McShane; 10 Grant Millington; 12 Cheyse Blair; 11 Oliver Holmes; 14 Nathan Massey. Subs (all used): 8 Liam Watts; 13 Adam Milner; 21 Jesse Sene-Lefao; 22 Daniel Smith.
Tries: Trueman (22), Olpherts (46, 72), McShane (50, 77), Turner (80); **Goals:** Richardson 4/6;
Field goal: O'Brien (99).
Rugby League & League Express Men of the Match:
Rovers: Matt Parcell; *Tigers:* Paul McShane.
Penalty count: 3-8; **Half-time:** 22-6;
Referee: Robert Hicks.

YORK CITY KNIGHTS 0 WIGAN WARRIORS 26

CITY KNIGHTS: 26 Myles Harrison; 22 Perry Whiteley; 30 Tyme Dow-Nikau; 3 Liam Salter; 5 Kieran Dixon; 1 Matty Marsh; 28 Danny Washbrook; 19 James Green; 9 Will Jubb; 13 Adam Cuthbertson; 21 Joe Porter; 12 Sam Scott; 20 Tim Spears. Subs: 24 Daniel Barcoe; 16 Marcus Stock; 25 AJ Towse; 8 Ronan Dixon (not used).
WARRIORS: 3 Zak Hardaker; 22 Jake Bibby; 11 Willie Isa; 28 Sam Halsall; 30 Umyla Hanley; 20 Harry Smith; 31 Jackson Hastings; 10 Joe Bullock; 9 Sam Powell (C); 8 Brad Singleton; 13 John Bateman; 15 Morgan Smithies; 14 Oliver Partington. Subs (all used): 19 Liam Byrne; 17 Tony Clubb; 21 Ethan Havard; 25 Joe Shorrocks.
Tries: Hardaker (20), Smith (32), Halsall (36), Hanley (51), Clubb (62); **Goals:** Hardaker 3/5.
Rugby League & League Express Men of the Match:
City Knights: Myles Harrison; *Warriors:* Zak Hardaker.
Penalty count: 8-4; **Half-time:** 0-14;
Referee: Marcus Griffiths.

Saturday 10th April 2021

SALFORD RED DEVILS 68 WIDNES VIKINGS 4

RED DEVILS: 1 Morgan Escare (D); 22 Rhys Williams; 3 Kallum Watkins; 24 Matthew Costello (D); 4 Krisnan Inu; 18 Chris Atkin; 6 Tui Lolohea; 25 Jack Ormondroyd; 29 Dec Patton; 8 Lee Mossop (C); 20 Harvey Livett; 12 Pauli Pauli; 26 Jack Wells. Subs (all used): 15 Oliver Roberts; 9 Andy Ackers; 28 Darcy Lussick (D); 10 Sebastine Ikahihifo.
Tries: Escare (13, 78), Costello (18, 21), Lolohea (36), Patton (43), Ackers (49), Ikahihifo (58), Watkins (63), Ormondroyd (73), Williams (75), Atkin (79);
Goals: Inu 10/12.
VIKINGS: 25 Daniel Hill; 5 Deon Cross; 3 Jake Spedding; 18 Lloyd Roby; 20 Owen Buckley; 6 Danny Craven; 7 Matty Smith; 14 Lee Jewitt; 23 Lewis Else; 11 Shane Grady; 12 Adam Lawton; 4 Steve Tyrer; 1 Jack Owens. Subs (all used): 8 Paul Clough; 17 Joe Lyons; 22 Josh Wilde; 24 Will Tilleke.
Try: Hill (39); **Goals:** Owens 0/1.
Rugby League & League Express Men of the Match:
Red Devils: Darcy Lussick; *Vikings:* Danny Craven.
Penalty count: 6-4; **Half-time:** 24-4;
Referee: Scott Mikalauskas.

ST HELENS 26 LEEDS RHINOS 18

SAINTS: 1 Lachlan Coote; 2 Tommy Makinson; 3 Kevin Naiqama; 18 Jack Welsby; 5 Regan Grace; 6 Jonny Lomax; 7 Theo Fages; 8 Alex Walmsley; 9 James Roby (C); 10 Matty Lees; 11 Joel Thompson; 12 James Bentley; 14 Sione Mata'utia. Subs (all used): 15 Louie McCarthy-Scarsbrook; 16 Kyle Amor; 17 Agnatius Paasi; 21 Lewis Dodd.
Tries: Makinson (2, 78), Grace (47, 61); **Goals:** Makinson 5/6.
RHINOS: 27 Jack Broadbent; 2 Tom Briscoe; 11 Alex Mellor; 21 Alex Sutcliffe; 24 Luke Briscoe; 12 Rhyse Martin; 17 Cameron Smith; 8 Mikolaj Oledzki; 9 Kruise Leeming; 10 Matt Prior (C); 22 Sam Walters; 25 James Donaldson; 13 Zane Tetevano. Subs (all used): 14 Brad Dwyer; 26 Jarrod O'Connor; 19 King Vuniyayawa (D); 31 Morgan Gannon (D).
Tries: Oledzki (10), Dwyer (65, 69); **Goals:** Martin 3/3.
Dismissal: Tetevano (44) - late challenge on Fages.
Rugby League & League Express Men of the Match:
Saints: Agnatius Paasi; *Rhinos:* Brad Dwyer.
Penalty count: 5-5; **Half-time:** 8-6; **Referee:** Ben Thaler.

CATALANS DRAGONS 26 WAKEFIELD TRINITY 6

DRAGONS: 29 Sam Tomkins; 2 Tom Davies; 3 Samisoni Langi; 4 Dean Whare; 5 Fouad Yaha; 6 James Maloney; 7 Josh Drinkwater; 8 Gil Dudson; 14 Alrix Da Costa; 10 Julian Bousquet; 11 Matt Whitley; 12 Mike McMeeken; 13 Benjamin Garcia (C). Subs (all used): 1 Arthur Mourgue; 16 Paul Seguier; 24 Jason Baitieri; 28 Sam Kasiano.
Tries: S Tomkins (16), Drinkwater (50), Davies (62), Dudson (66); **Goals:** Maloney 5/5.
TRINITY: 1 Max Jowitt; 18 Innes Senior; 4 Reece Lyne; 3 Bill Tupou; 2 Tom Johnstone; 6 Jacob Miller (C); 7 Mason Lino; 8 David Fifita; 23 Josh Wood; 12 Kelepi Tanginoa; 11 Matty Ashurst; 14 Jay Pitts; 13 Joe Westerman. Subs (all used): 19 Jordan Crowther; 17 Chris Green; 10 Tinirau Arona; 16 James Batchelor.
Try: Lino (26); **Goals:** Lino 1/1.
Rugby League & League Express Men of the Match:
Dragons: Sam Tomkins; *Trinity:* Jay Pitts.
Penalty count: 6-6; **Half-time:** 8-6;
Referee: Chris Kendall.
(at Totally Wicked Stadium, St Helens).

FEATHERSTONE ROVERS 14 HULL FC 34

ROVERS: 1 Craig Hall; 5 Gareth Gale; 4 Josh Hardcastle; 3 Kris Welham; 2 Ben Blackmore; 6 Tom Holmes; 7 Dane Chisholm; 20 Frankie Halton; 21 Dean Parata; 10 James Harrison; 11 Brett Ferres; 12 Brad Day; 27 Loui McConnell. Subs (all used): 9 Fa'amanu Brown; 31 Junior Moors; 18 Luke Cooper; 19 Callum Field.
Tries: Hardcastle (1), Ferres (46), Blackmore (68);
Goals: Hall 0/2, Chisholm 1/1.
HULL FC: 1 Jake Connor; 2 Bureta Faraimo; 4 Josh Griffin; 3 Carlos Tuimavave; 5 Mahe Fonua; 19 Ben McNamara; 9 Danny Houghton; 8 Scott Taylor (C); 14 Jordan Johnstone; 10 Tevita Satae; 11 Andre Savelio; 12 Manu Ma'u; 16 Jordan Lane. Subs (all used): 17 Brad Fash; 22 Josh Bowden; 24 Cameron Scott; 15 Joe Cator.
Tries: Faraimo (5), Tuimavave (7, 31), Griffin (18, 26), Johnstone (39); **Goals:** Connor 5/6.
Rugby League & League Express Men of the Match:
Rovers: Josh Hardcastle; *Hull FC:* Jake Connor.
Penalty count: 5-5; **Half-time:** 4-34; **Referee:** James Child.

Sunday 11th April 2021

SWINTON LIONS 8 WARRINGTON WOLVES 32

LIONS: 1 Mike Butt; 2 Richard Lepori; 3 Mitch Cox; 11 Rhodri Lloyd; 25 Luis Roberts; 6 Martyn Ridyard; 7 Jack Hansen; 8 Sam Brooks; 9 Luke Waterworth; 15 Louis Brogan; 19 Deane Meadows; 12 Nick Gregson; 13 Will Hope. Subs (all used): 20 Tayler Brown; 16 Paddy Jones; 18 Cobi Green; 26 Jordan Brown.
Try: Roberts (14); **Goals:** Ridyard 2/2.
WOLVES: 17 Matty Ashton; 2 Tom Lineham; 18 Jake Mamo; 4 Toby King; 5 Josh Charnley; 6 Blake Austin; 1 Stefan Ratchford; 8 Chris Hill (C); 9 Daryl Clark; 13 Joe Philbin; 11 Ben Currie; 22 Ellis Robson; 14 Jason Clark. Subs (all used): 19 Robbie Mulhern; 21 Rob Butler; 15 Matt Davis; 16 Danny Walker.
Tries: King (6, 32), Lineham (27), Austin (37), Ashton (67), Walker (73); **Goals:** Ratchford 4/6.
Rugby League & League Express Men of the Match:
Lions: Richard Lepori; *Wolves:* Toby King.
Penalty count: 5-9; **Half-time:** 8-20; **Referee:** Tom Grant.

LEIGH CENTURIONS 18 HUDDERSFIELD GIANTS 36

CENTURIONS: 6 Blake Wallace; 24 Keanan Brand; 3 Iain Thornley; 22 Craig Mullen; 5 Lewis Tierney; 30 Ben Reynolds; 1 Ryan Brierley; 8 Ben Flower (D); 9 Liam Hood (C); 20 Adam Sidlow; 11 Ben Hellewell; 18 Matty Gee; 21 Tyrone McCarthy. Subs (all used): 26 Nathan Peats (D); 12 Jordan Thompson; 10 Mark Ioane; 16 Nathaniel Peteru.
Tries: Thompson (27, 63), Peats (59); **Goals:** Reynolds 3/3.
Sin bin: Sidlow (65) - high tackle on Trout.
GIANTS: 5 Darnell McIntosh; 2 Jermaine McGillvary; 3 Jake Wardle; 21 Leroy Cudjoe; 27 Sam Wood; 6 Lee Gaskell; 16 Jack Cogger; 8 Luke Yates; 19 James Cunningham; 18 Jack Ashworth (D); 17 Chris McQueen; 11 Kenny Edwards; 13 Josh Jones. Subs (all used): 9 Adam O'Brien; 10 Michael Lawrence (C); 14 Matty English; 25 Owen Trout.
Tries: Edwards (7), Wood (13, 51), McGillvary (22, 46, 74), Gaskell (76); **Goals:** Jake Wardle 4/7, Gaskell 0/2.
Sin bin: Yates (33) - late challenge on Brierley.
Rugby League & League Express Men of the Match:
Centurions: Jordan Thompson; *Giants:* Jermaine McGillvary.
Penalty count: 5-8; **Half-time:** 6-20;
Referee: Liam Moore.

QUARTER FINALS

Friday 7th May 2021

CATALANS DRAGONS 6 WARRINGTON WOLVES 16

DRAGONS: 29 Sam Tomkins; 2 Tom Davies; 3 Samisoni Langi; 4 Dean Whare; 5 Fouad Yaha; 6 James Maloney; 7 Josh Drinkwater; 8 Gil Dudson; 9 Michael McIlorum; 10 Julian Bousquet; 22 Joel Tomkins; 12 Mike McMeeken; 13 Benjamin Garcia (C). Subs (all used): 14 Alrix Da Costa; 24 Jason Baitieri; 27 Joe Chan (D); 28 Sam Kasiano.
Try: McMeeken (62); **Goals:** Maloney 1/1.
Sin bin: Dudson (6) - high tackle.
WOLVES: 23 Josh Thewlis; 18 Jake Mamo; 3 Greg Inglis; 4 Toby King; 5 Josh Charnley; 6 Blake Austin; 7 Gareth Widdop; 8 Chris Hill; 9 Daryl Clark; 10 Mike Cooper; 11 Ben Currie; 12 Jack Hughes (C); 14 Jason Clark. Subs (all used): 13 Joe Philbin; 15 Matt Davis; 19 Robbie Mulhern; 20 Sitaleki Akauola.
Tries: D Clark (5, 27); **Goals:** Widdop 4/5.
Rugby League & League Express Men of the Match:
Dragons: Sam Tomkins; *Wolves:* Daryl Clark.
Penalty count: 6-6; **Half-time:** 0-14;
Referee: Liam Moore. *(at Emerald Headingley, Leeds).*

ST HELENS 23 HUDDERSFIELD GIANTS 18

SAINTS: 1 Lachlan Coote; 2 Tommy Makinson; 3 Kevin Naiqama; 4 Mark Percival; 5 Regan Grace; 6 Jonny Lomax; 7 Theo Fages; 8 Alex Walmsley; 9 James Roby (C); 15 Louie McCarthy-Scarsbrook; 11 Joel Thompson; 14 Sione Mata'utia; 20 Joe Batchelor. Subs (all used): 16 Kyle Amor; 17 Agnatius Paasi; 18 Jack Welsby; 19 Aaron Smith.
Tries: Grace (17, 53, 75), Percival (33); **Goals:** Coote 3/5;
Field goal: Fages (63).
GIANTS: 6 Lee Gaskell; 2 Jermaine McGillvary; 4 Ricky Leutele; 17 Chris McQueen; 5 Darnell McIntosh; 16 Jack Cogger; 7 Aidan Sezer (C); 8 Luke Yates; 19 James Cunningham; 10 Michael Lawrence; 11 Kenny Edwards; 13 Josh Jones; 15 Joe Greenwood. Subs (all used): 9 Adam O'Brien; 14 Matty English; 25 Owen Trout; 27 Sam Wood.
Tries: Lawrence (6), McIntosh (40, 67); **Goals:** Sezer 3/3.
Rugby League & League Express Men of the Match:
Saints: James Roby; *Giants:* Aidan Sezer.
Penalty count: 8-6; **Half-time:** 10-12;
Referee: James Child. *(at Emerald Headingley, Leeds).*

Saturday 8th May 2021

HULL FC 20 WIGAN WARRIORS 10

HULL FC: 21 Adam Swift; 24 Cameron Scott; 3 Carlos Tuimavave; 4 Josh Griffin; 5 Mahe Fonua; 6 Josh Reynolds; 7 Marc Sneyd; 10 Tevita Satae; 9 Danny Houghton (C); 13 Ligi Sao; 12 Manu Ma'u; 11 Andre Savelio; 16 Jordan Lane. Subs (all used): 20 Jack Brown; 15 Joe Cator; 14 Jordan Johnstone; 23 Connor Wynne.
Tries: Satae (13, 65), Swift (80); **Goals:** Sneyd 4/5
(last conversion attempt not taken).
Sin bin: Brown (34) - dangerous challenge.
WARRIORS: 3 Zak Hardaker; 22 Jake Bibby; 11 Willie Isa; 12 Liam Farrell (C); 1 Bevan French; 31 Jackson Hastings; 20 Harry Smith; 8 Brad Singleton; 9 Sam Powell; 19 Liam Byrne; 15 Morgan Smithies; 13 John Bateman; 14 Oliver Partington. Subs (all used): 2 Dom Manfredi; 10 Joe Bullock; 21 Ethan Havard; 25 Joe Shorrocks.
Tries: Bibby (10), Manfredi (78);
Goals: Hardaker 0/2, Smith 1/1.
Rugby League & League Express Men of the Match:
Hull FC: Tevita Satae; *Warriors:* Liam Farrell.
Penalty count: 3-5; **Half-time:** 8-4;
Referee: Robert Hicks. *(at Emerald Headingley, Leeds).*

CASTLEFORD TIGERS 19 SALFORD RED DEVILS 18
(after golden point extra-time)

TIGERS: 1 Niall Evalds; 2 Derrell Olpherts; 3 Peter Mata'utia; 4 Michael Shenton (C); 25 Jordan Turner; 6 Jake Trueman; 7 Danny Richardson; 15 George Griffin; 9 Paul McShane; 14 Nathan Massey; 11 Oliver Holmes; 10 Grant Millington; 13 Adam Milner. Subs (all used): 8 Liam Watts; 22 Daniel Smith; 28 Brad Martin; 31 Gareth O'Brien.
Tries: Smith (24), Mata'utia (39), Shenton (60);
Goals: Richardson 2/2, O'Brien 1/1; **Field goal:** O'Brien (83).
Sin bin: O'Brien (65) - professional foul;
Watts (74) - late challenge on Taylor.
RED DEVILS: 23 Dan Sarginson; 2 Ken Sio; 3 Kallum Watkins; 20 Harvey Livett; 22 Rhys Williams; 6 Tui Lolohea; 7 Kevin Brown; 8 Lee Mossop (C); 14 Danny Addy; 10 Sebastine Ikahihifo; 21 James Greenwood; 12 Pauli Pauli; 13 Elijah Taylor. Subs (all used): 11 Ryan Lannon; 16 Greg Burke; 18 Chris Atkin; 25 Jack Ormondroyd.
Tries: Livett (15, 35), Mossop (80); **Goals:** Livett 3/3.
Rugby League & League Express Men of the Match:
Tigers: Paul McShane; *Red Devils:* Harvey Livett.
Penalty count: 4-7; **Half-time:** 12-12;
Referee: Ben Thaler. *(at Emerald Headingley, Leeds).*

St Helens' Mark Percival looks for a way past Castleford's Grant Millington during the Challenge Cup Final

SEMI-FINALS

Saturday 5th June 2021

HULL FC 18 ST HELENS 33

HULL FC: 1 Jake Connor; 5 Mahe Fonua; 3 Carlos Tuimavave; 4 Josh Griffin; 21 Adam Swift; 6 Josh Reynolds; 7 Marc Sneyd (C); 13 Ligi Sao; 9 Danny Houghton; 10 Tevita Satae; 11 Andre Savelio; 12 Manu Ma'u; 16 Jordan Lane. Subs (all used): 22 Josh Bowden; 20 Jack Brown; 17 Brad Fash; 24 Cameron Scott.
Tries: Fonua (52), Houghton (66), Scott (71);
Goals: Sneyd 3/4.

SAINTS: 1 Lachlan Coote; 2 Tommy Makinson; 3 Kevin Naiqama; 18 Jack Welsby; 5 Regan Grace; 6 Jonny Lomax; 7 Theo Fages; 8 Alex Walmsley; 9 James Roby (C); 15 Louie McCarthy-Scarsbrook; 14 Sione Mata'utia; 11 Joel Thompson; 13 Morgan Knowles. Subs (all used): 16 Kyle Amor; 20 Joe Batchelor; 21 Lewis Dodd; 25 Dan Norman (D).
Tries: Grace (17, 75), Fages (25), Welsby (48), Coote (77);
Goals: Coote 6/7; **Field goal:** Fages (64).

Rugby Leaguer & League Express Men of the Match:
Hull FC: Carlos Tuimavave; *Saints:* Kevin Naiqama.
Penalty count: 4-5; **Half-time:** 2-14; **Referee:** Liam Moore.

CASTLEFORD TIGERS 35 WARRINGTON WOLVES 20

TIGERS: 1 Niall Evalds; 2 Derrell Olpherts; 3 Peter Mata'utia; 4 Michael Shenton (C); 25 Jordan Turner; 6 Jake Trueman; 31 Gareth O'Brien; 14 Nathan Massey; 9 Paul McShane; 24 Suaia Matagi; 11 Oliver Holmes; 21 Jesse Sene-Lefao; 13 Adam Milner. Subs (all used): 8 Liam Watts; 17 Alex Foster; 18 Jacques O'Neill; 20 James Clare.
Tries: O'Brien (16), Turner (24, 28, 57), Sene-Lefao (49), McShane (61); **Goals:** O'Brien 5/9;
Field goal: McShane (39).
Sin bin: O'Neill (53) - dangerous challenge.
WOLVES: 1 Stefan Ratchford; 2 Tom Lineham; 18 Jake Mamo; 4 Toby King; 5 Josh Charnley; 6 Blake Austin; 7 Gareth Widdop; 8 Chris Hill; 9 Daryl Clark; 10 Mike Cooper; 11 Ben Currie; 12 Jack Hughes (C); 15 Matt Davis. Subs (all used): 13 Joe Philbin; 19 Robbie Mulhern; 16 Danny Walker; 20 Sitaleki Akauola.
Tries: Currie (44), Mamo (46), King (55), Charnley (66);
Goals: Ratchford 0/2, Widdop 2/2.
Sin bin: Mamo (20) - professional foul.
Rugby Leaguer & League Express Men of the Match:
Tigers: Paul McShane; *Wolves:* Daryl Clark.
Penalty count: 5-4; **Half-time:** 19-0;
Referee: Chris Kendall.

Attendance: 4,000 *(both at Leigh Sports Village).*

FINAL

Saturday 17th July 2021

CASTLEFORD TIGERS 12 ST HELENS 26

TIGERS: 1 Niall Evalds; 2 Derrell Olpherts; 3 Peter Mata'utia; 4 Michael Shenton (C); 25 Jordan Turner; 6 Jake Trueman; 31 Gareth O'Brien; 15 George Griffin; 9 Paul McShane; 10 Grant Millington; 11 Oliver Holmes; 21 Jesse Sene-Lefao; 14 Nathan Massey. Subs (all used): 8 Liam Watts; 13 Adam Milner; 17 Alex Foster; 22 Daniel Smith.
Tries: Evalds (17), Trueman (25); **Goals:** O'Brien 2/2.
SAINTS: 1 Lachlan Coote; 2 Tommy Makinson; 3 Kevin Naiqama; 4 Mark Percival; 5 Regan Grace; 6 Jonny Lomax; 7 Theo Fages; 8 Alex Walmsley; 9 James Roby (C); 15 Louie McCarthy-Scarsbrook; 11 Joel Thompson; 20 Joe Batchelor; 13 Morgan Knowles. Subs (all used): 10 Matty Lees; 16 Kyle Amor; 17 Agnatius Paasi; 18 Jack Welsby.
Tries: Fages (10), Roby (42), Makinson (51), Amor (78);
Goals: Coote 5/7.

Rugby Leaguer & League Express Men of the Match:
Tigers: Niall Evalds; *Saints:* Lachlan Coote.
Penalty count: 4-6; **Half-time:** 12-6; **Referee:** Liam Moore;
Attendance: 40,000 *(at Wembley Stadium).*

2021 SEASON
Stats round-up

Gareth Gale

Craig Hall

Theerapol Ritson

Jack Miller

CHAMPIONSHIP *(Regular season & play-offs)*

TRIES

1	Gareth Gale	Featherstone Rovers	27
2	Craig Hall	Featherstone Rovers	26
3	Abbas Miski	London Broncos	18
4	Deon Cross	Widnes Vikings	17
5	Fa'amanu Brown	Featherstone Rovers	15
	Gideon Boafo	London Broncos	15
	Lachlan Walmsley	Whitehaven	15
8	Kieran Gill	Newcastle Thunder	14
	Mathieu Jussaume	Toulouse Olympique	14
	Andrew Bulman	Whitehaven	14

GOALS

1	Craig Hall	Featherstone Rovers	94
2	Mark Kheirallah	Toulouse Olympique	80
3	Chris Hankinson	London Broncos	79
4	Lachlan Walmsley	Whitehaven	71
5	Kieran Dixon	York City Knights	59
6	Tom Gilmore	Batley Bulldogs	53
	Josh Woods	Newcastle Thunder	53
8	Izaac Farrell	Sheffield Eagles	51
9	Danny Brough	Bradford Bulls	47
	Martyn Ridyard	Swinton Lions	47

POINTS

			T	G	FG	Pts
1	Craig Hall	Featherstone Rovers	26	94	0	292
2	Lachlan Walmsley	Whitehaven	15	71	0	202
3	Chris Hankinson	London Broncos	10	79	0	198
4	Mark Kheirallah	Toulouse Olympique	6	80	0	184
5	Kieran Dixon	York City Knights	11	59	0	162
6	Tom Gilmore	Batley Bulldogs	3	53	2	120
	Steve Tyrer	Widnes Vikings	8	44	0	120
8	Josh Woods	Newcastle Thunder	3	53	1	119
9	Izaac Farrell	Sheffield Eagles	4	51	0	118
10	Gareth Gale	Featherstone Rovers	27	0	0	108

LEAGUE 1 *(Regular season & play-offs)*

TRIES

1	Theerapol Ritson	Barrow Raiders	22
	Rob Massam	North Wales Crusaders	22
3	Brad Holroyd	Workington Town	18
4	Matty Chrimes	Hunslet	14
	Jack Miller	Keighley Cougars	14
6	Charlie Graham	Keighley Cougars	12
	Brenden Santi	Keighley Cougars	12
8	Matty Beharrell	Doncaster	11
	Jason Tali	Doncaster	11
	Patrick Ah Van	North Wales Crusaders	11
	Gav Rodden	North Wales Crusaders	11
	Matty Henson	Workington Town	11

GOALS

1	Jack Miller	Keighley Cougars	103
2	Carl Forber	Workington Town	76
3	Matty Beharrell	Doncaster	67
4	Tommy Johnson	North Wales Crusaders	66
5	Dan Coates	Coventry Bears	54
6	Neil Thorman	London Skolars	51
7	Dom Brambani	Hunslet	48
	Jamie Dallimore	Barrow Raiders	48
9	Will Ramsey	West Wales Raiders	28
10	Ryan Shaw	Barrow Raiders	27

POINTS

			T	G	FG	Pts
1	Jack Miller	Keighley Cougars	14	103	0	262
2	Matty Beharrell	Doncaster	11	67	1	179
3	Carl Forber	Workington Town	6	76	0	176
4	Tommy Johnson	North Wales Crusaders	10	66	0	172
5	Dan Coates	Coventry Bears	8	54	1	141
6	Jamie Dallimore	Barrow Raiders	5	48	1	117
7	Neil Thorman	London Skolars	0	51	0	102
8	Dom Brambani	Hunslet	1	48	0	100
9	Theerapol Ritson	Barrow Raiders	22	3	0	94
10	Rob Massam	North Wales Crusaders	22	0	0	88

LEADING SCORERS

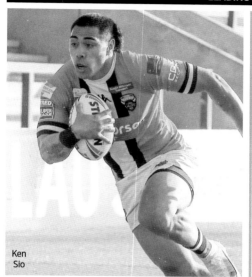

Ken
Sio

Regan
Grace

SUPER LEAGUE *(Regular season & play-offs)*

TRIES

1	Ken Sio	Salford Red Devils	19
2	Ryan Hall	Hull Kingston Rovers	16
	Jake Mamo	Warrington Wolves	16
4	Fouad Yaha	Catalans Dragons	15
5	Tom Davies	Catalans Dragons	14
	Regan Grace	St Helens	14
7	Jordan Turner	Castleford Tigers	13
	Adam Swift	Hull FC	13
	Kane Linnett	Hull Kingston Rovers	13
	Jack Welsby	St Helens	13
	Jake Bibby	Wigan Warriors	13

GOALS

1	James Maloney	Catalans Dragons	108
2	Rhyse Martin	Leeds Rhinos	85
3	Lachlan Coote	St Helens	80
4	Mason Lino	Wakefield Trinity	75
5	Stefan Ratchford	Warrington Wolves	71
6	Marc Sneyd	Hull FC	60
7	Jordan Abdull	Hull Kingston Rovers	47
8	Danny Richardson	Castleford Tigers	46
9	Krisnan Inu	Salford Red Devils	42
10	Oliver Russell	Huddersfield Giants	32

GOALS PERCENTAGE

			G	Att	%
1	Arthur Mourgue	Catalans Dragons	15	16	93.75
2	Mason Lino	Wakefield Trinity	75	84	89.28
3	James Maloney	Catalans Dragons	108	125	86.40
4	Gareth Widdop	Warrington Wolves	25	29	86.20
5	Ryan Brierley	Leigh Centurions	29	34	85.29
6	Stefan Ratchford	Warrington Wolves	71	85	83.52
7	Rhyse Martin	Leeds Rhinos	85	102	83.33
	Harvey Livett	Salford Red Devils	10	12	83.33
9	Danny Richardson	Castleford Tigers	46	56	82.14
10	Craig Mullen	Leigh Centurions	13	16	81.25

(10 minimum attempts to qualify)

POINTS

			T	G	FG	Pts
1	James Maloney	Catalans Dragons	5	108	5	241
2	Lachlan Coote	St Helens	7	80	0	188
3	Rhyse Martin	Leeds Rhinos	3	85	0	182
4	Mason Lino	Wakefield Trinity	5	75	1	171
5	Stefan Ratchford	Warrington Wolves	1	71	0	146
6	Marc Sneyd	Hull FC	0	60	2	122
7	Jordan Abdull	Hull Kingston Rovers	5	47	2	116
8	Danny Richardson	Castleford Tigers	1	46	3	99
9	Ryan Brierley	Leigh Centurions	10	29	0	98
10	Krisnan Inu	Salford Red Devils	3	42	0	96

CHALLENGE CUP

TRIES

1	Regan Grace	St Helens	7
2	Jordan Turner	Castleford Tigers	4
	Jack Owens	Widnes Vikings	4
	Steve Tyrer	Widnes Vikings	4
5	Paul McShane	Castleford Tigers	3
	Ben Blackmore	Featherstone Rovers	3
	James Harrison	Featherstone Rovers	3
	Jermaine McGillvary	Huddersfield Giants	3
	Tommy Makinson	St Helens	3
	Toby King	Warrington Wolves	3

GOALS

1	Lachlan Coote	St Helens	14
2	Jack Owens	Widnes Vikings	12
3	Krisnan Inu	Salford Red Devils	10
4	Craig Hall	Featherstone Rovers	9
	Martyn Ridyard	Swinton Lions	9

POINTS

			T	G	FG	Pts
1	Jack Owens	Widnes Vikings	4	12	0	40
2	Lachlan Coote	St Helens	1	14	0	32
3	Regan Grace	St Helens	7	0	0	28
4	Craig Hall	Featherstone Rovers	1	9	1	23
	Martyn Ridyard	Swinton Lions	1	9	1	23

LEADING SCORERS

James Maloney

ALL COMPETITIONS

TRIES

1	Craig Hall	Featherstone Rovers	28
2	Gareth Gale	Featherstone Rovers	27
3	Theerapol Ritson	Barrow Raiders	22
	Rob Massam	North Wales Crusaders	22
5	Regan Grace	St Helens	21
6	Ken Sio	Salford Red Devils	19
7	Abbas Miski	London Broncos	18
	Deon Cross	Widnes Vikings	18
	Brad Holroyd	Workington Town	18
10	Jordan Turner	Castleford Tigers	17
	Jake Mamo	Warrington Wolves	17
	Fa'amanu Brown	Featherstone Rovers	17

GOALS

1	James Maloney	Catalans Dragons	114
2	Craig Hall	Featherstone Rovers	113
3	Jack Miller	Keighley Cougars	104
4	Lachlan Coote	St Helens	94
5	Rhyse Martin	Leeds Rhinos	88
6	Chris Hankinson	London Broncos	83
7	Mark Kheirallah	Toulouse Olympique	80
8	Kieran Dixon	York City Knights	77
9	Mason Lino	Wakefield Trinity	76
	Carl Forber	Workington Town	76

POINTS

			T	G	FG	Pts
1	Craig Hall	Featherstone Rovers	28	113	1	339
2	Jack Miller	Keighley Cougars	14	104	0	264
3	James Maloney	Catalans Dragons	5	114	5	253
4	Lachlan Coote	St Helens	8	94	0	220
5	Lachlan Walmsley	Whitehaven	16	75	0	214
6	Chris Hankinson	London Broncos	10	83	0	206
7	Kieran Dixon	York City Knights	11	77	0	198
8	Rhyse Martin	Leeds Rhinos	3	88	0	188
9	Mark Kheirallah	Toulouse Olympique	6	80	0	184
10	Matty Beharrell	Doncaster	11	67	1	179

FIELD GOALS

1	James Maloney	Catalans Dragons	5
	Danny Brough	Bradford Bulls	5
3	Danny Richardson	Castleford Tigers	3
	Theo Fages	St Helens	3
	George Williams	Warrington Wolves	3
	Gregg McNally	Whitehaven	3

FINAL TABLES

SUPER LEAGUE

	P	W	D	L	F	A	Diff	%	Win %
Catalans Dragons	23	19	0	4	688	398	172.86		82.61
St Helens	21	16	0	5	548	229	239.30		76.19
Warrington Wolves	21	15	1	5	588	354	166.10		73.81
Wigan Warriors	25	15	0	10	387	385	100.52		60.00
Leeds Rhinos	24	13	0	11	556	440	126.36		54.17
Hull Kingston Rovers	20	10	0	10	497	458	108.52		50.00
Castleford Tigers	23	11	0	12	437	552	79.17		47.83
Hull FC	21	8	1	12	409	476	85.92		40.48
Huddersfield Giants	24	9	0	15	460	516	89.15		37.50
Wakefield Trinity	24	9	0	15	482	548	87.96		37.50
Salford Red Devils	22	7	0	15	402	584	68.84		31.82
Leigh Centurions	22	2	0	20	356	870	40.92		9.09

CHAMPIONSHIP

	P	W	D	L	F	A	Diff	%	Win %
Toulouse Olympique	14	14	0	0	698	124	562.90		100.00
Featherstone Rovers **	21	20	0	1	943	292	322.95		90.48
Halifax Panthers	21	13	0	8	528	354	149.15		61.90
Batley Bulldogs	21	13	0	8	561	411	136.50		61.90
Bradford Bulls	20	12	0	8	514	501	102.59		60.00
Whitehaven	22	12	1	9	502	524	95.80		56.82
London Broncos *	20	11	1	8	552	579	95.34		52.50
Widnes Vikings	21	9	1	11	494	534	92.51		45.24
York City Knights	20	9	0	11	502	477	105.24		45.00
Dewsbury Rams	21	8	1	12	360	608	59.21		40.48
Newcastle Thunder	20	7	1	12	431	627	68.74		37.50
Sheffield Eagles	20	5	3	12	420	665	63.16		32.50
Oldham	21	2	1	18	308	748	41.18		11.90
Swinton Lions	22	2	1	19	404	773	52.26		11.36

Deducted the equivalent of one win for failing to fulfil a fixture
**Deducted the equivalent of one win for breaching operational rules*

LEAGUE 1

	P	W	D	L	F	A	Diff	%	Win %
Barrow Raiders	17	13	1	3	596	275	216.73		79.41
Workington Town	15	10	1	4	471	310	151.94		70.00
North Wales Crusaders	17	11	0	6	539	410	131.46		64.71
Keighley Cougars	18	11	1	6	612	385	158.96		63.89
Doncaster	17	9	3	5	472	392	120.41		61.76
Hunslet	18	9	3	6	564	435	129.66		58.33
Rochdale Hornets	17	8	1	8	505	488	103.48		50.00
Coventry Bears	17	6	0	11	405	532	76.13		35.29
London Skolars	18	3	1	14	372	605	61.49		19.44
West Wales Raiders	18	0	1	17	238	942	25.27		2.78